LOCATION OF VIDEONOTES IN THE TEXT

Chapter 1
Compiling and Running a Java Program, p. 14
Using an IDE, p. 14
Your First Java Program, p. 28

Chapter 2
Displaying Console Output, p. 37
Declaring Variables, p. 44
Simple Math Expressions, p. 60
The Miles-per-Gallon Problem, p. 124

Chapter 3
Writing Classes and Creating Objects, p. 133
Initializing an Object with a Constructor, p. 155
The Personal Information Class Problem, p. 188

Chapter 4
The `if` Statement, p. 193
The `if-else` Statement, p. 202
The `if-else-if` Statement, p. 217
The Time Calculator Problem, p. 273

Chapter 5
The `while` Loop, p. 279
The Pennies for Pay Problem, p. 349

Chapter 6
Returning Objects from Methods, p. 389
Aggregation, p. 401
The `InventoryItem` Class Copy Constructor Problem, p. 442

Chapter 7
Accessing Array Elements in a Loop, p. 454
Passing an Array to a Method, p. 472
The Charge Account Validation Problem, p. 540

Chapter 8
The Sentence Capitalizer Problem, p. 599

Chapter 9
Inheritance, p. 605
Polymorphism, p. 646
The Employee and Production-worker Classes Problem, p. 675

Chapter 10
Handling Exceptions, p. 681
The Exception Project Problem, p. 737

Chapter 11
Creating a Simple GUI Application, p. 753
Handling Events, p. 763
The Monthly Sales Tax Problem, p. 836

Chapter 12
The `JList` Component, p. 842
The `JcomboBox` Component, p. 859
The Image Viewer Problem, p. 903

(continued on the next page)

LOCATION OF VIDEONOTES IN THE TEXT (continued) ▶

Chapter 13   Creating an Applet, p. 921
The House Applet Problem, p. 980

Chapter 14   Using Scene Builder to Create the Kilometer Converter GUI, p. 990
Learning More About the Main Application Class, p. 1002
Writing the Main Application Class For the Kilometer
Converter GUI, p. 1003
Learning More About the Controller Class, p. 1005
Registering the Controller Class to the Application's GUI, p. 1006
JavaFX RadioButtons, p. 1011
JavaFX CheckBoxes, p. 1019
The Retail Price Calculator Problem, p. 1034

Chapter 15   Reducing a Problem with Recursion, p. 1042
The Recursive Power Problem, p. 1065

STARTING OUT WITH

Java

Early Objects

FIFTH EDITION

STARTING OUT WITH

Early Objects

FIFTH EDITION

Tony Gaddis

Haywood Community College

Boston   Columbus   Indianapolis   New York   San Francisco   Upper Saddle River
Amsterdam   Cape Town   Dubai   London   Madrid   Milan   Munich   Paris   Montreal   Toronto
Delhi   Mexico City   São Paulo   Sydney   Hong Kong   Seoul   Singapore   Taipei   Tokyo

Vice President and Editorial Director, ECS:	*Marcia J. Horton*
Acquisitions Editor:	*Matt Goldstein*
Program Manager:	*Kayla Smith-Tarbox*
Executive Marketing Manager:	*Christy Lesko*
Marketing Assistant:	*Jon Bryant*
Permissions Project Manager:	*Karen Sanatar*
Senior Managing Editor:	*Scott Disanno*
Production Project Manager:	*Greg Dulles*
Operations Specialist:	*Linda Sager*
Cover Designer:	*Karen Noferi*
Cover Photo:	*© Natika/Fotolia*
Composition:	*Aptara®, Inc.*
Printer/Binder:	*Courier/Kendallville*
Cover Printer:	*Moore Langen*
Typeface:	*10/12.5 Sabon LT Std*

Pearson Education Ltd., *London*
Pearson Education Singapore, Pte. Ltd
Pearson Education Canada, Inc.
Pearson Education—Japan
Pearson Education Australia PTY, Limited

Pearson Education North Asia, Ltd., *Hong Kong*
Pearson Educación de Mexico, S.A. de C.V.
Pearson Education Malaysia, Pte. Ltd.
Pearson Education, Inc., *Upper Saddle River, New Jersey*

Library of Congress Cataloging-in-Publication

Gaddis, Tony.
   Starting out with Java : early objects/Tony Gaddis.—Fifth edition.
      pages cm
   Includes index.
   ISBN-13: 978-0-13-377674-4
   ISBN-10: 0-13-377674-3
   1. Java (Computer program language)   2. Object-oriented programming (Computer science) I. Title.
   QA76.73.J38G325 2014
   005.13'3—dc23

2014000221

10 9 8 7 6 5 4 3 2 1

ISBN-13: 978-0-13-377674-4
ISBN-10:   0-13-377674-3

Contents in Brief

Preface   xv

Chapter 1 **Introduction to Computers and Java**   1

Chapter 2 **Java Fundamentals**   31

Chapter 3 **A First Look at Classes and Objects**   129

Chapter 4 **Decision Structures**   193

Chapter 5 **Loops and Files**   279

Chapter 6 **A Second Look at Classes and Objects**   357

Chapter 7 **Arrays and the `ArrayList` Class**   449

Chapter 8 **Text Processing and Wrapper Classes**   547

Chapter 9 **Inheritance**   605

Chapter 10 **Exceptions and Advanced File I/O**   681

Chapter 11 **GUI Applications—Part 1**   739

Chapter 12 **GUI Applications—Part 2**   841

Chapter 13 **Applets and More**   909

Chapter 14 **Creating GUI Applications with JavaFX**   983

Chapter 15 **Recursion**   1039

Chapter 16 **Databases**   1067

Appendix A **Getting Started with Alice 2**   1163

Index   1189

Credits   1205

Appendixes B–M   Available on the book's online resource page

Case Studies 1–5   Available on the book's online resource page

Contents

Preface   xv

Chapter 1   Introduction to Computers and Java   1

1.1   Introduction. 1
1.2   Why Program?. 1
1.3   Computer Systems: Hardware and Software 2
1.4   Programming Languages. 6
1.5   What Is a Program Made of? 9
1.6   The Programming Process 16
1.7   Object-Oriented Programming 19
Review Questions and Exercises   24
Programming Challenge   28

Chapter 2   Java Fundamentals   31

2.1   The Parts of a Java Program. 31
2.2   The `System.out.print` and `System.out.println` Methods, and the
         Java API 37
2.3   Variables and Literals 43
2.4   Primitive Data Types 49
2.5   Arithmetic Operators 60
2.6   Combined Assignment Operators 69
2.7   Conversion between Primitive Data Types 70
2.8   Creating Named Constants with `final` 74
2.9   The `String` Class 76
2.10   Scope. 81
2.11   Comments. 83
2.12   Programming Style 87
2.13   Reading Keyboard Input 89
2.14   Dialog Boxes 97
2.15   The `System.out.printf` Method. 104
2.16   Common Errors to Avoid 116
Review Questions and Exercises   118
Programming Challenges   123

Chapter 3   A First Look at Classes and Objects   129

3.1   Classes 129
3.2   More about Passing Arguments 149
3.3   Instance Fields and Methods 152
3.4   Constructors 155
3.5   A BankAccount Class 161
3.6   Classes, Variables, and Scope 172
3.7   Packages and import Statements 173
3.8   Focus on Object-Oriented Design: Finding the Classes
         and Their Responsibilities 174
3.9   Common Errors to Avoid 183
Review Questions and Exercises   183
Programming Challenges   187

Chapter 4   Decision Structures   193

4.1   The if Statement 193
4.2   The if-else Statement 202
4.3   The Payroll Class 205
4.4   Nested if Statements 209
4.5   The if-else-if Statement 217
4.6   Logical Operators 222
4.7   Comparing string Objects 230
4.8   More about Variable Declaration and Scope 235
4.9   The Conditional Operator (Optional) 237
4.10   The switch Statement 238
4.11   Formatting Numbers with the DecimalFormat Class 248
4.12   Focus on Problem Solving: The SalesCommission Class 254
4.13   Generating Random Numbers with the Random Class 261
4.14   Common Errors to Avoid 267
Review Questions and Exercises   268
Programming Challenges   273

Chapter 5   Loops and Files   279

5.1   The Increment and Decrement Operators 279
5.2   The while Loop 283
5.3   Using the while Loop for Input Validation 290
5.4   The do-while Loop 293
5.5   The for Loop 296
5.6   Running Totals and Sentinel Values 307
5.7   Nested Loops 312
5.8   The break and continue Statements 320
5.9   Deciding Which Loop to Use 320
5.10   Introduction to File Input and Output 321
5.11   Common Errors to Avoid 341

Review Questions and Exercises   342
Programming Challenges   348

Chapter 6   A Second Look at Classes and Objects   357

6.1   Static Class Members 357
6.2   Overloaded Methods 364
6.3   Overloaded Constructors 369
6.4   Passing Objects as Arguments to Methods 376
6.5   Returning Objects from Methods 389
6.6   The `toString` Method 392
6.7   Writing an `equals` Method 396
6.8   Methods That Copy Objects 398
6.9   Aggregation 401
6.10   The `this` Reference Variable 414
6.11   Inner Classes 417
6.12   Enumerated Types 420
6.13   Garbage Collection 429
6.14   Focus on Object-Oriented Design: Class Collaboration 431
6.15   Common Errors to Avoid 435
Review Questions and Exercises   436
Programming Challenges   441

Chapter 7   Arrays and the `ArrayList` Class   449

7.1   Introduction to Arrays 449
7.2   Processing Array Contents 460
7.3   Passing Arrays as Arguments to Methods 472
7.4   Some Useful Array Algorithms and Operations 476
7.5   Returning Arrays from Methods 488
7.6   `String` Arrays 490
7.7   Arrays of Objects 494
7.8   The Sequential Search Algorithm 498
7.9   The Selection Sort and the Binary Search Algorithms 501
7.10   Two-Dimensional Arrays 509
7.11   Arrays with Three or More Dimensions 521
7.12   Command-Line Arguments and Variable-Length Argument Lists 522
7.13   The `ArrayList` Class 526
7.14   Common Errors to Avoid 534
Review Questions and Exercises   535
Programming Challenges   539

Chapter 8   Text Processing and Wrapper Classes   547

8.1   Introduction to Wrapper Classes 547
8.2   Character Testing and Conversion with the `Character` Class 548
8.3   More about `String` Objects 555

8.4   The `StringBuilder` Class 569
8.5   Tokenizing Strings 578
8.6   Wrapper Classes for the Numeric Data Types. 587
8.7   Focus on Problem Solving: The `TestScoreReader` Class. 591
8.8   Common Errors to Avoid 595
Review Questions and Exercises   595
Programming Challenges   599

Chapter 9   **Inheritance**   605

9.1   What Is Inheritance? 605
9.2   Calling the Superclass Constructor. 616
9.3   Overriding Superclass Methods 624
9.4   Protected Members 632
9.5   Classes That Inherit from Subclasses. 639
9.6   The `Object` Class 644
9.7   Polymorphism 646
9.8   Abstract Classes and Abstract Methods 651
9.9   Interfaces. 657
9.10   Common Errors to Avoid 668
Review Questions and Exercises   669
Programming Challenges   675

Chapter 10   **Exceptions and Advanced File I/O**   681

10.1   Handling Exceptions 681
10.2   Throwing Exceptions 704
10.3   Advanced Topics: Binary Files, Random Access Files, and Object
        Serialization 712
10.4   Common Errors to Avoid 728
Review Questions and Exercises   729
Programming Challenges   735

Chapter 11   **GUI Applications—Part 1**   739

11.1   Introduction. 739
11.2   Dialog Boxes 742
11.3   Creating Windows 753
11.4   Layout Managers 780
11.5   Radio Buttons and Check Boxes. 797
11.6   Borders 810
11.7   Focus on Problem Solving: Extending the `JPanel` Class 812
11.8   Splash Screens 826
11.9   Using Console Output to Debug a GUI Application. 827
11.10 Common Errors to Avoid 831
Review Questions and Exercises   831
Programming Challenges   836

Chapter 12   **GUI Applications—Part 2**   **841**

12.1   Read-Only Text Fields. 841
12.2   Lists 842
12.3   Combo Boxes 859
12.4   Displaying Images in Labels and Buttons 865
12.5   Mnemonics and Tool Tips 871
12.6   File Choosers and Color Choosers 873
12.7   Menus 877
12.8   More about Text Components: Text Areas and Fonts. 886
12.9   Sliders 891
12.10   Look and Feel. 895
12.11   Common Errors to Avoid 897
Review Questions and Exercises   898
Programming Challenges   903

Chapter 13   **Applets and More**   **909**

13.1   Introduction to Applets 909
13.2   A Brief Introduction to HTML. 911
13.3   Creating Applets with Swing 921
13.4   Using AWT for Portability. 929
13.5   Drawing Shapes. 934
13.6   Handling Mouse Events 954
13.7   `Timer` Objects. 965
13.8   Playing Audio. 969
13.9   Common Errors to Avoid 974
Review Questions and Exercises   974
Programming Challenges   980

Chapter 14   **Creating GUI Applications with JavaFX**   **983**

14.1   Introduction. 983
14.2   Scene Graphs. 985
14.3   Using Scene Builder to Create JavaFX Applications. 987
14.4   Writing the Application Code. 1001
14.5   RadioButtons and CheckBoxes. 1011
14.6   Displaying Images 1025
14.7   Common Errors to Avoid 1030
Review Questions and Exercises   1030
Programming Challenges   1034

Chapter 15   **Recursion**   **1039**

15.1   Introduction to Recursion. 1039
15.2   Solving Problems with Recursion 1042
15.3   Examples of Recursive Methods. 1046
15.4   A Recursive Binary Search Method. 1053

15.5   The Towers of Hanoi 1056
15.6   Common Errors to Avoid 1060
Review Questions and Exercises   1061
Programming Challenges   1064

Chapter 16   Databases   1067

16.1   Introduction to Database Management Systems 1067
16.2   Tables, Rows, and Columns 1073
16.3   Introduction to the SQL SELECT Statement. 1077
16.4   Inserting Rows 1098
16.5   Updating and Deleting Existing Rows 1101
16.6   Creating and Deleting Tables. 1110
16.7   Creating a New Database with JDBC 1114
16.8   Scrollable Result Sets 1115
16.9   Result Set Meta Data 1117
16.10 Displaying Query Results in a JTable 1120
16.11 Relational Data. 1131
16.12 Advanced Topics 1152
16.13 Common Errors to Avoid 1154
Review Questions and Exercises   1155
Programming Challenges   1160

Appendix A   Getting Started with Alice 2   1163

Index   1189

Credits   1205

**Available on the book's online resource page at
www.pearsonhighered.com/gaddis:**

Appendix B   The ASCII/Unicode Characters
Appendix C   Operator Precedence and Associativity
Appendix D   Java Key Words
Appendix E   Installing the JDK and JDK Documentation
Appendix F   Using the javadoc Utility
Appendix G   More about the Math Class
Appendix H   Packages
Appendix I   Working with Records and Random-Access Files
Appendix J   Installing Java DB
Appendix K   The QuickSort Algorithm
Appendix L   Answers to Checkpoints Questions
Appendix M   Answers to Odd-Numbered Review Questions
Case Study 1   The Amortization Class
Case Study 2   The PinTester Class
Case Study 3   Parallel Arrays
Case Study 4   The SerialNumber Class
Case Study 5   A Simple Text Editor Application

Preface

Welcome to *Starting Out with Java: Early Objects,* Fifth Edition. This book is intended for a one-semester or a two-quarter CS1 course. Although it is written for students with no prior programming background, even experienced students will benefit from its depth of detail.

Early Objects, Late Graphics

The approach taken by this text can be described as "early objects, late graphics." The student is introduced to object-oriented programming (OOP) early in the book. The fundamentals of control structures, classes, and the OOP paradigm are thoroughly covered before moving on to graphics and more powerful applications of the Java language.

As with all the books in the *Starting Out With* series, the hallmark of this text is its clear, friendly, and easy-to-understand writing. In addition, it is rich in example programs that are concise and practical.

New to this edition:

- **A New Chapter on JavaFX:** New to this edition is *Chapter 14: Creating GUI Applications with JavaFX.* JavaFX is the next-generation toolkit for creating GUIs and graphical applications in Java and is bundled with Java 7 and Java 8. This new chapter introduces the student to the JavaFX library and shows how to use Scene Builder (a free download from Oracle) to visually design GUIs. The chapter is written in such a way that it is independent from the existing chapters on Swing and AWT. The instructor can choose to skip the Swing and AWT chapters and go straight to JavaFX, or cover all of the GUI chapters.
- **Rewritten Database Chapter:** The database chapter, which is now Chapter 16, has been rewritten with more examples and more detailed explanations of various database operations.
- **Coverage of `System.out.printf` Has Been Expanded:** The section on `System.out.printf` in Chapter 2 has been completely rewritten and expanded to include diagrams and coverage of additional format specifiers.
- **`System.out.printf` Is Primarily Used For Formatting Console Output:** In this edition, `System.out.printf` is used as the primary method for formatting output in console programs. The `DecimalFormat` class is still introduced, but it is used to format numbers in GUI applications.

- **Discussion of Nested Loops Has Been Expanded:** In Chapter 4 the section on nested loops has been expanded to include an *In the Spotlight* section highlighting the use of nested loops to print patterns.
- **Usage of Random Numbers Has Been Expanded:** In Chapter 4 the section on random numbers has been expanded and now includes *In the Spotlight* sections demonstrating how random numbers can be used to simulate the rolling of dice.
- **New Motivational Example of Classes Has Been Added to Chapter 6:** In Chapter 6, a new motivational example of classes has been added. The example shows how a variation of the game of Cho-Han can be simulated with classes that represent the players, a dealer, and the dice.
- **Multi-Catch Exception Handling:** A discussion of multi-catch exception handling has been added to Chapter 10.
- **Equipping Swing GUI Applications with a Static `main` Method is Introduced Earlier:** In Chapter 11, *GUI Applications—Part 1*, the topic of equipping a GUI class with a static `main` method has been moved to a point very early in the chapter.
- **New Exercises and Programming Problems:** New, motivational programming problems have been added to many of the chapters.

Organization of the Text

The text teaches Java step-by-step. Each chapter covers a major set of topics and builds knowledge as students progress through the book. Although the chapters can be easily taught in their existing sequence, there is some flexibility. Figure P-1 shows chapter dependencies. Each box represents a chapter or a group of chapters. A solid-line arrow points from one chapter to the chapter that must be covered previously. A dotted-line arrow indicates that only a section or minor portion of the chapter depends on another chapter.

Brief Overview of Each Chapter

Chapter 1: Introduction to Computers and Java. This chapter provides an introduction to the field of computer science, and covers the fundamentals of hardware, software, and programming languages. The elements of a program, such as key words, variables, operators, and punctuation are discussed through the examination of a simple program. An overview of entering source code, compiling it, and executing it is presented. A brief history of Java is also given. The chapter concludes with a primer on OOP.

Chapter 2: Java Fundamentals. This chapter gets the student started in Java by introducing data types, identifiers, variable declarations, constants, comments, program output, and arithmetic operations. The conventions of programming style are also introduced. The student learns to read console input with the `Scanner` class, or as an option, through dialog boxes with `JOptionPane`.

Chapter 3: A First Look at Classes and Objects. This chapter introduces the student to classes. Once the student learns about fields and methods, UML diagrams are introduced as a design tool. The student learns to write simple `void` methods, as well as simple methods that return a value. Arguments and parameters are also discussed. Finally, the student learns how to write constructors, and the concept of the default constructor is discussed. A `BankAccount` class is presented as a case study, and a section on

Figure P-1 Chapter Dependencies

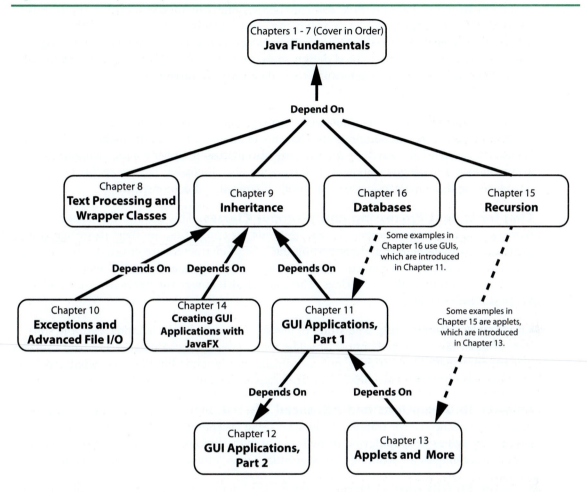

object-oriented design is included. This section leads the students through the process of identifying classes and their responsibilities within a problem domain. There is also a section that briefly explains packages and the import statement.

Chapter 4: Decision Structures. Here the student explores relational operators and relational expressions and is shown how to control the flow of a program with the if, if/else, and if/else if statements. The conditional operator and the switch statement are also covered. This chapter also discusses how to compare String objects with the equals, compareTo, equalsIgnoreCase, and compareToIgnoreCase methods. Formatting numeric output with the DecimalFormat class is covered. An object-oriented case study shows how lengthy algorithms can be decomposed into several methods.

Chapter 5: Loops and Files. This chapter covers Java's repetition control structures. The while loop, do-while loop, and for loop are taught, along with common uses for these devices. Counters, accumulators, running totals, sentinels, and other application-related topics are discussed. Simple file operations for reading and writing text files are also covered.

Chapter 6: A Second Look at Classes and Objects. This chapter shows students how to write classes with added capabilities. Static methods and fields, interaction between objects, passing objects as arguments, and returning objects from methods are discussed. Aggregation and the "has a" relationship is covered, as well as enumerated types. A section on object-oriented design shows how to use CRC (class, responsibilities, and collaborations) cards to determine the collaborations among classes.

Chapter 7: Arrays and the `ArrayList` Class. In this chapter students learn to create and work with single and multidimensional arrays. Numerous array-processing techniques are demonstrated, such as summing the elements in an array, finding the highest and lowest values, and sequentially searching an array are also discussed. Other topics, including ragged arrays and variable-length arguments (varargs), are also discussed. The `ArrayList` class is introduced, and Java's generic types are briefly discussed and demonstrated.

Chapter 8: Text Processing and Wrapper Classes. This chapter discusses the numeric and character wrapper classes. Methods for converting numbers to strings, testing the case of characters, and converting the case of characters are covered. Autoboxing and unboxing are also discussed. More `String` class methods are covered, including using the `split` method to tokenize strings. The chapter also covers the `StringBuilder` and `StringTokenizer` classes.

Chapter 9: Inheritance. The study of classes continues in this chapter with the subjects of inheritance and polymorphism. The topics covered include superclass and subclass constructors, method overriding, polymorphism and dynamic binding, protected and package access, class hierarchies, abstract classes and methods, and interfaces.

Chapter 10: Exceptions and Advanced File I/O. In this chapter the student learns to develop enhanced error trapping techniques using exceptions. Handling an exception is covered, as well as developing and throwing custom exceptions. This chapter also discusses advanced techniques for working with sequential access, random access, text, and binary files.

Chapter 11: GUI Applications—Part 1. This chapter presents the basics of developing graphical user interface (GUI) applications with Swing. Fundamental Swing components and the basic concepts of event-driven programming are covered.

Chapter 12: GUI Applications—Part 2. This chapter continues the study of GUI application development. More advanced components, as well as menu systems and look-and-feel, are covered.

Chapter 13: Applets and More. Here the student applies his or her knowledge of GUI development to the creation of applets. In addition to using Swing applet classes, Abstract Windowing Toolkit classes are also discussed for portability. Drawing simple graphical shapes is also discussed.

Chapter 14: Creating GUI Applications with JavaFX. This chapter introduces JavaFX, which is the next generation library for creating graphical applications in Java. This chapter also shows how to use Scene Builder, a free screen designer from Oracle, to visually design GUIs. This chapter is written in such a way that it is independent from the existing chapters on Swing and AWT. You can choose to skip Chapters 11, 12, and 13, and go straight to Chapter 14, or cover all of the GUI chapters.

Chapter 15: Recursion. This chapter presents recursion as a problem-solving technique. Numerous examples of recursion are demonstrated.

Chapter 16: Databases. This chapter introduces the student to database programming. The basic concepts of database management systems and SQL are first presented. Then the student learns to use JDBC to write database applications in Java. Relational data is covered, and numerous example programs are presented throughout the chapter.

Appendix A. Getting Started with Alice

Appendixes B–M and **Case Studies 1-5** are available on the book's online resource page at www.pearsonhighered.com/gaddis.

Features of the Text

Concept Statements Each major section of the text starts with a concept statement. This statement summarizes the ideas of the section.

Example Programs The text has an abundant number of complete example programs, each designed to highlight the topic currently being studied. In most cases, these are practical, real-world examples. Source code for these programs is provided so that students can run the programs themselves.

Program Output After each example program there is a sample of its screen output. This immediately shows the student how the program should function.

 Checkpoints

Checkpoints are questions placed throughout each chapter as a self-test study aid. Answers for all Checkpoint questions are found in Appendix L (available for download) so students can check how well they have learned a new topic. To download Appendix L, go to the Gaddis resource page at www.pearsonhighered.com/gaddis.

> **NOTE:** Notes appear at appropriate places throughout the text. They are short explanations of interesting or often misunderstood points relevant to the topic at hand.

> **WARNING!** Warnings are notes that caution the student about certain Java features, programming techniques, or practices that can lead to malfunctioning programs or lost data.

VidoeNotes. A series of online videos, developed specifically for this book, are available for viewing at www.pearsonhighered.com/gaddis. Icons appear throughout the text alerting the student to videos about specific topics.

Case Studies Case studies that simulate real-world applications appear in many chapters throughout the text, with complete code provided for each. These case studies are designed to highlight the major topics of the chapter in which they appear.

Review Questions and Exercises Each chapter presents a thorough and diverse set of review questions and exercises. They include Multiple Choice and True/False, Find the Error, Algorithm Workbench, and Short Answer.

Programming Challenges Each chapter offers a pool of programming challenges designed to solidify students' knowledge of topics at hand. In most cases the assignments present real-world problems to be solved.

 In the Spotlight. Many of the chapters provide an *In the Spotlight* section that presents a programming problem, along with detailed, step-by-step analysis showing the student how to solve it.

Supplements

Companion Website

Many student resources are available for this book from the book's Companion Website. The following items are available at www.pearsonhighered.com/gaddis using the Access Code bound into the front of the book:

- The source code for each example program in the book
- Access to the book's companion VideoNotes
- Appendixes B–M (listed in the Table of Contents)
- A collection of five valuable Case Studies (listed in the Table of Contents)
- Links to download the Java™ Development Kit
- Links to download numerous programming environments, including jGRASP™, Eclipse™, TextPad™, NetBeans™, JCreator, and DrJava

Online Practice and Assessment with MyProgrammingLab

MyProgrammingLab helps students fully grasp the logic, semantics, and syntax of programming. Through practice exercises and immediate, personalized feedback, MyProgrammingLab improves the programming competence of beginning students who often struggle with the basic concepts and paradigms of popular high-level programming languages.

A self-study and homework tool, a MyProgrammingLab course consists of hundreds of small practice problems organized around the structure of this textbook. For students, the system automatically detects errors in the logic and syntax of their code submissions and offers targeted hints that enable students to figure out what went wrong—and why. For instructors, a comprehensive gradebook tracks correct and incorrect answers and stores the code inputted by students for review.

MyProgrammingLab is offered to users of this book in partnership with Turing's Craft, the makers of the CodeLab interactive programming exercise system. For a full demonstration, to see feedback from instructors and students, or to get started using MyProgrammingLab in your course, visit www.myprogramminglab.com.

Instructor Resources

The following supplements are available to qualified instructors only. Visit the Pearson Education Instructor Resource Center (www.pearsonhighered.com/irc) for information on how to access them:

- Answers to all Review Questions in the text
- Solutions for all Programming Challenges in the text
- PowerPoint presentation slides for every chapter
- Computerized test bank

Acknowledgments

There have been many helping hands in the development and publication of this text. I would like to thank the following faculty reviewers for their helpful suggestions and expertise during the production of this text:

Rebecca Caldwell
Winston-Salem State University

Dan Dao
Richland College

Naser Heravi
College of Southern Nevada

Deborah Hughes
Lyndon State College

Nicole Jiao
South Texas College

Kurt Kominek
Northeast State Community College

Kevin Mess
College of Southern Nevada

Lisa Olivieri
Chestnut Hill College

Mark Swanson
Southeast Technical

Reviewers For Previous Editions

Ahmad Abuhejleh
*University of Wisconsin–
River Falls*

Colin Archibald
Valencia CC

Ijaz Awani
Savannah State University

Dr. Charles W. Bane
Tarleton State University

Dwight Barnett
Virginia Tech

Asoke Bhattacharyya
Saint Xavier University, Chicago

Marvin Bishop
Manhattan College

Heather Booth
University Tennessee—Knoxville

David Boyd
Valdosta University

Julius Brandstatter
Golden Gate University

Kim Cannon
Greenville Tech

James Chegwidden
Tarrant County College

Kay Chen
Bucks County Community College

Brad Chilton
Tarleton State University

Diane Christie
University of Wisconsin–Stout

Cara Cocking
Marquette University

Walter C. Daugherity
Texas A&M University

Michael Doherty
University of the Pacific

Jeanne M. Douglas
University of Vermont

Sander Eller
*California Polytechnic University—
Pomona*

Brooke Estabrook-Fishinghawk
Mesa Community College

Mike Fry
Lebanon Valley College

Georgia R. Grant
College of San Mateo

Chris Haynes
Indiana University

Ric Heishman
Northern Virginia Community College

Deedee Herrera
Dodge City Community College

Mary Hovik
Lehigh Carbon Community College

Brian Howard
DePauw University

Norm Jacobson
University of California at Irvine

Dr. Stephen Judd
University of Pennsylvania

Harry Lichtbach
Evergreen Valley College

Michael A. Long
California State University, Chico

Tim Margush
University of Akron

Blayne E. Mayfield
Oklahoma State University

Scott McLeod
Riverside Community College

Dean Mellas
Cerritos College

Georges Merx
San Diego Mesa College

Martin Meyers
California State University, Sacramento

Pati Milligan
Baylor University

Godfrey Muganda
North Central College

Steve Newberry
Tarleton State University

Lynne O'Hanlon
Los Angeles Pierce College

Merrill Parker
Chattaonooga State Technical Community College

Bryson R. Payne
North Georgia College and State University

Rodney Pearson
Mississippi State University

Peter John Polito
Springfield College

Charles Robert Putnam
California State University, Northridge

Dr. Y. B. Reddy
Grambling State University

Carolyn Schauble
Colorado State University

Bonnie Smith
Fresno City College

Daniel Spiegel
Kutztown University

Caroline St. Clair
North Central College

Karen Stanton
Los Medanos College

Peter H. Van Der Goes
Rose State College

Tuan A Vo
Mt. San Antonio College

Xiaoying Wang
University of Mississippi

Special thanks goes to Chris Rich for his assistance with the JavaFX chapter. I would like to thank my family for all the patience, love, and support they have shown me throughout this project. I would also like to thank everyone at Pearson Education for making the *Starting Out With* series so successful. I am extremely fortunate to have Matt Goldstein as my editor. I am also fortunate to work with Yez Alyan and the computer science marketing team at Pearson. They do a great job getting my books out to the academic community. I had a great production team led by Scott Disanno, Kayla Smith-Tarbox, and Gregory Dulles. Thanks to you all!

About the Author

Tony Gaddis is the principal author of the *Starting Out With* series of textbooks. Tony has nearly twenty years experience teaching computer science courses at Haywood Community College in North Carolina. He is a highly acclaimed instructor who was previously selected as the North Carolina Community College Teacher of the Year and has received the Teaching Excellence award from the National Institute for Staff and Organizational Development. Besides Java™ books, the Starting Out series includes introductory books using the C++ programming language, Microsoft® Visual Basic®, Microsoft® C#®, Python, Programming Logic and Design, Alice, and App Inventor, all published by Pearson.

TOPICS

1.1 Introduction
1.2 Why Program?
1.3 Computer Systems: Hardware and Software

1.4 Programming Languages
1.5 What Is a Program Made of?
1.6 The Programming Process
1.7 Object-Oriented Programming

1.1 Introduction

This book teaches programming using Java. Java is a powerful language that runs on practically every type of computer. It can be used to create large applications or small programs, known as applets, that are part of a Web site. Before plunging right into learning Java, however, this chapter will review the fundamentals of computer hardware and software and then take a broad look at computer programming in general.

1.2 Why Program?

CONCEPT: Computers can do many different jobs because they are programmable.

Every profession has tools that make the job easier to do. Carpenters use hammers, saws, and measuring tapes. Mechanics use wrenches, screwdrivers, and ratchets. Electronics technicians use probes, scopes, and meters. Some tools are unique and can be categorized as belonging to a single profession. For example, surgeons have certain tools that are designed specifically for surgical operations. Those tools probably aren't used by anyone other than surgeons. There are some tools, however, that are used in several professions. Screwdrivers, for instance, are used by mechanics, carpenters, and many others.

The computer is a tool used by so many professions that it cannot be easily categorized. It can perform so many different jobs that it is perhaps the most versatile tool ever made. To the accountant, computers balance books, analyze profits and losses, and prepare tax reports. To the factory worker, computers control manufacturing machines and track production. To the mechanic, computers analyze the various systems in an automobile and

1

pinpoint hard-to-find problems. The computer can do such a wide variety of tasks because it can be *programmed*. It is a machine specifically designed to follow instructions. Because of the computer's programmability, it doesn't belong to any single profession. Computers are designed to do whatever job their programs, or *software,* tell them to do.

Computer programmers do a very important job. They create software that transforms computers into the specialized tools of many trades. Without programmers, the users of computers would have no software, and without software, computers would not be able to do anything.

Computer programming is both an art and a science. It is an art because every aspect of a program should be carefully designed. Here are a few of the things that must be designed for any real-world computer program:

- The logical flow of the instructions
- The mathematical procedures
- The layout of the programming statements
- The appearance of the screens
- The way information is presented to the user
- The program's "user friendliness"
- Help systems and written documentation

There is also a science to programming. Because programs rarely work right the first time they are written, a lot of analyzing, experimenting, correcting, and redesigning is required. This demands patience and persistence of the programmer. Writing software demands discipline as well. Programmers must learn special languages such as Java because computers do not understand English or other human languages. Programming languages have strict rules that must be carefully followed.

Both the artistic and scientific nature of programming makes writing computer software like designing a car: Both cars and programs should be functional, efficient, powerful, easy to use, and pleasing to look at.

1.3   Computer Systems: Hardware and Software

CONCEPT: All computer systems consist of similar hardware devices and software components.

Hardware

Hardware refers to the physical components that a computer is made of. A computer, as we generally think of it, is not an individual device, but a system of devices. Like the instruments in a symphony orchestra, each device plays its own part. A typical computer system consists of the following major components:

- The central processing unit
- Main memory
- Secondary storage devices
- Input devices
- Output devices

The organization of a computer system is shown in Figure 1-1.

Figure 1-1   The organization of a computer system

Let's take a closer look at each of these devices.

The CPU

At the heart of a computer is its *central processing unit,* or *CPU.* The CPU's job is to fetch instructions, follow the instructions, and produce some resulting data. Internally, the central processing unit consists of two parts: the *control unit* and the *arithmetic and logic unit (ALU).* The control unit coordinates all of the computer's operations. It is responsible for determining where to get the next instruction and regulating the other major components of the computer with control signals. The arithmetic and logic unit, as its name suggests, is designed to perform mathematical operations. The organization of the CPU is shown in Figure 1-2.

Figure 1-2   The organization of the CPU

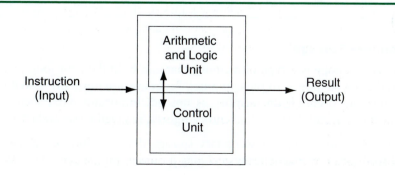

A program is a sequence of instructions stored in the computer's memory. When a computer is running a program, the CPU is engaged in a process known formally as the *fetch/decode/execute cycle*. The steps in the fetch/decode/execute cycle are as follows:

Fetch   The CPU's control unit fetches, from main memory, the next instruction in the sequence of program instructions.

Decode   The instruction is encoded in the form of a number. The control unit decodes the instruction and generates an electronic signal.

Execute   The signal is routed to the appropriate component of the computer (such as the ALU, a disk drive, or some other device). The signal causes the component to perform an operation.

These steps are repeated as long as there are instructions to perform.

Main Memory

Commonly known as *random-access memory*, or *RAM*, the computer's main memory is a device that holds data. Specifically, RAM holds the sequences of instructions in the programs that are running and the data those programs are using.

Memory is divided into sections that hold an equal amount of data. Each section is made of eight "switches" that may be either on or off. A switch in the on position usually represents the number 1, although a switch in the off position usually represents the number 0. The computer stores data by setting the switches in a memory location to a pattern that represents a character or a number. Each of these switches is known as a *bit*, which stands for *binary digit*. Each section of memory, which is a collection of eight bits, is known as a *byte*. Each byte is assigned a unique number known as an *address*. The addresses are ordered from lowest to highest. A byte is identified by its address in much the same way a post office box is identified by an address. Figure 1-3 shows a series of bytes with their addresses. In the illustration, sample data is stored in memory. The number 149 is stored in the byte at address 16, and the number 72 is stored in the byte at address 23.

RAM is usually a volatile type of memory, used only for temporary storage. When the computer is turned off, the contents of RAM are erased.

Figure 1-3   Memory bytes and their addresses

0	1	2	3	4	5	6	7	8	9
10	11	12	13	14	15	16 149	17	18	19
20	21	22	23 72	24	25	26	27	28	29

Secondary Storage

Secondary storage is a type of memory that can hold data for long periods of time—even when there is no power to the computer. Programs are normally stored in secondary memory and loaded into main memory as needed. Important data, such as word processing documents, payroll data, and inventory figures, is saved to secondary storage as well.

The most common type of secondary storage device is the *disk drive*. A traditional disk drive stores data by magnetically encoding it onto a spinning circular disk. *Solid-state drives*, which store data in solid-state memory, are increasingly becoming popular. A solid-state drive has no moving parts and operates faster than a traditional disk drive. Most computers have some sort of secondary storage device, either a traditional disk drive or a solid-state drive, mounted inside their case. External drives are also available that connect to one of the computer's communication ports. External drives can be used to create backup copies of important data or to move data to another computer.

In addition to external drives, many types of devices have been created for copying data and for moving it to other computers. *Universal Serial Bus drives*, or *USB drives,* are small devices that plug into the computer's USB port and appear to the system as a disk drive. These drives do not actually contain a disk, however. They store data in a special type of memory known as *flash memory.* USB drives are inexpensive, reliable, and small enough to be carried in your pocket.

Optical devices such as the *CD* (compact disc) and the *DVD* (digital versatile disc) are also popular for data storage. Data is not recorded magnetically on an optical disc, but is encoded as a series of pits on the disc surface. CD and DVD drives use a laser to detect the pits and thus read the encoded data. Optical discs hold large amounts of data, and because recordable CD and DVD drives are now commonplace, they make a good medium for creating backup copies of data.

Input Devices

Input is any data the computer collects from the outside world. The device that collects the data and sends it to the computer is called an *input device*. Common input devices are the keyboard, mouse, scanner, microphone, Webcam, and digital camera. Disk drives, optical drives, and USB drives can also be considered input devices because programs and data are retrieved from them and loaded into the computer's memory.

Output Devices

Output is any data the computer sends to the outside world. It might be a sales report, a list of names, or a graphic image. The data is sent to an output device, which formats and presents it. Common output devices are monitors and printers. Disk drives, USB drives, and CD/DVD recorders can also be considered output devices because the CPU sends data to them in order to be saved.

Software

As previously mentioned, software refers to the programs that run on a computer. There are two general categories of software: operating systems and application software. An *operating system* is a set of programs that manages the computer's hardware devices and controls their processes. Most all modern operating systems are multitasking, which means they are capable of running multiple programs at once. Through a technique called *time sharing,* a multitasking system divides the allocation of hardware resources and the attention of the CPU among all the executing programs. UNIX, Linux, and modern versions of Windows and Mac OS are multitasking operating systems.

Application software refers to programs that make the computer useful to the user. These programs solve specific problems or perform general operations that satisfy the needs of the user. Word processing, spreadsheet, and database programs are all examples of application software.

Checkpoint

1.1 Why is the computer used by so many different people, in so many different professions?

1.2 List the five major hardware components of a computer system.

1.3 Internally, the CPU consists of what two units?

1.4 Describe the steps in the fetch/decode/execute cycle.

1.5 What is a memory address? What is its purpose?

1.6 Explain why computers have both main memory and secondary storage.

1.7 What does the term "multitasking" mean?

 ## 1.4 Programming Languages

> **CONCEPT:** A program is a set of instructions a computer follows in order to perform a task. A programming language is a special language used to write computer programs.

What Is a Program?

Computers are designed to follow instructions. A computer program is a set of instructions that enable the computer to solve a problem or perform a task. For example, suppose we want the computer to calculate someone's gross pay. The following is a list of things the computer should do to perform this task.

1. Display a message on the screen: "How many hours did you work?"
2. Allow the user to enter the number of hours worked.
3. Once the user enters a number, store it in memory.
4. Display a message on the screen: "How much do you get paid per hour?"
5. Allow the user to enter an hourly pay rate.
6. Once the user enters a number, store it in memory.
7. Once both the number of hours worked and the hourly pay rate are entered, multiply the two numbers and store the result in memory.
8. Display a message on the screen that shows the amount of money earned. The message must include the result of the calculation performed in Step 7.

Collectively, these instructions are called an *algorithm*. An algorithm is a set of well-defined steps for performing a task or solving a problem. Notice that these steps are sequentially ordered. Step 1 should be performed before Step 2, and so forth. It is important that these instructions be performed in their proper sequence.

Although you and I might easily understand the instructions in the pay-calculating algorithm, it is not ready to be executed on a computer. A computer's CPU can only process instructions that are written in machine language. If you were to look at a machine language program, you would see a stream of binary numbers (numbers consisting of only 1s and 0s). The binary numbers form machine language instructions, which the CPU interprets as commands. Here is an example of what a machine language instruction might look like:

1011010000000101

As you can imagine, the process of encoding an algorithm in machine language is very tedious and difficult. In addition, each different type of CPU has its own machine language. If you wrote a machine language program for computer A and then wanted to run it on computer B, which has a different type of CPU, you would have to rewrite the program in computer B's machine language.

Programming languages, which use words instead of numbers, were invented to ease the task of programming. A program can be written in a programming language, which is much easier to understand than machine language, and then translated into machine language. Programmers use software to perform this translation. Many programming languages have been created. Table 1-1 lists a few of the well-known ones.

Table 1-1 Programming languages

Language	Description
BASIC	Beginners All-purpose Symbolic Instruction Code is a general-purpose, procedural programming language. It was originally designed to be simple enough for beginners to learn.
FORTRAN	FORmula TRANslator is a procedural language designed for programming complex mathematical algorithms.
COBOL	Common Business-Oriented Language is a procedural language designed for business applications.
Pascal	Pascal is a structured, general-purpose, procedural language designed primarily for teaching programming.
C	C is a structured, general-purpose, procedural language developed at Bell Laboratories.
C++	Based on the C language, C++ offers object-oriented features not found in C. C++ was also invented at Bell Laboratories.
C#	Pronounced "C sharp." It is a language invented by Microsoft for developing applications based on the Microsoft .NET platform.
Java	Java is an object-oriented language invented at Sun Microsystems and is now owned by Oracle. It may be used to develop stand-alone applications that operate on a single computer, applications that run over the Internet from a Web server, and applets that run in a Web browser.
JavaScript	JavaScript is a programming language that can be used in a Web site to perform simple operations. Despite its name, JavaScript is not related to Java.
Perl	A general-purpose programming language that is widely used on Internet servers.
PHP	A programming language used primarily for developing Web server applications and dynamic Web pages.
Python	Python is an object-oriented programming language that is used in both business and academia. Many popular Web sites have features that are developed in Python.
Ruby	Ruby is a simple but powerful object-oriented programming language. It can be used for a variety of purposes, from small utility programs to large Web applications.
Visual Basic	Visual Basic is a Microsoft programming language and software development environment that allows programmers to create Windows-based applications quickly.

A History of Java

In 1991 a team was formed at Sun Microsystems (a company that is now owned by Oracle) to speculate about the important technological trends that might emerge in the near future. The team, which was named the Green Team, concluded that computers would merge with consumer appliances. Their first project was to develop a handheld device named *7 (pronounced "star seven") that could be used to control a variety of home entertainment devices. In order for the unit to work, it had to use a programming language that could be processed by all the devices it controlled. This presented a problem because different brands of consumer devices use different processors, each with its own machine language.

Because no such universal language existed, James Gosling, the team's lead engineer, created one. Programs written in this language, which was originally named Oak, were not translated into the machine language of a specific processor, but were translated into an intermediate language known as *byte code.* Another program would then translate the byte code into machine language that could be executed by the processor in a specific consumer device.

Unfortunately, the technology developed by the Green Team was ahead of its time. No customers could be found, mostly because the computer-controlled consumer appliance industry was just beginning. But rather than abandoning their hard work and moving on to other projects, the team saw another opportunity: the Internet. The Internet is a perfect environment for a universal programming language such as Oak. It consists of numerous different computer platforms connected together in a single network.

To demonstrate the effectiveness of their language, which was renamed Java, the team used it to develop a Web browser. The browser, named HotJava, was able to download and run small Java programs known as applets. This gave the browser the capability to display animation and interact with the user. HotJava was demonstrated at the 1995 SunWorld conference before a wowed audience. Later the announcement was made that Netscape would incorporate Java technology into its Navigator browser. Other Internet companies rapidly followed, increasing the acceptance and the influence of the Java language. Today, Java is very popular for developing not only applets for the Internet, but also stand-alone applications.

Java Applications and Applets

There are two types of programs that may be created with Java: applications and applets. An application is a stand-alone program that runs on your computer. You have probably used several applications already, such as word processors, spreadsheets, database managers, and graphics programs. Although Java may be used to write these types of applications, other languages such as C, C++, and Visual Basic are also used.

In the previous section you learned that Java may also be used to create applets. The term *applet* refers to a small application, in the same way that the term *piglet* refers to a small pig. Unlike applications, an applet is designed to be transmitted over the Internet from a Web server, and then executed in a Web browser. Applets are important because they can be used to extend the capabilities of a Web page significantly.

Web pages are normally written in hypertext markup language (HTML). HTML is limited, however, because it merely describes the content and layout of a Web page. HTML does not have sophisticated abilities such as performing math calculations and interacting with the user. A Web designer can write a Java applet to perform operations that are normally performed by an application and embed it in a Web site. When someone visits the Web site, the applet is downloaded to the visitor's browser and executed.

Security

Any time content is downloaded from a Web server to a visitor's computer, security is an important concern. Because Java is a full-featured programming language, at first you might be suspicious of any Web site that transmits an applet to your computer. After all, couldn't a Java applet do harmful things, such as deleting the contents of the disk drive or transmitting private information to another computer? Fortunately, the answer is no. Web browsers run Java applets in a secure environment within your computer's memory and do not allow them to access resources, such as a disk drive, that are outside that environment.

1.5 What Is a Program Made of?

CONCEPT: There are certain elements that are common to all programming languages.

Language Elements

All programming languages have some things in common. Table 1-2 lists the common elements you will find in almost every language.

Table 1-2 The common elements of a programming language

Language Element	Description
Key Words	These are words that have a special meaning in the programming language. They may be used for their intended purpose only. Key words are also known as *reserved words*.
Operators	Operators are symbols or words that perform operations on one or more operands. An *operand* is usually an item of data, such as a number.
Punctuation	Most programming languages require the use of punctuation characters. These characters serve specific purposes, such as marking the beginning or ending of a statement, or separating items in a list.
Programmer-Defined Names	Unlike key words, which are part of the programming language, these are words or names that are defined by the programmer. They are used to identify storage locations in memory and parts of the program that are created by the programmer. Programmer-defined names are often called *identifiers*.
Syntax	These are rules that must be followed when writing a program. Syntax dictates how key words and operators may be used, and where punctuation symbols must appear.

Let's look at an example Java program and identify an instance of each of these elements. Code Listing 1-1 shows the code listing with each line numbered.

NOTE: The line numbers are not part of the program. They are included to help point out specific parts of the program.

Code Listing 1-1   `Payroll.java`

```
1   public class Payroll
2   {
3      public static void main(String[] args)
4      {
5         int hours = 40;
6         double grossPay, payRate = 25.0;
7
8         grossPay = hours * payRate;
9         System.out.println("Your gross pay is $" + grossPay);
10     }
11  }
```

Key Words (Reserved Words)

Two of Java's key words appear in line 1: `public` and `class`. In line 3 the words `public`, `static`, and `void` are all key words. The word `int` in line 5 and `double` in line 6 are also key words. These words, which are always written in lowercase, each have a special meaning in Java and can only be used for their intended purpose. As you will see, the programmer is allowed to make up his or her own names for certain things in a program. Key words, however, are reserved and cannot be used for anything other than their designated purpose. Part of learning a programming language is learning the commonly used key words, what they mean, and how to use them.

Table 1-3 shows a list of the Java key words.

Table 1-3   The Java key words

abstract	const	for	int	public	throw
assert	continue	final	interface	return	throws
boolean	default	finally	long	short	transient
break	do	float	native	static	true
byte	double	goto	new	strictfp	try
case	else	if	null	super	void
catch	enum	implements	package	switch	volatile
char	extends	import	private	synchronized	while
class	false	instanceof	protected	this	

Programmer-Defined Names

The words `hours`, `payRate`, and `grossPay` that appear in the program in lines 5, 6, 8, and 9 are programmer-defined names. They are not part of the Java language but are names made up by the programmer. In this particular program, these are the names of variables. As you will learn later in this chapter, variables are the names of memory locations that may hold data.

Operators

In line 8 the following line appears:

```
grossPay = hours * payRate;
```

The = and * symbols are both operators. They perform operations on items of data, known as operands. The * operator multiplies its two operands, which in this example are the variables hours and payRate. The = symbol is called the assignment operator. It takes the value of the expression that appears at its right and stores it in the variable whose name appears at its left. In this example, the = operator stores in the grossPay variable the result of the hours variable multiplied by the payRate variable. In other words, the statement says, "the grossPay variable is assigned the value of hours times payRate."

Punctuation

Notice that lines 5, 6, 8, and 9 end with a semicolon. A semicolon in Java is similar to a period in English: It marks the end of a complete sentence (or *statement,* as it is called in programming jargon). Semicolons do not appear at the end of every line in a Java program, however. There are rules that govern where semicolons are required and where they are not. Part of learning Java is learning where to place semicolons and other punctuation symbols.

Lines and Statements

Often, the contents of a program are thought of in terms of lines and statements. A *line* is just that—a single line as it appears in the body of a program. Code Listing 1-1 is shown with each of its lines numbered. Most of the lines contain something meaningful; however, line 7 is empty. Blank lines are only used to make a program more readable.

A statement is a complete instruction that causes the computer to perform some action. Here is the statement that appears in line 9 of Code Listing 1-1:

```
System.out.println("Your gross pay is $" + grossPay);
```

This statement causes the computer to display a message on the screen. Statements can be a combination of key words, operators, and programmer-defined names. Statements often occupy only one line in a program, but sometimes they are spread out over more than one line.

Variables

The most fundamental way that a Java program stores an item of data in memory is with a variable. A *variable* is a named storage location in the computer's memory. The data stored in a variable may change while the program is running (hence the name *variable*). Notice that in Code Listing 1-1 the programmer-defined names hours, payRate, and grossPay appear in several places. All three of these are the names of variables. The hours variable is used to store the number of hours the user has worked. The payRate variable stores the user's hourly pay rate. The grossPay variable holds the result of hours multiplied by payRate, which is the user's gross pay.

Variables are symbolic names made up by the programmer that represent locations in the computer's RAM. When data is stored in a variable, it is actually stored in RAM. Assume that a program has a variable named length. Figure 1-4 illustrates the way the variable name represents a memory location.

In Figure 1-4, the variable `length` is holding the value 72. The number 72 is actually stored in RAM at address 23, but the name `length` symbolically represents this storage location. If it helps, you can think of a variable as a box that holds data. In Figure 1-4, the number 72 is stored in the box named `length`. Only one item may be stored in the box at any given time. If the program stores another value in the box, it will take the place of the number 72.

Figure 1-4   A variable name represents a location in memory

0	1	2	3	4	5	6	7	8	9
10	11	12	13	14	15	16	17	18	19
20	21	22	23 72	24	25	26	27	28	29

length

The Compiler and the Java Virtual Machine

When a Java program is written, it must be typed into the computer and saved to a file. A *text editor,* which is similar to a word processing program, is used for this task. The Java programming statements written by the programmer are called *source code*, and the file they are saved in is called a *source file*. Java source files end with the *.java* extension.

After the programmer saves the source code to a file, he or she runs the Java compiler. A compiler is a program that translates source code into an executable form. During the translation process, the compiler uncovers any syntax errors that may be in the program. Syntax errors are mistakes that the programmer has made that violate the rules of the programming language. These errors must be corrected before the compiler can translate the source code. Once the program is free of syntax errors, the compiler creates another file that holds the translated instructions.

Most programming language compilers translate source code directly into files that contain machine language instructions. These files are called executable files because they may be executed directly by the computer's CPU. The Java compiler, however, translates a Java source file into a file that contains byte code instructions. Byte code instructions are not machine language and therefore cannot be directly executed by the CPU. Instead, they are executed by the Java Virtual Machine. The Java Virtual Machine (JVM) is a program that reads Java byte code instructions and executes them as they are read. For this reason, the JVM is often called an interpreter, and Java is often referred to as an interpreted language. Figure 1-5 illustrates the process of writing a Java program, compiling it to byte code, and running it.

Although Java byte code is not machine language for a CPU, it can be considered as machine language for the JVM. You can think of the JVM as a program that simulates a computer whose machine language is Java byte code.

Portability

The term *portable* means that a program may be written on one type of computer and then run on a wide variety of computers, with little or no modification necessary. Because Java byte code is the same on all computers, compiled Java programs are highly portable. In fact, a compiled Java program may be run on any computer that has a Java Virtual Machine.

Figure 1-5 Program development process

Figure 1-6 Java byte code may be run on any computer with a JVM

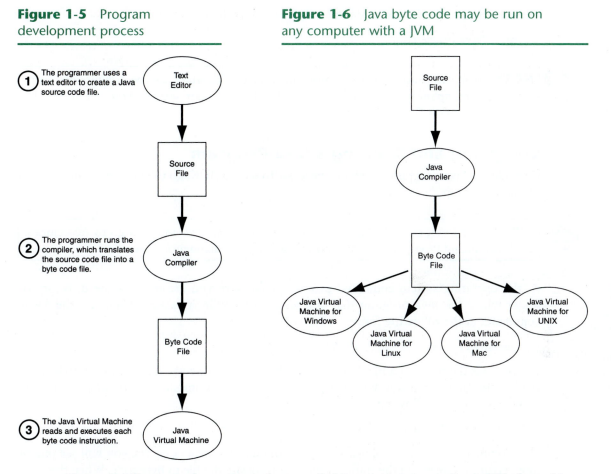

Figure 1-6 illustrates the concept of a compiled Java program running on Windows, Linux, Mac, and UNIX computers.

With most other programming languages, portability is achieved by the creation of a compiler for each type of computer that the language is to run on. For example, in order for the C++ language to be supported by Windows, Linux, and Mac computers, a separate C++ compiler must be created for each of those environments. Compilers are very complex programs and more difficult to develop than interpreters. For this reason, a JVM has been developed for many types of computers.

Java Software Editions

The software that you use to create Java programs is referred to as the *JDK* (Java Development Kit) or the *SDK* (Software Development Kit). These are the following different editions of the JDK available from Oracle:

- *Java SE*—The Java Standard Edition provides all the essential software tools necessary for writing Java applications and applets.
- *Java EE*—The Java Enterprise Edition provides tools for creating large business applications that employ servers and provide services over the Web.
- *Java ME*—The Java Micro Edition provides a small, highly optimized runtime environment for consumer products such as cell phones, pagers, and appliances.

These editions of Java may be downloaded from Oracle at:

http://java.oracle.com

> **NOTE:** You can follow the instructions in Appendix E, which can be downloaded from the book's companion Web site, to install the JDK on your system. You can access the book's companion Web site by going to www.pearsonhighered.com/gaddis.

Compiling and Running a Java Program

Compiling a Java program is a simple process. To use the JDK, go to your operating system's command prompt.

> **TIP:** In Windows, click the Start button, go to All Programs, and then go to Accessories. Click Command Prompt on the Accessories menu. A command prompt window should open.

VideoNote
Compiling
and
Running
a Java
Program

At the operating system command prompt, make sure you are in the same directory or folder where the Java program that you want to compile is located. Then, use the `javac` command, in the following form:

```
javac Filename
```

`Filename` is the name of a file that contains the Java source code. As mentioned earlier, this file has the *.java* extension. For example, if you want to compile the *Payroll.java* file, you would execute the following command:

```
javac Payroll.java
```

This command runs the compiler. If the file contains any syntax errors, you will see one or more error messages and the compiler will not translate the file to byte code. When this happens you must open the source file in a text editor and fix the error. Then you can run the compiler again. If the file has no syntax errors, the compiler will translate it to byte code. Byte code is stored in a file with the *.class* extension, so the byte code for the *Payroll.java* file will be stored in *Payroll.class*, which will be in the same directory or folder as the source file.

To run the Java program, you use the `java` command in the following form:

```
java ClassFilename
```

`ClassFilename` is the name of the *.class* file that you wish to execute. However, you do not type the *.class* extension. For example, to run the program that is stored in the *Payroll.class* file, you would enter the following command:

```
java Payroll
```

This command runs the Java interpreter (the JVM) and executes the program.

Integrated Development Environments

VideoNote
Using an
IDE

In addition to the command prompt programs, there are also several Java integrated development environments (IDEs). These environments consist of a text editor, compiler, debugger, and other utilities integrated into a package with a single set of menus. A program is compiled and executed with a single click of a button, or by selecting a single item from a menu. Figure 1-7 shows a screen from the NetBeans IDE.

Figure 1-7   An IDE

 Checkpoint

1.8   Describe the difference between a key word and a programmer-defined symbol.

1.9   Describe the difference between operators and punctuation symbols.

1.10   Describe the difference between a program line and a statement.

1.11   Why are variables called "variable"?

1.12   What happens to a variable's current contents when a new value is stored there?

1.13   What is a compiler?

1.14   What is a syntax error?

1.15   What is byte code?

1.16   What is the JVM?

1.6 The Programming Process

> **CONCEPT:** The programming process consists of several steps, which include design, creation, testing, and debugging activities.

Now that you have been introduced to what a program is, it's time to consider the process of creating a program. Quite often when inexperienced students are given programming assignments, they have trouble getting started because they don't know what to do first. If you find yourself in this dilemma, the following steps may help.

1. Clearly define what the program is to do.
2. Visualize the program running on the computer.
3. Use design tools to create a model of the program.
4. Check the model for logical errors.
5. Enter the code and compile it.
6. Correct any errors found during compilation. Repeat Steps 5 and 6 as many times as necessary.
7. Run the program with test data for input.
8. Correct any runtime errors found while running the program. Repeat Steps 5 through 8 as many times as necessary.
9. Validate the results of the program.

These steps emphasize the importance of planning. Just as there are good ways and bad ways to paint a house, there are good ways and bad ways to create a program. A good program always begins with planning. With the pay-calculating algorithm that was presented earlier in this chapter serving as our example, let's look at each of the steps in more detail.

1. Clearly define what the program is to do

This step commonly requires you to identify the purpose of the program, the data that is to be input, the processing that is to take place, and the desired output. Let's examine each of these requirements for the pay-calculating algorithm.

Purpose   To calculate the user's gross pay.

Input   Number of hours worked, hourly pay rate.

Process   Multiply number of hours worked by hourly pay rate. The result is the user's gross pay.

Output   Display a message indicating the user's gross pay.

2. Visualize the program running on the computer

Before you create a program on the computer, you should first create it in your mind. Try to imagine what the computer screen will look like while the program is running. If it helps, draw pictures of the screen, with sample input and output, at various points in the program. For instance, Figure 1-8 shows the screen we might want produced by a program that implements the pay-calculating algorithm.

Figure 1-8   Screen produced by the pay-calculating algorithm

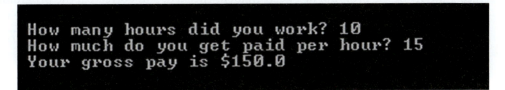

```
How many hours did you work? 10
How much do you get paid per hour? 15
Your gross pay is $150.0
```

In this step, you must put yourself in the shoes of the user. What messages should the program display? What questions should it ask? By addressing these concerns, you can determine most of the program's output.

3. Use design tools to create a model of the program

While planning a program, the programmer uses one or more design tools to create a model of the program. For example, *pseudocode* is a cross between human language and a programming language and is especially helpful when designing an algorithm. Although the computer can't understand pseudocode, programmers often find it helpful to write an algorithm in a language that's "almost" a programming language, but still very similar to natural language. For example, here is pseudocode that describes the pay-calculating algorithm:

> *Get payroll data.*
> *Calculate gross pay.*
> *Display gross pay.*

Although this pseudocode gives a broad view of the program, it does not reveal all the program's details. A more detailed version of the pseudocode follows:

> *Display "How many hours did you work?"*
> *Input hours.*
> *Display "How much do you get paid per hour?"*
> *Input rate.*
> *Store the value of hours times rate in the pay variable.*
> *Display the value in the pay variable.*

Notice that the pseudocode uses statements that look more like commands than the English statements that describe the algorithm in Section 1.4. The pseudocode even names variables and describes mathematical operations.

4. Check the model for logical errors

Logical errors are mistakes that cause the program to produce erroneous results. Once a model of the program is assembled, it should be checked for these errors. For example, if pseudocode is used, the programmer should trace through it, checking the logic of each step. If an error is found, the model can be corrected before the next step is attempted.

5. Enter the code and compile it

Once a model of the program has been created, checked, and corrected, the programmer is ready to write source code on the computer. The programmer saves the source code to a file and begins the process of compiling it. During this step the compiler will find any syntax errors that may exist in the program.

6. Correct any errors found during compilation. Repeat Steps 5 and 6 as many times as necessary

If the compiler reports any errors, they must be corrected. Steps 5 and 6 must be repeated until the program is free of compile-time errors.

7. Run the program with test data for input

Once an executable file is generated, the program is ready to be tested for runtime errors. A runtime error is an error that occurs while the program is running. These are usually logical errors, such as mathematical mistakes.

Testing for runtime errors requires that the program be executed with sample data or sample input. The sample data should be such that the correct output can be predicted. If the program does not produce the correct output, a logical error is present in the program.

8. Correct any runtime errors found while running the program. Repeat Steps 5 through 8 as many times as necessary

When runtime errors are found in a program, they must be corrected. You must identify the step where the error occurred and determine the cause. If an error is a result of incorrect logic (such as an improperly stated math formula), you must correct the statement or statements involved in the logic. If an error is due to an incomplete understanding of the program requirements, then you must restate the program purpose and modify the program model and source code. The program must then be saved, recompiled, and retested. This means Steps 5 though 8 must be repeated until the program reliably produces satisfactory results.

9. Validate the results of the program

When you believe you have corrected all the runtime errors, enter test data and determine if the program solves the original problem.

 Checkpoint

1.17 What four items should you identify when defining what a program is to do?

1.18 What does it mean to "visualize a program running"? What is the value of such an activity?

1.19 What is pseudocode?

1.20 Describe what a compiler does with a program's source code.

1.21 What is a runtime error?

1.22 Is a syntax error (such as misspelling a key word) found by the compiler or when the program is running?

1.23 What is the purpose of testing a program with sample data or input?

1.7 Object-Oriented Programming

CONCEPT: Java is an object-oriented programming (OOP) language. OOP is a method of software development that has its own practices, concepts, and vocabulary.

There are primarily two methods of programming in use today: procedural and object-oriented. The earliest programming languages were procedural, meaning a program was made of one or more procedures. A *procedure* is a set of programming statements that, together, perform a specific task. The statements might gather input from the user, manipulate data stored in the computer's memory, and perform calculations or any other operation necessary to complete its task.

Procedures typically operate on data items that are separate from the procedures. In a procedural program, the data items are commonly passed from one procedure to another, as shown in Figure 1-9.

Figure 1-9   Data is passed among procedures

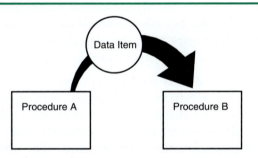

As you might imagine, the focus of procedural programming is on the creation of procedures that operate on the program's data. The separation of data and the code that operates on the data often leads to problems, however. For example, the data is stored in a particular format, which consists of variables and more complex structures that are created from variables. The procedures that operate on the data must be designed with that format in mind. But, what happens if the format of the data is altered? Quite often, a program's specifications change, resulting in a redesigned data format. When the structure of the data changes, the code that operates on the data must also be changed to accept the new format. This results in added work for programmers and a greater opportunity for bugs to appear in the code.

This has helped influence the shift from procedural programming to OOP. Whereas procedural programming is centered on creating procedures, object-oriented programming is centered on creating objects. An object is a software entity that contains data and procedures. The data contained in an object is known as the object's *attributes*. The procedures, or behaviors, that an object performs are known as the object's *methods*. The object is, conceptually, a self-contained unit consisting of data (attributes) and procedures (methods). This is illustrated in Figure 1-10.

OOP addresses the problem of code/data separation through encapsulation and data hiding. *Encapsulation* refers to the combining of data and code into a single object. *Data*

Figure 1-10   An object contains data and procedures

Figure 1-11   Code outside the object interacts with the object's methods

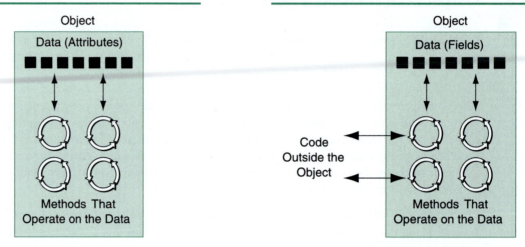

hiding refers to an object's ability to hide its data from code that is outside the object. Only the object's methods may then directly access and make changes to the object's data. An object typically hides its data, but allows outside code to access the methods that operate on the data. As shown in Figure 1-11, the object's methods provide programming statements outside the object indirect access to the object's data.

When an object's internal data is hidden from outside code and access to that data is restricted to the object's methods, the data is protected from accidental corruption. In addition, the programming code outside the object does not need to know about the format or internal structure of the object's data. The code only needs to interact with the object's methods. When a programmer changes the structure of an object's internal data, he or she also modifies the object's methods so they may properly operate on the data. The way in which outside code interacts with the methods, however, does not change.

Component Reusability

In addition to solving the problems of code and data separation, the use of OOP has also been encouraged by the trend of *component reusability*. A component is a software object that performs a specific, well-defined operation or that provides a particular service. The component is not a stand-alone program, but can be used by programs that need the component's service. For example, Sharon is a programmer who has developed a component for rendering three-dimensional (3D) images. She is a math whiz and knows a lot about computer graphics, so her component is coded to perform all the necessary 3D mathematical operations and handle the computer's video hardware. Tom, who is writing a program for an architectural firm, needs his application to display 3D images of buildings. Because he is working under a tight deadline and does not possess a great deal of knowledge about computer graphics, he can use Sharon's component to perform the 3D rendering (for a small fee, of course!).

Component reusability and OOP technology set the stage for large-scale computer applications to become systems of unique collaborating entities (components).

An Everyday Example of an Object

Think of your alarm clock as an object. It has the following attributes:

- The current second (a value in the range of 0–59)
- The current minute (a value in the range of 0–59)
- The current hour (a value in the range of 1–12)
- The time the alarm is set for (a valid hour and minute)
- Whether the alarm is on or off ("on" or "off")

As you can see, the attributes are merely data values that define the alarm clock's state. You, the user of the alarm clock object, cannot directly manipulate these attributes because they are *private*. To change an attribute's value, you must use one of the object's methods. Here are some of the alarm clock object's methods:

- Set time
- Set alarm time
- Turn alarm on
- Turn alarm off

Each method manipulates one or more of the attributes. For example, the "set time" method allows you to set the alarm clock's time. You activate the method by pressing a set of buttons on top of the clock. By using another set of buttons, you can activate the "set alarm time" method. In addition, another button allows you to execute the "turn alarm on" and "turn alarm off" methods. Notice that all of these methods can be activated by you, who are outside of the alarm clock. Methods that can be accessed by entities outside the object are known as *public methods*.

The alarm clock also has *private methods*, which are part of the object's private, internal workings. External entities (such as you, the user of the alarm clock) do not have direct access to the alarm clock's private methods. The object is designed to execute these methods automatically and hide the details from you. Here are the alarm clock object's private methods:

- Increment the current second
- Increment the current minute
- Increment the current hour
- Sound alarm

Every second the "increment the current second" method executes. This changes the value of the current second attribute. If the current second attribute is set to 59 when this method executes, the method is programmed to reset the current second to 0, and then cause the "increment current minute" method to execute. This method adds 1 to the current minute, unless it is set to 59. In that case, it resets the current minute to 0 and causes the "increment current hour" method to execute. (It might also be noted that the "increment current minute" method compares the new time to the alarm time. If the two times match and the alarm is turned on, the "sound alarm" method is executed.)

Classes and Objects

Now let us discuss how objects are created in software. Before an object can be created, it must be designed by a programmer. The programmer determines the attributes and methods that are necessary and then creates a class. A *class* is a collection of programming statements that specify the attributes and methods that a particular type of object may have. Think of a class as a "blueprint" that objects may be created from. So, a class is not an object, but a description of an object. When the program is running, it can use the class to create, in memory, as many objects as needed. Each object that is created from a class is called an *instance* of the class.

For example, Jessica is an entomologist (someone who studies insects), and she also enjoys writing computer programs. She designs a program to catalog different types of insects. In the program, she creates a class named Insect, which specifies attributes and methods for holding and manipulating data common to all types of insects. The Insect class is not an object, but a specification that objects may be created from. Next, she writes programming statements that create a housefly object, which is an instance of the Insect class. The housefly object is an entity that occupies computer memory and stores data about a housefly. It has the attributes and methods specified by the Insect class. Then she writes programming statements that create a mosquito object. The mosquito object is also an instance of the Insect class. It has its own area in memory and stores data about a mosquito. Although the housefly and mosquito objects are two separate entities in the computer's memory, they were both created from the Insect class. This means that each of the objects have the attributes and methods described by the Insect class. This is illustrated in Figure 1-12.

Figure 1-12   The housefly and mosquito objects are instances of the Insect class

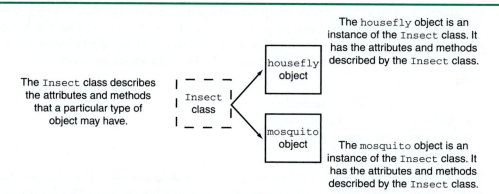

The Insect class describes the attributes and methods that a particular type of object may have.

Insect class

housefly object

The housefly object is an instance of the Insect class. It has the attributes and methods described by the Insect class.

mosquito object

The mosquito object is an instance of the Insect class. It has the attributes and methods described by the Insect class.

Inheritance

Sometimes a class is based on another class. This means that one class is a specialized case of the other. For example, consider a program that uses classes representing cars, trucks, and jet planes. Although those three types of objects in the real world are very different, they have some common characteristics: They are all modes of transportation, and they all carry some number of passengers. So, each of the three classes could be based on a Vehicle class that has the attributes and behaviors common to all of the classes. This is illustrated in Figure 1-13.

Figure 1-13   An example of inheritance

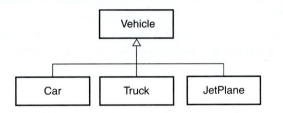

In OOP terminology, the Vehicle class is the *superclass*. The Car, Truck, and JetPlane classes are *subclasses*. Although the Vehicle class is very general in nature, the Car, Truck, and JetPlane classes are specialized. All of the attributes and behaviors of the Vehicle class are inherited by the Car, Truck, and JetPlane classes. The relationship between the classes implies that a Car is a Vehicle, a Truck is a Vehicle, and a JetPlane is a Vehicle.

In addition to inheriting the attributes and methods of the superclass, subclasses add their own. For example, the Car class might have attributes and methods that set and indicate whether it is a sedan or coupe, and the type of engine it has. The Truck class might have attributes and methods that set and indicate the maximum amount of weight it can carry, and the number of miles it can travel between refueling. The JetPlane class might have attributes and methods that set and indicate the plane's altitude and heading. These added capabilities make the subclasses more specialized than the superclass.

Software Engineering

The field of software engineering encompasses the whole process of crafting computer software. It includes designing, writing, testing, debugging, documenting, modifying, and maintaining complex software development projects. Like traditional engineers, software engineers use a number of tools in their craft. Here are a few examples:

- Program specifications
- Diagrams of screen output
- Diagrams representing classes, objects, and the flow of data
- Pseudocode
- Examples of expected input and desired output
- Special software designed for testing programs

Most commercial software applications are large and complex. Usually a team of programmers, not a single individual, develops them. It is important that the program requirements be thoroughly analyzed and divided into subtasks that are handled by individual teams, or individuals within a team.

Checkpoint

1.24   In procedural programming, what two parts of a program are typically separated?

1.25   What are an object's attributes?

1.26   What are an object's methods?

1.27   What is encapsulation?

1.28   What is data hiding?

Review Questions and Exercises

Multiple Choice

1. This part of the computer fetches instructions, carries out the operations commanded by the instructions, and produces some outcome or resultant information.
   a. memory
   b. CPU
   c. secondary storage
   d. input device

2. A byte is made up of eight
   a. CPUs
   b. addresses
   c. variables
   d. bits

3. Each byte is assigned a unique
   a. address
   b. CPU
   c. bit
   d. variable

4. This type of memory can hold data for long periods of time—even when there is no power to the computer.
   a. RAM
   b. primary storage
   c. secondary storage
   d. CPU storage

5. If you were to look at a machine language program, you would see _____.
   a. Java source code
   b. a stream of binary numbers
   c. English words
   d. circuits

6. This type of program is designed to be transmitted over the Internet and run in a Web browser.
   a. application
   b. applet
   c. machine language
   d. source code

7. These are words that have a special meaning in the programming language.
   a. punctuation
   b. programmer-defined names
   c. key words
   d. operators

8. These are symbols or words that perform operations on one or more operands.
   a. punctuation
   b. programmer-defined names
   c. key words
   d. operators

9. These characters serve specific purposes, such as marking the beginning or ending of a statement, or separating items in a list.
    a. punctuation
    b. programmer-defined names
    c. key words
    d. operators

10. These are words or names that are used to identify storage locations in memory and parts of the program that are created by the programmer.
    a. punctuation
    b. programmer-defined names
    c. key words
    d. operators

11. These are the rules that must be followed when writing a program.
    a. syntax
    b. punctuation
    c. key words
    d. operators

12. This is a named storage location in the computer's memory.
    a. class
    b. key word
    c. variable
    d. operator

13. The Java compiler generates _____.
    a. machine code
    b. byte code
    c. source code
    d. HTML

14. JVM stands for _____.
    a. Java Variable Machine
    b. Java Variable Method
    c. Java Virtual Method
    d. Java Virtual Machine

Find the Error

1. The following pseudocode algorithm has an error. The program is supposed to ask the user for the length and width of a rectangular room, and then display the room's area. The program must multiply the width by the length in order to determine the area. Find the error.

    area = width × length.
    Display "What is the room's width?"
    Input width.
    Display "What is the room's length?"
    Input length.
    Display area.

Algorithm Workbench

Write pseudocode algorithms for the programs described as follows:

1. **Available Credit**

   A program that calculates a customer's available credit should ask the user for the following:

   - The customer's maximum amount of credit
   - The amount of credit used by the customer

   Once these items have been entered, the program should calculate and display the customer's available credit. You can calculate available credit by subtracting the amount of credit used from the maximum amount of credit.

2. **Sales Tax**

   A program that calculates the total of a retail sale should ask the user for the following:

   - The retail price of the item being purchased
   - The sales tax rate

   Once these items have been entered, the program should calculate and display the following:

   - The sales tax for the purchase
   - The total of the sale

3. **Account Balance**

   A program that calculates the current balance in a savings account must ask the user for the following:

   - The starting balance
   - The total dollar amount of deposits made
   - The total dollar amount of withdrawals made
   - The monthly interest rate

   Once the program calculates the current balance, it should be displayed on the screen.

Predict the Result

The following are programs expressed as English statements. What would each display on the screen if they were actual programs?

1. The variable x starts with the value 0.
   The variable y starts with the value 5.
   Add 1 to x.
   Add 1 to y.
   Add x and y, and store the result in y.
   Display the value in y on the screen.

2. The variable a starts with the value 10.
   The variable b starts with the value 2.
   The variable c starts with the value 4.
   Store the value of a times b in a.

Store the value of b times c in c.
Add a and c, and store the result in b.
Display the value in b on the screen.

Short Answer

1. Both main memory and secondary storage are types of memory. Describe the difference between the two.

2. What type of memory is usually volatile?

3. What is the difference between operating system software and application software?

4. Indicate all the categories that the following operating systems belong to.

    System A   This system allows multiple users to run multiple programs simultaneously.

    System B   Only one user may access the system at a time, but multiple programs can be run simultaneously.

    System C   Only one user may access the system at a time, and only one program can be run on the system at a time.

5. Why must programs written in a high-level language be translated into machine language before they can be run?

6. Why is it easier to write a program in a high-level language than in machine language?

7. What is a source file?

8. What is the difference between a syntax error and a logical error?

9. What is an algorithm?

10. What is a compiler?

11. What is the difference between an application and an applet?

12. Why are Java applets safe to download and execute?

13. What must a computer have in order for it to execute Java programs?

14. What is the difference between machine language code and byte code?

15. Why does byte code make Java a portable language?

16. Is encapsulation a characteristic of procedural or object-oriented programming?

17. Why should an object hide its data?

18. What part of an object forms an interface through which outside code may access the object's data?

19. What is component reusability?

20. What is a class?

21. How is a class different from an object?

22. What object-oriented programming characteristic allows you to create a class that is a specialized version of another class?

23. What type of program do you use to write Java source code?

24. Will the Java compiler translate a source file that contains syntax errors?

25. What does the Java compiler translate Java source code to?

26. Assuming you have installed the Java JDK, what command would you type at the operating system command prompt to compile the program *LabAssignment.java*?

27. Assuming there are no syntax errors in the *LabAssignment.java* program when it is compiled, answer the following questions.
    a. What file will be produced?
    b. What will the file contain?
    c. What command would you type at the operating system command prompt to run the program?

Programming Challenge

1. Your First Java Program

This assignment will help you get acquainted with your Java development software. Here is the Java program you will enter:

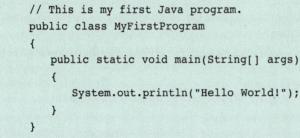

VideoNote
Your
First Java
Program

```java
// This is my first Java program.
public class MyFirstProgram
{
    public static void main(String[] args)
    {
        System.out.println("Hello World!");
    }
}
```

If You Are Using the JDK at the Command Prompt:

1. Use a text editor to type the source code exactly as it is shown. Be sure to place all the punctuation characters and be careful to match the case of the letters as they are shown. Save it to a file named *MyFirstProgram.java*.

2. After saving the program, go to your operating system's command prompt and change your current directory or folder to the one that contains the Java program you just created. Then use the following command to compile the program:

   `javac MyFirstProgram.java`

   If you typed the contents of the file exactly as shown, you shouldn't have any syntax errors. If you see error messages, open the file in the editor and compare your code to that shown. Correct any mistakes you have made, save the file, and run the compiler again. If you see no error messages, the file was successfully compiled.

3. Next, enter the following command to run the program:

   `java MyFirstProgram`

   Be sure to use the capitalization of `MyFirstProgram` exactly as it is shown here. You should see the message "Hello World!" displayed on the screen.

If You Are Using an IDE:

Because there are many Java IDEs, we cannot include specific instructions for all of these. The following are general steps that should apply to most of them. You will need to consult your IDE's documentation for specific instructions.

1. Start your Java IDE and perform any necessary setup operations, such as starting a new project and creating a new Java source file.

2. Use the IDE's text editor to type the source code exactly as it is shown. Be sure to place all the punctuation characters and be careful to match the case of the letters as they are shown. Save it to a file named *MyFirstProgram.java*.

3. After saving the program, use your IDE's command to compile the program. If you typed the contents of the file exactly as shown, you shouldn't have any syntax errors. If you see error messages, compare your code to that shown. Correct any mistakes you have made, save the file, and run the compiler again. If you see no error messages, the file was successfully compiled.

   Use your IDE's command to run the program. You should see the message "Hello World!" displayed.

TOPICS

2.1 The Parts of a Java Program
2.2 The `System.out.print` and `System.out.println` Methods, and the Java API
2.3 Variables and Literals
2.4 Primitive Data Types
2.5 Arithmetic Operators
2.6 Combined Assignment Operators
2.7 Conversion between Primitive Data Types

2.8 Creating Named Constants with `final`
2.9 The `String` Class
2.10 Scope
2.11 Comments
2.12 Programming Style
2.13 Reading Keyboard Input
2.14 Dialog Boxes
2.15 The `System.out.printf` Method
2.16 Common Errors to Avoid

2.1 The Parts of a Java Program

CONCEPT: A Java program has parts that serve specific purposes.

Java programs are made up of different parts. Your first step in learning Java is to learn what the parts are. We will begin by looking at a simple example, shown in Code Listing 2-1.

Code Listing 2-1 (`Simple.java`)

```java
1  // This is a simple Java program.
2
3  public class Simple
4  {
5     public static void main(String[] args)
6     {
7        System.out.println("Programming is great fun!");
8     }
9  }
```

31

> **TIP:** Remember, the line numbers shown in the program listings are not part of the program. The numbers are shown so we can refer to specific lines in the programs.

As mentioned in Chapter 1, the names of Java source code files end with *.java*. The program shown in Code Listing 2-1 is named *Simple.java*. Using the Sun Java compiler, this program may be compiled with the following command:

```
javac Simple.java
```

The compiler will create another file named *Simple.class*, which contains the translated Java byte code. This file can be executed with the following command:

```
java Simple
```

> **TIP:** Remember, you do not type the *.class* extension when using the java command.

The output of the program is as follows. This is what appears on the screen when the program runs.

Program Output

```
Programming is great fun!
```

Let's examine the program line by line. Here's the statement in line 1:

```
// This is a simple Java program.
```

Other than the two slash marks that begin this line, it looks pretty much like an ordinary sentence. The // marks the beginning of a comment. The compiler ignores everything from the double slash to the end of the line. That means you can type anything you want on that line and the compiler never complains. Although comments are not required, they are very important to programmers. Most programs are much more complicated than this example, and comments help explain what's going on.

Line 2 is blank. Programmers often insert blank lines in programs to make them easier to read. Line 3 reads:

```
public class Simple
```

This line is known as a *class header*, and it marks the beginning of a *class definition*. One of the uses of a class is to serve as a container for an application. As you progress through this book you will learn more and more about classes. For now, just remember that a Java program must have at least one class definition. This line of code consists of three words: public, class, and Simple. Let's take a closer look at each word.

- public is a Java key word, and it must be written in all lowercase letters. It is known as an *access specifier*, and it controls where the class may be accessed from. The public specifier means access to the class is unrestricted. (In other words, the class is "open to the public.")
- class, which must also be written in lowercase letters, is a Java key word that indicates the beginning of a class definition.

- `Simple` is the class name. This name was made up by the programmer. The class could have been called `Pizza`, or `Dog`, or anything else the programmer wanted. Programmer-defined names may be written in lowercase letters, uppercase letters, or a mixture of both.

In a nutshell, this line of code tells the compiler that a publicly accessible class named `Simple` is being defined. Here are two more points to know about classes:

- You may create more than one class in a file, but you may only have one `public class` per Java file.
- When a Java file has a `public` class, the name of the public class must be the same as the name of the file (without the *.java* extension). For instance, the program in Code Listing 2-1 has a `public class` named `Simple`, so it is stored in a file named *Simple.java*.

 NOTE: Java is a case-sensitive language. That means it regards uppercase letters as entirely different characters than their lowercase counterparts. The word `Public` is not the same as `public`, and `Class` is not the same as `class`. Some words in a Java program must be entirely in lowercase, while other words may use a combination of lower and uppercase characters. Later in this chapter you will see a list of all the Java key words, which must appear in lowercase.

Line 4 contains only a single character:

```
{
```

This is called a left brace, or an opening brace, and is associated with the beginning of the class definition. All of the programming statements that are part of the class are enclosed in a set of braces. If you glance at the last line in the program, line 9, you'll see the closing brace. Everything between the two braces is the *body* of the class named `Simple`. Here is the program code again; this time the body of the class definition is shaded.

```
// This is a simple Java program.
public class Simple
{
    public static void main(String[] args)
    {
        System.out.println("Programming is great fun!");
    }
}
```

WARNING! Make sure you have a closing brace for every opening brace in your program!

Line 5 reads:

```
public static void main(String[] args)
```

This line is known as a *method header*. It marks the beginning of a *method*. A method can be thought of as a group of one or more programming statements that collectively has a name. When creating a method, you must tell the compiler several things about it. That is why this line contains so many words. At this point, the only thing you should be concerned about is that the name of the method is main, and the rest of the words are required for the method to be properly defined. This is shown in Figure 2-1.

Recall from Chapter 1 that a stand-alone Java program that runs on your computer is known as an application. Every Java application must have a method named main. The main method is the starting point of an application.

Figure 2-1 The main method header

Name of the Method

```
public static void main (String[] args)
```

The other parts of this line are necessary
for the method to be properly defined.

 NOTE: For the time being, all the programs you will write will consist of a class with a main method whose header looks exactly like the one shown in Code Listing 2-1. As you progress through this book you will learn what public static void and (String[] args) mean. For now, just assume that you are learning a "recipe" for assembling a Java program.

Line 6 has another opening brace:

```
{
```

This opening brace belongs to the main method. Remember that braces enclose statements, and every opening brace must have an accompanying closing brace. If you look at line 8 you will see the closing brace that corresponds to this opening brace. Everything between these braces is the *body* of the main method.

Line 7 appears as follows:

```
System.out.println("Programming is great fun!");
```

To put it simply, this line displays a message on the screen. The message "Programming is great fun!" is printed without the quotation marks. In programming terms, the group of characters inside the quotation marks is called a *string literal*.

 NOTE: This is the only line in the program that causes anything to be printed on the screen. The other lines, like public class Simple and public static void main(String[] args), are necessary for the framework of your program, but they do not cause any screen output. Remember, a program is a set of instructions for the computer. If something is to be displayed on the screen, you must use a programming statement for that purpose.

At the end of the line is a *semicolon*. Just as a period marks the end of a sentence, a semicolon marks the end of a statement in Java. Not every line of code ends with a semicolon, however. Here is a summary of where you do not place a semicolon:

- Comments do not have to end with a semicolon because they are ignored by the compiler.
- Class headers and method headers do not end with a semicolon because they are terminated with a body of code inside braces.
- The brace characters, { and }, are not statements, so you do not place a semicolon after them.

It might seem that the rules for where to put a semicolon are not clear at all. For now, just concentrate on learning the parts of a program. You'll soon get a feel for where you should and should not use semicolons.

As has already been pointed out, lines 8 and 9 contain the closing braces for the main method and the class definition:

```
      }
   }
```

Before continuing, let's review the points we just covered, including some of the more elusive rules.

- Java is a case-sensitive language. It does not regard uppercase letters as being the same character as their lowercase equivalents.
- All Java programs must be stored in a file with a name that ends with *.java*.
- Comments are ignored by the compiler.
- A *.java* file may contain many classes, but may only have one public class. If a *.java* file has a public class, the class must have the same name as the file. For instance, if the file *Pizza.java* contains a public class, the class's name would be Pizza.
- Every Java application program must have a method named main.
- For every left brace, or opening brace, there must be a corresponding right brace, or closing brace.
- Statements are terminated with semicolons. This does not include comments, class headers, method headers, or braces.

In the sample program you encountered several special characters. Table 2-1 summarizes how they were used.

Table 2-1   Special characters

Characters	Name	Meaning
//	Double slash	Marks the beginning of a comment
( )	Opening and closing parentheses	Used in a method header
{ }	Opening and closing braces	Encloses a group of statements, such as the contents of a class or a method
" "	Quotation marks	Encloses a string of characters, such as a message that is to be printed on the screen
;	Semicolon	Marks the end of a complete programming statement

Checkpoint

2.1   The following program will not compile because the lines have been mixed up.

```
public static void main(String[] args)
}
// A crazy mixed up program
public class Columbus
{
System.out.println("In 1492 Columbus sailed the ocean blue.");
{
}
```

When the lines are properly arranged the program should display the following on the screen:

```
In 1492 Columbus sailed the ocean blue.
```

Rearrange the lines in the correct order. Test the program by entering it on the computer, compiling it, and running it.

2.2   When the program in Question 2.1 is saved to a file, what should the file be named?

2.3   Complete the following program skeleton so it displays the message "Hello World" on the screen.

```
public class Hello
{
    public static void main(String[] args)
    {
        // Insert code here to complete the program
    }
}
```

2.4   On paper, write a program that will display your name on the screen. Place a comment with today's date at the top of the program. Test your program by entering, compiling, and running it.

2.5   All Java source code filenames must end with _____.
   a.   a semicolon
   b.   *.class*
   c.   *.java*
   d.   none of the above

2.6   Every Java application program must have _____.
   a.   a method named `main`
   b.   more than one class definition
   c.   one or more comments

2.2 The `System.out.print` and `System.out.println` Methods, and the Java API

> **CONCEPT:** The `System.out.print` and `System.out.println` methods are used to display text output. They are part of the Java API, which is a collection of prewritten classes and methods for performing specific operations.

In this section you will learn how to write programs that produce output on the screen. The simplest type of output that a program can display on the screen is console output. *Console output* is merely plain text. When you display console output in a system that uses a graphical user interface, such as Windows or Mac OS, the output usually appears in a window similar to the one shown in Figure 2-2.

Figure 2-2 A console window

eoNote
splaying
onsole
utput

The word *console* is an old computer term. It comes from the days when the operator of a large computer system interacted with the system by typing on a terminal that consisted of a simple screen and keyboard. This terminal was known as the *console*. The console screen, which displayed only text, was known as the standard output device. Today, the term *standard output device* typically refers to the device that displays console output.

Performing output in Java, as well as many other tasks, is accomplished by using the Java API. The term API stands for *Application Programmer Interface*. The API is a standard library of prewritten classes for performing specific operations. These classes and their methods are available to all Java programs. The `print` and `println` methods are part of the API and provide ways for output to be displayed on the standard output device.

The program in Code Listing 2-1 (`Simple.java`) uses the following statement to print a message on the screen:

```java
System.out.println("Programming is great fun!");
```

System is a class that is part of the Java API. The System class contains objects and methods that perform system-level operations. One of the objects contained in the System class is named out. The out object has methods, such as print and println, for performing output on the system console, or standard output device. The hierarchical relationship among System, out, print, and println is shown in Figure 2-3.

Figure 2-3   Relationship among the System class, the out object, and the print and println methods

The System class holds the out object as well as other members.

The out object is a member of the System class.

print
The print method is a member of the out object.

println
The println method is a member of the out object.

Here is a brief summary of how it all works together:

- The System class is part of the Java API. It has member objects and methods for performing system-level operations, such as sending output to the console.
- The out object is a member of the System class. It provides methods for sending output to the screen.
- The print and println methods are members of the out object. They actually perform the work of writing characters on the screen.

This hierarchy explains why the statement that executes println is so long. The sequence System.out.println specifies that println is a member of out, which is a member of System.

NOTE: The period that separates the names of the objects is pronounced "dot." System.out.println is pronounced "system dot out dot print line."

The value that is to be displayed on the screen is placed inside the parentheses. This value is known as an *argument*. For example, the following statement executes the println method using the string "King Arthur" as its argument. This will print "King Arthur" on the screen. (The quotation marks are not displayed on the screen.)

```
System.out.println("King Arthur");
```

An important thing to know about the println method is that after it displays its message, it advances the cursor to the beginning of the next line. The next item printed on the screen will begin in this position. For example, look at the program in Code Listing 2-2.

Code Listing 2-2   **(TwoLines.java)**

```
 1   // This is another simple Java program.
 2
 3   public class TwoLines
 4   {
 5      public static void main(String[] args)
 6      {
 7         System.out.println("Programming is great fun!");
 8         System.out.println("I can't get enough of it!");
 9      }
10   }
```

Program Output

```
Programming is great fun!
I can't get enough of it!
```

Because each string was printed with separate println statements, they appear on separate lines.

The print Method

The print method, which is also part of the System.out object, serves a purpose similar to that of println—to display output on the screen. The print method, however, does not advance the cursor to the next line after its message is displayed. Look at Code Listing 2-3.

Code Listing 2-3   **(GreatFun.java)**

```
 1   // This is another simple Java program.
 2
 3   public class GreatFun
 4   {
 5      public static void main(String[] args)
 6      {
 7         System.out.print("Programming is ");
 8         System.out.println("great fun!");
 9      }
10   }
```

Program Output

```
Programming is great fun!
```

An important concept to understand about Code Listing 2-3 is that, although the output is broken up into two programming statements, this program will still display the message on one line. The data that you send to the print method is displayed in a continuous stream. Sometimes this can produce less-than-desirable results. The program in Code Listing 2-4 is an example.

Code Listing 2-4   (Unruly.java)

```
1   // An unruly printing program
2
3   public class Unruly
4   {
5      public static void main(String[] args)
6      {
7         System.out.print("These are our top sellers:");
8         System.out.print("Computer games");
9         System.out.print("Coffee");
10        System.out.println("Aspirin");
11     }
12  }
```

Program Output

```
These are our top sellers:Computer gamesCoffeeAspirin
```

The layout of the actual output looks nothing like the arrangement of the strings in the source code. First, even though the output is broken up into four lines in the source code (lines 7 through 10), it comes out on the screen as one line. Second, notice that some of the words that are displayed are not separated by spaces. The strings are displayed exactly as they are sent to the print method. If spaces are to be displayed, they must appear in the strings.

There are two ways to fix this program. The most obvious way is to use println methods instead of print methods. Another way is to use escape sequences to separate the output into different lines. An *escape sequence* starts with the backslash character (\) and is followed by one or more *control characters*. It allows you to control the way output is displayed by embedding commands within the string itself. The escape sequence that causes the output cursor to go to the next line is \n. Code Listing 2-5 illustrates its use.

Code Listing 2-5   (Adjusted.java)

```
1   // A well adjusted printing program
2
3   public class Adjusted
4   {
5      public static void main(String[] args)
6      {
```

```
 7          System.out.print("These are our top sellers:\n");
 8          System.out.print("Computer games\nCoffee\n");
 9          System.out.println("Aspirin");
10      }
11 }
```

Program Output

```
These are our top sellers:
Computer games
Coffee
Aspirin
```

The \n characters are called the newline escape sequence. When the print or println methods encounter \n in a string, they do not print the \n characters on the screen, but interpret them as a special command to advance the output cursor to the next line. There are several other escape sequences as well. For instance, \t is the tab escape sequence. When print or println encounters it in a string, it causes the output cursor to advance to the next tab position. Code Listing 2-6 shows it in use.

Code Listing 2-6   **(Tabs.java)**

```
 1  // Another well-adjusted printing program
 2
 3  public class Tabs
 4  {
 5      public static void main(String[] args)
 6      {
 7          System.out.print("These are our top sellers:\n");
 8          System.out.print("\tComputer games\n\tCoffee\n");
 9          System.out.println("\tAspirin");
10      }
11  }
```

Program Output

```
These are our top sellers:
        Computer games
        Coffee
        Aspirin
```

NOTE: Although you have to type two characters to write an escape sequence, they are stored in memory as a single character.

Table 2-2 lists the common escape sequences and describes them.

Table 2-2   Common escape sequences

Escape Sequence	Name	Description
\n	Newline	Advances the cursor to the next line for subsequent printing
\t	Horizontal tab	Causes the cursor to skip over to the next tab stop
\b	Backspace	Causes the cursor to back up, or move left, one position
\r	Return	Causes the cursor to go to the beginning of the current line, not the next line
\\	Backslash	Causes a backslash to be printed
\'	Single quote	Causes a single quotation mark to be printed
\"	Double quote	Causes a double quotation mark to be printed

> **WARNING!** Do not confuse the backslash (\) with the forward slash (/). An escape sequence will not work if you accidentally start it with a forward slash. Also, do not put a space between the backslash and the control character.

Checkpoint

2.7   The following program will not compile because the lines have been mixed up.

```
System.out.print("Success\n");
}
public class Success
{
System.out.print("Success\n");
public static void main(String[] args)
System.out.print("Success ");
}
// It's a mad, mad program.
System.out.println("\nSuccess");
{
```

When the lines are arranged properly the program should display the following output on the screen:

Program Output:

```
Success
Success Success

Success
```

Rearrange the lines in the correct order. Test the program by entering it on the computer, compiling it, and running it.

2.8   Study the following program and show what it will print on the screen.

```java
// The Works of Wolfgang
public class Wolfgang
{
    public static void main(String[] args)
    {
        System.out.print("The works of Wolfgang\ninclude ");
        System.out.print("the following");
        System.out.print("\nThe Turkish March ");
        System.out.print("and Symphony No. 40 ");
        System.out.println("in G minor.");
    }
}
```

2.9   On paper, write a program that will display your name on the first line; your street address on the second line; your city, state, and ZIP code on the third line; and your telephone number on the fourth line. Place a comment with today's date at the top of the program. Test your program by entering, compiling, and running it.

2.3   Variables and Literals

CONCEPT: A *variable* is a named storage location in the computer's memory. A *literal* is a value that is written into the code of a program.

As you discovered in Chapter 1, variables allow you to store and work with data in the computer's memory. Part of the job of programming is to determine how many variables a program will need and what types of data they will hold. The program in Code Listing 2-7 is an example of a Java program with a variable.

Code Listing 2-7   (Variable.java)

```java
1  // This program has a variable.
2
3  public class Variable
4  {
5     public static void main(String[] args)
6     {
7        int value;
8
9        value = 5;
10       System.out.print("The value is ");
11       System.out.println(value);
12    }
13 }
```

Program Output

```
The value is 5
```

Let's look more closely at this program. Here is line 7:

```
int value;
```

VideoNote
Declaring
Variables

This is called a variable declaration. Variables must be declared before they can be used. A variable declaration tells the compiler the variable's name and the type of data it will hold. This line indicates the variable's name is value. The word int stands for integer, so value will only be used to hold integer numbers. Notice that variable declarations end with a semicolon. The next statement in this program appears in line 9:

```
value = 5;
```

This is called an assignment statement. The equal sign is an operator that stores the value on its right (in this case 5) into the variable named on its left. After this line executes, the value variable will contain the value 5.

> **NOTE:** This line does not print anything on the computer screen. It runs silently behind the scenes.

Now look at lines 10 and 11:

```
System.out.print("The value is ");
System.out.println(value);
```

The statement in line 10 sends the string literal "The value is" to the print method. The statement in line 11 sends the name of the value variable to the println method. When you send a variable name to print or println, the variable's contents are displayed. Notice there are no quotation marks around value. Look at what happens in Code Listing 2-8.

Code Listing 2-8   (Variable2.java)

```
 1  // This program has a variable.
 2
 3  public class Variable2
 4  {
 5     public static void main(String[] args)
 6     {
 7        int value;
 8
 9        value = 5;
10        System.out.print("The value is ");
11        System.out.println("value");
12     }
13  }
```

Program Output

```
The value is value
```

When double quotation marks are placed around the word value it becomes a string literal, not a variable name. When string literals are sent to print or println, they are displayed exactly as they appear inside the quotation marks.

Displaying Multiple Items with the + Operator

When the + operator is used with strings, it is known as the *string concatenation operator*. To concatenate means to append, so the string concatenation operator appends one string to another. For example, look at the following statement:

```
System.out.println("This is " + "one string.");
```

This statement will print:

```
This is one string.
```

The + operator produces a string that is the combination of the two strings used as its operands. You can also use the + operator to concatenate the contents of a variable to a string. The following code shows an example:

```
number = 5;
System.out.println("The value is " + number);
```

The second line uses the + operator to concatenate the contents of the number variable with the string "The value is". Although number is not a string, the + operator converts its value to a string and then concatenates that value with the first string. The output that will be displayed is:

```
The value is 5
```

Sometimes the argument you use with print or println is too long to fit on one line in your program code. However, a string literal cannot begin on one line and end on another. For example, the following will cause an error:

```
// This is an error!
System.out.println("Enter a value that is greater than zero
                and less than 10.");
```

You can remedy this problem by breaking the argument up into smaller string literals and then using the string concatenation operator to spread them out over more than one line. Here is an example:

```
System.out.println("Enter a value that is " +
                "greater than zero and less " +
                "than 10.");
```

In this statement, the argument is broken up into three strings and joined using the + operator. The following example shows the same technique used when the contents of a variable are part of the concatenation:

```
sum = 249;
System.out.println("The sum of the three " +
                "numbers is " + sum);
```

Be Careful with Quotation Marks

As shown in Code Listing 2-8, placing quotation marks around a variable name changes the program's results. In fact, placing double quotation marks around anything that is not intended to be a string literal will create an error of some type. For example, in Code Listings 2-7 and 2-8, the number 5 was assigned to the variable value. It would have been an error to perform the assignment this way:

```
value = "5";      // Error!
```

In this statement, 5 is no longer an integer, but a string literal. Because value was declared an integer variable, you can only store integers in it. In other words, 5 and "5" are not the same thing.

The fact that numbers can be represented as strings frequently confuses students who are new to programming. Just remember that strings are intended for humans to read. They are to be printed on computer screens or paper. Numbers, however, are intended primarily for mathematical operations. You cannot perform math on strings, and before numbers can be displayed on the screen, first they must be converted to strings. (Fortunately, print and println handle the conversion automatically when you send numbers to them.) Don't fret if this still bothers you. Later in this chapter we will shed more light on the differences among numbers, characters, and strings by discussing their internal storage.

More about Literals

A literal is a value that is written in the code of a program. Literals are commonly assigned to variables or displayed. Code Listing 2-9 contains both literals and a variable.

Code Listing 2-9   (Literals.java)

```
 1   // This program has literals and a variable.
 2
 3   public class Literals
 4   {
 5      public static void main(String[] args)
 6      {
 7         int apples;
 8
 9         apples = 20;
10         System.out.println("Today we sold " + apples +
11                            " bushels of apples.");
12      }
13   }
```

Program Output

```
Today we sold 20 bushels of apples.
```

Of course, the variable in this program is `apples`. It is declared as an integer. Table 2-3 shows a list of the literals found in the program.

Table 2-3   Literals

Literal	Type of Literal
20	Integer literal
"Today we sold "	String literal
"bushels of apples."	String literal

Identifiers

An *identifier* is a programmer-defined name that represents some element of a program. Variable names and class names are examples of identifiers. You may choose your own variable names and class names in Java, as long as you do not use any of the Java key words. The *key words* make up the core of the language, and each has a specific purpose. Table 1-3 in Chapter 1 and Appendix B show a complete list of Java key words.

You should always choose names for your variables that give an indication of what they are used for. You may be tempted to declare variables with names like this:

```
int x;
```

The rather nondescript name, x, gives no clue as to what the variable's purpose is. Here is a better example.

```
int itemsOrdered;
```

The name `itemsOrdered` gives anyone reading the program an idea of what the variable is used for. This method of coding helps produce *self-documenting programs*, which means you get an understanding of what the program is doing just by reading its code. Because real-world programs usually have thousands of lines of code, it is important that they be as self-documenting as possible.

You have probably noticed the mixture of uppercase and lowercase letters in the name `itemsOrdered`. Although all of Java's key words must be written in lowercase, you may use uppercase letters in variable names. The reason the O in `itemsOrdered` is capitalized is to improve readability. Normally "items ordered" is used as two words. Variable names cannot contain spaces, however, so the two words must be combined. When "items" and "ordered" are stuck together, you get a variable declaration like this:

```
int itemsordered;
```

Capitalization of the letter O makes `itemsOrdered` easier to read. Typically, variable names begin with a lowercase letter, and after that, the first letter of each individual word that makes up the variable name is capitalized.

The following are some specific rules that must be followed with all identifiers:

- The first character must be one of the letters a–z, A–Z, an underscore (_), or a dollar sign ($).

- After the first character, you may use the letters a–z or A–Z, the digits 0–9, under-scores (_), or dollar signs ($).
- Uppercase and lowercase characters are distinct. This means `itemsOrdered` is not the same as `itemsordered`.
- Identifiers cannot include spaces.

NOTE: Although the $ is a legal identifier character, it is normally used for special purposes. So, don't use it in your variable names.

Table 2-4 shows a list of variable names and tells if each is legal or illegal in Java.

Table 2-4   Some variable names

Variable Name	Legal or Illegal?
dayOfWeek	Legal
3dGraph	Illegal because identifiers cannot begin with a digit
june1997	Legal
mixture#3	Illegal because identifiers may only use alphabetic letters, digits, underscores, or dollar signs
week day	Illegal because identifiers cannot contain spaces

Class Names

As mentioned before, it is standard practice to begin variable names with a lowercase letter, and then capitalize the first letter of each subsequent word that makes up the name. It is also a standard practice to capitalize the first letter of a class name, as well as the first letter of each subsequent word it contains. This helps differentiate the names of variables from the names of classes. For example, `payRate` would be a variable name, and `Employee` would be a class name.

Checkpoint

2.10   Examine the following program.

```
// This program uses variables and literals.

public class BigLittle
{
    public static void main(String[] args)
    {
        int little;
        int big;

        little = 2;
        big = 2000;
        System.out.println("The little number is " + little);
```

```
        System.out.println("The big number is " + big);
    }
}
```

List the variables and literals found in the program.

2.11   What will the following program display on the screen?

```
public class CheckPoint
{
    public static void main(String[] args)
    {
        int number;

        number = 712;
        System.out.println("The value is " + "number");
    }
}
```

2.4   Primitive Data Types

> **CONCEPT:** There are many different types of data. Variables are classified according to their data type, which determines the kind of data that may be stored in them.

Computer programs collect pieces of data from the real world and manipulate them in various ways. There are many different types of data. In the realm of numeric data, for example, there are whole and fractional numbers; negative and positive numbers; and numbers so large and others so small that they don't even have a name. Then there is textual information. Names and addresses, for instance, are stored as strings of characters. When you write a program you must determine what types of data it is likely to encounter.

Each variable has a *data type*, which is the type of data that the variable can hold. Selecting the proper data type is important because a variable's data type determines the amount of memory the variable uses and the way the variable formats and stores data. It is important to select a data type that is appropriate for the type of data that your program will work with. If you are writing a program to calculate the number of miles to a distant star, you need variables that can hold very large numbers. If you are designing software to record microscopic dimensions, you need variables that store very small and precise numbers. If you are writing a program that must perform thousands of intensive calculations, you want variables that can be processed quickly. The data type of a variable determines all of these factors.

Table 2-5 shows all of the Java *primitive data types* for holding numeric data.

Table 2-5   Primitive data types for numeric data

Data Type	Size	Range
byte	1 byte	Integers in the range of -128 to $+127$
short	2 bytes	Integers in the range of $-32{,}768$ to $+32{,}767$
int	4 bytes	Integers in the range of $-2{,}147{,}483{,}648$ to $+2{,}147{,}483{,}647$
long	8 bytes	Integers in the range of $-9{,}223{,}372{,}036{,}854{,}775{,}808$ to $+9{,}223{,}372{,}036{,}854{,}775{,}807$
float	4 bytes	Floating-point numbers in the range of $\pm 3.4 \times 10^{-38}$ to $\pm 3.4 \times 10^{38}$, with 7 digits of accuracy
double	8 bytes	Floating-point numbers in the range of $\pm 1.7 \times 10^{-308}$ to $\pm 1.7 \times 10^{308}$, with 15 digits of accuracy

The words listed in the left column of Table 2-5 are the key words that you use in variable declarations. A variable declaration takes the following general format:

```
DataType VariableName;
```

DataType is the name of the data type and *VariableName* is the name of the variable. Here are some examples of variable declarations:

```
byte inches;
int speed;
short month;
float salesCommission;
double distance;
```

The size column in Table 2-5 shows the number of bytes that a variable of each of the data types uses. For example, an int variable uses 4 bytes, and a double variable uses 8 bytes. The range column shows the ranges of numbers that may be stored in variables of each data type. For example, an int variable can hold numbers from $-2{,}147{,}483{,}648$ up to $+2{,}147{,}483{,}647$. One of the appealing characteristics of the Java language is that the sizes and ranges of all the primitive data types are the same on all computers.

NOTE: These data types are called "primitive" because you cannot use them to create objects. Recall from Chapter 1's discussion on object-oriented programming that an object has attributes and methods. With the primitive data types, you can only create variables, and a variable can only be used to hold a single value. Such variables do not have attributes or methods.

The Integer Data Types

The first four data types listed in Table 2-5, byte, int, short, and long, are all integer data types. An integer variable can hold whole numbers such as 7, 125, -14, and 6928. The program in Code Listing 2-10 shows several variables of different integer data types being used.

Code Listing 2-10   (`IntegerVariables.java`)

```java
1   // This program has variables of several of the integer types.
2
3   public class IntegerVariables
4   {
5      public static void main(String[] args)
6      {
7         int checking;   // Declare an int variable named checking.
8         byte miles;     // Declare a byte variable named miles.
9         short minutes;  // Declare a short variable named minutes.
10        long days;      // Declare a long variable named days.
11
12        checking = -20;
13        miles = 105;
14        minutes = 120;
15        days = 189000;
16        System.out.println("We have made a journey of " + miles +
17                           " miles.");
18        System.out.println("It took us " + minutes + " minutes.");
19        System.out.println("Our account balance is $" + checking);
20        System.out.println("About " + days + " days ago Columbus " +
21                           "stood on this spot.");
22     }
23  }
```

Program Output

```
We have made a journey of 105 miles.
It took us 120 minutes.
Our account balance is $-20
About 189000 days ago Columbus stood on this spot.
```

In most programs you will need more than one variable of any given data type. If a program uses three integers, `length`, `width`, and `area`, they could be declared separately, as follows:

```java
int length;
int width;
int area;
```

It is easier, however, to combine the three variable declarations:

```java
int length, width, area;
```

You can declare several variables of the same type, simply by separating their names with commas.

Integer Literals

When you write an integer literal in your program code, Java assumes it to be of the int data type. For example, in Code Listing 2-10, the literals −20, 105, 120, and 189000 are all treated as int values. You can force an integer literal to be treated as a long, however, by suffixing it with the letter L. For example, the value 57L would be treated as a long. You can use either an uppercase or lowercase L. The lowercase l looks too much like the number 1, so you should always use the uppercase L.

> **WARNING!** You cannot embed commas in numeric literals. For example, the following statement will cause an error:
>
> ```
>     number = 1,257,649;        // ERROR!
> ```
>
> This statement must be written as:
>
> ```
>     number = 1257649;          // Correct.
> ```

Floating-Point Data Types

Whole numbers are not adequate for many jobs. If you are writing a program that works with dollar amounts or precise measurements, you need a data type that allows fractional values. In programming terms, these are called *floating-point* numbers. Values such as 1.7 and −45.316 are floating-point numbers.

In Java there are two data types that can represent floating-point numbers. They are float and double. The float data type is considered a single precision data type. It can store a floating-point number with 7 digits of accuracy. The double data type is considered a double precision data type. It can store a floating-point number with 15 digits of accuracy. The double data type uses twice as much memory as the float data type, however. A float variable occupies 4 bytes of memory, whereas a double variable uses 8 bytes.

Code listing 2-11 shows a program that uses three double variables.

Code Listing 2-11   (Sale.java)

```java
 1  // This program demonstrates the double data type.
 2
 3  public class Sale
 4  {
 5     public static void main(String[] args)
 6     {
 7        double price, tax, total;
 8
 9        price = 29.75;
10        tax = 1.76;
11        total = 31.51;
12        System.out.println("The price of the item " +
13                           "is " + price);
14        System.out.println("The tax is " + tax);
```

```
15        System.out.println("The total is " + total);
16    }
17 }
```

Program Output

```
The price of the item is 29.75
The tax is 1.76
The total is 31.51
```

Floating-Point Literals

When you write a floating-point literal in your program code, Java assumes it to be of the double data type. For example, in Code Listing 2-11, the literals 29.75, 1.76, and 31.51 are all treated as double values. Because of this, a problem can arise when assigning a floating-point literal to a float variable. Java is a *strongly typed language*, which means that it only allows you to store values of compatible data types in variables. A double value is not compatible with a float variable because a double can be much larger or much smaller than the allowable range for a float. As a result, code such as the following will cause an error:

```
float number;
number = 23.5;            // Error!
```

You can force a double literal to be treated as a float, however, by suffixing it with the letter F or f. The preceding code can be rewritten in the following manner to prevent an error:

```
float number;
number = 23.5F;          // This will work.
```

 WARNING! If you are working with literals that represent dollar amounts, remember that you cannot embed currency symbols (such as $) or commas in the literal. For example, the following statement will cause an error:

```
grossPay = $1,257.00;    // ERROR!
```

This statement must be written as:

```
grossPay = 1257.00;      // Correct.
```

Scientific and E Notation

Floating-point literals can be represented in scientific notation. Take the number 47,281.97. In scientific notation this number is 4.728197×10^4. (10^4 is equal to 10,000, and $4.728197 \times 10,000$ is 47,281.97.)

Java uses E notation to represent values in scientific notation. In E notation, the number 4.728197×10^4 would be 4.728197E4. Table 2-6 shows other numbers represented in scientific and E notation.

Table 2-6 Floating-point representations

Decimal Notation	Scientific Notation	E Notation
247.91	2.4791×10^2	2.4791E2
0.00072	7.2×10^{-4}	7.2E-4
2,900,000	2.9×10^6	2.9E6

NOTE: The E can be uppercase or lowercase.

Code Listing 2-12 demonstrates the use of floating-point literals expressed in E notation.

Code Listing 2-12   (SunFacts.java)

```
 1  // This program uses E notation.
 2
 3  public class SunFacts
 4  {
 5     public static void main(String[] args)
 6     {
 7        double distance, mass;
 8
 9        distance = 1.495979E11;
10        mass = 1.989E30;
11        System.out.println("The Sun is " + distance +
12                           " meters away.");
13        System.out.println("The Sun's mass is " + mass +
14                           " kilograms.");
15     }
16  }
```

Program Output

```
The Sun is 1.495979E11 meters away.
The Sun's mass is 1.989E30 kilograms.
```

The boolean Data Type

The boolean data type allows you to create variables that may hold one of two possible values: true or false. Code Listing 2-13 demonstrates the declaration and assignment of a boolean variable.

Code Listing 2-13   `(TrueFalse.java)`

```
1   // A program for demonstrating boolean variables
2
3   public class TrueFalse
4   {
5      public static void main(String[] args)
6      {
7         boolean bool;
8
9         bool = true;
10        System.out.println(bool);
11        bool = false;
12        System.out.println(bool);
13     }
14  }
```

Program Output
```
true
false
```

Variables of the `boolean` data type are useful for evaluating conditions that are either true or false. You will not be using them until Chapter 3, however, so for now just remember the following things:

- `boolean` variables may only hold the values `true` or `false`.
- The contents of a `boolean` variable may not be copied to a variable of any type other than `boolean`.

The char Data Type

The `char` data type is used to store characters. A variable of the char data type can hold one character at a time. Character literals are enclosed in *single quotation marks*. The program in Code Listing 2-14 uses a `char` variable. While the program runs, the character literals 'A' and 'B' are assigned to the variable.

Code Listing 2-14   `(Letters.java)`

```
1   // This program demonstrates the char data type.
2
3   public class Letters
4   {
5      public static void main(String[] args)
6      {
7         char letter;
8
9         letter = 'A';
```

```
10          System.out.println(letter);
11          letter = 'B';
12          System.out.println(letter);
13      }
14  }
```

Program Output

```
A
B
```

It is important that you do not confuse character literals with string literals, which are enclosed in double quotation marks. String literals cannot be assigned to char variables.

Unicode

Characters are internally represented by numbers. Each printable character, as well as many nonprintable characters, is assigned a unique number. Java uses Unicode, which is a set of numbers that are used as codes for representing characters. Each Unicode number requires two bytes of memory, so char variables occupy two bytes. When a character is stored in memory, it is actually the numeric code that is stored. When the computer is instructed to print the value on the screen, it displays the character that corresponds with the numeric code.

You may want to refer to Appendix B, which shows a portion of the Unicode character set. Notice that the number 65 is the code for A, 66 is the code for B, and so on. Code Listing 2-15 demonstrates that when you work with characters, you are actually working with numbers.

Code Listing 2-15   (Letters2.java)

```
 1  // This program demonstrates the close relationship between
 2  // characters and integers.
 3
 4  public class Letters2
 5  {
 6      public static void main(String[] args)
 7      {
 8          char letter;
 9
10          letter = 65;
11          System.out.println(letter);
12          letter = 66;
13          System.out.println(letter);
14      }
15  }
```

Program Output

```
A
B
```

Figure 2-4 illustrates that when you think of the characters A, B, and C being stored in memory, it is really the numbers 65, 66, and 67 that are stored.

Figure 2-4   Characters and how they are stored in memory

These characters are stored in memory as...

Variable Assignment and Initialization

As you have already seen in several examples, a value is put into a variable with an *assignment statement*. For example, the following statement assigns the value 12 to the variable unitsSold:

```
unitsSold = 12;
```

The = symbol is called the assignment operator. Operators perform operations on data. The data that operators work with are called operands. The assignment operator has two operands. In the statement above, the operands are unitsSold and 12.

In an assignment statement, the name of the variable receiving the assignment must appear on the left side of the operator, and the value being assigned must appear on the right side. The following statement is incorrect:

```
12 = unitsSold;        // ERROR!
```

The operand on the left side of the = operator must be a variable name. The operand on the right side of the = symbol must be an expression that has a value. The assignment operator takes the value of the right operand and puts it in the variable identified by the left operand. Assuming that length and width are both int variables, the following code illustrates that the assignment operator's right operand may be a literal or a variable:

```
length = 20;
width = length;
```

It is important to note that the assignment operator only changes the contents of its left operand. The second statement assigns the value of the length variable to the width variable. After the statement has executed, length still has the same value, 20.

You may also assign values to variables as part of the declaration statement. This is known as *initialization*. Code Listing 2-16 shows how it is done.

The variable declaration statement in this program is in line 7:

```
int month = 2, days = 28;
```

Code Listing 2-16   (Initialize.java)

```
 1   // This program shows variable initialization.
 2
 3   public class Initialize
 4   {
 5      public static void main(String[] args)
 6      {
 7         int month = 2, days = 28;
 8
 9         System.out.println("Month " + month + " has " +
10                              days + " days.");
11      }
12   }
```

Program Output

```
Month 2 has 28 days.
```

This statement declares the month variable and initializes it with the value 2 and declares the days variable and initializes it with the value 28. As you can see, this simplifies the program and reduces the number of statements that must be typed by the programmer. Here are examples of other declaration statements that perform initialization:

```
double payRate = 25.52;
float interestRate = 12.9F;
char stockCode = 'D';
int customerNum = 459;
```

Of course, there are always variations on a theme. Java allows you to declare several variables and only initialize some of them. Here is an example of such a declaration:

```
int flightNum = 89, travelTime, departure = 10, distance;
```

The variable flightNum is initialized to 89, and departure is initialized to 10. The travelTime and distance variables remain uninitialized.

> **WARNING!** When a variable is declared inside a method, it must have a value stored in it before it can be used. If the compiler determines that the program might be using such a variable before a value has been stored in it, an error will occur. You can avoid this type of error by initializing the variable with a value.

Variables Hold Only One Value at a Time

Remember, a variable can hold only one value at a time. When you assign a new value to a variable, the new value takes the place of the variable's previous contents. For example, look at the following code.

```
int x = 5;
System.out.println(x);
x = 99;
System.out.println(x);
```

In this code, the variable x is initialized with the value 5 and its contents are displayed. Then the variable is assigned the value 99. This value overwrites the value 5 that was previously stored there. The code will produce the following output:

```
5
99
```

Checkpoint

2.12 Which of the following are illegal variable names and why?

```
x
99bottles
july97
theSalesFigureForFiscalYear98
r&d
grade_report
```

2.13 Is the variable name Sales the same as sales? Why or why not?

2.14 Refer to the Java primitive data types listed in Table 2-5 for this question.
   a. If a variable needs to hold whole numbers in the range 32 to 6,000, what primitive data type would be best?
   b. If a variable needs to hold whole numbers in the range −40,000 to +40,000, what primitive data type would be best?
   c. Which of the following literals use more memory? 22.1 or 22.1F?

2.15 How would the number 6.31×10^{17} be represented in E notation?

2.16 A program declares a float variable named number, and the following statement causes an error. What can be done to fix the error?

```
number = 7.4;
```

2.17 What values can boolean variables hold?

2.18 Write statements that do the following:
   a. Declare a char variable named letter.
   b. Assign the letter A to the letter variable.
   c. Display the contents of the letter variable.

2.19 What are the Unicode codes for the characters 'C', 'F', and 'W'? (You may need to refer to Appendix B.)

2.20 Which is a character literal, 'B' or "B"?

2.21 What is wrong with the following statement?

```
char letter = "Z";
```

2.5 Arithmetic Operators

> **CONCEPT:** There are many operators for manipulating numeric values and performing arithmetic operations.

VideoNote
Simple Math
Expressions

Java offers a multitude of operators for manipulating data. Generally, there are three types of operators: *unary*, *binary*, and *ternary*. These terms reflect the number of operands an operator requires.

Unary operators require only a single operand. For example, consider the following expression:

```
-5
```

Of course, we understand this represents the value negative five. We can also apply the operator to a variable, as follows:

```
-number
```

This expression gives the negative of the value stored in `number`. The minus sign, when used this way, is called the *negation operator*. Because it only requires one operand, it is a unary operator.

Binary operators work with two operands. The assignment operator is in this category. Ternary operators, as you may have guessed, require three operands. Java has only one ternary operator, which is discussed in Chapter 4.

Arithmetic operations are very common in programming. Table 2-7 shows the arithmetic operators in Java.

Table 2-7 Arithmetic operators

Operator	Meaning	Type	Example
+	Addition	Binary	`total = cost + tax;`
-	Subtraction	Binary	`cost = total - tax;`
*	Multiplication	Binary	`tax = cost * rate;`
/	Division	Binary	`salePrice = original / 2;`
%	Modulus	Binary	`remainder = value % 3;`

Each of these operators works as you probably expect. The addition operator returns the sum of its two operands. Here are some example statements that use the addition operator:

```
amount = 4 + 8;              // Assigns 12 to amount
total = price + tax;         // Assigns price + tax to total
number = number + 1;         // Assigns number + 1 to number
```

The subtraction operator returns the value of its right operand subtracted from its left operand. Here are some examples:

```
temperature = 112 - 14;        // Assigns 98 to temperature
sale = price - discount;       // Assigns price - discount to sale
number = number - 1;           // Assigns number - 1 to number
```

The multiplication operator returns the product of its two operands. Here are some examples:

```
markUp = 12 * 0.25;            // Assigns 3 to markUp
commission = sales * percent;  // Assigns sales * percent to commission
population = population * 2;    // Assigns population * 2 to population
```

The division operator returns the quotient of its left operand divided by its right operand. Here are some examples:

```
points = 100 / 20;            // Assigns 5 to points
teams = players / maxEach;    // Assigns players / maxEach to teams
half = number / 2;            // Assigns number / 2 to half
```

The modulus operator returns the remainder of a division operation involving two integers. The following statement assigns 2 to leftOver:

```
leftOver = 17 % 3;
```

Situations arise where you need to get the remainder of a division. Computations that detect odd numbers or are required to determine how many items are left over after division use the modulus operator.

The program in Code Listing 2-17 demonstrates some of these operators used in a simple payroll calculation.

Code Listing 2-17   (Wages.java)

```
1  // This program calculates hourly wages plus overtime.
2
3  public class Wages
4  {
5     public static void main(String[] args)
6     {
7        double regularWages;      // The calculated regular wages.
8        double basePay = 25;      // The base pay rate.
9        double regularHours = 40; // The hours worked less overtime.
10       double overtimeWages;     // Overtime wages
11       double overtimePay = 37.5; // Overtime pay rate
12       double overtimeHours = 10; // Overtime hours worked
13       double totalWages;        // Total wages
14
15       regularWages = basePay * regularHours;
16       overtimeWages = overtimePay * overtimeHours;
```

```
17          totalWages = regularWages + overtimeWages;
18          System.out.println("Wages for this week are $" +
19                         totalWages);
20    }
21 }
```

Program Output

Wages for this week are $1375.0

Code Listing 2-17 calculates the total wages an hourly paid worker earned in one week. As mentioned in the comments, there are variables for regular wages, base pay rate, regular hours worked, overtime wages, overtime pay rate, overtime hours worked, and total wages.

Line 15 in the program multiplies basePay times regularHours and stores the result, which is 1000, in regularWages:

```
regularWages = basePay * regularHours;
```

Line 16 multiplies overtimePay times overtimeHours and stores the result, which is 375, in overtimeWages:

```
overtimeWages = overtimePay * overtimeHours;
```

Line 17 adds the regular wages and the overtime wages and stores the result, 1375, in totalWages:

```
totalWages = regularWages + overtimeWages;
```

The println statement in lines 18 and 19 displays the message on the screen reporting the week's wages.

Integer Division

When both operands of the division operator are integers, the operator will perform *integer division*. This means the result of the division will be an integer as well. If there is a remainder, it will be discarded. For example, look at the following code:

```
double number;
number = 5 / 2;
```

This code divides 5 by 2 and assigns the result to the number variable. What will be stored in number? You would probably assume that 2.5 would be stored in number because that is the result your calculator shows when you divide 5 by 2. However, that is not what happens when the previous Java code is executed. Because the numbers 5 and 2 are both integers, the fractional part of the result will be thrown away, or *truncated*. As a result, the value 2 will be assigned to the number variable.

In the previous code, it doesn't matter that number is declared as a double because the fractional part of the result is discarded before the assignment takes place. In order for a division operation to return a floating-point value, one of the operands must be of a floating-point data type. For example, the previous code could be written as follows:

```
double number;
number = 5.0 / 2;
```

In this code, 5.0 is treated as a floating-point number, so the division operation will return a floating-point number. The result of the division is 2.5.

Operator Precedence

It is possible to build mathematical expressions with several operators. The following statement assigns the sum of 17, x, 21, and y to the variable answer:

```
answer = 17 + x + 21 + y;
```

Some expressions are not that straightforward, however. Consider the following statement:

```
outcome = 12 + 6 / 3;
```

What value will be stored in outcome? The 6 is used as an operand for both the addition and division operators. The outcome variable could be assigned either 6 or 14, depending on when the division takes place. The answer is 14 because the division operator has higher *precedence* than the addition operator.

Mathematical expressions are evaluated from left to right. When two operators share an operand, the operator with the highest precedence works first. Multiplication and division have higher precedence than addition and subtraction, so the statement above works like this:

1. 6 is divided by 3, yielding a result of 2
2. 12 is added to 2, yielding a result of 14

It could be diagrammed as shown in Figure 2-5.

Figure 2-5 Precedence illustrated

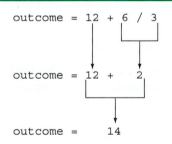

Table 2-8 shows the precedence of the arithmetic operators. The operators at the top of the table have higher precedence than the ones below it.

Table 2-8 Precedence of arithmetic operators (highest to lowest)

Highest Precedence →	– (unary negation)
	* / %
Lowest Precedence →	+ –

The multiplication, division, and modulus operators have the same precedence. The addition and subtraction operators have the same precedence. If two operators sharing an operand have the same precedence, they work according to their *associativity*. Associativity is either *left to right* or *right to left*. Table 2-9 shows the arithmetic operators and their associativity.

Table 2-9   Associativity of arithmetic operators

Operator	Associativity
– (unary negation)	Right to left
* / %	Left to right
+ –	Left to right

Table 2-10 shows some expressions and their values.

Table 2-10   Some expressions and their values

Expression	Value
5 + 2 * 4	13
10 / 2 – 3	2
8 + 12 * 2 – 4	28
4 + 17 % 2 – 1	4
6 – 3 * 2 + 7 – 1	6

Grouping with Parentheses

Parts of a mathematical expression may be grouped with parentheses to force some operations to be performed before others. In the statement below, the sum of a, b, c, and d is divided by 4.0.

```
average = (a + b + c + d) / 4.0;
```

Without the parentheses, however, d would be divided by 4 and the result added to a, b, and c. Table 2-11 shows more expressions and their values.

Table 2-11   More expressions and their values

Expression	Value
(5 + 2) * 4	28
10 / (5 – 3)	5
8 + 12 * (6 – 2)	56
(4 + 17) % 2 – 1	0
(6 – 3) * (2 + 7) / 3	9

In the Spotlight:
Calculating Percentages and Discounts

Determining percentages is a common calculation in computer programming. Although the % symbol is used in general mathematics to indicate a percentage, most programming languages (including Java) do not use the % symbol for this purpose. In a program, you have to convert a percentage to a floating-point number, just as you would if you were using a calculator. For example, 50 percent is written as 0.5 and 2 percent is written as 0.02.

Let's look at an example. Suppose you earn $6,000 per month and you are allowed to contribute a portion of your gross monthly pay to a retirement plan. You want to determine the amount of your pay that will go into the plan if you contribute 5 percent, 8 percent, or 10 percent of your gross wages. To make this determination you write a program like the one shown in Code Listing 2-18.

Code Listing 2-18   (Contribution.java)

```java
 1 // This program calculates the amount of pay that
 2 // will be contributed to a retirement plan if 5%,
 3 // 7%, or 10% of monthly pay is withheld.
 4
 5 public class Contribution
 6 {
 7    public static void main(String[] args)
 8    {
 9       // Variables to hold the monthly pay and
10       // the amount of contribution.
11       double monthlyPay = 6000.0;
12       double contribution;
13
14       // Calculate and display a 5% contribution.
15       contribution = monthlyPay * 0.05;
16       System.out.println("5 percent is $" +
17                          contribution +
18                          " per month.");
19
20       // Calculate and display a 8% contribution.
21       contribution = monthlyPay * 0.08;
22       System.out.println("8 percent is $" +
23                          contribution +
24                          " per month.");
25
26       // Calculate and display a 10% contribution.
27       contribution = monthlyPay * 0.1;
28       System.out.println("10 percent is $" +
29                          contribution +
30                          " per month.");
31    }
32 }
```

Program Output

```
5 percent is $300.0 per month.
8 percent is $480.0 per month.
10 percent is $600.0 per month.
```

Lines 11 and 12 declare two variables: monthlyPay and contribution. The monthlyPay variable, which is initialized with the value 6000.0, holds the amount of your monthly pay. The contribution variable holds the amount of a contribution to the retirement plan.

The statements in lines 15 through 18 calculate and display 5 percent of the monthly pay. The calculation is done in line 15, where the monthlyPay variable is multiplied by 0.05. The result is assigned to the contribution variable, which is then displayed by the statement in lines 16 through 18.

Similar steps are taken in lines 21 through 24, which calculate and display 8 percent of the monthly pay, and lines 27 through 30, which calculate and display 10 percent of the monthly pay.

Calculating a Percentage Discount

Another common calculation is determining a percentage discount. For example, suppose a retail business sells an item that is regularly priced at $59 and is planning to have a sale where the item's price will be reduced by 20 percent. You have been asked to write a program to calculate the sale price of the item.

To determine the sale price you perform two calculations:

- First, you get the amount of the discount, which is 20 percent of the item's regular price.
- Second, you subtract the discount amount from the item's regular price. This gives you the sale price.

Code Listing 2-19 shows how this is done in Java.

Code Listing 2-19   (Discount.java)

```
1 // This program calculates the sale price of an
2 // item that is regularly priced at $59, with
3 // a 20 percent discount subtracted.
4
5 public class Discount
6 {
7    public static void main(String[] args)
8    {
9       // Variables to hold the regular price, the
10      // amount of a discount, and the sale price.
11      double regularPrice = 59.0;
```

```
12          double discount;
13          double salePrice;
14
15          // Calculate the amount of a 20% discount.
16          discount = regularPrice * 0.2;
17
18          // Calculate the sale price by subtracting
19          // the discount from the regular price.
20          salePrice = regularPrice - discount;
21
22          // Display the results.
23          System.out.println("Regular price: $" + regularPrice);
24          System.out.println("Discount amount $" + discount);
25          System.out.println("Sale price: $" + salePrice);
26      }
27 }
```

Program Output

```
Regular price: $59.0
Discount amount $11.8
Sale price: $47.2
```

Lines 11 through 13 declare three variables. The `regularPrice` variable holds the item's regular price and is initialized with the value 59.0. The `discount` variable holds the amount of the discount once it is calculated. The `salePrice` variable holds the item's sale price.

Line 16 calculates the amount of the 20 percent discount by multiplying `regularPrice` by 0.2. The result is stored in the `discount` variable. Line 20 calculates the sale price by subtracting `discount` from `regularPrice`. The result is stored in the `salePrice` variable. The statements in lines 23 through 25 display the item's regular price, the amount of the discount, and the sale price.

The `Math` Class

The Java API provides a class named `Math`, which contains numerous methods that are useful for performing complex mathematical operations. In this section we will briefly look at the `Math.pow` and `Math.sqrt` methods.

The `Math.pow` Method

In Java, raising a number to a power requires the `Math.pow` method. Here is an example of how the `Math.pow` method is used:

```
result = Math.pow(4.0, 2.0);
```

The method takes two `double` arguments. It raises the first argument to the power of the second argument and returns the result as a `double`. In this example, 4.0 is raised to the power of 2.0. This statement is equivalent to the following algebraic statement:

result = 4^2

Here is another example of a statement using the `Math.pow` method. It assigns 3 times 6^3 to x:

```
x = 3 * Math.pow(6.0, 3.0);
```

And the following statement displays the value of 5 raised to the power of 4:

```
System.out.println(Math.pow(5.0, 4.0));
```

The `Math.sqrt` Method

The `Math.sqrt` method accepts a `double` value as its argument and returns the square root of the value. Here is an example of how the method is used:

```
result = Math.sqrt(9.0);
```

In this example the value 9.0 is passed as an argument to the `Math.sqrt` method. The method will return the square root of 9.0, which is assigned to the `result` variable. The following statement shows another example. In this statement the square root of 25.0 (which is 5.0) is displayed on the screen:

```
System.out.println(Math.sqrt(25.0));
```

> For more information about the `Math` class, see Appendix G, available on this book's online resource page at www.pearsonhighered.com/gaddis.

Checkpoint

2.22   Complete the following table by writing the value of each expression in the Value column.

```
Expression                          Value
------------------------------------------
6 + 3 * 5                           _____
12 / 2 - 4                          _____
9 + 14 * 2 - 6                      _____
5 + 19 % 3 - 1                      _____
(6 + 2) * 3                         _____
14 / (11 - 4)                       _____
9 + 12 * (8 - 3)                    _____
```

2.23   Is the division statement in the following code an example of integer division or floating-point division? What value will be stored in `portion`?

```
double portion;
portion = 70 / 3;
```

2.6 Combined Assignment Operators

CONCEPT: The combined assignment operators combine the assignment operator with the arithmetic operators.

Quite often, programs have assignment statements of the following form:

```
x = x + 1;
```

On the right side of the assignment operator, 1 is added to x. The result is then assigned to x, replacing the value that was previously there. Effectively, this statement adds 1 to x. Here is another example:

```
balance = balance + deposit;
```

Assuming that balance and deposit are variables, this statement assigns the value of balance + deposit to balance. The effect of this statement is that deposit is added to the value stored in balance. Here is another example:

```
balance = balance - withdrawal;
```

Assuming that balance and withdrawal are variables, this statement assigns the value of balance - withdrawal to balance. The effect of this statement is that withdrawal is subtracted from the value stored in balance.

If you have not seen these types of statements before, they might cause some initial confusion because the same variable name appears on both sides of the assignment operator. Table 2-12 shows other examples of statements written this way.

Table 2-12 Various assignment statements (assume x = 6 in each statement)

Statement	What It Does	Value of **x** after the Statement
x = x + 4;	Adds 4 to x	10
x = x - 3;	Subtracts 3 from x	3
x = x * 10;	Multiplies x by 10	60
x = x / 2;	Divides x by 2	3
x = x % 4	Assigns the remainder of x / 4 to x.	2

These types of operations are common in programming. For convenience, Java offers a special set of operators designed specifically for these jobs. Table 2-13 shows the *combined assignment operators*, also known as *compound operators*.

Table 2-13 Combined assignment operators

Operator	Example Usage	Equivalent to
+=	x += 5;	x = x + 5;
-=	y -= 2;	y = y - 2;
*=	z *= 10;	z = z * 10;
/=	a /= b;	a = a / b;
%=	c %= 3;	c = c % 3;

As you can see, the combined assignment operators do not require the programmer to type the variable name twice. The following statement:

```
balance = balance + deposit;
```

could be rewritten as

```
balance += deposit;
```

Similarly, the statement

```
balance = balance - withdrawal;
```

could be rewritten as

```
balance -= withdrawal;
```

 Checkpoint

2.24 Write statements using combined assignment operators to perform the following:
   a. Add 6 to x
   b. Subtract 4 from amount
   c. Multiply y by 4
   d. Divide total by 27
   e. Store in x the remainder of x divided by 7

 2.7 **Conversion between Primitive Data Types**

CONCEPT: Before a value can be stored in a variable, the value's data type must be compatible with the variable's data type. Java performs some conversions between data types automatically, but does not automatically perform any conversion that can result in the loss of data. Java also follows a set of rules when evaluating arithmetic expressions containing mixed data types.

Java is a *strongly typed* language. This means that before a value is assigned to a variable, Java checks the data types of the variable and the value being assigned to it to determine if they are compatible. For example, look at the following statements:

```
int x;
double y = 2.5;
x = y;
```

The assignment statement is attempting to store a double value (2.5) in an int variable. When the Java compiler encounters this line of code, it will respond with an error message. (The Sun JDK displays the message "possible loss of precision.")

Not all assignment statements that mix data types are rejected by the compiler, however. For instance, look at the following program segment:

```java
int x;
short y = 2;
x = y;
```

This assignment statement, which stores a short in an int, will work with no problems. So why does Java permit a short to be stored in an int, but does not permit a double to be stored in an int? The obvious reason is that a double can store fractional numbers and can hold values much larger than an int can hold. If Java were to permit a double to be assigned to an int, a loss of data would be likely.

Just like officers in the military, the primitive data types are ranked. One data type outranks another if it can hold a larger number. For example, a float outranks an int, and an int outranks a short. Figure 2-6 shows the numeric data types in order of their rank. The higher a data type appears in the list, the higher is its rank.

Figure 2-6 Primitive data type ranking

```
double      Highest Rank
float
long
int
short
byte        Lowest Rank
```

In assignment statements where values of lower-ranked data types are stored in variables of higher-ranked data types, Java automatically converts the lower-ranked value to the higher-ranked type. This is called a *widening conversion*. For example, the following code demonstrates a widening conversion, which takes place when an int value is stored in a double variable:

```java
double x;
int y = 10;
x = y;              // Performs a widening conversion
```

A *narrowing conversion* is the conversion of a value to a lower-ranked type. For example, converting a double to an int would be a narrowing conversion. Because narrowing conversions can potentially cause a loss of data, Java does not automatically perform them.

Cast Operators

The *cast operator* lets you manually convert a value, even if it means that a narrowing conversion will take place. Cast operators are unary operators that appear as a data type name enclosed in a set of parentheses. The operator precedes the value being converted. Here is an example:

```java
x = (int)number;
```

The cast operator in this statement is the word `int` inside the parentheses. It returns the value in `number`, converted to an `int`. This converted value is then stored in `x`. If number were a floating-point variable, such as a `float` or a `double`, the value that is returned would be *truncated*, which means the fractional part of the number is lost. The original value in the number variable is not changed, however.

Table 2-14 shows several statements using a cast operator.

Table 2-14 Example uses of cast operators

Statement	Description
`littleNum = (short)bigNum;`	The cast operator returns the value in `bigNum`, converted to a `short`. The converted value is assigned to the variable `littleNum`.
`x = (long)3.7;`	The cast operator is applied to the expression 3.7. The operator returns the value 3, which is assigned to the variable x.
`number = (int)72.567;`	The cast operator is applied to the expression 72.567. The operator returns 72, which is used to initialize the variable number.
`value = (float)x;`	The cast operator returns the value in x, converted to a `float`. The converted value is assigned to the variable `value`.
`value = (byte)number;`	The cast operator returns the value in number, converted to a `byte`. The converted value is assigned to the variable `value`.

Note that when a cast operator is applied to a variable, it does not change the contents of the variable. It only returns the value stored in the variable, converted to the specified data type.

Recall from our earlier discussion that when both operands of a division are integers, the operation will result in integer division. This means that the result of the division will be an integer, with any fractional part of the result thrown away. For example, look at the following code:

```
int pies = 10, people = 4;
double piesPerPerson;
piesPerPerson = pies / people;
```

Although 10 divided by 4 is 2.5, this code will store 2 in the `piesPerPerson` variable. Because both `pies` and `people` are int variables, the result will be an int, and the fractional part will be thrown away. We can modify the code with a cast operator, however, so it gives the correct result as a floating-point value:

```
piesPerPerson = (double)pies / people;
```

The variable `pies` is an int and holds the value 10. The expression `(double)pies` returns the value in `pies` converted to a `double`. This means that one of the division operator's operands is a double, so the result of the division will be a double. The statement could also have been written as follows:

```
piesPerPerson = pies / (double)people;
```

In this statement, the cast operator returns the value of the `people` variable converted to a `double`. In either statement, the result of the division is a `double`.

> **WARNING!** The cast operator can be applied to an entire expression enclosed in parentheses. For example, look at the following statement:
>
> ```
> piesPerPerson = (double)(pies / people);
> ```
>
> This statement does not convert the value in `pies` or `people` to a `double`, but converts the result of the expression `pies / people`. If this statement were used, an integer division operation would still have been performed. Here's why: The result of the expression `pies / people` is 2 (because integer division takes place). The value 2 converted to a `double` is 2.0. To prevent the integer division from taking place, one of the operands must be converted to a `double`.

Mixed Integer Operations

One of the nuances of the Java language is the way it internally handles arithmetic operations on `int`, `byte`, and `short` variables. When values of the `byte` or `short` data types are used in arithmetic expressions, they are temporarily converted to `int` values. The result of an arithmetic operation using only a mixture of `byte`, `short`, or `int` values will always be an `int`.

For example, assume that `b` and `c` in the following expression are `short` variables:

```
b + c
```

Although both `b` and `c` are `short` variables, the result of the expression `b + c` is an `int`. This means that when the result of such an expression is stored in a variable, the variable must be an `int` or higher data type. For example, look at the following code:

```
short firstNumber = 10,
      secondNumber = 20,
      thirdNumber;

// The following statement causes an error!
thirdNumber = firstNumber + secondNumber;
```

When this code is compiled, the following statement causes an error:

```
thirdNumber = firstNumber + secondNumber;
```

The error results from the fact that `thirdNumber` is a `short`. Although `firstNumber` and `secondNumber` are also `short` variables, the expression `firstNumber + secondNumber` results in an `int` value. The program can be corrected if `thirdNumber` is declared as an `int`, or if a cast operator is used in the assignment statement, as shown here:

```
thirdNumber = (short)(firstNumber + secondNumber);
```

Other Mixed Mathematical Expressions

In situations where a mathematical expression has one or more values of the `double`, `float`, or `long` data types, Java strives to convert all of the operands in the expression to the same data type. Let's look at the specific rules that govern evaluation of these types of expressions.

1. If one of an operator's operands is a `double`, the value of the other operand will be converted to a `double`. The result of the expression will be a `double`. For example, in the following statement assume that b is a `double` and c is an `int`:

   ```
   a = b + c;
   ```

   The value in c will be converted to a `double` prior to the addition. The result of the addition will be a `double`, so the variable a must also be a `double`.

2. If one of an operator's operands is a `float`, the value of the other operand will be converted to a `float`. The result of the expression will be a `float`. For example, in the following statement assume that x is a `short` and y is a `float`:

   ```
   z = x * y;
   ```

   The value in x will be converted to a `float` prior to the multiplication. The result of the multiplication will be a `float`, so the variable z must also be either a `double` or a `float`.

3. If one of an operator's operands is a `long`, the value of the other operand will be converted to a `long`. The result of the expression will be a `long`. For example, in the following statement assume that a is a `long` and b is a `short`:

   ```
   c = a - b;
   ```

   The variable b will be converted to a `long` prior to the subtraction. The result of the subtraction will be a `long`, so the variable c must also be a `long`, `float`, or `double`.

 Checkpoint

2.25 The following declaration appears in a program:

```
short totalPay, basePay = 500, bonus = 1000;
```

The following statement appears in the same program:

```
totalPay = basePay + bonus;
```

a. Will the statement compile properly or cause an error?
b. If the statement causes an error, why? How can you fix it?

2.26 The variable a is a `float` and the variable b is a `double`. Write a statement that will assign the value of b to a without causing an error when the program is compiled.

2.8 Creating Named Constants with `final`

CONCEPT: The `final` key word can be used in a variable declaration to make the variable a named constant. Named constants are initialized with a value, and that value cannot change during the execution of the program.

Assume that the following statement appears in a banking program that calculates data pertaining to loans:

```
amount = balance * 0.069;
```

In such a program, two potential problems arise. First, it is not clear to anyone other than the original programmer what 0.069 is. It appears to be an interest rate, but in some situations there are fees associated with loan payments. How can the purpose of this statement be determined without painstakingly checking the rest of the program?

The second problem occurs if this number is used in other calculations throughout the program and must be changed periodically. Assuming the number is an interest rate, what if the rate changes from 6.9 percent to 8.2 percent? The programmer would have to search through the source code for every occurrence of the number.

Both of these problems can be addressed by using named constants. A *named constant* is a variable whose value is read only and cannot be changed during the program's execution. You can create such a variable in Java by using the `final` key word in the variable declaration. The word `final` is written just before the data type. Here is an example:

```
final double INTEREST_RATE = 0.069;
```

This statement looks just like a regular variable declaration except that the word `final` appears before the data type, and the variable name is written in all uppercase letters. It is not required that the variable name appear in all uppercase letters, but many programmers prefer to write them this way so they are easily distinguishable from regular variable names.

An initialization value must be given when declaring a variable with the `final` modifier, or an error will result when the program is compiled. A compiler error will also result if there are any statements in the program that attempt to change the value of a `final` variable.

An advantage of using named constants is that they make programs more self-documenting. The following statement:

```
amount = balance * 0.069;
```

can be changed to read

```
amount = balance * INTEREST_RATE;
```

A new programmer can read the second statement and know what is happening. It is evident that balance is being multiplied by the interest rate. Another advantage to this approach is that widespread changes can easily be made to the program. Let's say the interest rate appears in a dozen different statements throughout the program. When the rate changes, the initialization value in the definition of the named constant is the only value that needs to be modified. If the rate increases to 8.2 percent, the declaration can be changed to the following:

```
final double INTEREST_RATE = 0.082;
```

The program is then ready to be recompiled. Every statement that uses `INTEREST_RATE` will use the new value.

The `Math.PI` Named Constant

The `Math` class, which is part of the Java API, provides a predefined named constant, `Math.PI`. This constant is assigned the value 3.14159265358979323846, which is an approximation of the mathematical value pi. For example, look at the following statement:

```
area = Math.PI * radius * radius;
```

Assuming the `radius` variable holds the radius of a circle, this statement uses the `Math.PI` constant to calculate the area of the circle.

> For more information about the `Math` class, see Appendix G, available on this book's online resource page at www.pearsonhighered.com/gaddis.

2.9 The String Class

CONCEPT: The `String` class allows you to create objects for holding strings. It also has various methods that allow you to work with strings.

You have already encountered strings and examined programs that display them on the screen, but let's take a moment to make sure you understand what a string is. A string is a sequence of characters. It can be used to represent any type of data that contains text, such as names, addresses, warning messages, and so forth. String literals are enclosed in double-quotation marks, such as the following:

```
"Hello World"
"Joe Mahoney"
```

Although programs commonly encounter strings and must perform a variety of tasks with them, Java does not have a primitive data type for storing them in memory. Instead, the Java API provides a class for handling strings. You use this class to create objects that are capable of storing strings and performing operations on them. Before discussing this class, let's briefly discuss how classes and objects are related.

Objects Are Created from Classes

Chapter 1 introduced you to objects as software entities that can contain attributes and methods. An object's attributes are data values that are stored in the object. An object's methods are procedures that perform operations on the object's attributes. Before an object can be created, however, it must be designed by a programmer. The programmer determines the attributes and methods that are necessary, and then creates a class that describes the object.

You have already seen classes used as containers for applications. A class can also be used to specify the attributes and methods that a particular type of object may have. Think of a class as a "blueprint" that objects may be created from. So a class is not an object, but a description of an object. When the program is running, it can use the class to create, in memory, as many objects as needed. Each object that is created from a class is called an *instance* of the class.

 TIP: Don't worry if these concepts seem a little fuzzy to you. As you progress through this book, the concepts of classes and objects will be reinforced again and again.

The String Class

The class that is provided by the Java API for handling strings is named String. The first step in using the String class is to declare a variable of the String class data type. Here is an example of a String variable declaration:

```
String name;
```

> **TIP:** The S in String is written in uppercase letters. By convention, the first character of a class name is always written in uppercase letters.

This statement declares name as a String variable. Remember that String is a class, not a primitive data type. Let's briefly look at the difference between primitive-type variables and class-type variables.

Primitive-Type Variables and Class-Type Variables

A variable of any type can be associated with an item of data. *Primitive-type variables* hold the actual data items with which they are associated. For example, assume that number is an int variable. The following statement stores the value 25 in the variable:

```
number = 25;
```

This is illustrated in Figure 2-7.

Figure 2-7   A primitive-type variable holds the data with which it is associated

The **number** variable holds the actual data with which it is associated.

```
25
```

A *class-type variable* does not hold the actual data item that it is associated with, but holds the memory address of the data item it is associated with. If name is a String class variable, then name can hold the memory address of a String object. This is illustrated in Figure 2-8.

Figure 2-8   A String class variable can hold the address of a String object

The name **variable** can hold the address of a String object.

When a class-type variable holds the address of an object, it is said that the variable references the object. For this reason, class-type variables are commonly known as *reference variables*.

Creating a `String` Object

Anytime you write a string literal in your program, Java will create a `String` object in memory to hold it. You can create a `String` object in memory and store its address in a `String` variable with a simple assignment statement. Here is an example:

```
name = "Joe Mahoney";
```

Here, the string literal causes a `String` object to be created in memory with the value "Joe Mahoney" stored in it. Then the assignment operator stores the address of that object in the name variable. After this statement executes, it is said that the name variable references a `String` object. This is illustrated in Figure 2-9.

Figure 2-9   The name variable holds the address of a `String` object

You can also use the = operator to initialize a `String` variable, as shown here:

```
String name = "Joe Mahoney";
```

This statement declares name as a `String` variable, creates a `String` object with the value "Joe Mahoney" stored in it and assigns the object's memory address to the name variable. Code Listing 2-20 shows `String` variables being declared, initialized, and then used in a println statement.

Code Listing 2-20   (`StringDemo.java`)

```java
 1  // A simple program demonstrating String objects.
 2
 3  public class StringDemo
 4  {
 5     public static void main(String[] args)
 6     {
 7        String greeting = "Good morning ";
 8        String name = "Herman";
 9
10        System.out.println(greeting + name);
11     }
12  }
```

Program Output

```
Good morning Herman
```

Because the String type is a class instead of a primitive data type, it provides numerous methods for working with strings. For example, the String class has a method named length that returns the length of the string stored in an object. Assuming the name variable references a String object, the following statement stores the length of its string in the variable stringSize (assume that stringSize is an int variable):

```
stringSize = name.length();
```

This statement calls the length method of the object that name refers to. To *call* a method means to execute it. The general form of a method call is as follows:

```
referenceVariable.method(arguments...)
```

referenceVariable is the name of a variable that references an object, *method* is the name of a method, and *arguments...* is zero or more arguments that are passed to the method. If no arguments are passed to the method, as is the case with the length method, a set of empty parentheses must follow the name of the method.

The String class's length method *returns* an int value. This means that the method sends an int value back to the statement that called it. This value can be stored in a variable, displayed on the screen, or used in calculations. Code Listing 2-21 demonstrates the length method.

Code Listing 2-21   **(StringLength.java)**

```java
 1  // This program demonstrates the String class's length method.
 2
 3  public class StringLength
 4  {
 5     public static void main(String[] args)
 6     {
 7        String name = "Herman";
 8        int stringSize;
 9
10        stringSize = name.length();
11        System.out.println(name + " has " + stringSize +
12                           " characters.");
13     }
14  }
```

Program Output

```
Herman has 6 characters.
```

 NOTE: The String class's length method returns the number of characters in the string, including spaces.

You will study the String class methods in detail in Chapter 10, but let's look at a few more examples now. In addition to length, Table 2-15 describes the charAt, toLowerCase, and toUpperCase methods.

Table 2-15   A few `String` class methods

Method	Description and Example

charAt(*index*)	The argument *index* is an int value and specifies a character position in the string. The first character is at position 0, the second character is at position 1, and so forth. The method returns the character at the specified position. The return value is of the type char.
	
	Example:
	<pre>char letter;
	String name = "Herman";
	letter = name.charAt(3);</pre>
	After this code executes, the variable letter will hold the character 'm'.

length()	This method returns the number of characters in the string. The return value is of the type int.
	
	Example:
	<pre>int stringSize;
	String name = "Herman";
	stringSize = name.length();</pre>
	After this code executes, the stringSize variable will hold the value 6.

toLowerCase()	This method returns a new string that is the lowercase equivalent of the string contained in the calling object.
	
	Example:
	<pre>String bigName = "HERMAN";
	String littleName = bigName.toLowerCase();</pre>
	After this code executes, the object referenced by littleName will hold the string "herman".

toUpperCase()	This method returns a new string that is the uppercase equivalent of the string contained in the calling object.
	
	Example:
	<pre>String littleName = "herman";
	String bigName = littleName.toUpperCase();</pre>
	After this code executes, the object referenced by bigName will hold the string "HERMAN".

The program in Code Listing 2-22 demonstrates these methods.

Code Listing 2-22   (**StringMethods.java**)

```
1   // This program demonstrates a few of the String methods.
2
3   public class StringMethods
4   {
5      public static void main(String[] args)
6      {
7         String message = "Java is Great Fun!";
```

```
8          String upper = message.toUpperCase();
9          String lower = message.toLowerCase();
10         char letter = message.charAt(2);
11         int stringSize = message.length();
12
13         System.out.println(message);
14         System.out.println(upper);
15         System.out.println(lower);
16         System.out.println(letter);
17         System.out.println(stringSize);
18     }
19 }
```

Program Output

```
Java is Great Fun!
JAVA IS GREAT FUN!
java is great fun!
v
18
```

 Checkpoint

2.27   Write a statement that declares a String variable named city. The variable should be initialized so it references an object with the string "San Francisco".

2.28   Assume that stringLength is an int variable. Write a statement that stores the length of the string referenced by the city variable (declared in Checkpoint 2.27) in stringLength.

2.29   Assume that oneChar is a char variable. Write a statement that stores the first character in the string referenced by the city variable (declared in Checkpoint 2.27) in oneChar.

2.30   Assume that upperCity is a String reference variable. Write a statement that stores the uppercase equivalent of the string referenced by the city variable (declared in Checkpoint 2.27) in upperCity.

2.31   Assume that lowerCity is a String reference variable. Write a statement that stores the lowercase equivalent of the string referenced by the city variable (declared in Checkpoint 2.27) in lowerCity.

2.10 Scope

CONCEPT: A variable's scope is the part of the program that has access to the variable.

Every variable has a *scope*. The scope of a variable is the part of the program where the variable may be accessed by its name. A variable is visible only to statements inside the variable's scope. The rules that define a variable's scope are complex, and you are only introduced to the concept here. In other chapters of the book we revisit this topic and expand on it.

So far, you have only seen variables declared inside the main method. Variables that are declared inside a method are called *local variables*. Later you will learn about variables that are declared outside a method, but for now, let's focus on the use of local variables.

A local variable's scope begins at the variable's declaration and ends at the end of the method in which the variable is declared. The variable cannot be accessed by statements that are outside this region. This means that a local variable cannot be accessed by code that is outside the method, or inside the method but before the variable's declaration. The program in Code Listing 2-23 shows an example.

Code Listing 2-23   (Scope.java)

```
 1   // This program can't find its variable.
 2
 3   public class Scope
 4   {
 5      public static void main(String[] args)
 6      {
 7         System.out.println(value);   // ERROR!
 8         int value = 100;
 9      }
10   }
```

The program does not compile because it attempts to send the contents of the variable value to println before the variable is declared. It is important to remember that the compiler reads your program from top to bottom. If it encounters a statement that uses a variable before the variable is declared, an error will result. To correct the program, the variable declaration must be written before any statement that uses it.

 NOTE: If you compile this program, the compiler will display an error message such as "cannot resolve symbol." This means that the compiler has encountered a name for which it cannot determine a meaning.

Another rule that you must remember about local variables is that you cannot have two local variables with the same name in the same scope. For example, look at the following method.

```
public static void main(String[] args)
{
   // Declare a variable named number and
   // display its value.
   int number = 7;
   System.out.println(number);
   // Declare another variable named number and
   // display its value.
```

```
    int number = 100;                // ERROR!!!
    System.out.println(number);      // ERROR!!!
}
```

This method declares a variable named number and initializes it with the value 7. The variable's scope begins at the declaration statement and extends to the end of the method. Inside the variable's scope a statement appears that declares another variable named number. This statement will cause an error because you cannot have two local variables with the same name in the same scope.

2.11 Comments

CONCEPT: Comments are notes of explanation that document lines or sections of a program. Comments are part of the program, but the compiler ignores them. They are intended for people who may be reading the source code.

Comments are short notes that are placed in different parts of a program, explaining how those parts of the program work. Comments are not intended for the compiler. They are intended for programmers to read to help them understand the code. The compiler skips all the comments that appear in a program.

As a beginning programmer, you might resist the idea of writing a lot of comments in your programs. After all, it's a lot more fun to write code that actually does something! However, it is crucial that you take the extra time to write comments. They will almost certainly save you time in the future when you have to modify or debug the program. Proper comments make even large and complex programs easy to read and understand.

In Java there are three types of comments: single-line comments, multiline comments, and documentation comments. Let's briefly discuss each one.

Single-Line Comments

You have already seen the first way to write comments in a Java program. You simply place two forward slashes (//) where you want the comment to begin. The compiler ignores everything from that point to the end of the line. Code Listing 2-24 shows that comments may be placed liberally throughout a program.

Code Listing 2-24   (`Comment1.java`)

```
1   // PROGRAM: Comment1.java
2   // Written by Herbert Dorfmann
3   // This program calculates company payroll
4
5   public class Comment1
6   {
7      public static void main(String[] args)
```

```
 8    {
 9        double payRate;      // Holds the hourly pay rate
10        double hours;        // Holds the hours worked
11        int employeeNumber;  // Holds the employee number
12
13        // The remainder of this program is omitted.
14    }
15 }
```

In addition to telling who wrote the program and describing the purpose of variables, comments can also be used to explain complex procedures in your code.

Multiline Comments

The second type of comment in Java is the multiline comment. *Multiline comments* start with /* (a forward slash followed by an asterisk) and end with */ (an asterisk followed by a forward slash). Everything between these markers is ignored. Code Listing 2-25 illustrates how multiline comments may be used.

Code Listing 2-25   (`Comment2.java`)

```
 1 /*
 2     PROGRAM: Comment2.java
 3     Written by Herbert Dorfmann
 4     This program calculates company payroll
 5 */
 6
 7 public class Comment2
 8 {
 9     public static void main(String[] args)
10     {
11         double payRate;      // Holds the hourly pay rate
12         double hours;        // Holds the hours worked
13         int employeeNumber;  // Holds the employee number
14
15         // The remainder of this program is omitted.
16     }
17 }
```

Unlike a comment started with //, a multiline comment can span several lines. This makes it more convenient to write large blocks of comments because you do not have to mark every line. Consequently, the multiline comment is inconvenient for writing single-line comments because you must type both a beginning and ending comment symbol.

Remember the following advice when using multiline comments:

- Be careful not to reverse the beginning symbol with the ending symbol.
- Be sure not to forget the ending symbol.

Many programmers use asterisks or other characters to draw borders or boxes around their comments. This helps to visually separate the comments from surrounding code. These are called block comments. Table 2-16 shows four examples of block comments.

Table 2-16   Block comments

```
/**                                    //*********************************
 *   This program demonstrates the     //   This program demonstrates the *
 *   way to write comments.            //   way to write comments.        *
 */                                    //*********************************

/////////////////////////////////      //-----------------------------------
//   This program demonstrates the     //   This program demonstrates the
//   way to write comments.            //   way to write comments.
/////////////////////////////////      //-----------------------------------
```

Documentation Comments

The third type of comment is known as a documentation comment. *Documentation comments* can be read and processed by a program named javadoc, which comes with the Sun JDK. The purpose of the javadoc program is to read Java source code files and generate attractively formatted HTML files that document the source code. If the source code files contain any documentation comments, the information in the comments becomes part of the HTML documentation, which may be viewed in a Web browser.

Any comment that starts with /** and ends with */ is considered a documentation comment. Normally you write a documentation comment just before a class header, giving a brief description of the class. You also write a documentation comment just before each method header, giving a brief description of the method. For example, Code Listing 2-26 shows a program with documentation comments. This program has a documentation comment just before the class header, and just before the main method header.

Code Listing 2-26   (Comment3.java)

```java
 1  /**
 2      This class creates a program that calculates company payroll.
 3  */
 4
 5  public class Comment3
 6  {
 7      /**
 8          The main method is the program's starting point.
 9      */
10
11      public static void main(String[] args)
12      {
```

```
13        double payRate;        // Holds the hourly pay rate
14        double hours;          // Holds the hours worked
15        int employeeNumber;    // Holds the employee number
16
17        // The Remainder of This Program is Omitted.
18    }
19 }
```

You run the `javadoc` program from the operating system command prompt. Here is the general format of the `javadoc` command:

```
javadoc SourceFile.java
```

`SourceFile.java` is the name of a Java source code file, including the `.java` extension. The file will be read by `javadoc`, and documentation will be produced for it. For example, the following command will produce documentation for the *Comment3.java* source code file, which is shown in Code Listing 2-26:

```
javadoc Comment3.java
```

After this command executes, several documentation files will be created in the same directory as the source code file. One of these files will be named *index.html*. Figure 2-10 shows the *index.html* file being viewed in Internet Explorer. Notice that the text written in the documentation comments appears in the file.

Figure 2-10 Documentation generated by `javadoc`

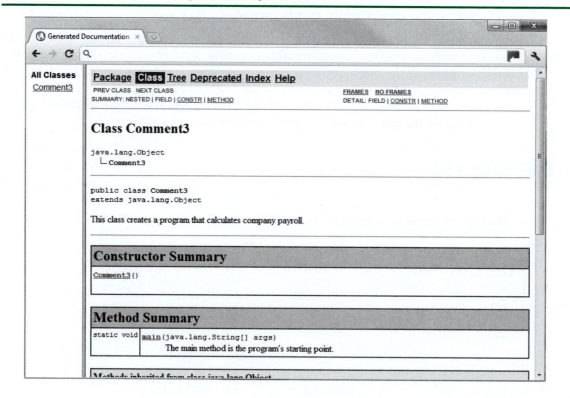

If you look at the JDK documentation, which are HTML files that you view in a Web browser, you will see that they are formatted in the same way as the files generated by javadoc. A benefit of using javadoc to document your source code is that your documentation will have the same professional look and feel as the standard Java documentation.

> You can learn more about documentation comments and the javadoc utility by reading Appendix F, available on this book's online resource page at www.pearsonhighered.com/gaddis. From this point forward in the book we will use simple block style comments and single-line comments in the example source code.

Checkpoint

2.32 How do you write a single-line comment? How do you write a multiline comment? How do you write a documentation comment?

2.33 How are documentation comments different from other types of comments?

2.12 Programming Style

CONCEPT: Programming style refers to the way a programmer uses spaces, indentations, blank lines, and punctuation characters to visually arrange a program's source code.

In Chapter 1, you learned that syntax rules govern the way a language may be used. The syntax rules of Java dictate how and where to place key words, semicolons, commas, braces, and other elements of the language. The compiler checks for syntax errors, and if there are none, generates byte code.

When the compiler reads a program it processes it as one long stream of characters. The compiler doesn't care that each statement is on a separate line, or that spaces separate operators from operands. Humans, on the other hand, find it difficult to read programs that aren't written in a visually pleasing manner. Consider Code Listing 2-27 for example.

Code Listing 2-27   (Compact.java)

```
1   public class Compact {public static void main(String [] args){int
2   shares=220; double averagePrice=14.67; System.out.println(
3   "There were "+shares+" shares sold at $"+averagePrice+
4   " per share.");}}
```

Program Output

```
There were 220 shares sold at $14.67 per share.
```

Although the program is syntactically correct (it doesn't violate any rules of Java), it is very difficult to read. The same program is shown in Code Listing 2-28, written in a more understandable style.

Code Listing 2-28 (Readable.java)

```
1 // This example is much more readable than Compact.java.
2
3 public class Readable
4 {
5    public static void main(String[] args)
6    {
7       int shares = 220;
8       double averagePrice = 14.67;
9
10      System.out.println("There were " + shares
11                         + " shares sold at $"
12                         + averagePrice + " per share.");
13   }
14 }
```

Program Output

There were 220 shares sold at $14.67 per share.

The term *programming style* usually refers to the way source code is visually arranged. It includes techniques for consistently putting spaces and indentations in a program so visual cues are created. These cues quickly tell a programmer important information about a program.

For example, notice in Code Listing 2-28 that inside the class's braces each line is indented, and inside the main method's braces each line is indented again. It is a common programming style to indent all the lines inside a set of braces, as shown in Figure 2-11.

Figure 2-11 Indentation

```
// This example is much more readable than Compact.java.

public class Readable
{
INDENT▸public static void main(String[] args)
INDENT▸{
INDENT▸INDENT▸int shares = 220;
INDENT▸INDENT▸double averagePrice = 14.67;

INDENT▸INDENT▸System.out.println("There were " + shares
INDENT▸INDENT▸ Extra spaces inserted here  + " shares sold at $"
INDENT▸INDENT▸ Extra spaces inserted here  + averagePrice + " per share.");
INDENT▸}
}
```

Another aspect of programming style is how to handle statements that are too long to fit on one line. Notice that the `println` statement is spread out over three lines. Extra spaces are inserted at the beginning of the statement's second and third lines, which indicate that they are continuations.

When declaring multiple variables of the same type with a single statement, it is a common practice to write each variable name on a separate line with a comment explaining the variable's purpose. Here is an example:

```
int fahrenheit,     // To hold the Fahrenheit temperature
    celsius,        // To hold the Celsius temperature
    kelvin;         // To hold the Kelvin temperature
```

You may have noticed in the example programs that a blank line is inserted between the variable declarations and the statements that follow them. This is intended to separate the declarations visually from the executable statements.

There are many other issues related to programming style. They will be presented throughout the book.

2.13 Reading Keyboard Input

CONCEPT: Objects of the `Scanner` class can be used to read input from the keyboard.

Previously we discussed the `System.out` object and how it refers to the standard output device. The Java API has another object, `System.in`, which refers to the standard input device. The *standard input device* is normally the keyboard. You can use the `System.in` object to read keystrokes that have been typed at the keyboard. However, using `System.in` is not as simple and straightforward as using `System.out` because the `System.in` object reads input only as `byte` values. This isn't very useful because programs normally require values of other data types as input. To work around this, you can use the `System.in` object in conjunction with an object of the `Scanner` class. The `Scanner` class is designed to read input from a source (such as `System.in`) and it provides methods that you can use to retrieve the input formatted as primitive values or strings.

First, you create a `Scanner` object and connect it to the `System.in` object. Here is an example of a statement that does just that:

```
Scanner keyboard = new Scanner(System.in);
```

Let's dissect the statement into two parts. The first part of the statement,

```
Scanner keyboard
```

declares a variable named `keyboard`. The data type of the variable is `Scanner`. Because `Scanner` is a class, the `keyboard` variable is a class type variable. Recall from our discussion on `String` objects that a class type variable holds the memory address of an object. Therefore, the `keyboard` variable will be used to hold the address of a `Scanner` object. The second part of the statement is as follows:

```
= new Scanner(System.in);
```

The first thing we see in this part of the statement is the assignment operator (=). The assignment operator will assign something to the `keyboard` variable. After the assignment operator we see the word `new`, which is a Java key word. The purpose of the `new` key word is to create an object in memory. The type of object that will be created is listed next. In this case, we see `Scanner(System.in)` listed after the `new` key word. This specifies that a `Scanner` object should be created, and it should be connected to the `System.in` object. The memory address of the object is assigned (by the = operator) to the variable `keyboard`. After the statement executes, the `keyboard` variable will reference the `Scanner` object that was created in memory.

Figure 2-12 points out the purpose of each part of this statement. Figure 2-13 illustrates how the `keyboard` variable references an object of the `Scanner` class.

Figure 2-12 The parts of the statement

Figure 2-13 The `keyboard` variable references a `Scanner` object

 NOTE: In the preceding code, we chose `keyboard` as the variable name. There is nothing special about the name `keyboard`. We simply chose that name because we will use the variable to read input from the keyboard.

The `Scanner` class has methods for reading strings, bytes, integers, `long` integers, `short` integers, `floats`, and `doubles`. For example, the following code uses an object of the `Scanner` class to read an `int` value from the keyboard and assign the value to the `number` variable.

```
int number;
Scanner keyboard = new Scanner(System.in);
System.out.print("Enter an integer value: ");
number = keyboard.nextInt();
```

The last statement shown here calls the `Scanner` class's `nextInt` method. The `nextInt` method formats an input value as an `int`, and then returns that value. Therefore, this statement formats the input that was entered at the keyboard as an `int`, and then returns it. The value is assigned to the `number` variable.

Table 2-17 lists several of the `Scanner` class's methods and describes their use.

Table 2-17   Some of the `Scanner` class methods

Method	Example and Description

nextByte	**Example Usage:**
	```byte x;```
	```Scanner keyboard = new Scanner(System.in);```
	```System.out.print("Enter a byte value: ");```
	```x = keyboard.nextByte();```
	
	Description: Returns input as a byte.

nextDouble	**Example Usage:**
	```double number;```
	```Scanner keyboard = new Scanner(System.in);```
	```System.out.print("Enter a double value: ");```
	```number = keyboard.nextDouble();```
	
	Description: Returns input as a double.

nextFloat	**Example Usage:**
	```float number;```
	```Scanner keyboard = new Scanner(System.in);```
	```System.out.print("Enter a float value: ");```
	```number = keyboard.nextFloat();```
	
	Description: Returns input as a float.

nextInt	**Example Usage:**
	```int number;```
	```Scanner keyboard = new Scanner(System.in);```
	```System.out.print("Enter an integer value: ");```
	```number = keyboard.nextInt();```
	
	Description: Returns input as an int.

nextLine	**Example Usage:**
	```String name;```
	```Scanner keyboard = new Scanner(System.in);```
	```System.out.print("Enter your name: ");```
	```name = keyboard.nextLine();```
	
	Description: Returns input as a String.

(continued)

Table 2-17 Some of the Scanner class methods (continued)

Method	Example and Description

nextLong	**Example Usage:**
	`long number;`
	`Scanner keyboard = new Scanner(System.in);`
	`System.out.print("Enter a long value: ");`
	`number = keyboard.nextLong();`
	Description: Returns input as a long.

nextShort	**Example Usage:**
	`short number;`
	`Scanner keyboard = new Scanner(System.in);`
	`System.out.print("Enter a short value: ");`
	`number = keyboard.nextShort();`
	Description: Returns input as a short.

Using the import Statement

There is one last detail about the Scanner class that you must know before you will be ready to use it. The Scanner class is not automatically available to your Java programs. Any program that uses the Scanner class should have the following statement near the beginning of the file, before any class definition:

```
import java.util.Scanner;
```

This statement tells the Java compiler where in the Java library to find the Scanner class and makes it available to your program.

Code Listing 2-29 shows the Scanner class being used to read a String, an int, and a double.

Code Listing 2-29   (Payroll.java)

```
 1  import java.util.Scanner;  // Needed for the Scanner class
 2
 3  /**
 4   *    This program demonstrates the Scanner class.
 5   */
 6
 7  public class Payroll
 8  {
 9      public static void main(String[] args)
10      {
11          String name;        // To hold a name
12          int hours;          // Hours worked
13          double payRate;     // Hourly pay rate
14          double grossPay;    // Gross pay
```

```
15
16          // Create a Scanner object to read input.
17          Scanner keyboard = new Scanner(System.in);
18
19          // Get the user's name.
20          System.out.print("What is your name? ");
21          name = keyboard.nextLine();
22
23          // Get the number of hours worked this week.
24          System.out.print("How many hours did you work this week? ");
25          hours = keyboard.nextInt();
26
27          // Get the user's hourly pay rate.
28          System.out.print("What is your hourly pay rate? ");
29          payRate = keyboard.nextDouble();
30
31          // Calculate the gross pay.
32          grossPay = hours * payRate;
33
34          // Display the resulting information.
35          System.out.println("Hello " + name);
36          System.out.println("Your gross pay is $" + grossPay);
37       }
38  }
```

Program Output with Example Input Shown in Bold

What is your name? **Joe Mahoney [Enter]**
How many hours did you work this week? **40 [Enter]**
What is your hourly pay rate? **20 [Enter]**
Hello Joe Mahoney
Your gross pay is $800.0

NOTE: Notice that each Scanner class method that we used waits for the user to press the [Enter] key before it returns a value. When the [Enter] key is pressed, the cursor automatically moves to the next line for subsequent output operations.

Reading a Character

Sometimes you will want to read a single character from the keyboard. For example, your program might ask the user a yes/no question and specify that he or she type Y for yes or N for no. The Scanner class does not have a method for reading a single character, however. The approach that we will use in this book for reading a character is to use the Scanner class's nextLine method to read a string from the keyboard, and then use the String class's charAt method to extract the first character of the string. This will be the character that the user entered at the keyboard. Here is an example:

```
String input;    // To hold a line of input
char answer;     // To hold a single character

// Create a Scanner object for keyboard input.
Scanner keyboard = new Scanner(System.in);

// Ask the user a question.
System.out.print("Are you having fun? (Y=yes, N=no) ");
input = keyboard.nextLine();   // Get a line of input.
answer = input.charAt(0)       // Get the first character.
```

The input variable references a String object. The last statement in this code calls the String class's charAt method to retrieve the character at position 0, which is the first character in the string. After this statement executes, the answer variable will hold the character that the user typed at the keyboard.

Mixing Calls to nextLine with Calls to Other Scanner Methods

When you call one of the Scanner class's methods to read a primitive value, such as nextInt or nextDouble, and then call the nextLine method to read a string, an annoying and hard-to-find problem can occur. For example, look at the program in Code Listing 2-30.

Code Listing 2-30   (InputProblem.java)

```
 1  import java.util.Scanner;  // Needed for the Scanner class
 2
 3  /**
 4   *   This program has a problem reading input.
 5   */
 6
 7  public class InputProblem
 8  {
 9     public static void main(String[] args)
10     {
11        String name;    // To hold the user's name
12        int age;        // To hold the user's age
13        double income;  // To hold the user's income
14
15        // Create a Scanner object to read input.
16        Scanner keyboard = new Scanner(System.in);
17
18        // Get the user's age.
19        System.out.print("What is your age? ");
20        age = keyboard.nextInt();
21
```

```
22          // Get the user's income
23          System.out.print("What is your annual income? ");
24          income = keyboard.nextDouble();
25
26          // Get the user's name.
27          System.out.print("What is your name? ");
28          name = keyboard.nextLine();
29
30          // Display the information back to the user.
31          System.out.println("Hello " + name + ". Your age is " +
32                             age + " and your income is $" +
33                             income);
34      }
35  }
```

Program Output with Example Input Shown in Bold

What is your age? **24 [Enter]**
What is your annual income? **50000.00 [Enter]**
What is your name? Hello. Your age is 24 and your income is $50000.0

Notice in the example output that the program first allows the user to enter his or her age. The statement in line 20 reads an `int` from the keyboard and stores the value in the `age` variable. Next, the user enters his or her income. The statement in line 24 reads a `double` from the keyboard and stores the value in the `income` variable. Then the user is asked to enter his or her name, but it appears that the statement in line 28 is skipped. The name is never read from the keyboard. This happens because of a slight difference in behavior between the `nextLine` method and the other `Scanner` class methods.

When the user types keystrokes at the keyboard, those keystrokes are stored in an area of memory that is sometimes called the *keyboard buffer*. Pressing the [Enter] key causes a new-line character to be stored in the keyboard buffer. In the example running of the program in Code Listing 2-30, the user was asked to enter his or her age, and the statement in line 20 called the `nextInt` method to read an integer from the keyboard buffer. Notice that the user typed 24 and then pressed the [Enter] key. The `nextInt` method read the value 24 from the keyboard buffer, and then stopped when it encountered the newline character. So the value 24 was read from the keyboard buffer, but the newline character was not read. The newline character remained in the keyboard buffer.

Next, the user was asked to enter his or her annual income. The user typed 50000.00 and then pressed the [Enter] key. When the `nextDouble` method in line 24 executed, it first encountered the newline character that was left behind by the `nextInt` method. This does not cause a problem because the `nextDouble` method is designed to skip any leading newline characters it encounters. It skips over the initial newline, reads the value 50000.00 from the keyboard buffer, and stops reading when it encounters the next newline character. This newline character is then left in the keyboard buffer.

Next, the user is asked to enter his or her name. In line 28 the nextLine method is called. The nextLine method, however, is not designed to skip over an initial newline character. If a newline character is the first character that the nextLine method encounters, then nothing will be read. Because the nextDouble method, back in line 24, left a newline character in the keyboard buffer, the nextLine method will not read any input. Instead, it will immediately terminate, and the user will not be given a chance to enter his or her name.

Although the details of this problem might seem confusing, the solution is easy. The program in Code Listing 2-31 is a modification of Code Listing 2-30, with the input problem fixed.

Code Listing 2-31   **(CorrectedInputProblem.java)**

```
 1 import java.util.Scanner;  // Needed for the Scanner class
 2
 3 /**
 4  *    This program correctly read numeric and string input.
 5  */
 6
 7 public class CorrectedInputProblem
 8 {
 9    public static void main(String[] args)
10    {
11       String name;    // To hold the user's name
12       int age;        // To hold the user's age
13       double income; // To hold the user's income
14
15       // Create a Scanner object to read input.
16       Scanner keyboard = new Scanner(System.in);
17
18       // Get the user's age.
19       System.out.print("What is your age? ");
20       age = keyboard.nextInt();
21
22       // Get the user's income
23       System.out.print("What is your annual income? ");
24       income = keyboard.nextDouble();
25
26       // Consume the remaining newline.
27       keyboard.nextLine();
28
29       // Get the user's name.
30       System.out.print("What is your name? ");
31       name = keyboard.nextLine();
32
33       // Display the information back to the user.
```

```
34          System.out.println("Hello " + name + ". Your age is " +
35                          age + " and your income is $" +
36                          income);
37     }
38 }
```

Program Output with Example Input Shown in Bold

What is your age? **24 [Enter]**
What is your annual income? **50000.00 [Enter]**
What is your name? **Mary Simpson [Enter]**
Hello Mary Simpson. Your age is 24 and your income is $50000.0

Notice that after the user's income is read by the nextDouble method in line 24, the nextLine method is called in line 27. The purpose of this call is to consume, or remove, the newline character that remains in the keyboard buffer. Then, in line 31, the nextLine method is called again. This time it correctly reads the user's name.

NOTE: Notice that in line 27, where we consume the remaining newline character, we do not assign the method's return value to any variable. This is because we are simply calling the method to remove the newline character, and we do not need to keep the method's return value.

2.14 Dialog Boxes

CONCEPT: The JOptionPane class allows you to quickly display a dialog box, which is a small graphical window displaying a message or requesting input.

A *dialog box* is a small graphical window that displays a message to the user or requests input. You can quickly display dialog boxes with the JOptionPane class. In this section we will discuss the following types of dialog boxes and how you can display them using JOptionPane:

- Message Dialog   A dialog box that displays a message; an OK button is also displayed
- Input Dialog   A dialog box that prompts the user for input and provides a text field where input is typed; an OK button and a Cancel button are also displayed

Figure 2-14 shows an example of each type of dialog box.

Figure 2-14 A message dialog and an input dialog

Message dialog

Input dialog

The JOptionPane class is not automatically available to your Java programs. Any program that uses the JOptionPane class must have the following statement near the beginning of the file:

```java
import javax.swing.JOptionPane;
```

This statement tells the compiler where to find the JOptionPane class and makes it available to your program.

Displaying Message Dialogs

The showMessageDialog method is used to display a message dialog. Here is a statement that calls the method:

```java
JOptionPane.showMessageDialog(null, "Hello World");
```

The first argument is only important in programs that display other graphical windows. You will learn more about this in Chapter 7. Until then, we will always pass the key word null as the first argument. This causes the dialog box to be displayed in the center of the screen. The second argument is the message that we wish to display in the dialog box. This code will cause the dialog box in Figure 2-15 to appear. When the user clicks the OK button, the dialog box will close.

Figure 2-15 Message dialog

Displaying Input Dialogs

An input dialog is a quick and simple way to ask the user to enter data. You use the JOptionPane class's showInputDialog method to display an input dialog. The following code calls the method:

```
String name;
name = JOptionPane.showInputDialog("Enter your name.");
```

The argument passed to the method is a message to display in the dialog box. This statement will cause the dialog box shown in Figure 2-16 to be displayed in the center of the screen. If the user clicks the OK button, name will reference the string value entered by the user into the text field. If the user clicks the Cancel button, name will reference the special value null.

Figure 2-16   Input dialog

An Example Program

The program in Code Listing 2-32 demonstrates how to use both types of dialog boxes. This program uses input dialogs to ask the user to enter his or her first, middle, and last names, and then displays a greeting with a message dialog. When this program executes, the dialog boxes shown in Figure 2-17 will be displayed, one at a time.

Code Listing 2-32   **(NamesDialog.java)**

```java
 1  import javax.swing.JOptionPane;
 2
 3  /**
 4   *  This program demonstrates using dialogs
 5   *  with JOptionPane.
 6   */
 7
 8  public class NamesDialog
 9  {
10     public static void main(String[] args)
11     {
12        String firstName;  // The user's first name
13        String middleName; // The user's middle name
14        String lastName;   // The user's last name
15
```

```
16          // Get the user's first name.
17          firstName =
18              JOptionPane.showInputDialog("What is " +
19                                          "your first name? ");
20
21          // Get the user's middle name.
22          middleName =
23              JOptionPane.showInputDialog("What is " +
24                                          "your middle name? ");
25
26          // Get the user's last name.
27          lastName =
28              JOptionPane.showInputDialog("What is " +
29                                          "your last name? ");
30
31          // Display a greeting
32          JOptionPane.showMessageDialog(null, "Hello " +
33                          firstName + " " + middleName +
34                          " " + lastName);
35          System.exit(0);
36      }
37  }
```

Notice the last statement in the `main` method:

```
System.exit(0);
```

This statement causes the program to end and is required if you use the `JOptionPane` class to display dialog boxes. Unlike a console program, a program that uses `JOptionPane` does not automatically stop executing when the end of the `main` method is reached because the `JOptionPane` class causes an additional task to run in the JVM. If the `System.exit` method is not called, this task, also known as a *thread*, will continue to execute, even after the end of the `main` method has been reached.

The `System.exit` method requires an integer argument. This argument is an exit code that is passed back to the operating system. Although this code is usually ignored, it can be used outside the program to indicate whether the program ended successfully or as the result of a failure. The value 0 traditionally indicates that the program ended successfully.

Converting String Input to Numbers

Unlike the `Scanner` class, the `JOptionPane` class does not have different methods for reading values of different data types as input. The `showInputDialog` method always returns the user's input as a `String`, even if the user enters numeric data. For example, if the user enters the number 72 into an input dialog, the `showInputDialog` method will return the string `"72"`. This can be a problem if you wish to use the user's input in a math operation because, as you know, you cannot perform math on strings. In such a case, you must convert the input to a numeric value. To convert a string value to a numeric value, you use one of the methods listed in Table 2-18.

Figure 2-17 Dialog boxes displayed by the `NamesDialog` program

The first dialog box appears as shown here. The user types Joe and clicks OK.

The second dialog box appears, as shown here. In this example the user types Clondike and clicks OK.

The third dialog box appears, as shown here. In this example the user types Mahoney and clicks OK.

The fourth dialog box appears, as shown here, displaying a greeting.

Table 2-18 Methods for converting strings to numbers

Method	Use This Method to ...	Example Code
`Byte.parseByte`	Convert a string to a byte.	`byte num;` `num = Byte.parseByte(str);`
`Double.parseDouble`	Convert a string to a double.	`double num;` `num = Double.parseDouble(str);`
`Float.parseFloat`	Convert a string to a float.	`float num;` `num = Float.parseFloat(str);`
`Integer.parseInt`	Convert a string to an int.	`int num;` `num = Integer.parseInt(str);`
`Long.parseLong`	Convert a string to a long.	`long num;` `num = Long.parseLong(str);`
`Short.parseShort`	Convert a string to a short.	`short num;` `num = Short.parseShort(str);`

NOTE: The methods in Table 2-18 are part of Java's wrapper classes, which you will learn more about in Chapter 8.

Here is an example of how you would use the `Integer.parseInt` method to convert the value returned from the `JOptionPane.showInputDialog` method to an int:

```
int number;
String str;
str = JOptionPane.showInputDialog("Enter a number.");
number = Integer.parseInt(str);
```

After this code executes, the `number` variable will hold the value entered by the user, converted to an int. Here is an example of how you would use the `Double.parseDouble` method to convert the user's input to a double:

```
double price;
String str;
str = JOptionPane.showInputDialog("Enter the retail price.");
price = Double.parseDouble(str);
```

After this code executes, the `price` variable will hold the value entered by the user, converted to a double. Code Listing 2-33 shows a complete program. This is a modification of the `Payroll.java` program in Code Listing 2-29. When this program executes, the dialog boxes shown in Figure 2-18 will be displayed, one at a time.

Code Listing 2-33 **(PayrollDialog.java)**

```
 1   import javax.swing.JOptionPane;
 2
 3   /**
 4    *  This program demonstrates using dialogs
 5    *  with JOptionPane.
 6    */
 7
 8   public class PayrollDialog
 9   {
10     public static void main(String[] args)
11     {
12        String inputString;      // For reading input
13        String name;             // The user's name
14        int hours;               // The number of hours worked
15        double payRate;          // The user's hourly pay rate
16        double grossPay;         // The user's gross pay
17
18        // Get the user's name.
19        name = JOptionPane.showInputDialog("What is " +
20                                           "your name? ");
21
22        // Get the hours worked.
23        inputString =
24          JOptionPane.showInputDialog("How many hours " +
25                                      "did you work this week? ");
26
```

```
27          // Convert the input to an int.
28          hours = Integer.parseInt(inputString);
29
30          // Get the hourly pay rate.
31          inputString =
32            JOptionPane.showInputDialog("What is your " +
33                                        "hourly pay rate? ");
34
35          // Convert the input to a double.
36          payRate = Double.parseDouble(inputString);
37
38          // Calculate the gross pay.
39          grossPay = hours * payRate;
40
41          // Display the results.
42          JOptionPane.showMessageDialog(null, "Hello " +
43                        name + ". Your gross pay is $" +
44                        grossPay);
45
46          // End the program.
47          System.exit(0);
48      }
49 }
```

Figure 2-18 Dialog boxes displayed by `PayrollDialog.java`

The first dialog box appears as shown here. The user enters his or her name and then clicks OK.

The second dialog box appears, as shown here. The user enters the number of hours worked and then clicks OK.

The third dialog box appears, as shown here. The user enters his or her hourly pay rate and then clicks OK.

The fourth dialog box appears, as shown here.

Checkpoint

2.34 What is the purpose of the following types of dialog boxes?
Message dialog
Input dialog

2.35 Write code that will display each of the dialog boxes shown in Figure 2-19.

2.36 Write code that displays an input dialog asking the user to enter his or her age. Convert the input value to an `int` and store it in an `int` variable named `age`.

2.37 What `import` statement do you write in a program that uses the `JOptionPane` class?

Figure 2-19 Dialog boxes for Checkpoint 2.35

a)
```
Message                    [x]
   (i)   Greetings Earthling.

              OK
```

b)
```
Input                      [x]
  ?    Enter a number.
       [                    ]

         OK      Cancel
```

2.15 The `System.out.printf` Method

CONCEPT: The `System.out.printf` method allows you to format output in a variety of ways.

When you display numbers with the `System.out.println` or `System.out.print` methods, you have little control over the way the numbers appear. For example, a value of the `double` data type can be displayed with as many as 15 decimal places, as demonstrated by the following code:

```
double number = 10.0 / 6.0;
System.out.println(number);
```

This code will display:

```
1.666666666666667
```

Quite often, you want to format numbers so they are displayed in a particular way. For example, you might want to round a floating-point number to a specific number of decimal places, or insert comma separators to make a number easier to read. Fortunately, Java gives you a way to do just that, and more, with the `System.out.printf` method. The method's general format is as follows:

```
System.out.printf(FormatString, ArgumentList)
```

In the general format, *FormatString* is a string that contains text and/or special formatting specifiers. *ArgumentList* is a list of zero or more additional arguments, which will be formatted according to the format specifiers listed in the format string.

The simplest way you can use the `System.out.printf` method is with only a format string, and no additional arguments. Here is an example:

```
System.out.printf("I love Java programming.");
```

The format string in this example is `"I love Java programming"`. This method call does not perform any special formatting; however, it simply prints the string `"I love Java programming."`. Using the method in this fashion is exactly like using the `System.out.print` method.

In most cases you will call the `System.out.printf` method in the following manner:

- The format string will contain one or more format specifiers. A *format specifier* is a placeholder for a value that will be inserted into the string when it is displayed.
- After the format string, one or more additional arguments will appear. Each of the additional arguments will correspond to a format specifier that appears inside the format string.

The following code shows an example:

```
double sales = 12345.67;
System.out.printf("Our sales is %f for the day.\n", sales);
```

Notice the following characteristics of the `System.out.printf` method call:

- Inside the format string, the `%f` is a format specifier. The letter `f` indicates that a floating-point value will be inserted into the string when it is displayed.
- Following the format string, the `sales` variable is passed as an argument. This argument corresponds to the `%f` format specifier that appears inside the format string.

When the `System.out.printf` method executes, the `%f` will not be displayed on the screen. In its place, the value of the `sales` argument will be displayed. Here is the output of the code:

```
Our sales is 12345.670000 for the day.
```

The diagram in Figure 2-20 shows how the `sales` variable corresponds to the `%f` format specifier.

Figure 2-20   The value of the `sales` variable is displayed in the place of the `%f` format specifier

```
System.out.printf("Our sales are %f for the day.\n", sales);
```

Here is another example:

```
double temp1 = 72.5, temp2 = 83.7;
System.out.printf("The temperatures are %f and %f degrees.\n", temp1, temp2);
```

First, notice that this example uses two %f format specifiers in the format string. Also notice that the two additional arguments appear after the format string. The value of the first argument, temp1, will be printed in place of the first %f, and the value of the second argument, temp2, will be printed in place of the second %f. The code will produce the following output:

```
The temperatures are 72.500000 and 83.700000 degrees.
```

There is a one-to-one correspondence between the format specifiers and the arguments that appear after the format string. The diagram in Figure 2-21 shows how the first format specifier corresponds to the first argument after the format string (the temp1 variable), and the second format specifier corresponds to the second argument after the format string (the temp2 variable).

Figure 2-21 The format specifiers and their corresponding arguments

The following code shows another example:

```
double value1 = 3.0;
double value2 = 6.0;
double value3 = 9.0;
System.out.printf("%f %f %f\n", value1, value2, value3);
```

In the System.out.printf method call, there are three format specifiers and three additional arguments after the format string. This code will produce the following output:

```
3.000000 6.000000 9.000000
```

The diagram in Figure 2-22 shows how the format specifiers correspond to the arguments that appear after the format string.

Figure 2-22 The format specifiers and their corresponding arguments

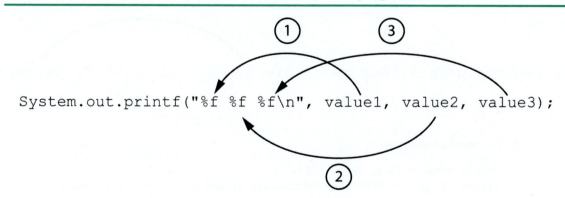

The previous examples demonstrated how to format floating-point numbers with the `%f` format specifier. The letter f in the format specifier is a *conversion character* that indicates the data type of the argument that is being formatted. You use the f conversion character with any argument that is a `float` or a `double`.

If you want to format an integer value, you must use the `%d` format specifier. The d conversion character stands for decimal integer, and it can be used with arguments of the `int`, `short`, and `long` data types. Here is an example that displays an `int`:

```
int hours = 40;
System.out.printf("I worked %d hours this week.\n", hours);
```

In this example, the `%d` format specifier corresponds with the `hours` argument. This code will display the following:

```
I worked 40 hours this week.
```

Here is an example that displays two `int` values:

```
int dogs = 2;
int cats = 4;
System.out.printf("We have %d dogs and %d cats.\n", dogs, cats);
```

This code will display the following:

```
We have 2 dogs and 4 cats.
```

Keep in mind that `%f` must be used with floating-point values, and `%d` must be used with integer values. Otherwise, an error will occur at runtime.

Format Specifier Syntax

In the previous examples you saw how format specifiers correspond to the arguments that appear after the format string. Now you can learn how to use format specifiers to actually format the values that they correspond to. When displaying numbers, the general syntax for writing a format specifier is:

```
%[flags][width][.precision]conversion
```

The items that appear inside brackets are optional. Here is a summary of each item:

- `%`—All format specifiers begin with a `%` character.
- *flags*—After the `%` character, one or more optional flags may appear. Flags cause the value to be formatted in a variety of ways.
- *width*—After any flags, you can optionally specify the minimum field width for the value.
- *.precision*—If the value is a floating-point number, after the minimum field width, you can optionally specify the precision. This is the number of decimal places that the number should be rounded to.
- *conversion*—All format specifiers must end with a conversion character, such as f for floating-point, or d for decimal integer.

Let's take a closer look at each of the optional items, beginning with precision.

Precision

You probably noticed in the previous examples that the `%f` format specifier causes floating-point values to be displayed with six decimal places. You can change the number of decimal places that are displayed, as shown in the following example:

```
double temp = 78.42819;
System.out.printf("The temperature is %.2f degrees.\n", temp);
```

Notice that this example doesn't use the regular `%f` format specifier, but uses `%.2f` instead. The `.2` that appears between the `%` and the `f` specifies the *precision* of the displayed value. It will cause the value of the `temp` variable to be rounded to two decimal places. This code will produce the following output:

```
The temperature is 78.43 degrees.
```

The following example displays the same value, rounded to one decimal place:

```
double temp = 78.42819;
System.out.printf("The temperature is %.1f degrees.\n", temp);
```

This code will produce the following output:

```
The temperature is 78.4 degrees.
```

The following code shows another example:

```
double value1 = 123.45678;
double value2 = 123.45678;
double value3 = 123.45678;
System.out.printf("%.1f %.2f %.3f\n", value1, value2, value3);
```

In this example, `value1` is rounded to one decimal place, `value2` is rounded to two decimal places, and `value3` is rounded to three decimal places. This code will produce the following output:

```
123.5 123.46 123.457
```

Keep in mind that you can specify precision only with floating-point values. If you specify a precision with the `%d` format specifier, an error will occur at runtime.

Specifying a Minimum Field Width

A format specifier can also include a *minimum field width*, which is the minimum number of spaces that should be used to display the value. The following example prints a floating-point number in a field that is 20 spaces wide:

```
double number = 12345.6789;
System.out.printf("The number is:%20f\n", number);
```

Notice that the number 20 appears in the format specifier, between the `%` and the `f`. This code will produce the following output:

```
The number is:         12345.678900
```

In this example, the 20 that appears inside the `%f` format specifier indicates that the number should be displayed in a field that is a minimum of 20 spaces wide. This is illustrated in Figure 2-23.

Figure 2-23   The number is displayed in a field that is 20 spaces wide

```
The number is:              12345.678900
```

The number is displayed in a
field that is 20 spaces wide.

In this case, the number that is displayed is shorter than the field that it is displayed in. The number 12345.678900 uses only 12 spaces on the screen, but it is displayed in a field that is 20 spaces wide. When this is the case, the number will be right justified in the field. If a value is too large to fit in the specified field width, the field is automatically enlarged to accommodate it. The following example prints a floating-point number in a field that is only one space wide:

```
double number = 12345.6789;
System.out.printf("The number is:%1f\n", number);
```

The value of the number variable requires more than one space, however, so the field width is expanded to accommodate the entire number. This code will produce the following output:

```
The number is:12345.678900
```

You can specify a minimum field width for integers, as well as floating-point values. The following example displays an integer with a minimum field width of six characters:

```
int number = 200;
System.out.printf("The number is:%6d", number);
```

This code will display the following:

```
The number is:   200
```

Combining Minimum Field Width and Precision in the Same Format Specifier

When specifying the minimum field width and the precision of a floating-point number in the same format specifier, remember that the field width must appear first, followed by the precision. For example, the following code displays a number in a field of 12 spaces, rounded to two decimal places:

```
double number = 12345.6789;
System.out.printf("The number is:%12.2f\n", number);
```

This code will produce the following output:

```
The number is:    12345.68
```

Field widths can help when you need to print numbers aligned in columns. For example, look at Code Listing 2-34. Each of the variables is displayed in a field that is eight spaces wide, and rounded to two decimal places. The numbers appear aligned in a column.

Code Listing 2-34 (Columns.java)

```
 1  /**
 2   *  This program displays a variety of
 3   *  floating-point numbers in a column
 4   *  with their decimal points aligned.
 5   */
 6
 7  public class Columns
 8  {
 9     public static void main(String[] args)
10     {
11        // Declare a variety of double variables.
12        double num1 = 127.899;
13        double num2 = 3465.148;
14        double num3 = 3.776;
15        double num4 = 264.821;
16        double num5 = 88.081;
17        double num6 = 1799.999;
18
19        // Display each variable in a field of
20        // 8 spaces with 2 decimal places.
21        System.out.printf("%8.2f\n", num1);
22        System.out.printf("%8.2f\n", num2);
23        System.out.printf("%8.2f\n", num3);
24        System.out.printf("%8.2f\n", num4);
25        System.out.printf("%8.2f\n", num5);
26        System.out.printf("%8.2f\n", num6);
27     }
28  }
```

Program Output

```
 127.90
3465.15
   3.78
 264.82
  88.08
1800.00
```

Flags

There are several optional flags that you can insert into a format specifier to cause a value to be formatted in a particular way. In this book, we will use flags for the following purposes:

- To display numbers with comma separators
- To pad numbers with leading zeros
- To left justify numbers

If you use a flag in a format specifier, you must write the flag before the field width and the precision.

Comma Separators

Large numbers are easier to read if they are displayed with comma separators. You can format a number with comma separators by inserting a comma (,) flag into the format specifier. Here is an example:

```
double amount = 1234567.89;
System.out.printf("%,f\n", amount);
```

This code will produce the following output:

```
1,234,567.890000
```

Quite often, you will want to format a number with comma separators, and round the number to a specific number of decimal places. You can accomplish this by inserting a comma, followed by the precision value, into the %f format specifier, as shown in the following example:

```
double sales = 28756.89;
System.out.printf("Sales for the month are %,.2f\n", sales);
```

This code will produce the following output:

```
Sales for the month are 28,756.89
```

Code Listing 2-35 demonstrates how the comma separator and a precision of two decimal places can be used to format a number as a currency amount.

Code Listing 2-35   **(CurrencyFormat.java)**

```
 1  /**
 2   *  This program demonstrates how to use the System.out.printf
 3   *  method to format a number as currency.
 4   */
 5
 6  public class CurrencyFormat
 7  {
 8     public static void main(String[] args)
 9     {
10        double monthlyPay = 5000.0;
11        double annualPay = monthlyPay * 12;
12        System.out.printf("Your annual pay is $%,.2f\n", annualPay);
13     }
14  }
```

Program Output

```
Your annual pay is $60,000.00
```

The following example displays a floating-point number with comma separators, in a field of 15 spaces, rounded to two decimal places:

```java
double amount = 1234567.8901;
System.out.printf("%,15.2f\n", amount);
```

This code will produce the following output:

```
  1,234,567.89
```

The following example displays an int with a minimum field width of six characters:

```java
int number = 200;
System.out.printf("The number is:%6d", number);
```

This code will display the following:

```
The number is:   200
```

The following example displays an int with comma separators, with a minimum field width of 10 characters:

```java
int number = 20000;
System.out.printf("The number is:%,10d", number);
```

This code will display the following:

```
The number is:    20,000
```

Padding Numbers with Leading Zeros

Sometimes, when a number is shorter than the field in which it is displayed, you want to pad the number with leading zeros. If you insert a 0 flag into a format specifier, the resulting number will be padded with leading zeros, if it is shorter than the field width. The following code shows an example:

```java
double number = 123.4;
System.out.printf("The number is:%08.1f\n", number);
```

This code will produce the following output:

```
The number is:000123.4
```

The diagram in Figure 2-24 shows the purpose of each part of the format specifier in the previous example.

Figure 2-24   Format specifier that pads with leading zeros

The following example displays an int padded with leading zeros, with a minimum field width of seven characters:

```
int number = 1234;
System.out.printf("The number is:%07d", number);
```

This code will display the following:

```
The number is:0001234
```

The program in Code Listing 2-36 shows another example. This program displays a variety of floating-point numbers with leading zeros, in a field of nine spaces, rounded to two decimal places.

Code Listing 2-36   (LeadingZeros.java)

```
 1 /**
 2  *  This program displays numbers padded with leading zeros.
 3  */
 4
 5 public class LeadingZeros
 6 {
 7    public static void main(String[] args)
 8    {
 9       // Declare a variety of double variables.
10       double number1 = 1.234;
11       double number2 = 12.345;
12       double number3 = 123.456;
13
14       // Display each variable with leading
15       // zeros, in a field of 9 spaces, rounded
16       // to 2 decimal places.
17       System.out.printf("%09.2f\n", number1);
18       System.out.printf("%09.2f\n", number2);
19       System.out.printf("%09.2f\n", number3);
20    }
21 }
```

Program Output

```
000001.23
000012.35
000123.46
```

Left-Justified Numbers

By default, when a number is shorter than the field in which it is displayed, the number is right-justified within that field. If you want a number to be left-justified within its field, you insert a minus sign (-) flag into the format specifier. Code Listing 2-37 shows an example.

Code Listing 2-37   `(LeftJustified.java)`

```
 1   /**
 2    *  This program displays a variety of
 3    *  numbers left-justified in columns.
 4    */
 5
 6   public class LeftJustified
 7   {
 8      public static void main(String[] args)
 9      {
10         // Declare a variety of int variables.
11         int num1 = 123;
12         int num2 = 12;
13         int num3 = 45678;
14         int num4 = 456;
15         int num5 = 1234567;
16         int num6 = 1234;
17
18         // Display each variable left-justified
19         // in a field of 8 spaces.
20         System.out.printf("%-8d%-8d\n", num1, num2);
21         System.out.printf("%-8d%-8d\n", num3, num4);
22         System.out.printf("%-8d%-8d\n", num5, num6);
23      }
24   }
```

Program Output

```
123      12
45678    456
1234567  1234
```

Formatting String Arguments

If you wish to print a string argument, use the `%s` format specifier. Here is an example:

```
String name = "Ringo";
System.out.printf("Your name is %s\n", name);
```

This code produces the following output:

```
Your name is Ringo
```

You can also use a field width when printing strings. For example, look at the following code:

```
String name1 = "George";
String name2 = "Franklin";
String name3 = "Jay";
String name4 = "Ozzy";
```

```
String name5 = "Carmine";
String name6 = "Dee";
System.out.printf("%10s%10s\n", name1, name2);
System.out.printf("%10s%10s\n", name3, name4);
System.out.printf("%10s%10s\n", name5, name6);
```

The `%10s` format specifier prints a string in a field that is 10 spaces wide. This code displays the values of the variables in a table with three rows and two columns. Each column has a width of 10 spaces. Here is the output of the code:

```
    George   Franklin
       Jay       Ozzy
    Carmine        Dee
```

Notice that the strings are right-justified. You can use the minus flag (-) to left-justify a string within its field. The following code demonstrates:

```
String name1 = "George";
String name2 = "Franklin";
String name3 = "Jay";
String name4 = "Ozzy";
String name5 = "Carmine";
String name6 = "Dee";
System.out.printf("%-10s%-10s\n", name1, name2);
System.out.printf("%-10s%-10s\n", name3, name4);
System.out.printf("%-10s%-10s\n", name5, name6);
```

Here is the output of the code:

```
George    Franklin
Jay       Ozzy
Carmine   Dee
```

The following example shows how you can print arguments of different data types:

```
int hours = 40;
double pay = hours * 25;
String name = "Jay";
System.out.printf("Name: %s, Hours: %d, Pay: $%,.2f\n",
                  name, hours, pay);
```

In this example, we are displaying a `String`, an `int`, and a `double`. The code will produce the following output:

```
Name: Jay, Hours: 40, Pay: $1,000.00
```

NOTE: The format specifiers we have shown in this section are the basic ones. Java provides much more powerful format specifiers for more complex formatting needs. The API documentation gives an overview of them all.

Checkpoint

2.38   Assume the following variable declaration exists in a program:

        double number = 1234567.456;

Write a statement that uses System.out.printf to display the value of the number variable formatted as:

        1,234,567.46

2.39   Assume the following variable declaration exists in a program:

        double number = 123.456;

Write a statement that uses System.out.printf to display the value of the number variable rounded to one decimal place, in a field that is 10 spaces wide. (Do not use comma separators.)

2.40   Assume the following variable declaration exists in a program:

        double number = 123.456;

Write a statement that uses System.out.printf to display the value of the number variable padded with leading zeros, in a field that is eight spaces wide, rounded to one decimal place. (Do not use comma separators.)

2.41   Assume the following variable declaration exists in a program:

        int number = 123456;

Write a statement that uses System.out.printf to display the value of the number variable in a field that is 10 spaces wide, with comma separators.

2.42   Assume the following variable declaration exists in a program:

        double number = 123456.789;

Write a statement that uses System.out.printf to display the value of the number variable left-justified, with comma separators, in a field that is 20 spaces wide, rounded to two decimal places.

2.43   Assume the following declaration exists in a program:

        String name = "James";

Write a statement that uses System.out.printf to display the value of name in a field that is 20 spaces wide.

 2.16   Common Errors to Avoid

The following list describes several errors that are commonly made when learning this chapter's topics.

- **Mismatched braces, quotation marks, or parentheses.** In this chapter you saw that the statements making up a class definition are enclosed in a set of braces. Also, you saw that the statements in a method are also enclosed in a set of braces. For every opening brace, there must be a closing brace in the proper location. The same is true of double-quotation marks that enclose string literals and single quotation marks that enclose character literals. Also, in a statement that uses parentheses, such as a mathematical expression, you must have a closing parenthesis for every opening parenthesis.

- **Misspelling key words.** Java will not recognize a key word that has been misspelled.

- **Using capital letters in key words.** Remember that Java is a case-sensitive language, and all key words are written in lowercase. Using an uppercase letter in a key word is the same as misspelling the key word.
- **Using a key word as a variable name.** The key words are reserved for special uses; they cannot be used for any other purpose.
- **Using inconsistent spelling of variable names.** Each time you use a variable name, it must be spelled exactly as it appears in its declaration statement.
- **Using inconsistent case of letters in variable names.** Because Java is a case-sensitive language, it distinguishes between uppercase and lowercase letters. Java will not recognize a variable name that is not written exactly as it appears in its declaration statement.
- **Inserting a space in a variable name.** Spaces are not allowed in variable names. Instead of using a two-word name such as `gross pay`, use one word, such as `grossPay`.
- **Forgetting the semicolon at the end of a statement.** A semicolon appears at the end of each complete statement in Java.
- **Assigning a `double` literal to a `float` variable.** Java is a strongly typed language, which means that it only allows you to store values of compatible data types in variables. All floating-point literals are treated as `doubles`, and a `double` value is not compatible with a `float` variable. A floating-point literal must end with the letter `f` or `F` in order to be stored in a `float` variable.
- **Using commas or other currency symbols in numeric literals.** Numeric literals cannot contain commas or currency symbols, such as the dollar sign.
- **Unintentionally performing integer division.** When both operands of a division statement are integers, the statement will result in an integer. If there is a remainder, it will be discarded.
- **Forgetting to group parts of a mathematical expression.** If you use more than one operator in a mathematical expression, the expression will be evaluated according to the order of operations. If you wish to change the order in which the operators are used, you must use parentheses to group part of the expression.
- **Inserting a space in a combined assignment operator.** A space cannot appear between the two operators that make a combined assignment operator.
- **Using a variable to receive the result of a calculation when the variable's data type is incompatible with the data type of the result.** A variable that receives the result of a calculation must be of a data type that is compatible with the data type of the result.
- **Incorrectly terminating a multiline comment or a documentation comment.** Multiline comments and documentation comments are terminated by the `*/` characters. Forgetting to place these characters at a comment's desired ending point, or accidentally switching the `*` and the `/`, will cause the comment not to have an ending point.
- **Forgetting to use the correct `import` statement in a program that uses the `Scanner` class or the `JOptionPane` class.** In order for the `Scanner` class to be available to your program, you must have the import java.util.Scanner; statement near the top of your program file. In order for the `JOptionPane` class to be available to your program, you must have the import javax.swing.JOptionPane; statement near the top of the program file.
- **When using an input dialog to read numeric input, not converting the `showInputDialog` method's return value to a number.** The `showInputDialog` method always returns the user's input as a string. If the user enters a numeric value, it must be converted to a number before it can be used in a math statement.

Review Questions and Exercises

Multiple Choice and True/False

1. Every complete statement ends with a _____.
   a. period
   b. parenthesis
   c. semicolon
   d. ending brace

2. The following data

   ```
   72
   'A'
   "Hello World"
   2.8712
   ```

   are all examples of _____.
   a. variables
   b. literals
   c. strings
   d. none of these

3. A group of statements, such as the contents of a class or a method, are enclosed in _____.
   a. braces {}
   b. parentheses ()
   c. brackets []
   d. any of these will do

4. Which of the following are *not* valid assignment statements? (Indicate all that apply.)
   a. `total = 9;`
   b. `72 = amount;`
   c. `profit = 129`
   d. `letter = 'W';`

5. Which of the following are not valid `println` statements? (Indicate all that apply.)
   a. `System.out.println + "Hello World";`
   b. `System.out.println("Have a nice day");`
   c. `out.System.println(value);`
   d. `println.out(Programming is great fun);`

6. The negation operator is _____.
   a. unary
   b. binary
   c. ternary
   d. none of these

7. This key word is used to declare a named constant.
   a. `constant`
   b. `namedConstant`
   c. `final`
   d. `concrete`

8. These characters mark the beginning of a multiline comment.
   a. `//`
   b. `/*`
   c. `*/`
   d. `/**`

9. These characters mark the beginning of a single-line comment.
   a. `//`
   b. `/*`
   c. `*/`
   d. `/**`

10. These characters mark the beginning of a documentation comment.
    a. `//`
    b. `/*`
    c. `*/`
    d. `/**`

11. Which `Scanner` class method would you use to read a string as input?
    a. `nextString`
    b. `nextLine`
    c. `readString`
    d. `getLine`

12. Which `Scanner` class method would you use to read a double as input?
    a. `nextDouble`
    b. `getDouble`
    c. `readDouble`
    d. None of these; you cannot read a `double` with the `Scanner` class

13. You can use this class to display dialog boxes.
    a. `JOptionPane`
    b. `BufferedReader`
    c. `InputStreamReader`
    d. `DialogBox`

14. When Java converts a lower-ranked value to a higher-ranked type, it is called a _____.
    a. 4-bit conversion
    b. escalating conversion
    c. widening conversion
    d. narrowing conversion

15. This type of operator lets you manually convert a value, even if it means that a narrowing conversion will take place.
    a. cast
    b. binary
    c. uploading
    d. dot

16. **True or False:** A left brace in a Java program is always followed by a right brace later in the program.

17. **True or False:** A variable must be declared before it can be used.

18. **True or False:** Variable names may begin with a number.

19. **True or False:** You cannot change the value of a variable whose declaration uses the `final` key word.

20. **True or False:** Comments that begin with `//` can be processed by `javadoc`.

21. **True or False:** If one of an operator's operands is a `double` and the other operand is an `int`, Java will automatically convert the value of the `double` to an `int`.

Predict the Output

What will the following code segments print on the screen?

1.
```java
int freeze = 32, boil = 212;
freeze = 0;
boil = 100;
System.out.println(freeze + "\n"+ boil + "\n");
```

2.
```java
int x = 0, y = 2;
x = y * 4;
System.out.println(x + "\n" + y + "\n");
```

3.
```java
System.out.print("I am the incredible");
System.out.print("computing\nmachine");
System.out.print("\nand I will\namaze\n)";
System.out.println("you.");
```

4.
```java
System.out.print("Be careful\n)";
System.out.print("This might/n be a trick ");
System.out.println("question.");
```

5.
```java
int a, x = 23;
a = x % 2;
System.out.println(x + "\n" + a);
```

Find the Error

There are a number of syntax errors in the following program. Locate as many as you can.

```java
*/   What's wrong with this program? /*
public MyProgram
{
    public static void main(String[] args);
    }
        int a, b, c      \\ Three integers
        a = 3
        b = 4
        c = a + b
        System.out.println('The value of c is' + C);
    {
```

Algorithm Workbench

1. Show how the `double` variables `temp`, `weight`, and `age` can be declared in one statement.

2. Show how the int variables months, days, and years may be declared in one statement, with months initialized to 2 and years initialized to 3.

3. Write assignment statements that perform the following operations with the variables a, b, and c.

    a. Adds 2 to a and stores the result in b
    b. Multiplies b times 4 and stores the result in a
    c. Divides a by 3.14 and stores the result in b
    d. Subtracts 8 from b and stores the result in a
    e. Stores the character 'K' in c
    f. Stores the Unicode code for 'B' in c

4. Assume the variables result, w, x, y, and z are all integers, and that $w = 5$, $x = 4$, $y = 8$, and $z = 2$. What value will be stored in result in each of the following statements?

    a. result = x + y;
    b. result = z * 2;
    c. result = y / x;
    d. result = y - z;
    e. result = w % 2;

5. How would each of the following numbers be represented in E notation?

    a. 3.287×10^6
    b. -9.7865×10^{12}
    c. 7.65491×10^{-3}

6. Modify the following program so it prints two blank lines between each line of text.

```java
public class
{
    public static void main(String[] args)
    {
        System.out.print("This is line 1.");
        System.out.print("This is line 2.");
        System.out.print("This is line 3.");
        System.out.print("This is line 4.");
        System.out.println("This is line 5.");
    }
}
```

7. What will the following code output?

```java
int apples = 0, bananas = 2, pears = 10;
apples += 10;
bananas *= 10;
pears /= 10;
System.out.println(apples + " " +
                   bananas + " " +
                   pears);
```

8. What will the following code output?

```java
double d = 12.9;
int i = (int)d;
System.out.println(i);
```

9. What will the following code output?

```java
String message = "Have a great day!";
System.out.println(message.charAt(5));
```

10. What will the following code output?

```java
String message = "Have a great day!";
System.out.println(message.toUpperCase());
System.out.println(message);
```

11. Convert the following pseudocode to Java code. Be sure to declare the appropriate variables.

Store 20 in the speed variable.
Store 10 in the time variable.
Multiply speed by time and store the result in the distance variable.
Display the contents of the distance variable.

12. Convert the following pseudocode to Java code. Be sure to define the appropriate variables.

Store 172.5 in the force variable.
Store 27.5 in the area variable.
Divide area by force and store the result in the pressure variable.
Display the contents of the pressure variable.

13. Write the code to set up all the necessary objects for reading keyboard input. Then write code that asks the user to enter his or her desired annual income. Store the input in a `double` variable.

14. Write the code to display a dialog box that asks the user to enter his or her desired annual income. Store the input in a `double` variable.

15. A program has a `float` variable named `total` and a `double` variable named `number`. Write a statement that assigns `number` to `total` without causing an error when compiled.

Short Answer

1. Is the following comment a single-line style comment or a multiline style comment?

   ```java
   /* This program was written by M. A. Codewriter */
   ```

2. Is the following comment a single-line style comment or a multiline style comment?

   ```java
   // This program was written by M. A. Codewriter
   ```

3. Describe what the term *self-documenting program* means.

4. What is meant by "case sensitive"? Why is it important for a programmer to know that Java is a case-sensitive language?

5. Briefly explain how the `print` and `println` methods are related to the `System` class and the `out` object.

6. What does a variable declaration tell the Java compiler about a variable?

7. Why are variable names like x not recommended?

8. What things must be considered when deciding on a data type to use for a variable?

9. Briefly describe the difference between variable assignment and variable initialization.

10. What is the difference between comments that start with the `//` characters and comments that start with the `/*` characters?

11. Briefly describe what programming style means. Why should your programming style be consistent?

12. Assume that a program uses the named constant `PI` to represent the value 3.14. The program uses the named constant in several statements. What is the advantage of using the named constant instead of the actual value 3.14 in each statement?

13. Assume the file *SalesAverage.java* is a Java source file that contains documentation comments. Assuming you are in the same folder or directory as the source code file, what command would you enter at the operating system command prompt to generate the HTML documentation files?

14. An expression adds a `byte` variable and a `short` variable. Of what data type will the result be?

Programming Challenges

1. Name, Age, and Annual Income

Write a program that declares the following:

- a `String` variable named `name`
- an `int` variable named `age`
- a `double` variable named `annualPay`

Store your age, name, and desired annual income as literals in these variables. The program should display these values on the screen in a manner similar to the following:

```
My name is Joe Mahoney, my age is 26 and
I hope to earn $100000.0 per year.
```

2. Name and Initials

Write a program that has the following `String` variables: `firstName`, `middleName`, and `lastName`. Initialize these with your first, middle, and last names. The program should also have the following `char` variables: `firstInitial`, `middleInitial`, and `lastInitial`. Store your first, middle, and last initials in these variables. The program should display the contents of these variables on the screen.

3. Personal Information

Write a program that displays the following information, each on a separate line:

- Your name
- Your address, with city, state, and ZIP

- Your telephone number
- Your college major

Although these items should be displayed on separate output lines, use only a single `println` statement in your program.

4. Star Pattern

Write a program that displays the following pattern:

```
   *
  ***
 *****
*******
 *****
  ***
   *
```

5. Cookie Calories

A bag of cookies holds 40 cookies. The calorie information on the bag claims that there are 10 servings in the bag and that a serving equals 300 calories. Write a program that lets the user enter the number of cookies he or she actually ate and then reports the number of total calories consumed.

6. Sales Prediction

The East Coast sales division of a company generates 65 percent of total sales. Based on that percentage, write a program that will predict how much the East Coast division will generate if the company has $8.3 million in sales this year.

Hint: Use the value 0.65 to represent 65 percent.

7. Land Calculation

One acre of land is equivalent to 43,560 square feet. Write a program that calculates the number of acres in a tract of land with 389,767 square feet.

Hint: Divide the size of the tract of land by the size of an acre to get the number of acres.

8. Sales Tax

Write a program that will ask the user to enter the amount of a purchase. The program should then compute the state and county sales tax. Assume the state sales tax is 5.5 percent and the county sales tax is 2 percent. The program should display the amount of the purchase, the state sales tax, the county sales tax, the total sales tax, and the total of the sale (which is the sum of the amount of purchase plus the total sales tax).

Hint: Use the value 0.02 to represent 2 percent, and 0.055 to represent 5.5 percent.

VideoNote
The Miles-per-Gallon Problem

9. Miles-per-Gallon

A car's miles-per-gallon (MPG) can be calculated with the following formula:

MPG = Miles driven / Gallons of gas used

Write a program that asks the user for the number of miles driven and the gallons of gas used. It should calculate the car's MPG and display the result on the screen.

10. Test Average

Write a program that asks the user to enter three test scores. The program should display each test score, as well as the average of the scores.

11. Male and Female Percentages

Write a program that asks the user for the number of males and the number of females registered in a class. The program should display the percentage of males and females in the class.

Hint: Suppose there are 8 males and 12 females in a class. There are 20 students in the class. The percentage of males can be calculated as 8 ÷ 20 = 0.4, or 40%. The percentage of females can be calculated as 12 ÷ 20 = 0.6, or 60%.

12. String Manipulator

Write a program that asks the user to enter the name of his or her favorite city. Use a `String` variable to store the input. The program should display the following:

- The number of characters in the city name
- The name of the city in all uppercase letters
- The name of the city in all lowercase letters
- The first character in the name of the city

13. Restaurant Bill

Write a program that computes the tax and tip on a restaurant bill. The program should ask the user to enter the charge for the meal. The tax should be 7.5 percent of the meal charge. The tip should be 18 percent of the total after adding the tax. Display the meal charge, tax amount, tip amount, and total bill on the screen.

14. Stock Commission

Kathryn bought 1000 shares of stock at a price of $25.50 per share. She must pay her stock broker a 2 percent commission for the transaction. Write a program that calculates and displays the following:

- The amount paid for the stock alone (without the commission)
- The amount of the commission
- The total amount paid (for the stock plus the commission)

15. Ingredient Adjuster

A cookie recipe calls for the following ingredients:

- 1.5 cups of sugar
- 1 cup of butter
- 2.75 cups of flour

The recipe produces 48 cookies with these amounts of the ingredients. Write a program that asks the user how many cookies he or she wants to make and then displays the number of cups of each ingredient needed for the specified number of cookies.

16. Energy Drink Consumption

A soft-drink company recently surveyed 15,000 of its customers and found that approximately 18 percent of those surveyed purchase one of more energy drinks per week. Of those customers who purchase energy drinks, approximately 58 percent of them prefer citrus-flavored energy drinks. Write a program that displays the following:

- The approximate number of customers in the survey who purchase one or more energy drinks per week
- The approximate number of customers in the survey who prefer citrus-flavored energy drinks

17. Word Game

Write a program that plays a word game with the user. The program should ask the user to enter the following:

- His or her name
- His or her age
- The name of a city
- The name of a college
- A profession
- A type of animal
- A pet's name

After the user has entered these items, the program should display the following story, inserting the user's input into the appropriate locations:

> There once was a person named **NAME** who lived in **CITY**. At the age of **AGE**, **NAME** went to college at **COLLEGE**. **NAME** graduated and went to work as a **PROFESSION**. Then, **NAME** adopted a(n) **ANIMAL** named **PETNAME**. They both lived happily ever after!

18. Stock Transaction Program

Last month Joe purchased some stock in Acme Software, Inc. Here are the details of the purchase:

- The number of shares that Joe purchased was 1,000.
- When Joe purchased the stock, he paid $32.87 per share.
- Joe paid his stockbroker a commission that amounted to 2% of the amount he paid for the stock.

Two weeks later Joe sold the stock. Here are the details of the sale:

- The number of shares that Joe sold was 1,000.
- He sold the stock for $33.92 per share.
- He paid his stockbroker another commission that amounted to 2% of the amount he received for the stock.

Write a program that displays the following information:

- The amount of money Joe paid for the stock.
- The amount of commission Joe paid his broker when he bought the stock.
- The amount that Joe sold the stock for.
- The amount of commission Joe paid his broker when he sold the stock.
- Display the amount of profit that Joe made after selling his stock and paying the two commissions to his broker. (If the amount of profit that your program displays is a negative number, then Joe lost money on the transaction.)

3

A First Look at Classes and Objects

TOPICS

3.1 Classes
3.2 More about Passing Arguments
3.3 Instance Fields and Methods
3.4 Constructors
3.5 A BankAccount Class
3.6 Classes, Variables, and Scope

3.7 Packages and `import` Statements
3.8 Focus on Object-Oriented Design: Finding the Classes and Their Responsibilities
3.9 Common Errors to Avoid

3.1 Classes

CONCEPT: A class is the blueprint for an object. It specifies the attributes and methods that a particular type of object has. From the class, one or more objects may be created.

Have you ever driven a car? If so, you know that a car is made of a lot of components. A car has a steering wheel, an accelerator pedal, a brake pedal, a gear shifter, a speedometer, and numerous other devices that the driver interacts with. There are also a lot of components under the hood, such as the engine, the battery, the radiator, and so forth. A car is not just one single object, but rather a collection of objects that work together.

This same notion also applies to computer programming. Most programming languages that are used today are object-oriented. When you use an object-oriented language, such as Java, you create programs that are made of objects. In programming, an object isn't a physical device, however, like a steering wheel or a brake pedal. Instead, it's a software component that exists in the computer's memory and performs a specific task. In software, an object has two general capabilities:

- An object can store data. The data stored in an object are commonly called *attributes*, or *fields*.
- An object can perform operations. The operations that an object can perform are called *methods*.

Objects are very important in Java; for example, if you need to store a string in memory, you use a `String` object, and if you need to read input from the keyboard, you use a `Scanner` object. When a program needs the services of a particular type of object, it creates that object in memory and then calls that object's methods as necessary.

Strings as Objects

Chapter 2 introduced you to the Java primitive data types: `byte`, `short`, `int`, `long`, `char`, `float`, `double`, and `boolean`. You use these data types to create variables, which are storage locations in the computer's memory. A primitive data type is called "primitive" because a variable created with a primitive data type has no built-in capabilities other than storing a value.

Chapter 2 also introduced you to the `String` class, which allows you to create `String` objects. In addition to storing strings, `String` objects have numerous methods that perform operations on the strings they hold. As a review, let's look at an example. Consider the following statement:

```
String cityName = "Charleston";
```

For each string literal that appears in a Java program, a `String` object is created in memory to hold it. The string literal "Charleston" that appears in this statement causes a `String` object to be created and initialized with the string "Charleston". This statement also declares a variable named `cityName` that references the `String` object. This means that the `cityName` variable holds the `String` object's memory address. This is illustrated in Figure 3-1.

Figure 3-1   The `cityName` variable references a `String` object

Assume that the same program has an `int` variable named `stringSize`. Look at the following statement.

```
stringSize = cityName.length();
```

This statement calls the `String` class's `length` method, which returns the length of a string. The expression `cityName.length()` returns the length of the string referenced by `cityName`. After this statement executes, the `stringSize` variable will contain the value 10, which is the length of the string "Charleston".

As you saw in Chapter 2, the `String` class has other methods in addition to `length`. This illustrates one of the differences between an object created from a class and a variable created from a primitive data type. Class objects normally have methods that perform useful operations on their data. Primitive variables, however, only store data and have no methods. Any operations performed on a primitive variable must be written in code that is external to the variable.

Classes and Instances

Objects are very useful, but they don't just magically appear in your program. Before a specific type of object can be used by a program, that object has to be created in memory. And, before an object can be created in memory, you must have a class for the object.

A *class* is code that describes a particular type of object. It specifies the data that an object can hold (the object's attributes) and the actions that an object can perform (the object's methods). You can think of a class as a code "blueprint" that can be used to create a particular type of object. It serves a similar purpose as the blueprint for a house. The blueprint itself is not a house, but is a detailed description of a house. When we use the blueprint to build an actual house, we could say we are building an instance of the house described by the blueprint. If we so desire, we can build several identical houses from the same blueprint. Each house is a separate instance of the house described by the blueprint. This idea is illustrated in Figure 3-2.

Figure 3-2   A blueprint and houses built from the blueprint

Blueprint that describes a house

Instances of the house described by the blueprint

So, a class is not an object, but a description of an object. When a program is running, it can use the class to create as many objects as needed. Each object is considered an *instance* of the class. All of the objects that are created from the same class will have the attributes and methods described by the class. For example, we can create several objects from the String class, as demonstrated with the following code:

```
String person = "Jenny";
String pet = "Fido";
String favoriteColor = "Blue";
```

As illustrated in Figure 3-3, this code creates three String objects in memory, which are referenced by the person, pet, and favoriteColor variables.

Figure 3-3   Three variables referencing three `String` objects

The `person` variable holds the address of a `String` object. | address ⟶ | A `String` object | `"Jenny"`

The `pet` variable holds the address of a `String` object. | address ⟶ | A `String` object | `"Fido"`

The `favoriteColor` variable holds the address of a `String` object. | address ⟶ | A `String` object | `"Blue"`

Although each of the three `String` objects holds different data, they are all identical in design. For example, we can call the `length` method for each of the objects as shown here.

```
stringSize = person.length();
stringSize = pet.length();
stringSize = favoriteColor.length();
```

Because each of the three objects is an instance of the `String` class, each has the attributes and methods specified by the `String` class.

Building a Simple Class Step by Step

In this section we will write a class named `Rectangle`. Each object that is created from the `Rectangle` class will be able to hold data about a rectangle. Specifically, a `Rectangle` object will have the following attributes:

- `length`. The `length` attribute will hold the rectangle's length.
- `width`. The `width` attribute will hold the rectangle's width.

The `Rectangle` class will also have the following methods:

- `setLength`. The `setLength` method will store a value in the `length` attribute.
- `setWidth`. The `setWidth` method will store a value in the `width` attribute.
- `getLength`. The `getLength` method will return the value in the `length` attribute.
- `getWidth`. The `getWidth` method will return the value in the `width` attribute.
- `getArea`. The `getArea` method will return the area of the rectangle, which is the result of its length multiplied by its width.

When designing a class it is often helpful to draw a UML diagram. *UML* stands for *Unified Modeling Language*. It provides a set of standard diagrams for graphically depicting object-oriented systems. Figure 3-4 shows the general layout of a UML diagram for a class. Notice that the diagram is a box that is divided into three sections. The top section is where you write the name of the class. The middle section holds a list of the class's attributes. The bottom section holds a list of the class's methods.

Figure 3-4   General layout of a UML diagram for a class

Class name goes here ⟶
Attributes are listed here ⟶
Methods are listed here ⟶

Following this layout, Figure 3-5 shows a UML diagram for our `Rectangle` class. Throughout this book we frequently use UML diagrams to illustrate classes.

Figure 3-5   UML diagram for the `Rectangle` class

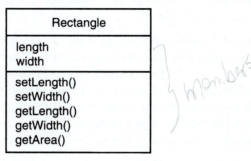

Rectangle
length width
setLength() setWidth() getLength() getWidth() getArea()

Writing the Code for a Class

Now that we have identified the attributes and methods that we want the `Rectangle` class to have, let's write the Java code. First, we use an editor to create a new file named *Rectangle. java*. In the *Rectangle.java* file we will start by writing a general class "skeleton" as follows.

```java
public class Rectangle
{

}
```

The key word `public`, which appears in the first line, is an access specifier. An *access specifier* indicates how the class may be accessed. The `public` access specifier indicates that the class will be publicly available to code that is written outside the *Rectangle.java* file. Almost all of the classes that we will write in this book will be `public`.

Following the access specifier is the key word `class`, followed by `Rectangle`, which is the name of the class. On the next line an opening brace appears, which is followed by a closing brace. The contents of the class, which are the attributes and methods, will be written inside these braces. The general format of a class definition is:

```
AccessSpecifier class Name
{
      Members
}
```

In general terms, the attributes and methods that belong to a class are referred to as the class's *members*.

VideoNote
Writing Classes and Creating Objects

Writing the Code for the Class Attributes

Let's continue writing our `Rectangle` class by filling in the code for some of its members. First we will write the code for the class's two attributes, `length` and `width`. We will use variables of the `double` data type for these attributes. The new lines of code are shown in bold, as follows.

```java
public class Rectangle
{
    private double length;
    private double width;
}
```

These two lines of code that we have added declare the variables `length` and `width`. Notice that both declarations begin with the key word `private`, preceding the data type. The key word `private` is an access specifier. It indicates that these variables may not be accessed by statements outside the class.

Recall from our discussion in Chapter 1 on object-oriented programming that an object can perform data hiding, which means that critical data stored inside the object is protected from code outside the object. In Java, a class's private members are hidden and can be accessed only by methods that are members of the same class. When an object's internal data is hidden from outside code and access to that data is restricted to the object's methods, the data is protected from accidental corruption. It is a common practice in object-oriented programming to make all of a class's attributes private and to provide access to those attributes through methods.

When writing classes, you will primarily use the `private` and `public` access specifiers for class members. Table 3-1 summarizes these access specifiers.

Table 3-1   Summary of the `private` and `public` Access Specifiers for Class Members

Access Specifier	Description
private	When the `private` access specifier is applied to a class member, the member cannot be accessed by code outside the class. The member can be accessed only by methods that are members of the same class.
public	When the `public` access specifier is applied to a class member, the member can be accessed by code inside the class or outside.

You can optionally initialize an attribute with a value. For example, the following statements declare `length` and `width` and initialize them with the values 10 and 12, respectively:

```java
private double length = 10;
private double width = 12;
```

If you do not provide initialization values for numeric attributes, they will be automatically initialized with 0. We will discuss default initialization in greater detail later in this chapter.

Before moving on, we should introduce the term field. In Java, a *field* is a class member that holds data. In our `Rectangle` class, the `length` and `width` variables are both fields.

TIP: We have referred to `length` and `width` both as attributes and fields. Don't let this confuse you. The term "attribute" is a generic OOP term that refers to an item of data held by an object. The term "field" is a Java-specific term that refers to a member of a class that holds data. In Java, you use fields as attributes.

Writing the `setLength` Method

Now we will begin writing the class methods. We will start with the `setLength` method. This method will allow code outside the class to store a value in the `length` field. Code Listing 3-1 shows the `Rectangle` class at this stage of its development. The `setLength` method is in lines 16 through 19. (If you have downloaded the book's source code from www. pearsonhighered.com/gaddis, you will find this file in the folder *Chapter 03\Rectangle Class Phase 1*.)

Code Listing 3-1   (`Rectangle.java`)

```
 1   /**
 2    * Rectangle class, Phase 1
 3    * Under Construction!
 4    */
 5
 6   public class Rectangle
 7   {
 8      private double length;
 9      private double width;
10
11      /**
12       * The setLength method accepts an argument
13       * that is stored in the length field.
14       */
15
16      public void setLength(double len)
17      {
18         length = len;
19      }
20   }
```

In lines 11 through 14 we write a block comment that gives a brief description of the method. It's important to always write comments that describe a class's methods so that in the future, anyone reading the code will better understand it. The definition of the method appears after the block comment in lines 16 through 19. The first line of the method definition, which appears in line 16, is known as the *method header*. It appears as:

```
public void setLength(double len)
```

The method header has several parts. Let's look at each one.

- `public`. The key word `public` is an access specifier. It indicates that the method may be called by statements outside the class.
- `void`. This is the method's return type. The key word `void` indicates that the method returns no data to the statement that called it.
- `setLength`. This is the name of the method.
- `(double len)`. This is the declaration of a parameter variable. A parameter variable holds the value of an argument that is passed to the method. The parameter variable's name is `len`, and it is of the `double` data type.

Figure 3-6 labels each part of the header for the setLength method.

Figure 3-6 Header for the setLength method

After the header, the body of the method appears inside a set of braces:

```
{
    length = len;
}
```

This method has only one statement, which assigns the value of len to the length field. When the method executes, the len parameter variable will hold the value of an argument that is passed to the method. That value is assigned to the length field.

Before adding the other methods to the class, it might help if we demonstrate how the setLength method works. First, notice that the Rectangle class does not have a main method. This class is not a complete program, but is a blueprint that Rectangle objects may be created from. Other programs will use the Rectangle class to create objects. The programs that create and use these objects will have their own main methods. We can demonstrate the class's setLength method by saving the current contents of the *Rectangle.java* file and then creating the program shown in Code Listing 3-2. (If you have downloaded the book's source code from www.pearsonhighered.com/gaddis, you will find this file in the folder *Chapter 03\Rectangle Class Phase 1.*)

Code Listing 3-2   (LengthDemo.java)

```
 1  /**
 2   * This program demonstrates the Rectangle class's
 3   * setLength method.
 4   */
 5
 6  public class LengthDemo
 7  {
 8      public static void main(String[] args)
 9      {
10          Rectangle box = new Rectangle();
11
12          System.out.println("Sending the value 10.0 to "
13                              + "the setLength method.");
14          box.setLength(10.0);
15          System.out.println("Done.");
16      }
17  }
```

The program in Code Listing 3-2 must be saved as *LengthDemo.java* in the same folder or directory as the file *Rectangle.java*. The following command can then be used with the Sun JDK to compile the program:

```
javac LengthDemo.java
```

When the compiler reads the source code for *LengthDemo.java* and sees that a class named Rectangle is being used, it looks in the current folder or directory for the file *Rectangle.class*. That file does not exist, however, because we have not yet compiled *Rectangle.java*. So, the compiler searches for the file *Rectangle.java* and compiles it. This creates the file *Rectangle.class*, which makes the Rectangle class available. The compiler then finishes compiling *LengthDemo.java*. The resulting *LengthDemo.class* file may be executed with the following command:

```
java LengthDemo
```

The output of the program is as follows.

Program Output

```
Sending the value 10.0 to the setLength method.
Done.
```

Let's look at each statement in this program's main method. In line 10 the program uses the following statement to create a Rectangle class object and associate it with a variable:

```
Rectangle box = new Rectangle();
```

Let's dissect the statement into two parts. The first part of the statement,

```
Rectangle box
```

declares a variable named box. The data type of the variable is Rectangle. (Because the word Rectangle is not the name of a primitive data type, Java assumes it to be the name of a class.) Recall from Chapter 2 that a variable of a class type is a reference variable, and it holds the memory address of an object. When a reference variable holds an object's memory address, it is said that the variable references the object. So, the variable box will be used to reference a Rectangle object. The second part of the statement is:

```
= new Rectangle();
```

This part of the statement uses the key word new, which creates an object in memory. After the word new, the name of a class followed by a set of parentheses appears. This specifies the class that the object should be created from. In this case, an object of the Rectangle class is created. The memory address of the object is then assigned (by the = operator) to the variable box. After the statement executes, the variable box will reference the object that was created in memory. This is illustrated in Figure 3-7.

Figure 3-7 The box variable references a Rectangle class object

Notice that Figure 3-7 shows the `Rectangle` object's `length` and `width` fields set to 0. All of a class's numeric fields are initialized to 0 by default.

> **TIP:** The parentheses in this statement are required. It would be an error to write the statement as:
>
> ```
> Rectangle box = new Rectangle;    // ERROR!!
> ```

Lines 12 and 13 call the `println` method to display a message on the screen:

```
System.out.println("Sending the value 10.0 to "
                 + "the setLength method.");
```

Line 14 calls the `box` object's `setLength` method. As you have already seen from our examples with the `String` class, you use the dot operator (a period) to access the members of a class object. Recall from Chapter 2 that the general form of a method call is

```
refVariable.method(arguments...)
```

where *refVariable* is the name of a variable that references an object, `method` is the name of a method, and `arguments...` is zero or more arguments that are passed to the method. An argument is a value that is passed into a method. Here is the statement in line 14 that calls the `setLength` method:

```
box.setLength(10.0);
```

This statement passes the argument 10.0 to the `setLength` method. When the method executes, the value 10.0 is copied into the `len` parameter variable. This is illustrated in Figure 3-8.

Figure 3-8   The argument 10.0 is copied into the `len` parameter variable

In the `setLength` method, the parameter variable `len` contains the value 10.0. The method assigns the value of `len` to the `length` field and then terminates. Figure 3-9 shows the state of the `box` object after the method executes.

Figure 3-9   The state of the `box` object after the `setLength` method executes

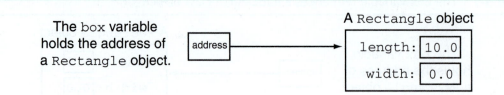

When passing an argument to a method, the argument's data type must be compatible with the parameter variable's data type. Otherwise, an error will occur. For example, the len parameter in the setLength method is a double variable. You cannot pass an argument that cannot be automatically converted to the double data type. So, the following statement would cause an error because the argument is a string:

```
box.setLength("10.0");    // ERROR!
```

Writing the setWidth Method

Now that we've seen how the setLength method works, let's add the setWidth method to the Rectangle class. The setWidth method is similar to setLength. It accepts an argument, which is assigned to the width field. Code Listing 3-3 shows the updated Rectangle class. The setWidth method is in lines 26 through 29. (If you have downloaded the book's source code from www.pearsonhighered.com/gaddis, you will find this file in the folder *Chapter 03\ Rectangle Class Phase 2*.)

Code Listing 3-3   (Rectangle.java)

```
1   /**
2    * Rectangle class, Phase 2
3    * Under Construction!
4    */
5
6   public class Rectangle
7   {
8       private double length;
9       private double width;
10
11      /**
12       * The setLength method accepts an argument
13       * that is stored in the length field.
14       */
15
16      public void setLength(double len)
17      {
18          length = len;
19      }
20
21      /**
22       * The setWidth method accepts an argument
23       * that is stored in the width field.
24       */
25
26      public void setWidth(double w)
27      {
28          width = w;
29      }
30  }
```

The setWidth method has a parameter variable named w. When an argument is passed to the method, the argument's value is copied into the w variable. The value of the w variable is then assigned to the width field. For example, assume that box references a Rectangle object and the following statement is executed:

```
box.setWidth(20.0);
```

After this statement executes, the box object's width field will be set to 20.0.

Writing the getLength and getWidth Methods

Because the length and width fields are private, we wrote the setLength and setWidth methods to allow code outside the Rectangle class to store values in the fields. We must also write methods that allow code outside the class to get the values that are stored in these fields. That's what the getLength and getWidth methods will do. The getLength method will return the value stored in the length field, and the getWidth method will return the value stored in the width field.

Here is the code for the getLength method:

```
public double getLength()
{
    return length;;
}
```

Notice that instead of the word void, the header uses the word double for the method's return type. This means that the method returns a value of the double data type. Also notice that no parameter variables are declared inside the parentheses. This means that the method does not accept arguments. The parentheses are still required, however.

Inside the method, the following statement appears:

```
return length;
```

This is called a *return statement*. The value that appears after the key word return is sent back to the statement that called the method. This statement sends the value that is stored in the length field. For example, assume that size is a double variable and that box references a Rectangle object, and the following statement is executed:

```
size = box.getLength();
```

This statement assigns the value that is returned from the getLength method to the size variable. After this statement executes, the size variable will contain the same value as the box object's length field. This is illustrated in Figure 3-10.

Figure 3-10 The value returned from getLength is assigned to size

> **NOTE:** No arguments are passed to the getLength method. You must still write the parentheses, however, even when no arguments are passed.

The getWidth method is similar to getLength. The code for the method follows.

```java
public double getWidth()
{
    return width;
}
```

This method returns the value that is stored in the width field. For example, assume that size is a double variable and that box references a Rectangle object, and the following statement is executed:

```java
size = box.getWidth();
```

This statement assigns the value that is returned from the getWidth method to the size variable. After this statement executes, the size variable will contain the same value as the box object's width field.

Code Listing 3-4 shows the Rectangle class with all of the members we have discussed so far. The code for the getLength and getWidth methods is shown in lines 31 through 49. (If you have downloaded the book's source code from www.pearsonhighered.com/gaddis, you will find this file in the folder *Chapter 03\Rectangle Class Phase 3*.)

Code Listing 3-4   (`Rectangle.java`)

```java
 1  /**
 2   * Rectangle class, Phase 3
 3   * Under Construction!
 4   */
 5
 6  public class Rectangle
 7  {
 8      private double length;
 9      private double width;
10
11      /**
12       * The setLength method accepts an argument
13       * that is stored in the length field.
14       */
15
16      public void setLength(double len)
17      {
18          length = len;
19      }
20
21      /**
22       * The setWidth method accepts an argument
23       * that is stored in the width field.
24       */
```

```
25
26      public void setWidth(double w)
27      {
28         width = w;
29      }
30
31      /**
32       * The getLength method returns the value
33       * stored in the length field.
34       */
35
36      public double getLength()
37      {
38         return length;
39      }
40
41      /**
42       * The getWidth method returns the value
43       * stored in the width field.
44       */
45
46      public double getWidth()
47      {
48         return width;
49      }
50   }
```

Before continuing we should demonstrate how these methods work. Look at the program in Code Listing 3-5. (If you have downloaded the book's source code from www.pearsonhighered .com/gaddis, you will find this file in the folder *Chapter 03\Rectangle Class Phase 3*.)

Code Listing 3-5   (`LengthWidthDemo.java`)

```
1   /**
2    * This program demonstrates the Rectangle class's
3    * setLength, setWidth, getLength, and getWidth methods.
4    */
5
6   public class LengthWidthDemo
7   {
8      public static void main(String[] args)
9      {
10         Rectangle box = new Rectangle();
11
12         box.setLength(10.0);
13         box.setWidth(20.0);
```

```
14          System.out.println("The box's length is "
15                         + box.getLength());
16          System.out.println("The box's width is "
17                         + box.getWidth());
18     }
19  }
```

Program Output

```
The box's length is 10.0
The box's width is 20.0
```

Let's take a closer look at the program. First, this program creates a `Rectangle` object, which is referenced by the `box` variable. Then the following statements, in lines 12 and 13, execute:

```
box.setLength(10.0);
box.setWidth(20.0);
```

After these statements execute, the box object's `length` field is set to 10.0, and its `width` field is set to 20.0. The state of the object is shown in Figure 3-11.

Figure 3-11   State of the box object

Next, the following statement, in lines 14 and 15, executes:

```
System.out.println("The box's length is "
                   + box.getLength());
```

This statement calls the `box.getLength()` method, which returns the value 10.0. The following message is displayed on the screen:

```
The box's length is 10.0
```

Then the statement in lines 16 and 17 executes.

```
System.out.println("The box's width is "
                   + box.getWidth());
```

This statement calls the `box.getWidth()` method, which returns the value 20.0. The following message is displayed on the screen:

```
The box's width is 20.0
```

Writing the `getArea` Method

The last method we will write for the `Rectangle` class is `getArea`. This method returns the area of a rectangle, which is its length multiplied by its width. Here is the code for the `getArea` method:

```java
public double getArea()
{
    return length * width;
}
```

This method returns the result of the mathematical expression `length * width`. For example, assume that `area` is a `double` variable and that `box` references a `Rectangle` object, and the following code is executed:

```java
box.setLength(10.0);
box.setWidth(20.0);
area = box.getArea();
```

The last statement assigns the value that is returned from the `getArea` method to the `area` variable. After this statement executes, the `area` variable will contain the value 200.0.

Code Listing 3-6 shows the `Rectangle` class with all of the members we have discussed so far. The `getArea` method appears in lines 56 through 59. (If you have downloaded the book's source code from www.pearsonhighered.com/gaddis, you will find this file in the folder *Chapter 03\Rectangle Class Phase 4.*)

Code Listing 3-6   (`Rectangle.java`)

```java
1  /**
2   * Rectangle class, Phase 4
3   * Under Construction!
4   */
5
6  public class Rectangle
7  {
8      private double length;
9      private double width;
10
11     /**
12      * The setLength method accepts an argument
13      * that is stored in the length field.
14      */
15
16     public void setLength(double len)
17     {
18         length = len;
19     }
20
21     /**
22      * The setWidth method accepts an argument
23      * that is stored in the width field.
24      */
25
```

```
26      public void setWidth(double w)
27      {
28         width = w;
29      }
30
31      /**
32       * The getLength method returns the value
33       * stored in the length field.
34       */
35
36      public double getLength()
37      {
38         return length;
39      }
40
41      /**
42       * The getWidth method returns the value
43       * stored in the width field.
44       */
45
46      public double getWidth()
47      {
48         return width;
49      }
50
51      /**
52       * The getArea method returns the value of the
53       * length field times the width field.
54       */
55
56      public double getArea()
57      {
58         return length * width;
59      }
60   }
```

The program in Code Listing 3-7 demonstrates all the methods of the Rectangle class, including getArea. (If you have downloaded the book's source code from www.pearsonhighered.com/gaddis, you will find this file in the folder *Chapter 03\Rectangle Class Phase 4*.)

Code Listing 3-7   (`RectangleDemo.java`)

```
1   /**
2    * This program demonstrates the Rectangle class's
3    * setLength, setWidth, getLength, getWidth, and
4    * getArea methods.
5    */
6
7   public class RectangleDemo
```

```
 8  {
 9      public static void main(String[] args)
10      {
11          // Create a Rectangle object.
12          Rectangle box = new Rectangle();
13
14          // Set the length to 10 and width to 20.
15          box.setLength(10.0);
16          box.setWidth(20.0);
17
18          // Display the length, width, and area.
19          System.out.println("The box's length is "
20                              + box.getLength());
21          System.out.println("The box's width is "
22                              + box.getWidth());
23          System.out.println("The box's area is "
24                              + box.getArea());
25      }
26  }
```

Program Output

```
The box's length is 10.0
The box's width is 20.0
The box's area is 200.0
```

Accessor and Mutator Methods

As mentioned earlier, it is a common practice to make all of a class's fields private and to provide public methods for accessing and changing those fields. This ensures that the object owning those fields is in control of all changes being made to them. A method that gets a value from a class's field but does not change it is known as an *accessor method*. A method that stores a value in a field or in some other way changes the value of a field is known as a *mutator method*. In the Rectangle class the methods getLength and getWidth are accessors, and the methods setLength and setWidth are mutators.

> **NOTE:** Mutator methods are sometimes called "setters" and accessor methods are sometimes called "getters."

The Importance of Data Hiding

Data hiding is an important concept in object-oriented programming. An object hides its internal data from code that is outside the class that the object is an instance of. Only the class's methods may directly access and make changes to the object's internal data. You hide an object's internal data by making the class's fields private and making the methods that access those fields public.

As a beginning student, you might be wondering why you would want to hide the data that is inside the classes you create. As you learn to program, you will be the user of your own classes, so it might seem that you are putting forth a great effort to hide data from yourself. If you write software in industry, however, the classes that you create will be used as components in large software systems, and programmers other than yourself will be using your classes. By hiding a class's data, and allowing it to be accessed only through the class's methods, you can better ensure that the class will operate as you intended it to.

Avoiding Stale Data

Recall that the `Rectangle` class has the methods `getLength`, `getWidth`, and `getArea`. The `getLength` and `getWidth` methods return the values stored in fields, but the `getArea` method returns the result of a calculation. You might be wondering why the area of the rectangle is not stored in a field, like the length and the width. The area is not stored in a field because it could potentially become stale. When the value of an item is dependent on other data and that item is not updated when the other data is changed, it is said that the item has become *stale*. If the area of the rectangle were stored in a field, the value of the field would become incorrect as soon as either the `length` or `width` field changed.

When designing a class, you should take care not to store in a field calculated data that could potentially become stale. Instead, provide a method that returns the result of the calculation.

Showing Access Specification in UML Diagrams

In Figure 3-5 we presented a UML diagram for the `Rectangle` class. The diagram listed all of the members of the class but did not indicate which members were private and which were public. In a UML diagram, you have the option to place a - character before a member name to indicate that it is private, or a + character to indicate that it is public. Figure 3-12 shows the UML diagram modified to include this notation.

Figure 3-12   UML diagram for the `Rectangle` class

```
           Rectangle
   ┌─────────────────────┐
   │ Rectangle           │
   ├─────────────────────┤
   │ - length            │
   │ - width             │
   ├─────────────────────┤
   │ + setLength()       │
   │ + setWidth()        │
   │ + getLength()       │
   │ + getWidth()        │
   │ + getArea()         │
   └─────────────────────┘
```

Data Type and Parameter Notation in UML Diagrams

The Unified Modeling Language also provides notation that you can use to indicate the data types of fields, methods, and parameters. To indicate the data type of a field, place a colon followed by the name of the data type after the name of the field. For example, the `length` field in the `Rectangle` class is a `double`. It could be listed as follows in the UML diagram:

```
- length : double
```

The return type of a method can be listed in the same manner: After the method's name, place a colon followed by the return type. The `Rectangle` class's `getLength` method returns a `double`, so it could be listed as follows in the UML diagram:

```
+ getLength() : double
```

Parameter variables and their data types may be listed inside a method's parentheses. For example, the Rectangle class's setLength method has a double parameter named len, so it could be listed as follows in the UML diagram:

```
+ setLength(len : double) : void
```

Figure 3-13 shows a UML diagram for the Rectangle class with parameter and data type notation.

Figure 3-13   UML diagram for the Rectangle class with parameter and data type notation

Rectangle
- length : double - width : double
+ setLength(len : double) : void + setWidth(w : double) : void + getLength() : double + getWidth() : double + getArea() : double

Layout of Class Members

Notice that in the Rectangle class, the field variables are declared first and then the methods are defined. You are not required to write field declarations before the method definitions. In fact, some programmers prefer to write the definitions for the public methods first and then write the declarations for the private fields last. Regardless of which style you use, you should be consistent. In this book we always write the field declarations first, followed by the method definitions. Figure 3-14 shows this layout.

Figure 3-14   Typical layout of class members

```
public class ClassName
{
```
>   Field declarations

>   Method definitions
```
}
```

Checkpoint

3.1   In this chapter, we use the metaphor of a blueprint and houses that are created from the blueprint to describe classes and objects. In this metaphor, are classes the blueprint or the houses?

3.2   Describe a way that variables of the primitive data types are different from objects.

3.3   When a variable is said to reference an object, what is actually stored in the variable?

3.4   A string literal, such as "Joe", causes what type of object to be created?

3.5   Look at the UML diagram in Figure 3-15 and answer the following questions.
    a.   What is the name of the class?
    b.   What are the attributes?
    c.   What are the methods?
    d.   What are the private members?
    e.   What are the public members?

3.6   Assume that `limo` is a variable that references an instance of the class depicted in Figure 3-15. Write a statement that calls `setMake` and passes the argument "Cadillac".

Figure 3-15   UML diagram

```
            Car
-------------------------
- make
- yearModel
-------------------------
+ setMake()
+ setYearModel()
+ getMake()
+ getYearModel()
```

3.7   What does the key word `new` do?

3.8   What is a parameter variable?

3.9   What is an accessor? What is a mutator?

3.10   What is a stale data item?

3.2 More about Passing Arguments

CONCEPT: A method can have multiple parameter variables, allowing you to pass multiple arguments to the method. When an argument is passed to a method, it is passed by value. This means that the parameter variable holds a copy of the value passed to it. Changes made to the parameter variable do not affect the argument.

Passing Multiple Arguments

Often it is useful to pass more than one argument into a method. For example, the `Rectangle` class has two separate methods for setting the `length` and `width` fields: `setLength` and `setWidth`. Setting the `length` and `width` fields using these methods requires two method calls. We could add another method that accepts two arguments, one for the length and one for the width, making it possible to set both the `length` and the `width` fields with one method call. Here is such a method:

```
public void set(double len, double w)
{
    length = len;
    width = w;
}
```

Two parameter variables, len and w, are declared inside the parentheses in the method header. This requires us to pass two arguments to the method when we call it. For example, assume that box references a Rectangle object and the following statement is executed.

```
box.set(10.0, 20.0);
```

This statement passes the value 10.0 into the len parameter and the value 20.0 into the w parameter, as illustrated in Figure 3-16.

Figure 3-16   Multiple arguments passed to the set method

Notice that the arguments are passed to the parameter variables in the order that they appear in the method call. In other words, the first argument is passed into the first parameter, and the second argument is passed into the second parameter. For example, the following method call would pass 15.0 into the len parameter and 30.0 into the w parameter:

```
box.set(15.0, 30.0);
```

The program in Code Listing 3-8 demonstrates passing two arguments to the set method. In this program, variables that are declared in the main method are passed as the arguments. (If you have downloaded the book's source code from www.pearsonhighered.com/gaddis, you will find this file, along with a modified version of the Rectangle class, in the folder *Chapter 03\Rectangle Class Phase 5.*)

Code Listing 3-8   **(MultipleArgs.java)**

```
 1  import java.util.Scanner;  // Needed for the Scanner class
 2
 3  /**
 4   * This program demonstrates how to pass
 5   * multiple arguments to a method.
 6   */
 7
 8  public class MultipleArgs
 9  {
10     public static void main(String[] args)
11     {
12        double boxLength, // To hold the box's length
13               boxWidth;  // To hold the box's width
14
```

```
15          // Create a Scanner object for keyboard input.
16          Scanner keyboard = new Scanner(System.in);
17
18          // Create a Rectangle object.
19          Rectangle box = new Rectangle();
20
21          // Get the box's length.
22          System.out.print("What is the box's length? ");
23          boxLength = keyboard.nextDouble();
24
25          // Get the box's width.
26          System.out.print("What is the box's width? ");
27          boxWidth = keyboard.nextDouble();
28
29          // Pass boxLength and boxWidth to the set method.
30          box.set(boxLength, boxWidth);
31
32          // Display the box's length, width, and area.
33          System.out.println("The box's length is "
34                              + box.getLength());
35          System.out.println("The box's width is "
36                              + box.getWidth());
37          System.out.println("The box's area is "
38                              + box.getArea());
39      }
40  }
```

Program Output with Example Input Shown in Bold

```
What is the box's length? 10.0 [Enter]
What is the box's width? 20.0 [Enter]
The box's length is 10.0
The box's width is 20.0
The box's area is 200.0
```

In the program, the user enters values that are stored in the boxLength and boxWidth variables. The following statement, in line 30, calls the set method, passing the boxLength and boxWidth variables as arguments.

```
box.set(boxLength, boxWidth);
```

When this statement executes, the value stored in the boxLength variable is passed into the len parameter, and the value stored in the boxWidth variable is passed into the w parameter.

Arguments Are Passed by Value

In Java, all arguments of the primitive data types are *passed by value*, which means that a copy of an argument's value is passed into a parameter variable. A method's parameter variables are separate and distinct from the arguments that are listed inside the parentheses of a method call. If a parameter variable is changed inside a method, it has no effect on the original argument.

3.3 Instance Fields and Methods

CONCEPT: Each instance of a class has its own set of fields, which are known as instance fields. You can create several instances of a class and store different values in each instance's fields. The methods that operate on an instance of a class are known as instance methods.

The program in Code Listing 3-7 creates one instance of the Rectangle class. It is possible to create many instances of the same class, each with its own data. For example, the *RoomAreas.java* program in Code Listing 3-9 creates three instances of the Rectangle class, referenced by the variables kitchen, bedroom, and den.

Code Listing 3-9 (RoomAreas.java)

```java
 1  import java.util.Scanner;  // Needed for the Scanner class
 2
 3  /**
 4   * This program creates three instances of the
 5   * Rectangle class.
 6   */
 7
 8  public class RoomAreas
 9  {
10     public static void main(String[] args)
11     {
12        double number,      // To hold numeric input
13               totalArea;   // The total area of all rooms
14
15        // Create a Scanner object for keyboard input.
16        Scanner keyboard = new Scanner(System.in);
17
18        // Create three Rectangle objects.
19        Rectangle kitchen = new Rectangle();
20        Rectangle bedroom = new Rectangle();
21        Rectangle den = new Rectangle();
22
23        // Get and store the dimensions of the kitchen.
24        System.out.print("What is the kitchen's length? ");
25        number = keyboard.nextDouble();
26        kitchen.setLength(number);
27        System.out.print("What is the kitchen's width? ");
28        number = keyboard.nextDouble();
29        kitchen.setWidth(number);
30
```

```
31          // Get and store the dimensions of the bedroom.
32          System.out.print("What is the bedroom's length? ");
33          number = keyboard.nextDouble();
34          bedroom.setLength(number);
35          System.out.print("What is the bedroom's width? ");
36          number = keyboard.nextDouble();
37          bedroom.setWidth(number);
38
39          // Get and store the dimensions of the den.
40          System.out.print("What is the den's length? ");
41          number = keyboard.nextDouble();
42          den.setLength(number);
43          System.out.print("What is the den's width? ");
44          number = keyboard.nextDouble();
45          den.setWidth(number);
46
47          // Calculate the total area of the rooms.
48          totalArea = kitchen.getArea() + bedroom.getArea()
49                        + den.getArea();
50
51          // Display the total area of the rooms.
52          System.out.println("The total area of the rooms is "
53                             + totalArea);
54      }
55  }
```

Program Output with Example Input Shown in Bold

```
What is the kitchen's length? 10 [Enter]
What is the kitchen's width? 14 [Enter]
What is the bedroom's length? 15 [Enter]
What is the bedroom's width? 12 [Enter]
What is the den's length? 20 [Enter]
What is the den's width? 30 [Enter]
The total area of the rooms is 920.0
```

In the program, the code in lines 19 through 21 creates three objects, each an instance of the Rectangle class:

```
Rectangle kitchen = new Rectangle();
Rectangle bedroom = new Rectangle();
Rectangle den = new Rectangle();
```

Figure 3-17 illustrates how the kitchen, bedroom, and den variables reference the objects.

In the example session with the program, the user enters 10 and 14 as the length and width of the kitchen, 15 and 12 as the length and width of the bedroom, and 20 and 30 as the length and width of the den. Figure 3-18 shows the states of the objects after these values are stored in them.

Figure 3-17   The kitchen, bedroom, and den variables reference Rectangle objects

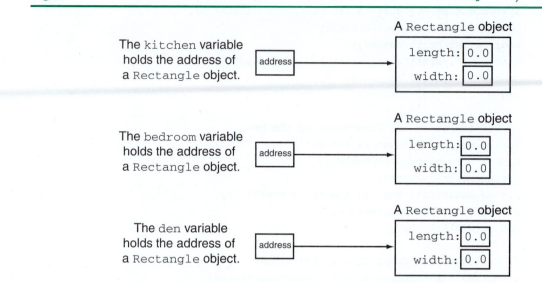

Figure 3-18   States of the objects after data has been stored in them

Notice from Figure 3-18 that each instance of the Rectangle class has its own length and width variables. For this reason, the variables are known as *instance variables*, or *instance fields*. Every instance of a class has its own set of instance fields and can store its own values in those fields.

The methods that operate on an instance of a class are known as *instance methods*. All of the methods in the Rectangle class are instance methods because they perform operations on specific instances of the class. For example, look at line 26 in the *RoomsAreas.java* program:

```
kitchen.setLength(number);
```

This statement calls the setLength method which stores a value in the kitchen object's length field. Now look at line 34 in the same program.

```
bedroom.setLength(number);
```

This statement also calls the setLength method, but this time it stores a value in the bedroom object's length field. Likewise, line 42 calls the setLength method to store a value in the den object's length field:

```
den.setLength(number);
```

The setLength method stores a value in a specific instance of the Rectangle class. This is true of all of the methods that are members of the Rectangle class.

 Checkpoint

3.11   Assume that r1 and r2 are variables that reference Rectangle objects, and the following statements are executed:

```
r1.setLength(5.0);
r2.setLength(10.0);
r1.setWidth(20.0);
r2.setWidth(15.0);
```

Fill in the boxes in Figure 3-19 that represent each object's length and width fields.

Figure 3-19   Fill in the boxes for each field

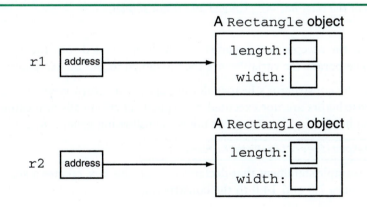

3.4   Constructors

CONCEPT: A constructor is a method that is automatically called when an object is created.

A constructor is a method that is automatically called when an instance of a class is created. Constructors normally perform initialization or setup operations, such as storing initial values in instance fields.

Note
lizing an
ct with a
structor

A constructor method has the same name as the class. For example, Code Listing 3-10 shows the first few lines of a new version of the Rectangle class. In this version of the class, a constructor has been added. (If you have downloaded the book's source code from www.pearsonhighered.com/gaddis, you will find this file in the folder *Chapter 03\ Rectangle Class Phase 6.*)

Code Listing 3-10 `(Rectangle.java)`

```
 1  /**
 2   * Rectangle class, Phase 6
 3   */
 4
 5  public class Rectangle
 6  {
 7     private double length;
 8     private double width;
 9
10     /**
11      * Constructor
12      */
13
14     public Rectangle(double len, double w)
15     {
16        length = len;
17        width = w;
18     }
```
... The remainder of the class has not changed and is not shown.

This constructor accepts two arguments, which are passed into the `len` and `w` parameter variables. The parameter variables are then assigned to the `length` and `width` fields.

Notice that the constructor's header doesn't specify a return type—not even `void`. This is because constructors are not executed by explicit function calls and cannot return a value. The method header for a constructor takes the following general form:

> *AccessSpecifier ClassName(Arguments...)*

Here is an example statement that declares the variable `box`, creates a `Rectangle` object, and passes the values 7.0 and 14.0 to the constructor.

```
Rectangle box = new Rectangle(7.0, 14.0);
```

After this statement executes, `box` will reference a `Rectangle` object whose `length` field is set to 7.0 and whose `width` field is set to 14.0. The program in Code Listing 3-11 demonstrates the `Rectangle` class constructor. (If you have downloaded the book's source code from www.pearsonhighered.com/gaddis, you will find this file in the folder *Chapter 03\ Rectangle Class Phase 6.*)

Code Listing 3-11 `(ConstructorDemo.java)`

```
 1  /**
 2   * This program demonstrates the Rectangle class's
 3   * constructor.
 4   */
 5
 6  public class ConstructorDemo
```

```
 7  {
 8      public static void main(String[] args)
 9      {
10          Rectangle box = new Rectangle(5.0, 15.0);
11
12          System.out.println("The box's length is "
13                                  + box.getLength());
14          System.out.println("The box's width is "
15                                  + box.getWidth());
16          System.out.println("The box's area is "
17                                  + box.getArea());
18      }
19  }
```

Program Output

```
The box's length is 5.0
The box's width is 15.0
The box's area is 75.0
```

The program in Code Listing 3-11 uses the new key word to create a Rectangle object as part of the box variable's declaration statement. Recall that the new key word can be used in a simple assignment statement as well. For example, the following statement can be used to declare box as a Rectangle variable.

```
    Rectangle box;
```

Then, the following statement can be used to create a Rectangle object and pass the values 7.0 and 14.0 to its constructor.

```
    box = new Rectangle(7.0, 14.0);
```

The *RoomConstructor.java* program in Code Listing 3-12 uses this technique. It is a modification of the *RoomAreas.java* program presented earlier in this chapter. (If you have downloaded the book's source code from www.pearsonhighered.com/gaddis, you will find this file in the folder *Chapter 03\Rectangle Class Phase 6*.)

Code Listing 3-12   (RoomConstructor.java)

```
 1  import java.util.Scanner;  // Needed for the Scanner class
 2
 3  /**
 4   * This program creates three instances of the Rectangle
 5   * class and passes arguments to the constructor.
 6   */
 7
 8  public class RoomConstructor
 9  {
10      public static void main(String [] args)
11      {
12          double roomLength,    // To hold a room's length
13                 roomWidth,     // To hold a room's width
14                 totalArea;     // To hold the total area
```

```
15
16          // Declare Rectangle variables to reference
17          // objects for the kitchen, bedroom, and den.
18          Rectangle kitchen, bedroom, den;
19
20          // Create a Scanner object for keyboard input.
21          Scanner keyboard = new Scanner(System.in);
22
23          // Get and store the dimensions of the kitchen.
24          System.out.print("What is the kitchen's length? ");
25          roomLength = keyboard.nextDouble();
26          System.out.print("What is the kitchen's width? ");
27          roomWidth = keyboard.nextDouble();
28          kitchen = new Rectangle(roomLength, roomWidth);
29
30          // Get and store the dimensions of the bedroom.
31          System.out.print("What is the bedroom's length? ");
32          roomLength = keyboard.nextDouble();
33          System.out.print("What is the bedroom's width? ");
34          roomWidth = keyboard.nextDouble();
35          bedroom = new Rectangle(roomLength, roomWidth);
36
37          // Get and store the dimensions of the den.
38          System.out.print("What is the den's length? ");
39          roomLength = keyboard.nextDouble();
40          System.out.print("What is the den's width? ");
41          roomWidth = keyboard.nextDouble();
42          den = new Rectangle(roomLength, roomWidth);
43
44          // Calculate the total area of the rooms.
45          totalArea = kitchen.getArea() + bedroom.getArea()
46                      + den.getArea();
47
48          // Display the total area of the rooms.
49          System.out.println("The total area of the rooms is "
50                      + totalArea);
51      }
52  }
```

Program Output with Example Input Shown in Bold

```
What is the kitchen's length? 10 [Enter]
What is the kitchen's width? 14 [Enter]
What is the bedroom's length? 15 [Enter]
What is the bedroom's width? 12 [Enter]
What is the den's length? 20 [Enter]
What is the den's width? 30 [Enter]
The total area of the rooms is 920.0
```

In the program, the following statement in line 18 declares `kitchen`, `bedroom`, and `den` as `Rectangle` variables:

```
Rectangle kitchen, bedroom, den;
```

These variables do not yet reference instances of the `Rectangle` class, however. Because these variables do not yet hold an object's address, they are *uninitialized reference variables*. These variables cannot be used until they reference objects. The following statement, which appears in line 28, creates a `Rectangle` object, passes the `roomLength` and `roomWidth` variables as arguments to the constructor, and assigns the object's address to the `kitchen` variable.

```
kitchen = new Rectangle(roomLength, roomWidth);
```

After this statement executes, the kitchen variable will reference the `Rectangle` object. Similar statements also appear later in the program that cause the `bedroom` and `den` variables to reference objects.

The Default Constructor

When an object is created, its constructor is always called. But what if we do not write a constructor in the object's class? If you do not write a constructor in a class, Java automatically provides one when the class is compiled. The constructor that Java provides is known as the default constructor. The default constructor doesn't accept arguments. It sets all of the class's numeric fields to 0, `boolean` fields to `false`, and `char` fields to the Unicode value 0. If the object has any fields that are reference variables, the default constructor sets them to the special value `null`, which means that they do not reference anything.

The *only* time that Java provides a default constructor is when you do not write your own constructor for a class. For example, at the beginning of this chapter we developed the `Rectangle` class without writing a constructor for it. When we compiled the class, the compiler generated a default constructor that set both the `length` and `width` fields to 0.0. Assume that the following code uses that version of the class to create a `Rectangle` object:

```
// We wrote no constructor for the Rectangle class.
Rectangle r = new Rectangle();  // Calls the default constructor
```

When we created `Rectangle` objects using that version of the class, we did not pass any arguments to the default constructor, because the default constructor doesn't accept arguments.

Later we added our own constructor to the class. The constructor that we added accepts arguments for the `length` and `width` fields. When we compiled the class at that point, Java did not provide a default constructor. The constructor that we added became the only constructor that the class had. When we create `Rectangle` objects with that version of the class, we *must* pass the length and width arguments to the constructor. Using that version of the class, the following statement would cause an error because we have not provided arguments for the constructor.

```
// Now we wrote our own constructor for the Rectangle class.
Rectangle box = new Rectangle();  // Error! Must now pass arguments.
```

Because we have added our own constructor, which requires two arguments, the class no longer has a default constructor.

No-Arg Constructors

A constructor that does not accept arguments is known as a *no-arg constructor*. The default constructor doesn't accept arguments, so it is considered a no-arg constructor. In addition, you can write your own no-arg constructor. For example, suppose we wrote the following constructor for the `Rectangle` class:

```
public Rectangle()
{
    length = 1.0;
    width = 1.0;
}
```

If we were using this constructor in our `Rectangle` class, we would not pass any arguments when creating a `Rectangle` object. The following code shows an example. After this code executes, the `Rectangle` object's `length` and `width` fields would both be set to 1.0.

```
// Now we have written our own no-arg constructor.
Rectangle r = new Rectangle();  // Calls the no-arg constructor
```

Showing Constructors in a UML Diagram

There is more than one accepted way of showing a class's constructor in a UML diagram. In this book, we simply show a constructor just as any other method, except we list no return type. Figure 3-20 shows a UML diagram for the `Rectangle` class with the constructor listed.

Figure 3-20   UML diagram for the `Rectangle` class showing the constructor

```
┌─────────────────────────────────────────┐
│                Rectangle                 │
├─────────────────────────────────────────┤
│ - length : double                        │
│ - width : double                         │
├─────────────────────────────────────────┤
│ + Rectangle(len : double, w : double)    │
│ + setLength(len : double) : void         │
│ + setWidth(w : double) : void            │
│ + getLength() : double                   │
│ + getWidth() : double                    │
│ + getArea() : double                     │
└─────────────────────────────────────────┘
```

The `String` Class Constructor

You create primitive variables with simple declaration statements, and you create objects with the new operator. There is one class, however, that can be instantiated without the new operator: the `String` class. Because string operations are so common, Java allows you to create `String` objects in the same way that you create primitive variables. Here is an example:

```
String name = "Joe Mahoney";
```

This statement creates a `String` object in memory, initialized with the string literal `"Joe Mahoney"`. The object is referenced by the `name` variable. If you wish, you can use the new operator to create a `String` object and initialize the object by passing a string literal to the constructor, as shown here:

```
String name = new String("Joe Mahoney");
```

> **NOTE:** String objects are a special case in Java. Because they are so commonly used, Java provides numerous shortcut operations with String objects that are not possible with objects of other types. In addition to creating a String object without using the new operator, you can use the = operator to assign values to String objects, you can use the + operator to concatenate strings, and so forth. Chapter 9 discusses several of the String class methods.

Checkpoint

3.12 How is a constructor named?

3.13 What is a constructor's return type?

3.14 Assume that the following is a constructor, which appears in a class.

```
ClassAct(int number)
{
    item = number;
}
```

   a. What is the name of the class that this constructor appears in?
   b. Write a statement that creates an object from the class and passes the value 25 as an argument to the constructor.

3.5 A BankAccount Class

The Rectangle class discussed in the previous section allows you to create objects that describe rectangles. Now we will look at a class that is modeled after a more tangible object: a bank account. Objects that are created from this class will simulate bank accounts, allowing us to perform operations such as making deposits, making withdrawals, calculating and adding interest, and getting the current balance. A UML diagram for the BankAccount class is shown in Figure 3-21.

Figure 3-21 UML diagram for the BankAccount class

Here is a summary of the BankAccount class's fields:

- balance is a double that holds an account's current balance.
- interestRate is a double that holds the monthly interest rate for an account. The monthly interest rate is the annual interest rate divided by 12. For example, if the

annual interest rate is 3 percent, then the monthly interest rate is 0.25 percent. We would store this value as 0.0025 in the interestRate field.

- interest is a double that holds the amount of interest earned for an account.

Here is a summary of the class's methods:

- The constructor has two parameter variables: startBalance and intRate. Both parameters are doubles. When the constructor executes, the account's starting balance is passed into the startBalance parameter, and the account's monthly interest rate is passed into the intRate parameter. The constructor assigns startBalance to the balance field and intRate to the interestRate field. Additionally, the constructor assigns 0.0 to the interest field.
- The deposit method has a parameter, amount, that is a double. When the method is called, an amount that is to be deposited into the account is passed into this parameter. The value of the parameter is then added to the value in the balance field.
- The withdraw method has a parameter, amount, that is a double. When the method is called, an amount that is to be withdrawn from the account is passed into this parameter. The value of the parameter is then subtracted from the value in the balance field.
- The addInterest method multiplies the interestRate field by the balance field to determine the monthly interest for the account. The amount of interest is assigned to the interest field and added to the value in the balance field.
- The getBalance method returns the value in the balance field, which is the current account balance.
- The getInterest method returns the value in the interest field, which is the amount of interest earned the last time the addInterest method was called.

Code Listing 3-13 shows the code for the BankAccount class, which is stored in the *BankAccount.java* file.

Code Listing 3-13   (BankAccount.java)

```
1  /**
2   * BankAccount class
3   * This class simulates a bank account.
4   */
5
6  public class BankAccount
7  {
8     private double balance;      // Account balance
9     private double interestRate; // Interest rate
10    private double interest;      // Interest earned
11
12    /**
13     * The constructor initializes the balance
14     * and interestRate fields with the values
15     * passed to startBalance and intRate. The
16     * interest field is assigned 0.0.
17     */
18
```

```
19      public BankAccount(double startBalance,
20                          double intRate)
21      {
22         balance = startBalance;
23         interestRate = intRate;
24         interest = 0.0;
25      }
26
27      /**
28       * The deposit method adds the parameter
29       * amount to the balance field.
30       */
31
32      public void deposit(double amount)
33      {
34         balance += amount;
35      }
36
37      /**
38       * The withdraw method subtracts the
39       * parameter amount from the balance
40       * field.
41       */
42
43      public void withdraw(double amount)
44      {
45         balance -= amount;
46      }
47
48      /**
49       * The addInterest method adds the
50       * interest for the month to the balance field.
51       */
52
53      public void addInterest()
54      {
55         interest = balance * interestRate;
56         balance += interest;
57      }
58
59      /**
60       * The getBalance method returns the
61       * value in the balance field.
62       */
63
64      public double getBalance()
65      {
66         return balance;
67      }
68
```

```
69       /**
70        * The getInterest method returns the
71        * value in the interest field.
72        */
73
74       public double getInterest()
75       {
76          return interest;
77       }
78   }
```

The *AccountTest.java* program, shown in Code Listing 3-14, demonstrates the BankAccount class.

Code Listing 3-14   (`AccountTest.java`)

```java
 1   import java.util.Scanner;   // Needed for the Scanner class
 2
 3   /**
 4    * This program demonstrates the BankAccount class.
 5    */
 6
 7   public class AccountTest
 8   {
 9      public static void main(String[] args)
10      {
11         BankAccount account;      // To reference a BankAccount object
12         double balance,           // The account's starting balance
13                interestRate,      // The monthly interest rate
14                pay,               // The user's pay
15                cashNeeded;        // The amount of cash to withdraw
16
17         // Create a Scanner object for keyboard input.
18         Scanner keyboard = new Scanner(System.in);
19
20         // Get the starting balance.
21         System.out.print("What is your account's "
22                     + "starting balance? ");
23         balance = keyboard.nextDouble();
24
25         // Get the monthly interest rate.
26         System.out.print("What is your monthly interest rate? ");
27         interestRate = keyboard.nextDouble();
28
29         // Create a BankAccount object.
30         account = new BankAccount(balance, interestRate);
31
```

```
32          // Get the amount of pay for the month.
33          System.out.print("How much were you paid this month? ");
34          pay = keyboard.nextDouble();
35
36          // Deposit the user's pay into the account.
37          System.out.println("We will deposit your pay "
38                             + "into your account.");
39          account.deposit(pay);
40          System.out.println("Your current balance is $"
41                             + account.getBalance());
42
43          // Withdraw some cash from the account.
44          System.out.print("How much would you like "
45                             + "to withdraw? ");
46          cashNeeded = keyboard.nextDouble();
47          account.withdraw(cashNeeded);
48
49          // Add the monthly interest to the account.
50          account.addInterest();
51
52          // Display the interest earned and the balance.
53          System.out.println("This month you have earned $"
54                             + account.getInterest()
55                             + " in interest.");
56          System.out.println("Now your balance is $"
57                             + account.getBalance());
58      }
59  }
```

Program Output with Example Input Shown in Bold

```
What is your account's starting balance? 500 [Enter]
What is your monthly interest rate? 0.045 [Enter]
How much were you paid this month? 1000 [Enter]
We will deposit your pay into your account.
Your current balance is $1500.0
How much would you like to withdraw? 900 [Enter]
This month you have earned $27.0 in interest.
Now your balance is $627.0
```

Let's look at some of the details of this program. First, some variables are declared with the following statements, which appear in lines 11 through 15:

```
BankAccount account;    // To reference a BankAccount object
double balance,         // The account's starting balance
       interestRate,    // The monthly interest rate
       pay,             // The user's pay
       cashNeeded;      // The amount of cash to withdraw
```

The first variable declared is account. This is a variable that will be used later in the program to reference a BankAccount object. Note that the new key word is not used in this statement, so the variable does not yet reference an object. Then, the variables balance, interestRate, pay, and cashNeeded are declared. These will hold values that are input by the user.

Next, the following code appears in lines 20 through 27:

```
// Get the starting balance.
System.out.print("What is your account's "
                  + "starting balance? ");
balance = keyboard.nextDouble();

// Get the monthly interest rate.
System.out.print("What is your monthly interest rate? ");
interestRate = keyboard.nextDouble();
```

This code asks the user to enter his or her account's starting balance and the monthly interest rate. These values are stored in the balance and interestRate variables. Then, the following code appears in lines 29 through 30:

```
// Create a BankAccount object.
account = new BankAccount(balance, interestRate);
```

The statement shown in line 30 uses the new key word to create a BankAccount object. The balance and interestRate variables are passed as arguments. Next, the following code appears in lines 32 through 41:

```
// Get the amount of pay for the month.
System.out.print("How much were you paid this month? ");
pay = keyboard.nextDouble();

// Deposit the user's pay into the account.
System.out.println("We will deposit your pay "
                   + "into your account.");
account.deposit(pay);
System.out.println("Your current balance is $"
                   + account.getBalance());
```

First, this code asks the user to enter his or her pay for the month. The input is stored in the pay variable. The account object's deposit method is called, and the pay variable is passed as an argument. Here is the code for the deposit method, which appears in the BankAccount class in lines 32 through 35:

```
public void deposit(double amount)
{
    balance += amount;
}
```

The value in pay is passed into the amount parameter variable. Then, the statement in this method uses a combined assignment operator to add amount to the value already in balance. This statement is the same as:

```
balance = balance + amount;
```

Back in the AccountTest program, the account object's getBalance method is then called in line 41 to get the current balance, which is displayed on the screen. Next, the following code appears in lines 43 through 47:

```
// Withdraw some cash from the account.
System.out.print("How much would you like "
                    + "to withdraw? ");
cashNeeded = keyboard.nextDouble();
account.withdraw(cashNeeded);
```

This code asks the user for the amount to withdraw from the account, and the input is stored in the cashNeeded variable. This variable is then passed as an argument to the account object's withdraw method. Here is the code for the withdraw method, which appears in the BankAccount class, in lines 43 through 46:

```
public void withdraw(double amount)
{
    balance -= amount;
}
```

The value in cashNeeded is passed into the amount parameter variable. Then, the statement in line 45 uses a combined assignment operator to subtract amount from the value already in balance. This statement is the same as:

```
balance = balance - amount;
```

Back in the AccountTest program, the following code appears in lines 49 through 57:

```
// Add the monthly interest to the account.
account.addInterest();

// Display the interest earned and the balance.
System.out.println("This month you have earned $"
                    + account.getInterest()
                    + " in interest.");
System.out.println("Now your balance is $"
                    + account.getBalance());
```

Line 50 calls the account object's addInterest method, which calculates an amount of interest, assigns that amount to the object's interest field, and adds that amount to the object's balance field. Then, the object's getInterest and getBalance methods are called to get the amount of interest and the current balance, which are displayed.

In the Spotlight:

Creating the `CellPhone` Class

Wireless Solutions, Inc., is a business that sells cell phones and wireless service. You are a programmer in the company's IT department, and your team is designing a program to manage all of the cell phones that are in inventory. You have been asked to design a class that represents a cell phone. The data that should be kept as fields in the class are as follows:

- The name of the phone's manufacturer is assigned to the `manufact` field.
- The phone's model number is assigned to the `model` field.
- The phone's retail price is assigned to the `retailPrice` field.

The class will also have the following methods:

- A constructor that accepts arguments for the manufacturer, model number, and retail price.
- A `setManufact` method that accepts an argument for the manufacturer. This method allows us to change the value of the `manufact` field after the object has been created, if necessary.
- A `setModel` method that accepts an argument for the model. This method allows us to change the value of the `model` field after the object has been created, if necessary.
- A `setRetailPrice` method that accepts an argument for the retail price. This method allows us to change the value of the `retailPrice` field after the object has been created, if necessary.
- A `getManufact` method that returns the phone's manufacturer.
- A `getModel` method that returns the phone's model number.
- A `getRetailPrice` method that returns the phone's retail price.

Figure 3-22 shows a UML diagram for the class. Code Listing 3-15 shows the class definition.

Figure 3-22   UML diagram for the `CellPhone` class

```
                    CellPhone

 - manufact : String
 - model : String
 - retailPrice : double

 + CellPhone(man : String, mod : String,
                  price : double);
 + setManufact(man : String) : void
 + setModel(mod : String) : void
 + setRetailPrice(price : double) : void
 + getManufact() : String
 + getModel() : String
 + getRetailPrice() : double
```

Code Listing 3-15   (`CellPhone.java`)

```java
 1  /**
 2   *  The CellPhone class represents a cell phone.
 3   */
 4
 5  public class CellPhone
 6  {
 7     // Fields
 8     private String manufact;    // Manufacturer
 9     private String model;       // Model
10     private double retailPrice; // Retail price
11
12     /**
13      *  The constructor accepts arguments for
14      *  the phone's manufacturer, model number,
15      *  and retail price.
16      */
17
18     public CellPhone(String man, String mod, double price)
19     {
20        manufact = man;
21        model = mod;
22        retailPrice = price;
23     }
24
25     /**
26      *  The setManufact method accepts an argument for
27      *  the phone's manufacturer name.
28      */
29
30     public void setManufact(String man)
31     {
32        manufact = man;
33     }
34
35     /**
36      *  The setModelNumber method accepts an argument
37      *  for the phone's model number.
38      */
39
40     public void setMod(String mod)
41     {
42        model = mod;
43     }
44
45     /**
46      *  The setRetailPrice method accepts an argument
47      *  for the phone's retail price.
48      */
49
```

```
50      public void setRetailPrice(double price)
51      {
52         retailPrice = price;
53      }
54
55      /**
56       *  The getManufact method returns the name of
57       *  the phone's manufacturer.
58       */
59
60      public String getManufact()
61      {
62         return manufact;
63      }
64
65      /**
66       *  The getModel method returns the phone's
67       *  model number.
68       */
69
70      public String getModel()
71      {
72         return model;
73      }
74
75      /**
76       *  The getRetailPrice method returns the
77       *  phone's retail price.
78       */
79
80      public double getRetailPrice()
81      {
82         return retailPrice;
83      }
84 }
```

The CellPhone class will be used by several programs that your team is developing. To perform a simple test of the class, you write the program shown in Code Listing 3-16. This is a simple program that prompts the user for the phone's manufacturer, model number, and retail price. An instance of the CellPhone class is created and the data is assigned to its attributes.

Code Listing 3-16   (CellPhoneTest.java)

```
1 import java.util.Scanner;
2
3 /**
4  *  This program runs a simple test
5  *  of the CellPhone class.
```

```
 6   */
 7
 8  public class CellPhoneTest
 9  {
10     public static void main(String[] args)
11     {
12         String testMan;    // To hold a manufacturer
13         String testMod;    // To hold a model number
14         double testPrice;  // To hold a price
15
16         // Create a Scanner object for keyboard input.
17         Scanner keyboard = new Scanner(System.in);
18
19         // Get the manufacturer name.
20         System.out.print("Enter the manufacturer: ");
21         testMan = keyboard.nextLine();
22
23         // Get the model number.
24         System.out.print("Enter the model number: ");
25         testMod = keyboard.nextLine();
26
27         // Get the retail price.
28         System.out.print("Enter the retail price: ");
29         testPrice = keyboard.nextDouble();
30
31         // Create an instance of the CellPhone class,
32         // passing the data that was entered as arguments
33         // to the constructor.
34         CellPhone phone = new CellPhone(testMan, testMod, testPrice);
35
36         // Get the data from the phone and display it.
37         System.out.println();
38         System.out.println("Here is the data that you provided:");
39         System.out.println("Manufacturer: " + phone.getManufact());
40         System.out.println("Model number: " + phone.getModel());
41         System.out.println("Retail price: " + phone.getRetailPrice());
42     }
43 }
```

Program Output with Example Input Shown in Bold

```
Enter the manufacturer: Acme Electronics [Enter]
Enter the model number: M1000 [Enter]
Enter the retail price: 299.99 [Enter]

Here is the data that you provided:
Manufacturer: Acme Electronics
Model Number: M1000
Retail Price: $299.99
```

3.6   Classes, Variables, and Scope

CONCEPT: Instance fields are visible to all of the class's instance methods. Local variables, including parameter variables, are visible only to statements in the method where they are declared.

Recall from Chapter 2 that a variable's scope is the part of a program where the variable can be accessed by its name. A variable's name is visible only to statements inside the variable's scope. The location of a variable's declaration determines the variable's scope. So far you have seen variables declared in the following locations:

- **Inside a method.** Variables declared inside a method are known as local variables.
- **Inside a class, but not inside any method.** Variables that are declared inside a class, but not inside any method are known as fields.
- **Inside the parentheses of a method header.** Variables that are declared inside the parentheses of a method header are known as parameter variables.

The following list summarizes the scope for each of these types of variables.

- **Local variables.** A local variable's scope is the method in which it is declared, from the variable's declaration to the end of the method. Only statements in this area can access the variable.
- **Fields.** For now we will define a field's scope as the entire class in which it is declared. A field can be accessed by the methods that are members of the same class as the field. (To be completely accurate, an instance field may be accessed by any instance method that is a member of the same class. In Chapter 7, we discuss non-instance class members.)
- **Parameter variables.** A parameter variable's scope is the method in which it is declared. Only statements inside the method can access the parameter variable.

Shadowing

In Chapter 2 you saw that you cannot have two local variables with the same name in the same scope. This applies to parameter variables as well. A parameter variable is, in essence, a local variable. So, you cannot give a parameter variable and a local variable in the same method the same name.

However, you can have a local variable or a parameter variable with the same name as a field. When you do, the name of the local or parameter variable *shadows* the name of the field. This means that the field name is hidden by the name of the local or parameter variable.

For example, assume that the Rectangle class's setLength method had been written in the following manner.

```
public void setLength(double len)
{
    int length;              // Local variable

    length = len;
}
```

In this code a local variable is given the same name as the field. Therefore, the local variable's name shadows the field's name. When the statement `length = len;` is executed, the value of `len` is assigned to the local variable `length`, not to the field. The unintentional shadowing of field names can cause elusive bugs, so you need to be careful not to give local variables the same names as fields.

3.7 Packages and `import` Statements

CONCEPT: The classes in the Java API are organized into packages. An `import` statement tells the compiler in which package a class is located.

In Chapter 2 you were introduced to the Java API, which is a standard library of prewritten classes. Each class in the Java API is designed for a specific purpose, and you can use the classes in your own programs. You've already used a few classes from the API, such as the `String` class, the `Scanner` class, and the `JOptionPane` class.

All of the classes in the Java API are organized into packages. A *package* is simply a group of related classes. Each package also has a name. For example, the `Scanner` class is in the `java.util` package.

Many of the classes in the Java API are not automatically available to your program. Quite often, you have to *import* an API class in order to use it. You use the `import` key word to import a class. For example, the following statement is required to import the `Scanner` class:

```
import java.util.Scanner;
```

This statement tells the compiler that the `Scanner` class is located in the `java.util` package. Without this statement, the compiler will not be able to locate the `Scanner` class, and the program will not compile.

Explicit and Wildcard `import` Statements

There are two types of `import` statements: explicit and wildcard. An *explicit import* statement identifies the package location of a single class. For example, the following statement explicitly identifies the location of the `Scanner` class:

```
import java.util.Scanner;
```

The `java.util` package has several other classes in it as well as the `Scanner` class. For example, in Chapter 7 we will study the `ArrayList` class, and in Chapter 8 we will study the `StringTokenizer` class. Both of these classes are part of the `java.util` package. If a program needs to use the `Scanner` class, the `ArrayList` class, and the `StringTokenizer` class, it will have to import all three of these classes. One way to do this is to write explicit `import` statements for each class, as shown here:

```
import java.util.Scanner;
import java.util.ArrayList;
import java.util.StringTokenizer;
```

Another way to import all of these classes is to use a wildcard `import` statement. A *wildcard import* statement tells the compiler to import all of the classes in a package. Here is an example:

```
import java.util.*;
```

The `.*` that follows the package name tells the compiler to import all the classes that are part of the `java.util` package. Using a wildcard `import` statement does not affect the performance or the size of your program. It merely tells the compiler that you want to make every class in a particular package available to your program.

The `java.lang` Package

The Java API has one package, `java.lang`, that is automatically imported into every Java program. This package contains general classes, such as `String` and `System`, that are fundamental to the Java programming language. You do not have to write an `import` statement for any class that is part of the `java.lang` package.

Other API Packages

There are numerous packages in the Java API. Table 3-2 lists a few of them.

Table 3-2   A few of the standard Java packages

Package	Description
java.applet	Provides the classes necessary to create an applet.
java.awt	Provides classes for the Abstract Windowing Toolkit. These classes are used in drawing images and creating graphical user interfaces.
java.io	Provides classes that perform various types of input and output.
java.lang	Provides general classes for the Java language. This package is automatically imported.
java.net	Provides classes for network communications.
java.security	Provides classes that implement security features.
java.sql	Provides classes for accessing databases using structured query language.
java.text	Provides various classes for formatting text.
java.util	Provides various utility classes.
javax.swing	Provides classes for creating graphical user interfaces.

For more details about packages, see Appendix H, available on this book's online resource page at www.pearsonhighered.com/gaddis.

3.8 Focus on Object-Oriented Design: Finding the Classes and Their Responsibilities

CONCEPT: One of the first steps in creating an object-oriented application is determining the classes that are necessary, and their responsibilities within the application.

So far you have learned the basics of writing a class, creating an object from the class, and using the object to perform operations. Although this knowledge is necessary to create an object-oriented application, it is not the first step. The first step is to analyze the problem that you are trying to solve and determine the classes that you will need. In this section we will discuss a simple technique for finding the classes in a problem and determining their responsibilities.

Finding the Classes

When developing an object-oriented application, one of your first tasks is to identify the classes that you will need to create. Typically, your goal is to identify the different types of real-world objects that are present in the problem, and then create classes for those types of objects within your application.

Over the years, software professionals have developed numerous techniques for finding the classes in a given problem. One simple and popular technique involves the following steps.

1. Get a written description of the problem domain.
2. Identify all the nouns (including pronouns and noun phrases) in the description. Each of these is a potential class.
3. Refine the list to include only the classes that are relevant to the problem.

Let's take a closer look at each of these steps.

Writing a Description of the Problem Domain

The *problem domain* is the set of real-world objects, parties, and major events related to the problem. If you adequately understand the nature of the problem you are trying to solve, you can write a description of the problem domain yourself. If you do not thoroughly understand the nature of the problem, you should have an expert write the description for you.

For example, suppose we are programming an application that the manager of Joe's Automotive Shop will use to print service quotes for customers. Here is a description that an expert, perhaps Joe himself, might have written:

> Joe's Automotive Shop services foreign cars and specializes in servicing cars made by Mercedes, Porsche, and BMW. When a customer brings a car to the shop, the manager gets the customer's name, address, and telephone number. The manager then determines the make, model, and year of the car and gives the customer a service quote. The service quote shows the estimated parts charges, estimated labor charges, sales tax, and total estimated charges.

The problem domain description should include any of the following:

- Physical objects such vehicles, machines, or products
- Any role played by a person, such as manager, employee, customer, teacher, student, etc.
- The results of a business event, such as a customer order, or in this case a service quote
- Recordkeeping items, such as customer histories and payroll records

Identify All of the Nouns

The next step is to identify all of the nouns and noun phrases. (If the description contains pronouns, include them too.) Here's another look at the previous problem domain description. This time the nouns and noun phrases appear in bold.

> **Joe's Automotive Shop** services **foreign cars** and specializes in servicing **cars** made by **Mercedes**, **Porsche**, and **BMW**. When a **customer** brings a **car** to the **shop**, the **manager** gets the **customer's** **name**, **address**, and **telephone number**. The **manager** then determines the **make**, **model**, and **year** of the **car** and gives the **customer** a **service quote**. The **service quote** shows the **estimated parts charges**, **estimated labor charges**, **sales tax**, and **total estimated charges**.

Notice that some of the nouns are repeated. The following list shows all of the nouns without duplicating any of them.

address	foreign cars	Porsche
BMW	Joe's Automotive Shop	sales tax
car	make	service quote
cars	manager	shop
customer	Mercedes	telephone number
estimated labor charges	model	total estimated charges
estimated parts charges	name	year

Refining the List of Nouns

The nouns that appear in the problem description are merely candidates to become classes. It might not be necessary to make classes for them all. The next step is to refine the list to include only the classes that are necessary to solve the particular problem at hand. We will look at the common reasons that a noun can be eliminated from the list of potential classes.

1. Some of the nouns really mean the same thing.

In this example, the following sets of nouns refer to the same thing:

- **cars and foreign cars**
  These all refer to the general concept of a car.

- **Joe's Automotive Shop and shop**
  Both of these refer to the company "Joe's Automotive Shop."

We can settle on a single class for each of these. In this example we will arbitrarily eliminate **foreign cars** from the list, and use the word **cars**. Likewise we will eliminate **Joe's Automotive Shop** from the list and use the word **shop**. The updated list of potential classes is:

address

BMW

car

cars

customer

estimated labor charges

estimated parts charges

~~foreign cars~~

~~Joe's Automotive Shop~~

make

manager

Mercedes

model

name

Porsche

sales tax

service quote

shop

telephone number

total estimated charges

year

Because **cars** and **foreign** cars mean the same thing in this problem, we have eliminated **foreign cars**. Also, because **Joe's Automotive Shop** and **shop** mean the same thing, we have eliminated **Joe's Automotive Shop**.

2. **Some nouns might represent items that we do not need to be concerned with in order to solve the problem.**

A quick review of the problem description reminds us of what our application should do: print a service quote. In this example we can eliminate two unnecessary classes from the list:

- We can cross **shop** off the list because our application needs to be concerned only with individual service quotes. It doesn't need to work with or determine any company-wide information. If the problem description asked us to keep a total of all the service quotes, then it would make sense to have a class for the shop.
- We will not need a class for the **manager** because the problem statement does not direct us to process any information about the manager. If there were multiple shop managers, and the problem description had asked us to record which manager generated each service quote, then it would make sense to have a class for the manager.

The updated list of potential classes at this point is:

address

BMW

car

cars

customer

estimated labor charges

estimated parts charges

~~foreign cars~~

~~Joe's Automotive Shop~~

make

~~manager~~

Mercedes

model

name

Porsche

sales tax

service quote

~~shop~~

telephone number

total estimated charges

year

Our problem description does not direct us to process any information about the **shop**, or any information about the **manager**, so we have eliminated those from the list.

3. **Some of the nouns might represent objects, not classes.**

We can eliminate **Mercedes, Porsche,** and **BMW** as classes because, in this example, they all represent specific cars and can be considered instances of a **cars** class. Also, we can eliminate the word **car** from the list. In the description it refers to a specific car brought to the shop by a customer. Therefore, it would also represent an instance of a **cars** class. At this point the updated list of potential classes is:

address

~~BMW~~

~~car~~

cars

customer

estimated labor charges

estimated parts charges

~~foreign cars~~

~~Joe's Automotive Shop~~

~~manager~~

make

~~Mercedes~~

model

name

~~Porsche~~

sales tax

service quote

~~shop~~

telephone number

total estimated charges

year

We have eliminated **Mercedes, Porsche, BMW,** and **car** because they are all instances of a **cars** class. That means that these nouns identify objects, not classes.

> **TIP:** Some object-oriented designers take note of whether a noun is plural or singular. Sometimes a plural noun will indicate a class and a singular noun will indicate an object.

4. **Some of the nouns might represent simple values that can be stored in a primitive variable and do not require a class.**

Remember, a class contains fields and methods. Fields are related items that are stored within an object of the class, and define the object's state. Methods are actions or behaviors that may be performed by an object of the class. If a noun represents a type of item that would not have any identifiable fields or methods, then it can probably be eliminated from the list. To help determine whether a noun represents an item that would have fields and methods, ask the following questions about it:

- Would you use a group of related values to represent the item's state?
- Are there any obvious actions to be performed by the item?

If the answers to both of these questions are no, then the noun probably represents a value that can be stored in a primitive variable. If we apply this test to each of the nouns that remain in our list, we can conclude that the following are probably not classes: **address, estimated labor charges, estimated parts charges, make, model, name, sales tax, telephone number, total estimated charges** and **year**. These are all simple string or numeric values that can be stored in primitive variables. Here is the updated list of potential classes:

~~address~~

~~BMW~~

~~car~~

cars

customer

~~estimated labor charges~~

~~estimated parts charges~~

~~foreign cars~~

~~Joe's Automotive Shop~~

~~make~~

~~manager~~

~~Mercedes~~

~~model~~

~~name~~

~~Porsche~~

~~sales tax~~

service quote

~~shop~~

~~telephone number~~

~~total estimated charges~~

~~year~~

We have eliminated **address, estimated labor charges, estimated parts charges, make, model, name, sales tax, telephone number, total estimated charges,** and **year** as classes because they represent simple values that can be stored in primitive variables.

As you can see from the list, we have eliminated everything except **cars**, **customer**, and **service quote**. This means that in our application, we will need classes to represent cars, customers, and service quotes. Ultimately, we will write a `Car` class, a `Customer` class, and a `ServiceQuote` class.

Identifying a Class's Responsibilities

Once the classes have been identified, the next task is to identify each class's responsibilities. A class's *responsibilities* are

- the things that the class is responsible for knowing
- the actions that the class is responsible for doing

When you have identified the things that a class is responsible for knowing, then you have identified the class's attributes. These values will be stored in fields. Likewise, when you have identified the actions that a class is responsible for doing, you have identified its methods.

It is often helpful to ask the questions, "In the context of this problem, what must the class know? What must the class do?" The first place to look for the answers is in the description of the problem domain. Many of the things that a class must know and do will be mentioned. Some class responsibilities, however, might not be directly mentioned in the problem domain, so brainstorming is often required. Let's apply this methodology to the classes we previously identified from our problem domain.

The `Customer` class

In the context of our problem domain, what must the `Customer` class know? The description directly mentions the following items, which are all attributes of a customer:

- the customer's name
- the customer's address
- the customer's telephone number

These are all values that can be represented as strings and stored in the class's fields. The `Customer` class can potentially know many other things. One mistake that can be made at this point is to identify too many things that an object is responsible for knowing. In some applications, a `Customer` class might know the customer's email address. This particular problem domain does not mention that the customer's email address is used for any purpose, so we should not include it as a responsibility.

Now let's identify the class's methods. In the context of our problem domain, what must the `Customer` class do? The only obvious actions are:

- create an object of the `Customer` class
- set and get the customer's name
- set and get the customer's address
- set and get the customer's telephone number

From this list we can see that the `Customer` class will have a constructor, as well as accessor and mutator methods, for each of its fields. Figure 3-23 shows a UML diagram for the `Customer` class.

Figure 3-23   UML diagram for the `Customer` class

```
                    Customer
        - name : String
        - address : String
        - phone : String
        + Customer()
        + setName(n : String) : void
        + setAddress(a : String) : void
        + setPhone(p : String) : void
        + getName() : String
        + getAddress() : String
        + getPhone() : String
```

The `Car` Class

In the context of our problem domain, what must an object of the `Car` class know? The following items are all attributes of a car, and are mentioned in the problem domain:

- the car's make
- the car's model
- the car's year

Now let's identify the class's methods. In the context of our problem domain, what must the `Car` class do? Once again, the only obvious actions are the standard set of methods that we will find in most classes (constructors, accessors, and mutators). Specifically, the actions are:

- create an object of the `Car` class
- set and get the car's make
- set and get the car's model
- set and get the car's year

Figure 3-24 shows a UML diagram for the `Car` class at this point.

Figure 3-24   UML diagram for the `Car` class

```
                    Car
        - make : String
        - model : String
        - year : int
        + Car()
        + setMake(m : String) : void
        + setModel(m : String) : void
        + setYear(y : int) : void
        + getMake() : String
        + getModel() : String
        + getYear() : int
```

The ServiceQuote Class

In the context of our problem domain, what must an object of the ServiceQuote class know? The problem domain mentions the following items:

- the estimated parts charges
- the estimated labor charges
- the sales tax
- the total estimated charges

Careful thought and a little brainstorming will reveal that two of these items are the results of calculations: sales tax and total estimated charges. These items are dependent on the values of the estimated parts and labor charges. In order to avoid the risk of holding stale data, we will not store these values in fields. Rather, we will provide methods that calculate these values and return them. The other methods that we will need for this class are a constructor and the accessors and mutators for the estimated parts charges and estimated labor charges fields. Figure 3-25 shows a UML diagram for the ServiceQuote class.

Figure 3-25   UML diagram for the ServiceQuote class

```
+-----------------------------------------+
|              ServiceQuote               |
+-----------------------------------------+
| - partsCharges : double                 |
| - laborCharges : double                 |
+-----------------------------------------+
| + ServiceQuote()                        |
| + setPartsCharges(c : double) :         |
|       void                              |
| + setLaborCharges(c : double) :         |
|       void                              |
| + getPartsCharges() : double            |
| + getLaborCharges() : double            |
| + getSalesTax() : double                |
| + getTotalCharges() : double            |
+-----------------------------------------+
```

This Is Only the Beginning

You should look at the process that we have discussed in this section merely as a starting point. It's important to realize that designing an object-oriented application is an iterative process. It may take you several attempts to identify all of the classes that you will need and determine all of their responsibilities. As the design process unfolds, you will gain a deeper understanding of the problem, and consequently you will see ways to improve the design.

Checkpoint

3.15   What is a problem domain?

3.16   When designing an object-oriented application, who should write a description of the problem domain?

3.17   How do you identify the potential classes in a problem domain description?

3.18   What are a class's responsibilities?

3.19   What two questions should you ask to determine a class's responsibilities?

3.20   Will all of a class's actions always be directly mentioned in the problem domain description?

3.9 Common Errors to Avoid

The following list describes several errors that are commonly made when learning this chapter's topics.

- **Putting a semicolon at the end of a method header.** A semicolon never appears at the end of a method header.
- **Declaring a variable to reference an object, but forgetting to use the new key word to create the object.** Declaring a variable to reference an object does not create an object. You must use the new key word to create the object.
- **Forgetting the parentheses that must appear after the class name, which appears after the new key word.** The name of a class appears after the new key word, and a set of parentheses appears after the class name. You must write the parentheses even if no arguments are passed to the constructor.
- **Forgetting to provide arguments when a constructor requires them.** When using a constructor that has parameters, you must provide arguments for them.
- **Forgetting the parentheses in a method call.** You must write the parentheses after the name of the method in a statement that calls the method, even if no arguments are passed to the method.
- **Forgetting to pass arguments to methods that require them.** If a method has parameters, you must provide arguments when calling the method.
- **In a method, unintentionally declaring a local variable with the same name as a field of the same class.** When a method's local variable has the same name as a field in the same class, the local variable's name shadows the field's name.
- **Passing an argument to a method that is incompatible with the parameter variable's data type.** An argument that is passed to a method must be of a data type that is compatible with the parameter variable receiving it.
- **Using a variable to receive a method's return value when the variable's data type is incompatible with the data type of the return value.** A variable that receives a method's return value must be of a data type that is compatible with the data type of the return value.

Review Questions and Exercises

Multiple Choice and True/False

1. This is a collection of programming statements that specify the attributes and methods that a particular type of object can have.
   a. class
   b. method
   c. parameter
   d. instance

2. A class is analogous to a
   a. blueprint
   b. house
   c. architect
   d. attribute

3. An object is a(n)
   a. blueprint
   b. attribute
   c. variable
   d. instance

4. This is a member of a class that holds data.
   a. method
   b. instance
   c. field
   d. constructor

5. This key word causes an object to be created in memory.
   a. `create`
   b. `new`
   c. `object`
   d. `construct`

6. This key word causes a value to be sent back from a method to the statement that called it.
   a. `send`
   b. `return`
   c. `value`
   d. `public`

7. This is a method that gets a value from a class's field, but does not change it.
   a. accessor
   b. constructor
   c. void
   d. mutator

8. This is a method that stores a value in a field or in some other way changes the value of a field.
   a. accessor
   b. constructor
   c. void
   d. mutator

9. When the value of an item is dependent on other data, and that item is not updated when the other data is changed, what has the value become?
   a. bitter
   b. stale
   c. asynchronous
   d. moldy

10. This is a method that is automatically called when an instance of a class is created.
    a. accessor
    b. constructor
    c. void
    d. mutator

11. When a local variable has the same name as a field, the local variable's name does this to the field's name.
    a. shadows
    b. complements
    c. deletes
    d. merges with

12. If you do not write a constructor for a class, this is automatically provided for the class.
    a. accessor method
    b. default instance
    c. default constructor
    d. predefined constructor

13. A class's responsibilities are
    a. the objects created from the class
    b. things the class knows
    c. actions the class performs
    d. Both b and c

14. **True or False:** The occurrence of a string literal in a Java program causes a `String` object to be created in memory, initialized with the string literal.

15. **True or False:** When passing an argument to a method, the argument's data type must be compatible with the parameter variable's data type.

16. **True or False:** When passing multiple arguments to a method, the order in which the arguments are passed is not important.

17. **True or False:** Each instance of a class has its own set of instance fields.

18. **True or False:** When you write a constructor for a class, it still has the default constructor that Java automatically provides.

19. **True or False:** To find the classes needed for an object-oriented application, you identify all of the verbs in a description of the problem domain.

Find the Error

1. Find the error in the following class.

```
public class MyClass
{
    private int x;
    private double y;

    public void MyClass(int a, double b)
    {
      x = a;
      y = b;
    }
}
```

2. Assume that the following method is a member of a class. Find the error.

```
public void total(int value1, value2, value3)
{
    return value1 + value2 + value3;
}
```

3. The following statement attempts to create a `Rectangle` object. Find the error.

```
Rectangle box = new Rectangle;
```

Algorithm Workbench

1. Design a class named `Pet`, which should have the following attributes:

   - **name**. The name attribute holds the name of a pet.
   - **animal**. The animal attribute holds the type of animal that a pet is. Example values are "Dog", "Cat", and "Bird".
   - **age**. The age attribute holds the pet's age.

   The `Pet` class should also have the following methods:

   - **setName**. The setName method stores a value in the name attribute.
   - **setAnimal**. The setAnimal method stores a value in the animal attribute.
   - **setAge**. The setAge method stores a value in the age attribute.
   - **getName**. The getName method returns the value of the name attribute.
   - **getAnimal**. The getAnimal method returns the value of the animal attribute.
   - **getAge**. The getAge method returns the value of the age attribute.

     a. Draw a UML diagram of the class. Be sure to include notation showing each attribute's and method's access specification and data type. Also include notation showing any method parameters and their data types.
     b. Write the Java code for the `Pet` class.

2. Look at the following partial class definition, and then respond to the questions that follow it.

```
public class Book
{
    private String title;
    private String author;
    private String publisher;
    private int copiesSold;
}
```

   a. Write a constructor for this class. The constructor should accept an argument for each of the fields.
   b. Write accessor and mutator methods for each field.
   c. Draw a UML diagram for the class, including the methods you have written.

3. Look at the following description of a problem domain:

   The bank offers the following types of accounts to its customers: savings accounts, checking accounts, and money market accounts. Customers are allowed to deposit money into an account (thereby increasing its balance), withdraw money from an account (thereby decreasing its balance), and earn interest on the account. Each account has an interest rate.

Assume that you are writing an application that will calculate the amount of interest earned for a bank account.

a. Identify the potential classes in this problem domain.
b. Refine the list to include only the necessary class or classes for this problem.
c. Identify the responsibilities of the class or classes.

Short Answer

1. What is the difference between a class and an instance of the class?

2. A contractor uses a blueprint to build a set of identical houses. Are classes analogous to the blueprint or the houses?

3. What is an accessor method? What is a mutator method?

4. Is it a good idea to make fields private? Why or why not?

5. If a class has a private field, what has access to the field?

6. What is the purpose of the `new` key word?

7. Assume a program named *MailList.java* is stored in the `DataBase` folder on your hard drive. The program creates objects of the `Customer` and `Account` classes. Describe the steps that the compiler goes through in locating and compiling the `Customer` and `Account` classes.

8. Explain what is meant by the phrase "pass by value."

9. Why are constructors useful for performing "start-up" operations?

10. What is the difference between a field and an attribute?

11. What is the difference between an argument and a parameter variable?

12. Under what circumstances does Java automatically provide a default constructor for a class?

13. What do you call a constructor that accepts no arguments?

Programming Challenges

1. Employee Class

Write a class named `Employee` that has the following fields:

- **name**. The `name` field is a `String` object that holds the employee's name.
- **idNumber**. The `idNumber` is an `int` variable that holds the employee's ID number.
- **department**. The `department` field is a `String` object that holds the name of the department where the employee works.
- **position**. The `position` field is a `String` object that holds the employee's job title.

Write appropriate mutator methods that store values in these fields and accessor methods that return the values in these fields. Once you have the written the class, write a separate program that creates three `Employee` objects to hold the following data.

Name	ID Number	Department	Position
Susan Meyers	47899	Accounting	Vice President
Mark Jones	39119	IT	Programmer
Joy Rogers	81774	Manufacturing	Engineer

The program should store this data in the three objects and then display the data for each employee on the screen.

2. Car Class

Write a class named Car that has the following fields:

- **yearModel.** The yearModel field is an int that holds the car's year model.
- **make.** The make field is a String object that holds the make of the car.
- **speed.** The speed field is an int that holds the car's current speed.

In addition, the class should have the following methods.

- **Constructor.** The constructor should accept the car's year model and make as arguments. These values should be assigned to the object's yearModel and make fields. The constructor should also assign 0 to the speed field.
- **Accessor.** The appropriate accessor methods get the values stored in an object's yearModel, make, and speed fields.
- **accelerate.** The accelerate method should add 5 to the speed field each time it is called.
- **brake.** The brake method should subtract 5 from the speed field each time it is called.

Demonstrate the class in a program that creates a Car object, and then calls the accelerate method five times. After each call to the accelerate method, get the current speed of the car and display it. Then, call the brake method five times. After each call to the brake method, get the current speed of the car and display it.

3. Personal Information Class

Design a class that holds the following personal data: name, address, age, and phone number. Write appropriate accessor and mutator methods. Demonstrate the class by writing a program that creates three instances of it. One instance should hold your information, and the other two should hold your friends' or family members' information.

VideoNote
The Personal
Information
Class Problem

4. Temperature Class

Write a Temperature class that will hold a temperature in Fahrenheit and provide methods to get the temperature in Fahrenheit, Celsius, and Kelvin. The class should have the following field:

- **ftemp**—A double that holds a Fahrenheit temperature.

The class should have the following methods:

- **Constructor**—The constructor accepts a Fahrenheit temperature (as a double) and stores it in the ftemp field.
- **setFahrenheit**—The setFahrenheit method accepts a Fahrenheit temperature (as a double) and stores it in the ftemp field.
- **getFahrenheit**—Returns the value of the ftemp field, as a Fahrenheit temperature (no conversion required).
- **getCelsius**—Returns the value of the ftemp field converted to Celsius.
- **getKelvin**—Returns the value of the ftemp field converted to Kelvin.

Use the following formula to convert the Fahrenheit temperature to Celsius:

$$Celsius = (5/9) \times (Fahrenheit - 32)$$

Use the following formula to convert the Fahrenheit temperature to Kelvin:

$$Kelvin = ((5/9) \times (Fahrenheit - 32)) + 273$$

Demonstrate the `Temperature` class by writing a separate program that asks the user for a Fahrenheit temperature. The program should create an instance of the `Temperature` class, with the value entered by the user passed to the constructor. The program should then call the object's methods to display the temperature in Celsius and Kelvin.

5. `RetailItem` Class

Write a class named `RetailItem` that holds data about an item in a retail store. The class should have the following fields:

- `description`. The `description` field is a `String` object that holds a brief description of the item.
- `unitsOnHand`. The `unitsOnHand` field is an `int` variable that holds the number of units currently in inventory.
- `price`. The `price` field is a `double` that holds the item's retail price.

Write appropriate mutator methods that store values in these fields and accessor methods that return the values in these fields. Once you have written the class, write a separate program that creates three `RetailItem` objects and stores the following data in them.

Description		Units On Hand	Price
Item #1	Jacket	12	59.95
Item #2	Designer Jeans	40	34.95
Item #3	Shirt	20	24.95

6. `Payroll` Class

Design a `Payroll` class that has fields for an employee's name, ID number, hourly pay rate, and number of hours worked. Write the appropriate accessor and mutator methods and a constructor that accepts the employee's name and ID number as arguments. The class should also have a method that returns the employee's gross pay, which is calculated as the number of hours worked multiplied by the hourly pay rate. Write a program that demonstrates the class by creating a `Payroll` object, then asking the user to enter the data for an employee. The program should display the amount of gross pay earned.

7. Widget Factory

Design a class for a widget manufacturing plant. The class should have a method whose argument is the number of widgets that must be produced. The class should have another method that calculates how many days it will take to produce the number of widgets. (Assume that 10 widgets can be produced each hour. The plant operates two shifts of eight hours each per day.)

Demonstrate the class by writing a separate program that creates an instance of the class. The program should pass a number of widgets to the object and call the object's method that displays the number of days it will take to produce that many widgets.

8. TestScores Class

Design a TestScores class that has fields to hold three test scores. The class should have accessor and mutator methods for the test score fields and a method that returns the average of the test scores. Demonstrate the class by writing a separate program that creates an instance of the class. The program should ask the user to enter three test scores, which are stored in the TestScores object. Then the program should display the average of the scores, as reported by the TestScores object.

9. Circle Class

Write a Circle class that has the following fields:

- radius: a double
- PI: a final double initialized with the value 3.14159

The class should have the following methods:

- **Constructor.** Accepts the radius of the circle as an argument.
- **setRadius.** A mutator method for the radius field.
- **getRadius.** An accessor method for the radius field.
- **getArea.** Returns the area of the circle, which is calculated as

    area = PI * radius * radius

- **getDiameter.** Returns the diameter of the circle, which is calculated as

    diameter = radius * 2

- **getCircumference.** Returns the circumference of the circle, which is calculated as

    circumference = 2 * PI * radius

Write a program that demonstrates the Circle class by asking the user for the circle's radius, creating a Circle object, and then reporting the circle's area, diameter, and circumference.

10. Pet Class

Design a class named Pet, which should have the following fields:

- **name.** The name field holds the name of a pet.
- **type.** The type field holds the type of animal that a pet is. Example values are "Dog", "Cat", and "Bird".
- **age.** The age field holds the pet's age.

The Pet class should also have the following methods:

- **setName.** The setName method stores a value in the name field.
- **setType.** The setType method stores a value in the type field.

- **setAge.** The setAge method stores a value in the age field.
- **getName.** The getName method returns the value of the name field.
- **gettype.** The getType method returns the value of the type field.
- **getAge.** The getAge method returns the value of the age field.

Once you have designed the class, design a program that creates an object of the class and prompts the user to enter the name, type, and age of his or her pet. This data should be stored in the object. Use the object's accessor methods to retrieve the pet's name, type, and age and display this data on the screen.

4 Decision Structures

TOPICS

4.1 The if Statement
4.2 The if-else Statement
4.3 The Payroll Class
4.4 Nested if Statements
4.5 The if-else-if Statement
4.6 Logical Operators
4.7 Comparing String Objects
4.8 More about Variable Declaration and Scope

4.9 The Conditional Operator (Optional)
4.10 The switch Statement
4.11 Formatting Numbers with the DecimalFormat Class
4.12 Focus on Problem Solving: The SalesCommission Class
4.13 Generating Random Numbers with the Random Class
4.14 Common Errors to Avoid

4.1 The if Statement

CONCEPT: The if statement is used to create a decision structure, which allows a program to have more than one path of execution. The if statement causes one or more statements to execute only when a **boolean** expression is true.

VideoNote
The if
Statement

In all the methods you have written so far, the statements are executed one after the other, in the order they appear. You might think of sequentially executed statements as the steps you take as you walk down a road. To complete the journey, you must start at the beginning and take each step, one after the other, until you reach your destination. This is illustrated in Figure 4-1.

Figure 4-1   Sequence structure

```java
public class SquareArea
{

   public static void main(String[] args)
   {
      double length, width, area;

Step 1 ──────▶ length = 10;
Step 2 ──────▶ width = 5;
Step 3 ──────▶ area = length * width;
Step 4 ──────▶ System.out.print("The area is " + area);
   }


}
```

The type of code in Figure 4-1 is called a *sequence structure* because the statements are executed in sequence, without branching off in another direction. Programs often need more than one path of execution, however. Many algorithms require a program to execute some statements only under certain circumstances. This can be accomplished with a *decision structure*.

In a decision structure's simplest form, a specific action is taken only when a condition exists. If the condition does not exist, the action is not performed. The flowchart in Figure 4-2 shows the logic of a decision structure. The diamond symbol represents a yes/no question or a true/false condition. If the answer to the question is yes (or if the condition is true), the program flow follows one path that leads to an action being performed. If the answer to the question is no (or the condition is false), the program flow follows another path that skips the action.

Figure 4-2   Simple decision structure logic

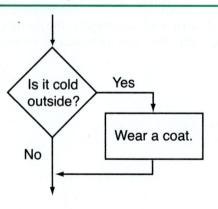

In the flowchart, the action "Wear a coat" is performed only when it is cold outside. If it is not cold outside, the action is skipped. The action "Wear a coat" is *conditionally executed* because it is performed only when a certain condition (cold outside) exists. Figure 4-3 shows a more elaborate flowchart, where three actions are taken only when it is cold outside.

Figure 4-3   Three-action decision structure logic

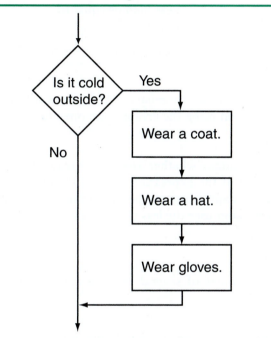

One way to code a decision structure in Java is with the if statement. Here is the general format of the if statement:

```
if (BooleanExpression)
    statement;
```

The if statement is simple in the way it works: The `BooleanExpression` that appears inside the parentheses must be a boolean expression. A *boolean expression* is one that is either true or false. If the boolean expression is true, the very next *statement* is executed. Otherwise, it is skipped. The *statement* is *conditionally executed* because it executes only under the condition that the expression in the parentheses is true.

Using Relational Operators to Form Conditions

Typically, the condition that is tested by an if statement is formed with a relational operator. A *relational operator* determines whether a specific relationship exists between two values. For example, the greater than operator (>) determines whether one value is greater than another. The equal to operator (==) determines whether two values are equal. Table 4-1 lists all of the Java relational operators.

Table 4-1 Relational operators

Relational Operators (in Order of Precedence)	Meaning
>	Greater than
<	Less than
>=	Greater than or equal to
<=	Less than or equal to
==	Equal to
!=	Not equal to

All of the relational operators are binary, which means they use two operands. Here is an example of an expression using the greater than operator:

```
length > width
```

This expression determines whether `length` is greater than `width`. If `length` is greater than `width`, the value of the expression is `true`. Otherwise, the value of the expression is `false`. Because the expression can be only `true` or `false`, it is a `boolean` expression. The following expression uses the less than operator to determine whether `length` is less than `width`:

```
length < width
```

Table 4-2 shows examples of several `boolean` expressions that compare the variables `x` and `y`.

Table 4-2 `boolean` expressions using relational operators

Expression	Meaning
x > y	Is x greater than y?
x < y	Is x less than y?
x >= y	Is x greater than or equal to y?
x <= y	Is x less than or equal to y?
x == y	Is x equal to y?
x != y	Is x not equal to y?

Two of the operators, `>=` and `<=`, test for more than one relationship. The `>=` operator determines whether the operand on its left is greater than or equal to the operand on the right. Assuming that a is 4, b is 6, and c is 4, both of the expressions `b >= a` and `a >= c` are true and `a >= 5` is false. When using this operator, the `>` symbol must precede the `=` symbol, and there is no space between them. The `<=` operator determines whether the operand on its left is less than or equal to the operand on its right. Once again, assuming that a is 4, b is 6, and c is 4, both `a <= c` and `b <= 10` are true, but `b <= a` is false. When using this operator, the `<` symbol must precede the `=` symbol, and there is no space between them.

The == operator determines whether the operand on its left is equal to the operand on its right. If both operands have the same value, the expression is true. Assuming that a is 4, the expression a == 4 is true and the expression a == 2 is false. Notice the equality operator is two = symbols together. Don't confuse this operator with the assignment operator, which is one = symbol.

The != operator is the not equal operator. It determines whether the operand on its left is not equal to the operand on its right, which is the opposite of the == operator. As before, assuming a is 4, b is 6, and c is 4, both a != b and b != c are true because a is not equal to b and b is not equal to c. However, a != c is false because a is equal to c.

Putting It All Together

Let's look at an example of the if statement:

```java
if (sales > 50000)
    bonus = 500.0;
```

This statement uses the > operator to determine whether sales is greater than 50,000. If the expression sales > 50000 is true, the variable bonus is assigned 500.0. If the expression is false, however, the assignment statement is skipped. The program in Code Listing 4-1 shows another example. The user enters three test scores and the program calculates their average. If the average is greater than 95, the program congratulates the user on obtaining a high score.

Code Listing 4-1   (AverageScore.java)

```java
 1  import java.util.Scanner;   // Needed for the Scanner class
 2
 3  /**
 4   * This program demonstrates the if statement.
 5   */
 6
 7  public class AverageScore
 8  {
 9     public static void main(String[] args)
10     {
11        double score1,      // Score #1
12               score2,      // Score #2
13               score3,      // Score #3
14               average;     // Average score
15
16        // Create a Scanner object to read input.
17        Scanner keyboard = new Scanner(System.in);
18
19        System.out.println("This program averages "
20                           + "3 test scores.");
21
```

```
22          // Get the first score.
23          System.out.print("Enter score #1: ");
24          score1 = keyboard.nextDouble();
25
26          // Get the second score.
27          System.out.print("Enter score #2: ");
28          score2 = keyboard.nextDouble ();
29
30          // Get the third score.
31          System.out.print("Enter score #3: ");
32          score3 = keyboard.nextDouble ();
33
34          // Calculate and display the average score.
35          average = (score1 + score2 + score3) / 3.0;
36          System.out.println("The average is " + average);
37
38          // If the average is higher than 95, congratulate
39          // the user.
40          if (average > 95)
41              System.out.println("That's a great score!");
42      }
43  }
```

Program Output with Example Input Shown in Bold

```
This program averages 3 test scores.
Enter score #1: 82 [Enter]
Enter score #2: 76 [Enter]
Enter score #3: 91 [Enter]
The average is 83.0
```

Program Output with Example Input Shown in Bold

```
This program averages 3 test scores.
Enter score #1: 97 [Enter]
Enter score #2: 94 [Enter]
Enter score #3: 100 [Enter]
The average is 97.0
That's a great score!
```

The if statement in lines 40 and 41 cause the congratulatory message to be printed:

```
if (average > 95)
    System.out.println("That's a great score!");
```

Figure 4-4 shows the logic of this if statement.

Figure 4-4   Logic of the if statements

Table 4-3 shows other examples of if statements and their outcomes.

Table 4-3   Other examples of if statements

Statement	Outcome
`if (hours > 40)` `    overTime = true;`	If hours is greater than 40, assigns true to the boolean variable overTime.
`if (value < 32)` `    System.out.println("Invalid number");`	If value is less than 32, displays the message "Invalid number"

Programming Style and the if Statement

Even though an if statement usually spans more than one line, it is really one long statement. For instance, the following if statements are identical except for the style in which they are written:

```
if (average > 95)
   System.out.println("That's a great score!");

if (average > 95) System.out.println("That's a great score!");
```

In both of these examples, the compiler considers the if statement and the conditionally executed statement as one unit, with a semicolon properly placed at the end. Indentions and spacing are for the human readers of a program, not the compiler. Here are two important style rules you should adopt for writing if statements:

- The conditionally executed statement should appear on the line after the if statement.
- The conditionally executed statement should be indented one level from the if statement.

In most editors, each time you press the tab key, you are indenting one level. By indenting the conditionally executed statement, you are causing it to stand out visually. This is so you can tell at a glance what part of the program the `if` statement executes. This is a standard way of writing `if` statements and is the method you should use.

Be Careful with Semicolons

You do not put a semicolon after the `if (BooleanExpression)` portion of an `if` statement, as illustrated in Figure 4-5. This is because the `if` statement isn't complete without its conditionally executed statement.

Figure 4-5   Do not prematurely terminate an `if` statement with a semicolon

If you prematurely terminate an `if` statement with a semicolon, the compiler will not display an error message, but will assume that you are placing a *null statement* there. The null statement, which is an empty statement that does nothing, will become the conditionally executed statement. The statement that you intended to be conditionally executed will be disconnected from the `if` statement and will always execute.

For example, look at the following code:

```
int x = 0, y = 10;

// The following if statement is prematurely
// terminated with a semicolon.
if (x > y);
    System.out.println(x + " is greater than " + y);
```

This code will always display the message "0 is greater than 10". The `if` statement in this code is prematurely terminated with a semicolon. Because the `println` statement is not connected to the `if` statement, it will always execute.

Having Multiple Conditionally Executed Statements

The previous examples of the `if` statement conditionally execute a single statement. The `if` statement can also conditionally execute a group of statements, as long as they are enclosed in a set of braces. Enclosing a group of statements inside braces creates a *block* of statements. Here is an example:

```
if (sales > 50000)
{
 bonus = 500.0;
 commissionRate = 0.12;
 daysOff += 1;
}
```

If `sales` is greater than 50,000, this code will execute all three of the statements inside the braces, in the order they appear. If the braces were accidentally left out, however, the `if` statement conditionally executes only the very next statement. Figure 4-6 illustrates this.

Figure 4-6   An `if` statement missing its braces

```
                         if (sales > 50000)
                             bonus = 500.0;  ◄──────────   Only this statement is
                                                           conditionally executed.
  These statements are  ──►commissionRate = 0.12;
  always executed.      ──►daysOff += 1;
```

Flags

A *flag* is a `boolean` variable that signals when some condition exists in the program. When the flag variable is set to `false`, it indicates the condition does not yet exist. When the flag variable is set to `true`, it means the condition does exist.

For example, suppose a program similar to the previous test averaging program has a `boolean` variable named `highScore`. The variable might be used to signal that a high score has been achieved by the following code.

```
if (average > 95)
    highScore = true;
```

Later, the same program might use code similar to the following to test the `highScore` variable, in order to determine if a high score has been achieved.

```
if (highScore)
    System.out.println("That's a high score!");
```

You will find flag variables useful in many circumstances, and we will come back to them in future chapters.

Comparing Characters

You can use the relational operators to test character data as well as numbers. For example, the following code segment uses the `==` operator to compare the contents of the `char` variable `myLetter` to the character `'A'`.

```
char myLetter = 'A';
if (myLetter == 'A')
    System.out.println("That is the letter A.");
```

The `!=` operator can also be used with characters to test for inequality. For example, the following statement determines whether the `char` variable `myLetter` is not equal to the letter `'A'`.

```
if (myLetter != 'A')
    System.out.println("That is not the letter A.");
```

You can also use the `>`, `<`, `>=`, and `<=` operators to compare characters. Computers do not actually store characters, such as A, B, C, and so forth, in memory. Instead, they store numeric codes that represent the characters. Recall from Chapter 2 that Java uses Unicode, which is a set of numbers that represents all the letters of the alphabet (both lowercase and uppercase), the printable digits 0 through 9, punctuation symbols, and special characters. When a character is stored in memory, it is actually the Unicode number that is stored. When the computer is instructed to print the value on the screen, it displays the character that corresponds with the numeric code.

> **NOTE:** Unicode is an international encoding system that is extensive enough to represent all the characters of all the world's alphabets.

In Unicode, letters are arranged in alphabetic order. Because 'A' comes before 'B', the numeric code for the character 'A' is less than the code for the character 'B'. (The code for 'A' is 65 and the code for 'B' is 66. Appendix B lists the codes for all of the printable English characters.) In the following `if` statement, the `boolean` expression `'A' < 'B'` is true.

```
if ('A' < 'B')
    System.out.println("A is less than B.");
```

In Unicode, the uppercase letters come before the lowercase letters, so the numeric code for 'A' (65) is less than the numeric code for 'a' (97). In addition, the space character (code 32) comes before all the alphabetic characters.

Checkpoint

4.1 Write an `if` statement that assigns 0 to x when y is equal to 20.

4.2 Write an `if` statement that multiplies payRate by 1.5 if hours is greater than 40.

4.3 Write an `if` statement that assigns 0.2 to commission if sales is greater than or equal to 10000.

4.4 Write an `if` statement that sets the variable fees to 50 if the `boolean` variable max is true.

4.5 Write an `if` statement that assigns 20 to the variable y and assigns 40 to the variable z if the variable x is greater than 100.

4.6 Write an `if` statement that assigns 0 to the variable b and assigns 1 to the variable c if the variable a is less than 10.

4.7 Write an `if` statement that displays "Goodbye" if the variable myCharacter contains the character 'D'.

4.2 The `if-else` Statement

CONCEPT: The `if-else` statement will execute one group of statements if its `boolean` expression is true, or another group if its `boolean` expression is false.

The `if-else` statement is an expansion of the `if` statement. Here is its general format:

```
if (BooleanExpression)
    statement or block
else
    statement or block
```

Like the `if` statement, a boolean expression is evaluated. If the expression is `true`, a statement or block of statements is executed. If the expression is `false`, however, a separate group of statements is executed. The program in Code Listing 4-2 uses the `if-else` statement to handle a classic programming problem: division by zero. Division by zero is mathematically impossible to perform and in Java it causes an error to occur at runtime.

Code Listing 4-2   (`Division.java`)

```java
 1  import java.util.Scanner;  // Needed for the Scanner class
 2
 3  /**
 4   * This program demonstrates the if-else statement.
 5   */
 6
 7  public class Division
 8  {
 9      public static void main(String[] args)
10      {
11          int number1, number2;   // Two numbers
12          double quotient;        // The quotient of two numbers
13
14          // Create a Scanner object to read input.
15          Scanner keyboard = new Scanner(System.in);
16
17          // Get two numbers from the user.
18          System.out.print("Enter an integer: ");
19          number1 = keyboard.nextInt();
20          System.out.print("Enter another integer: ");
21          number2 = keyboard.nextInt();
22
23          // Determine whether division by zero will occur.
24          if (number2 == 0)
25          {
26              // Error - division by zero.
27              System.out.println("Division by zero is not possible.");
28              System.out.println("Please run the program again and ");
29              System.out.println("enter a number other than zero.");
30          }
31          else
32          {
```

```
33              // Perform the division and display the quotient.
34              quotient = (double) number1 / number2;
35              System.out.print("The quotient of " + number1);
36              System.out.print(" divided by " + number2);
37              System.out.println(" is " + quotient);
38          }
39      }
40  }
```

Program Output with Example Input Shown in Bold

Enter an integer: **10 [Enter]**
Enter another integer: **0 [Enter]**
Division by zero is not possible.
Please run the program again and
enter a number other than zero.

Program Output with Example Input Shown in Bold

Enter an integer: **10 [Enter]**
Enter another integer: **5 [Enter]**
The quotient of 10 divided by 5 is 2.0

The value of `number2` is tested before the division is performed. If the user entered 0, the block of statements controlled by the `if` clause executes, displaying a message that indicates the program cannot perform a division by zero. Otherwise, the `else` clause takes control, which divides `number1` by `number2` and displays the result. Figure 4-7 shows the logic of the `if-else` statement.

Figure 4-7   Logic of the `if-else` statement

 Checkpoint

4.8   Write an `if-else` statement that assigns 20 to the variable y if the variable x is greater than 100. Otherwise, it should assign 0 to the variable y.

4.9   Write an `if-else` statement that assigns 1 to x when y is equal to 100. Otherwise it should assign 0 to x.

4.10 Write an if-else statement that assigns 0.1 to commission unless sales is greater than or equal to 50000.0, in which case it assigns 0.2 to commission.

4.11 Write an if-else statement that assigns 0 to the variable b and assigns 1 to the variable c if the variable a is less than 10. Otherwise, it should assign –99 to the variable b and assign 0 to the variable c.

4.3 The Payroll Class

In this section we will examine a Payroll class that determines an employee's gross pay. The gross pay is calculated as the number of hours worked multiplied by the hourly pay rate. The class also has the ability to calculate overtime pay if more than 40 hours were worked. The employee earns 1.5 times his or her regular hourly pay rate for all hours over 40. Figure 4-8 shows a UML diagram for the Payroll class.

Figure 4-8 UML diagram for the Payroll class

```
┌─────────────────────────────────────────┐
│                 Payroll                  │
├─────────────────────────────────────────┤
│ - hoursWorked : double                   │
│ - payRate : double                       │
├─────────────────────────────────────────┤
│ + Payroll()                              │
│ + setHoursWorked(hours : double) :       │
│   void                                   │
│ + setPayRate(rate : double) : void       │
│ + getHoursWorked() : double              │
│ + getPayRate() : double                  │
│ + getGrossPay() : double                 │
└─────────────────────────────────────────┘
```

Here is a summary of the class's fields.

- hoursWorked is a double that holds the number of hours the employee has worked.
- payRate is a double that holds the employee's hourly pay rate.

Here is a summary of the class's methods.

- A constructor initializes the fields to 0.0.
- setHoursWorked is a mutator method that accepts an argument and stores the argument's value in the hoursWorked field.
- setPayRate is a mutator method that accepts an argument and stores the argument's value in the payRate field.
- getHoursWorked is an accessor method that returns the value in the hoursWorked field.
- getPayRate is an accessor method that returns the value in the payRate field.
- The getGrossPay method calculates and returns the employee's gross pay. If the number of hours worked is greater than 40, the method adds overtime pay to the gross pay.

Code Listing 4-3 shows the code for the Payroll class, which is stored in the file Payroll.java.

Code Listing 4-3   **(Payroll.java)**

```
1   /**
2    * This class holds values for hours worked and the
3    * hourly pay rate. It calculates the gross pay and
4    * adds additional pay for overtime.
5    */
6
7   public class Payroll
8   {
9      private double hoursWorked; // Number of hours worked
10     private double payRate;     // The hourly pay rate
11
12     /**
13      * The constructor initializes the hoursWorked and
14      * payRate fields to 0.0.
15      */
16
17     public Payroll()
18     {
19        hoursWorked = 0.0;
20        payRate = 0.0;
21     }
22
23     /**
24      * The setHoursWorked method accepts an argument
25      * that is stored in the hoursWorked field.
26      */
27
28     public void setHoursWorked(double hours)
29     {
30        hoursWorked = hours;
31     }
32
33     /**
34      * The setPayRate method accepts an argument that
35      * is stored in the payRate field.
36      */
37
38     public void setPayRate(double rate)
39     {
40        payRate = rate;
41     }
42
43     /**
44      * The getHoursWorked method returns the hoursWorked
45      * field.
46      */
47
```

```
48      public double getHoursWorked()
49      {
50         return hoursWorked
51      }
52
53      /**
54       * The getPayRate method returns the payRate field.
55       */
56
57      public double getPayRate()
58      {
59         return payRate;
60      }
61
62      /**
63       * The getGrossPay method calculates and returns the
64       * gross pay. Overtime pay is also included.
65       */
66
67      public double getGrossPay()
68      {
69         double grossPay,      // Holds the gross pay
70                overtimePay;   // Holds pay for overtime
71
72         // Determine whether the employee worked more
73         // than 40 hours.
74         if (hoursWorked > 40)
75         {
76            // Calculate regular pay for the first 40 hours.
77            grossPay = 40 * payRate;
78
79            // Calculate overtime pay at 1.5 times the regular
80            // hourly pay rate.
81            overtimePay = (hoursWorked - 40) * (payRate * 1.5);
82
83            // Add the overtime pay to the regular pay.
84            grossPay += overtimePay;
85         }
86         else
87         {
88            // No overtime worked.
89            grossPay = payRate * hoursWorked;
90         }
91
92         return grossPay;
93      }
94  }
```

Notice that the getGrossPay method uses an if-else statement in lines 74 through 90 to control how the gross pay is calculated. If the hoursWorked field is greater than 40, the gross pay is calculated with the overtime pay included. Otherwise, the gross pay is calculated simply as `payRate` times `hoursWorked`. The program shown in Code Listing 4-4 demonstrates the `Payroll` class.

Code Listing 4-4   (`GrossPay.java`)

```java
 1  import java.util.Scanner;  // Needed for the Scanner class
 2
 3  /**
 4   * This program uses the Payroll class to
 5   * calculate an employee's gross pay.
 6   */
 7
 8  public class GrossPay
 9  {
10     public static void main(String[] args)
11     {
12        double hours,  // To hold hours worked
13               rate;   // To hold the hourly pay rate
14
15        // Create a Scanner object to read input.
16        Scanner keyboard = new Scanner(System.in);
17
18        // Create a Payroll object.
19        Payroll employee = new Payroll();
20
21        // Get the number of hours worked.
22        System.out.print("How many hours did the "
23                        + "employee work? ");
24        hours = keyboard.nextDouble();
25
26        // Get the hourly pay rate.
27        System.out.print("What is the employee's "
28                        + "hourly pay rate? ");
29        rate = keyboard.nextDouble();
30
31        // Store the data.
32        employee.setHoursWorked(hours);
33        employee.setPayRate(rate);
34
35        // Display the gross pay.
36        System.out.println("The employee's gross pay "
37                        + "is $" + employee.getGrossPay());
38     }
39  }
```

Program Output with Example Input Shown in Bold

```
How many hours did the employee work? 30 [Enter]
What is the employee's hourly pay rate? 20 [Enter]
The employee's gross pay is $600.0
```

Program Output with Example Input Shown in Bold

```
How many hours did the employee work? 50 [Enter]
What is the employee's hourly pay rate? 10 [Enter]
The employee's gross pay is $550.0
```

4.4 Nested if Statements

CONCEPT: To test more than one condition, an `if` statement can be nested inside another `if` statement.

Sometimes an `if` statement must be nested inside another `if` statement. For example, consider a banking program that determines whether a bank customer qualifies for a special, low interest rate on a loan. To qualify, two conditions must exist: (1) the customer's salary must be at least $50,000, and (2) the customer must have must have held his or her current job for at least 2 years. Figure 4-9 shows a flowchart for an algorithm that could be used in such a program.

Figure 4-9   Logic of nested `if` statements

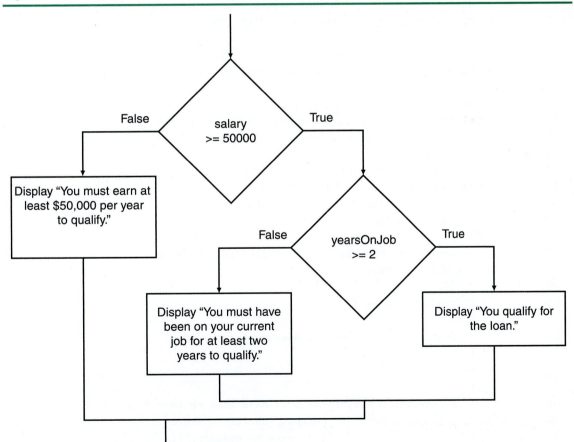

If we follow the flow of execution in the flowchart, we see that the expression salary >= 50000 is tested. If this expression is false, there is no need to perform further tests; we know that the customer does not qualify for the special interest rate. If the expression is true, however, we need to test the second condition. This is done with a nested decision structure that tests the expression yearsOnJob >= 2. If this expression is true, then the customer qualifies for the special interest rate. If this expression is false, then the customer does not qualify. Code Listing 4-5 shows the complete program.

Code Listing 4-5   (LoanQualifier.java)

```java
 1   import java.util.Scanner;
 2
 3   /**
 4    * This program demonstrates a nested if statement.
 5    */
 6
 7   public class LoanQualifier
 8   {
 9      public static void main(String[] args)
10      {
11         double salary;        // Annual salary
12         double yearsOnJob;    // Years at current job
13
14         // Create a Scanner object for keyboard input.
15         Scanner keyboard = new Scanner(System.in);
16
17         // Get the user's annual salary.
18         System.out.print("Enter your annual salary: ");
19         salary = keyboard.nextDouble();
20
21         // Get the number of years at the current job.
22         System.out.print("Enter the number of years "
23                          + "at your current job: ");
24         yearsOnJob = keyboard.nextDouble();
25
26         // Determine whether the user qualifies for the loan.
27         if (salary >= 50000)
28         {
29            if (yearsOnJob >= 2)
30            {
31               System.out.println("You qualify for the loan.");
32            }
33            else
34            {
35               System.out.println("You must have been on your "
36                          + "current job for at least "
37                          + "two years to qualify.");
38            }
```

```
39              }
40          else
41          {
42                  System.out.println("You must earn at least "
43                                  + "$50,000 per year to qualify.");
44          }
45      }
46  }
```

Program Output with Example Input Shown in Bold

Enter your annual salary: **55000.00 [Enter]**
Enter the number of years at your current job: **1 [Enter]**
You must have been on your current job for at least two years to qualify.

Program Output with Example Input Shown in Bold

Enter your annual salary: **25000.00 [Enter]**
Enter the number of years at your current job: **5 [Enter]**
You must earn at least $30,000 per year to qualify.

Program Output with Example Input Shown in Bold

Enter your annual salary: **55000.00 [Enter]**
Enter the number of years at your current job: **5 [Enter]**
You qualify for the loan.

The first if statement (which begins in line 27) conditionally executes the second one (which begins in line 29). The only way the program will execute the second if statement is if the salary variable contains a value that is greater than or equal to 50,000. When this is the case, the second if statement tests the yearsOnJob variable. If it contains a value that is greater than or equal to 2, the program displays a message informing the user that he or she qualifies for the loan.

It should be noted that the braces used in the if statements in this program are not required. The statements could have been written as follows:

```
if (salary >= 50000)
    if (yearsOnJob >= 2)
        System.out.println("You qualify for the loan.");
    else
        System.out.println("You must have been on your "
                        + "current job for at least "
                        + "two years to qualify.");
else
        System.out.println("You must earn at least "
                        + "$50,000 per year to qualify.");
```

Not only do the braces make the statements easier to read, they also help in debugging code. When debugging a program with nested if-else statements, it is important to know to which `if` clause each `else` clause belongs. The rule for matching `else` clauses with `if` clauses is this: an `else` clause goes with the closest previous `if` clause that doesn't already have its own `else` clause. This is easy to see when the conditionally executed statements are enclosed in braces and are properly indented, as shown in Figure 4-10. Each `else` clause lines up with the `if` clause it belongs to. These visual cues are important because nested `if` statements can be very long and complex.

Figure 4-10   Alignment of `if` and `else` clauses

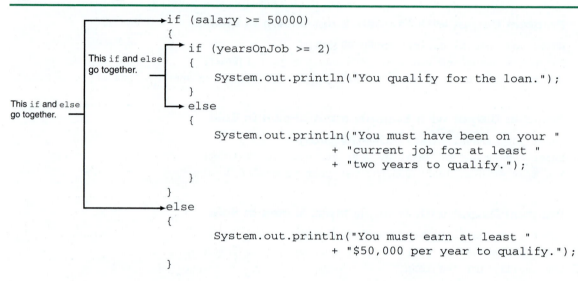

```java
if (salary >= 50000)
{
    if (yearsOnJob >= 2)
    {
        System.out.println("You qualify for the loan.");
    }
    else
    {
        System.out.println("You must have been on your "
                    + "current job for at least "
                    + "two years to qualify.");
    }
}
else
{
    System.out.println("You must earn at least "
                    + "$50,000 per year to qualify.");
}
```

This `if` and `else` go together.

This `if` and `else` go together.

Testing a Series of Conditions

In the previous example you saw how a program can use nested decision structures to test more than one condition. It is not uncommon for a program to have a series of conditions to test and then to perform an action, depending on which condition is true. One way to accomplish this it to have a decision structure with numerous other decision structures nested inside it. For example, consider the program presented in the following *In the Spotlight* section.

In the Spotlight:
Multiple Nested Decision Structures

Suppose one of your professors uses the following 10-point grading scale for exams:

Test Score	Grade
90 and above	A
80–89	B
70–79	C
60–69	D
Below 60	F

Your professor has asked you to write a program that will allow the user to enter a test score and then display the grade for that score. Here is the algorithm that you will use:

Ask the user to enter a test score.
Determine the grade in the following manner:
If the score is less than 60, then the grade is F.
  Otherwise, if the score is less than 70, then the grade is D.
    Otherwise, if the score is less than 80, then the grade is C.
      Otherwise, if the score is less than 90, then the grade is B.
        Otherwise, the grade is A.

The process of determining the grade will require several nested decisions structures, as shown in Figure 4-11.

Figure 4-11   Nested decision structure to determine a grade

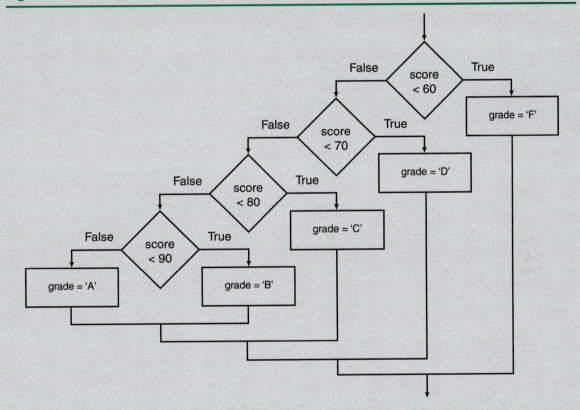

You decide to create a class named TestGrade that will determine the letter grade for a given numeric test score. Figure 4-12 shows the UML diagram for the class. Here is a summary of the class's fields and methods:

- **score**: A private int field to hold a numeric test score
- **Constructor**: Accepts an argument for the score field
- **setScore**: Mutator method that accepts an argument for the score field
- **getScore**: Accessor method that returns the value of the score field
- **getLetterGrade**: A method that uses the nested decision structures shown in Figure 4-11 to determine a letter grade for the score, and returns that grade as a char.

Figure 4-12 UML Diagram for the `TestGrade` class

```
┌─────────────────────────────────┐
│            TestGrade            │
├─────────────────────────────────┤
│ - score : int                   │
├─────────────────────────────────┤
│ + TestGrade(s: int)             │
│ + setScore(s : int) : void      │
│ + getScore() : int              │
│ + getLetterGrade() : char       │
└─────────────────────────────────┘
```

To use the `TestScore` class, you simply create an instance of it, passing a numeric test score as an argument to the constructor. You can the call the `getLetterGrade` method to get the letter grade for that test score. Code Listing 4-6 shows the code for the class. The nested decision structures appears in lines 48 through 76. Code Listing 4-7 shows a complete program that demonstrates the class.

Code Listing 4-6   (`TestGrade.java`)

```java
 1  /**
 2   * The TestGrade class determines a letter grade
 3   * based on a numeric test score.
 4   */
 5
 6  public class TestGrade
 7  {
 8     private int score;
 9
10     /**
11      * The constructor accepts an argument
12      * for the score field.
13      */
14
15     public TestGrade(int s)
16     {
17        score = s;
18     }
19
20     /**
21      * The setScore method accepts an argument
22      * for the score field.
23      */
24
25     public void SetScore(int s)
26     {
27        score = s;
28     }
29
30     /**
31      * The getScore method returns the score field.
```

```
32        */
33
34       public int getScore()
35       {
36          return score;
37       }
38
39       /**
40        * The getLetterGrade returns the letter
41        * grade for the test score.
42        */
43
44       public char getLetterGrade()
45       {
46          char grade;
47
48          if (score < 60)
49          {
50             grade = 'F';
51          }
52          else
53          {
54             if (score < 70)
55             {
56                grade = 'D';
57             }
58             else
59             {
60                if (score < 80)
61                {
62                   grade = 'C';
63                }
64                else
65                {
66                   if (score < 90)
67                   {
68                      grade = 'B';
69                   }
70                   else
71                   {
72                      grade = 'A';
73                   }
74                }
75             }
76          }
77
78          return grade;
79       }
80    }
```

Code Listing 4-7   (TestResults.java)

```java
 1  import java.util.Scanner;  // Needed for the Scanner class
 2
 3  /**
 4   * This program uses the TestGrade class to determine
 5   * a letter grade for a numeric test score.
 6   */
 7
 8  public class TestResults
 9  {
10     public static void main(String[] args)
11     {
12        int testScore;      // To hold a test score
13        char letterGrade;   // To hold a letter grade
14
15        // Create a Scanner object to read input.
16        Scanner keyboard = new Scanner(System.in);
17
18        // Get the numeric test score.
19        System.out.print("Enter your numeric test score and "
20                        + "I will tell you the grade: ");
21        testScore = keyboard.nextInt();
22
23        // Create a TestGrade object with the numeric score.
24        TestGrade test = new TestGrade(testScore);
25
26        // Get the letter grade.
27        letterGrade = test.getLetterGrade();
28
29        // Display the grade.
30        System.out.print("Your grade is "
31                        + test.getLetterGrade());
32     }
33  }
```

Program Output with Example Input Shown in Bold

Enter your numeric test score and I will tell you the grade: **80 [Enter]**
Your grade is B

Program Output with Example Input Shown in Bold

Enter your numeric test score and I will tell you the grade: **72 [Enter]**
Your grade is C

✔ **Checkpoint**

4.12 Write nested `if` statements that perform the following test: If `amount1` is greater than 10 and `amount2` is less than 100, display the greater of the two.

4.13 Write code that tests the variable `x` to determine whether it is greater than 0. If `x` is greater than 0, the code should test the variable `y` to determine whether it is less than 20. If `y` is less than 20, the code should assign 1 to the variable `z`. If `y` is not less than 20, the code should assign 0 to the variable `z`.

4.5 The `if-else-if` Statement

CONCEPT: The `if-else-if` statement tests a series of conditions. It is often simpler to test a series of conditions with the `if-else-if` statement than with a set of nested `if-else` statements.

Even though the `TestGrade` class is a simple example (see Code Listing 4-6), the logic of the nested decision structure in lines 48 through 76 is fairly complex. You can alternatively test a series of conditions using the `if-else-if` statement. The `if-else-if` statement makes certain types of nested decision logic simpler to write. Here is the general format of the `if-else-if` statement:

```
if (expression_1)
{
    statement
    statement
    etc.
}
```
If expression_1 is true these statements are executed, and the rest of the structure is ignored.

```
else if (expression_2)
{
    statement
    statement
    etc.
}
```
Otherwise, if eexpression_2 is true these statements are executed, and the rest of the structure is ignored.

Insert as many `else if` clauses as necessary

```
else
{
    statement
    statement
    etc.
}
```
These statements are executed if none of the expressions above are true.

When the statement executes, *expression_1* is tested. If *expression_1* is true, the block of statements that immediately follows is executed, and the rest of the structure is ignored. If *expression_1* is false, however, the program jumps to the very next else if clause and tests *expression_2*. If it is true, the block of statements that immediately follows is executed, and then the rest the structure is ignored. This process continues, from the top of the structure to the bottom, until one of the expressions is found to be true. If none of the expressions are true, the last else clause takes over, and the block of statements immediately following it is executed.

The last else clause, which does not have an if statement following it, is referred to as the *trailing else*. The trailing else is optional, but in most cases you will use it.

 NOTE: The general format shows braces surrounding each block of conditionally executed statements. As with other forms of the if statement, the braces are required only when more than one statement is conditionally executed.

The TestGrade2 class shown in Code Listing 4-8 demonstrates the if-else-if statement. This class is a modification of the TestGrade class shown in Code Listing 4-6, which appears in the previous *In the Spotlight* section.

Code Listing 4-8 (TestGrade2.Java)

```
1   /**
2    * The TestGrade2 class determines a letter grade
3    * based on a numeric test score.
4    */
5
6   public class TestGrade2
7   {
8      private int score;
9
10     /**
11      * The constructor accepts an argument
12      * for the score field.
13      */
14
15     public TestGrade2(int s)
16     {
17        score = s;
18     }
19
20     /**
21      * The setScore method accepts an argument
22      * for the score field.
23      */
24
25     public void SetScore(int s)
26     {
27        score = s;
```

```
28       }
29
30       /**
31        * The getScore method returns the score field.
32        */
33
34       public int getScore()
35       {
36          return score;
37       }
38
39       /**
40        * The getLetterGrade returns the letter
41        * grade for the test score.
42        */
43
44       public char getLetterGrade()
45       {
46          char grade;
47
48          if (score < 60)
49              grade = 'F';
50          else if (score < 70)
51              grade = 'D';
52          else if (score < 80)
53              grade = 'C';
54          else if (score < 90)
55              grade = 'B';
56          else
57              grade = 'A';
58
59          return grade;
60       }
61  }
```

Let's analyze how the if-else if statement in lines 48 through 57 works. First, the expression score < 60 is tested in line 48:

```
→ if (score < 60)
        grade = 'F';
   else if (score < 70)
        grade = 'D';
   else if (score < 80)
        grade = 'C';
   else if (score < 90)
        grade = 'B';
   else
        grade = 'A';
```

If score is less than 60, the grade variable is assigned 'F' and the rest of the if-else if statement is skipped. If score is not less than 60, the else clause in line 50 takes over and causes the next if statement to be executed:

```
if (score < 60)
    grade = 'F';
else if (score < 70)
    grade = 'D';
else if (score < 80)
    grade = 'C';
else if (score < 90)
    grade = 'B';
else
    grade = 'A';
```

The first if statement handled all the grades less than 60, so when this if statement executes, score will have a value of 60 or greater. If score is less than 70, the grade variable is assigned 'D' and the rest of the if-else if statement is skipped. This chain of events continues until one of the expressions is found to be true or the last else clause at the end of the statement is encountered. Notice the alignment and indentation that is used with the if-else if statement: The starting if clause, the else if clauses, and the trailing else clause are all aligned, and the conditionally executed statements are indented.

The if-else-if Statement Compared to a Nested Decision Structure

You never have to use the if-else-if statement because its logic can be coded with nested if-else statements. However, a long series of nested if-else statements has two particular disadvantages when you are debugging code:

- The code can grow complex and become difficult to understand.
- Because indenting is important in nested statements, a long series of nested if-else statements can become too long to be displayed on the computer screen without horizontal scrolling. Also, long statements tend to wrap around when printed on paper, making the code even more difficult to read.

The logic of an if-else-if statement is usually easier to follow than that of a long series of nested if-else statements. And, because all the clauses are aligned in an if-else-if statement, the lengths of the lines in the statement tend to be shorter.

Checkpoint

4.14 What will the following program display?

```
public class CheckPoint
{
    public static void main(String[] args)
    {
        int funny = 7, serious = 15;
```

```
        funny = serious % 2;
        if (funny != 1)
        {
            funny = 0;
            serious = 0;
        }
        else if (funny == 2)
        {
            funny = 10;
            serious = 10;
        }
        else
        {
            funny = 1;
            serious = 1;
        }
        System.out.println(funny + " " + serious);
    }
}
```

4.15 The following program is used in a bookstore to determine how many discount coupons a customer gets. Complete the table that appears after the program.

```
import java.util.Scanner;
public class CheckPoint
{
    public static void main(String[] args)
    {
        int books, coupons;

        Scanner keyboard = new Scanner(System.in);
        System.out.print("How many books are being purchased? ");
        books = keyboard.nextInt();

        if (books < 1)
            coupons = 0;
        else if (books < 3)
            coupons = 1;
        else if (books < 5)
            coupons = 2;
        else
            coupons = 3;

        System.out.println("Number of coupons: "
                            + coupons);
    }
}
```

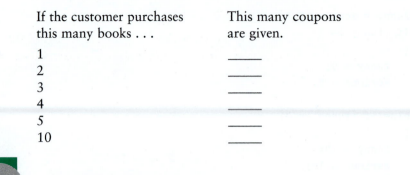

If the customer purchases this many books . . .	This many coupons are given.
1	_____
2	_____
3	_____
4	_____
5	_____
10	_____

4.6 Logical Operators

CONCEPT: Logical operators connect two or more relational expressions into one or reverse the logic of an expression.

Java provides two binary logical operators, `&&` and `||`, which are used to combine two `boolean` expressions into a single expression. It also provides the unary `!` operator, which reverses the truth of a `boolean` expression. Table 4-4 describes these logical operators.

Table 4-4 Logical Operators

Operator	Meaning	Effect
`&&`	AND	Connects two `boolean` expressions into one. Both expressions must be true for the overall expression to be true.
`||`	OR	Connects two `boolean` expressions into one. One or both expressions must be true for the overall expression to be true. It is only necessary for one to be true, and it does not matter which one.
`!`	NOT	The `!` operator reverses the truth of a `boolean` expression. If it is applied to an expression that is true, the operator returns false. If it is applied to an expression that is false, the operator returns true.

Table 4-5 shows examples of several `boolean` expressions that use logical operators.

Table 4-5 boolean expressions using logical operators

Expression	Meaning
`x > y && a < b`	Is x greater than y AND is a less than b?
`x == y || x == z`	Is x equal to y OR is x equal to z?
`!(x > y)`	Is the expression x > y NOT true?

Let's take a close look at each of these operators.

The && Operator

The && operator is known as the logical AND operator. It takes two boolean expressions as operands and creates a boolean expression that is true only when both subexpressions are true. Here is an example of an if statement that uses the && operator:

```
if (temperature < 20 && minutes > 12)
{
    System.out.println("The temperature is in the "
                        + "danger zone.");
}
```

In this statement the two boolean expressions temperature < 20 and minutes > 12 are combined into a single expression. The message will be displayed only if temperature is less than 20 AND minutes is greater than 12. If either boolean expression is false, the entire expression is false and the message is not displayed.

Table 4-6 shows a truth table for the && operator. The truth table lists all the possible combinations of values that two expressions may have, and the resulting value returned by the && operator connecting the two expressions.

Table 4-6   Truth table for the && operator

Expression	Resulting Value
true && false	false
false && true	false
false && false	false
true && true	true

As the table shows, both subexpressions must be true for the && operator to return a true value.

The && operator performs *short-circuit evaluation*. Here's how it works: If the expression on the left side of the && operator is false, the expression on the right side will not be checked. Because the entire expression is false if only one of the subexpressions is false, it would waste CPU time to check the remaining expression. So, when the && operator finds that the expression on its left is false, it short-circuits and does not evaluate the expression on its right.

The && operator can be used to simplify programs that otherwise would use nested if statements. Code Listing 4-9 shows another loan qualifying program. This one is written to use the && operator.

Code Listing 4-9   (LogicalAnd.java)

```
1  import java.util.Scanner;  // Needed for the Scanner class
2
3  /**
4   * This program demonstrates the logical && operator.
5   */
6
```

```
 7   public class LogicalAnd
 8   {
 9      public static void main(String[] args)
10      {
11         double salary;        // Annual salary
12         double yearsOnJob;    // Years at current job
13
14         // Create a Scanner object for keyboard input.
15         Scanner keyboard = new Scanner(System.in);
16
17         // Get the user's annual salary.
18         System.out.print("Enter your annual salary: ");
19         salary = keyboard.nextDouble();
20
21         // Get the number of years at the current job.
22         System.out.print("Enter the number of years "
23                          + "at your current job: ");
24         yearsOnJob = keyboard.nextDouble();
25
26         // Determine whether the user qualifies for the loan.
27         if (salary >= 50000 && yearsOnJob >= 2)
28         {
29             System.out.println("You qualify for the loan.");
30         }
31         else
32         {
33             System.out.println("You do not qualify.");
34         }
35      }
36   }
```

Program Output with Example Input Shown in Bold

Enter your annual salary: **55000.00 [Enter]**
Enter the number of years at your current job: **1 [Enter]**
You do not qualify.

Program Output with Example Input Shown in Bold

Enter your annual salary: **55000.00 [Enter]**
Enter the number of years at your current job: **4 [Enter]**
You qualify for the loan.

The message "You qualify for the loan." is displayed only when both the expressions salary >= 50000 and yearsOnJob >= 2 are true. If either of these expressions is false, the message "You do not qualify." is displayed.

You can also use logical operators with `boolean` variables. For example, assuming that `isValid` is a `boolean` variable, the following `if` statement determines whether `isValid` is true and x is greater than 90.

```
if (isValid && x > 90)
```

The || Operator

The || operator is known as the logical OR operator. It takes two `boolean` expressions as operands and creates a `boolean` expression that is true when either of the subexpressions are true. Here is an example of an `if` statement that uses the || operator:

```
if (temperature < 20 || temperature > 100)
{
    System.out.println("The temperature is in the "
                    + "danger zone.");
}
```

The message will be displayed if `temperature` is less than 20 OR `temperature` is greater than 100. If either relational test is true, the entire expression is true. Table 4-7 shows a truth table for the || operator.

Table 4-7   Truth table for the || operator

Expression	Resulting Value
`true || false`	`true`
`false || true`	`true`
`false || false`	`false`
`true || true`	`true`

All it takes for an OR expression to be `true` is for one of the subexpressions to be `true`. It doesn't matter if the other subexpression is `false` or `true`. Like the `&&` operator, the || operator performs short-circuit evaluation. If the subexpression on the left side of the || operator is `true`, the expression on the right side will not be checked. Because it is only necessary for one of the subexpressions to be `true`, it would waste CPU time to check the remaining expression.

The program in Code Listing 4-10 is a different version of the previous program, shown in Code Listing 4-9. This version uses the || operator to determine whether `salary >= 50000` is true OR `yearsOnJob >= 2` is true. If either expression is true, then the person qualifies for the loan.

Code Listing 4-10   **(LogicalOr.java)**

```
1   import java.util.Scanner;   // Needed for the Scanner class
2
3   /**
4    * This program demonstrates the logical || operator.
5    */
```

```
 6
 7  public class LogicalOr
 8  {
 9     public static void main(String[] args)
10     {
11        double salary;        // Annual salary
12        double yearsOnJob;    // Years at current job
13
14        // Create a Scanner object for keyboard input.
15        Scanner keyboard = new Scanner(System.in);
16
17        // Get the user's annual salary.
18        System.out.print("Enter your annual salary: ");
19        salary = keyboard.nextDouble();
20
21        // Get the number of years at the current job.
22        System.out.print("Enter the number of years "
23                       + "at your current job: ");
24        yearsOnJob = keyboard.nextDouble();
25
26        // Determine whether the user qualifies for the loan.
27        if (salary >= 50000 || yearsOnJob >= 2)
28        {
29           System.out.println("You qualify for the loan.");
30        }
31        else
32        {
33           System.out.println("You do not qualify.");
34        }
35     }
36  }
```

Program Output with Example Input Shown in Bold

Enter your annual salary: **20000.00 [Enter]**
Enter the number of years at your current job: **7 [Enter]**
You qualify for the loan.

Program Output with Example Input Shown in Bold

Enter your annual salary: **55000.00 [Enter]**
Enter the number of years at your current job: **1 [Enter]**
You qualify for the loan.

Program Output with Example Input Shown in Bold

Enter your annual salary: **20000.00 [Enter]**
Enter the number of years at your current job: **1 [Enter]**
You do not qualify.

The ! Operator

The ! operator performs a logical NOT operation. It is a unary operator that takes a boolean expression as its operand and reverses its logical value. In other words, if the expression is true, the ! operator returns false, and if the expression is false, it returns true. Here is an if statement using the ! operator:

```
if (!(temperature > 100))
    System.out.println("This is below the maximum temperature.");
```

First, the expression (temperature > 100) is tested and a value of either true or false is the result. Then the ! operator is applied to that value. If the expression (temperature > 100) is true, the ! operator returns false. If the expression (temperature > 100) is false, the ! operator returns true. The previous code is equivalent to asking: "Is the temperature not greater than 100?"

Table 4-8 shows a truth table for the ! operator.

Table 4-8   Truth table for the ! operator

Expression	Resulting Value
!true	false
!false	true

The Precedence and Associativity of Logical Operators

Like other operators, the logical operators have orders of precedence and associativity. Table 4-9 shows the precedence of the logical operators, from highest to lowest.

Table 4-9   Logical operators in order of precedence

!
&&
||

The ! operator has a higher precedence than many of Java's other operators. You should always enclose its operand in parentheses unless you intend to apply it to a variable or a simple expression with no other operators. For example, consider the following expressions (assume x is an int variable with a value stored in it):

```
!(x > 2)
```

```
!x > 2
```

The first expression applies the ! operator to the expression x > 2. It is asking "is x not greater than 2?" The second expression, however, attempts to apply the ! operator to x only. It is asking "is the logical complement of x greater than 2?" Because the ! operator can be applied only to boolean expressions, this statement would cause a compiler error.

The && and || operators rank lower in precedence than the relational operators, so precedence problems are less likely to occur. If you are unsure, however, it doesn't hurt to use parentheses anyway.

(a > b) && (x < y)	*is the same as*	a > b && x < y
(x == y) || (b > a)	*is the same as*	x == y || b > a

The logical operators evaluate their expressions from left to right. In the following expression, a < b is evaluated before y == z.

```
a < b || y == z
```

In the following expression, y == z is evaluated first, however, because the && operator has higher precedence than ||.

```
a < b || y == z && m > j
```

This expression is equivalent to:

```
(a < b) || ((y == z) && (m > j))
```

Table 4-10 shows the precedence of all the operators we have discussed so far. This table includes the assignment, arithmetic, relational, and logical operators.

Table 4-10 Precedence of all operators discussed so far

Order of Precedence	Operators	Description
1	- !	Unary negation, logical not
2	* / %	Multiplication, division, modulus
3	+ -	Addition, subtraction
4	< > <= >=	Less than, greater than, less than or equal to, greater than or equal to
5	== !=	Equal to, not equal to
6	&&	Logical AND
7	||	Logical OR
8	= += -= *= /= %=	Assignment and combined assignment

Checking Numeric Ranges with Logical Operators

Sometimes you will need to write code that determines whether a numeric value is within a specific range of values or outside a specific range of values. When determining whether a number is inside a range, it's best to use the && operator. For example, the following if statement checks the value in x to determine whether it is in the range of 20 through 40:

```
if (x >= 20 && x <= 40)
    System.out.println(x + " is in the acceptable range.");
```

The `boolean` expression in the `if` statement will be `true` only when x is greater than or equal to 20 AND less than or equal to 40. The value in x must be within the range of 20 through 40 for this expression to be `true`.

When determining whether a number is outside a range, the `||` operator is best to use. The following statement determines whether x is outside the range of 20 through 40:

```
if (x < 20 || x > 40)
    System.out.println(x + " is outside the acceptable range.");
```

It's important not to get the logic of these logical operators confused. For example, the `boolean` expression in the following `if` statement would never test `true`:

```
if (x < 20 && x > 40)
    System.out.println(x + " is outside the acceptable range.");
```

Obviously, x cannot be less than 20 and at the same time be greater than 40.

Checkpoint

4.16 The following truth table shows various combinations of the values `true` and `false` connected by a logical operator. Complete the table by indicating if the result of such a combination is `true` or `false`.

Logical Expression	Result (`true` or `false`)
true && false	
true && true	
false && true	
false && false	
true || false	
true || true	
false || true	
false || false	
!true	
!false	

4.17 Assume the variables a = 2, b = 4, and c = 6. Indicate by circling the T or F if each of the following conditions is true or false.

```
a == 4 || b > 2          T        F
6 <= c && a > 3          T        F
1 != b && c != 3         T        F
a >= -1 || a <= b        T        F
!(a > 2)                 T        F
```

4.18 Write an `if` statement that prints the message `"The number is valid"` if the variable speed is within the range 0 through 200.

4.19 Write an `if` statement that prints the message `"The number is not valid"` if the variable speed is outside the range 0 through 200.

4.7   Comparing `String` Objects

CONCEPT: You should not use relational operators to compare `String` objects. Instead you should use an appropriate `String` method.

You saw in the preceding sections how numeric values can be compared using the relational operators. You should not use the relational operators to compare `String` objects, however. Remember, a `String` variable holds the memory address of a `String` object. When you use a relational operator to compare two `String` variables, you are comparing the memory addresses that the variables contain, not the contents of the `String` objects that the variables reference.

To determine whether two `String` objects are equal, you should use the `String` class's `equals` method. The general form of the method is

> *StringReference1*.equals(*StringReference2*)

StringReference1 is a variable that references a `String` object, and *StringReference2* is another variable that references a `String` object. The method returns `true` if the two strings are equal, or `false` if they are not equal. Here is an example:

```
if (name1.equals(name2))
```

Assuming that `name1` and `name2` reference `String` objects, the expression in the `if` statement will return `true` if they are the same, or `false` if they are not the same. The program in Code Listing 4-11 demonstrates.

Code Listing 4-11   (GoodStringCompare.java)

```java
 1  import java.util.Scanner;  // Needed for the Scanner class
 2
 3  /**
 4   * This program correctly compares two String objects using
 5   * the equals method.
 6   */
 7
 8  public class GoodStringCompare
 9  {
10      public static void main(String[] args)
11      {
12          String name1, name2, name3; // Three names
13
14          // Create a Scanner object to read input.
15          Scanner keyboard = new Scanner(System.in);
16
17          // Get a name.
18          System.out.print("Enter a name: ");
19          name1 = keyboard.nextLine();
```

```
20
21        // Get a second name.
22        System.out.print("Enter a second name: ");
23        name2 = keyboard.nextLine();
24
25        // Get a third name.
26        System.out.print("Enter a third name: ");
27        name3 = keyboard.nextLine();
28
29        // Compare name1 and name2
30        if (name1.equals(name2))
31        {
32            System.out.println(name1 + " and " + name2
33                                + " are the same.");
34        }
35        else
36        {
37            System.out.println(name1 + " and " + name2
38                                + " are NOT the same.");
39        }
40
41        // Compare name1 and name3
42        if (name1.equals(name3))
43        {
44            System.out.println(name1 + " and " + name3
45                                + " are the same.");
46        }
47        else
48        {
49            System.out.println(name1 + " and " + name3
50                                + " are NOT the same.");
51        }
52    }
53 }
```

Program Output with Example Input Shown in Bold
```
Enter a name: Mark [Enter]
Enter a second name: Mark [Enter]
Enter a third name: Mary [Enter]
Mark and Mark are the same.
Mark and Mary are NOT the same.
```

You can also compare `String` objects to string literals. Simply pass the string literal as the argument to the `equals` method, as shown here:

```
if (name1.equals("Mark"))
```

To determine if two strings are not equal, simply apply the ! operator to the equals method's return value. Here is an example:

```
if (!name1.equals("Mark"))
```

The boolean expression in this if statement performs a not-equal-to operation. It determines whether the object referenced by name1 is not equal to "Mark".

The String class also provides the compareTo method, which can be used to determine whether one string is greater than, equal to, or less than another string. The general form of the method is:

```
StringReference.compareTo(OtherString)
```

StringReference is a variable that references a String object, and OtherString is either another variable that references a String object or a string literal. The method returns an integer value that can be used in the following manner:

- If the method's return value is negative, the string referenced by StringReference (the calling object) is less than the OtherString argument.
- If the method's return value is 0, the two strings are equal.
- If the method's return value is positive, the string referenced by StringReference (the calling object) is greater than the OtherString argument.

For example, assume that name1 and name2 are variables that reference String objects. The following if statement uses the compareTo method to compare the strings.

```
if (name1.compareTo(name2) == 0)
    System.out.println("The names are the same.");
```

Also, the following expression compares the string referenced by name1 to the string literal "Joe".

```
if (name1.compareTo("Joe") == 0)
    System.out.println("The names are the same.");
```

The program in Code Listing 4-12 more fully demonstrates the compareTo method.

Code Listing 4-12   (StringCompareTo.java)

```
 1  import java.util.Scanner;  // Needed for the Scanner class
 2
 3  /**
 4   * This program compares two String objects using
 5   * the compareTo method.
 6   */
 7
 8  public class StringCompareTo
 9  {
10     public static void main(String[] args)
11     {
12        String name1, name2;  // To hold two names
13
```

```
14          // Create a Scanner object to read input.
15          Scanner keyboard = new Scanner(System.in);
16
17          // Get a name.
18          System.out.print("Enter a name: ");
19          name1 = keyboard.nextLine();
20
21          // Get another name.
22          System.out.print("Enter another name: ");
23          name2 = keyboard.nextLine();
24
25          // Compare the names.
26          if (name1.compareTo(name2) < 0)
27          {
28              System.out.println(name1 + " is less than " + name2);
29          }
30          else if (name1.compareTo(name2) == 0)
31          {
32              System.out.println(name1 + " is equal to " + name2);
33          }
34          else if (name1.compareTo(name2) > 0)
35          {
36              System.out.println(name1 + " is greater than " + name2);
37          }
38      }
39  }
```

Program Output with Example Input Shown in Bold

```
Enter a name: Mary [Enter]
Enter another name: Mark [Enter]
Mary is greater than Mark
```

Let's take a closer look at this program. When you use the compareTo method to compare two strings, the strings are compared character by character. This is often called a *lexicographical comparison*. The program uses the compareTo method to compare the strings "Mary" and "Mark", beginning with the first, or leftmost characters. This is illustrated in Figure 4-13.

Figure 4-13   String comparison of "Mary" and "Mark"

Here is how the comparison takes place:

1. The "M" in "Mary" is compared with the "M" in "Mark." Because these are the same, the next characters are compared.
2. The "a" in "Mary" is compared with the "a" in "Mark." Because these are the same, the next characters are compared.
3. The "r" in "Mary" is compared with the "r" in "Mark." Because these are the same, the next characters are compared.
4. The "y" in "Mary" is compared with the "k" in "Mark." Because these are not the same, the two strings are not equal. The character "y" is greater than "k", so it is determined that "Mary" is greater than "Mark."

If one of the strings in a comparison is shorter in length than the other, Java can compare only the corresponding characters. If the corresponding characters are identical, then the shorter string is considered less than the longer string. For example, suppose the strings "High" and "Hi" were being compared. The string "Hi" would be considered less than "High" because it is shorter in length.

Ignoring Case in String Comparisons

The equals and compareTo methods perform case-sensitive comparisons, which means that uppercase letters are not considered the same as their lowercase counterparts. In other words, "A" is not the same as "a". This can obviously lead to problems when you want to perform case-insensitive comparisons.

The String class provides the equalsIgnoreCase and compareToIgnoreCase methods. These methods work like the equals and compareTo methods, except the case of the characters in the strings is ignored. For example, the program in Code Listing 4-13 asks the user to enter the "secret word," which is similar to a password. The secret word is "PROSPERO", and the program performs a case-insensitive string comparison to determine whether the user has entered it.

Code Listing 4-13   (SecretWord.java)

```java
 1  import java.util.Scanner;  // Needed for the Scanner class
 2
 3  /**
 4   * This program demonstrates a case-insensitive string comparison.
 5   */
 6
 7  public class SecretWord
 8  {
 9     public static void main(String[] args)
10     {
11        String input;     // To hold the user's input
12
13        // Create a Scanner object to read input.
14        Scanner keyboard = new Scanner(System.in);
15
```

```
16              // Prompt the user to enter the secret word.
17              System.out.print("Enter the secret word: ");
18              input = keyboard.nextLine();
19
20              // Determine if the user entered the secret word.
21              if (input.equalsIgnoreCase("PROSPERO"))
22              {
23                 System.out.println("Congratulations! You know the "
24                                   + "secret word!");
25              }
26              else
27              {
28                 System.out.println("Sorry, that is NOT the "
29                                   + "secret word!");
30              }
31          }
32  }
```

Program Output with Example Input Shown in Bold

Enter the secret word: **Ferdinand [Enter]**
Sorry, that is NOT the secret word!

Program Output with Example Input Shown in Bold

Enter the secret word: **Prospero [Enter]**
Congratulations! You know the secret word!

See the file *CompareWithoutCase.java* for an example demonstrating the `compareToIgnore-Case` method. (The book's source code is available at www.pearsonhighered.com/gaddis.)

 Checkpoint

4.20   Assume the variable `name` references a `String` object. Write an `if` statement that displays "Do I know you?" if the `String` object contains "Timothy".

4.21   Assume the variables `name1` and `name2` reference two different `String` objects, containing different strings. Write code that displays the strings referenced by these variables in alphabetical order.

4.22   Modify the statement you wrote in response to Checkpoint 4.20 so it performs a case-insensitive comparison.

4.8 More about Variable Declaration and Scope

CONCEPT: The scope of a variable is limited to the block in which it is declared.

Recall from Chapter 2 that a local variable is a variable that is declared inside a method. Java allows you to create local variables just about anywhere in a method. For example, look at the program in Code Listing 4-14. The main method declares two String reference variables: firstName and lastName. Notice that the declarations of these variables appear near the code that first uses the variables.

Code Listing 4-14   (VariableScope.java)

```java
 1  import java.util.Scanner;
 2
 3  /**
 4   *  This program demonstrates how variables may be declared
 5   *  in various locations throughout a program.
 6   */
 7
 8  public class VariableScope
 9  {
10     public static void main(String[] args)
11     {
12        // Create a Scanner object for keyboard input.
13        Scanner keyboard = new Scanner(System.in);
14
15        // Get the user's first name.
16        System.out.print("Enter your first name: ");
17        String firstName;
18        firstName = keyboard.nextLine();
19
20        // Get the user's last name.
21        System.out.print("Enter your last name: ");
22        String lastName;
23        lastName = keyboard.nextLine();
24
25        // Display a message.
26        System.out.println("Hello " + firstName
27                                 + " " + lastName);
28     }
29  }
```

Although it is a common practice to declare all of a method's local variables at the beginning of the method, it is possible to declare them at later points. Sometimes programmers declare certain variables near the part of the program where they are used in order to make their purpose more evident.

NOTE: When a program is running and it enters the section of code that constitutes a variable's scope, it is said that the variable "comes into scope." This simply means the variable is now visible and the program can reference it. Likewise, when a variable "leaves scope" it cannot be used.

4.9 The Conditional Operator (Optional)

CONCEPT: You can use the conditional operator to create short expressions that work like `if-else` statements.

The *conditional operator* is powerful and unique. Because it takes three operands, it is considered a ternary operator. The conditional operator provides a shorthand method of expressing a simple `if-else` statement. The operator consists of the question mark (?) and the colon (:). You use the operator to write a conditional expression, in the following format:

```
BooleanExpresion ? Value1 : Value2;
```

The `BooleanExpression` is like the `boolean` expression in the parentheses of an `if` statement. If the `BooleanExpression` is true, then the value of the conditional expression is `Value1`. Otherwise, the value of the conditional expression is `Value2`. Here is an example of a statement using the conditional operator:

```
y = x < 0 ? 10 : 20;
```

This preceding statement performs the same operation as the following `if-else` statement:

```
if (x < 0)
    y = 10;
else
    y = 20;
```

The conditional operator gives you the ability to pack decision-making power into a concise line of code. With a little imagination it can be applied to many other programming problems. For instance, consider the following statement:

```
System.out.println("Your grade is: " + (score < 60 ? "Fail." : "Pass."));
```

Converted to an `if-else` statement, it would be written as follows:

```
if (score < 60)
    System.out.println("Your grade is: Fail.");
else
    System.out.println("Your grade is: Pass.");
```

NOTE: The parentheses are placed around the conditional expression because the + operator has higher precedence than the ?: operator. Without the parentheses, the + operator would concatenate the value in `score` with the string `"Your grade is: "`.

Checkpoint

4.23 Rewrite the following `if-else` statements as conditional expressions.

```
a.  if (x > y)
        z = 1;
    else
        z = 20;
```

b.
```
if (temp > 45)
    population = base * 10;
else
    population = base * 2;
```

c.
```
if (hours > 40)
    wages *= 1.5;
else
    wages *= 1;
```

d.
```
if (result >= 0)
    System.out.println("The result is positive.)";
else
    System.out.println("The result is negative.")
```

4.10 The switch Statement

CONCEPT: The switch statement lets the value of a variable or expression determine where the program will branch to.

The *switch statement* is a *multiple alternative decision structure*. It allows you to test the value of a variable or an expression and then use that value to determine which statement or set of statements to execute. Figure 4-14 shows an example of how a multiple alternative decision structure looks in a flowchart.

Figure 4-14 A multiple alternative decision structure

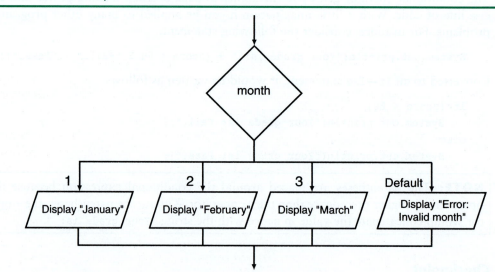

In the flowchart, the diamond symbol shows month, which is the name of a variable. If the month variable contains the value 1, the program displays *January*. If the month variable contains the value 2, the program displays *February*. If the month variable contains the value 3, the program displays *March*. If the month variable contains none of these values, the action that is labeled Default is executed. In this case, the program displays *Error: Invalid month*.

Here is the general format of a switch statement in Java:

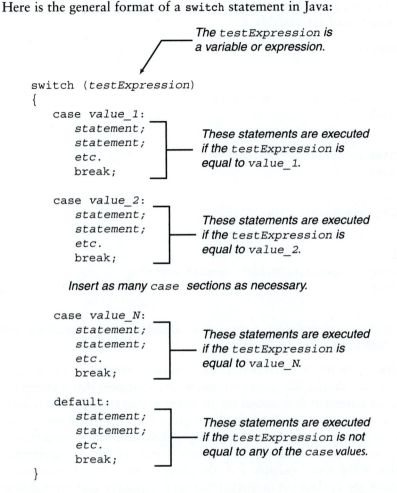

The testExpression is a variable or expression.

```
switch (testExpression)
{
    case value_1:
        statement;
        statement;
        etc.
        break;

    case value_2:
        statement;
        statement;
        etc.
        break;
```

These statements are executed if the testExpression is equal to value_1.

These statements are executed if the testExpression is equal to value_2.

Insert as many case sections as necessary.

```
    case value_N:
        statement;
        statement;
        etc.
        break;

    default:
        statement;
        statement;
        etc.
        break;
}
```

These statements are executed if the testExpression is equal to value_N.

These statements are executed if the testExpression is not equal to any of the case values.

The first line of the statement starts with the word switch, followed by a *testExpression*, which is enclosed in parentheses. The *testExpression* is a variable or an expression that gives a char, byte, short, int, or string value. (If you are using a version of Java prior to Java 7, the *testExpression* cannot be a string.)

Beginning at the next line is a block of code enclosed in curly braces. Inside this block of code are one or more case sections. A case section begins with the word case, followed by a value, followed by a colon. Each case section contains one or more statements, followed by a break statement. After all the case sections, an optional default section appears.

When the switch statement executes, it compares the value of the *testExpression* with the values that follow each of the case statements (from top to bottom). When it finds a case value that matches the *testExpression*'s value, the program branches to the case statement. The statements that follow the case statement are executed, until a break statement is encountered. At that point program jumps out of the switch statement. If the *testExpression* does not match any of the case values, the program branches to the default statement and executes the statements that immediately following it.

NOTE: Each of the case values must be unique.

For example, the following code performs the same operation as the flowchart in Figure 4-14. Assume `month` is an `int` variable.

```
switch (month)
{
    case 1:
        System.out.println("January");
        break;

    case 2:
        System.out.println("February");
        break;

    case 3:
        System.out.println("March");
        break;

    default:
        System.out.println("Error: Invalid month");
        break;
}
```

In this example, the *testExpression* is the `month` variable. The `month` variable is evaluated and one of the following actions takes place:

- If the value in the `month` variable is 1, the program branches to the `case 1:` section and executes the `System.out.println("January")` statement that immediately follows it. The `break` statement then causes the program to exit the `switch` statement.
- If the value in the `month` variable is 2, the program branches to the `case 2:` section and executes the `System.out.println("February")` statement that immediately follows it. The `break` statement then causes the program to exit the `switch` statement.
- If the value in the `month` variable is 3, the program branches to the `case 3:` section and executes the `System.out.println("March")` statement that immediately follows it. The `break` statement then causes the program to exit the `switch` statement.
- If the value in the `month` variable is not 1, 2, or 3, the program branches to the `default:` section and executes the `System.out.println("Error: Invalid month")` statement that immediately follows it.

The `switch` statement can be used as an alternative to an `if-else-if` statement that tests the same variable or expression to several different values. For example, the previously shown `switch` statement works like this `if-else-if` statement:

```
if (month == 1)
{
    System.out.println("January");
}
else if (month == 2)
{
    System.out.println("February");
}
```

```
        else if (month == 3)
        {
            System.out.println("March");
        }
        else
        {
            System.out.println("Error: Invalid month");
        }
```

> **NOTE:** The default section is optional. If you leave it out, however, the program has nowhere to branch to if the *testExpression* does not match any of the case values.

The program in Code Listing 4-15 shows how a simple switch statement works.

Code Listing 4-15   (SwitchDemo.java)

```java
 1  import java.util.Scanner;  // Needed for the Scanner class
 2
 3  /**
 4   * This program demonstrates the switch statement.
 5   */
 6
 7  public class SwitchDemo
 8  {
 9     public static void main(String[] args)
10     {
11        String input; // To hold keyboard input
12        char choice;  // To store the user's choice
13
14        // Create a Scanner object to read input.
15        Scanner keyboard = new Scanner(System.in);
16
17        // Ask the user to enter A, B, or C.
18        System.out.print("Enter A, B, or C: ");
19        input = keyboard.nextLine();
20        choice = input.charAt(0);  // Get the first char
21
22        // Determine which character the user entered.
23        switch (choice)
24        {
25           case 'A':
26              System.out.println("You entered A.");
27              break;
28           case 'B':
29              System.out.println("You entered B.");
30              break;
```

```
31              case 'C':
32                  System.out.println("You entered C.");
33                  break;
34              default:
35                  System.out.println("That's not A, B, or C!");
36          }
37      }
38  }
```

Program Output with Example Input Shown in Bold

Enter A, B, or C: **B [Enter]**
You entered B.

Program Output with Example Input Shown in Bold

Enter A, B, or C: **F [Enter]**
That's not A, B, or C!

Notice the break statements that appear in lines 27, 30, and 33. The case statements show the program where to start executing in the block and the break statements show the program where to stop. Without the break statements, the program would execute all of the lines from the matching case statement to the end of the block.

NOTE: The default section (or the last case section if there is no default) does not need a break statement. Some programmers prefer to put one there anyway for consistency.

The program in Code Listing 4-16 is a modification of Code Listing 4-15, without the break statements.

Code Listing 4-16   (NoBreaks.java)

```
 1  import java.util.Scanner;  // Needed for the Scanner class
 2
 3  /**
 4   * This program demonstrates a switch statement
 5   * without any break statements.
 6   */
 7
 8  public class NoBreaks
 9  {
10      public static void main(String[] args)
11      {
12          String input; // To hold keyboard input
13          char choice;   // To store the user's choice
14
15          // Create a Scanner object to read input.
16          Scanner keyboard = new Scanner(System.in);
```

```
17
18          // Ask the user to enter A, B, or C.
19          System.out.print("Enter A, B, or C: ");
20          input = keyboard.nextLine();
21          choice = input.charAt(0);   // Get the first char
22
23          // Determine which character the user entered.
24          switch (choice)
25          {
26             case 'A':
27                System.out.println("You entered A.");
28             case 'B':
29                System.out.println("You entered B.");
30             case 'C':
31                System.out.println("You entered C.");
32             default:
33                System.out.println("That's not A, B, or C!");
34          }
35       }
36  }
```

Program Output with Example Input Shown in Bold

Enter A, B, or C: **A [Enter]**
You entered A.
You entered B.
You entered C.
That's not A, B, or C!

Program Output with Example Input Shown in Bold

Enter A, C, or C: **C [Enter]**
You entered C.
That's not A, B, or C!

Without the break statement, the program "falls through" all of the statements below the one with the matching case expression. Sometimes this is what you want. For instance, the program in Code Listing 4-17 asks the user to select a grade of pet food. The available choices are A, B, and C. The switch statement will recognize either upper or lowercase letters.

Code Listing 4-17   (PetFood.java)

```
1  import java.util.Scanner;  // Needed for the Scanner class
2
3  /**
4   * This program demonstrates a switch statement.
5   */
6
```

```
 7  public class PetFood
 8  {
 9      public static void main(String[] args)
10      {
11          String input;     // To hold keyboard input
12          char feedGrade;   // To hold the feed grade
13
14          // Create a Scanner object to read input.
15          Scanner keyboard = new Scanner(System.in);
16
17          // Get the desired pet food grade.
18          System.out.println("Our pet food is available in "
19                          + "three grades:");
20          System.out.print("A, B, and C. Which do you want "
21                          + "pricing for? ");
22          input = keyboard.nextLine();
23          feedGrade = input.charAt(0);  // Get the first char.
24
25          // Determine the grade that was entered.
26          switch(feedGrade)
27          {
28            case 'a':
29            case 'A':
30                System.out.println("30 cents per lb.");
31                break;
32            case 'b':
33            case 'B':
34                System.out.println("20 cents per lb.");
35                break;
36            case 'c':
37            case 'C':
38                System.out.println("15 cents per lb.");
39                break;
40            default:
41                System.out.println("Invalid choice.");
42          }
43      }
44  }
```

Program Output with Example Input Shown in Bold

```
Our dog food is available in three grades:
A, B, and C. Which do you want pricing for? b [Enter]
20 cents per lb.
```

Program Output with Example Input Shown in Bold

```
Our dog food is available in three grades:
A, B, and C. Which do you want pricing for? B [Enter]
20 cents per lb.
```

When the user enters 'a' the corresponding case has no statements associated with it, so the program falls through to the next case, which corresponds with 'A'.

```
case 'a':
case 'A':
    System.out.println("30 cents per lb.");
    break;
```

The same technique is used for 'b' and 'c'.

If you are using a version of Java prior to Java 7, a switch statement's *testExpression* can be a char, byte, short, or int value. Beginning with Java 7, however, the *testExpression* can also be a string. The program in Code Listing 4-18 demonstrates.

Code Listing 4-18   **(Seasons.java)**

```
 1  import java.util.Scanner;
 2
 3  /**
 4   *  This program translates the English names of
 5   *  the seasons into Spanish.
 6   */
 7
 8  public class Seasons
 9  {
10      public static void main(String[] args)
11      {
12          String input;
13
14          // Create a Scanner object for keyboard input.
15          Scanner keyboard = new Scanner(System.in);
16
17          // Get a day from the user.
18          System.out.print("Enter the name of a season: ");
19          input = keyboard.nextLine();
20
21          // Translate the season to Spanish.
22          switch (input)
23          {
24              case "spring":
25                  System.out.println("la primavera");
26                  break;
27              case "summer":
28                  System.out.println("el verano");
29                  break;
30              case "autumn":
31              case "fall":
32                  System.out.println("el otono");
33                  break;
```

```
34              case "winter":
35                  System.out.println("el invierno");
36                  break;
37              default:
38                  System.out.println("Please enter one of these words:\n"
39                          + "spring, summer, autumn, fall, or winter.");
40          }
41      }
42  }
```

Program Output with Example Input Shown in Bold

```
Enter the name of a season: summer [Enter]
el verano
```

Program Output with Example Input Shown in Bold

```
Enter the name of a season: fall [Enter]
el otono
```

Checkpoint

4.24   Complete the following program skeleton by writing a switch statement that displays "one" if the user has entered 1, "two" if the user has entered 2, and "three" if the user has entered 3. If a number other than 1, 2, or 3 is entered, the program should display an error message.

```
import java.util.Scanner;
public class CheckPoint
{
    public static void main(String[] args)
    {
        int userNum;

        Scanner keyboard = new Scanner(System.in);
        System.out.print("Enter one of the numbers " +
                    "1, 2, or 3: ");
        userNum = keyboard.nextInt();
        //
        // Write the switch statement here.
        //
    }
}
```

4.25   Rewrite the following if-else-if statement as a switch statement.

```
if (selection == 'A')
    System.out.println("You selected A.");
else if (selection == 'B')
    System.out.println("You selected B.");
```

```
    else if (selection == 'C')
        System.out.println("You selected C.");
    else if (selection == 'D')
        System.out.println("You selected D.");
    else
        System.out.println("Not good with letters, eh?");
```

4.26   Explain why you cannot convert the following if-else-if statement into a switch statement.

```
if (temp == 100)
    x = 0;
else if (population > 1000)
    x = 1;
else if (rate < .1)
    x = -1;
```

4.27   What is wrong with the following switch statement?

```
// This code has errors!!!
switch (temp)
{
    case temp < 0 :
        System.out.println("Temp is negative.");
        break;
    case temp == 0:
        System.out.println("Temp is zero.");
        break;
    case temp > 0 :
        System.out.println("Temp is positive.");
        break;
}
```

4.28   What will the following code display?

```
int funny = 7, serious = 15;
funny = serious * 2;
switch (funny)
{
    case 0 :
        System.out.println("That is funny.");
        break;
    case 30:
        System.out.println("That is serious.");
        break;
    case 32:
        System.out.println("That is seriously funny.");
        break;
    default:
        System.out.println(funny);
}
```

4.11 Formatting Numbers with the DecimalFormat Class

CONCEPT: The DecimalFormat class can be used to format the appearance of floating-point numbers rounded to a specified number of decimal places.

In Chapter 2 you learned how to format console output with the System.out.printf method. However, if you want to display formatted output in a graphical interface, such as a Message dialog, you will need to use a different approach. In this section we will discuss the DecimalFormat class, which can be used to format numbers, regardless of whether they are displayed in the console window or in a Message dialog.

The DecimalFormat class is part of the Java API, but it is not automatically available to your programs. To use the DecimalFormat class you must have the following import statement at the top of your program:

```
import java.text.DecimalFormat;
```

This statement makes the class available to your program. Then, in the part of the program where you want to format a number, you create a DecimalFormat object. Here is an example:

```
DecimalFormat formatter = new DecimalFormat("#0.00");
```

This statement creates an instance of the DecimalFormat class. After the statement executes, the formatter variable will reference the object. Notice the characters in the string that is passed to the constructor. The # character specifies that a digit should be displayed in this position if it is present. If there is no digit in this position, no digit should be displayed. The 0 character also specifies that a digit should be displayed in this position if it is present. However, if there is no digit present in this position, a 0 should be displayed. Also, notice that there are two zeros after the decimal point. This indicates that numbers should be rounded to two decimal places.

To use the DecimalFormat object to format a number, you call its format method and pass the number you wish to format as an argument. (You can pass either a floating-point value or an integer value to the method.) The method returns a string containing the formatted number. For example, look at the program in Code Listing 4-19.

Code Listing 4-19   (Format1.java)

```
1  import javax.swing.JOptionPane;
2  import java.text.DecimalFormat;
3
4  /**
5   * This program uses the DecimalFormat class to display
6   * formatted numbers in a message dialog.
7   */
8
9  public class Format1
```

```
10  {
11     public static void main(String[] args)
12     {
13        double number1 = 0.166666666666667;
14        double number2 = 1.666666666666667;
15        double number3 = 16.666666666666667;
16        double number4 = 166.666666666666667;
17
18        // Create a DecimalFormat object.
19        DecimalFormat formatter = new DecimalFormat("#0.00");
20
21        // Display the formatted variable contents.
22        JOptionPane.showMessageDialog(null, formatter.format(number1));
23        JOptionPane.showMessageDialog(null, formatter.format(number2));
24        JOptionPane.showMessageDialog(null, formatter.format(number3));
25        JOptionPane.showMessageDialog(null, formatter.format(number4));
26     }
27  }
```

Figure 4-15   Output of Code Listing 4-19

This is displayed by the statement in line 22. ⟶ (0.17)

This is displayed by the statement in line 23. ⟶ (1.67)

This is displayed by the statement in line 24. ⟶ (16.67)

This is displayed by the statement in line 25. ⟶ (166.67)

Notice the subtle difference between the output of the # character and the 0 character in the formatting pattern:

- If the number contains a digit in the position of a # character in the formatting pattern, the digit will be displayed. Otherwise, no digit will be displayed.
- If the number contains a digit in the position of a 0 character in the formatting pattern, the digit will be displayed. Otherwise, a 0 will be displayed.

For example, look at the program in Code Listing 4-20. This is the same program as shown in Code Listing 4-19, but using a different format pattern. The program's output is shown in Figure 4-16.

Code Listing 4-20   (Format2.java)

```
 1   import javax.swing.JOptionPane;
 2   import java.text.DecimalFormat;
 3
 4   /**
 5    *  This program uses the DecimalFormat class to display
 6    *  formatted numbers in a message dialog.
 7    */
 8
 9   public class Format2
10   {
11      public static void main(String[] args)
12      {
13         double number1 = 0.166666666666667;
14         double number2 = 1.666666666666667;
15         double number3 = 16.666666666666667;
16         double number4 = 166.666666666666667;
17
18         // Create a DecimalFormat object.
19         DecimalFormat formatter = new DecimalFormat("00.00");
20
21         // Display the formatted variable contents.
22         JOptionPane.showMessageDialog(null, formatter.format(number1));
23         JOptionPane.showMessageDialog(null, formatter.format(number2));
24         JOptionPane.showMessageDialog(null, formatter.format(number3));
25         JOptionPane.showMessageDialog(null, formatter.format(number4));
26      }
27   }
```

Figure 4-16 Output of Code Listing 4-20

This is displayed by the
statement in line 22. ———

This is displayed by the
statement in line 23. ———

This is displayed by the
statement in line 24. ———

This is displayed by the
statement in line 25. ———

You can insert a comma into the format pattern to create grouping separators in formatted numbers. The program in Code Listing 4-21 demonstrates. The program's output is shown in Figure 4-17.

Code Listing 4-21   **(Format3.java)**

```
1   import javax.swing.JOptionPane;
2   import java.text.DecimalFormat;
3
4   /**
5    *  This program uses the DecimalFormat class to display
6    *  formatted numbers in a message dialog.
7    */
8
9   public class Format3
10  {
11     public static void main(String[] args)
12     {
13        double number1  = 123.899;
14        double number2  = 1233.899;
15        double number3  = 12345.899;
16        double number4  = 123456.899;
17        double number5  = 1234567.899;
18
```

```
19          // Create a DecimalFormat object.
20          DecimalFormat formatter = new DecimalFormat("#,##0.00");
21
22          // Display the formatted variable contents.
23          JOptionPane.showMessageDialog(null, formatter.format(number1));
24          JOptionPane.showMessageDialog(null, formatter.format(number2));
25          JOptionPane.showMessageDialog(null, formatter.format(number3));
26          JOptionPane.showMessageDialog(null, formatter.format(number4));
27          JOptionPane.showMessageDialog(null, formatter.format(number5));
28      }
29  }
```

Figure 4-17 Output of Code Listing 4-21

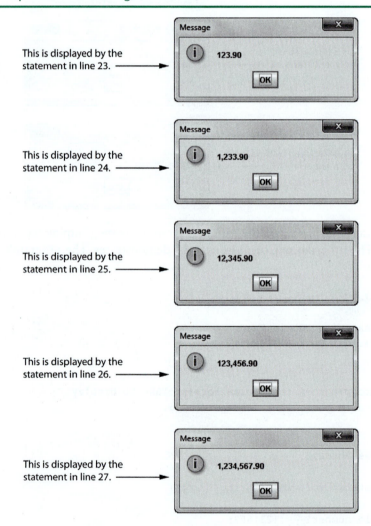

This is displayed by the statement in line 23. → Message 123.90 OK

This is displayed by the statement in line 24. → Message 1,233.90 OK

This is displayed by the statement in line 25. → Message 12,345.90 OK

This is displayed by the statement in line 26. → Message 123,456.90 OK

This is displayed by the statement in line 27. → Message 1,234,567.90 OK

You can also format numbers as percentages by writing the % character at the last position in the format pattern. This causes a number to be multiplied by 100, and the % character is appended to its end. The program in Code Listing 4-22 demonstrates. The program's output is shown in Figure 4-18.

Code Listing 4-22   **(Format4.java)**

```java
 1  import javax.swing.JOptionPane;
 2  import java.text.DecimalFormat;
 3
 4  /**
 5   *  This program uses the DecimalFormat class to display
 6   *  formatted numbers in a message dialog.
 7   */
 8
 9  public class Format4
10  {
11     public static void main(String[] args)
12     {
13        double number1  = 0.12;
14        double number2  = 0.05;
15
16        // Create a DecimalFormat object.
17        DecimalFormat formatter = new DecimalFormat("#0%");
18
19        // Display the formatted variable contents.
20        JOptionPane.showMessageDialog(null, formatter.format(number1));
21        JOptionPane.showMessageDialog(null, formatter.format(number2));
22     }
23  }
```

Figure 4-18   Output of Code Listing 4-22

This is displayed by the statement in line 20.

This is displayed by the statement in line 21.

Checkpoint

4.29   Assume that the `double` variable `number` holds the value 459.6329. What format pattern would you use with a `DecimalFormat` object to display the number as 00459.633?

4.30   Assume that the `double` variable `number` holds the value 0.179. What format pattern would you use with a `DecimalFormat` object to display the number as .18?

4.31   Assume that the `double` variable `number` holds the value 7634869.1. What format pattern would you use with a `DecimalFormat` object to display the number as 7,634,869.10?

4.12 Focus on Problem Solving: The `SalesCommission` Class

In this section we will examine a case study that implements many of the topics discussed in this chapter. In addition we will discuss how a lengthy algorithm can be decomposed into several shorter methods.

Hal's Home Computer Emporium is a retail seller of personal computers. Hal's sales staff work strictly on commission. At the end of the month, each salesperson's commission is calculated according to Table 4-11.

Table 4-11   Sales Commission Rates

Sales this Month	Commission Rate
less than $10,000	5%
$10,000–14,999	10%
$15,000–17,999	12%
$18,000–21,999	14%
$22,000 or more	16%

For example, a salesperson with $16,000 in monthly sales will earn a 12% commission ($1,920.00). Another salesperson with $20,000 in monthly sales will earn a 14% commission ($2,800.00).

Because the staff gets paid once per month, Hal allows each employee to take up to $1,500 per month in advance. When sales commissions are calculated, the amount of each employee's advanced pay is subtracted from the commission. If any salesperson's commissions are less than the amount of their advance, they must reimburse Hal for the difference.

Here are two examples: Beverly and John have $21,400 and $12,600 in sales, respectively. Beverly's commission is $2,996, and John's commission is $1,260. Both Beverly and John took $1,500 in advanced pay. At the end of the month, Beverly gets a check for $1,496, but John must pay $240 back to Hal.

Now we will examine a program that eases the task of calculating the end-of-month commission. The core of the program will be a `SalesCommission` class that holds the primary data for a salesperson, determines the rate of commission, and calculates the salesperson's pay. Figure 4-19 shows a UML diagram for the class.

Figure 4-19   UML diagram for the SalesCommission class

```
┌─────────────────────────────────────────┐
│              SalesCommission             │
├─────────────────────────────────────────┤
│ - sales : double                         │
│ - rate : double                          │
│ - commission : double                    │
│ - advance : double                       │
│ - pay : double                           │
├─────────────────────────────────────────┤
│ + SalesCommission(s : double,           │
│                    a : double)          │
│ - setRate() : void                       │
│ - calculatePay() : void                  │
│ + getPay() : double                      │
│ + getCommission() : double               │
│ + getRate() : double                     │
│ + getAdvance() : double                  │
│ + getSales() : double                    │
└─────────────────────────────────────────┘
```

Table 4-12 lists and describes the class's fields.

Table 4-12   SalesCommission class fields

Field	Description
sales	A double variable to hold a salesperson's total monthly sales.
rate	A double variable to hold the salesperson's commission rate.
commission	A double variable to hold the commission.
advance	A double variable to hold the amount of advanced pay the salesperson has drawn.
pay	A double variable to hold the salesperson's amount of gross pay.

Table 4-13 lists and describes the class's methods.

Table 4-13   SalesCommission class methods

Method	Description
Constructor	The constructor accepts two arguments: the amount of sales that a salesperson has made and the amount of advanced pay that salesperson has drawn. The method assigns these values to the sales and advance fields and then calls the calculatePay method.
setRate	A private method that sets the rate of commission, based on the amount of sales made by the salesperson. This method is called from the calculatePay method.
calculatePay	A private method that calculates the salesperson's commission and actual pay. This method is called from the constructor.

(continued)

Table 4-13 `SalesCommission` class methods (continued)

Method	Description
`getPay`	Returns as a double the amount of gross pay due the salesperson, which is the amount of commission minus advanced pay.
`getComission`	Returns as a double the amount of commission earned by the salesperson.
`getRate`	Returns as a double the rate of commission for the amount of sales made by the salesperson.
`getAdvance`	Returns as a double the amount of advanced pay drawn by the salesperson.
`getSales`	Returns as a double the amount of sales made by the salesperson.

Code Listing 4-23 shows the code for the class.

Code Listing 4-23 (`SalesCommission.java`)

```
 1  /**
 2   * This class calculates a salesperson's gross
 3   * pay based on the amount of sales.
 4   */
 5
 6  public class SalesCommission
 7  {
 8     private double sales,      // Monthly sales
 9                    rate,       // Rate of commission
10                    commission, // Amount of commission
11                    advance,    // Advanced pay
12                    pay;        // Amount to pay
13
14
15     /**
16      * The constructor uses two parameters to accept
17      * arguments: s and a. The value in s is assigned to
18      * the sales field and the value in a is assigned to
19      * the advance field. The calculatePay method is called.
20      */
21
22     public SalesCommission(double s, double a)
23     {
24        sales = s;
25        advance = a;
26        calculatePay();
27     }
28
29     /**
30      * The setRate method sets the rate of commission,
31      * based on the amount of sales. This method is called
```

```
32        * from the calculatePay method.
33        */
34
35       private void setRate()
36       {
37          if (sales < 10000)
38             rate = 0.05;
39          else if (sales < 15000)
40             rate = 0.1;
41          else if (sales < 18000)
42             rate = 0.12;
43          else if (sales < 22000)
44             rate = 0.14;
45          else
46             rate = 0.16;
47       }
48
49       /**
50        * The calculatePay method calculates the salesperson's
51        * commission and amount of actual pay.
52        */
53
54       private void calculatePay()
55       {
56          setRate();
57          commission = sales * rate;
58          pay = commission - advance;
59       }
60
61       /**
62        * The getPay method returns the pay field.
63        */
64
65       public double getPay()
66       {
67          return pay;
68       }
69
70       /**
71        * The getCommission method returns the commission field.
72        */
73
74       public double getCommission()
75       {
76          return commission;
77       }
78
79       /**
80        * The getRate method returns the rate field.
81        */
```

```
82
83      public double getRate()
84      {
85         return rate;
86      }
87
88      /**
89       * The getAdvance method returns the advance field.
90       */
91
92      public double getAdvance()
93      {
94         return advance;
95      }
96
97      /**
98       * The getSales method returns the sales field.
99       */
100
101     public double getSales()
102     {
103        return sales;
104     }
105  }
```

Private Methods and Algorithm Decomposition

Notice that the class has two private methods: setRate and calculatePay. When a method is declared as private, it can be called only from other methods that are members of the same class. Sometimes a class will contain methods that are necessary for internal processing, but not useful to code outside of the class. These methods are usually declared as private.

In the case of the SalesCommission class, the setRate and calculatePay methods are part of an algorithm that has been *decomposed*. Decomposing an algorithm usually means breaking it into several short methods, each performing a specific task. For example, look at the SalesCommission class's constructor, which appears in lines 22 through 27. Notice that in line 26, the constructor calls the calculatePay method. Then, in line 56 the calculatePay method calls the setRate method, which appears in lines 35 through 47.

All three of these methods, the constructor, calculatePay, and setRate, form the pieces of a single algorithm. The entire algorithm could have been written in the constructor, which would then look something like this:

```
// The entire algorithm written in the constructor!
public void SalesCommission(double s, double a)
{
    sales = s;
    advance = a;
```

```
            if (sales < 10000)
                rate = 0.05;
            else if (sales < 15000)
                rate = 0.1;
            else if (sales < 18000)
                rate = 0.12;
            else if (sales < 22000)
                rate = 0.14;
            else
                rate = 0.16;
            commission = sales * rate;
            pay = commission - advance;
    }
```

Can you see how decomposing this algorithm into three methods improves the code? First, it isolates the related tasks into separate methods: The constructor assigns initial values to the sales and advance fields; the setRate method determines the commission rate; and the calculatePay method calculates the salesperson's gross pay. Second, code that is broken up into small, related chunks is easier to read and debug than one long method that performs many tasks.

The Main Program

The main program code is shown in Code Listing 4-24. First, it gets the amount of sales and advanced pay for a salesperson as input from the user. It then creates an instance of the SalesCommission class and passes this data to the class's constructor. The program then reads the resultant pay data from the SalesCommission object and displays it on the screen.

Code Listing 4-24   (**HalsCommission.java**)

```java
1   import java.util.Scanner;
2   import java.text.DecimalFormat;
3
4   /**
5    * This program calculates a salesperson's gross
6    * pay at Hal's Computer Emporium.
7    */
8
9   public class HalsCommission
10  {
11      public static void main(String[] args)
12      {
13          double sales,       // To hold amount of sales
14                  advancePay;  // To hold advance pay
15
16          // Create DecimalFormat objects for dollar amounts
17          // and percentages.
18          DecimalFormat dollar = new DecimalFormat("#,##0.00");
19          DecimalFormat percent = new DecimalFormat("#0%");
20
```

```
21          // Create a Scanner object to read input.
22          Scanner keyboard = new Scanner(System.in);
23
24          System.out.println("This program will display a "
25                            + "pay report for a salesperson.");
26          System.out.println("Enter the following information:");
27
28          // Ask the user for sales & Advanced Pay
29          System.out.print("Amount of sales: $");
30          sales = keyboard.nextDouble();
31          System.out.print("Amount of advanced pay: $");
32          advancePay = keyboard.nextDouble();
33
34          // Create an instance of the SalesCommission
35          // class and pass the data to the constructor.
36          SalesCommission payInfo =
37                  new SalesCommission(sales, advancePay);
38
39          // Display the pay report for the salesperson.
40          System.out.println("\nPay Report");
41          System.out.println("-------------------------");
42          System.out.println("Sales: $"
43                  + dollar.format(payInfo.getSales()));
44          System.out.println("Commission rate: "
45                  + percent.format(payInfo.getRate()));
46          System.out.println("Commission: $"
47                  + dollar.format(payInfo.getCommission()));
48          System.out.println("Advanced pay: $"
49                  + dollar.format(payInfo.getAdvance()));
50          System.out.println("Remaining pay: $"
51                  + dollar.format(payInfo.getPay()));
52      }
53  }
```

Program Output with Example Input Shown in Bold

```
This program will display a pay report for a salesperson.
Enter the following information:
Amount of sales: $19600 [Enter]
Amount of advanced pay: $1000 [Enter]


Pay Report
-------------------------
Sales: $19,600.00
Commission rate: 14%
Commission: $2,744.00
Advanced pay: $1,000.00
Remaining pay: $1,744.00
```

4.13 Generating Random Numbers with the Random Class

CONCEPT: Random numbers are used in a variety of applications. Java provides the Random class, which you can use in to generate random numbers.

Random numbers are useful for lots of different programming tasks. The following are just a few examples:

- Random numbers are commonly used in games, such as computer games that let the player roll dice use random numbers to represent the values of the dice. Programs that show cards being drawn from a shuffled deck use random numbers to represent the face values of the cards.
- Random numbers are useful in simulation programs. In some simulations, the computer must randomly decide how a person, animal, insect, or other living being will behave. Formulas can be constructed in which a random number is used to determine various actions and events that take place in the program.
- Random numbers are useful in statistical programs that must randomly select data for analysis.
- Random numbers are commonly used in computer security to encrypt sensitive data.

The Java API provides a class named Random that you can use to generate random numbers. The class is part of the java.util package, so any program that uses it will need an import statement such as

```java
import java.util.Random;
```

You create an object from the Random class with a statement such as this:

```java
Random randomNumbers = new Random();
```

This statement does the following:

- It declares a variable named randomNumbers. The data type is the Random class.
- The expression new Random() creates an instance of the Random class.
- The equal sign assigns the address of the Random class to the randomNumbers variable.

After this statement executes, the randomNumbers variable references a Random object. Once you have created a Random object, you can call its nextInt method to get a random integer number. The following code shows an example:

```java
// Declare an int variable.
int number;

// Create a Random object.
Random randomNumbers = new Random();

// Get a random integer and assign it to number.
number = randomNumbers.nextInt();
```

After this code executes, the number variable contains a random integer. If you call the nextInt method with no arguments, as shown in this example, the returned integer is somewhere between −2,147,483,648 and +2,147,483,647. Alternatively, you can pass an argument that specifies an upper limit to the generated number's range. In the following statement, the value assigned to number is somewhere between 0 and 99:

```
number = randomNumbers.nextInt(100);
```

You can add or subtract a value to shift the numeric range upward or downward. In the following statement, we call the nextInt method to get a random number in the range of 0 through 9, and then we add 1 to it. So, the number assigned to number is somewhere in the range of 1 through 10:

```
number = randomNumbers.nextInt(10) + 1;
```

The following statement shows another example. It assigns a random integer between −50 and +49 to number:

```
number = randomNumbers.nextInt(100) - 50
```

The Random class has other methods for generating random numbers, and Table 4-14 summarizes several of them.

Table 4-14 Some of the Random class's methods

Method	Description
nextDouble()	Returns the next random number as a double. The number will be within the range of 0.0 and 1.0.
nextFloat()	Returns the next random number as a float. The number will be within the range of 0.0 and 1.0.
nextInt()	Returns the next random number as an int. The number will be within the range of an int, which is −2,147,483,648 to +2,147,483,647.
nextInt(int n)	This method accepts an integer argument, n. It returns a random number as an int. The number will be within the range of 0 and, not including n.
nextLong()	Returns the next random number as a long. The number will be within the range of a long, which is −9,223,372,036,854,775,808 to +9,223,372,036,854,775,807.

The program in Code Listing 4-25 demonstrates using the Random class.

Code Listing 4-25   (MathTutor.java)

```
1   import java.util.Scanner; // Needed for Scanner class
2   import java.util.Random;  // Needed for Random class
3
4   /**
5    * This program demonstrates the Random class.
6    */
7
8   public class MathTutor
9   {
10      public static void main(String[] args)
11      {
```

```
12          int number1;        // First number
13          int number2;        // Second number
14          int sum;            // Sum of numbers
15          int userAnswer;     // User's answer
16
17          // Create a Scanner object for keyboard input.
18          Scanner keyboard = new Scanner(System.in);
19
20          // Create a Random object.
21          Random randomNumbers = new Random();
22
23          // Get two random numbers.
24          number1 =   randomNumbers.nextInt(100);
25          number2 =   randomNumbers.nextInt(100);
26
27          // Display an addition problem.
28          System.out.println("What is the answer to " +
29                              "the following problem?");
30          System.out.print(number1  + " + " +
31                              number2  + " = ? ");
32
33          // Calculate the answer.
34          sum = number1  + number2;
35
36          // Get the user's answer.
37          userAnswer = keyboard.nextInt();
38
39          // Display the user's results.
40          if (userAnswer == sum)
41             System.out.println("Correct!");
42          else
43          {
44             System.out.println("Sorry, wrong answer. " +
45                              "The correct answer is " +
46                              sum);
47          }
48       }
49  }
```

Program Output with Example Input Shown in Bold

```
What is the answer to the following problem?
52 + 19 = ? 71 [Enter]
Correct!
```

Program Output with Example Input Shown in Bold

```
What is the answer to the following problem?
27 + 73 = ? 101 [Enter]
Sorry, wrong answer. The correct answer is 100
```

In the Spotlight:
Simulating Dice with Objects

Dice traditionally have six sides, representing the values 1-6. Some games, however, use specialized dice that have a different number of sides. For example, the fantasy role-playing game *Dungeons and Dragons*® uses dice with 4, 6, 8, 10, 12, and 20 sides.

Suppose you are writing a program that needs to roll simulated dice with various numbers of sides. A simple approach would be to write a Die class with a constructor that accepts the number of sides as an argument. The class would also have appropriate methods for rolling the die, and getting the die's value. Figure 4-20 shows the UML diagram for such a class, and Code Listing 4-26 shows the code.

Figure 4-20   UML diagram for the Die class

Die
- sides : int - value : int
+ Die(numSides : int) + roll() : void + getSides() : int + getValue() : int

Code Listing 4-26   (Die.java)

```java
 1   import java.util.Random;
 2
 3   /**
 4    *  The Die class simulates a die with a specified number of sides.
 5    */
 6
 7   public class Die
 8   {
 9      private int sides;    // Number of sides
10      private int value;    // The die's value
11
12      /**
13       *  The constructor performs an initial
14       *  roll of the die. The number of sides
15       *  for the die is passed as an argument.
16       */
17
18      public Die(int numSides)
```

```
19      {
20         sides = numSides;
21         roll();
22      }
23
24      /**
25       *  The roll method simulates the rolling of
26       *  the die.
27       */
28
29      public void roll()
30      {
31         // Create a Random object.
32         Random rand = new Random();
33
34         // Get a random value for the die.
35         value = rand.nextInt(sides) + 1;
36      }
37
38      /**
39       *  The getSides method returns the
40       *  number of sides for the die.
41       */
42
43      public int getSides()
44      {
45         return sides;
46      }
47
48      /**
49       *  The getValue method returns the
50       *  value of the die.
51       */
52
53      public int getValue()
54      {
55         return value;
56      }
57   }
```

Let's take a closer look at the code for the class:

Lines 9 and 10: These statements declare two int fields. The sides field will hold the number of sides that the die has, and the value field will hold the value of the die once it has been rolled.

Lines 18–22: This is the constructor. Notice that the constructor has a parameter for the number of sides. The parameter is assigned to the sides field in line 20. Line 21 calls the roll method, which simulates the rolling of the die.

Lines 29–36: This is the `roll` method, which simulates the rolling of the die. In line 32 a `Random` object is created, and it is referenced by the `rand` variable. Line 35 uses the `Random` object to get a random number that is in the appropriate range for this particular die. For example, if the `sides` field is set to 6, the expression `rand.nextInt(sides) + 1` will return a random integer in the range of 1 through 6. The random number is assigned to the `value` field.

Lines 43–46: This is the `getSides` method, an accessor that returns the `sides` field.

Lines 53–56: This is the `getValue` method, an accessor that returns the `value` field.

The program in Code Listing 4-27 demonstrates the class. It creates two instances of the `Die` class: one with 6 sides and the other with 12 sides. It then simulates rolling the dice.

Code Listing 4-27   (DiceDemo.java)

```java
1   /**
2    *  This program simulates the rolling of dice.
3    */
4
5   public class DiceDemo
6   {
7      public static void main(String[] args)
8      {
9         final int DIE1_SIDES = 6;  // Number of sides for die #1
10        final int DIE2_SIDES = 12; // Number of sides for die #2
11
12        // Create two instances of the Die class.
13        Die die1  = new Die(DIE1_SIDES);
14        Die die2  = new Die(DIE2_SIDES);
15
16        // Display initial information.
17        System.out.println("This simulates the rolling of a " +
18                            DIE1_SIDES + " sided die and a " +
19                            DIE2_SIDES + " sided die.");
20
21        // Roll the dice.
22        System.out.println("Rolling the dice.");
23        die1.roll();
24        die2.roll();
25
26        // Display the values of the dice.
27        System.out.println(die1.getValue() + " " +
28                            die2.getValue());
29     }
30  }
```

Program Output

```
This simulates the rolling of a 6 sided die and a 12 sided die.
Rolling the dice.
5   10
```

Let's take a closer look at the program:

Lines 9–10:	These statements declare two constants. DIE1_SIDES is the number of sides for the first die (6), DIE2_SIDES is the number of sides for the second die (12).
Lines 13–14:	These statements create two instances of the Die class. Notice that DIE1_SIDES, which is 6, is passed to the constructor in line 13, and DIE2_SIDES, which is 12, is passed to the constructor in line 14. As a result, die1 will reference a Die object with 6 sides, and die2 will reference a Die object with 12 sides.
Lines 17–19:	This statement displays information about the program.
Lines 23–24:	These statements call the Die objects' roll method to simulate rolling the dice.
Lines 27–28:	This statement displays the value of the dice.

4.14 Common Errors to Avoid

The following list describes several errors that are commonly made when learning this chapter's topics.

- **Using = instead of == to compare primitive values.** Remember, = is the assignment operator and == tests for equality.
- **Using == instead of the equals method to compare String objects.** You cannot use the == operator to compare the contents of a String object with another string. Instead you must use the equals or compareTo methods.
- **Forgetting to enclose an if statement's boolean expression in parentheses.** Java requires that the boolean expression being tested by an if statement be enclosed in a set of parentheses. An error will result if you omit the parentheses or use any other grouping characters.
- **Writing a semicolon at the end of an if clause.** When you write a semicolon at the end of an if clause, Java assumes that the conditionally executed statement is a null or empty statement.
- **Forgetting to enclose multiple conditionally executed statements in braces.** Normally the if statement conditionally executes only one statement. To conditionally execute more than one statement, you must enclose them in braces.
- **Omitting the trailing else in an if-else-if statement.** This is not a syntax error, but can lead to logical errors. If you omit the trailing else from an if-else-if statement, no code will be executed if none of the statement's boolean expressions are true.
- **Not writing complete boolean expressions on both sides of a logical && or || operator.** You must write a complete boolean expression on both sides of a logical && or || operator. For example, the expression x > 0 && < 10 is not valid because < 10 is not a complete expression. The expression should be written as x > 0 && x < 10.
- **Trying to perform case-insensitive string comparisons with the String class's equals and compareTo methods.** To perform case-insensitive string comparisons, use the String class's equalsIgnoreCase and compareToIgnoreCase methods.
- **Using an invalid testExpression in a switch statement.** The switch statement can evaluate char, byte, short, or int expressions. Beginning with Java 7, string expressions can also be evaluated.

- **Forgetting to write a colon at the end of a `case` statement.** A colon must appear after the `CaseExpression` in each case statement.
- **Forgetting to write a `break` statement in a `case` section.** This is not a syntax error, but it can lead to logical errors. The program does not branch out of a `switch` statement until it reaches a `break` statement or the end of the `switch` statement.
- **Forgetting to write a `default` section in a `switch` statement.** This is not a syntax error, but can lead to a logical error. If you omit the `default` section, no code will be executed if none of the case values match the `testExpression`.
- **Reversing the `?` and the `:` when using the conditional operator.** When using the conditional operator, the `?` character appears first in the conditional expression, then the `:` character.

Review Questions and Exercises

Multiple Choice and True/False

1. The `if` statement is an example of a
   a. sequence structure.
   b. decision structure.
   c. pathway structure.
   d. class structure.

2. This type of expression has a value of either `true` or `false`.
   a. `binary` expression
   b. `decision` expression
   c. `unconditional` expression
   d. `boolean` expression

3. `>`, `<`, and `==` are
   a. relational operators.
   b. logical operators.
   c. conditional operators.
   d. ternary operators.

4. `&&`, `||`, and `!` are
   a. relational operators.
   b. logical operators.
   c. conditional operators.
   d. ternary operators.

5. This is an empty statement that does nothing.
   a. missing statement
   b. virtual statement
   c. null statement
   d. conditional statement

6. To create a block of statements, you enclose the statements in these.
   a. parentheses `( )`
   b. square brackets `[ ]`
   c. angled brackets `<>`
   d. braces `{ }`

7. This is a `boolean` variable that signals when some condition exists in the program.
   a. flag
   b. signal
   c. sentinel
   d. siren

8. How does the character "A" compare to the character "B"?
   a. "A" is greater than "B"
   b. "A" is less than "B"
   c. "A" is equal to "B"
   d. You cannot compare characters.

9. This is an `if` statement that appears inside another `if` statement.
   a. nested `if` statement
   b. tiered `if` statement
   c. dislodged `if` statement
   d. structured `if` statement

10. An `else` always clause goes with
    a. the closest previous `if` clause that doesn't already have its own `else` clause.
    b. the closest `if` clause.
    c. the `if` clause that is randomly selected by the compiler.
    d. none of these

11. When determining whether a number is inside a range, it's best to use this operator.
    a. `&&`
    b. `!`
    c. `||`
    d. `? :`

12. This determines whether two different `String` objects contain the same string.
    a. the `==` operator
    b. the `=` operator
    c. the `equals` method
    d. the `stringCompare` method

13. The conditional operator takes this many operands.
    a. one
    b. two
    c. three
    d. four

14. This section of a `switch` statement is branched to if none of the `case` values match the *testExpression*.
    a. `else`
    b. `default`
    c. `case`
    d. `otherwise`

15. **True or False:** The `=` operator and the `==` operator perform the same operation.

16. **True or False:** A conditionally executed statement should be indented one level from the `if` clause.

17. **True or False:** All lines in a conditionally executed block should be indented one level.

18. **True or False:** When an `if` statement is nested in the `if` clause of another statement, the only time the inner `if` statement is executed is when the `boolean` expression of the outer `if` statement is `true`.

19. **True or False:** When an `if` statement is nested in the `else` clause of another statement, the only time the inner `if` statement is executed is when the `boolean` expression of the outer `if` statement is true.

20. **True or False:** The scope of a variable is limited to the block in which it is defined.

Find the Error

Find the errors in the following code.

1.
```
// Warning! This code contains ERRORS!
if (x == 1);
    y = 2;
else if (x == 2);
    y = 3;
else if (x == 3);
    y = 4;
```

2.
```
// Warning! This code contains an ERROR!
if (average = 100)
    System.out.println("Perfect Average!");
```

3.
```
// Warning! This code contains ERRORS!
if (num2  == 0)
    System.out.println("Division by zero is not possible.");
    System.out.println("Please run the program again ");
    System.out.println("and enter a number besides zero.");
else
    Quotient = num1 / num2;
    System.out.print("The quotient of " + Num1);
    System.out.print(" divided by " + Num2  + " is ");
    System.out.println(Quotient);
```

4.
```
// Warning! This code contains ERRORS!
switch (score)
{
    case (score > 90):
        grade = 'A';
        break;
    case(score > 80):
        grade = 'b';
        break;
    case(score > 70):
        grade = 'C';
        break;
    case (score > 60):
        grade = 'D';
        break;
    default:
        grade = 'F';
}
```

5. The following statement should determine whether x is not greater than 20. What is wrong with it?

   ```
   if (!x > 20)
   ```

6. The following statement should determine whether count is within the range of 0 through 100. What is wrong with it?

   ```
   if (count >= 0 || count <= 100)
   ```

7. The following statement should determine whether count is outside the range of 0 through 100. What is wrong with it?

   ```
   if (count < 0 && count > 100)
   ```

8. The following statement should assign 0 to z if a is less than 10, otherwise it should assign 7 to z. What is wrong with it?

   ```
   z = (a < 10) : 0 ? 7;
   ```

9. Assume that partNumber references a String object. The following if statement should perform a case-insensitive comparison.

   ```
   if (partNumber.equals("BQ789W4"))
       available = true;
   ```

Algorithm Workbench

1. Write an if statement that assigns 100 to x when y is equal to 0.

2. Write an if-else statement that assigns 0 to x when y is equal to 10. Otherwise it should assign 1 to x.

3. Using the following chart, write an if-else-if statement that assigns .10, .15, or .20 to commission, depending on the value in sales.

Sales	Commission Rate
Up to $10,000	10%
$10,000 to $15,000	15%
Over $15,000	20%

4. Write an if statement that sets the variable hours to 10 when the flag variable minimum is equal to true.

5. Write nested if statements that perform the following tests: If amount1 is greater than 10 and amount2 is less than 100, display the greater of the two.

6. Write an if statement that prints the message "The number is valid" if the variable grade is within the range 0 through 100.

7. Write an if statement that prints the message "The number is valid" if the variable temperature is within the range −50 through 150.

8. Write an if statement that prints the message "The number is not valid" if the variable hours is outside the range 0 through 80.

9. Write an if-else statement that displays the String objects title1 and title2 in alphabetical order.

10.   Convert the following `if-else-if` statement into a `switch` statement:

```
if (choice == 1)
{
   System.out.println("You selected 1.");
}
else if (choice == 2 || choice == 3)
{
   System.out.println("You selected 2 or 3.");
}
else if (choice == 4)
{
   System.out.println("You selected 4.");
}
else
{
   System.out.println("Select again please.");
}
```

11.   Match the conditional expression with the `if-else` statement that performs the same operation.

a. q = x < y ? a + b : x * 2;
b. q = x < y ? x * 2 : a + b;
c. x < y ? q = 0 : q = 1;

```
_____       if (x < y)
                q = 0;
            else
                q = 1;

_____       if (x < y)
                q = a + b;
            else
                q = x * 2;

_____       if (x < y)
                q = x * 2;
            else
                q = a + b;
```

12.   Assume that the `double` variable number holds the value 0.0329. What format pattern would you use with the `DecimalFormat` class to display the number as 00000.033?

13.   Assume that the `double` variable number holds the value 0.0329. What format pattern would you use with the `DecimalFormat` class to display the number as 0.03?

14.   Assume that the `double` variable number holds the value 456198736.3382. What format pattern would you use with the `DecimalFormat` class to display the number as 456,198,736.34?

Short Answer

1.   Explain what is meant by the term "conditionally executed."

2.   Explain why a misplaced semicolon can cause an `if` statement to operate incorrectly.

3. Why is it good advice to indent all the statements inside a set of braces?

4. What happens when you compare two `String` objects with the `==` operator?

5. Explain the purpose of a flag variable. Of what data type should a flag variable be?

6. What risk does a programmer take when not placing a trailing `else` at the end of an `if-else-if` statement?

7. Briefly describe how the `&&` operator works.

8. Briefly describe how the `||` operator works.

9. Why are the relational operators called "relational"?

10. How do you use `private` methods in a class to decompose an algorithm?

Programming Challenges

1. Roman Numerals

Write a program that prompts the user to enter a number within the range of 1 through 10. The program should display the Roman numeral version of that number. If the number is outside the range of 1–10, the program should display an error message.

VideoNote
The Time
Calculator
Problem

2. Time Calculator

Write a program that asks the user to enter a number of seconds.

- There are 60 seconds in a minute. If the number of seconds entered by the user is greater than or equal to 60, the program should display the number of minutes in that many seconds.
- There are 3,600 seconds in an hour. If the number of seconds entered by the user is greater than or equal to 3,600, the program should display the number of hours in that many seconds.
- There are 86,400 seconds in a day. If the number of seconds entered by the user is greater than or equal to 86,400, the program should display the number of days in that many seconds.

3. `TestScores` Class

Design a `TestScores` class that has fields to hold three test scores. (If you have already written the `TestScores` class for Programming Challenge 8 of Chapter 3, you can modify it.) The class constructor should accept three test scores as arguments and assign these arguments to the test score fields. The class should also have accessor methods for the test score fields, a method that returns the average of the test scores, and a method that returns the letter grade that is assigned for the test score average. Use the grading scheme in the following table.

Test Score Average	Letter Grade
90–100	A
80–89	B
70–79	C
60–69	D
Below 60	F

4. Software Sales

A software company sells a package that retails for $99. Quantity discounts are given according to the following table:

Quantity	Discount
10–19	20%
20–49	30%
50–99	40%
100 or more	50%

Design a class that stores the number of units sold and has a method that returns the total cost of the purchase.

5. BankCharges Class

A bank charges $10 per month plus the following check fees for a commercial checking account:

$.10 for each check if less than 20 checks were written
$.08 for each check if 20 through 39 checks were written
$.06 for each check if 40 through 59 checks were written
$.04 for each check if 60 or more checks were written

The bank also charges an extra $15 if the account balance falls below $400 (before any check fees are applied). Design a class that stores the ending balance of an account and the number of checks written. It should also have a method that returns the bank's service fees for the month.

6. ShippingCharges Class

The Fast Freight Shipping Company charges the following rates:

Weight of Package (in kilograms)	Rate per 500 Miles Shipped
2 Kg or less	$1.10
Over 2 Kg but not more than 6 Kg	$2.20
Over 6 Kg but not more than 10 Kg	$3.70
Over 10 Kg	$4.80

The shipping charges per 500 miles are not prorated. For example, if a 2 Kg package is shipped 550 miles, the charges would be $2.20.

Design a class that stores the weight of a package and has a method that returns the shipping charges.

7. FatGram Class

Design a class with a method that stores the number of calories and fat grams in a food item. The class should have a method that returns the percentage of the calories that come from fat. One gram of fat has 9 calories, so:

Calories from fat = fat grams * 9

The percentage of calories from fat can be calculated as:

Calories from fat ÷ total calories

Demonstrate the class in a program that asks the user to enter the number of calories and the number of fat grams for a food item. The program should display the percentage of calories that come from fat. If the calories from fat are less than 30% of the total calories of the food, it should also display a message indicating the food is low in fat.

Because the number of calories from fat cannot be greater than the total number of calories, if the user enters a number for the calories from fat that is greater than the total number of calories, the program should display an error message indicating that the numbers are invalid.

8. Running the Race

Design a class that stores the names of three runners and the time, in minutes, it took each of them to finish a race. The class should have methods that return the name of the runner in 1st, 2nd, or 3rd place.

9. The Speed of Sound

The following table shows the approximate speed of sound in air, water, and steel.

Medium	Speed
Air	1100 feet per second
Water	4900 feet per second
Steel	16,400 feet per second

Design a class that stores in a `distance` field the distance, in feet, traveled by a sound wave. The class should have the appropriate accessor and mutator methods for this field. In addition, the class should have the following methods:

- **getSpeedInAir**. This method should return the number of seconds it would take a sound wave to travel, in air, the distance stored in the `distance` field. The formula to calculate the amount of time it will take the sound wave to travel the specified distance in air is:

  Time = distance/1100

- **getSpeedInWater**. This method should return the number of seconds it would take a sound wave to travel, in water, the distance stored in the `distance` field. The formula to calculate the amount of time it will take the sound wave to travel the specified distance in water is:

  Time = distance/4900

- **getSpeedInSteel**. This method should return the number of seconds it would take a sound wave to travel, in steel, the distance stored in the `distance` field. The formula to calculate the amount of time it will take the sound wave to travel the specified distance in air is:

  Time = distance/16400

Write a program to demonstrate the class. The program should display a menu allowing the user to select air, water, or steel. Once the user has made a selection, he or she should be asked to enter the distance a sound wave will travel in the selected medium. The program will then display the amount of time it will take. Check that the user has selected one of the available choices from the menu.

10. Freezing and Boiling Points

The following table lists the freezing and boiling points of several substances in Fahrenheit.

Substance	Freezing Point	Boiling Point
Ethyl Alcohol	–173	172
Oxygen	–362	–306
Water	32	212

Design a class that stores a temperature in a temperature field and has the appropriate accessor and mutator methods for the field. The class should also have the following methods:

- **isEthylFreezing.** This method should return the boolean value true if the temperature stored in the temperature field is at or below the freezing point of ethyl alcohol. Otherwise, the method should return false.

- **isEthylBoiling.** This method should return the boolean value true if the temperature stored in the temperature field is at or above the boiling point of ethyl alcohol. Otherwise, the method should return false.

- **isOxygenFreezing.** This method should return the boolean value true if the temperature stored in the temperature field is at or below the freezing point of oxygen. Otherwise, the method should return false.

- **isOxygenBoiling.** This method should return the boolean value true if the temperature stored in the temperature field is at or above the boiling point of oxygen. Otherwise, the method should return false.

- **isWaterFreezing.** This method should return the boolean value true if the temperature stored in the temperature field is at or below the freezing point of water. Otherwise, the method should return false.

- **isWaterBoiling.** This method should return the boolean value true if the temperature stored in the temperature field is at or above the boiling point of water. Otherwise, the method should return false.

Write a program that demonstrates the class. The program should ask the user to enter a temperature and then display a list of the substances that will freeze at that temperature and those that will boil at that temperature. For example, if the temperature is −20, the class should report that water will freeze and oxygen will boil at that temperature.

11. Mobile Service Provider

A mobile phone service provider has three different subscription packages for its customers:

Package A: For $39.99 per month 450 minutes are provided. Additional minutes are $0.45 per minute.

Package B: For $59.99 per month 900 minutes are provided. Additional minutes are $0.40 per minute.

Package C: For $69.99 per month unlimited minutes are provided.

Design a class that calculates a customer's monthly bill. It should store the letter of the package the customer has purchased (A, B, or C) and the number of minutes that were used. It should have a method that returns the total charges. Demonstrate the class in a program that asks the user to select a package and enter the number of minutes used. The program should display the total charges.

12. Mobile Service Provider, Part 2

Modify the program you wrote for Programming Challenge 11 so it also calculates and displays the amount of money Package A customers would save if they purchased packages B or C, and the amount of money package B customers would save if they purchased package C. If there would be no savings, no message should be printed.

13. Body Mass Index

Write a program that calculates and displays a person's body mass index (BMI). The BMI is often used to determine whether a person is overweight or underweight for his or her height. A person's BMI is calculated with the following formula:

$$BMI = weight \times 703/height^2$$

where *weight* is measured in pounds and *height* is measured in inches. The program should display a message indicating whether the person has optimal weight, is underweight, or is overweight. A person's weight is considered to be optimal if his or her BMI is between 18.5 and 25. If the BMI is less than 18.5, the person is considered to be underweight. If the BMI value is greater than 25, the person is considered to be overweight.

14. Days in a Month

Write a class named `MonthDays`. The class's constructor should accept two arguments:

- An integer for the month (1 = January, 2 February, etc).
- An integer for the year

The class should have a method named `getNumberOfDays` that returns the number of days in the specified month. The method should use the following criteria to identify leap years:

1. Determine whether the year is divisible by 100. If it is, then it is a leap year if and if only it is divisible by 400. For example, 2000 is a leap year but 2100 is not.
2. If the year is not divisible by 100, then it is a leap year if and if only it is divisible by 4. For example, 2008 is a leap year but 2009 is not.

Demonstrate the class in a program that asks the user to enter the month (letting the user enter an integer in the range of 1 through 12) and the year. The program should then display the number of days in that month. Here is a sample run of the program:

```
Enter a month (1-12): 2 [Enter]
Enter a year: 2008 [Enter]
29 days
```

15. Book Club Points

Serendipity Booksellers has a book club that awards points to its customers based on the number of books purchased each month. The points are awarded as follows:

- If a customer purchases 0 books, he or she earns 0 points.
- If a customer purchases 1 book, he or she earns 5 points.
- If a customer purchases 2 books, he or she earns 15 points.
- If a customer purchases 3 books, he or she earns 30 points.
- If a customer purchases 4 or more books, he or she earns 60 points.

Write a program that asks the user to enter the number of books that he or she has purchased this month and then displays the number of points awarded.

16. Magic Dates

The date June 10, 1960, is special because when we write it in the following format, the month times the day equals the year.

6/10/60

Design a class named MagicDate. The class constructor should accept, as integers, values for a month, a day, and a year. The class should also have a method named isMagic that returns true if the date passed to the constructor is magic, or false otherwise.

Write a program that asks the user to enter a month, a day, and a two-digit year as integers. The program should create an instance of the MagicDate class to determine whether the date entered by the user is a magic date. If it is, the program should display a message saying the date is magic. Otherwise it should display a message saying the date is not magic.

17. Hot Dog Cookout Calculator

Assume that hot dogs come in packages of 10, and hot dog buns come in packages of 8. Write a program that calculates the number of packages of hot dogs and the number of packages of hot dog buns needed for a cookout, with the minimum amount of leftovers. The program should ask the user for the number of people attending the cookout, and the number of hot dogs each person will be given. The program should display:

- The minimum number of packages of hot dogs required
- The minimum number of packages of buns required
- The number of hot dogs that will be left over
- The number of buns that will be left over

18. Roulette Wheel Colors

On a roulette wheel, the pockets are numbered from 0 to 36. The colors of the pockets are as follows:

- Pocket 0 is green.
- For pockets 1 through 10, the odd numbered pockets are red and the even numbered pockets are black.
- For pockets 11 through 18, the odd numbered pockets are black and the even numbered pockets are red.
- For pockets 19 through 28, the odd numbered pockets are red and the even numbered pockets are black.
- For pockets 29 through 36, the odd numbered pockets are black and the even numbered pockets are red.

Write a class named RoulettePocket. The class's constructor should accept a pocket number. The class should have a method named getPocketColor that returns the pocket's color, as a string.

Demonstrate the class in a program that asks the user to enter a pocket number, and displays whether the pocket is green, red, or black. The program should display an error message if the user enters a number that is outside the range of 0 through 36.

5 Loops and Files

TOPICS

5.1 The Increment and Decrement Operators

5.2 The while Loop

5.3 Using the while Loop for Input Validation

5.4 The do-while Loop

5.5 The for Loop

5.6 Running Totals and Sentinel Values

5.7 Nested Loops

5.8 The break and continue Statements

5.9 Deciding Which Loop to Use

5.10 Introduction to File Input and Output

5.11 Common Errors to Avoid

5.1 The Increment and Decrement Operators

CONCEPT: ++ and -- are operators that add and subtract one from their operands.

VideoNote
The while Loop

To increment a value means to increase it by one, and to decrement a value means to decrease it by one. Both of the following statements increment the variable number:

```
number = number + 1;
number += 1;
```

And number is decremented in both of the following statements:

```
number = number - 1;
number -= 1;
```

Java provides a set of simple unary operators designed just for incrementing and decrementing variables. The increment operator is ++ and the decrement operator is --. The following statement uses the ++ operator to increment number.

```
number++;
```

And the following statement decrements number.

```
number--;
```

NOTE: The expression number++ is pronounced "number plus plus," and number-- is pronounced "number minus minus."

The program in Code Listing 5-1 demonstrates the ++ and -- operators.

Code Listing 5-1   (`IncrementDecrement.java`)

```
 1  /**
 2   * This program demonstrates the ++ and -- operators.
 3   */
 4
 5  public class IncrementDecrement
 6  {
 7     public static void main(String[] args)
 8     {
 9        int number = 4;
10
11        // Display the value in number.
12        System.out.println("number is " + number);
13        System.out.println("I will increment number.");
14
15        // Increment number.
16        number++;
17
18        // Display the value in number.
19        System.out.println("Now, number is " + number);
20        System.out.println("I will decrement number.");
21
22        // Decrement number.
23        number--;
24
25        // Display the value in number.
26        System.out.println("Now, number is " + number);
27     }
28  }
```

Program Output

```
number is 4
I will increment number.
Now, number is 5
I will decrement number.
Now, number is 4
```

The statements in Code Listing 5-1 show the increment and decrement operators used in *postfix mode*, which means the operator is placed after the variable. The operators also work in *prefix mode*, where the operator is placed before the variable name:

```
++number;
--number;
```

In both postfix and prefix mode, these operators add one to or subtract one from their operand. Code Listing 5-2 demonstrates this.

Code Listing 5-2   (`Prefix.java`)

```java
 1  /**
 2   * This program demonstrates the ++ and -- operators
 3   * in prefix mode.
 4   */
 5
 6  public class Prefix
 7  {
 8      public static void main(String[] args)
 9      {
10          int number = 4;
11
12          // Display the value in number.
13          System.out.println("number is " + number);
14          System.out.println("I will increment number.");
15
16          // Increment number.
17          ++number;
18
19          // Display the value in number.
20          System.out.println("Now, number is " + number);
21          System.out.println("I will decrement number.");
22
23          // Decrement number.
24          --number;
25
26          // Display the value in number.
27          System.out.println("Now, number is " + number);
28      }
29  }
```

Program Output

```
number is 4
I will increment number.
Now, number is 5
I will decrement number.
Now, number is 4
```

The Difference between Postfix and Prefix Modes

In Code Listings 5-1 and 5-2, the statements number++ and ++number both increment the variable number, while the statements number-- and --number both decrement the variable number. In these simple statements it doesn't matter whether the operator is used in postfix or prefix mode. The difference is important, however, when these operators are used in statements that do more than just incrementing or decrementing. For example, look at the following code:

```
number = 4;
System.out.println(number++);
```

The statement calling the `println` method is doing two things: (1) displaying the value of `number` and (2) incrementing `number`. But which happens first? The `println` method will display a different value if `number` is incremented first than if `number` is incremented last. The answer depends upon the mode of the increment operator.

Postfix mode causes the increment to happen after the value of the variable is used in the expression. In the previously shown statement, the `println` method will display 4 and then `number` will be incremented to 5. Prefix mode, however, causes the increment to happen first. Here is an example:

```
number = 4;
System.out.println(++number);
```

In these statements, `number` is incremented to 5, then `println` will display 5. For another example, look at the following code:

```
int x = 1, y;
y = x++;        // Postfix increment
```

The first statement declares the variable x (initialized with the value 1) and the variable y. The second statement does two things:

- It assigns the value of x to the variable y.
- The variable x is incremented.

The value that will be stored in y depends on when the increment takes place. Because the ++ operator is used in postfix mode, it acts after the assignment takes place. So, this code will store 1 in y. After the code has executed, x will contain 2. Let's look at the same code, but with the ++ operator used in prefix mode:

```
int x = 1, y;
y = ++x;        // Prefix increment
```

The first statement declares the variable x (initialized with the value 1) and the variable y. The second statement does two things:

- The variable x is incremented.
- The value of x is assigned to the variable y.

Because the operator is used in prefix mode, it acts on the variable before the assignment takes place. So, this code will store 2 in y. After the code has executed, x will also contain 2.

Checkpoint

5.1 What will the following program segments display?

a.
```
x = 2;
y = x++;
System.out.println(y);
```

b. ```
    x = 2;
    System.out.println(x++);
    ```
c.  ```
    x = 2;
    System.out.println(--x);
    ```
d. ```
    x = 8;
    y = x--;
    System.out.println(y);
    ```

# 5.2 The while Loop

**CONCEPT:**  A loop is a part of a program that repeats.

In Chapter 4 you were introduced to the concept of control structures, which direct the flow of a program. A *loop* is a control structure that causes a statement or group of statements to repeat. Java has three looping control structures: the while loop, the do-while loop, and the for loop. The difference between each of these is how they control the repetition. In this section we will focus on the while loop.

The while loop has two important parts: (1) a boolean expression that is tested for a true or false value and (2) a statement or block of statements that is repeated as long as the expression is true. Figure 5-1 shows the logic of a while loop.

**Figure 5-1**   Logic of a while loop

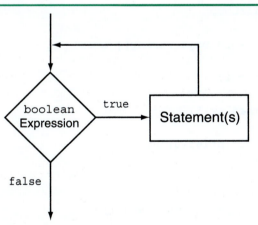

Here is the general format of the while loop:

```
while (BooleanExpression)
    statement;
```

The first line shown in the format is sometimes called the *loop header*. It consists of the key word while followed by a boolean expression enclosed in parentheses. The *BooleanExpression* is tested, and if it is true, the *statement* is executed. Then, the *BooleanExpression* is tested again. If it is true, the *statement* is executed. This cycle repeats until the boolean expression is false. The statement that is repeated is known as
```

the *body* of the loop. It is also considered a conditionally executed statement because it is only executed under the condition that the `boolean` expression is true.

Notice there is no semicolon at the end of the loop header. Like the `if` statement, the `while` loop is not complete without the conditionally executed statement that follows it.

If you wish the `while` loop to repeat a block of statements, the format is:

```
while (BooleanExpression)
{
    statement;
    statement;
    // Place as many statements here
    // as necessary.
}
```

The `while` loop works like an `if` statement that executes over and over. As long as the expression in the parentheses is true, the conditionally executed statement or block will repeat. The program in Code Listing 5-3 uses the `while` loop to print "Hello" five times.

Code Listing 5-3   (WhileLoop.java)

```
 1  /**
 2   * This program demonstrates the while loop.
 3   */
 4
 5  public class WhileLoop
 6  {
 7     public static void main(String[] args)
 8     {
 9        int number = 1;
10
11        while (number <= 5)
12        {
13           System.out.println("Hello");
14           number++;
15        }
16
17        System.out.println("That's all!");
18     }
19  }
```

Program Output
```
Hello
Hello
Hello
Hello
Hello
That's all!
```

Let's take a closer look at this program. In line 9, an integer variable, number, is declared and initialized with the value 1. In line 11, the while loop begins with this statement:

```
while (number <= 5)
```

This statement tests the variable number to determine whether it is less than or equal to 5. If it is, then the statements in the body of the loop, which are in lines 13 and 14, are executed:

```
System.out.println("Hello");
number++;
```

The first statement in the body of the loop (line 13) prints the word "Hello". The second statement (line 14) uses the increment operator to add one to number. This is the last statement in the body of the loop, so after it executes, the loop starts over. It tests the boolean expression again, and if it is true, the statements in the body of the loop are executed. This cycle repeats until the boolean expression number <= 5 is false. This is illustrated in Figure 5-2.

Figure 5-2   The while Loop

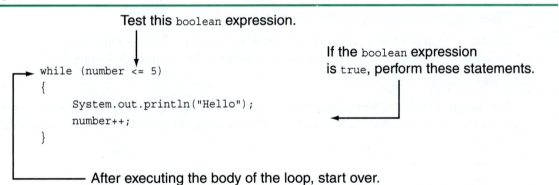

Each repetition of a loop is known as an *iteration*. This loop will perform five iterations because the variable number is initialized with the value 1, and it is incremented each time the body of the loop is executed. When the expression number <= 5 is tested and found to be false, the loop will terminate and the program will resume execution at the statement that immediately follows the loop. Figure 5-3 shows the logic of this loop.

Figure 5-3   Logic of the example `while` loop

In this example, the `number` variable is referred to as the *loop control variable* because it controls the number of times that the loop iterates.

The `while` Loop Is a Pretest Loop

The `while` loop is known as a *pretest* loop, which means it tests its expression before each iteration. Notice the variable declaration of `number` in line 9 of Code Listing 5-3:

```
int number = 1;
```

The `number` variable is initialized with the value 1. If `number` had been initialized with a value that is greater than 5, as shown in the following program segment, the loop would never execute:

```
int number = 6;
while (number <= 5)
{
    System.out.println("Hello");
    number++;
}
```

An important characteristic of the `while` loop is that the loop will never iterate if the boolean expression is `false` to start with. If you want to be sure that a `while` loop executes the first time, you must initialize the relevant data in such a way that the boolean expression starts out as `true`.

Infinite Loops

In all but rare cases, loops must contain within themselves a way to terminate. This means that something inside the loop must eventually make the boolean expression `false`. The loop in Code Listing 5-3 stops when the variable `number` is no longer less than or equal to 5.

If a loop does not have a way of stopping, it is called an infinite loop. An infinite loop continues to repeat until the program is interrupted. Here is an example of an infinite loop:

```
int number = 1;
while (number <= 5)
{
    System.out.println("Hello");
}
```

This is an infinite loop because it does not contain a statement that changes the value of the number variable. Each time the boolean expression is tested, number will contain the value 1.

It's also possible to create an infinite loop by accidentally placing a semicolon after the first line of the while loop. Here is an example:

```
int number = 1;
while (number <= 5);   // This semicolon is an ERROR!
{
    System.out.println("Hello");
    number++;
}
```

The semicolon at the end of the first line is assumed to be a null statement and disconnects the while statement from the block that comes after it. To the compiler, this loop looks like:

```
while (number <= 5);
```

This while loop will forever execute the null statement, which does nothing. The program will appear to have "gone into space" because there is nothing to display screen output or show activity.

Don't Forget the Braces with a Block of Statements

If you're using a block of statements, don't forget to enclose all of the statements in a set of braces. If the braces are accidentally left out, the while statement conditionally executes only the very next statement. For example, look at the following code:

```
int number = 1;
// This loop is missing its braces!
while (number <= 5)
    System.out.println("Hello");
    number++;
```

In this code the number++ statement is not in the body of the loop. Because the braces are missing, the while statement only executes the statement that immediately follows it. This loop will execute infinitely because there is no code in its body that changes the number variable.

Programming Style and the while Loop

It's possible to create loops that look like this:

```
while (number != 99) number = keyboard.nextInt();
```

as well as this:

```
while (number <= 5) { System.out.println("Hello"); number++; }
```

Avoid this style of programming. The programming style you should use with the `while` loop is similar to that of the `if` statement:

- If there is only one statement repeated by the loop, it should appear on the line after the `while` statement and be indented one additional level. The statement can optionally appear inside a set of braces.
- If the loop repeats a block, each line inside the braces should be indented.

This programming style should visually set the body of the loop apart from the surrounding code. In general, you'll find a similar style being used with the other types of loops presented in this chapter.

In the Spotlight:

Designing a program with a `while` Loop

A project currently underway at Chemical Labs, Inc., requires that a substance be continually heated in a vat. A technician must check the substance's temperature every 15 minutes. If the substance's temperature does not exceed 102.5 degrees Celsius, then the technician does nothing. However, if the temperature is greater than 102.5 degrees Celsius, the technician must turn down the vat's thermostat, wait 5 minutes, and check the temperature again. The technician repeats these steps until the temperature does not exceed 102.5 degrees Celsius. The director of engineering has asked you to write a program that guides the technician through this process.

Here is the algorithm:

1. *Prompt the user to enter the substance's temperature.*
2. *Repeat the following steps as long as the temperature is greater than 102.5 degrees Celsius:*
   a. *Tell the technician to turn down the thermostat, wait 5 minutes, and check the temperature again.*
   b. *Prompt the user to enter the substance's temperature.*
3. *After the loop finishes, tell the technician that the temperature is acceptable and to check it again in 15 minutes.*

After reviewing this algorithm, you realize that steps 2(a) and 2(b) should not be performed if the test condition (temperature is greater than 102.5) is false to begin with. The `while` loop will work well in this situation because it will not execute even once if its condition is false. Code Listing 5-4 shows the program.

Code Listing 5-4   (`CheckTemperature.java`)

```
1  import java.util.Scanner;
2
3  /**
4   * This program asists a technician in the process
5   * of checking a substance's temperature.
```

```
 6    */
 7
 8   public class CheckTemperature
 9   {
10      public static void main(String[] args)
11      {
12          final double MAX_TEMP = 102.5;  // Maximum temperature
13          double temperature;             // To hold the temperature
14
15          // Create a Scanner object for keyboard input.
16          Scanner keyboard = new Scanner(System.in);
17
18          // Get the current temperature.
19          System.out.print("Enter the substance's Celsius temperature: ");
20          temperature = keyboard.nextDouble();
21
22          // As long as necessary, instruct the technician
23          // to adjust the temperature.
24          while (temperature > MAX_TEMP)
25          {
26              System.out.println("The temperature is too high. Turn the");
27              System.out.println("thermostat down and wait 5 minutes.");
28              System.out.println("Then, take the Celsius temperature again");
29              System.out.print("and enter it here: ");
30              temperature = keyboard.nextDouble();
31          }
32
33          // Remind the technician to check the temperature
34          // again in 15 minutes.
35          System.out.println("The temperature is acceptable.");
36          System.out.println("Check it again in 15 minutes.");
37      }
38  }
```

Program Output with Example Input Shown in Bold

Enter the substance's Celsius temperature: **104.7 [Enter]**
The temperature is too high. Turn the
thermostat down and wait 5 minutes.
Then take the Celsius temperature again
and enter it here: **103.2 [Enter]**
The temperature is too high. Turn the
thermostat down and wait 5 minutes.
Then take the Celsius temperature again
and enter it here: **102.1 [Enter]**
The temperature is acceptable.
Check it again in 15 minutes.

Checkpoint

5.2 How many times will `"Hello World"` be printed in the following program segment?

```
int count = 10;
while (count < 1)
{
    System.out.println("Hello World");
    count++;
}
```

5.3 How many times will `"I love Java programming!"` be printed in the following program segment?

```
int count = 0;
while (count < 10)
    System.out.println("Hello World");
    System.out.println("I love Java programming!");
```

5.3 Using the `while` Loop for Input Validation

CONCEPT: The `while` loop can be used to create input routines that repeat until acceptable data is entered.

Perhaps the most famous saying of the computer industry is "garbage in, garbage out." The integrity of a program's output is only as good as its input, so you should try to make sure garbage does not go into your programs. *Input validation* is the process of inspecting data given to a program by the user and determining if it is valid. A good program should give clear instructions about the kind of input that is acceptable and should not assume the user has followed those instructions.

The `while` loop is especially useful for validating input. If an invalid value is entered, a loop can require that the user reenter it as many times as necessary. For example, look at the following code, which asks the user to enter a number in the range of 1 through 100:

```
Scanner keyboard = new Scanner(System.in);
System.out.print("Enter a number in the "
                + "range of 1 through 100: ");
number = keyboard.nextInt();
// Validate the input.
while (number < 1 || number > 100)
{
    System.out.println("That number is invalid.");
    System.out.print("Enter a number in the "
                + "range of 1 through 100: ");
    number = keyboard.nextInt();
}
```

This code first allows the user to enter a number. This takes place just before the loop. If the input is valid, the loop will not execute. If the input is invalid, however, the loop will display an error message and require the user to enter another number. The loop will continue to execute until the user enters a valid number. The general logic of performing input validation is shown in Figure 5-4.

Figure 5-4   Input validation logic

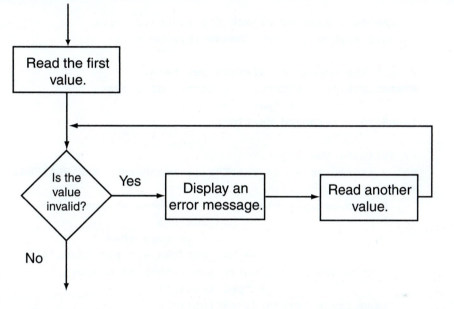

The read operation that takes place just before the loop is called a *priming read*. It provides the first value for the loop to test. Subsequent values are obtained by the loop.

The program in Code Listing 5-5 calculates the number of soccer teams a youth league may create, based on a given number of players and a maximum number of players per team. The program uses `while` loops to validate all of the user input.

Code Listing 5-5   (`SoccerTeams.java`)

```java
 1   import java.util.Scanner;
 2
 3   /**
 4    * This program calculates the number of soccer teams
 5    * that a youth league may create from the number of
 6    * available players. Input validation is demonstrated
 7    * with while loops.
 8    */
 9
10   public class SoccerTeams
11   {
```

```
12      public static void main(String[] args)
13      {
14         final int MIN_PLAYERS = 9,   // Minimum players per team
15                   MAX_PLAYERS = 15; // Maximum players per team
16         int players,                 // Number of available players
17             teamSize,                // Number of players per team
18             teams,                   // Number of teams
19             leftOver;                // Number of left over players
20
21         // Create a scanner object for keyboard input.
22         Scanner keyboard = new Scanner(System.in);
23
24         // Get the number of players per team.
25         System.out.print("Enter the number of players "
26                        + "per team: ");
27         teamSize = keyboard.nextInt();
28
29         // Validate the input.
30         while (teamSize < MIN_PLAYERS || teamSize > MAX_PLAYERS)
31         {
32             System.out.println("You should have at least "
33                               + MIN_PLAYERS
34                               + " but no more than "
35                               + MAX_PLAYERS + " per team.");
36             System.out.print("Enter the number of players "
37                            + "per team: ");
38             teamSize = keyboard.nextInt();
39         }
40
41         // Get the available number of players.
42         System.out.print("Enter the available number of players: ");
43         players = keyboard.nextInt();
44
45         // Validate the input.
46         while (players < 0)
47         {
48             System.out.println("Please do not enter a negative "
49                               + "number.");
50             System.out.print("Enter the available number "
51                            + "of players: ");
52             players = keyboard.nextInt();
53         }
54
55         // Calculate the number of teams.
56         teams = players / teamSize;
57
58         // Calculate the number of left over players.
59         leftOver = players % teamSize;
```

```
60
61          // Display the results.
62          System.out.println("There will be " + teams + " teams "
63                              + "with " + leftOver
64                              + " players left over.");
65      }
66  }
```

Program Output with Example Input Shown in Bold

```
Enter the number of players per team: 4 [Enter]
You should have at least 9 but no more than 15 per team.
Enter the number of players per team: 12 [Enter]
Enter the available number of players: −142 [Enter]
Please do not enter a negative number.
Enter the available number of players: 142 [Enter]
There will be 11 teams with 10 players left over.
```

 Checkpoint

5.4   Write an input validation loop that asks the user to enter a number in the range of 10 through 25.

5.5   Write an input validation loop that asks the user to enter 'Y', 'y', 'N', or 'n'.

5.6   Write an input validation loop that asks the user to enter "Yes" or "No".

5.4   The do-while Loop

CONCEPT: The do-while loop is a posttest loop, which means its boolean expression is tested after each iteration.

The do-while loop looks something like an inverted while loop. Here is the do-while loop's format when the body of the loop contains only a single statement:

```
do
    statement;
while (BooleanExpression);
```

Here is the format of the do-while loop when the body of the loop contains multiple statements:

```
do
{
    statement;
    statement;
    // Place as many statements here
    // as necessary.
} while (BooleanExpression);
```

NOTE: The do-while loop must be terminated with a semicolon.

The do-while loop is a posttest loop. This means it does not test its boolean expression until it has completed an iteration. As a result, the do-while loop always performs at least one iteration, even if the boolean expression is false to begin with. This differs from the behavior of a while loop, which you will recall is a pretest loop. For example, in the following while loop the println statement will not execute at all:

```java
int x = 1;
while (x < 0)
    System.out.println(x);
```

But the println statement in the following do-while loop will execute once because the do-while loop does not evaluate the expression x < 0 until the end of the iteration.

```java
int x = 1;
do
    System.out.println(x);
while (x < 0);
```

Figure 5-5 illustrates the logic of the do-while loop.

Figure 5-5 Logic of the do-while loop

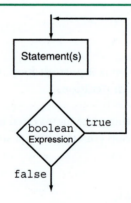

You should use the do-while loop when you want to make sure the loop executes at least once. For example, the program in Code Listing 5-6 averages a series of three test scores for a student. After the average is displayed, it asks the user if he or she wants to average another set of test scores. The program repeats as long as the user enters Y for yes.

Code Listing 5-6   (`TestAverage1.java`)

```java
 1   import java.util.Scanner;
 2
 3   /**
 4    * This program demonstrates a user-controlled loop.
 5    */
 6
 7   public class TestAverage1
 8   {
 9      public static void main(String[] args)
10      {
11         String input;                    // To hold keyboard input
12         double score1, score2, score3; // Three test scores
13         double average;                  // Average test score
14         char repeat;                     // Holds 'y' or 'n'
15
16         // Create a Scanner object for keyboard input.
17         Scanner keyboard = new Scanner(System.in);
18
19         System.out.println("This program calculates the average "
20                           + "of three test scores.");
21
22         do
23         {
24            // Get the three test scores.
25            System.out.print("Enter score #1: ");
26            score1 = keyboard.nextDouble();
27            System.out.print("Enter score #2: ");
28            score2 = keyboard.nextDouble();
29            System.out.print("Enter score #3: ");
30            score3 = keyboard.nextDouble();
31
32            // Calculate and print the average test score.
33            average = (score1 + score2 + score3) / 3.0;
34            System.out.println("The average is " + average);
35            System.out.println();
36
37            // Does the user want to average another set?
38            System.out.println("Would you like to average "
39                              + "another set of test scores?");
40            System.out.print("Enter Y for yes or N for no: ");
41            input = keyboard.next();   // Read a string.
42            repeat = input.charAt(0);  // Get the first char.
43
44         } while (repeat == 'Y' || repeat == 'y');
45      }
46   }
```

Program Output with Example Input Shown in Bold

```
This program calculates the average of three test scores.
Enter score #1: 89 [Enter]
Enter score #2: 90 [Enter]
Enter score #3: 97 [Enter]
The average is 92.0

Would you like to average another set of test scores?
Enter Y for yes or N for no: Y [Enter]
Enter score #1: 78 [Enter]
Enter score #2: 65 [Enter]
Enter score #3: 88 [Enter]
The average is 77.0

Would you like to average another set of test scores?
Enter Y for yes or N for no: N [Enter]
```

When this program was written, the programmer had no way of knowing the number of times the loop would iterate. This is because the loop asks the user if he or she wants to repeat the process. This type of loop is known as a *user-controlled loop* because it allows the user to decide the number of iterations.

5.5 The for Loop

CONCEPT: The for loop is ideal for performing a known number of iterations.

In general, there are two categories of loops: conditional loops and count-controlled loops. A *conditional loop* executes as long as a particular condition exists. For example, an input validation loop executes as long as the input value is invalid. When you write a conditional loop, you have no way of knowing the number of times it will iterate.

Sometimes you do know the exact number of iterations that a loop must perform. A loop that repeats a specific number of times is known as a *count-controlled loop*. For example, if a loop asks the user to enter the sales amounts for each month in the year, it will iterate twelve times. In essence, the loop counts to 12 and asks the user to enter a sales amount each time it makes a count.

A count-controlled loop must possess three elements:

1. It must initialize a control variable to a starting value.
2. It must test the control variable by comparing it to a maximum value. When the control variable reaches its maximum value, the loop terminates.
3. It must update the control variable during each iteration. This is usually done by incrementing the variable.

In Java, the `for` loop is ideal for writing count-controlled loops. It is specifically designed to initialize, test, and update a loop control variable. Here is the general format of the `for` loop when used to repeat a single statement:

```
for (Initialization; Test; Update)
   statement;
```

The format of the `for` loop when used to repeat a block is:

```
for (Initialization; Test; Update)
{
   statement;
   statement;
   // Place as many statements here
   // as necessary.
}
```

The first line of the `for` loop is known as the *loop header*. After the key word `for`, there are three expressions inside the parentheses, separated by semicolons. (Notice there is no semicolon after the third expression.) The first expression is the *initialization expression*. It is normally used to initialize a control variable to its starting value. This is the first action performed by the loop, and it is only done once. The second expression is the *test expression*. This is a `boolean` expression that controls the execution of the loop. As long as this expression is `true`, the body of the `for` loop will repeat. The `for` loop is a pretest loop, so it evaluates the test expression before each iteration. The third expression is the *update expression*. It executes at the end of each iteration. Typically, this is a statement that increments the loop's control variable.

Here is an example of a simple `for` loop that prints "Hello" five times:

```
for (count = 1; count <= 5; count++)
    System.out.println("Hello");
```

In this loop, the initialization expression is `count = 1`, the test expression is `count <= 5`, and the update expression is `count++`. The body of the loop has one statement, which is the `println` statement. Figure 5-6 illustrates the sequence of events that take place during the loop's execution. Notice that Steps 2 through 4 are repeated as long as the test expression is `true`.

Figure 5-6   Sequence of events in the `for` loop

Step 1: Perform the initialization expression.

Step 2: Evaluate the test expression. If it is `true`, go to step 3. Otherwise, terminate the loop.

```
for (count = 1; count <= 5; count++)
    System.out.println("Hello");
```

Step 3: Execute the body of the loop.

Step 4: Perform the update expression, then go back to step 2.

Figure 5-7 shows the loop's logic in the form of a flowchart.

Figure 5-7   Logic of the `for` loop

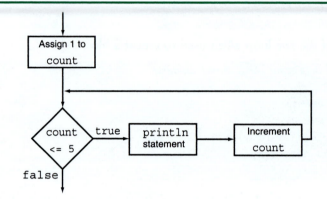

Notice how the control variable, `count`, is used to control the number of times that the loop iterates. During the execution of the loop, this variable takes on the values 1 through 5, and when the test expression `count <= 5` is false, the loop terminates. Because this variable keeps a count of the number of iterations, it is often called a *counter variable*.

Also notice that the `count` variable is used only in the loop header, to control the number of loop iterations. It is not used for any other purpose. It is also possible to use the control variable within the body of the loop. For example, look at the following code:

```
for (number = 1; number <= 10; number++)
    System.out.print(number + " ");
```

The control variable in this loop is `number`. In addition to controlling the number of iterations, it is also used in the body of the loop. This loop will produce the following output:

```
1 2 3 4 5 6 7 8 9 10
```

As you can see, the loop displays the contents of the `number` variable during each iteration. The program in Code Listing 5-7 shows another example of a `for` loop that uses its control variable within the body of the loop. This program displays a table showing the numbers 1 through 10 and their squares.

Code Listing 5-7   (`Squares.java`)

```
 1  /**
 2   * This program demonstrates the for loop.
 3   */
 4
 5  public class Squares
 6  {
 7      public static void main(String[] args)
 8      {
 9          int number; // Loop control variable
```

```
10
11          System.out.println("Number     Number Squared");
12          System.out.println("-----------------------");
13
14          for (number = 1; number <= 10; number++)
15          {
16              System.out.println(number + "\t\t"
17                                  + number * number);
18          }
19      }
20  }
```

Program Output

Number	Number Squared
1	1
2	4
3	9
4	16
5	25
6	36
7	49
8	64
9	81
10	100

Figure 5-8 illustrates the sequence of events performed by this for loop.

Figure 5-8   Sequence of events with the for loop in Code Listing 5-7

Figure 5-9 shows the logic of the loop.

Figure 5-9   Logic of the `for` loop in Code Listing 5-7

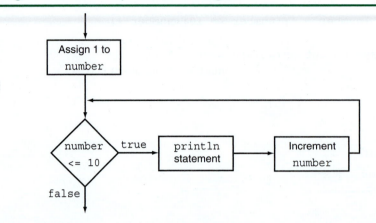

The `for` Loop Is a Pretest Loop

Because the `for` loop tests its `boolean` expression before it performs an iteration, it is a pretest loop. It is possible to write a `for` loop in such a way that it will never iterate. Here is an example:

```
for (count = 11; count <= 10; count++)
    System.out.println("Hello");
```

Because the variable `count` is initialized to a value that makes the `boolean` expression `false` from the beginning, this loop terminates as soon as it begins.

Avoid Modifying the Control Variable in the Body of the `for` Loop

Be careful not to place a statement that modifies the control variable in the body of the `for` loop. All modifications of the control variable should take place in the update expression, which is automatically executed at the end of each iteration. If a statement in the body of the loop also modifies the control variable, the loop will probably not terminate when you expect it to. The following loop, for example, increments x twice for each iteration:

```
for (x = 1; x <= 10; x++)
{
    System.out.println(x);
    x++;
}
```

Other Forms of the Update Expression

You are not limited to using increment statements in the update expression. Here is a loop that displays all the even numbers from 2 through 100 by adding 2 to its counter:

```
for (number = 2; number <= 100; number += 2)
    System.out.println(number);
```

And here is a loop that counts backward from 10 down to 0:

```
for (number = 10; number >= 0; number--)
    System.out.println(number);
```

Declaring a Variable in the `for` Loop's Initialization Expression

Not only may the control variable be initialized in the initialization expression, it may be declared there as well. The following code shows an example. This is a modified version of the loop in Code Listing 5-7.

```
for (int number = 1; number <= 10; number++)
{
        System.out.println(number + "\t\t"
                              + number * number);
}
```

In this loop, the variable `number` is both declared and initialized in the initialization expression. If the control variable is used only in the loop, it makes sense to declare it in the loop header. This makes the variable's purpose more clear.

When a variable is declared in the initialization expression of a `for` loop, the scope of the variable is limited to the loop. This means you cannot access the variable in statements outside the loop. For example, the following program segment will not compile because the last `println` statement cannot access the variable `count`.

```
for (int count = 1; count <= 10; count++)
    System.out.println(count);
System.out.println("count is now " + count);    // ERROR!
```

Creating a User Controlled `for` Loop

Sometimes you want the user to determine the maximum value of the control variable in a `for` loop, and therefore determine the number of times the loop iterates. For example, look at the program in Code Listing 5-8. It is a modification of Code Listing 5-7. Instead of displaying the numbers 1 through 10 and their squares, this program allows the user to enter the maximum value to display.

Code Listing 5-8   (`UserSquares.java`)

```
 1   import java.util.Scanner;
 2
 3   /**
 4    * This program demonstrates a user-controlled
 5    * for loop.
 6    */
 7
 8   public class UserSquares
 9   {
```

```
10        public static void main(String[] args)
11        {
12           int number,     // Loop control variable
13               maxValue;  // Maximum value to display
14
15           // Create a Scanner object for keyboard input.
16           Scanner keyboard = new Scanner(System.in);
17
18           System.out.println("I will display a table of "
19                            + "numbers and their squares.");
20
21           // Get the maximum value to display.
22           System.out.print("How high should I go? ");
23           maxValue = keyboard.nextInt();
24
25           // Display the table.
26           System.out.println("Number    Number Squared");
27           System.out.println("-----------------------");
28
29           for (number = 1; number <= maxValue; number++)
30           {
31              System.out.println(number + "\t\t"
32                                + number * number);
33           }
34        }
35   }
```

Program Output with Example Input Shown in Bold

```
I will display a table of numbers and their squares.
How high should I go? 7 [Enter]
Number        Number Squared
------------------------------

1                 1
2                 4
3                 9
4                16
5                25
6                36
7                49
```

In lines 22 and 23, which are before the loop, this program asks the user to enter the highest value to display. This value is stored in the maxValue variable:

```
System.out.print("How high should I go? ");
maxValue = keyboard.nextInt();
```

In line 29, the for loop's test expression uses this value as the upper limit for the control variable:

```
for (number = 1; number <= maxValue; number++)
```

In this loop, the number variable takes on the values 1 through maxValue, and then the loop terminates.

Using Multiple Statements in the Initialization and Update Expressions

It is possible to execute more than one statement in the initialization expression and the update expression. When using multiple statements in either of these expressions, simply separate the statements with commas. For example, look at the loop in the following code, which has two statements in the initialization expression.

```
int x, y;
for (x = 1, y = 1; x <= 5; x++)
{
    System.out.println(x + " plus " + y
                        + " equals "
                        + (x + y));
}
```

This loop's initialization expression is:

```
x = 1, y = 1
```

This initializes two variables, x and y. The output produced by this loop is:

```
1 plus 1 equals 2
2 plus 1 equals 3
3 plus 1 equals 4
4 plus 1 equals 5
5 plus 1 equals 6
```

We can further modify the loop to execute two statements in the update expression. Here is an example:

```
int x, y;
for (x = 1, y = 1; x <= 5; x++, y++)
{
    System.out.println(x + " plus " + y
                        + " equals "
                        + (x + y));
}
```

The loop's update expression is:

```
x++, y++
```

This update expression increments both the x and y variables. The output produced by this loop is:

```
1 plus 1 equals 2
2 plus 2 equals 4
3 plus 3 equals 6
4 plus 4 equals 8
5 plus 5 equals 10
```

Connecting multiple statements with commas works well in the initialization and update expressions, but don't try to connect multiple boolean expressions this way in the test expression. If you wish to combine multiple boolean expressions in the test expression, you must use the && or || operators.

In the Spotlight:
Designing a Count-Controlled for Loop

Your friend Amanda just inherited a European sports car from her uncle. Amanda lives in the United States, and she is afraid she will get a speeding ticket because the car's speedometer indicates kilometers per hour. She has asked you to write a program that displays a table of speeds in kilometers per hour with their values converted to miles per hour. The formula for converting kilometers per hour (KPH) to miles per hour (MPH) is

MPH = KPH * 0.6214

The table that your program displays should show speeds from 60 kilometers per hour through 130 kilometers per hour, in increments of 10, along with their values converted to miles per hour. The table should look something like this:

KPH	MPH
60	37.3
70	43.5
80	49.7
.	
.	
.	
130	80.8

After thinking about this table of values, you decide that you will write the following code:

- A class named SpeedConverter that can perform the conversion from kilometers per hour to miles per hour.
- A program that creates an instance of the SpeedConverter class and uses that object to convert the sequence of kilometer per hour speeds to miles per hour.

The SpeedConverter class, which is shown in Code Listing 5-9, has only one method named getMPH. The method, which appears in lines 18 through 21, accepts a speed in kilometers per hour as an argument, and it returns that speed converted to miles per hour.

Code Listing 5-9   (SpeedConverter.java)

```
1   /**
2    * The SpeedConverter class converts speeds
3    * in KPH (kilometers per hour) to MPH (miles
4    * per hour).
5    */
6
7   public class SpeedConverter
8   {
9      // Factor to convert MPH to KPH
10     final double CONVERSION_FACTOR = 0.6214;
11
12     /**
13      * The getMPH method accepts a speed in
14      * KPH as an argument and returns that
15      * speed converted to MPH.
16      */
17
18     public double getMPH(double kph)
19     {
20        return kph * CONVERSION_FACTOR;
21     }
22  }
```

As previously mentioned, the program that displays the table of speeds creates an instance of the SpeedConverter class. In the program, you decide to write a for loop that uses a counter variable to hold the kilometer-per-hour speeds. The counter's starting value is 60 and its ending value is 130, and you need to add 10 to the counter variable after each iteration. Inside the loop you will call the SpeedConverter class's getMPH method, passing the counter variable as an argument. The method will return the speed converted to miles per hour. Code Listing 5-10 shows the code.

Code Listing 5-10   (SpeedTable.java)

```
1   /**
2    * This program displays a table of speeds in
3    * kph converted to mph.
4    */
5
6   public class SpeedTable
7   {
8      public static void main(String[] args)
9      {
10        // Constants
11        final int STARTING_KPH = 60; // Starting speed
12        final int MAX_KPH = 130;     // Maximum speed
13        final int INCREMENT = 10;    // Speed increment
14
```

```
15              // Variables
16              int kph;        // To hold the speed in kph
17              double mph;     // To hold the speed in mph
18
19              // Create an instance of the SpeedConverter class.
20              SpeedConverter converter = new SpeedConverter();
21
22              // Display the table headings.
23              System.out.println("KPH\t\tMPH");
24              System.out.println("----------------");
25
26              // Display the speeds.
27              for (kph = STARTING_KPH; kph <= MAX_KPH; kph += INCREMENT)
28              {
29                  // Get the mph.
30                  mph = converter.getMPH(kph);
31
32                  // Display the speeds in kph and mph.
33                  System.out.printf("%d\t\t%.1f\n", kph, mph);
34              }
35          }
36  }
```

Program Output

```
KPH             MPH
----------------
60              37.3
70              43.5
80              49.7
90              55.9
100             62.1
110             68.4
120             74.6
130             80.8
```

 Checkpoint

5.7 Name the three expressions that appear inside the parentheses in the for loop's header.

5.8 You want to write a for loop that displays "I love to program" 50 times. Assume that you will use a control variable named count.
   a. What initialization expression will you use?
   b. What test expression will you use?
   c. What update expression will you use?
   d. Write the loop.

5.9 What will the following program segments display?
   a. for (int count = 0; count < 6; count++)
        System.out.println(count + count);

b. ```
for (int value = -5; value < 5; value++)
    System.out.println(value);
```

c. ```
for (int x = 5; x <= 14; x += 3)
    System.out.println(x);
    System.out.println(x);
```

5.10 Write a for loop that displays your name 10 times.

5.11 Write a for loop that displays all of the odd numbers, 1 through 49.

5.12 Write a for loop that displays every fifth number, zero through 100.

5.6 Running Totals and Sentinel Values

CONCEPT: A running total is a sum of numbers that accumulates with each iteration of a loop. The variable used to keep the running total is called an accumulator. A sentinel is a value that signals when the end of a list of values has been reached.

Many programming tasks require you to calculate the total of a series of numbers. For example, suppose you are writing a program that calculates a business's total sales for a week. The program reads the sales for each day as input and calculates the total of those numbers.

Programs that calculate the total of a series of numbers typically use two elements:

- A loop that reads each number in the series.
- A variable that accumulates the total of the numbers as they are read.

The variable that is used to accumulate the total of the numbers is called an *accumulator*. It is often said that the loop keeps a *running total* because it accumulates the total as it reads each number in the series. Figure 5-10 shows the general logic of a loop that calculates a running total.

Figure 5-10 Logic for calculating a running total

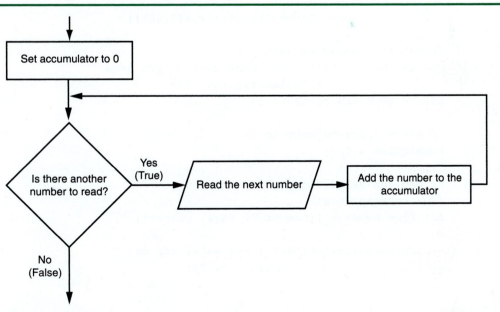

When the loop finishes, the accumulator will contain the total of the numbers that were read by the loop. Notice that the first step in the flowchart is to set the accumulator variable to 0. This is a critical step. Each time the loop reads a number, it adds it to the accumulator. If the accumulator starts with any value other than 0, it will not contain the correct total when the loop finishes.

Let's look at a program that calculates a running total. Code Listing 5-11 calculates a company's total sales over a period of time by taking daily sales figures as input and calculating a running total of them as they are gathered.

Code Listing 5-11   (TotalSales.java)

```java
 1   import java.util.Scanner;
 2   import java.text.DecimalFormat;
 3
 4   /**
 5    * This program calculates a running total.
 6    */
 7
 8   public class TotalSales
 9   {
10      public static void main(String[] args)
11      {
12         int days;          // The number of days
13         double sales;      // A day's sales figure
14         double totalSales; // Accumulator
15
16         // Create a Scanner object for keyboard input.
17         Scanner keyboard = new Scanner(System.in);
18
19         // Create a DecimalFormat object.
20         DecimalFormat dollar =
21                     new DecimalFormat("#,##0.00");
22
23         // Get the number of days.
24         System.out.print("For how many days do you have "
25                     + "sales figures? ");
26         days = keyboard.nextInt();
27
28         // Set the accumulator to 0.
29         totalSales = 0.0;
30
31         // Get the sales figures and calculate
32         // a running total.
33         for (int count = 1; count <= days; count++)
34         {
35            System.out.print("Enter the sales for day "
36                     + count + ": ");
```

```
37                sales = keyboard.nextDouble();
38                totalSales += sales;   // Add sales to total.
39             }
40
41          // Display the total sales.
42          System.out.println("The total sales are $"
43                              + dollar.format(totalSales));
44       }
45    }
```

Program Output with Example Input Shown in Bold

```
For how many days do you have sales figures? 5 [Enter]
Enter the sales for day 1: 687.59 [Enter]
Enter the sales for day 2: 563.22 [Enter]
Enter the sales for day 3: 896.35 [Enter]
Enter the sales for day 4: 743.29 [Enter]
Enter the sales for day 5: 926.72 [Enter]
The total sales are $3,817.17
```

Let's take a closer look at this program. In lines 24 through 26 the user is asked to enter the number of days that he or she has sales figures for. The number of days is read from the keyboard and assigned to the days variable. Next, in line 29, the totalSales variable is assigned 0.0.

In general programming terms, the totalSales variable is referred to as an accumulator. An *accumulator* is a variable initialized with a starting value, which is usually zero, and then accumulates a sum of numbers by having the numbers added to it. As you will see, it is critical that the accumulator is set to zero before values are added to it.

Next, the for loop that appears in lines 33 through 39 executes:

```
for (int count = 1; count <= days; count++)
{
    System.out.print("Enter the sales for day "
                     + count + ": ");
    sales = keyboard.nextDouble();
    totalSales += sales;   // Add sales to total.
}
```

The user enters the daily sales figures, which are assigned to the sales variable. The contents of sales is then added to the totalSales variable. Because totalSales was initially assigned 0.0, after the first iteration it will be set to the same value as sales. After each subsequent iteration, totalSales will be increased by the amount in sales. After the loop has finished, totalSales will contain the total of all the daily sales figures entered. Now it should be clear why we assigned 0.0 to totalSales before the loop executed. If totalSales started at any other value, the total would be incorrect.

Using a Sentinel Value

The program in Code Listing 5-11 requires the user to know in advance the number of days he or she has sales figures for. Sometimes the user has a list of input values that is very long and doesn't know the number of items there are. In other cases, the user might be entering values from several lists, and it is impractical to require that every item in every list be counted.

A technique that can be used in these situations is to ask the user to enter a sentinel value at the end of the list. A *sentinel value* is a special value that cannot be mistaken as a member of the list and signals that there are no more values to be entered. When the user enters the sentinel value, the loop terminates.

The program in Code Listing 5-12 shows an example. It calculates the total points earned by a soccer team over a series of games. It allows the user to enter the series of game points, then –1 to signal the end of the list.

Code Listing 5-12   (SoccerPoints.java)

```java
 1  import java.util.Scanner;
 2
 3  /**
 4   * This program calculates the total number of points a
 5   * soccer team has earned over a series of games. The user
 6   * enters a series of point values, then -1 when finished.
 7   */
 8
 9  public class SoccerPoints
10  {
11     public static void main(String[] args)
12     {
13        int points,          // Game points
14            totalPoints = 0;  // Accumulator
15
16        // Create a Scanner object for keyboard input.
17        Scanner keyboard = new Scanner(System.in);
18
19        // Display general instructions.
20        System.out.println("Enter the number of points your team");
21        System.out.println("has earned for each game this season.");
22        System.out.println("Enter -1 when finished.");
23        System.out.println();
24
25        // Get the first number of points.
26        System.out.print("Enter game points or -1 to end: ");
27        points = keyboard.nextInt();
28
29        // Accumulate the points until -1 is entered.
30        while (points != -1)
31        {
```

```
32            // Add points to totalPoints.
33            totalPoints += points;
34
35            // Get the next number of points.
36            System.out.print("Enter game points or -1 to end: ");
37            points = keyboard.nextInt();
38        }
39
40        // Display the total number of points.
41        System.out.println("The total points are " +
42                            totalPoints);
43    }
44 }
```

Program Output with Example Input Shown in Bold

```
Enter the number of points your team
has earned for each game this season.
Enter -1 when finished.

Enter game points or -1 to end: 7 [Enter]
Enter game points or -1 to end: 9 [Enter]
Enter game points or -1 to end: 4 [Enter]
Enter game points or -1 to end: 6 [Enter]
Enter game points or -1 to end: 8 [Enter]
Enter game points or -1 to end: -1 [Enter]
The total points are 34
```

The value –1 was chosen for the sentinel because it is not possible for a team to score negative points. Notice that this program performs a priming read to get the first value. This makes it possible for the loop to immediately terminate if the user enters –1 as the first value. Also note that the sentinel value is not included in the running total.

Checkpoint

5.13   Write a for loop that repeats seven times, asking the user to enter a number. The loop should also calculate the sum of the numbers entered.

5.14   In the following program segment, which variable is the loop control variable (also known as the counter variable) and which is the accumulator?

```
int a, x = 0, y = 0;
Scanner keyboard = new Scanner(System.in);
while (x < 10)
{
    System.out.print("Enter a number: ");
    a = keyboard.nextInt();
    y += a;
}
System.out.println("The sum is " + y);
```

5.15   Why should you be careful when choosing a sentinel value?

5.7 Nested Loops

CONCEPT: A loop that is inside another loop is called a nested loop.

Nested loops are necessary when a task performs a repetitive operation and that task itself must be repeated. A clock is a good example of something that works like a nested loop. The second hand, minute hand, and hour hand all spin around the face of the clock. Each time the hour hand increments, the minute hand has incremented 60 times. Each time the minute hand increments, the second hand has incremented 60 times.

The program in Code Listing 5-13 uses nested loops to simulate a clock.

Code Listing 5-13   (Clock.java)

```
1   /**
2    *  This program uses nested loops to simulate a clock.
3    */
4
5   public class Clock
6   {
7      public static void main(String[] args)
8      {
9         // Simulate the clock.
10        for (int hours = 1; hours <= 12; hours++)
11        {
12           for (int minutes = 0; minutes <= 59; minutes++)
13           {
14              for (int seconds = 0; seconds <= 59; seconds++)
15              {
16                 System.out.printf("%02d:%02d:%02d\n", hours, minutes, seconds);
17              }
18           }
19        }
20     }
21  }
```

Program Output

```
01:00:00
01:00:01
01:00:02
01:00:03
```

(The loop continues to count . . .)

```
12:59:57
12:59:58
12:59:59
```

The innermost loop will iterate 60 times for each single iteration of the middle loop. The middle loop will iterate 60 times for each single iteration of the outermost loop. When the outermost loop has iterated 12 times, the middle loop will have iterated 720 times and the innermost loop will have iterated 43,200 times.

The simulated clock example brings up a few points about nested loops:

- An inner loop goes through all of its iterations for each iteration of an outer loop.
- Inner loops complete their iterations before outer loops do.
- To get the total number of iterations of a nested loop, multiply the number of iterations of all the loops.

The program in Code Listing 5-14 is another test-averaging program. It asks the user for the number of students and the number of test scores per student. A nested inner loop asks for all the test scores for one student, iterating once for each test score. The outer loop iterates once for each student.

Code Listing 5-14   (**TestAverages2.java**)

```java
 1   import java.util.Scanner;
 2
 3   /**
 4    * This program demonstrates a user-controlled loop.
 5    */
 6
 7   public class TestAverages2
 8   {
 9      public static void main(String[] args)
10      {
11         int numStudents;    // Number of students
12         int numTests;       // Number of tests per student
13         double score;       // Test score
14         double total;       // Accumulator for test scores
15         double average;     // Average test score
16
17         // Create a Scanner object for keyboard input.
18         Scanner keyboard = new Scanner(System.in);
19
20         System.out.println("This program averages test scores.");
21
```

```
22          // Get the number of students.
23          System.out.print("How many students do you have? ");
24          numStudents = keyboard.nextInt();
25
26          // Get the number of test scores per student.
27          System.out.print("How many test scores per student? ");
28          numTests = keyboard.nextInt();
29
30          // Process all the students.
31          for (int student = 1; student <= numStudents; student++)
32          {
33             // Set the accumulator to zero.
34             total = 0.0;
35
36             // Get the test scores for a student.
37             for (int test = 1; test <= numTests; test++)
38             {
39                System.out.print("Enter score " + test
40                           + " for student " + student + ": ");
41                score = keyboard.nextDouble();
42                total += score;  // Add score to total.
43             }
44
45             // Calculate and display the average.
46             average = total / numTests;
47             System.out.println("The average score for student "
48                           + student + " is " + average);
49             System.out.println();
50          }
51       }
52    }
```

Program Output with Example Input Shown in Bold

```
This program averages test scores.
How many students do you have? 2 [Enter]
How many test scores per student? 3 [Enter]
Enter score 1 for student 1: 78 [Enter]
Enter score 2 for student 1: 86 [Enter]
Enter score 3 for student 1: 91 [Enter]
The average score for student 1 is 85.0

Enter score 1 for student 2: 97 [Enter]
Enter score 2 for student 2: 88 [Enter]
Enter score 3 for student 2: 91 [Enter]
The average score for student 2 is 92.0
```

In the Spotlight:

Using Nested Loops to Print Patterns

One interesting way to learn about nested loops is to use them to display patterns on the screen. Let's look at a simple example. Suppose we want to print asterisks on the screen in the following rectangular pattern:

```
* * * * * *

* * * * * *

* * * * * *

* * * * * *

* * * * * *

* * * * * *

* * * * * *

* * * * * *
```

If you think of this pattern as having rows and columns, you can see that it has eight rows, and each row has six columns. The following code can be used to display one row of asterisks:

```java
final int COLS = 6;
for (int col = 0; col < COLS; col++)
{
    System.out.print("*");
}
```

If we run this code in a program, it will produce the following output:

```
******
```

To complete the entire pattern, we need to execute this loop eight times. We can place the loop inside another loop that iterates eight times, as shown here:

```java
1    final int COLS = 6;
2    final int ROWS = 8;
3    for (int row = 0; row < ROWS; row++)
4    {
5        for (int col = 0; col < COLS; col++)
6        {
7            System.out.print("*");
8        }
9        System.out.println();
10   }
```

The outer loop iterates eight times. Each time it iterates, the inner loop iterates six times. (Notice that in line 9, after each row has been printed, we call the `System.out.println()` method. We have to do that to advance the screen cursor to the next line at the end of each row. Without that statement, all the asterisks will be printed in one long row on the screen.)

We could easily write a program that prompts the user for the number of rows and columns, as shown in Code Listing 5-15.

Code Listing 5-15   (RectangularPattern.java)

```java
 1  import java.util.Scanner;
 2
 3  /**
 4   *  This program displays a rectangular pattern
 5   *  of asterisks.
 6   */
 7
 8  public class RectangularPattern
 9  {
10     public static void main(String[] args)
11     {
12        int rows, cols;
13
14        // Create a Scanner object for keyboard input.
15        Scanner keyboard = new Scanner(System.in);
16
17        // Get the number of rows and columns.
18        System.out.print("How many rows? ");
19        rows = keyboard.nextInt();
20        System.out.print("How many columns? ");
21        cols = keyboard.nextInt();
22
23        for (int r = 0; r < rows; r++)
24        {
25           for (int c = 0; c < cols; c++)
26           {
27              System.out.print("*");
28           }
29           System.out.println();
30        }
31     }
32  }
```

Program Output

```
How many rows? 5 [Enter]
How many columns? 10 [Enter]
**********
**********
**********
**********
**********
```

Let's look at another example. Suppose you want to print asterisks in a pattern that looks like the following triangle:

```
*
**
***
****
*****
******
*******
********
```

Once again, think of the pattern as being arranged in rows and columns. The pattern has a total of eight rows. In the first row, there is one column. In the second row, there are two columns. In the third row, there are three columns. This continues to the eighth row, which has eight columns. Code Listing 5-16 shows the program that produces this pattern.

Code Listing 5-16   **(TrianglePattern.java)**

```java
 1   import java.util.Scanner;
 2
 3   /**
 4    *  This program displays a triangle pattern.
 5    */
 6
 7   public class TrianglePattern
 8   {
 9      public static void main(String[] args)
10      {
11         final int BASE_SIZE = 8;
12
13         for (int r = 0; r < BASE_SIZE; r++)
14         {
15            for (int c = 0; c < (r+1); c++)
16            {
17               System.out.print("*");
18            }
19            System.out.println();
20         }
21      }
22   }
```

Program Output

```
*
**
***
****
*****
******
*******
********
```

The outer loop (which begins in line 13) will iterate eight times. As the loop iterates, the variable r will be assigned the values 0 through 7.

For each iteration of the outer loop, the inner loop will iterate r+1 times. So,

- During the outer loop's 1st iteration, the variable r is assigned 0. The inner loop iterates one time, printing one asterisk.
- During the outer loop's 2nd iteration, the variable r is assigned 1. The inner loop iterates two times, printing two asterisks.
- During the outer loop's 3rd iteration, the variable r is assigned 2. The inner loop iterates three times, printing three asterisks.
- And so forth.

Let's look at another example. Suppose you want to display the following stairstep pattern:

The pattern has six rows. In general, we can describe each row as having some number of spaces followed by a # character. Here's a row-by-row description:

First row:	0 spaces followed by a # character.
Second row:	1 space followed by a # character.
Third row:	2 spaces followed by a # character.
Fourth row:	3 spaces followed by a # character.
Fifth row:	4 spaces followed by a # character.
Sixth row:	5 spaces followed by a # character.

To display this pattern, we can write code containing a pair of nested loops that work in the following manner:

- The outer loop will iterate six times. Each iteration will perform the following:
  - The inner loop will display the correct number of spaces, side-by-side.
  - Then, a # character will be displayed.

Code Listing 5-17 shows the Java code.

Code Listing 5-17   `(StairStepPattern.java)`

```java
 1  import java.util.Scanner;
 2
 3  /**
 4   *  This program displays a stairstep pattern.
 5   */
 6
 7  public class StairStepPattern
 8  {
 9      public static void main(String[] args)
10      {
11          final int NUM_STEPS = 6;
12
13          for (int r = 0; r < NUM_STEPS; r++)
14          {
15              for (int c = 0; c < r; c++)
16              {
17                  System.out.print(" ");
18              }
19              System.out.println("#");
20          }
21      }
22  }
```

Program Output

```
#
 #
  #
   #
    #
     #
```

The outer loop (which begins in line 13) will iterate six times. As the loop iterates, the variable r will be assigned the values 0 through 5.

For each iteration of the outer loop, the inner loop will iterate r times. So,

- During the outer loop's 1st iteration, the variable r is assigned 0. The inner loop will not execute at this time.
- During the outer loop's 2nd iteration, the variable r is assigned 1. The inner loop iterates one time, printing one space.
- During the outer loop's 3rd iteration, the variable r is assigned 2. The inner loop iterates two times, printing two spaces.
- And so forth.

5.8 The break and continue Statements

CONCEPT: The break statement causes a loop to terminate early. The continue statement causes a loop to stop its current iteration and begin the next one.

The break statement, which was used with the switch statement in Chapter 4, can also be placed inside a loop. When it is encountered, the loop stops and the program jumps to the statement immediately following the loop. Although it is perfectly acceptable to use the break statement in a switch statement, it is considered "taboo" to use it in a loop. This is because it bypasses the normal condition that is required to terminate the loop, and it makes code difficult to understand and debug. For this reason, you should avoid using the break statement in a loop when possible.

The continue statement causes the current iteration of a loop to immediately end. When continue is encountered, all the statements in the body of the loop that appear after it are ignored, and the loop prepares for the next iteration. In a while loop, this means the program jumps to the boolean expression at the top of the loop. As usual, if the expression is still true, the next iteration begins. In a do-while loop, the program jumps to the boolean expression at the bottom of the loop, which determines whether the next iteration will begin. In a for loop, continue causes the update expression to be executed, and then the test expression is evaluated.

The continue statement should also be avoided. Like the break statement, it bypasses the loop's logic and makes the code difficult to understand and debug.

5.9 Deciding Which Loop to Use

CONCEPT: Although most repetitive algorithms can be written with any of the three types of loops, each works best in different situations.

Each of Java's three loops is ideal to use in different situations. Here's a short summary of when each loop should be used.

- **The while loop.** The while loop is a pretest loop. It is ideal in situations where you do not want the loop to iterate if the condition is false from the beginning. It is also ideal if you want to use a sentinel value to terminate the loop.
- **The do-while loop.** The do-while loop is a posttest loop. It is ideal in situations where you always want the loop to iterate at least once.
- **The for loop.** The for loop is a pretest loop that has built-in expressions for initializing, testing, and updating. These expressions make it very convenient to use a loop control variable as a counter. The for loop is ideal in situations where the exact number of iterations is known.

5.10 Introduction to File Input and Output

CONCEPT: The Java API provides several classes that you can use for writing data to a file and reading data from a file. To write data to a file, you can use the `PrintWriter` class, and optionally, the `FileWriter` class. To read data from a file, you can use the `Scanner` class and the `File` class.

The programs you have written so far require you to reenter data each time the program runs. This is because the data stored in variables and objects in RAM disappear once the program stops running. To retain data between the times it runs, a program must have a way of saving the data.

Data may be saved in a file, which is usually stored on a computer's disk. Once the data is saved in a file, it will remain there after the program stops running. The data can then be retrieved and used at a later time. In general, there are three steps taken when a file is used by a program:

1. The file must be *opened*. When the file is opened, a connection is created between the file and the program.
2. Data is then written to the file or read from the file.
3. When the program is finished using the file, the file must be *closed*.

In this section we will discuss how to write Java programs that read data from files and write data to files. The terms *input file* and *output file* are commonly used. An *input file* is a file that a program reads data from. It is called an input file because the data stored in it serves as input to the program. An *output file* is a file that a program writes data to. It is called an output file because the program stores output in the file.

In general, there are two types of files: text and binary. A *text file* contains plain text and may be opened in a text editor such as Notepad. A *binary file* contains unformatted binary data, and you cannot view its contents with a text editor. In this chapter we will discuss how to work with text files. Binary files are discussed in Chapter 10.

In this section we will discuss a number of classes from the Java API that you will use to work with files. To use these classes, you will place the following import statement near the top of your program:

```
import java.io.*;
```

Using the PrintWriter Class to Write Data to a File

To write data to a file you will create an instance of the `PrintWriter` class. The `PrintWriter` class allows you to open a file for writing. It also allows you to write data to the file using the same `print` and `println` methods that you have been using to display data on the screen. You pass the name of the file that you wish to open, as a string, to the `PrintWriter` class's constructor. For example, the following statement creates a `PrintWriter` object and passes the file name *StudentData.txt* to the constructor.

```
PrintWriter outputFile = new PrintWriter("StudentData.txt");
```

This statement will create an empty file named *StudentData.txt* and establish a connection between it and the `PrintWriter` object referenced by `outputFile`. The file will be created in the current directory or folder.

You may also pass a reference to a `String` object as an argument to the `PrintWriter` constructor. For example, in the following code the user specifies the name of the file.

```
Scanner keyboard = new Scanner(System.in);
System.out.print("Enter the filename: ");
String filename = keyboard.nextLine();
PrintWriter outputFile = new PrintWriter(filename);
```

 WARNING! If the file that you are opening with the `PrintWriter` object already exists, it will be erased and an empty file by the same name will be created.

Once you have created an instance of the `PrintWriter` class and opened a file, you can write data to the file using the `print` and `println` methods. You already know how to use `print` and `println` with `System.out` to display data on the screen. They are used the same way with a `PrintWriter` object to write data to a file. For example, assuming that `outputFile` references a `PrintWriter` object, the following statement writes the string `"Jim"` to the file.

```
outputFile.println("Jim");
```

When the program is finished writing data to the file, it must close the file. To close the file, use the `PrintWriter` class's `close` method. Here is an example of the method's use:

```
outputFile.close();
```

Your application should always close files when finished with them. This is because the system creates one or more buffers when a file is opened. A *buffer* is a small "holding section" of memory. When a program writes data to a file, that data is first written to the buffer. When the buffer is filled, all the information stored there is written to the file. This technique increases the system's performance because writing data to memory is faster than writing it to a disk. The `close` method writes any unsaved data remaining in the file buffer.

Once a file is closed, the connection between it and the `PrintWriter` object is removed. To perform further operations on the file, it must be opened again.

More About the `PrintWriter` Class's `println` Method

The `PrintWriter` class's `println` method writes a line of data to a file. For example, assume an application creates a file and writes three students' first names and their test scores to the file with the following code.

```
PrintWriter outputFile = new PrintWriter("StudentData.txt");
outputFile.println("Jim");
outputFile.println(95);
outputFile.println("Karen");
outputFile.println(98);
outputFile.println("Bob");
outputFile.println(82);
outputFile.close();
```

The `println` method writes data to the file and then writes a newline character immediately after the data. You can visualize the data written to the file in the following manner:

Jim*<newline>*95*<newline>*Karen*<newline>*98*<newline>*Bob*<newline>*82*<newline>*

The newline characters are represented here as *<newline>*. You do not actually see the newline characters, but when the file is opened in a text editor such as Notepad, its contents will appear as shown in Figure 5-11. As you can see from the figure, each newline character causes the data that follows it to be displayed on a new line.

Figure 5-11   File contents displayed in Notepad

In addition to separating the contents of a file into lines, the newline character also serves as a delimiter. A *delimiter* is an item that separates other items. When you write data to a file using the `println` method, newline characters will separate the individual items of data. Later you will see that the individual items of data in a file must be separated for them to be read from the file.

The `PrintWriter` Class's `print` Method

The `print` method is used to write an item of data to a file without writing the newline character. For example, look at the following code:

```
String name = "Jeffrey Smith";
String phone = "554-7864";
int idNumber = 47895;
PrintWriter outputFile = new PrintWriter("PersonalData.txt");
outputFile.print(name + " ");
outputFile.print(phone + " ");
outputFile.println(idNumber);
outputFile.close();
```

This code uses the `print` method to write the contents of the `name` object to the file, followed by a space (`" "`). Then it uses the `print` method to write the contents of the `phone` object to the file, followed by a space. Then it uses the `println` method to write the contents of the `idNumber` variable, followed by a newline character. Figure 5-12 shows the contents of the file displayed in Notepad.

Figure 5-12 Contents of file displayed in Notepad

Adding a `throws` Clause to the Method Header

When an unexpected event occurs in a Java program, it is said that the program throws an exception. For now, you can think of an *exception* as a signal indicating that the program cannot continue until the unexpected event has been dealt with. For example, suppose you create a `PrintWriter` object and pass the name of a file to its constructor. The `PrintWriter` object attempts to create the file, but unexpectedly, the disk is full and the file cannot be created. Obviously the program cannot continue until this situation has been dealt with, so an exception is thrown, which causes the program to suspend normal execution.

When an exception is thrown, the method that is executing must either deal with the exception or throw it again. If the `main` method throws an exception, the program halts and an error message is displayed. Because `PrintWriter` objects are capable of throwing exceptions, we must either write code that deals with the possible exceptions or allow our methods to rethrow the exceptions when they occur. In Chapter 10 you will learn all about exceptions and how to respond to them, but for now, we will simply allow our methods to rethrow any exceptions that might occur.

To allow a method to rethrow an exception that has not been dealt with, you simply write a `throws` clause in the method header. The `throws` clause must indicate the type of exception that might be thrown. Here is an example:

```
public static void main(String[] args) throws IOException
```

This header indicates that the `main` method is capable of throwing an exception of the `IOException` type. This is the type of exception that `PrintWriter` objects are capable of throwing. So, any method that uses `PrintWriter` objects and does not respond to their exceptions must have this `throws` clause listed in its header.

In addition, any method that calls a method that uses a `PrintWriter` object should have a `throws IOException` clause in its header. For example, suppose the `main` method does not perform any file operations, but calls a method named `buildFile` that opens a file and writes data to it. Both the `buildFile` and `main` methods should have a `throws IOException` clause in their headers. Otherwise a compiler error will occur.

An Example Program

Let's look at an example program that writes data to a file. The program in Code Listing 5-18 writes the names of your friends to a file.

Code Listing 5-18   `(FileWriteDemo.java)`

```java
 1  import java.util.Scanner;    // Needed for Scanner
 2  import java.io.*;            // Needed for PrintWriter and IOException
 3
 4  /**
 5   *  This program writes data to a file.
 6   */
 7
 8  public class FileWriteDemo
 9  {
10     public static void main(String[] args) throws IOException
11     {
12        String filename;       // File name
13        String friendName;     // Friend's name
14        int numFriends;        // Number of friends
15
16        // Create a Scanner object for keyboard input.
17        Scanner keyboard = new Scanner(System.in);
18
19        // Get the number of friends.
20        System.out.print("How many friends do you have? ");
21        numFriends = keyboard.nextInt();
22
23        // Consume the remaining newline character.
24        keyboard.nextLine();
25
26        // Get the filename.
27        System.out.print("Enter the filename: ");
28        filename = keyboard.nextLine();
29
30        // Open the file.
31        PrintWriter outputFile = new PrintWriter(filename);
32
33        // Get data and write it to the file.
34        for (int i = 1; i <= numFriends; i++)
35        {
36           // Get the name of a friend.
37           System.out.print("Enter the name of friend "+
38                            "number " + i + ": ");
39           friendName = keyboard.nextLine();
40
41           // Write the name to the file.
42           outputFile.println(friendName);
43        }
44
45        // Close the file.
46        outputFile.close();
```

```
47              System.out.println("Data written to the file.");
48      }
49  }
```

Program Output with Example Input Shown in Bold

```
How many friends do you have? 5 [Enter]
Enter the filename: MyFriends.txt [Enter]
Enter the name of friend number 1: Joe [Enter]
Enter the name of friend number 2: Rose [Enter]
Enter the name of friend number 3: Greg [Enter]
Enter the name of friend number 4: Kirk [Enter]
Enter the name of friend number 5: Renee [Enter]
Data written to the file.
```

The import statement in line 2 is necessary because this program uses the PrintWriter class and because the main method header, in line 10, has a throws IOException clause. We need this clause in the main method header because objects of the PrintWriter class can potentially throw an IOException.

This program asks the user to enter the number of friends he or she has (in lines 20 through 21), then a name for the file that will be created (in lines 27 and 28). The filename variable references the name of the file, and is used in the following statement, in line 31:

```
PrintWriter outputFile = new PrintWriter(filename);
```

This statement opens the file and creates a PrintWriter object that can be used to write data to the file. The for loop in lines 34 through 43 performs an iteration for each friend that the user has, each time asking for the name of a friend. The user's input is referenced by the friendName variable. Once the name is entered, it is written to the file with the following statement, which appears in line 42:

```
outputFile.println(friendName);
```

After the loop finishes, the file is closed in line 46. After the program is executed with the input shown in the example run, the file *MyFriends.txt* will be created. If we open the file in Notepad, we will see its contents as shown in Figure 5-13.

Figure 5-13 Contents of the file displayed in Notepad

Review

Before moving on, let's review the basic steps necessary when writing a program that writes data to a file:

1. You need the `import java.io.*;` statement in the top section of your program.
2. Because we have not yet learned how to respond to exceptions, any method that uses a `PrintWriter` object must have a `throws IOException` clause in its header.
3. You create a `PrintWriter` object and pass the name of the file as a string to the constructor.
4. You use the `PrintWriter` class's `print` and `println` methods to write data to the file.
5. When finished writing to the file, you use the `PrintWriter` class's `close` method to close the file.

Appending Data to a File

When you pass the name of a file to the `PrintWriter` constructor and the file already exists, it will be erased and a new empty file with the same name will be created. Sometimes, however, you want to preserve an existing file and append new data to its current contents. Appending to a file means writing new data to the end of the data that already exists in the file.

To append data to an existing file, you first create an instance of the `FileWriter` class. You pass two arguments to the `FileWriter` constructor: a string containing the name of the file and the `boolean` value `true`. Here is an example:

```
FileWriter fwriter = new FileWriter("MyFriends.txt", true);
```

This statement creates a `FileWriter` object and opens the file *MyFriends.txt* for writing. Any data written to the file will be appended to the file's existing contents. (If the file does not exist, it will be created.)

You still need to create a `PrintWriter` object so you can use the `print` and `println` methods to write data to the file. When you create the `PrintWriter` object, you pass a reference to the `FileWriter` object as an argument to the `PrintWriter` constructor. For example, look at the following code:

```
FileWriter fwriter = new FileWriter("MyFriends.txt", true);
PrintWriter outputFile = new PrintWriter(fwriter);
```

This creates a `PrintWriter` object that can be used to write data to the file *MyFriends.txt*. Any data written to the file will be appended to the file's existing contents. For example, assume the file *MyFriends.txt* exists and contains the following data:

```
Joe
Rose
Greg
Kirk
Renee
```

The following code opens the file and appends additional data to its existing contents:

```
FileWriter fwriter = new FileWriter("MyFriends.txt", true);
PrintWriter outputFile = new PrintWriter(fwriter);
```

```
outputFile.println("Bill");
outputFile.println("Steven");
outputFile.println("Sharon");
outputFile.close();
```

After this code executes, the *MyFriends.txt* file will contain the following data:

```
Joe
Rose
Greg
Kirk
Renee
Bill
Steven
Sharon
```

NOTE: The `FileWriter` class also throws an `IOException` if the file cannot be opened for any reason.

Specifying the File Location

When you open a file you may specify its path along with its file name. On a Windows computer, paths contain backslash characters. Remember that when a single backslash character appears in a string literal, it marks the beginning of an escape sequence such as `"\n"`. Two backslash characters in a string literal represent a single backslash. So, when you provide a path in a string literal and the path contains backslash characters, you must use two backslash characters in the place of each single backslash character.

For example, the path `"E:\\Names.txt"` specifies that *Names.txt* is in the root folder of drive E:, and the path `"C:\\MyData\\Data.txt"` specifies that *Data.txt* is in the `\MyData` folder on drive C:. In the following statement, the file *Pricelist.txt* is created in the root folder of drive A:.

```
PrintWriter outputFile = new PrintWriter("A:\\PriceList.txt");
```

You only need to use double backslashes if the file's path is in a string literal. If your program asks the user to enter a path into a `String` object, which is then passed to the `PrintWriter` or `FileWriter` constructor, the user does not have to enter double backslashes.

TIP: Java allows you to substitute forward slashes for backslashes in a Windows path. For example, the path `"C:\\MyData\\Data.txt"` could be written as `"C:/MyData/Data.txt"`. This eliminates the need to use double backslashes.

On a UNIX or Linux computer, you can provide a path without any modifications. Here is an example:

```
PrintWriter outputFile = new PrintWriter("/home/rharrison/names.txt");
```

Reading Data from a File

In Chapter 2 you learned how to use the Scanner class to read input from the keyboard. To read keyboard input, recall that we create a Scanner object, passing System.in to the Scanner class constructor. Here is an example:

```
Scanner keyboard = new Scanner(System.in);
```

Recall that the System.in object represents the keyboard. Passing System.in as an argument to the Scanner constructor specifies that the keyboard is the Scanner object's source of input.

You can also use the Scanner class to read input from a file. Instead of passing System.in to the Scanner class constructor, you pass a reference to a File object. Here is an example:

```
File myFile = new File("Customers.txt");
Scanner inputFile = new Scanner(myFile);
```

The first statement creates an instance of the File class. The File class is in the Java API and is used to represent a file. Notice that we have passed the string "Customers.txt" to the constructor. This creates a File object that represents the file *Customers.txt*. In the second statement we pass a reference to this File object as an argument to the Scanner class constructor. This creates a Scanner object that uses the file *Customers.txt* as its source of input. You can then use the same Scanner class methods that you learned about in Chapter 2 to read items from the file. (See Table 2-17 for a list of commonly used methods.) When you are finished reading from the file, you use the Scanner class's close method to close the file. For example, assuming the variable inputFile references a Scanner object, the following statement closes the file that is the object's source of input:

```
inputFile.close();
```

Reading Lines from a File with the nextLine Method

The Scanner class's nextLine method reads a line of input and returns the line as a String. The program in Code Listing 5-19 demonstrates how the nextLine method can be used to read a line from a file. This program asks the user to enter a file name. It then displays the first line in the file on the screen.

Code Listing 5-19   (ReadFirstLine.java)

```java
 1  import java.util.Scanner;    // Needed for Scanner
 2  import java.io.*;            // Needed for File and IOException
 3
 4  /**
 5   *  This program reads the first line from a file.
 6   */
 7
 8  public class ReadFirstLine
 9  {
10     public static void main(String[] args) throws IOException
11     {
12        // Create a Scanner object for keyboard input.
```

```
13              Scanner keyboard = new Scanner(System.in);
14
15              // Get the file name.
16              System.out.print("Enter the name of a file: ");
17              String filename = keyboard.nextLine();
18
19              // Open the file.
20              File file = new File(filename);
21              Scanner inputFile = new Scanner(file);
22
23              // Read the first line from the file.
24              String line = inputFile.nextLine();
25
26              // Display the line.
27              System.out.println("The first line in the file is:");
28              System.out.println(line);
29
30              // Close the file.
31              inputFile.close();
32      }
33  }
```

Program Output with Example Input Shown in Bold

Enter the name of a file: **MyFriends.txt [Enter]**
The first line in the file is:
Joe

This program gets the name of a file from the user in line 17. A `File` object is created in line 20 to represent the file, and a `Scanner` object is created in line 21 to read data from the file. Line 24 reads a line from the file. After this statement executes, the `line` variable references a `String` object holding the line that was read from the file. The line is displayed on the screen in line 28, and the file is closed in line 31.

Notice that this program creates two separate `Scanner` objects. The `Scanner` object created in line 13 reads data from the keyboard, and the `Scanner` object created in line 21 reads data from a file.

When a file is opened for reading, a special value known as a *read position* is internally maintained for that file. A file's read position marks the location of the next item that will be read from the file. When a file is opened, its read position is set to the first item in the file. When the item is read, the read position is advanced to the next item in the file. As subsequent items are read, the internal read position advances through the file. For example, consider the file *Quotation.txt*, shown in Figure 5-14. As you can see from the figure, the file has three lines.

Figure 5-14   File with three lines

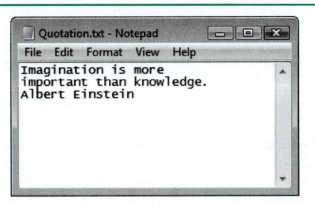

You can visualize that the data is stored in the file in the following manner:

```
Imagination is more<newline>important than knowledge<newline>
Albert Einstein<newline>
```

Suppose a program opens the file with the following code.

```
File file = new File("Quotation.txt");
Scanner inputFile = new Scanner(file);
```

When this code opens the file, its read position is at the beginning of the first line, as illustrated in Figure 5-15.

Figure 5-15   Initial read position

Read position ⟶ **Imagination is more**
important than knowledge.
Albert Einstein

Now, suppose the program uses the following statement to read a line from the file:

```
String str = inputFile.nextLine();
```

This statement will read a line from the file, beginning at the current read position. After the statement executes, the object referenced by `str` will contain the string "Imagination is more". The file's read position will be advanced to the next line, as illustrated in Figure 5-16.

Figure 5-16   Read position after first line is read

Imagination is more
Read position ⟶ **important than knowledge.**
Albert Einstein

If the `nextLine` method is called again, the second line will be read from the file and the file's read position will be advanced to the third line. After all the lines have been read, the read position will be at the end of the file.

> **NOTE:** The string returned from the `nextLine` method will not contain the newline character.

Adding a `throws` Clause to the Method Header

When you pass a `File` object reference to the `Scanner` class constructor, the constructor will throw an exception of the `IOException` type if the specified file is not found. So, you will need to write a `throws IOException` clause in the header of any method that passes a `File` object reference to the `Scanner` class constructor.

Detecting the End of a File

Quite often a program must read the contents of a file without knowing the number of items stored in the file. For example, the *MyFriends.txt* file created by the program in Code Listing 5-18 can have any number of names stored in it. This is because the program asks the user for the number of friends that he or she has. If the user enters 5 for the number of friends, the program creates a file with five names in it. If the user enters 100, the program creates a file with 100 names in it.

The `Scanner` class has a method named `hasNext` that can be used to determine whether the file has more data that can be read. You call the `hasNext` method before you call any other methods to read from the file. If there is more data that can be read from the file, the `hasNext` method returns `true`. If the end of the file has been reached and there is no more data to read, the `hasNext` method returns `false`.

Code Listing 5-20 shows an example. The program reads the file containing the names of your friends, which was created by the program in Code Listing 5-18.

Code Listing 5-20   (FileReadDemo.java)

```
 1  import java.util.Scanner;    // Needed for Scanner
 2  import java.io.*;            // Needed for File and IOException
 3
 4  /**
 5   *  This program reads data from a file.
 6   */
 7
 8  public class FileReadDemo
 9  {
10     public static void main(String[] args) throws IOException
11     {
12        // Create a Scanner object for keyboard input.
13        Scanner keyboard = new Scanner(System.in);
14
```

```
15           // Get the filename.
16           System.out.print("Enter the filename: ");
17           String filename = keyboard.nextLine();
18
19           // Open the file.
20           File file = new File(filename);
21           Scanner inputFile = new Scanner(file);
22
23           // Read lines from the file until no more are left.
24           while (inputFile.hasNext())
25           {
26              // Read the next name.
27              String friendName = inputFile.nextLine();
28
29              // Display the last name read.
30              System.out.println(friendName);
31           }
32
33           // Close the file.
34           inputFile.close();
35        }
36  }
```

Program Output with Example Input Shown in Bold

```
Enter the filename: MyFriends.txt [Enter]
Joe
Rose
Greg
Kirk
Renee
```

The file is opened and a Scanner object to read it is created in line 21. The loop in lines 24 through 31 reads all of the lines from the file and displays them. In line 24 the loop calls the Scanner object's hasNext method. If the method returns true, then the file has more data to read. In that case, the next line is read from the file in line 27 and is displayed in line 30. The loop repeats until the hasNext method returns false in line 24. Figure 5-17 shows the logic of reading a file until the end is reached.

Figure 5-17 Logic of reading a file until the end is reached

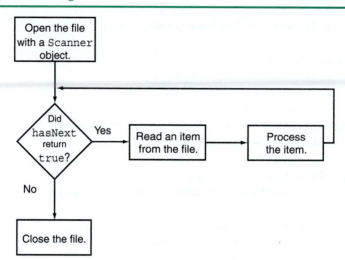

Reading Primitive Values from a File

Recall from Chapter 2 that the Scanner class provides methods for reading primitive values. These methods are named nextByte, nextDouble, nextFloat, nextInt, nextLong, and nextShort. Table 2-18 gives more information on each of these methods, which can be used to read primitive values from a file. The FileSum class in Code Listing 5-21 demonstrates how the nextDouble method can be used to read floating-point values from a file.

Code Listing 5-21 (FileSum.java)

```java
1   import java.util.Scanner;     // Needed for Scanner
2   import java.io.*;             // Needed for File and IOException
3
4   /**
5    * This class reads a series of numbers from a file and
6    * accumulates their sum.
7    */
8
9   public class FileSum
10  {
11     private double sum;    // Accumulator
12
13     /**
14      * The constructor accepts a file name as its argument.
15      * The file is opened, the numbers read from it, and
16      * their sum is stored in the sum field.
17      */
18
19     public FileSum(String filename) throws IOException
20     {
```

```
21          String str;  // To hold a line read from the file
22
23          // Create the necessary objects for file input.
24          File file = new File(filename);
25          Scanner inputFile = new Scanner(file);
26
27          // Initialize the accumulator.
28          sum = 0.0;
29
30          // Read all of the values from the file and
31          // calculate their total.
32          while (inputFile.hasNext())
33          {
34             // Read a value from the file.
35             double number = inputFile.nextDouble();
36
37             // Add the number to sum.
38             sum = sum + number;
39          }
40
41          // Close the file.
42          inputFile.close();
43       }
44
45       /**
46        * The getSum method returns the value in the sum field.
47        */
48
49       public double getSum()
50       {
51          return sum;
52       }
53    }
```

Program Output

```
The sum of the numbers in Numbers.txt is 41.4
```

The purpose of the FileSum class is to read the contents of a file that contains a series of numbers. The constructor, which begins at line 19, accepts a file name as its argument. The file is opened in line 25. The loop in lines 32 through 39 processes all of the numbers in the file. Line 35 reads a double and assigns it to the number variable. Line 38 adds number to the sum field. When this loop finishes, the sum field will contain the total of all the numbers read from the file. The getSum method, in lines 49 through 52, returns the value stored in the sum field.

To test this class, suppose the file *Numbers.txt* exists with the contents shown in Figure 5-18. The program in Code Listing 5-22 creates a FileSum object, passing the file's name, "Numbers.txt", to the constructor. The getSum method is then called to get the sum of the numbers.

Figure 5-18 Contents of `Numbers.txt`

```
Numbers.txt - Notepad
File  Edit  Format  View  Help
8.7
7.9
3.0
9.2
12.6
```

Code Listing 5-22 (`FileSumDemo.java`)

```java
 1  import java.io.*;  // Required for IOException
 2
 3  /**
 4   * This program demonstrates the FileSum class.
 5   */
 6
 7  public class FileSumDemo
 8  {
 9     public static void main(String[] args) throws IOException
10     {
11        // Create an instance of the FileSum class.
12        FileSum fs = new FileSum("Numbers.txt");
13
14        // Display the sum of the values in Numbers.txt.
15        System.out.println("The sum of the numbers in "+
16                           "Numbers.txt is "+
17                           fs.getSum());
18     }
19  }
```

Program Output

```
The sum of the numbers in Numbers.txt is 41.4
```

Review

Let's quickly review the steps necessary when writing a program that reads data from a file:

1. You will need the `import java.util.Scanner;` statement in the top section of your program, so you can use the `Scanner` class. You will also need the `import java.io.*;` statement in the top section of your program. This is required by the `File` class and the `IOException class`.

2. Because we have not yet learned how to respond to exceptions, any method that uses a `Scanner` object to open a file must have a `throws IOException` clause in its header.
3. You create a `File` object and pass the name of the file as a string to the constructor.
4. You create a `Scanner` object and pass a reference to the `File` object as an argument to the constructor.
5. You use the `Scanner` class's `nextLine` method to read a line from the file. The method returns the line of data as a string. To read primitive values, use methods such as `nextInt`, `nextDouble`, and so on.
6. Call the `Scanner` class's `hasNext` method to determine whether there is more data to read from the file. If the method returns `true`, then there is more data to read. If the method returns `false`, you have reached the end of the file.
7. When finished writing to the file, you use the `Scanner` class's `close` method to close the file.

Checking for a File's Existence

It's usually a good idea to make sure that a file exists before you try to open it for input. If you attempt to open a file for input and the file does not exist, the program will throw an exception and halt. For example, the program you saw in Code Listing 5-20 will throw an exception at line 21 if the file being opened does not exist. Here is an example of the error message that will be displayed when this happens:

```
Exception in thread "main" java.io.FileNotFoundException: MyFriends.txt (The
system cannot find the file specified)
    at java.io.FileInputStream.open(Native Method)
    at java.io.FileInputStream.<init>(FileInputStream.java:106)
    at java.util.Scanner.<init>(Scanner.java:636)
    at FileReadDemo.main(FileReadDemo.java:21)
```

Rather than allowing the exception to be thrown and permitting this cryptic error message to be displayed, your program can check for the file's existence before it attempts to open the file. If the file does not exist, the program can display a more user-friendly error message and gracefully shut down.

After you create a `File` object representing the file that you want to open, you can use the `File` class's `exists` method to determine whether the file exists. The method returns `true` if the file exists, or `false` if the file does not exist. Code Listing 5-23 shows how to use the method. This is a modification of the *FileReadDemo* program in Code Listing 5-20. This version of the program checks for the existence of the file before it attempts to open it.

Code Listing 5-23   **(FileReadDemo2.java)**

```java
1   import java.util.Scanner;    // Needed for Scanner
2   import java.io.*;            // Needed for File and IOException
3
4   /**
5    *  This program reads data from a file.
6    */
7
```

```
 8  public class FileReadDemo2
 9  {
10     public static void main(String[] args) throws IOException
11     {
12        // Create a Scanner object for keyboard input.
13        Scanner keyboard = new Scanner(System.in);
14
15        // Get the filename.
16        System.out.print("Enter the filename: ");
17        String filename = keyboard.nextLine();
18
19        // Make sure the file exists.
20        File file = new File(filename);
21        if (!file.exists())
22        {
23           // Display an error message.
24           System.out.println("The file " + filename +
25                                  " does not exist.");
26
27           // Exit the program.
28           System.exit(0);
29        }
30
31        // Open the file.
32        Scanner inputFile = new Scanner(file);
33
34        // Read lines from the file until no more are left.
35        while (inputFile.hasNext())
36        {
37           // Read the next name.
38           String friendName = inputFile.nextLine();
39
40           // Display the last name read.
41           System.out.println(friendName);
42        }
43
44        // Close the file.
45        inputFile.close();
46     }
47  }
```

Program Output (Assuming *badfile.txt* Does Not Exist)

```
Enter the filename: badfile.txt [Enter]
The file badfile.txt does not exist.
```

In line 20 the program creates a `File` object to represent the file. In line 21, the `if` statement calls the `file.exists()` method. Notice the use of the `!` operator. If the method returns `false`, indicating that the file does not exist, the code in lines 23 through 28 executes. The statement in lines 24 and 25 displays an error message, and line 28 calls the `System.exit(0)` method, which shuts the program down.

The previous example shows you how to make sure that a file exists before trying to open it for input. But, when you are opening a file for output, sometimes you want to make sure the file does *not* exist. When you use a `PrintWriter` object to open a file, the file will be erased if it already exists. If you do not want to erase the existing file, you have to check for its existence before creating the `PrintWriter` object. Code Listing 5-24 shows you how to use the `File` class's `exists` method in this type of situation. This is a modification of the program you saw in Code Listing 5-18.

Code Listing 5-24   (FileWriteDemo2.java)

```java
 1  import java.io.*;          // Needed for File and IOException
 2  import java.util.Scanner; // Needed for Scanner
 3
 4  /**
 5   *  This program writes data to a file. It makes sure the
 6   *  specified file does not exist before opening it.
 7   */
 8
 9  public class FileWriteDemo2
10  {
11     public static void main(String[] args) throws IOException
12     {
13        String filename;       // File name
14        String friendName;     // Friend's name
15        int numFriends;        // Number of friends
16
17        // Create a Scanner object for keyboard input.
18        Scanner keyboard = new Scanner(System.in);
19
20        // Get the number of friends.
21        System.out.print("How many friends do you have? ");
22        numFriends = keyboard.nextInt();
23
24        // Consume the remaining newline character.
25        keyboard.nextLine();
26
27        // Get the filename.
28        System.out.print("Enter the filename: ");
29        filename = keyboard.nextLine();
30
31        // Make sure the file does not exist.
32        File file = new File(filename);
```

```
33          if (file.exists())
34          {
35             // Display an error message.
36             System.out.println("The file " + filename +
37                                " already exists.");
38
39             // Exit the program.
40             System.exit(0);
41          }
42
43          // Open the file.
44          PrintWriter outputFile = new PrintWriter(file);
45
46          // Get data and write it to the file.
47          for (int i = 1; i <= numFriends; i++)
48          {
49             // Get the name of a friend.
50             System.out.print("Enter the name of friend " +
51                              "number " + i + ": ");
52             friendName = keyboard.nextLine();
53
54             // Write the name to the file.
55             outputFile.println(friendName);
56          }
57
58          // Close the file.
59          outputFile.close();
60          System.out.println("Data written to the file.");
61       }
62    }
```

Program Output with Example Input Shown in Bold

```
How many friends do you have? 2 [Enter]
Enter the filename: MyFriends.txt [Enter]
The file MyFriends.txt already exists.
```

Line 32 creates a File object representing the file. The if statement in line 33 calls the file.exists() method. If the method returns true, then the file exists. In this case the code in lines 35 through 40 executes. This code displays an error message and shuts the program down. If the file does not exist, the rest of the program executes.

Notice that in line 44 we pass a reference to the File object to the PrintWriter constructor. In previous programs that created an instance PrintWriter, we passed a file name to the constructor. If you have a reference to a File object that represents the file you wish to open, as we do in this program, you have the option of passing it to the PrintWriter constructor.

Checkpoint

5.16   What is the difference between an input file and an output file?

5.17   What `import` statement will you need in a program that performs file operations?

5.18   What class do you use to write data to a file?

5.19   Write code that does the following: Opens a file named *MyName.txt*, writes your first name to the file, and then closes the file.

5.20   What classes do you use to read data from a file?

5.21   Write code that does the following: Opens a file named *MyName.txt*, reads the first line from the file and displays it, and then closes the file.

5.22   You are opening an existing file with for output. How do you open the file without erasing it and at the same time make sure that new data written to the file is appended to the end of the file's existing data?

5.23   What clause must you write in the header of a method that performs a file operation?

See the Amortization Class Case Study for an in-depth example using this chapter's topics. The case study is available on this book's online resource page at www.pearsonhighered .com/gaddis.

5.11 Common Errors to Avoid

The following list describes several errors that are commonly made when learning this chapter's topics.

- **Using the increment or decrement operator in the wrong mode.** When the increment or decrement operator is placed in front of (to the left of) its operand, it is used in prefix mode. When either of these operators are placed behind (to the right of) their operand, they are used in postfix mode.
- **Forgetting to enclose the `boolean` expression in a `while` loop or a `do-while` loop inside parentheses.**
- **Placing a semicolon at the end of a `while` or `for` loop's header.** When you write a semicolon at the end of a `while` or `for` loop's header, Java assumes that the conditionally executed statement is a `null` or empty statement. This usually results in an infinite loop.
- **Forgetting to write the semicolon at the end of the `do-while` loop.** The do-while loop must be terminated with a semicolon.
- **Forgetting to enclose multiple statements in the body of a loop in braces.** Normally a loop conditionally executes only one statement. To conditionally execute more than one statement, you must place the statements in braces.
- **Using commas instead of semicolons to separate the initialization, test, and update expressions in a `for` loop.**
- **Forgetting to write code in the body of a `while` or `do-while` loop that modifies the loop control variable.** If a `while` or do-while loop's `boolean` expression never becomes `false`, the loop will repeat indefinitely. You must have code in the body of the loop that modifies the loop control variable so that the `boolean` expression will at some point become `false`.

- **Using a sentinel value that can also be a valid data value.** Remember, a sentinel is a special value that cannot be mistaken as a member of a list of data items and signals that there are no more data items from the list to be processed. If you choose as a sentinel a value that might also appear in the list, the loop will prematurely terminate if it encounters the value in the list.
- **Forgetting to initialize an accumulator to zero.** For an accumulator to keep a correct running total, it must be initialized to zero before any values are added to it.

Review Questions and Exercises

Multiple Choice and True/False

1. What will the `println` statement in the following program segment display?
   ```
   int x = 5;
   System.out.println(x++);
   ```
   a. 5
   b. 6
   c. 0
   d. None of these

2. What will the `println` statement in the following program segment display?
   ```
   int x = 5;
   System.out.println(++x);
   ```
   a. 5
   b. 6
   c. 0
   d. None of these

3. In the expression `number++`, the `++` operator is in what mode?
   a. prefix
   b. pretest
   c. postfix
   d. posttest

4. What is each repetition of a loop known as?
   a. cycle
   b. revolution
   c. orbit
   d. iteration

5. This is a variable that controls the number of iterations performed by a loop.
   a. loop control variable
   b. accumulator
   c. iteration register variable
   d. repetition meter

6. The `while` loop is this type of loop.
   a. pretest
   b. posttest
   c. prefix
   d. postfix

7. The `do-while` loop is this type of loop.
   a. pretest
   b. posttest
   c. prefix
   d. postfix

8. The `for` loop is this type of loop.
   a. pretest
   b. posttest
   c. prefix
   d. postfix

9. This type of loop has no way of ending and repeats until the program is interrupted.
   a. indeterminate
   b. interminable
   c. infinite
   d. timeless

10. This type of loop always executes at least one time.
    a. while
    b. do-while
    c. for
    d. Any of these

11. This expression is executed by the `for` loop only once, regardless of the number of iterations.
    a. initialization expression
    b. test expression
    c. update expression
    d. preincrement expression

12. This is a variable that keeps a running total.
    a. sentinel
    b. sum
    c. total
    d. accumulator

13. This a special value that signals when there are no more items from a list of items to be processed. This value cannot be mistaken as an item from the list.
    a. sentinel
    b. flag
    c. signal
    d. accumulator

14. To open a file for writing, you use the following class.
    a. `PrintWriter`
    b. `FileOpen`
    c. `OutputFile`
    d. `FileReader`

15. To open a file for reading, you use the following classes.
    a. `File` and `Writer`
    b. `File` and `Output`
    c. `File` and `Input`
    d. `File` and `Scanner`

16. When a program is finished using a file, it should do this.
    a. Erase the file
    b. Close the file
    c. Throw an exception
    d. Reset the read position

17. This class allows you to use the `print` and `println` methods to write data to a file.
    a. `File`
    b. `FileReader`
    c. `OutputFile`
    d. `PrintWriter`

18. This class allows you to read a line from a file.
    a. `FileWriter`
    b. `Scanner`
    c. `InputFile`
    d. `FileReader`

19. **True or False:** The `while` loop is a pretest loop.

20. **True or False:** The `do-while` loop is a pretest loop.

21. **True or False:** The `for` loop is a posttest loop.

22. **True or False:** It is not necessary to initialize accumulator variables.

23. **True or False:** One limitation of the `for` loop is that only one variable may be initialized in the initialization expression.

24. **True or False:** A variable may be defined in the initialization expression of the `for` loop.

25. **True or False:** In a nested loop, the inner loop goes through all of its iterations for every single iteration of the outer loop.

26. **True or False:** To calculate the total number of iterations of a nested loop, add the number of iterations of all the loops.

Find the Error

Find the errors in the following code.

1.
```java
// This code contains ERRORS!
// It adds two numbers entered by the user.
int num1, num2;
String input;
char again;

Scanner keyboard = new Scanner(System.in);
while (again == 'y' || again == 'Y')
   System.out.print("Enter a number: ");
   num1 = keyboard.nextInt();
   System.out.print("Enter another number: ";
   num2 = keyboard.nextInt();
   System.out.println("Their sum is "+ (num1 + num2));
   System.out.println("Do you want to do this again? ");
```

```
       keyboard.nextLine();   // Consume remaining newline
       input = keyboard.nextLine();
       again = input.charAt(0);
```

2. ```
   // This code contains ERRORS!
   int count = 1, total;
   while (count <= 100)
       total += count;
   System.out.print("The sum of the numbers 1 - 100 is ");
   System.out.println(total);
   ```

3. ```
   // This code contains ERRORS!
   Scanner keyboard = new Scanner(System.in);
   int choice, num1, num2;
   do
   {
       System.out.print("Enter a number: ");
       num1 = keyboard.nextInt();
       System.out.print("Enter another number: ");
       num2 = keyboard.nextInt();
       System.out.println("Their sum is " + (num1 + num2));
       System.out.println("Do you want to do this again? ");
       System.out.print("1 = yes, 0 = no  ");
       choice = keyboard.nextInt();
   } while (Choice = 1)
   ```

4. ```
   // This code contains ERRORS!
   // Print the numbers 1 through 10.
   for (int count = 1, count <= 10, count++;)
   {
       System.out.println(count);
       count++;
   }
   ```

Algorithm Workbench

1. Write a `while` loop that lets the user enter a number. The number should be multiplied by 10 and the result stored in the variable `product`. The loop should iterate as long as `product` contains a value less than 100.

2. Write a `do-while` loop that asks the user to enter two numbers. The numbers should be added and the sum displayed. The user should be asked if he or she wishes to perform the operation again. If so, the loop should repeat, otherwise it should terminate.

3. Write a `for` loop that displays the following set of numbers:

   ```
   0, 10, 20, 30, 40, 50 . . . 1000
   ```

4. Write a loop that asks the user to enter a number. The loop should iterate 10 times and keep a running total of the numbers entered.

5. Write a `for` loop that calculates the total of the following series of numbers:

   $$\frac{1}{30} + \frac{2}{29} + \frac{3}{28} + \cdots \frac{30}{1}$$
   ```

6. Write a nested loop that displays 10 rows of '#' characters. There should be 15 '#' characters in each row.

7. Write nested loops to draw this pattern:

```
*******
******
*****
****
***
**
*
```

8. Write nested loops to draw this pattern:

```
##
# #
#  #
#   #
#    #
#     #
```

9. Complete the following program so it performs the following actions 10 times:

   • Generates a random number that is either 0 or 1.
   • Displays either the word "Yes" or the word "No" depending on the random number that was generated.

   ```java
   // Write the necessary import statement(s) here.

   public class ReviewQuestion
   {
       public static void main(String[] args)
       {
           // Write the necessary code here.
       }
   }
   ```

10. Convert the while loop in the following code segment to a do-while loop:

    ```java
    Scanner keyboard = new Scanner(System.in);
    int x = 1;
    while (x > 0)
    {
        System.out.print("Enter a number: ");
        x = keyboard.nextInt();
    }
    ```

11. Convert the do-while loop in the following code segment to a while loop:

    ```java
    Scanner keyboard = new Scanner(System.in);
    String input;
    char sure;
    do
    {
        System.out.print("Are you sure you want to quit? ");
        input = keyboard.next();
        sure = input.charAt(0);
    } while (sure != 'Y' && sure != 'N');
    ```

12. Convert the `while` loop in the following code segment to a `for` loop:

```
int count = 0;
while (count < 50)
{
    System.out.println("count is " + count);
    count++;
}
```

13. Convert the following `for` loop to a `while` loop:

```
for (int x = 50; x > 0; x--)
{
    System.out.println(x + " seconds to go.");
}
```

14. Write an input validation loop that asks the user to enter a number in the range of 1 through 5.

15. Write an input validation loop that asks the user to enter the words "yes" or "no".

16. Write code that does the following: Opens a file named *numberList.txt*, uses a loop to write the numbers 1 through 100 to the file, and then closes the file.

17. Write code that does the following: Opens the *numberList.txt* file created by the code in Question 13, reads all of the numbers from the file and displays them, and then closes the file.

18. Modify the code you wrote in Question 14 so it adds all of the numbers read from the file and displays their total.

19. Write code that opens a file named *numberList.txt* for writing, but does not erase the file's contents if it already exists.

Short Answer

1. Briefly describe the difference between the prefix and postfix modes used by the increment and decrement operators.

2. Why should you indent the statements in the body of a loop?

3. Describe the difference between pretest loops and posttest loops.

4. Why are the statements in the body of a loop called conditionally executed statements?

5. Describe the difference between the `while` loop and the `do-while` loop.

6. Which loop should you use in situations where you wish the loop to repeat until the Boolean expression is false, and the loop should not execute if the test expression is false to begin with?

7. Which loop should you use in situations where you wish the loop to repeat until the Boolean expression is false, but the loop should execute at least one time?

8. Which loop should you use when you know the number of required iterations?

9. Why is it critical that accumulator variables be properly initialized?

10. What is an infinite loop? Write the code for an infinite loop.

11. Describe a programming problem that would require the use of an accumulator.

12. What does it mean to let the user control a loop?

13. What is the advantage of using a sentinel?

14. Why must the value chosen for use as a sentinel be carefully selected?

15. Describe a programming problem requiring the use of nested loops.

16. How does a file buffer increase a program's performance?

17. Why should a program close a file when finished using it?

18. What is a file's read position? Where is the read position when a file is first opened for reading?

19. When writing data to a file, what is the difference between the `print` and the `println` methods?

20. What does the `Scanner` class's `hasNext` method return when the end of the file has been reached?

21. What is a potential error that can occur when a file is opened for reading?

22. What does it mean to append data to a file?

23. How do you open a file so that new data will be written to the end of the file's existing data?

Programming Challenges

1. Sum of Numbers

Write a program that asks the user for a positive nonzero integer value. The program should use a loop to get the sum of all the integers from 1 up to the number entered. For example, if the user enters 50, the loop will find the sum of 1, 2, 3, 4, . . . , 50.

2. Distance Traveled

The distance a vehicle travels can be calculated as follows:

$$Distance = Speed * Time$$

For example, if a train travels 40 miles per hour (mph) for three hours, the distance traveled is 120 miles.

Design a class that stores the speed of a vehicle (in miles per hour) and the number of hours it has traveled. It should have a method named `getDistance` that returns the distance, in miles, that the vehicle has traveled.

Demonstrate the class in a program that uses a loop to display the distance a vehicle has traveled for each hour of a time period specified by the user. For example, if a vehicle is traveling at 40 mph for a three-hour time period, it should display a report similar to the one shown here.

```
Hour            Distance Traveled
--------------------------------------------
1                       40
2                       80
3                      120
```

Input Validation: Do not accept a negative number for speed, and do not accept any value less than one for time traveled.

3. Distance File

Modify the program you wrote for Programming Challenge 2 (Distance Traveled) so it writes the report to a file instead of the screen. Open the file in Notepad or another text editor to confirm the output.

VideoNote
The Pennies for Pay Problem

4. Pennies for Pay

Write a program that calculates how much a person would earn over a period of time if his or her salary is one penny the first day, two pennies the second day, and continues to double each day. The program should display a table showing the salary for each day, and then show the total pay at the end of the period. The output should be displayed in a dollar amount, not the number of pennies.

Input Validation: Do not accept a number less than one for the number of days worked.

5. Hotel Occupancy

A hotel's occupancy rate is calculated as follows:

$$Occupancy\ rate\ =\ number\ of\ rooms\ occupied\ \div\ total\ number\ of\ rooms$$

Write a program that calculates the occupancy rate for each floor of a hotel. The program should start by asking for the number of floors that the hotel has. A loop should then iterate once for each floor. During each iteration, the loop should ask the user for the number of rooms on the floor and how many of them are occupied. After all the iterations, the program should display the number of rooms the hotel has, the number that are occupied, the number that are vacant, and the occupancy rate for the hotel.

Input Validation: Do not accept a value less than 1 for the number of floors. Do not accept a number less than 10 for the number of rooms on a floor.

6. Population

Write a class that will predict the size of a population of organisms. The class should store the starting number of organisms, their average daily population increase (as a percentage), and the number of days they will multiply. The class should have a method that uses a loop to display the size of the population for each day.

Test the class in a program that asks the user for the starting size of the population, their average daily increase, and the number of days they will multiply. The program should display the daily population.

Input Validation: Do not accept a number less than 2 for the starting size of the population. Do not accept a negative number for average daily population increase. Do not accept a number less than 1 for the number of days they will multiply.

7. Average Rainfall

Write a program that uses nested loops to collect data and calculate the average rainfall over a period of years. The program should first ask for the number of years. The outer loop will iterate once for each year. The inner loop will iterate twelve times, once for each month. Each iteration of the inner loop will ask the user for the inches of rainfall for that month.

After all iterations, the program should display the number of months, the total inches of rainfall, and the average rainfall per month for the entire period.

Input Validation: Do not accept a number less than 1 for the number of years. Do not accept negative numbers for the monthly rainfall.

8. The Greatest and Least of These

Write a program with a loop that lets the user enter a series of integers. The user should enter −99 to signal the end of the series. After all the numbers have been entered, the program should display the largest and smallest numbers entered.

9. Payroll Report

Design a `Payroll` class that stores an employee's ID number, gross pay, state tax, federal tax, and FICA withholdings. The class should have a method that calculates the employee's net pay, as follows:

net pay = gross pay − state tax − federal tax − FICA withholdings

Use the class in a program that displays a weekly payroll report. A loop in the program should ask the user for the employee ID number, gross pay, state tax, federal tax, and FICA withholdings and should pass these values to an instance of the `Payroll` class. The net pay should be displayed. The loop should terminate when 0 is entered for the employee number. After the data is entered, the program should display totals for gross pay, state tax, federal tax, FICA withholdings, and net pay.

Input Validation: Do not accept negative numbers for any of the items entered. Do not accept values for state, federal, or FICA withholdings that are greater than the gross pay. If the state tax + federal tax + FICA withholdings for any employee are greater than gross pay, print an error message, and ask the user to reenter the data for that employee.

10. `SavingsAccount` Class

Design a `SavingsAccount` class that stores a savings account's annual interest rate and balance. The class constructor should accept the amount of the savings account's starting balance. The class should also have methods for subtracting the amount of a withdrawal, adding the amount of a deposit, and adding the amount of monthly interest to the balance. The monthly interest rate is the annual interest rate divided by 12. To add the monthly interest to the balance, multiply the monthly interest rate by the balance and add the result to the balance.

Test the class in a program that calculates the balance of a savings account at the end of a period of time. It should ask the user for the annual interest rate, the starting balance, and the number of months that have passed since the account was established. A loop should then iterate once for every month, performing the following:

    a. Ask the user for the amount deposited into the account during the month. Use the class method to add this amount to the account balance.

    b. Ask the user for the amount withdrawn from the account during the month. Use the class method to subtract this amount from the account balance.

    c. Use the class method to calculate the monthly interest.

After the last iteration, the program should display the ending balance, the total amount of deposits, the total amount of withdrawals, and the total interest earned.

11. Deposit and Withdrawal Files

Use Notepad or another text editor to create a text file named *Deposits.txt*. The file should contain the following numbers, one per line:

```
100.00
125.00
78.92
37.55
```

Next, create a text file named *Withdrawals.txt*. The file should contain the following numbers, one per line:

```
29.88
110.00
27.52
50.00
12.90
```

The numbers in the *Deposits.txt* file are the amounts of deposits that were made to a savings account during the month, and the numbers in the *Withdrawals.txt* file are the amounts of withdrawals that were made during the month. Write a program that creates an instance of the SavingsAccount class that you wrote in Programming Challenge 10. The starting balance for the object is 500.00. The program should read the values from the *Deposits.txt* file and use the object's method to add them to the account balance. The program should read the values from the *Withdrawals.txt* file and use the object's method to subtract them from the account balance. The program should call the class method to calculate the monthly interest, and then display the ending balance and the total interest earned.

12. Bar Chart

Write a program that asks the user to enter today's sales for five stores. The program should then display a bar chart comparing each store's sales. Create each bar in the bar chart by displaying a row of asterisks. Each asterisk should represent $100 of sales. Here is an example of the program's output.

```
Enter today's sales for store 1: 1000 [Enter]
Enter today's sales for store 2: 1200 [Enter]
Enter today's sales for store 3: 1800 [Enter]
Enter today's sales for store 4: 800 [Enter]
Enter today's sales for store 5: 1900 [Enter]
SALES BAR CHART
Store 1: **********
Store 2: ************
Store 3: ******************
Store 4: ********
Store 5: *******************
```

13. Centigrade to Fahrenheit Table

Write a program that displays a table of the centigrade temperatures 0 through 20 and their Fahrenheit equivalents. The formula for converting a temperature from centigrade to Fahrenheit is

$$F = \frac{9}{5} C + 32$$

where *F* is the Fahrenheit temperature and *C* is the centigrade temperature. Your program must use a loop to display the table.

14. `FileDisplay` Class

Write a class named `FileDisplay` with the following methods:

- Constructor: The class's constructor should take the name of a file as an argument.
- `displayHead`: This method should display only the first five lines of the file's contents. If the file contains less than five lines, it should display the file's entire contents.
- `displayContents`: This method should display the entire contents of the file, the name of which was passed to the constructor.
- `displayWithLineNumbers`: This method should display the contents of the file, the name of which was passed to the constructor. Each line should be preceded with a line number followed by a colon. The line numbering should start at 1.

15. `UpperCaseFile` Class

Write a class named `UpperCaseFile`. The class's constructor should accept two file names as arguments. The first file should be opened for reading and the second file should be opened for writing. The class should read the contents of the first file, change all characters to uppercase, and store the results in the second file. The second file will be a copy of the first file, except all the characters will be uppercase. Use Notepad or another text editor to create a simple file that can be used to test the class.

16. Budget Analysis

Write a program that asks the user to enter the amount that he or she has budgeted for a month. A loop should then prompt the user to enter each of his or her expenses for the month and keep a running total. When the loop finishes, the program should display the amount that the user is over or under budget.

17. Random Number Guessing Game

Write a program that generates a random number and asks the user to guess what the number is. If the user's guess is higher than the random number, the program should display "Too high, try again." If the user's guess is lower than the random number, the program should display "Too low, try again." The program should use a loop that repeats until the user correctly guesses the random number.

18. Random Number Guessing Game Enhancement

Enhance the program that you wrote for Programming Challenge 17 so it keeps a count of the number of guesses that the user makes. When the user correctly guesses the random number, the program should display the number of guesses.

19. Square Display

Write a program that asks the user for a positive integer no greater than 15. The program should then display a square on the screen using the character 'x'. The number entered by the user will be the length of each side of the square. For example, if the user enters 5, the program should display the following:

```
XXXXX
XXXXX
XXXXX
XXXXX
XXXXX
```

If the user enters 8, the program should display the following:

```
XXXXXXXX
XXXXXXXX
XXXXXXXX
XXXXXXXX
XXXXXXXX
XXXXXXXX
XXXXXXXX
XXXXXXXX
```

20. Coin-Toss Simulator

Write a class named `Coin`. The `Coin` class should have the following field:

- A `String` named `sideUp`. The `sideUp` field will hold either "heads" or "tails" indicating the side of the coin that is facing up.

The `Coin` class should have the following methods:

- A no-arg constructor that calls the `toss` method, described next.
- A `void` method named `toss` that simulates the tossing of the coin. When the `toss` method is called, it generates a random number in the range of 0 through 1. If the random number is 0, then it sets the `sideUp` field to "heads". If the random number is 1, then it sets the `sideUp` field to "tails".
- A method named `getSideUp` that returns the value of the `sideUp` field.

Write a program that demonstrates the `Coin` class. The program should create an instance of the class and display the side that is initially facing up. Then, use a loop to toss the coin 20 times. Each time the coin is tossed, display the side that is facing up. The program should keep count of the number of times a head is facing up and the number of times a tail is facing up and display those values after the loop finishes.

21. Tossing Coins for a Dollar

For this assignment you will create a game program using the `Coin` class from Programming Challenge 20. The program should have three instances of the `Coin` class: one representing a quarter, one representing a dime, and one representing a nickel.

When the game begins, your starting balance is $0. During each round of the game, the program will toss the simulated coins. When a coin is tossed, the value of the coin is added to your balance if it lands heads-up. For example, if the quarter lands heads-up, 25 cents is added to your balance. Nothing is added to your balance for coins that land tails-up. The game is over when your balance reaches one dollar or more. If your balance is exactly one dollar, you win the game. You lose if your balance exceeds one dollar.

22. Dice Game

Write a program that uses the Die class that was presented in Chapter 4 to play a simple dice game between the computer and the user. The program should create two instances of the Die class (each a six-sided die). One Die object is the computer's die, and the other Die object is the user's die.

The program should have a loop that iterates 10 times. Each time the loop iterates, it should roll both dice. The die with the highest value wins. (In case of a tie, there is no winner for that particular roll of the dice.)

As the loop iterates, the program should keep count of the number of times the computer wins and the number of times that the user wins. After the loop performs all of its iterations, the program should display who was the grand winner, the computer or the user.

23. Fishing Game Simulation

Write a program that uses the Die class that was presented in Chapter 4 to simulate a fishing game. In this game, a six-sided die is rolled to determine what the user has caught. Each possible item is worth a certain number of fishing points. The points will remain hidden until the user is finished fishing, and then a message is displayed congratulating the user depending on the number of fishing points gained.

Here are some suggestions for the game's design:

- Each round of the game is performed as an iteration of a loop that repeats as long as the player wants to fish for more items.
- At the beginning of each round, the program will ask the user whether or not they want to continue fishing.
- The program simulates the rolling of a six-sided die. (Use the Die class that was demonstrated in Chapter 4.)
- Each item that can be caught is represented by a number generated from the die. For example, 1 for "a huge fish", 2 for "an old shoe", 3 for "a little fish", and so on.
- Each item the user catches is worth a different amount of points.
- The loop keeps a running total of the user's fishing points.
- After the loop has finished, the total number of fishing points is displayed, along with a message that varies depending on the number of points earned.

24. A Game of 21

Write a program that uses the Die class that was presented in Chapter 4 to write a program that lets the user play against the computer in a variation of the popular blackjack card game. In this variation of the game, two six-sided dice are used instead of cards. The dice are rolled, and the player tries to beat the computer's hidden total without going over 21.

Here are some suggestions for the game's design:

- Each round of the game is performed as an iteration of a loop that repeats as long as the player agrees to roll the dice, and the player's total does not exceed 21.
- At the beginning of each round, the program will ask the user whether he or she wants to roll the dice to accumulate points.

- During each round, the program simulates the rolling of two six-sided dice. It rolls the dice first for the computer, and then it asks the user if he or she wants to roll. (Use the `Die` class that was demonstrated in Chapter 4 to simulate the dice).
- The loop keeps a running total of both the computer and the user's points.
- The computer's total should remain hidden until the loop has finished.
- After the loop has finished, the computer's total is revealed, and whoever the player with the most points without going over 21 wins.

25. ESP Game

Write a program that tests your ESP (extrasensory perception). The program should randomly select the name of a color from the following list of words:

Red, Green, Blue, Orange, Yellow

To select a word, the program can generate a random number. For example, if the number is 0, the selected word is *Red*, if the number is 1, the selected word is *Green*, and so forth.

Next, the program should ask the user to enter the color that the computer has selected. After the user has entered his or her guess, the program should display the name of the randomly selected color. The program should repeat this 10 times and then display the number of times the user correctly guessed the selected color.

26. Slot Machine Simulation

A slot machine is a gambling device that the user inserts money into and then pulls a lever (or presses a button). The slot machine then displays a set of random images. If two or more of the images match, the user wins an amount of money that the slot machine dispenses back to the user.

Create a program that simulates a slot machine. When the program runs, it should do the following:

- Ask the user to enter the amount of money he or she wants to enter into the slot machine.
- Instead of displaying images, have the program randomly select a word from the following list:

  Cherries, Oranges, Plums, Bells, Melons, Bars

  To select a word, the program can generate a random number in the range of 0 through 5. If the number is 0, the selected word is *Cherries*, if the number is 1, the selected word is *Oranges*, and so forth. The program should randomly select a word from this list three times and display all three of the words.
- If none of the randomly selected words match, the program informs the user that he or she has won $0. If two of the words match, the program informs the user that he or she has won two times the amount entered. If three of the words match, the program informs the user that he or she has won three times the amount entered.
- The program asks if the user wants to play again. If so, these steps are repeated. If not, the program displays the total amount of money entered into the slot machine and the total amount won.

6

A Second Look at Classes and Objects

TOPICS

6.1   Static Class Members
6.2   Overloaded Methods
6.3   Overloaded Constructors
6.4   Passing Objects as Arguments to Methods
6.5   Returning Objects from Methods
6.6   The toString Method
6.7   Writing an equals Method
6.8   Methods That Copy Objects

6.9   Aggregation
6.10 The this Reference Variable
6.11 Inner Classes
6.12 Enumerated Types
6.13 Garbage Collection
6.14 Focus on Object-Oriented Design: Object Collaboration
6.15 Common Errors to Avoid

6.1   Static Class Members

CONCEPT: A static class member belongs to the class, not objects instantiated from the class.

A Quick Review of Instance Fields and Instance Methods

Recall from Chapter 3 that each instance of a class has its own set of fields, which are known as instance fields. You can create several instances of a class and store different values in each instance's fields. For example, the Rectangle class that we created in Chapter 3 has a length field and a width field. Let's say that box references an instance of the Rectangle class and execute the following statement:

```
box.setLength(10);
```

This statement stores the value 10 in the length field that belongs to the instance referenced by box. You can think of instance fields as belonging to an instance of a class.

You will also recall that classes may have instance methods as well. When you call an instance method, it performs an operation on a specific instance of the class. For example, assuming that box references an instance of the Rectangle class, look at the following statement:

```
x = box.getLength();
```

This statement calls the getLength method, which returns the value of the length field that belongs to a specific instance of the Rectangle class, the one referenced by box. Both instance fields and instance methods are associated with a specific instance of a class, and they cannot be used until an instance of the class is created.

Static Members

It is possible to create a field or method that does not belong to any instance of a class. Such members are known as *static fields* and *static methods*. When a value is stored in a static field, it is not stored in an instance of the class. In fact, an instance of the class doesn't even have to exist for values to be stored in the class's static fields. Likewise, static methods do not operate on the fields that belong to any instance of the class. Instead, they can operate only on static fields. In this section, we will take a closer look at static members. First we will examine static fields.

Static Fields

When a field is declared static, there will be only one copy of the field in memory, regardless of the number of instances of the class that might exist. A single copy of a class's static field is shared by all instances of the class. For example, the Countable class shown in Code Listing 6-1 uses a static field to keep count of the number of instances of the class that are created.

Code Listing 6-1   (Countable.java)

```
 1  /**
 2   * This class demonstrates a static field.
 3   */
 4
 5  public class Countable
 6  {
 7     private static int instanceCount = 0;
 8
 9     /**
10      * The constructor increments the static
11      * field instanceCount. This keeps track
12      * of the number of instances of this
13      * class that are created.
14      */
15
16     public Countable()
17     {
18        instanceCount++;
19     }
20
21     /**
22      * The getInstanceCount method returns
23      * the value in the instanceCount field,
24      * which is the number of instances of
```

```
25          * this class that have been created.
26          */
27
28         public int getInstanceCount()
29         {
30            return instanceCount;
31         }
32   }
```

First, notice the declaration of the static field named `instanceCount` in line 7. A static field is created by placing the key word `static` after the access specifier and before the field's data type. Notice that we have explicitly initialized the `instanceCount` field with the value 0. This initialization only takes place once, regardless of the number of instances of the class that are created.

NOTE: Java automatically stores 0 in all uninitialized numeric static member variables. The `instanceCount` field in this class is explicitly initialized so it is clear to anyone reading the code that the field starts with the value 0.

Next, look at the constructor, which appears in lines 16 through 19. The statement in line 18 uses the ++ operator to increment the `instanceCount` field. Each time an instance of the `Countable` class is created, the constructor will be called and the `instanceCount` field will be incremented. As a result, the `instanceCount` field will contain the number of instances of the `Countable` class that have been created. The `getInstanceCount` method, which appears in lines 28 through 31, can be used to retrieve this value. The program in Code Listing 6-2 demonstrates this class.

Code Listing 6-2   (`StaticDemo.java`)

```
1    /**
2     * This program demonstrates the Countable class.
3     */
4
5    public class StaticDemo
6    {
7       public static void main(String [] args)
8       {
9           int objectCount;
10
11          // Create three instances of the
12          // Countable class.
13          Countable object1 = new Countable();
14          Countable object2 = new Countable();
15          Countable object3 = new Countable();
16
17          // Get the number of instances from
```

or Countable

```
18          // the class's static field.
19          objectCount = object1.getInstanceCount();
20          System.out.println(objectCount + " instances "
21                          + "of the class were created.");
22    }
23  }
```

Program Output

```
3 instances of the class were created.
```

The program creates three instances of the Countable class, referenced by the variables object1, object2, and object3. Although there are three instances of the class, there is only one copy of the static field. This is illustrated in Figure 6-1.

Figure 6-1   All instances of the class share the static field

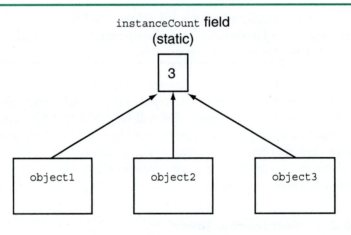

In line 19, the program calls the getInstanceCount method to retrieve the number of instances that have been created. Although the program calls the getInstanceCount method from object1, the same value would be returned from any of the objects.

Static Methods

When a class contains a static method, it isn't necessary for an instance of the class to be created to execute the method. The program in Code Listing 6-3 shows an example of a class with static methods.

Code Listing 6-3   (Metric.java)

```
1  /**
2   * This class demonstrates static methods.
```

```
3    */
4
5    public class Metric
6    {
7       /**
8        * The milesToKilometers method converts miles
9        * to kilometers. A distance in miles should be
10       * passed into the miles parameter. The method
11       * returns the equivalent distance in kilometers.
12       */
13
14      public static double milesToKilometers(double miles)
15      {
16         return miles * 1.609;
17      }
18
19      /**
20       * The kilometersToMiles method converts kilometers
21       * to miles. A distance in kilometers should be
22       * passed into the kilometers parameter. The method
23       * returns the equivalent distance in miles.
24       */
25
26      public static double kilometersToMiles(double kilometers)
27      {
28         return kilometers / 1.609;
29      }
30   }
```

A static method is created by placing the key word `static` after the access specifier in the method header. The `Metric` class has two static methods: `milesToKilometers` and `kilometersToMiles`. Because they are declared as `static`, they belong to the class and may be called without any instances of the class being in existence. You simply write the name of the class before the dot operator in the method call. Here is an example:

```
kilos = Metric.milesToKilometers(10.0);
```

This statement calls the `milesToKilometers` method, passing the value `10.0` as an argument. Notice that the method is not called from an instance of the class, but is called directly from the `Metric` class. Code Listing 6-4 shows a program that uses the `Metric` class.

Code Listing 6-4   (`MetricDemo.java`)

```
1    import java.util.Scanner;
2    import java.text.DecimalFormat;
3
4    /**
```

```
 5    * This program demonstrates the Metric class.
 6    */
 7
 8   public class MetricDemo
 9   {
10      public static void main(String[] args)
11      {
12         double miles,  // A distance in miles
13                kilos;  // A distance in kilometers
14
15         // Create a Scanner object for keyboard input.
16         Scanner keyboard = new Scanner(System.in);
17
18         // Create a DecimalFormat object for
19         // output formatting.
20         DecimalFormat fmt = new DecimalFormat("0.00");
21
22         // Get a distance in miles.
23         System.out.print("Enter a distance in miles: ");
24         miles = keyboard.nextDouble();
25
26         // Convert the distance to kilometers.
27         kilos = Metric.milesToKilometers(miles);
28         System.out.println(fmt.format(miles)
29                    + " miles equals " + fmt.format(kilos)
30                    + " kilometers.");
31
32         // Get a distance in kilometers.
33         System.out.print("Enter a distance in kilometers: ");
34         kilos = keyboard.nextDouble();
35
36         // Convert the distance to kilometers.
37         miles = Metric.kilometersToMiles(kilos);
38         System.out.println(fmt.format(kilos)
39                    + " kilometers equals " + fmt.format(miles)
40                    + " miles.");
41      }
42   }
```

Program Output with Example Input Shown in Bold

```
Enter a distance in miles: 10 [Enter]
10.00 miles equals 16.09 kilometers.
Enter a distance in kilometers: 100 [Enter]
100.00 kilometers equals 62.15 miles.
```

Static methods are convenient for many tasks because they can be called directly from the class, as needed. They are most often used to create utility classes that perform operations on data, but have no need to collect and store data. The `Metric` class is a good example. It is used as a container to hold methods that convert miles to kilometers and vice versa, but is not intended to store any data.

If a class has both static members and instance members, keep the following points in mind.

- An instance method can refer to a static variable in the same class. You saw this demonstrated in the `Countable` class in Code Listing 6-1.
- An instance method can call a static method.
- It is not necessary to create an object to execute a static method. However, an instance method or an instance variable can be referred to only in the context of an object. Because a static method can be executed without an object of the class being in existence, a static method cannot refer to an instance variable or an instance method of the same class—that is, unless the static method has an object reference. For example, a static method could create an object of the class, and then use the object reference to call instance methods or refer to instance variables.

The `Math` Class

The Java `Math` class is a collection of static methods for performing specific mathematical operations. In Chapter 2 you were introduced to the `Math.pow` method, which returns the value of a number raised to a power. For example, the following statement raises 5 to the 10th power and assigns the result to the `result` variable:

```
result = Math.pow(5.0, 10.0);
```

The `Math` class also has a method named `sqrt` that returns the square root of its argument. For example, in the following statement the `Math.sqrt` method returns the square root of the value stored in the `number` variable, and assigns the result to the `result` variable:

```
result = Math.sqrt(number);
```

The `Math.sqrt` method accepts a `double` argument, and returns a `double`. The `Math` class also has a static `final` variable named `PI`, which is set to the mathematical constant pi, or π. It is defined as 3.14159265358979323846. The following statement uses `Math.PI` in a calculation.

```
circumference = Math.PI * diameter;
```

> The `Math` class has other static members. For more information see Appendix F, available on this book's online resource page at www.pearsonhighered.com/gaddis.

 Checkpoint

6.1　What is the difference between an instance member variable and a static member variable?

6.2　What action is possible with a static method that isn't possible with an instance method?

6.3　Describe the limitation of static methods.

6.2 Overloaded Methods

CONCEPT: Two or more methods in a class may have the same name as long as their signatures are different.

Sometimes you will need to perform an operation in different ways, perhaps using items of different data types. For example, consider the following two methods, squareInt and squareDouble.

```java
public static int squareInt(int number)
{
     return number * number;
}
public static double squareDouble(double number)
{
     return number * number;
}
```

Both of these methods accept an argument and return the square of that argument. The squareInt method accepts an int and the squareDouble method accepts a double. Although this approach will work, a better solution is to use method overloading. In *method overloading*, multiple methods have the same name, but use different parameters.

For example, Code Listing 6-5 shows the MyMath class. This class has two methods named square. Both methods do the same thing: return the square of their argument. One version of the method accepts an int argument and the other accepts a double.

Code Listing 6-5   (MyMath.java)

```java
 1  /**
 2   * This class overloads the square method.
 3   */
 4
 5  public class MyMath
 6  {
 7     public static int square(int number)
 8     {
 9        return number * number;
10     }
11
12     public static double square(double number)
13     {
14        return number * number;
15     }
16  }
```

The program in Code Listing 6-6 uses both square methods.

Code Listing 6-6   (`OverloadingDemo.java`)

```java
 1  import java.util.Scanner;
 2
 3  /**
 4   * This program uses the MyMath class to
 5   * demonstrate overloaded methods.
 6   */
 7
 8  public class OverloadingDemo
 9  {
10      public static void main(String[] args)
11      {
12          int iNumber;
13          double dNumber;
14
15          // Create a Scanner object for keyboard input.
16          Scanner keyboard = new Scanner(System.in);
17
18          // Get an integer and display its square.
19          System.out.print("Enter an integer: ");
20          iNumber = keyboard.nextInt();
21          System.out.println("That number's square is "
22                          + MyMath.square(iNumber));
23
24          // Get a double and display its square.
25          System.out.print("Enter a double: ");
26          dNumber = keyboard.nextDouble();
27          System.out.println("That number's square is "
28                          + MyMath.square(dNumber));
29      }
30  }
```

Program Output with Example Input Shown in Bold

```
Enter an integer: 5 [Enter]
That number's square is 25
Enter a double: 1.2 [Enter]
That number's square is 1.44
```

The process of matching a method call with the correct method is known as *binding*. When an overloaded method is being called, Java uses the method's name and parameter list to determine which method to bind the call to. In Code Listing 6-6, when an `int` argument is passed to `square`, the version of the method that has an `int` parameter is called. Likewise, when a `double` argument is passed to `square`, the version with a `double` parameter is called.

Method Signatures

Java uses a method's signature to distinguish it from other methods of the same name. A method's *signature* consists of the method's name and the data types of the method's parameters, in the order that they appear. For example, here are the signatures of the `square` methods that appear in the `MyMath` class:

```
square(int)


square(double)
```

Note that the method's return type is not part of the signature. For example, the `square` method cannot be overloaded in the following manner:

```
public static int square(int number)
{
    return number * number;
}


// ERROR! The following method's parameter list does
// not differ from the previous square method.

public static double square(int number)
{
    return number * number;
}
```

Although these methods have different return values, their signatures are the same. For this reason, an error message will be issued when a class containing these methods is compiled.

Overloading is also convenient when there are similar methods that use a different number of parameters. For example, Code Listing 6-7 shows the `Pay` class, which uses two methods, each named `getWeeklyPay`. These methods return an employee's gross weekly pay. One version of the method returns the weekly pay for an hourly paid employee. It uses an `int` parameter for the number of hours worked and a `double` parameter for the hourly pay rate. The other version of the method returns the weekly pay for a salaried employee. It uses a `double` parameter for the yearly salary. Code Listing 6-8 illustrates the use of the `Pay` class.

Code Listing 6-7   (`Pay.java`)

```
1   /**
2    * This class uses overloaded methods to return an employee's
3    * weekly salary.
4    */
5
6   public class Pay
7   {
8      /**
9       * The following method calculates the gross weekly pay of
10      * an hourly paid employee. The parameter hours holds the
11      * number of hours worked. The parameter payRate holds the
12      * hourly pay rate. The method returns the weekly salary.
13      */
14
15     public static double getWeeklyPay(int hours, double payRate)
16     {
17        return hours * payRate;
18     }
19
20     /**
21      * The following method overloads the getWeeklyPay method.
22      * It calculates the gross weekly pay of a salaried
23      * employee. The parameter holds the employee's yearly
24      * salary. The method returns the weekly salary.
25      */
26
27     public static double getWeeklyPay(double yearlySalary)
28     {
29        return yearlySalary / 52;
30     }
31  }
```

Code Listing 6-8   (`WeeklyPay.java`)

```
1   import java.util.Scanner;
2   import java.text.DecimalFormat;
3
4   /**
5    * This program uses the Pay class to determine an
6    * employee's weekly pay. It can process hourly paid
7    * or salaried employees.
8    */
9
```

```
10   public class WeeklyPay
11   {
12      public static void main(String[] args)
13      {
14         String selection;   // The user's selection, H or S
15         int hours;          // The number of hours worked
16         double hourlyRate;  // The hourly pay rate
17         double yearly;      // The yearly salary
18
19         // Create a Scanner object for keyboard input.
20         Scanner keyboard = new Scanner(System.in);
21
22         // Create a DecimalFormat object for output formatting.
23         DecimalFormat dollar = new DecimalFormat("#,##0.00");
24
25         // Determine whether the employee is hourly paid or salaried.
26         System.out.println("Do you want to calculate the " +
27                            "weekly salary of an hourly paid");
28         System.out.println("or a salaried employee?");
29         System.out.print("Enter H for hourly or S for salaried: ");
30         selection = keyboard.nextLine();
31
32         // Determine and display the weekly pay.
33         switch(selection.charAt(0))
34         {
35            case 'H':
36            case 'h':
37               System.out.print("How many hours were worked? ");
38               hours = keyboard.nextInt();
39               System.out.print("What is the hourly pay rate? ");
40               hourlyRate = keyboard.nextDouble();
41               System.out.println("The weekly gross pay is $" +
42                  dollar.format(Pay.getWeeklyPay(hours, hourlyRate)));
43               break;
44
45            case 'S':
46            case 's':
47               System.out.print("What is the annual salary? ");
48               yearly = keyboard.nextDouble();
49               System.out.println("The weekly gross pay is $" +
50                        dollar.format(Pay.getWeeklyPay(yearly)));
51               break;
52
53            default:
54               System.out.println("Invalid selection.");
55         }
56      }
57   }
```

Program Output with Example Input Shown in Bold

```
Do you want to calculate the weekly salary of an hourly paid
or a salaried employee?
Enter H for hourly or S for salaried: h [Enter]
How many hours were worked? 40 [Enter]
What is the hourly pay rate? 26.50 [Enter]
The weekly gross pay is $1,060.00
```

Program Output with Example Input Shown in Bold

```
Do you want to calculate the weekly salary of an hourly paid
or a salaried employee?
Enter H for hourly or S for salaried: s [Enter]
What is the annual salary? 65000.00 [Enter]
The weekly gross pay is $1,250.00
```

6.3 Overloaded Constructors

CONCEPT: More than one constructor may be defined for a class.

A class's constructor may be overloaded in the same manner as other methods. The rules for overloading constructors are the same for overloading other methods: Each version of the constructor must have a different signature. As long as each constructor has a unique signature, the compiler can tell them apart. For example, recall the Rectangle class from Chapter 3. We added a constructor to the class that accepts two arguments, which are assigned to the length and width fields. Code Listing 6-9 shows how the class can be modified with the addition of another constructor.

Code Listing 6-9   (Rectangle.java)

```java
1   /**
2    * Rectangle class
3    */
4
5   public class Rectangle
6   {
7       private double length;
8       private double width;
9
10      /**
11       * Constructor
12       */
13
```

```
14        public Rectangle()
15        {
16           length = 0.0;
17           width = 0.0;
18        }
19
20        /**
21         * Overloaded constructor
22         */
23
24        public Rectangle(double len, double w)
25        {
26           length = len;
27           width = w;
28        }
```
The remainder of the class has not been changed, so it is not shown.

The first constructor accepts no arguments, and assigns 0.0 to the length and width fields.
The second constructor accepts two arguments which are assigned to the length and width
fields. The program in Code Listing 6-10 demonstrates both of these constructors.

Code Listing 6-10   (TwoRectangles.java)

```
 1  /**
 2   * This program demonstrates both of the Rectangle
 3   * class's constructors.
 4   */
 5
 6  public class TwoRectangles
 7  {
 8     public static void main(String[] args)
 9     {
10        // Declare two Rectangle variables, but don't
11        // create instances of the class yet.
12
13        Rectangle box1, box2;
14
15        // Create a Rectangle object and use the
16        // first constructor.
17
18        box1 = new Rectangle();
19        System.out.println("The box1 object's length "
20                           + "and width are "
21                           + box1.getLength() + " and "
22                           + box1.getWidth());
23
```

```
24          // Create another Rectangle object and use
25          // the second constructor.
26
27          box2 = new Rectangle(5.0, 10.0);
28          System.out.println("The box2 object's length "
29                          + "and width are "
30                          + box2.getLength() + " and "
31                          + box2.getWidth());
32     }
33  }
```

Program Output

```
The box1 object's length and width are 0.0 and 0.0
The box2 object's length and width are 5.0 and 10.0
```

This program declares two `Rectangle` variables, `box1` and `box2`. The statement in line 18 creates the first `Rectangle` object. Because the statement passes no arguments to the constructor, the first constructor is executed:

```
public Rectangle()
{
    length = 0.0;
     width = 0.0;
}
```

This is verified by a call to `System.out.println` in lines 19 through 22, which displays the contents of the `length` and `width` fields as 0.0. Here is the statement in line 27, which creates the second `Rectangle` object:

```
box2 = new Rectangle(5.0, 10.0);
```

Because this statement passes two `double` arguments to the constructor, the second constructor is called:

```
public Rectangle(double len, double w)
{
    length = len;
    width = w;
}
```

The call to `System.out.println` statement in lines 28 through 31 verifies that the content of the `length` field is 5.0 and the `width` field is 10.0.

The Default Constructor Revisited

Recall from Chapter 3 that if you do not write a constructor for a class, Java automatically provides one. The constructor that Java provides is known as the default constructor. It sets all of the class's numeric fields to 0 and `boolean` fields to `false`. If the class has any fields that are reference variables, the default constructor sets them to the value `null`, which means they do not reference anything.

Java provides a default constructor only when you do not write any constructors for a class. If a class has a constructor that accepts arguments, but it does not also have a no-arg constructor (a constructor that does not accept arguments), you cannot create an instance of the class without passing arguments to the constructor. Therefore, any time you write a constructor for a class, you should also write a no-arg constructor if you want to be able to create instances of the class without passing arguments to the constructor.

The `InventoryItem` Class

Let's look at a class that uses multiple constructors. The `InventoryItem` class holds simple data about an item in an inventory. A description of the item is stored in the `description` field and the number of units on hand is stored in the `units` field. Figure 6-2 shows a UML diagram for the class.

Figure 6-2 UML diagram for the `InventoryItem` class

```
┌─────────────────────────────────────┐
│            InventoryItem             │
├─────────────────────────────────────┤
│ - description : String               │
│ - units : int                        │
├─────────────────────────────────────┤
│ + InventoryItem()                    │
│ + InventoryItem(d : String)          │
│ + InventoryItem(d : String, u : int) │
│ + setDescription(d : String) : void  │
│ + setUnits(u : int) : void           │
│ + getDescription() : String          │
│ + getUnits() : int                   │
└─────────────────────────────────────┘
```

The code for the class is shown in Code Listing 6-11.

Code Listing 6-11 (`InventoryItem.java`)

```java
 1  /**
 2   * This class uses three constructors.
 3   */
 4
 5  public class InventoryItem
 6  {
 7     private String description;  // Item description
 8     private int units;           // Units on-hand
 9
10     /**
11      * No-arg constructor
12      */
13
14     public InventoryItem()
```

```
15      {
16          description = "";
17          units = 0;
18      }
19
20      /**
21       * The following constructor accepts a
22       * String argument that is assigned to the
23       * description field.
24       */
25
26      public InventoryItem(String d)
27      {
28          description = d;
29          units = 0;
30      }
31
32      /**
33       * The following constructor accepts a
34       * String argument that is assigned to the
35       * description field, and an int argument
36       * that is assigned to the units field.
37       */
38
39      public InventoryItem(String d, int u)
40      {
41          description = d;
42          units = u;
43      }
44
45      /**
46       * The setDescription method assigns its
47       * argument to the description field.
48       */
49
50      public void setDescription(String d)
51      {
52          description = d;
53      }
54
55      /**
56       * The setUnits method assigns its argument
57       * to the units field.
58       */
59
60      public void setUnits(int u)
61      {
62          units = u;
```

```
63        }
64
65        /**
66         * The getDescription method returns the
67         * value in the description field.
68         */
69
70        public String getDescription()
71        {
72           return description;
73        }
74
75        /**
76         * The getUnits method returns the value in
77         * the units field.
78         */
79
80        public int getUnits()
81        {
82           return units;
83        }
84  }
```

The first constructor in the InventoryItem class, in lines 14 through 18, is the no-arg constructor. It assigns an empty string ("") to the description field and assigns 0 to the units field. The second constructor, in lines 26 through 30, accepts a String argument, d, which is assigned to the description field, and assigns 0 to the units field. The third constructor, in lines 39 through 43, accepts a String argument, d, which is assigned to the description field and an int argument, u, which is assigned to the units field. The program in Code Listing 6-12 demonstrates the class.

Code Listing 6-12   (InventoryDemo.java)

```
1   /**
2    * This program demonstrates the InventoryItem class's
3    * three constructors.
4    */
5
6   public class InventoryDemo
7   {
8      public static void main(String[] args)
9      {
10        // Variables to reference 3 instances of
11        // the InventoryItem class.
12        InventoryItem item1, item2, item3;
13
```

```
14          // Instantiate item1 and use the
15          // no-arg constructor.
16          item1 = new InventoryItem();
17          System.out.println("Item 1:");
18          System.out.println("Description: "
19                              + item1.getDescription());
20          System.out.println("Units: " + item1.getUnits());
21          System.out.println();
22
23
24          // Instantiate item2 and use the
25          // second constructor.
26          item2 = new InventoryItem("Wrench");
27          System.out.println("Item 2:");
28          System.out.println("Description: "
29                              + item2.getDescription());
30          System.out.println("Units: " + item2.getUnits());
31          System.out.println();
32
33          // Instantiate item3 and use the
34          // third constructor.
35          item3 = new InventoryItem("Hammer", 20);
36          System.out.println("Item 3:");
37          System.out.println("Description: "
38                              + item3.getDescription());
39          System.out.println("Units: " + item3.getUnits());
40      }
41  }
```

Program Output

```
Item 1:
Description:
Units: 0

Item 2:
Description: Wrench
Units: 0

Item 3:
Description: Hammer
Units: 20
```

 Checkpoint

6.4   Is it required that overloaded methods have different return values, different parameter lists, or both?

6.5   What is a method's signature?

6.6   What will the following program display?

```java
public class CheckPoint
{
    public static void main(String[] args)
    {
        message(1.2);
        message(1);
    }

    public static void message(int x)
    {
        System.out.print("This is the first version ");
        System.out.println("of the method.");
    }

    public static void message(double x)
    {
        System.out.print("This is the second version ");
        System.out.println("of the method.");
    }
}
```

6.7   How many default constructors may a class have?

6.4   Passing Objects as Arguments to Methods

CONCEPT: To pass an object as a method argument, you pass an object reference.

In Chapter 3 we discussed how primitive variables can be passed as arguments to methods. You can also pass objects as arguments to methods. For example, look at Code Listing 6-13.

Code Listing 6-13   (`PassObject.java`)

```java
 1  /**
 2   * This program passes an object as an argument.
 3   */
 4
 5  public class PassObject
 6  {
 7      public static void main(String[] args)
 8      {
 9          // Create an InventoryItem object.
10          InventoryItem item = new InventoryItem("Wrench", 20);
11
12          // Pass the object to the DisplayItem method.
```

```
13            displayItem(item);
14      }
15
16      /**
17       * The following method accepts an InventoryItem
18       * object as an argument and displays its contents.
19       */
20
21      public static void displayItem(InventoryItem i)
22      {
23          System.out.println("Description: " + i.getDescription());
24          System.out.println("Units: " + i.getUnits());
25      }
26  }
```

Program Output

```
Description: Wrench
Units: 20
```

When an object is passed as an argument, it is actually a reference to the object that is passed. In this program's main method, the item variable is an InventoryItem reference variable. Its value is passed as an argument to the displayItem method. The displayItem method has a parameter variable, i, also an InventoryItem reference variable, which receives the argument.

Recall that a reference variable holds the memory address of an object. When the displayItem method is called, the address that is stored in item is passed into the i parameter variable. This is illustrated in Figure 6-3. This means that when the displayItem method is executing, item and i both reference the same object. This is illustrated in Figure 6-4.

Figure 6-3   Passing a reference as an argument

Figure 6-4   Both `item` and `i` reference the same object

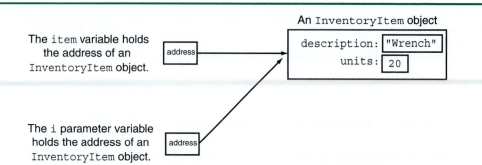

Recall from Chapter 3 that when a variable is passed as an argument to a method, it is said to be *passed by value*. This means that a copy of the variable's value is passed into the method's parameter. When the method changes the contents of the parameter variable, it does not affect the contents of the actual variable that was passed as an argument. When a reference variable is passed as an argument to a method, however, the method has access to the object that the variable references. As you can see from Figure 6-4, the `displayItem` method has access to the same `InventoryItem` object that the `item` variable references. When a method receives a reference variable as an argument, it is possible for the method to modify the contents of the object referenced by the variable. This is demonstrated in Code Listing 6-14.

Code Listing 6-14   **(PassObject2.java)**

```
1   /**
2    * This program passes an object as an argument.
3    * The object is modified by the receiving method.
4    */
5
6   public class PassObject2
7   {
8      public static void main(String [] args)
9      {
10        // Create an InventoryItem object.
11        InventoryItem item = new InventoryItem("Wrench", 20);
12
13        // Display the object's contents.
14        System.out.println("The contents of item are:");
15        System.out.println("Description: "
16                              + item.getDescription()
17                              + "  Units: " + item.getUnits());
18
19        // Pass the object to the ChangeItem method.
20        changeItem(item);
21
22        // Display the object's contents again.
23        System.out.println();
24        System.out.println("Now the contents of item are:");
25        System.out.println("Description: "
```

```
26                              + item.getDescription()
27                              + "  Units: " + item.getUnits());
28      }
29
30      /**
31       * The following method accepts an InventoryItem
32       * object as an argument and changes its contents.
33       */
34
35      public static void changeItem(InventoryItem i)
36      {
37         i.setDescription("Hammer");
38         i.setUnits(5);
39      }
40   }
```

Program Output

```
The contents of item are:
Description: Wrench  Units: 20

Now the contents of item are:
Description: Hammer  Units: 5
```

When writing a method that receives a reference as an argument, you must take care not to accidentally modify the contents of the object that is passed.

In the Spotlight:
Simulating the Game of Cho-Han

Cho-Han is a traditional Japanese gambling game in which a dealer uses a cup to roll two six-sided dice. The cup is placed upside down on a table so the value of the dice is concealed. Players then wager on whether the sum of the dice values is even (Cho) or odd (Han). The winner, or winners, take all of the wagers, or the house takes them if there are no winners.

We will develop a program that simulates a simplified variation of the game. The simulated game will have a dealer and two players. The players will not wager money, but will simply guess whether the sum of the dice values is even (Cho) or odd (Han). One point will be awarded to the player, or players, correctly guessing the outcome. The game is played for five rounds, and the player with the most points is the grand winner.

In the program, we will use the Die class that was introduced in Chapter 4. We will create two instances of the class to represent two six-sided dice. In addition to the Die class, we will write the following classes:

- **Dealer class:** We will create an instance of this class to represent the dealer. It will have the ability to roll the dice, report the value of the dice, and report whether the total dice value is Cho or Han.

- Player class: We will create two instances of this class to represent the players. Instances of the Player class can store the player's name, make a guess between Cho or Han, and be awarded points.

First, let's look at the Dealer class. Figure 6-5 shows a UML diagram for the class, and Code Listing 6-15 shows the code.

Figure 6-5   UML diagram for the Dealer class

```
                    ┌─────────────────────────────┐
                    │            Dealer           │
                    ├─────────────────────────────┤
                    │ - die1Value : int           │
                    │ - die2Value : int           │
                    ├─────────────────────────────┤
                    │ + Dealer()                  │
                    │ + rollDice() : void         │
                    │ + getChoOrHan() : String    │
                    │ + getDie1Value() : int      │
                    │ + getDie2Value() : int      │
                    └─────────────────────────────┘
```

Code Listing 6-15   (Dealer.java)

```java
 1  /**
 2   *   Dealer class for the game of Cho-Han
 3   */
 4
 5  public class Dealer
 6  {
 7      private int die1Value;  // The value of die #1
 8      private int die2Value;  // The value of die #2
 9
10      /**
11       * Constructor
12       */
13
14      public Dealer()
15      {
16          die1Value = 0;
17          die2Value = 0;
18      }
19
20      /**
21       *   The rollDice method rolls the dice and saves
22       *   their values.
23       */
24
25      public void rollDice()
26      {
```

```
27          final int SIDES = 6; // Number of sides for the dice
28
29          // Create the two dice. (This also rolls them.)
30          Die die1 = new Die(SIDES);
31          Die die2 = new Die(SIDES);
32
33          // Record their values.
34          die1Value = die1.getValue();
35          die2Value = die2.getValue();
36      }
37
38      /**
39       *  The getChoOrHan method returns the result of the dice
40       *  roll. If the sum of the dice is even, the method returns
41       *  "Cho (even)". Otherwise, it returns "Han (odd)".
42       */
43
44      public String getChoOrHan()
45      {
46          String result; // To hold the result
47
48          // Get the sum of the dice.
49          int sum = die1Value + die2Value;
50
51          // Determine even or odd.
52          if (sum % 2 == 0)
53              result = "Cho (even)";
54          else
55              result = "Han (odd)";
56
57          // Return the result.
58          return result;
59      }
60
61      /**
62       *  The getDie1Value method returns the value of
63       *  die #1.
64       */
65
66      public int getDie1Value()
67      {
68          return die1Value;
69      }
70
71      /**
72       *  The getDie2Value method returns the value of
73       *  die #2.
74       */
```

```
75
76      public int getDie2Value()
77      {
78         return die2Value;
79      }
80   }
```

Let's take a closer look at the code for the `Dealer` class:

- Lines 7 and 8 declare the fields `die1Value` and `die2Value`. These fields will hold the value of the two dice after they have been rolled.
- The constructor, in lines 14 through 18, initializes the `die1Value` and `die2Value` fields to 0.
- The `rollDice` method, in lines 25 through 36, simulates the rolling of the dice. Lines 30 and 31 create two `Die` objects. Recall that the `Die` class constructor performs an initial roll of the die, so there is no need to call the `Die` objects' `roll` method. Lines 34 and 35 save the value of the dice in the `die1Value` and `die2Value` fields.
- The `getChoOrHan` method, in lines 44 through 59, returns a string indicating whether the sum of the dice is Cho (even) or Han (odd).
- The `getDie1Value` method, in lines 66 through 69, returns the value of first die (stored in the `die1Value` field).
- The `getDie2Value` method, in lines 76 through 79, returns the value of second die (stored in the `die2Value` field).

Now let's look at the `Player` class. Figure 6-6 shows a UML diagram for the class, and Code Listing 6-16 shows the code.

Figure 6-6 UML diagram for the `Player` class

Code Listing 6-16   (`Player.java`)

```
1   import java.util.Random;
2
3   /**
4    *  Player class for the game of Cho-Han
5    */
```

```
 6
 7   public class Player
 8   {
 9      private String name;     // The player's name
10      private String guess;    // The player's guess
11      private int points;      // The player's points
12
13      /**
14       *  Constructor
15       *  Accepts the player's name as an argument
16       */
17
18      public Player(String playerName)
19      {
20         name = playerName;
21         guess = "";
22         points = 0;
23      }
24
25      /**
26       *  The makeGuess method causes the player to guess
27       *  either "Cho (even)" or "Han (odd)".
28       */
29
30      public void makeGuess()
31      {
32         // Create a Random object.
33         Random rand = new Random();
34
35         // Get a random number, either 0 or 1.
36         int guessNumber = rand.nextInt(2);
37
38         // Convert the random number to a guess of
39         // either "Cho (even)" or "Han (odd)".
40         if (guessNumber == 0)
41            guess = "Cho (even)";
42         else
43            guess = "Han (odd)";
44      }
45
46      /**
47       *  The addPoints method adds a specified number of
48       *  points to the player's current balance. The number
49       *  of points is passed as an argument.
50       */
51
52      public void addPoints(int newPoints)
53      {
```

```
54              points += newPoints;
55          }
56
57      /**
58          The getName method returns the player's name.
59      */
60
61      public String getName()
62      {
63          return name;
64      }
65
66      /**
67          The getGuess method returns the player's guess.
68      */
69
70      public String getGuess()
71      {
72          return guess;
73      }
74
75      /**
76          The getPoints method returns the player's points
77      */
78
79      public int getPoints()
80      {
81          return points;
82      }
83  }
```

Here's a summary of the code for the `Player` class:

- Lines 9 through 11 declare the field's `name`, `guess`, and `points`. These fields will hold the player's name, the player's guess, and the number of points the player has earned.
- The constructor, in lines 18 through 23, accepts an argument for the player's name, which is assigned to the `name` field. The `guess` field is assigned an empty string, and the `points` field is set to 0.
- The `makeGuess` method, in lines 30 through 44, causes the player to make a guess. The method generates a random number that is either a 0 or a 1. The `if` statement that begins at line 40 assigns the string "Cho (even)" to the `guess` field if the random number is 0, or it assigns the string "Han (odd)" to the `guess` field if the random number is 1.
- The `addPoints` method, in lines 52 through 55, adds the number of points specified by the argument to the player's point field.
- The `getName` method, in lines 61 through 64, returns the player's name.
- The `getGuess` method, in lines 70 through 73, returns the player's guess.
- The `getPoints` method, in lines 79 through 82, returns the player's points.

Code Listing 6-17 shows the program that uses these classes to simulate the game. The main method simulates five rounds of the game, displaying the results of each round, and then displays the overall game results.

Code Listing 6-17   (`ChoHan.java`)

```java
 1  import java.util.Scanner;
 2
 3  public class ChoHan
 4  {
 5     public static void main(String[] args)
 6     {
 7        final int MAX_ROUNDS = 5;   // Number of rounds
 8        String player1Name;         // First player's name
 9        String player2Name;         // Second player's name
10
11        // Create a Scanner object for keyboard input.
12        Scanner keyboard = new Scanner(System.in);
13
14        // Get the player's names.
15        System.out.print("Enter the first player's name: ");
16        player1Name = keyboard.nextLine();
17        System.out.print("Enter the second player's name: ");
18        player2Name = keyboard.nextLine();
19
20        // Create the dealer.
21        Dealer dealer = new Dealer();
22
23        // Create the two players.
24        Player player1 = new Player(player1Name);
25        Player player2 = new Player(player2Name);
26
27        // Play the rounds.
28        for (int round = 0; round < MAX_ROUNDS; round++)
29        {
30           System.out.println("-----------------------------");
31           System.out.printf("Now playing round %d.\n", round + 1);
32
33           // Roll the dice.
34           dealer.rollDice();
35
36           // The players make their guesses.
37           player1.makeGuess();
38           player2.makeGuess();
39
40           // Determine the winner of this round.
41           roundResults(dealer, player1, player2);
```

```
42          }
43
44          // Display the grand winner.
45          displayGrandWinner(player1, player2);
46      }
47
48      /**
49       *   The roundResults method determines the results of
50       *   the current round. The parameters are:
51       *   dealer: The Dealer object
52       *   player1: Player #1 object
53       *   player2: Player #2 object
54       */
55
56      public static void roundResults(Dealer dealer, Player player1,
57                                        Player player2)
58      {
59          // Show the dice values.
60          System.out.printf("The dealer rolled %d and %d.\n",
61                              dealer.getDie1Value(), dealer.getDie2Value());
62          System.out.printf("Result: %s\n", dealer.getChoOrHan());
63
64          // Check each player's guess and award points.
65          checkGuess(player1, dealer);
66          checkGuess(player2, dealer);
67      }
68
69      /**
70       *   The checkGuess method checks a player's guess against
71       *   the dealer's result. The parameters are:
72       *   player: The Player object to check.
73       *   dealer: The Dealer object.
74       */
75
76      public static void checkGuess(Player player, Dealer dealer)
77      {
78          final int POINTS_TO_ADD = 1; // Points to award winner
79          String guess = player.getGuess();             // Player's guess
80          String choHanResult = dealer.getChoOrHan(); // Cho or Han
81
82          // Display the player's guess.
83          System.out.printf("The player %s guessed %s.\n",
84                              player.getName(), player.getGuess());
85
86          // Award points if the player guessed correctly.
87          if (guess.equalsIgnoreCase(choHanResult))
88          {
89              player.addPoints(POINTS_TO_ADD);
```

```
 90              System.out.printf("Awarding %d point(s) to %s.\n",
 91                          POINTS_TO_ADD, player.getName());
 92       }
 93    }
 94
 95    /**
 96     *  The displayGrandWinner method displays the game's grand winner.
 97     *  The parameters are:
 98     *  player1: Player #1
 99     *  player2: Player #2
100     */
101
102    public static void displayGrandWinner(Player player1, Player player2)
103    {
104       System.out.println("-----------------------------");
105       System.out.println("Game over. Here are the results:");
106       System.out.printf("%s: %d points.\n", player1.getName(),
107                          player1.getPoints());
108       System.out.printf("%s: %d points.\n", player2.getName(),
109                          player2.getPoints());
110
111       if (player1.getPoints() > player2.getPoints())
112          System.out.println(player1.getName() + " is the grand winner!");
113       else if (player2.getPoints() > player1.getPoints())
114          System.out.println(player2.getName() + " is the grand winner!");
115       else
116          System.out.println("Both players are tied!");
117    }
118 }
```

Program Output with Example Input Shown in Bold

```
Enter the first player's name: Chelsea [Enter]
Enter the second player's name: Chris [Enter]

Now playing round 1.
The dealer rolled 3 and 6.
Result: Han (odd)
The player Chelsea guessed Han (odd).
Awarding 1 point(s) to Chelsea.
The player Chris guessed Han (odd).
Awarding 1 point(s) to Chris.

Now playing round 2.
The dealer rolled 4 and 5.
Result: Han (odd)
The player Chelsea guessed Cho (even).
The player Chris guessed Cho (even).
```

```
Now playing round 3.
The dealer rolled 5 and 6.
Result: Han (odd)
The player Chelsea guessed Cho (even).
The player Chris guessed Han (odd).
Awarding 1 point(s) to Chris.

Now playing round 4.
The dealer rolled 1 and 6.
Result: Han (odd)
The player Chelsea guessed Cho (even).
The player Chris guessed Cho (even).

Now playing round 5.
The dealer rolled 6 and 6.
Result: Cho (even)
The player Chelsea guessed Han (odd).
The player Chris guessed Cho (even).
Awarding 1 point(s) to Chris.

Game over. Here are the results:
Chelsea: 1 points.
Chris: 3 points.
Chris is the grand winner!
```

Let's look at the code. Here is a summary of the main method:

- Lines 7 through 9 make the following declarations: MAX_ROUNDS—the number of rounds to play, player1Name—to hold the name of player #1, and player2Name—to hold the name of player #2.
- Lines 15 through 18 prompt the user to enter the players' names.
- Line 21 creates an instance of the Dealer class. The object represents the dealer and is referenced by the dealer variable.
- Line 24 creates an instance of the Player class. The object represents player #1 and is referenced by the player1 variable. Notice that player1Name is passed as an argument to the constructor.
- Line 25 creates another instance of the Player class. The object represents player #2 and is referenced by the player2 variable. Notice that player2Name is passed as an argument to the constructor.
- The for loop that begins in line 28 iterates five times, causing the simulation of five rounds of the game. The loop performs the following actions:
  - Line 34 causes the dealer to roll the dice.
  - Line 37 causes player #1 to make a guess (Cho or Han).
  - Line 38 causes player #2 to make a guess (Cho or Han).
  - Line 41 passes the dealer, player1, and player2 objects to the roundResults method. The method displays the results of this round.
- Line 45 passes the player1 and player2 objects to the displayGrandWinner method, which displays the grand winner of the game.

The roundResults method, which displays the results of a round, appears in lines 56 through 67. Here is a summary of the method:

- The method accepts references to the dealer, player1, and player2 objects as arguments.
- The statement in lines 60 through 61 displays the value of the two dice.
- Line 62 calls the dealer object's getChoOrHan method to display the results, Cho or Han.
- Line 65 calls the checkGuess method, passing the player1 and dealer objects as arguments. The checkGuess method compares a player's guess to the dealer's result (Cho or Han), and awards points to the player if the guess is correct.
- Line 66 calls the checkGuess method, passing the player2 and dealer objects as arguments.

The checkGuess method, which compares a player's guess to the dealer's result, awarding points to the player for a correct guess, appears in lines 76 through 93. Here is a summary of the method:

- The method accepts references to a Player object and the Dealer object as arguments.
- Line 78 declares the constant POINTS_TO_ADD, set to the value 1, which is the number of points to add to the player's balance if the player's guess is correct.
- Line 79 assigns the player's guess to the String object guess.
- Line 80 assigns the dealer's results (Cho or Han) to the String object choHanResult.
- The statement in lines 83 through 84 displays the player's name and guess.
- The if statement in line 87 compares the player's guess to the dealer's result. If they match, then the player guessed correctly, and line 89 awards points to the player.

The displayGrandWinner method, which displays the grand winner of the game, appears in lines 102 through 117. Here is a summary of the method:

- The method accepts references to the player1 and player2 objects.
- The statements in lines 106 through 109 display both players' names and points.
- The if-else-if statement that begins in line 111 determines which of the two players has the highest score, and displays that player's name as the grand winner. If both players have the same score, a tie is declared.

Checkpoint

6.8 When an object is passed as an argument to a method, what is actually passed?

6.9 When an argument is passed by value, the method has a copy of the argument and does not have access to the original argument. Is this still true when an object is passed to a method?

6.10 Recall the Rectangle class shown earlier in this chapter. Write a method that accepts a Rectangle object as its argument and displays the object's length and width fields on the screen.

6.5 Returning Objects from Methods

CONCEPT: A method can return a reference to an object.

VideoNote
Returning Objects from Methods

Just as methods can be written to return an int, double, float, or other primitive data type, they can also be written to return a reference to an object. For example, the program in Code Listing 6-18 uses a method, getData, which returns a reference to an InventoryItem object.

Code Listing 6-18 `(ReturnObject.java)`

```java
 1  import java.util.Scanner;
 2
 3  /**
 4   * This program demonstrates how a method can return
 5   * a reference to an object.
 6   */
 7
 8  public class ReturnObject
 9  {
10     public static void main(String[] args)
11     {
12        // Declare a variable that will be used to
13        // reference an InventoryItem object.
14        InventoryItem item;
15
16        // The getData method will return a reference
17        // to an InventoryItem object.
18
19        item = getData();
20
21        // Display the object's data.
22        System.out.println("Here is the data you entered:");
23        System.out.println("Description: "
24                           + item.getDescription()
25                           + "  Units: " + item.getUnits());
26
27     }
28
29     /**
30      * The getData method gets an item's description
31      * and number of units from the user. The method
32      * returns an InventoryItem object containing
33      * the data that was entered.
34      */
35
36     public static InventoryItem getData()
37     {
38        String desc;    // To hold the description
39        int units;      // To hold the units
40
41        // Create a Scanner object for keyboard input.
42        Scanner keyboard = new Scanner(System.in);
43
44        // Get the item description.
45        System.out.print("Enter an item description: ");
```

```
46          desc = keyboard.nextLine();
47
48          // Get the number of units.
49          System.out.print("Enter a number of units: ");
50          units = keyboard.nextInt();
51
52          // Create an InventoryItem object and return
53          // a reference to it.
54          return new InventoryItem(desc, units);
55      }
56  }
```

Program Output with Example Input Shown in Bold
Enter an item description: **Pliers [Enter]**
Enter a number of units: **25 [Enter]**
Here is the data you entered:
Description: Pliers   Units: 25

Notice in line 36 that the getData method has the return data type of InventoryItem. Figure 6-7 shows the method's return type, which is listed in the method header.

Figure 6-7 The getData method header

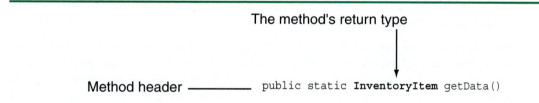

A return type of InventoryItem means the method returns a reference to an InventoryItem object when it terminates. The following statement, which appears in line 19 in the main method, assigns the getData method's return value to item:

```
item = getData();
```

After this statement executes, the item variable will reference the InventoryItem object that was returned from the getData method.

Now let's look at the getData method. First, the method declares two local variables, desc and units. These variables are used to hold an item description and a number of units, as entered by the user in lines 46 and 50. The last statement in the getData method is the following return statement, which appears in line 54:

```
return new InventoryItem(desc, units);
```

This statement uses the new key word to create an InventoryItem object, passing desc and units as arguments to the constructor. The address of the object is then returned from the method.

6.11   Recall the `Rectangle` class shown earlier in this chapter. Write a method that returns a reference to a `Rectangle` object. The method should store the user's input in the object's `length` and `width` fields before returning it.

6.6   The toString Method

> **CONCEPT:** Most classes can benefit from having a method named **toString**, which is implicitly called under certain circumstances. Typically, the method returns a string that represents the state of an object.

So far you've seen many examples in which an object is created and then its contents are used in messages displayed on the screen. Previously you saw the following statement in lines 23 through 25 of Code Listing 6-18:

```
System.out.println("Description: "
        + item.getDescription()
        + "  Units: " + item.getUnits());
```

Recall that `item` references an `InventoryItem` object. In this statement, the `System.out.println` method displays a string showing the values of the object's `description` and `units` fields. Assuming that the object's `description` field is set to "Pliers" and the `units` field is set to 25, the output of this statement will look like this:

```
Description: Pliers  Units: 25
```

In this statement, the argument passed to `System.out.println` is a string, which is put together from several pieces. The concatenation operator (+) joins the pieces together. The first piece is the string literal `"Description: "`. To this, the value returned from the `getDescription` method is concatenated, followed by the string literal `"  Units: "`, followed by the value returned from the `getUnits` method. The resulting string represents the current state of the object.

Creating a string that represents the state of an object is such a common task that many programmers equip their classes with a method that returns such a string. In Java, it is standard practice to name this method `toString`. Let's look at an example of a class that has a `toString` method. Figure 6-8 shows the UML diagram for the `Stock` class, which holds data about a company's stock.

Figure 6-8   UML diagram for the `Stock` class

Stock
- symbol : String - sharePrice : double
+ Stock(sym : String, price : double) + getSymbol() : String + getSharePrice() : double + toString() : String

Java also implicitly calls an object's toString method any time you concatenate an object of the class with a string. For example, the following code would implicitly call the xyzCompany object's toString method:

```
Stock xyzCompany = new Stock ("XYZ", 9.62);
System.out.println("The stock data is:\n" + xyzCompany);
```

This code would produce the following output:

```
The stock data is:
Trading symbol: XYZ
Share price: 9.62
```

Code Listing 6-20 shows a complete program demonstrating the Stock class's toString method. (If you have downloaded the book's source code, you will find this file in the folder *Chapter 06\Stock Class Phase 1*.)

Code Listing 6-20   **(StockDemo1.java)**

```
 1  /**
 2   * This program demonstrates the Stock class's
 3   * toString method.
 4   */
 5
 6  public class StockDemo1
 7  {
 8     public static void main(String[] args)
 9     {
10        // Create a Stock object for the XYZ Company.
11        // The trading symbol is XYZ and the current
12        // price per share is $9.62.
13        Stock xyzCompany = new Stock ("XYZ", 9.62);
14
15        // Display the object's values.
16        System.out.println(xyzCompany);
17     }
18  }
```

Program Output

```
Trading symbol: XYZ
Share price: 9.62
```

 NOTE: Every class automatically has a toString method that returns a string containing the object's class name, followed by the @ symbol, followed by an integer unique to the object. This method is called when necessary if you have not provided your own toString method. You will learn more about this in Chapter 9.

6.7   Writing an equals Method

CONCEPT: You cannot determine whether two objects contain the same data by comparing them with the == operator. Instead, the class must have a method such as equals for comparing the contents of objects.

Recall from Chapter 4 that the String class has a method named equals that determines whether two strings are equal. You can write an equals method for any of your own classes as well.

In fact, you must write an equals method (or one that works like it) for a class in order to determine whether two objects of the class contain the same values. This is because you cannot use the == operator to compare the contents of two objects. For example, the following code might appear to compare the contents of two Stock objects, but in reality it does not.

```
// Create two Stock objects with the same values.
Stock company1 = new Stock("XYZ", 9.62);
Stock company2 = new Stock("XYZ", 9.62);

// Use the == operator to compare the objects.
// (This is a mistake.)
if (company1 == company2)
    System.out.println("Both objects are the same.");
else
    System.out.println("The objects are different.");
```

When you use the == operator with reference variables, the operator compares the memory addresses that the variables contain, not the contents of the objects referenced by the variables. This is illustrated in Figure 6-9.

Figure 6-9   The if statement tests the contents of the reference variables, not the contents of the objects that the variables reference

Because the two variables reference different objects in memory, they will contain different addresses. Therefore, the result of the boolean expression company1 == company2 is false and the code reports that the objects are not the same. Instead of using the == operator to compare the two Stock objects, we should write an equals method that compares the contents of the two objects.

If you have downloaded the book's source code, in the folder *Chapter 06\Stock Class Phase 2* you will find a revision of the Stock class. This version of the class has an equals method. The code for the method follows. (No other part of the class has changed, so only the equals method is shown.)

```java
public boolean equals(Stock object2)
{
    boolean status;

    // Determine whether this object's symbol and
    // sharePrice fields are equal to object2's
    // symbol and sharePrice fields.
    if (symbol.equals(object2.symbol) && sharePrice == object2.sharePrice)
        status = true;   // Yes, the objects are equal.
    else
        status = false; // No, the objects are not equal.

    // Return the value in status.
    return status;
}
```

The equals method accepts a Stock object as its argument. The parameter variable object2 will reference the object that was passed as an argument. The if statement performs the following comparison: If the symbol field of the calling object is equal to the symbol field of object2, and the sharePrice field of the calling object is equal to the sharePrice field of object2, then the two objects contain the same values. In this case, the local variable status (a boolean) is set to true. Otherwise, status is set to false. Finally, the method returns the value of the status variable.

Notice that the method can access object2's symbol and sharePrice fields directly. Because object2 references a Stock object, and the equals method is a member of the Stock class, the method is allowed to access object2's private fields.

The program in Code Listing 6-21 demonstrates the equals method. (If you have downloaded the book's source code, you will find this file in the folder *Chapter 06\Stock Class Phase 2*.)

Code Listing 6-21   **(StockCompare.java)**

```java
1  /**
2   * This program uses the Stock class's equals
3   * method to compare two Stock objects.
4   */
5
```

```
6   public class StockCompare
7   {
8      public static void main(String[] args)
9      {
10        // Create two Stock objects with the same values.
11        Stock company1 = new Stock("XYZ", 9.62);
12        Stock company2 = new Stock("XYZ", 9.62);
13
14        // Use the equals method to compare the objects.
15        if (company1.equals(company2))
16           System.out.println("Both objects are the same.");
17        else
18           System.out.println("The objects are different.");
19     }
20  }
```

Program Output

Both objects are the same.

If you want to be able to compare the objects of a given class, you should always write an equals method for the class.

 NOTE: Every class automatically has an equals method that works the same as the == operator. This method is called when necessary if you have not provided your own equals method. You will learn more about this in Chapter 9.

6.8 Methods That Copy Objects

CONCEPT: You can simplify the process of duplicating objects by equipping a class with a method that returns a copy of an object.

You cannot make a copy of an object with a simple assignment statement as you would with a primitive variable. For example, look at the following code:

```
Stock company1 = new Stock("XYZ", 9.62);
Stock company2 = company1;
```

The first statement creates a Stock object and assigns its address to the company1 variable. The second statement assigns company1 to company2. This does not make a copy of the object referenced by company1. Rather, it makes a copy of the address that is stored in company1 and stores that address in company2. After this statement executes, both the company1 and company2 variables will reference the same object. This is illustrated in Figure 6-10.

Figure 6-10   Both variables reference the same object

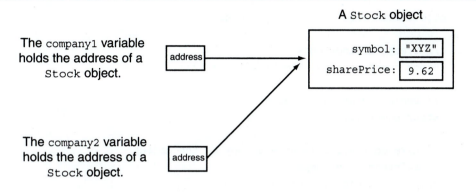

This type of assignment operation is called a *reference copy* because only the object's address is copied, not the actual object itself. To copy the object itself, you must create a new object and then set the new object's fields to the same values as the fields of the object being copied. This process can be simplified by equipping the class with a method that performs this operation. The method then returns a reference to the duplicate object.

If you have downloaded the book's source code, in the folder *Chapter 06\Stock Class Phase 3* you will find a revision of the Stock class. This version of the class has a method named copy that returns a copy of a Stock object. The code for the method follows. (No other part of the class has changed, so only the copy method is shown.)

```java
public Stock copy()
{
    // Create a new Stock object and initialize it
    // with the same data held by the calling object.
    Stock copyObject = new Stock(symbol, sharePrice);

    // Return a reference to the new object.
    return copyObject;
}
```

The copy method creates a new Stock object and passes the calling object's symbol and sharePrice fields as arguments to the constructor. This makes the new object a copy of the calling object. The program in Code Listing 6-22 demonstrates the copy method. (If you have downloaded the book's source code, you will find this file in the folder *Chapter 06\Stock Class Phase 3*.)

Code Listing 6-22   **(ObjectCopy.java)**

```java
1   /**
2    * This program uses the Stock class's copy method
3    * to create a copy of a Stock object.
4    */
5
```

```
 6   public class ObjectCopy
 7   {
 8      public static void main(String[] args)
 9      {
10         // Create a Stock object.
11         Stock company1 = new Stock("XYZ", 9.62);
12
13         // Declare a Stock variable.
14         Stock company2;
15
16         // Make company2 reference a copy of the object
17         // referenced by company1.
18         company2 = company1.copy();
19
20         // Display the contents of both objects.
21         System.out.println("Company 1:\n" + company1);
22         System.out.println();
23         System.out.println("Company 2:\n" + company2);
24
25         // Confirm that we actually have two objects.
26         if (company1 == company2)
27         {
28            System.out.println("The company1 and company2 "
29                   + "variables reference the same object.");
30         }
31         else
32         {
33            System.out.println("The company1 and company2 "
34                   + "variables reference different objects.");
35         }
36      }
37   }
```

Program Output

```
Company 1:
Trading symbol: XYZ
Share price: 9.62

Company 2:
Trading symbol: XYZ
Share price: 9.62
The company1 and company2 variables reference different objects.
```

Copy Constructors

Another way to create a copy of an object is to use a copy constructor. A *copy constructor* is simply a constructor that accepts an object of the same class as an argument. It makes the object that is being created a copy of the object that was passed as an argument.

If you have downloaded the book's source code, in the folder *Chapter 06\Stock Class Phase 4* you will find another revision of the `Stock` class. This version of the class has a copy constructor. The code for the copy constructor follows. (No other part of the class has changed, so only the copy constructor is shown.)

```java
public Stock(Stock object2)
{
    symbol = object2.symbol;
    sharePrice = object2.sharePrice;
}
```

Notice that the constructor accepts a `Stock` object as an argument. The parameter variable `object2` will reference the object passed as an argument. The constructor copies the values in `object2`'s `symbol` and `sharePrice` fields to the `symbol` and `sharePrice` fields of the object being created.

The following code segment demonstrates the copy constructor. It creates a `Stock` object referenced by the variable `company1`. Then it creates another `Stock` object referenced by the variable `company2`. The object referenced by `company2` is a copy of the object referenced by `company1`.

```java
// Create a Stock object.
Stock company1 = new Stock("XYZ", 9.62);
// Create another Stock object that is a copy of the company1 object.
Stock company2 = new Stock(company1);
```

6.9 Aggregation

CONCEPT: Aggregation occurs when an instance of a class is a field in another class.

VideoNote
Aggregation

In real life, objects are frequently made of other objects. A house, for example, is made of door objects, window objects, wall objects, and much more. It is the combination of all these objects that makes a house object.

When designing software, it sometimes makes sense to create an object from other objects. For example, suppose you need an object to represent a course that you are taking in college. You decide to create a `Course` class, which will hold the following information:

- The course name
- The instructor's last name, first name, and office number
- The textbook's title, author, and publisher

In addition to the course name, the class will hold items related to the instructor and the textbook. You could put fields for each of these items in the `Course` class. However, a good design principle is to separate related items into their own classes. In this example, an `Instructor` class could be created to hold the instructor-related data and a `TextBook` class could be created to hold the textbook-related data. Instances of these classes could then be used as fields in the `Course` class.

Figure 6-11   UML diagram for the `Instructor` class

```
┌─────────────────────────────────────────────┐
│                  Instructor                  │
├─────────────────────────────────────────────┤
│ - lastName : String                          │
│ - firstName : String                         │
│ - officeNumber : String                      │
├─────────────────────────────────────────────┤
│ + Instructor(lname : String, fname : String, │
│              office : String)                │
│ + Instructor(object2 : Instructor)           │
│ + set(lname : String, fname : String,        │
│        office : String) : void               │
│ + toString() : String                        │
└─────────────────────────────────────────────┘
```

Let's take a closer look at how this might be done. Figure 6-11 shows a UML diagram for the `Instructor` class. To keep things simple, the class has only the following methods:

- A constructor that accepts arguments for the instructor's last name, first name, and office number
- A copy constructor
- A set method that can be used to set all of the class's fields
- A `toString` method

The code for the `Instructor` class is shown in Code Listing 6-23.

Code Listing 6-23   (`Instructor.java`)

```java
1   /**
2    * This class stores information about an instructor.
3    */
4
5   public class Instructor
6   {
7      private String lastName,      // Last name
8                     firstName,     // First name
9                     officeNumber;  // Office number
10
11     /**
12      * This constructor accepts arguments for the
13      * last name, first name, and office number.
14      */
15
16     public Instructor(String lname, String fname,
17                       String office)
18     {
19        lastName = lname;
20        firstName = fname;
21        officeNumber = office;
22     }
```

```
23
24       /**
25        * Copy constructor
26        */
27
28       public Instructor(Instructor object2)
29       {
30          lastName = object2.lastName;
31          firstName = object2.firstName;
32          officeNumber = object2.officeNumber;
33       }
34
35       /**
36        * The set method sets each field.
37        */
38
39       public void set(String lname, String fname,
40                       String office)
41       {
42          lastName = lname;
43          firstName = fname;
44          officeNumber = office;
45       }
46
47       /**
48        * The toString method returns a string containing
49        * the instructor information.
50        */
51
52       public String toString()
53       {
54          // Create a string representing the object.
55          String str = "Last Name: " + lastName
56                       + "\nFirst Name: " + firstName
57                       + "\nOffice Number: " + officeNumber;
58
59          // Return the string.
60          return str;
61       }
62    }
```

Figure 6-12 shows a UML diagram for the TextBook class. As before, we want to keep the class simple. The only methods it has are a constructor, a copy constructor, a set method, and a toString method. The code for the TextBook class is shown in Code Listing 6-24.

Figure 6-12 UML diagram for the TextBook class

```
                        TextBook
        - title : String
        - author : String
        - publisher : String

        + TextBook(textTitle : String, auth : String,
                        pub : String)
        + TextBook(object2 : TextBook)
        + set(textTitle : String, auth : String,
              pub : String) : void
        + toString() : String
```

Code Listing 6-24   **(TextBook.java)**

```java
 1   /**
 2    * This class stores information about a textbook.
 3    */
 4
 5   public class TextBook
 6   {
 7      private String title,     // Title of the book
 8                     author,    // Author's last name
 9                     publisher; // Name of publisher
10
11      /**
12       * This constructor accepts arguments for the
13       * title, author, and publisher.
14       */
15
16      public TextBook(String textTitle, String auth,
17                      String pub)
18      {
19         title = textTitle;
20         author = auth;
21         publisher = pub;
22      }
23
24      /**
25       * Copy constructor
26       */
27
28      public TextBook(TextBook object2)
29      {
30         title = object2.title;
31         author = object2.author;
32         publisher = object2.publisher;
33      }
```

```
34
35      /**
36       * The set method sets each field.
37       */
38
39      public void set(String textTitle, String auth,
40                      String pub)
41      {
42         title = textTitle;
43         author = auth;
44         publisher = pub;
45      }
46
47      /**
48       * The toString method returns a string containing
49       * the textbook information.
50       */
51
52      public String toString()
53      {
54         // Create a string representing the object.
55         String str = "Title: " + title
56                      + "\nAuthor: " + author
57                      + "\nPublisher: " + publisher;
58
59         // Return the string.
60         return str;
61      }
62  }
```

Figure 6-13 shows a UML diagram for the Course class. Notice that the Course class has an Instructor object and a TextBook object as fields. Making an instance of one class a field in another class is called object aggregation. The word *aggregate* means "a whole that is made of constituent parts." In this example, the Course class is an aggregate class because it is made of constituent objects.

Figure 6-13   UML diagram for the Course class

When an instance of one class is a member of another class, it is said that there is a "has a" relationship between the classes. For example, the relationships that exist among the Course, Instructor, and TextBook classes can be described as follows:

- The course *has an* instructor.
- The course *has a* textbook.

The "has a" relationship is sometimes called a *whole–part relationship* because one object is part of a greater whole. The code for the Course class is shown in Code Listing 6-25.

Code Listing 6-25   (Course.java)

```java
 1  /**
 2   * This class stores information about a course.
 3   */
 4
 5  public class Course
 6  {
 7     private String courseName;     // Name of the course
 8     private Instructor instructor; // The instructor
 9     private TextBook textBook;     // The textbook
10
11     /**
12      * This constructor accepts arguments for the
13      * course name, instructor, and textbook.
14      */
15
16     public Course(String name, Instructor instr,
17                   TextBook text)
18     {
19        // Assign the courseName.
20        courseName = name;
21
22        // Create a new Instructor object, passing
23        // instr as an argument to the copy constructor.
24        instructor = new Instructor(instr);
25
26        // Create a new TextBook object, passing
27        // text as an argument to the copy constructor.
28        textBook = new TextBook(text);
29     }
30
31     /**
32      * getName method
33      */
34
```

```
35      public String getName()
36      {
37         return courseName;
38      }
39
40      /**
41       * getInstructor method
42       */
43
44      public Instructor getInstructor()
45      {
46         // Return a copy of the instructor object.
47         return new Instructor(instructor);
48      }
49
50      /**
51       * getTextBook method
52       */
53
54      public TextBook getTextBook()
55      {
56         // Return a copy of the textBook object.
57         return new TextBook(textBook);
58      }
59
60      /**
61       * The toString method returns a string containing
62       * the course information.
63       */
64
65      public String toString()
66      {
67         // Create a string representing the object.
68         String str = "Course name: " + courseName
69                         + "\nInstructor Information:\n"
70                         + instructor
71                         + "\nTextbook Information:\n"
72                         + textBook;
73
74         // Return the string.
75         return str;
76      }
77   }
```

The program in Code Listing 6-26 demonstrates the Course class.

Code Listing 6-26   (CourseDemo.java)

```
1   /**
2    * This program demonstrates the Course class.
3    */
4
5   public class CourseDemo
6   {
7      public static void main(String[] args)
8      {
9         // Create an Instructor object.
10        Instructor myInstructor =
11           new Instructor("Kramer", "Shawn", "RH3010");
12
13        // Create a TextBook object.
14        TextBook myTextBook =
15           new TextBook("Starting Out with Java",
16                        "Gaddis", "Addison-Wesley");
17
18        // Create a Course object.
19        Course myCourse =
20           new Course("Intro to Java", myInstructor,
21                      myTextBook);
22
23        // Display the course information.
24        System.out.println(myCourse);
25     }
26  }
```

Program Output

```
Course name: Intro to Java
Instructor Information:
Last Name: Kramer
First Name: Shawn
Office Number: RH3010
Textbook Information:
Title: Starting Out with Java
Author: Gaddis
Publisher: Addison-Wesley
```

Aggregation in UML Diagrams

You show aggregation in a UML diagram by connecting two classes with a line that has an open diamond at one end. The diamond is closest to the class that is the aggregate. Figure 6-14 shows a UML diagram depicting the relationship among the Course, Instructor, and TextBook classes. The open diamond is closest to the Course class because it is the aggregate (the whole).

Figure 6-14   UML diagram showing aggregation

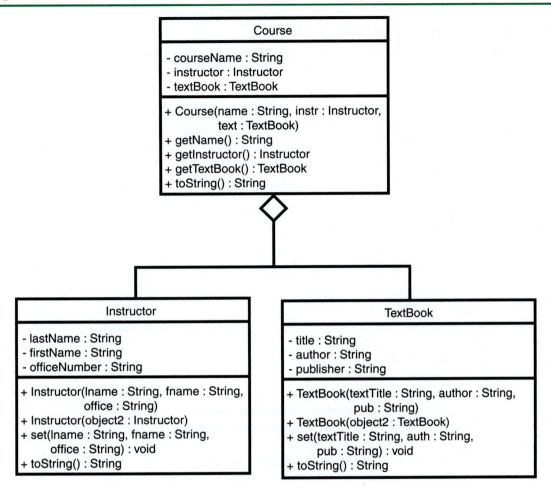

Security Issues with Aggregate Classes

When writing an aggregate class, you should be careful not to unintentionally create "security holes" that can allow code outside the class to modify private data inside the class. We will focus on two specific practices that can help prevent security holes in your classes:

- **Perform Deep Copies When Creating Field Objects**
  An aggregate object contains references to other objects. When you make a copy of the aggregate object, it is important that you also make copies of the objects it references. This is known as a *deep copy*. If you make a copy of an aggregate object, but only make a reference copy of the objects it references, then you have performed a *shallow copy*.
- **Return Copies of Field Objects, not the Original Objects**
  When a method in the aggregate class returns a reference to a field object, return a reference to a copy of the field object.

Let's discuss each of these practices in more depth.

Perform Deep Copies when Creating Field Objects

Let's take a closer look at the `Course` class in Code Listing 6-25. First, notice the arguments that the constructor accepts in lines 16 and 17:

- A reference to a `String` containing the name of the course is passed into the `name` parameter.
- A reference to an `Instructor` object is passed into the `instr` parameter.
- A reference to a `TextBook` object is passed into the `text` parameter.

Next, notice that the constructor does not merely assign `instr` to the `instructor` field. Instead, in line 24 it creates a new `Instructor` object for the `instructor` field and passes `instr` to the copy constructor. Here is the statement:

```
instructor = new Instructor(instr);
```

This statement creates a copy of the object referenced by `instr`. The `instructor` field will reference the copy.

When a class has a field that is an object, it is possible that a shallow copy operation will create a security hole. For example, suppose the `Course` constructor had been written like this:

```
// Bad constructor!
public Course(String name, Instructor instr, TextBook text)
{
    // Assign the courseName.
    courseName = name;

    // Assign the instructor (Reference copy)
    instructor = instr;   // Causes security hole!

    // Assign the textBook (Reference copy)
    textBook = text;      // Causes security hole!
}
```

In this example, the `instructor` and `textBook` fields are merely assigned the addresses of the objects passed into the constructor. This can cause problems because there may be variables outside the `Course` object that also contain references to these `Instructor` and `TextBook` objects. These outside variables would provide direct access to the `Course` object's private data.

At this point you might be wondering why a deep copy was not also done for the `courseName` field. In line 20 the `Course` constructor performs a reference copy, simply assigning the address of the `String` object referenced by `name` to the `courseName` field. This is permissible because `String` objects are immutable. An immutable object does not provide a way to change its contents. Even if variables outside the `Course` class reference the same object that `courseName` references, the object cannot be changed.

Return Copies of Field Objects, Not the Original Objects

When a method in an aggregate class returns a reference to a field object, it should return a reference to a copy of the field object, not the field object itself. For example, look at the `getInstructor` method in the `Course` class. The code is shown here:

```java
public Instructor getInstructor()
{
    // Return a copy of the instructor object.
    return new Instructor(instructor);
}
```

Notice that the `return` statement uses the `new` key word to create a new `Instructor` object, passing the `instructor` field to the copy constructor. The object that is created is a copy of the object referenced by `instructor`. The address of the copy is then returned. This is preferable to simply returning a reference to the field object itself. For example, suppose the method had been written this way:

```java
// Bad method
public Instructor getInstructor()
{
    // Return a reference to the instructor object.
    return instructor; // WRONG! Causes a security hole.
}
```

This method returns the value stored in the `instructor` field, which is the address of an `Instructor` object. Any variable that receives the address can then access the `Instructor` object. This means that code outside the `Course` object can change the values held by the `Instructor` object. This is a security hole because the `Instructor` object is a private field! Only code inside the `Course` class should be allowed to access it.

> **NOTE:** It is permissible to return a reference to a `String` object, even if the `String` object is a private field. This is because `String` objects are immutable.

Avoid Using `null` References

Recall from Chapter 3 that by default a reference variable that is an instance field is initialized to the value `null`. This indicates that the variable does not reference an object. Because a `null` reference variable does not reference an object, you cannot use it to perform an operation that would require the existence of an object. For example, a `null` reference variable cannot be used to call a method. If you attempt to perform an operation with a `null` reference variable, the program will terminate. For example, look at the `FullName` class in Code Listing 6-27.

Code Listing 6-27 (FullName.java)

```java
 1  /**
 2   * This class stores a person's first, last, and middle names.
 3   * The class is dangerous because it does not prevent operations
 4   * on null reference fields.
 5   */
 6
 7  public class FullName
 8  {
 9     private String lastName,    // To hold a last name
10                    firstName,   // To hold a first name
11                    middleName;  // To hold a middle name
12
13     /**
14      * The following method sets the lastName field.
15      */
16
17     public void setLastName(String str)
18     {
19        lastName = str;
20     }
21
22     /**
23      * The following method sets the firstName field.
24      */
25
26     public void setFirstName(String str)
27     {
28        firstName = str;
29     }
30
31     /**
32      * The following method sets the middleName field.
33      */
34
35     public void setMiddleName(String str)
36     {
37        middleName = str;
38     }
39
40     /**
41      * The following method returns the length of the
42      * full name.
43      */
44
45     public int getLength()
```

```
46        {
47            return lastName.length() + firstName.length()
48                    + middleName.length();
49        }
50
51        /**
52         * The following method returns the full name.
53         */
54
55        public String toString()
56        {
57            return firstName + " " + middleName + " "
58                    + lastName;
59        }
60    }
```

First, notice that the class has three String reference variables as fields: lastName, firstName, and middleName. Second, notice that the class does not have a programmer-defined constructor. When an instance of this class is created, the lastName, firstName, and middleName fields will be initialized to null by the default constructor. Third, notice that the getLength method uses the lastName, firstName, and middleName variables to call the String class's length method in lines 47 and 48. Nothing is preventing the length method from being called while any or all of these reference variables are set to null. The program in Code Listing 6-28 demonstrates this.

Code Listing 6-28   (NameTester.java)

```
1   /**
2    * This program creates a FullName object, and then calls the
3    * object's getLength method before values are established for
4    * its reference fields. As a result, this program will crash.
5    */
6
7   public class NameTester
8   {
9       public static void main(String[] args)
10      {
11          // Create a FullName object.
12          FullName name = new FullName();
13
14          // Display the length of the name.
15          System.out.println(name.getLength());
16      }
17  }
```

This program will crash[1] when you run it because the getLength method is called before the name object's fields are made to reference String objects. One way to prevent the program from crashing is to use if statements in the getLength method to determine whether any of the fields are set to null. Here is an example:

```java
public int getLength()
{
    int len = 0;

    if (lastName != null)
        len += lastName.length();

    if (firstName != null)
        len += firstName.length();

    if (middleName != null)
        len += middleName.length();

    return len;
}
```

Another way to handle this problem is to write a no-arg constructor that assigns values to the reference fields. Here is an example:

```java
public FullName()
{
    lastName = "";
    firstName = "";
    middleName = "";
}
```

Checkpoint

6.12   Consider the following statement: "A car has an engine." If this statement refers to classes, what is the aggregate class?

6.13   Why is it not safe to return a reference to an object that is a private field? Does this also hold true for String objects that are private fields? Why or why not?

6.14   A class has a reference variable as an instance field. Is it advisable to use the reference variable to call a method prior to assigning it the address of an object? Why or why not?

6.10   The this Reference Variable

CONCEPT: The this key word is the name of a reference variable that an object can use to refer to itself. It is available to all nonstatic methods.

[1]Actually, the program throws an exception. Exceptions are discussed in Chapter 10.

The key word `this` is the name of a reference variable that an object can use to refer to itself. For example, recall the `Stock` class presented earlier in this chapter. The class has the following `equals` method that compares the calling `Stock` object to another `Stock` object that is passed as an argument:

```java
public boolean equals(Stock object2)
{
   boolean status;

   // Determine whether this object's symbol and
   // sharePrice fields are equal to object2's
   // symbol and sharePrice fields.
   if (symbol.equals(object2.symbol) &&
      sharePrice == object2.sharePrice)
      status = true;   // Yes, the objects are equal.
   else
      status = false; // No, the objects are not equal.

   // Return the value in status.
   return status;
}
```

When this method is executing, the `this` variable contains the address of the calling object. We could rewrite the `if` statement as follows, and it would perform the same operation (the changes appear in bold):

```java
if (this.symbol.equals(object2.symbol) &&
    this.sharePrice == object2.sharePrice)
```

The `this` reference variable is available to all of a class's nonstatic methods.

Using `this` to Overcome Shadowing

One common use of the `this` key word is to overcome the shadowing of a field name by a parameter name. Recall from Chapter 3 that if a method's parameter has the same name as a field in the same class, then the parameter name shadows the field name. For example, look at the constructor in the `Stock` class:

```java
public Stock(String sym, double price)
{
   symbol = sym;
   sharePrice = price;
}
```

This method uses the parameter `sym` to accept an argument assigned to the `symbol` field, and the parameter `price` to accept an argument assigned to the `sharePrice` field. Sometimes it is difficult (and even time-consuming) to think of a good parameter name that is different from a field name. To avoid this problem, many programmers give parameters the same names as the fields to which they correspond, and then use the `this` key word to refer to the field names. For example the `Stock` class's constructor could be written as follows:

```
public Stock(String symbol, double sharePrice)
{
    this.symbol = symbol;
    this.sharePrice = sharePrice;
}
```

Although the parameter names `symbol` and `sharePrice` shadow the field names `symbol` and `sharePrice`, the `this` key word overcomes the shadowing. Because `this` is a reference to the calling object, the expression `this.symbol` refers to the calling object's `symbol` field, and the expression `this.sharePrice` refers to the calling object's `sharePrice` field.

Using `this` to Call an Overloaded Constructor from Another Constructor

You learned in Chapter 3 that a constructor is automatically called when an object is created. You also learned that you cannot call a constructor explicitly, as you do other methods. However, there is one exception to this rule: You can use the `this` key word to call one constructor from another constructor in the same class.

To illustrate this, recall the `Stock` class presented earlier in this chapter. It has the following constructor:

```
public Stock(String sym, double price)
{
    symbol = sym;
    sharePrice = price;
}
```

This constructor accepts arguments that are assigned to the `symbol` and `sharePrice` fields. Let's suppose we also want a constructor that only accepts an argument for the `symbol` field, and assigns 0.0 to the `sharePrice` field. Here's one way to write the constructor:

```
public Stock(String sym)
{
    this(sym, 0.0);
}
```

This constructor simply uses the `this` variable to call the first constructor. It passes the value in `sym` as the first argument and 0.0 as the second argument. The result is that the `symbol` field is assigned the value in `sym` and the `sharePrice` field is assigned 0.0.

Remember the following rules about using `this` to call a constructor:

- `this` can only be used to call a constructor from another constructor in the same class.
- It *must* be the first statement in the constructor that is making the call. If it is not the first statement, a compiler error will result.

Checkpoint

6.15 Look at the following code. (You might want to review the Stock class presented earlier in this chapter.)

```
Stock stock1 = new Stock("XYZ", 9.65);
Stock stock2 = new Stock("SUNW", 7.92);
```

While the equals method is executing as a result of the following statement, what object does this reference?

```
if (stock2.equals(stock1))
    System.out.println("The stocks are the same.");
```

6.11 Inner Classes

CONCEPT: An inner class is a class that is defined inside another class definition.[2]

All of the classes you have written so far have been stored separately in their own source files. Java also allows you to write a class definition inside of another class definition. A class that is defined inside of another class is called an *inner class*.[2] Code Listing 6-29 shows an example of a class with an inner class. The program in Code Listing 6-30 demonstrates the classes.

Code Listing 6-29   **(RetailItem.java)**

```
 1  import java.text.DecimalFormat;
 2
 3  /**
 4   * This class uses an inner class.
 5   */
 6
 7  public class RetailItem
 8  {
 9     private String description;  // Item description
10     private int itemNumber;      // Item number
11     private CostData cost;       // Cost data
12
13     /**
14      * RetailItem class constructor
15      */
16
17     public RetailItem(String desc, int itemNum,
18                       double wholesale, double retail)
19     {
```

[2]When the class defined inside another class is written with the static modifier, it is known as a nested class, not an inner class. We do not discuss nested classes in this book.

```
20          description = desc;
21          itemNumber = itemNum;
22          cost = new CostData(wholesale, retail);
23       }
24
25       /**
26        * RetailItem class toString method
27        */
28
29       public String toString()
30       {
31          String str;   // To hold a descriptive string.
32
33          // Create a DecimalFormat object to format output.
34          DecimalFormat dollar = new DecimalFormat("#,##0.00");
35
36          // Create a string describing the item.
37          str = "Description: " + description
38              + "\nItem Number: " + itemNumber
39              + "\nWholesale Cost: $"
40              + dollar.format(cost.wholesale)
41              + "\nRetail Price: $"
42              + dollar.format(cost.retail);
43
44          // Return the string.
45          return str;
46       }
47
48       /**
49        * CostData Inner Class
50        */
51
52       private class CostData
53       {
54          public double wholesale,   // Wholesale cost
55                        retail;      // Retail price
56
57          /**
58           * CostData class constructor
59           */
60
61          public CostData(double w, double r)
62          {
63             wholesale = w;
64             retail = r;
65          }
66       }
67    }
```

Code Listing 6-30   (`InnerClassDemo.java`)

```
1  /**
2   * This program demonstrates the RetailItem class,
3   * which has an inner class.
4   */
5
6  public class InnerClassDemo
7  {
8     public static void main(String[] args)
9     {
10        // Create a RetailItem object.
11        RetailItem item = new RetailItem("Candy bar", 17789,
12                                         0.75, 1.5);
13
14        // Display the item's information.
15        System.out.println(item);
16     }
17  }
```

Program Output

```
Description: Candy bar
Item Number: 17789
Wholesale Cost: $0.75
Retail Price: $1.50
```

The `RetailItem` class is an aggregate class. It has as a field an instance of the `CostData` class. Notice that the `CostData` class is defined inside of the `RetailItem` class. The `RetailItem` class is the outer class and the `CostData` class is the inner class.

An inner class is visible only to code inside the outer class. This means that the use of the inner class is restricted to the outer class. Only code in the outer class may create an instance of the inner class.

One unusual aspect of the `CostData` class is that its fields, `wholesale` and `retail`, are declared as `public`. Although Chapter 3 warns against making a field public, it is permissible in the case of inner classes. This is because the inner class's members are not accessible to code outside the outer class. Even though the `CostData` class's fields are public, only code in the `RetailItem` class can access its members. In effect, the `CostData` class's public members are like private members of the `RetailItem` class. The following points summarize the accessibility issues between inner and outer classes.

- An outer class can access the public members of an inner class.
- A private inner class is not visible or accessible to code outside the outer class.
- An inner class can access the private members of the outer class.

Although you will not write inner classes very often, you can use them to create classes that are visible and accessible only to specific other classes. Later in this book we will use inner classes in graphics programs.

> **NOTE:** When a class with an inner class is compiled, byte code for the inner class will be stored in a separate file. The file's name will consist of the name of the outer class, followed by a $ character, followed by the name of the inner class, followed by `.class`. For example, the byte code for the `CostData` class in Code Listing 6-29 would be stored in the file `RetailItem$CostData.class`.

6.12 Enumerated Types

CONCEPT: An enumerated data type consists of a set of predefined values. You can use the data type to create variables that can hold only the values that belong to the enumerated data type.

You've already learned the concept of data types and how they are used with primitive variables. For example, a variable of the `int` data type can hold integer values within a certain range. You cannot assign floating-point values to an `int` variable because only `int` values may be assigned to `int` variables. A data type defines the values that are legal for any variable of that data type.

Sometimes it is helpful to create your own data type that has a specific set of legal values. For example, suppose you wanted to create a data type named `Day`, and the legal values in that data type were the names of the days of the week (Sunday, Monday, and so on). When you create a variable of the `Day` data type, you can only store the names of the days of the week in that variable. Any other values would be illegal. In Java, such a type is known as an *enumerated data type*.

You use the enum key word to create your own data type and specify the values that belong to that type. Here is an example of an enumerated data type declaration:

```
enum Day { SUNDAY, MONDAY, TUESDAY, WEDNESDAY,
           THURSDAY, FRIDAY, SATURDAY }
```

An enumerated data type declaration begins with the key word enum, followed by the name of the type, followed by a list of identifiers inside braces. The example declaration creates an enumerated data type named `Day`. The identifiers SUNDAY, MONDAY, TUESDAY, WEDNESDAY, THURSDAY, FRIDAY, and SATURDAY, which are listed inside the braces, are known as enum *constants*. They represent the values that belong to the `Day` data type. Here is the general format of an enumerated type declaration:

```
enum TypeName { One or more enum constants }
```

Note that the enum constants are not enclosed in quotation marks; therefore, they are not strings. enum constants must be legal Java identifiers.

> **TIP:** When making up names for enum constants, it is not required that they be written in all uppercase letters. We could have written the `Day` type's enum constants as sunday, monday, and so forth. Because they represent constant values, however, the standard convention is to write them in all uppercase letters.

Once you have created an enumerated data type in your program, you can declare variables of that type. For example, the following statement declares `workDay` as a variable of the `Day` type:

```
Day workDay;
```

Because `workDay` is a `Day` variable, the only values that we can legally assign to it are the enum constants `Day.SUNDAY`, `Day.MONDAY`, `Day.TUESDAY`, `Day.WEDNESDAY`, `Day.THURSDAY`, `Day.FRIDAY`, and `Day.SATURDAY`. If we try to assign any value other than one of the `Day` type's enum constants, a compiler error will result. For example, the following statement assigns the value `Day.WEDNESDAY` to the `workDay` variable.

```
Day workDay = Day.WEDNESDAY;
```

Notice that we assigned `Day.WEDNESDAY` instead of just `WEDNESDAY`. The name `Day.WEDNESDAY` is the *fully qualified name* of the `Day` type's `WEDNESDAY` constant. Under most circumstances you must use the fully qualified name of an enum constant.

Enumerated Types Are Specialized Classes

When you write an enumerated type declaration, you are actually creating a special kind of class. In addition, the enum constants that you list inside the braces are actually objects of the class. In the previous example, `Day` is a class, and the enum constants `Day.SUNDAY`, `Day.MONDAY`, `Day.TUESDAY`, `Day.WEDNESDAY`, `Day.THURSDAY`, `Day.FRIDAY`, and `Day.SATURDAY` are all instances of the `Day` class. When we assigned `Day.WEDNESDAY` to the `workDay` variable, we were assigning the address of the `Day.WEDNESDAY` object to the variable. This is illustrated in Figure 6-15.

Figure 6-15   The `workDay` variable references the `Day.WEDNESDAY` object

enum constants, which are actually objects, come automatically equipped with a few methods. One of them is the `toString` method. The `toString` method simply returns the name of the calling enum constant as a string. For example, assuming that the `Day` type has been declared as previously shown, both of the following code segments display the string

WEDNESDAY. (Recall that the toString method is implicitly called when an object is passed to System.out.println).

```
// This code displays WEDNESDAY.
Day workDay = Day.WEDNESDAY;
System.out.println(workDay);
```

```
// This code also displays WEDNESDAY.
System.out.println(Day.WEDNESDAY);
```

enum constants also have a method named ordinal. The ordinal method returns an integer value representing the constant's ordinal value. The constant's *ordinal value* is its position in the enum declaration, with the first constant being at position 0. Figure 6-16 shows the ordinal values of each of the constants declared in the Day data type.

Figure 6-16   The Day enumerated data type and the ordinal positions of its enum constants.

For example, assuming that the Day type has been declared as previously shown, look at the following code segment.

```
Day lastWorkDay = Day.FRIDAY;
System.out.println(lastWorkDay.ordinal());
System.out.println(Day.MONDAY.ordinal());
```

The ordinal value for Day.FRIDAY is 5 and the ordinal value for Day.MONDAY is 1, so this code will display:

```
5
1
```

The last enumerated data type methods that we will discuss here are equals and compareTo. The equals method accepts an object as its argument and returns true if that object is equal to the calling enum constant. For example, assuming that the Day type has been declared as previously shown, the following code segment will display "The two are the same":

```
Day myDay = Day.TUESDAY;
if (myDay.equals(Day.TUESDAY))
    System.out.println("The two are the same.");
```

The compareTo method is designed to compare enum constants of the same type. It accepts an object as its argument and returns

- a negative integer value if the calling enum constant's ordinal value is less than the argument's ordinal value
- zero if the calling enum constant is the same as the argument
- a positive integer value if the calling enum constant's ordinal value is greater than the argument's ordinal value

For example, assuming that the Day type has been declared as previously shown, the following code segment will display "FRIDAY is greater than MONDAY":

```
Day myDay = Day.FRIDAY;
if (myDay.compareTo(Day.MONDAY) > 0)
    System.out.println(myDay + " is greater than "
                        + Day.MONDAY);
```

One place to declare an enumerated type is inside a class. If you declare an enumerated type inside a class, it cannot be inside a method. Code Listing 6-31 shows an example. It demonstrates the Day enumerated type.

Code Listing 6-31   (EnumDemo.java)

```java
 1  /**
 2   * This program demonstrates an enumerated type.
 3   */
 4
 5  public class EnumDemo
 6  {
 7     // Declare the Day enumerated type.
 8     enum Day { SUNDAY, MONDAY, TUESDAY, WEDNESDAY,
 9                THURSDAY, FRIDAY, SATURDAY }
10
11     public static void main(String[] args)
12     {
13        // Declare a Day variable and assign it a value.
14        Day workDay = Day.WEDNESDAY;
15
16        // The following statement displays WEDNESDAY.
17        System.out.println(workDay);
18
19        // The following statement displays the ordinal
20        // value for Day.SUNDAY, which is 0.
21        System.out.println("The ordinal value for "
22                           + Day.SUNDAY + " is "
23                           + Day.SUNDAY.ordinal());
24
25        // The following statement displays the ordinal
26        // value for Day.SATURDAY, which is 6.
27        System.out.println("The ordinal value for "
28                           + Day.SATURDAY + " is "
29                           + Day.SATURDAY.ordinal());
30
31        // The following statement compares two enum constants.
32        if (Day.FRIDAY.compareTo(Day.MONDAY) > 0)
33           System.out.println(Day.FRIDAY + " is greater than "
34                              + Day.MONDAY);
```

```
35          else
36              System.out.println(Day.FRIDAY + " is NOT greater than "
37                                  + Day.MONDAY);
38      }
39 }
```

Program Output

```
WEDNESDAY
The ordinal value for SUNDAY is 0
The ordinal value for SATURDAY is 6
FRIDAY is greater than MONDAY
```

You can also write an enumerated type declaration inside its own file. If you do, the filename must match the name of the type. For example, if we stored the Day type in its own file, we would name the file Day.java. This makes sense because enumerated data types are specialized classes. For example, look at Code Listing 6-32. This file, CarType.java, contains the declaration of an enumerated data type named CarType. When it is compiled, a byte code file named CarType.class will be generated.

Code Listing 6-32   **(CarType.java)**

```
1  /**
2   * CarType enumerated data type
3   */
4
5  enum CarType { PORSCHE, FERRARI, JAGUAR }
```

Also look at Code Listing 6-33. This file, CarColor.java, contains the declaration of an enumerated data type named CarColor. When it is compiled, a byte code file named CarColor.class will be generated.

Code Listing 6-33   **(CarColor.java)**

```
1  /**
2   * CarColor enumerated data type
3   */
4
5  enum CarColor { RED, BLACK, BLUE, SILVER }
```

Code Listing 6-34 shows the SportsCar class, which uses these enumerated types. Code Listing 6-35 demonstrates the class.

Code Listing 6-34   **(SportsCar.java)**

```java
1   import java.text.DecimalFormat;
2
3   /**
4    * SportsCar class
5    */
6
7   public class SportsCar
8   {
9      private CarType make;      // The car's make
10     private CarColor color;    // The car's color
11     private double price;      // The car's price
12
13     /**
14      * The constructor accepts arguments for the
15      * car's make, color, and price.
16      */
17
18     public SportsCar(CarType aMake, CarColor aColor,
19                       double aPrice)
20     {
21        make = aMake;
22        color = aColor;
23        price = aPrice;
24     }
25
26     /**
27      * getMake method
28      */
29
30     public CarType getMake()
31     {
32        return make;
33     }
34
35     /**
36      * getColor method
37      */
38
39     public CarColor getColor()
40     {
41        return color;
42     }
43
```

```
44    /**
45     * getPrice method
46     */
47
48    public double getPrice()
49    {
50        return price;
51    }
52
53    /**
54     *  toString method
55     */
56
57    public String toString()
58    {
59        // Create a DecimalFormat object for
60        // dollar formatting.
61        DecimalFormat dollar = new DecimalFormat("#,##0.00");
62
63        // Create a string representing the object.
64        String str = "Make: " + make +
65                     "\nColor: " + color +
66                     "\nPrice: $" + dollar.format(price);
67
68        // Return the string.
69        return str;
70    }
71 }
```

Code Listing 6-35   (SportsCarDemo.java)

```
1  /**
2   * This program demonstrates the SportsCar class.
3   */
4
5  public class SportsCarDemo
6  {
7     public static void main(String[] args)
8     {
9        // Create a SportsCar object.
10       SportsCar yourNewCar = new SportsCar(CarType.PORSCHE,
11                                    CarColor.RED, 100000);
12
13       // Display the object's values.
14       System.out.println(yourNewCar);
15    }
16 }
```

Program Output

```
Make: PORSCHE
Color: RED
Price: $100,000.00
```

Switching on an Enumerated Type

Java allows you to test an enum constant with a switch statement. For example, look at the program in Code Listing 6-36. It creates a SportsCar object, and then uses a switch statement to test the object's make field.

Code Listing 6-36   (SportsCarDemo2.java)

```java
 1  /**
 2   * This program shows that you can switch on an
 3   * enumerated type.
 4   */
 5
 6  public class SportsCarDemo2
 7  {
 8     public static void main(String[] args)
 9     {
10        // Create a SportsCar object.
11        SportsCar yourNewCar = new SportsCar(CarType.PORSCHE,
12                                  CarColor.RED, 100000);
13
14        // Get the car make and switch on it.
15        switch (yourNewCar.getMake())
16        {
17          case PORSCHE :
18             System.out.println("Your car was made in Germany.");
19             break;
20          case FERRARI :
21             System.out.println("Your car was made in Italy.");
22             break;
23          case JAGUAR :
24             System.out.println("Your car was made in England.");
25             break;
26          default:
27             System.out.println("I'm not sure where that car "
28                              + "was made.");
29        }
30     }
31  }
```

Program Output

```
Your car was made in Germany.
```

In line 15 the switch statement tests the value returned from the yourNewCar.getMake() method. This method returns a CarType enumerated constant. Based upon the value returned from the method, the program then branches to the appropriate case statement. Notice in the case statements that the enumerated constants are not fully qualified. In other words, we had to write PORSCHE, FERRARI, and JAGUAR instead of CarType.PORSCHE, CarType.FERRARI, and CarType.JAGUAR. If you give a fully qualified enum constant name as a case expression, a compiler error will result.

> **TIP:** Notice that the switch statement in Code Listing 6-37 has a default section, even though it has a case statement for every enum constant in the CarType type. This will handle things in the event that more enum constants are added to the CarType file. This type of planning is an example of "defensive" programming.

Checkpoint

6.16   Look at the following statement, which declares an enumerated data type.

        enum Flower { ROSE, DAISY, PETUNIA }

   a.   What is the name of the data type?
   b.   What is the ordinal value for the enum constant ROSE? For DAISY? For PETUNIA?
   c.   What is the fully qualifed name of the enum constant ROSE? Of DAISY? Of PETUNIA?
   d.   Write a statement that declares a variable of this enumerated data type. The variable should be named flora. Initialize the variable with the PETUNIA constant.

6.17   Assume that the following enumerated data type has been declared.

        enum Creatures{ HOBBIT, ELF, DRAGON }

   What will the following code display?

        System.out.println(Creatures.HOBBIT + " "
                        + Creatures.ELF + " "
                        + Creatures.DRAGON);

6.18   Assume that the following enumerated data type has been declared.

        enum Letters { Z, Y, X }

   What will the following code display?

        if (Letters.Z.compareTo(Letters.X) > 0)
            System.out.println("Z is greater than X.");
        else
            System.out.println("Z is not greater than X.");

6.13 Garbage Collection

CONCEPT: The Java Virtual Machine periodically runs a process known as the garbage collector, which removes unreferenced objects from memory.

When an object is no longer needed, it should be destroyed so the memory it uses can be freed for other purposes. Fortunately, you do not have to destroy objects after you are finished using them. The JVM periodically performs a process known as garbage collection, which automatically removes unreferenced objects from memory. For example, look at the following code:

```java
// Declare two InventoryItem reference variables.
InventoryItem item1, item2;

// Create an object and reference it with item1.
item1 = new InventoryItem("Wrench", 20);

// Reference the same object with item2.
item2 = item1;

// Store null in item1 so it no longer references the object.
item1 = null;

// The object is still referenced by item2, though.
// Store null in item2 so it no longer references the object.
item2 = null;

// Now the object is no longer referenced, so it can be removed
// by the garbage collector.
```

This code uses two reference variables, item1 and item2. An InventoryItem object is created and referenced by item1. Then, item1 is assigned to item2, which causes item2 to reference the same object as item1. This is illustrated in Figure 6-17.

Figure 6-17   Both item1 and item2 reference the same object

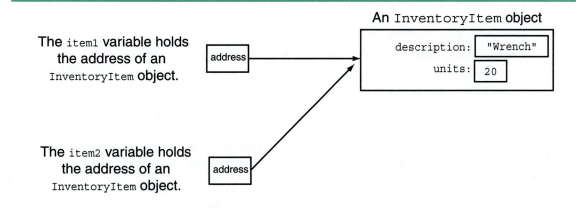

Next, the `null` value is assigned to `item1`. This removes the address of the object from the `item1` variable, causing it to no longer reference the object. Figure 6-18 illustrates this.

Figure 6-18 The object is only referenced by the `item2` variable

The object is still accessible, however, because it is referenced by the `item2` variable. The next statement assigns `null` to `item2`. This removes the object's address from `item2`, causing it to no longer reference the object. Figure 6-19 illustrates this. Because the object is no longer accessible, it will be removed from memory the next time the garbage collector process runs.

Figure 6-19 The object is no longer referenced

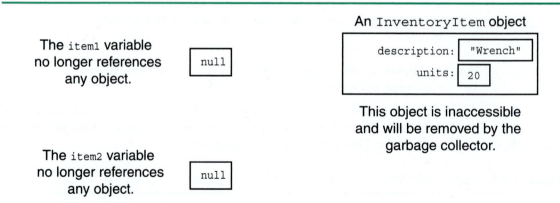

The `finalize` Method

If a class has a method named `finalize`, it is called automatically just before an instance of the class is destroyed by the garbage collector. If you wish to execute code just before an object is destroyed, you can create a `finalize` method in the class and place the code there. The `finalize` method accepts no arguments and has a `void` return type.

NOTE: The garbage collector runs periodically, and you cannot predict exactly when it will execute. Therefore, you cannot know exactly when an object's `finalize` method will execute.

6.14 Focus on Object-Oriented Design: Class Collaboration

CONCEPT: It is common for classes to interact, or collaborate, with each other to perform their operations. Part of the object-oriented design process is identifying the collaborations between classes.

In an object-oriented application it is common for objects of different classes to collaborate. This simply means that objects interact with each other. Sometimes one object will need the services of another object to fulfill its responsibilities. For example, let's say an object needs to read a number from the keyboard and then format the number to appear as a dollar amount. The object might use the services of a Scanner object to read the number from the keyboard, and then use the services of a DecimalFormat object to format the number. In this example, the object is collaborating with objects created from classes in the Java API. The objects that you create from your own classes can also collaborate with each other.

If one object is to collaborate with another object, then it must know something about the other object's class methods and how to call them. For example, suppose we were to write a class named StockPurchase, which uses an object of the Stock class (presented earlier in this chapter) to simulate the purchase of a stock. The StockPurchase class is responsible for calculating the cost of the stock purchase. To do that, it must know how to call the Stock class's getSharePrice method to get the price per share of the stock. Code Listing 6-37 shows an example of the StockPurchase class. (If you have downloaded the book's source code, you will find this file in the folder *Chapter 06\StockPurchase Class.*)

Code Listing 6-37   (`StockPurchase.java`)

```
 1  /**
 2   * The StockPurchase class represents a stock purchase.
 3   */
 4
 5  public class StockPurchase
 6  {
 7     private Stock stock;   // The stock that was purchased
 8     private int shares;    // Number of shares owned
 9
10     /**
11      * The constructor accepts arguments for the
12      * stock and number of shares.
13      */
14
15     public StockPurchase(Stock stockObject, int numShares)
16     {
17        // Create a copy of the object referenced by
18        // stockObject.
19        stock = new Stock(stockObject);
20        shares = numShares;
21     }
```

```
22
23      /**
24       * getStock method
25       */
26
27      public Stock getStock()
28      {
29          // Return a copy of the object referenced by stock.
30          return new Stock(stock);
31      }
32
33      /**
34       * getShares method
35       */
36
37      public int getShares()
38      {
39          return shares;
40      }
41
42      /**
43       * The getCost method returns the cost of the
44       * stock purchase.
45       */
46
47      public double getCost()
48      {
49          return shares * stock.getSharePrice();
50      }
51  }
```

The constructor for this class accepts a `Stock` object representing the stock being purchased and an `int` representing the number of shares to purchase. In line 19 we see the first collaboration: the `StockPurchase` constructor makes a copy of the `Stock` object by using the `Stock` class's copy constructor. The copy constructor is used again in the `getStock` method, in line 30, to return a copy of the `Stock` object.

The next collaboration takes place in the `getCost` method. This method calculates and returns the cost of the stock purchase. In line 49 it calls the `Stock` class's `getSharePrice` method to determine the stock's price per share. The program in Code Listing 6-38 demonstrates this class. (If you have downloaded the book's source code, you will find this file in the folder *Chapter 06\StockPurchase Class*.)

Code Listing 6-38   (`StockTrader.java`)

```java
1   import java.util.Scanner;
2   import java.text.DecimalFormat;
3
4   /**
5    * This program allows you to purchase shares of XYZ
6    * company's stock.
7    */
8
9   public class StockTrader
10  {
11     public static void main(String[] args)
12     {
13        int sharesToBuy;   // Number of shares to buy.
14
15        // Create a Stock object for the company stock.
16        // The trading symbol is XYZ and the stock is
17        // currently $9.62 per share.
18        Stock xyzCompany = new Stock("XYZ", 9.62);
19
20        // Create a Scanner object for keyboard input.
21        Scanner keyboard = new Scanner(System.in);
22
23        // Create a DecimalFormat object to format numbers
24        // as dollar amounts.
25        DecimalFormat dollar = new DecimalFormat("#,##0.00");
26
27        // Display the current share price.
28        System.out.println("XYZ Company's stock is currently $"
29                    + dollar.format(xyzCompany.getSharePrice())
30                    + " per share.");
31
32        // Get the number of shares to purchase.
33        System.out.print("How many shares do you want to buy? ");
34        sharesToBuy = keyboard.nextInt();
35
36        // Create a StockPurchase object for the transaction.
37        StockPurchase buy =
38                    new StockPurchase(xyzCompany, sharesToBuy);
39
40        // Display the cost of the transaction.
41        System.out.println("Cost of the stock: $"
42                            + dollar.format(buy.getCost()));
43     }
44  }
```

Program Output with Example Input Shown in Bold

```
XYZ Company's stock is currently $9.62 per share.
How many shares do you want to buy? 100 [Enter]
Cost of the stock: $962.00
```

Determining Class Collaborations with CRC Cards

During the object-oriented design process, you can determine many of the collaborations that will be necessary between classes by examining the responsibilities of the classes. In Chapter 3, Section 3.7, we discussed the process of finding the classes and their responsibilities. Recall from that section that a class's responsibilities are

- the things that the class is responsible for knowing
- the actions that the class is responsible for doing

Often you will determine that the class must collaborate with another class to fulfill one or more of its responsibilities. One popular method of discovering a class's responsibilities and collaborations is by creating CRC cards. CRC stands for class, responsibilities, and collaborations.

You can use simple index cards for this procedure. Once you have gone through the process of finding the classes (which is discussed in Chapter 3, Section 3.8), set aside one index card for each class. At the top of the index card, write the name of the class. Divide the rest of the card into two columns. In the left column, write each of the class's responsibilities. As you write each responsibility, think about whether the class needs to collaborate with another class to fulfill that responsibility. Ask yourself questions such as:

- Will an object of this class need to get data from another object to fulfill this responsibility?
- Will an object of this class need to request another object to perform an operation to fulfill this responsibility?

If collaboration is required, write the name of the collaborating class in the right column, next to the responsibility that requires it. If no collaboration is required for a responsibility, simply write "None" in the right column, or leave it blank. Figure 6-20 shows an example CRC card for the StockPurchase class.

Figure 6-20   CRC Card

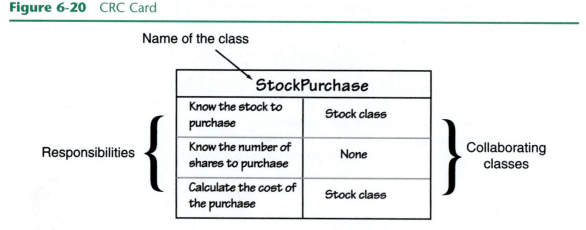

StockPurchase	
Know the stock to purchase	Stock class
Know the number of shares to purchase	None
Calculate the cost of the purchase	Stock class

Name of the class

Responsibilities

Collaborating classes

From the CRC card shown in the figure, we can see that the StockPurchase class has the following responsibilities and collaborations:

- Responsibility: To know the stock to purchase
  Collaboration: The Stock class
- Responsibility: To know the number of shares to purchase
  Collaboration: None
- Responsibility: To calculate the cost of the purchase
  Collaboration: The Stock class

When you have completed a CRC card for each class in the application, you will have a good idea of each class's responsibilities and how the classes must interact.

6.15 Common Errors to Avoid

The following list describes several errors that are commonly made when learning this chapter's topics.

- **Trying to overload methods by giving them different return types.** Overloaded methods must have unique parameter lists.
- **Forgetting to write a no-arg constructor for a class that you want to be able to create instances of without passing arguments to the constructor.** If you write a constructor that accepts arguments, you must also write a no-arg constructor for the same class if you want to be able to create instances of the class without passing arguments to the constructor.
- **In a method that accepts an object as an argument, writing code that accidentally modifies the object.** When a reference variable is passed as an argument to a method, the method has access to the object that the variable references. When writing a method that receives a reference variable as an argument, you must take care not to accidentally modify the contents of the object referenced by the variable.
- **Allowing a null reference to be used.** Because a null reference variable does not reference an object, you cannot use it to perform an operation that would require the existence of an object. For example, a null reference variable cannot be used to call a method. If you attempt to perform an operation with a null reference variable, the program will terminate. This can happen when a class has a reference variable as a field, and it is not properly initialized with the address of an object.
- **Forgetting to use the fully qualified name of an enum constant.** Under most circumstances you must use the fully qualified name of an enum constant. One exception to this is when the enum constant is used as a case expression in a switch statement.
- **Attempting to refer to an instance field or instance method in a static method.** Static methods can refer only to other class members that are static.

Review Questions and Exercises

Multiple Choice and True/False

1. This type of method cannot access any nonstatic member variables in its own class.
   a. instance
   b. void
   c. static
   d. nonstatic

2. Two or more methods in a class may have the same name, as long as this is different.
   a. their return values
   b. their access specifier
   c. their signatures
   d. their memory address

3. The process of matching a method call with the correct method is known as
   a. matching
   b. binding
   c. linking
   d. connecting

4. When an object is passed as an argument to a method, this is actually passed.
   a. a copy of the object
   b. the name of the object
   c. a reference to the object
   d. None of these. You cannot pass an object.

5. If you write this method for a class, Java will automatically call it any time you concatenate an object of the class with a string.
   a. toString
   b. plusString
   c. stringConvert
   d. concatString

6. Making an instance of one class a field in another class is called
   a. nesting
   b. class fielding
   c. aggregation
   d. concatenation

7. This is the name of a reference variable that is always available to an instance method and refers to the object that is calling the method.
   a. callingObject
   b. this
   c. me
   d. instance

8. This enum method returns the position of an enum constant in the declaration.
   a. position
   b. location
   c. ordinal
   d. toString

9. Assuming the following declaration exists:
   enum Seasons { SPRING, WINTER, SUMMER, FALL }
   what is the fully qualified name of the FALL constant?
   a. FALL
   b. enum.FALL
   c. FALL.Seasons
   d. Seasons.FALL

10. You cannot use the fully qualified name of an enum constant for this.
    a. a switch expression
    b. a case expression
    c. an argument to a method
    d. all of these

11. A class that is defined inside of another class is called a(n)
    a. inner class
    b. folded class
    c. hidden class
    d. unknown class

12. The JVM periodically performs this process, which automatically removes unreferenced objects from memory.
    a. memory cleansing
    b. memory deallocation
    c. garbage collection
    d. object expungement

13. If a class has this method, it is called automatically just before an instance of the class is destroyed by the JVM
    a. finalize
    b. destroy
    c. remove
    d. housekeeper

14. CRC stands for
    a. Class, Return value, Composition
    b. Class, Responsibilities, Collaborations
    c. Class, Responsibilities, Composition
    d. Compare, Return, Continue

15. **True or False:** A static member method may refer to nonstatic member variables of the same class at any time.

16. **True or False:** All static member variables are initialized to –1 by default.

17. **True or False:** A class may not have more than one constructor.

18. **True or False:** When an object is passed as an argument to a method, the method can access the argument.

19. **True or False:** A method cannot return a reference to an object.

20. **True or False:** A private class that is defined inside another class is not visible to code outside the outer class.

21. **True or False:** You can declare an enumerated data type inside a method.

22. **True or False:** Enumerated data types are actually special types of classes.

23. **True or False:** enum constants have a toString method.

Find the Error

Each of the following class definitions has errors. Find as many as you can.

1.
```java
public class MyClass
{
    private int x;
    private double y;

    public static void setValues(int a, double b)
    {
        x = a;
        y = b;
    }
}
```

2.
```java
public class TwoValues
{
    private int x, y;

    public TwoValues()
    {
        x = 0;
    }

    public TwoValues()
    {
        x = 0;
        y = 0;
    }
}
```

3.
```java
public class MyMath
{
    public static int square(int number)
    {
        return number * number;
    }

    public static double square(int number)
    {
        return number * number;
    }
}
```

4. Assume the following declaration exists.

    ```
    enum Coffee { MEDIUM, DARK, DECAF }
    ```

    Find the error(s) in the following switch statement.

    ```
    // This code has errors!
    Coffee myCup = DARK;
    switch (myCup)
    {
        case Coffee.MEDIUM :
            System.out.println("Mild flavor.");
            break;
        case Coffee.DARK :
            System.out.println("strong flavor.");
            break;
        case Coffee.DECAF :
            System.out.println("Won't keep you awake.");
            break;
        default:
            System.out.println("Never heard of it.");
    }
    ```

Algorithm Workbench

1. Consider the following class declaration:

    ```
    public class Circle
    {
        private double radius;

        private void getArea()
        {
            return Math.PI * radius * radius;
        }

        private double getRadius()
        {
            return radius;
        }
    }
    ```

    a. Write a no-arg constructor for this class. It should assign the radius field the value 0.
    b. Write an overloaded constructor for this class. It should accept an argument copied into the radius member variable.
    c. Write a toString method for this class. The method should return a string containing the radius and area of the circle.

   d. Write an equals method for this class. The method should accept a Circle object as an argument. It should return true if the argument object contains the same data as the calling object, or false otherwise.

   e. Write a greaterThan method for this class. The method should accept a Circle object as an argument. It should return true if the argument object has an area greater than the area of the calling object, or false otherwise.

2. A pet store sells dogs, cats, birds, and hamsters. Write a declaration for an enumerated data type that can represent the types of pets the store sells.

Short Answer

1. Describe one thing you cannot do with a static method.

2. Why are static methods useful in creating utility classes?

3. Consider the following class declaration:

```java
public class Thing
{
    private int x;
    private int y;
    private static int z = 0;

    public Thing()
    {
        x = z;
        y = z;
    }

    public static void putThing(int a)
    {
        z = a;
    }
}
```

Assume a program containing the class declaration defines three Thing objects with the following statements:

```java
Thing one = new Thing();
Thing two = new Thing();
Thing three = new Thing();
```

   a. How many separate instances of the x member exist?
   b. How many separate instances of the y member exist?
   c. How many separate instances of the z member exist?
   d. What value will be stored in the x and y members of each object?
   e. Write a statement that will call the putThing method.

4. When the same name is used for two or more methods in the same class, how does Java tell them apart?

5. How does method overloading improve the usefulness of a class?

6. Describe the difference in the way variables and class objects are passed as arguments to a method.

7. If you do not write an `equals` method for a class, Java provides one. Describe the behavior of the `equals` method that Java automatically provides.

8. A "has a" relationship can exist between classes. What does this mean?

9. What happens if you attempt to call a method using a reference variable that is set to `null`?

10. Is it advisable or not advisable to write a method that returns a reference to an object that is a private field? What is the exception to this?

11. What is the `this` key word?

12. Look at the following declaration.

    ```
    enum Color { RED, ORANGE, GREEN, BLUE }
    ```

    a. What is the name of the data type declared by this statement?
    b. What are the enum constants for this type?
    c. Write a statement that defines a variable of this type and initializes it with a valid value.

13. Assuming the following enum declaration exists:

    ```
    enum Dog { POODLE, BOXER, TERRIER }
    ```

    What will the following statements display?

    ```
    a. System.out.println(Dog.POODLE + "\n"
                        + Dog.BOXER + "\n"
                        + Dog.TERRIER);

    b. System.out.println(Dog.POODLE.ordinal() + "\n"
                        + Dog.BOXER.ordinal() + "\n"
                        + Dog.TERRIER.ordinal());

    c. Dog myDog = Dog.BOXER;
       if (myDog.compareTo(Dog.TERRIER) > 0)
          System.out.println(myDog + " is greater than "
                        + Dog.TERRIER);
       else
          System.out.println(myDog + " is NOT greater than "
                        + Dog.TERRIER);
    ```

14. Under what circumstances does an object become a candidate for garbage collection?

Programming Challenges

1. Area Class

Write a class that has three overloaded static methods for calculating the areas of the following geometric shapes.

- circles
- rectangles
- cylinders

Here are the formulas for calculating the area of the shapes.

Area of a circle: $Area = \pi r^2$

where π is Math.PI and r is the circle's radius

Area of a rectangle: $Area = Width \times Length$

Area of a cylinder: $Area = \pi r^2 h$

where π is Math.PI, r is the radius of the cylinder's base, and h is the cylinder's height

Because the three methods are to be overloaded, they should each have the same name, but different parameter lists. Demonstrate the class in a complete program.

VideoNote
The
InventoryItem
Class Copy
Constructor
Problem

2. InventoryItem **Class Copy Constructor**

Add a copy constructor to the InventoryItem class. This constructor should accept an InventoryItem object as an argument. The constructor should assign to the description field the value in the argument's description field and assign to the units field the value in the argument's units field. As a result, the new object will be a copy of the argument object.

3. Carpet Calculator

The Westfield Carpet Company has asked you to write an application that calculates the price of carpeting for rectangular rooms. To calculate the price, you multiply the area of the floor (width times length) by the price per square foot of carpet. For example, the area of floor that is 12 feet long and 10 feet wide is 120 square feet. To cover that floor with carpet that costs $8 per square foot would cost $960. ($12 \times 10 \times 8 = 960$.)

First, you should create a class named RoomDimension that has two fields: one for the length of the room and one for the width. The RoomDimension class should have a method that returns the area of the room. (The area of the room is the room's length multiplied by the room's width.)

Next you should create a RoomCarpet class that has a RoomDimension object as a field. It should also have a field for the cost of the carpet per square foot. The RoomCarpet class should have a method that returns the total cost of the carpet.

Figure 6-21 is a UML diagram showing possible class designs and depicting the relationships between the classes. Once you have written these classes, use them in an application that asks the user to enter the dimensions of a room and the price per square foot of the desired carpeting. The application should display the total cost of the carpet.

Figure 6-21   UML diagram for Programming Challenge 3

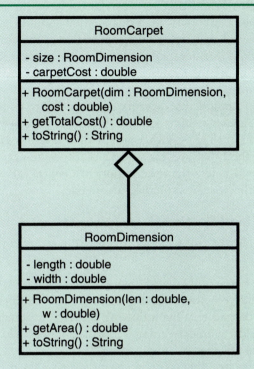

4. LandTract Class

Make a LandTract class that has two fields: one for the tract's length and one for the width. The class should have a method that returns the tract's area, as well as an equals method and a toString method. Demonstrate the class in a program that asks the user to enter the dimensions for two tracts of land. The program should display the area of each tract of land and indicate whether the tracts are of equal size.

5. Month class

Write a class named Month. The class should have an int field named monthNumber that holds the number of the month. For example,

January would be 1, February would be 2, and so forth. In addition, provide the following methods:

- A no-arg constructor that sets the monthNumber field to 1.
- A constructor that accepts the number of the month as an argument. It should set the monthNumber field to the value passed as the argument. If a value less than 1 or greater than 12 is passed, the constructor should set monthNumber to 1.
- A constructor that accepts the name of the month, such as "January" or "February", as an argument. It should set the monthNumber field to the correct corresponding value.
- A setMonthNumber method that accepts an int argument, which is assigned to the monthNumber field. If a value less than 1 or greater than 12 is passed, the method should set monthNumber to 1.

- A `getMonthNumber` method that returns the value in the `monthNumber` field.
- A `getMonthName` method that returns the name of the month. For example, if the `monthNumber` field contains 1, then this method should return "January".
- A `toString` method that returns the same value as the `getMonthName` method.
- An `equals` method that accepts a `Month` object as an argument. If the argument object holds the same data as the calling object, this method should return `true`. Otherwise, it should return `false`.
- A `greaterThan` method that accepts a `Month` object as an argument. If the calling object's `monthNumber` field is greater than the argument's `monthNumber` field, this method should return `true`. Otherwise, it should return `false`.
- A `lessThan` method that accepts a `Month` object as an argument. If the calling object's `monthNumber` field is less than the argument's `monthNumber` field, this method should return `true`. Otherwise, it should return `false`.

6. `Employee` Class Modification

In Programming Challenge 1 of Chapter 3 you wrote an `Employee` class. Add the following to the class:

- A constructor that accepts the following values as arguments and assigns them to the appropriate fields: employee's name, employee's ID number, department, and position.
- A constructor that accepts the following values as arguments and assigns them to the appropriate fields: employee's name and ID number. The `department` and `position` fields should be assigned an empty string (`""`).
- A no-arg constructor that assigns empty strings (`""`) to the `name`, `department`, and `position` fields, and 0 to the `idNumber` field.

Write a program that tests and demonstrates these constructors.

7. `RetailItem` Class Modification

Modify this chapter's `RetailItem` class (which uses an inner class named `CostData`) to include accessor and mutator methods for getting and setting an item's wholesale and retail cost. Demonstrate the methods in a program.

8. `CashRegister` Class

Write a `CashRegister` class that can be used with the `RetailItem` class that you modified in Programming Challenge 7. The `CashRegister` class should simulate the sale of a retail item. It should have a constructor that accepts a `RetailItem` object as an argument. The constructor should also accept an integer that represents the quantity of items being purchased. In addition, the class should have the following methods:

- The `getSubtotal` method should return the subtotal of the sale, which is the quantity multiplied by the retail cost. This method must get the retail cost from the `RetailItem` object that was passed as an argument to the constructor.
- The `getTax` method should return the amount of sales tax on the purchase. The sales tax rate is 6% of a retail sale.
- The `getTotal` method should return the total of the sale, which is the subtotal plus the sales tax.

Demonstrate the class in a program that asks the user for the quantity of items being purchased, and then displays the sale's subtotal, amount of sales tax, and total.

9. Sales Receipt File

Modify the program you wrote in Programming Challenge 8 to create a file containing a sales receipt. The program should ask the user for the quantity of items being purchased, and then generate a file with contents similar to the following:

```
SALES RECEIPT
Unit Price: $10.00
Quantity: 5
Subtotal: $50.00
Sales Tax: $ 3.00
Total: $53.00
```

10. Parking Ticket Simulator

For this assignment you will design a set of classes that work together to simulate a police officer issuing a parking ticket. The classes you should design are:

- **The `ParkedCar` Class:** This class should simulate a parked car. The class's responsibilities are:
  - To know the car's make, model, color, license number, and the number of minutes that the car has been parked
- **The `ParkingMeter` Class:** This class should simulate a parking meter. The class's only responsibility is:
  - To know the number of minutes of parking time that has been purchased
- **The `ParkingTicket` Class:** This class should simulate a parking ticket. The class's responsibilities are:
  - To report the make, model, color, and license number of the illegally parked car
  - To report the amount of the fine, which is $25 for the first hour or part of an hour that the car is illegally parked, plus $10 for every additional hour or part of an hour that the car is illegally parked
  - To report the name and badge number of the police officer issuing the ticket
- **The `PoliceOfficer` Class:** This class should simulate a police officer inspecting parked cars. The class's responsibilities are:
  - To know the police officer's name and badge number
  - To examine a `ParkedCar` object and a `ParkingMeter` object, and determine whether the car's time has expired
  - To issue a parking ticket (generate a `ParkingTicket` object) if the car's time has expired

Write a program that demonstrates how these classes collaborate.

11. Geometry Calculator

Design a `Geometry` class with the following methods:

- A static method that accepts the radius of a circle and returns the area of the circle. Use the following formula:

    $Area = \pi r^2$

    Use `Math.PI` for π and the radius of the circle for r.

- A static method that accepts the length and width of a rectangle and returns the area of the rectangle. Use the following formula:

$$Area = Length \times Width$$

- A static method that accepts the length of a triangle's base and the triangle's height. The method should return the area of the triangle. Use the following formula:

$$Area = Base \times Height \times 0.5$$

The methods should display an error message if negative values are used for the circle's radius, the rectangle's length or width, or the triangle's base or height.

Next, write a program to test the class, which displays the following menu and responds to the user's selection:

```
Geometry Calculator
1. Calculate the Area of a Circle
2. Calculate the Area of a Rectangle
3. Calculate the Area of a Triangle
4. Quit


Enter your choice (1-4):
```

Display an error message if the user enters a number outside the range of 1 through 4 when selecting an item from the menu.

12. Car-Instrument Simulator

For this assignment you will design a set of classes that work together to simulate a car's fuel gauge and odometer. The classes you will design are as follows:

- The FuelGauge Class: This class simulate a fuel gauge. It's responsibilities are
  - To know the car's current amount of fuel, in gallons.
  - To report the car's current amount of fuel, in gallons.
  - To be able to increment the amount of fuel by 1 gallon. This simulates putting fuel in the car. (The car can hold a maximum of 15 gallons.)
  - To be able to decrement the amount of fuel by 1 gallon, if the amount of fuel is greater than 0 gallons. This simulates burning fuel as the car runs.
- The Odometer Class: This class simulates the car's odometer. It's responsibilities are
  - To know the car's current mileage.
  - To report the car's current mileage.
  - To be able to increment the current mileage by 1 mile. The maximum mileage the odometer can store is 999,999 miles. When this amount is exceeded, the odometer resets the current mileage to 0.
  - To be able to work with a FuelGuage object. It should decrease the FuelGauge object's current amount of fuel by 1 gallon for every 24 miles traveled. (The car's fuel economy is 24 miles per gallon.)

Demonstrate the classes by creating instances of each. Simulate filling the car up with fuel, and then run a loop that increments the odometer until the car runs out of fuel. During each loop iteration, print the car's current mileage and amount of fuel.

13. First to One Game

This game is meant for two or more players. In the game, each player starts out with 50 points, as each player takes a turn rolling a pair of dice; the amount generated by the dice is subtracted from the player's points. The first player with exactly one point remaining wins. If a player's remaining points minus the amount generated by the dice results in a value less than one, then the amount should be added to the player's points. (As an alternative, the game can be played with a set number turns. In this case, the player with the amount of points closest to one, when all rounds have been played, wins.)

Write a program that simulates the game being played by two players. Use the Die class that was presented in Chapter 4 to simulate the dice. Write a Player class to simulate the players.

14. Heads or Tails Game

This game is meant for two or more players. In this game, the players take turns flipping a coin. Before the coin is flipped, players should guess if the coin will land headsup or tailsup. If a player guesses correctly, then that player is awarded a point. If a player guesses incorrectly, then that player will lose a point. The first player to score five points is the winner.

Write a program that simulates the game being played by two players. Use the Coin class that you wrote as an assignment in Chapter 5 (Programming Challenge 20) to simulate the coin. Write a Player class to simulate the players.

Arrays and the **ArrayList** Class

TOPICS

7.1 Introduction to Arrays
7.2 Processing Array Contents
7.3 Passing Arrays as Arguments to Methods
7.4 Some Useful Array Algorithms and Operations
7.5 Returning Arrays from Methods
7.6 String Arrays
7.7 Arrays of Objects

7.8 The Sequential Search Algorithm
7.9 The Selection Sort and the Binary Search Algorithms
7.10 Two-Dimensional Arrays
7.11 Arrays with Three or More Dimensions
7.12 Command-Line Arguments and Variable-Length Argument Lists
7.13 The ArrayList Class
7.14 Common Errors to Avoid

7.1 Introduction to Arrays

> **CONCEPT:** An array can hold multiple values of the same data type simultaneously.

The primitive variables you have worked with so far are designed to hold only one value at a time. Each of the variable declarations in Figure 7-1 causes only enough memory to be reserved to hold one value of the specified data type.

An array, however, is an object that can store a group of values, all of the same type. For example, suppose a weather-related application records the high temperature each day for a week. It would record a total of seven values, one for each day. All of these values would be doubles. That application could store the values in an array of seven doubles. Or, suppose a sales-related application records the number of items sold each month for a year. It would record a total of 12 values, one for each month. All of these values would be ints. That application could store the values in an array of 12 ints.

Creating and using an array in Java is similar to creating and using any other type of object: You declare a reference variable and use the new key word to create an instance of the array in memory. Here is an example of a statement that declares an array reference variable:

```
int[] numbers;
```

Figure 7-1 Variable declarations and their memory allocations

```
int count;
```
Enough memory to
hold one `int`.

| 1234 |

```
double number;
```
Enough memory to
hold one `double`.

| 1234.55 |

```
char letter;
```
Enough memory to
hold one `char`.

| A |

This statement declares numbers as an array reference variable. The numbers variable can reference an array of `int` values. Notice that this statement looks like a regular `int` variable declaration except for the set of brackets that appear after the word `int`. The brackets indicate that this variable is a reference to an `int` array. Declaring an array reference variable does not create an array. The next step in the process is to use the `new` key word to create an array and assign its address to the numbers variable. The following statement shows an example.

```
numbers = new int[6];
```

The number inside the brackets is the array's *size declarator*. It indicates the number of *elements*, or values, the array can hold. When this statement is executed, numbers will reference an array that can hold six elements, each one an `int`. This is depicted in Figure 7-2.

Figure 7-2 The numbers array

numbers **variable**

numbers **references an array with enough memory for 6 int values**

Element 0   Element 1   Element 2   Element 3   Element 4   Element 5

As with any other type of object, it is possible to declare a reference variable and create an instance of an array with one statement. Here is an example:

```
int[] numbers = new int[6];
```

Arrays of any data type can be declared. The following are all valid array declarations:

```
float[] temperatures = new float[100];
char[] letters = new char[41];
long[] units = new long[50];
double[] sizes = new double[1200];
```

An array's size declarator must be a nonnegative integer expression. It can be either a literal value, as shown in the previous examples, or a variable. It is a common practice to use a `final` variable as a size declarator. Here is an example:

```
final int ARRAY_SIZE = 6;
int[] numbers = new int[ARRAY_SIZE];
```

This practice makes programs easier to maintain. As you will see, programs that use an array often refer to its size. When we store the size of an array in a variable, we can use the variable instead of a literal number when we refer to the size of the array. If we ever need to change the array's size, we need only to change the value of the variable. The variable should be `final` so its contents cannot be changed during the program's execution.

NOTE: Once an array is created, its size cannot be changed.

Accessing Array Elements

Although an array has only one name, the elements in the array may be accessed and used as individual variables. This is possible because each element is assigned a number known as a *subscript*. A subscript is used as an index to pinpoint a specific element within an array. The first element is assigned the subscript 0, the second element is assigned 1, and so forth. The six elements in the `numbers` array (described earlier) would have the subscripts 0 through 5. This is shown in Figure 7-3.

Figure 7-3 Subscripts for the `numbers` array

The `numbers` array has six elements, numbered 0 through 5.

Subscript numbering always starts at 0. The subscript of the last element in an array is one less than the total number of elements in the array. This means that for the `numbers` array, which has six elements, 5 is the subscript for the last element.

Each element in the `numbers` array, when accessed by its subscript, can be used as an `int` variable. Here is an example of a statement that stores the number 20 in the first element of the array:

```
numbers[0] = 20;
```

NOTE: The expression `numbers[0]` is pronounced "numbers sub zero." You would read this assignment statement as "numbers sub zero is assigned twenty."

Figure 7-4 illustrates the contents of the numbers array after the previously shown statement assigns 20 to numbers[0].

Figure 7-4   Contents of the array after 20 is assigned to numbers[0]

numbers[0] numbers[1] numbers[2] numbers[3] numbers[4] numbers[5]

| 20 | 0 | 0 | 0 | 0 | 0 |

> **NOTE:**   By default, Java initializes array elements with 0. In Figure 7-4, values have not been stored in elements 1 through 5, so they are shown as 0s.

The following statement stores the integer 30 in numbers[3], which is the fourth element of the numbers array:

```
numbers[3] = 30;
```

Figure 7-5 illustrates the contents of the array after this statement executes.

Figure 7-5   Contents of the array after 30 is assigned to numbers[3]

numbers[0] numbers[1] numbers[2] numbers[3] numbers[4] numbers[5]

| 20 | 0 | 0 | 30 | 0 | 0 |

By this point you should understand the difference between the array size declarator and a subscript. The number inside the brackets in a statement that uses the new key word to create an array is the size declarator. It indicates the number of elements that the array has. The number inside the brackets in an assignment statement or any statement that works with the contents of an array is a subscript. It is used to access a specific element in the array.

Inputting and Outputting Array Contents

If you want to input values into an array, you must input the values one at a time into the individual array elements. For example, if you have an array with five elements, then inputting values into the array will require five input operations, one for each element. The same is true for outputting the contents of an array. If you want to display the contents of an array with five elements, then you must display the contents of each individual array element.

Code Listing 7-1 gives an example of inputting and outputting an array's contents. Values are read from the keyboard and stored in an array. The value of each element is then displayed.

Code Listing 7-1   `(ArrayDemo1.java)`

```java
 1  import java.util.Scanner;
 2
 3  /**
 4   * This program shows values being read into an array's
 5   * elements and then displayed.
 6   */
 7
 8  public class ArrayDemo1
 9  {
10      public static void main(String[] args)
11      {
12          final int NUM_EMPLOYEES = 3;  // Number of employees
13
14          // Create an array to hold employee hours.
15          int[] hours = new int[NUM_EMPLOYEES];
16
17          // Create a Scanner object for keyboard input.
18          Scanner keyboard = new Scanner(System.in);
19
20          System.out.println("Enter the hours worked by "
21                      + NUM_EMPLOYEES + " employees.");
22
23          // Get employee 1's hours.
24          System.out.print("Employee 1: ");
25          hours[0] = keyboard.nextInt();
26
27          // Get employee 2's hours.
28          System.out.print("Employee 2: ");
29          hours[1] = keyboard.nextInt();
30
31          // Get employee 3's hours.
32          System.out.print("Employee 3: ");
33          hours[2] = keyboard.nextInt();
34
35          // Display the values in the array.
36          System.out.println("The hours you entered are:");
37          System.out.println(hours[0]);
38          System.out.println(hours[1]);
39          System.out.println(hours[2]);
40      }
41  }
```

Program Output with Example Input
```
Enter the hours worked by 3 employees.
Employee 1: 40 [Enter]
Employee 2: 20 [Enter]
Employee 3: 15 [Enter]
The hours you entered are:
40
20
15
```

Figure 7-6 shows the contents of the hours array with the values entered by the user in the example output.

Figure 7-6 Contents of the hours array

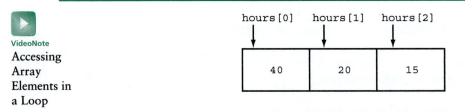

VideoNote
Accessing
Array
Elements in
a Loop

Subscript numbers can be stored in variables. This makes it possible to use a loop to "cycle through" or "walk through" an entire array, performing the same operation on each element. For example, Code Listing 7-1 could be simplified by using two for loops: one for inputting the values into the array and the other for displaying the contents of the array. This is shown in Code Listing 7-2.

Code Listing 7-2   (`ArrayDemo2.java`)

```java
1   import java.util.Scanner;
2
3   /**
4    * This program shows an array being processed with loops.
5    */
6
7   public class ArrayDemo2
8   {
9       public static void main(String[] args)
10      {
11          final int NUM_EMPLOYEES = 3; // Number of employees
12
13          // Create an array to hold employee hours.
14          int[] hours = new int[NUM_EMPLOYEES];
15
```

```
16            // Create a Scanner object for keyboard input.
17            Scanner keyboard = new Scanner(System.in);
18
19            System.out.println("Enter the hours worked by "
20                        + NUM_EMPLOYEES + " employees.");
21
22            // Cycle through the array, getting each
23            // employee's hours.
24            for (int index = 0; index < NUM_EMPLOYEES; index++)
25            {
26                System.out.print("Employee " + (index + 1) + ": ");
27                hours[index] = keyboard.nextInt();
28            }
29
30            // Cycle through the array displaying each element.
31            System.out.println("The hours you entered are:");
32            for (int index = 0; index < NUM_EMPLOYEES; index++)
33                System.out.println(hours[index]);
34    }
35 }
```

Program Output with Example Input Shown in Bold
```
Enter the hours worked by 3 employees.
Employee 1: 40 [Enter]
Employee 2: 20 [Enter]
Employee 3: 15 [Enter]
The hours you entered are:
40
20
15
```

Let's take a closer look at the first loop in this program, which appears in lines 24 through 28. Notice that the loop's control variable, index, is used as a subscript in line 27:

```
hours[index] = keyboard.nextInt();
```

The variable index starts at 0. During the loop's first iteration, the user's input is stored in hours[0]. Then, index is incremented, so its value becomes 1. During the next iteration, the user's input is stored in hours[1]. This continues until values have been stored in all of the elements of the array. Notice that the loop correctly starts and ends the control variable with valid subscript values (0 through 2), as illustrated in Figure 7-7. This ensures that only valid subscripts are used.

Figure 7-7 Annotated loop

The variable `index` starts at 0, which
is the first valid subscript value.

The loop ends before the
variable `index` reaches 3, which
is the first invalid subscript value.

```java
for (int index = 0; index < NUM_EMPLOYEES; index++)
{
    System.out.print("Employee " + (index + 1) + ": ");
    hours[index] = keyboard.nextInt();
}
```

Java Performs Bounds Checking

Java performs array bounds checking, which means that it does not allow a statement to use a subscript outside the range of valid subscripts for an array. For example, the following code creates an array with 10 elements. The valid subscripts for the array are 0 through 9.

```java
final int ARRAY_SIZE = 10;
int[] values = new int[ARRAY_SIZE];
```

Java will not allow a statement to use a subscript less than 0 or greater than 9 with this array. Bounds checking occurs at runtime. The Java compiler does not display an error message when it processes a statement that uses an invalid subscript. Instead, when the statement executes, the program throws an exception and terminates. (Exceptions are discussed in Chapter 10.) For instance, the program in Code Listing 7-3 declares a three-element array, but attempts to store four values in the array.

Code Listing 7-3   (`InvalidSubscript.java`)

```java
1   /**
2    * This program uses an invalid subscript with an array.
3    */
4
5   public class InvalidSubscript
6   {
7      public static void main(String[] args)
8      {
9         // Create an array with three elements.
10        int[] values = new int[3];
11
12        System.out.println("I will attempt to store four "
13                         + "numbers in a 3-element array.");
14
15        for (int index = 0; index < 4; index++)
16        {
```

```
17              System.out.println("Now processing element " + index);
18              values[index] = 10;
19          }
20      }
21  }
```

Program Output

```
I will attempt to store four numbers in a 3-element array.
Now processing element 0
Now processing element 1
Now processing element 2
Now processing element 3
Exception in thread "main" java.lang.ArrayIndexOutOf BoundsException: 3
        at InvalidSubscript.main(InvalidSubscript.java:18)
```

When the program attempted to store a value in values[3], it halted and an error message was displayed.

 NOTE: The error message you see may be different, depending on your system.

Watch Out for Off-by-One Errors

Because array subscripts start at 0 rather than 1, you have to be careful not to perform an *off-by-one error*. For example, look at the following code:

```
// This code has an off-by-one error.
final int ARRAY_SIZE = 100;
int[] numbers = new int[ARRAY_SIZE];
for (int index = 1; index <= ARRAY_SIZE; index++)
    numbers[index] = 99;
```

The intent of this code is to create an array of integers with 100 elements, and store the value 99 in each element. However, this code has an off-by-one error. The loop uses its control variable, index, as a subscript with the numbers array. During the loop's execution, the variable index takes on the values 1 through 100, when it should take on the values 0 through 99. As a result, the first element, which is at subscript 0, is skipped. In addition, the loop attempts to use 100 as a subscript during the last iteration. Because 100 is an invalid subscript, the program will throw an exception and halt.

Array Initialization

When you create an array, Java allows you to initialize its elements with values. Here is an example:

```
int[] days = {31, 28, 31, 30, 31, 30, 31, 31, 30, 31, 30, 31};
```

This statement declares the reference variable days, creates an array in memory, and stores initial values in the array's elements. The series of values inside the braces and separated with commas is called an *initialization list*. These values are stored in the array elements in the order they appear in the list. (The first value, 31, is stored in days[0], the second value, 28, is stored in days[1], and so forth.) Note that you do not use the new key word when you use an initialization list. Java automatically creates the array and stores the values in the initialization list in it.

The Java compiler determines the size of the array by the number of items in the initialization list. Because there are 12 items in the example statement's initialization list, the array will have 12 elements. Figure 7-8 shows the contents of the array after the initialization. The program in Code Listing 7-4 demonstrates the array.

Figure 7-8 The contents of the array after the initialization

Code Listing 7-4   (`ArrayInitialization.java`)

```java
 1  /**
 2   * This program shows an array being initialized.
 3   */
 4
 5  public class ArrayInitialization
 6  {
 7     public static void main(String[] args)
 8     {
 9        final int MONTHS = 12;   // Number of months
10
11        // Create and initialize an array.
12        int[] days = { 31, 28, 31, 30, 31, 30,
13                       31, 31, 30, 31, 30, 31 };
14
15        // Display the days in each month.
16        for (int index = 0; index < MONTHS; index++)
17        {
18           System.out.println("Month " + (index + 1)
19                 + " has " + days[index] + " days.");
20        }
21     }
22  }
```

Program Output

```
Month 1 has 31 days.
Month 2 has 28 days.
Month 3 has 31 days.
Month 4 has 30 days.
Month 5 has 31 days.
Month 6 has 30 days.
Month 7 has 31 days.
Month 8 has 31 days.
Month 9 has 30 days.
Month 10 has 31 days.
Month 11 has 30 days.
Month 12 has 31 days.
```

Java allows you to spread the initialization list across multiple lines. Both of the following array declarations are equivalent:

```java
double[] coins = { 0.05, 0.1, 0.25, 0.5, 1.0 };

double[] coins = { 0.05,
                   0.1,
                   0.25,
                0.5,
                   1.0 };
```

Alternate Array Declaration Notation

Java allows you to use two different styles when declaring array reference variables. The first style is the one that we have used in this book, with the brackets immediately following the data type, as shown here:

```java
int[] numbers;
```

In the second style the brackets are placed after the variable name, as shown here:

```java
int numbers[];
```

Both of these statements accomplish the same thing: They declare that numbers is a reference to an int array. The difference between the two styles is noticed when more than one variable is declared in the same statement. For example, look at the following statement.

```java
int[] numbers, codes, scores;
```

This statement declares three variables: numbers, codes, and scores. All three are references to int arrays. This makes perfect sense because int[] is the data type for all the variables declared in the statement. Now look at the following statement, which uses the alternate notation.

```java
int numbers[], codes, scores;
```

This statement declares the same three variables, but only numbers is a reference to an int array. The codes and scores variables are regular int variables. This is because int is the data type for all the variables declared in the statement, and only `numbers` is followed by the brackets. To declare all three of these variables as references to `int` arrays using the alternate notation, you need to write a set of brackets after each variable name. Here is an example:

```java
int numbers[], codes[], scores[];
```

The first style is the standard notation for most Java programmers, so we will continue to use that style in this book.

Checkpoint

7.1 Write statements that create the following arrays.
  a. A 100-element `int` array referenced by the variable `employeeNumbers`.
  b. A 25-element `double` array referenced by the variable `payRates`.
  c. A 14-element `float` array referenced by the variable `miles`.
  d. A 1000-element `char` array referenced by the variable `letters`.

7.2 What's wrong with the following array declarations?

```java
int[] readings = new int[-1];
double[] measurements = new double[4.5];
```

7.3 What would the valid subscript values be in a four-element array of `doubles`?

7.4 What is the difference between an array's size declarator and a subscript?

7.5 What does it mean for a subscript to be out-of-bounds?

7.6 What happens in Java when a program tries to use a subscript that is out-of-bounds?

7.7 What is the output of the following code?

```java
int[] values = new int[5];

for (int count = 0; count < 5; count++)
    values[count] = count + 1;

for (int count = 0; count < 5; count++)
    System.out.println(values[count]);
```

7.8 Write a statement that creates and initializes a `double` array with the following values: 1.7, 6.4, 8.9, 3.1, and 9.2. How many elements are in the array?

7.2 Processing Array Contents

CONCEPT: Individual array elements are processed like any other type of variable.

Working with an individual array element is no different than working with a variable. For example, the following statement multiplies `hours[3]` by the variable `payRate`. The result is stored in the variable `grossPay`.

```java
grossPay = hours[3] * payRate;
```

The following are examples of preincrement and postincrement operations on array elements:

```
int[] score = {7, 8, 9, 10, 11};
++score[2]; // Preincrement operation
score[4]++; // Postincrement operation
```

When using increment and decrement operators, be careful not to use the operator on the subscript when you intend to use it on the array element. For example, the following statement decrements the variable count, but does nothing to amount[count]:

```
amount[count--];
```

Code Listing 7-5 demonstrates the use of array elements in a simple mathematical statement. A loop steps through each element of the array, using the elements to calculate the gross pay of five employees.

Code Listing 7-5   **(PayArray.java)**

```
1   import java.util.Scanner;
2   import java.text.DecimalFormat;
3
4   /**
5    * This program stores in an array the hours worked by
6    * five employees who all make the same hourly wage.
7    */
8
9   public class PayArray
10  {
11     public static void main(String[] args)
12     {
13        final int NUM_EMPLOYEES = 5; // Number of employees
14        double payRate,              // Hourly pay rate
15               grossPay;             // Gross pay
16
17        // Create an array for employee hours.
18        int[] hours = new int[NUM_EMPLOYEES];
19
20        // Create a Scanner object for keyboard input.
21        Scanner keyboard = new Scanner(System.in);
22
23        System.out.println("Enter the hours worked by " +
24                           NUM_EMPLOYEES + " employees who " +
25                           "all earn the same hourly rate.");
26
27        // Get each employee's hours worked.
28        for (int index = 0; index < NUM_EMPLOYEES; index++)
29        {
30           System.out.print("Employee #" + (index + 1) + ": ");
31           hours[index] = keyboard.nextInt();
```

```
32            }
33
34            // Get the hourly pay rate.
35            System.out.print("Enter each employee's hourly rate: ");
36            payRate = keyboard.nextDouble();
37
38            // Create a DecimalFormat object to format numbers.
39            DecimalFormat dollar = new DecimalFormat("#,##0.00");
40
41            // Display each employee's gross pay.
42            System.out.println("Gross pay for each employee:");
43            for (int index = 0; index < NUM_EMPLOYEES; index++)
44            {
45                grossPay = hours[index] * payRate;
46                System.out.println("Employee #" + (index + 1)
47                           + ": $" + dollar.format(grossPay));
48            }
49      }
50 }
```

Program Output with Example Input Shown in Bold

```
Enter the hours worked by 5 employees who all earn the same hourly rate.
Employee #1: 10 [Enter]
Employee #2: 20 [Enter]
Employee #3: 30 [Enter]
Employee #4: 40 [Enter]
Employee #5: 50 [Enter]
Enter each employee's hourly rate: 10 [Enter]
Gross pay for each employee:
Employee #1: $100.00
Employee #2: $200.00
Employee #3: $300.00
Employee #4: $400.00
Employee #5: $500.00
```

In line 45 of the program, the following statement assigns the value of `hours[index]` times `payRate` to the `grossPay` variable:

```
grossPay = hours[index] * payRate;
```

Array elements may also be used in relational expressions. For example, the following `if` statement determines whether `cost[20]` is less than `cost[0]`:

```
if (cost[20] < cost[0])
```

And the following `while` loop iterates as long as `value[count]` does not equal 0:

```
while (value[count] != 0)
{
    Statements
}
```

Code Listing 7-6, a modification of Code Listing 7-5, includes overtime wages in the gross pay. If an employee works more than 40 hours, an overtime pay rate of 1.5 times the regular pay rate is used for the excess hours.

Code Listing 7-6   (`Overtime.java`)

```java
1   import java.util.Scanner;
2   import java.text.DecimalFormat;
3
4   /**
5    * This program stores in an array the hours worked by
6    * five employees who all make the same hourly wage.
7    * Overtime wages are paid for hours greater than 40.
8    */
9
10  public class Overtime
11  {
12     public static void main(String[] args)
13     {
14        final int NUM_EMPLOYEES = 5;  // Number of employees
15        double payRate,               // Hourly pay rate
16               grossPay,              // Gross pay
17               overtime;              // Overtime wages
18
19        // Create an array for employee hours.
20        int[] hours = new int[NUM_EMPLOYEES];
21
22        // Create a Scanner object for keyboard input.
23        Scanner keyboard = new Scanner(System.in);
24
25        System.out.println("Enter the hours worked by " +
26                           NUM_EMPLOYEES + " employees who " +
27                           "all earn the same hourly rate.");
28
29        // Get each employee's hours worked.
30        for (int index = 0; index < NUM_EMPLOYEES; index++)
31        {
32           System.out.print("Employee #" + (index + 1) + ": ");
33           hours[index] = keyboard.nextInt();
34        }
35
36        // Get the hourly pay rate.
37        System.out.print("Enter the hourly rate for "
38                         + " each employee: ");
39        payRate = keyboard.nextDouble();
40
41        // Create a DecimalFormat object to format output.
```

```
42            DecimalFormat dollar = new DecimalFormat("#,##0.00");
43
44            // Display each employee's gross pay.
45            System.out.println("Here is the gross pay for "
46                                + "each employee:");
47            for (int index = 0; index < NUM_EMPLOYEES; index++)
48            {
49                if (hours[index] > 40)
50                {
51                    // Calculate base pay
52                    grossPay = 40 * payRate;
53
54                    // Calculate overtime pay
55                    overtime = (hours[index] - 40) * (1.5 * payRate);
56
57                    // Add base pay and overtime pay
58                    grossPay += overtime;
59                }
60                else
61                    grossPay = hours[index] * payRate;
62
63                System.out.println("Employee #" + (index + 1)
64                                    + ": $" + dollar.format(grossPay));
65            }
66        }
67  }
```

Program Output with Example Input Shown in Bold

```
Enter the hours worked by 5 employees who all earn the same hourly rate.
Employee #1: 10 [Enter]
Employee #2: 40 [Enter]
Employee #3: 60 [Enter]
Employee #4: 50 [Enter]
Employee #5: 30 [Enter]
Enter the hourly rate for each employee: 10 [Enter]
Here is the gross pay for each employee:
Employee #1: $100.0
Employee #2: $400.0
Employee #3: $700.0
Employee #4: $550.0
Employee #5: $300.0
```

As the second `for` loop in Code Listing 7-6 is stepping through the array, it tests each element with the following `if` statement in line 49:

```
if (hours[index] > 40)
```

If the array element is greater than 40, an overtime formula is used to calculate the employee's gross pay.

Array Length

Each array in Java has a public field named `length`. This field contains the number of elements in the array. For example, consider an array created by the following statement:

```
double[] temperatures = new double[25];
```

Because the `temperatures` array has 25 elements, the following statement would assign 25 to the variable `size`.

```
size = temperatures.length;
```

The `length` field can be useful when processing the entire contents of an array. For example, the following loop steps through an array and displays the contents of each element. The array's `length` field is used in the test expression as the upper limit for the loop control variable:

```
for (int index = 0; index < temperatures.length; index++)
    System.out.println(temperatures[index]);
```

WARNING! Be careful not to cause an off-by-one error when using the `length` field as the upper limit of a subscript. The `length` field contains the number of elements that an array has. The largest subscript that an array has is `length` − 1.

NOTE: You cannot change the value of an array's `length` field.

The Enhanced `for` Loop

Java provides a specialized version of the `for` loop that, in many circumstances, simplifies array processing. It is known as the *enhanced for loop*. Here is the general format of the enhanced `for` loop:

```
for (dataType elementVariable : array)
    statement;
```

The enhanced `for` loop is designed to iterate once for every element in an array. Each time the loop iterates, it copies an array element to a variable. Let's look at the syntax more closely:

- *dataType elementVariable* is a variable declaration. This variable will receive the value of a different array element during each loop iteration. During the first loop iteration, it receives the value of the first element; during the second iteration, it receives the value of the second element, and so on. This variable must be of the same data type as the array elements, or a type that the elements can automatically be converted to.
- *array* is the name of an array that you wish the loop to operate on. The loop will iterate once for every element in the array.
- *statement* is a statement that executes during a loop iteration.

For example, assume that we have the following array declaration:

```
int[] numbers = { 3, 6, 9 };
```

We can use the following enhanced `for` loop to display the contents of the `numbers` array:

```
for (int val : numbers)
    System.out.println(val);
```

Because the `numbers` array has three elements, this loop will iterate three times. The first time it iterates, the `val` variable will receive the value in `numbers[0]`. During the second iteration, `val` will receive the value in `numbers[1]`. During the third iteration, `val` will receive the value in `numbers[2]`. The code's output will be as follows:

```
3
6
9
```

If you need to execute more than one statement in the enhanced `for` loop, simply enclose the block of statements in a set of braces. Here is an example:

```
int[] numbers = { 3, 6, 9 };
for (int val : numbers)
{
    System.out.print("The next value is ");
    System.out.println(val);
}
```

This code will produce the following output:

```
The next value is 3
The next value is 6
The next value is 9
```

The Enhanced `for` Loop versus the Traditional `for` Loop

When you need to access the values stored in an array, from the first element to the last element, the enhanced `for` loop is simpler to use than the traditional `for` loop. With the enhanced `for` loop you do not have to be concerned about the size of the array, and you do not have to create an "index" variable to hold subscripts. However, there are circumstances in which the enhanced `for` loop is not adequate. You cannot use the enhanced `for` loop if

- you need to change the contents of an array element
- you need to work through the array elements in reverse order
- you need to access some of the array elements, but not all of them
- you need to simultaneously work with two or more arrays within the loop
- you need to refer to the subscript number of a particular element

In any of these circumstances, you should use the traditional `for` loop to process the array.

Letting the User Specify an Array's Size

Java allows you to use an integer variable to specify an array's size declarator. This makes it possible to allow the user to specify an array's size. The following code shows an example. (Assume that `keyboard` references a `Scanner` object.)

```
int size;
int[] numbers;
```

```
System.out.print("How many numbers do you have? ");
size = keyboard.nextInt();
numbers = new int[size];
```

Code Listing 7-7 demonstrates this, as well as the use of the length field. It stores a number of test scores in an array and then displays them.

Code Listing 7-7   (DisplayTestScores.java)

```
 1   import java.util.Scanner;
 2
 3   /**
 4    * This program demonstrates how the user may specify an
 5    * array's size.
 6    */
 7
 8   public class DisplayTestScores
 9   {
10      public static void main(String[] args)
11      {
12         int numTests;   // Number of tests
13         int[] tests;    // To reference an array of scores
14
15         // Create a Scanner object for keyboard input.
16         Scanner keyboard = new Scanner(System.in);
17
18         // Get the number of test scores.
19         System.out.print("How many tests do you have? ");
20         numTests = keyboard.nextInt();
21
22         // Create an array to hold that number of scores.
23         tests = new int[numTests];
24
25         // Get the individual test scores.
26         for (int index = 0; index < tests.length; index++)
27         {
28            System.out.print("Enter test score "
29                             + (index + 1) + ": ");
30            tests[index] = keyboard.nextInt();
31         }
32
33         // Display the test scores.
34         System.out.println();
35         System.out.println("Here are the scores you entered:");
36         for (int index = 0; index < tests.length; index++)
37            System.out.println(tests[index]);
38      }
39   }
```

Program Output with Example Input Shown in Bold
```
How many tests do you have? 5 [Enter]
Enter test score 1: 72 [Enter]
Enter test score 2: 85 [Enter]
Enter test score 3: 81 [Enter]
Enter test score 4: 94 [Enter]
Enter test score 5: 99 [Enter]
Here are the scores you entered:
72 85 81 94 99
```

This program allows the user to determine the size of the array. The statement in line 23 creates the array, using the `numTests` variable to determine its size. The program then uses two `for` loops. The first, in lines 26 through 31, allows the user to input each test score, and the second, in lines 36 through 37, displays all of the test scores. Both loops use the `length` member to control their number of iterations.

Reassigning Array Reference Variables

It is possible to reassign an array reference variable to a different array, as demonstrated by the following code.

```java
// Create an array referenced by the numbers variable.
int[] numbers = new int[10];
// Reassign numbers to a new array.
numbers = new int[5];
```

The first statement creates a ten-element integer array and assigns its address to the `numbers` variable. This is illustrated in Figure 7-9.

Figure 7-9 The `numbers` variable references a ten-element array

The second statement then creates a five-element integer array and assigns its address to the `numbers` variable. The address of the five-element array takes the place of the address of the ten-element array. After this statement executes, the `numbers` variable references the five-element array instead of the ten-element array. This is illustrated in Figure 7-10.

Figure 7-10 The `numbers` variable references a five-element array

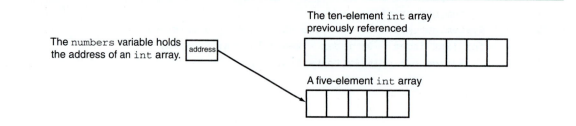

Because the ten-element array is no longer referenced, it becomes a candidate for garbage collection. The next time the garbage collector runs, the array will be destroyed.

Copying Arrays

Because an array is an object, there is a distinction between an array and the variable that references it. The array and the reference variable are two separate entities. This is important to remember when you wish to copy the contents of one array to another. You might be tempted to write something like the following code, thinking that you are copying an array.

```java
int[] array1 = { 2, 4, 6, 8, 10 };
int[] array2 = array1;   // This does not copy array1.
```

The first statement creates an array and assigns its address to the array1 variable. The second statement assigns array1 to array2. This does not make a copy of the array referenced by array1. Rather, it makes a copy of the address stored in array1 and stores it in array2. After this statement executes, both the array1 and array2 variables will reference the same array. Recall from Chapter 6 that this is called a reference copy. This is illustrated in Figure 7-11.

Figure 7-11 Both array1 and array2 reference the same array

Code Listing 7-8 demonstrates the assigning of an array's address to two reference variables. Regardless of which variable the program uses, it is working with the same array.

Code Listing 7-8   (SameArray.java)

```java
1  /**
2   * This program demonstrates that two variables can
3   * reference the same array.
4   */
5
6  public class SameArray
7  {
8     public static void main(String[] args)
9     {
10        int[] array1 = { 2, 4, 6, 8, 10 };
```

```
11              int[] array2 = array1;
12
13              // Change one of the elements using array1.
14              array1[0] = 200;
15
16              // Change one of the elements using array2.
17              array2[4] = 1000;
18
19              // Display all the elements using array1
20              System.out.println("The contents of array1:");
21              for (int value : array1)
22                  System.out.print(value + " ");
23              System.out.println();
24
25              // Display all the elements using array2
26              System.out.println("The contents of array2:");
27              for (int value : array2)
28                  System.out.print(value + " ");
29              System.out.println();
30      }
31  }
```

Program Output

```
The contents of array1:
200 4 6 8 1000
The contents of array2:
200 4 6 8 1000
```

The program in Code Listing 7-8 illustrates that you cannot copy an array by merely assigning one array reference variable to another. Instead, you must copy the individual elements of one array to another. Usually, this is best done with a loop, such as:

```
final int ARRAY_SIZE = 5;
int[] firstArray = {5, 10, 15, 20, 25 };
int[] secondArray = new int[ARRAY_SIZE];

for (int index = 0; index < firstArray.length; index++)
    secondArray[index] = firstArray[index];
```

The loop in this code copies each element of `firstArray` to the corresponding element of `secondArray`. This is demonstrated by Code Listing 7-9, which is a modification of the program in Code Listing 7-8. This version of the program makes a copy of the array referenced by `array1`.

Code Listing 7-9 (CopyArray.java)

```
1  /**
2   * This program demonstrates how to copy an array.
3   */
```

```
4
5  public class CopyArray
6  {
7     public static void main(String[] args)
8     {
9        final int ARRAY_SIZE = 5;   // Sizes of the arrays.
10       int[] array1 = { 2, 4, 6, 8, 10 };
11       int[] array2 = new int[ARRAY_SIZE];
12
13       // Make array 2 reference a copy of array1.
14       for (int index = 0; index < array1.length; index++)
15          array2[index] = array1[index];
16
17       // Change one of the elements of array1.
18       array1[0] = 200;
19
20       // Change one of the elements of array2.
21       array2[4] = 1000;
22
23       // Display all the elements using array1
24       System.out.println("The contents of array1:");
25       for (int value : array1)
26          System.out.print(value + " ");
27       System.out.println();
28
29       // Display all the elements using array2
30       System.out.println("The contents of array2:");
31       for (int value : array2)
32          System.out.print(value + " ");
33       System.out.println();
34    }
35 }
```

Program Output

```
The contents of array1:
200 4 6 8 10
The contents of array2:
2 4 6 8 1000
```

 Checkpoint

7.9   Look at the following statements.

```
int[] numbers1 = { 1, 3, 6, 9 };
int[] numbers2 = { 2, 4, 6, 8 };
int result;
```

Write a statement that multiplies element 0 of the numbers1 array by element 3 of the numbers2 array and assigns the result to the result variable.

7.10 A program uses a variable named array that references an array of integers. You do not know the number of elements in the array. Write a for loop that stores −1 in each element of the array.

7.11 A program has the following declaration:

```
double[] values;
```

Write code that asks the user for the size of the array and then creates an array of the specified size, referenced by the values variable.

7.12 Look at the following statements.

```
final int ARRAY_SIZE = 7;
int[] a = { 1, 2, 3, 4, 5, 6, 7 };
int[] b = new int[ARRAY_SIZE];
```

Write code that copies the a array to the b array. The code must perform a deep copy.

7.3 Passing Arrays as Arguments to Methods

CONCEPT: An array can be passed as an argument to a method. To pass an array, you pass the value in the variable that references the array.

VideoNote
Passing an
Array to a
Method

Quite often you'll want to write methods that process the data in arrays. As you will see, methods can be written to store values in an array, display an array's contents, total all of an array's elements, calculate their average, and so forth. Usually, such methods accept an array as an argument.

When a single element of an array is passed to a method, it is handled like any other variable. For example, Code Listing 7-10 shows a loop that passes each element of the array numbers to the method showValue.

Code Listing 7-10   (`PassElements.java`)

```
 1  /**
 2   * This program demonstrates passing individual array
 3   * elements as arguments to a method.
 4   */
 5
 6  public class PassElements
 7  {
 8     public static void main(String[] args)
 9     {
10        // Create an array.
11        int[] numbers = {5, 10, 15, 20, 25, 30, 35, 40};
12
13        // Pass each element to the ShowValue method.
14        for (int index = 0; index < numbers.length; index++)
15           showValue(numbers[index]);
```

```
16      }
17
18  /**
19   * The showValue method displays its argument.
20   */
21
22      public static void showValue(int n)
23      {
24          System.out.print(n + " ");
25      }
26  }
```

Program Output

5 10 15 20 25 30 35 40

The loop in lines 14 through 15 calls the showValue method, once for each element in the array. Each time the method is called, an array element is passed to it as an argument. The showValue method has an int parameter variable named n that receives the argument. The method simply displays the contents of n. If the method were written to accept the entire array as an argument, however, the parameter would have to be set up differently. In the following method definition, the parameter array is declared as an array reference variable. This indicates that the argument will be an array, not a single value.

```
public static void showArray(int[] array)
{
    for (int value : array)
        System.out.print(value + " ");
}
```

When you pass an array as an argument, you simply pass the value in the variable that references the array, as shown here:

```
showArray(numbers);
```

When an entire array is passed into a method, it is passed just as an object is passed: The actual array itself is not passed, but a reference to the array is passed into the parameter. Consequently, this means the method has direct access to the original array. This is illustrated in Figure 7-12.

Figure 7-12 An array reference passed as an argument

Code Listing 7-11 shows the showArray method in use and another method, getValues. The getValues method accepts an array as an argument. It asks the user to enter a value for each element.

Code Listing 7-11   (`PassArray.java`)

```
 1  import java.util.Scanner;
 2
 3  /**
 4   * This program demonstrates passing an array as an
 5   * argument to a method.
 6   */
 7
 8  public class PassArray
 9  {
10     public static void main(String[] args)
11     {
12        final int ARRAY_SIZE = 4;    // Size of the array
13
14        // Create an array.
15        int[] numbers = new int[ARRAY_SIZE];
16
17        // Pass the array to the getValues method.
18        getValues(numbers);
19
20        System.out.println("Here are the numbers "
21                             + "that you entered:");
```

```
22
23            // Pass the array to the showArray method.
24            showArray(numbers);
25        }
26
27        /**
28         * The getValues method accepts an array as its
29         * argument. The user is asked to enter a value
30         * for each element.
31         */
32
33        private static void getValues(int[] array)
34        {
35            // Create a Scanner object for keyboard input.
36            Scanner keyboard = new Scanner(System.in);
37
38            System.out.println("Enter a series of "
39                        + array.length + " numbers.");
40
41            // Read values into the array.
42            for (int index = 0; index < array.length; index++)
43            {
44                System.out.print("Number " + (index + 1) + ": ");
45                array[index] = keyboard.nextInt();
46            }
47        }
48
49        /**
50         * The showArray method accepts an array as
51         * an argument displays its contents.
52         */
53
54        public static void showArray(int[] array)
55        {
56            // Display the array elements.
57            for (int value : array)
58                System.out.print(value + " ");
59        }
60    }
```

Program Output with Example Input Shown in Bold

```
Enter a series of 4 numbers.
Number 1: 2 [Enter]
Number 2: 4 [Enter]
Number 3: 6 [Enter]
Number 4: 8 [Enter]
Here are the numbers that you entered:
2 4 6 8
```

Checkpoint

7.13 Look at the following method header:

```
public static void myMethod(double[] array)
```

The following code shows an array declaration:

```
final int ARRAY_SIZE = 100;
double[] numbers = new double[ARRAY_SIZE];
```

Write a statement that passes the numbers array to the `myMethod` method.

7.14 Write a static method named `zero` that accepts an `int` array as an argument and stores the value 0 in each element.

7.4 Some Useful Array Algorithms and Operations

CONCEPT: In this section you will see various algorithms written in Java that perform useful operations on arrays.

Comparing Arrays

In the previous section you saw that you cannot copy an array by simply assigning its reference variable to another array's reference variable. In addition, you cannot use the `==` operator to compare two array reference variables and determine whether the arrays are equal. For example, the following code appears to compare two arrays, but in reality it does not.

```
int[] firstArray = { 5, 10, 15, 20, 25  };
int[] secondArray = { 5, 10, 15, 20, 25  };
if (firstArray == secondArray)          // This is a mistake.
    System.out.println("The arrays are the same.");
else
    System.out.println("The arrays are not the same.");
```

Recall from Chapter 6 that when you use the `==` operator with reference variables, the operator compares the memory addresses that the variables contain, not the contents of the objects referenced by the variables. Because the two array variables in this code reference different objects in memory, they will contain different addresses. Therefore, the result of the boolean expression `firstArray == secondArray` is `false`, and the code reports that the arrays are not the same.

To compare the contents of two arrays, you must compare the elements of the two arrays. For example, look at the following code.

```
int[] firstArray = { 2, 4, 6, 8, 10 };
int[] secondArray = { 2, 4, 6, 8, 10 };
boolean arraysEqual = true;   // Flag variable
int index = 0;                // Loop control variable

// First determine whether the arrays are the same size.
if (firstArray.length != secondArray.length)
    arraysEqual = false;
```

```
// Next determine whether the elements contain the same data.
while (arraysEqual && index < firstArray.length)
{
    if (firstArray[index] != secondArray[index])
        arraysEqual = false;
    index++;
}

if (arraysEqual)
    System.out.println("The arrays are equal.");
else
    System.out.println("The arrays are not equal.");
```

This code determines whether `firstArray` and `secondArray` contain the same values. A `boolean` flag variable, `arraysEqual`, which is initialized to true, is used to signal whether the arrays are equal. Another variable, `index`, which is initialized to 0, is used as a loop control variable.

First, this code determines whether the two arrays are the same length. If they are not the same length, then the arrays cannot be equal, so the flag variable `arraysEqual` is set to `false`. Then a `while` loop begins. The loop executes as long as `arraysEqual` is true and the control variable `index` is less than `firstArray.length`. During each iteration, it compares a different set of corresponding elements in the arrays. When it finds two corresponding elements that have different values, the flag variable `arraysEqual` is set to `false`. After the loop finishes, an `if` statement examines the `arraysEqual` variable. If the variable is `true`, then the arrays are equal and a message indicating so is displayed. Otherwise, they are not equal, so a different message is displayed.

Summing the Values in a Numeric Array

To sum the values in an array you must use a loop with an accumulator variable. The loop adds the value in each array element to the accumulator. For example, assume that the following code appears in a program and that values have been stored in the units array.

```
final int ARRAY_SIZE = 25;
int[] units = new int[ARRAY_SIZE];
```

The following loop adds the values of each element of the units array to the `total` variable. When the code is finished, `total` will contain the sum of all of the units array's elements.

```
int total = 0;              // Initialize accumulator
for (int index = 0; index < units.length; index++)
    total += units[index];
```

You can also use an enhanced `for` loop to sum the contents of an array, as shown here:

```
int total = 0;              // Initialize accumulator
for (int value : units)
    total += value;
```

Getting the Average of the Values in a Numeric Array

The first step in calculating the average of all the values in an array is to sum the values. The second step is to divide the sum by the number of elements in the array. Assume that the following statement appears in a program and that values have been stored in the `scores` array.

```
final int ARRAY_SIZE = 10;
double[] scores = new double[ARRAY_SIZE];
```

The following code calculates the average of the values in the `scores` array. When the code completes, the average will be stored in the `average` variable.

```
double total = 0;      // Initialize accumulator
double average;        // Will hold the average
// Add up all the values in the array.
for (int index = 0; index < scores.length; index++)
   total += scores[index];
// Calculate the average.
average = total / scores.length;
```

Notice that the last statement, which divides `total` by `scores.length`, is not inside the loop. This statement should only execute once, after the loop has finished its iterations.

Finding the Highest and Lowest Values in a Numeric Array

The algorithms for finding the highest and lowest values in an array are very similar. First, let's look at code for finding the highest value in an array. Assume that the following statement exists in a program and that values have been stored in the `numbers` array.

```
final int ARRAY_SIZE = 50;
int[] numbers = new int[ARRAY_SIZE];
```

The code to find the highest value in the array is as follows:

```
int highest = numbers[0];
for (int index = 1; index < numbers.length; index++)
{
   if (numbers[index] > highest)
     highest = numbers[index];
}
```

First we copy the value in the first array element to the variable `highest`. Then the loop compares all of the remaining array elements, beginning at subscript 1, to the value in `highest`. Each time it finds a value in the array greater than `highest`, it copies that value to `highest`. When the loop has finished, `highest` will contain the highest value in the array.

The following code finds the lowest value in the array. As you can see, it is nearly identical to the code for finding the highest value.

```
int lowest = numbers[0];
for (int index = 1; index < numbers.length; index++)
{
   if (numbers[index] < lowest)
       lowest = numbers[index];
}
```

When the loop has finished, `lowest` will contain the lowest value in the array.

The `SalesData` Class

To demonstrate these algorithms, look at the `SalesData` class shown in Code Listing 7-12. The class keeps sales amounts for any number of days in an array, which is a private field. Public methods are provided that return the total, average, highest, and lowest amounts of sales. The program in Code Listing 7-13 demonstrates the class.

Code Listing 7-12   (`SalesData.java`)

```java
 1   /**
 2    * This class keeps the sales figures for a number of
 3    * days in an array and provides methods for getting
 4    * the total and average sales, and the highest and
 5    * lowest amounts of sales.
 6    */
 7
 8   public class SalesData
 9   {
10      private double[] sales; // References the sales data
11
12      /**
13       * The constructor accepts an array as an argument.
14       * The elements in the argument array are copied
15       * to the sales array.
16       */
17
18      public SalesData(double[] s)
19      {
20         // Create a new array the same length as s.
21         sales = new double[s.length];
22
23         // Copy the values in s to sales.
24         for (int index = 0; index < s.length; index++)
25            sales[index] = s[index];
26      }
27
28      /**
29       * The getTotal method returns the total of the
30       * elements in the sales array.
31       */
32
33      public double getTotal()
34      {
35         double total = 0.0;    // Accumulator
36
37         // Add up all the values in the sales array.
38         for (double value : sales)
39            total += value;
40
41         // Return the total.
42         return total;
43      }
```

```
44
45      /**
46       * The getAverage method returns the average of the
47       * elements in the sales array.
48       */
49
50      public double getAverage()
51      {
52         return getTotal() / sales.length;
53      }
54
55      /**
56       * The getHighest method returns the highest value
57       * stored in the sales array.
58       */
59
60      public double getHighest()
61      {
62         // Store the first value in the sales array in
63         // the variable highest.
64         double highest = sales[0];
65
66         // Search the array for the highest value.
67         for (int index = 1; index < sales.length; index++)
68         {
69            if (sales[index] > highest)
70               highest = sales[index];
71         }
72
73         // Return the highest value.
74         return highest;
75      }
76
77      /**
78       * The getLowest method returns the lowest value
79       * stored in the sales array.
80       */
81
82      public double getLowest()
83      {
84         // Store the first value in the sales array in
85         // the variable lowest.
86         double lowest = sales[0];
87
88         // Search the array for the lowest value.
89         for (int index = 1; index < sales.length; index++)
90         {
91            if (sales[index] < lowest)
92               lowest = sales[index];
93         }
94
95         // Return the lowest value.
96         return lowest;
97      }
98   }
```

Code Listing 7-13   (`Sales.java`)

```java
 1   import java.util.Scanner;
 2   import java.text.DecimalFormat;
 3
 4   /**
 5    * This program gathers sales amounts for the week.
 6    * It uses the SalesData class to display the total,
 7    * average, highest, and lowest sales amounts.
 8    */
 9
10   public class Sales
11   {
12      public static void main(String[] args)
13      {
14         final int ONE_WEEK = 7; // Number of array elements
15
16         // Create an array to hold the sales numbers
17         // for one week.
18         double[] sales = new double[ONE_WEEK];
19
20         // Get the week's sales figures and store them
21         // in the sales array.
22         getValues(sales);
23
24         // Create a SalesData object initialized with the
25         // sales array.
26         SalesData week = new SalesData(sales);
27
28         // Create a DecimalFormat object for output formatting.
29         DecimalFormat dollar = new DecimalFormat("#,##0.00");
30
31         // Display the total, average, highest, and lowest
32         // sales amounts for the week.
33         System.out.println();
34         System.out.println("The total sales were $"
35                     + dollar.format(week.getTotal()));
36         System.out.println("The average sales were $"
37                     + dollar.format(week.getAverage()));
38         System.out.println("The highest sales were $"
39                     + dollar.format(week.getHighest()));
40         System.out.println("The lowest sales were $"
41                     + dollar.format(week.getLowest()));
42      }
43
44      /**
45       * The following method accepts an array as its
46       * argument. The user is asked to enter sales
47       * amounts for each element.
48       */
49
50      private static void getValues(double[] array)
51      {
52         // Create a Scanner object for keyboard input.
53         Scanner keyboard = new Scanner(System.in);
```

```
54
55          System.out.println("Enter the sales for each of "
56                            + "the following days.");
57
58          // Get the sales for each day in the week.
59          for (int index = 0; index < array.length; index++)
60          {
61              System.out.print("Day " + (index + 1) + ": ");
62              array[index] = keyboard.nextDouble();
63          }
64      }
65  }
```

Program Output with Example Input Shown in Bold

```
Enter the sales for each of the following days.
Day 1: 2374.55 [Enter]
Day 2: 1459.04 [Enter]
Day 3: 1762.99 [Enter]
Day 4: 1207.82 [Enter]
Day 5: 2798.53 [Enter]
Day 6: 2207.64 [Enter]
Day 7: 2194.51 [Enter]
The total sales were $14,005.08
The average sales were $2,000.73
The highest sales were $2,798.53
The lowest sales were $1,207.82
```

In the Spotlight:
Creating an Object that Processes an Array

Dr. LaClaire gives a set of exams during the semester in her chemistry class. At the end of the semester she drops each student's lowest test score before averaging the remaining scores. She has asked you to write a program that will read a student's test scores as input and calculate the average with the lowest score dropped.

The following pseudocode shows the steps for calculating the average of a set of test scores with the lowest score dropped:

Calculate the total of the scores.

Find the lowest score.

Subtract the lowest score from the total. This gives the adjusted total.

Divide the adjusted total by (number of scores − 1). This is the average.

You decide to create a class named `Grader`, with a constructor that accepts a `double` array of test scores. The `Grader` class will have a method named `getLowestScore` that returns the lowest score in the array and a method named `getAverage` that returns the average of the test scores with the lowest score dropped. Figure 7-13 shows a UML diagram for the class.

Figure 7-13   UML diagram for the Grader class

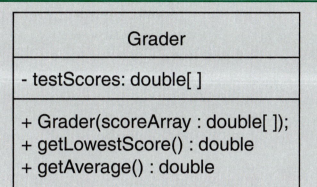

Code Listing 7-14 shows the code for the class.

Code Listing 7-14   (Grader.java)

```
1  /**
2   *  The Grader class calculates the average
3   *  of an array of test scores, with the
4   *  lowest score dropped.
5   */
6
7  public class Grader
8  {
9     // The testScores field is a variable
10    // that will reference an array
11    // of test scores.
12    private double[] testScores;
13
14    /**
15     * The constructor accepts an array of
16     * test scores as an argument.
17     */
18
19    public Grader(double[] scoreArray)
20    {
21       // Assign the array argument to
22       // the testScores field.
23       testScores = scoreArray;
24    }
25
26    /**
27     * The getLowestScore method returns
28     * the lowest test score.
29     */
30
31    public double getLowestScore()
```

```
32      {
33          double lowest;    // To hold the lowest score
34
35          // Get the first test score in the array.
36          lowest = testScores[0];
37
38          // Step through the rest of the array. When
39          // a value less than lowest is found, assign
40          // it to lowest.
41          for (int index = 1; index < testScores.length; index++)
42          {
43              if (testScores[index] < lowest)
44                  lowest = testScores[index];
45          }
46
47          // Return the lowest test score.
48          return lowest;
49      }
50
51      /**
52       * The getAverage method returns the average of the
53       * test scores with the lowest score dropped.
54       */
55
56      public double getAverage()
57      {
58          double total = 0;    // To hold the score total
59          double lowest;       // To hold the lowest score
60          double average;      // To hold the average
61
62          // If the array contains less than two test
63          // scores, display an error message and set
64          // average to 0.
65          if (testScores.length < 2)
66          {
67              System.out.println("ERROR: You must have at " +
68                                  "least two test scores!");
69              average = 0;
70          }
71          else
72          {
73              // First, calculate the total of the scores.
74              for (double score : testScores)
75                  total += score;
76
77              // Next, get the lowest score.
78              lowest = getLowestScore();
79
80              // Subtract the lowest score from the total.
81              total -= lowest;
```

```
82
83              // Get the adjusted average.
84              average = total / (testScores.length - 1);
85          }
86
87          // Return the adjusted average.
88          return average;
89      }
90  }
```

- Line 12 declares a field named testScores, which is used to reference a double array of test scores.
- The constructor appears in lines 19 through 24. It accepts a double array as an argument, which is assigned to the testScores field.
- The getLowestScore method appears in lines 31 through 49. It finds the lowest value in the testScores array and returns that value.
- The getAverage method appears in lines 56 through 89. This method first determines if there are fewer than two elements in the testScores array (in line 65). If that is the case, we cannot drop the lowest score, so an error message is displayed and the average variable is set to 0. Otherwise, the code in lines 73 through 84 calculates the average of the test scores with the lowest score dropped and assigns that value to the average variable. Line 88 returns the value of the average variable.

Code Listing 7-15 shows the program that Dr. LaClaire will use to calculate a student's adjusted average. The program gets a series of test scores, stores those scores in an array, and uses an instance of the Grader class to calculate the average.

Code Listing 7-15   (CalcAverage.java)

```
1   import java.util.Scanner;
2
3   /**
4    * This program gets a set of test scores and
5    * uses the Grader class to calculate the average
6    * with the lowest score dropped.
7    */
8
9   public class CalcAverage
10  {
11      public static void main(String[] args)
12      {
13          int numScores;    // To hold the number of scores
14
15          // Create a Scanner object for keyboard input.
16          Scanner keyboard = new Scanner(System.in);
17
18          // Get the number of test scores.
19          System.out.print("How many test scores do you have? ");
20          numScores = keyboard.nextInt();
```

```
21
22          // Create an array to hold the test scores.
23          double[] scores = new double[numScores];
24
25          // Get the test scores and store them
26          // in the scores array.
27          for (int index = 0; index < numScores; index++)
28          {
29              System.out.print("Enter score #"
30                              + (index + 1) + ": ");
31              scores[index] = keyboard.nextDouble();
32          }
33
34          // Create a Grader object, passing the
35          // scores array as an argument to the
36          // constructor.
37          Grader myGrader = new Grader(scores);
38
39          // Display the adjusted average.
40          System.out.println("Your adjusted average is "
41                              + myGrader.getAverage());
42
43          // Display the lowest score.
44          System.out.println("Your lowest test score was "
45                              + myGrader.getLowestScore());
46      }
47  }
```

Program Output with Example Input Shown in Bold

```
How many test scores do you have? 4 [Enter]
Enter scores #1: 100 [Enter]
Enter scores #2: 100 [Enter]
Enter scores #3: 40 [Enter]
Enter scores #4: 100 [Enter]
Your adjusted average is 100.0
Your lowest test score was 40.0
```

Partially Filled Arrays

Sometimes you need to store a series of items in an array, but you don't know the number of items that there are. As a result, you don't know the exact number of elements needed for the array. One solution is to make the array large enough to hold the largest possible number of items. This can lead to another problem, however: If the actual number of items stored in the array is less than the number of elements, the array will be only partially filled. When you process a partially filled array, you must only process the elements that contain valid data items.

A partially filled array is normally used with an accompanying integer variable that holds the number of items stored in the array. For example, suppose a program uses the following code to create an array with 100 elements, and an `int` variable named `count` that will hold the number of items stored in the array:

```java
final int ARRAY_SIZE = 100;
int[] array = new int[ARRAY_SIZE];
int count = 0;
```

Each time we add an item to the array, we must increment `count`. The following code demonstrates:

```java
Scanner keyboard = new Scanner(System.in);
System.out.print("Enter a number or -1 to quit: ");
number = keyboard.nextInt();
while (number != -1 && count < array.length)
{
    array[count] = number;
    count++;
    System.out.print("Enter a number or -1 to quit: ");
    number = keyboard.nextInt();
}
```

Each iteration of this sentinel-controlled loop allows the user to enter a number to be stored in the array, or −1 to quit. The `count` variable is used as the subscript of the next available element in the array, and then incremented. When the user enters −1, or `count` reaches the size of the array, the loop stops. The following code displays all of the valid items in the array:

```java
for (int index = 0; index < count; index++)
{
    System.out.println(array[index]);
}
```

Notice that this code uses `count` to determine the maximum array subscript to use.

> **NOTE:** If a partially filled array is passed as an argument to a method, the variable that holds the count of items in the array must also be passed as an argument. Otherwise, the method will not be able to determine the number of items stored in the array.

Working with Arrays and Files

Saving the contents of an array to a file is a straightforward procedure: Use a loop to step through each element of the array, writing its contents to the file. For example, assume a program defines an array as follows:

```java
int[] numbers = { 10, 20, 30, 40, 50 };
```

The following code opens a file named *Values.txt* and writes the contents of each element of the `numbers` array to the file.

```java
int[] numbers = { 10, 20, 30, 40, 50 };


// Open the file.
PrintWriter outputFile = new PrintWriter("Values.txt");
```

```
// Write the array elements to the file.
for (int index = 0; index < numbers.length; index++)
    outputFile.println(numbers[index]);

// Close the file.
outputFile.close();
```

The following code demonstrates how to open the *Values.txt* file and read its contents back into the numbers array.

```
final int SIZE = 5;
int[] numbers = new int[SIZE];
int index = 0;  // Loop control variable

// Open the file.
File file = new File("Values.txt");
Scanner inputFile = new Scanner(file);

// Read the file contents into the array.
while (inputFile.hasNext() && index < numbers.length)
{
    numbers[index] = inputFile.nextInt();
    index++;
}

// Close the file.
inputFile.close();
```

The file is opened, then a while loop reads all of the values from the file into the numbers array. The loop repeats as long as inputFile.hasNext() returns true, and index is less than numbers.length. The inputFile.hasNext() method is called to make sure there is a value remaining in the file. This prevents an error in case the file does not contain enough values to fill the array. The second condition (index < numbers.length) prevents the loop from writing outside the array boundaries.

7.5 Returning Arrays from Methods

CONCEPT: In addition to accepting arrays as arguments, methods may also return arrays.

A method can return a reference to an array. To do so, the return type of the method must be declared properly. For example, look at the following method definition:

```
public static double[] getArray()
{
    double[] array = { 1.2, 2.3, 4.5, 6.7, 8.9 };
    return array;
}
```

The getArray method is a public static method that returns an array of doubles. Notice that the return type listed in the method header is double[ ]. The method header is illustrated in Figure 7-14. It indicates that the method returns a reference to a double array.

Figure 7-14   Array reference return type

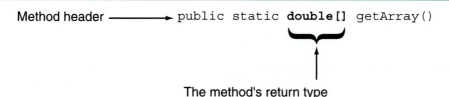

Method header ──────────► `public static` **`double[]`** `getArray()`

The method's return type

Inside the method an array of doubles is created, initialized with some values, and referenced by the array variable. The return statement then returns the array variable. By returning the array variable, the method is returning a reference to the array. The method's return value can be stored in any compatible reference variable, as demonstrated in Code Listing 7-16.

Code Listing 7-16   **(ReturnArray.java)**

```
 1  /**
 2   * This program demonstrates how a reference to an
 3   * array can be returned from a method.
 4   */
 5
 6  public class ReturnArray
 7  {
 8     public static void main(String[] args)
 9     {
10        double[] values;
11
12        // Let values reference the array returned
13        // from the getArray method.
14        values = getArray();
15
16        // Display the values in the array.
17        for (double num : values)
18           System.out.println(num);
19     }
20
21     /**
22      * The getArray method returns a reference to
23      * an array of doubles.
24      */
25
26     public static double[] getArray()
```

```
27      {
28          double[] array = { 1.2, 2.3, 4.5, 6.7, 8.9 };
29          return array;
30      }
31  }
```

Program Output

```
1.2   2.3   4.5   6.7   8.9
```

The statement in line 14 assigns the array created in `getArray` to the array variable `values`. The `for` loop in lines 17 through 18 then displays the value of each element of the `values` array.

We could easily modify the `getArray` method to create an array of a specified size and fill it with values entered by the user. The following shows an example.

```java
public static double[] getArray(int size)
{
    // Create an array of the specified size.
    double[] array = new double[size];

    // Create a Scanner object for keyboard input.
    Scanner keyboard = new Scanner(System.in);

    System.out.println("Enter a series of "
                        + array.length + " numbers.");

    // Get values from the user for the array.
    for (int index = 0; index < array.length; index++)
    {
        System.out.print("Number " + (index + 1) + ": ");
        array[index] = keyboard.nextInt();
    }

    // Return the array.
    return array;
}
```

7.6   String Arrays

CONCEPT: An array of `String` objects may be created, but if the array is uninitialized, each `String` in the array must be created individually.

Java also allows you to create arrays of `String` objects. Here is a statement that creates an array of String objects initialized with values.

```java
String[] names = { "Bill", "Susan", "Steven", "Jean" };
```

In memory, an array of String objects is arranged differently than an array of a primitive data type. To use a String object, you must have a reference to the String object. So, an array of String objects is really an array of references to String objects. Figure 7-15 illustrates how the names variable will reference an array of references to String objects.

Figure 7-15   The names variable references a String array

Each element in the names array is a reference to a String object. The names[0] element references a String object containing "Bill", the names[1] element references a String object containing "Susan", and so forth. The program in Code Listing 7-17 demonstrates an array of String objects.

Code Listing 7-17   **(MonthDays.java)**

```
1   /**
2    * This program demonstrates an array of String objects.
3    */
4
5   public class MonthDays
6   {
7      public static void main(String[] args)
8      {
9         // Create an array of Strings containing the names
10        // of the months.
11        String[] months = { "January", "February", "March",
12                            "April", "May", "June", "July",
13                            "August", "September", "October",
14                            "November", "December" };
15
16        // Create an array of ints containing the numbers
17        // of days in each month.
18        int[] days = { 31, 28, 31, 30, 31, 30, 31,
19                       31, 30, 31, 30, 31 };
20
```

```
21          // Display the months and the days in each.
22          for (int index = 0; index < months.length; index++)
23          {
24              System.out.println(months[index] + " has "
25                                  + days[index] + " days.");
26          }
27      }
28  }
```

Program Output

```
January has 31 days.
February has 28 days.
March has 31 days.
April has 30 days.
May has 31 days.
June has 30 days.
July has 31 days.
August has 31 days.
September has 30 days.
October has 31 days.
November has 30 days.
December has 31 days.
```

As with the primitive data types, an initialization list automatically causes an array of `String` objects to be created in memory. If you do not provide an initialization list, you must use the new key word to create the array. Here is an example:

```
final int ARRAY_SIZE = 4;
String[] names = new String[ARRAY_SIZE];
```

This statement creates an array of four references to `String` objects, as shown in Figure 7-16. Notice that the array is an array of four uninitialized `String` references. Because they do not reference any objects, they are set to `null`.

Figure 7-16   An uninitialized `String` array

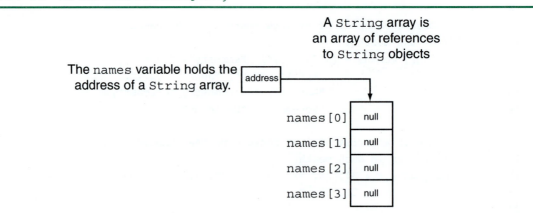

When you create an uninitialized array of `String` objects, you must assign a value to each element in the array. Here is an example:

```
final int ARRAY_SIZE = 4;
String[] names = new String[ARRAY_SIZE];
names[0] = "Bill";
names[1] = "Susan";
names[2] = "Steven";
names[3] = "Jean";
```

After these statements execute, each element of the names array will reference a `String` object.

Calling `String` Methods from an Array Element

Recall from Chapter 2 that `String` objects have several methods. For example, the `toUpperCase` method returns the uppercase equivalent of a `String` object. Because each element of a `String` array is a `String` object, you can use an element to call a `String` method. For example, the following statement calls the `toUpperCase` method from element 0 of the names array.

```
System.out.println(names[0].toUpperCase());
```

The program in Code Listing 7-18 uses a loop to call the `toUpperCase` method from each element of the names array.

Code Listing 7-18   (`StringArrayMethods.java`)

```
 1  /**
 2   * This program demonstrates the toUpperCase method
 3   * being called from the elements of a String array.
 4   */
 5
 6  public class StringArrayMethods
 7  {
 8     public static void main(String[] args)
 9     {
10        // Create an array of Strings.
11        String[] names = { "Bill", "Susan",
12                           "Steven", "Jean" };
13
14        // Display each string in the names array
15        // in uppercase.
16        for (int index = 0; index < names.length; index++)
17           System.out.println(names[index].toUpperCase());
18     }
19  }
```

Program Output

```
BILL
SUSAN
STEVEN
JEAN
```

TIP: Arrays have a field named `length` and `String` objects have a method named `length`. When working with `String` arrays, do not confuse the two. The following loop displays the length of each string held in a `String` array. Note that the loop uses both the array's `length` field and each element's `length` method.

```
for (int index = 0; index < names.length; index++)
    System.out.println(names[index].length());
```

Because the array's `length` member is a field, you do not write a set of parentheses after its name. You do write the parentheses after the name of the `String` class's `length` method.

Checkpoint

7.15 a. Write a statement that declares a `String` array initialized with the following strings: "Mercury", "Venus", "Earth", and "Mars".

      b. Write a loop that displays the contents of each element in the array you declared in Checkpoint 7.15a.

      c. Write a loop that displays the first character of the strings stored in each element of the array you declared in Checkpoint 7.15a. (Hint: Use the `String` class's `charAt` method discussed in Chapter 2.)

7.7   Arrays of Objects

CONCEPT: You may create arrays of objects that are instances of classes that you have written.

Like any other data type, you can create arrays of class objects. For example, recall the `InventoryItem` class that was introduced in Chapter 6. An array of `InventoryItem` objects could be created to represent a business's inventory records. Here is a statement that declares an array of five `InventoryItem` objects:

```
final int NUM_ITEMS = 5;
InventoryItem[] inventory = new InventoryItem[NUM_ITEMS];
```

The variable that references the array is named inventory. As with `String` arrays, each element in this array is a reference variable, as illustrated in Figure 7-17.

Figure 7-17   The inventory variable references an array of references

Notice from the figure that each element of the array is initialized with the null value. This indicates that the array elements do not yet reference objects. You must create the objects that each element will reference. The following code uses a loop to create objects for each element.

```
for (int index = 0; index < inventory.length; index++)
    inventory[index] = new InventoryItem();
```

In this code, the no-arg constructor is called for each object. Recall that the InventoryItem class has a no-arg constructor that assigns an empty string ("") to the description field and 0 to the units field. After the loop executes, each element of the inventory array will reference an object, as shown in Figure 7-18.

Figure 7-18   Each element of the array references an object

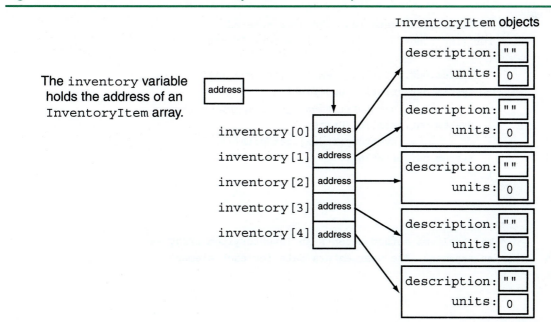

Objects in an array are accessed with subscripts, just like any other data type in an array. For example, the following code calls the `setDescription` and `setUnits` methods of the element `inventory[2]`:

```
inventory[2].setDescription("Wrench");
inventory[2].setUnits(20);
```

Code Listing 7-19 shows a complete program that uses an array of objects.

Code Listing 7-19   (`ObjectArray.java`)

```java
 1  import java.util.Scanner;
 2
 3  /**
 4   * This program works with an array of InventoryItem objects.
 5   */
 6
 7  public class ObjectArray
 8  {
 9     public static void main(String[] args)
10     {
11        final int NUM_ITEMS = 3;   // Number of items
12
13        // Create an InventoryItem array.
14        InventoryItem[] inventory = new InventoryItem[NUM_ITEMS];
15
16        // Call the getItems method to get data for each element.
17        getItems(inventory);
18
19        System.out.println("You entered the following:");
20
21        // Display the data that the user entered.
22        for (int index = 0; index < inventory.length; index++)
23        {
24           System.out.println("Item " + (index + 1));
25           System.out.println("Description: "
26                     + inventory[index].getDescription());
27           System.out.println("Units: "
28                     + inventory[index].getUnits());
29           System.out.println();
30        }
31     }
32
33     /**
34      * The getItems method accepts an InventoryItem array as
35      * an argument. The user enters data for each element.
36      */
```

```
37
38      private static void getItems(InventoryItem[] array)
39      {
40          String description;  // Item description
41          int units;           // Number of units on hand
42
43          // Create a Scanner object for keyboard input.
44          Scanner keyboard = new Scanner(System.in);
45
46          System.out.println("Enter data for " + array.length
47                             + " inventory items.");
48
49          // Get data for the array.
50          for (int index = 0; index < array.length; index++)
51          {
52              // Get an item's description.
53              System.out.print("Enter the description for "
54                             + "item " + (index + 1) + ": ");
55              description = keyboard.nextLine();
56
57              // Get the number of units.
58              System.out.print("Enter the units for "
59                             + "item " + (index + 1) + ": ");
60              units = keyboard.nextInt();
61
62              // Consume the remaining newline.
63              keyboard.nextLine();
64
65              // Create an InventoryItem object initialized with
66              // the data and store the object in the array.
67              array[index] = new InventoryItem(description, units);
68
69              // Display a blank line before going on.
70              System.out.println();
71          }
72      }
73  }
```

Program Output with Example Input Shown in Bold

```
Enter data for 3 inventory items.
Enter the description for item 1: Wrench [Enter]
Enter the units for item 1: 20 [Enter]

Enter the description for item 2: Hammer [Enter]
Enter the units for item 2: 15 [Enter]

Enter the description for item 3: Pliers [Enter]
Enter the units for item 3: 18 [Enter]
```

```
You entered the following:
Item 1
Description: Wrench
Units: 20

Item 2
Description: Hammer
Units: 15

Item 3
Description: Pliers
Units: 18
```

 Checkpoint

7.16 Recall that we discussed a `Rectangle` class in Chapter 3. Write code that declares a `Rectangle` array with five elements. Instantiate each element with a `Rectangle` object. Use the `Rectangle` constructor to initialize each object with values for the `length` and `width` fields.

7.8 The Sequential Search Algorithm

CONCEPT: A search algorithm is a method of locating a specific item in a larger collection of data. This section discusses the sequential search algorithm, which is a simple technique for searching the contents of an array.

It is very common for programs not only to store and process information stored in arrays, but to search arrays for specific items. This section shows you how to use the simplest of all search algorithms, the sequential search.

The *sequential search algorithm* uses a loop to sequentially step through an array, starting with the first element. It compares each element with the value being searched for and stops when the value is found or the end of the array is encountered. If the value being searched for is not in the array, the algorithm unsuccessfully searches to the end of the array.

The `SearchArray` class shown in Code Listing 7-20 uses a static method, `sequentialSearch`, to find a value in an integer array. The argument array is searched for an occurrence of the number stored in `value`. If the number is found, its array subscript is returned. Otherwise, −1 is returned, indicating the value did not appear in the array.

Code Listing 7-20 (`SearchArray.java`)

```
1   /**
2    * This class's sequentialSearch method searches an
3    * int array for a specified value.
4    */
5
```

```
 6  public class SearchArray
 7  {
 8     /**
 9      * The sequentialSearch method searches array for
10      * value. If value is found in array, the element's
11      * subscript is returned. Otherwise, -1 is returned.
12      */
13
14     public static int sequentialSearch(int[] array, int value)
15     {
16        int index,       // Loop control variable
17            element;      // Element the value is found at
18        boolean found;   // Flag indicating search results
19
20        // Element 0 is the starting point of the search.
21        index = 0;
22
23        // Store the default values for element and found.
24        element = -1;
25        found = false;
26
27        // Search the array.
28        while (!found && index < array.length)
29        {
30           // Does this element have the value?
31           if (array[index] == value)
32           {
33              found = true;     // Indicate the value is found.
34              element = index;  // Save the subscript of the value.
35           }
36
37           // Increment index so we can look at the next element.
38           index++;
39        }
40
41        // Return either the subscript of the value (if found)
42        // or -1 to indicate the value was not found.
43        return element;
44     }
45  }
```

 NOTE: The reason −1 is returned when the search value is not found in the array is because −1 is not a valid subscript.

Code Listing 7-21 is a complete program that uses the SearchArray class. It searches the five-element array tests to find a score of 100.

Code Listing 7-21   (`TestSearch.java`)

```java
 1  /**
 2   * This program demonstrates the SearchArray class's
 3   * sequentialSearch method.
 4   */
 5
 6  public class TestSearch
 7  {
 8     public static void main(String[] args)
 9     {
10        int results;  // Results of the search
11
12        // Create an array of values.
13        int[] tests = { 87, 75, 98, 100, 82 };
14
15        // Search the array for the value 100.
16        results = SearchArray.sequentialSearch(tests, 100);
17
18        // Determine whether 100 was found in the array.
19        if (results == -1)
20        {
21           // -1 indicates the value was not found.
22           System.out.println("You did not earn 100 "
23                             + "on any test.");
24        }
25        else
26        {
27           // results holds the subscript of the value 100.
28           System.out.println("You earned 100 on "
29                             + "test " + (results + 1));
30        }
31     }
32  }
```

Program Output

```
You earned 100 on test 4
```

See the `PinTester` Class Case Study for another example using arrays. Also, see the Case Study on Parallel Arrays to learn about another programming technique using arrays. These case studies are available on the book's online resource page at www.pearsonhighered.com/gaddis.

7.9 The Selection Sort and the Binary Search Algorithms

> **CONCEPT:** A sorting algorithm is used to arrange data into some order. A search algorithm is a method of locating a specific item in a larger collection of data. The selection sort and the binary search are popular sorting and searching algorithms.

The Selection Sort Algorithm

Often the data in an array must be sorted in some order. Customer lists, for instance, are commonly sorted in alphabetical order. Student grades might be sorted from highest to lowest. Product codes could be sorted so all the products of the same color are stored together. In this section we explore how to write a sorting algorithm. A *sorting algorithm* is a technique for scanning through an array and rearranging its contents in some specific order. The algorithm that we will explore is called the *selection sort*.

The *selection sort* works like this: The smallest value in the array is located and moved to element 0. Then the next smallest value is located and moved to element 1. This process continues until all of the elements have been placed in their proper order. Let's see how the selection sort works when arranging the elements of the following array in Figure 7-19.

Figure 7-19 Values in an array

The selection sort scans the array, starting at element 0, and locates the element with the smallest value. The contents of this element are then swapped with the contents of element 0. In this example, the 1 stored in element 5 is swapped with the 5 stored in element 0. After the exchange, the array would appear as shown in Figure 7-20.

Figure 7-20 Values in array after first swap

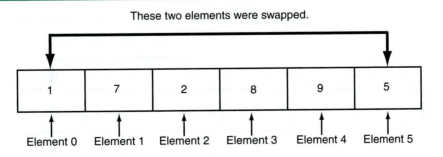

The algorithm then repeats the process, but because element 0 already contains the smallest value in the array, it can be left out of the procedure. This time, the algorithm begins the scan at element 1. In this example, the contents of element 2 are exchanged with that of element 1. The array would then appear as shown in Figure 7-21.

Figure 7-21 Values in array after second swap

Once again the process is repeated, but this time the scan begins at element 2. The algorithm will find that element 5 contains the next smallest value. This element's value is swapped with that of element 2, causing the array to appear as shown in Figure 7-22.

Figure 7-22 Values in array after third swap

Next, the scanning begins at element 3. Its value is swapped with that of element 5, causing the array to appear as shown in Figure 7-23.

Figure 7-23 Values in array after fourth swap

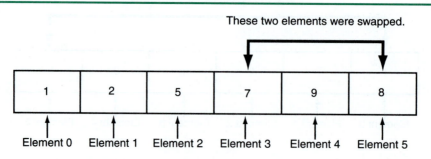

At this point there are only two elements left to sort. The algorithm finds that the value in element 5 is smaller than that of element 4, so the two are swapped. This puts the array in its final arrangement as shown in Figure 7-24.

Figure 7-24   Values in array after fifth swap

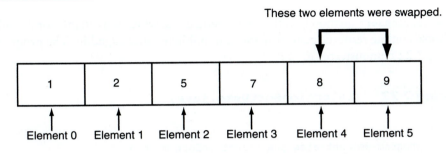

Here is the selection sort algorithm in pseudocode:

> For startScan *is each subscript in array from 0 through the next-to-last subscript*
>> Set minIndex *variable to* startScan.
>> Set minValue *variable to* array[startScan].
>> For index *is each subscript in array from (*startScan + 1*) through the last subscript*
>>> If array[index] *is less than* minValue
>>>> Set minValue *to* array[index].
>>>> Set minIndex *to index.*
>>> End If.
>>> Increment index.
>> End For.
>> Set array[minIndex] *to* array[startScan].
>> Set array[startScan] *to* minValue.
> End For.

The following static method performs a selection sort on an integer array. The array that is passed as an argument is sorted in ascending order.

```java
public static void selectionSort(int[] array)
{
    int startScan, index, minIndex, minValue;
    for (startScan = 0; startScan < (array.length-1); startScan++)
    {
        minIndex = startScan;
        minValue = array[startScan];
        for(index = startScan + 1; index < array.length; index++)
        {
            if (array[index] < minValue)
            {
                minValue = array[index];
                minIndex = index;
```

```
                    }
                }
                array[minIndex] = array[startScan];
                array[startScan] = minValue;
            }
        }
```

The selectionSort method is in the ArrayTools class, which is available for download from the book's online resource page at www.pearsonhighered.com/gaddis. The program in Code Listing 7-22 demonstrates it.

Code Listing 7-22   (SelectionSortDemo.java)

```
 1   /**
 2    * This program demonstrates the selectionSort method
 3    * in the ArrayTools class.
 4    */
 5
 6   public class SelectionSortDemo
 7   {
 8      public static void main(String[] arg)
 9      {
10         // Create an array of unsorted values.
11         int[] values = {5, 7, 2, 8, 9, 1};
12
13         // Display the unsorted array.
14         System.out.println("The unsorted values are:");
15         for (int index = 0; index < values.length; index++)
16            System.out.print(values[index] + " ");
17         System.out.println();
18
19         // Sort the array.
20         ArrayTools.selectionSort(values);
21
22         // Display the sorted array.
23         System.out.println("The sorted values are:");
24         for (int index = 0; index < values.length; index++)
25            System.out.print(values[index] + " ");
26      }
27   }
```

Program Output

```
The unsorted values are:
5 7 2 8 9 1
The sorted values are:
1 2 5 7 8 9
```

The Binary Search Algorithm

This chapter previously presented the sequential search algorithm for searching an array. The advantage of the sequential search is its simplicity. It is easy to understand and implement. Furthermore, it doesn't require the data in the array to be stored in any particular order. Its disadvantage, however, is its inefficiency. If the array being searched contains 20,000 elements, the algorithm will have to look at all 20,000 elements to find a value stored in the last element. In an average case, an item is just as likely to be found near the end of the array as near the beginning. Typically, for an array of N items, the sequential search will locate an item in N/2 attempts. If an array has 50,000 elements, the sequential search will make a comparison with 25,000 of them in a typical case.

This is assuming, of course, that the search item is consistently found in the array. (N/2 is the average number of comparisons. The maximum number of comparisons is always N.) When the sequential search fails to locate an item, it must make a comparison with every element in the array. As the number of failed search attempts increases, so does the average number of comparisons. Obviously, the sequential search should not be used on large arrays if speed is important.

The *binary search* is a clever algorithm that is much more efficient than the sequential search. Its only requirement is that the values in the array must be sorted in ascending order. Instead of testing the array's first element, this algorithm starts with the element in the middle. If that element happens to contain the desired value, then the search is over. Otherwise, the value in the middle element is either greater than or less than the value being searched for. If it is greater, then the desired value (if it is in the list) will be found somewhere in the first half of the array. If it is less, then the desired value (again, if it is in the list) will be found somewhere in the last half of the array. In either case, half of the array's elements have been eliminated from further searching.

If the desired value wasn't found in the middle element, the procedure is repeated for the half of the array that potentially contains the value. For instance, if the last half of the array is to be searched, the algorithm tests *its* middle element. If the desired value isn't found there, the search is narrowed to the quarter of the array that resides before or after that element. This process continues until the value being searched for is either found, or there are no more elements to test. Here is the pseudocode for a method that performs a binary search on an array:

> *Set* first *to 0.*
> *Set* last *to the last subscript in the array.*
> *Set* position *to −1.*
> *Set* found *to false.*
> *While* found *is not true and* first *is less than or equal to* last
>> *Set* middle *to the subscript halfway between* array[first] *and* array[last].
>> *If* array[middle] *equals the desired value*
>>> *Set* found *to true.*
>>> *Set* position *to* middle.
>> *Else If* array[middle] *is greater than the desired value*
>>> *Set* last *to* middle −1.
>> *Else*
>>> *Set* first *to* middle +1.
>> *End If.*
> *End While.*
> *Return* position.

This algorithm uses three variables to mark positions within the array: `first`, `last`, and `middle`. The `first` and `last` variables mark the boundaries of the portion of the array currently being searched. They are initialized with the subscripts of the array's `first` and `last` elements. The subscript of the element halfway between `first` and `last` is calculated and stored in the `middle` variable. If the element in the middle of the array does not contain the search value, the `first` or `last` variables are adjusted so that only the top or bottom half of the array is searched during the next iteration. This cuts the portion of the array being searched in half each time the loop fails to locate the search value.

The following static method performs a binary search on an integer array. The first parameter, `array`, is searched for an occurrence of the number stored in `value`. If the number is found, its array subscript is returned. Otherwise, -1 is returned, indicating the value did not appear in the array.

```java
public static int binarySearch(int[] array, int value)
{
    int first,          // First array element
        last,           // Last array element
        middle,         // Midpoint of search
        position;       // Position of search value
    boolean found;      // Flag

    // Set the inital values.
    first = 0;
    last = array.length - 1;
    position = -1;
    found = false;

    // Search for the value.
    while (!found && first <= last)
    {
        middle = (first + last) / 2;    // Calculate midpoint
        if (array[middle] == value)     // If value is found at mid
        {
            found = true;
            position = middle;
        }
        else if (array[middle] > value) // If value is in lower half
            last = middle - 1;
        else
            first = middle + 1;         // If value is in upper half
    }

    // Return the position of the item, or -1
    // if it was not found.
    return position;
}
```

The binarySearch method is in the ArrayTools class, which available for download from the book's online resource page at www.pearsonhighered.com/gaddis. The program in Code Listing 7-23 demonstrates it. Note that the values in the array are already sorted in ascending order.

Code Listing 7-23   (BinarySearchDemo.java)

```java
 1  import java.util.Scanner;
 2
 3  /**
 4   * This program demonstrates the binary search method in
 5   * the ArrayTools class.
 6   */
 7
 8  public class BinarySearchDemo
 9  {
10      public static void main(String[] args)
11      {
12          int result,        // Result of the search
13              searchValue;   // Value to search for
14          String again;      // Indicates whether to search again
15
16          // Create a Scanner object for keyboard input.
17          Scanner keyboard = new Scanner(System.in);
18
19          // The values in the following array are sorted
20          // in ascending order.
21          int numbers[] = {101, 142, 147, 189, 199, 207, 222,
22                           234, 289, 296, 310, 319, 388, 394,
23                           417, 429, 447, 521, 536, 600};
24
25          do
26          {
27              // Get a value to search for.
28              System.out.print("Enter a value to search for: ");
29              searchValue = keyboard.nextInt();
30
31              // Search for the value
32              result = ArrayTools.binarySearch(numbers, searchValue);
33
34              // Display the results.
35              if (result == -1)
36                  System.out.println(searchValue + " was not found.");
37              else
38              {
39                  System.out.println(searchValue + " was found at "
40                                      + "element " + result);
41              }
```

```
42
43              // Consume the remaining newline.
44              keyboard.nextLine();
45
46              // Does the user want to search again?
47              System.out.print("Do you want to search again? (Y or N): ");
48              again = keyboard.nextLine();
49
50          } while (again.charAt(0) == 'y' || again.charAt(0) == 'Y');
51      }
52  }
```

Program Output with Example Input Shown in Bold

```
Enter a value to search for: 296 [Enter]
296 was found at element 9
Do you want to search again? (Y or N): y [Enter]
Enter a value to search for: 600 [Enter]
600 was found at element 19
Do you want to search again? (Y or N): y [Enter]
Enter a value to search for: 101 [Enter]
101 was found at element 0
Do you want to search again? (Y or N): y [Enter]
Enter a value to search for: 207 [Enter]
207 was found at element 5
Do you want to search again? (Y or N): y [Enter]
Enter a value to search for: 999 [Enter]
999 was not found.
Do you want to search again? (Y or N): n [Enter]
```

 Checkpoint

7.17 What value in an array does the selection sort algorithm look for first?
When the selection sort finds this value, what does it do with it?

7.18 How many times will the selection sort swap the smallest value in an array with another value?

7.19 Describe the difference between the sequential search and the binary search.

7.20 On average, with an array of 20,000 elements, how many comparisons will the sequential search perform? (Assume the items being searched for are consistently found in the array.)

7.21 If a sequential search is performed on an array, and it is known that some items are searched for more frequently than others, how can the contents of the array be reordered to improve the average performance of the search?

7.10 Two-Dimensional Arrays

CONCEPT: A two-dimensional array is an array of arrays. It can be thought of as having rows and columns.

An array is useful for storing and working with a set of data. Sometimes, though, it's necessary to work with multiple sets of data. For example, in a grade-averaging program a teacher might record all of one student's test scores in an array of `doubles`. If the teacher has 30 students, that means she'll need 30 arrays to record the scores for the entire class. Instead of defining 30 individual arrays, however, it would be better to define a two-dimensional array.

The arrays that you have studied so far are one-dimensional arrays. They are called *one-dimensional* because they can only hold one set of data. Two-dimensional arrays, which are sometimes called *2D arrays*, can hold multiple sets of data. Although a two-dimensional array is actually an array of arrays, it's best to think of it as having rows and columns of elements, as shown in Figure 7-25. This figure shows an array of test scores, having three rows and four columns.

Figure 7-25   Rows and columns

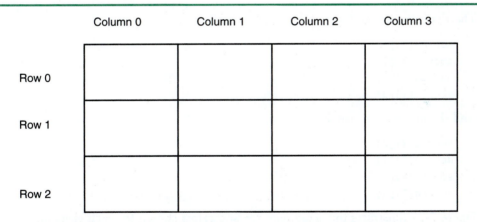

The array depicted in the figure has three rows (numbered 0 through 2) and four columns (numbered 0 through 3). There are a total of 12 elements in the array.

To declare a two-dimensional array, two sets of brackets and two size declarators are required: The first one is for the number of rows and the second one is for the number of columns. Here is an example declaration of a two-dimensional array with three rows and four columns:

```
double[][] scores = new double[3][4];
```

The two sets of brackets in the data type indicate that the `scores` variable will reference a two-dimensional array. The numbers 3 and 4 are size declarators. The first size declarator specifies the number of rows, and the second size declarator specifies the number of columns. Notice that each size declarator is enclosed in its own set of brackets. This is illustrated in Figure 7-26.

Figure 7-26 Declaration of a two-dimensional array

As with one-dimensional arrays, it is a common practice to use `final` variables as the size declarators for two-dimensional arrays. Here is an example:

```
final int ROWS = 3;
final int COLS = 4;
double[][] scores = new double[ROWS][COLS];
```

When processing the data in a two-dimensional array, each element has two subscripts: one for its row and another for its column. In the `scores` array, the elements in row 0 are referenced as

```
scores[0][0]
scores[0][1]
scores[0][2]
scores[0][3]
```

The elements in row 1 are

```
scores[1][0]
scores[1][1]
scores[1][2]
scores[1][3]
```

And the elements in row 2 are

```
scores[2][0]
scores[2][1]
scores[2][2]
scores[2][3]
```

Figure 7-27 illustrates the array with the subscripts shown for each element.

Figure 7-27 Subscripts for each element of the scores array

The `scores` variable holds the address of a 2D array of doubles.		column 0	column 1	column 2	column 3
address →	row 0	scores[0][0]	scores[0][1]	scores[0][2]	scores[0][3]
	row 1	scores[1][0]	scores[1][1]	scores[1][2]	scores[1][3]
	row 2	scores[2][0]	scores[2][1]	scores[2][2]	scores[2][3]

To access one of the elements in a two-dimensional array, you must use both subscripts. For example, the following statement stores the number 95 in `scores[2][1]`.

```
scores[2][1] = 95;
```

Programs that process two-dimensional arrays can do so with nested loops. For example, the following code prompts the user to enter a score, once for each element in the `scores` array.

```
final int ROWS = 3;
final int COLS = 4;
double[][] scores = new double[ROWS][COLS];
for (int row = 0; row < ROWS; row++)
{
    for (int col = 0; col < COLS; col++)
    {
        System.out.print("Enter a score: ");
        number = keyboard.nextDouble();
        scores[row][col] = number;
    }
}
```

And the following code displays all the elements in the `scores` array.

```
for (int row = 0; row < ROWS; row++)
{
    for (int col = 0; col < COLS; col++)
    {
        System.out.println(scores[row][col]);
    }
}
```

The program in Code Listing 7-24 uses a two-dimensional array to store corporate sales data. The array has three rows (one for each division of the company) and four columns (one for each quarter).

Code Listing 7-24   **(CorpSales.java)**

```
1   import java.util.Scanner;
2
3   /**
4    * This program demonstrates a two-dimensional array.
5    */
6
7   public class CorpSales
8   {
9       public static void main(String[] args)
10      {
11          final int DIVS = 3;        // Three divisions in the company
```

```
12          final int QTRS = 4;        // Four quarters
13          double totalSales = 0.0;   // Accumulator
14
15          // Create an array to hold the sales for each
16          // division, for each quarter.
17          double[][] sales = new double[DIVS][QTRS];
18
19          // Create a Scanner object for keyboard input.
20          Scanner keyboard = new Scanner(System.in);
21
22          // Display an introduction.
23          System.out.println("This program will calculate the " +
24                              "total sales of");
25          System.out.println("all the company's divisions. " +
26                              "Enter the following sales data:");
27
28          // Nested loops to fill the array with quarterly
29          // sales figures for each division.
30          for (int div = 0; div < DIVS; div++)
31          {
32             for (int qtr = 0; qtr < QTRS; qtr++)
33             {
34                System.out.printf("Division %d, Quarter %d: $",
35                                  (div + 1), (qtr + 1));
36                sales[div][qtr] = keyboard.nextDouble();
37             }
38             System.out.println();   // Print blank line.
39          }
40
41          // Nested loops to add all the elements of the array.
42          for (int div = 0; div < DIVS; div++)
43          {
44             for (int qtr = 0; qtr < QTRS; qtr++)
45             {
46                totalSales += sales[div][qtr];
47             }
48          }
49
50          // Display the total sales.
51          System.out.printf("Total company sales: $%,.2f\n",
52                            totalSales);
53       }
54    }
```

Program Output with Example Input Shown in Bold

```
This program will calculate the total sales of
all the company's divisions. Enter the following sales data:

Division 1, Quarter 1: $35698.77 [Enter]
Division 1, Quarter 2: $36148.63 [Enter]
Division 1, Quarter 3: $31258.95 [Enter]
Division 1, Quarter 4: $30864.12 [Enter]

Division 2, Quarter 1: $41289.64 [Enter]
Division 2, Quarter 2: $43278.52 [Enter]
Division 2, Quarter 3: $40927.18 [Enter]
Division 2, Quarter 4: $42818.98 [Enter]

Division 3, Quarter 1: $28914.56 [Enter]
Division 3, Quarter 2: $27631.52 [Enter]
Division 3, Quarter 3: $30596.64 [Enter]
Division 3, Quarter 4: $29834.21 [Enter]

Total company sales: $419,261.72
```

Look at the array declaration in line 17. As mentioned earlier, the array has three rows (one for each division) and four columns (one for each quarter) to store the company's sales data. The row subscripts are 0, 1, and 2, and the column subscripts are 0, 1, 2, and 3. Figure 7-28 illustrates how the quarterly sales data is stored in the array.

Figure 7-28   Division and quarter data stored in the `sales` array

Initializing a Two-Dimensional Array

When initializing a two-dimensional array, you enclose each row's initialization list in its own set of braces. Here is an example:

```
int[][] numbers = { {1, 2, 3}, {4, 5, 6}, {7, 8, 9} };
```

As with one-dimensional arrays, you do not use the `new` key word when you provide an initialization list. Java automatically creates the array and fills its elements with the initialization values. In this example, the initialization values for row 0 are {1, 2, 3}, the initialization values for row 1 are {4, 5, 6}, and the initialization values for row 2 are {7, 8, 9}. So, this statement declares an array with three rows and three columns. The same statement could also be written as:

```
int[][] numbers = { {1, 2, 3},
                    {4, 5, 6},
                    {7, 8, 9} };
```

In either case, the values are assigned to the `numbers` array in the following manner:

```
numbers[0][0] is set to 1
numbers[0][1] is set to 2
numbers[0][2] is set to 3
numbers[1][0] is set to 4
numbers[1][1] is set to 5
numbers[1][2] is set to 6
numbers[2][0] is set to 7
numbers[2][1] is set to 8
numbers[2][2] is set to 9
```

Figure 7-29 illustrates the array initialization.

Figure 7-29   The numbers array

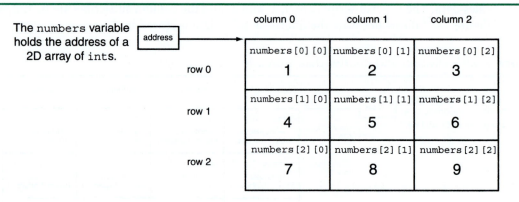

The `length` Field in a Two-Dimensional Array

A one-dimensional array has a `length` field that holds the number of elements in the array. A two-dimensional array, however, has multiple `length` fields. It has a `length` field that holds the number of rows, and then each row has a `length` field that holds the number of columns. This makes sense when you think of a two-dimensional array as an array of one-dimensional arrays. Figure 7-29 shows the numbers array depicted in rows and columns. Figure 7-30 shows another way of thinking of the numbers array: As an array of arrays.

Figure 7-30   The numbers array is an array of arrays

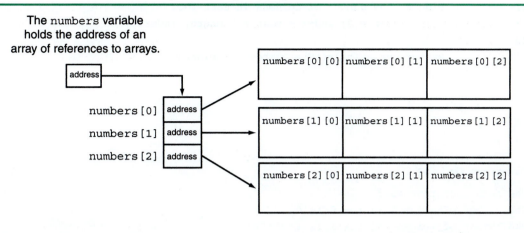

As you can see from the figure, the `numbers` variable references a one-dimensional array with three elements. Each of the three elements is a reference to another one-dimensional array. The elements in the array referenced by `numbers[0]` are `numbers[0][0]`, `numbers[0][1]`, and `numbers[0][2]`. This pattern continues with `numbers[1]` and `numbers[2]`. The figure shows a total of four arrays. Each of the arrays in the figure has its own `length` field. The program in Code Listing 7-25 uses these `length` fields to display the number of rows and columns in a two-dimensional array.

Code Listing 7-25   (Lengths.java)

```java
 1  /**
 2   * This program uses the length fields of a 2D array
 3   * to display the number of rows and the number of
 4   * columns in each row.
 5   */
 6
 7  public class Lengths
 8  {
 9     public static void main(String[] args)
10     {
11        // Declare a 2D array with 3 rows
12        // and 4 columns.
13        int[][] numbers = { { 1,  2,  3,  4  },
14                            { 5,  6,  7,  8  },
15                            { 9, 10, 11, 12 } };
16
17        // Display the number of rows.
18        System.out.println("The number of rows is "
19                              + numbers.length);
```

```
20
21          // Display the number of columns in each row.
22          for (int index = 0; index < numbers.length; index++)
23          {
24             System.out.println("The number of columns "
25                                  + "in row " + index + " is "
26                                  + numbers[index].length);
27          }
28       }
29  }
```

Program Output

```
The number of rows is 3
The number of columns in row 0 is 4
The number of columns in row 1 is 4
The number of columns in row 2 is 4
```

Displaying All the Elements of a Two-Dimensional Array

As you have seen in previous example programs, a pair of nested loops can be used to display all the elements of a two-dimensional array. For example, the following code creates the numbers array with three rows and four columns, and then displays all the elements in the array.

```java
int[][] numbers = { { 1,  2,  3,  4  },
                    { 5,  6,  7,  8  },
                    { 9, 10, 11, 12 } };

for (int row = 0; row < 3; row++)
{
   for (int col = 0; col < 4; col++)
      System.out.println(numbers[row][col]);
}
```

Although this code will display all of the elements, it is limited in the following way: The loops are specifically written to display an array with three rows and four columns. A better approach is to use the array's length fields for the upper limit of the subscripts in the loop test expressions. Here are the modified loops:

```java
for (int row = 0; row < numbers.length; row++)
{
   for (int col = 0; col < numbers[row].length; col++)
      System.out.println(numbers[row][col]);
}
```

Let's take a closer look at the header for the outer loop:

```java
for (int row = 0; row < numbers.length; row++)
```

This loop controls the subscript for the `number` array's rows. Because `numbers.length` holds the number of rows in the array, we have used it as the upper limit for the row subscripts. Here is the header for the inner loop:

```
for (int col = 0; col < numbers[row].length; col++)
```

This loop controls the subscript for the `number` array's columns. Because each row's `length` field holds the number of columns in the row, we have used it as the upper limit for the column subscripts. By using the `length` fields in algorithms that process two-dimensional arrays, you can write code that works with arrays of any number of rows and columns.

Summing All the Elements of a Two-Dimensional Array

To sum all the elements of a two-dimensional array, you can use a pair of nested loops to add the contents of each element to an accumulator. The following code shows an example:

```
int[][] numbers = { { 1,   2,   3,   4 },
                    { 5,   6,   7,   8 },
                    { 9,  10,  11,  12 } };
int total;          // Accumulator

total = 0;          // Start the accumulator at 0.

// Sum the array elements.
for (int row = 0; row < numbers.length; row++)
{
    for (int col = 0; col < numbers[row].length; col++)
        total += numbers[row][col];
}

// Display the sum.
System.out.println("The total is " + total);
```

Summing the Rows of a Two-Dimensional Array

Sometimes you may need to calculate the sum of each row in a two-dimensional array. For example, suppose a two-dimensional array is used to hold a set of test scores for a set of students. Each row in the array is a set of test scores for one student. To get the sum of a student's test scores (perhaps so an average may be calculated), you use a loop to add all the elements in one row. The following code shows an example:

```
int[][] numbers = { { 1,   2,   3,   4 },
                    { 5,   6,   7,   8 },
                    { 9,  10,  11,  12 } };
int total;          // Accumulator

for (int row = 0; row < numbers.length; row++)
{
    // Set the accumulator to 0.
    total = 0;
```

```
   // Sum a row.
   for (int col = 0; col < numbers[row].length; col++)
      total += numbers[row][col];

   // Display the row's total.
   System.out.println("Total of row " + row +
                     " is " + total);
}
```

Notice that the `total` variable, which is used as an accumulator, is set to zero just before the inner loop executes. This is because the inner loop sums the elements of a row and stores the sum in `total`. Therefore, the `total` variable must be set to zero before each iteration of the inner loop.

Summing the Columns of a Two-Dimensional Array

Sometimes you may need to calculate the sum of each column in a two-dimensional array. For example, suppose a two-dimensional array is used to hold a set of test scores for a set of students, and you wish to calculate the class average for each of the test scores. To do this, you calculate the average of each column in the array. This is accomplished with a set of nested loops. The outer loop controls the column subscript and the inner loop controls the row subscript. The inner loop calculates the sum of a column, which is stored in an accumulator. The following code demonstrates:

```
int[][] numbers = { { 1,   2,   3,   4 },
                    { 5,   6,   7,   8 },
                    { 9, 10, 11, 12 } };
int total;        // Accumulator

for (int col = 0; col < numbers[0].length; col++)
{
    // Set the accumulator to 0.
    total = 0;

    // Sum a column.
    for (int row = 0; row < numbers.length; row++)
       total += numbers[row][col];

    // Display the column's total.
    System.out.println("Total of column " + col +
                      " is " + total);
}
```

Passing Two-Dimensional Arrays to Methods

When a two-dimensional array is passed to a method, the parameter must be declared as a reference to a two-dimensional array. The following method header shows an example.

```
private static void showArray(int[][] array)
```

This method's parameter, array, is declared as a reference to a two-dimensional int array. Any two-dimensional int array can be passed as an argument to the method. Code Listing 7-26 demonstrates two such methods.

Code Listing 7-26   (Pass2Darray.java)

```java
1  /**
2   * This class demonstrates methods that accept a two-
3   * dimensional array as an argument.
4   */
5
6  public class Pass2Darray
7  {
8     public static void main(String[] args)
9     {
10       // Create a 2D array of integers.
11       int[][] numbers = { { 1,  2,  3,  4  },
12                           { 5,  6,  7,  8  },
13                           { 9, 10, 11, 12  } };
14
15       System.out.println("Here are the values in "
16                          + "the array.");
17
18       // Pass the numbers array to the showArray method.
19       // This will display the array's contents.
20       showArray(numbers);
21
22       // Display the sum of the array's values.
23       // Note the call to the arraySum method, with the
24       // array being passed as an argument.
25       System.out.println("The sum of the values is "
26                          + arraySum(numbers));
27    }
28
29    /**
30     * The showArray method accepts a two-dimensional
31     * int array and displays its contents.
32     */
33
34    private static void showArray(int[][] array)
35    {
36       for (int row = 0; row < array.length; row++)
37       {
38          for (int col = 0; col < array[row].length; col++)
39             System.out.print(array[row][col] + " ");
40          System.out.println();
41       }
```

```
42        }
43
44        /**
45         * The arraySum method accepts a two-dimensional
46         * int array and returns the sum of its contents.
47         */
48
49        private static int arraySum(int[][] array)
50        {
51            int total = 0;    // Accumulator
52
53            for (int row = 0; row < array.length; row++)
54            {
55                for (int col = 0; col < array[row].length; col++)
56                    total += array[row][col];
57            }
58
59            return total;
60        }
61  }
```

Program Output

```
Here are the values in the array.
1 2 3 4
5 6 7 8
9 10 11 12
The sum of the values is 78
```

Ragged Arrays

Because the rows in a two-dimensional array are also arrays, each row can have its own length. When the rows of a two-dimensional array are of different lengths, the array is known as a *ragged array*. You create a ragged array by first creating a two-dimensional array with a specific number of rows, but no columns. Here is an example:

```
int[][] ragged = new int[4][];
```

This statement partially creates a two-dimensional array. The array can have four rows, but the rows have not yet been created. Next, you create the individual rows as shown in the following code.

```
ragged[0] = new int[3];    // Row 0 has 3 columns.
ragged[1] = new int[4];    // Row 1 has 4 columns.
ragged[2] = new int[5];    // Row 2 has 5 columns.
ragged[3] = new int[6];    // Row 3 has 6 columns.
```

This code creates the four rows. Row 0 has three columns, row 1 has four columns, row 2 has five columns, and row 3 has six columns. The following code displays the number of columns in each row.

```
for (int index = 0; index < ragged.length; index++)
{
    System.out.println("The number of columns "
                    + "in row " + index + " is " + ragged[index].length);
}
```

This code will display the following output:

```
The number of columns in row 0 is 3
The number of columns in row 1 is 4
The number of columns in row 2 is 5
The number of columns in row 3 is 6
```

7.11 Arrays with Three or More Dimensions

CONCEPT: Java does not limit the number of dimensions that an array may have. It is possible to create arrays with multiple dimensions, to model data that occurs in multiple sets.

Java allows you to create arrays with virtually any number of dimensions. Here is an example of a three-dimensional array declaration:

```
double[][][] seats = new double[3][5][8];
```

This array can be thought of as three sets of five rows, with each row containing eight elements. The array might be used to store the prices of seats in an auditorium, where there are eight seats in a row, five rows in a section, and a total of three sections.

Figure 7-31 illustrates the concept of a three-dimensional array as "pages" of two-dimensional arrays.

Figure 7-31 A three-dimensional array

Arrays with more than three dimensions are difficult to visualize, but can be useful in some programming problems. For example, in a factory warehouse where cases of widgets are stacked on pallets, an array with four dimensions could be used to store a part number for each widget. The four subscripts of each element could represent the pallet number, case number, row number, and column number of each widget. Similarly, an array with five dimensions could be used if there were multiple warehouses.

Checkpoint

7.22 A video rental store keeps videos on 50 racks with 10 shelves each. Each shelf holds 25 videos. Declare a three-dimensional array large enough to represent the store's storage system.

7.12 Command-Line Arguments and Variable-Length Argument Lists

CONCEPT: When you invoke a Java program from the operating system command line, you can specify arguments that are passed into the **main** method of the program. In addition, you can write a method that takes a variable number of arguments. When the method runs, it can determine the number of arguments that were passed to it and act accordingly.

Command-Line Arguments

Every program you have seen in this book and every program you have written uses a static main method with a header that looks like this:

```
public static void main(String[] args)
```

Inside the parentheses of the method header is the declaration of a parameter named args. This parameter is an array name. As its declaration indicates, it is used to reference an array of Strings. The array that is passed into the args parameter comes from the operating system command line. For example, look at Code Listing 7-27.

Code Listing 7-27   (`CommandLine.java`)

```
1  /**
2   * This program displays the arguments passed to
3   * it from the operating system command line.
4   */
5
6  public class CommandLine
7  {
8     public static void main(String [] args)
9     {
```

```
10          for (int i = 0; i < args.length; i++)
11              System.out.println(args[i]);
12      }
13  }
```

If this program is compiled and then executed with the command

```
java CommandLine How does this work?
```

its output will be

```
How
does
this
work?
```

Any items typed on the command line, separated by spaces, after the name of the class are considered one or more arguments to be passed into the main method. In the previous example, four arguments are passed into args. The word "How" is passed into args[0], "does" is passed into args[1], "this" is passed into args[2], and "work?" is passed into args[3]. The for loop in main simply displays each argument.

NOTE: It is not required that the name of main's parameter array be args. You can name it anything you wish. It is a standard convention, however, for the name args to be used.

Variable-Length Argument Lists

Java provides a mechanism known as *variable-length argument lists,* which makes it possible to write a method that takes a variable number of arguments. In other words, you can write a method that accepts any number of arguments when it is called. When the method runs, it can determine the number of arguments that were passed to it and act accordingly.

For example, suppose we need to write a method named sum that can accept any number of int values and then return the sum of those values. We might call the method as shown here:

```
result = sum(10, 20);
```

Here we pass two arguments to the method: 10 and 20. After this code executes, the value 30 would be stored in the result variable. But the method does not have to accept two arguments each time it is called. We could call the method again with a different number of arguments, as shown here:

```
int firstVal = 1, secondVal = 2, thirdVal = 3, fourthVal = 4;
result = sum(firstVal, secondVal, thirdVal, fourthVal);
```

Here we pass four arguments to the method: firstVal (which is set to 1), secondVal (which is set to 2), thirdVal (which is set to 3), and fourthVal (which is set to 4). After this code executes, the value 10 would be stored in the `result` variable. Here's the code for the `sum` method:

```
public static int sum(int... numbers)
{
    int total = 0;   // Accumulator

    // Add all the values in the numbers array.
    for (int val : numbers)
        total += val;

    // Return the total.
    return total;
}
```

Notice the declaration of the `numbers` parameter in the method header. The ellipsis (three periods) that follows the data type indicates that `numbers` is a special type of parameter known as a `vararg` *parameter*. A `vararg` parameter can take a variable number of arguments.

In fact, `vararg` parameters are actually arrays. In the `sum` method, the `numbers` parameter is an array of `int`s. All of the arguments passed to the `sum` method are stored in the elements of the `numbers` array. As you can see from the code, the method uses the enhanced `for` loop to step through the elements of the `numbers` array, adding up the values stored in its elements. (The *VarargsDemo1.java* program, available for download from the book's online resource page, demonstrates the `sum` method.)

You can also write a method to accept a variable number of object references as arguments. For example, the program in Code Listing 7-28 shows a method that accepts a variable number of references to `InventoryItem` objects. The method returns the total of the objects' units fields.

Code Listing 7-28   (`VarargsDemo2.java`)

```
 1  /**
 2   * This program demonstrates a method that accepts
 3   * a variable number of arguments (varargs).
 4   */
 5
 6  public class VarargsDemo2
 7  {
 8     public static void main(String[] args)
 9     {
10        int total;   // To hold the total units
11
12        // Create an InventoryItem object with 10 units.
13        InventoryItem item1 = new InventoryItem("Soap", 10);
14
15        // Create an InventoryItem object with 20 units.
16        InventoryItem item2 = new InventoryItem("Shampoo", 20);
17
```

```
18          // Create an InventoryItem object with 30 units.
19          InventoryItem item3 = new InventoryItem("Toothpaste", 30);
20
21          // Call the method with one argument.
22          total = totalUnits(item1);
23          System.out.println("Total: " + total);
24
25          // Call the method with two arguments.
26          total = totalUnits(item1, item2);
27          System.out.println("Total: " + total);
28
29          // Call the method with three arguments.
30          total = totalUnits(item1, item2, item3);
31          System.out.println("Total: " + total);
32     }
33
34     /**
35      * The totalUnits method takes a variable number
36      * of InventoryItem objects and returns the total
37      * of their units.
38      */
39
40     public static int totalUnits(InventoryItem... items)
41     {
42        int total = 0;   // Accumulator
43
44        // Add all the values in the numbers array.
45        for (InventoryItem itemObject : items)
46           total += itemObject.getUnits();
47
48        // Return the total.
49        return total;
50     }
51  }
```

Program Output

```
Total: 10
Total: 30
Total: 60
```

You can write a method to accept a mixture of fixed arguments and a variable-length argument list. For example, suppose you want to write a method named courseAverage that accepts the name of a course as a String, and a variable-length list of test scores as doubles. We could write the method header as:

```
public static void courseAverage(String course, double... scores)
```

This method has a regular `String` parameter named `course`, and a vararg parameter named `scores`. When we call this method, we always pass a `String` argument, then a list of `double` values. (This method is demonstrated in the program *VarargsDemo3.java*, which is available for download from the book's online resource page at www.pearsonhighered.com/gaddis.) Note that when a method accepts a mixture of fixed arguments and a variable-length argument list, the vararg parameter must be the last one declared.

> **NOTE:** You can also pass an array to a vararg parameter. This is demonstrated in the program *VarargsDemo4.java*, which is available for download from the book's online resource page at www.pearsonhighered.com/gaddis.

7.13 The `ArrayList` Class

CONCEPT: `ArrayList` is a class in the Java API that is similar to an array and allows you to store objects. Unlike an array, an `ArrayList` object's size is automatically adjusted to accommodate the number of items being stored in it.

The Java API provides a class named `ArrayList`, which can be used for storing and retrieving objects. Once you create an `ArrayList` object, you can think of it as a container for holding other objects. An `ArrayList` object is similar to an array of objects, but offers many advantages over an array. Here are a few:

- An `ArrayList` object automatically expands as items are added to it.
- In addition to adding items to an `ArrayList`, you can remove items as well.
- An `ArrayList` object automatically shrinks as items are removed from it.

The `ArrayList` class is in the `java.util` package, so the following `import` statement is required:

```
import java.util.ArrayList;
```

Creating and Using an `ArrayList` Object

Here is an example of how you create an `ArrayList` object:

```
ArrayList<String> nameList = new ArrayList<String>();
```

This statement creates a new `ArrayList` object and stores its address in the `nameList` variable. Notice that in this example the word `String` is written inside angled brackets, `<>`, immediately after the word `ArrayList`. This specifies that the `ArrayList` can hold `String` objects. If we try to store any other type of object in this `ArrayList`, an error occurs. (Later in this section you will see an example that creates an `ArrayList` for holding other types of objects.)

To add items to the `ArrayList` object, you use the `add` method. For example, the following statements add a series of `String` objects to `nameList`:

```
nameList.add("James");
nameList.add("Catherine");
nameList.add("Bill");
```

After these statements execute, nameList will hold three references to String objects. The first will reference "James", the second will reference "Catherine", and the third will reference "Bill".

The items stored in an ArrayList have a corresponding index. The index specifies the item's location in the ArrayList, so it is much like an array subscript. The first item that is added to an ArrayList is stored at index 0. The next item that is added to the ArrayList is stored at index 1, and so forth. After the previously shown statements execute, "James" will be stored at index 0, "Catherine" will be stored at index 1, and "Bill" will be stored at index 2.

The ArrayList class has a size method that reports the number of items stored in an ArrayList. It returns the number of items as an int. For example, the following statement uses the method to display the number of items stored in nameList:

```java
System.out.println("The ArrayList has " +
                   nameList.size() +
                   " objects stored in it.");
```

Assuming that nameList holds the Strings "James", "Catherine", and "Bill", the following statement will display:

```
The ArrayList has 3 objects stored in it.
```

The ArrayList class's get method returns the item stored at a specific index. You pass the index as an argument to the method. For example, the following statement will display the item stored at index 1 of nameList:

```java
System.out.println(nameList.get(1));
```

The program in Code Listing 7-29 demonstrates the topics discussed so far.

Code Listing 7-29   (ArrayListDemo1.java)

```java
 1  import java.util.ArrayList; // Needed for ArrayList class
 2
 3  /**
 4   *  This program demonstrates an ArrayList.
 5   */
 6
 7  public class ArrayListDemo1
 8  {
 9     public static void main(String[] args)
10     {
11        // Create an ArrayList to hold some names.
12        ArrayList<String> nameList = new ArrayList<String>();
13
14        // Add some names to the ArrayList.
15        nameList.add("James");
16        nameList.add("Catherine");
17        nameList.add("Bill");
18
```

```
19              // Display the size of the ArrayList.
20              System.out.println("The ArrayList has " +
21                              nameList.size() +
22                              " objects stored in it.");
23
24              // Now display the items in nameList.
25              for (int index = 0; index < nameList.size(); index++)
26                  System.out.println(nameList.get(index));
27          }
28      }
```

Program Output

```
The ArrayList has 3 objects stored in it.
James
Catherine
Bill
```

Notice in line 25 that the for loop uses the value returned from nameList's size method to control the number of times the loop iterates. This is to prevent a bounds checking error from occurring. The last item stored in an ArrayList will have an index that is 1 less than the size of the ArrayList. If you pass a value larger than this to the get method, an error will occur.

Using the Enhanced for Loop with an ArrayList

Earlier in this chapter you saw how the enhanced for loop can be used to iterate over each element in an array. You can also use the enhanced for loop to iterate over each item in an ArrayList. Code Listing 7-30 demonstrates. The enhanced for loop is used in lines 26 and 27 to display all the items stored in the ArrayList.

Code Listing 7-30   **(ArrayDemo2.java)**

```
1  import java.util.ArrayList; // Needed for ArrayList class
2
3  /**
4   * This program demonstrates how the enhanced for loop
5   * can be used with an ArrayList.
6   */
7
8  public class ArrayListDemo2
9  {
10     public static void main(String[] args)
11     {
12         // Create an ArrayList to hold some names.
13         ArrayList<String> nameList = new ArrayList<String>();
14
```

```
15        // Add some names to the ArrayList.
16        nameList.add("James");
17        nameList.add("Catherine");
18        nameList.add("Bill");
19
20        // Display the size of the ArrayList.
21        System.out.println("The ArrayList has " +
22                           nameList.size() +
23                           " objects stored in it.");
24
25        // Now display the items in nameList.
26        for (String name : nameList)
27           System.out.println(name);
28     }
29  }
```

Program Output

```
The ArrayList has 3 objects stored in it.
James
Catherine
Bill
```

The ArrayList Class's toString method

The ArrayList class has a toString method that returns a string representing all of the items stored in an ArrayList object. For example, suppose we have set up the nameList object as previously shown, with the Strings "James", "Catherine", and "Bill". We could use the following statement to display all of the names:

```
System.out.println(nameList);
```

The contents of the ArrayList will be displayed in the following manner:

```
[James, Catherine, Bill]
```

Removing an Item from an ArrayList

The ArrayList class has a remove method that removes an item at a specific index. You pass the index as an argument to the method. The program in Code Listing 7-31 demonstrates.

Code Listing 7-31   (ArrayListDemo3.java)

```
1  import java.util.ArrayList; // Needed for ArrayList class
2
3  /**
4   *  This program demonstrates an ArrayList.
5   */
6
7  public class ArrayListDemo3
```

```
8  {
9     public static void main(String[] args)
10    {
11       // Create an ArrayList to hold some names.
12       ArrayList<String> nameList = new ArrayList<String>();
13
14       // Add some names to the ArrayList.
15       nameList.add("James");
16       nameList.add("Catherine");
17       nameList.add("Bill");
18
19       // Display the items in nameList and their indices.
20       for (int index = 0; index < nameList.size(); index++)
21       {
22          System.out.println("Index: " + index + " Name: " +
23                              nameList.get(index));
24       }
25
26       // Now remove the item at index 1.
27       nameList.remove(1);
28
29       System.out.println("The item at index 1 is removed. " +
30                           "Here are the items now.");
31
32       // Display the items in nameList and their indices.
33       for (int index = 0; index < nameList.size(); index++)
34       {
35          System.out.println("Index: " + index + " Name: " +
36                              nameList.get(index));
37       }
38    }
39 }
```

Program Output

```
Index: 0 Name: James
Index: 1 Name: Catherine
Index: 2 Name: Bill
The item at index 1 is removed. Here are the items now.
Index: 0 Name: James
Index: 1 Name: Bill
```

When the item at index 1 was removed (in line 27), the item that was previously stored at index 2 was shifted in position to index 1. When an item is removed from an `ArrayList`, the items that come after it are shifted downward in position to fill the empty space. This means that the index of each item after the removed item will be decreased by one.

Note that an error will occur if you call the remove method with an invalid index.

Inserting an Item

The add method, as previously shown, adds an item at the last position in an ArrayList object. The ArrayList class has an overloaded version of the add method that allows you to add an item at a specific index. This causes the item to be inserted into the ArrayList object at a specific position. The program in Code Listing 7-32 demonstrates.

Code Listing 7-32   **(ArrayListDemo4.java)**

```java
 1  import java.util.ArrayList; // Needed for ArrayList class
 2
 3  /**
 4   *  This program demonstrates inserting an item.
 5   */
 6
 7  public class ArrayListDemo4
 8  {
 9     public static void main(String[] args)
10     {
11        // Create an ArrayList to hold some names.
12        ArrayList<String> nameList = new ArrayList<String>();
13
14        // Add some names to the ArrayList.
15        nameList.add("James");
16        nameList.add("Catherine");
17        nameList.add("Bill");
18
19        // Display the items in nameList and their indices.
20        for (int index = 0; index < nameList.size(); index++)
21        {
22           System.out.println("Index: " + index + " Name: " +
23                                 nameList.get(index));
24        }
25
26        // Now insert an  item at index 1.
27        nameList.add(1, "Mary");
28
29        System.out.println("Mary was added at index 1. " +
30                                 "Here are the items now.");
31
32        // Display the items in nameList and their indices.
33        for (int index = 0; index < nameList.size(); index++)
34        {
35           System.out.println("Index: " + index + " Name: " +
36                                 nameList.get(index));
37        }
38     }
39  }
```

Program Output

```
Index: 0 Name: James
Index: 1 Name: Catherine
Index: 2 Name: Bill
Mary was added at index 1. Here are the items now.
Index: 0 Name: James
Index: 1 Name: Mary
Index: 2 Name: Catherine
Index: 3 Name: Bill
```

When a new item was added at index 1 (in line 27), the item that was previously stored at index 1 was shifted in position to index 2. When an item is added at a specific index, the items that come after it are shifted upward in position to accommodate the new item. This means that the index of each item after the new item will be increased by one.

Note that an error will occur if you call the `add` method with an invalid index.

Replacing an Item

The `ArrayList` class's `set` method can be used to replace an item at a specific index with another item. For example, the following statement will replace the item currently at index 1 with the string "Becky":

```
nameList.set(1, "Becky");
```

> This is demonstrated in the program *ArrayListDemo5.java*, which is available for download from the book's online resource page at www.pearsonhighered.com/gaddis. Note that an error will occur if you specify an invalid index.

Capacity

Previously you learned that an `ArrayList` object's size is the number of items stored in the `ArrayList` object. When you add an item to the `ArrayList` object, its size increases by one, and when you remove an item from the `ArrayList` object, its size decreases by one.

An `ArrayList` object also has a *capacity*, which is the number of items it can store without having to increase its size. When an `ArrayList` object is first created, using the no-arg constructor, it has an initial capacity of 10 items. This means that it can hold up to 10 items without having to increase its size. When the eleventh item is added, the `ArrayList` object must increase its size to accommodate the new item. You can specify a different starting capacity, if you desire, by passing an `int` argument to the `ArrayList` constructor. For example, the following statement creates an `ArrayList` object with an initial capacity of 100 items:

```
ArrayList<String> list = new ArrayList<String>(100);
```

All the examples we have looked at so far use `ArrayList` objects to hold `Strings`. You can create an `ArrayList` to hold any type of object. For example, the following statement creates an `ArrayList` that can hold `InventoryItem` objects:

```
ArrayList<InventoryItem> list = new ArrayList<InventoryItem>();
```

By specifying `InventoryItem` inside the angled brackets, we are declaring that the `ArrayList` can hold only `InventoryItem` objects. Code Listing 7-33 demonstrates such an `ArrayList`.

Code Listing 7-33   (`ArrayListDemo6.java`)

```
 1   import java.util.ArrayList;    // Needed for the ArrayList class
 2
 3   /**
 4    * This program demonstrates how to use a cast operator
 5    * with the ArrayList class's get method.
 6    */
 7
 8   public class ArrayListDemo6
 9   {
10      public static void main(String[] args)
11      {
12         // Create an ArrayList to hold InventoryItem objects.
13         ArrayList<InventoryItem> list = new ArrayList<InventoryItem>();
14
15         // Add three InventoryItem objects to the ArrayList.
16         list.add(new InventoryItem("Nuts", 100));
17         list.add(new InventoryItem("Bolts", 150));
18         list.add(new InventoryItem("Washers", 75));
19
20         // Display each item.
21         for (int index = 0; index < list.size(); index++)
22         {
23            InventoryItem item = (InventoryItem)list.get(index);
24            System.out.println("Item at index " + index +
25                            "\nDescription: " + item.getDescription() +
26                            "\nUnits: " + item.getUnits());
27         }
28      }
29   }
```

Program Output

```
Item at index 0
Description: Nuts
Units: 100
Item at index 1
Description: Bolts
Units: 150
Item at index 2
Description: Washers
Units: 75
```

Using the Diamond Operator for Type Inference (Java 7)

Beginning with Java 7, you can simplify the instantiation of an `ArrayList` by using the *diamond operator* (<>). For example, in this chapter you have seen several programs that create an `ArrayList` object with a statement such as this:

```
ArrayList<String> list = new ArrayList<String>();
```

Notice that the data type (in this case, `String`) appears between the angled brackets in two locations: first in the part that declares the reference variable and then again in the part that calls the `ArrayList` constructor. Beginning in Java 7, you are no longer required to write the data type in the part of the statement that calls the `ArrayList` constructor. Instead, you can simply write a set of empty angled brackets, as shown here:

```
ArrayList<String> list = new ArrayList<>();
```

The set of empty angled brackets (<>), the diamond operator, causes the compiler to infer the required data type from the reference variable declaration. Here is another example:

```
ArrayList<InventoryItem> list = new ArrayList<>();
```

This creates an `ArrayList` that can hold `InventoryItem` objects. Keep in mind that type inference was introduced in Java 7. If you are using a previous version of the Java language, you will have to use the more lengthy form of the declaration statement to create an `ArrayList`.

 Checkpoint

7.23   What `import` statement must you include in your code to use the `ArrayList` class?

7.24   Write a statement that creates an `ArrayList` object and assigns its address to a variable named `frogs`.

7.25   Write a statement that creates an `ArrayList` object and assigns its address to a variable named `lizards`. The `ArrayList` should be able to store `String` objects only.

7.26   How do you add items to an `ArrayList` object?

7.27   How do you remove an item from an `ArrayList` object?

7.28   How do you retrieve a specific item from an `ArrayList` object?

7.29   How do you insert an item at a specific location in an `ArrayList` object?

7.30   How do you determine an `ArrayList` object's size?

7.31   What is the difference between an `ArrayList` object's size and its capacity?

 ## 7.14 Common Errors to Avoid

The following list describes several errors that are commonly made when learning this chapter's topics.

- **Using an invalid subscript.** Java does not allow you to use a subscript value that is outside the range of valid subscripts for an array.

- **Confusing the contents of an integer array element with the element's subscript.** An element's subscript and the value stored in the element are not the same thing. The subscript identifies an element, which holds a value.
- **Causing an off-by-one error.** When processing arrays, the subscripts start at 0 and end at 1 less than the number of elements in the array. Off-by-one errors are commonly caused when a loop uses an initial subscript of 1 and/or uses a maximum subscript that is equal to the number of elements in the array.
- **Using the = operator to copy an array.** Assigning one array reference variable to another with the = operator merely copies the address in one variable to the other. To copy an array, you should copy the individual elements of one array to another.
- **Using the == operator to compare two arrays.** You cannot use the == operator to compare two array reference variables and determine whether the arrays are equal. When you use the == operator with reference variables, the operator compares the memory addresses that the variables contain, not the contents of the objects referenced by the variables.
- **Reversing the row and column subscripts when processing a two-dimensional array.** When thinking of a two-dimensional array as having rows and columns, the first subscript accesses a row and the second subscript accesses a column. If you reverse these subscripts, you will access the wrong element.

Review Questions and Exercises

Multiple Choice and True/False

1. This indicates in an array declaration the number of elements that an array is to have.
   a. subscript
   b. size declarator
   c. element sum
   d. reference variable

2. Each element of an array is accessed by a number known as a(n)
   a. subscript
   b. size declarator
   c. address
   d. specifier

3. The first subscript in an array is always
   a. 1
   b. 0
   c. −1
   d. 1 less than the number of elements

4. The last subscript in an array is always
   a. 100
   b. 0
   c. −1
   d. 1 less than the number of elements

5. Array bounds checking happens
   a. when the program is compiled
   b. when the program is saved
   c. when the program runs
   d. when the program is loaded into memory

6. This array field holds the number of elements that the array has.
   a. `size`
   b. `elements`
   c. `length`
   d. `width`

7. This search algorithm steps through an array, comparing each item with the search value.
   a. binary search
   b. sequential search
   c. selection search
   d. iterative search

8. This search algorithm repeatedly divides the portion of an array being searched in half.
   a. binary search
   b. sequential search
   c. selection search
   d. iterative search

9. This is the *maximum* number of comparisons performed by the sequential search on an array of N elements (assuming the search values are consistently found).
   a. $2N$
   b. N
   c. N^2
   d. $N/2$

10. When initializing a two-dimensional array, you enclose each row's initialization list in these.
    a. braces
    b. parentheses
    c. brackets
    d. quotation marks

11. To store an item in an `ArrayList` object, use this method.
    a. `store`
    b. `insert`
    c. `add`
    d. `get`

12. To insert an item at a specific location in an `ArrayList` object, use this method.
    a. `store`
    b. `insert`
    c. `add`
    d. `get`

13. To delete an item from an `ArrayList` object, use this method.
    a. `remove`
    b. `delete`
    c. `erase`
    d. `get`

14. To determine the number of items stored in an `ArrayList` object, use this method.
    a. `size`
    b. `capacity`
    c. `items`
    d. `length`

15. **True or False:** Java does not allow a statement to use a subscript that is outside the range of valid subscripts for an array.

16. **True or False:** An array's size declarator can be a negative integer expression.

17. **True or False:** Both of the following declarations are legal and equivalent:

    ```
    int[] numbers;
    int numbers[];
    ```

18. **True or False:** The subscript of the last element in a single-dimensional array is one less than the total number of elements in the array.

19. **True or False:** The values in an initialization list are stored in the array in the order they appear in the list.

20. **True or False:** The Java compiler does not display an error message when it processes a statement that uses an invalid subscript.

21. **True or False:** When an array is passed to a method, the method has access to the original array.

22. **True or False:** The first size declarator in the declaration of a two-dimensional array represents the number of columns. The second size declarator represents the number of rows.

23. **True or False:** A two-dimensional array has multiple `length` fields.

24. **True or False:** An `ArrayList` automatically expands in size to accommodate the items stored in it.

Find the Error

1. `int[] collection = new int[-20];`

2. `int[] hours = 8, 12, 16;`

3.
   ```
   int[] table = new int[10];
   Scanner keyboard = new Scanner(System.in);
   for (int x = 1; x <= 10; x++)
   {
       System.out.print("Enter the next value: ");
       table[x] = keyboard.nextInt();
   }
   ```

4.
   ```
   String[] names = { "George", "Susan" };
   int totalLength = 0;
   for (int i = 0; i < names.length(); i++)
       totalLength += names[i].length;
   ```

5.
   ```
   String[] words = { "Hello", "Goodbye" };
   System.out.println(words.toUpperCase());
   ```

Algorithm Workbench

1. The variable `names` references an integer array with 20 elements. Write a `for` loop that prints each element of the array.

2. The variables `numberArray1` and `numberArray2` reference arrays that each have 100 elements. Write code that copies the values in `numberArray1` to `numberArray2`.

3. a. Write a statement that declares a `String` array initialized with the following strings: "Einstein", "Newton", "Copernicus", and "Kepler".
   b. Write a loop that displays the contents of each element in the array you declared in Part a.
   c. Write code that displays the total length of all the strings in the array you declared in Part a.

4. In a program you need to store the populations of 12 countries.

   a. Define two arrays that may be used in parallel to store the names of the countries and their populations.
   b. Write a loop that uses these arrays to print each country's name and its population.

5. In a program you need to store the identification numbers of 10 employees (as integers) and their weekly gross pay (as `double` values).

   a. Define two arrays that may be used in parallel to store the 10 employee identification numbers and gross pay amounts.
   b. Write a loop that uses these arrays to print each of the employees' identification number and weekly gross pay.

6. Declare and create a two-dimensional `int` array named `grades`. It should have 30 rows and 10 columns.

7. Write code that calculates the average of all the elements in the `grades` array that you declared in Question 6.

8. Look at the following array declaration.

   ```
   int[][] numberArray = new int[9][11];
   ```

   a. Write a statement that assigns 145 to the first column of the first row of this array.
   b. Write a statement that assigns 18 to the last column of the last row of this array.

9. The `values` variable references a two-dimensional `double` array with 10 rows and 20 columns. Write code that sums all the elements in the array and stores the sum in the variable `total`.

10. An application uses a two-dimensional array declared as follows.

    ```
    int[][] days = new int[29][5];
    ```

    a. Write code that sums each row in the array and displays the results.
    b. Write code that sums each column in the array and displays the results.

11. Write code that creates an `ArrayList` object that can hold `String` objects. Add the names of three cars to the `ArrayList`, then display the contents of the `ArrayList`.

Short Answer

1. What is the difference between an array size declarator and a subscript?

2. Look at the following array definition.

    ```
    int[] values = new int[10];
    ```

    a. How many elements does the array have?
    b. What is the subscript of the first element in the array?
    c. What is the subscript of the last element in the array?

3. In the following array definition

    ```
    int[] values = { 4, 7, 6, 8, 2 };
    ```

    what does each of the following code segments display?

    ```
    System.out.println(values[4]);        a. _____
    ```

    ```
    x = values[2] + values[3];
    System.out.println(x);                b. _____
    ```

    ```
    x = ++values[1];
    System.out.println(x);                c. _____
    ```

4. How do you define an array without providing a size declarator?

5. Assuming that `array1` and `array2` are both array reference variables, why is it not possible to assign the contents of the array referenced by `array2` to the array referenced by `array1` with the following statement?

    ```
    array1 = array2;
    ```

6. The following statement creates an `InventoryItem` array:

    ```
    InventoryItem[] items = new InventoryItem[10];
    ```

    Is it okay or not okay to execute the following statements?

    ```
    items[0].setDescription("Hammer");
    ```

    ```
    items[0].setUnits(10);
    ```

7. If a sequential search method is searching for a value that is stored in the last element of a 10,000-element array, how many elements will the search code have to examine to locate the value?

8. Look at the following array definition.

    ```
    double[][] sales = new double[8][10];
    ```

    a. How many rows does the array have?
    b. How many columns does the array have?
    c. How many elements does the array have?
    d. Write a statement that stores a number in the last column of the last row in the array.

Programming Challenges

1. Rainfall Class

Write a `RainFall` class that stores the total rainfall for each of 12 months into an array of `doubles`. The program should have methods that return the following:

- total rainfall for the year
- the average monthly rainfall

- the month with the most rain
- the month with the least rain

Demonstrate the class in a complete program.

Input Validation: Do not accept negative numbers for monthly rainfall figures.

2. Payroll Class

Write a `Payroll` class that uses the following arrays as fields:

- **`employeeId`.** An array of seven integers to hold employee identification numbers. The array should be initialized with the following numbers:

      5658845 4520125 7895122 8777541
      8451277 1302850 7580489

- **`hours`.** An array of seven integers to hold the number of hours worked by each employee
- **`payRate`.** An array of seven `doubles` to hold each employee's hourly pay rate
- **`wages`.** An array of seven `doubles` to hold each employee's gross wages

The class should relate the data in each array through the subscripts. For example, the number in element 0 of the `hours` array should be the number of hours worked by the employee whose identification number is stored in element 0 of the `employeeId` array. That same employee's pay rate should be stored in element 0 of the `payRate` array.

In addition to the appropriate accessor and mutator methods, the class should have a method that accepts an employee's identification number as an argument and returns the gross pay for that employee.

Demonstrate the class in a complete program that displays each employee number and asks the user to enter that employee's hours and pay rate. It should then display each employee's identification number and gross wages.

Input Validation: Do not accept negative values for hours or numbers less than 6.00 for pay rate.

3. Charge Account Validation

Create a class with a method that accepts a charge account number as its argument. The method should determine whether the number is valid by comparing it to the following list of valid charge account numbers.

    5658845   4520125   7895122   8777541   8451277   1302850
    8080152   4562555   5552012   5050552   7825877   1250255
    1005231   6545231   3852085   7576651   7881200   4581002

These numbers should be stored in an array. Use either a sequential search or a binary search to locate the number passed as an argument. If the number is in the array, the method should return `true`, indicating the number is valid. If the number is not in the array, the method should return `false`, indicating the number is invalid.

Write a program that tests the class by asking the user to enter a charge account number. The program should display a message indicating whether the number is valid or invalid.

4. Larger Than *n*

In a program, write a method that accepts two arguments: an array and a number *n*. Assume that the array contains integers. The method should display all of the numbers in the array that are greater than the number *n*.

5. Charge Account Modification

Modify the charge account validation class that you wrote for Programming Challenge 3 so it reads the list of valid charge account numbers from a file. Use Notepad or another text editor to create the file.

6. Driver's License Exam

The local driver's license office has asked you to write a program that grades the written portion of the driver's license exam. The exam has 20 multiple choice questions. Here are the correct answers:

1. B	6. A	11. B	16. C
2. D	7. B	12. C	17. C
3. A	8. A	13. D	18. B
4. A	9. C	14. A	19. D
5. C	10. D	15. D	20. A

A student must correctly answer 15 of the 20 questions to pass the exam.

Write a class named `DriverExam` that holds the correct answers to the exam in an array field. The class should also have an array field that holds the student's answers. The class should have the following methods:

- `passed`. Returns `true` if the student passed the exam, or `false` if the student failed
- `totalCorrect`. Returns the total number of correctly answered questions
- `totalIncorrect`. Returns the total number of incorrectly answered questions
- `questionsMissed`: An int array containing the question numbers of the questions that the student missed

Demonstrate the class in a complete program that asks the user to enter a student's answers, and then displays the results returned from the `DriverExam` class's methods.

Input Validation: Only accept the letters A, B, C, or D as answers.

7. Quarterly Sales Statistics

Write a program that lets the user enter four quarterly sales figures for six divisions of a company. The figures should be stored in a two-dimensional array. Once the figures are entered, the program should display the following data for each quarter:

- A list of the sales figures by division
- Each division's increase or decrease from the previous quarter (this will not be displayed for the first quarter)
- The total sales for the quarter
- The company's increase or decrease from the previous quarter (this will not be displayed for the first quarter)
- The average sales for all divisions that quarter
- The division with the highest sales for that quarter

Input Validation: Do not accept negative numbers for sales figures.

8. Grade Book

A teacher has five students who have taken four tests. The teacher uses the following grading scale to assign a letter grade to a student, based on the average of his or her four test scores.

Test Score	Letter Grade
90–100	A
80–89	B
70–79	C
60–69	D
0–59	F

Write a class that uses a `String` array (or an `ArrayList` object) to hold the five students' names, an array of five characters to hold the five students' letter grades, and five arrays of four `double`s each to hold each student's set of test scores. The class should have methods that return a specific student's name, average test score, and a letter grade based on the average.

Demonstrate the class in a program that allows the user to enter each student's name and his or her four test scores. It should then display each student's average test score and letter grade.

Input validation: Do not accept test scores less than zero or greater than 100.

9. Grade Book Modification

Modify the grade book application in Programming Challenge 7 so it drops each student's lowest score when determining the test score averages and letter grades.

10. Lottery Application

Write a `Lottery` class that simulates a lottery. The class should have an array of five integers named `lotteryNumbers`. The constructor should generate a random number in the range of 0 through 9 for each element in the array. Refer to Chapter 4's discussion of the `Random` class for generating random numbers. The class should also have a method that accepts an array of five integers that represent a person's lottery picks. The method is to compare the corresponding elements in the two arrays and return the number of digits that match. For example, the following shows the `lotteryNumbers` array and the user's array with sample numbers stored in each. There are two matching digits (elements 2 and 4).

`lotteryNumbers` array:

User's array:

4	2	9	7	3

In addition, the class should have a method that returns a copy of the `lotteryNumbers` array.

Demonstrate the class in a program that asks the user to enter five numbers. The program should display the number of digits that match the randomly generated lottery numbers. If all of the digits match, display a message proclaiming the user a grand prize winner.

11. `ArrayOperations` Class

Write a class name `ArrayOperations` with the following static methods:

- `getTotal`. This method should accept a one-dimensional array as its argument and return the total of the values in the array. Write overloaded versions of this method that work with `int`, `float`, `double`, and `long` arrays.
- `getAverage`. This method should accept a one-dimensional array as its argument and return the average of the values in the array. Write overloaded versions of this method that work with `int`, `float`, `double`, and `long` arrays.
- `getHighest`. This method should accept a one-dimensional array as its argument and return the highest value in the array. Write overloaded versions of this method that work with `int`, `float`, `double`, and `long` arrays.
- `getLowest`. This method should accept a one-dimensional array as its argument and return the lowest value in the array. Write overloaded versions of this method that work with `int`, `float`, `double`, and `long` arrays.

Demonstrate the class in a complete program with test data stored in arrays of various data types.

12. Number Analysis Class

Write a class with a constructor that accepts a file name as its argument. Assume the file contains a series of numbers, each written on a separate line. The class should read the contents of the file into an array, and then display the following data:

- The lowest number in the array
- The highest number in the array
- The total of the numbers in the array
- The average of the numbers in the array

The student source code folder `Chapter 07` contains a text file named `Numbers.txt`. This file contains 12 random numbers. Write a program that tests the class by using this file.

13. Name Search

If you have downloaded this book's source code (the companion Web site is available at www.pearsonhighered.com/gaddis) you will find the following files in the Chapter 7 folder:

- GirlNames.txt—This file contains a list of the 200 most popular names given to girls born in the U.S. from the year 2000 to 2009.
- BoyNames.txt—This file contains a list of the 200 most popular names given to girls born in the U.S. from the year 2000 to 2009.

Write a program that reads the contents of the two files into two separate arrays, or `ArrayLists`. The user should be able to enter a boy's name, a girl's name, or both, and the application will display messages indicating whether the names were among the most popular.

14. Population Data

If you have downloaded this book's source code (the companion Web site is available at www.pearsonhighered.com/gaddis), you will find a file named USPopulation.txt in the Chapter 7 folder. The file contains the midyear population of the U.S., in thousands, during the years 1950 to 1990. The first line in the file contains the population for 1950, the second line contains the population for 1951, and so forth.

Write a program that reads the file's contents into an array, or an `ArrayList`. The program should display the following data:

- The average annual change in population during the time period
- The year with the greatest increase in population during the time period
- The year with the smallest increase in population during the time period

15. World Series Champions

If you have downloaded this book's source code (the companion Web site is available at www.pearsonhighered.com/gaddis), you will find a file named WorldSeriesWinners.txt. This file contains a chronological list of the World Series winning teams from 1903 to 2009. (The first line in the file is the name of the team that won in 1903, and the last line is the name of the team that won in 2009. Note that the World Series was not played in 1904 or 1994, so the file contains no entries for those years)

Write a program that lets the user enter the name of a team, and then displays the number of times that team has won the World Series in the time period from 1903 to 2009.

> **TIP:** Read the contents of the WorldSeriesWinners.txt file into an array, or an `ArrayList`. When the user enters the name of a team, the program should step through the array or `ArrayList` counting the number of times the selected team appears.

16. `2DArrayOperations` Class

Write a class named `2DArrayOperations` with the following static methods:

- `getTotal`. This method should accept a two-dimensional array as its argument and return the total of all the values in the array. Write overloaded versions of this method that work with `int`, `float`, `double`, and `long` arrays.
- `getAverage`. This method should accept a two-dimensional array as its argument and return the average of all the values in the array. Write overloaded versions of this method that work with `int`, `float`, `double`, and `long` arrays.
- `getRowTotal`. This method should accept a two-dimensional array as its first argument and an integer as its second argument. The second argument should be the subscript of a row in the array. The method should return the total of the values in the specified row. Write overloaded versions of this method that work with `int`, `float`, `double`, and `long` arrays.
- `getColumnTotal`. This method should accept a two-dimensional array as its first argument and an integer as its second argument. The second argument should be the subscript of a column in the array. The method should return the total of the values in the specified column. Write overloaded versions of this method that work with `int`, `float`, `double`, and `long` arrays.

- getHighestInRow. This method should accept a two-dimensional array as its first argument and an integer as its second argument. The second argument should be the subscript of a row in the array. The method should return the highest value in the specified row of the array. Write overloaded versions of this method that work with int, float, double, and long arrays.
- getLowestInRow. This method should accept a two-dimensional array as its first argument and an integer as its second argument. The second argument should be the subscript of a row in the array. The method should return the lowest value in the specified row of the array. Write overloaded versions of this method that work with int, float, double, and long arrays.

Demonstrate the class in a complete program with test data stored in two-dimensional arrays of various data types.

17. Search Benchmarks

Modify the sequentialSearch and binarySearch methods presented in this chapter so they keep a count of and display on the screen the number of comparisons they make before finding the value they are searching for. Then write a program that has an array of at least 20 integers. It should call the sequentialSearch method to locate at least five of the values. Then it should call the binarySearch method to locate the same values. On average, which method makes the fewest comparisons?

18. Phone Book ArrayList

Write a class named PhoneBookEntry that has fields for a person's name and phone number. The class should have a constructor and appropriate accessor and mutator methods. Then write a program that creates at least five PhoneBookEntry objects and stores them in an ArrayList. Use a loop to display the contents of each object in the ArrayList.

19. Trivia Game

In this programming challenge you will create a simple trivia game for two players. The program will work like this:

- Starting with player 1, each player gets a turn at answering 5 trivia questions. (There are a total of 10 questions, 5 for each player.) When a question is displayed, four possible answers are also displayed. Only one of the answers is correct, and if the player selects the correct answer, he or she earns a point.
- After answers have been selected for all the questions, the program displays the number of points earned by each player and declares the player with the highest number of points the winner.

You are to design a Question class to hold the data for a trivia question. The Question class should have fields for the following data:

- A trivia question
- Possible answer #1
- Possible answer #2
- Possible answer #3
- Possible answer #4
- The number of the correct answer (1, 2, 3, or 4)

The `Question` class should have appropriate constructor(s), accessor, and mutator methods.

The program should create an array of 10 `Question` objects, one for each trivia question. (If you prefer, you can use an `ArrayList` instead of an array.) Make up your own trivia questions on the subject or subjects of your choice for the objects.

20. Lo Shu Magic Square

The Lo Shu Magic Square is a grid with 3 rows and 3 columns shown in Figure 7-32. The Lo Shu Magic Square has the following properties:

- The grid contains the numbers 1 through 9 exactly.
- The sum of each row, each column, and each diagonal all add up to the same number. This is shown in Figure 7-33.

In a program you can simulate a magic square using a two-dimensional array. Write a method that accepts a two-dimensional array as an argument and determines whether the array is a Lo Shu Magic Square. Test the method in a program.

Figure 7-32 Lo Shu Magic Square

Figure 7-33 Row, column, and diagonal sums in the Lo Shu Magic Square

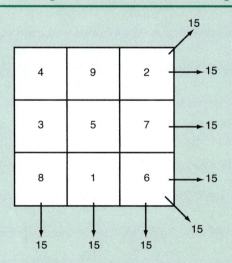

8 Text Processing and Wrapper Classes

TOPICS

8.1 Introduction to Wrapper Classes

8.2 Character Testing and Conversion with the Character Class

8.3 More about String Objects

8.4 The StringBuilder Class

8.5 Tokenizing Strings

8.6 Wrapper Classes for the Numeric Data Types

8.7 Focus on Problem Solving: The TestScoreReader Class

8.8 Common Errors to Avoid

8.1 Introduction to Wrapper Classes

CONCEPT: Java provides wrapper classes for the primitive data types. The wrapper class for a given primitive type contains not only a value of that type, but also methods that perform operations related to the type.

Recall from Chapter 2 that the primitive data types are called "primitive" because they are not created from classes. Instead of instantiating objects, you create variables from the primitive data types, and variables do not have attributes or methods. They are designed simply to hold a single value in memory.

Java also provides wrapper classes for all of the primitive data types. A *wrapper class* is a class that is "wrapped around" a primitive data type and allows you to create objects instead of variables. In addition, these wrapper classes provide methods that perform useful operations on primitive values.

Although these wrapper classes can be used to create objects instead of variables, few programmers use them that way. One reason is because the wrapper classes are immutable, which means that once you create an object, you cannot change the object's value. Another reason is because they are not as easy to use as variables for simple operations. For example, to get the value stored in an object you must call a method, whereas variables can be used directly in assignment statements, passed as arguments to the print and println methods, and so forth.

Although it is not normally useful to create objects from the wrapper classes, they do provide static methods that are very useful. We examine several of Java's wrapper classes in this chapter. We begin by looking at the `Character` class, which is the wrapper class for the char data type.

8.2   Character Testing and Conversion with the `Character` Class

CONCEPT: The `Character` class is a wrapper class for the `char` data type. It provides numerous methods for testing and converting character data.

The `Character` class is part of the `java.lang` package, so no `import` statement is necessary to use this class. The class provides several static methods for testing the value of a char variable. Some of these methods are listed in Table 8-1. Each of the methods accepts a single char argument and returns a `boolean` value.

Table 8-1   Some static `Character` class methods for testing char values

Method	Description
boolean isDigit(char *ch*)	Returns true if the argument passed into *ch* is a digit from 0 through 9. Otherwise returns false.
boolean isLetter(char *ch*)	Returns true if the argument passed into *ch* is an alphabetic letter. Otherwise returns false.
boolean isLetterOrDigit(char *ch*)	Returns true if the character passed into *ch* contains a digit (0 through 9) or an alphabetic letter. Otherwise returns false.
boolean isLowerCase(char *ch*)	Returns true if the argument passed into *ch* is a lowercase letter. Otherwise returns false.
boolean isUpperCase(char *ch*)	Returns true if the argument passed into *ch* is an uppercase letter. Otherwise returns false.
boolean isSpaceChar(char *ch*)	Returns true if the argument passed into *ch* is a space character. Otherwise returns false.
boolean isWhiteSpace(char *ch*)	Returns true if the argument passed into *ch* is a whitespace character (a space, tab, or newline character). Otherwise returns false.

The program in Code Listing 8-1 demonstrates many of these methods.

Code Listing 8-1 **(CharacterTest.java)**

```
1   import java.util.Scanner;
2
3   /**
4    * This program demonstrates some of the Character class's
5    * character testing methods.
6    */
7
8   public class CharacterTest
9   {
10     public static void main(String[] args)
11     {
12        String inputLine;    // A line of input
13        char inputChar;      // A character
14
15        // Create a Scanner object for keyboard input.
16        Scanner keyboard = new Scanner(System.in);
17
18        // Get a character from the user.
19        System.out.print("Enter a character: ");
20        inputLine = keyboard.nextLine();
21        inputChar = inputLine.charAt(0);
22
23        // Test the character.
24        if (Character.isLetter(inputChar))
25           System.out.println("Letter");
26
27        if (Character.isDigit(inputChar))
28           System.out.println("Digit");
29
30        if (Character.isLowerCase(inputChar))
31           System.out.println("Lowercase letter");
32
33        if (Character.isUpperCase(inputChar))
34           System.out.println("Uppercase letter");
35
36        if (Character.isSpaceChar(inputChar))
37           System.out.println("Space");
38
39        if (Character.isWhitespace(inputChar))
40           System.out.println("Whitespace");
41     }
42  }
```

Program Output with Example Input Shown in Bold

```
Enter a character: a [Enter]
Letter
Lowercase letter
```

Program Output with Example Input Shown in Bold

```
Enter a character: A [Enter]
Letter
Uppercase letter
```

Program Output with Example Input Shown in Bold

```
Enter a character: 4 [Enter]
Digit
```

Program Output with Example Input Shown in Bold

```
Enter a character: [Space] [Enter]
Space
Whitespace character
```

Program Output with Example Input Shown in Bold

```
Enter any character: [Tab] [Enter]
Whitespace character
```

Code Listing 8-2 shows a more practical application of the character testing methods. It tests a string to determine whether it is a seven-character customer number in the proper format.

Code Listing 8-2   (`CustomerNumber.java`)

```
 1  import java.util.Scanner;
 2
 3  /**
 4   * This program tests a customer number to determine
 5   * whether it is in the proper format.
 6   */
 7
 8  public class CustomerNumber
 9  {
10     public static void main(String[] args)
11     {
12        String customer;  // To hold a customer number
13
```

```
14          // Create a Scanner object for keyboard input.
15          Scanner keyboard = new Scanner(System.in);
16
17          System.out.println("Enter a customer number in "
18                             + "the form LLLNNNN");
19          System.out.print("(LLL = letters and NNNN "
20                             + "= numbers): ");
21
22          // Get a customer number from the user.
23          customer = keyboard.nextLine();
24
25          // Determine whether it is valid.
26          if (isValid(customer))
27          {
28             System.out.println("That's a valid customer "
29                                + "number.");
30          }
31          else
32          {
33             System.out.println("That is not the proper "
34                                + "format.");
35             System.out.println("Here is an example: "
36                                + "ABC1234");
37          }
38       }
39
40       /**
41        * The isValid method accepts a String as its argument
42        * and tests its contents for a valid customer number.
43        */
44
45       private static boolean isValid(String custNumber)
46       {
47          boolean goodSoFar = true;   // Flag
48          int index = 0;              // Loop control variable
49
50          // Is the string the correct length?
51          if (custNumber.length() != 7)
52             goodSoFar = false;
53
54          // Test the first three characters for letters.
55          while (goodSoFar && index < 3)
56          {
57             if (!Character.isLetter(custNumber.charAt(index)))
58                goodSoFar = false;
59             index++;
60          }
61
```

```
62          // Test the last four characters for digits.
63          while (goodSoFar && index < 7)
64          {
65              if (!Character.isDigit(custNumber.charAt(index)))
66                  goodSoFar = false;
67              index++;
68          }
69
70          // Return the results
71          return goodSoFar;
72      }
73  }
```

Program Output with Example Input Shown in Bold

```
Enter a customer number in the form LLLNNNN
(LLL = letters and NNNN = numbers): RQS4567 [Enter]
That's a valid customer number.
```

Program Output with Example Input Shown in Bold

```
Enter a customer number in the form LLLNNNN
(LLL = letters and NNNN = numbers): AX467T9 [Enter]
That is not the proper format.
Here is an example: ABC1234
```

In this program, the customer number is expected to be seven characters in length and consist of three alphabetic letters followed by four numeric digits. The isValid method, in lines 45 through 72, accepts a String argument that will be tested. In lines 47 and 48 two local variables are declared: goodSoFar, a boolean that is initialized as true; and index, an int, that is initialized as 0. The goodSoFar variable is a flag that will be set to false immediately when the method determines the customer number is not in a valid format. The index variable is a loop control variable.

In line 51 the isValid method tests the length of the custNumber argument. If the argument is not seven characters long, it is not valid, and the goodSoFar variable is set to false in line 52. Next the method uses the while loop in lines 55 through 60 to validate the first three characters. Recall from Chapter 2 that the String class's charAt method returns a character at a specific position in a string (position numbering starts at 0). Inside the loop, the if statement in line 57 uses the Character.isLetter method to test the characters at positions 0, 1, and 2 in the custNumber string. If any of these characters are not letters, the goodSoFar variable is set to false (in line 58) and the loop terminates.

Next the method uses the while loop in lines 63 through 68 to validate the last four characters. Inside the loop, the if statement in line 65 uses the Character.isDigit method to test the characters at positions 3, 4, 5, and 6 in the custNumber string. If any of these characters are not digits, the goodSoFar variable is set to false (in line 66) and the loop terminates.

Last, in line 71, the method returns the value of the goodSoFar variable.

Character Case Conversion

The Character class also provides the static methods listed in Table 8-2 for converting the case of a character. Each method accepts a char argument and returns a char value.

Table 8-2   Some Character class methods for case conversion

Method	Description
char toLowerCase(char ch)	Returns the lowercase equivalent of the argument passed to ch.
char toUpperCase(char ch)	Returns the uppercase equivalent of the argument passed to ch.

If the toLowerCase method's argument is an uppercase character, the method returns the lowercase equivalent. For example, the following statement will display the character a on the screen:

```
System.out.println(Character.toLowerCase('A'));
```

If the argument is already lowercase, the toLowerCase method returns it unchanged. The following statement also causes the lowercase character a to be displayed:

```
System.out.println(Character.toLowerCase('a'));
```

If the toUpperCase method's argument is a lowercase character, the method returns the uppercase equivalent. For example, the following statement will display the character A on the screen:

```
System.out.println(Character.toUpperCase('a'));
```

If the argument is already uppercase, the toUpperCase method returns it unchanged.

Any nonletter argument passed to toLowerCase or toUpperCase is returned as it is. Each of the following statements displays the method argument without any change:

```
System.out.println(Character.toLowerCase('*'));
System.out.println(Character.toLowerCase('$'));
System.out.println(Character.toUpperCase('&'));
System.out.println(Character.toUpperCase('%'));
```

The program in Code Listing 8-3 demonstrates the toUpperCase method in a loop that asks the user to enter Y or N.

Code Listing 8-3   (CircleArea.java)

```
 1  import java.util.Scanner;
 2
 3  /**
 4   *  This program demonstrates the Character
 5   *  class's toUpperCase method.
 6   */
 7
```

```
 8  public class CircleArea
 9  {
10     public static void main(String[] args)
11     {
12         double radius; // The circle's radius
13         double area;   // The circle's area
14         String input;  // To hold a line of input
15         char choice;   // To hold a single character
16
17         // Create a Scanner object to read keyboard input.
18         Scanner keyboard = new Scanner(System.in);
19
20         do
21         {
22             // Get the circle's radius.
23             System.out.print("Enter the circle's radius: ");
24             radius = keyboard.nextDouble();
25
26             // Consume the remaining newline character.
27             keyboard.nextLine();
28
29             // Calculate and display the area.
30             area = Math.PI * radius * radius;
31             System.out.printf("The area is %.2f.\n", area);
32
33             // Repeat this?
34             System.out.print("Do you want to do this " +
35                              "again? (Y or N) ");
36             input = keyboard.nextLine();
37             choice = input.charAt(0);
38
39         } while (Character.toUpperCase(choice) == 'Y');
40     }
41  }
```

Program Output with Example Input Shown in Bold

```
Enter the circle's radius: 10 [Enter]
The area is 314.16.
Do you want to do this again? (Y or N) y [Enter]
Enter the circle's radius: 15 [Enter]
The area is 706.86.
Do you want to do this again? (Y or N) n [Enter]
```

Checkpoint

8.1   Write a statement that converts the contents of the char variable big to lowercase. The converted value should be assigned to the variable little.

8.2   Write an if statement that displays the word "digit" if the char variable ch contains a numeric digit. Otherwise, it should display "Not a digit."

8.3   What is the output of the following statement?

```
System.out.println(Character.toUpperCase(Character.toLowerCase('A')));
```

8.4   Write a loop that asks the user "Do you want to repeat the program or quit? (R/Q)". The loop should repeat until the user has entered an R or Q (either upper case or lowercase).

8.5   What will the following code display?

```
char var = '$';
System.out.println(Character.toUpperCase(var));
```

8.6   Write a loop that counts the number of uppercase characters that appear in the String object str.

8.3   More about String Objects

CONCEPT: The String class provides several methods for searching and working with String objects.

Searching for Substrings

The String class provides several methods that search for a string inside of a string. The term *substring* commonly is used to refer to a string that is part of another string. Table 8-3 summarizes some of these methods. Each of the methods in Table 8-3 returns a boolean value indicating whether the string was found.

Let's take a closer look at each of these methods.

The startsWith and endsWith Methods

The startsWith method determines whether the calling object's string begins with a specified substring. For example, the following code determines whether the string "Four score and seven years ago" begins with "Four". The method returns true if the string does begin with the specified substring, or false otherwise.

```
String str = "Four score and seven years ago";
if (str.startsWith("Four"))
    System.out.println("The string starts with Four.");
else
    System.out.println("The string does not start with Four.");
```

In the code, the method call `str.startsWith("Four")` returns true because the string does begin with "Four". The `startsWith` method performs a case-sensitive comparison, so the method call `str.startsWith("four")` would return `false`.

The `endsWith` method determines whether the calling string ends with a specified substring. For example, the following code determines whether the string "Four score and seven years ago" ends with "ago". The method returns `true` if the string does end with the specified substring or `false` otherwise.

```
String str = "Four score and seven years ago";
if (str.endsWith("ago"))
    System.out.println("The string ends with ago.");
else
    System.out.println("The string does not end with ago.");
```

Table 8-3 `String` methods that search for a substring

Method	Description
`boolean startsWith(String str)`	This method returns true if the calling string begins with the string passed into *str*. Otherwise it returns false.
`boolean endsWith(String str)`	This method returns true if the calling string ends with the string passed into *str*. Otherwise it returns false.
`boolean regionMatches(int start, String str, int start2, int n)`	This method returns true if a specified region of the calling string matches a specified region of the string passed into *str*. The *start* parameter indicates the starting position of the region within the calling string. The *start2* parameter indicates the starting position of the region within *str*. The *n* parameter indicates the number of characters in both regions.
`boolean regionMatches(boolean ignoreCase, int start, String str, int start2, int n)`	This overloaded version of the *regionMatches* method has an additional parameter, *ignoreCase*. If true is passed into this parameter, the method ignores the case of the calling string and *str* when comparing the regions. If *false* is passed into the *ignoreCase* parameter, the comparison is case sensitive.

In the code, the method call `str.endsWith("ago")` returns true because the string does end with "ago". The `endsWith` method also performs a case-sensitive comparison, so the method call `str.endsWith("Ago")` would return `false`.

The program in Code Listing 8-4 demonstrates a search algorithm that uses the startsWith method. The program searches an array of strings for an element that starts with a specified string.

Code Listing 8-4   (PersonSearch.java)

```
1   import java.util.Scanner;
2
3   /**
4    * This program uses the startsWith method to search using
5    * a partial string.
6    */
7
8   public class PersonSearch
9   {
10     public static void main(String[] args)
11     {
12        String lookUp;  // To hold a lookup string
13
14        // Create an array of names.
15        String[] people = { "Cutshaw, Will", "Davis, George",
16                            "Davis, Jenny", "Russert, Phil",
17                            "Russell, Cindy", "Setzer, Charles",
18                            "Smart, Kathryn", "Smith, Chris",
19                            "Smith, Brad", "Williams, Jean" };
20
21        // Create a Scanner object for keyboard input.
22        Scanner keyboard = new Scanner(System.in);
23
24        // Get a partial name to search for.
25        System.out.print("Enter the first few characters of " +
26                        "the last name to look up: ");
27        lookUp = keyboard.nextLine();
28
29        // Display all of the names that begin with the
30        // string entered by the user.
31        System.out.println("Here are the names that match:");
32        for (String person : people)
33        {
34           if (person.startsWith(lookUp))
35              System.out.println(person);
36        }
37     }
38  }
```

Program Output with Example Input Shown in Bold

```
Enter the first few characters of the last name to look up: Davis [Enter]
Here are the names that match:
Davis, George
Davis, Jenny
```

Program Output with Example Input Shown in Bold

```
Enter the first few characters of the last name to look up: Russ [Enter]
Here are the names that match:
Russert, Phil
Russell, Cindy
```

The `regionMatches` Methods

The `String` class provides overloaded versions of the `regionMatches` method, which determines whether specified regions of two strings match. The following code demonstrates.

```
String str = "Four score and seven years ago";
String str2 = "Those seven years passed quickly";
if (str.regionMatches(15, str2, 6, 11))
    System.out.println("The regions match.");
else
    System.out.println("The regions do not match.");
```

This code will display "The regions match." The specified region of the `str` string begins at position 15, and the specified region of the `str2` string begins at position 6. Both regions consist of 11 characters. The specified region in the `str` string is "seven years" and the specified region in the `str2` string is also "seven years". Because the two regions match, the `regionMatches` method in this code returns `true`. This version of the `regionMatches` method performs a case-sensitive comparison. An overloaded version accepts an additional argument indicating whether to perform a case-insensitive comparison. The following code demonstrates.

```
String str = "Four score and seven years ago";
String str2 = "THOSE SEVEN YEARS PASSED QUICKLY";

if (str.regionMatches(true, 15, str2, 6, 11))
    System.out.println("The regions match.");
else
    System.out.println("The regions do not match.");
```

This code will also display "The regions match." The first argument passed to this version of the `regionMatches` method can be `true` or `false`, indicating whether a case-insensitive comparison should be performed. In this example, `true` is passed, so case will be ignored when the regions "seven years" and "SEVEN YEARS" are compared.

Each of these methods indicates by a `boolean` return value whether a substring appears within a string. The `String` class also provides methods that not only search for items within a string, but report the location of those items. Table 8-4 describes overloaded versions of the `indexOf` and `lastIndexOf` methods.

Table 8-4   String methods for getting a character or substring's location

Method	Description
`int indexOf(char ch)`	Searches the calling String object for the character passed into `ch`. If the character is found, the position of its first occurrence is returned. Otherwise, −1 is returned.
`int indexOf(char ch, int start)`	Searches the calling String object for the character passed into `ch`, beginning at the position passed into `start` and going to the end of the string. If the character is found, the position of its first occurrence is returned. Otherwise, −1 is returned.
`int indexOf(String str)`	Searches the calling String object for the string passed into `str`. If the string is found, the beginning position of its first occurrence is returned. Otherwise, −1 is returned.
`int indexOf(String str, int start)`	Searches the calling String object for the string passed into `str`. The search begins at the position passed into `start` and goes to the end of the string. If the string is found, the beginning position of its first occurrence is returned. Otherwise, −1 is returned.
`int lastIndexOf(char ch)`	Searches the calling String object for the character passed into `ch`. If the character is found, the position of its last occurrence is returned. Otherwise, −1 is returned.
`int lastIndexOf(char ch, int start)`	Searches the calling String object for the character passed into `ch`, beginning at the position passed into `start`. The search is conducted backward through the string, to position 0. If the character is found, the position of its last occurrence is returned. Otherwise, −1 is returned.
`int lastIndexOf(String str)`	Searches the calling String object for the string passed into `str`. If the string is found, the beginning position of its last occurrence is returned. Otherwise, −1 is returned.
`int lastIndexOf(String str, int start)`	Searches the calling String object for the string passed into `str`, beginning at the position passed into `start`. The search is conducted backward through the string, to position 0. If the string is found, the beginning position of its last occurrence is returned. Otherwise, −1 is returned.

Finding Characters with the `indexOf` and `lastIndexOf` Methods

The `indexOf` and `lastIndexOf` methods can search for either a character or a substring within the calling string. If the item being searched for is found, its position is returned. Otherwise −1 is returned. Here is an example of code using two of the methods to search for a character:

```java
String str = "Four score and seven years ago";
int first, last;

first = str.indexOf('r');
last = str.lastIndexOf('r');

System.out.println("The letter r first appears at " +
                   "position " + first);

System.out.println("The letter r last appears at " +
                   "position " + last);
```

This code produces the following output:

```
The letter r first appears at position 3
The letter r last appears at position 24
```

The following code shows another example. It uses a loop to show the positions of each letter "r" in the string.

```java
String str = "Four score and seven years ago";
int position;

System.out.println("The letter r appears at the " +
                   "following locations:");
position = str.indexOf('r');
while (position != -1)
{
    System.out.println(position);
    position = str.indexOf('r', position + 1);
}
```

This code will produce the following output:

```
The letter r appears at the following locations:
3
8
24
```

The following code is very similar, but it uses the `lastIndexOf` method and shows the positions in reverse order.

```java
String str = "Four score and seven years ago";
int position;

System.out.println("The letter r appears at the " +
                   "following locations.");
```

```
position = str.lastIndexOf('r');
while (position != -1)
{
    System.out.println(position);
    position = str.lastIndexOf('r', position - 1);
}
```

This code will produce the following output:

```
The letter r appears at the following locations.
24
8
3
```

Finding Substrings with the `indexOf` and `lastIndexOf` Methods

The `indexOf` and `lastIndexOf` methods can also search for substrings within a string. The following code shows an example. It displays the starting positions of each occurrence of the word "and" within a string.

```
String str = "and a one and a two and a three";
int position;

System.out.println("The word and appears at the " +
                   "following locations.");
position = str.indexOf("and");
while (position != -1)
{
    System.out.println(position);
    position = str.indexOf("and", position + 1);
}
```

This code produces the following output:

```
The word and appears at the following locations.
0
10
20
```

The following code also displays the same results, but in reverse order.

```
String str = "and a one and a two and a three";
int position;

System.out.println("The word and appears at the " +
                   "following locations.");
position = str.lastIndexOf("and");
while (position != -1)
{
    System.out.println(position);
    position = str.lastIndexOf("and", position - 1);
}
```

This code produces the following output:

```
The word and appears at the following locations.
20
10
0
```

Extracting Substrings

The `String` class provides several methods that allow you to retrieve a substring from a string. The methods we will examine are listed in Table 8-5.

Table 8-5 `String` methods for extracting substrings

Method	Description
`String substring(int start)`	This method returns a copy of the substring that begins at *start* and goes to the end of the calling object's string.
`String substring(int start, int end)`	This method returns a copy of a substring. The argument passed into *start* is the substring's starting position, and the argument passed into *end* is the substring's ending position. The character at the *start* position is included in the substring, but the character at the *end* position is not included.
`void getChars(int start, int end, char[] array, int arrayStart)`	This method extracts a substring from the calling object and stores it in a `char` array. The argument passed into start is the substring's starting position, and the argument passed into end is the substring's ending position. The character at the start position is included in the substring, but the character at the end position is not included. (The last character in the substring ends at end − 1.) The characters in the substring are stored as elements in the array that is passed into the `array` parameter. The `arrayStart` parameter specifies the starting subscript within the array where the characters are to be stored.
`char[] toCharArray()`	This method returns all of the characters in the calling object as a `char` array.

The `substring` Methods

The `substring` method returns a copy of a substring from the calling object. There are two overloaded versions of this method. The first version accepts an `int` argument that is the starting position of the substring. The method returns a string consisting of all the characters from the starting position to the end of the string. The character at the starting position is part of the substring. Here is an example of the method's use.

```
String fullName = "Cynthia Susan Smith";
String lastName = fullName.substring(14);
System.out.println("The full name is " + fullName);
System.out.println("The last name is " + lastName);
```

This code will produce the following output:

```
The full name is Cynthia Susan Smith
The last name is Smith
```

Keep in mind that the substring method returns a new String object that holds a copy of the substring. When this code executes, the fullName and lastName variables will reference two different String objects as shown in Figure 8-1.

Figure 8-1   The fullName and lastName variables reference separate objects

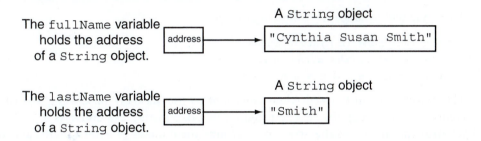

The second version of the method accepts two int arguments. The first specifies the substring's starting position and the second specifies the substring's ending position. The character at the starting position is included in the substring, but the character at the ending position is not. Here is an example of how the method is used:

```
String fullName = "Cynthia Susan Smith";
String middleName = fullName.substring(8, 13);
System.out.println("The full name is " + fullName);
System.out.println("The middle name is " + middleName);
```

The code will produce the following output:

```
The full name is Cynthia Susan Smith
The middle name is Susan
```

The getChars and toCharArray Methods

The getChars and toCharArray methods both convert the calling String object to a char array. The getChars method can be used to convert a substring, whereas the toCharArray method converts the entire string. Here is an example of how the getChars method might be used:

```
String fullName = "Cynthia Susan Smith";
char[] nameArray = new char[5];
fullName.getChars(8, 13, nameArray, 0);
System.out.println("The full name is " + fullName);
System.out.println("The values in the array are:");
for (int i = 0; i < nameArray.length; i++)
    System.out.print(nameArray[i] + " ");
```

This code stores the individual characters of the substring "Susan" in the elements of the nameArray array, beginning at element 0. The code will produce the following output:

```
The full name is Cynthia Susan Smith
The values in the array are:
S u s a n
```

The `toCharArray` method returns a reference to a `char` array that contains all of the characters in the calling object. Here is an example:

```
String fullName = "Cynthia Susan Smith";
char[] nameArray;
nameArray = fullName.toCharArray();
System.out.println("The full name is " + fullName);
System.out.println("The values in the array are:");
for (int i = 0; i < nameArray.length; i++)
      System.out.print(nameArray[i] + " ");
```

This code will produce the following output:

```
The full name is Cynthia Susan Smith
The values in the array are:
C y n t h i a   S u s a n   S m i t h
```

These methods can be used when you want to use an array processing algorithm on the contents of a `String` object. The program in Code Listing 8-5 converts a `String` object to an array and then uses the array to determine the number of letters, digits, and whitespace characters in the string.

Code Listing 8-5   (`StringAnalyzer.java`)

```
 1  import java.util.Scanner;
 2
 3  /**
 4   * This program displays the number of letters, digits, and
 5   * whitespace characters in a string.
 6   */
 7
 8  public class StringAnalyzer
 9  {
10     public static void main(String[] args)
11     {
12        String str;          // To hold the input as a string
13        char[] array;        // To hold the input as an array
14        int letters = 0,     // Total number of alphabetic letters
15            digits = 0,      // Total number of digits
16            whitespaces = 0; // Total number of whitespace characters
17
18        // Create a Scanner object for keyboard input.
19        Scanner keyboard = new Scanner(System.in);
20
21        // Get a string from the user.
22        System.out.print("Enter a string: ");
23        str = keyboard.nextLine();
24
25        // Convert the string to a char array.
26        array = str.toCharArray();
27
```

```
28          // Analyze the characters.
29          for (int i = 0; i < array.length; i++)
30          {
31             if (Character.isLetter(array[i]))
32                letters++;
33             else if (Character.isDigit(array[i]))
34                digits++;
35             else if (Character.isWhitespace(array[i]))
36                whitespaces++;
37          }
38
39          // Display the results.
40          System.out.println("That string contains " +
41                             letters + " letters, " +
42                             digits + " digits, and " +
43                             whitespaces +
44                             " whitespace characters.");
45       }
46    }
```

Program Output with Example Input Shown in Bold

Enter a string: **99 red balloons [Enter]**
That string contains 11 letters, 2 digits, and 2 whitespace characters.

Methods That Return a Modified String

The String class methods listed in Table 8-6 return a modified copy of a String object.

Table 8-6 Methods that return a modified copy of a String object

Method	Description
String concat(String *str*)	This method returns a copy of the calling String object with the contents of *str* concatenated to it.
String replace(char *oldChar*, char *newChar*)	This method returns a copy of the calling String object, in which all occurrences of the character passed into *oldChar* have been replaced by the character passed into *newChar*.
String trim()	This method returns a copy of the calling String object, in which all leading and trailing whitespace characters have been deleted.

The concat method performs the same operation as the + operator when used with strings. For example, look at the following code, which uses the + operator:

```
String fullName,
       firstName = "Timothy ",
       lastName = "Haynes";
fullName = firstName + lastName;
```

Equivalent code can also be written with the `concat` method. Here is an example:

```
String fullName,
       firstName = "Timothy ",
       lastName = "Haynes";
fullName = firstName.concat(lastName);
```

The `replace` method returns a copy of a `String` object, where every occurrence of a specified character has been replaced with another character. For example, look at the following code.

```
String str1 = "Tom Talbert Tried Trains";
String str2;
str2 = str1.replace('T', 'D');
System.out.println(str1);
System.out.println(str2);
```

In this code, the `replace` method will return a copy of the `str1` object with every occurrence of the letter "T" replaced with the letter "D". The code will produce the following output:

```
Tom Talbert Tried Trains
Dom Dalbert Dried Drains
```

Remember that the `replace` method does not modify the contents of the calling `String` object, but returns a modified copy of it. After the previous code executes, the `str1` and `str2` variables will reference different `String` objects.

The `trim` method returns a copy of a `String` object with all leading and trailing whitespace characters deleted. A *leading* whitespace character is one that appears at the beginning, or left side, of a string. For example, the following string has three leading whitespace characters:

```
"   Hello"
```

A *trailing* whitespace character is one that appears at the end, or right side, of a string, after the nonspace characters. For example, the following string has three trailing whitespace characters:

```
"Hello   "
```

Here is an example:

```
String greeting1 = "   Hello   ";
String greeting2;
greeting2 = greeting1.trim();
System.out.println("*" + greeting1 + "*");
System.out.println("*" + greeting2 + "*");
```

In this code, the first statement assigns the string "   Hello   " (with three leading spaces and three trailing spaces) to the `greeting1` variable. The `trim` method is called, which returns a copy of the string with the leading and trailing spaces removed. The code will produce the following output:

```
*   Hello   *
*Hello*
```

One common use of the `trim` method is to remove any leading or trailing spaces that the user might have entered while inputting data.

The Static `valueOf` Methods

The `String` class has several overloaded versions of a method named `valueOf`. This method accepts a value of any primitive data type as its argument and returns a string representation of the value. Table 8-7 describes these methods.

Table 8-7   Some of the `String` class's `valueOf` methods

Method	Description
`String valueOf(boolean b)`	If the `boolean` argument passed to *b* is `true`, the method returns the string "true". If the argument is `false`, the method returns the string "false".
`String valueOf(char c)`	This method returns a string containing the character passed into *c*.
`String valueOf(char[] array)`	This method returns a string that contains all of the elements in the char array passed into *array*.
`String valueOf(char[] array, int subscript, int count)`	This method returns a string that contains part of the elements in the char array passed into *array*. The argument passed into *subscript* is the starting subscript and the argument passed into *count* is the number of elements.
`String valueOf(double number)`	This method returns the string representation of the double argument passed into *number*.
`String valueOf(float number)`	This method returns the string representation of the float argument passed into *number*.
`String valueOf(int number)`	This method returns the string representation of the `int` argument passed into *number*.
`String valueOf(long number)`	This method returns the string representation of the `long` argument passed into *number*.

The following code demonstrates several of these methods.

```
boolean b = true;
char[] letters = { 'a', 'b', 'c', 'd', 'e' };
double d = 2.4981567;
int i = 7;

System.out.println(String.valueOf(b));
System.out.println(String.valueOf(letters));
System.out.println(String.valueOf(letters, 1, 3));
System.out.println(String.valueOf(d));
System.out.println(String.valueOf(i));
```

This code will produce the following output:

```
true
abcde
bcd
2.4981567
7
```

Checkpoint

8.7 Write a method that accepts a `String` object as an argument and returns `true` if the argument ends with the substring "ger". Otherwise, the method should return `false`.

8.8 Modify the method you wrote for Checkpoint 8.7 so it performs a case-insensitive test. The method should return `true` if the argument ends with "ger" in any possible combination of upper and lowercase letters.

8.9 Look at the following declaration:

```
String cafeName = "Broadway Cafe";
String str;
```

Which of the following methods would you use to make `str` reference the string `"Broadway"`?

```
startsWith
regionMatches
substring
indexOf
```

8.10 What is the difference between the `indexOf` and `lastIndexOf` methods?

8.11 What is the difference between the `getChars` and `substring` methods?

8.12 The + operator, when used with strings, performs the same operation as what `String` method?

8.13 What is the difference between the `getChars` and `toCharArray` methods?

8.14 Look at the following code.

```
String str1 = "To be, or not to be";
String str2 = str1.replace('o', 'u');
System.out.println(str1);
System.out.println(str2);
```

You hear a fellow student claim that the code will display the following:

```
Tu be ur nut tu be
Tu be ur nut tu be
```

Is your fellow student right or wrong? Why?

8.15 What will the following code display?

```
String str1 = "William ",
       str2 = " the ",
       str3 = " Conqueror";
System.out.println(str1.trim() + str2.trim() +
                   str3.trim());
```

8.16 Assume that a program has the following declarations:

```
double number = 9.47;
String str;
```

Write a statement that assigns a string representation of the number variable to `str`.

8.4 The StringBuilder Class

> **CONCEPT:** The StringBuilder class is similar to the String class, except that you can change the contents of StringBuilder objects. The StringBuilder class also provides several useful methods that the String class does not have.

The StringBuilder class is similar to the String class. The main difference between the two is that you can change the contents of a StringBuilder object, but you cannot change the contents of a String object. Recall from Chapter 6 that String objects are immutable. This means that once you set the contents of a String object, you cannot change the string value that it holds. For example, look at the following code.

```
String name;
name = "George";
name = "Sally";
```

The first statement creates the name variable. The second creates a String object containing the string "George" and assigns its address to the name variable. Although we cannot change the contents of the String object, we can make the name variable reference a different String object. That's what the third statement does: It creates another String object containing the string "Sally", and assigns its address to name. This is illustrated by Figure 8-2.

Figure 8-2   The String object containing "George" is no longer referenced

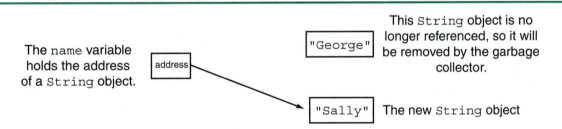

Unlike String objects, StringBuilder objects have methods that allow you to modify their contents without creating a new object in memory. You can change specific characters, insert characters, delete characters, and perform other operations. The StringBuilder object will grow or shrink in size, as needed, to accommodate the changes.

The fact that String objects are immutable is rarely a problem, but you might consider using StringBuilder objects if your program needs to make a lot of changes to one or more strings. This will improve the program's efficiency by reducing the number of String objects that must be created and then removed by the garbage collector. Now let's look at the StringBuilder class's constructors and methods.

The `StringBuilder` Constructors

Table 8-8 lists three of the `StringBuilder` constructors.

Table 8-8 StringBuilder Constructors

Constructor	Description
StringBuilder()	This constructor accepts no arguments. It gives the object enough storage space to hold 16 characters, but no characters are stored in it.
StringBuilder(int *length*)	This constructor gives the object enough storage space to hold *length* characters, but no characters are stored in it.
StringBuilder(String *str*)	This constructor initializes the object with the string in *str*. The object's initial storage space will be the length of the string plus 16.

The first two constructors create empty `StringBuilder` objects of a specified size. The first constructor makes the `StringBuilder` object large enough to hold 16 characters, and the second constructor makes the object large enough to hold `length` characters. Remember, `StringBuilder` objects automatically resize themselves, so it is not a problem if you later want to store a larger string in the object. The third constructor accepts a `String` object as its argument and assigns the object's contents to the `StringBuilder` object. Here is an example of its use:

```
StringBuilder city = new StringBuilder("Charleston");
System.out.println(city);
```

This code creates a `StringBuilder` object and assigns its address to the `city` variable. The object is initialized with the string "Charleston". As demonstrated by this code, you can pass a `StringBuilder` object to the `println` and `print` methods.

One limitation of the `StringBuilder` class is that you cannot use the assignment operator to assign strings to `StringBuilder` objects. For example, the following code will not work:

```
StringBuilder city = "Charleston";   // ERROR!!! Will not work!
```

Instead of using the assignment operator you must use the `new` key word and a constructor, or one of the `StringBuilder` methods, to store a string in a `StringBuilder` object.

Other `StringBuilder` Methods

The `StringBuilder` class provides many of the same methods as the `String` class. Table 8-9 lists several of the `StringBuilder` methods that work exactly like their `String` class counterparts.

Table 8-9 Methods that are common to the `String` and `StringBuilder` classes

```
char charAt(int position)
void getChars(int start, int end, char[] array, int arrayStart)
int indexOf(String str)
int indexOf(String str, int start)
int lastIndexOf(String str)
int lastIndexOf(String str, int start)
int length()
String substring(int start)
String substring(int start, int end)
```

In addition, the `StringBuilder` class provides several methods that the `String` class does not have. Let's look at a few of them.

The `append` Methods

The `StringBuilder` class has several overloaded versions of a method named append. These methods accept an argument that may be of any primitive data type, a char array, or a `String` object. They append a string representation of their argument to the calling object's current contents. Because there are so many overloaded versions of append, we will examine the general form of a typical call to the method:

```
object.append(item);
```

After the method is called, a string representation of item will be appended to object's contents. The following code shows some of the append methods being used.

```
StringBuilder str = new StringBuilder();

// Append values to the object.
str.append("We sold ");          // Append a String object.
str.append(12);                  // Append an int.
str.append(" doughnuts for $");  // Append another String.
str.append(15.95);               // Append a double.

// Display the object's contents.
System.out.println(str);
```

This code will produce the following output:

```
We sold 12 doughnuts for $15.95
```

For more variations of the append method, see the Java API documentation.

The `insert` Methods

The `StringBuilder` class also has several overloaded versions of a method named insert, which inserts a value into the calling object's string. These methods accept two arguments:

an int that specifies the position in the calling object's string where the insertion should begin, and the value to be inserted. The value to be inserted can be of any primitive data type, a char array, or a String object. Because there are so many overloaded versions of insert, we will examine the general form of a typical call to the method.

```
object.insert(start, item);
```

In the general form, *start* is the starting position of the insertion and *item* is the item to be inserted. The following code shows an example:

```
StringBuilder str = new StringBuilder("New City");
str.insert(4, "York ");
System.out.println(str);
```

The first statement creates a StringBuilder object initialized with the string "New City". The second statement inserts the string "York " into the StringBuilder object, beginning at position 4. The characters that are currently in the object beginning at position 4 are moved to the right. In memory, the StringBuilder object is automatically expanded in size to accommodate the inserted characters. If these statements were in a complete program and we ran it, we would see New York City displayed on the screen.

The following code shows how a char array can be inserted into a StringBuilder object:

```
char cArray[] = { '2', '0', ' ' };
StringBuilder str = new StringBuilder("In July we sold cars.");
str.insert(16, cArray);
System.out.println(str);
```

The first statement declares a char array named cArray containing the characters '2', '0', and ' '. The second statement creates a StringBuilder object initialized with the string "In July we sold cars." The third statement inserts the characters in cArray into the StringBuilder object, beginning at position 16. The characters that are currently in the object beginning at position 16 are moved to the right. If these statements were in a complete program and we ran it, we would see In July we sold 20 cars. displayed on the screen.

The replace Method

The StringBuilder class has a replace method that differs slightly from the String class's replace method. Whereas the String class's replace method replaces the occurrences of one character with another character, the StringBuilder class's replace method replaces a specified substring with a string. Here is the general form of a call to this method:

```
object.replace(start, end, str);
```

In the general form, *start* is an int that specifies the starting position of a substring in the calling object, and *end* is an int that specifies the ending position of the substring. (The starting position is included in the substring, but the ending position is not.) The str parameter is a String object. After the method executes, the substring will be replaced with str. Here is an example:

```
StringBuilder str =
    new StringBuilder("We moved from Chicago to Atlanta.");
str.replace(14, 21, "New York");
System.out.println(str);
```

The replace method in this code replaces the word "Chicago" with "New York". The code will produce the following output:

```
We moved from New York to Atlanta.
```

The delete, deleteCharAt, and setCharAt Methods

The delete and deleteCharAt methods are used to delete a substring or a character from a StringBuilder object. The setCharAt method changes a specified character to another value. Table 8-10 describes these methods.

Table 8-10   The StringBuilder class's delete and deleteCharAt methods

Method	Description
StringBuilder delete(int *start*, int *end*)	The *start* parameter is an int that specifies the starting position of a substring in the calling object, and the *end* parameter is an int that specifies the ending position of the substring. (The starting position is included in the substring, but the ending position is not.) The method will delete the substring.
StringBuilder deleteCharAt(int *position*)	The *position* parameter specifies the location of a character that will be deleted.
void setCharAt(int *position*, char *ch*)	This method changes the character at *position* to the value passed into *ch*.

The following code demonstrates both of these methods.

```java
StringBuilder str =
        new StringBuilder("I ate 100 blueberries!");

// Display the StringBuilder object.
System.out.println(str);

// Delete the '0'.
str.deleteCharAt(8);

// Delete "blue".
str.delete(9, 13);

// Display the StringBuilder object.
System.out.println(str);

// Change the '1' to '5'
str.setCharAt(6, '5');

// Display the StringBuilder object.
System.out.println(str);
```

This code will produce the following output.

```
I ate 100 blueberries!
I ate 10 berries!
I ate 50 berries!
```

Although the `StringBuilder` methods presented in this section generally are the most useful, there are others that we haven't covered. Refer to the Java API documentation for more details.

The `toString` Method

If you need to convert a `StringBuilder` object to a regular string, you can call the object's `toString` method. The following code shows an example of a `StringBuilder` object's contents being assigned to a `String` variable:

```
StringBuilder strb = new StringBuilder("This is a test.");
String str = strb.toString();
```

In the Spotlight:
Formatting and Unformatting Telephone Numbers

Telephone numbers in the United States are commonly formatted to appear in the following manner:

```
(XXX)XXX-XXXX
```

In the format, `x` represents a digit. The three digits that appear inside the parentheses are the area code. The three digits following the area code are the prefix, and the four digits after the hyphen are the line number. Here is an example:

```
(919)555-1212
```

Although the parentheses and the hyphen make the number easier for people to read, those characters are unnecessary for processing by a computer. In a computer system, a telephone number is commonly stored as an unformatted series of digits, as shown here:

```
9195551212
```

A program that works with telephone numbers usually needs to unformat numbers that have been entered by the user. This means that the parentheses and the hyphen must be removed prior to storing the number in a file or processing it in some other way. In addition, such programs need the ability to format a number so it contains the parentheses and the hyphen before displaying it on the screen or printing it on paper.

Code Listing 8-6 shows a class named `Telephone` that contains the following static methods:

- `isFormatted`—This method accepts a `String` argument and returns `true` if the argument is formatted as `(XXX)XXX-XXXX`. If the argument is not formatted this way, the method returns `false`.
- `unformat`—This method accepts a `String` argument. If the argument is formatted as `(XXX)XXX-XXXX`, the method returns an unformatted version of the argument with the parentheses and the hyphen removed. Otherwise, the method returns the original argument.

- format—This method's purpose is to format sequence of digits as (XXX)XXX-XXXX. The sequence of digits is passed as a String argument. If the argument is 10 characters in length, then the method returns the argument with parentheses and a hyphen inserted. Otherwise, the method returns the original argument.

The program in Code Listing 8-7 demonstrates the Telephone class.

Code Listing 8-6   **(Telephone.java)**

```java
 1   /**
 2    * The Telephone class provides static methods
 3    * for formatting and unformatting US telephone
 4    * numbers.
 5    */
 6
 7   public class Telephone
 8   {
 9      // These constant fields hold the valid lengths of
10      // strings that are formatted and unformatted.
11      public final static int FORMATTED_LENGTH = 13;
12      public final static int UNFORMATTED_LENGTH = 10;
13
14      /**
15       * The isFormatted method accepts a string argument
16       * and determines whether it is properly formatted as
17       * a US telephone number in the following manner:
18       * (XXX)XXX-XXXX
19       * If the argument is properly formatted, the method
20       * returns true, otherwise false.
21       */
22
23      public static boolean isFormatted(String str)
24      {
25         boolean valid;  // Flag to indicate valid format
26
27         // Determine whether str is properly formatted.
28         if (str.length() == FORMATTED_LENGTH &&
29             str.charAt(0) == '(' &&
30             str.charAt(4) == ')' &&
31             str.charAt(8) == '-')
32             valid = true;
33         else
34             valid = false;
35
36         // Return the value of the valid flag.
37         return valid;
38      }
39
40      /**
41       * The unformat method accepts a string containing
42       * a telephone number formatted as:
43       * (XXX)XXX-XXXX.
44       * If the argument is formatted in this way, the
```

```
45          * method returns an unformatted string where the
46          * parentheses and hyphen have been removed. Otherwise,
47          * it returns the original argument.
48          */
49
50         public static String unformat(String str)
51         {
52             // Create a StringBuilder initialized with str.
53             StringBuilder strb = new StringBuilder(str);
54
55             // If the argument is properly formatted, then
56             // unformat it.
57             if (isFormatted(str))
58             {
59                 // First, delete the left paren at position 0.
60                 strb.deleteCharAt(0);
61
62                 // Next, delete the right paren. Because of the
63                 // previous deletion it is now located at
64                 // position 3.
65                 strb.deleteCharAt(3);
66
67                 // Next, delete the hyphen. Because of the
68                 // previous deletions it is now located at
69                 // position 6.
70                 strb.deleteCharAt(6);
71             }
72
73             // Return the unformatted string.
74             return strb.toString();
75         }
76
77         /**
78          * The format method formats a string as:
79          * (XXX)XXX-XXXX.
80          * If the length of the argument is UNFORMATTED_LENGTH
81          * the method returns the formatted string. Otherwise,
82          * it returns the original argument.
83          */
84
85         public static String format(String str)
86         {
87             // Create a StringBuilder initialized with str.
88             StringBuilder strb = new StringBuilder(str);
89
90             // If the argument is the correct length, then
91             // format it.
92             if (str.length() == UNFORMATTED_LENGTH)
93             {
94                 // First, insert the left paren at position 0.
95                 strb.insert(0, "(");
96
97                 // Next, insert the right paren at position 4.
98                 strb.insert(4, ")");
```

```
 99
100             // Next, insert the hyphen at position 8.
101             strb.insert(8, "-");
102         }
103
104         // Return the formatted string.
105         return strb.toString();
106     }
107 }
```

Code Listing 8-7   (TelephoneTester.java)

```
 1  import java.util.Scanner;
 2
 3  /**
 4   * This program demonstrates the Telephone
 5   * class's static methods.
 6   */
 7
 8  public class TelephoneTester
 9  {
10      public static void main(String[] args)
11      {
12          String phoneNumber;   // To hold a phone number
13
14          // Create a Scanner object for keyboard input.
15          Scanner keyboard = new Scanner(System.in);
16
17          // Get an unformatted telephone number.
18          System.out.print("Enter an unformatted telephone number: ");
19          phoneNumber = keyboard.nextLine();
20
21          // Format the telephone number.
22          System.out.println("Formatted: " +
23                  Telephone.format(phoneNumber));
24
25          // Get a formatted telephone number.
26          System.out.println("Enter a telephone number formatted as");
27          System.out.print("(XXX)XXX-XXXX : ");
28          phoneNumber = keyboard.nextLine();
29
30          // Unformat the telephone number.
31          System.out.println("Unformatted: " +
32                  Telephone.unformat(phoneNumber));
33      }
34  }
```

Program Output with Example Input Shown in Bold

```
Enter an unformatted telephone number: 9195551212 [Enter]
Formatted: (919)555-1212
Enter a telephone number formatted as
(XXX)XXX-XXXX: (828)555-1212 [Enter]
Unformatted: 8285551212
```

> **NOTE:** The Java API provides a class named `StringBuffer` that is essentially the same as the `StringBuilder` class, with the same constructors and the same methods. The difference is that the methods in the `StringBuffer` class are *synchronized*. This means that the `StringBuffer` class is safe to use in a multithreaded application. Multithreaded programming is beyond the scope of this book, but in a nutshell, a *multithreaded application* is one that concurrently runs multiple threads of execution. In such an application, more than one thread can access the same objects in memory at the same time. In multithreaded applications, the methods must be synchronized, to prevent the possibility of data corruption.
>
> Because synchronization requires extra steps to be performed, the `StringBuffer` class is slower than the `StringBuilder` class. In an application where the object will not be accessed by multiple threads, you should use the `StringBuilder` class to get the best performance. In an application where multiple threads will be accessing the object, you should use the `StringBuffer` class to ensure that its data does not become corrupted.

Checkpoint

8.17 The `String` class is immutable. What does this mean?

8.18 In a program that makes lots of changes to strings, would it be more efficient to use `String` objects or `StringBuilder` objects? Why?

8.19 Look at the following statement:

```
String city = "Asheville";
```

Rewrite this statement so that `city` is a `StringBuilder` object instead of a `String` object.

8.20 You wish to add a string to the end of the existing contents of a `StringBuilder` object. What method do you use?

8.21 You wish to insert a string into the existing contents of a `StringBuilder` object. What method do you use?

8.22 You wish to delete a specific character from the existing contents of a `StringBuilder` object. What method do you use?

8.23 You wish to change a specific character in a `StringBuilder` object. What method do you use?

8.24 How does the `StringBuilder` class's `replace` method differ from the `String` class's `replace` method?

8.5 Tokenizing Strings

CONCEPT: Tokenizing a string is a process of breaking a string down into its components, which are called tokens. The **StringTokenizer** class and the **String** class's **split** method can be used to tokenize strings.

Sometimes a string will contain a series of words or other items of data separated by spaces or other characters. For example, look at the following string.

```
"peach raspberry strawberry vanilla"
```

This string contains the following four items of data: `peach`, `raspberry`, `strawberry`, and `vanilla`. In programming terms, items such as these are known as *tokens*. Notice that a space appears between the items. The character that separates tokens is known as a *delimiter*. Here is another example:

```
"17;92;81;12;46;5"
```

This string contains the following tokens: `17`, `92`, `81`, `12`, `46`, and `5`. Notice that a semicolon appears between each item. The semicolon is used as a delimiter. Some programming problems require you to read a string that contains a list of items and then extract all of the tokens from the string for processing. For example, look at the following string that contains a date:

```
"11-22-2011"
```

The tokens in this string are `11`, `22`, and `2011`, and the delimiter is the hyphen character. Perhaps a program needs to extract the month, day, and year from such a string. Another example is an operating system pathname, such as the following:

```
/home/rsullivan/data
```

The tokens in this string are `home`, `rsullivan`, and `data`, and the delimiter is the / character. Perhaps a program needs to extract all of the directory names from such a pathname.

The process of breaking a string into tokens is known as *tokenizing*. In this section we will discuss two of Java's tools for tokenizing strings: the `StringTokenizer` class and the `String` class's `split` method.

The `StringTokenizer` Class

The Java API provides a class, `StringTokenizer`, that allows you to tokenize a string. The class is part of the `java.util` package, so you need the following `import` statement in any program that uses it:

```
import java.util.StringTokenizer;
```

When you create an instance of the `StringTokenizer` class, you pass a string as an argument to one of the constructors. The tokens will be extracted from this string. Table 8-11 summarizes the class's three constructors.

Table 8-11 The StringTokenizer constructors

Constructor	Description
StringTokenizer(String *str*)	The string to be tokenized is passed into str. Whitespace characters (space, tab, and newline) are used as delimiters.
StringTokenizer(String *str*, String *delimiters*)	The string to be tokenized is passed into str. The characters in delimiters will be used as delimiters.
StringTokenizer(String *str*, String *delimiters*, Boolean *returnDelimeters*)	The string to be tokenized is passed into str. The characters in delimiters will be used as delimiters. If the returnDelimiters parameter is set to true, the delimiters will be included as tokens. If this parameter is set to false, the delimiters will not be included as tokens.

The first constructor uses whitespace characters as delimiters. The following statement instantiates a StringTokenizer object and uses this constructor.

```
StringTokenizer strTokenizer = new StringTokenizer("2 4 6 8");
```

The second constructor accepts a second argument, which is a string containing one or more characters that are to be used as delimiters. The following statement creates an object using this constructor. It specifies that the - character is to be used as a delimiter.

```
StringTokenizer strTokenizer = new StringTokenizer("8-14-2011", "-");
```

The third constructor accepts a second argument, which is a string containing one or more characters that are to be used as delimiters, and a third argument, which indicates whether the delimiters should be included as tokens. The following statement creates an object using this constructor. It specifies that the - character is to be used as a delimiter and that the delimiters are to be included as tokens.

```
StringTokenizer strTokenizer =
            new StringTokenizer("8-14-2011", "-", true);
```

 NOTE: The first two constructors do not include the delimiter characters as tokens.

Extracting Tokens

Once you have created a StringTokenizer object, you can use its methods to extract tokens from the string you passed to the constructor. Table 8-12 lists some of the StringTokenizer methods.

Table 8-12   Some of the `StringTokenizer` methods

Method	Description
`int countTokens()`	This method returns the number of tokens left in the string.
`boolean hasMoreTokens()`	This method returns `true` if there are more tokens left in the string. Otherwise it returns `false`.
`String nextToken()`	This method returns the next token found in the string.

The following code demonstrates how all of the tokens can be extracted from a `StringTokenizer` object. The loop executes as long as there are tokens left to extract.

```
StringTokenizer strTokenizer = new StringTokenizer("One Two Three");
while (strTokenizer.hasMoreTokens())
{
    System.out.println(strTokenizer.nextToken());
}
```

This code will produce the following output:

```
One
Two
Three
```

The `DateComponent` class in Code Listing 8-8 uses a `StringTokenizer` object. Its constructor accepts a string containing a date in the form MONTH/DAY/YEAR. It extracts the month, day, and year and stores these values in the `month`, `day`, and `year` fields. The methods `getMonth`, `getDay`, and `getYear` can then be used to retrieve the values. The program in Code Listing 8-9 demonstrates the class.

Code Listing 8-8   (`DateComponent.java`)

```
 1  import java.util.StringTokenizer;
 2
 3  /**
 4   * The DateComponent class extracts the month, day, and
 5   * year from a string containing a date.
 6   */
 7
 8  public class DateComponent
 9  {
10     private String month, // To hold a month
11                    day,   // To hold a day
12                    year;  // To hold a year
13
14     /**
15      * The constructor accepts a string containing a date
16      * in the form MONTH/DAY/YEAR. It extracts the month,
```

```
17        * day, and year from the string.
18        */
19
20       public DateComponent(String dateStr)
21       {
22          // Create a StringTokenizer object. The string to
23          // tokenize is dateStr, and "/" is the delimiter.
24          StringTokenizer strTokenizer =
25                     new StringTokenizer(dateStr, "/");
26
27          // Get the first token, which is the month.
28          month = strTokenizer.nextToken();
29
30          // Get the next token, which is the day.
31          day = strTokenizer.nextToken();
32
33          // Get the next token, which is the year.
34          year = strTokenizer.nextToken();
35       }
36
37       /**
38        * The getMonth method returns the month field.
39        */
40
41       public String getMonth()
42       {
43          return month;
44       }
45
46       /**
47        * The getDay method returns the day field.
48        */
49
50       public String getDay()
51       {
52          return day;
53       }
54
55       /**
56        * The getYear method returns the year field.
57        */
58
59       public String getYear()
60       {
61          return year;
62       }
63   }
```

Code Listing 8-9   `(DateTester.java)`

```
 1  /**
 2   * This program demonstrates the DateComponent class.
 3   */
 4
 5  public class DateTester
 6  {
 7     public static void main(String[] args)
 8     {
 9        // Create a string containing a date.
10        String date = "10/23/2014";
11
12        // Create a DateComponent object, initialized
13        // with the date.
14        DateComponent dc = new DateComponent(date);
15
16        // Display the components of the date.
17        System.out.println("Here's the date: " + date);
18        System.out.println("The month is " + dc.getMonth());
19        System.out.println("The day is " + dc.getDay());
20        System.out.println("The year is " + dc.getYear());
21     }
22  }
```

Program Output

```
Here's the date: 10/23/2014
The month is 10
The day is 23
The year is 2014
```

Using Multiple Delimiters

Some situations require that you use multiple characters as delimiters in the same string. For example, look at the following email address:

```
joe@gaddisbooks.com
```

This string uses two delimiters: @ (the at symbol) and . (the period). To extract the tokens from this string we must specify both characters as delimiters to the constructor. Here is an example:

```
StringTokenizer strTokenizer =
        new StringTokenizer("joe@gaddisbooks.com", "@.");
while (strTokenizer.hasMoreTokens())
{
   System.out.println(strTokenizer.nextToken());
}
```

This code will produce the following output:

```
joe
gaddisbooks
com
```

Trimming a String Before Tokenizing

When you are tokenizing a string that was entered by the user, and you are using characters other than whitespaces as delimiters, you will probably want to trim the string before tokenizing it. Otherwise, if the user enters leading whitespace characters, they will become part of the first token. Likewise, if the user enters trailing whitespace characters, they will become part of the last token. For example look at the following code:

```java
// Create a string with leading and trailing whitespaces.
String str = "   one;two;three   ";
// Tokenize the string using the semicolon as a delimiter.
StringTokenizer strTokenizer = new StringTokenizer(str, ";");
// Display the tokens.
while (strTokenizer.hasMoreTokens())
{
    System.out.println("*" + strTokenizer.nextToken() + "*");
}
```

This code will produce the following output:

```
*   one*
*two*
*three   *
```

To prevent leading and/or trailing whitespace characters from being included in the first and last tokens, use the String class's trim method to remove them. Here is the same code, modified to use the trim method.

```java
String str = "   one;two;three   ";
StringTokenizer strTokenizer =
            new StringTokenizer(str.trim(), ";");
while (strTokenizer.hasMoreTokens())
{
    System.out.println("*" + strTokenizer.nextToken() + "*");
}
```

This code will produce the following output:

```
*one*
*two*
*three*
```

See the SerialNumber Class Case Study, available on this book's online resource page at www.pearsonhighered.com/gaddis, for another example using the StringTokenizer class.

The `String` Class's `split` Method

The `String` class has a method named `split` that tokenizes a string and returns an array of `String` objects. Each element in the array is one of the tokens. The following code, which is taken from the program *SplitDemo1.java* (in the book's source code), shows an example of the method's use.

```
// Create a String to tokenize.
String str = "one two three four";
// Get the tokens from the string.
String[] tokens = str.split(" ");
// Display each token.
for (String s : tokens)
    System.out.println(s);
```

The argument passed to the `split` method indicates the delimiter. In this example a space is used as the delimiter. The code will produce the following output:

```
one
two
three
four
```

The argument that you pass to the `split` method is a *regular expression*. A regular expression is a string that specifies a pattern of characters. Regular expressions can be powerful tools and are commonly used to search for patterns that exist in strings, files, or other collections of text. A complete discussion of regular expressions is outside the scope of this book. However, we will discuss some basic uses of regular expressions for the purpose of tokenizing strings.

In the previous example we passed a string containing a single space to the `split` method. This specified that the space character was the delimiter. The `split` method also allows you to use multi-character delimiters. This means you are not limited to a single character as a delimiter. Your delimiters can be entire words, if you wish. The following code, which is taken from the program *SplitDemo2.java* (in the book's source code), demonstrates.

```
// Create a string to tokenize.
String str = "one and two and three and four";
// Get the tokens, using " and " as the delimiter.
String[] tokens = str.split(" and ");
// Display the tokens.
for (String s : tokens)
    System.out.println(s);
```

This code will produce the following output:

```
one
two
three
four
```

The previous code demonstrated multi-character delimiters (delimiters containing multiple characters). You can also specify a series of characters where each individual character is a delimiter. In our discussion of the `StringTokenizer` class we used the following string as an example requiring multiple delimiters:

```
joe@gaddisbooks.com
```

This string uses two delimiters: @ (the "at" character) and . (the period). To specify that both the @ character and the . character are delimiters, we must enclose them in brackets inside our regular expression. The regular expression will look like this:

```
"[@.]"
```

Because the @ and . characters are enclosed in brackets, they will each be considered as a delimiter. The following code, which is taken from the program *SplitDemo3.java* (in the book's source code), demonstrates.

```java
// Create a string to tokenize.
String str = "joe@gaddisbooks.com";
// Get the tokens, using @ and . as delimiters.
String[] tokens = str.split("[@.]");
// Display the tokens.
for (String s : tokens)
    System.out.println(s);
```

This code will produce the following output:

```
joe
gaddisbooks
com
```

 Checkpoint

8.25 Look at the following string.

```
"apples pears bananas"
```

This string contains three tokens. What are they?

What character is the delimiter?

8.26 Look at the following code.

```java
StringTokenizer st = new StringTokenizer("one two three four");
int x = st.countTokens();
String stuff = st.nextToken();
```

What value will be stored in x?

What value will the `stuff` variable reference?

8.27 Look at the following string:

```
"/home/rjones/mydata.txt"
```

a. Write the declaration of a `StringTokenizer` object that can be used to extract the following tokens from the string: home, rjones, mydata, and txt.

b. Write code using the `String` class's `split` method that can be used to extract the same tokens specified in part a.

8.28   Look at the following string:

```
"dog$cat@bird%squirrel"
```

Write code using the `String` class's `split` method that can be used to extract the following tokens from the string: dog, cat, bird, and squirrel.

8.6 Wrapper Classes for the Numeric Data Types

CONCEPT: The Java API provides wrapper classes for each of the numeric data types. These classes have methods that perform useful operations involving primitive numeric values.

Earlier in this chapter, we discussed the `Character` wrapper class and some of its static methods. The Java API also provides wrapper classes for all of the numeric primitive data types, as listed in Table 8-13. These wrapper classes have numerous static methods that perform useful operations.

Table 8-13   Wrapper classes for the numeric primitive data types

Wrapper Class	Primitive Type It Applies To
Byte	byte
Double	double
Float	float
Integer	int
Long	long
Short	short

The Parse Methods

In some programming problems a string containing a number, such as "127.89", must be converted to a numeric data type so it can be mathematically processed. Each of the numeric wrapper classes has a static method that converts a string to a number. For example, the `Integer` class has a method that converts a string to an `int`, the `Double` class has a method that converts a string to a `double`, and so forth. These methods are known as *parse methods* because their names begin with the word "parse." Table 8-14 lists each wrapper class's parse method.

Table 8-14   The parse methods

Wrapper Class	Parse Method
Byte	byte parseByte(String str)
Double	double parseDouble(String str)
Float	float parseFloat(String str)
Integer	int parseInt(String str)
Long	long parseLong(String str)
Short	short parseShort(String str)

The following code demonstrates how to use the parse methods.

```
byte bVar = Byte.parseByte("1");           // Store 1 in bVar.
int iVar = Integer.parseInt("2599");       // Store 2599 in iVar.
short sVar = Short.parseShort("10");       // Store 10 in sVar.
long lVar = Long.parseLong("15908");       // Store 15908 in lVar.
float fVar = Float.parseFloat("12.3");     // Store 12.3 in fVar.
double dVar = Double.parseDouble("7945.6"); // Store 7945.6 in dVar.
```

Of course, you can pass `String` objects as arguments to these methods too, as shown here:

```
String str = "2599";
int iVar = Integer.parseInt(str);          // Store 2599 in iVar.
```

The Static `toString` Methods

Each of the numeric wrapper classes has a static `toString` method that converts a number to a string. The method accepts the number as its argument and returns a string representation of that number. The following code demonstrates.

```
int i = 12;
double d = 14.95;
String str1 = Integer.toString(i);
String str2 = Double.toString(d);
```

The `toBinaryString`, `toHexString`, and `toOctalString` Methods

The `toBinaryString`, `toHexString`, and `toOctalString` methods are static members of the `Integer` and `Long` wrapper classes. These methods accept an integer as an argument and return a string representation of that number converted to binary, hexadecimal, or octal. The following code demonstrates these methods.

```
int number = 14;
System.out.println(Integer.toBinaryString(number));
System.out.println(Integer.toHexString(number));
System.out.println(Integer.toOctalString(number));
```

This code will produce the following output:

```
1110
e
16
```

The `MIN_VALUE` and `MAX_VALUE` Constants

The numeric wrapper classes each have a set of static `final` variables named `MIN_VALUE` and `MAX_VALUE`. These variables hold the minimum and maximum values for a particular data type. For example, `Integer.MAX_VALUE` holds the maximum value that an `int` can hold. For example, the following code displays the minimum and maximum values for an `int`:

```
System.out.println("The minimum value for an " +
                   "int is " + Integer.MIN_VALUE);
System.out.println("The maximum value for an " +
                   "int is " + Integer.MAX_VALUE);
```

Autoboxing and Unboxing

It is possible to create objects from the wrapper classes. One way is to pass an initial value to the constructor, as shown here:

```
Integer number = new Integer(7);
```

This creates an `Integer` object initialized with the value 7, referenced by the variable `number`. Another way is to simply declare a wrapper class variable, and then assign a primitive value to it. For example, look at the following code:

```
Integer number;
number = 7;
```

The first statement in this code declares an `Integer` variable named `number`. It does not create an `Integer` object, just a variable. The second statement is a simple assignment statement. It assigns the primitive value 7 to the variable. You might suspect that this will cause an error. After all, `number` is a reference variable, not a primitive variable. However, because `number` is a wrapper class variable, Java performs an autoboxing operation. *Autoboxing* is Java's process of automatically "boxing up" a value inside an object. When this assignment statement executes, Java boxes up the value 7 inside an `Integer` object, and then assigns the address of that object to the `number` variable.

Unboxing is the opposite of boxing. It is the process of converting a wrapper class object to a primitive type. The following code demonstrates an unboxing operation:

```
Integer myInt = 5;           // Autoboxes the value 5
int primitiveNumber;
primitiveNumber = myInt;     // Unboxes the object
```

The first statement in this code declares `myInt` as an `Integer` reference variable. The primitive value 5 is autoboxed, and the address of the resulting object is assigned to the `myInt` variable. The second statement declares `primitiveNumber` as an `int` variable. The third statement assigns the `myInt` object to `primitiveNumber`. When this statement executes, Java automatically unboxes the `myInt` wrapper class object and stores the resulting value, which is 5, in `primitiveNumber`.

Although you rarely need to create an instance of a wrapper class, Java's autoboxing and unboxing features make some operations more convenient. Occasionally, you will find yourself in a situation where you want to perform an operation using a primitive variable, but the operation can be used only with an object. For example, recall the `ArrayList` class that we discussed in Chapter 7. An `ArrayList` is an array-like object that can be used to store other objects. You cannot, however, store primitive values in an `ArrayList`. It is intended for objects only. If you compile the following statement, an error will occur.

```
ArrayList<int> list = new ArrayList<int>(); // ERROR!
```

However, you can store wrapper class objects in an `ArrayList`. If we need to store `int` values in an `ArrayList`, we have to specify that the `ArrayList` will hold `Integer` objects. Here is an example:

```
ArrayList<Integer> list = new ArrayList<Integer>(); // Okay.
```

This statement declares that `list` references an `ArrayList` that can hold `Integer` objects. One way to store an `int` value in the `ArrayList` is to instantiate an `Integer` object, initialize it with the desired `int` value, and then pass the `Integer` object to the `ArrayList`'s add method. Here is an example.

```
ArrayList<Integer> list = new ArrayList<Integer>();
Integer myInt = 5;
list.add(myInt);
```

However, Java's autoboxing and unboxing features make it unnecessary to create the `Integer` object. If you add an `int` value to the `ArrayList`, Java will autobox the value. The following code works without any problems.

```
ArrayList<Integer> list = new ArrayList<Integer>();
list.add(5);
```

When the value 5 is passed to the add method, Java boxes the value up in an `Integer` object. When necessary, Java also unboxes values that are retrieved from the `ArrayList`. The following code demonstrates.

```
ArrayList<Integer> list = new ArrayList<Integer>();
list.add(5);
int primitiveNumber = list.get(0);
```

The last statement in this code retrieves the item at index 0. Because the item is being assigned to an `int` variable, Java unboxes it and stores the primitive value in the `int` variable.

 Checkpoint

8.29 Write a statement that converts the following string to a `double` and stores it in the `double` variable number.

```
String str = "894.56";
```

8.30 Write a statement that converts the following integer to a string and stores it in the String object referenced by `str`.

```
int i = 99;
```

8.31   What wrapper class methods convert a number from decimal to another numbering system? What wrapper classes are these methods a member of?

8.32   What is the purpose of the MIN_VALUE and MAX_VALUE variables that are members of the numeric wrapper classes?

8.7   Focus on Problem Solving: The TestScoreReader Class

Professor Harrison keeps her students' test scores in a Microsoft Excel spreadsheet. Figure 8-3 shows a set of five test scores for five students. Each column holds a test score and each row represents the scores for one student.

Figure 8-3   Microsoft Excel spreadsheet

	A	B	C	D	E	F
1	87	79	91	82	94	
2	72	79	81	74	88	
3	94	92	81	89	96	
4	77	56	67	81	79	
5	79	82	85	81	90	
6						

In addition to manipulating the scores in Excel, Dr. Harrison wants to write a Java application that accesses them. Excel, like many commercial applications, has the ability to export data to a text file. When the data in a spreadsheet is exported, each row is written to a line, and the values in the cells are separated by commas. For example, when the data shown in Figure 8-3 is exported, it will be written to a text file in the following format:

```
87,79,91,82,94
72,79,81,74,88
94,92,81,89,96
77,56,67,81,79
79,82,85,81,90
```

This is called the *comma separated value* file format. When you save a spreadsheet in this format, Excel saves it to a file with the .csv extension. Dr. Harrison decides to export her spreadsheet to a .csv file, and then write a Java program that reads the file. The program will use the String class's split method to extract the test scores from each line, and a wrapper class to convert the tokens to numeric values. As an experiment, she writes the TestScoreReader class shown in Code Listing 8-10.

Code Listing 8-10   (TestScoreReader.java)

```java
1   import java.util.Scanner; // For Scanner
2   import java.io.*;          // For File and IOException
3
4   /**
5    *  The TestScoreReader class reads test scores as
6    *  tokens from a file and calculates the average
```

```
 7     *   of each line of scores.
 8     */
 9
10    public class TestScoreReader
11    {
12       private Scanner inputFile;
13       private String line;
14
15       /**
16        *   The constructor opens a file to read
17        *   the grades from.
18        */
19
20       public TestScoreReader(String filename)
21                               throws IOException
22       {
23          File file = new File(filename);
24          inputFile = new Scanner(file);
25       }
26
27       /**
28        *   The readNextLine method reads the next line
29        *   from the file.
30        */
31
32       public boolean readNextLine() throws IOException
33       {
34          boolean lineRead; // Flag variable
35
36          // Determine whether there is more to read.
37          lineRead = inputFile.hasNext();
38
39          // If so, read the next line.
40          if (lineRead)
41             line = inputFile.nextLine();
42
43          return lineRead;
44       }
45
46       /**
47        *   The getAverage method calculates the average
48        *   of the last set of test scores read from the file.
49        */
50
51       public double getAverage()
52       {
53          int total = 0;     // Accumulator
54          double average;    // The average test score
```

```
55
56          // Tokenize the last line read from the file.
57          String[] tokens = line.split(",");
58
59          // Calculate the total of the test scores.
60          for (String str : tokens)
61          {
62              total += Integer.parseInt(str);
63          }
64
65          // Calculate the average of the scores.
66          // Use a cast to avoid integer division.
67          average = (double) total / tokens.length;
68
69          // Return the average.
70          return average;
71      }
72
73      /**
74       *  The close method closes the file.
75       */
76
77      public void close() throws IOException
78      {
79          inputFile.close();
80      }
81  }
```

The constructor accepts the name of a file as an argument and opens the file. The readNextLine method reads a line from the file and stores it in the line field. The method returns true if a line was successfully read from the file, or false if there are no more lines to read. The getAverage method tokenizes the last line read from the file, converts the tokens to double values, and calculates the average of the values. The average is returned. The program in Code Listing 8-11 uses the TestScoreReader class to open the file Grades.csv and get the averages of the test scores it contains.

Code Listing 8-11   (TestAverages.java)

```
1  import java.io.*;     // Needed for IOException
2
3  /**
4   * This program uses the TestScoreReader class to read
5   * test scores from a file and get their averages.
6   */
7
8  public class TestAverages
```

```
 9  {
10      public static void main(String[] args)
11                      throws IOException
12      {
13          double average;          // To hold an average
14          int studentNumber = 1;   // To count students
15
16          // Create a TestScoreReader object.
17          TestScoreReader scoreReader =
18                  new TestScoreReader("Grades.csv");
19
20          // Process the file contents.
21          while (scoreReader.readNextLine())
22          {
23              // Get this student's average.
24              average = scoreReader.getAverage();
25
26              // Display this student's average.
27              System.out.println("Average for student number " +
28                                  studentNumber + " is " +
29                                  average);
30
31              // Increment the student number.
32              studentNumber++;
33          }
34
35          // Close the file.
36          scoreReader.close();
37          System.out.println("No more scores.");
38      }
39  }
```

Program Output

```
Average for student number 1 is 86.6
Average for student number 2 is 78.8
Average for student number 3 is 90.4
Average for student number 4 is 72.0
Average for student number 5 is 83.4
No more scores.
```

Dr. Harrison's class works properly, and she decides that she can expand it to perform other, more complex, operations.

8.8 Common Errors to Avoid

The following list describes several errors that are commonly made when learning this chapter's topics.

- **Using static wrapper class methods as if they were instance methods.** Many of the most useful wrapper class methods are static, and you should call them directly from the class.
- **Trying to use `String` comparison methods such as `startsWith` and `endsWith` for case-insensitive comparisons.** Most of the `String` comparison methods are case sensitive. Only the `regionMatches` method performs a case-insensitive comparison.
- **Thinking of the first position of a string as 1.** Many of the `String` and `StringBuilder` methods accept a character position within a string as an argument. Remember, the position numbers in a string start at zero. If you think of the first position in a string as 1, you will cause an off-by-one error.
- **Thinking of the ending position of a substring as part of the substring.** Methods such as `getChars` accept the starting and ending position of a substring as arguments. The character at the *start* position is included in the substring, but the character at the *end* position is not included. (The last character in the substring ends at *end* − 1.)
- **Extracting more tokens from a `StringTokenizer` object than exist.** Trying to extract more tokens than exist from a `StringTokenizer` object will cause an error. You can use the `countTokens` method to determine the number of tokens and the `hasMoreTokens` method to determine whether there are any more unread tokens.

Review Questions and Exercises

Multiple Choice and True/False

1. The `isDigit`, `isLetter`, and `isLetterOrDigit` methods are members of this class.
   a. `String`
   b. `Char`
   c. `Character`
   d. `StringBuilder`

2. This method converts a character to uppercase.
   a. `makeUpperCase`
   b. `toUpperCase`
   c. `isUpperCase`
   d. `upperCase`

3. The `startsWith`, `endsWith`, and `regionMatches` methods are members of this class.
   a. `String`
   b. `Char`
   c. `Character`
   d. `StringTokenizer`

4. The `indexOf` and `lastIndexOf` methods are members of this class.
   a. `String`
   b. `Integer`
   c. `Character`
   d. `StringTokenizer`

5.   The substring, getChars, and toCharArray methods are members of this class.
       a. String
       b. Float
       c. Character
       d. StringTokenizer

6.   This String class method performs the same operation as the + operator when used on strings.
       a. add
       b. join
       c. concat
       d. plus

7.   The String class has several overloaded versions of a method that accepts a value of any primitive data type as its argument and returns a string representation of the value. The name of the method is
       a. stringValue
       b. valueOf
       c. getString
       d. valToString

8.   If you do not pass an argument to the StringBuilder constructor, the object will have enough memory to store this many characters.
       a. 16
       b. 1
       c. 256
       d. Unlimited

9.   This is one of the methods that are common to both the String and StringBuilder classes.
       a. append
       b. insert
       c. delete
       d. length

10.   To change the value of a specific character in a StringBuilder object, use this method.
       a. changeCharAt
       b. setCharAt
       c. setChar
       d. change

11.   To delete a specific character in a StringBuilder object, use this method.
       a. deleteCharAt
       b. removeCharAt
       c. removeChar
       d. expunge

12.   The character that separates tokens in a string is known as a
       a. separator
       b. tokenizer
       c. delimiter
       d. terminator

13. This `StringTokenizer` method returns `true` if there are more tokens to be extracted from a string.
    a. `moreTokens`
    b. `tokensLeft`
    c. `getToken`
    d. `hasMoreTokens`

14. Each of the numeric wrapper classes has a static method that converts a string to a number. All of these methods begin with this word.
    a. `convert`
    b. `toString`
    c. `parse`
    d. `toNumber`

15. These static `final` variables are members of the numeric wrapper classes and hold the minimum and maximum values for a particular data type.
    a. `MIN_VALUE` and `MAX_VALUE`
    b. `MIN` and `MAX`
    c. `MINIMUM` and `MAXIMUM`
    d. `LOWEST` and `HIGHEST`

16. **True or False:** Character testing methods, such as `isLetter`, accept strings as arguments and test each character in the string.

17. **True or False:** If the `toUpperCase` method's argument is already uppercase, it is returned as is, with no changes.

18. **True or False:** If the `toLowerCase` method's argument is already lowercase, it will be inadvertently converted to uppercase.

19. **True or False:** The `startsWith` and `endsWith` methods are case sensitive.

20. **True or False:** There are two versions of the `regionMatches` method: one that is case sensitive and one that can be case insensitive.

21. **True or False:** The `indexOf` and `lastIndexOf` methods find characters, but cannot find substrings.

22. **True or False:** The `String` class's `replace` method can replace individual characters, but not substrings.

23. **True or False:** The `StringBuilder` class's `replace` method can replace individual characters, but not substrings.

24. **True or False:** You can use the = operator to assign a string to a `StringBuilder` object.

25. **True or False:** To get the value of a wrapper class object, you must call a method.

Find the Error

Find the error in each of the following code segments.

1.
```
int number = 99;
String str;
// Convert number to a string.
str.valueOf(number);
```

2.
```
// Store a name in a StringBuilder object.
StringBuilder name = "Joe Schmoe";
```

3.
```
int number;
String str = "99";
// Convert str to an int.
number = str.parseInt();
```

4.
```
// Change the very first character of a
// StringBuilder object to 'Z'.
str.setCharAt(1, 'Z');
```

5.
```
// Tokenize a string that is delimited
// with semicolons. The string has three tokens.
StringTokenizer strTokenizer =
        new StringTokenizer("One;Two;Three");
// Extract the three tokens from the string.
while (strTokenizer.hasMoreTokens())
{
    System.out.println(strTokenizer.nextToken());
}
```

Algorithm Workbench

1. The following if statement determines whether choice is equal to 'Y' or 'y'.

   ```
   if (choice == 'Y' || choice == 'y')
   ```

   Rewrite this statement so it makes only one comparison and does not use the || operator. (Hint: Use either the toUpperCase or toLowerCase methods.)

2. Write a loop that counts the number of space characters that appear in the String object str.

3. Write a loop that counts the number of digits that appear in the String object str.

4. Write a loop that counts the number of lowercase characters that appear in the String object str.

5. Write a method that accepts a String object as an argument and returns true if the argument ends with the substring ".com". Otherwise, the method should return false.

6. Modify the method you wrote for question 5 so it performs a case-insensitive test. The method should return true if the argument ends with ".com" in any possible combination of upper and lowercase letters.

7. Write a method that accepts a StringBuilder object as an argument and converts all occurrences of the lowercase letter "t" in the object to uppercase.

8. Look at the following string:

   ```
   "cookies>milk>fudge:cake:ice cream"
   ```

   a. Write code using a StringTokenizer object that extracts the following tokens from the string and displays them: cookies, milk, fudge, cake, and ice cream.

   b. Write code using the String class's split method that extracts the same tokens as the code you wrote for part a.

9. Assume that d is a double variable. Write an if statement that assigns d to the int variable i if the value in d is not larger than the maximum value for an int.

10. Write code that displays the contents of the `int` variable `i` in binary, hexadecimal, and octal.

11. Look at the following declaration statements.

```
String str = "237.89";
double value;
```

Write a statement that converts the string referenced by `str` to a `double` and stores the result in `value`.

Short Answer

1. Why should you use `StringBuilder` objects instead of `String` objects in a program that makes lots of changes to strings?

2. A program reads a string as input from the user for the purpose of tokenizing it. Why is it a good idea to trim the string before tokenizing it?

3. Each of the numeric wrapper classes has a "parse" method. What do these methods do?

4. Each of the numeric wrapper classes has a static `toString` method. What do these methods do?

5. How can you determine the minimum and maximum values that can be stored in a variable of a given data type?

Programming Challenges

1. Backward String

Write a method that accepts a `String` object as an argument and displays its contents backward. For instance, if the string argument is "gravity" the method should display "ytivarg". Demonstrate the method in a program that asks the user to input a string and then passes it to the method.

2. Word Counter

Write a method that accepts a `String` object as an argument and returns the number of words it contains. For instance, if the argument is "Four score and seven years ago" the method should return the number 6. Demonstrate the method in a program that asks the user to input a string and then passes it to the method. The number of words in the string should be displayed on the screen.

3. Sentence Capitalizer

oNote
e Sentence
pitalizer
blem

Write a method that accepts a `String` object as an argument and returns a copy of the string with the first character of each sentence capitalized. For instance, if the argument is "hello. my name is Joe. what is your name?" the method should return the string, "Hello. My name is Joe. What is your name?" Demonstrate the method in a program that asks the user to input a string and then passes it to the method. The modified string should be displayed on the screen.

4. Vowels and Consonants

Write a class with a constructor that accepts a `String` object as its argument. The class should have a method that returns the number of vowels in the string, and another method that returns the number of consonants in the string. Demonstrate the class in a program that performs the following steps:

1. The user is asked to enter a string.
2. The program displays the following menu:
   a. Count the number of vowels in the string
   b. Count the number of consonants in the string
   c. Count both the vowels and consonants in the string
   d. Enter another string
   e. Exit the program
3. The program performs the operation selected by the user and repeats until the user selects e, to exit the program.

5. Password Verifier

Imagine you are developing a software package for an online shopping site that requires users to enter their own passwords. Your software requires that users' passwords meet the following criteria:

- The password should be at least six characters long.
- The password should contain at least one uppercase and at least one lowercase letter.
- The password should have at least one digit.

Write a class that verifies that a password meets the stated criteria. Demonstrate the class in a program that allows the user to enter a password and then displays a message indicating whether it is valid or not.

6. Telemarketing Phone Number List

Write a program that has two parallel arrays of `String` objects. One of the arrays should hold people's names and the other should hold their phone numbers. Here are sample contents of both arrays.

`name` Array Sample Contents	`phone` Array Sample Contents
`"Harrison, Rose"`	`"555-2234"`
`"James, Jean"`	`"555-9098"`
`"Smith, William"`	`"555-1785"`
`"Smith, Brad"`	`"555-9224"`

The program should ask the user to enter a name or the first few characters of a name to search for in the array. The program should display all of the names that match the user's input and their corresponding phone numbers. For example, if the user enters "Smith," the program should display the following names and phone numbers from the list:

```
Smith, William: 555-1785
Smith, Brad: 555-9224
```

7. Check Writer

Write a program that displays a simulated paycheck. The program should ask the user to enter the date, the payee's name, and the amount of the check. It should then display a simulated check with the dollar amount spelled out, as shown here:

	Date: 11/24/2014
Pay to the Order of: John Phillips	$1920.85
One thousand nine hundred twenty and 85 cents	

8. Sum of Numbers in a String

Write a program that asks the user to enter a series of numbers separated by commas. Here is an example of valid input:

```
7,9,10,2,18,6
```

The program should calculate and display the sum of all the numbers.

9. Sum of Digits in a String

Write a program that asks the user to enter a series of single digit numbers with nothing separating them. The program should display the sum of all the single digit numbers in the string. For example, if the user enters 2514, the method should return 12, which is the sum of 2, 5, 1, and 4. The program should also display the highest and lowest digits in the string. (*Hint: Convert the string to an array.*)

10. Word Counter

Write a program that asks the user for the name of a file. The program should display the number of words that the file contains.

11. Sales Analysis

If you have downloaded the book's source code from www.pearsonhighered.com/gaddis, you will find the file *SalesData.txt* in the *Chapter 08* folder. This file contains the dollar amount of sales that a retail store made each day for a number of weeks. Each line in the file contains seven numbers, which are the sales numbers for one week. The numbers are separated by a comma. The following line is an example from the file:

```
1245.67,1490.07,1679.87,2378.46,1783.92,1468.99,2059.77
```

Write a program that opens the file and processes its contents. The program should display the following:

- The total sales for each week
- The average daily sales for each week
- The total sales for all of the weeks
- The average weekly sales
- The week number that had the highest amount of sales
- The week number that had the lowest amount of sales

12. Miscellaneous String Operations

Write a class with the following static methods:

wordCount. This method should accept a String object as an argument and return the number of words contained in the object.

arrayToString. This method accepts a char array as an argument and converts it to a String object. The method should return a reference to the String object.

mostFrequent. This method accepts a String object as an argument and returns the character that occurs most frequently in the object.

replaceSubstring. This method accepts three String objects as arguments. Let's call them *string1*, *string2*, and *string3*. It searches *string1* for all occurrences of *string2*. When it finds an occurrence of *string2*, it replaces it with *string3*. For example, suppose the three arguments have the following values:

```
string1:  "the dog jumped over the fence"
string2:  "the"
string3:  "that"
```

With these three arguments, the method would return a String object with the value "that dog jumped over that fence".

Demonstrate each of these methods in a complete program.

13. Alphabetic Telephone Number Translator

Many companies use telephone numbers such as 555-GET-FOOD so the number is easier for their customers to remember. On a standard telephone, the alphabetic letters are mapped to numbers in the following fashion:

A, B, and C = 2
D, E, and F = 3
G, H, and I = 4
J, K, and L = 5
M, N, and O = 6
P, Q, R, and S = 7
T, U, and V = 8
W, X, Y, and Z = 9

Write an application that asks the user to enter a 10-character telephone number in the format XXX-XXX-XXXX. The application should display the telephone number with any alphabetic characters that appeared in the original translated to their numeric equivalent. For example, if the user enters 555-GET-FOOD, the application should display 555-438-3663.

14. Word Separator

Write a program that accepts as input a sentence in which all the words are run together, but the first character of each word is uppercase. Convert the sentence to a string in which the words are separated by spaces and only the first word starts with an uppercase letter. For example the string "StopAndSmellTheRoses." would be converted to "Stop and smell the roses."

15. Pig Latin

Write a program that reads a sentence as input and converts each word to "Pig Latin". In one version of Pig Latin you convert a word by removing the first letter, placing that letter at the end of the word, and then appending "ay" to the word. Here is an example:

English: I SLEPT MOST OF THE NIGHT

Pig Latin: IAY LEPTSAY OSTMAY FOAY HETAY IGHTNAY

16. Morse Code Converter

Write a program that asks the user to enter a string and then converts that string to Morse code. Morse code is a code where each letter of the English alphabet, each digit, and various punctuation characters are represented by a series of dots and dashes. Table 8-15 shows part of the code.

Table 8-15   Morse code

Character	Code	Character	Code	Character	Code	Character	Code
space	space	6	-....	G	--.	Q	--.-
comma	--..--	7	--...	H	....	R	.-.
period	.-.-.-	8	---..	I	..	S	...
question mark	..--..	9	----.	J	.---	T	-
0	-----	A	.-	K	-.-	U	..-
1	.----	B	-...	L	.-..	V	...-
2	..---	C	-.-.	M	--	W	.--
3	...--	D	-..	N	-.	X	-..-
4	....-	E	.	O	---	Y	-.--
5	.....	F	..-.	P	.--.	Z	--..

9 Inheritance

TOPICS

9.1 What Is Inheritance?
9.2 Calling the Superclass Constructor
9.3 Overriding Superclass Methods
9.4 Protected Members
9.5 Classes That Inherit from Subclasses
9.6 The Object Class

9.7 Polymorphism
9.8 Abstract Classes and Abstract Methods
9.9 Interfaces
9.10 Common Errors to Avoid

9.1 What Is Inheritance?

CONCEPT: Inheritance allows a new class to be based on an existing class. The new class inherits the members of the class it is based on.

VideoNote
Inheritance

Generalization and Specialization

In the real world you can find many objects that are specialized versions of other more general objects. For example, the term "insect" describes a very general type of creature with numerous characteristics. Because grasshoppers and bumblebees are insects, they have all the general characteristics of an insect. In addition, they have special characteristics of their own. For example, the grasshopper has its jumping ability, and the bumblebee has its stinger. Grasshoppers and bumblebees are specialized versions of an insect. This is illustrated in Figure 9-1.

Figure 9-1 Bumblebees and grasshoppers are specialized versions of an insect

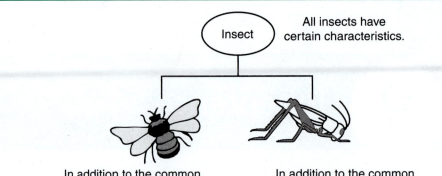

Insect — All insects have certain characteristics.

In addition to the common insect characteristics, the bumblebee has its own unique characteristics such as the ability to sting.

In addition to the common insect characteristics, the grasshopper has its own unique characteristics such as the ability to jump.

Inheritance and the "Is a" Relationship

When one object is a specialized version of another object, there is an *"is a" relationship* between them. For example, a grasshopper *is an* insect. Here are a few other examples of the "is a" relationship.

- A poodle *is a* dog.
- A car *is a* vehicle.
- A flower *is a* plant.
- A rectangle *is a* shape.
- A football player *is an* athlete.

When an "is a" relationship exists between objects, it means that the specialized object has all of the characteristics of the general object, plus additional characteristics that make it special. In object-oriented programming, *inheritance* is used to create an "is a" relationship among classes. This allows you to extend the capabilities of a class by creating another class that is a specialized version of it.

Inheritance involves a superclass and a subclass. The *superclass* is the general class and the *subclass* is the specialized class. (Superclasses are also called *base classes*, and subclasses are also called *derived classes*.) You can think of the subclass as an extended version of the superclass. The subclass inherits fields and methods from the superclass without any of them being rewritten. Furthermore, new fields and methods can be added to the subclass to make it more specialized than the superclass.

Let's look at an example of how inheritance can be used. Most teachers assign various graded activities for their students to complete. A graded activity can be given a numeric score such as 70, 85, 90, and so on, and a letter grade such as A, B, C, D or F. Figure 9-2 shows a UML diagram for the GradedActivity class, which is designed to hold the numeric score of a graded activity. The setScore method sets a numeric score, and the getScore method returns the numeric score. The getGrade method returns the letter grade that corresponds to the numeric score. Notice that the class does not have a programmer-defined constructor, so Java will automatically generate a default constructor for it. This will be a point of discussion later. Code Listing 9-1 shows the code for the class, and the program in Code Listing 9-2 demonstrates the class.

Figure 9-2   UML diagram for the `GradedActivity` class

```
┌─────────────────────────────────┐
│         GradedActivity          │
├─────────────────────────────────┤
│ - score : double                │
├─────────────────────────────────┤
│ + setScore(s : double) : void   │
│ + getScore() : double           │
│ + getGrade() : char             │
└─────────────────────────────────┘
```

Code Listing 9-1   `(GradedActivity.java)`

```java
 1  /**
 2   * A class that holds a grade for a graded activity.
 3   */
 4
 5  public class GradedActivity
 6  {
 7     private double score;  // Numeric score
 8
 9     /**
10      * The setScore method stores its argument in
11      * the score field.
12      */
13
14     public void setScore(double s)
15     {
16        score = s;
17     }
18
19     /**
20      * The getScore method returns the score field.
21      */
22
23     public double getScore()
24     {
25        return score;
26     }
27
28     /**
29      * The getGrade method returns a letter grade
30      * determined from the score field.
31      */
32
33     public char getGrade()
34     {
35        char letterGrade;  // To hold the grade
36
```

```
37          if (score >= 90)
38              letterGrade = 'A';
39          else if (score >= 80)
40              letterGrade = 'B';
41          else if (score >= 70)
42              letterGrade = 'C';
43          else if (score >= 60)
44              letterGrade = 'D';
45          else
46              letterGrade = 'F';
47
48          return letterGrade;
49      }
50  }
```

Code Listing 9-2 (GradeDemo.java)

```
1   import java.util.Scanner;
2
3   /**
4    * This program demonstrates the GradedActivity class.
5    */
6
7   public class GradeDemo
8   {
9       public static void main(String[] args)
10      {
11          double testScore;   // To hold a test score
12
13          // Create a Scanner object for keyboard input.
14          Scanner keyboard = new Scanner(System.in);
15
16          // Create a GradedActivity object.
17          GradedActivity grade = new GradedActivity();
18
19          // Get a test score from the user.
20          System.out.print("Enter a numeric test score: ");
21          testScore = keyboard.nextDouble();
22
23          // Set the GradedActivity object's score.
24          grade.setScore(testScore);
25
26          // Display the letter grade for that score.
27          System.out.println("The grade for that test is " +
28                              grade.getGrade());
29      }
30  }
```

Program Output with Example Input Shown in Bold

```
Enter a numeric test score: 89 [Enter]
The grade for that test is B
```

Program Output with Example Input Shown in Bold

```
Enter a numeric test score: 75 [Enter]
The grade for that test is C
```

The `GradedActivity` class represents the general characteristics of a student's graded activity. Many different types of graded activities exist, however, such as quizzes, midterm exams, final exams, lab reports, essays, and so on. Because the numeric scores might be determined differently for each of these graded activities, we can create subclasses to handle each one. For example, a `FinalExam` class could inherit from the `GradedActivity` class. Figure 9-3 shows the UML diagram for such a class, and Code Listing 9-3 shows its code. It has fields for the number of questions on the exam (`numQuestions`), the number of points each question is worth (`pointsEach`), and the number of questions missed by the student (`numMissed`).

Figure 9-3   UML diagram for the `FinalExam` class

Code Listing 9-3   (`FinalExam.java`)

```java
 1  /**
 2   * This class determines the grade for a final exam.
 3   */
 4
 5  public class FinalExam extends GradedActivity
 6  {
 7     private int numQuestions;  // Number of questions
 8     private double pointsEach; // Points for each question
 9     private int numMissed;     // Number of questions missed
10
11     /**
12      * The constructor accepts as arguments the number
13      * of questions on the exam and the number of
14      * questions the student missed.
15      */
```

```
16
17      public FinalExam(int questions, int missed)
18      {
19         double numericScore;   // To calculate the numeric score
20
21         // Set the numQuestions and numMissed fields.
22         numQuestions = questions;
23         numMissed = missed;
24
25         // Calculate the points for each question and
26         // the numeric score for this exam.
27         pointsEach = 100.0 / questions;
28         numericScore = 100.0 - (missed * pointsEach);
29
30         // Call the superclass's setScore method to
31         // set the numeric score.
32         setScore(numericScore);
33      }
34
35      /**
36       * The getPointsEach method returns the pointsEach
37       * field.
38       */
39
40      public double getPointsEach()
41      {
42         return pointsEach;
43      }
44
45      /**
46       * The getNumMissed method returns the numMissed
47       * field.
48       */
49
50      public int getNumMissed()
51      {
52         return numMissed;
53      }
54   }
```

The only new notation in this class declaration is in the class header (in line 5), which is shown in Figure 9-4.

Figure 9-4   First line of the `FinalExam` class declaration

Class being declared   Superclass
(the subclass)

The `extends` key word indicates that this class inherits from another class (a superclass). The name of the superclass is listed after the word `extends`. So, this line of code indicates that `FinalExam` is the name of the class being declared and `GradedActivity` is the name of the superclass it inherits from.

As you read this line, it communicates the fact that the `FinalExam` class extends the `GradedActivity` class. This makes sense because a subclass is an extension of its superclass. If we want to express the relationship between the two classes, we can say that a `FinalExam` is a `GradedActivity`.

Because the `FinalExam` class inherits from the `GradedActivity` class, it inherits all of the public members of the `GradedActivity` class. Here is a list of the members of the `FinalExam` class:

Fields:

`int numQuestions;`	Declared in `FinalExam`
`double pointsEach;`	Declared in `FinalExam`
`int numMissed;`	Declared in `FinalExam`

Methods:

Constructor	Declared in `FinalExam`
`getPointsEach`	Declared in `FinalExam`
`getNumMissed`	Declared in `FinalExam`
`setScore`	Inherited from `GradedActivity`
`getScore`	Inherited from `GradedActivity`
`getGrade`	Inherited from `GradedActivity`

Notice that the `GradedActivity` class's `score` field is not listed among the members of the `FinalExam` class. That is because the `score` field is private. Private members of the superclass cannot be accessed by the subclass, so technically speaking, they are not inherited. When an object of the subclass is created, the private members of the superclass exist in memory, but only methods in the superclass can access them. They are truly private to the superclass.

You will also notice that the superclass's constructor is not listed among the members of the `FinalExam` class. It makes sense that superclass constructors are not inherited because their purpose is to construct objects of the superclass. In the next section we discuss in more detail how superclass constructors operate.

To see how inheritance works in this example, let's take a closer look at the `FinalExam` constructor. The constructor accepts two arguments: the number of test questions on the exam, and the number of questions missed by the student. These values are assigned to the `numQuestions` and `numMissed` fields in lines 22 and 23. Then, the number of points for each question is calculated in line 27, and the numeric test score is calculated in line 28. The last statement in the constructor, in line 32, reads:

```
setScore(numericScore);
```

This is a call to the setScore method. Although no setScore method appears in the FinalExam class, the method is inherited from the GradedActivity class. The program in Code Listing 9-4 demonstrates the FinalExam class.

Code Listing 9-4 (FinalExamDemo.java)

```java
1   import java.util.Scanner;
2
3   /**
4    *  This program demonstrates the FinalExam class, which
5    *  inherits from the GradedActivity class.
6    */
7
8   public class FinalExamDemo
9   {
10     public static void main(String[] args)
11     {
12        int questions,  // Number of questions
13            missed;     // Number of questions missed
14
15        // Create a Scanner object for keyboard input.
16        Scanner keyboard = new Scanner(System.in);
17
18        // Get the number of questions on the final exam.
19        System.out.print("How many questions are on " +
20                         "the final exam? ");
21        questions = keyboard.nextInt();
22
23        // Get the number of questions the student missed.
24        System.out.print("How many questions did the " +
25                         "student miss? ");
26        missed = keyboard.nextInt();
27
28        // Create a FinalExam object.
29        FinalExam exam = new FinalExam(questions, missed);
30
31        // Display the test results.
32        System.out.println("Each question counts " +
33                            exam.getPointsEach() +
34                            " points.");
35        System.out.println("The exam score is " +
36                            exam.getScore());
37        System.out.println("The exam grade is " +
38                            exam.getGrade());
39     }
40  }
```

Program Output with Example Input Shown in Bold

```
How many questions are on the final exam? 20 [Enter]
How many questions did the student miss? 3 [Enter]
Each question counts 5.0 points.
The exam score is 85.0
The exam grade is B
```

In line 29 this program creates an instance of the `FinalExam` class and assigns its address to the exam variable. When a `FinalExam` object is created in memory, it has not only the members declared in the `FinalExam` class, but the members declared in the `GradedActivity` class as well. Notice that in lines 36 and 38 two public methods of the `GradedActivity` class, `getScore` and `getGrade`, are directly called, using the object referenced by exam. When a class inherits from another class, the public members of the superclass become public members of the subclass. In this program the `getScore` and `getGrade` methods can be called from the exam object because they are public members of the object's superclass.

As mentioned before, the private members of the superclass (in this case, the `score` field) cannot be accessed by the subclass. When the exam object is created in memory, a `score` field exists, but only the methods defined in the superclass, `GradedActivity`, can access it. It is truly private to the superclass. Because the `FinalExam` constructor cannot directly access the `score` field, it must call the superclass's `setScore` method (which is public) to store a value in it.

Inheritance in UML Diagrams

You show inheritance in a UML diagram by connecting two classes with a line that has an open arrowhead at one end. The arrowhead points to the superclass. Figure 9-5 shows a UML diagram depicting the relationship between the `GradedActivity` and `FinalExam` classes.

Figure 9-5 UML diagram showing inheritance

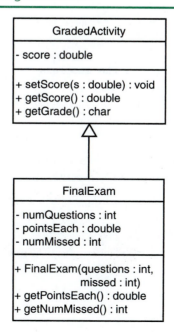

The Superclass's Constructor

As was mentioned earlier, the GradedActivity class has only one constructor, which is the default constructor that Java automatically generated for it. When a FinalExam object is created, the GradedActivity class's default constructor is executed just before the FinalExam constructor is executed. In an inheritance relationship, the superclass constructor always executes before the subclass constructor.

Code Listing 9-5 shows a class, SuperClass1, that has a programmer-defined no-arg constructor. The constructor simply displays the message "This is the superclass constructor." Code Listing 9-6 shows SubClass1, which inherits from SuperClass1. This class also has a programmer-defined no-arg constructor, which displays the message "This is the subclass constructor."

Code Listing 9-5   (SuperClass1.java)

```
1   public class SuperClass1
2   {
3      // Constructor
4      public SuperClass1()
5      {
6         System.out.println("This is the superclass " +
7                            "constructor.");
8      }
9   }
```

Code Listing 9-6   (SubClass1.java)

```
1   public class SubClass1 extends SuperClass1
2   {
3      // Constructor
4      public SubClass1()
5      {
6         System.out.println("This is the subclass " +
7                            "constructor.");
8      }
9   }
```

The program in Code Listing 9-7 creates a SubClass1 object. As you can see from the program output, the superclass constructor executes first, followed by the subclass constructor.

Code Listing 9-7   (`ConstructorDemo1.java`)

```java
 1  /**
 2   * This program demonstrates the order in which superclass
 3   * and subclass constructors are called.
 4   */
 5
 6  public class ConstructorDemo1
 7  {
 8     public static void main(String[] args)
 9     {
10        SubClass1 obj = new SubClass1();
11     }
12  }
```

Program Output

```
This is the superclass constructor.
This is the subclass constructor.
```

Inheritance Does Not Work in Reverse

In an inheritance relationship, the subclass inherits members from the superclass, not the other way around. This means it is not possible for a superclass to call a subclass's method. For example, if we create a `GradedActivity` object, it cannot call the `getPointsEach` or the `getNumMissed` methods because they are members of the `FinalExam` class.

Checkpoint

9.1 Here is the first line of a class declaration. What is the name of the superclass? What is the name of the subclass?

```java
public class Truck extends Vehicle
```

9.2 Look at the following class declarations, and answer the questions that follow them.

```java
public class Shape
{
    private double area;

    public void setArea(double a)
    {
        area = a;
    }
    public double getArea()
    {
        return area;
    }
}
```

```
public class Circle extends Shape
{
    private double radius;

    public void setRadius(double r)
    {
        radius = r;
        setArea(Math.PI * r * r);
    }

    public double getRadius()
    {
        return radius;
    }
}
```

   a.   Which class is the superclass? Which class is the subclass?

   b.   Draw a UML diagram showing the relationship between these two classes.

   c.   When a `Circle` object is created, what are its public members?

   d.   What members of the `Shape` class are not accessible to the `Circle` class's methods?

   e.   Assume a program has the following declarations:

```
Shape s = new Shape();
Circle c = new Circle();
```

      Indicate whether the following statements are legal or illegal:

```
c.setRadius(10.0);
s.setRadius(10.0);
System.out.println(c.getArea());
System.out.println(s.getArea());
```

9.3   Class B inherits from class A. Describe the order in which the class's constructors execute when a class B object is created.

9.2 Calling the Superclass Constructor

CONCEPT: The super key word refers to an object's superclass. You can use the super key word to call a superclass constructor.

In the previous section, you learned that a superclass's default constructor or no-arg constructor is automatically called just before the subclass's constructor executes. But what if the superclass does not have a default constructor or a no-arg constructor? Or, what if the superclass has multiple overloaded constructors and you want to make sure a specific one is called? In either of these situations, you use the super key word to explicitly call a superclass constructor. The super key word refers to an object's superclass and can be used to access members of the superclass.

Code Listing 9-8 shows a class, SuperClass2, which has a no-arg constructor and a constructor that accepts an int argument. Code Listing 9-9 shows SubClass2, which inherits from SuperClass2. This class's constructor uses the super key word to call the superclass's constructor and pass an argument to it.

Code Listing 9-8   `(SuperClass2.java)`

```
1   public class SuperClass2
2   {
3      // No-arg constructor
4      public SuperClass2()
5      {
6         System.out.println("This is the superclass " +
7                            "no-arg constructor.");
8      }
9
10     // Constructor #2
11     public SuperClass2(int arg)
12     {
13        System.out.println("The following argument was " +
14                           "passed to the superclass " +
15                           "constructor: " + arg);
16     }
17  }
```

Code Listing 9-9   `(SubClass2.java)`

```
1   public class SubClass2 extends SuperClass2
2   {
3      // Constructor
4      public SubClass2()
5      {
6         // Call the superclass constructor.
7         super(10);
8
9         // Display a message.
10        System.out.println("This is the subclass " +
11                           "constructor.");
12     }
13  }
```

In the SubClass2 constructor, the statement in line 7 calls the superclass constructor and passes the argument 10 to it. Here are three guidelines you should remember about calling a superclass constructor:

- The super statement that calls the superclass constructor can be written only in the subclass's constructor. You cannot call the superclass constructor from any other method.
- The super statement that calls the superclass constructor must be the first statement in the subclass's constructor. This is because the superclass's constructor must execute before the code in the subclass's constructor executes.

- If a subclass constructor does not explicitly call a superclass constructor, Java will automatically call the superclass's default constructor, or no-arg constructor, just before the code in the subclass's constructor executes. This is equivalent to placing the following statement at the beginning of a subclass constructor:

```
super();
```

The program in Code Listing 9-10 demonstrates these classes.

Code Listing 9-10   (`ConstructorDemo2.java`)

```
1  /**
2   * This program demonstrates how a superclass constructor
3   * can be called with the super key word.
4   */
5
6  public class ConstructorDemo2
7  {
8     public static void main(String[] args)
9     {
10        SubClass2 obj = new SubClass2();
11     }
12  }
```

Program Output

```
The following argument was passed to the superclass constructor: 10
This is the subclass constructor.
```

Let's look at a more meaningful example. Recall the `Rectangle` class that was introduced in Chapter 3. Figure 9-6 shows a UML diagram for the class.

Figure 9-6   UML diagram for the `Rectangle` class

Rectangle
- length : double - width : double
+ Rectangle(len : double, w : double) + setLength(len : double) : void + setWidth(w : double) : void + getLength() : double + getWidth() : double + getArea() : double

Here is part of the class's code:

```java
public class Rectangle
{
    private double length;
    private double width;
    /**
     * Constructor
     */
    public Rectangle(double len, double w)
    {
        length = len;
        width = w;
    }
    (Other methods follow . . .)
}
```

Next we will design a `Cube` class, which inherits from the `Rectangle` class. The `Cube` class is designed to hold data about cubes, which not only have a length, width, and area (the area of the base), but a height, surface area, and volume as well. A UML diagram showing the inheritance relationship between the `Cube` and `Rectangle` classes is shown in Figure 9-7, and the code for the `Cube` class is shown in Code Listing 9-11.

Figure 9-7   UML diagram for the `Rectangle` and `Cube` classes

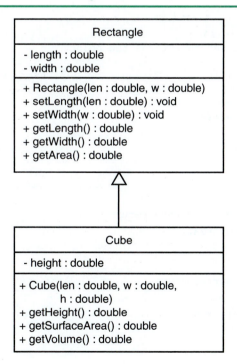

Code Listing 9-11   (Cube.java)

```
1  /**
2   *  This class holds data about a cube.
3   */
4
5  public class Cube extends Rectangle
6  {
7     private double height;  // The height of the cube
8
9     /**
10     *  The constructor accepts the cube's length,
11     *  width, and height as arguments.
12     */
13
14    public Cube(double len, double w, double h)
15    {
16       // Call the superclass constructor to
17       // initialize length and width.
18       super(len, w);
19
20       // Initialize height.
21       height = h;
22    }
23
24    /**
25     *  The getHeight method returns the height
26     *  field.
27     */
28
29    public double getHeight()
30    {
31       return height;
32    }
33
34    /**
35     *  The getSurfaceArea method returns the
36     *  cube's surface area.
37     */
38
39    public double getSurfaceArea()
40    {
41       return getArea() * 6;
42    }
43
44    /**
45     *  The getVolume method returns the volume of
46     *  the cube.
47     */
```

```
48
49      public double getVolume()
50      {
51          return getArea() * height;
52      }
53  }
```

The `Cube` constructor accepts arguments for the parameters `w`, `len`, and `h`. The values that are passed to `w` and `len` are subsequently passed as arguments to the `Rectangle` constructor in line 18. When the `Rectangle` constructor finishes, the remaining code in the `Cube` constructor is executed. The program in Code Listing 9-12 demonstrates the class.

Code Listing 9-12   **(CubeDemo.java)**

```
1   import java.util.Scanner;
2
3   /**
4    *  This program demonstrates passing arguments to a
5    *  superclass constructor.
6    */
7
8   public class CubeDemo
9   {
10      public static void main(String[] args)
11      {
12          double length,    // To hold a length
13                 width,     // To hold a width
14                 height;    // To hold a height
15
16          // Create a Scanner object for keyboard input.
17          Scanner keyboard = new Scanner(System.in);
18
19          // Get the dimensions of a cube from the user.
20          System.out.println("Enter the following dimensions " +
21                             "of a cube: ");
22          System.out.print("Length: ");
23          length = keyboard.nextDouble();
24          System.out.print("Width: ");
25          width = keyboard.nextDouble();
26          System.out.print("Height: ");
27          height = keyboard.nextDouble();
28
29          // Create a cube object and pass the dimensions
30          // to the constructor.
31          Cube myCube = new Cube(length, width, height);
32
```

```
33          // Display the properties of the cube.
34          System.out.println();
35          System.out.println("Here are the properties of " +
36                             "the cube.");
37          System.out.println("Length: " + myCube.getLength());
38          System.out.println("Width: " + myCube.getWidth());
39          System.out.println("Height: " + myCube.getHeight());
40          System.out.println("Base Area: " + myCube.getArea());
41          System.out.println("Surface Area: " +
42                             myCube.getSurfaceArea());
43          System.out.println("Volume: " + myCube.getVolume());
44      }
45  }
```

Program Output with Example Input Shown in Bold

```
Enter the following dimensions of a cube:
Length: 10 [Enter]
Width: 15 [Enter]
Height: 12 [Enter]
Here are the properties of the cube.
Length: 10.0
Width: 15.0
Height: 12.0
Base Area: 150.0
Surface Area: 900.0
Volume: 1800.0
```

When the Superclass Has No Default or No-Arg Constructor

Recall from Chapter 3 that Java provides a default constructor for a class only when you provide no constructors for the class. This makes it possible to have a class with no default constructor. The Rectangle class we just looked at is an example. It has a constructor that accepts two arguments. Because we have provided this constructor, the Rectangle class does not have a default constructor. In addition, we have not written a no-arg constructor for the class.

If a superclass does not have a default constructor and does not have a no-arg constructor, then a class that inherits from it *must* call one of the constructors that the superclass does have. If it does not, an error will result when the subclass is compiled.

Summary of Constructor Issues in Inheritance

We have covered a number of important issues that you should remember about constructors in an inheritance relationship. The following list summarizes them.

- The superclass constructor always executes before the subclass constructor.
- You can write a super statement that calls a superclass constructor, but only in the subclass's constructor. You cannot call the superclass constructor from any other method.

- If a super statement that calls a superclass constructor appears in a subclass constructor, it must be the first statement.
- If a subclass constructor does not explicitly call a superclass constructor, Java will automatically call `super()` just before the code in the subclass's constructor executes.
- If a superclass does not have a default constructor and does not have a no-arg constructor, then a class that inherits from it *must* call one of the constructors that the superclass does have.

Checkpoint

9.4   Look at the following classes:

```java
public class Ground
{
   public Ground()
   {
      System.out.println("You are on the ground.");
   }
}
public class Sky extends Ground
{
   public Sky()
   {
      System.out.println("You are in the sky.");
   }
}
```

What will the following program display?

```java
public class Checkpoint
{
   public static void main(String[] args)
   {
      Sky object = new Sky();
   }
}
```

9.5   Look at the following classes:

```java
public class Ground
{
   public Ground()
   {
      System.out.println("You are on the ground.");
   }
   public Ground(String groundColor)
   {
      System.out.println("The ground is " +
                         groundColor);
   }
```

```
    }
public class Sky extends Ground
{
   public Sky()
   {
      System.out.println("You are in the sky.");
   }
   public Sky(String skyColor)
   {
      super("green");
      System.out.println("The sky is " + skyColor);
   }
}
```

What will the following program display?

```
public class Checkpoint
{
   public static void main(String[] args)
   {
      Sky object = new Sky("blue");
   }
}
```

9.3 Overriding Superclass Methods

CONCEPT: A subclass may have a method with the same signature as a superclass method. In such a case, the subclass method overrides the superclass method.

Sometimes a subclass inherits a method from its superclass, but the method is inadequate for the subclass's purpose. Because the subclass is more specialized than the superclass, it is sometimes necessary for the subclass to replace inadequate superclass methods with more suitable ones. This is known as *method overriding*.

For example, recall the GradedActivity class that was presented earlier in this chapter. This class has a setScore method that sets a numeric score and a getGrade method that returns a letter grade based on that score. But, suppose a teacher wants to curve a numeric score before the letter grade is determined. For example, Dr. Harrison determines that in order to curve the grades in her class she must multiply each student's score by a certain percentage. This gives an adjusted score that is used to determine the letter grade. To satisfy this need we can design a new class, CurvedActivity, which inherits from the GradedActivity class and has its own specialized version of the setScore method. The setScore method in the subclass *overrides* the setScore method in the superclass. Figure 9-8 shows a UML diagram depicting the relationship between the GradedActivity class and the CurvedActivity class.

Figure 9-8   The GradedActivity and CurvedActivity classes

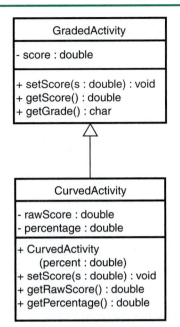

Table 9-1 summarizes the CurvedActivity class's fields, and Table 9-2 summarizes the class's methods.

Table 9-1   CurvedActivity class fields

Field	Description
rawScore	This field holds the student's unadjusted score.
percentage	This field holds the value that the unadjusted score must be multiplied by to get the curved score.

Table 9-2   CurvedActivity class methods

Method	Description
Constructor	The constructor accepts a double argument that is the curve percentage. This value is assigned to the percentage field and the rawScore field is assigned 0.0.
setScore	This method accepts a double argument that is the student's unadjusted score. The method stores the argument in the rawScore field, then passes the result of rawScore * percentage as an argument to the superclass's setScore method.
getRawScore	This method returns the value in the rawScore field.
getPercentage	This method returns the value in the percentage field.

Code Listing 9-13 shows the code for the `CurvedActivity` class.

Code Listing 9-13 `(CurvedActivity.java)`

```java
 1  /**
 2   * This class computes a curved grade. It inherits
 3   * from the GradedActivity class.
 4   */
 5
 6  public class CurvedActivity extends GradedActivity
 7  {
 8     double rawScore,      // Unadjusted score
 9            percentage;    // Curve percentage
10
11     /**
12      * The constructor accepts the curve percentage
13      * as an argument.
14      */
15
16     public CurvedActivity(double percent)
17     {
18        percentage = percent;
19        rawScore = 0.0;
20     }
21
22     /**
23      * The setScore method overrides the superclass
24      * setScore method. This version accepts the
25      * unadjusted score as an argument. That score
26      * is multiplied by the curve percentage and the
27      * result is sent as an argument to the
28      * superclass's setScore method.
29      */
30
31     public void setScore(double s)
32     {
33        rawScore = s;
34        super.setScore(rawScore * percentage);
35     }
36
37     /**
38      * The getRawScore method returns the rawScore
39      * field.
40      */
41
42     public double getRawScore()
```

```
43     {
44         return rawScore;
45     }
46
47     /**
48      * The getPercentage method returns the
49      * percentage field.
50      */
51
52     public double getPercentage()
53     {
54         return percentage;
55     }
56 }
```

Let's take a closer look at the CurvedActivity class's setScore method, which appears in lines 31 through 35. Recall from Chapter 6 that a method's *signature* consists of the method's name and the data types of the method's parameters, in the order that they appear. Notice that this method has the same signature as the setScore method in the superclass, GradedActivity. In order for a subclass method to override a superclass method, it must have the same signature. When an object of the subclass invokes the method, it invokes the subclass's version of the method, not the superclass's.

The setScore method in the CurvedActivity class accepts an argument, which is the student's unadjusted numeric score. This value is stored in the rawScore field. Then the following statement, in line 34, is executed:

```
super.setScore(rawScore * percentage);
```

As you already know, the super key word refers to the object's superclass. This statement calls the superclass's version of the setScore method with the result of the expression rawScore * percentage passed as an argument. This is necessary because the superclass's score field is private, and the subclass cannot access it directly. In order to store a value in the superclass's score field, the subclass must call the superclass's setScore method. A subclass may call an overridden superclass method by prefixing its name with the super key word and a dot (.). The program in Code Listing 9-14 demonstrates this class.

Code Listing 9-14   (CurvedActivityDemo.java)

```
1  import java.util.Scanner;
2
3  /**
4   * This program demonstrates the CurvedActivity class,
5   * which inherits from the GradedActivity class.
6   */
7
8  public class CurvedActivityDemo
9  {
```

```
10       public static void main(String[] args)
11       {
12          double score,              // Raw score
13              curvePercent;          // Curve percentage
14
15          // Create a Scanner object for keyboard input.
16          Scanner keyboard = new Scanner(System.in);
17
18          // Get the unadjusted exam score.
19          System.out.print("Enter the student's raw " +
20                          "numeric score: ");
21          score = keyboard.nextDouble();
22
23          // Get the curve percentage.
24          System.out.print("Enter the curve percentage: ");
25          curvePercent = keyboard.nextDouble();
26
27          // Create a CurvedActivity object.
28          CurvedActivity curvedExam =
29                      new CurvedActivity(curvePercent);
30
31          // Set the exam score.
32          curvedExam.setScore(score);
33
34          // Display the test results.
35          System.out.println("The raw score is " +
36                              curvedExam.getRawScore() +
37                              " points.");
38          System.out.println("The curved score is " +
39                              curvedExam.getScore());
40          System.out.println("The exam grade is " +
41                              curvedExam.getGrade());
42      }
43  }
```

Program Output with Example Input Shown in Bold

```
Enter the student's raw numeric score: 87 [Enter]
Enter the curve percentage: 1.06 [Enter]
The raw score is 87.0 points.
The curved score is 92.22
The exam grade is A
```

This program uses the curvedExam variable to reference a CurvedActivity object. The statement in line 32 calls the setScore method. Because curvedExam references a CurvedActivity object, this statement calls the CurvedActivity class's setScore method, not the superclass's version.

Even though a subclass may override a method in the superclass, superclass objects still call the superclass version of the method. For example, the following code creates an object of the GradedActivity class and calls the setScore method:

```
GradedActivity regularExam = new GradedActivity();
regularExam.setScore(85);
```

Because regularExam references a GradedActivity object, this code calls the GradedActivity class's version of the setScore method.

Overloading vs. Overriding

There is a distinction between overloading a method and overriding a method. Recall from Chapter 6 that overloading is when a method has the same name as one or more other methods, but a different parameter list. Although overloaded methods have the same name, they have different signatures. When a method overrides another method, however, they both have the same signature.

Both overloading and overriding can take place in an inheritance relationship. You already know that overloaded methods can appear within the same class. In addition, a method in a subclass can overload a method in the superclass. If class A is the superclass and class B is the subclass, a method in class B can overload a method in class A, or another method in class B. Overriding, on the other hand, can take place only in an inheritance relationship. If class A is the superclass and class B is the subclass, a method in class B can override a method in class A. However, a method cannot override another method in the same class. The following list summarizes the distinction between overloading and overriding.

- If two methods have the same name but different signatures, they are overloaded. This is true where the methods are in the same class or where one method is in the superclass and the other method is in the subclass.
- If a method in a subclass has the same signature as a method in the superclass, the subclass method overrides the superclass method.

The distinction between overloading and overriding is important because it can affect the accessibility of superclass methods in a subclass. When a subclass overloads a superclass method, both methods can be called with a subclass object. However, when a subclass overrides a superclass method, only the subclass's version of the method can be called with a subclass object. For example, look at the SuperClass3 class in Code Listing 9-15. It has two overloaded methods named showValue. One of the methods accepts an int argument and the other accepts a String argument.

Code Listing 9-15   (SuperClass3.java)

```
1  public class SuperClass3
2  {
3     /**
4      *  The following method displays an int.
5      */
6
```

```
 7       public void showValue(int arg)
 8       {
 9          System.out.println("SUPERCLASS: The int " +
10                                   "argument was " + arg);
11       }
12
13       /**
14        *  The following method displays a String.
15        */
16
17       public void showValue(String arg)
18       {
19          System.out.println("SUPERCLASS: The String " +
20                                   "argument was " + arg);
21       }
22    }
```

Now look at the SubClass3 class in Code Listing 9-16. It inherits from the SuperClass3 class.

Code Listing 9-16   (SubClass3.java)

```
 1   public class SubClass3 extends SuperClass3
 2   {
 3      /**
 4       *  The following method overrides one of
 5       *  the superclass methods.
 6       */
 7
 8      public void showValue(int arg)
 9      {
10         System.out.println("SUBCLASS: The int " +
11                                  "argument was " + arg);
12      }
13
14      /**
15       *  The following method overloads the base
16       *  class methods.
17       */
18
19      public void showValue(double arg)
20      {
21         System.out.println("SUBCLASS: The double " +
22                                  "argument was " + arg);
23      }
24   }
```

Notice that SubClass3 also has two methods named showValue. The first one accepts an int argument. This method overrides one of the superclass methods because they have the same signature. The second showValue method accepts a double argument. This method overloads the other showValue methods because none of the others have the same signature. Although there is a total of four showValue methods in these classes, only three of them can be called from a SubClass3 object. This is demonstrated in Code Listing 9-17.

Code Listing 9-17   (ShowValueDemo.java)

```
1   /**
2    * This program demonstrates the methods in the
3    * SuperClass3 and SubClass3 classes.
4    */
5
6   public class ShowValueDemo
7   {
8      public static void main(String[] args)
9      {
10         SubClass3 myObject = new SubClass3();
11
12         myObject.showValue(10);       // Pass an int.
13         myObject.showValue(1.2);      // Pass a double.
14         myObject.showValue("Hello");  // Pass a String.
15      }
16   }
```

Program Output

```
SUBCLASS: The int argument was 10
SUBCLASS: The double argument was 1.2
SUPERCLASS: The String argument was Hello
```

When an int argument is passed to showValue, the subclass's method is called because it overrides the superclass method. In order to call the overridden superclass method, we would have to use the super key word in the subclass method. Here is an example:

```
public void showValue(int arg)
{
   super.showValue(arg);   // Call the superclass method.
   System.out.println("SUBCLASS: The int " +
                      "argument was " + arg);
}
```

Preventing a Method from Being Overridden

When a method is declared with the `final` modifier, it cannot be overridden in a subclass. The following method header is an example that uses the `final` modifier:

```
public final void message()
```

If a subclass attempts to override a `final` method, the compiler generates an error. This technique can be used to make sure that a particular superclass method is used by subclasses and not a modified version of it.

Checkpoint

9.6   Under what circumstances would a subclass need to override a superclass method?

9.7   How can a subclass method call an overridden superclass method?

9.8   If a method in a subclass has the same signature as a method in the superclass, does the subclass method overload or override the superclass method?

9.9   If a method in a subclass has the same name as a method in the superclass, but uses a different parameter list, does the subclass method overload or override the superclass method?

9.10   How do you prevent a method from being overridden?

9.4 Protected Members

CONCEPT: Protected members of a class can be accessed by methods in a subclass, and by methods in the same package as the class.

Until now you have used two access specifications within a class: `private` and `public`. Java provides a third access specification, `protected`. A protected member of a class can be directly accessed by methods of the same class or methods of a subclass. In addition, protected members can be accessed by methods of any class that are in the same package as the protected member's class. A protected member is not quite private, because it can be accessed by some methods outside the class. Protected members are not quite public either because access to them is restricted to methods in the same class, subclasses, and classes in the same package as the member's class. A protected member's access is somewhere between private and public.

Let's look at a class with a protected member. Code Listing 9-18 shows the `GradedActivity2` class, which is a modification of the `GradedActivity` class presented earlier. In this class, the `score` field has been made protected instead of private.

Code Listing 9-18   (`GradedActivity2.java`)

```
1  /**
2   * A class that holds a grade for a graded activity.
3   */
4
```

```
 5   public class GradedActivity2
 6   {
 7      protected double score;  // Numeric score
 8
 9      /**
10       * The setScore method stores its argument in
11       * the score field.
12       */
13
14      public void setScore(double s)
15      {
16         score = s;
17      }
18
19      /**
20       * The getScore method returns the score field.
21       */
22
23      public double getScore()
24      {
25         return score;
26      }
27
28      /**
29       * The getGrade method returns a letter grade
30       * determined from the score field.
31       */
32
33      public char getGrade()
34      {
35         char letterGrade;   // To hold the grade
36
37         if (score >= 90)
38            letterGrade = 'A';
39         else if (score >= 80)
40            letterGrade = 'B';
41         else if (score >= 70)
42            letterGrade = 'C';
43         else if (score >= 60)
44            letterGrade = 'D';
45         else
46            letterGrade = 'F';
47
48         return letterGrade;
49      }
50   }
```

Because the score field is declared as protected, any class that inherits from this class has direct access to it. The FinalExam2 class, shown in Code Listing 9-19, is an example. This class is a modification of the FinalExam class, which was presented earlier. This class has a new method, adjustScore, which directly accesses the superclass's score field. If the contents of score have a fractional part of .5 or greater, the method rounds score up to the next whole number. The adjustScore method is called from the constructor.

Code Listing 9-19   (FinalExam2.java)

```java
 1  /**
 2   * This class determines the grade for a final exam. The
 3   * numeric score is rounded up to the next whole number
 4   * if its fractional part is .5 or greater.
 5   */
 6
 7  public class FinalExam2 extends GradedActivity2
 8  {
 9     private int numQuestions;   // Number of questions
10     private double pointsEach; // Points for each question
11     private int numMissed;      // Number of questions missed
12
13     /**
14      * The constructor accepts as arguments the number
15      * of questions on the exam and the number of
16      * questions the student missed.
17      */
18
19     public FinalExam2(int questions, int missed)
20     {
21        double numericScore;   // To hold the numeric score
22
23        // Set the numQuestions and numMissed fields.
24        numQuestions = questions;
25        numMissed = missed;
26
27        // Calculate the points for each question and
28        // the numeric score for this exam.
29        pointsEach = 100.0 / questions;
30        numericScore = 100.0 - (missed * pointsEach);
31
32        // Call the superclass's setScore method to
33        // set the numeric score.
34        setScore(numericScore);
35        adjustScore();
36     }
```

```
37
38      /**
39       * The getPointsEach method returns the pointsEach
40       * field.
41       */
42
43      public double getPointsEach()
44      {
45          return pointsEach;
46      }
47
48      /**
49       * The getNumMissed method returns the numMissed
50       * field.
51       */
52
53      public int getNumMissed()
54      {
55          return numMissed;
56      }
57
58      /**
59       * The adjustScore method adjusts a numeric score.
60       * If score is within 0.5 points of the next whole
61       * number, it rounds the score up.
62       */
63
64      private void adjustScore()
65      {
66          double fraction;  // Fractional part of a score
67
68          // Get the fractional part of the score.
69          fraction = score - (int) score;
70
71          // If the fractional part is 0.5 or greater,
72          // round the score up to the next whole number.
73          if (fraction >= 0.5)
74              score = score + (1.0 - fraction);
75      }
76  }
```

The program in Code Listing 9-20 demonstrates the class.

Code Listing 9-20   (`ProtectedDemo.java`)

```java
 1  import java.util.Scanner;
 2
 3  /**
 4   * This program demonstrates the FinalExam2 class, which
 5   * inherits from the GradedActivity2 class.
 6   */
 7
 8  public class ProtectedDemo
 9  {
10     public static void main(String[] args)
11     {
12        int questions,   // Number of questions
13            missed;      // Number of questions missed
14
15        // Create a Scanner object for keyboard input.
16        Scanner keyboard = new Scanner(System.in);
17
18        // Get the number of questions on the final exam.
19        System.out.print("How many questions are on " +
20                         "the final exam? ");
21        questions = keyboard.nextInt();
22
23        // Get the number of questions the student missed.
24        System.out.print("How many questions did the " +
25                         "student miss? ");
26        missed = keyboard.nextInt();
27
28        // Create a FinalExam2 object.
29        FinalExam2 exam =
30                   new FinalExam2(questions, missed);
31
32        // Display the test results.
33        System.out.println("Each question counts " +
34                           exam.getPointsEach() +
35                           " points.");
36        System.out.println("The exam score is " +
37                           exam.getScore());
38        System.out.println("The exam grade is " +
39                           exam.getGrade());
40     }
41  }
```

Program Output with Example Input Shown in Bold

```
How many questions are on the final exam? 40 [Enter]
How many questions did the student miss? 5 [Enter]
Each question counts 2.5 points.
The exam score is 88.0
The exam grade is B
```

In the example running of the program, the student missed 5 out of 40 questions. The unadjusted numeric score would be 87.5, but the `adjustScore` method rounded the `score` field up to 88.

Protected class members can be denoted in a UML diagram with the # symbol. Figure 9-9 shows a UML diagram for the `GradedActivity2` class, with the score field denoted as protected.

Figure 9-9   UML diagram for the `GradedActivity2` class

```
┌─────────────────────────────┐
│      GradedActivity2         │
├─────────────────────────────┤
│ # score : double            │
├─────────────────────────────┤
│ + setScore(s : double) : void│
│ + getScore() : double       │
│ + getGrade() : char         │
└─────────────────────────────┘
```

Although making a class member protected instead of private might make some tasks easier, you should avoid this practice when possible. This is because any class that inherits from the class, or is in the same package, has unrestricted access to the protected member. It is always better to make all fields private and then provide public methods for accessing those fields.

Package Access

If you do not provide an access specifier for a class member, the class member is given *package access* by default. This means that any method in the same package can access the member. Here is an example:

```
public class Circle
{
    double radius;
    int centerX, centerY;

    (Method definitions follow . . .)
}
```

In this class, the radius, centerX, and centerY fields were not given an access specifier, so the compiler grants them package access. Any method in the same package as the Circle class can directly access these members.

There is a subtle difference between protected access and package access. Protected members can be accessed by methods in the same package or in a subclass. This is true even if the subclass is in a different package. Members with package access, however, cannot be accessed by subclasses that are in a different package.

It is more likely that you will give package access to class members by accident than by design, because it is easy to forget the access specifier. Although there are circumstances under which package access can be helpful, you should normally avoid it. Be careful to always specify an access specifier for class members.

Tables 9-3 and 9-4 summarize how each of the access specifiers affect a class member's accessibility within and outside of the class's package.

Table 9-3   Accessibility from within the class's package

Access Modifier	Accessible to a subclass inside the same package?	Accessible to all other classes in the same package?
default (no modifier)	Yes	Yes
public	Yes	Yes
protected	Yes	Yes
private	No	No

Table 9-4   Accessibility from outside the class's package

Access Modifier	Accessible to a subclass outside the package?	Accessible to all other classes outside the package?
default (no modifier)	No	No
public	Yes	Yes
protected	Yes	No
private	No	No

 Checkpoint

9.11   When a class member is declared as protected, what code can access it?

9.12   What is the difference between private members and protected members?

9.13   Why should you avoid making class members protected when possible?

9.14   What is the difference between private access and package access?

9.15   Why is it easy to give package access to a class member by accident?

9.5 Classes That Inherit from Subclasses

CONCEPT: A superclass can also inherit from another class.

Sometimes it is desirable to establish a chain of inheritance in which one class inherits from a second class, which in turn inherits from a third class, as illustrated by Figure 9-10. In some cases, this chaining of classes goes on for many layers.

Figure 9-10 A chain of inheritance

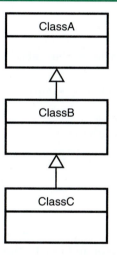

In Figure 9-10, ClassC inherits ClassB's members, including the ones that ClassB inherited from ClassA. Let's look at an example of such a chain of inheritance. Consider the PassFailActivity class, shown in Code Listing 9-21, which inherits from the GradedActivity class. The class is intended to determine a letter grade of "P" for passing, or "F" for failing.

Code Listing 9-21   (PassFailActivity.java)

```
1  /**
2   * This class holds a numeric score and determines
3   * whether the score is passing or failing.
4   */
5
6  public class PassFailActivity extends GradedActivity
7  {
8     private double minPassingScore;  // Minimum passing score
9
10    /**
11     * The constructor accepts the minimum passing
12     * score as its argument.
13     */
```

```
14
15      public PassFailActivity(double mps)
16      {
17         minPassingScore = mps;
18      }
19
20      /**
21       * The getGrade method returns a letter grade
22       * determined from the score field. This
23       * method overrides the superclass method.
24       */
25
26      public char getGrade()
27      {
28         char letterGrade; // To hold the letter grade
29
30         if (super.getScore() >= minPassingScore)
31            letterGrade = 'P';
32         else
33            letterGrade = 'F';
34
35         return letterGrade;
36      }
37   }
```

The `PassFailActivity` constructor, in lines 15 through 18, accepts a `double` argument that is the minimum passing grade for the activity. This value is stored in the `minPassingScore` field. The `getGrade` method in lines 26 through 36, which overrides the superclass method, returns a grade of `"P"` if the numeric score is greater than or equal to `minPassingScore`. Otherwise, the method returns a grade of `"F"`.

Suppose we wish to extend this class with another class that is even more specialized. For example, the `PassFailExam` class, shown in Code Listing 9-22, determines a passing or failing grade for an exam. It has fields for the number of questions on the exam (`numQuestions`), the number of points each question is worth (`pointsEach`), and the number of questions missed by the student (`numMissed`).

Code Listing 9-22   (`PassFailExam.java`)

```
1  /**
2   * This class determines a passing or failing grade for
3   * an exam.
4   */
5
6  public class PassFailExam extends PassFailActivity
7  {
```

```
 8      private int numQuestions;    // Number of questions
 9      private double pointsEach;  // Points for each question
10      private int numMissed;       // Number of questions missed
11
12      /**
13       * The constructor accepts as arguments the number
14       * of questions on the exam, the number of
15       * questions the student missed, and the minimum
16       * passing score.
17       */
18
19      public PassFailExam(int questions, int missed,
20                          double minPassing)
21      {
22         // Call the superclass constructor.
23         super(minPassing);
24
25         // Declare a local variable for the numeric score.
26         double numericScore;
27
28         // Set the numQuestions and numMissed fields.
29         numQuestions = questions;
30         numMissed = missed;
31
32         // Calculate the points for each question and
33         // the numeric score for this exam.
34         pointsEach = 100.0 / questions;
35         numericScore = 100.0 - (missed * pointsEach);
36
37         // Call the superclass's setScore method to
38         // set the numeric score.
39         setScore(numericScore);
40      }
41
42      /**
43       * The getPointsEach method returns the pointsEach
44       * field.
45       */
46
47      public double getPointsEach()
48      {
49         return pointsEach;
50      }
51
52      /**
53       * The getNumMissed method returns the numMissed
54       * field.
55       */
```

```
56
57     public int getNumMissed()
58     {
59        return numMissed;
60     }
61  }
```

The PassFailExam class inherits the PassFailActivity class's members, including the ones that PassFailActivity inherited from GradedActivity. The program in Code Listing 9-23 demonstrates the class.

Code Listing 9-23 (PassFailExamDemo.java)

```java
1   import java.util.Scanner;
2
3   /**
4    *  This program demonstrates the PassFailExam class.
5    */
6
7   public class PassFailExamDemo
8   {
9      public static void main(String[] args)
10     {
11        int questions,     // Number of questions
12            missed;        // Number of questions missed
13        double minPassing; // Minimum passing score
14
15        // Create a Scanner object for keyboard input.
16        Scanner keyboard = new Scanner(System.in);
17
18        // Get the number of questions on the exam.
19        System.out.print("How many questions are " +
20                         "on the exam? ");
21        questions = keyboard.nextInt();
22
23        // Get the number of questions the student missed.
24        System.out.print("How many questions did the " +
25                         "student miss? ");
26        missed = keyboard.nextInt();
27
28        // Get the minimum passing score.
29        System.out.print("What is the minimum " +
30                         "passing score? ");
31        minPassing = keyboard.nextInt();
32
33        // Create a PassFailExam object.
```

```
34          PassFailExam exam =
35               new PassFailExam(questions, missed, minPassing);
36
37          // Display the test results.
38          System.out.println("Each question counts " +
39                              exam.getPointsEach() +
40                              " points.");
41          System.out.println("The exam score is " +
42                              exam.getScore());
43          System.out.println("The exam grade is " +
44                              exam.getGrade());
45     }
46  }
```

Program Output with Example Input Shown in Bold

```
How many questions are on the exam? 100 [Enter]
How many questions did the student miss? 25 [Enter]
What is the minimum passing score? 60 [Enter]
Each question counts 1.0 points.
The exam score is 75.0
The exam grade is P
```

Figure 9-11 shows a UML diagram depicting the inheritance relationship among the GradedActivity, PassFailActivity, and PassFailExam classes.

Figure 9-11   The GradedActivity, PassFailActivity, and PassFailExam classes

Class Hierarchies

Classes often are depicted graphically in a *class hierarchy*. Like a family tree, a class hierarchy shows the inheritance relationships among classes. Figure 9-12 shows a class hierarchy for the `GradedActivity`, `FinalExam`, `PassFailActivity`, and `PassFailExam` classes. The more general classes are toward the top of the tree and the more specialized classes are toward the bottom.

Figure 9-12 Class hierarchy

9.6 The `Object` Class

CONCEPT: The Java API has a class named `Object`, which all other classes directly or indirectly inherit from.

Every class in Java, including the ones in the API and the classes that you create, directly or indirectly inherit from a class named `Object`, which is part of the `java.lang` package. Here's how it happens: When a class does not use the `extends` key word to inherit from another class, Java automatically extends it from the `Object` class. For example, look at the following class declaration:

```
public class MyClass
{
    (Member Declarations . . .)
}
```

This class does not explicitly extend any other class, so Java treats it as though it were written as:

```
public class MyClass extends Object
{
    (Member Declarations . . .)
}
```

Ultimately, every class inherits from the `Object` class. Figure 9-13 shows how the `PassFailExam` class ultimately inherits from `Object`.

Figure 9-13   The line of inheritance from `Object` to `PassFailExam`

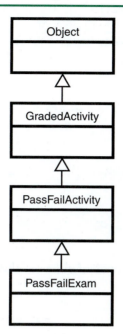

Because every class directly or indirectly inherits from the `Object` class, every class inherits the `Object` class's members. Two of the most useful are the `toString` and `equals` methods. In Chapter 6 you learned that every object has a `toString` and an `equals` method, and now you know why! It is because those methods are inherited from the `Object` class.

In the `Object` class, the `toString` method returns a string containing the object's class name, followed by the @ character, followed by the object's hexadecimal hashcode. (An object's hashcode is an integer that is unique to the object.) The `equals` method accepts the address of an object as its argument and returns `true` if it is the same as the calling object's address. This is demonstrated in Code Listing 9-24.

Code Listing 9-24   **(ObjectMethods.java)**

```
1   /**
2    *  This program demonstrates the toString and equals
3    *  methods that are inherited from the Object class.
4    */
5
6   public class ObjectMethods
7   {
8      public static void main(String[] args)
9      {
10        // Create two objects.
11        PassFailExam exam1 = new PassFailExam(0, 0, 0);
12        PassFailExam exam2 = new PassFailExam(0, 0, 0);
13
14        // Send the objects to println, which will
15        // call the toString method.
```

```
16          System.out.println(exam1);
17          System.out.println(exam2);
18
19          // Test the equals method.
20          if (exam1.equals(exam2))
21              System.out.println("The two are the same.");
22          else
23              System.out.println("The two are not the same.");
24      }
25  }
```

Program Output

```
PassFailExam@45a877
PassFailExam@1372a1a
The two are not the same.
```

If you wish to change the behavior of either of these methods for a given class, you must override them in the class.

Checkpoint

9.16   Look at the following class definition:

```
public class ClassD extends ClassB
{
    (Member Declarations . . .)
}
```

Because ClassD inherits from ClassB, is it true that ClassD does not inherit from the Object class? Why or why not?

9.17   When you create a class, it automatically has a toString method and an equals method. Why?

9.7   Polymorphism

VideoNote
Polymorphism

CONCEPT: A reference variable can reference objects of classes that inherit from the variable's class.

Look at the following statement that declares a reference variable named exam.

```
GradedActivity exam;
```

This statement tells us that the exam variable's data type is GradedActivity. Therefore, we can use the exam variable to reference a GradedActivity object, as shown in the following statement.

```
exam = new GradedActivity();
```

The GradedActivity class is also used as the superclass for the FinalExam class. Because of the "is-a" relationship between a superclass and a subclass, an object of the FinalExam class is not just a `FinalExam` object. It is also a `GradedActivity` object. (A final exam *is a* graded activity.) Because of this relationship, we can use a `GradedActivity` variable to reference a `FinalExam` object. For example, look at the following statement:

```
GradedActivity exam = new FinalExam(50, 7);
```

This statement declares exam as a `GradedActivity` variable. It creates a `FinalExam` object and stores the object's address in the exam variable. This statement is perfectly legal and will not cause an error message because a `FinalExam` object is also a `GradedActivity` object.

This is an example of polymorphism. The term *polymorphism* means the ability to take many forms. In Java, a reference variable is *polymorphic* because it can reference objects of types different from its own, as long as those types are related to its type through inheritance. All of the following declarations are legal because the `FinalExam`, `PassFailActivity`, and `PassFailExam` classes inherit from `GradedActivity`.

```
GradedActivity exam1 = new FinalExam(50, 7);
GradedActivity exam2 = new PassFailActivity(70);
GradedActivity exam3 = new PassFailExam(100, 10, 70);
```

Although a `GradedActivity` variable can reference objects of any class that inherits from `GradedActivity`, there is a limit to what the variable can do with those objects. Recall that the `GradedActivity` class has three methods: `setScore`, `getScore`, and `getGrade`. So, a `GradedActivity` variable can be used to call only those three methods, regardless of the type of object the variable references. For example, look at the following code.

```
GradedActivity exam = new PassFailExam(100, 10, 70);
System.out.println(exam.getScore());       // This works.
System.out.println(exam.getGrade());       // This works.
System.out.println(exam.getPointsEach());  // ERROR! Won't work.
```

In this code, exam is declared as a `GradedActivity` variable and is assigned the address of a `PassFailExam` object. The `GradedActivity` class has only the `setScore`, `getScore`, and `getGrade` methods, so those are the only methods that the exam variable knows how to execute. The last statement in this code is a call to the `getPointsEach` method, which is defined in the `PassFailExam` class. Because the exam variable knows only about methods in the `GradedActivity` class, it cannot execute this method.

Polymorphism and Dynamic Binding

When a superclass variable references a subclass object, a potential problem exists. What if the subclass has overridden a method in the superclass, and the variable makes a call to that method? Does the variable call the superclass's version of the method, or the subclass's version? For example, look at the following code.

```
GradedActivity exam = new PassFailActivity(60);
exam.setScore(70);
System.out.println(exam.getGrade());
```

Recall that the `PassFailActivity` class inherits from the `GradedActivity` class, and it overrides the `getGrade` method. When the last statement calls the `getGrade` method, does it call the `GradedActivity` class's version (which returns "A", "B", "C", "D", or "F") or does it call the `PassFailActivity` class's version (which returns "P" or "F")?

Recall from Chapter 6 that the process of matching a method call with the correct method definition is known as binding. Java performs *dynamic binding* or *late binding* when a variable contains a polymorphic reference. This means that the Java Virtual Machine determines at runtime which method to call, depending on the type of object that the variable references. So, it is the object's type that determines which method is called, not the variable's type. In this case, the exam variable references a PassFailActivity object, so the PassFailActivity class's version of the getGrade method is called. The last statement in this code will display a grade of P.

The program in Code Listing 9-25 demonstrates polymorphic behavior. It declares an array of GradedActivity variables, and then assigns the addresses of objects of various types to the elements of the array.

Code Listing 9-25   (Polymorphic.java)

```java
1  /**
2   *  This program demonstrates polymorphic behavior.
3   */
4
5  public class Polymorphic
6  {
7     public static void main(String[] args)
8     {
9        // Create an array of GradedActivity references.
10       GradedActivity[] tests = new GradedActivity[3];
11
12       // The first test is a regular exam with a
13       // numeric score of 95.
14       tests[0] = new GradedActivity();
15       tests[0].setScore(95);
16
17       // The second test is a pass/fail test. The
18       // student missed 5 out of 20 questions, and the
19       // minimum passing grade is 60.
20       tests[1] = new PassFailExam(20, 5, 60);
21
22       // The third test is the final exam. There were
23       // 50 questions and the student missed 7.
24       tests[2] = new FinalExam(50, 7);
25
26       // Display the grades.
27       for (int index = 0; index < tests.length; index++)
28       {
29          System.out.println("Test " + (index+ 1) + ": " +
30                             "score " + tests[index].getScore() +
31                             ", grade " + tests[index].getGrade());
32       }
33    }
34 }
```

Program Output

```
Test 1: score 95.0, grade A
Test 2: score 75.0, grade P
Test 3: score 86.0, grade B
```

You can also use parameters to polymorphically accept arguments to methods. For example, look at the following method.

```java
public static void displayGrades(GradedActivity g)
{
    System.out.println("Score " + g.getScore() +
                       ", grade " + g.getGrade());
}
```

This method's parameter, g, is a GradedActivity variable. But, it can be used to accept arguments of any type that inherits from GradedActivity. For example, the following code passes objects of the FinalExam, PassFailActivity, and PassFailExam classes to the method.

```java
GradedActivity exam1 = new FinalExam(50, 7);
GradedActivity exam2 = new PassFailActivity(70);
GradedActivity exam3 = new PassFailExam(100, 10, 70);
displayGrades(exam1);   // Pass a FinalExam object.
displayGrades(exam2);   // Pass a PassFailActivity object.
displayGrades(exam3);   // Pass a PassFailExam object.
```

The "Is-a" Relationship Does Not Work in Reverse

It is important to note that the "is-a" relationship does not work in reverse. Although the statement "a final exam is a graded activity" is true, the statement "a graded activity is a final exam" is not true. This is because not all graded activities are final exams. Likewise, not all GradedActivity objects are FinalExam objects. So, the following code will not work.

```java
GradedActivity activity = new GradedActivity();
FinalExam exam = activity;    // ERROR!
```

You cannot assign the address of a GradedActivity object to a FinalExam variable. This makes sense because FinalExam objects have capabilities that go beyond those of a GradedActivity object. Interestingly, the Java compiler will let you make such an assignment if you use a type cast, as shown here:

```java
GradedActivity activity = new GradedActivity();
FinalExam exam = (FinalExam) activity;  // Will compile but not run.
```

But, the program will crash when the assignment statement executes.

The instanceof Operator

There is an operator in Java named instanceof that you can use to determine whether an object is an instance of a particular class. Here is the general form of an expression that uses the instanceof operator.

```
refVar instanceof ClassName
```

In the general form, *refVar* is a reference variable and *ClassName* is the name of a class. This is the form of a boolean expression that will return true if the object referenced by *refVar* is an instance of *ClassName*. Otherwise, the expression returns false. For example, the if statement in the following code determines whether the reference variable activity references a GradedActivity object:

```
GradedActivity activity = new GradedActivity();
if (activity instanceof GradedActivity)
    System.out.println("Yes, activity is a GradedActivity.");
else
    System.out.println("No, activity is not a GradedActivity.");
```

This code will display "Yes, activity is a GradedActivity."

The instanceof operator understands the "is-a" relationship that exists when a class inherits from another class. For example, look at the following code.

```
FinalExam exam = new FinalExam(20, 2);
if (exam instanceof GradedActivity)
    System.out.println("Yes, exam is a GradedActivity.");
else
    System.out.println("No, exam is not a GradedActivity.");
```

Even though the object referenced by exam is a FinalExam object, this code will display "Yes, exam is a GradedActivity." The instanceof operator returns true because FinalExam is a subclass of GradedActivity.

Checkpoint

9.18   Recall the Rectangle and Cube classes discussed earlier, as shown in Figure 9-14.

Figure 9-14   Rectangle and Cube classes

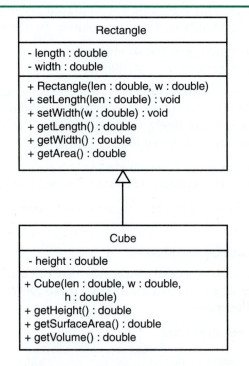

a. Is the following statement legal or illegal? If it is illegal, why?

```
Rectangle r = new Cube(10, 12, 5);
```

b. If you determined that the statement in Part a is legal, are the following statements legal or illegal? (Indicate legal or illegal for each statement.)

```
System.out.println(r.getLength());
System.out.println(r.getWidth());
System.out.println(r.getHeight());
System.out.println(r.getSurfaceArea());
```

c. Is the following statement legal or illegal? If it is illegal, why?

```
Cube c = new Rectangle(10, 12);
```

9.8 Abstract Classes and Abstract Methods

CONCEPT: An abstract class is not instantiated, but other classes inherit from it. An abstract method has no body and must be overridden in a subclass.

An *abstract method* is a method that appears in a superclass, but expects to be overridden in a subclass. An abstract method has only a header and no body. Here is the general format of an abstract method header.

```
AccessSpecifier abstract ReturnType MethodName(ParameterList);
```

Notice that the key word `abstract` appears in the header, and that the header ends with a semicolon. There is no body for the method. Here is an example of an abstract method header:

```
public abstract void setValue(int value);
```

When an abstract method appears in a class, the method must be overridden in a subclass. If a subclass fails to override the method, an error will result. Abstract methods are used to ensure that a subclass implements the method.

When a class contains an abstract method, you cannot create an instance of the class. Abstract methods are commonly used in abstract classes. An *abstract class* is not instantiated itself, but serves as a superclass for other classes. The abstract class represents the generic or abstract form of all the classes that inherit from it.

For example, consider a factory that manufactures airplanes. The factory does not make a generic airplane, but makes three specific types of airplanes: two different models of prop-driven planes and one commuter jet model. The computer software that catalogs the planes might use an abstract class named `Airplane`. That class has members representing the common characteristics of all airplanes. In addition, the software has classes for each of the three specific airplane models the factory manufactures. These classes all inherit from the `Airplane` class, and they have members representing the unique characteristics of each type of plane. The `Airplane` class is never instantiated, but is used as a superclass for the other classes.

A class becomes abstract when you place the `abstract` key word in the class definition. Here is the general format:

```
public abstract class ClassName
```

For example, look at the following abstract class Student shown in Code Listing 9-26. It holds data common to all students, but does not hold all the data needed for students of specific majors.

Code Listing 9-26   (Student.java)

```java
 1  /**
 2   * The Student class is an abstract class that holds
 3   * general data about a student. Classes representing
 4   * specific types of students should inherit from
 5   * this class.
 6   */
 7
 8  public abstract class Student
 9  {
10     private String name;      // Student name
11     private String idNumber;  // Student ID
12     private int yearAdmitted; // Year student was admitted
13
14     /**
15      * The Constructor accepts as arguments the
16      * student's name, ID number, and the year
17      * admitted.
18      */
19
20     public Student(String n, String id, int year)
21     {
22        name = n;
23        idNumber = id;
24        yearAdmitted = year;
25     }
26
27     /**
28      *  toString method
29      */
30
31     public String toString()
32     {
33        String str;
34
35        str = "Name: " + name
36              + "\nID Number: " + idNumber
37              + "\nYear Admitted: " + yearAdmitted;
38
39        return str;
40     }
```

```
41
42      /**
43       * The getRemainingHours method is abstract.
44       * It must be overridden in a subclass.
45       */
46
47      public abstract int getRemainingHours();
48  }
```

The Student class contains fields for storing a student's name, ID number, and year admitted. It also has a constructor, a toString method, and an abstract method named getRemainingHours.

This abstract method must be overridden in classes that inherit from the Student class. The idea behind this method is for it to return the number of hours remaining for a student to take in his or her major. It was made abstract because this class is intended to be the base for other classes that represent students of specific majors. For example, a CompSciStudent class might hold the data for a computer science student, and a BiologyStudent class might hold the data for a biology student. Computer science students must take courses in different disciplines than those taken by biology students. It stands to reason that the CompSciStudent class will calculate the number of hours remaining to be taken in a different manner than the BiologyStudent class. Let's look at an example of the CompSciStudent class, which is shown in Code Listing 9-27.

Code Listing 9-27   (CompSciStudent.java)

```
1  /**
2   * This class holds data for a computer science student.
3   */
4
5  public class CompSciStudent extends Student
6  {
7      // Constants for the math, computer science, and
8      // general education hours required for graduation.
9      private final int MATH_HOURS = 20,
10                       CS_HOURS = 40,
11                       GEN_ED_HOURS = 60;
12
13      private int mathHours,  // Math hours taken
14                  csHours,    // Comp. sci. hours taken
15                  genEdHours; // General ed hours taken
16
17      /**
18       * The Constructor accepts as arguments the
19       * student's name, ID number, and the year
20       * admitted.
21       */
```

```
22
23      public CompSciStudent(String n, String id, int year)
24      {
25         super(n, id, year);
26      }
27
28      /**
29       * The setMathHours method accepts a value for
30       * the number of math hours taken.
31       */
32
33      public void setMathHours(int math)
34      {
35         mathHours = math;
36      }
37
38      /**
39       * The setCsHours method accepts a value for
40       * the number of computer science hours taken.
41       */
42
43      public void setCsHours(int cs)
44      {
45         csHours = cs;
46      }
47
48      /**
49       * The setGenEdHours method accepts a value for
50       * the number of general education hours taken.
51       */
52
53      public void setGenEdHours(int genEd)
54      {
55         genEdHours = genEd;
56      }
57
58      /**
59       * toString method
60       */
61
62      public String toString()
63      {
64         String str; // To hold a string
65
```

```
66          // Create a string representing this computer
67          // science student's hours taken.
68          str = super.toString() +
69                "\nMajor: Computer Science" +
70                "\nMath Hours Taken: " + mathHours +
71                "\nComputer Science Hours Taken: " + csHours +
72                "\nGeneral Ed Hours Taken: " + genEdHours;
73
74          // Return the string.
75          return str;
76       }
77
78       /**
79        * The getRemainingHours method returns the
80        * the number of hours remaining to be taken.
81        */
82
83       public int getRemainingHours()
84       {
85          int reqHours,        // Total required hours
86              remainingHours;  // Remaining hours
87
88          // Calculate the total required hours.
89          reqHours = MATH_HOURS + CS_HOURS + GEN_ED_HOURS;
90
91          // Calculate the remaining hours.
92          remainingHours = reqHours - (mathHours + csHours
93                           + genEdHours);
94
95          // Return the remaining hours.
96          return remainingHours;
97       }
98    }
```

The CompSciStudent class, which inherits from the Student class, declares the following final integer fields in lines 9 through 11: MATH_HOURS, CS_HOURS, and GEN_ED_HOURS. These fields hold the required number of math, computer science, and general education hours for a computer science student. It also declares the following fields in lines 13 through 15: mathHours, csHours, and genEdHours. These fields hold the number of math, computer science, and general education hours taken by the student. Mutator methods are provided to store values in these fields. In addition, the class overrides the toString method and the abstract getRemainingHours method. The program in Code Listing 9-28 demonstrates the class.

Code Listing 9-28   (CompSciStudentDemo.java)

```
 1  /**
 2   * This program demonstrates the CompSciStudent class.
 3   */
 4
 5  public class CompSciStudentDemo
 6  {
 7     public static void main(String[] args)
 8     {
 9        // Create a CompSciStudent object.
10        CompSciStudent csStudent =
11           new CompSciStudent("Jennifer Haynes",
12                                "167W98337", 2011);
13
14        // Store values for Math, CS, and General Ed hours.
15        csStudent.setMathHours(12);
16        csStudent.setCsHours(20);
17        csStudent.setGenEdHours(40);
18
19        // Display the student's data.
20        System.out.println(csStudent);
21
22        // Display the number of remaining hours.
23        System.out.println("Hours remaining: " +
24                               csStudent.getRemainingHours());
25     }
26  }
```

Program Output

```
Name: Jennifer Haynes
ID Number: 167W98337
Year Admitted: 2011
Major: Computer Science
Math Hours Taken: 12
Computer Science Hours Taken: 20
General Ed Hours Taken: 40
Hours remaining: 48
```

Remember the following points about abstract methods and classes:

- Abstract methods and abstract classes are defined with the abstract key word.
- Abstract methods have no body, and their header must end with a semicolon.
- An abstract method must be overridden in a subclass.
- When a class contains an abstract method, it cannot be instantiated. It must serve as a superclass.
- An abstract class cannot be instantiated. It must serve as a superclass.

Abstract Classes in UML

Abstract classes are drawn like regular classes in UML, except the name of the class and the names of abstract methods are shown in italics. For example, Figure 9-15 shows a UML diagram for the Student class.

Figure 9-15   UML Diagram for the Student class

```
                    Student

- name : String
- idNumber: String
- yearAdmitted: int

+ Student(n : String, id : String,
            year : int)
+ toString() : String
+ getRemainingHours() : int
```

 Checkpoint

9.19   What is the purpose of an abstract method?

9.20   If a subclass extends a superclass with an abstract method, what must you do in the subclass?

9.21   What is the purpose of an abstract class?

9.22   If a class is defined as abstract, what can you not do with the class?

9.9 Interfaces

CONCEPT: An interface specifies behavior for a class.

In the previous section you learned that an abstract class cannot be instantiated, but is intended to serve as a superclass. You also learned that an abstract method has no body and must be overridden in a subclass. An *interface* is similar to an abstract class that has all abstract methods. It cannot be instantiated, and all of the methods listed in an interface must be written elsewhere. The purpose of an interface is to specify behavior for other classes.

An interface looks similar to a class, except the key word `interface` is used instead of the key word `class`, and the methods that are specified in an interface have no bodies, only headers that are terminated by semicolons. Here is the general format of an interface definition:

```
public interface InterfaceName
{
    (Method headers . . .)
}
```

For example, Code Listing 9-29 shows an interface named `Relatable`, which is intended to be used with the `GradedActivity` class presented earlier. This interface has three method headers: `equals`, `isGreater`, and `isLess`. Notice that each method accepts a `GradedActivity` object as its argument. Also notice that no access specifier is used with the method headers, because all methods specified by an interface are public.

Code Listing 9-29   (Relatable.java)

```
1  /**
2   *  Relatable interface
3   */
4
5  public interface Relatable
6  {
7     boolean equals(GradedActivity g);
8     boolean isGreater(GradedActivity g);
9     boolean isLess(GradedActivity g);
10 }
```

In order for a class to use an interface, it must *implement* the interface. This is accomplished with the `implements` key word. For example, suppose we have a class named `FinalExam3` that inherits from the `GradedActivity` class and implements the `Relatable` interface. The first line of its definition would look like this:

```
public class FinalExam3 extends GradedActivity implements Relatable
```

When a class implements an interface, it must provide all of the methods that are listed in the interface, with the exact signatures specified. In other words, it must override all of the methods specified by the interface. In addition, the methods must have the same return type specified in the interface. So, the `FinalExam3` class must provide an `equals` method, an `isGreater` method, and an `isLess` method, all of which accept a `GradedActivity` object as an argument and return a `boolean` value.

You might have guessed that the `Relatable` interface is named "Relatable" because it specifies methods that, presumably, make relational comparisons with `GradedActivity` objects. The intent is to make any class that implements this interface "relatable" with `GradedActivity` objects by ensuring that it has an `equals`, an `isGreater`, and an `isLess` method that perform relational comparisons. But, the interface specifies only the signatures for these methods, not what the methods should do. Although the programmer of a class that implements the `Relatable` interface can choose what those methods do, he or she should provide methods that comply with this intent.

Code Listing 9-30 shows the complete code for the `FinalExam3` class, which implements the `Relatable` interface. The `equals`, `isGreater`, and `isLess` methods compare the calling object with the object passed as an argument. The program in Code Listing 9-31 demonstrates the class.

Code Listing 9-30   `(FinalExam3.java)`

```java
 1  /**
 2   *  This class determines the grade for a final exam.
 3   */
 4
 5  public class FinalExam3 extends GradedActivity
 6                          implements Relatable
 7  {
 8     private int numQuestions;      // Number of questions
 9     private double pointsEach;     // Points for each question
10     private int numMissed;         // Number of questions missed
11
12     /**
13      * The constructor accepts as arguments the number
14      * of questions on the exam and the number of
15      * questions the student missed.
16      */
17
18     public FinalExam3(int questions, int missed)
19     {
20        double numericScore;          // To hold the numeric score
21
22        // Set the numQuestions and numMissed fields.
23        numQuestions = questions;
24        numMissed = missed;
25
26        // Calculate the points for each question and
27        // the numeric score for this exam.
28        pointsEach = 100.0 / questions;
29        numericScore = 100.0 - (missed * pointsEach);
30
31        // Call the superclass's setScore method to
32        // set the numeric score.
33        setScore(numericScore);
34     }
35
36     /**
37      * The getPointsEach method returns the pointsEach
38      * field.
39      */
40
41     public double getPointsEach()
42     {
43        return pointsEach;
44     }
45
```

```
46      /**
47       * The getNumMissed method returns the numMissed
48       * field.
49       */
50
51      public int getNumMissed()
52      {
53         return numMissed;
54      }
55
56      /**
57       * The equals method returns true if the calling
58       * object's score is equal to the argument's
59       * score.
60       */
61
62      public boolean equals(GradedActivity g)
63      {
64         boolean status; // Result of comparison
65
66         if (this.getScore() == g.getScore())
67            status = true;
68         else
69            status = false;
70
71         return status;
72      }
73
74      /**
75       * The isGreater method returns true if the calling
76       * object's score is greater than the argument's
77       * score.
78       */
79
80      public boolean isGreater(GradedActivity g)
81      {
82         boolean status; // Result of comparison
83
84         if (this.getScore() > g.getScore())
85            status = true;
86         else
87            status = false;
88
89         return status;
90      }
91
```

```
 92      /**
 93       * The isLess method returns true if the calling
 94       * object's score is less than the argument's
 95       * score.
 96       */
 97
 98      public boolean isLess(GradedActivity g)
 99      {
100         boolean status; // Result of comparison
101
102         if (this.getScore() < g.getScore())
103            status = true;
104         else
105            status = false;
106
107         return status;
108      }
109   }
```

Code Listing 9-31   (`InterfaceDemo.java`)

```
 1   /**
 2    * This program demonstrates the FinalExam3 class which
 3    * implements the Relatable interface.
 4    */
 5
 6   public class InterfaceDemo
 7   {
 8      public static void main(String[] args)
 9      {
10         // Exam #1 had 100 questions and the student
11         // missed 20 questions.
12         FinalExam3 exam1 = new FinalExam3(100, 20);
13
14         // Exam #2 had 100 questions and the student
15         // missed 30 questions.
16         FinalExam3 exam2 = new FinalExam3(100, 30);
17
18         // Display the exam scores.
19         System.out.println("Exam 1: " + exam1.getScore());
20         System.out.println("Exam 2: " + exam2.getScore());
21
22         // Compare the exam scores.
23         if (exam1.equals(exam2))
24            System.out.println("The exam scores are equal.");
25
```

```
26          if (exam1.isGreater(exam2))
27              System.out.println("The Exam 1 score is the highest.");
28
29          if (exam1.isLess(exam2))
30              System.out.println("The Exam 1 score is the lowest.");
31      }
32  }
```

Program Output

```
Exam 1: 80.0
Exam 2: 70.0
The Exam 1 score is the highest.
```

Fields in Interfaces

An interface can contain field declarations, but all fields in an interface are treated as `final` and `static`. Because they automatically become `final`, you must provide an initialization value. For example, look at the following interface definition:

```
public interface Doable
{
    int FIELD1 = 1,
        FIELD2 = 2;
    (Method headers . . .)
}
```

In this interface, `FIELD1` and `FIELD2` are `final static int` variables. Any class that implements this interface has access to these variables.

Implementing Multiple Interfaces

You might be wondering why we need both abstract classes and interfaces because they are so similar to each other. The reason is that a class can directly inherit from only one superclass, but Java allows a class to implement multiple interfaces. When a class implements multiple interfaces, it must provide the methods specified by all of them.

To specify multiple interfaces in a class definition, simply list the names of the interfaces, separated by commas, after the `implements` key word. Here is the first line of an example of a class that implements multiple interfaces:

```
public class MyClass implements Interface1,
                                Interface2,
                                Interface3
```

This class implements three interfaces: `Interface1`, `Interface2`, and `Interface3`.

Interfaces in UML

In a UML diagram, an interface is drawn like a class, except the interface name and the method names are italicized, and the <<interface>> tag is shown above the interface name. The relationship between a class and an interface is known as a *realization relationship* (the class realizes the interfaces). You show a realization relationship in a UML diagram by connecting a class and an interface with a dashed line that has an open arrowhead at one end. The arrowhead points to the interface. This depicts the realization relationship. Figure 9-16 shows a UML diagram depicting the relationships among the GradedActivity class, the FinalExam3 class, and the Relatable interface.

Figure 9-16   Realization relationship in a UML diagram

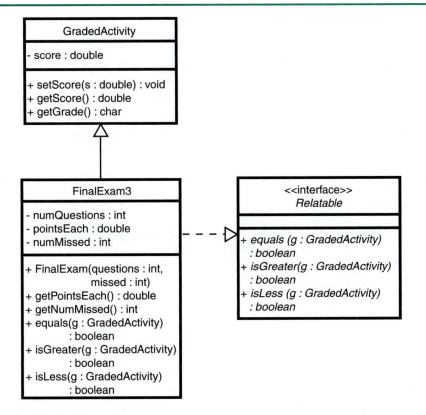

Polymorphism and Interfaces

Just as you can create reference variables of a class type, Java allows you to create reference variables of an interface type. An interface reference variable can reference any object that implements that interface, regardless of its class type. This is another example of polymorphism. For example, look at the RetailItem interface in Code Listing 9-32.

Code Listing 9-32   **(RetailItem.java)**

```
1  /**
2   * RetailItem interface
3   */
4
5  public interface RetailItem
6  {
7      public double getRetailPrice();
8  }
```

This interface specifies only one method: `getRetailPrice`. Both the `CompactDisc` and `DvdMovie` classes, shown in Code Listings 9-33 and 9-34, implement this interface.

Code Listing 9-33 (`CompactDisc.java`)

```java
 1  /**
 2   * Compact Disc class
 3   */
 4
 5  public class CompactDisc implements RetailItem
 6  {
 7     private String title;        // The CD's title
 8     private String artist;       // The CD's artist
 9     private double retailPrice;  // The CD's retail price
10
11     /**
12      * Constructor
13      */
14
15     public CompactDisc(String cdTitle, String cdArtist,
16                        double cdPrice)
17     {
18        title = cdTitle;
19        artist = cdArtist;
20        retailPrice = cdPrice;
21     }
22
23     /**
24      * getTitle method
25      */
26
27     public String getTitle()
28     {
29        return title;
30     }
31
32     /**
33      * getArtist method
34      */
35
36     public String getArtist()
37     {
38        return artist;
39     }
40
```

```
41      /**
42       * getRetailPrice method (Required by the RetailItem
43       * interface)
44       */
45
46      public double getRetailPrice()
47      {
48         return retailPrice;
49      }
50   }
```

Code Listing 9-34   (DvdMovie.java)

```
1   /**
2    * DvdMovie class
3    */
4
5   public class DvdMovie implements RetailItem
6   {
7      private String title;          // The DVD's title
8      private int runningTime;       // Running time in minutes
9      private double retailPrice;    // The DVD's retail price
10
11     /**
12      * Constructor
13      */
14
15     public DvdMovie(String dvdTitle, int runTime,
16                     double dvdPrice)
17     {
18        title = dvdTitle;
19        runningTime = runTime;
20        retailPrice = dvdPrice;
21     }
22
23     /**
24      * getTitle method
25      */
26
27     public String getTitle()
28     {
29        return title;
30     }
31
```

```
32      /**
33       * getRunningTime method
34       */
35
36      public int getRunningTime()
37      {
38          return runningTime;
39      }
40
41      /**
42       * getRetailPrice method (Required by the RetailItem
43       * interface)
44       */
45
46      public double getRetailPrice()
47      {
48          return retailPrice;
49      }
50  }
```

Because they implement the RetailItem interface, objects of these classes can be referenced by a RetailItem reference variable. The following code demonstrates.

```
RetailItem item1 = new CompactDisc("Songs From the Heart",
                                   "Billy Nelson",
                                   18.95);
RetailItem item2 = new DvdMovie("Planet X",
                                102,
                                22.95);
```

In this code, two RetailItem reference variables, item1 and item2, are declared. The item1 variable references a CompactDisc object and the item2 variable references a DvdMovie object. This is possible because both the CompactDisc and DvdMovie classes implement the RetailItem interface. When a class implements an interface, an inheritance relationship known as *interface inheritance* is established. Because of this inheritance relationship, a CompactDisc object *is a* RetailItem, and likewise, a DvdMovie object *is a* RetailItem. Therefore, we can create RetailItem reference variables and have them reference CompactDisc and DvdMovie objects.

The program in Code Listing 9-35 demonstrates how an interface reference variable can be used as a method parameter.

Code Listing 9-35   (PolymorphicInterfaceDemo.java)

```
1 /**
2  *  This program demonstrates that an interface type may
3  *  be used to create a polymorphic reference.
4  */
5
```

```
 6 public class PolymorphicInterfaceDemo
 7 {
 8    public static void main(String[] args)
 9    {
10       // Create a CompactDisc object.
11       CompactDisc cd =
12             new CompactDisc("Greatest Hits",
13                                "Joe Looney Band",
14                                18.95);
15       // Create a DvdMovie object.
16       DvdMovie movie =
17             new DvdMovie("Wheels of Fury",
18                             137, 12.95);
19
20       // Display the CD's title.
21       System.out.println("Item #1: " +
22                             cd.getTitle());
23
24       // Display the CD's price.
25       showPrice(cd);
26
27       // Display the DVD's title.
28       System.out.println("Item #2: " +
29                             movie.getTitle());
30
31       // Display the DVD's price.
32       showPrice(movie);
33    }
34
35    /**
36     *  The showPrice method displays the price
37     *  of the RetailItem object that is passed
38     *  as an argument.
39     */
40
41    private static void showPrice(RetailItem item)
42    {
43       System.out.printf("Price: $%,.2f\n", item.getRetailPrice());
44    }
45 }
```

Program Output

```
Item #1: Greatest Hits
Price: $18.95
Item #2: Wheels of Fury
Price: $12.95
```

There are some limitations to using interface reference variables. As previously mentioned, you cannot create an instance of an interface. The following code will cause a compiler error:

```
RetailItem item = new RetailItem();  // ERROR! Will not compile!
```

In addition, when an interface variable references an object, you can use the interface variable to call only the methods that are specified in the interface. For example, look at the following code:

```
// Reference a CompactDisc object with a RetailItem variable.
RetailItem item = new CompactDisc("Greatest Hits",
                                  "Joe Looney Band",
                                  18.95);
// Call the getRetailPrice method...
System.out.println(item.getRetailPrice());  // OK, this works.
// Attempt to call the getTitle method...
System.out.println(item.getTitle());  // ERROR! Will not compile!
```

The last line of code will not compile because the `RetailItem` interface specifies only one method: `getRetailPrice`. So, we cannot use a `RetailItem` reference variable to call any other method.[1]

 Checkpoint

9.23   What is the purpose of an interface?

9.24   How is an interface similar to an abstract class?

9.25   How is an interface different from an abstract class, or any class?

9.26   If an interface has fields, how are they treated?

9.27   Write the first line of a class named `Customer`, which implements an interface named `Relatable`.

9.28   Write the first line of a class named `Employee`, which implements `interfaces` named `Payable` and `Listable`.

 9.10   Common Errors to Avoid

The following list describes several errors that are commonly made when learning this chapter's topics.

- **Attempting to directly access a private superclass member from a subclass.** Private superclass members cannot be directly accessed by a method in a subclass. The subclass must call a public or protected superclass method in order to access the superclass's private members.

---

[1]Actually, it is possible to cast an interface reference variable to the type of the object it references, and then call methods that are members of that type. The syntax is somewhat awkward, however. The statement that causes the compiler error in the example code could be rewritten as:

```
System.out.println(((CompactDisc)item).getTitle());
```

- **Forgetting to explicitly call a superclass constructor when the superclass has no default constructor or programmer-defined no-arg constructor.** When a superclass does not have a default constructor or a no-arg constructor, the subclass's constructor must explicitly call one of the constructors that the superclass does have.
- **Allowing the superclass's default constructor or no-arg constructor to be implicitly called when you intend to call another superclass constructor.** If a subclass's constructor does not explicitly call a superclass constructor, Java automatically calls super().
- **Forgetting to precede a call to an overridden superclass method with super.** When a subclass method calls an overridden superclass method, it must precede the method call with the key word super and a dot (.). Failing to do so results in the subclass's version of the method being called.
- **Forgetting a class member's access specifier.** When you do not give a class member an access specifier, it is granted package access by default. This means that any method in the same package can access the member.
- **Writing a body for an abstract method.** An abstract method cannot have a body. It must be overridden in a subclass.
- **Forgetting to terminate an abstract method's header with a semicolon.** An abstract method header does not have a body, and it must be terminated with a semicolon.
- **Failing to override an abstract method.** An abstract method must be overridden in a subclass.
- **Overloading an abstract method instead of overriding it.** Overloading is not the same as overriding. When a superclass has an abstract method, the subclass must have a method with the same signature as the abstract method.
- **Trying to instantiate an abstract class.** You cannot create an instance of an abstract class.
- **Implementing an interface but forgetting to override all of its methods.** When a class implements an interface, all of the methods specified by the interface must be overridden in the class.
- **Overloading an interface method instead of overriding it.** As previously mentioned, overloading is not the same as overriding. When a class implements an interface, the class must have methods with the same signature as the methods specified in the interface.

Review Questions and Exercises

Multiple Choice and True/False

1. In an inheritance relationship, this is the general class.
   a. subclass
   b. superclass
   c. derived class
   d. child class

2. In an inheritance relationship, this is the specialized class.
   a. superclass
   b. base class
   c. subclass
   d. parent class

3. This key word indicates that a class inherits from another class.
   a. `derived`
   b. `specialized`
   c. `based`
   d. `extends`

4. A subclass does not have access to these superclass members.
   a. public
   b. private
   c. protected
   d. all of these

5. This key word refers to an object's superclass.
   a. `super`
   b. `base`
   c. `this`
   d. `parent`

6. In a subclass constructor, a call to the superclass constructor must
   a. appear as the very first statement.
   b. appear as the very last statement.
   c. appear between the constructor's header and the opening brace.
   d. not appear.

7. The following is an explicit call to the superclass's default constructor.
   a. `default();`
   b. `class();`
   c. `super();`
   d. `base();`

8. A method in a subclass having the same signature as a method in the superclass is an example of
   a. overloading
   b. overriding
   c. composition
   d. an error

9. A method in a subclass having the same name as a method in the superclass but a different signature, is an example of
   a. overloading
   b. overriding
   c. composition
   d. an error

10. These superclass members are accessible to subclasses and classes in the same package.
    a. private
    b. public
    c. protected
    d. all of these

11. All classes directly or indirectly inherit from this class.
    a. `Object`
    b. `Super`
    c. `Root`
    d. `Java`

12. With this type of binding, the Java Virtual Machine determines at runtime which method to call, depending on the type of the object that a variable references.
    a. static
    b. early
    c. flexible
    d. dynamic

13. When a class implements an interface, it must
    a. overload all of the methods listed in the interface
    b. provide all of the methods that are listed in the interface, with the exact signatures specified
    c. not have a constructor
    d. be an abstract class

14. Fields in an interface are
    a. `final`
    b. `static`
    c. both `final` and `static`
    d. not allowed

15. Abstract methods must be
    a. overridden
    b. overloaded
    c. deleted and replaced with real methods
    d. declared as private

16. Abstract classes cannot
    a. be used as superclasses
    b. have abstract methods
    c. be instantiated
    d. have fields

17. **True or False:** Constructors are not inherited.

18. **True or False:** In a subclass, a call to the superclass constructor can be written only in the subclass constructor.

19. **True or False:** If a subclass constructor does not explicitly call a superclass constructor, Java will not call any of the superclass's constructors.

20. **True or False:** An object of a superclass can access members declared in a subclass.

21. **True or False:** The superclass constructor always executes before the subclass constructor.

22. **True or False:** When a method is declared with the `final` modifier, it must be overridden in a subclass.

23. **True or False:** A superclass has a member with package access. A class that is outside the superclass's package but inherits from the superclass can access this member.

24. **True or False:** A superclass reference variable can reference an object of a class that inherits from the superclass.

25. **True or False:** A subclass reference variable can reference an object of the superclass.

26. **True or False:** When a class contains an abstract method, the class cannot be instantiated.

27. **True or False:** A class can implement only one interface.

28. **True or False:** By default all members of an interface are public.

Find the Error

Find the error in each of the following code segments.

1.
```java
// Superclass
public class Vehicle
{
    (Member declarations . . . )
}
// Subclass
public class Car expands Vehicle
{
    (Member declarations . . . )
}
```

2.
```java
// Superclass
public class Vehicle
{
    private double cost;
    (Other methods . . . )
}
// Subclass
public class Car extends Vehicle
{
    public Car(double c)
    {
        cost = c;
    }
}
```

3.
```java
// Superclass
public class Vehicle
{
    private double cost;
    public Vehicle(double c)
    {
        cost = c;
    }
    (Other methods . . . )
}
// Subclass
public class Car extends Vehicle
{
    private int passengers;
    public Car(int p)
    {
        passengers = c;
    }
    (Other methods . . . )
}
```

```
4.  // Superclass
    public class Vehicle
    {
        public abstract double getMilesPerGallon();
        (Other methods . . . )
    }
    // Subclass
    public class Car extends Vehicle
    {
        private int mpg;

        public int getMilesPerGallon();
        {
            return mpg;
        }
        (Other methods . . . )
    }
```

Algorithm Workbench

1. Write the first line of the definition for a Poodle class. The class should inherit from the Dog class.

2. Look at the following code which is the first line of a class definition:

    `public class Tiger extends Felis`

    In what order will the class constructors execute?

3. Write the declaration for class B. The class's members should be:

    - m, an integer. This variable should not be accessible to code outside the class or to any class that inherits from class B.
    - n, an integer. This variable should be accessible only to classes that inherit from class B or in the same package as class B.
    - setM, getM, setN, and getN. These are the mutator and accessor methods for the member variables m and n. These methods should be accessible to code outside the class.
    - calc. This is a public abstract method.

    Next write the declaration for class D, which inherits from class B. The class's members should be:

    - q, a double. This variable should not be accessible to code outside the class.
    - r, a double. This variable should be accessible to any class that extends class D or in the same package.
    - setQ, getQ, setR, and getR. These are the mutator and accessor methods for the member variables q and r. These methods should be accessible to code outside the class.
    - calc, a public method that overrides the superclass's abstract calc method. This method should return the value of q times r.

4. Write the statement that calls a superclass constructor and passes the arguments x, y, and z.

5. A superclass has the following method:

```
public void setValue(int v)
{
    value = v;
}
```

Write a statement that can appear in a subclass that calls this method, passing 10 as an argument.

6. A superclass has the following abstract method:

```
public abstract int getValue();
```

Write an example of a getValue method that can appear in a subclass.

7. Write the first line of the definition for a Stereo class. The class should inherit from the SoundSystem class, and it should implement the CDplayable, TunerPlayable, and CassettePlayable interfaces.

8. Write an interface named Nameable that specifies the following methods:

```
public void setName(String n)
public String getName()
```

Short Answer

1. What is an "is-a" relationship?

2. A program uses two classes: Animal and Dog. Which class is the superclass and which is the subclass?

3. What is the superclass and what is the subclass in the following line?

```
public class Pet extends Dog
```

4. What is the difference between a protected class member and a private class member?

5. Can a subclass ever directly access the private members of its superclass?

6. Which constructor is called first, that of the subclass or the superclass?

7. What is the difference between overriding a superclass method and overloading a superclass method?

8. Reference variables can be polymorphic. What does this mean?

9. When does dynamic binding take place?

10. What is an abstract method?

11. What is an abstract class?

12. What are the differences between an abstract class and an interface?

Programming Challenges

1. `Employee` and `ProductionWorker` Classes

Design a class named `Employee`. The class should keep the following information in fields:

- Employee name
- Employee number in the format XXX–L, where each X is a digit within the range 0–9 and the L is a letter within the range A–M.
- Hire date

Write one or more constructors and the appropriate accessor and mutator methods for the class.

Next, write a class named `ProductionWorker` that inherits from the `Employee` class. The `ProductionWorker` class should have fields to hold the following information:

- Shift (an integer)
- Hourly pay rate (a `double`)

The workday is divided into two shifts: day and night. The shift field will be an integer value representing the shift that the employee works. The day shift is shift 1 and the night shift is shift 2. Write one or more constructors and the appropriate accessor and mutator methods for the class. Demonstrate the classes by writing a program that uses a `ProductionWorker` object.

2. `ShiftSupervisor` Class

In a particular factory a shift supervisor is a salaried employee who supervises a shift. In addition to a salary, the shift supervisor earns a yearly bonus when his or her shift meets production goals. Design a `ShiftSupervisor` class that inherits from the `Employee` class you created in Programming Challenge 1. The `ShiftSupervisor` class should have a field that holds the annual salary and a field that holds the annual production bonus that a shift supervisor has earned. Write one or more constructors and the appropriate accessor and mutator methods for the class. Demonstrate the class by writing a program that uses a `ShiftSupervisor` object.

3. `TeamLeader` Class

In a particular factory, a team leader is an hourly paid production worker who leads a small team. In addition to hourly pay, team leaders earn a fixed monthly bonus. Team leaders are required to attend a minimum number of hours of training per year. Design a `TeamLeader` class that inherits from the `ProductionWorker` class you designed in Programming Challenge 1. The `TeamLeader` class should have fields for the monthly bonus amount, the required number of training hours, and the number of training hours that the team leader has attended. Write one or more constructors and the appropriate accessor and mutator methods for the class. Demonstrate the class by writing a program that uses a `TeamLeader` object.

4. `Essay` Class

Design an `Essay` class that inherits from the `GradedActivity` class presented in this chapter. The `Essay` class should determine the grade a student receives on an essay. The student's essay score can be up to 100 and is determined in the following manner:

    Grammar: 30 points
    Spelling: 20 points
    Correct length: 20 points
    Content: 30 points

Demonstrate the class in a simple program.

5. Course Grades

In a course, a teacher gives the following tests and assignments:

- A **lab activity** that is observed by the teacher and assigned a numeric score.
- A **pass/fail exam** that has 10 questions. The minimum passing score is 70.
- An **essay** that is assigned a numeric score.
- A **final exam** that has 50 questions.

Write a class named `CourseGrades`. The class should have a `GradedActivity` array named `grades` as a field. The array should have four elements, one for each of the assignments previously described. The class should have the following methods:

`setLab:` This method should accept a `GradedActivity` object as its argument. This object should already hold the student's score for the lab activity. Element 0 of the `grades` field should reference this object.

`setPassFailExam:` This method should accept a `PassFailExam` object as its argument. This object should already hold the student's score for the pass/fail exam. Element 1 of the `grades` field should reference this object.

`setEssay:` This method should accept an `Essay` object as its argument. (See Programming Challenge 4 for the `Essay` class. If you have not completed Programming Challenge 4, use a `GradedActivity` object instead.) This object should already hold the student's score for the essay. Element 2 of the `grades` field should reference this object.

`setFinalExam:` This method should accept a `FinalExam` object as its argument. This object should already hold the student's score for the final exam. Element 3 of the `grades` field should reference this object.

`toString:` This method should return a string that contains the numeric scores and grades for each element in the `grades` array.

Demonstrate the class in a program.

6. `Analyzable` Interface

Modify the `CourseGrades` class you created in Programming Challenge 5 so it implements the following interface:

```
public interface Analyzable
{
    double getAverage();
    GradedActivity getHighest();
    GradedActivity getLowest();
}
```

The `getAverage` method should return the average of the numeric scores stored in the `grades` array. The `getHighest` method should return a reference to the element of the `grades` array that has the highest numeric score. The `getLowest` method should return a reference to the element of the `grades` array that has the lowest numeric score. Demonstrate the new methods in a complete program.

7. `Person` and `Customer` **Classes**

Design a class named `Person` with fields for holding a person's name, address, and telephone number. Write one or more constructors and the appropriate mutator and accessor methods for the class's fields.

Next, design a class named `Customer`, which inherits from the `Person` class. The `Customer` class should have a field for a customer number and a `boolean` field indicating whether the customer wishes to be on a mailing list. Write one or more constructors and the appropriate mutator and accessor methods for the class's fields. Demonstrate an object of the `Customer` class in a simple program.

8. `PreferredCustomer` **Class**

A retail store has a preferred customer plan where customers can earn discounts on all their purchases. The amount of a customer's discount is determined by the amount of the customer's cumulative purchases in the store, as follows:

- When a preferred customer spends $500, he or she gets a 5% discount on all future purchases.
- When a preferred customer spends $1,000, he or she gets a 6% discount on all future purchases.
- When a preferred customer spends $1,500, he or she gets a 7% discount on all future purchases.
- When a preferred customer spends $2,000 or more, he or she gets a 10% discount on all future purchases.

Design a class named `PreferredCustomer`, which inherits from the `Customer` class you created in Programming Challenge 7. The `PreferredCustomer` class should have fields for the amount of the customer's purchases and the customer's discount level. Write one or more constructors and the appropriate mutator and accessor methods for the class's fields. Demonstrate the class in a simple program.

9. `BankAccount` and `SavingsAccount` **Classes**

Design an abstract class named `BankAccount` to hold the following data for a bank account:

- Balance
- Number of deposits this month
- Number of withdrawals
- Annual interest rate
- Monthly service charges

The class should have the following methods:

Constructor:	The constructor should accept arguments for the balance and annual interest rate.
`deposit`:	A method that accepts an argument for the amount of the deposit. The method should add the argument to the account balance. It should also increment the variable holding the number of deposits.
`withdraw`:	A method that accepts an argument for the amount of the withdrawal. The method should subtract the argument from the balance. It should also increment the variable holding the number of withdrawals.

calcInterest: A method that updates the balance by calculating the monthly interest earned by the account, and adding this interest to the balance. This is performed by the following formulas:

Monthly Interest Rate = (Annual Interest Rate/12)
*Monthly Interest = Balance * Monthly Interest Rate*
Balance = Balance + Monthly Interest

monthlyProcess: A method that subtracts the monthly service charges from the balance, calls the `calcInterest` method, and then sets the variables that hold the number of withdrawals, number of deposits, and monthly service charges to zero.

Next, design a `SavingsAccount` class that extends the `BankAccount` class. The `SavingsAccount` class should have a status field to represent an active or inactive account. If the balance of a savings account falls below $25, it becomes inactive. (The `status` field could be a `boolean` variable.) No more withdrawals can be made until the balance is raised above $25, at which time the account becomes active again. The savings account class should have the following methods:

withdraw: A method that determines whether the account is inactive before a withdrawal is made. (No withdrawal will be allowed if the account is not active.) A withdrawal is then made by calling the superclass version of the method.

deposit: A method that determines whether the account is inactive before a deposit is made. If the account is inactive and the deposit brings the balance above $25, the account becomes active again. The deposit is then made by calling the superclass version of the method.

monthlyProcess: Before the superclass method is called, this method checks the number of withdrawals. If the number of withdrawals for the month is more than 4, a service charge of $1 for each withdrawal above 4 is added to the superclass field that holds the monthly service charges. (Don't forget to check the account balance after the service charge is taken. If the balance falls below $25, the account becomes inactive.)

10. `Ship`, `CruiseShip`, and `CargoShip` Classes

Design a `Ship` class that the following members:

- A field for the name of the ship (a string)
- A field for the year that the ship was built (a string)
- A constructor and appropriate accessors and mutators
- A `toString` method that displays the ship's name and the year it was built

Design a `CruiseShip` class that extends the `Ship` class. The `CruiseShip` class should have the following members:

- A field for the maximum number of passengers (an int)
- A constructor and appropriate accessors and mutators

- A toString method that overrides the toString method in the base class. The CruiseShip class's toString method should display only the ship's name and the maximum number of passengers.

Design a CargoShip class that extends the Ship class. The CargoShip class should have the following members:

- A field for the cargo capacity in tonnage (an int)
- A constructor and appropriate accessors and mutators
- A toString method that overrides the toString method in the base class. The CargoShip class's toString method should display only the ship's name and the ship's cargo capacity.

Demonstrate the classes in a program that has a Ship array. Assign various Ship, CruiseShip, and CargoShip objects to the array elements. The program should then step through the array, calling each object's toString method. (See Code Listing 9-25 as an example.)

10 Exceptions and Advanced File I/O

TOPICS

10.1 Handling Exceptions

10.2 Throwing Exceptions

10.3 Advanced Topics: Binary Files, Random Access Files, and Object Serialization

10.4 Common Errors to Avoid

10.1 Handling Exceptions

CONCEPT: An exception is an object that is generated as the result of an error or an unexpected event. To prevent exceptions from crashing your program, you must write code that detects and handles them.

VideoNote
Handling
Exceptions

There are many error conditions that can occur while a Java application is running that will cause it to halt execution. By now you have probably experienced this many times. For example, look at the program in Code Listing 10-1. This program attempts to read beyond the bounds of an array.

Code Listing 10-1   (BadArray.java)

```
1   /**
2    *  This program causes an error and crashes.
3    */
4
5   public class BadArray
6   {
7      public static void main(String[] args)
8      {
9         // Create an array with three elements.
10        int[] numbers = { 1, 2, 3 };
11
```

```
12          // Attempt to read beyond the bounds
13          // of the array.
14          for (int index = 0; index <= 3; index++)
15              System.out.println(numbers[index]);
16      }
17  }
```

Program Output

```
1
2
3
Exception in thread "main" java.lang.ArrayIndexOutOfBoundsException
        at BadArray.main(BadArray.java:15)
```

The `numbers` array in this program has only three elements, with the subscripts 0 though 2. The program crashes when it tries to read the element at `numbers[3]` and displays the error message that you see at the end of the program output. This message indicates that an exception occurred, and it gives some information about it. An *exception* is an object that is generated in memory as the result of an error or an unexpected event. When an exception is generated, it is said to have been "thrown." Unless an exception is detected by the application and dealt with, it causes the application to halt.

To detect that an exception has been thrown and prevent it from halting your application, Java allows you to create exception handlers. An *exception handler* is a section of code that gracefully responds to exceptions when they are thrown. The process of intercepting and responding to exceptions is called *exception handling*. If your code does not handle an exception when it is thrown, the *default exception handler* deals with it, as shown in Code Listing 10-1. The default exception handler prints an error message and crashes the program.

The error that caused the exception to be thrown in Code Listing 10-1 is easy to avoid. If the loop were written properly, it would not have tried to read outside the bounds of the array. Some errors, however, are caused by conditions that are outside the application and cannot be avoided. For example, suppose an application creates a file on the disk and the user deletes it. Later the application attempts to open the file to read from it, and because it does not exist, an error occurs. As a result, an exception is thrown.

Exception Classes

As previously mentioned, an exception is an object. Exception objects are created from classes in the Java API. The API has an extensive hierarchy of exception classes. A small part of the hierarchy is shown in Figure 10-1.

Figure 10-1   Part of the exception class hierarchy

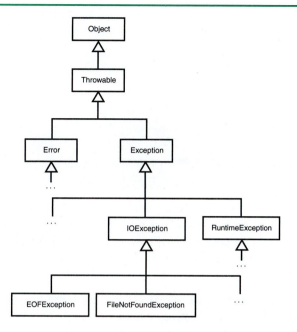

As you can see, all of the classes in the hierarchy inherit from the `Throwable` class. Just below the `Throwable` class are the classes `Error` and `Exception`. The `Error` class is intended to be a superclass for exceptions that are thrown when a critical error occurs, such as an internal error in the Java Virtual Machine or running out of memory. Your applications should not try to handle these errors because they are the result of a serious condition.

All of the exceptions that you will handle are instances of classes that inherit from `Exception`. Figure 10-1 shows two of these classes: `IOException` and `RuntimeException`. These classes also serve as superclasses. `IOException` serves as a superclass for exceptions that are related to input and output operations. `RuntimeException` serves as a superclass for exceptions that result from programming errors, such as an out-of-bounds array subscript.

The chart in Figure 10-1 shows two of the classes that inherit from the `IOException` class: `EOFException` and `FileNotFoundException`. These are examples of classes that exception objects are created from. An `EOFException` object is thrown when an application attempts to read beyond the end of a file, and a `FileNotFoundException` object is thrown when an application tries to open a file that does not exist.

NOTE: The exception classes are in packages in the Java API. For example, `FileNotFoundException` is in the `java.io` package. When you handle an exception that is not in the `java.lang` package, you will need the appropriate `import` statement.

Handling an Exception

To handle an exception, you use a *try* statement. We will look at several variations of the try statement, beginning with the following general format.

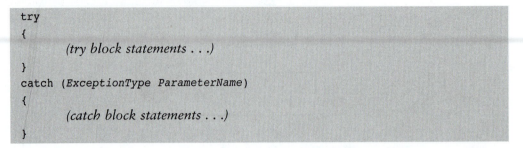

```
try
{
       (try block statements . . .)
}
catch (ExceptionType ParameterName)
{
       (catch block statements . . .)
}
```

First the key word `try` appears. Next, a block of code appears inside braces, which are required. This block of code is known as a *try block*. A *try block* is one or more statements that are executed and can potentially throw an exception. You can think of the code in the try block as being "protected" because the application will not halt if the try block throws an exception.

After the try block, a `catch` clause appears. A `catch` clause begins with the key word `catch`, followed by the code *(ExceptionType ParameterName)*. This is a parameter variable declaration, where *ExceptionType* is the name of an exception class and *ParameterName* is a variable name. If code in the try block throws an exception of the *ExceptionType* class, then the parameter variable will reference the exception object. In addition, the code that immediately follows the `catch` clause is executed. The code that immediately follows the `catch` clause is known as a *catch block*. Once again, the braces are required.

Let's look at an example of code that uses a `try` statement. The statement inside the following try block attempts to open the file *MyFile.txt*. If the file does not exist, the `Scanner` object throws an exception of the `FileNotFoundException` class. This code is designed to handle that exception if it is thrown.

```
try
{
    File file = new File("MyFile.txt");
    Scanner inputFile = new Scanner(file);
}
catch (FileNotFoundException e)
{
    System.out.println("File not found.");
}
```

Let's look closer. First, the code in the try block is executed. If this code throws an exception, the Java Virtual Machine searches for a catch clause that can deal with the exception. In order for a catch clause to be able to deal with an exception, its parameter must be of a type that is compatible with the exception's type. Here is this code's catch clause:

```
catch (FileNotFoundException e)
```

This catch clause declares a reference variable named e as its parameter. The e variable can reference an object of the FileNotFoundException class. So, this catch clause can deal with an exception of the FileNotFoundException class. If the code in the try block throws an exception of the FileNotFoundException class, the e variable will reference the exception object and the code in the catch block will execute. In this case, the message "File not found." will be printed. After the catch block is executed, the program will resume with the code that appears after the entire try/catch construct.

NOTE: The Java API documentation lists all of the exceptions that can be thrown from each method.

Code Listing 10-2 shows a program that asks the user to enter a file name, then opens the file. If the file does not exist, an error message is printed.

Code Listing 10-2   (OpenFile.java)

```java
1   import java.io.*;           // For File class and FileNotFoundException
2   import java.util.Scanner;   // For the Scanner class
3
4   /**
5    * This program demonstrates how a FileNotFoundException
6    * exception can be handled.
7    */
8
9   public class OpenFile
10  {
11     public static void main(String[] args)
12     {
13        // Create a Scanner object for keyboard input.
14        Scanner keyboard = new Scanner(System.in);
15
16        // Get a file name from the user.
17        System.out.print("Enter the name of a file: ");
18        String fileName = keyboard.nextLine();
19
20        // Attempt to open the file.
21        try
22        {
23           // Create a File object representing the file.
24           File file = new File(fileName);
25
26           // Create a Scanner object to read the file.
27           // If the file does not exist, the following
28           // statement will throw a FileNotFoundException.
29           Scanner inputFile = new Scanner(file);
30
```

```
31                  // If the file was successfully opened, the
32                  // following statement will execute.
33                  System.out.println("The file was found.");
34          }
35          catch (FileNotFoundException e)
36          {
37                  // If the file was not found, the following
38                  // statement will execute.
39                  System.out.println("File not found.");
40          }
41
42          System.out.println("Done.");
43      }
44  }
```

Program Output with Example Input Shown in Bold

(Assume that BadFile.txt does not exist.)
Enter the name of a file: **BadFile.txt [Enter]**
File not found.
Done.

Program Output with Example Input Shown in Bold

(Assume that GoodFile.txt does exist.)
Enter the name of a file: **GoodFile.txt [Enter]**
The file was found.
Done.

Look at the first example run of the program. The user entered *BadFile.txt* as the file name. In line 24, inside the try block, a File object is created and this name is passed to the File constructor. In line 29 a reference to the File object is passed to the Scanner constructor. Because *BadFile.txt* does not exist, an exception of the FileNotFoundException class is thrown by the Scanner class constructor. When the exception is thrown, the program immediately exits the try block, skipping the remaining lines in the block (lines 30 through 33). The program jumps to the catch clause in line 35, which has a FileNotFoundException parameter, and executes the catch block that follows it. Figure 10-2 illustrates this sequence of events.

Figure 10-2 Sequence of events with an exception

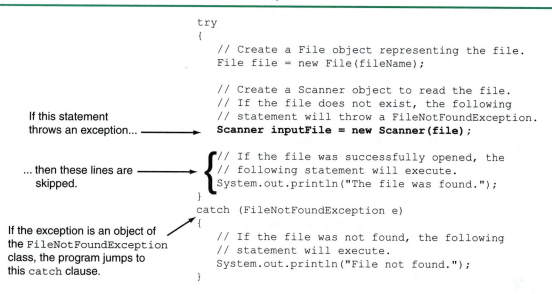

```
try
{
    // Create a File object representing the file.
    File file = new File(fileName);

    // Create a Scanner object to read the file.
    // If the file does not exist, the following
    // statement will throw a FileNotFoundException.
    Scanner inputFile = new Scanner(file);

    // If the file was successfully opened, the
    // following statement will execute.
    System.out.println("The file was found.");
}
catch (FileNotFoundException e)
{
    // If the file was not found, the following
    // statement will execute.
    System.out.println("File not found.");
}
```

If this statement throws an exception...

... then these lines are skipped.

If the exception is an object of the `FileNotFoundException` class, the program jumps to this `catch` clause.

Notice that after the catch block executes, the program resumes at the statement that immediately follows the `try/catch` construct. This statement prints the message "Done."

Now look at the second example run of the program. In this case, the user entered *GoodFile.txt*, which is the name of a file that exists. No exception was thrown in the try block, so the program skips the `catch` clause and its catch block and jumps directly to the statement that follows the `try/catch` construct. This statement prints the message "Done." Figure 10-3 illustrates this sequence of events.

Figure 10-3 Sequence of events with no exception

```
try
{
    // Create a File object representing the file.
    File file = new File(fileName);

    // Create a Scanner object to read the file.
    // If the file does not exist, the following
    // statement will throw a FileNotFoundException.
    Scanner inputFile = new Scanner(file);

    // If the file was successfully opened, the
    // following statement will execute.
    System.out.println("The file was found.");
}
catch (FileNotFoundException e)
{
    // If the file was not found, the following
    // statement will execute.
    System.out.println("File not found.");
}

System.out.println("Done.");
```

If no exception is thrown in the try block, the program jumps to the statement that immediately follows the `try/catch` construct.

Retrieving the Default Error Message

Each exception object has a method named getMessage that can be used to retrieve the default error message for the exception. This is the same message that is displayed when the exception is not handled and the application halts. The program in Code Listing 10-3 demonstrates the getMessage method. This is a modified version of the program in Code Listing 10-2.

Code Listing 10-3   (ExceptionMessage.java)

```java
 1  import java.io.*; // For File class and FileNotFoundException
 2  import java.util.Scanner; // For the Scanner class
 3
 4  /**
 5   *  This program demonstrates how the default error message
 6   *  can be retrieved from an exception object.
 7   */
 8
 9  public class ExceptionMessage
10  {
11     public static void main(String[] args)
12     {
13        // Create a Scanner object for keyboard input.
14        Scanner keyboard = new Scanner(System.in);
15
16        // Get a file name from the user.
17        System.out.print("Enter the name of a file: ");
18        String fileName = keyboard.nextLine();
19
20        // Attempt to open the file.
21        try
22        {
23           // Create a File object representing the file.
24           File file = new File(fileName);
25
26           // Create a Scanner object to read the file.
27           // If the file does not exist, the following
28           // statement will throw a FileNotFoundException.
29           Scanner inputFile = new Scanner(file);
30
31           // If the file was successfully opened, the
32           // following statement will execute.
33           System.out.println("The file was found.");
34        }
35        catch (FileNotFoundException e)
36        {
37           // If the file was not found, the following
38           // statement will execute. It displays the
39           // default error message.
40           System.out.println(e.getMessage());
41        }
```

```
42
43          System.out.println("Done.");
44      }
45  }
```

Program Output with Example Input Shown in Bold

(Assume that BadFile.txt does not exist.)

Enter the name of a file: **BadFile.txt [Enter]**
BadFile.txt (The system cannot find the file specified)
Done.

Code Listing 10-4 shows another example. This program forces the parseInt method of the Integer wrapper class to throw an exception.

Code Listing 10-4   **(ParseIntError.java)**

```
 1  /**
 2   *  This program demonstrates how the Integer.parseInt
 3   *  method throws an exception.
 4   */
 5
 6  public class ParseIntError
 7  {
 8      public static void main(String[] args)
 9      {
10          String str = "abcde";
11          int number;
12
13          try
14          {
15              // Try to convert str to an int.
16              number = Integer.parseInt(str);
17          }
18          catch (NumberFormatException e)
19          {
20              System.out.println("Conversion error: "
21                                  + e.getMessage());
22          }
23      }
24  }
```

Program Output

Conversion error: For input string: "abcde"

The numeric wrapper classes' "parse" methods all throw an exception of the NumberFormatException type if the string being converted does not contain a convertible numeric value. As you can see from the program, the exception's `getMessage` method returns a string containing the value that could not be converted.

Polymorphic References to Exceptions

Recall from Chapter 9 that a reference variable of a superclass type can reference objects that inherit from that superclass. This is called polymorphism. When handling exceptions, you can use a polymorphic reference as a parameter in the `catch` clause. For example, all of the exceptions that we have dealt with inherit from the `Exception` class. So, a `catch` clause that uses a parameter variable of the `Exception` type is capable of catching any exception that inherits from the `Exception` class. For example, the try statement in Code Listing 10-4 could be written as follows:

```
try
{
    // Try to convert str to an int.
    number = Integer.parseInt(str);
}
catch (Exception e)
{
    System.out.println("The following error occurred: "
                        + e.getMessage());
}
```

Although the `Integer` class's `parseInt` method throws a `NumberFormatException` object, this code still works because the `NumberFormatException` class inherits from the `Exception` class.

Handling Multiple Exceptions

The programs we have studied so far test only for a single type of exception. In many cases, however, the code in the try block will be capable of throwing more than one type of exception. In such a case, you need to write a `catch` clause for each type of exception that could potentially be thrown.

For example, the program in Code Listing 10-5 reads the contents of a file named *SalesData.txt*. Each line in the file contains the sales amount for one month, and the file has several lines. Here are the contents of the file:

```
24987.62
26978.97
32589.45
31978.47
22781.76
29871.44
```

The program in Code Listing 10-5 reads each number from the file and adds it to an accumulator variable. The try block contains code that can throw different types of exceptions. For example, the `Scanner` class's constructor can throw a `FileNotFoundException` if the file is not found, and the `Scanner` class's `nextDouble` method can throw an `InputMismatchException` (which is in the `java.util` package) if it reads a nonnumeric value from the file. To handle these exceptions, the try statement has two `catch` clauses.

Code Listing 10-5   (`SalesReport.java`)

```java
1    import java.io.*;    // For File class and FileNotFoundException
2    import java.util.*; // For Scanner and InputMismatchException
3    import java.text.DecimalFormat;  // For the DecimalFormat class
4
5    /**
6     *  This program demonstrates how multiple exceptions can
7     *  be caught with one try statement.
8     */
9
10   public class SalesReport
11   {
12      public static void main(String[] args)
13      {
14         String filename = "SalesData.txt"; // File name
15         int months = 0;                     // Month counter
16         double oneMonth;                    // One month's sales
17         double totalSales = 0.0;            // Total sales
18         double averageSales;                // Average sales
19
20         // Create a DecimalFormat object to format output.
21         DecimalFormat dollar =
22                     new DecimalFormat("#,##0.00");
23
24         try
25         {
26            // Open the file.
27            File file = new File(filename);
28            Scanner inputFile = new Scanner(file);
29
30            // Process the contents of the file.
31            while (inputFile.hasNext())
32            {
33               // Get a month's sales amount.
34               oneMonth = inputFile.nextDouble();
35
36               // Accumulate the amount.
37               totalSales += oneMonth;
38
39               // Increment the month counter
40               months++;
41            }
42
43            // Close the file.
44            inputFile.close();
45
```

```
46                 // Calculate the average.
47                 averageSales = totalSales / months;
48
49                 // Display the results.
50                 System.out.println("Number of months: " + months);
51                 System.out.println("Total Sales: $" +
52                                   dollar.format(totalSales));
53                 System.out.println("Average Sales: $" +
54                                   dollar.format(averageSales));
55            }
56            catch(FileNotFoundException e)
57            {
58                 // The file was not found.
59                 System.out.println("The file " + filename +
60                                   " does not exist.");
61            }
62            catch(InputMismatchException e)
63            {
64                 // Thrown by the Scanner class's nextDouble
65                 // method when a nonnumeric value is found.
66                 System.out.println("Nonnumeric data " +
67                                    "found in the file:" +
68                                    e.getMessage());
69            }
70       }
71  }
```

Program Output

```
Number of months: 6
Total Sales: $169,187.71
Average Sales: $28,197.95
```

When an exception is thrown by code in the try block, the JVM begins searching the try statement for a catch clause that can handle it. It searches the catch clauses from top to bottom and passes control of the program to the first catch clause with a parameter that is compatible with the exception.

Using Exception Handlers to Recover from Errors

The program in Code Listing 10-5 demonstrates how a try statement can have several catch clauses in order to handle different types of exceptions. However, the program does not use the exception handlers to recover from any of the errors. Regardless of whether the file is not found or a nonnumeric item is encountered in the file, this program still halts. The program in Code Listing 10-6 is a better example of effective exception handling. It attempts to recover from as many of the exceptions as possible.

Code Listing 10-6   (`SalesReport2.java`)

```java
 1   import java.io.*;     // For File class and FileNotFoundException
 2   import java.util.*;   // For Scanner and InputMismatchException
 3   import java.text.DecimalFormat; // For the DecimalFormat class
 4
 5   /**
 6    *  This program demonstrates how exception handlers can
 7    *  be used to recover from errors.
 8    */
 9
10   public class SalesReport2
11   {
12      public static void main(String[] args)
13      {
14         String filename = "SalesData.txt"; // File name
15         int months = 0;                     // Month counter
16         double oneMonth;                    // One month's sales
17         double totalSales = 0.0;            // Total sales
18         double averageSales;                // Average sales
19
20         // Create a DecimalFormat object.
21         DecimalFormat dollar =
22                 new DecimalFormat("#,##0.00");
23
24         // Attempt to open the file by calling the
25         // openfile method.
26         Scanner inputFile = openFile(filename);
27
28         // If the openFile method returned null, then
29         // the file was not found. Get a new file name.
30         while (inputFile == null)
31         {
32            Scanner keyboard = new Scanner(System.in);
33            System.out.print("ERROR: " + filename +
34                             " does not exist.\n" +
35                             "Enter another file name: ");
36            filename = keyboard.nextLine();
37            inputFile = openFile(filename);
38         }
39
40         // Process the contents of the file.
41         while (inputFile.hasNext())
42         {
43            try
44            {
45               // Get a month's sales amount.
46               oneMonth = inputFile.nextDouble();
47
```

```
48                // Accumulate the amount.
49                totalSales += oneMonth;
50
51                // Increment the month counter.
52                months++;
53            }
54          catch(InputMismatchException e)
55          {
56                // Display an error message.
57                // Nonnumeric data was encountered.
58                System.out.println("Nonnumeric data " +
59                                    "encountered in the file: " +
60                                    e.getMessage());
61
62                System.out.println("The invalid record " +
63                                    "will be skipped.");
64
65                // Skip past the invalid data.
66                inputFile.nextLine();
67            }
68        }
69
70      // Close the file.
71      inputFile.close();
72
73      // Calculate the average.
74      averageSales = totalSales / months;
75
76      // Display the results.
77      System.out.println("Number of months: " + months);
78      System.out.println("Total Sales: $" +
79                          dollar.format(totalSales));
80      System.out.println("Average Sales: $" +
81                          dollar.format(averageSales));
82    }
83
84    /**
85     *  The openFile method opens the file with the name specified
86     *  by the argument. A reference to a Scanner object is
87     *  returned.
88     */
89
90    public static Scanner openFile(String filename)
91    {
92      Scanner scan;
93
94      // Attempt to open the file.
95      try
96      {
```

```
 97                File file = new File(filename);
 98                scan = new Scanner(file);
 99            }
100            catch(FileNotFoundException e)
101            {
102                scan = null;
103            }
104
105            return scan;
106        }
107    }
```

Let's look at how this program recovers from a `FileNotFoundException`. The `openFile` method, in lines 90 through 106, accepts a file name as its argument. The method creates a `File` object (passing the file name to the constructor) and a `Scanner` object. If the `Scanner` class constructor throws a `FileNotFoundException`, the method returns `null`. Otherwise, it returns a reference to the `Scanner` object. In the `main` method, a loop is used in lines 30 through 38 to ask the user for a different file name in the event that the `openFile` method returns null.

Now let's look at how the program recovers from unexpectedly encountering a nonnumeric item in the file. The statement in line 46, which calls the `Scanner` class's `nextDouble` method, is wrapped in a `try` statement that catches the `InputMismatchException`. If this exception is thrown by the `nextDouble` method, the catch block in lines 54 through 67 displays a message indicating that a nonnumeric item was encountered and that the invalid record will be skipped. The invalid data is then read from the file with the `nextLine` method in line 66. Because the statement `months++` in line 52 is in the try block, it will not be executed when the exception occurs, so the number of months will still be correct. The loop continues processing with the next line in the file.

Let's look at some examples of how the program recovers from these errors. Suppose we rename the *SalesData.txt* file to *SalesInfo.txt*. Here is an example running of the program.

Program Output with Example Input Shown in Bold

```
ERROR: SalesData.txt does not exist.
Enter another file name: SalesInfo.txt [Enter]
Number of months: 6
Total Sales: $169,187.71
Average Sales: $28,197.95
```

Now, suppose we change the name of the file back to *SalesData.txt* and edit its contents as follows:

```
24987.62
26978.97
abc
31978.47
22781.76
29871.44
```

Notice that the third item is no longer a number. Here is the output of the program:

Program Output

```
Nonnumeric data encountered in the file: For input string: "abc"
The invalid record will be skipped.
Number of months: 5
Total Sales: $136,598.26
Average Sales: $27,319.65
```

Handle Each Exception Only Once in a `try` Statement

Not including polymorphic references, a `try` statement can have only one `catch` clause for each specific type of exception. For example, the following `try` statement will cause the compiler to issue an error message because it handles a `NumberFormatException` object with two `catch` clauses.

```
try
{
      number = Integer.parseInt(str);
}
catch (NumberFormatException e)
{
      System.out.println("Bad number format.");
}
// ERROR!!! NumberFormatException has already been caught!
catch (NumberFormatException e)
{
      System.out.println(str + " is not a number.");
}
```

Sometimes you can cause this error by using polymorphic references. For example, look at Figure 10-4, which shows an inheritance hierarchy for the `NumberFormatException` class.

Figure 10-4   Inheritance hierarchy for the `NumberFormatException` class

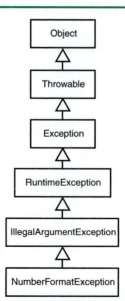

As you can see from the figure, the `NumberFormatException` class inherits from the `IllegalArgumentException` class. Now look at the following code.

```
try
{
     number = Integer.parseInt(str);
}
catch (IllegalArgumentException e)
{
     System.out.println("Bad number format.");
}
// This will also cause an error.
catch (NumberFormatException e)
{
     System.out.println(str + " is not a number.");
}
```

The compiler issues an error message regarding the second `catch` clause, reporting that `NumberFormatException` has already been caught. This is because the first `catch` clause, which catches `IllegalArgumentException` objects, will polymorphically catch `NumberFormatException` objects.

When in the same `try` statement you are handling multiple exceptions and some of the exceptions are related to each other through inheritance, then you should handle the more specialized exception classes before the more general exception classes. We can rewrite the previous code as follows, with no errors.

```
try
{
     number = Integer.parseInt(str);
}
catch (NumberFormatException e)
{
     System.out.println(str + " is not a number.");
}
catch (IllegalArgumentException e)
{
     System.out.println("Bad number format.");
}
```

The `finally` Clause

The try statement may have an optional `finally` clause, which must appear after all of the catch clauses. Here is the general format of a try statement with a `finally` clause:

```
try
{
          (try block statements . . .)
}
```

```
catch (ExceptionType ParameterName)
{
        (catch block statements . . .)
}
finally
{
        (finally block statements . . .)

}
```

The *finally block* is one or more statements that are always executed after the try block has executed and after any catch blocks have executed if an exception was thrown. The statements in the finally block execute whether an exception occurs or not. For example, the following code opens a file of doubles and reads its contents. The outer try statement opens the file and has a catch clause that catches the FileNotFoundException. The inner try statement reads values from the file and has a catch clause that catches the InputMismatchException. The finally block closes the file regardless of whether an InputMismatchException occurs.

```
try
{
    // Open the file.
    File file = new File(filename);
    Scanner inputFile = new Scanner(file);

    try
    {
        // Read and display the file's contents.
        while (inputFile.hasNext())
        {
            System.out.println(inputFile.nextDouble());
        }
    }
    catch (InputMismatchException e)
    {
        System.out.println("Invalid data found.");
    }
    finally
    {
        // Close the file.
        inputFile.close();
    }
}
catch (FileNotFoundException e)
{
    System.out.println("File not found.");
}
```

The Stack Trace

Quite often, a method will call another method, which will call yet another method. For example, method A calls method B, which calls method C. The *call stack* is an internal list of all the methods that are currently executing.

When an exception is thrown by a method that is executing under several layers of method calls, it is sometimes helpful to know which methods were responsible for the method being called. A *stack trace* is a list of all the methods in the call stack. It indicates the method that was executing when an exception occurred and all of the methods that were called in order to execute that method. For example, look at the program in Code Listing 10-7. It has three methods: main, myMethod, and produceError. The main method calls myMethod, which calls produceError. The produceError method causes an exception by passing an invalid position number to the String class's charAt method. The exception is not handled by the program, but is dealt with by the default exception handler.

Code Listing 10-7   (StackTrace.java)

```java
 1  /**
 2   * This program demonstrates the stack trace that is
 3   * produced when an exception is thrown.
 4   */
 5
 6  public class StackTrace
 7  {
 8     public static void main(String[] args)
 9     {
10        System.out.println("Calling myMethod...");
11        myMethod();
12        System.out.println("Method main is done.");
13     }
14
15     /**
16      * myMethod
17      */
18
19     public static void myMethod()
20     {
21        System.out.println("Calling produceError...");
22        produceError();
23        System.out.println("myMethod is done.");
24     }
25
26     /**
27      * produceError
28      */
29
30     public static void produceError()
```

```
31      {
32          String str = "abc";
33
34          // The following statement will cause an error.
35          System.out.println(str.charAt(3));
36          System.out.println("produceError is done.");
37      }
38  }
```

Program Output

```
Calling myMethod...
Calling produceError...
Exception in thread "main" java.lang.StringIndexOutOfBoundsException:
String index out of range: 3
    at java.lang.String.charAt(String.java:687)
    at StackTrace.produceError(StackTrace.java:35)
    at StackTrace.myMethod(StackTrace.java:22)
    at StackTrace.main(StackTrace.java:11)
```

When the exception occurs, the error message shows a stack trace listing the methods that were called in order to produce the exception. The first method that is listed, charAt, is the method that is responsible for the exception. The next method, produceError, is the method that called charAt. The next method, myMethod, is the method that called produceError. The last method, main, is the method that called myMethod. The stack trace shows the chain of methods that were called when the exception was thrown.

 NOTE: All exception objects have a printStackTrace method, inherited from the Throwable class, that prints a stack trace.

Handling Multiple Exceptions with One catch Clause (Introduced in Java 7)

In versions of Java prior to Java 7, each catch clause can handle only one type of exception. Beginning in Java 7, however, a catch clause can handle more than one type of exception. This can reduce a lot of duplicated code in a try statement that needs to catch multiple exceptions, but performs the same operation for each one. For example, suppose we have the following try statement in a program:

```
try
{
    (try block statements ...)
}
catch(NumberFormatException ex)
{
    respondToError();
}
catch(IOException ex)
```

```
    {
        respondToError();
    }
```

This try statement has two catch clauses: one that handles a NumberFormatException, and another that handles an IOException. Notice that both catch blocks do the same thing: they call a method named respondToError. Since both catch blocks perform the same operation, the catch clauses can be combined into a single catch clause that handles both types of exception, as shown here:

```
    try
    {
        (try block statements...)
    }
    catch(NumberFormatException | IOException ex)
    {
        respondToError();
    }
```

Notice in the catch clause that the exception types are separated by a | symbol, which is the same symbol used as the logical OR operator. You can think of this as meaning that the clause will catch a NumberFormatException or an IOException. The following code shows a catch clause that handles three types of exceptions:

```
    try
    {
        (try block statements...)
    }
    catch(NumberFormatException | IOException | InputMismatchException ex)
    {
        respondToError();
    }
```

In this code, the catch clause will handle a NumberFormatException, or an IOException, or an InputMismatchException.

The ability to catch multiple types of exceptions with a single catch clause is known as *multi-catch* and was introduced in Java 7. Code Listing 10-8 shows a complete program that uses multi-catch. The catch clause in line 34 can handle a FileNotFoundException or an InputMismatchException.

Code Listing 10-8   (MultiCatch.java)

```
 1  import java.io.*;    // For File class and FileNotFoundException
 2  import java.util.*;  // For Scanner and InputMismatchException
 3
 4  /**
 5   *  This program demonstrates how multiple exceptions can
 6   *  be caught with a single catch clause.
 7   */
 8
 9  public class MultiCatch
10  {
```

```
11     public static void main(String[] args)
12     {
13        int number;     // To hold a number from the file
14
15        try
16        {
17           // Open the file.
18           File file = new File("Numbers.txt");
19           Scanner inputFile = new Scanner(file);
20
21           // Process the contents of the file.
22           while (inputFile.hasNext())
23           {
24              // Get a number from the file.
25              number = inputFile.nextInt();
26
27              // Display the number.
28              System.out.println(number);
29           }
30
31           // Close the file.
32           inputFile.close();
33        }
34        catch(FileNotFoundException | InputMismatchException ex)
35        {
36           // Display an error message.
37           System.out.println("Error processing the file.");
38        }
39     }
40  }
```

> **NOTE:** If you are using a version of Java prior to Java 7, you cannot use multi-catch.

When an Exception Is Not Caught

When an exception is thrown, it cannot be ignored. It must be handled by the program, or by the default exception handler. When the code in a method throws an exception, the normal execution of that method stops and the JVM searches for a compatible exception handler inside the method. If there is no code inside the method to handle the exception, then control of the program is passed to the previous method in the call stack (that is, the method that called the offending method). If that method cannot handle the exception, then control is passed again, up the call stack, to the previous method. This continues until control reaches the main method. If the main method does not handle the exception, then the program is halted and the default exception handler handles the exception.

This was the case for the program in Code Listing 10-7. Because the produceError method did not handle the exception, control was passed back to myMethod. It didn't handle the exception either, so control was passed back to main. Because main didn't handle the exception, the program halted and the default exception handler displayed the error messages.

Checked and Unchecked Exceptions

In Java, there are two categories of exceptions: unchecked and checked. *Unchecked exceptions* are those that inherit from the Error class or the RuntimeException class. Recall that the exceptions that inherit from Error are thrown when a critical error occurs, such as running out of memory. You should not handle these exceptions because the conditions that cause them can rarely be dealt with in the program. Also recall that RuntimeException serves as a superclass for exceptions that result from programming errors, such as an out-of-bounds array subscript. It is best not to handle these exceptions either, because they can be avoided with properly written code. So, you should not handle unchecked exceptions.

All of the remaining exceptions (that is, those that do *not* inherit from Error or RuntimeException) are *checked exceptions*. These are the exceptions that you should handle in your program. If the code in a method can potentially throw a checked exception, then that method must meet one of the following requirements:

- It must handle the exception, or
- It must have a throws clause listed in the method header.

The throws clause informs the compiler of the exceptions that could get thrown from a method. For example, look at the following method.

```java
// This method will not compile!
public void displayFile(String name)
{
    // Open the file.
    File file = new File(name);
    Scanner inputFile = new Scanner(file);

    // Read and display the file's contents.
    while (inputFile.hasNext())
    {
        System.out.println(inputFile.nextLine());
    }

    // Close the file.
    inputFile.close();
}
```

The code in this method is capable of throwing a FileNotFoundException, which is a checked exception. Because the method does not handle this exception, it must have a throws clause in its header or it will not compile.

The key word throws is written at the end of the method header, followed by a list of the types of exceptions that the method can throw. Here is the revised method header:

```java
public void displayFile(String name) throws FileNotFoundException
```

The throws clause tells the compiler that this method can throw a FileNotFoundException. (If there is more than one type of exception, you separate them with commas.)

Now you know why you wrote a `throws` clause on any method that performed file operations in the previous chapters. We did not handle any of the checked exceptions that `Scanner` objects can throw, so we had to inform the compiler that our methods might pass them up the call stack.

✔ Checkpoint

10.1 Briefly describe what an exception is.

10.2 What does it mean to "throw" an exception?

10.3 If an exception is thrown and the program does not handle it, what happens?

10.4 Other than the `Object` class, what class do all exceptions inherit from?

10.5 What is the difference between exceptions that inherit from the `Error` class and exceptions that inherit from the `Exception` class?

10.6 What is the difference between a try block and a catch block?

10.7 After the catch block has handled the exception, where does program execution resume?

10.8 How do you retrieve an error message from an exception?

10.9 If multiple exceptions can be thrown by code in a try block, how does the JVM know which `catch` clause it should pass the control of the program to?

10.10 When does the code in a finally block execute?

10.11 What is the call stack? What is a stack trace?

10.12 A program's `main` method calls method A, which calls method B. None of these methods perform any exception handling. The code in method B throws an exception. Describe what happens.

10.13 What are the differences between a checked and an unchecked exception?

10.14 When are you required to have a `throws` clause in a method header?

10.2 Throwing Exceptions

CONCEPT: You can write code that throws one of the standard Java exceptions, or an instance of a custom exception class that you have designed.

You can use the `throw` statement to manually throw an exception. The general format of the `throw` statement is:

```
throw new ExceptionType(MessageString);
```

The `throw` statement causes an exception object to be created and thrown. In this general format, *ExceptionType* is an exception class name and *MessageString* is an optional `String` argument passed to the exception object's constructor. The *MessageString* argument contains a custom error message that can be retrieved from the exception object's `getMessage` method. If you do not pass a message to the constructor, the exception will have a `null` message. Here is an example of a `throw` statement:

```
throw new Exception("Out of fuel");
```

This statement creates an object of the Exception class and passes the string "Out of fuel" to the object's constructor. The object is then thrown, which causes the exception-handling process to begin.

> **NOTE:** Don't confuse the throw statement with the throws clause. The throw statement causes an exception to be thrown. The throws clause informs the compiler that a method throws one or more exceptions.

Recall the InventoryItem class from Chapter 6. This class holds simple data about an item in an inventory. A description of the item is stored in the description field and the number of units on hand is stored in the units field. Figure 10-5 shows a UML diagram for the class.

Figure 10-5　UML diagram for the InventoryItem class

```
┌─────────────────────────────────────┐
│            InventoryItem             │
├─────────────────────────────────────┤
│ - description: String                │
│ - units: int                         │
├─────────────────────────────────────┤
│ + InventoryItem()                    │
│ + InventoryItem(d : String)          │
│ + InventoryItem(d : String, u : int) │
│ + setDescription(d : String) : void  │
│ + setUnits(u : int) : void           │
│ + getDescription() : String          │
│ + getUnits() : int                   │
└─────────────────────────────────────┘
```

The second constructor accepts a String argument for the description field. The third constructor accepts a String argument for the description field and an int argument for the units field. Suppose we want to prevent invalid data from being passed to the constructors. For example, we want to prevent an empty string from being passed into the description field and a negative number from being passed into the units field. One way to accomplish this is to have the constructors throw an exception when invalid data is passed as arguments.

Here is the code for the second constructor, written to throw an exception when an empty string is passed as the argument:

```java
public InventoryItem(String d)
{
   if (d.equals(""))
   {
      throw new IllegalArgumentException("Description "
                  + "is an empty string.");
   }
   description = d;
   units = 0;
}
```

This constructor throws an `IllegalArgumentException` if the `d` parameter contains an empty string. The message "Description is an empty string" is passed to the exception object's constructor. When we catch this exception, we can retrieve the message by calling the object's `getMessage` method. The `IllegalArgumentException` class was chosen for this error condition because it seems like the most appropriate exception to throw in response to an illegal argument being passed to the constructor. (`IllegalArgumentException` inherits from `RuntimeException`, which inherits from `Exception`.)

Here is the code for the third constructor, written to throw an exception when an empty string is passed as the `d` parameter or a negative number is passed into the `u` parameter:

```java
public InventoryItem(String d, int u)
{
    if (d.equals(""))
    {
        throw new IllegalArgumentException("Description "
                    + "is an empty string.");
    }
    if (u < 0)
        throw new IllegalArgumentException("Units is negative.");
    description = d;
    units = u;
}
```

 NOTE: Because the `IllegalArgumentException` class inherits from the `RuntimeException` class, it is unchecked. If we had chosen a checked exception class, we would have to put a `throws` clause in each of these constructor's headers.

The program in Code Listing 10-9 demonstrates how these constructors work.

Code Listing 10-9   (`InventoryDemo.java`)

```java
 1  /**
 2   *  This program demonstrates how the InventoryItem class
 3   *  throws exceptions.
 4   */
 5
 6  public class InventoryDemo
 7  {
 8      public static void main(String[] args)
 9      {
10          InventoryItem item;
11
```

```
12          // Try to assign an empty string to the
13          // description field.
14          try
15          {
16              item = new InventoryItem("");
17          }
18          catch (IllegalArgumentException e)
19          {
20              System.out.println(e.getMessage());
21          }
22
23          // Again, try to assign an empty string to
24          // the description field.
25          try
26          {
27              item = new InventoryItem("", 5);
28          }
29          catch (IllegalArgumentException e)
30          {
31              System.out.println(e.getMessage());
32          }
33
34          // Try to assign a negative number to the
35          // units field.
36          try
37          {
38              item = new InventoryItem("Wrench", -1);
39          }
40          catch (IllegalArgumentException e)
41          {
42              System.out.println(e.getMessage());
43          }
44      }
45  }
```

Program Output

```
Description is an empty string.
Description is an empty string.
Units is negative.
```

Creating Your Own Exception Classes

To meet the needs of a specific class or application, you can create your own exception classes by extending the `Exception` class or one of its subclasses.

Let's look at an example that uses programmer-defined exceptions. Recall the `BankAccount` class from Chapter 3. This class holds the data for a bank account. A UML diagram for the class is shown in Figure 10-6.

Figure 10-6   UML diagram for the `BankAccount` class

There are a number of errors that could cause a `BankAccount` object to incorrectly perform its duties. Here are some specific examples:

- A negative starting balance is passed to the constructor.
- A negative interest rate is passed to the constructor.
- A negative number is passed to the `deposit` method.
- A negative number is passed to the `withdraw` method.
- The amount passed to the `withdraw` method exceeds the account's balance.

We can create our own exceptions that represent each of these error conditions. Then we can rewrite the class so it throws one of our custom exceptions when any of these errors occur. Let's start by creating an exception class for a negative starting balance. Code Listing 10-10 shows an exception class named `NegativeStartingBalance`.

Code Listing 10-10   (`NegativeStartingBalance.java`)

```
 1  /**
 2   *  NegativeStartingBalance exceptions are thrown by
 3   *  the BankAccount class when a negative starting
 4   *  balance is passed to the constructor.
 5   */
 6
 7  public class NegativeStartingBalance extends Exception
 8  {
```

```
 9      /**
10       *  No-arg constructor
11       */
12
13      public NegativeStartingBalance()
14      {
15          super("Error: Negative starting balance");
16      }
17
18      /**
19       *  The following constructor accepts the amount
20       *  that was given as the starting balance.
21       */
22
23      public NegativeStartingBalance(double amount)
24      {
25          super("Error: Negative starting balance: " +
26                  amount);
27      }
28  }
```

Notice that this class inherits from the Exception class. It has two constructors. The no-arg constructor passes the string "Error: Negative starting balance" to the superclass constructor. This is the error message that is retrievable from an object's getMessage method. The second constructor accepts the starting balance as a double argument. This amount is used to pass a more detailed error message containing the starting balance amount to the superclass.

A similar class can be written to handle negative interest rates. Code Listing 10-11 shows the NegativeInterestRate class. This class is also derived from the Exception class.

Code Listing 10-11   **(NegativeInterestRate.java)**

```
 1  /**
 2   *  NegativeInterestRate exceptions are thrown by the
 3   *  BankAccount class when a negative interest rate is
 4   *  passed to the constructor.
 5   */
 6
 7  public class NegativeInterestRate extends Exception
 8  {
 9      /**
10       *  No-arg constructor
11       */
12
13      public NegativeInterestRate()
14      {
```

```
15          super("Error: Negative interest rate");
16      }
17
18      /**
19       *  The following constructor accepts the amount that
20       *  was given as the interest rate.
21       */
22
23      public NegativeInterestRate(double amount)
24      {
25          super("Error: Negative interest rate: " + amount);
26      }
27  }
```

The `BankAccount` constructor can now be rewritten, as follows, to throw a `NegativeStartingBalance` exception when a negative value is passed as the starting balance, or a `NegativeInterestRate` exception when a negative number is passed as the interest rate.

```
public BankAccount(double startBalance,
                   double intRate) throws NegativeStartingBalance,
                                          NegativeInterestRate
{
    if (startBalance < 0)
        throw new NegativeStartingBalance(startBalance);
    if (intRate < 0)
        throw new NegativeInterestRate(intRate);

    balance = startBalance;
    interestRate = intRate;
    interest = 0.0;
}
```

Note that both `NegativeStartingBalance` and `NegativeInterestRate` inherit from the `Exception` class. This means that both classes are checked exception classes. Because of this, the constructor header must have a `throws` clause listing these exception types.

The program in Code Listing 10-12 demonstrates this constructor by forcing it to throw the exceptions.

Code Listing 10-12   (`AccountTest.java`)

```
1  /**
2   * This program demonstrates how the BankAccount
3   * class constructor throws custom exceptions.
4   */
5
6  public class AccountTest
7  {
```

```
 8      public static void main(String[] args)
 9      {
10         // Force a NegativeStartingBalance exception.
11         try
12         {
13             BankAccount account = new BankAccount(-1, 0.04);
14         }
15         catch(NegativeStartingBalance e)
16         {
17             System.out.println(e.getMessage());
18         }
19         catch(NegativeInterestRate e)
20         {
21             System.out.println(e.getMessage());
22         }
23
24         // Force a NegativeInterestRate exception.
25         try
26         {
27             BankAccount account = new BankAccount(100, -0.04);
28         }
29         catch(NegativeStartingBalance e)
30         {
31             System.out.println(e.getMessage());
32         }
33         catch(NegativeInterestRate e)
34         {
35             System.out.println(e.getMessage());
36         }
37     }
38 }
```

Program Output

```
Error: Negative starting balance: -1.0
Error: Negative interest rate: -0.04
```

 Checkpoint

10.15 What does the throw statement do?

10.16 What is the purpose of the argument that is passed to an exception object's constructor? What happens if you do not pass an argument to the constructor?

10.17 What is the difference between the throw statement and the throws clause?

10.18 If a method has a throw statement, does it always have to have a throws clause in its header? Why or why not?

10.19 If you are writing a custom exception class, how can you make sure it is checked? How can you make sure it is unchecked?

10.3 Advanced Topics: Binary Files, Random Access Files, and Object Serialization

CONCEPT: A file that contains raw binary data is known as a binary file. The content of a binary file is not formatted as text and not meant to be opened in a text editor. A random access file is a file that allows a program to read data from any location within the file, or write data to any location within the file. Object serialization is the process of converting an object to a series of bytes and saving them to a file. Deserialization is the process of reconstructing a serialized object.

Binary Files

All the files you've been working with so far have been text files. That means the data stored in the files has been formatted as text. Even a number, when stored in a text file with the print or println method, is converted to text. For example, consider the following program segment:

```
PrintWriter outputFile = new PrintWriter("Number.txt");
int x = 1297;
outputFile.print(x);
```

The last statement writes the contents of the variable x to the *Number.txt* file. When the number is written, however, it is stored as the characters '1', '2', '9', and '7'. This is illustrated in Figure 10-7.

Figure 10-7 The number 1297 expressed as characters

1297 expressed as characters.

'1'	'2'	'9'	'7'

When a number such as 1297 is stored in the computer's memory, it isn't stored as text, however. It is formatted as a binary number. Figure 10-8 shows how the number 1297 is stored in memory, in an int variable, using binary. Recall that int variables occupy four bytes.

Figure 10-8 The number 1297 as a binary number, as it is stored in memory

1297 as a binary number.

00000000	00000000	00000101	00010001

The binary representation of the number shown in Figure 10-8 is the way the raw data is stored in memory. In fact, this is sometimes called the *raw binary format*. Data can be stored in a file in its raw binary format. A file that contains binary data is often called a *binary file*.

Storing data in its binary format is more efficient than storing it as text because there are fewer conversions to take place. In addition, there are some types of data that should be stored only in its raw binary format. Images are an example. However, when data is stored in a binary file, you cannot open the file in a text editor such as Notepad. When a text editor opens a file, it assumes the file contains text.

Writing Data to a Binary File

To write data to a binary file you must create objects from the following classes:

FileOutputStream	This class allows you to open a file for writing binary data and establish a connection with it. It provides only basic functionality for writing bytes to the file, however.
DataOutputStream	This class allows you to write data of any primitive type or String objects to a binary file The DataOutputStream class by itself cannot directly access a file, however. It is used in conjunction with a FileOutputStream object that has a connection to a file.

You wrap a DataOutputStream object around a FileOutputStream object to write data to a binary file. The following code shows how a file named *MyInfo.dat* can be opened for binary output.

```
FileOutputStream fstream = new FileOutputStream("MyInfo.dat");
DataOutputStream outputFile = new DataOutputStream(fstream);
```

The first line creates an instance of the FileOutputStream class, which has the ability to open a file for binary output and establish a connection with it. You pass the name of the file that you wish open, as a string, to the constructor. The second line creates an instance of the DataOutputStream object that is connected to the FileOutputStream referenced by fstream. The result of this statement is that the outputFile variable will reference an object that is able to write binary data to the *MyInfo.dat* file.

> **WARNING!** If the file that you are opening with the FileOutputStream object already exists, it will be erased and an empty file by the same name will be created.

> **NOTE:** The FileOutputStream constructor throws an IOException if an error occurs when it attempts to open the file.

If there is no reason to reference the FileOutputStream object, these statements can be combined into one, as follows:

```
DataOutputStream outputFile =
    new DataOutputStream(new FileOutputStream("MyInfo.dat"));
```

Once the `DataOutputStream` object has been created, you can use it to write binary data to the file. Table 10-1 lists some of the `DataOutputStream` methods. Note that each of the methods listed in the table throws an `IOException` if an error occurs.

Table 10-1 Some of the `DataOutputStream` methods

Method	Description
void close()	Closes the file.
void writeBoolean(boolean b)	Writes the boolean value passed to *b* to the file.
void writeByte(byte b)	Writes the byte value passed to *b* to the file.
void writeChar(int c)	This method accepts an int which is assumed to be a character code. The character it represents is written to the file as a two-byte Unicode character.
void writeDouble(double d)	Writes the double value passed to *d* to the file.
void writeFloat(float f)	Writes the float value passed to *f* to the file.
void writeInt(int i)	Writes the int value passed to *i* to the file.
void writeLong(long num)	Writes the long value passed to *num* to the file.
void writeShort(short s)	Writes the short value passed to *s* to the file.
void writeUTF(String str)	Writes the String object passed to *str* to the file using the Unicode Text Format.

The program in Code Listing 10-13 shows a simple demonstration. An array of int values is written to the file *Numbers.dat*.

Code Listing 10-13   (WriteBinaryFile.java)

```java
1   import java.io.*;
2
3   /**
4    * This program opens a binary file and writes the contents
5    * of an int array to the file.
6    */
7
8   public class WriteBinaryFile
9   {
10     public static void main(String[] args) throws IOException
11     {
12        // Create an array of integers.
13        int[] numbers = { 2, 4, 6, 8, 10, 12, 14 };
14
```

```
15        // Open a binary file for output.
16        FileOutputStream fstream =
17                      new FileOutputStream("Numbers.dat");
18        DataOutputStream outputFile =
19                      new DataOutputStream(fstream);
20
21        System.out.println("Writing to the file...");
22
23        // Write the array elements to the binary file.
24        for (int i = 0; i < numbers.length; i++)
25           outputFile.writeInt(numbers[i]);
26
27        // Close the file.
28        outputFile.close();
29        System.out.println("Done.");
30     }
31 }
```

Program Output

```
Writing to the file...
Done.
```

Reading Data from a Binary File

To open a binary file for input, you use the following classes:

FileInputStream	This class allows you to open a file for reading binary data and establish a connection with it. It provides only the basic functionality for reading bytes from the file, however.
DataInputStream	This class allows you to read data of any primitive type, or String objects, from a binary file. The DataInputStream class by itself cannot directly access a file, however. It is used in conjunction with a FileInputStream object that has a connection to a file.

To open a binary file for input, you wrap a DataInputStream object around a FileInputStream object. The following code shows the file *MyInfo.dat* can be opened for binary input.

```
FileInputStream fstream = new FileInputStream("MyInfo.dat");
DataInputStream inputFile = new DataInputStream(fstream);
```

The following code, which combines these two statements into one, can also be used:

```
DataInputStream inputFile =
        new DataInputStream(new FileInputStream("MyInfo.dat"));
```

The FileInputStream constructor will throw a FileNotFoundException if the file named by the string argument cannot be found. Once the DataInputStream object has been created, you can use it to read binary data from the file. Table 10-2 lists some of the DataInputStream methods. Note that each of the read methods listed in the table throws an EOFException if the end of the file has already been reached.

Table 10-2 Some of the `DataInputStream` methods

Method	Description
`void close()`	Closes the file.
`boolean readBoolean()`	Reads a `boolean` value from the file and returns it.
`byte readByte()`	Reads a `byte` value from the file and returns it.
`char readChar()`	Reads a `char` value from the file and returns it. The character is expected to be stored as a two-byte Unicode character, as written by the `DataOutputStream` class's `writeChar` method.
`double readDouble()`	Reads a `double` value from the file and returns it.
`float readFloat()`	Reads a `float` value from the file and returns it.
`int readInt()`	Reads an `int` value from the file and returns it.
`long readLong()`	Reads a `long` value from the file and returns it.
`short readShort()`	Reads a `short` value from the file and returns it.
`String readUTF()`	Reads a string from the file and returns it as a `String` object. The string must have been written with the `DataOutputStream` class's `writeUTF` method.

The program in Code Listing 10-14 opens the *Numbers.dat* file that was created by the program in Code Listing 10-13. The numbers are read from the file and displayed on the screen. Notice that the program must catch the `EOFException` in order to determine when the file's end has been reached.

Code Listing 10-14   (`ReadBinaryFile.java`)

```
 1  import java.io.*;
 2
 3  /**
 4   *  This program opens a binary file, then reads and displays
 5   *  the contents.
 6   */
 7
 8  public class ReadBinaryFile
 9  {
10     public static void main(String[] args) throws IOException
11     {
12        int number;              // To hold a number
13        boolean endOfFile = false; // End of file flag
14
15        // Open Numbers.dat as a binary file.
16        FileInputStream fstream =
17                 new FileInputStream("Numbers.dat");
18        DataInputStream inputFile =
19                 new DataInputStream(fstream);
```

```
20
21          System.out.println("Reading numbers from the file:");
22
23          // Read data from the file.
24          while (!endOfFile)
25          {
26              try
27              {
28                  number = inputFile.readInt();
29                  System.out.print(number + " ");
30              }
31              catch (EOFException e)
32              {
33                  endOfFile = true;
34              }
35          }
36
37          // Close the file.
38          inputFile.close();
39          System.out.println("\nDone.");
40      }
41  }
```

Program Output

```
Reading numbers from the file:
2 4 6 8 10 12 14
Done.
```

Writing and Reading Strings

To write a string to a binary file you should use the DataOutputStream class's writeUTF method. This method writes its String argument in a format known as *UTF-8 encoding*. Here's how the encoding works: Just before writing the string, this method writes a two-byte integer indicating the number of bytes that the string occupies. Then, it writes the string's characters in Unicode. (UTF stands for Unicode Text Format.)

When the DataInputStream class's readUTF method reads from the file, it expects the first two bytes to contain the number of bytes that the string occupies. It then reads that many bytes and returns them as a String.

For example, assuming that outputFile references a DataOutputStream object, the following code uses the writeUTF method to write a string:

```
String name = "Chloe";
outputFile.writeUTF(name);
```

Assuming that inputFile references a DataInputStream object, the following statement uses the readUTF method to read a UTF-8 encoded string from the file:

```
String name = inputFile.readUTF();
```

Remember that the readUTF method will correctly read a string only when the string was written with the writeUTF method.

> **NOTE:** The book's source code, available at www.pearsonhighered.com/gaddis, contains the example programs WriteUTF.java and ReadUTF.java, which demonstrate writing and reading strings using these methods.

Appending Data to an Existing Binary File

If you pass the name of an existing file to the FileOutputStream constructor, it will be erased and a new empty file with the same name will be created. Sometimes, however, you want to preserve an existing file and append new data to its current contents. The FileOutputStream constructor takes an optional second argument which must be a boolean value. If the argument is true, the file will not be erased if it already exists and new data will be written to the end of the file. If the argument is false, the file will be erased if it already exists. For example, the following code opens the file *MyInfo.dat* for output. If the file exists, it will not be deleted, and any data written to the file will be appended to the existing data.

```
FileOutputStream fstream = new FileOutputStream("MyInfo.dat", true);
DataOutputStream outputFile = new DataOutputStream(fstream);
```

Random Access Files

All of the programs that you have created to access files so far have performed *sequential file access*. With sequential access, when a file is opened for input, its read position is at the very beginning of the file. This means that the first time data is read from the file, the data will be read from its beginning. As the reading continues, the file's read position advances sequentially through the file's contents.

The problem with sequential file access is that in order to read a specific byte from the file, all the bytes that precede it must be read first. For instance, if a program needs data stored at the hundredth byte of a file, it will have to read the first 99 bytes to reach it. If you've ever listened to a cassette tape player, you understand sequential access. To listen to a song at the end of the tape, you have to listen to all the songs that are before it, or fast-forward over them. There is no way to immediately jump to that particular song.

Although sequential file access is useful in many circumstances, it can slow a program down tremendously. If the file is very large, locating data buried deep inside it can take a long time. Alternatively, Java allows a program to perform *random file access*. In random file access, a program can immediately jump to any location in the file without first reading the preceding bytes. The difference between sequential and random file access is like the difference between a cassette tape and a compact disc. When listening to a CD, there is no need to listen to or fast-forward over unwanted songs. You simply jump to the track that you want to listen to. This is illustrated in Figure 10-9.

Figure 10-9   Sequential access vs. random access

Items in a sequential access file are accessed one after the other.

Items in a random access file are accessed in any order.

To create and work with random access files in Java, you use the `RandomAccessFile` class, which is in the `java.io` package. The general format of the class constructor is:

```
RandomAccessFile(String filename, String mode)
```

The first argument is the name of the file. The second argument is a string indicating the mode in which you wish to use the file. The two modes are `"r"` for reading, and `"rw"` for reading and writing. When a file is opened with `"r"` as the mode, the program can only read from the file. When a file is opened with `"rw"` as the mode, the program can read from the file and write to it. Here are some examples of statements that open files using the `RandomAccessFile` class:

```
// Open a file for random reading.
RandomAccessFile randomFile = new RandomAccessFile("MyData.dat", "r");

// Open a file for random reading and writing.
RandomAccessFile randomFile = new RandomAccessFile("MyData.dat", "rw");
```

Here are some important points to remember about the two modes:

- If you open a file in `"r"` mode and the file does not exist, a `FileNotFoundException` will be thrown.
- If you open a file in `"r"` mode and try to write to it, an `IOException` will be thrown.
- If you open an existing file in `"rw"` mode, it will not be deleted. The file's existing contents will be preserved.
- If you open a file in `"rw"` mode and the file does not exist, it will be created.

Reading and Writing with the `RandomAccessFile` Class

A file that is opened or created with the `RandomAccessFile` class is treated as a binary file. In fact, the `RandomAccessFile` class has the same methods as the `DataOutputStream` class for writing data, and the same methods as the `DataInputStream` class for reading data. In fact, you can use the `RandomAccessFile` class to sequentially process a binary file. For example, the program in Code Listing 10-15 opens a file named *Letters.dat* and writes all of the letters of the alphabet to the file.

Code Listing 10-15   (WriteLetters.java)

```java
 1  import java.io.*;
 2
 3  /**
 4   *  This program uses a RandomAccessFile object to create
 5   *  the file Letters.dat. The letters of the alphabet are
 6   *  written to the file.
 7   */
 8
 9  public class WriteLetters
10  {
11     public static void main(String[] args) throws IOException
12     {
13        // The letters array has all 26 letters of the alphabet.
14        char[] letters = { 'a', 'b', 'c', 'd', 'e', 'f', 'g',
15                           'h', 'i', 'j', 'k', 'l', 'm', 'n',
16                           'o', 'p', 'q', 'r', 's', 't', 'u',
17                           'v', 'w', 'x', 'y', 'z' };
18
19        System.out.println("Opening the file.");
20
21        // Open a file for reading and writing.
22        RandomAccessFile randomFile =
23                    new RandomAccessFile("Letters.dat", "rw");
24
25        System.out.println("Writing data to the file...");
26
27        // Sequentially write the letters array to the file.
28        for (int i = 0; i < letters.length; i++)
29           randomFile.writeChar(letters[i]);
30
31        // Close the file.
32        randomFile.close();
33        System.out.println("Done.");
34     }
35  }
```

Program Output

```
Opening the file.
Writing data to the file...
Done.
```

After this program executes, the letters of the alphabet will be stored in the *Letters.dat* file. Because the writeChar method was used, the letters will each be stored as two-byte characters. This fact will be important to know later when we want to read the characters from the file.

The File Pointer

The `RandomAccessFile` class treats a file as a stream of bytes. The bytes are numbered, with the first byte being byte 0. The last byte's number is one less than the number of bytes in the file. These byte numbers are similar to an array's subscripts, and are used to identify locations in the file.

Internally, the `RandomAccessFile` class keeps a long integer value known as the file pointer. The *file pointer* holds the byte number of a location in the file. When a file is first opened, the file pointer is set to 0. This causes it to "point" to the first byte in the file. When an item is read from the file, it is read from the byte that the file pointer points to. Reading also causes the file pointer to advance to the byte just beyond the item that was read. For example, let's say the file pointer points to byte 0 and an `int` is read from the file with the `readInt` method. An `int` is four bytes in size, so four bytes will be read from the file, starting at byte 0. After the value is read, the file pointer will be advanced to byte number 4, which is the fifth byte in the file. If another item is immediately read, the reading will begin at byte number 4. If the file pointer refers to a byte number that is beyond the end of the file, an `EOFException` is thrown when a read operation is performed.

Writing also takes place at the location pointed to by the file pointer. If the file pointer points to the end of the file when a write operation is performed, then the data will be written to the end of the file. However, if the file pointer holds the number of a byte within the file, at a location where data is already stored, then a write operation will cause data to be written over the existing data at that location.

Not only does the `RandomAccessFile` class let you read and write data, but it also allows you to move the file pointer. This means that you can immediately read data from any byte location in the file. It also means that you can write data to any location in the file, over existing data. To move the file pointer, you use the `seek` method. Here is the method's general format:

```
void seek(long position)
```

The argument is the number of the byte that you want to move the file pointer to. For example, look at the following code.

```
RandomAccessFile file = new RandomAccessFile("MyInfo.dat", "r");
file.seek(99);
byte b = file.readByte();
```

This code opens the file *MyInfo.dat* for reading. The `seek` method is called to move the file pointer to byte number 99 (which is the 100th byte in the file). Then, the `readByte` method is called to read byte number 99 from the file. After that statement executes, the file pointer will be advanced by one byte, so it will point to byte 100. Suppose we continue processing the same file with the following code:

```
file.seek(49);
int i = file.readInt();
```

First, the `seek` method moves the file pointer to byte number 49 (which is the 50th byte in the file). Then, the `readInt` method is called. This reads an `int` from the file. An `int` is four bytes in size, so this statement reads four bytes, beginning at byte number 49. After the statement executes the file pointer will be advanced by four bytes, so it will point to byte 53.

Although a file might contain chars, ints, doubles, strings, and so forth, the RandomAccessFile class sees it only as a stream of bytes. The class is unaware of the data types of the data stored in the file, and it cannot determine where one item of data ends and another begins. When you write a program that reads data from a random access file, it is your responsibility to know how the data is structured.

For example, recall that the program in Code Listing 10-14 wrote the letters of the alphabet to the *Letters.dat* file. Let's say the first letter is character 0, the second letter is character 1, and so forth. Suppose we want to read character 5 (the sixth letter in the file). At first, we might be tempted to try the following code:

```
// Open the file for reading.
RandomAccessFile randomFile =
                new RandomAccessFile("Letters.dat", "r");
// Move the file pointer to byte 5, which is the 6th byte.
randomFile.seek(5);
// Read the character.
char ch = randomFile.readChar();
// What will this display?
System.out.println("The sixth letter is " + ch);
```

Although this code will compile and run, you might be surprised at the result. Recall that the writeChar method writes a character as two bytes. Because each character occupies two bytes in the file, the sixth character begins at byte 10, not byte 5. This is illustrated in Figure 10-10. In fact, if we try to read a character starting at byte 5, we will read garbage because byte 5 is not at the beginning of a character.

Figure 10-10   Layout of the *Letters.dat* file

To determine the position of a character in the file, we must take each character's size into account. The following code will correctly read and display the sixth character. To determine the character's starting byte number, it multiplies the size of a character by the number of the character we want to locate.

```
final int CHAR_SIZE = 2;    // Each char uses two bytes
// Move the file pointer to character 5.
randomFile.seek(CHAR_SIZE * 5);
// Read the character.
char ch = randomFile.readChar();
// This will display the correct character.
System.out.println("The sixth character is " + ch);
```

The program in Code Listing 10-16 demonstrates further. It randomly reads characters 5, 10, and 3 from the file.

Code Listing 10-16   (ReadRandomLetters.java)

```java
1  import java.io.*;
2
3  /**
4   * This program uses the RandomAccessFile class
5   * to open the file Letters.dat and randomly read
6   * letters from different locations.
7   */
8
9  public class ReadRandomLetters
10 {
11    public static void main(String[] args) throws IOException
12    {
13       final int CHAR_SIZE = 2;    // 2 byte characters
14       long byteNum;               // For the byte number
15       char ch;                    // To hold a character
16
17       // Open the file for reading.
18       RandomAccessFile randomFile =
19                 new RandomAccessFile("Letters.dat", "r");
20
21       // Move to character 5. This is the sixth character
22       // from the beginning of the file.
23       byteNum = CHAR_SIZE * 5;
24       randomFile.seek(byteNum);
25
26       // Read the character stored at this location
27       // and display it. Should be the letter f.
28       ch = randomFile.readChar();
29       System.out.println(ch);
30
31       // Move to character 10 (the 11th character),
32       // read the character and display it.
33       // Should be the letter k.
34       byteNum = CHAR_SIZE * 10;
35       randomFile.seek(byteNum);
36       ch = randomFile.readChar();
37       System.out.println(ch);
38
39       // Move to character 3 (the fourth character),
40       // read the character and display it.
41       // Should be the letter d.
```

```
42              byteNum = CHAR_SIZE * 3;
43              randomFile.seek(byteNum);
44              ch = randomFile.readChar();
45              System.out.println(ch);
46
47              // Close the file.
48              randomFile.close();
49          }
50      }
```

Program Output

```
f
k
d
```

Appendix I *Working with Records and Random Access Files* is available on this book's online resource page at www.pearsonhighered.com/gaddis.

Object Serialization

In the previous section you saw how an object's fields can be retrieved and saved to a file as fields in a record. If an object contains other types of objects as fields, however, the process of saving its contents can become complicated. Fortunately, Java allows you to *serialize* objects, which is a simpler way of saving objects to a file.

When an object is serialized, it is converted into a series of bytes that contain the object's data. If the object is set up properly, even the other objects that it might contain as fields are automatically serialized. The resulting set of bytes can be saved to a file for later retrieval.

In order for an object to be serialized, its class must implement the Serializable interface. The Serializable interface, which is in the java.io package, has no methods or fields. It is used only to let the Java compiler know that objects of the class might be serialized. In addition, if a class contains objects of other classes as fields, those classes must also implement the Serializable interface, in order to be serialized.

For example, the book's source code contains a modified version of the InventoryItem class named InventoryItem2. The only modification to the class is that it implements the Serializable interface. Here are the modified lines of code from the file:

```
import java.io.Serializable;

public class InventoryItem2 implements Serializable
```

This new code tells the compiler that we want to be able to serialize objects of the InventoryItem2 class. But what about the class's description field, which is String object? The String class, as well as many others in the Java API, also implement the Serializable interface. So, the InventoryItem2 class is ready for serialization.

To write a serialized object to a file, you use an `ObjectOutputStream` object. The `ObjectOutputStream` class is designed to perform the serialization process (converting an object to a series of bytes). To write the bytes to a file, you must also use an output stream object, such as `FileOutputStream`. Here is an example:

```
FileOutputStream outStream =
        new FileOutputStream("Objects.dat");
ObjectOutputStream objectOutputFile =
        new ObjectOutputStream(outStream);
```

To serialize an object and write it to the file, use the `ObjectOutputStream` class's `writeObject` method, as shown here:

```
InventoryItem2 item = new InventoryItem2("Wrench", 20);
objectOutputFile.writeObject(item);
```

The `writeObject` method throws an `IOException` if an error occurs.

The process of reading a serialized object's bytes and constructing an object from them is known as *deserialization*. To deserialize an object you use an `ObjectInputStream` object, along with a `FileInputStream` object. Here is an example of how to set the objects up:

```
FileInputStream inStream =
        new FileInputStream("Objects.dat");
ObjectInputStream objectInputFile =
        new ObjectInputStream(inStream);
```

To read a serialized object from the file, use the `ObjectInputStream` class's `readObject` method. Here is an example:

```
InventoryItem2 item;
item = (InventoryItem2) objectInputFile.readObject();
```

The `readObject` method returns the deserialized object. Notice that you must cast the return value to the desired class type. (The `readObject` method throws a number of different exceptions if an error occurs. See the API documentation for more information.)

The following programs demonstrate how to serialize and deserialize objects. The program in Code Listing 10-17 serializes three `InventoryItem2` objects, and the program in Code Listing 10-18 deserializes them.

Code Listing 10-17   (SerializeObjects.java)

```
 1   import java.util.Scanner;
 2   import java.io.*;
 3
 4   /**
 5    *  This program serializes the objects in an array of
 6    *  InventoryItem2 objects.
 7    */
 8
 9   public class SerializeObjects
10   {
```

```
11    public static void main(String[] args) throws IOException
12    {
13       final int NUM_ITEMS = 3;   // Number of items
14       String description;        // Item description
15       int units;                 // Units on hand
16
17       // Create a Scanner object for keyboard input.
18       Scanner keyboard = new Scanner(System.in);
19
20       // Create an array to hold InventoryItem objects.
21       InventoryItem2[] items =
22                    new InventoryItem2[NUM_ITEMS];
23
24       // Get data for the InventoryItem objects.
25       System.out.println("Enter data for " + NUM_ITEMS +
26                         " inventory items.");
27
28       for (int i = 0; i < items.length; i++)
29       {
30          // Get the item description.
31          System.out.print("Enter an item description: ");
32          description = keyboard.nextLine();
33
34          // Get the number of units.
35          System.out.print("Enter the number of units: ");
36          units = keyboard.nextInt();
37
38          // Consume the remaining newline.
39          keyboard.nextLine();
40
41          // Create an InventoryItem2 object in the array.
42          items[i] = new InventoryItem2(description, units);
43       }
44
45       // Create the stream objects.
46       FileOutputStream outStream =
47             new FileOutputStream("Objects.dat");
48       ObjectOutputStream objectOutputFile =
49             new ObjectOutputStream(outStream);
50
51       // Write the serialized objects to the file.
52       for (int i = 0; i < items.length; i++)
53       {
54          objectOutputFile.writeObject(items[i]);
55       }
56
```

```
57        // Close the file.
58        objectOutputFile.close();
59        System.out.println("The serialized objects were written to the " +
60                           "Objects.dat file.");
61    }
62 }
```

Program Output with Example Input Shown in Bold

```
Enter data for 3 inventory items.
Enter an item description: Wrench [Enter]
Enter the number of units: 20 [Enter]
Enter an item description: Hammer [Enter]
Enter the number of units: 15 [Enter]
Enter an item description: Pliers [Enter]
Enter the number of units: 12 [Enter]
The serialized objects were written to the Objects.dat file.
```

Code Listing 10-18   (DeserializeObjects.java)

```
1  import java.io.*;
2
3  /**
4   *  This program deserializes the objects in the Objects.dat
5   *  file and stores them in an array.
6   */
7
8  public class DeserializeObjects
9  {
10    public static void main(String[] args) throws Exception
11    {
12       final int NUM_ITEMS = 3;   // Number of items
13
14       // Create the stream objects.
15       FileInputStream inStream =
16             new FileInputStream("Objects.dat");
17       ObjectInputStream objectInputFile =
18             new ObjectInputStream(inStream);
19
20       // Create an array to hold InventoryItem objects.
21       InventoryItem2[] items = new InventoryItem2[NUM_ITEMS];
22
23       // Read the serialized objects from the file.
24       for (int i = 0; i < items.length; i++)
25       {
26          items[i] =
27                (InventoryItem2) objectInputFile.readObject();
28       }
```

```
29
30          // Close the file.
31          objectInputFile.close();
32
33          // Display the objects.
34          for (int i = 0; i < items.length; i++)
35          {
36              System.out.println("Item " + (i + 1));
37              System.out.println("   Description: " +
38                                      items[i].getDescription());
39              System.out.println("   Units: " +
40                                      items[i].getUnits());
41          }
42      }
43  }
```

Program Output

```
Item 1
   Description: Wrench
   Units: 20
Item 2
   Description: Hammer
   Units: 15
Item 3
   Description: Pliers
   Units: 12
```

 Checkpoint

10.20 What is the difference between a text file and a binary file?

10.21 What classes do you use to write output to a binary file? To read from a binary file?

10.22 What is the difference between sequential and random access?

10.23 What class do you use to work with random access files?

10.24 What are the two modes that a random access file can be opened in? Explain the difference between them.

10.25 What must you do to a class in order to serialize objects of that class?

 10.4 Common Errors to Avoid

The following list describes several errors that are commonly made when learning this chapter's topics.

- **Assuming that all statements inside a try block will execute.** When an exception is thrown, the try block is exited immediately. This means that statements appearing in the try block after the offending statement will not be executed.

- **Getting the `try`, `catch`, and `finally` clauses out of order.** In a try statement, the try clause must appear first, followed by all of the catch clauses, followed by the optional finally clause.

- **Writing two `catch` clauses that handle the same exception in the same `try` statement.** You cannot have more than one catch clause per exception type in the same try statement.

- **When catching multiple exceptions that are related to one another through inheritance, listing the more general exceptions first.** When in the same try statement you are handling multiple exceptions, and some of the exceptions are related to each other through inheritance, then you should handle the more specialized exception classes before the more general exception classes. Otherwise, an error will occur because the compiler thinks you are handling the same exception more than once.

- **Forgetting to write a `throws` clause on a method that can throw a checked exception but does not handle the exception.** If a method is capable of throwing a checked exception but does not handle the exception, it must have a throws clause in its header that specifies the exception.

- **Calling a method but not handling an exception that it might throw.** You must either handle all of the checked exceptions that a method can throw, or list them in the calling method's throws clause.

- **In a custom exception class, forgetting to pass an error message to the superclass's constructor.** If you do not pass an error message to the superclass's constructor, the exception object will have a null error message.

- **Serializing an object with members that are not serializable.** If a class has fields that are objects of other classes, those classes must implement the `Serializable` interface in order to be serialized.

Review Questions and Exercises

Multiple Choice and True/False

1. When an exception is generated, it is said to have been
   a. built
   b. thrown
   c. caught
   d. killed

2. This is a section of code that gracefully responds to exceptions.
   a. exception generator
   b. exception manipulator
   c. exception handler
   d. exception monitor

3. If your code does not handle an exception when it is thrown, it is dealt with by this.
   a. default exception handler
   b. the operating system
   c. system debugger
   d. default exception generator

4. All exception classes inherit from this class.
   a. `Error`
   b. `RuntimeException`
   c. `JavaException`
   d. `Throwable`

5. `FileNotFoundException` inherits from
   a. `Error`
   b. `IOException`
   c. `JavaException`
   d. `FileException`

6. You can think of this code as being "protected" because the application will not halt if it throws an exception.
   a. try block
   b. catch block
   c. finally block
   d. protected block

7. This method can be used to retrieve the error message from an exception object.
   a. `errorMessage`
   b. `errorString`
   c. `getError`
   d. `getMessage`

8. The numeric wrapper classes' "parse" methods all throw an exception of this type.
   a. `ParseException`
   b. `NumberFormatException`
   c. `IOException`
   d. `BadNumberException`

9. This is one or more statements that are always executed after the try block has executed and after any catch blocks have executed if an exception was thrown.
   a. try block
   b. catch block
   c. finally block
   d. protected block

10. This is an internal list of all the methods that are currently executing.
    a. invocation list
    b. call stack
    c. call list
    d. list trace

11. This method can be called from any exception object, and it shows the chain of methods that were called when the exception was thrown.
    a. `printInvocationList`
    b. `printCallStack`
    c. `printStackTrace`
    d. `printCallList`

12. These are exceptions that inherit from the `Error` class or the `RuntimeException` class.
    a. unrecoverable exceptions
    b. unchecked exceptions
    c. recoverable exceptions
    d. checked exceptions

13. All exceptions that do *not* inherit from the `Error` class or the `RuntimeException` class are
    a. unrecoverable exceptions
    b. unchecked exceptions
    c. recoverable exceptions
    d. checked exceptions

14. This informs the compiler of the exceptions that could get thrown from a method.
    a. `throws` clause
    b. parameter list
    c. `catch` clause
    d. method return type

15. You use this statement to manually throw an exception.
    a. `try`
    b. `generate`
    c. `throw`
    d. `System.exit(0)`

16. This is the process of converting an object to a series of bytes that represent the object's data.
    a. Serialization
    b. Deserialization
    c. Dynamic conversion
    d. Casting

17. **True or False:** You are not required to catch exceptions that inherit from the `RuntimeException` class.

18. **True or False:** When an exception is thrown by code inside a try block, all of the statements in the try block are always executed.

19. **True or False:** `IOException` serves as a superclass for exceptions that are related to programming errors, such as an out-of-bounds array subscript.

20. **True or False:** You cannot have more than one `catch` clause per `try` statement.

21. **True or False:** When an exception is thrown, the JVM searches the `try` statement's `catch` clauses from top to bottom and passes control of the program to the first `catch` clause with a parameter that is compatible with the exception.

22. **True or False:** Not including polymorphic references, a `try` statement can have only one `catch` clause for each specific type of exception.

23. **True or False:** When in the same `try` statement you are handling multiple exceptions and some of the exceptions are related to each other through inheritance, you should handle the more general exception classes before the more specialized exception classes.

24. **True or False:** The `throws` clause causes an exception to be thrown.

Find the Error

Find the error in each of the following code segments.

1.
```java
catch (FileNotFoundException e)
{
    System.out.println("File not found.");
}
try
{
    File file = new File("MyFile.txt");
    Scanner inputFile = new Scanner(file);
}
```

2.
```java
// Assume inputFile references a Scanner object.
try
{
    input = inputFile.nextInt();
}
finally
{
    inputFile.close();
}
catch (InputMismatchException e)
{
    System.out.println(e.getMessage());
}
```

3.
```java
try
{
    number = Integer.parseInt(str);
}
catch (Exception e)
{
    System.out.println(e.getMessage());
}
catch (IllegalArgumentException e)
{
    System.out.println("Bad number format.");
}
catch (NumberFormatException e)
{
    System.out.println(str + " is not a number.");
}
```

Algorithm Workbench

1. Look at the following program and tell what the program will output when run.

```java
public class ExceptionTest
{
    public static void main(String[] args)
    {
        int number;
        String str;

        try
        {
            str = "xyz";
            number = Integer.parseInt(str);
            System.out.println("A");
        }
        catch(NumberFormatException e)
        {
            System.out.println("B");
        }
        catch(IllegalArgumentException e)
        {
            System.out.println("C");
        }

        System.out.println("D");
    }
}
```

2. Look at the following program and tell what the program will output when run.

```java
public class ExceptionTest
{
    public static void main(String[] args)
    {
        int number;
        String str;

        try
        {
            str = "xyz";
            number = Integer.parseInt(str);
            System.out.println("A");
        }
        catch(NumberFormatException e)
        {
            System.out.println("B");
        }
```

```
            catch(IllegalArgumentException e)
            {
                System.out.println("C");
            }
            finally
            {
                System.out.println("D");
            }
            System.out.println("E");
        }
    }
```

3. Write a method that searches a numeric array for a specified value. The method should return the subscript of the element containing the value if it is found in the array. If the value is not found, the method should throw an exception of the `Exception` class with the error message "Element not found".

4. Write a statement that throws an `IllegalArgumentException` with the error message "Argument cannot be negative".

5. Write an exception class that can be thrown when a negative number is passed to a method.

6. Write a statement that throws an instance of the exception class that you created in Question 5.

7. The method `getValueFromFile` is public and returns an int. It accepts no arguments. The method is capable of throwing an `IOException` and a `FileNotFoundException`. Write the header for this method.

8. Write a `try` statement that calls the `getValueFromFile` method described in Question 7. Be sure to handle all the exceptions that the method can throw.

9. Write a statement that creates an object that can be used to write binary data to the file *Configuration.dat*.

10. Assume that the reference variable r refers to a serializable object. Write code that serializes the object to the file *ObjectData.dat*.

Short Answer

1. What is meant when it is said that an exception is thrown?

2. What does it mean to catch an exception?

3. What happens when an exception is thrown, but the `try` statement does not have a `catch` clause that is capable of catching it?

4. What is the purpose of a `finally` clause?

5. Where does execution resume after an exception has been thrown and caught?

6. When multiple exceptions are caught in the same `try` statement and some of them are related through inheritance, does the order in which they are listed matter?

7. What types of objects can be thrown?

8. When are you required to have a `throws` clause in a method header?

9.   What is the difference between a checked exception and an unchecked exception?

10. What is the difference between the throw statement and the throws clause?

11. What is the difference between a text file and a binary file?

12. What is the difference between a sequential access file and a random access file?

13. What happens when you serialize an object? What happens when you deserialize an object?

Programming Challenges

1. TestScores Class

Write a class named TestScores. The class constructor should accept an array of test scores as its argument. The class should have a method that returns the average of the test scores. If any test score in the array is negative or greater than 100, the class should throw an IllegalArgumentException. Demonstrate the class in a program.

2. TestScores Class Custom Exception

Write an exception class named InvalidTestScore. Modify the TestScores class you wrote in Programming Challenge 1 so it throws an InvalidTestScore exception if any of the test scores in the array are invalid.

3. RetailItem Exceptions

Programming Challenge 4 of Chapter 3 required you to write a RetailItem class that held data pertaining to a retail item. Write an exception class that can be instantiated and thrown when a negative number is given for the price. Write another exception class that can be instantiated and thrown when a negative number is given for the units on hand. Demonstrate the exception classes in a program.

4. Month Class Exceptions

Programming Challenge 5 of Chapter 6 required you to write a Month class that holds information about the month. Write exception classes for the following error conditions:

- A number less than 1 or greater than 12 is given for the month number.
- An invalid string is given for the name of the month.

Modify the Month class so it throws the appropriate exception when either of these errors occurs. Demonstrate the classes in a program.

5. Payroll Class Exceptions

Programming Challenge 5 of Chapter 3 required you to write a Payroll class that calculates an employee's payroll. Write exception classes for the following error conditions:

- An empty string is given for the employee's name.
- An invalid value is given for the employee's ID number. If you implemented this field as a string, then an empty string would be invalid. If you implemented this field as a numeric variable, then a negative number or zero would be invalid.
- An invalid number is given for the number of hours worked. This would be a negative number or a number greater than 84.

- An invalid number is given for the hourly pay rate. This would be a negative number or a number greater than 25.

Modify the `Payroll` class so it throws the appropriate exception when any of these errors occurs. Demonstrate the exception classes in a program.

6. FileArray Class

Design a class that has a static method named `writeArray`. The method should take two arguments: the name of a file and a reference to an `int` array. The file should be opened as a binary file, the contents of the array should be written to the file, and then the file should be closed.

Write a second method in the class named `readArray`. The method should take two arguments: the name of a file and a reference to an `int` array. The file should be opened, data should be read from the file and stored in the array, and then the file should be closed. Demonstrate both methods in a program.

7. File Encryption Filter

File encryption is the science of writing the contents of a file in a secret code. Your encryption program should work like a filter, reading the contents of one file, modifying the data into a code, and then writing the coded contents out to a second file. The second file will be a version of the first file, but written in a secret code.

Although there are complex encryption techniques, you should come up with a simple one of your own. For example, you could read the first file one character at a time, and add 10 to the character code of each character before it is written to the second file.

8. File Decryption Filter

Write a program that decrypts the file produced by the program in Programming Challenge 7. The decryption program should read the contents of the coded file, restore the data to its original state, and write it to another file.

9. TestScores Modification for Serialization

Modify the `TestScores` class that you created for Programming Challenge 1 to be serializable. Write a program that creates an array of at least five `TestScore` objects and serializes them. Write another program that deserializes the objects from the file.

10. Bank Account Random File

 NOTE: To do this assignment, be sure to read Appendix I, available on this book's online resource page at www.pearsonhighered.com/gaddis.

One of the example classes you saw in this chapter was the `BankAccount` class. Write a `BankAccountFile` class that manages a random access file of `BankAccount` object records. The class should read and write records, and move the file pointer to any location within the file. (The class should be similar to the `InventoryItemFile` class, which is presented in Appendix I.) In a program or programs demonstrate how to create records, randomly look at records, and randomly modify records.

ideoNote
he Exception
roject Problem

11. Exception Project

This assignment assumes you have completed Programming Challenge 1 of Chapter 9 (`Employee` and `ProductionWorker` Classes). Modify the `Employee` and `ProductionWorker` classes so they throw exceptions when the following errors occur:

- The `Employee` class should throw an exception named `InvalidEmployeeNumber` when it receives an employee number that is less than 0 or greater than 9999.
- The `ProductionWorker` class should throw an exception named `InvalidShift` when it receives an invalid shift.
- The `ProductionWorker` class should throw an exception named `InvalidPayRate` when it receives a negative number for the hourly pay rate.

Write a test program that demonstrates how each of these exception conditions work.

11 GUI Applications—Part 1

TOPICS

11.1   Introduction
11.2   Dialog Boxes
11.3   Creating Windows
11.4   Layout Managers
11.5   Radio Buttons and Check Boxes
11.6   Borders

11.7   Focus on Problem Solving: Extending the `JPanel` Class
11.8   Splash Screens
11.9   Using Console Output to Debug a GUI Application
11.10 Common Errors to Avoid

11.1 Introduction

CONCEPT: In Java, you use the Java Foundation Classes (JFC) to create a graphical user interface for your application. Within the JFC you use the Abstract Windowing Toolkit (AWT) or Swing classes to create a graphical user interface.

In this chapter we discuss the basics of creating a Java application with a *graphical user interface* or *GUI* (pronounced "gooey"). A GUI is a graphical window or a system of graphical windows presented by an application for interaction with the user. In addition to accepting input from the keyboard, GUIs typically accept input from a mouse as well.

A window in a GUI commonly consists of several *components* that present data to the user and/or allow interaction with the application. Some of the common GUI components are buttons, labels, text fields, check boxes, and radio buttons. Figure 11-1 shows an example of a window with a variety of components. Table 11-1 describes the components that appear in the window.

Figure 11-1 Various GUI components

Table 11-1 Some GUI components

Component	Description
Label	An area that can display text.
Text field	An area in which the user may type a single line of input from the keyboard.
Combo box	A component that displays a drop-down list of items from which the user may select. A combo box also provides a text field in which the user may type input. It is called a combo box because it is the combination of a list and a text field.
Check box	A component that has a box that may be checked or unchecked.
List	A list from which the user may select an item.
Radio button	A component that can be either selected or deselected. Radio buttons usually appear in groups and allow the user to select one of several options.
Slider	A component that allows the user to select a value by moving a slider along a track.
Button	A button that can cause an action to occur when it is clicked.

The JFC, AWT, and Swing

Java programmers use the *Java Foundation Classes (JFC)* to create GUI applications. The JFC consists of several sets of classes, many of which are beyond the scope of this book. The two sets of JFC classes that we focus on are the AWT and Swing classes. First, we discuss the differences between these two.

Java has been equipped, since its earliest version, with a set of classes for drawing graphics and creating graphical user interfaces. These classes are part of the *Abstract Windowing Toolkit (AWT)*. The AWT allows programmers to create applications and applets that interact with the user via windows and other GUI components.

Programmers are limited in what they can do with the AWT, however. This is because the AWT does not actually draw user interface components on the screen. Instead, the AWT communicates with another layer of software, known as the *peer classes*, which directs the underlying operating system to draw its own built-in components. Each version of Java developed for a particular operating system has its own set of peer classes. Although this means that Java programs have a look consistent with other applications on the same system, it also leads to some problems.

One problem is that not all operating systems offer the same set of GUI components. For example, one operating system might provide a sophisticated slider bar component that is not found on any other platform. Other operating systems might have their own unique components as well. For the AWT to retain its portability, it has to offer only those components that are common to all the operating systems that support Java.

Another problem is in the behavior of components across various operating systems. A component on one operating system might have slightly different behavior than the same component on a different operating system. In addition, the peer classes for some operating systems reportedly have bugs. As a result, programmers cannot be completely sure how their AWT programs will behave on different operating systems until they test each one.

A third problem is that programmers cannot easily extend the AWT components. Because these components rely on the appearance and behavior of the underlying operating system components, there is little that can be done by the programmer to change their properties.

To remedy these problems, Swing was introduced with the release of Java 2. *Swing* is a library of classes that do not replace the AWT, but provide an improved alternative for creating GUI applications and applets. Very few of the Swing classes rely on an underlying system of peer classes. Instead, Swing draws most of its own components. This means that Swing components can have a consistent look and predictable behavior on any operating system.[1] In addition, Swing components can be easily extended. The Swing library provides many sophisticated components that are not found in the AWT. In this chapter and in Chapter 12 we primarily use Swing to develop GUI applications. In Chapter 13 we use AWT to develop applets.

> **NOTE:** AWT components are commonly called heavyweight components because they are coupled with their underlying peers. Very few of the Swing components are coupled with peers, so they are called lightweight components.

The `javax.swing` and `java.awt` Packages

In this chapter we use the Swing classes for all of the graphical components that we create in our GUIs. The Swing classes are part of the `javax.swing` package. (Take note of the letter x that appears after the word java.) We also use some of the AWT classes to determine when events, such as the clicking of a mouse, take place in our applications. The AWT classes are part of the `java.awt` package. (Note that there is no x after java in this package name.)

---

[1]This does not mean that Swing applications cannot have the look of a specific operating system. The programmer may choose from a variety of "look and feel" themes.

Event-Driven Programming

Programs that operate in a GUI environment must be *event-driven*. An *event* is an action that takes place within a program, such as the clicking of a button. Part of writing a GUI application is creating event listeners. An *event listener* is an object that automatically executes one of its methods when a specific event occurs. If you wish for an application to perform an operation when a particular event occurs, you must create an event listener object that responds when that event takes place.

11.2 Dialog Boxes

CONCEPT: The `JOptionPane` class allows you to quickly display a dialog box, which is a small graphical window displaying a message or requesting input.

Chapter 2 presented an optional section on using the `JOptionPane` class to display dialog boxes. A *dialog box* is a small graphical window that displays a message to the user or requests input. In this section we review the basics of using `JOptionPane` and learn about additional capabilities of the class.

NOTE: If you skipped the optional `JOptionPane` section in Chapter 2, there is no need to go back and read it. This section presents a comprehensive discussion.

You can quickly display a variety of dialog boxes with the `JOptionPane` class. We discuss the following types of dialog boxes and how you can display them using `JoptionPane`.

Message Dialog   This is a dialog box that displays a message. An OK button is also displayed.

Input Dialog   This is a dialog box that prompts the user for input. It provides a text field where input is typed. An OK button and a Cancel button are also displayed.

Confirm Dialog   This is a dialog box that asks the user a Yes/No question. A Yes button, a No button, and a Cancel button are displayed.

Figure 11-2 shows an example of each type of dialog box.

The `JOptionPane` class, which is in the `javax.swing` package, provides static methods to display each type of dialog box.

More about Message Dialogs

The `showMessageDialog` method is used to display a message dialog. There are several overloaded versions of this method. Table 11-2 describes two of the versions.

Figure 11-2 Message box, input box, and confirm box

Message Box

Input Box

Confirm Box

Table 11-2 The showMessageDialog Method

Method	Description
void showMessageDialog(Component parent, Object message	This method displays a message dialog. The argument passed into *parent* is a reference to the graphical component that the dialog box should be displayed within. If you pass null to this parameter, the dialog box appears in the center of the screen. The object passed to the *message* parameter contains the message that is to be displayed.
void showMessageDialog(Component parent, Object message, String title, int messageType)	This method displays a message dialog. The argument passed into *parent* is a reference to the graphical component that the dialog box should be displayed within. If you pass null to this parameter, the dialog box appears in the center of the screen. The object passed to the *message* parameter contains the message to be displayed. The string passed to the *title* parameter is displayed in the dialog box's title bar. The value passed to *messageType* indicates the type of icon to display in the message box.

Here is a statement that calls the first version of the method:

```
JOptionPane.showMessageDialog(null, "Hello World");
```

The first argument can be a reference to a graphical component. The dialog box is displayed inside that component. In this statement we pass null as the first argument. This causes the dialog box to be displayed in the center of the screen. The second argument is the message that we wish to display. This code causes the dialog box in Figure 11-3 to appear.

Figure 11-3 Message dialog box

Notice that by default the dialog box in Figure 11-3 has the string "Message" displayed in its title bar, and an information icon (showing the letter "i") is displayed. You can control the text displayed in the title bar and the type of icon displayed with the second version of the showMessageDialog method. Here is an example:

```
JOptionPane.showMessageDialog(null, "Invalid Data",
                    "My Message Box",
                    JOptionPane.ERROR_MESSAGE);
```

In this method call, the third argument is a string displayed in the dialog box's title bar. The fourth argument is a constant that specifies the type of message being displayed, which determines the type of icon that appears in the dialog box. The constant JOptionPane.ERROR_MESSAGE specifies that an error icon is to be displayed. This statement displays the dialog box shown in Figure 11-4.

Figure 11-4 Message dialog with specified title and icon

The constants that you may use for the message type are JOptionPane.ERROR_MESSAGE, JOptionPane.INFORMATION_MESSAGE, JOptionPane.WARNING_MESSAGE, JOptionPane.QUESTION_MESSAGE, and JOptionPane.PLAIN_MESSAGE. The following statements call the method with each type of message. Figure 11-5 shows the dialog boxes displayed by these messages.

```
// Display an error message.
JOptionPane.showMessageDialog(null, "Error Message",
                                    "Error",
                                    JOptionPane.ERROR_MESSAGE);
// Display an information message.
JOptionPane.showMessageDialog(null, "Information Message",
                                    "Information",
                                    JOptionPane.INFORMATION_MESSAGE);
// Display a warning message.
JOptionPane.showMessageDialog(null, "Warning Message",
                                    "Warning",
                                    JOptionPane.WARNING_MESSAGE);
// Display a question message.
JOptionPane.showMessageDialog(null, "Question Message",
                                    "Question",
                                    JOptionPane.QUESTION_MESSAGE);
// Display a plain message.
JOptionPane.showMessageDialog(null, "Plain Message",
                                    "Message",
                                    JOptionPane.PLAIN_MESSAGE);
```

Figure 11-5   Different types of messages

If the previous code was written into a program just as it appears and then executed, the five dialog boxes shown in Figure 11-5 would be displayed one at a time. The user would have to click the OK button on the first dialog box to close it before the second dialog box would appear. The same would be true for all of the dialog boxes that follow. The dialog boxes displayed by the `JOptionPane` class are modal dialog boxes. A *modal dialog box* suspends execution of any other statements until the dialog box is closed. For example, when the `JOptionPane.showMessageDialog` method is called, the statements that appear after the method call do not execute until the user closes the message box. This is illustrated in Figure 11-6.

Figure 11-6   Execution of statements after displaying a modal dialog box

```
statement;
statement;
JOptionPane.showMessageDialog(null, "Hello World");
statement;
statement;
statement;            These statements will not
                      execute until the message
                      box is closed.
```

More about Input Dialogs

An input dialog is a quick and simple way to ask the user to enter data. Table 11-3 describes two overloaded versions of the static `showInputDialog` method, which displays an input dialog.

Table 11-3   The `showInputDialog` Method

Method	Description
String showInputDialog (Object *message*)	This method displays an input dialog that provides a text field for the user to type input. The object passed to the *message* parameter contains the message to be displayed. If the user clicks on the OK button, this method returns the string entered by the user. If the user clicks on the Cancel button, this method returns *null*.
String showInputDialog (Component *parent*, Object *message*, String *title*, int *messageType*	This method displays an input dialog that provides a text input field for the user to type input. The argument passed into *parent* is a reference to the graphical component that the dialog box should be displayed within. If you pass *null* to this parameter, the dialog box appears in the center of the screen. The object passed to the *message* parameter contains the message to be displayed. The string passed to the *title* parameter is displayed in the dialog box's title bar. The value passed to *messageType* indicates the type of icon to display in the message box. If the user clicks on the OK button, this method returns the string entered by the user. If the user clicks on the Cancel button, this method returns *null*.

The following code calls the first version of the showInputDialog method:

```
String name;
name = JOptionPane.showInputDialog("Enter your name.");
```

The argument passed to the method is the message to display. This statement causes the dialog box shown in Figure 11-7 to be displayed in the center of the screen. If the user clicks on the OK button, name references the string value entered by the user into the text field. If the user clicks on the Cancel button, name references null.

Figure 11-7   Input dialog box

By default, the input dialog box has the string "Input" in its title bar and displays a question icon. The second version of the method shown in Table 11-3 allows you to control the text displayed in the input dialog's title bar and the type of icon displayed. It takes the same arguments as the second version of the showMessageDialog method in Table 11-2. Here is an example:

```
String value;
value = JOptionPane.showInputDialog(null, "Enter the value again.",
                            "Enter Carefully!",
                            JOptionPane.WARNING_MESSAGE);
```

This statement displays the input dialog shown in Figure 11-8. If the user clicks on the OK button, value references the string value entered by the user into the text field. If the user clicks on the Cancel button, value references null.

Figure 11-8   Input dialog box

Displaying Confirm Dialogs

A confirm dialog box typically asks the user a yes or no question. By default a Yes button, a No button, and a Cancel button are displayed. The showConfirmDialog method is used to display a confirm dialog box. There are several overloaded versions of this method. Table 11-4 describes two of them.

Table 11-4 The `showConfirmDialog` Method

Method	Description
`int showConfirmDialog(Component parent, Object message)`	The argument passed into *parent* is a reference to the graphical component that the dialog box should be displayed within. If you pass `null` to this parameter, the dialog box appears in the center of the screen. The object passed to the *message* parameter contains the message to be displayed. The method returns an integer that represents the button clicked by the user.
`int showConfirmDialog(Component parent, Object message, String title, int optionType)`	The argument passed into *parent* is a reference to the graphical component that the dialog box should be displayed within. If you pass `null` to this parameter, the dialog box appears in the center of the screen. The object passed to the *message* parameter contains the message to be displayed. The string passed to the *title* parameter is displayed in the dialog box's title bar. The value passed to *optionType* indicates the types of buttons to display in the dialog box. The method returns an integer that represents the button clicked by the user.

The following code calls the first version of the method:

```
int value;
value = JOptionPane.showConfirmDialog(null, "Are you sure?");
```

The first argument can be a reference to a graphical component, and the dialog box is displayed inside that component. In this statement we pass `null`, which causes the dialog box to be displayed in the center of the screen. The second argument is the message that we wish to display. This code causes the dialog box in Figure 11-9 to appear.

Figure 11-9 Confirm dialog box

By default the confirm dialog box displays "Select an Option" in its title bar, a Yes button, a No button, and a Cancel button. The `showConfirmDialog` method returns an integer that represents the button clicked by the user. You can determine which button the user clicked by comparing the method's return value to one of the following constants: `JOptionPane.YES_OPTION`, `JOptionPane.NO_OPTION`, or `JOptionPane.CANCEL_OPTION`. Here is an example:

```
int value;
value = JOptionPane.showConfirmDialog(null, "Are you sure?");
if (value == JOptionPane.YES_OPTION)
{
    If the user clicked Yes, the code here is executed.
}
else if (value == JOptionPane.NO_OPTION)
{
    If the user clicked No, the code here is executed.
}
else if (value == JOptionPane.CANCEL_OPTION)
{
    If the user clicked Cancel, the code here is executed.
}
```

The second version of the method shown in Table 11-4 allows you to control the text displayed in the confirm dialog's title bar and the type of buttons displayed. The first three arguments are the same as those used for the second version of the `showMessageDialog` method in Table 11-2. The fourth argument specifies the types of buttons to appear in the dialog box. You may use one of the following constants: `JOptionPane.YES_NO_OPTION` or `JOptionPane.YES_NO_CANCEL_OPTION`. For example, the following code displays a confirm dialog box with only a Yes button and a No button, as shown in Figure 11-10:

```
int value;
value = JOptionPane.showConfirmDialog(null, "Are you sure?",
            "Please Confirm", JOptionPane.YES_NO_OPTION);
```

Figure 11-10   Confirm dialog box with a Yes button and a No button

An Example Program

The program in Code Listing 11-1 displays each of the types of dialog boxes we have discussed. It asks the user to enter three test scores, then displays the average of the scores.

Code Listing 11-1 (`TestAverageDialog.java`)

```java
1    import javax.swing.JOptionPane;
2
3    /**
4     * This program demonstrates different types of
5     * dialog boxes.
6     */
7
8    public class TestAverageDialog
9    {
10      public static void main(String[] args)
11      {
12         int score1, score2, score3; // Three test scores
13         String strInput;            // String input
14         double average;             // Average test score
15         int repeat;                 // Confirm dialog button clicked
16
17         do
18         {
19            // Get the first test score.
20            strInput = JOptionPane.showInputDialog(null,
21                                   "Enter score #1.");
22            score1 = Integer.parseInt(strInput);
23
24            // Get the second test score.
25            strInput = JOptionPane.showInputDialog(null,
26                                   "Enter score #2.");
27            score2 = Integer.parseInt(strInput);
28
29            // Get the third test score.
30            strInput = JOptionPane.showInputDialog(null,
31                                   "Enter score #3.");
32            score3 = Integer.parseInt(strInput);
33
34            // Calculate and display the average test score.
35            average = (score1 + score2 + score3) / 3.0;
36            JOptionPane.showMessageDialog(null,
37                           "The average is " + average);
38
39            // Does the user want to average another set?
40            repeat = JOptionPane.showConfirmDialog(null,
41                        "Would you like to average another " +
42                        "set of test scores?", "Please Confirm.",
43                        JOptionPane.YES_NO_OPTION);
44
45         } while (repeat == JOptionPane.YES_OPTION);
46
```

```
47          System.exit(0);
48      }
49  }
```

When this program executes, the dialog boxes shown in Figure 11-11 are displayed, one at a time.

Figure 11-11 Dialog boxes displayed by the `TestAverageDialog` program

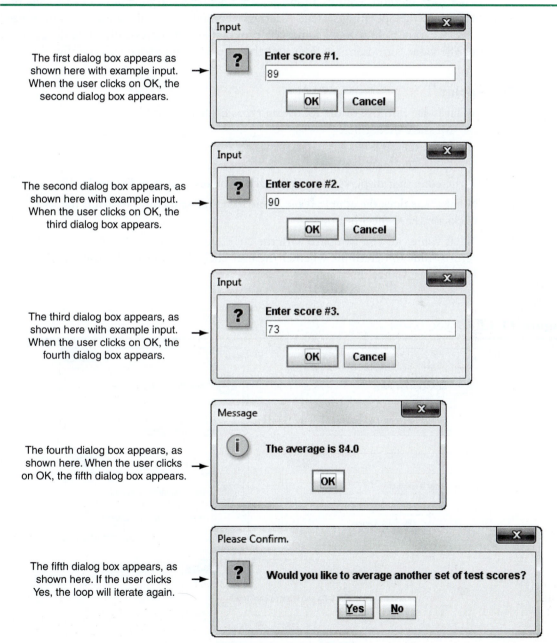

The first dialog box appears as shown here with example input. When the user clicks on OK, the second dialog box appears.

The second dialog box appears, as shown here with example input. When the user clicks on OK, the third dialog box appears.

The third dialog box appears, as shown here with example input. When the user clicks on OK, the fourth dialog box appears.

The fourth dialog box appears, as shown here. When the user clicks on OK, the fifth dialog box appears.

The fifth dialog box appears, as shown here. If the user clicks Yes, the loop will iterate again.

Notice the last statement in this program, in line 47:

```
System.exit(0);
```

This statement causes the program to end and is required in any GUI program. Unlike a console program, a GUI program does not automatically stop executing when the end of the main method is reached. This is because Swing generates a *thread,* which is a task running in the JVM. If the System.exit method is not called, this thread continues to execute, even after the end of the main method has been reached.

The System.exit method requires an integer argument. This argument is an *exit code* that is passed back to the operating system. Although this code is usually ignored, it can be used outside the program to indicate whether the program ended successfully or as the result of a failure. The value 0 traditionally indicates that the program ended successfully.

 Checkpoint

11.1   What is the purpose of the following types of dialog boxes?
  Message dialog box
  Input dialog box
  Confirm dialog box

11.2   Write code that displays each of the dialog boxes shown in Figure 11-12.

11.3   What value does the JOptionPane.showInputDialog method return if the user clicks on the Cancel button?

11.4   What value can you compare with the JOptionPane.showConfirmDialog method's return value to determine whether the user clicked on the Yes button? the No button? the Cancel button?

Figure 11-12   Dialog boxes

a) Message — Greetings Earthling — OK

b) Error — That Does Not Compute! — OK

c) Input — Enter a number. — OK Cancel

d) Select an Option — Do you want to continue? — Yes No Cancel

e) Please Confirm — Do you want to continue? — Yes No

11.3 Creating Windows

CONCEPT: You can use Swing classes to create windows containing various GUI components.

The JOptionPane dialog boxes allow you to easily display messages, gather input, and get answers to yes or no questions. If an application is to provide a full graphical user interface, however, much more is needed. Often, applications need one or more windows with various components that allow the user to enter and/or select data and interact with the application. For example, the window that is displayed in Figure 11-1 has several different components within it.

A window is a component, but because a window contains other components, it is considered a container. A *container* is simply a component that holds other components. In GUI terminology, a container that can be displayed as a window is known as a *frame*. A frame is a basic window that has a border around it, a title bar, and a set of buttons for minimizing, maximizing, and closing the window. In a Swing application, you create a frame from the JFrame class. There are a number of steps involved in creating a window, so let's look at an example. The program in Code Listing 11-2 displays the window shown in Figure 11-13.

Code Listing 11-2   **(SimpleWindow.java)**

```java
1   import javax.swing.*;  // Needed for Swing classes
2
3   /**
4    * This program displays a simple window with a title. The
5    * application exits when the user clicks the close button.
6    */
7
8   public class SimpleWindow
9   {
10     public static void main(String[] args)
11     {
12       final int WINDOW_WIDTH = 350,   // Window width in pixels
13                 WINDOW_HEIGHT = 250;  // Window height in pixels
14
15       // Create a window with a title.
16       JFrame window = new JFrame("A Simple Window");
17
18       // Set the size of the window.
19       window.setSize(WINDOW_WIDTH, WINDOW_HEIGHT);
20
21       // Specify what happens when the close button is clicked.
22       window.setDefaultCloseOperation(JFrame.EXIT_ON_CLOSE);
23
```

when OK is clicked after thank you message

```
24          // Display the window.
25          window.setVisible(true);
26     }
27 }
```

Figure 11-13   Window displayed by `SimpleWindow.java`

The window shown in Figure 11-13 was produced on a system running Windows. Notice that the window has a border and a title bar with "A Simple Window" displayed in it. In addition, it has the standard Windows buttons in the upper-right corner, a minimize button, a maximize button, and a close button. These standard features are sometimes referred to as *decorations*. If you run this program, you will see the window displayed on your screen. When you click on the close button, the window disappears and the program terminates.

Let's take a closer look at the code. First, notice the `import` statement in line 1. We need this because `JFrame`, as well as the other Swing classes, are part of the `javax.swing` package.

In lines 12 and 13 the two constants `WINDOW_WIDTH` and `WINDOW_HEIGHT` are declared. We use these constants later in the program to set the size of the window to 350 pixels wide by 250 pixels high. A *pixel* is one of the small dots that make up a screen display; the resolution of your monitor is measured in pixels. For example, if your monitor's resolution is 1024 by 768, that means the width of your screen is 1024 pixels, and the height of your screen is 768 pixels.

In line 16 we create an instance of the `JFrame` class with the following statement:

```
JFrame window = new JFrame("A Simple Window");
```

This statement creates a `JFrame` object in memory and assigns its address to the `window` variable. The string passed to the constructor appears in the window's title bar when it is displayed. This statement does not display the window on the screen, however. A `JFrame` is initially invisible.

In line 19 we call the `JFrame` object's `setSize` method to set the window's size. The two arguments passed to `setSize` specify the window's width and height in pixels. In this program we pass the constants `WINDOW_WIDTH` and `WINDOW_HEIGHT`, which we declared earlier, to set the size of the window to 350 pixels by 250 pixels.

In line 22 we specify the action that we wish to take place when the user clicks on the close button, which appears in the upper-right corner of the window. There are a number of actions that can take place when the user clicks on the close button. The `setDefaultCloseOperation` method takes an `int` argument that specifies the action. In this statement, we pass the constant `JFrame.EXIT_ON_CLOSE`, which causes the application to end with a `System.exit` method call. If we had passed `JFrame.HIDE_ON_CLOSE`, the window would be hidden from view, but the application would not end. The default action is `JFrame.HIDE_ON_CLOSE`.

In line 25, we call our `JFrame` object's `setVisible` method to display the window. The `setVisible` method takes a `boolean` argument. If the argument is `true`, the window is made visible. If the argument is `false`, the window is hidden.

Extending the `JFrame` Class

The program in Code Listing 11-2 performs a very simple operation: It creates an instance of the `JFrame` class and displays it. Most of the time, your GUI applications will be much more involved than this. As you progress through this chapter, you will add numerous components and capabilities to the windows that you create.

Instead of creating an instance of the `JFrame` class, a better technique is to create a new class that inherits from the `JFrame` class. For example, look at the `SimpleWindow2` class in Code Listing 11-3.

Code Listing 11-3   (`SimpleWindow2.java`)

```
1   import javax.swing.*;     // Needed for Swing classes
2
3   /**
4    * This class inherits from the JFrame class. Its constructor
5    * displays a simple window with a title. The application
6    * exits when the user clicks the close button.
7    */
8
9   public class SimpleWindow2 extends JFrame
10  {
11      public SimpleWindow2()
12      {
13          // Call the JFrame constructor and pass the title.
14          super("A Simple Window");
15
16          final int WINDOW_WIDTH = 350,   // Window width in pixels
17                    WINDOW_HEIGHT = 250;  // Window height in pixels
18
```

```
19          // Set the size of this window.
20          setSize(WINDOW_WIDTH, WINDOW_HEIGHT);
21
22          // Specify what happens when the close button is clicked.
23          setDefaultCloseOperation(JFrame.EXIT_ON_CLOSE);
24
25          // Display the window.
26          setVisible(true);
27       }
28  }
```

Notice the class header in line 9, which reads:

```
public class SimpleWindow2 extends JFrame
```

This indicates that SimpleWindow2 inherits from the JFrame class. Recall from Chapter 9 that inheritance establishes an "is a" relationship between classes. Because SimpleWindow2 inherits from JFrame, we can say that a SimpleWindow2 object is a JFrame.

Now look at line 14, in the constructor:

```
super("A Simple Window");
```

This statement calls the JFrame constructor and passes "A Simple Window" as an argument. This establishes the text to be displayed in the title bar. Recall that when a subclass uses the super key word to call the superclass constructor, it must be the first statement in the subclass's constructor (other than comments).

The rest of the constructor calls superclass methods to set the size of the window, establish the action that takes place when the close button is clicked, and make the window visible. All that is necessary to display the window is to create an instance of the SimpleWindow2 class, as shown in the program in Code Listing 11-4. When this program runs, the window previously shown in Figure 11-13 is displayed.

Code Listing 11-4   (`SimpleWindow2Demo.java`)

```
1  /**
2   * This program creates an instance of the
3   * SimpleWindow2 class.
4   */
5
6  public class SimpleWindow2Demo
7  {
8     public static void main(String[] args)
9     {
10        SimpleWindow2 myWindow = new SimpleWindow2();
11     }
12  }
```

Equipping GUI Classes with a `main` Method

You know that a Java application always starts execution with a static method named `main`. The previous example consists of two separate files:

- `SimpleWindow2.java`: This file contains the `SimpleWindow2` class, which defines a GUI window. (See Code Listing 11-3.)
- `SimpleWindow2Demo.java`: This file contains a static `main` method that creates an object of the GUI window class, thus displaying it. (See Code Listing 11-4.)

The purpose of the `SimpleWindow2Demo.java` file is simply to create an instance of the `SimpleWindow2` class. It is possible to eliminate the second file, `SimpleWindow2Demo.java`, by writing the static `main` method directly into the `SimpleWindow2.java` file. The `EmbeddedMain` class in Code Listing 11-5 shows an example.

Code Listing 11-5   (`EmbeddedMain.java`)

```java
 1  import javax.swing.*;  // Needed for Swing classes
 2
 3  /**
 4   *  This class inherits from the JFrame class. Its constructor
 5   *  displays a simple window with a title. The application
 6   *  exits when the user clicks the close button.
 7   */
 8
 9  public class EmbeddedMain extends JFrame
10  {
11     /**
12      *    Constructor
13      */
14
15     public EmbeddedMain()
16     {
17        // Call the JFrame constructor and pass the title.
18        super("A Simple Window");
19
20        final int WINDOW_WIDTH = 350,    // Window width in pixels
21                  WINDOW_HEIGHT = 250;   // Window height in pixels
22
23        // Set the size of this window.
24        setSize(WINDOW_WIDTH, WINDOW_HEIGHT);
25
26        // Specify what happens when the close button is clicked.
27        setDefaultCloseOperation(JFrame.EXIT_ON_CLOSE);
28
29        // Display the window.
30        setVisible(true);
31     }
32
```

```
33      /**
34       * The main method creates an instance of the EmbeddedMain
35       * class, which causes it to display its window.
36       */
37
38      public static void main(String[] args)
39      {
40          EmbeddedMain em = new EmbeddedMain();
41      }
42  }
43
```

The `EmbeddedMain` class contains its own static `main` method (in lines 38 through 41) which creates an instance of the class. Notice that the `main` method has exactly the same header as any other static `main` method that we have written. We can compile the *EmbeddedMain. java* file and then run the resulting *.class* file. When we do, we see the window that was previously shown in Figure 11-13.

Notice that in line 40 the `main` method declares a variable named `em` to reference the instance of the class. Once the instance is created, however, the variable is not used again. Because we do not need the variable, we can instantiate the class *anonymously* as shown here:

```
public static void main(String[] args)
{
    new EmbeddedMain();
}
```

In this version of the method, an instance of the `EmbeddedMain` class is created in memory, but its address is not assigned to any reference variable.

Adding Components to a Window

Swing provides numerous components that can be added to a window. Three fundamental components are the label, the text field, and the button. These are summarized in Table 11-5.

Table 11-5   Label, text field, and button controls

Component	Swing Class	Description
Label	`JLabel`	An area that can display text.
Text field	`JTextField`	An area in which the user may type a single line of input from the keyboard.
Button	`JButton`	A button that can cause an action to occur when it is clicked.

In Swing, labels are created with the `JLabel` class, text fields are created with the `JTextField` class, and buttons are created with the `JButton` class. To demonstrate these components, we will build a simple GUI application: The Kilometer Converter. This application will present a window in which the user will be able to enter a distance in kilometers, and then click on a button to see that distance converted to miles. The conversion formula is:

Miles = Kilometers $\times$ 0.6214

When designing a GUI application, it is usually helpful to draw a sketch depicting the window you are creating. Figure 11-14 shows a sketch of what the Kilometer Converter application's window will look like. As you can see from the sketch, the window will have a label, a text field, and a button. When the user clicks on the button, the distance in miles will be displayed in a separate `JOptionPane` dialog box.

Figure 11-14   Sketch of the Kilometer Converter window

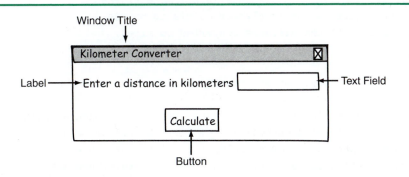

Content Panes and Panels

Before we start writing code, you should be familiar with content panes and panels. A *content pane* is a container that is part of every `JFrame` object. You cannot see the content pane and it does not have a border, but any component added to a `JFrame` must be added to its content pane.

A *panel* is also a container that can hold GUI components. Unlike `JFrame` objects, panels cannot be displayed by themselves. However, they are commonly used to hold and organize collections of related components. With Swing, you create panels with the `JPanel` class. In our Kilometer Converter application, we will create a panel to hold the label, text field, and button. We will then add the panel to the `JFrame` object's content pane. This is illustrated in Figure 11-15.

Figure 11-15   A panel is added to the content pane

Code Listing 11-6 shows the initial code for the `KiloConverterWindow` class. We will be adding to this code as we develop the application. (This file is stored in the student source code folder *Chapter 11\KiloConverter Phase 1*.)

Code Listing 11-6 **(KiloConverter.java)**

```java
 1   import javax.swing.*;
 2
 3   /**
 4    *  The KiloConverter class displays a JFrame that
 5    *  lets the user enter a distance in kilometers. When
 6    *  the Calculate button is clicked, a dialog box is
 7    *  displayed with the distance converted to miles.
 8    */
 9
10   public class KiloConverter extends JFrame
11   {
12      private JPanel panel;                    // To reference a panel
13      private JLabel messageLabel;             // To reference a label
14      private JTextField kiloTextField;        // To reference a text field
15      private JButton calcButton;              // To reference a button
16      private final int WINDOW_WIDTH = 310;    // Window width
17      private final int WINDOW_HEIGHT = 100;   // Window height
18
19      /**
20       *  Constructor
21       */
22
23      public KiloConverter()
24      {
25         // Call the JFrame constructor.
26         super("Kilometer Converter");
27
28         // Set the size of the window.
29         setSize(WINDOW_WIDTH, WINDOW_HEIGHT);
30
31         // Specify what happens when the close button is clicked.
32         setDefaultCloseOperation(JFrame.EXIT_ON_CLOSE);
33
34         // Build the panel and add it to the frame.
35         buildPanel();
36
37         // Add the panel to the frame's content pane.
38         add(panel);
39
40         // Display the window.
41         setVisible(true);
42      }
43
```

```
44        /**
45         *  The buildPanel method adds a label, text field, and
46         *  and a button to a panel.
47         */
48
49        private void buildPanel()
50        {
51           // Create a label to display instructions.
52           messageLabel = new JLabel("Enter a distance " +
53                                     "in kilometers");
54
55           // Create a text field 10 characters wide.
56           kiloTextField = new JTextField(10);
57
58           // Create a button with the caption "Calculate".
59           calcButton = new JButton("Calculate");
60
61           // Create a JPanel object and let the panel
62           // field reference it.
63           panel = new JPanel();
64
65           // Add the label, text field, and button
66           // components to the panel.
67           panel.add(messageLabel);
68           panel.add(kiloTextField);
69           panel.add(calcButton);
70        }
71
72        /**
73         *  main method
74         */
75
76        public static void main(String[] args)
77        {
78           new KiloConverter();
79        }
80  }
```

Let's take a closer look at this class. First, notice in line 10 that the class inherits from JFrame. The clause extends JFrame specifies that this class is a subclass of the JFrame class.

In line 12 we declare a JPanel reference variable named panel, which we will use to reference the panel that will hold the other components. In line 13 we declare a JLabel variable named messageLabel. This variable will reference a JLabel object that displays a message instructing the user to enter a distance in kilometers. In line 14 we declare a JTextField variable named kiloTextField. This variable will reference a JTextField object that will hold a value typed by the user. In line 15 we declare a JButton variable named calcButton. This variable will reference a JButton object that will calculate and display the kilometers converted to miles when clicked. The `WINDOW_WIDTH` and `WINDOW_HEIGHT` constants, which are declared in lines 16 and 17, hold the width and height of the window.

Now let's look at the constructor. In line 26 the `JFrame` constructor is called to set the text for the window's title bar. In line 29 the `JFrame` class's `setSize` method is called to establish the size of the window. `WINDOW_WIDTH` and `WINDOW_HEIGHT` are passed as arguments. In line 32 the `JFrame` class's `setDefaultCloseOperation` method is called to establish the action that should occur when the window's Close button is clicked.

The next statement, which is in line 35, is a call to this class's `buildPanel` method. The purpose of the `buildPanel` method is to create a panel, a label, a text field, and a button. The label, text field, and button are then added to the panel.

The statement in lines 52 and 53 creates a `JLabel` object and assigns its address to the `messageLabel` variable. The string that is passed to the `JLabel` constructor is the text that will be displayed in the label. The statement in line 56 creates a `JTextField` object and assigns its address to the `kiloTextField` variable. The argument that is passed to the constructor is the width of the text field in columns. One column is enough space to hold the letter "m," which is the widest letter in the alphabet. The statement in line 59 creates a `JButton` object and assigns its address to the `calcButton` variable. The string that is passed as an argument to the `JButton` constructor is the text that will be displayed on the button.

In line 63 the method creates a `JPanel` object and assigns its address to the `panel` variable. A `JPanel` object is used to hold other components. You add a component to a `JPanel` with the `JPanel` class's `add` method. The code in lines 67 through 69 adds the objects referenced by the `messageLabel`, `kiloTextField`, and `calcButton` variables to the `JPanel` object.

At this point, the panel is fully constructed in memory. The `buildPanel` method ends, and control returns to the class constructor. The next statement to execute in the constructor is line 38. This statement calls the `JFrame` class's `add` method, passing the `panel` variable as an argument. The `JFrame` class's `add` method adds an object to the `JFrame` object's content pane. This method adds the `JPanel` object referenced by the `panel` variable to the content pane.

The last statement in the constructor is in line 41. It calls the `JFrame` class's `setVisible` method to display the window on the screen.

The class has a static `main` method, which appears in lines 76 through 79. Line 78 creates an instance of the `KiloConverter` class. When this program is executed, the window shown in Figure 11-16 is displayed on the screen. (This file is also stored in the student source code folder *Chapter 11\KiloConverter Phase 1*.)

Figure 11-16 Kilometer Converter window

Figure 11-17 shows the window again, this time pointing out each of the components.

Figure 11-17   Components in the Kilometer Converter window

Although you can type input into the text field, the application does nothing when you click on the Calculate button. That is because we have not written an event handler that will execute when the button is clicked. That's the next step.

> **TIP:** Recall that the size of the window in the `KiloConverter` class is set to 320 pixels wide by 100 pixels high. This is set with the `WINDOW_WIDTH` and `WINDOW_HEIGHT` constants. Figures 11-16 and 11-17 show the window as it appears on a system with a video resolution of 1024 by 768 pixels. If your video resolution is lower than this, the window might not appear exactly as shown in the figures. If this is the case, you can increase the values of the `WINDOW_WIDTH` and `WINDOW_HEIGHT` constants and recompile the program. This will be true for other GUI applications in this book as well.

Handling Events with Action Listeners

An *event* is an action that takes place within a program, such as the clicking of a button. When an event takes place, the component responsible for the event creates an event object in memory. The *event object* contains information about the event. The component that generated the event object is known as the *event source*. For example, when the user clicks on a button, the `JButton` component generates an event object. The `JButton` component that generated the event object is the event source.

But what happens to the event object once it is generated by a source component? It's possible that the source component is connected to one or more event listeners. An *event listener* is an object that responds to events. If the source component is connected to an event listener, then the event object is passed to a specific method in the event listener. The method then performs any actions that it was programmed to perform in response to the event. This process is sometimes referred to as *event firing*.

When you are writing a GUI application, it is your responsibility to write the classes for the event listeners that your application needs. You then create instances of the event listener classes and connect them to the appropriate components. For example, let's examine the steps necessary to create an event listener that responds when the user clicks on the Calculate button in our Kilometer Converter application.

There are different types of events that can occur within an application. `JButton` components generate *action events*, so we must write an *action listener* class. When you write an action listener class, it must meet the following requirements:

- It must implement the `ActionListener` interface.
- It must have a method named `actionPerformed`. This method must take an argument of the `ActionEvent` type.

NOTE: The `ActionListener` interface is in the `java.awt.event` package, so you must have an `import` statement for that package in your source code.

Once we have written an action listener class, we must create an object of that class, and then connect the action listener object with the `JButton` component. When a `JButton` component generates an event, it automatically executes the `actionPerformed` method of the action listener object it is connected to, passing the event object as an argument. This is illustrated in Figure 11-18.

Figure 11-18 A `JButton` component firing an action event

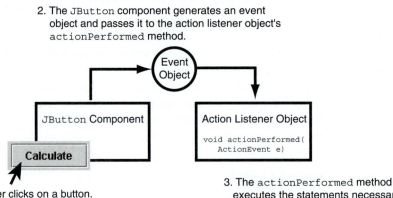

2. The `JButton` component generates an event object and passes it to the action listener object's `actionPerformed` method.

Event Object

JButton Component

Calculate

Action Listener Object

void actionPerformed(
    ActionEvent e)

1. The user clicks on a button.

3. The `actionPerformed` method executes the statements necessary to handle the event.

A common technique for writing an event listener class is to write it as a private inner class inside the class that creates the GUI. Here is the code for an action listener class that we will add to the `KiloConverterWindow` class:

```java
private class CalcButtonListener implements ActionListener
{
    public void actionPerformed(ActionEvent e)
    {
        String str;     // To hold text entered
        double miles;   // To hold miles

        // Get the number of kilometers entered in the
        // text field. The input is a string.
        str = kiloTextField.getText();

        // Convert the kilometers to miles.
        miles = Double.parseDouble(str) * 0.6214;

        // Display a message dialog showing the miles.
        JOptionPane.showMessageDialog(null, str +
                " kilometers is " + miles + " miles.");
    }
}
```

You can name your event listener classes anything you want to. The name of this class is `CalcButtonListener` and it implements the `ActionListener` interface. Recall that an interface specifies methods that an implementing class must have. The `ActionListener` interface only specifies one method: `actionPerformed`. Here is the header for the `actionPerformed` method:

```
void actionPerformed(ActionEvent e)
```

The `actionPerformed` method has one parameter, e, which is an `ActionEvent` object. This parameter receives the event object when the method is called. Although we do not use the e parameter in this method, we still have to list it inside the method header's parentheses because it is required by the `ActionListener` interface.

This method declares two local variables: `str`, a reference to a `String` object; and `miles`, a double. Next, the following statement is executed:

```
str = kiloTextField.getText();
```

`JTextField` objects have a `getText` method that returns the text contained in the text field. This will be any value entered into the text field by the user. The value is returned as a string. So, this statement retrieves any value entered by the user into the text field and assigns it to `str`.

Here is the next statement:

```
miles = Double.parseDouble(str) * 0.6214;
```

This statement converts the value in `str` to a double, and then multiplies it by 0.6214. This will convert the number of kilometers entered by the user to miles. The result is stored in the `miles` variable. The last statement uses `JOptionPane` to display a dialog box showing the distance converted to miles:

```
JOptionPane.showMessageDialog(null, str +
        " kilometers is " + miles + " miles.");
```

Registering the Action Listener

Now that we have written the action listener class, we must create an object from the class and connect the object to the `JButton` component. The process of connecting an event listener object to a component is called *registering* the event listener. `JButton` components have a method named `addActionListener`, which is used for registering event listeners. In the `KiloConverterWindow` class, the following statement can be used to create a `CalcButtonListener` object and register that object with the `calcButton` object:

```
calcButton.addActionListener(new CalcButtonListener());
```

You pass the address of an action listener object as the argument to the `addActionListener` method. This statement uses the expression new `CalcButtonListener()` to create an instance of the `CalcButtonListener` class. The address of that instance is then passed to the `addActionListener` method. Now, when the user clicks on the Calculate button, the `CalcButtonListener` object's `actionPerformed` method will be executed.

Code Listing 11-7 shows the `KiloConverterWindow` class with the new code added. The new code is shown in bold. (This file is stored in the student source code folder *Chapter 11\ KiloConverter Phase 2.*)

Code Listing 11-7 **(KiloConverter.java)**

```java
 1  import javax.swing.*;    // Needed for Swing classes
 2  import java.awt.event.*; // Needed for ActionListener Interface
 3
 4  /**
 5   *  The KiloConverter class displays a JFrame that
 6   *  lets the user enter a distance in kilometers. When
 7   *  the Calculate button is clicked, a dialog box is
 8   *  displayed with the distance converted to miles.
 9   */
10
11  public class KiloConverter extends JFrame
12  {
13     private JPanel panel;                // To reference a panel
14     private JLabel messageLabel;         // To reference a label
15     private JTextField kiloTextField;    // To reference a text field
16     private JButton calcButton;          // To reference a button
17     private final int WINDOW_WIDTH = 310;  // Window width
18     private final int WINDOW_HEIGHT = 100; // Window height
19
20     /**
21      *  Constructor
22      */
23
24     public KiloConverter()
25     {
26        // Set Call the JFrame constructor.
27        super("Kilometer Converter");
28
29        // Set the size of the window.
30        setSize(WINDOW_WIDTH, WINDOW_HEIGHT);
31
32        // Specify what happens when the close button is clicked.
33        setDefaultCloseOperation(JFrame.EXIT_ON_CLOSE);
34
35        // Build the panel and add it to the frame.
36        buildPanel();
37
38        // Add the panel to the frame's content pane.
39        add(panel);
40
41        // Display the window.
42        setVisible(true);
43     }
44
```

```
45    /**
46     *   The buildPanel method adds a label, text field, and
47     *   and a button to a panel.
48     */
49
50    private void buildPanel()
51    {
52       // Create a label to display instructions.
53       messageLabel = new JLabel("Enter a distance " +
54                                    "in kilometers");
55
56       // Create a text field 10 characters wide.
57       kiloTextField = new JTextField(10);
58
59       // Create a button with the caption "Calculate".
60       calcButton = new JButton("Calculate");
61
62       // Add an action listener to the button.
63       calcButton.addActionListener(new CalcButtonListener());
64
65       // Create a JPanel object and let the panel
66       // field reference it.
67       panel = new JPanel();
68
69       // Add the label, text field, and button
70       // components to the panel.
71       panel.add(messageLabel);
72       panel.add(kiloTextField);
73       panel.add(calcButton);
74    }
75
76    /**
77     * CalcButtonListener is an action listener class for
78     * the Calculate button.
79     */
80
81    private class CalcButtonListener implements ActionListener
82    {
83       /**
84        *   The actionPerformed method executes when the user
85        *   clicks on the Calculate button.
86        *   The ActionEvent parameter is required.
87        */
88
89       public void actionPerformed(ActionEvent e)
90       {
91          final double CONVERSION = 0.6214;
92          String input;  // To hold the user's input
93          double miles;  // The number of miles
```

```
94
95              // Get the text entered by the user into the
96              // text field.
97              input = kiloTextField.getText();
98
99              // Convert the input to miles.
100             miles = Double.parseDouble(input) * CONVERSION;
101
102             // Display the result.
103             JOptionPane.showMessageDialog(null, input +
104                     " kilometers is " + miles + " miles.");
105         }
106     }
107
108     /**
109      *  main method
110      */
111
112     public static void main(String[] args)
113     {
114         new KiloConverter();
115     }
116 }
```

First, notice that we've added the `import java.awt.event.*;` statement in line 2. This is necessary for our program to use the `ActionListener` interface. Next, look at the following code in line 81:

```
private class CalcButtonListener implements ActionListener
```

This is the header for an inner class that we will use to create event listener objects. The name of this class is `CalcButtonListener`, and it implements the `ActionListener` interface. We could have named the class anything we wanted to, but because it will handle the `JButton` component's action events, it must implement the `ActionListener` interface. The class has one method, `actionPerformed`, which is required by the `ActionListener` interface. The header for the `actionPerformed` method appears in line 89 as follows:

```
public void actionPerformed(ActionEvent e)
```

This method will be executed when the user clicks the `JButton` component. It has one parameter, e, which is an `ActionEvent` object. This parameter receives the event object that is passed to the method when it is called. Although we do not actually use the e parameter in this method, we still have to list it inside the method header's parentheses because it is required by the `ActionListener` interface.

The `actionPerformed` method declares a constant for the conversion factor in line 91 and two local variables in lines 92 and 93: input, a reference to a `String` object; and miles, a double. The following statement appears in line 97:

```
input = kiloTextField.getText();
```

All `JTextField` objects have a `getText` method that returns the text contained in the text field. This will be any value entered into the text field by the user. The value is returned as a string. So, this statement retrieves any value entered by the user into the text field and assigns it to `input`.

The following statement appears in line 100:

```
miles = Double.parseDouble(input) * CONVERSION;
```

This statement converts the value in `input` to a `double` and then multiplies it by the constant `CONVERSION`, which is set to 0.6214. This will convert the number of kilometers entered by the user to miles. The result is stored in the `miles` variable. The method's last statement, in lines 103 and 104, uses `JOptionPane` to display a dialog box showing the distance converted to miles as follows:

```
JOptionPane.showMessageDialog(null, input +
        " kilometers is " + miles + " miles.");
```

Writing an action listener class is only part of the process of handling a `JButton` component's action events. We must also create an object from the class and then register the object with the `JButton` component. When we register the action listener object with the `JButton` component, we are creating a connection between the two objects.

`JButton` components have a method named `addActionListener`, which is used for registering action event listeners. In line 63, which is in the `buildPanel` method, the following statement creates a `CalcButtonListener` object and registers that object with the `calcButton` object:

```
calcButton.addActionListener(new CalcButtonListener());
```

You pass the address of an action listener object as the argument to the `addActionListener` method. This statement uses the expression `new CalcButtonListener()` to create an instance of the `CalcButtonListener` class. The address of that instance is then passed to the `addActionListener` method. Now, when the user clicks the Calculate button, the `CalcButtonListener` object's `actionPerformed` method will be executed.

> **TIP:** Instead of the one statement in line 63, we could have written the following two statements:
>
> ```
> CalcButtonListener listener = new CalcButtonListener();
> calcButton.addActionListener(listener);
> ```
>
> The first statement shown here declares a `CalcButtonListener` variable named `listener`, creates a new `CalcButtonListener` object, and assigns the object's address to the `listener` variable. The second statement passes the address in `listener` to the `addActionListener` method. These two statements accomplish the same thing as the one statement in line 63, but it declares a variable, `listener` that we will not use again in the program. A better way is to use the one statement that appears in line 63 as follows:
>
> ```
> calcButton.addActionListener(new CalcButtonListener());
> ```
>
> Recall that the new key word creates an object and returns the object's address. This statement uses the new key word to create a `CalcButtonListener` object and passes the object's address directly to the `addActionListener` method. Because we do not need to refer to the object again in the program, we do not assign the object's address to a variable. It is known as an *anonymous object*.

When this program is executed, the first window shown in Figure 11-19 is displayed on the screen. If the user enters 2 in the text field and clicks the Calculate button, the second window shown in the figure (a dialog box) appears. To exit the application, the user clicks the OK button on the dialog box, and then clicks the close button in the upper-right corner of the main window.

Figure 11-19 Windows displayed by the `KiloConverter` class

More about the Event Object

The `ActionEvent` argument that is passed to an action listener's `actionPerformed` method is the event object that was generated in response to an event. Earlier it was mentioned that the event object contains information about the event. In the `CalcButtonListener` class that we wrote, we did not use the event object because we did not need to know anything about the event. We only needed to perform a calculation and display a message when the event occurred.

If you wish, you can retrieve certain information about the event by calling one of the event object's methods. Two of the `ActionEvent` methods are listed in Table 11-6.

Table 11-6 `ActionEvent` Methods

Method	Description
`String getActionCommand()`	Returns the action command for this event as a `String`.
`Object getSource()`	Returns a reference to the object that generated this event.

The first method listed in the table, `getActionCommand`, returns the action command that is associated with the event. By default, the action command is the text that appears on the `JButton` component that generated the event. For example, suppose a `JButton` component is created with the following statement:

```
JButton cancelButton = new JButton("Cancel");
```

When this component generates an event, the action command will be set to "Cancel". This method can also be used to determine which button was clicked when several buttons share the same action listener class.

To demonstrate, look at the class in Code Listing 11-8. It displays a window with three buttons. The buttons have the text "Button 1", "Button 2", and "Button 3". All three buttons use the same event listener class, which uses the action command to determine which button was clicked.

Code Listing 11-8   (`EventObject.java`)

```
 1  import javax.swing.*;     // Needed for Swing classes
 2  import java.awt.event.*; // Needed for event listener interface
 3
 4  /**
 5   *  This class demonstrates how to retrieve the action command
 6   *  from an event object.
 7   */
 8
 9  public class EventObject extends JFrame
10  {
11     private JButton button1;              // Button 1
12     private JButton button2;              // Button 2
13     private JButton button3;              // Button 3
14     private JPanel panel;                 // A panel to hold components
15     private final int WINDOW_WIDTH = 300; // Window width
16     private final int WINDOW_HEIGHT = 70; // Window height
17
18     /**
19      *  Constructor
20      */
21
22     public EventObject()
23     {
24        // Set the title bar text.
25        super("Event Object Demonstration");
26
27        // Set the size of the window.
28        setSize(WINDOW_WIDTH, WINDOW_HEIGHT);
29
30        // Specify what happens when the close button is clicked.
31        setDefaultCloseOperation(JFrame.EXIT_ON_CLOSE);
32
33        // Create the three buttons.
34        button1 = new JButton("Button 1");
35        button2 = new JButton("Button 2");
36        button3 = new JButton("Button 3");
37
38        // Register an event listener with all 3 buttons.
39        button1.addActionListener(new ButtonListener());
40        button2.addActionListener(new ButtonListener());
41        button3.addActionListener(new ButtonListener());
42
```

```
43          // Create a panel and add the buttons to it.
44          panel = new JPanel();
45          panel.add(button1);
46          panel.add(button2);
47          panel.add(button3);
48
49          // Add the panel to the content pane.
50          add(panel);
51
52          // Display the window.
53          setVisible(true);
54      }
55
56      /**
57       *  Private inner class that handles the event when
58       *  the user clicks a button.
59       */
60
61      private class ButtonListener implements ActionListener
62      {
63          public void actionPerformed(ActionEvent e)
64          {
65              // Get the action command.
66              String actionCommand = e.getActionCommand();
67
68              // Determine which button was clicked and display
69              // a message.
70              if (actionCommand.equals("Button 1"))
71              {
72                  JOptionPane.showMessageDialog(null, "You clicked " +
73                                              "the first button.");
74              }
75              else if (actionCommand.equals("Button 2"))
76              {
77                  JOptionPane.showMessageDialog(null, "You clicked " +
78                                              "the second button.");
79              }
80              else if (actionCommand.equals("Button 3"))
81              {
82                  JOptionPane.showMessageDialog(null, "You clicked " +
83                                              "the third button.");
84              }
85          }
86      }
87
```

```
88       /**
89        *   main method
90        */
91
92       public static void main(String[] args)
93       {
94           new EventObject();
95       }
96   }
```

This application uses the same action listener class for all three buttons. In lines 39 through 41, we create and register three separate instances of the `ButtonListener` class with the three buttons, as follows:

```
button1.addActionListener(new ButtonListener());
button2.addActionListener(new ButtonListener());
button3.addActionListener(new ButtonListener());
```

Figure 11-20 shows the output of the application when the user clicks Button 1, Button 2, and Button 3.

Figure 11-20   Output of `EventObjectWindow` class

> **TIP:** The text displayed on a button is the default action command. You can change the action command by calling the JButton class's setActionCommand method. For example, assuming that myButton references a JButton component, the following statement would change the component's action command to "The button was clicked":
>
>   myButton.setActionCommand("The button was clicked");
>
> Changing a JButton component's action command does not change the text that is displayed on the button.

The getSource Method

The second ActionEvent method listed in Table 11-6, getSource, returns a reference to the component that is the source of the event. As with the getActionCommand method, if you have several buttons and use objects of the same action listener class to respond to their events, you can use the getSource method to determine which button was clicked. For example, the ButtonListener class's actionPerformed method in Code Listing 11-8 could have been written as follows.

```java
public void actionPerformed(ActionEvent e)
{
    // Determine which button was clicked and display
    // a message.
    if (e.getSource() == button1)
    {
        JOptionPane.showMessageDialog(null, "You clicked " +
                                       "the first button.");
    }
    else if (e.getSource() == button2)
    {
        JOptionPane.showMessageDialog(null, "You clicked " +
                                       "the second button.");
    }
    else if (e.getSource() == button3)
    {
        JOptionPane.showMessageDialog(null, "You clicked " +
                                       "the third button.");
    }
}
```

This code is taken from the file *EventObjectWindow2.java*, which is part of the book's source code. You can run *EventObjectWindowDemo2.java* to see it in action.

How the Components Fit in the Swing and AWT Class Hierarchy

Now that you have seen some of the fundamental GUI components, let's look at how they fit into the class hierarchy. Figure 11-21 shows the parts of the Swing and AWT class hierarchy that contain the JFrame, JPanel, JLabel, JTextField, and JButton classes. Because of the inheritance relationships that exist, there are many other classes in the figure as well.

Figure 11-21   Part of the Swing and AWT class hierarchy

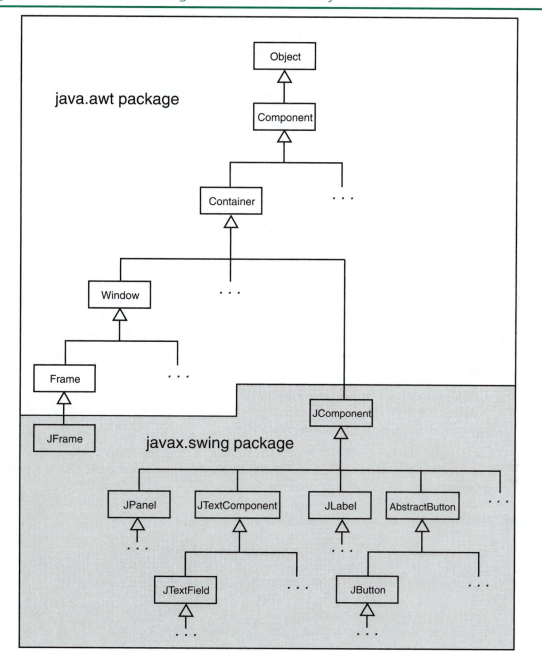

The classes in the unshaded top part of the figure are AWT classes and are in the java.awt package. The classes in the shaded bottom part of the figure are Swing classes and are in the javax.swing package. Notice that all of the components we have dealt with are ultimately derived from the Component class.

Background and Foreground Colors

Any class that inherits from the `Component` class will have methods named `setBackground` and `setForeground`. You call these methods to change a component's color. The background color is the color of the component itself, and the foreground color is the color of text that might be displayed on the component.

The argument that you pass to the `setBackground` and `setForeground` methods is a color code. The `Color` class, which is part of the `java.awt` package, has several predefined constants for colors. They are listed in Table 11-7.

Table 11-7 Color Class Constants

Color.BLACK	Color.BLUE
Color.CYAN	Color.DARK_GRAY
Color.GRAY	Color.GREEN
Color.LIGHT_GRAY	Color.MAGENTA
Color.ORANGE	Color.PINK
Color.RED	Color.WHITE
Color.YELLOW	

For example, the following code creates a button with the text "OK" displayed on it. The `setBackground` and `setForeground` methods are called to make the button blue and the text yellow.

```
JButton okButton = new JButton("OK");
okButton.setBackground(Color.BLUE);
okButton.setForeground(Color.YELLOW);
```

The class in Code Listing 11-9 displays a window with a label and three buttons. When the user clicks on a button, it changes the background color of the panel that contains the components and the foreground color of the label.

Code Listing 11-9   **(ColorWindow.java)**

```
 1  import javax.swing.*;      // Needed for Swing classes
 2  import java.awt.*;         // Needed for Color class
 3  import java.awt.event.*;   // Needed for event listener interface
 4
 5  /**
 6   *  This class demonstrates how to set the background color of
 7   *  a panel and the foreground color of a label.
 8   */
 9
10  public class ColorWindow extends JFrame
11  {
12      private JLabel messageLabel;     // To display a message
13      private JButton redButton;       // Changes color to red
14      private JButton blueButton;      // Changes color to blue
15      private JButton yellowButton;    // Changes color to yellow
16      private JPanel panel;            // A panel to hold components
```

```java
17        private final int WINDOW_WIDTH = 200; // Window width
18        private final int WINDOW_HEIGHT = 125; // Window height
19
20        /**
21         *  Constructor
22         */
23
24        public ColorWindow()
25        {
26           // Set the title bar text.
27           super("Colors");
28
29           // Set the size of the window.
30           setSize(WINDOW_WIDTH, WINDOW_HEIGHT);
31
32           // Specify an action for the close button.
33           setDefaultCloseOperation(JFrame.EXIT_ON_CLOSE);
34
35           // Create a label.
36           messageLabel = new JLabel("Click a button to " +
37                                     "select a color.");
38
39           // Create the three buttons.
40           redButton = new JButton("Red");
41           blueButton = new JButton("Blue");
42           yellowButton = new JButton("Yellow");
43
44           // Register an event listener with all 3 buttons.
45           redButton.addActionListener(new RedButtonListener());
46           blueButton.addActionListener(new BlueButtonListener());
47           yellowButton.addActionListener(new YellowButtonListener());
48
49           // Create a panel and add the components to it.
50           panel = new JPanel();
51           panel.add(messageLabel);
52           panel.add(redButton);
53           panel.add(blueButton);
54           panel.add(yellowButton);
55
56           // Add the panel to the content pane.
57           add(panel);
58
59           // Display the window.
60           setVisible(true);
61        }
62
63        /**
64         *  Private inner class that handles the event when
65         *  the user clicks the Red button.
66         */
67
```

```
68      private class RedButtonListener implements ActionListener
69      {
70         public void actionPerformed(ActionEvent e)
71         {
72            // Set the panel's background to red.
73            panel.setBackground(Color.RED);
74
75            // Set the label's text to blue.
76            messageLabel.setForeground(Color.BLUE);
77         }
78      }
79
80      /**
81       *  Private inner class that handles the event when
82       *  the user clicks the Blue button.
83       */
84
85      private class BlueButtonListener implements ActionListener
86      {
87         public void actionPerformed(ActionEvent e)
88         {
89            // Set the panel's background to blue.
90            panel.setBackground(Color.BLUE);
91
92            // Set the label's text to yellow.
93            messageLabel.setForeground(Color.YELLOW);
94         }
95      }
96
97      /**
98       *  Private inner class that handles the event when
99       *  the user clicks the Yellow button.
100      */
101
102     private class YellowButtonListener implements ActionListener
103     {
104        public void actionPerformed(ActionEvent e)
105        {
106           // Set the panel's background to yellow.
107           panel.setBackground(Color.YELLOW);
108
109           // Set the label's text to black.
110           messageLabel.setForeground(Color.BLACK);
111        }
112     }
113
114     /**
115      *  main method
116      */
117
```

```
118      public static void main(String[] args)
119      {
120         new ColorWindow();
121      }
122  }
```

Notice that this class has three action listener classes, one for each button. The action listener classes are RedButtonListener, BlueButtonListener, and YellowButtonListener. The following statements, in lines 45 through 47, register instances of these classes with the appropriate button components:

```
redButton.addActionListener(new RedButtonListener());
blueButton.addActionListener(new BlueButtonListener());
yellowButton.addActionListener(new YellowButtonListener());
```

When you run the program, the window shown in Figure 11-22 appears.

Figure 11-22   The window produced by the ColorWindow class

The window components first appear in their default colors.

When the user clicks the Red button, the panel turns red and the label turns blue.

When the user clicks the Blue button, the panel turns blue and the label turns yellow.

When the user clicks the Yellow button, the panel turns yellow and the label turns black.

Changing the Background Color of a JFrame Object's Content Pane

Recall that a JFrame object has a content pane, which is a container for all the components that are added to the JFrame. When you add a component to a JFrame object, you are actually adding it to the object's content pane. In the example shown in this section, we added a label and some buttons to a panel, and then added the panel to the JFrame object's content pane. When we changed the background color, we changed the background color of the panel. In this example, the color of the content pane does not matter because it is completely filled up by the panel. The color of the panel covers up the color of the content pane.

In some cases, where you have not filled up the JFrame object's content pane with a panel, you might want to change the background color of the content pane. If you wish to change the background color of a JFrame object's content pane, you must call the content pane's setBackground method, not the JFrame object's setBackground method. For example, in a class that extends the JFrame class, the following statement can be used to change the content pane's background to blue:

```
getContentPane().setBackground(Color.blue);
```

In this statement, the getContentPane method is called to get a reference to the JFrame object's content pane. This reference is then used to call the content pane's setBackground method. As a result, the content pane's background color will change to blue.

 Checkpoint

11.5   What is a frame? How do you create a frame with Swing?

11.6   How do you set a frame's size?

11.7   How do you display a frame on the screen?

11.8   What is a content pane?

11.9   What is the difference between a frame and a panel?

11.10   What is an event listener?

10.11   If you are writing an event listener class for a JButton component, what interface must the class implement? What method must the class have? When is this method executed?

10.12   How do you register an event listener with a JButton component?

10.13   How do you change the background color of a component? How do you change the color of text displayed by a label or a button?

11.4 Layout Managers

CONCEPT: A layout manager is an object that governs the positions and sizes of components in a container. The layout manager automatically repositions and, in some cases, resizes the components when the container is resized.

An important part of designing a GUI application is determining the layout of the components displayed in the application's windows. The term *layout* refers to the positioning and sizing of components. In Java, you do not normally specify the exact location of a component within a window. Instead, you let a layout manager control the positions of components for you. A *layout manager* is an object that has its own rules about how components are to be positioned and sized, and it makes adjustments when necessary. For example, when the user resizes a window, the layout manager determines where the components should be moved to.

To use a layout manager with a group of components, you must place the components in a container, and then create a layout manager object. The layout manager object and the container work together. In this chapter we discuss the three layout managers described in Table 11-8. The classes for these layout managers are in the java.awt package.

Table 11-8 Layout Managers

Layout Manager	Description
FlowLayout	Arranges components in rows. This is the default layout manager for JPanel objects.
BorderLayout	Arranges components in five regions: north, south, east, west, and center. This is the default layout manager for a JFrame object's content pane.
GridLayout	Arranges components in a grid with rows and columns.

Adding a Layout Manager to a Container

Recall from Figure 11-21 that the Container class is one of the superclasses that many components such as JPanel are derived from. Any component that inherits from the Container class can have a layout manager added to it. This includes a JFrame object's content pane, which is actually an instance of the Container class.

You add a layout manager to a container by calling the setLayout method, which is inherited from the Container class, and passing a reference to a layout manager object as the argument. For example, the following code creates a JPanel object, then sets a BorderLayout object as its layout manager:

```
JPanel panel = new JPanel();
panel.setLayout(new BorderLayout());
```

You can call the setLayout method directly from a JFrame object to set a layout manager for its content pane. For example, the following code might appear in the constructor of a class that inherits from JFrame. It sets a FlowLayout object as the layout manager for the content pane.

```
setLayout(new FlowLayout());
```

Once you establish a layout manager for a container, the layout manager governs the positions and sizes of the components that are added to the container.

The FlowLayout Manager

The FlowLayout manager arranges components in rows. This is the default layout manager for JPanel objects. Here are some rules that the FlowLayout manager follows:

- You can add multiple components to a container that uses a FlowLayout manager.
- When you add components to a container that uses a FlowLayout manager, the components appear horizontally, from left to right, in the order that they were added to the component.
- When there is no more room in a row but more components are added, the new components "flow" to the next row.

For example, the FlowWindow class shown in Code Listing 11-10 inherits from JFrame. This class creates a 200 pixel wide by 105 pixel high window. In the constructor, the content pane's setLayout method is called to give the content pane a FlowLayout manager. Then, three buttons are created and added directly to the content pane. The main method creates an instance of the FlowWindow class, which displays the window.

Code Listing 11-10 **(FlowWindow.java)**

```java
 1  import java.awt.*;        // Needed for the FlowLayout manager
 2  import javax.swing.*;
 3
 4  /**
 5   * This class demonstrates how to use a FlowLayout manager
 6   * with a JFrame object's content pane.
 7   */
 8
 9  public class FlowWindow extends JFrame
10  {
11     private final int WINDOW_WIDTH = 200;   // Window width
12     private final int WINDOW_HEIGHT = 105;  // Window height
13
14     /**
15      * Constructor
16      */
17
18     public FlowWindow()
19     {
20        // Set the title bar text.
21        super("Flow Layout");
22
23        // Set the size of the window.
24        setSize(WINDOW_WIDTH, WINDOW_HEIGHT);
25
26        // Specify what happens when the close button is clicked.
27        setDefaultCloseOperation(JFrame.EXIT_ON_CLOSE);
28
29        // Add a FlowLayout manager to the content pane.
30        setLayout(new FlowLayout());
31
32        // Create three buttons.
33        JButton button1 = new JButton("Button 1");
34        JButton button2 = new JButton("Button 2");
35        JButton button3 = new JButton("Button 3");
36
37        // Add the three buttons to the content pane.
38        add(button1);
39        add(button2);
40        add(button3);
41
42        // Display the window.
43        setVisible(true);
44     }
45
```

```
46      /**
47       * The main method creates an instance of the
48       * FlowWindow class, causing it to display its window.
49       */
50
51      public static void main(String[] args)
52      {
53          new FlowWindow();
54      }
55  }
```

Figure 11-23 shows the window that is displayed. Notice that the buttons appear from left to right in the order they were added to the content pane. Because there's only enough room for the first two buttons in the first row, the third button is positioned in the second row. By default, the content of each row is centered and there is a five-pixel gap between the components.

Figure 11-23   The window displayed by the `FlowWindow` class

![The window displayed by the FlowWindow class showing a Flow Layout window with Button 1 and Button 2 on the first row and Button 3 centered on the second row]

If the user resizes the window, the layout manager repositions the components according to its rules. Figure 11-24 shows the appearance of the window in three different sizes.

Figure 11-24   The arrangement of the buttons after resizing

Adjusting the `FlowLayout` Alignment

The `FlowLayout` manager allows you to align components in the center of each row or along the left or right edges of each row. An overloaded constructor allows you to pass one of the following constants as an argument to set an alignment: `FlowLayout.CENTER`, `FlowLayout.LEFT`, or `FlowLayout.RIGHT`. Here is an example that sets left alignment:

```
setLayout(new FlowLayout(FlowLayout.LEFT));
```

Figure 11-25 shows examples of windows that use a `FlowLayout` manager with left, center, and right alignment.

Figure 11-25 Left, center, and right alignment

Adjusting the `FlowLayout` Component Gaps

By default, the `FlowLayout` manager inserts a gap of five pixels between components, both horizontally and vertically. You can adjust this gap by passing values for the horizontal and vertical gaps as arguments to an overloaded `FlowLayout` constructor. The constructor has the following format:

```
FlowLayout(int alignment, int horizontalGap, int verticalGap)
```

You pass one of the alignment constants discussed in the previous section to the *alignment* parameter. The *horizontalGap* parameter is the number of pixels to separate components horizontally, and the *verticalGap* parameter is the number of pixels to separate components vertically. Here is an example of the constructor call:

```
setLayout(new FlowLayout(FlowLayout.LEFT, 10, 7));
```

This statement causes components to be left aligned with a horizontal gap of 10 pixels and a vertical gap of seven pixels.

The `BorderLayout` Manager

The `BorderLayout` manager divides a container into five regions. The regions are known as north, south, east, west, and center. The arrangement of these regions is shown in Figure 11-26.

Figure 11-26 The regions of a `BorderLayout` manager

When a component is placed into a container managed by a `BorderLayout` manager, the component must be placed into one of these five regions. Only one component at a time may be placed into a region.

When adding a component to the container, you specify the region by passing one of the following constants as a second argument to the container's add method: `BorderLayout.NORTH`, `BorderLayout.SOUTH`, `BorderLayout.EAST`, `BorderLayout.WEST`, or `BorderLayout.CENTER`.

For example, look at the following code:

```
JPanel panel = new JPanel();
JButton button = new JButton("Click Me");
panel.setLayout(new BorderLayout());
panel.add(button, BorderLayout.NORTH);
```

The first statement creates a `JPanel` object, referenced by the `panel` variable. The second statement creates a `JButton` object, referenced by the `button` variable. The third statement sets the `JPanel` object's layout manager to a `BorderLayout` object. The fourth statement adds the `JButton` object to the `JPanel` object's north region.

If you do not pass a second argument to the `add` method, specifying the region to add the component to, the component will be added to the center region.

Here are some rules that the `BorderLayout` manager follows:

- Each region can hold only one component at a time.
- When a component is added to a region, it is stretched so it fills up the entire region.

Look at the `BorderWindow` class shown in Code Listing 11-11, which inherits from `JFrame`. This class creates a 400 pixel wide by 300 pixel high window. In the constructor, the `setLayout` method is called to give the content pane a `BorderLayout` manager. Then, five buttons are created and each is added to a different region. The `main` method creates an instance of the `BorderWindow` class, which displays the window.

Code Listing 11-11 **(BorderWindow.java)**

```java
 1  import java.awt.*;      // Needed for BorderLayout
 2  import javax.swing.*;
 3
 4  /**
 5   * This class demonstrates the BorderLayout manager.
 6   */
 7
 8  public class BorderWindow extends JFrame
 9  {
10     private final int WINDOW_WIDTH = 400;   // Width
11     private final int WINDOW_HEIGHT = 300;  // Height
12
13     /**
14      * Constructor
15      */
16
17     public BorderWindow()
18     {
19        // Set the title bar text.
20        super("Border Layout");
21
22        // Set the size of the window.
23        setSize(WINDOW_WIDTH, WINDOW_HEIGHT);
24
25        // Specify what happens when the close button is clicked.
26        setDefaultCloseOperation(JFrame.EXIT_ON_CLOSE);
27
28        // Add a BorderLayout manager to the content pane.
29        setLayout(new BorderLayout());
30
31        // Create five buttons.
32        JButton button1 = new JButton("North Button");
33        JButton button2 = new JButton("South Button");
34        JButton button3 = new JButton("East Button");
35        JButton button4 = new JButton("West Button");
36        JButton button5 = new JButton("Center Button");
37
38        // Add the five buttons to the content pane.
39        add(button1, BorderLayout.NORTH);
40        add(button2, BorderLayout.SOUTH);
41        add(button3, BorderLayout.EAST);
42        add(button4, BorderLayout.WEST);
43        add(button5, BorderLayout.CENTER);
44
```

```
45          // Display the window.
46          setVisible(true);
47      }
48
49      /**
50       * The main method creates an instance of the
51       * BorderWindow class, causing it to display its window.
52       */
53
54      public static void main(String[] args)
55      {
56          new BorderWindow();
57      }
58  }
```

 NOTE: A `JFrame` object's content pane is automatically given a `BorderLayout` manager. We have explicitly added it in Code Listing 11-11 so it is clear that we are using a `BorderLayout` manager.

Figure 11-27 shows the window that is displayed. Normally the size of a button is just large enough to accommodate the text that is displayed on the button. Notice that the buttons displayed in this window did not retain their normal size. Instead, they were stretched to fill all of the space in their regions. If the user resizes the window, the sizes of the components will be changed as well. This is shown in Figure 11-28.

Figure 11-27   The window displayed by the `BorderWindow` class

![Window titled "Border Layout" with five buttons arranged in border layout: North Button across the top, West Button on the left, Center Button in the middle, East Button on the right, and South Button across the bottom.]

Figure 11-28 The window resized

Here are the rules that govern how a `BorderLayout` manager resizes components:

- A component placed in the north or south regions may be resized horizontally so it fills up the entire region.
- A component placed in the east or west regions may be resized vertically so it fills up the entire region.
- A component placed in the center region may be resized both horizontally and vertically so it fills up the entire region.

TIP: You do not have to place a component in every region of a border layout. To achieve the desired positioning, you might want to place components in only a few of the layout regions. In Chapter 12 you will see examples of applications that do this.

By default there is no gap between the regions. You can use an overloaded version of the `BorderLayout` constructor to specify horizontal and vertical gaps, however. Here is the constructor's format:

```
BorderLayout(int horizontalGap, int verticalGap)
```

The `horizontalGap` parameter is the number of pixels to separate the regions horizontally, and the `verticalGap` parameter is the number of pixels to separate the regions vertically. Here is an example of the constructor call:

```
setLayout(new BorderLayout(5, 10));
```

This statement causes the regions to appear with a horizontal gap of five pixels and a vertical gap of ten pixels.

Nesting Panels Inside a Container's Regions

You might think that the BorderLayout manager is limiting because it allows only one component per region, and the components placed in its regions are automatically resized to fill up any extra space. These limitations are easy to overcome, however, by adding components to panels and then nesting the panels inside the regions.

For example, suppose we wish to modify the BorderWindow class in Code Listing 11-11 so the buttons retain their original size. We can accomplish this by placing each button in a JPanel object and then adding the JPanel objects to the content pane's five regions. This is illustrated in Figure 11-29. As a result, the BorderLayout manager resizes the JPanel objects to fill up the space in the regions, not the buttons contained within the JPanel objects.

Figure 11-29   Nesting JPanel objects inside each region

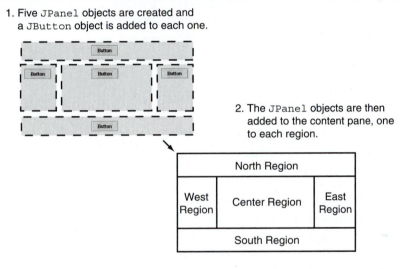

1. Five JPanel objects are created and a JButton object is added to each one.

2. The JPanel objects are then added to the content pane, one to each region.

The BorderPanelWindow class in Code Listing 11-12 demonstrates this technique. This class also introduces a new way of sizing windows. Notice that the constructor does not explicitly set the size of the window with the setSize method. Instead, it calls the pack method just before calling the setVisible method. The pack method is inherited from JFrame (which inherits it from the Window class) and it automatically sizes the window to accommodate the components contained within it. The main method creates an instance of the BorderPanelWindow class, which displays the window shown in Figure 11-30.

Code Listing 11-12   (**BorderPanelWindow.java**)

```
1   import java.awt.*;     // Needed for BorderLayout
2   import javax.swing.*;
3
4   /**
5    * This class demonstrates how JPanels can be nested
6    * inside each region of a content pane governed by
7    * a BorderLayout manager.
8    */
```

```
 9
10   public class BorderPanelWindow extends JFrame
11   {
12      /**
13       * Constructor
14       */
15
16      public BorderPanelWindow()
17      {
18         // Set the title bar text.
19         super("Border Layout");
20
21         // Specify an action for the close button.
22         setDefaultCloseOperation(JFrame.EXIT_ON_CLOSE);
23
24         // Add a BorderLayout manager to the content pane.
25         setLayout(new BorderLayout());
26
27         // Create five panels.
28         JPanel panel1 = new JPanel();
29         JPanel panel2 = new JPanel();
30         JPanel panel3 = new JPanel();
31         JPanel panel4 = new JPanel();
32         JPanel panel5 = new JPanel();
33
34         // Create five buttons.
35         JButton button1 = new JButton("North Button");
36         JButton button2 = new JButton("South Button");
37         JButton button3 = new JButton("East Button");
38         JButton button4 = new JButton("West Button");
39         JButton button5 = new JButton("Center Button");
40
41         // Add the buttons to the panels.
42         panel1.add(button1);
43         panel2.add(button2);
44         panel3.add(button3);
45         panel4.add(button4);
46         panel5.add(button5);
47
48         // Add the five panels to the content pane.
49         add(panel1, BorderLayout.NORTH);
50         add(panel2, BorderLayout.SOUTH);
51         add(panel3, BorderLayout.EAST);
52         add(panel4, BorderLayout.WEST);
53         add(panel5, BorderLayout.CENTER);
54
```

```
55        // Pack and display the window.
56        pack();
57        setVisible(true);
58    }
59
60    /**
61     * The main method creates an instance of the
62     * BorderPanelWindow class, causing it to display
63     * its window.
64     */
65
66    public static void main(String[] args)
67    {
68     new BorderPanelWindow();
69    }
70  }
```

Figure 11-30 Window displayed by the `BorderPanelWindow` class

> **NOTE:** There are multiple layout managers at work in the `BorderPanelWindow` class. The content pane uses a `BorderLayout` manager, and each of the `JPanel` objects use a `FlowLayout` manager.

The `GridLayout` Manager

The `GridLayout` manager creates a grid with rows and columns, much like a spreadsheet. As a result, the container managed by a `GridLayout` object is divided into equally sized cells. Figure 11-31 illustrates a container with three rows and five columns. This means that the container is divided into 15 cells.

Figure 11-31 The GridLayout manager divides a container into cells

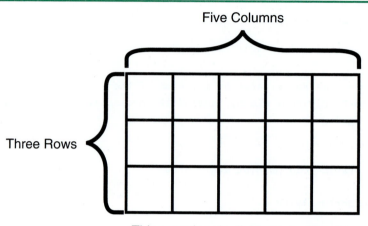

Five Columns

Three Rows

This container is divided into 15 cells.

Here are some rules that the GridLayout manager follows:

- Each cell can hold only one component.
- All of the cells are the same size. This is the size of the largest component placed within the layout.
- A component placed in a cell is automatically resized to fill up any extra space.

You pass the number of rows and columns that a container should have as arguments to the GridLayout constructor. Here is the general format of the constructor:

```
GridLayout(int rows, int columns)
```

The following statement creates a GridLayout manager and passes it as an argument to the setLayout method:

```
setLayout(new GridLayout(2, 3));
```

This statement gives the container two rows and three columns, for a total of six cells. You can pass 0 as an argument for the rows or the columns, but not both. Passing 0 for both arguments will cause an IllegalArgumentException to be thrown.

When adding components to a container that is governed by the GridLayout manager, you cannot specify a cell. Instead, the components are assigned to cells in the order they are added. The first component added to the container is assigned to the first cell, which is in the upper-left corner. As other components are added, they are assigned to the remaining cells in the first row, from left to right. When the first row is filled up, components are assigned to the cells in the second row, and so forth.

The GridWindow class shown in Code Listing 11-13 demonstrates. It creates a 400 pixel wide by 200 pixel high window, governed by a GridLayout manager. The content pane is divided into two rows and three columns, and a button is added to each cell. The main method creates an instance of the class that displays the window shown in Figure 11-32.

Code Listing 11-13   (`GridWindow.java`)

```java
 1  import java.awt.*;       // Needed for GridLayout
 2  import javax.swing.*;
 3
 4  /**
 5   * This class demonstrates the GridLayout manager.
 6   */
 7
 8  public class GridWindow extends JFrame
 9  {
10     private final int WINDOW_WIDTH = 400;   // Width
11     private final int WINDOW_HEIGHT = 200;  // Height
12
13     /**
14      * Constructor
15      */
16
17     public GridWindow()
18     {
19        // Set the title bar text.
20        super("Grid Layout");
21
22        // Set the size of the window.
23        setSize(WINDOW_WIDTH, WINDOW_HEIGHT);
24
25        // Specify an action for the close button.
26        setDefaultCloseOperation(JFrame.EXIT_ON_CLOSE);
27
28        // Add a GridLayout manager to the content pane.
29        setLayout(new GridLayout(2, 3));
30
31        // Create six buttons.
32        JButton button1 = new JButton("Button 1");
33        JButton button2 = new JButton("Button 2");
34        JButton button3 = new JButton("Button 3");
35        JButton button4 = new JButton("Button 4");
36        JButton button5 = new JButton("Button 5");
37        JButton button6 = new JButton("Button 6");
38
39        // Add the six buttons to the content pane.
40        add(button1); // Goes into row 1, column 1
41        add(button2); // Goes into row 1, column 2
42        add(button3); // Goes into row 1, column 3
43        add(button4); // Goes into row 2, column 1
44        add(button5); // Goes into row 2, column 2
45        add(button6); // Goes into row 2, column 3
```

```
46
47        // Display the window.
48        setVisible(true);
49    }
50
51    /**
52     * The main method creates an instance of the
53     * GridWindow class, causing it to display its window.
54     */
55
56    public static void main(String[] args)
57    {
58        new GridWindow();
59    }
60 }
```

Figure 11-32 Window displayed by the `GridWindow` class

As previously mentioned, the `GridLayout` manager limits each cell to only one component and resizes components to fill up all of the space in a cell. To get around these limitations you can nest panels inside the cells and add other components to the panels. For example, the `GridPanelWindow` class shown in Code Listing 11-14 is a modification of the `GridWindow` class. It creates six panels and adds a button and a label to each panel. These panels are then added to the content pane's cells. The `main` method creates an instance of the class that displays the window shown in Figure 11-33.

Code Listing 11-14   `(GridPanelWindow.java)`

```
1   import java.awt.*;
2   import javax.swing.*;
3
4   /**
5    * This class demonstrates how panels may be added
6    * to the cells created by a GridLayout manager.
7    */
8
9   public class GridPanelWindow extends JFrame
10  {
11     private final int WINDOW_WIDTH = 400;  // Width
12     private final int WINDOW_HEIGHT = 200; // Height
13
14     /**
15      * Constructor
16      */
17
18     public GridPanelWindow()
19     {
20        // Set the title bar text.
21        super("Grid Layout");
22
23        // Set the size of the window.
24        setSize(WINDOW_WIDTH, WINDOW_HEIGHT);
25
26        // Specify an action for the close button.
27        setDefaultCloseOperation(JFrame.EXIT_ON_CLOSE);
28
29        // Add a GridLayout manager to the content pane.
30        setLayout(new GridLayout(2, 3));
31
32        // Create six buttons.
33        JButton button1 = new JButton("Button 1");
34        JButton button2 = new JButton("Button 2");
35        JButton button3 = new JButton("Button 3");
36        JButton button4 = new JButton("Button 4");
37        JButton button5 = new JButton("Button 5");
38        JButton button6 = new JButton("Button 6");
39
40        // Create six labels.
41        JLabel label1 = new JLabel("This is cell 1.");
42        JLabel label2 = new JLabel("This is cell 2.");
43        JLabel label3 = new JLabel("This is cell 3.");
44        JLabel label4 = new JLabel("This is cell 4.");
45        JLabel label5 = new JLabel("This is cell 5.");
46        JLabel label6 = new JLabel("This is cell 6.");
```

```
47
48        // Create six panels.
49        JPanel panel1 = new JPanel();
50        JPanel panel2 = new JPanel();
51        JPanel panel3 = new JPanel();
52        JPanel panel4 = new JPanel();
53        JPanel panel5 = new JPanel();
54        JPanel panel6 = new JPanel();
55
56        // Add the labels to the panels.
57        panel1.add(label1);
58        panel2.add(label2);
59        panel3.add(label3);
60        panel4.add(label4);
61        panel5.add(label5);
62        panel6.add(label6);
63
64        // Add the buttons to the panels.
65        panel1.add(button1);
66        panel2.add(button2);
67        panel3.add(button3);
68        panel4.add(button4);
69        panel5.add(button5);
70        panel6.add(button6);
71
72        // Add the panels to the content pane.
73        add(panel1); // Goes into row 1, column 1
74        add(panel2); // Goes into row 1, column 2
75        add(panel3); // Goes into row 1, column 3
76        add(panel4); // Goes into row 2, column 1
77        add(panel5); // Goes into row 2, column 2
78        add(panel6); // Goes into row 2, column 3
79
80        // Display the window.
81        setVisible(true);
82    }
83
84    /**
85     * The main method creates an instance of the
86     * GridPanelWindow class, causing it to display
87     * its window.
88     */
89
90    public static void main(String[] args)
91    {
92        new GridPanelWindow();
93    }
94 }
```

Figure 11-33   Window displayed by the `GridPanelWindow` class

Because we have containers nested inside the content pane, there are multiple layout managers at work in the `GridPanelWindow` class. The content pane uses a `GridLayout` manager, and each of the `JPanel` objects use a `FlowLayout` manager.

Checkpoint

11.14 How do you add a layout manager to a container?

11.15 Which layout manager divides a container into regions known as north, south, east, west, and center?

11.16 Which layout manager arranges components in a row, from left to right, in the order they were added to the container?

11.17 Which layout manager arranges components in rows and columns?

11.18 How many components can you have at one time in a `BorderLayout` region? In a `GridLayout` cell?

11.19 How do you prevent the `BorderLayout` manager from resizing a component that has been placed in its region?

11.20 How can you cause a `JFrame` object's content pane to be automatically sized to accommodate the components contained within it?

11.21 What is the default layout manager for a `JFrame` object's content pane? For a `JPanel` object?

11.5 Radio Buttons and Check Boxes

CONCEPT: Radio buttons normally appear in groups of two or more and allow the user to select one of several possible options. Check boxes, which may appear alone or in groups, allow the user to make yes/no or on/off selections.

Radio Buttons

Radio buttons are useful when you want the user to select one choice from several possible options. Figure 11-34 shows a group of radio buttons.

Figure 11-34   Radio buttons

Figure 11-34   Radio buttons

A radio button may be selected or deselected. Each radio button has a small circle that appears filled-in when the radio button is selected and appears empty when the radio button is deselected. You use the `JRadioButton` class to create radio buttons. Here are the general formats of two `JRadioButton` constructors.

```
JRadioButton(String text)
JRadioButton(String text, boolean selected)
```

The first constructor shown creates a deselected radio button. The argument passed to the *text* parameter is the string displayed next to the radio button. For example, the following statement creates a radio button with the text "Choice 1" displayed next to it. The radio button initially appears deselected.

```
JRadioButton radio1 = new JRadioButton("Choice 1");
```

The second constructor takes an additional `boolean` argument, which is passed to the *selected* parameter. If `true` is passed as the `selected` argument, the radio button initially appears selected. If `false` is passed, the radio button initially appears deselected. For example, the following statement creates a radio button with the text "Choice 1" displayed next to it. The radio button initially appears selected.

```
JRadioButton radio1 = new JRadioButton("Choice 1", true);
```

Radio buttons normally are grouped together. When a set of radio buttons are grouped together, only one of the radio buttons in the group may be selected at any time. Clicking on a radio button selects it and automatically deselects any other radio button in the same group. Because only one radio button in a group can be selected at any given time, the buttons are said to be *mutually exclusive*.

> **NOTE:** The name radio button refers to the old car radios that had push buttons for selecting stations. Only one of the buttons could be pushed in at a time. When you pushed a button in, it automatically popped out any other button that was pushed in.

Grouping with the `ButtonGroup` class

Once you have created the `JRadioButton` objects that you wish to appear in a group, you must create an instance of the `ButtonGroup` class, and then add the `JRadioButton` objects to it. The `ButtonGroup` object creates the mutually exclusive relationship between the radio buttons that it contains. The following code shows an example:

```
// Create three radio buttons.
JRadioButton radio1 = new JRadioButton("Choice 1", true);
JRadioButton radio2 = new JRadioButton("Choice 2");
JRadioButton radio3 = new JRadioButton("Choice 3");

// Create a ButtonGroup object.
ButtonGroup group = new ButtonGroup();

// Add the radio buttons to the ButtonGroup object.
group.add(radio1);
group.add(radio2);
group.add(radio3);
```

Although you add radio buttons to a `ButtonGroup` object, `ButtonGroup` objects are not containers like `JPanel` objects, or content frames. The function of a `ButtonGroup` object is to deselect all the other radio buttons when one of them is selected. If you wish to add the radio buttons to a panel or a content frame, you must add them individually, as shown here:

```
// Add the radio buttons to the JPanel referenced by panel.
panel.add(radio1);
panel.add(radio2);
panel.add(radio3);
```

Responding to Radio Button Events

Just like `JButton` objects, `JRadioButton` objects generate an action event when they are clicked. To respond to an action event, you must write an action listener class. To demonstrate, we will look at the `MetricConverter` class, which is similar to the `KiloConverterWindow` class presented earlier.

The `MetricConverter` class presents a window in which the user can enter a distance in kilometers, and then click on radio buttons to see that distance converted to miles, feet, or inches. The conversion formulas are:

Miles = Kilometers × 0.6214
Feet = Kilometers × 3281.0
Inches = Kilometers × 39370.0

Figure 11-35 shows a sketch of what the window will look like. As you can see from the sketch, the window will have a label, a text field, and three radio buttons. When the user clicks on one of the radio buttons, the distance will be converted to the selected units and displayed in a separate `JOptionPane` dialog box.

Figure 11-35   Metric Converter window

The MetricConverter class is shown in Code Listing 11-15. The main method creates an instance of the class and displays the window shown at the top of Figure 11-36. The figure also shows the dialog boxes displayed when the user clicks on any of the radio buttons.

Code Listing 11-15   **(MetricConverter.java)**

```
 1   import java.awt.*;
 2   import java.awt.event.*;
 3   import javax.swing.*;
 4
 5   /**
 6    * The MetricConverter class lets the user enter a distance
 7    * in kilometers. Radio buttons can be selected to convert
 8    * the kilometers to miles, feet, or inches.
 9    */
10
11   public class MetricConverter extends JFrame
12   {
13      private JPanel panel;                    // A panel to hold components
14      private JLabel messageLabel;             // A message to the user
15      private JTextField kiloTextField;        // To hold user input
16      private JRadioButton milesButton;        // Miles conversion button
17      private JRadioButton feetButton;         // Feet conversion button
18      private JRadioButton inchesButton;       // Inches conversion button
19      private ButtonGroup radioButtonGroup;    // To group radio buttons
20      private final int WINDOW_WIDTH = 400;    // Window width
21      private final int WINDOW_HEIGHT = 100;   // Window height
22
23      /**
24       * Constructor
25       */
26
27      public MetricConverter()
28      {
29         // Call the JFrame constructor.
30         super("Metric Converter");
31
32         // Set the size of the window.
33         setSize(WINDOW_WIDTH, WINDOW_HEIGHT);
34
35         // Specify an action for the close button.
36         setDefaultCloseOperation(JFrame.EXIT_ON_CLOSE);
37
38         // Build the panel.
39         buildPanel();
40
```

```
41          // Add the panel to the frame's content pane.
42          add(panel);
43
44          // Display the window.
45          setVisible(true);
46      }
47
48      /**
49       * The buildPanel method adds a label, text field, and
50       * three radio buttons to a panel.
51       */
52
53      private void buildPanel()
54      {
55          // Create the label, text field, and radio buttons.
56          messageLabel = new JLabel("Enter a distance in kilometers");
57          kiloTextField = new JTextField(10);
58          milesButton = new JRadioButton("Convert to miles");
59          feetButton = new JRadioButton("Convert to feet");
60          inchesButton = new JRadioButton("Convert to inches");
61
62          // Group the radio buttons.
63          radioButtonGroup = new ButtonGroup();
64          radioButtonGroup.add(milesButton);
65          radioButtonGroup.add(feetButton);
66          radioButtonGroup.add(inchesButton);
67
68          // Add action listeners to the radio buttons.
69          milesButton.addActionListener(new RadioButtonListener());
70          feetButton.addActionListener(new RadioButtonListener());
71          inchesButton.addActionListener(new RadioButtonListener());
72
73          // Create a panel and add the components to it.
74          panel = new JPanel();
75          panel.add(messageLabel);
76          panel.add(kiloTextField);
77          panel.add(milesButton);
78          panel.add(feetButton);
79          panel.add(inchesButton);
80      }
81
82      /**
83       * Private inner class that handles the event when
84       * the user clicks one of the radio buttons.
85       */
86
```

```
 87        private class RadioButtonListener implements ActionListener
 88        {
 89           public void actionPerformed(ActionEvent e)
 90           {
 91              String input;              // To hold input
 92              String convertTo = "";     // What we are converting to
 93              double result = 0.0;       // To hold the conversion
 94
 95              // Get input from the text field.
 96              input = kiloTextField.getText();
 97
 98              // Determine the button that was clicked and
 99              // perform the selected conversion.
100              if (e.getSource() == milesButton)
101              {
102                 convertTo = " miles.";
103                 result = Double.parseDouble(input) * 0.6214;
104              }
105              else if (e.getSource() == feetButton)
106              {
107                 convertTo = " feet.";
108                 result = Double.parseDouble(input) * 3281.0;
109              }
110              else if (e.getSource() == inchesButton)
111              {
112                 convertTo = " inches.";
113                 result = Double.parseDouble(input) * 39370.0;
114              }
115
116              // Display the converted distance.
117              JOptionPane.showMessageDialog(null, input +
118                    " kilometers is " + result + convertTo);
119           }
120        }
121
122        /**
123         * The main method creates an instance of the
124         * MetricConverter class, causing it to display
125         * its window.
126         */
127
128        public static void main(String[] args)
129        {
130           new MetricConverter();
131        }
132     }
```

Figure 11-36   Window and dialog boxes displayed by the `MetricConverter` class

This window appears first. The user enters 2 into the text field.

This dialog box appears when the user clicks the "Convert to miles" radio button.

This dialog box appears when the user clicks the "Convert to feet" radio button.

This dialog box appears when the user clicks the "Convert to inches" radio button.

Determining in Code Whether a Radio Button Is Selected

In many applications you will merely want to know if a radio button is selected. The `JRadioButton` class's `isSelected` method returns a `boolean` value indicating whether the radio button is selected. If the radio button is selected, the method returns `true`. Otherwise, it returns `false`. In the following code, the `radio` variable references a radio button. The `if` statement calls the `isSelected` method to determine whether the radio button is selected.

```
if (radio.isSelected())
{
    // Code here executes if the radio
    // button is selected.
}
```

Selecting a Radio Button in Code

It is also possible to select a radio button in code with the `JRadioButton` class's `doClick` method. When the method is called, the radio button is selected just as if the user had clicked on it. As a result, an action event is generated. In the following statement, the `radio` variable references a radio button. When this statement executes, the radio button will be selected.

```
radio.doClick();
```

Check Boxes

A *check box* appears as a small box with a label appearing next to it. The window shown in Figure 11-37 has three check boxes.

Figure 11-37   Check boxes

Like radio buttons, check boxes may be selected or deselected at run time. When a check box is selected, a small check mark appears inside the box. Although check boxes are often displayed in groups, they are not usually grouped in a `ButtonGroup` like radio buttons are. This is because check boxes are not normally used to make mutually exclusive selections. Instead, the user is allowed to select any or all of the check boxes displayed in a group.

You create a check box with the `JCheckBox` class. Here are the general formats of two `JCheckBox` constructors.

```
JCheckBox(String text)
JCheckBox(String text, boolean selected)
```

The first constructor shown creates a deselected radio check box. The argument passed to the `text` parameter is the string displayed next to the check box. For example, the following statement creates a check box with the text "Macaroni" displayed next to it. The radio check box initially appears deselected.

```
JCheckBox check1 = new JCheckBox("Macaroni");
```

The second constructor takes an additional `boolean` argument, which is passed to the `selected` parameter. If `true` is passed as the `selected` argument, the radio check box initially appears selected. If `false` is passed, the check box initially appears deselected. For example, the following statement creates a check box with the text "Macaroni" displayed next to it. The radio check box initially appears selected.

```
JCheckBox check1 = new JCheckBox("Macaroni", true);
```

Responding to Check Box Events

When a `JCheckBox` object is selected or deselected, it generates an *item event*. You handle item events in a manner similar to the way you handle the action events generated by `JButton` and `JRadioButton` objects. First, you write an *item listener* class, which must meet the following requirements:

- It must implement the `ItemListener` interface.
- It must have a method named `itemStateChanged`. This method must take an argument of the `ItemEvent` type.

NOTE: The `ItemListener` interface is in the `java.awt.event` package, so you must have an import statement for that package in your source code.

Once you have written an item listener class, you must create an object of that class, and then register the item listener object with the `JCheckBox` component. When a `JCheckBox` component generates an event, it automatically executes the `itemStateChanged` method of the item listener object registered to it, passing the event object as an argument.

Determining in Code Whether a Check Box Is Selected

As with `JRadioButton`, you use the `isSelected` method to determine whether a `JCheckBox` component is selected. The method returns a `boolean` value. If the check box is selected, the method returns `true`. Otherwise, it returns `false`. In the following code, the `checkBox` variable references a `JCheckBox` component. The `if` statement calls the `isSelected` method to determine whether the check box is selected.

```
if (checkBox.isSelected())
{
    // Code here executes if the check
    // box is selected.
}
```

The `ColorCheckBoxWindow` class, shown in Code Listing 11-16, demonstrates how check boxes are used. The `main` method creates an instance of the class, which displays the window shown in Figure 11-38. When the "Yellow background" check box is selected, the background color of the content pane, the label, and the check boxes turns yellow. When this check box is deselected, the background colors go back to light gray. When the "Red foreground" check box is selected, the color of the text displayed in the label and the check boxes turns red. When this check box is deselected, the foreground colors go back to black.

Code Listing 11-16   (`ColorCheckBoxWindow.java`)

```java
 1  import java.awt.*;
 2  import java.awt.event.*;
 3  import javax.swing.*;
 4
 5  /**
 6   * The ColorCheckBoxWindow class demonstrates how check boxes
 7   * can be used.
 8   */
 9
10  public class ColorCheckBoxWindow extends JFrame
11  {
12     private JLabel messageLabel;         // A message
13     private JCheckBox yellowCheckBox;    // To select yellow
14     private JCheckBox redCheckBox;       // To select red
15     private final int WINDOW_WIDTH = 300;  // Width
16     private final int WINDOW_HEIGHT = 100; // Height
17
```

```
18      /**
19       * Constructor
20       */
21
22      public ColorCheckBoxWindow()
23      {
24          // Call the JFrame constructor.
25          super("Color Check Boxes");
26
27          // Set the size of the window.
28          setSize(WINDOW_WIDTH, WINDOW_HEIGHT);
29
30          // Specify an action for the close button.
31          setDefaultCloseOperation(JFrame.EXIT_ON_CLOSE);
32
33          // Create a label displaying a message to the user.
34          messageLabel = new JLabel("Select the check boxes " +
35                                    "to change colors.");
36
37          // Create the check boxes.
38          yellowCheckBox = new JCheckBox("Yellow background");
39          redCheckBox = new JCheckBox("Red foreground");
40
41          // Add an item listener to the check boxes.
42          yellowCheckBox.addItemListener(new CheckBoxListener());
43          redCheckBox.addItemListener(new CheckBoxListener());
44
45          // Add a FlowLayout manager to the content pane.
46          setLayout(new FlowLayout());
47
48          // Add the label and check boxes to the content pane.
49          add(messageLabel);
50          add(yellowCheckBox);
51          add(redCheckBox);
52
53          // Display the window.
54          setVisible(true);
55      }
56
57      /**
58       * Private inner class that handles the event when
59       * the user clicks one of the check boxes.
60       */
61
62      private class CheckBoxListener implements ItemListener
63      {
64          public void itemStateChanged(ItemEvent e)
65          {
```

```
66              // Determine whether yellowCheckBox was clicked.
67              if (e.getSource() == yellowCheckBox)
68              {
69                 // Is yellowCheckBox selected?
70                 if (yellowCheckBox.isSelected())
71                 {
72                    // Set the content pane background to yellow.
73                    getContentPane().setBackground(Color.YELLOW);
74                    // Set the yellowCheckBox background to yellow.
75                    yellowCheckBox.setBackground(Color.YELLOW);
76                    // Set the redCheckBox background to yellow.
77                    redCheckBox.setBackground(Color.YELLOW);
78                 }
79                 else
80                 {
81                    // Set the content pane background to gray.
82                    getContentPane().setBackground(Color.LIGHT_GRAY);
83                    // Set the yellowCheckBox background to gray.
84                    yellowCheckBox.setBackground(Color.LIGHT_GRAY);
85                    // Set the redCheckBox background to gray.
86                    redCheckBox.setBackground(Color.LIGHT_GRAY);
87                 }
88              }
89              // Determine whether redCheckBox was clicked.
90              else if (e.getSource() == redCheckBox)
91              {
92                 // Is redCheckBox selected?
93                 if (redCheckBox.isSelected())
94                 {
95                    // Set the label text to red.
96                    messageLabel.setForeground(Color.RED);
97                    // Set the yellowCheckBox text to red.
98                    yellowCheckBox.setForeground(Color.RED);
99                    // Set the redCheckBox text to red.
100                   redCheckBox.setForeground(Color.RED);
101                }
102                else
103                {
104                   // Set the label text to black.
105                   messageLabel.setForeground(Color.BLACK);
106                   // Set the yellowCheckBox text to black.
107                   yellowCheckBox.setForeground(Color.BLACK);
108                   // Set the redCheckBox text to black.
109                   redCheckBox.setForeground(Color.BLACK);
110                }
111             }
112          }
113       }
```

```
114
115    /**
116     * The main method creates an instance of the
117     * ColorCheckBoxWindow class, displaying its window.
118     */
119
120    public static void main(String[] args)
121    {
122       new ColorCheckBoxWindow();
123    }
124 }
```

Figure 11-38 Window displayed by the `ColorCheckBoxWindow` class

Selecting a Check Box in Code

As with radio buttons, it is possible to check boxes in code with the `JCheckBox` class's `doClick` method. When the method is called, the check box is selected just as if the user had clicked on it. As a result, an item event is generated. In the following statement, the `checkBox` variable references a `JCheckBox` object. When this statement executes, the check box will be selected.

```
checkBox.doClick();
```

The AWT and Swing Class Hierarchy Revisited

Figure 11-39 shows the locations of the `JRadioButton` and `JCheckBox` classes in the Swing and AWT class hierarchy.

Checkpoint

11.22 You want the user to be able to select only one item from a group of items. Which type of component would you use for the items, radio buttons or check boxes?

11.23 You want the user to be able to select any number of items from a group of items. Which type of component would you use for the items, radio buttons or check boxes?

11.24 What is the purpose of a `ButtonGroup` object?

11.25 Do you normally add radio buttons, check boxes, or both to a `ButtonGroup` object?

11.26 What type of event does a radio button generate when the user clicks on it?

11.27 What type of event does a check box generate when the user clicks on it?

11.28 How do you determine in code whether a radio button is selected?

11.29 How do you determine in code whether a check box is selected?

Figure 11-39   `JRadioButton` and `JCheckBox` locations in the Swing and AWT class hierarchy

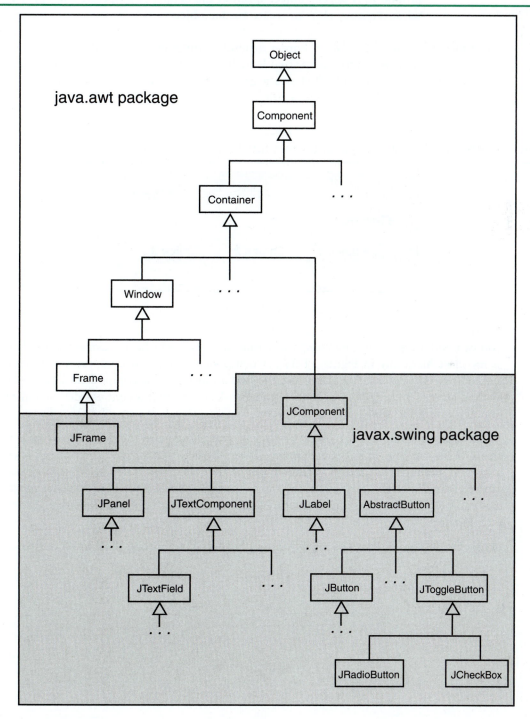

11.6 Borders

CONCEPT: A component can appear with several different styles of borders around it. A `Border` object specifies the details of a border. You use the `BorderFactory` class to create `Border` objects.

Sometimes it is helpful to place a border around a component or a group of components. You can give windows a more organized look by grouping related components inside borders. For example, Figure 11-40 shows a group of check boxes enclosed in a border. In addition, notice that the border has a title.

Figure 11-40 A group of check boxes with a titled border

You can add a border to any component that inherits from the `JComponent` class. (See the Swing class hierarchy in Figure 11-39.) A component derived from `JComponent` inherits a method named `setBorder`, which is used to add a border to the component. The `setBorder` method accepts a `Border` object as its argument. A `Border` object contains detailed information describing the appearance of a border.

Rather than creating `Border` objects yourself, you should use the `BorderFactory` class to create them for you. The `BorderFactory` class, which is part of the `javax.swing` package, has static methods that return various types of borders. Table 11-9 describes borders that can be created with the `BorderFactory` class. The table also lists the `BorderFactory` methods that can be called to create the borders. Note that there are several overloaded versions of each method.

In this chapter we discuss specifically empty borders, line borders, and titled borders.

Table 11-9   Borders produced by the `BorderFactory` class

Border	`BorderFactory` Method	Description
Compound border	createCompoundBorder	A border that has two parts: an inside edge and an outside edge. The inside and outside edges can be any of the other borders.
Empty border	createEmptyBorder	A border that contains only empty space.
Etched border	createEtchedBorder	A border with a 3D appearance that looks "etched" into the background.
Line border	createLineBorder	A border that appears as a line.
Lowered bevel border	createLoweredBevelBorder	A border that looks like beveled edges. It has a 3D appearance that gives the illusion of being sunken into the surrounding background.
Matte border	createMatteBorder	A line border that can have edges of different thicknesses.
Raised bevel border	createRaisedBevelBorder	A border that looks like beveled edges. It has a 3D appearance that gives the illusion of being raised above the surrounding background.
Titled border	createTitledBorder	An etched border with a title.

Empty Borders

An empty border is simply empty space around the edges of a component. To create an empty border, call the `BorderFactory` class's `createEmptyBorder` method. Here is the method's general format:

```
createEmptyBorder(int top, int left, int bottom, int right)
```

The arguments passed into *top*, *left*, *bottom*, and *right* specify in pixels the size of the border's top, left, bottom, and right edges. The method returns a reference to a `Border` object. Here is an example of a statement that uses the method. Assume that the `panel` variable references a `JPanel` object.

```
panel.setBorder(BorderFactory.createEmptyBorder(5, 5, 5, 5));
```

After this statement executes, the `JPanel` referenced by `panel` will have an empty border of five pixels around each edge.

Line Borders

A line border is a line of a specified color and thickness that appears around the edges of a component. To create a line border, call the `BorderFactory` class's `createLineBorder` method. Here is the method's general format:

```
createLineBorder(Color color, int thickness)
```

The arguments passed into *color* and *thickness* specify the color of the line and the size of the line in pixels. The method returns a reference to a Border object. Here is an example of a statement that uses the method. Assume that the panel variable references a JPanel object.

```
panel.setBorder(BorderFactory.createLineBorder(Color.RED, 1));
```

After this statement executes, the JPanel referenced by panel will have a red line border that is one pixel thick around its edges.

Titled Borders

A titled border is an etched border with a title displayed on it. To create a titled border, call the BorderFactory class's createTitledBorder method. Here is the method's general format:

```
createTitledBorder(String title)
```

The argument passed into *title* is the text to be displayed as the border's title. The method returns a reference to a Border object. Here is an example of a statement that uses the method. Assume that the panel variable references a JPanel object.

```
panel.setBorder(BorderFactory.createTitledBorder("Choices"));
```

After this statement executes, the JPanel referenced by panel will have an etched border with the title "Choices" displayed on it.

 Checkpoint

11.30 For a component to have a border, what class must it inherit from?

11.31 What method do you use to set a border around a component?

11.32 What is the preferred way of creating a Border object?

11.7 Focus on Problem Solving: Extending the JPanel Class

CONCEPT: By writing a class that inherits from JPanel you can create a custom panel component that can hold other components and their related code.

In the applications that you have studied so far in this chapter, we have written classes that inherit from the JFrame class. The subclass is a specialized version of the JFrame class, and its constructor creates the panels, buttons, and all of the other components needed. This approach works well for simple applications. But for applications that use many components, this approach can be cumbersome. Bundling all of the code and event listeners for a large number of components into a single class can lead to a large and complex class. A better approach is to encapsulate smaller groups of related components and their event listeners into their own classes.

A commonly used technique is to write a class that inherits from the JPanel class. This allows you to create your own specialized panel component, which can contain other components and related code such as event listeners. A complex application that uses numerous components can be constructed from several specialized panel components. In this section we will examine such an application.

The Brandi's Bagel House Application

Brandi's Bagel House has a bagel and coffee delivery service for the businesses in the neighborhood. Customers may call in and order white and whole wheat bagels with a variety of toppings. In addition, customers may order three different types of coffee. (Delivery for coffee alone is not available, however.) Here is a complete price list:

Bagels: White bagel $1.25, whole wheat bagel $1.50
Toppings: Cream cheese $0.50, butter $0.25, peach jelly $0.75, blueberry jam $0.75
Coffee: Regular coffee $1.25, decaf coffee $1.25, cappuccino $2.00

Brandi, the owner, needs an "order calculator" application that her staff can use to calculate the price of an order as it is called in. The application should display the subtotal, the amount of a 6% sales tax, and the total of the order. Figure 11-41 shows a sketch of the application's window. The user selects the type of bagel, toppings, and coffee, then clicks on the Calculate button. A dialog box appears displaying the subtotal, amount of sales tax, and total. The user can exit the application by either clicking on the Exit button or the standard close button in the upper-right corner.

Figure 11-41   Sketch of the Order Calculator window

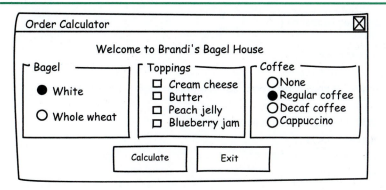

The layout shown in the sketch can be achieved using a `BorderLayout` manager with the window's content pane. The label that displays "Welcome to Brandi's Bagel House" is in the north region, the radio buttons for the bagel types are in the west region, the check boxes for the toppings are in the center region, the radio buttons for the coffee selection are in the east region, and the Calculate and Exit buttons are in the south region. To construct this window we create the following specialized panel classes that inherit from `JPanel`:

- **GreetingsPanel**. This panel contains the label that appears in the window's north region.
- **BagelPanel**. This panel contains the radio buttons for the types of bagels.
- **ToppingsPanel**. This panel contains the check boxes for the types of bagels.
- **CoffeePanel**. This panel contains the radio buttons for the coffee selections.

(We will not create a specialized panel for the Calculate and Exit buttons. The reason is explained later.) After these classes have been created, we can create objects from them and add the objects to the correct regions of the window's content pane. Let's take a closer look at each of these classes.

The `GreetingPanel` Class

The `GreetingPanel` class holds the label displaying the text "Welcome to Brandi's Bagel House". Code Listing 11-17 shows the class, which inherits from `JPanel`.

Code Listing 11-17   (`GreetingPanel.java`)

```java
1   import javax.swing.*;
2
3   /**
4    * The GreetingPanel class is a specialized JPanel class.
5    * It displays a greeting for the application window.
6    */
7
8   public class GreetingPanel extends JPanel
9   {
10     /**
11      * Constructor
12      */
13
14     public GreetingPanel()
15     {
16        // Create the label.
17        JLabel greeting =
18           new JLabel("Welcome to Brandi's Bagel House");
19
20        // Add the label to this panel.
21        add(greeting);
22     }
23  }
```

An instance of this class is a `JPanel` component that displays a label with the text "Welcome to Brandi's Bagel House". Figure 11-42 shows how the component will appear when it is placed in the window's north region.

Figure 11-42   Appearance of the `GreetingPanel` component

Welcome to Brandi's Bagel House

The `BagelPanel` Class

The `BagelPanel` class holds the radio buttons for the types of bagels. Notice that this panel uses a `GridLayout` manager with two rows and one column. Code Listing 11-18 shows the class, which inherits from `JPanel`.

Code Listing 11-18   `(BagelPanel.java)`

```
1   import java.awt.*;
2   import javax.swing.*;
3
4   /**
5    * The BagelPanel class allows the user to select either
6    * a white or whole wheat bagel.
7    */
8
9   public class BagelPanel extends JPanel
10  {
11      // The following constants are used to indicate
12      // the cost of each type of bagel.
13      public final double WHITE_BAGEL = 1.25;
14      public final double WHEAT_BAGEL = 1.50;
15
16      // The following variables will reference radio
17      // buttons for white and whole wheat bagels.
18      private JRadioButton whiteBagel;
19      private JRadioButton wheatBagel;
20
21      // The following variable will reference a
22      // ButtonGroup object to group the radio buttons.
23      private ButtonGroup bg;
24
25      /**
26       * Constructor
27       */
28
29      public BagelPanel()
30      {
31          // Create a GridLayout manager with
32          // two rows and one column.
33          setLayout(new GridLayout(2, 1));
34
35          // Create the radio buttons.
36          whiteBagel = new JRadioButton("White", true);
37          wheatBagel = new JRadioButton("Wheat");
38
39          // Group the radio buttons.
40          bg = new ButtonGroup();
41          bg.add(whiteBagel);
42          bg.add(wheatBagel);
43
44          // Add a border around the panel.
45          setBorder(BorderFactory.createTitledBorder("Bagel"));
46
```

```
47              // Add the radio buttons to this panel.
48              add(whiteBagel);
49              add(wheatBagel);
50          }
51
52          /**
53           * The getBagelCost method returns the cost of
54           * the selected bagel.
55           */
56
57          public double getBagelCost()
58          {
59              // The following variable will hold the cost
60              // of the selected bagel.
61              double bagelCost = 0.0;
62
63              // Determine which bagel is selected.
64              if (whiteBagel.isSelected())
65                  bagelCost = WHITE_BAGEL;
66              else
67                  bagelCost = WHEAT_BAGEL;
68
69              // Return the cost of the selected bagel.
70              return bagelCost;
71          }
72      }
```

Notice that the whiteBagel radio button is automatically selected when it is created. This is the default choice. This class does not have an inner event listener class because we do not want to execute any code when the user selects a bagel. Instead, we want this class to be able to report the cost of the selected bagel. That is the purpose of the getBagelCost method, which returns the cost of the selected bagel as a double. (This method is called by the Calculate button's event listener.) Figure 11-43 shows how the component appears when it is placed in the window's west region.

Figure 11-43 Appearance of the BagelPanel component

The `ToppingPanel` Class

The `ToppingPanel` class holds the check boxes for the available toppings. Code Listing 11-19 shows the class, which inherits from `JPanel`.

Code Listing 11-19   (`ToppingPanel.java`)

```java
1   import java.awt.*;
2   import javax.swing.*;
3
4   /**
5    *  The ToppingPanel class allows the user to select
6    *  the toppings for the bagel.
7    */
8
9   public class ToppingPanel extends JPanel
10  {
11     // The following constants are used to indicate
12     // the cost of toppings.
13     public final double CREAM_CHEESE = 0.50;
14     public final double BUTTER = 0.25;
15     public final double PEACH_JELLY = 0.75;
16     public final double BLUEBERRY_JAM = 0.75;
17
18     // Check boxes for the available toppings.
19     private JCheckBox creamCheese;      // Cream cheese
20     private JCheckBox butter;           // Butter
21     private JCheckBox peachJelly;       // Peach jelly
22     private JCheckBox blueberryJam;     // Blueberry jam
23
24     /**
25      * Constructor
26      */
27
28     public ToppingPanel()
29     {
30        // Create a GridLayout manager with
31        // four rows and one column.
32        setLayout(new GridLayout(4, 1));
33
34        // Create the check boxes.
35        creamCheese = new JCheckBox("Cream cheese");
36        butter = new JCheckBox("Butter");
37        peachJelly = new JCheckBox("Peach jelly");
38        blueberryJam = new JCheckBox("Blueberry jam");
39
```

```
40          // Add a border around the panel.
41          setBorder(BorderFactory.createTitledBorder("Toppings"));
42
43          // Add the check boxes to this panel.
44          add(creamCheese);
45          add(butter);
46          add(peachJelly);
47          add(blueberryJam);
48       }
49
50       /**
51        *  The getToppingCost method returns the cost of
52        *  the selected toppings.
53        */
54
55       public double getToppingCost()
56       {
57          // The following variable will hold the cost
58          // of the selected topping.
59          double toppingCost = 0.0;
60
61          // Determine which of the toppings are selected.
62          // More than one may be selected.
63          if (creamCheese.isSelected())
64             toppingCost += CREAM_CHEESE;
65          if (butter.isSelected())
66             toppingCost += BUTTER;
67          if (peachJelly.isSelected())
68             toppingCost += PEACH_JELLY;
69          if (blueberryJam.isSelected())
70             toppingCost += BLUEBERRY_JAM;
71
72          // Return the topping cost.
73          return toppingCost;
74       }
75    }
```

As with the BagelPanel class, this class does not have an inner event listener class because we do not want to execute any code when the user selects a topping. Instead, we want this class to be able to report the total cost of all the selected toppings. That is the purpose of the getToppingCost method, which returns the cost of all the selected toppings as a double. (This method is called by the Calculate button's event listener.) Figure 11-44 shows how the component appears when it is placed in the window's center region.

Figure 11-44   Appearance of the `ToppingPanel` component

The `CoffeePanel` Class

The `CoffeePanel` class holds the radio buttons for the available coffee selections. Code Listing 11-20 shows the class, which inherits from `JPanel`.

Code Listing 11-20   (`CoffeePanel.java`)

```
 1  import java.awt.*;
 2  import javax.swing.*;
 3
 4  /**
 5   * The CoffeePanel class allows the user to select coffee
 6   */
 7
 8  public class CoffeePanel extends JPanel
 9  {
10     // The following constants are used to indicate
11     // the cost of coffee.
12     public final double NO_COFFEE = 0.0;
13     public final double REGULAR_COFFEE = 1.25;
14     public final double DECAF_COFFEE = 1.25;
15     public final double CAPPUCCINO = 2.00;
16
17     // Radio buttons for the available coffees.
18     private JRadioButton noCoffee;      // No coffee
19     private JRadioButton regularCoffee; // Regular coffee
20     private JRadioButton decafCoffee;   // Decaf
21     private JRadioButton cappuccino;    // Cappuccino
22
23     // The following variable will reference a
24     // ButtonGroup object to group the radio buttons.
25     private ButtonGroup bg;
26
27     /**
28      * Constructor
29      */
30
```

```
31      public CoffeePanel()
32      {
33         // Create a GridLayout manager with
34         // four rows and one column.
35         setLayout(new GridLayout(4, 1));
36
37         // Create the radio buttons.
38         noCoffee = new JRadioButton("None");
39         regularCoffee = new JRadioButton("Regular coffee", true);
40         decafCoffee = new JRadioButton("Decaf coffee");
41         cappuccino = new JRadioButton("Cappuccino");
42
43         // Group the radio buttons and add them to this panel.
44         bg = new ButtonGroup();
45         bg.add(noCoffee);
46         bg.add(regularCoffee);
47         bg.add(decafCoffee);
48         bg.add(cappuccino);
49
50         // Add a border around the panel.
51         setBorder(BorderFactory.createTitledBorder("Coffee"));
52
53         // Add the radio buttons to this panel.
54         add(noCoffee);
55         add(regularCoffee);
56         add(decafCoffee);
57         add(cappuccino);
58      }
59
60      /**
61       * The getCoffeeCost method returns the cost of
62       * the selected coffee.
63       */
64
65      public double getCoffeeCost()
66      {
67         // The following variable will hold the cost
68         // of the selected coffee.
69         double coffeeCost = 0.0;
70
71         // Determine which coffee is selected.
72         if (noCoffee.isSelected())
73            coffeeCost = NO_COFFEE;
74         else if (regularCoffee.isSelected())
75            coffeeCost = REGULAR_COFFEE;
76         else if (decafCoffee.isSelected())
77            coffeeCost = DECAF_COFFEE;
78         else if (cappuccino.isSelected())
79            coffeeCost = CAPPUCCINO;
```

```
80
81          // Return the coffee cost.
82          return coffeeCost;
83      }
84  }
```

As with the `BagelPanel` and `ToppingPanel` classes, this class does not have an inner event listener class because we do not want to execute any code when the user selects coffee. Instead, we want this class to be able to report the cost of the selected coffee. The `getCoffeeCost` method returns the cost of the selected coffee as a `double`. (This method is called by the Calculate button's event listener.) Figure 11-45 shows how the component appears when it is placed in the window's east region.

Figure 11-45   Appearance of the `CoffeePanel` component

Putting It All Together

The last step in creating this application is to write a class that builds the application's window and adds the Calculate and Exit buttons. This class, which we name `OrderCalculatorGUI`, inherits from `JFrame` and uses a `BorderLayout` manager with its content pane. Figure 11-46 shows how instances of the `GreetingPanel`, `BagelPanel`, `ToppingPanel`, and `CoffeePanel` classes are placed in the content pane.

Figure 11-46   Placement of the custom panels

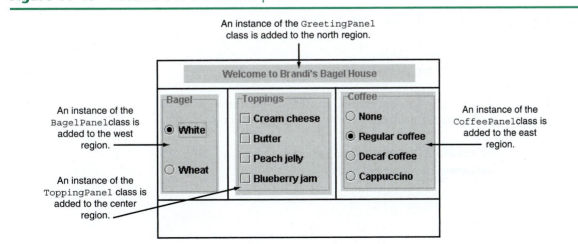

We have not created a custom panel class to hold the Calculate and Exit buttons. The reason is that the Calculate button's event listener must call the `getBagelCost`, `getToppingCost`, and `getCoffeeCost` methods. To call those methods, the event listener must have access to the `BagelPanel`, `ToppingPanel`, and `CoffeePanel` objects that are created in the `OrderCalculatorGUI` class. So, the `OrderCalculatorGUI` class itself creates the buttons. The code for the `OrderCalculatorGUI` class is shown in Code Listing 11-21.

Code Listing 11-21   **(OrderCalculatorGUI.java)**

```java
 1   import javax.swing.*;
 2   import java.awt.*;
 3   import java.awt.event.*;
 4   import java.text.DecimalFormat;
 5
 6   /**
 7    * The OrderCalculatorGUI class creates the GUI for the
 8    * Brandi's Bagel House application.
 9    */
10
11   public class OrderCalculatorGUI extends JFrame
12   {
13      private BagelPanel bagels;          // Bagel panel
14      private ToppingPanel toppings;      // Topping panel
15      private CoffeePanel coffee;         // Coffee panel
16      private GreetingPanel banner;       // To display a greeting
17      private JPanel buttonPanel;         // To hold the buttons
18      private JButton calcButton;         // To calculate the cost
19      private JButton exitButton;         // To exit the application
20      private final double TAX_RATE = 0.06; // Sales tax rate
21
22      /**
23       * Constructor
24       */
25
26      public OrderCalculatorGUI()
27      {
28         // Display a title.
29         super("Order Calculator");
30
31         // Specify an action for the close button.
32         setDefaultCloseOperation(JFrame.EXIT_ON_CLOSE);
33
34         // Create a BorderLayout manager.
35         setLayout(new BorderLayout());
36
```

```java
37          // Create the custom panels.
38          banner = new GreetingPanel();
39          bagels = new BagelPanel();
40          toppings = new ToppingPanel();
41          coffee = new CoffeePanel();
42
43          // Create the button panel.
44          buildButtonPanel();
45
46          // Add the components to the content pane.
47          add(banner, BorderLayout.NORTH);
48          add(bagels, BorderLayout.WEST);
49          add(toppings, BorderLayout.CENTER);
50          add(coffee, BorderLayout.EAST);
51          add(buttonPanel, BorderLayout.SOUTH);
52
53          // Pack the contents of the window and display it.
54          pack();
55          setVisible(true);
56       }
57
58       /**
59        * The buildButtonPanel method builds the button panel.
60        */
61
62       private void buildButtonPanel()
63       {
64          // Create a panel for the buttons.
65          buttonPanel = new JPanel();
66
67          // Create the buttons.
68          calcButton = new JButton("Calculate");
69          exitButton = new JButton("Exit");
70
71          // Register the action listeners.
72          calcButton.addActionListener(new CalcButtonListener());
73          exitButton.addActionListener(new ExitButtonListener());
74
75          // Add the buttons to the button panel.
76          buttonPanel.add(calcButton);
77          buttonPanel.add(exitButton);
78       }
79
80       /**
81        * Private inner class that handles the event when
82        * the user clicks the Calculate button.
83        */
84
```

```
 85        private class CalcButtonListener implements ActionListener
 86        {
 87           public void actionPerformed(ActionEvent e)
 88           {
 89              // Variables to hold the subtotal, tax, and total
 90              double subtotal, tax, total;
 91
 92              // Calculate the subtotal.
 93              subtotal = bagels.getBagelCost() +
 94                         toppings.getToppingCost() +
 95                         coffee.getCoffeeCost();
 96
 97              // Calculate the sales tax.
 98              tax = subtotal * TAX_RATE;
 99
100              // Calculate the total.
101              total = subtotal + tax;
102
103              // Create a DecimalFormat object to format output.
104              DecimalFormat dollar = new DecimalFormat("0.00");
105
106              // Display the charges.
107              JOptionPane.showMessageDialog(null, "Subtotal: $" +
108                          dollar.format(subtotal) + "\n" +
109                        "Tax: $" + dollar.format(tax) + "\n" +
110                        "Total: $" + dollar.format(total));
111           }
112        }
113
114        /**
115         * Private inner class that handles the event when
116         * the user clicks the Exit button.
117         */
118
119        private class ExitButtonListener implements ActionListener
120        {
121           public void actionPerformed(ActionEvent e)
122           {
123               System.exit(0);
124           }
125        }
126
127        /**
128         * main method
129         */
130
```

```
131      public static void main(String[] args)
132      {
133        new OrderCalculatorGUI();
134      }
135   }
```

When the application runs, the window shown in Figure 11-47 appears. Figure 11-48 shows the JOptionPane dialog box that is displayed when the user selects a wheat bagel with cream cheese, butter, and decaf coffee.

Figure 11-47 The Order Calculator window

Figure 11-48 The subtotal, tax, and total displayed

11.8 Splash Screens

CONCEPT: A splash screen is a graphic image that is displayed while an application loads into memory and starts up.

Most major applications display a splash screen, which is a graphic image that is displayed while the application is loading into memory. Splash screens usually show company logos and keep the user's attention while the application starts up. Splash screens are particularly important for large applications that take a long time to load, because they assure the user that the program is not malfunctioning.

Beginning with Java 6, you can display splash screens with your Java applications. First, you have to use a graphics program to create the image that you want to display. Java supports splash screens in the GIF, PNG, or JPEG formats. (If you are using Windows, you can create images with Microsoft Paint, which supports all of these formats.)

To display the splash screen you use the `java` command in the following way when you run the application:

```
java -splash:GraphicFileName ClassFileName
```

GraphicFileName is the name of the file that contains the graphic image, and *ClassFileName* is the name of the `class` file that you are running. For example, in the book's source code, in the same folder as the Brandi's Bagel House application, you will find a file named `BrandiLogo.jpg`. This image, which is shown in Figure 11-49, is a logo for the Brandi's Bagel House application. To display the splash screen when the application starts, you would use the following command:

```
java -splash:BrandiLogo.jpg Bagel
```

When you run this command, the graphic file will immediately be displayed in the center of the screen. It will remain displayed until the application's window appears.

Figure 11-49   Splash screen for the Brandi's Bagel House application

11.9 Using Console Output to Debug a GUI Application

CONCEPT: When debugging a GUI application, you can use `System.out.println` to send diagnostic messages to the console.

When an application is not performing correctly, programmers sometimes write statements that display *diagnostic messages* into the application. For example, if an application is not giving the correct result for a calculation, diagnostic messages can be displayed at various points in the program's execution showing the values of all the variables used in the calculation. If the trouble is caused by a variable that has not been properly initialized, or that has not been assigned the correct value, the diagnostic messages reveal this problem. This helps the programmer to see what is going on "under the hood" while an application is running.

The `System.out.println` method can be a valuable tool for displaying diagnostic messages in a GUI application. Because the `System.out.println` method sends its output to the console, diagnostic messages can be displayed without interfering with the application's GUI windows.

Code Listing 11-22 shows an example. This is a modified version of the `KiloConverterWindow` class, discussed earlier in this chapter. Inside the `actionPerformed` method, which is in the `CalcButtonListener` inner class, calls to the `System.out.println` method have been written. The lines containing the calls are shown in bold. These calls display the value that the application has retrieved from the text field, and is working with in its calculation. (This file is stored in the student source code folder *Chapter 11\KiloConverter Phase 3*.)

Code Listing 11-22   (`KiloConverterWindow.java`)

```java
1   import javax.swing.*;
2   import java.awt.event.*;
3
4   /**
5    * This version of the KiloConverterWindow class
6    * displays debugging messages to the console window.
7    */
8
9   public class KiloConverterWindow extends JFrame
10  {
11     private JPanel panel;            // A panel container
12     private JLabel messageLabel;     // A message to display
13     private JTextField kiloTextField; // To hold user input
14     private JButton calcButton;      // Performs calculation
15     private final int WINDOW_WIDTH = 320;  // Window width
16     private final int WINDOW_HEIGHT = 100; // Window height
17
18     /**
19      * Constructor
20      */
21
```

```
22        public KiloConverterWindow()
23        {
24           // Call the JFrame constructor.
25           super("Kilometer Converter");
26
27           // Set the size of the window.
28           setSize(WINDOW_WIDTH, WINDOW_HEIGHT);
29
30           // Specify what happens when the close
31           // button is clicked.
32           setDefaultCloseOperation(JFrame.EXIT_ON_CLOSE);
33
34           // Build the panel and add it to the frame.
35           buildPanel();
36
37           // Add the panel to the frame's content pane.
38           add(panel);
39
40           // Display the window.
41           setVisible(true);
42        }
43
44        /**
45         * The buildPanel method adds a label, text field, and
46         * a button to a panel.
47         */
48
49        private void buildPanel()
50        {
51           // Create the label, text field, and button components.
52           messageLabel = new JLabel("Enter a distance in kilometers");
53           kiloTextField = new JTextField(10);
54           calcButton = new JButton("Calculate");
55
56           // Add an action listener to the button.
57           calcButton.addActionListener(new CalcButtonListener());
58
59           // Create a panel to hold the components.
60           panel = new JPanel();
61
62           // Add the label, text field, and button to the panel.
63           panel.add(messageLabel);
64           panel.add(kiloTextField);
65           panel.add(calcButton);
66        }
67
```

```
68        /**
69         * Private inner class that handles the event when
70         * the user clicks the calculate button.
71         */
72
73        private class CalcButtonListener implements ActionListener
74        {
75           public void actionPerformed(ActionEvent e)
76           {
77              String str;   // To hold text entered
78              double miles; // To hold miles
79
80              // Get the number of kilometers entered in the
81              // text field. The input is a string.
82              str = kiloTextField.getText();
83
84              // For debugging, display the text entered, and
85              // its value converted to a double.
86              System.out.println("Reading " + str +
87                                 " from the text field.");
88              System.out.println("Converted value: " +
89                                 Double.parseDouble(str));
90
91              // Convert the kilometers to miles.
92              miles = Double.parseDouble(str) * 0.6214;
93
94              // Display a message dialog showing the miles.
95              JOptionPane.showMessageDialog(null, str +
96                        " kilometers is " + miles + " miles.");
97
98              // For debugging, display a message indicating
99              // the application is ready for more input.
100             System.out.println("Ready for the next input.");
101          }
102       }
103
104       /**
105        * The main method creates an instance of the
106        * KiloConverterWindow class, which displays
107        * a window on the screen.
108        */
109
110       public static void main(String[] args)
111       {
112          new KiloConverterWindow();
113       }
114 }
```

Let's take a closer look. In lines 86 through 87 a message is displayed to the console showing the value that was read from the text field. In lines 88 through 89 another message is displayed showing the value after it is converted to a `double`. Then, in line 100, a message is displayed indicating that the application is ready for its next input. Figure 11-50 shows an example session with the application on a computer running Windows. Both the console window and the application windows are shown.

Figure 11-50 Messages displayed to the console during the application's execution

1. A command is typed in the console window to execute the application. The application's window appears.

2. The user types a value into the text field and clicks the Calculate button. Debugging messages appear in the console window, and a message dialog appears showing the value converted to miles.

3. The user dismisses the dialog box and a message is displayed in the console window indicating that the application is ready for the next input.

The messages displayed to the console are meant only for the programmer to see while he or she is debugging the application. Once the programmer is satisfied that the application is running correctly, the calls to `System.out.println` can be taken out.

11.10 Common Errors to Avoid

The following list describes several errors that are commonly made when learning this chapter's topics.

- **Misspelling the name of the `javax.swing` package in an `import` statement.** Swing components are part of the javax.swing package. Don't forget the letter x that appears after java.
- **Forgetting to specify the action taken when the user clicks on a `JFrame`'s close button.** By default, a window is hidden from view when the close button is clicked, but the application is not terminated. If you wish to exit the application when a JFrame's close button is clicked, you must call the setDefaultCloseOperation method and pass JFrame.EXIT_ON_CLOSE as the argument.
- **Forgetting to write an event listener for each event you wish an application to respond to.** To respond to an event, you must write an event listener of the proper type registered to the component that generates the event.
- **Forgetting to register an event listener.** Even if you write an event listener, it will not execute unless it has been registered with the correct component.
- **When writing the `actionPerformed` method in an action listener class, not using the exact signature required by the `ActionListener` interface.** The signature of the actionPerformed method in the ActionListener interface specifies that it accepts one argument, which is an ActionEvent object. If you provide a different parameter list, you have not overridden the method as required.
- **Placing components directly into the regions of a container governed by a `BorderLayout` manager when you do not want the components resized or you want to add more than one component per region.** If you do not want the components that you place in a BorderLayout region to be resized, place them in a JPanel component and then add the JPanel component to the region.
- **Placing components directly into the cells of a container governed by a `GridLayout` manager when you do not want the components resized or you want to add more than one component per cell.** If you do not want the components that you place in a GridLayout cell to be resized, place them in a JPanel component, and then add the JPanel component to the cell.
- **Forgetting to add `JRadioButton` components to a `ButtonGroup` object.** A mutually exclusive relationship is created between radio buttons only when they are added to a ButtonGroup object.

Review Questions and Exercises

Multiple Choice and True/False

1. To display a message box in the center of the screen, you pass this as the first argument to the JOptionPane.showMessageDialog method.
   a. JOptionPane.CENTER
   b. The X and Y coordinates of the screen's center
   c. null
   d. 0

2. This type of dialog box suspends execution of any other statements until the dialog box is closed.
   a. private
   b. modal
   c. dominant
   d. system

3. The `JOptionPane.showInputDialog` method returns this if the user clicks on the OK button.
   a. `null`
   b. `JOptionPane.OK_BUTTON`
   c. `0`
   d. the value entered into the dialog box's text field

4. The `JOptionPane.showInputDialog` method returns this if the user clicks on the Cancel button.
   a. `null`
   b. `JOptionPane.CANCEL_BUTTON`
   c. `0`
   d. `-1`

5. The `JOptionPane.showConfirmDialog` method returns this if the user clicks on the Yes button.
   a. `null`
   b. `JOptionPane.YES_OPTION`
   c. `1`
   d. `JOptionPane.YES_BUTTON`

6. This is required in a GUI application to stop the program's execution.
   a. an exception
   b. a call to the `JSystem.stop` method
   c. the end of the `main` method must be reached
   d. a call to the `System.exit` method

7. With Swing, you use this class to create a frame.
   a. `Frame`
   b. `SwingFrame`
   c. `JFrame`
   d. `JavaFrame`

8. Swing components are part of this package.
   a. `java.swing`
   b. `javax.swing`
   c. `java.awt.swing`
   d. `java.graphics.swing`

9. This is the part of a `JFrame` object that holds the components that have been added to the `JFrame` object.
   a. content pane
   b. viewing area
   c. component array
   d. object collection

10. This is a `JPanel` object's default layout manager.
    a. `BorderLayout`
    b. `GridLayout`
    c. `FlowLayout`
    d. None

11. This is the default layout manager for a `JFrame` object's content pane.
    a. `BorderLayout`
    b. `GridLayout`
    c. `FlowLayout`
    d. None

12. If a container is governed by a `BorderLayout` manager and you add a component to it, but you do not pass the second argument specifying the region, this is the region in which the component will be added.
    a. north
    b. south
    c. east
    d. center

13. Components in this/these regions of a `BorderLayout` manager are resized horizontally so they fill up the entire region.
    a. north and south
    b. east and west
    c. center only
    d. north, south, east, and west

14. Components in this/these regions of a `BorderLayout` manager are resized vertically so they fill up the entire region.
    a. north and south
    b. east and west
    c. center only
    d. north, south, east, and west

15. Components in this/these regions of a `BorderLayout` manager are resized both horizontally and vertically so they fill up the entire region.
    a. north and south
    b. east and west
    c. center only
    d. north, south, east, and west.

16. This is the default alignment of a `FlowLayout` manager.
    a. left
    b. center
    c. right
    d. no alignment

17. Adding radio button components to this type of object creates a mutually exclusive relationship between them.
    a. `MutualExclude`
    b. `RadioGroup`
    c. `LogicalGroup`
    d. `ButtonGroup`

18. Any component that inherits from this class can have a border around it.
    a. `Container`
    b. `Object`
    c. `JComponent`
    d. `JFrame`

19. You use this class to create `Border` objects.
    a. `BorderFactory`
    b. `BorderMaker`
    c. `BorderCreator`
    d. `BorderSource`

20. **True or False:** A `JOptionPane` confirm dialog box has a text field for the user to enter input.

21. **True or False:** Only one type of icon may be displayed in a `JOptionPane` message box.

22. **True or False:** A panel cannot be displayed by itself.

23. **True or False:** You can place multiple components inside a `GridLayout` cell.

24. **True or False:** You can place multiple components inside a `BorderLayout` region.

25. **True or False:** You can place multiple components inside a container governed by a `FlowLayout` manager.

26. **True or False:** You can place a panel inside a region governed by a `BorderLayout` manager.

27. **True or False:** A component placed in a `GridLayout` manager's cell will not be resized to fill up any extra space in the cell.

28. **True or False:** You normally add `JCheckBox` components to a `ButtonGroup` object.

29. **True or False:** A mutually exclusive relationship is automatically created between all `JRadioButton` components that are in the same container.

30. **True or False:** You can write a class that inherits from the `JPanel` class.

Find the Error

1. The following statement is in a class that uses Swing components.

   ```
   import java.swing.*;
   ```

2. The following is an inner class that will be registered as an action listener for a `JButton` component.

   ```
   private class ButtonListener implements ActionListener
   {
       public void actionPerformed()
       {
           // Code appears here.
       }
   }
   ```

3. The intention of the following statement is to give the `panel` object a `GridLayout` manager with 10 columns and 5 rows.

   ```
   panel.setLayout(new GridLayout(10, 5));
   ```

4. The `panel` variable references a `JPanel` governed by a `BorderLayout` manager. The following statement attempts to add the button component to the north region of `panel`.

```
panel.add(button, NORTH);
```

5. The `panel` variable references a `JPanel` object. The intention of the following statement is to create a titled border around `panel`.

```
panel.setBorder(new BorderFactory("Choices"));
```

Algorithm Workbench

1. Write a statement that displays a default message dialog box with the message "Have a nice day."

2. Write a statement that displays a message dialog box with the message "Have a nice day." The text "Greeting" should appear in the dialog box's title bar. No icon should be displayed in the dialog box.

3. Write code that displays an input dialog asking the user to enter the temperature. If the user enters 50 or less, the code should display a message dialog box with the message "A bit cold!" If the user enters a value between 50 and 80, the code should display a message dialog box with the message "Nice day!" If the user enters 80 or greater, the code should display a message dialog box with the message "A bit warm!"

4. The variable `myWindow` references a `JFrame` object. Write a statement that sets the size of the object to 500 pixels wide and 250 pixels high.

5. The variable `myWindow` references a `JFrame` object. Write a statement that causes the application to end when the user clicks on the `JFrame` object's close button.

6. The variable `myWindow` references a `JFrame` object. Write a statement that displays the object's window on the screen.

7. The variable `myButton` references a `JButton` object. Write the code to set the object's background color to white and foreground color to red.

8. Assume that a class inherits from the `JFrame` class. Write code that can appear in the class constructor, which gives the content pane a `FlowLayout` manager. Components added to the content pane should be aligned with the left edge of each row.

9. Assume that a class inherits from the `JFrame` class. Write code that can appear in the class constructor, which gives the content pane a `GridLayout` manager with five rows and 10 columns.

10. Assume that the variable `panel` references a `JPanel` object that uses a `BorderLayout` manager. In addition, the variable `button` references a `JButton` object. Write code that adds the `button` object to the `panel` object's west region.

11. Write code that creates three radio buttons with the text "Option 1", "Option 2", and "Option 3". The radio button that displays the text "Option 1" should be initially selected. Make sure these components are grouped so that a mutually exclusive relationship exists between them.

12. Assume that `panel` references a `JPanel` object. Write code that creates a two-pixel thick blue line border around it.

Short Answer

1. When using an input dialog box, how do you determine the input entered by the user?

2. What is the difference between an input dialog box and a confirm dialog box?

3. Why doesn't a GUI application stop executing when the end of the main method is reached?

4. If you do not change the default close operation, what happens when the user clicks on the close button on a JFrame object?

5. Why is it sometimes necessary to place a component inside a panel and then place the panel inside a container governed by a BorderLayout manager?

6. In what type of situation would you present a group of items to the user with radio buttons? With check boxes?

7. How can you create a specialized panel component that can be used to hold other components and their related code?

Programming Challenges

1. Retail Price Calculator

Create a GUI application where the user enters the wholesale cost of an item and its markup percentage into text fields. (For example, if an item's wholesale cost is $5 and its markup percentage is 100%, then its retail price is $10.) The application should have a button that displays the item's retail price when clicked.

2. Monthly Sales Tax

VideoNote
The Monthly
Sales Tax
Problem

A retail company must file a monthly sales tax report listing the total sales for the month, and the amount of state and county sales tax collected. The state sales tax rate is 4% and the county sales tax rate is 2%. Create a GUI application that allows the user to enter the total sales for the month into a text field. From this figure, the application should calculate and display the following:

- The amount of county sales tax
- The amount of state sales tax
- The total sales tax (county plus state)

In the application's code, represent the county tax rate (0.02) and the state tax rate (0.04) as named constants.

3. Property Tax

A county collects property taxes on the assessment value of property, which is 60% of the property's actual value. If an acre of land is valued at $10,000, its assessment value is $6,000. The property tax is then $0.64 for each $100 of the assessment value. The tax for the acre assessed at $6,000 will be $38.40. Create a GUI application that displays the assessment value and property tax when a user enters the actual value of a property.

4. Travel Expenses

Create a GUI application that calculates and displays the total travel expenses of a business person on a trip. Here is the information that the user must provide:

- Number of days on the trip
- Amount of airfare, if any
- Amount of car rental fees, if any
- Number of miles driven, if a private vehicle was used
- Amount of parking fees, if any
- Amount of taxi charges, if any
- Conference or seminar registration fees, if any
- Lodging charges, per night

The company reimburses travel expenses according to the following policy:

- $37 per day for meals
- Parking fees, up to $10.00 per day
- Taxi charges up to $20.00 per day
- Lodging charges up to $95.00 per day
- If a private vehicle is used, $0.27 per mile driven

The application should calculate and display the following:

- Total expenses incurred by the businessperson
- The total allowable expenses for the trip
- The excess that must be paid by the businessperson, if any
- The amount saved by the businessperson if the expenses were under the total allowed

5. Theater Revenue

A movie theater only keeps a percentage of the revenue earned from ticket sales. The remainder goes to the movie company. Create a GUI application that allows the user to enter the following data into text fields:

- Price per adult ticket
- Number of adult tickets sold
- Price per child ticket
- Number of child tickets sold

The application should calculate and display the following data for one night's box office business at a theater:

- **Gross revenue for adult tickets sold.** This is the amount of money taken in for all adult tickets sold.
- **Net revenue for adult tickets sold.** This is the amount of money from adult ticket sales left over after the payment to the movie company has been deducted.
- **Gross revenue for child tickets sold.** This is the amount of money taken in for all child tickets sold.
- **Net revenue for child tickets sold.** This is the amount of money from child ticket sales left over after the payment to the movie company has been deducted.
- **Total gross revenue.** This is the sum of gross revenue for adult and child tickets sold.
- **Total net revenue.** This is the sum of net revenue for adult and child tickets sold.

Assume the theater keeps 20% of its box office receipts. Use a constant in your code to represent this percentage.

6. Joe's Automotive

Joe's Automotive performs the following routine maintenance services:

- Oil change—$26.00
- Lube job—$18.00
- Radiator flush—$30.00
- Transmission flush—$80.00
- Inspection—$15.00
- Muffler replacement—$100.00
- Tire rotation—$20.00

Joe also performs other nonroutine services and charges for parts and for labor ($20 per hour). Create a GUI application that displays the total for a customer's visit to Joe's.

7. Long Distance Calls

A long-distance provider charges the following rates for telephone calls:

Rate Category	Rate per Minute
Daytime (6:00 a.m. through 5:59 p.m.)	$0.07
Evening (6:00 p.m. through 11:59 p.m.)	$0.12
Off-Peak (12:00 a.m. through 5:59 a.m.)	$0.05

Create a GUI application that allows the user to select a rate category (from a set of radio buttons), and enter the number of minutes of the call into a text field. A dialog box should display the charge for the call.

8. Latin Translator

Look at the following list of Latin words and their meanings.

Latin	English
sinister	left
dexter	right
medium	center

Write a GUI application that translates the Latin words to English. The window should have three buttons, one for each Latin word. When the user clicks a button, the program displays the English translation in a label.

9. Miles-per-Gallon Calculator

Write a GUI application that calculates a car's gas mileage. The application should let the user enter the number of gallons of gas the car holds, and the number of miles it can be driven on a full tank. When a *Calculate MPG* button is clicked, the application should display the number of miles that the car may be driven per gallon of gas. Use the following formula to calculate miles per gallon:

$$MPG = \frac{miles}{gallons}$$

10. Celsius to Fahrenheit

Write a GUI application that converts Celsius temperatures to Fahrenheit temperatures. The user should be able to enter a Celsius temperature, click a button, and then see the equivalent Fahrenheit temperature. Use the following formula to make the conversion:

$$F = \frac{9}{5} C + 32$$

where *F* is the Fahrenheit temperature and *C* is the Celsius temperature.

TOPICS

12.1	Read-Only Text Fields	12.7	Menus
12.2	Lists	12.8	More about Text Components: Text
12.3	Combo Boxes		Areas and Fonts
12.4	Displaying Images in Labels and Buttons	12.9	Sliders
12.5	Mnemonics and Tool Tips	12.10	Look and Feel
12.6	File Choosers and Color Choosers	12.11	Common Errors to Avoid

12.1 Read-Only Text Fields

CONCEPT: A read-only text field displays text that can be changed by code in the application, but cannot be edited by the user.

A *read-only text field* is not a new component, but a different way to use the JTextField component. The JTextField component has a method named setEditable, which has the following general format:

```
setEditable(boolean editable)
```

You pass a boolean argument to this method. By default a text field is editable, which means that the user can enter data into it. If you call the setEditable method and pass false as the argument, then the text field becomes read-only. This means it is not editable by the user. Figure 12-1 shows a window that has three read-only text fields.

Figure 12-1   A window with three read-only text fields

841

The following code could be used to create the read-only text fields shown in the figure.

```
// Create a read-only text field for the subtotal.
JTextField subtotalTextField = new JTextField(10);
subtotalTextField.setEditable(false);

// Create a read-only text field for the sales tax.
JTextField taxTextField = new JTextField(10);
taxTextField.setEditable(false);

// Create a read-only text field for the total.
JTextField totalTextField = new JTextField(10);
totalTextField.setEditable(false);
```

A read-only text field is like a label with a border drawn around it. You can use the setText method to display data inside it. Here is an example:

```
subtotalTextField.setText("100.00");
taxTextField.setText("6.00");
totalTextField.setText("106.00");
```

This code causes the text fields to appear as shown in Figure 12-2.

Figure 12-2   Read-only text fields with data displayed

12.2 Lists

CONCEPT: A list component displays a list of items and allows the user to select an item from the list.

VideoNote
The JList
Component

A *list* is a component that displays a list of items and also allows the user to select one or more items from the list. Java provides the JList component for creating lists. Figure 12-3 shows an example. The JList component in the figure shows a list of names. At run time, the user may select an item in the list, which causes the item to appear highlighted. In the figure, the first name is selected.

When you create an instance of the JList class, you pass an array of objects to the constructor. Here is the general format of the constructor call:

```
JList (Object[] array)
```

Figure 12-3   A JList component

The JList component uses the array to create the list of items. In this text we always pass an array of String objects to the JList constructor. For example, the list component shown in Figure 12-3 could be created with the following code:

```
String[] names = { "Bill", "Geri", "Greg", "Jean",
                   "Kirk", "Phillip", "Susan" };
JList nameList = new JList(names);
```

Selection Modes

The JList component can operate in any of the following selection modes:

- **Single Selection Mode.** In this mode only one item can be selected at a time. When an item is selected, any other item that is currently selected is deselected.
- **Single Interval Selection Mode.** In this mode multiple items can be selected, but they must be in a single interval. An interval is a set of contiguous items.
- **Multiple Interval Selection Mode.** In this mode, multiple items may be selected with no restrictions. This is the default selection mode.

Figure 12-4 shows an example of a list in each type of selection mode.

Figure 12-4   Selection modes

Single selection mode allows only one item to be selected at a time.

Single interval selection mode allows a single interval of contiguous items to be selected.

Multiple interval selection mode allows multiple items to be selected with no restrictions.

The default mode is multiple interval selection. To keep our applications simple, we will use single selection mode for now. You change a `JList` component's selection mode with the `setSelectionMode` method. The method accepts an `int` argument that determines the selection mode.

The `ListSelectionModel` class, which is in the `javax.swing` package, provides the following constants that you can use as arguments to the `setSelectionMode` method:

- `ListSelectionModel.SINGLE_SELECTION`
- `ListSelectionModel.SINGLE_INTERVAL_SELECTION`
- `ListSelectionModel.MULTIPLE_INTERVAL_SELECTION`

Assuming that `nameList` references a `JList` component, the following statement sets the component to single selection mode:

```
nameList.setSelectionMode(ListSelectionModel.SINGLE_SELECTION);
```

Responding to List Events

When an item in a `JList` object is selected, it generates a *list selection event*. You handle list selection events with a list selection listener class, which must meet the following requirements:

- It must implement the `ListSelectionListener` interface.
- It must have a method named `valueChanged`. This method must take an argument of the `ListSelectionEvent` type.

NOTE: The `ListSelectionListener` interface is in the `javax.swing.event` package, so you must have an `import` statement for that package in your source code.

Once you have written a list selection listener class, you create an object of that class and then pass it as an argument to the `JList` component's `addListSelectionListener` method. When the `JList` component generates an event, it automatically executes the `valueChanged` method of the list selection listener object, passing the event object as an argument. You will see an example in a moment.

Retrieving the Selected Item

You may use either the `getSelectedValue` method or the `getSelectedIndex` method to determine which item in a list is currently selected. The `getSelectedValue` method returns a reference to the item that is currently selected. For example, assume that `nameList` references the `JList` component shown earlier in Figure 12-3. The following code retrieves a reference to the name that is currently selected and assigns it to the `selectedName` variable.

```
String selectedName;
selectedName = (String) nameList.getSelectedValue();
```

Note that the return value of the `getSelectedValue` method is an `Object` reference. In this code we had to cast the return value to the `String` type to store it in the `selectedName` variable. If no item in the list is selected, the method returns `null`.

The `getSelectedIndex` method returns the index of the selected item, or –1 if no item is selected. Internally, the items stored in a list are numbered. Each item's number is called its *index*. The first item (which is the item stored at the top of the list) has the index 0, the second item has the index 1, and so forth. You can use the index of the selected item to retrieve the item from an array. For example, assume that the following code was used to build the nameList component shown in Figure 12-3:

```
String[] names = { "Bill", "Geri", "Greg", "Jean",
                   "Kirk", "Phillip", "Susan" };
JList nameList = new JList(names);
```

Because the names array holds the values displayed in the namesList component, the following code could be used to determine the selected item:

```
int index;
String selectedName;
index = nameList.getSelectedIndex();
if (index != -1)
    selectedName = names[index];
```

The ListWindow class shown in Code Listing 12-1 demonstrates the concepts we have discussed so far. It uses a JList component with a list selection listener. When an item is selected from the list, it is displayed in a read-only text field. The main method creates an instance of the ListWindow class, which displays the window shown on the left in Figure 12-5. After the user selects October from the list, the window appears as that shown on the right in the figure.

Code Listing 12-1   (ListWindow.java)

```
 1   import java.awt.*;
 2   import javax.swing.event.*;
 3   import javax.swing.*;
 4
 5   /**
 6    *  This class demonstrates the List Component.
 7    */
 8
 9   public class ListWindow extends JFrame
10   {
11      private JPanel monthPanel;          // To hold components
12      private JPanel selectedMonthPanel;  // To hold components
13      private JList monthList;            // A list of months
14      private JTextField selectedMonth;   // The selected month
15      private JLabel label;               // To display a message
16
17      // The following array holds the values that will be
18      // displayed in the monthList list component.
19      private String[] months = { "January", "February", "March",
20               "April", "May", "June", "July", "August",
21               "September", "October", "November", "December" };
22
23      /**
24       *  Constructor
25       */
```

```
26
27      public ListWindow()
28      {
29         // Call the JFrame constructor.
30         super("List Demo");
31
32         // Specify an action for the close button.
33         setDefaultCloseOperation(JFrame.EXIT_ON_CLOSE);
34
35         // Create a BorderLayout manager for the content pane.
36         setLayout(new BorderLayout());
37
38         // Build the month and selectedMonth panels.
39         buildMonthPanel();
40         buildSelectedMonthPanel();
41
42         // Add the panels to the content pane.
43         add(monthPanel, BorderLayout.CENTER);
44         add(selectedMonthPanel, BorderLayout.SOUTH);
45
46         // Pack and display the window.
47         pack();
48         setVisible(true);
49      }
50
51      /**
52       *  The buildMonthPanel method adds a list containing
53       *  the names of the months to a panel.
54       */
55
56      private void buildMonthPanel()
57      {
58         // Create a panel to hold the list.
59         monthPanel = new JPanel();
60
61         // Create the list.
62         monthList = new JList(months);
63
64         // Set the selection mode to single selection.
65         monthList.setSelectionMode(ListSelectionModel.SINGLE_SELECTION);
66
67         // Register the list selection listener.
68         monthList.addListSelectionListener(new ListListener());
69
70         // Add the list to the panel.
71         monthPanel.add(monthList);
72      }
73
74      /**
75       *  The buildSelectedMonthPanel method adds an uneditable
```

```
76          *  text field to a panel.
77          */
78
79         private void buildSelectedMonthPanel()
80         {
81            // Create a panel to hold the text field.
82            selectedMonthPanel = new JPanel();
83
84            // Create the label.
85            label = new JLabel("You selected: ");
86
87            // Create the text field.
88            selectedMonth = new JTextField(10);
89
90            // Make the text field uneditable.
91            selectedMonth.setEditable(false);
92
93            // Add the label and text field to the panel.
94            selectedMonthPanel.add(label);
95            selectedMonthPanel.add(selectedMonth);
96         }
97
98         /**
99          *  Private inner class that handles the event when
100         *  the user selects an item from the list.
101         */
102
103        private class ListListener implements ListSelectionListener
104        {
105           public void valueChanged(ListSelectionEvent e)
106           {
107              // Get the selected string from the list.
108              String selection = (String) monthList.getSelectedValue();
109
110              // Store the selected string in the text field.
111              selectedMonth.setText(selection);
112           }
113        }
114
115        /**
116         *  The main method creates an instance of the ListWindow
117         *  class, which causes it to display its window.
118         */
119
120        public static void main(String[] args)
121        {
122           new ListWindow();
123        }
124     }
```

Figure 12-5 Window displayed by the `ListWindow` class

Window as initially displayed.

Window after the user selects October.

List Demo	List Demo
January	January
February	February
March	March
April	April
May	May
June	June
July	July
August	August
September	September
October	October
November	November
December	December
You selected:	You selected: October

Placing a Border around a List

As with other components, you can use the `setBorder` method, which was discussed in Chapter 11, to draw a border around a `JList`. For example the following statement can be used to draw a black 1-pixel thick line border around the `monthList` component:

```
monthList.setBorder(BorderFactory.createLineBorder(Color.BLACK, 1));
```

This code will cause the list to appear as shown in Figure 12-6.

Figure 12-6 List with a line border

List Demo
January
February
March
April
May
June
July
August
September
October
November
December
You selected:

Adding a Scroll Bar to a List

By default, a list component is large enough to display all of the items it contains. Sometimes a list component contains too many items to be displayed at once, however. Most GUI applications display a scroll bar on list components that contain a large number of items. The user simply uses the scroll bar to scroll through the list of items.

List components do not automatically display a scroll bar. To display a scroll bar on a list component, you must follow these general steps.

1. Set the number of visible rows for the list component.
2. Create a scroll pane object and add the list component to it.
3. Add the scroll pane object to any other containers, such as panels.

Let's take a closer look at how these steps can be used to apply a scroll bar to the list component created in the following code.

```
String[] names = { "Bill", "Geri", "Greg", "Jean",
                   "Kirk", "Phillip", "Susan" };
JList nameList = new JList(names);
```

First, we establish the size of the list component. You do this with the `JList` class's `setVisibleRowCount` method. The following statement sets the number of visible rows in the `nameList` component to three:

```
nameList.setVisibleRowCount(3);
```

This statement causes the `nameList` component to display only three items at a time.

Next, we create a scroll pane object and add the list component to it. A *scroll pane object* is a container that displays scroll bars on any component it contains. In Java we use the `JScrollPane` class to create a scroll pane object. We pass the object that we wish to add to the scroll pane as an argument to the `JScrollPane` constructor. The following statement demonstrates:

```
JScrollPane scrollPane = new JScrollPane(nameList);
```

This statement creates a `JScrollPane` object and adds the `nameList` component to it.

Next we add the scroll pane object to any other containers necessary for our GUI. For example, the following code adds the scroll pane to a `JPanel`, which is then added to the `JFrame` object's content pane.

```
// Create a panel and add the scroll pane to it.
JPanel panel = new JPanel();
panel.add(scrollPane);

// Add the panel to this JFrame object's contentPane.
add(panel);
```

When the list component is displayed, it will appear as shown in Figure 12-7.

Although the list component only displays three items at a time, the user can scroll through all of the items it contains.

Figure 12-7 List component with a scroll bar

The `ListWindowWithScroll` class shown in Code Listing 12-2 is a modification of the `ListWindow` class. In this class, the `monthList` component shows only six items at a time, but displays a scroll bar. The statements shown in bold (in lines 71 through 78) are the new lines used to add the scroll bar to the list. The `main` method creates an instance of the class, which displays the window shown in Figure 12-8.

Code Listing 12-2   (`ListWindowWithScroll.java`)

```
 1  import java.awt.*;
 2  import javax.swing.event.*;
 3  import javax.swing.*;
 4
 5  /**
 6   *  This class demonstrates the List Component with a
 7   *  scroll pane.
 8   */
 9
10  public class ListWindowWithScroll extends JFrame
11  {
12     private JPanel monthPanel;          // To hold components
13     private JPanel selectedMonthPanel;  // To hold components
14     private JList monthList;            // A list of months
15     private JTextField selectedMonth;   // The selected month
16     private JLabel label;               // To display a message
17
18     // The following array holds the values that will be
19     // displayed in the monthList list component.
20     private String[] months = { "January", "February", "March",
21              "April", "May", "June", "July", "August",
22              "September", "October", "November", "December" };
23
24     /**
25      *  Constructor
26      */
27
```

```
28      public ListWindowWithScroll()
29      {
30         // Call the JFrame constructor.
31         super("List Demo");
32
33         // Specify an action for the close button.
34         setDefaultCloseOperation(JFrame.EXIT_ON_CLOSE);
35
36         // Create a BorderLayout manager for the content pane.
37         setLayout(new BorderLayout());
38
39         // Build the month and selectedMonth panels.
40         buildMonthPanel();
41         buildSelectedMonthPanel();
42
43         // Add the panels to the content pane.
44         add(monthPanel, BorderLayout.CENTER);
45         add(selectedMonthPanel, BorderLayout.SOUTH);
46
47         // Pack and display the window.
48         pack();
49         setVisible(true);
50      }
51
52      /**
53       *  The buildMonth Panel method adds a list containing
54       *  the names of the months to a panel.
55       */
56
57      private void buildMonthPanel()
58      {
59         // Create a panel to hold the list.
60         monthPanel = new JPanel();
61
62         // Create the list.
63         monthList = new JList(months);
64
65         // Set the selection mode to single selection.
66         monthList.setSelectionMode(ListSelectionModel.SINGLE_SELECTION);
67
68         // Register the list selection listener.
69         monthList.addListSelectionListener(new ListListener());
70
71         // Set the number of visible rows to 6.
72         monthList.setVisibleRowCount(6);
73
74         // Add the list to a scroll pane.
75         JScrollPane scrollPane = new JScrollPane(monthList);
```

```
 76
 77            // Add the scroll pane to the panel.
 78            monthPanel.add(scrollPane);
 79        }
 80
 81        /**
 82         *  The buildSelectedMonth Panel method adds an uneditable
 83         *  test field to a panel.
 84         */
 85
 86        private void buildSelectedMonthPanel()
 87        {
 88            // Create a panel to hold the text field.
 89            selectedMonthPanel = new JPanel();
 90
 91            // Create the label.
 92            label = new JLabel("You selected: ");
 93
 94            // Create the text field.
 95            selectedMonth = new JTextField(10);
 96
 97            // Make the text field uneditable.
 98            selectedMonth.setEditable(false);
 99
100            // Add the label and text field to the panel.
101            selectedMonthPanel.add(label);
102            selectedMonthPanel.add(selectedMonth);
103        }
104
105        /**
106         *  Private inner class that handles the event when
107         *  the user selects an item from the list.
108         */
109
110        private class ListListener implements ListSelectionListener
111        {
112            public void valueChanged(ListSelectionEvent e)
113            {
114                // Get the selected string from the list.
115                String selection = (String) monthList.getSelectedValue();
116
117                // Store the selected string in the text field.
118                selectedMonth.setText(selection);
119            }
120        }
121
122        /**
123         *  The main method creates an instance of the class,
```

```
124        *  which causes it to display its window.
125        */
126
127     public static void main(String[] args)
128     {
129        new ListWindowWithScroll();
130     }
131  }
```

Figure 12-8 List component with scroll bars

NOTE: By default, when a `JList` component is added to a `JScrollPane` object, the scroll bar is only displayed when there are more items in the list than there are visible rows.

NOTE: When a `JList` component is added to a `JScrollPane` object, a border will automatically appear around the list.

Adding Items to an Existing `JList` Component

The `JList` class's `setListData` method allows you to store items in an existing `JList` component. Here is the method's general format:

```
Void setListData(Object[] data)
```

The argument passed into `data` is an array of objects that will become the items displayed in the `JList` component. Any items currently displayed in the component will be replaced by the new items.

In addition to replacing the existing items in a list, you can use this method to add items to an empty list. You can create an empty list by passing no argument to the `JList` constructor. Here is an example:

```
JList nameList = new JList();
```

This statement creates an empty `JList` component referenced by the `nameList` variable. You can then add items to the list, as shown here:

```
String[] names = { "Bill", "Geri", "Greg", "Jean",
                   "Kirk", "Phillip", "Susan" };
nameList.setListData(names);
```

Multiple Selection Lists

For simplicity, the previous examples used a `JList` component in single selection mode. Recall that the two other selection modes are single interval and multiple interval. Both of these modes allow the user to select multiple items. Let's take a closer look at each of these modes.

Single Interval Selection Mode

You put a `JList` component in single interval selection mode by passing the constant `ListSelectionModel.SINGLE_INTERVAL_SELECTION` to the component's `setSelectionMode` method. In single interval selection mode, single or multiple items can be selected. An interval is a set of contiguous items. (See Figure 12-4 to see an example of an interval.)

To select an interval of items, you select the first item in the interval by clicking on it. You then select the last item in the interval by holding down the Shift key while clicking on it. All of the items that appear in the list from the first item through the last item are selected.

In single interval selection mode, the `getSelectedValue` method returns the first item in the selected interval. The `getSelectedIndex` method returns the index of the first item in the selected interval. To get the entire selected interval, use the `getSelectedValues` method. This method returns an array of objects. The array will hold the items in the selected interval. You can also use the `getSelectedIndices` method, which returns an array of `int` values. The values in the array will be the indices of all the selected items in the list.

Multiple Interval Selection Mode

You put a `JList` component in multiple interval selection mode by passing the constant `ListSelectionModel.MULTIPLE_INTERVAL_SELECTION` to the component's `setSelectionMode` method. In multiple interval selection mode, multiple items can be selected and the items do not have to be in the same interval. (See Figure 12-4 for an example.)

In multiple interval selection mode the user can select single items or intervals. When the user holds down the Ctrl key while clicking on an item, it selects the item without deselecting any items that are currently selected. This allows the user to select multiple items that are not in an interval.

In multiple interval selection mode, the `getSelectedValue` method returns the first selected item. The `getSelectedIndex` method returns the index of the first selected item. The `getSelectedValues` method returns an array of objects containing the items that are selected. The `getSelectedIndices` method returns an `int` array containing the indices of all the selected items in the list.

The `MultipleIntervalSelection` class, shown in Code Listing 12-3, demonstrates a `JList` component used in multiple interval selection mode. The main method creates an instance of the class that displays the window shown on the left in Figure 12-9. When the user selects items from the top `JList` component and then clicks on the Get Selections button, the selected items appear in the bottom `JList` component.

Code Listing 12-3   (`MultipleIntervalSelection.java`)

```
 1   import java.awt.*;
 2   import java.awt.event.*;
 3   import javax.swing.*;
 4
 5   /**
 6    *  This class demonstrates the List component in
 7    *  multiple interval selection mode.
 8    */
 9
10   public class MultipleIntervalSelection extends JFrame
11   {
12      private JList monthList;            // List of months
13      private JList selectedMonthList;    // Selected months
14      private JButton button;             // To get selected items
15      private JPanel monthPanel;          // To hold components
16      private JPanel selectedMonthPanel;  // To hold components
17      private JPanel buttonPanel;         // To hold the button
18
19
20      // The following array holds the values that will be
21      // displayed in the monthList list component.
22      private String[] months = { "January", "February", "March",
23                "April", "May", "June", "July", "August",
24                "September", "October", "November", "December" };
25
26      /**
27       *  Constructor
28       */
29
30      public MultipleIntervalSelection()
31      {
32         // Call the JFrame constructor.
33         super("List Demo");
34
35         // Specify an action for the close button.
36         setDefaultCloseOperation(JFrame.EXIT_ON_CLOSE);
37
```

```
38          // Create a BorderLayout manager for the content pane.
39          setLayout(new BorderLayout());
40
41          // Build the panels.
42          buildMonthPanel();
43          buildSelectedMonthsPanel();
44          buildButtonPanel();
45
46          // Add the panels to the content pane.
47          add(monthPanel, BorderLayout.NORTH);
48          add(selectedMonthPanel, BorderLayout.CENTER);
49          add(buttonPanel, BorderLayout.SOUTH);
50
51          // Pack and display the window.
52          pack();
53          setVisible(true);
54      }
55
56      /**
57       *  The buildMonthPanel method adds a list containing the
58       *  names of the months to a panel.
59       */
60
61      private void buildMonthPanel()
62      {
63          // Create a panel to hold the list.
64          monthPanel = new JPanel();
65
66          // Create the list.
67          monthList = new JList(months);
68
69          // Set the list to multiple interval selection mode.
70          monthList.setSelectionMode(
71              ListSelectionModel.MULTIPLE_INTERVAL_SELECTION);
72
73          // Set the number of visible rows to 6.
74          monthList.setVisibleRowCount(6);
75
76          // Add the list to a scroll pane.
77          JScrollPane monthListScrollPane =
78                          new JScrollPane(monthList);
79
80          // Add the scroll pane to the panel.
81          monthPanel.add(monthListScrollPane);
82      }
83
```

```
 84        /**
 85         *   The buildSelectedMonthsPanel method adds a list to
 86         *   a panel. This will hold the selected months.
 87         */
 88
 89        private void buildSelectedMonthsPanel()
 90        {
 91           // Create a panel to hold the list.
 92           selectedMonthPanel = new JPanel();
 93
 94           // Create the list.
 95           selectedMonthList = new JList();
 96
 97           // Set the number of visible rows to 6.
 98           selectedMonthList.setVisibleRowCount(6);
 99
100           // Add the list to a scroll pane.
101           JScrollPane selectedMonthScrollPane =
102                        new JScrollPane(selectedMonthList);
103
104           // Add the scroll pane to the panel.
105           selectedMonthPanel.add(selectedMonthScrollPane);
106        }
107
108        /**
109         *   The buildButtonPanel method adds a button to a panel.
110         */
111
112        private void buildButtonPanel()
113        {
114           // Create a panel to hold the button.
115           buttonPanel = new JPanel();
116
117           // Create the button.
118           button = new JButton("Get Selections");
119
120           // Add an action listener to the button.
121           button.addActionListener(new ButtonListener());
122
123           // Add the button to the panel.
124           buttonPanel.add(button);
125        }
126
127        /**
128         *   Private inner class that handles the event when
129         *   the user clicks the "Get Selections" button.
130         */
131
```

```
132        private class ButtonListener implements ActionListener
133        {
134           public void actionPerformed(ActionEvent e)
135           {
136              // Get all the items that were selected.
137              Object[] selections = monthList.getSelectedValues();
138
139              // Display the items in selectedMonthList.
140              selectedMonthList.setListData(selections);
141           }
142        }
143
144        /**
145         *  The main method creates an instance of the class,
146         *  which causes it to display its window.
147         */
148
149        public static void main(String[] args)
150        {
151           new MultipleIntervalSelection();
152        }
153     }
```

Figure 12-9   The window displayed by the `MultipleIntervalSelection` class

This is the window as it
is intially displayed.

This is the window after the user has
selected some items from the top list
and clicked the Get Selections button.

12.3 Combo Boxes

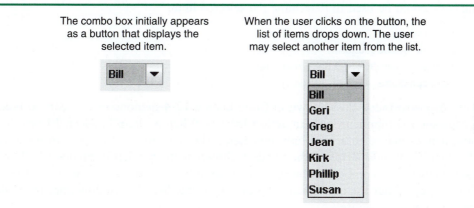

CONCEPT: A combo box allows the user to select an item from a drop-down list.

VideoNote
The JcomboBox Component

A combo box presents a list of items that the user may select from. Unlike a list component, a combo box presents its items in a drop-down list. You use the JComboBox class, which is in the javax.swing package, to create a combo box. You pass an array of objects to be displayed as the items in the drop-down list to the constructor. Here is an example:

```
String[] names = { "Bill", "Geri", "Greg", "Jean",
                   "Kirk", "Phillip", "Susan" };
JComboBox nameBox = new JComboBox(names);
```

When displayed, the combo box created by this code will initially appear as the button shown on the left in Figure 12-10. The button displays the item that is currently selected. Notice that the first item in the list is automatically selected when the combo box is first displayed. When the user clicks on the button, the drop-down list appears, and the user may select another item.

Figure 12-10 A combo box

The combo box initially appears as a button that displays the selected item.

When the user clicks on the button, the list of items drops down. The user may select another item from the list.

Bill ▼

Bill ▼

Bill
Geri
Greg
Jean
Kirk
Phillip
Susan

As you can see, a combo box is a combination of two components. In the case of the combo box shown in Figure 12-10, it is the combination of a button and a list. This is where the name "combo box" comes from.

Responding to Combo Box Events

When an item in a JComboBox object is selected, it generates an action event. As with JButton components, you handle action events with an action event listener class that must have an actionPerformed method. When the user selects an item in a combo box, the combo box executes its action event listener's actionPerformed method, passing an ActionEvent object as an argument.

Retrieving the Selected Item

There are two methods in the `JComboBox` class that you can use to determine which item in a list is currently selected: `getSelectedItem` and `getSelectedIndex`. The `getSelectedItem` method returns a reference to the item that is currently selected. For example, assume that `nameBox` references the `JComboBox` component shown earlier in Figure 12-10. The following code retrieves a reference to the name that is currently selected and assigns it to the `selectedName` variable.

```
String selectedName;
selectedName = (String) nameBox.getSelectedItem();
```

The return value of the `getSelectedItem` method is an `Object` reference. In this code we had to cast the return value to the `String` type to store it in the `selectedName` variable.

The `getSelectedIndex` method returns the index of the selected item. As with `JList` components, the items stored in a combo box are numbered with indices that start at 0. You can use the index of the selected item to retrieve the item from an array. For example, assume that the following code was used to build the `nameBox` component shown in Figure 12-10:

```
String[] names = { "Bill", "Geri", "Greg", "Jean",
                   "Kirk", "Phillip", "Susan" };
JComboBox nameBox = new JComboBox(names);
```

Because the `names` array holds the values displayed in the `namesBox` component, the following code could be used to determine the selected item:

```
int index;
String selectedName;
index = nameBox.getSelectedIndex();
selectedName = names[index];
```

The `ComboBoxWindow` class shown in Code Listing 12-4 demonstrates a combo box. It uses a `JComboBox` component with an action listener. When an item is selected from the combo box, it is displayed in a read-only text field. The `main` method creates an instance of the class, which initially displays the window shown at the top left in Figure 12-11. When the user clicks on the combo box button, the drop-down list appears as shown in the top right of the figure. After the user selects Espresso from the list, the window appears as shown at the bottom of the figure.

Code Listing 12-4   (`ComboBoxWindow.java`)

```
 1  import java.awt.*;
 2  import java.awt.event.*;
 3  import javax.swing.*;
 4
 5  /**
 6   *  This class demonstrates a combo box.
 7   */
 8
 9  public class ComboBoxWindow extends JFrame
10  {
```

```
11      private JPanel coffeePanel;          // To hold components
12      private JPanel selectedCoffeePanel;  // To hold components
13      private JComboBox coffeeBox;          // List of coffees
14      private JLabel label;                 // To display a message
15      private JTextField selectedCoffee;   // The selected coffee
16
17      // The following array holds the values that will be
18      // displayed in the coffeeBox combo box.
19      private String[] coffee = { "Regular Coffee", "Dark Roast",
20                                  "Cappuccino", "Espresso", "Decaf"};
21
22      /**
23       *  Constructor
24       */
25
26      public ComboBoxWindow()
27      {
28          // Call the JFrame constructor.
29          super("Combo Box Demo");
30
31          // Specify an action for the close button.
32          setDefaultCloseOperation(JFrame.EXIT_ON_CLOSE);
33
34          // Create a BorderLayout manager for the content pane.
35          setLayout(new BorderLayout());
36
37          // Build the panels.
38          buildCoffeePanel();
39          buildSelectedCoffeePanel();
40
41          // Add the panels to the content pane.
42          add(coffeePanel, BorderLayout.CENTER);
43          add(selectedCoffeePanel, BorderLayout.SOUTH);
44
45          // Pack and display the window.
46          pack();
47          setVisible(true);
48      }
49
50      /**
51       *  The buildCoffeePanel method adds a combo box with the
52       *  types of coffee to a panel.
53       */
54
55      private void buildCoffeePanel()
56      {
```

```
 57            // Create a panel to hold the combo box.
 58            coffeePanel = new JPanel();
 59
 60            // Create the combo box
 61            coffeeBox = new JComboBox(coffee);
 62
 63            // Register an action listener.
 64            coffeeBox.addActionListener(new ComboBoxListener());
 65
 66            // Add the combo box to the panel.
 67            coffeePanel.add(coffeeBox);
 68         }
 69
 70         /**
 71          *  The buildSelectedCoffeePanel method adds a read-only
 72          *  text field to a panel.
 73          */
 74
 75         private void buildSelectedCoffeePanel()
 76         {
 77            // Create a panel to hold the text field.
 78            selectedCoffeePanel = new JPanel();
 79
 80            // Create the label.
 81            label = new JLabel("You selected: ");
 82
 83            // Create the uneditable text field.
 84            selectedCoffee = new JTextField(10);
 85            selectedCoffee.setEditable(false);
 86
 87            // Add the label and text field to the panel.
 88            selectedCoffeePanel.add(label);
 89            selectedCoffeePanel.add(selectedCoffee);
 90         }
 91
 92         /**
 93          *  Private inner class that handles the event when
 94          *  the user selects an item from the combo box.
 95          */
 96
 97         private class ComboBoxListener implements ActionListener
 98         {
 99            public void actionPerformed(ActionEvent e)
100            {
101               String selection = (String) coffeeBox.getSelectedItem();
102               selectedCoffee.setText(selection);
103            }
104         }
```

```
105
106     /**
107      *  The main method creates an instance of the class,
108      *  which causes it to display its window.
109      */
110
111     public static void main(String[] args)
112     {
113        new ComboBoxWindow();
114     }
115  }
```

Figure 12-11   The window displayed by the `ComboBoxWindow` class

This is the window that initially appears.

When the user clicks on the combo box button, the drop-down list appears.

The item selected by the user appears in the read-only text field.

Editable Combo Boxes

There are two types of combo boxes: uneditable and editable. The default type of combo box is uneditable. An *uneditable combo box* combines a button with a list and allows the user to only select items from its list. This is the type of combo box used in the previous examples.

An editable combo box combines a text field and a list. In addition to selecting items from the list, the user may also type input into the text field. You make a combo box editable by calling the component's `setEditable` method, passing `true` as the argument. Here is an example:

```
String[] names = { "Bill", "Geri", "Greg", "Jean",
                   "Kirk", "Phillip", "Susan" };
JComboBox nameBox = new JComboBox(names);
nameBox.setEditable(true);
```

When displayed, the combo box created by this code initially appears as shown on the left in Figure 12-12. An editable combo box appears as a text field with a small button displaying an arrow joining it. The text field displays the item that is currently selected. When the user clicks on the button, the drop-down list appears as shown in the center of the figure. The user may select an item from the list. Alternatively, the user may type a value into the text field, as shown on the right of the figure. The user is not restricted to the values that appear in the list, and may type any input into the text field.

Figure 12-12   An editable combo box

The editable combo box initially appears as a text field that displays the selected item. A small button with an arrow appears next to the text field.

When the user clicks on the button, the list of items drops down. The user may select another item from the list.

Alternatively, the user may type input into the text field. The user may type a value that does not appear in the list.

| Bill ▼ |

| Bill ▼ |
| Bill |
| Geri |
| Greg |
| Jean |
| Kirk |
| Phillip |
| Susan |

| Sharon ▼ |

You can use the `getSelectedItem` method to retrieve a reference to the item that is currently selected. This method returns the item that appears in the combo box's text field, so it may or may not be an item that appears in the combo box's list.

The `getSelectedIndex` method returns the index of the selected item. However, if the user has entered a value in the text field that does not appear in the list, this method will return −1.

Checkpoint

12.1   How do you make a text field read-only? In code, how do you store text in a text field?

12.2   What is the index of the first item stored in a `JList` or a `JComboBox` component? If one of these components holds twelve items, what is the index of the twelfth item?

12.3   How do you retrieve the selected item from a `JList` component? How do you get the index of the selected item?

12.4   How do you cause a scroll bar to be displayed with a `JList` component?

12.5   How do you retrieve the selected item from a `JComboBox` component? How do you get the index of the selected item?

12.6   What is the difference between an uneditable and an editable combo box? Which of these is the default for a combo box?

12.4 Displaying Images in Labels and Buttons

CONCEPT: Images may be displayed in labels and buttons. You use the `ImageIcon` class to get an image from a file.

In addition to displaying text in a label, you can also display an image. For example, Figure 12-13 shows a window with two labels. The top label displays a smiley face image and no text. The bottom label displays a smiley face image and text.

Figure 12-13   Labels displaying an image icon

To display an image, you first create an instance of the `ImageIcon` class, which can read the contents of an image file. The `ImageIcon` class is part of the `javax.swing` package. The constructor accepts a `String` argument that is the name of an image file. The supported file types are JPEG, GIF, and PNG. The name can also contain path information. Here is an example:

```
ImageIcon image = new ImageIcon("Smiley.gif");
```

This statement creates an `ImageIcon` object that reads the contents of the file `Smiley.gif`. Because no path was given, it is assumed that the file is in the current directory or folder. Here is an example that uses a path.

```
ImageIcon image = new ImageIcon("C:\\Chapter 12\\Images\\Smiley.gif");
```

Next, you can display the image in a label by passing the `ImageIcon` object as an argument to the `JLabel` constructor. Here is the general format of the constructor:

```
JLabel(Icon image)
```

The argument passed to the image parameter can be an `ImageIcon` object or any object that implements the `Icon` interface. Here is an example:

```
ImageIcon image = new ImageIcon("Smiley.gif");
JLabel label = new JLabel(image);
```

This creates a label with an image, but no text. You can also create a label with both an image and text. An easy way to do this is to create the label with text, as usual, and then use the JLabel class's setIcon method to add an image to the label. The setIcon method accepts an ImageIcon object as its argument. Here is an example:

```
JLabel label = new JLabel("Have a nice day!");
label.setIcon(image);
```

The text will be displayed to the right of the image. The JLabel class also has the following constructor:

```
JLabel(String text, Icon image, int horizontalAlignment)
```

The first argument is the text to be displayed, the second argument is the image to be displayed, and the third argument is an int that specifies the horizontal alignment of the label contents. You should use the constants SwingConstants.LEFT, SwingConstants.CENTER, or SwingConstants.RIGHT to specify the horizontal alignment. Here is an example:

```
ImageIcon image = new ImageIcon("Smiley.gif");
JLabel label = new JLabel("Have a nice day!",
                          image,
                          SwingConstants.RIGHT);
```

You can also display images in buttons, as shown in Figure 12-14.

Figure 12-14   Buttons displaying an image icon

The process of creating a button with an image is similar to that of creating a label with an image. You use an ImageIcon object to read the image file, then pass the ImageIcon object as an argument to the JButton constructor. To create a button with an image and no text, pass only the ImageIcon object to the constructor. Here is an example:

```
// Create a button with an image, but no text.
ImageIcon image = new ImageIcon("Smiley.gif");
JButton button = new JButton(image);
```

To create a button with an image and text, pass a String and an ImageIcon object to the constructor. Here is an example:

```
// Create a button with an image and text.
ImageIcon image = new ImageIcon("Smiley.gif");
JButton button = new JButton("Have a nice day!", image);
```

To add an image to an existing button, pass an `ImageIcon` object to the button's `setIcon` method. Here is an example:

```
// Create a button with an image and text.
JButton button = new JButton("Have a nice day!");
ImageIcon image = new ImageIcon("Smiley.gif");
button.setIcon(image);
```

You're not limited to small graphical icons when placing images in labels or buttons. For example, the `MyCatImage` class in Code Listing 12-5 displays a digital photograph in a label when the user clicks on a button. The main method creates an instance of the class, which displays the window shown at the left in Figure 12-15. When the user clicks on the Get Image button, the window displays the image shown at the right of the figure.

Code Listing 12-5   (`MyCatImage.java`)

```
 1   import java.awt.*;
 2   import java.awt.event.*;
 3   import javax.swing.*;
 4
 5   /**
 6    *  This class demonstrates how to use an ImageIcon
 7    *  and a JLabel to display an image.
 8    */
 9
10   public class MyCatImage extends JFrame
11   {
12      private JLabel imageLabel;   // Holds an image
13      private JButton button;      // Gets an image
14      private JPanel imagePanel;   // To hold the label
15      private JPanel buttonPanel;  // To hold a button
16
17
18      /**
19       *  Constructor
20       */
21
22      public MyCatImage()
23      {
24         // Call the JFrame constructor.
25         super("My Cat");
26
27         // Specify an action for the close button.
28         setDefaultCloseOperation(JFrame.EXIT_ON_CLOSE);
29
30         // Create a BorderLayout manager for the content pane.
31         setLayout(new BorderLayout());
32
```

```
33          // Build the panels.
34          buildImagePanel();
35          buildButtonPanel();
36
37          // Add the panels to the content pane.
38          add(imagePanel, BorderLayout.CENTER);
39          add(buttonPanel, BorderLayout.SOUTH);
40
41          // Pack and display the window.
42          pack();
43          setVisible(true);
44      }
45
46      /**
47       *  The buildImagePanel method adds a label to a panel.
48       */
49
50      private void buildImagePanel()
51      {
52          // Create a panel.
53          imagePanel = new JPanel();
54
55          // Create a label.
56          imageLabel = new JLabel("Click the button to see an " +
57                                  "image of my cat.");
58
59          // Add the label to the panel.
60          imagePanel.add(imageLabel);
61      }
62
63      /**
64       *  The buildButtonPanel method adds a button
65       *  to a panel.
66       */
67
68      private void buildButtonPanel()
69      {
70          // Create a panel.
71          buttonPanel = new JPanel();
72
73          // Get the smiley face image.
74          ImageIcon smileyImage = new ImageIcon("Smiley.gif");
75
76          // Create a button.
77          button = new JButton("Get Image");
78          button.setIcon(smileyImage);
79
```

```
 80            // Register an action listener with the button.
 81            button.addActionListener(new ButtonListener());
 82
 83            // Add the button to the panel.
 84            buttonPanel.add(button);
 85        }
 86
 87        /**
 88         *  Private inner class that handles the event when
 89         *  the user clicks the button.
 90         */
 91
 92        private class ButtonListener implements ActionListener
 93        {
 94            public void actionPerformed(ActionEvent e)
 95            {
 96                // Read the image file into an ImageIcon object.
 97                ImageIcon catImage = new ImageIcon("Cat.jpg");
 98
 99                // Display the image in the label.
100                imageLabel.setIcon(catImage);
101
102                // Remove the text from the label.
103                imageLabel.setText(null);
104
105                // Pack the frame again to accommodate the
106                // new size of the label.
107                pack();
108            }
109        }
110
111        /**
112         *  This program creates an instance of the MyCatImage
113         *  class that causes it to display its window.
114         */
115
116        public static void main(String[] args)
117        {
118            new MyCatImage();
119        }
120    }
```

Figure 12-15 Window displayed by the `MyCatImage` class

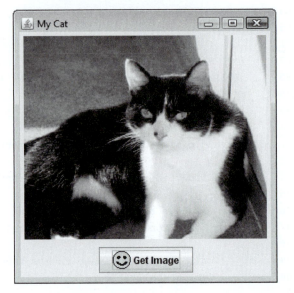

This window initially appears.

When the user clicks the Get Image button, this image appears.

Let's take a closer look at the `MyCatImage` class. After some initial setup, in lines 24 through 31, the constructor calls the `buildImagePanel` method in line 34. In line 53 this method creates a `JPanel` component, referenced by the `imagePanel` variable, and in lines 56 through 57 it creates a `JLabel` component, referenced by the `imageLabel` variable. This is the label that will display the image when the user clicks on the button. The last statement in the method, in line 60, adds the `imageLabel` component to the `imagePanel` panel.

Back in the constructor, line 35 calls the `buildButtonPanel` method, which creates the Get Image button and adds it to a panel. An instance of the `ButtonListener` inner class is also registered as the button's action listener. Let's look at the `ButtonListener` class's `actionPerformed` method. This method is executed when the user clicks on the Get Image button. In line 97 an `ImageIcon` object is created from the file `Cat.jpg`. This file is in the same directory as the class. In line 100 the `imageLabel` component's `setIcon` method is called, with `catImage` passed as an argument. This stores the image in the label. In line 103 the `imageLabel` component's `setText` method is called, with " " passed as an argument. This removes the text that is currently displayed in the label.

Line 107 then calls the `JFrame` class's `pack` method. When the image was loaded into the `JLabel` component, the component resized itself to accommodate its new contents. The `JFrame` that encloses the window does not automatically resize itself, so we must call the `pack` method. This forces the `JFrame` to resize itself.

Checkpoint

12.7 How do you store an image in a `JLabel` component? How do you store both an image and text in a `JLabel` component?

12.8 How do you store an image in a `JButton` component? How do you store both an image and text in a `JButton` component?

12.9 What method do you use to store an image in an existing `JLabel` or `JButton` component?

12.5 Mnemonics and Tool Tips

CONCEPT: A mnemonic is a key that you press while holding down the Alt key to interact with a component. A tool tip is text that is displayed in a small box when the user holds the mouse cursor over a component.

Mnemonics

A *mnemonic* is a key on the keyboard that you press in combination with the Alt key to quickly access a component such as a button. These are sometimes referred to as shortcut keys, or hot keys. When you assign a mnemonic to a button, the user can click on the button by holding down the Alt key and pressing the mnemonic key. Although users can interact with components with either the mouse or their mnemonic keys, those who are quick with the keyboard usually prefer to use mnemonic keys instead of the mouse.

You assign a mnemonic to a component through the component's `setMnemonic` method, which is inherited from the `AbstractButton` class. The method's general format is:

```
void setMnemonic(int key)
```

The argument that you pass to the method is an integer code that represents the key you wish to assign as a mnemonic. The `KeyEvent` class, which is in the `java.awt.event` package, has predefined constants that you can use. These constants take the form `KeyEvent.VK_x`, where x is a key on the keyboard. For example, to assign the A key as a mnemonic, you would use `KeyEvent.VK_A`. (The letters VK in the constants stand for "virtual key.") Here is an example of code that creates a button with the text "Exit" and assigns the X key as the mnemonic.

```
JButton exitButton = new JButton("Exit");
exitButton.setMnemonic(KeyEvent.VK_X);
```

The user may click on this button by pressing Alt+X on the keyboard. (This means holding down the Alt key and pressing X.)

If the letter chosen as the mnemonic is in the component's text, the first occurrence of that letter will appear underlined when the component is displayed. For example, the button created with the previous code has the text "Exit". Because X was chosen as the mnemonic, the letter x will appear underlined, as shown in Figure 12-16.

Figure 12-16 Button with the mnemonic X

If the mnemonic is a letter that does not appear in the component's text, then no letter will appear underlined.

> **NOTE:** The KeyEvent class also has constants for symbols. For example, the constant for the ! symbol is VK_EXCLAMATION_MARK, and the constant for the & symbol is VK_AMPERSAND. See the Java API documentation for the KeyEvent class for a list of all the constants.

You can also assign mnemonics to radio buttons and check boxes, as shown in the following code.

```java
// Create three radio buttons and assign mnemonics.
JRadioButton rb1 = new JRadioButton("Breakfast");
rb1.setMnemonic(KeyEvent.VK_B);
JRadioButton rb2 = new JRadioButton("Lunch");
rb2.setMnemonic(KeyEvent.VK_L);
JRadioButton rb3 = new JRadioButton("Dinner");
rb3.setMnemonic(KeyEvent.VK_D);
// Create three check boxes and assign mnemonics.
JCheckBox cb1 = new JCheckBox("Monday");
cb1.setMnemonic(KeyEvent.VK_M);
JCheckBox cb2 = new JCheckBox("Wednesday");
cb2.setMnemonic(KeyEvent.VK_W);
JCheckBox cb3 = new JCheckBox("Friday");
cb3.setMnemonic(KeyEvent.VK_F);
```

This code will create the components shown in Figure 12-17.

Figure 12-17   Radio buttons and check boxes with mnemonics assigned

Tool Tips

A *tool tip* is text that is displayed in a small box when the user holds the mouse cursor over a component. The box usually gives a short description of what the component does. Most GUI applications use tool tips as a way of providing immediate and concise help to the user. For example, Figure 12-18 shows a button with its tool tip displayed.

Figure 12-18   Button with tool tip displayed

You assign a tool tip to a component with the `setToolTipText` method, which is inherited from the `JComponent` class. Here is the method's general format.

```
void setToolTipText(String text)
```

The `String` that is passed as an argument is the text that will be displayed in the component's tool tip. For example, the following code creates the Exit button shown in Figure 12-18 and its associated tool tip:

```
JButton exitButton = new JButton("Exit");
exitButton.setMnemonic(KeyEvent.VK_X);
exitButton.setToolTipText("Click here to exit.");
```

Checkpoint

12.10 What is a mnemonic? How do you assign a mnemonic to a component?

12.11 What is a tool tip? How do you assign a tool tip to a component?

12.6 File Choosers and Color Choosers

CONCEPT: Java provides components that equip your applications with standard dialog boxes for opening files, saving files, and selecting colors.

File Choosers

A file chooser is a specialized dialog box that allows the user to browse for a file and select it. Figure 12-19 shows an example of a file chooser dialog box.

Figure 12-19 A file chooser dialog box for opening a file

You create an instance of the `JFileChooser` class, which is part of the `javax.swing` package, to display a file chooser dialog box. The class has several constructors. We will focus on two of them, which have the following general formats:

```
JFileChooser()
JFileChooser(String path)
```

The first constructor shown takes no arguments. This constructor uses the default directory as the starting point for all of its dialog boxes. If you are using Windows, this will probably be the "My Documents" folder under your account. If you are using UNIX, this will be your login directory. The second constructor takes a `String` argument containing a valid path. This path will be the starting point for the object's dialog boxes.

A `JFileChooser` object can display two types of predefined dialog boxes: an open file dialog box and a save file dialog box. Figure 12-19 shows an example of an open file dialog box. It lets the user browse for an existing file to open. A save file dialog box, as shown in Figure 12-20, is employed when the user needs to browse to a location to save a file. Both of these dialog boxes appear the same, except the open file dialog box displays "Open" in its title bar, and the save file dialog box displays "Save." There is no difference in the way they operate.

Figure 12-20   A save file dialog box

Displaying a File Chooser Dialog Box

To display an open file dialog box, use the `showOpenDialog` method. The method's general format is:

```
int showOpenDialog(Component parent)
```

The argument can be either `null` or a reference to a component. If you pass `null`, the dialog box is normally centered in the screen. If you pass a reference to a component, such as `JFrame`, the dialog box is displayed over the component.

To display a save file dialog box, use the `showSaveDialog` method. The method's general format is:

```
int showSaveDialog(Component parent)
```

Once again, the argument can be either `null` or a reference to a component. Both the `showOpenDialog` and `showSaveDialog` methods return an integer that indicates the action taken by the user to close the dialog box. You can compare the return value to one of the following constants:

- **JFileChooser.CANCEL_OPTION.** This return value indicates that the user clicked on the Cancel button.
- **JFileChooser.APPROVE_OPTION.** This return value indicates that the user clicked on the Open or Save button.
- **JFileChooser.ERROR_OPTION.** This return value indicates that an error occurred, or the user clicked on the standard close button on the window to dismiss it.

If the user selected a file, you can use the `getSelectedFile` method to determine the file that was selected. The `getSelectedFile` method returns a `File` object, which contains data about the selected file. The `File` class is part of the `java.io` package. You can then use the `File` object's `getPath` method to get the path and file name as a `String`. Here is an example:

```
JFileChooser fileChooser = new JFileChooser();
int status = fileChooser.showOpenDialog(null);
if (status == JFileChooser.APPROVE_OPTION)
{
    File selectedFile = fileChooser.getSelectedFile();
    String filename = selectedFile.getPath();
    JOptionPane.showMessageDialog(null, "You selected " + filename);
}
```

Color Choosers

A color chooser is a specialized dialog box that allows the user to select a color from a predefined palette of colors. Figure 12-21 shows an example of a color chooser. By clicking the HSB tab you can select a color by specifying its hue, saturation, and brightness. By clicking the RGB tab you can select a color by specifying its red, green, and blue components.

Figure 12-21 A color chooser dialog box

You use the JColorChooser class, which is part of the javax.swing package, to display a color chooser dialog box. You do not create an instance of the class, however. It has a static method named showDialog, with the following general format:

```
Color showDialog(Component parent, String title, Color initial)
```

The first argument can be either null or a reference to a component. If you pass null, the dialog box is normally centered in the screen. If you pass a reference to a component, such as JFrame, the dialog box is displayed over the component. The second argument is text that is displayed in the dialog box's title bar. The third argument indicates the color that appears initially selected in the dialog box. This method returns the color selected by the user. The following code is an example. This code allows the user to select a color, and then that color is assigned as a panel's background color.

```
JPanel panel = new JPanel();
Color selectedColor;
selectedColor = JColorChooser.showDialog(null,
                "Select a Background Color", Color.BLUE);
panel.setBackground(selectedColor);
```

12.7 Menus

CONCEPT: Java provides classes for creating systems of drop-down menus. Menus can contain menu items, checked menu items, radio button menu items, and other menus.

In the GUI applications you have studied so far, the user initiates actions by clicking on components such as buttons. When an application has several operations for the user to choose from, a menu system is more commonly used than buttons. A *menu system* is a collection of commands organized in one or more drop-down menus. Before learning how to construct a menu system, you must learn about the basic items found in a typical menu system. Look at the example menu system in Figure 12-22.

Figure 12-22 Example menu system

The menu system in the figure consists of the following items:

- **Menu Bar.** At the top of the window, just below the title bar, is a menu bar. The *menu bar* lists the names of one or more menus. The menu bar in Figure 12-22 shows the names of two menus: File and Edit.
- **Menu.** A *menu* is a drop-down list of menu items. The user may activate a menu by clicking on its name on the menu bar. In the figure, the Edit menu has been activated.
- **Menu Item.** A *menu item* can be selected by the user. When a menu item is selected, some type of action is usually performed.
- **Check box menu item.** A *check box menu item* appears with a small box beside it. The item may be selected or deselected. When it is selected, a check mark appears in the box. When it is deselected, the box appears empty. Check box menu items are normally used to turn an option on or off. The user toggles the state of a check box menu item each time he or she selects it.

- **Radio button menu item.** A *radio button menu item* may be selected or deselected. A small circle appears beside it that is filled in when the item is selected and appears empty when the item is deselected. Like a check box menu item, a radio button menu item can be used to turn an option on or off. When a set of radio button menu items are grouped with a `ButtonGroup` object, only one of them can be selected at a time. When the user selects a radio button menu item, the one that was previously selected is deselected.
- **Submenu.** A menu within a menu is called a *submenu*. Some of the commands on a menu are actually the names of submenus. You can tell when a command is the name of a submenu because a small right arrow appears to its right. Activating the name of a submenu causes the submenu to appear. For example, in Figure 12-22, clicking on the Sort command causes a submenu to appear.
- **Separator bar.** A separator bar is a horizontal bar used to separate groups of items on a menu. Separator bars are only used as a visual aid and cannot be selected by the user.

A menu system is constructed with the following classes:

JMenuItem. Use this class to create a regular menu item. A `JMenuItem` component generates an action event when the user selects it.

JCheckBoxMenuItem. Use this class to create a check box menu item. The class's `isSelected` method returns `true` if the item is selected, or `false` otherwise. A `JCheckBoxMenuItem` component generates an action event when the user selects it.

JRadioButtonMenuItem. Use this class to create a radio button menu item. `JRadioButtonMenuItem` components can be grouped together in a `ButtonGroup` object so that only one of them can be selected at a time. The class's `isSelected` method returns `true` if the item is selected, or `false` otherwise. A `JRadioButtonMenuItem` component generates an action event when the user selects it.

JMenu. Use this class to create a menu. A `JMenu` component can contain `JMenuItem`, `JCheckBoxMenuItem`, and `JRadioButton` components, as well as other `JMenu` components. A submenu is a `JMenu` component that is inside another `JMenu` component.

JMenuBar. Use this class to create a menu bar. A `JMenuBar` object can contain `JMenu` components.

All of these classes are in the `javax.swing` package. A menu system is a `JMenuBar` component that contains one or more `JMenu` components. Each `JMenu` component can contain `JMenuItem`, `JRadioButtonMenuItem`, and `JCheckBoxMenuItem` components, as well as other `JMenu` components. The classes contain all of the code necessary to operate the menu system.

To see an example of an application that uses a menu system, look at the `MenuWindow` class shown in Code Listing 12-6. The class displays the window shown in Figure 12-23.

Code Listing 12-6   (`MenuWindow.java`)

```
1   import java.awt.*;
2   import java.awt.event.*;
3   import javax.swing.*;
4
```

```java
5   /**
6    *  The MenuWindow class demonstrates a menu system.
7    */
8
9   public class MenuWindow extends JFrame
10  {
11     private JLabel messageLabel;            // To display a message
12     private final int LABEL_WIDTH = 400;    // The label's width
13     private final int LABEL_HEIGHT = 200;   // The label's height
14
15     // The following variables will reference menu components.
16     private JMenuBar menuBar;                // The menu bar
17     private JMenu fileMenu;                  // The File menu
18     private JMenu textMenu;                  // The Text menu
19     private JMenuItem exitItem;              // An item to exit the application
20     private JRadioButtonMenuItem blackItem; // To make the text black
21     private JRadioButtonMenuItem redItem;   // To make the text red
22     private JRadioButtonMenuItem blueItem;  // To make the text blue
23     private JCheckBoxMenuItem visibleItem;  // To toggle visibility
24
25     /**
26      *  Constructor
27      */
28
29     public MenuWindow()
30     {
31        // Call the JFrame constructor.
32        super("Example Menu System");
33
34        // Specify an action for the close button.
35        setDefaultCloseOperation(JFrame.EXIT_ON_CLOSE);
36
37        // Create the message label and set its size and color.
38        messageLabel = new JLabel("Use the Text menu to " +
39                    "change my color and make me invisible.",
40                    SwingConstants.CENTER);
41        messageLabel.setPreferredSize(
42                    new Dimension(LABEL_WIDTH, LABEL_HEIGHT));
43        messageLabel.setForeground(Color.BLACK);
44
45        // Add the label to the content pane.
46        add(messageLabel);
47
48        // Build the menu bar.
49        buildMenuBar();
```

```
50
51          // Pack and display the window.
52          pack();
53          setVisible(true);
54      }
55
56      /**
57       *  The buildMenuBar method builds the menu bar.
58       */
59
60      private void buildMenuBar()
61      {
62          // Create the menu bar.
63          menuBar = new JMenuBar();
64
65          // Create the file and text menus.
66          buildFileMenu();
67          buildTextMenu();
68
69          // Add the file and text menus to the menu bar.
70          menuBar.add(fileMenu);
71          menuBar.add(textMenu);
72
73          // Set the window's menu bar.
74          setJMenuBar(menuBar);
75      }
76
77      /**
78       *  The buildFileMenu method builds the File menu
79       *  and returns a reference to its JMenu object.
80       */
81
82      private void buildFileMenu()
83      {
84          // Create an Exit menu item.
85          exitItem = new JMenuItem("Exit");
86          exitItem.setMnemonic(KeyEvent.VK_X);
87          exitItem.addActionListener(new ExitListener());
88
89          // Create a JMenu object for the File menu.
90          fileMenu = new JMenu("File");
91          fileMenu.setMnemonic(KeyEvent.VK_F);
92
93          // Add the Exit menu item to the File menu.
94          fileMenu.add(exitItem);
95      }
96
97      /**
```

```
 98          * The buildTextMenu method builds the Text menu
 99          * and returns a reference to its JMenu object.
100          */
101
102         private void buildTextMenu()
103         {
104            // Create the radio button menu items to change the color
105            // of the text. Add an action listener to each one.
106            blackItem = new JRadioButtonMenuItem("Black", true);
107            blackItem.setMnemonic(KeyEvent.VK_B);
108            blackItem.addActionListener(new ColorListener());
109
110            redItem = new JRadioButtonMenuItem("Red");
111            redItem.setMnemonic(KeyEvent.VK_R);
112            redItem.addActionListener(new ColorListener());
113
114            blueItem = new JRadioButtonMenuItem("Blue");
115            blueItem.setMnemonic(KeyEvent.VK_U);
116            blueItem.addActionListener(new ColorListener());
117
118            // Create a button group for the radio button items.
119            ButtonGroup group = new ButtonGroup();
120            group.add(blackItem);
121            group.add(redItem);
122            group.add(blueItem);
123
124            // Create a check box menu item to make the text
125            // visible or invisible.
126            visibleItem = new JCheckBoxMenuItem("Visible", true);
127            visibleItem.setMnemonic(KeyEvent.VK_V);
128            visibleItem.addActionListener(new VisibleListener());
129
130            // Create a JMenu object for the Text menu.
131            textMenu = new JMenu("Text");
132            textMenu.setMnemonic(KeyEvent.VK_T);
133
134            // Add the menu items to the Text menu.
135            textMenu.add(blackItem);
136            textMenu.add(redItem);
137            textMenu.add(blueItem);
138            textMenu.addSeparator();    // Add a separator bar.
139            textMenu.add(visibleItem);
140         }
141
142         /**
143          * Private inner class that handles the event that
144          * is generated when the user selects Exit from
145          * the File menu.
```

```
146        */
147
148        private class ExitListener implements ActionListener
149        {
150          public void actionPerformed(ActionEvent e)
151          {
152             System.exit(0);
153          }
154        }
155
156      /**
157       * Private inner class that handles the event that
158       * is generated when the user selects a color from
159       * the Text menu.
160       */
161
162        private class ColorListener implements ActionListener
163        {
164          public void actionPerformed(ActionEvent e)
165          {
166             // Determine which color was selected and
167             // act accordingly.
168             if (blackItem.isSelected())
169                messageLabel.setForeground(Color.BLACK);
170             else if (redItem.isSelected())
171                messageLabel.setForeground(Color.RED);
172             else if (blueItem.isSelected())
173                messageLabel.setForeground(Color.BLUE);
174          }
175        }
176
177      /**
178       * Private inner class that handles the event that
179       * is generated when the user selects Visible from
180       * the Text menu.
181       */
182
183        private class VisibleListener implements ActionListener
184        {
185          public void actionPerformed(ActionEvent e)
186          {
187             // Determine whether Visible is selected and
188             // act accordingly.
189             if (visibleItem.isSelected())
190                messageLabel.setVisible(true);
191             else
192                messageLabel.setVisible(false);
193          }
194        }
```

```
195
196      /**
197       * The main method creates an instance of the MenuWindow
198       * class, which causes it to display its window.
199       */
200
201      public static void main(String[] args)
202      {
203          new MenuWindow();
204      }
205  }
```

Figure 12-23   Window displayed by the `MenuWindow` class

The class demonstrates how a label appears in different colors. Notice that the window has a menu bar with two menus: File and Text. Figure 12-24 shows a sketch of the menu system. When the user opens the Text menu, he or she can select a color using the radio button menu items and the label will change to the selected color. The Text menu also has a Visible item, which is a check box menu item. When this item is selected (checked), the label is visible. When this item is deselected (unchecked), the label is invisible.

Figure 12-24   Sketch of the `MenuWindow` class's menu system

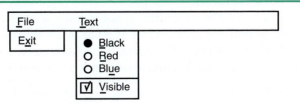

Let's take a closer look at the `MenuWindow` class. Before we examine how the menu system is constructed, the code in lines 38 through 43 should be explained. Lines 38 through 40 create the `messageLabel` component and align its text in the label's center. Then, in lines 41 and 42, the `setPreferredSize` method is called. The `setPreferredSize` method is inherited from the `JComponent` class, and it establishes a component's preferred size. It is called the *preferred size* because the layout manager adjusts the component's size when necessary. Normally, a label's preferred size is determined automatically, depending on its contents. We want to make this label larger, however, so the window will be larger when it is packed around the label.

The `setPreferredSize` method accepts a `Dimension` object as its argument. A `Dimension` object specifies a component's width and height. The first argument to the `Dimension` class constructor is the component's width, and the second argument is the component's height. In this class, the `LABEL_WIDTH` and `LABEL_HEIGHT` constants are defined with the values 400 and 200, respectively. So, this statement sets the label's preferred size to 400 pixels wide by 200 pixels high. (The `Dimension` class is part of the `java.awt` package.) Notice from Figure 12-23 that this code does not affect the size of the text displayed in the label, only the size of the label component.

To create the menu system, the constructor calls the `buildMenuBar` method in line 49. Inside this method, the statement in line 63 creates a `JMenuBar` component and assigns its address to the `menuBar` variable. The `JMenuBar` component acts as a container for `JMenu` components. The menu bar in this application has two menus: File and Text.

Next, the statement in line 66 calls the `buildFileMenu` method. The `buildFileMenu` method creates the File menu, which has only one item: Exit. The statement in line 85 creates a `JMenuItem` component for the Exit item, which is referenced by the `exitItem` variable. The `String` that is passed to the `JMenuItem` constructor is the text that will appear on a menu for this menu item. The statement in line 86 assigns the x key as a mnemonic to the `exitItem` component. Then, line 87 creates an action listener for the component (an instance of `ExitListener`, a private inner class), which causes the application to end.

Next, line 90 creates a `JMenu` object for the File menu. Notice that the name of the menu is passed as an argument to the `JMenu` constructor. Line 91 assigns the F key to the File menu as a mnemonic.

The last statement in the `buildFileMenu` method, in line 94, adds `exitItem` to the `fileMenu` component.

Back in the `buildMenuBar` method, the statement in line 67 calls the `buildTextMenu` method. The `buildTextMenu` method builds the Text menu, which has three radio button menu items (Black, Red, and Blue), a separator bar, and a check box menu item (Visible). The code in lines 106 through 116 creates the radio button menu items, assigns mnemonic keys to them, and adds an action listener to each.

The `JRadioButtonItem` constructor accepts a `String` argument, which is the menu item's text. By default, a radio button menu item is not initially selected. The constructor can also accept an optional second argument, which is a `boolean` value indicating whether the item should be initially selected. Notice that in line 106, `true` is passed as the second argument to the `JRadioButtonItem` constructor. This causes the Black menu item to be initially selected.

Next, in lines 119 through 122, a button group is created and the radio button menu items are added to it. As with `JRadioButton` components, `JRadioButtonMenuItem` components may be grouped in a `ButtonGroup` object. As a result, only one of the grouped menu items may be selected at a time. When one is selected, any other menu item in the group is deselected.

Next, the Visible item, a check box menu item, is created in line 126. Notice that `true` is passed as the second argument to the constructor. This causes the item to be initially selected. A mnemonic key is assigned in line 127, and an action listener is added to the component in line 128.

Line 131 creates a `JMenu` component for the Text menu, and line 132 assigns a mnemonic key to it. Lines 135 through 137 add the `blackItem`, `redItem`, and `blueItem` radio button menu items to the Text menu. In line 138 the `addSeparator` method is called to add a separator bar to the menu. Because the `addSeparator` method is called just after the `blueItem` component is added and just before the `visibleItem` component is added, it will appear between the Blue and Visible items on the menu. Line 139 adds the Visible item to the Text menu.

Back in the `buildMenuBar` method, in lines 70 and 71, the File menu and Text menu are added to the menu bar. In line 74, the `setJMenuBar` method is called, passing `menuBar` as an argument. The `setJMenuBar` method is a `JFrame` method that places a menu bar in a frame. You pass a `JMenuBar` component as the argument. When the `JFrame` is displayed, the menu bar will appear at its top.

Figure 12-25 shows how the class's window appears with the File menu and the Text menu opened. Selecting a color from the Text menu causes an instance of the `ColorListener` class to execute its `actionPerformed` method, which changes the color of the text. Selecting the Visible item causes an instance of the `VisibleListener` class to execute its `actionPerformed` method, which toggles the label's visibility.

Figure 12-25 The window with the File menu and Text menu opened

The window with the File menu opened.

The window with the Text menu opened.

Checkpoint

12.12 Briefly describe each of the following menu system items.
   a.   Menu bar
   b.   Menu item
   c.   Check box menu item
   d.   Radio button menu item
   e.   Submenu
   f.   Separator bar

12.13 What class do you use to create a regular menu item? What do you pass to the class constructor?

12.14 What class do you use to create a radio button menu item? What do you pass to the class constructor? How do you cause it to be initially selected?

12.15 How do you create a relationship between radio button menu items so that only one may be selected at a time?

12.16 What class do you use to create a check box menu item? What do you pass to the class constructor? How do you cause it to be initially selected?

12.17 What class do you use to create a menu? What do you pass to the class constructor?

12.18 What class do you use to create a menu bar?

12.19 How do you place a menu bar in a `JFrame`?

12.20 What type of event do menu items generate when selected by the user?

12.21 How do you change the size of a component such as a `JLabel` after it has been created?

12.22 What arguments do you pass to the `Dimension` class constructor?

 12.8   More about Text Components: Text Areas and Fonts

CONCEPT: A text area is a multiline text field that can accept several lines of text input. Components that inherit from the `JComponent` class have a `setFont` method that allows you to change the font and style of the component's text.

Text Areas

In Chapter 11 you were introduced to the `JTextField` class, which is used to create text fields. A text field is a component that allows the user to enter a single line of text. A text area is like a text field that can accept multiple lines of input. You use the `JTextArea` class to create a text area. Here is the general format of two of the class's constructors:

```
JTextArea(int rows, int columns)
JTextArea(String text, int rows, int columns)
```

In both constructors, *rows* is the number of rows or lines of text that the text area is to display, and *columns* is the number of columns or characters to be displayed per line. In the second constructor, *text* is a string that the text area will initially display. For example, the following statement creates a text area with 20 rows and 40 columns:

```
JTextArea textInput = new JTextArea(20, 40);
```

The following statement creates a text area with 10 rows and 20 columns that will initially display the text stored in the String object info:

```
JTextArea textInput = new JTextArea(info, 20, 40);
```

As with the JTextField class, the JTextArea class provides the getText and setText methods for getting and setting the text contained in the component. For example, the following statement gets the text stored in the textInput text area and stores it in the String object userText:

```
String userText = textInput.getText();
```

The following statement stores the text that is in the String object info in the textInput text area:

```
textInput.setText(info);
```

JTextArea components do not automatically display scroll bars. To display scroll bars on a JTextArea component, you must add it to the scroll pane. As you already know, you create a scroll pane with the JScrollPane class. Here is an example of code that creates a text area and adds it to a scroll pane.

```
JTextArea textInput = new JTextArea(20, 40);
JScrollPane scrollPane = new JScrollPane(textInput);
```

The JScrollPane object displays both vertical and horizontal scroll bars on a text area. By default, the scroll bars are not displayed until they are needed; however, you can alter this behavior with two of the JScrollPane class's methods. The setHorizontalScrollBarPolicy method takes an int argument that specifies when a horizontal scroll bar should appear in the scroll pane. You can pass one of the following constants as an argument:

- **JScrollPane.HORIZONTAL_SCROLLBAR_AS_NEEDED.** This is the default setting. A horizontal scroll bar is displayed only when there is not enough horizontal space to display the text contained in the text area.
- **JScrollPane.HORIZONTAL_SCROLLBAR_NEVER.** This setting prevents a horizontal scroll bar from being displayed on the text area.
- **JScrollPane.HORIZONTAL_SCROLLBAR_ALWAYS.** With this setting, a horizontal scroll bar is always displayed, even when it is not needed.

The setVerticalScrollBarPolicy method also takes an int argument, which specifies when a vertical scroll bar should appear in the scroll pane. You can pass one of the following constants as an argument:

- **JScrollPane.VERTICAL_SCROLLBAR_AS_NEEDED.** This is the default setting. A vertical scroll bar is displayed only when there is not enough vertical space to display the text contained in the text area.

- **JScrollPane.VERTICAL_SCROLLBAR_NEVER.** This setting prevents a vertical scroll bar from being displayed on the text area.
- **JScrollPane.VERTICAL_SCROLLBAR_ALWAYS.** With this setting, a vertical scroll bar is always displayed, even when it is not needed.

For example, the following code specifies that a vertical scroll bar should always appear on a scroll pane's component, but a horizontal scroll bar should not appear.

```
scrollPane.setHorizontalScrollBarPolicy(
                JScrollPane.HORIZONTAL_SCROLLBAR_NEVER);
scrollPane.setVerticalScrollBarPolicy(
                JScrollPane.VERTICAL_SCROLLBAR_ALWAYS);
```

Figure 12-26 shows a text area without scroll bars, a text area with a vertical scroll bar, and a text area with both a horizontal and a vertical scroll bar.

Figure 12-26   Text areas with and without scroll bars

By default, JTextArea components do not perform *line wrapping*. This means that when text is entered into the component and the end of a line is reached, the text does not wrap around to the next line. If you want line wrapping, you use the JTextArea class's setLineWrap method to turn it on. The method accepts a boolean argument. If you pass true, then line wrapping is turned on. If you pass false, line wrapping is turned off. Here is an example of a statement that turns a text area's line wrapping on:

```
textInput.setLineWrap(true);
```

There are two different styles of line wrapping: word wrapping and character wrapping. When *word wrapping* is performed, the line breaks always occur between words, never in the middle of a word. When character wrapping is performed, lines are broken between characters. This means that lines can be broken in the middle of a word. You specify the style of line wrapping that you prefer with the JTextArea class's setWrapStyleWord method. This method accepts a boolean argument. If you pass true, then the text area will perform word wrapping. If you pass false, the text area will perform character wrapping. The default style is character wrapping.

Fonts

The appearance of a component's text is determined by the text's font, style, and size. The font is the name of the typeface—the style can be plain, bold, and/or italic—and the size is the size of the text in points. To change the appearance of a component's text you use the component's `setFont` method, which is inherited from the `JComponent` class. The general format of the method is:

```
void setFont(Font appearance)
```

You pass a `Font` object as an argument to this method. The `Font` class constructor has the following general format:

```
Font(String fontName, int style, int size);
```

The first argument is the name of a font. Although the fonts that are available vary from system to system, Java guarantees that you will have Dialog, DialogInput, Monospaced, SansSerif, and Serif. Figure 12-27 shows an example of each of these.

Figure 12-27   Examples of fonts

The second argument to the `Font` constructor is an `int` that represents the style of the text. The `Font` class provides the following constants that you can use: `Font.PLAIN`, `Font.BOLD`, and `Font.ITALIC`. The third argument is the size of the text in points. (There are 72 points per inch, so a 72-point font would have a height of one inch. Ten- and 12-point fonts are normally used for most applications.) Here is an example of a statement that changes the text of a label to a 24-point bold Serif font:

```
label.setFont(new Font("Serif", Font.BOLD, 24));
```

You can combine styles by mathematically adding them. For example, the following statement changes a label's text to a 24-point bold and italic Serif font:

```
label.setFont(new Font("Serif", Font.BOLD + Font.Italic, 24));
```

Figure 12-28 shows an example of the Serif font in plain, bold, italic, and bold plus italic styles. The following code was used to create the labels:

```
JLabel label1 = new JLabel("Serif Plain", SwingConstants.CENTER);
label1.setFont(new Font("Serif", Font.PLAIN, 24));

JLabel label2 = new JLabel("Serif Bold", SwingConstants.CENTER);
label2.setFont(new Font("Serif", Font.BOLD, 24));

JLabel label3 = new JLabel("Serif Italic", SwingConstants.CENTER);
label3.setFont(new Font("Serif", Font.ITALIC, 24));

JLabel label4 = new JLabel("Serif Bold + Italic",
                            SwingConstants.CENTER);
label4.setFont(new Font("Serif", Font.BOLD + Font.ITALIC, 24));
```

Figure 12-28 Examples of Serif plain, bold, italic, and bold plus italic

 Checkpoint

12.23 What arguments do you pass to the `JTextArea` constructor?

12.24 How do you retrieve the text that is stored in a `JTextArea` component?

12.25 Does the `JTextArea` component automatically display scroll bars? If not, how do you accomplish this?

12.26 What is line wrapping? What are the two styles of line wrapping? How do you turn a `JTextArea` component's line wrapping on? How do you select a line wrapping style?

12.27 What type of argument does a component's `setFont` method accept?

12.28 What are the arguments that you pass to the `Font` class constructor?

See the Simple Text Editor Case Study for an in-depth example using menus and other topics from this chapter. The case study is available on this book's online resource page at www.pearsonhighered.com/gaddis.

12.9 Sliders

CONCEPT: A slider is a component that allows the user to graphically adjust a number within a range of values.

Sliders, which are created from the `JSlider` class, display an image of a "slider knob" that can be dragged along a track. Sliders can be horizontally or vertically oriented, as shown in Figure 12-29.

Figure 12-29   A horizontal and a vertical slider

A slider is designed to represent a range of numeric values. At one end of the slider is the range's minimum value and at the other end is the range's maximum value. Both of the sliders shown in Figure 12-29 represent a range of 0 through 50. Sliders hold a numeric value in a field, and as the user moves the knob along the track, the numeric value is adjusted accordingly. Notice that the sliders in Figure 12-29 have accompanying tick marks. At every tenth value, a major tick mark is displayed along with a label indicating the value at that tick mark. Between the major tick marks are minor tick marks, which in this example are displayed at every second value. The appearance of tick marks, their spacing, and the appearance of labels can be controlled through methods in the `JSlider` class. The `JSlider` constructor has the following general format:

```
JSlider(int orientation, int minValue,
        int maxValue, int initialValue)
```

The first argument is an `int` specifying the slider's orientation. You should use one of the constants `JSlider.HORIZONTAL` or `JSlider.VERTICAL`. The second argument is the minimum value of the slider's range, and the third argument is the maximum value of the slider's range. The fourth argument is the initial value of the slider, which determines the initial position of the slider's knob. For example, the following code could be used to create the sliders shown in Figure 12-29:

```
JSlider slider1 = new JSlider(JSlider.HORIZONTAL, 0, 50, 25);
JSlider slider2 = new JSlider(JSlider.VERTICAL, 0, 50, 25);
```

You set the major and minor tick mark spacing with the methods `setMajorTickSpacing` and `setMinorTickSpacing`. Each of these methods accepts an `int` argument that specifies the intervals of the tick marks. For example, the following code sets the `slider1` object's major tick mark spacing at 10, and its minor tick mark spacing at 2:

```
slider1.setMajorTickSpacing(10);
slider1.setMinorTickSpacing(2);
```

If the `slider1` component's range is 0 through 50, then these statements would cause major tick marks to be displayed at values 0, 10, 20, 30, 40, and 50. Minor tick marks would be displayed at values 2, 4, 6, and 8, then at values 12, 14, 16, and 18, and so forth.

By default, tick marks are not displayed, and setting their spacing does not cause them to be displayed. You display tick marks by calling the `setPaintTicks` method, which accepts a `boolean` argument. If you pass `true`, then tick marks are displayed. If you pass `false`, they are not displayed. Here is an example:

```
slider1.setPaintTicks(true);
```

By default, labels are not displayed either. You display numeric labels on the slider component by calling the `setPaintLabels` method, which accepts a `boolean` argument. If you pass `true`, then numeric labels are displayed at the major tick marks. If you pass `false`, labels are not displayed. Here is an example:

```
slider1.setPaintLabels(true);
```

When the knob's position is moved, the slider component generates a *change event*. To handle the change event, you must write a *change listener* class. When you write a change listener class, it must meet the following requirements:

- It must implement the `ChangeListener` interface. This interface is in the `javax.swing.event` package.
- It must have a method named `stateChanged`. This method must take an argument of the `ChangeEvent` type.

To retrieve the current value stored in a `JSlider`, use the `getValue` method. This method returns the slider's value as an `int`. Here is an example:

```
currentValue = slider1.getValue();
```

The class shown in Code Listing 12-7 demonstrates the `JSlider` component. This class displays the window shown in Figure 12-30. Two temperatures are initially shown: 32.0 degrees Fahrenheit and 0.0 degrees Celsius. A slider, which has the range of 0 through 100, allows you to adjust the Celsius temperature and immediately see the Fahrenheit conversion. The `main` method creates an instance of the class and displays the window.

Code Listing 12-7   `(TempConverter.java)`

```
1   import java.awt.*;
2   import javax.swing.event.*;
3   import javax.swing.*;
4   import java.text.DecimalFormat;
5
6   /**
7    *  This class displays a window with a slider component. The
8    *  user can convert the Celsius temperatures from 0 through
9    *  100 to Fahrenheit by moving the slider.
10   */
11
12  public class TempConverter extends JFrame
13  {
14     private JTextField fahrenheitTemp; // Displays Fahrenheit
15     private JTextField celsiusTemp;    // Displays Celsius
16     private JPanel fpanel;             // Holds Fahrenheit
17     private JPanel cpanel;             // Holds Celsius
18     private JPanel sliderPanel;        // Holds the slider
19     private JSlider slider;            // Adjusts temperature
20
21     /**
22      *  Constructor
23      */
24
25     public TempConverter()
26     {
27        // Call the JFrame constructor.
28        super("Temperatures");
29
30        // Specify an action for the close button.
31        setDefaultCloseOperation(JFrame.EXIT_ON_CLOSE);
32
33        // Create the labels.
34        JLabel label1 = new JLabel("Fahrenheit: ");
35        JLabel label2 = new JLabel("Celsius: ");
36
37        // Create the read-only text fields.
38        fahrenheitTemp = new JTextField("32.0", 10);
39        fahrenheitTemp.setEditable(false);
40        celsiusTemp = new JTextField("0.0", 10);
41        celsiusTemp.setEditable(false);
42
43        // Create the slider.
44        slider = new JSlider(JSlider.HORIZONTAL, 0, 100, 0);
45        slider.setMajorTickSpacing(20);
```

```
46              slider.setMinorTickSpacing(5);
47              slider.setPaintTicks(true);
48              slider.setPaintLabels(true);
49              slider.addChangeListener(new SliderListener());
50
51              // Create panels and place the components in them.
52              fpanel = new JPanel();
53              fpanel.add(label1);
54              fpanel.add(fahrenheitTemp);
55              cpanel = new JPanel();
56              cpanel.add(label2);
57              cpanel.add(celsiusTemp);
58              sliderPanel = new JPanel();
59              sliderPanel.add(slider);
60
61              // Create a layout manager for the content pane.
62              setLayout(new GridLayout(3, 1));
63
64              // Add the panels to the content pane.
65              add(fpanel);
66              add(cpanel);
67              add(sliderPanel);
68
69              // Pack and display the frame.
70              pack();
71              setVisible(true);
72           }
73
74           /**
75            *  Private inner class to handle the change events
76            *  that are generated when the slider is moved.
77            */
78
79           private class SliderListener implements ChangeListener
80           {
81              public void stateChanged(ChangeEvent e)
82              {
83                 double fahrenheit, celsius;
84                 DecimalFormat fmt = new DecimalFormat("0.0");
85
86                 celsius = slider.getValue();
87                 fahrenheit = (9.0 / 5.0) * celsius + 32.0;
88                 celsiusTemp.setText(Double.toString(celsius));
89                 fahrenheitTemp.setText(fmt.format(fahrenheit));
90              }
91           }
92
```

```
93      /**
94       *   The main method creates an instance of the
95       *   TempConverter class.
96       */
97
98      public static void main(String[] args)
99      {
100         new TempConverter();
101     }
102 }
```

Figure 12-30   Window displayed by the `TempConverter` class

Checkpoint

12.29 What type of event does a `JSlider` generate when its slider knob is moved?

12.30 What `JSlider` methods do you use to perform each of these operations?
   a.   Establish the spacing of major tick marks.
   b.   Establish the spacing of minor tick marks.
   c.   Cause tick marks to be displayed.
   d.   Cause labels to be displayed.

12.10 Look and Feel

CONCEPT: A GUI application's appearance is determined by its look and feel. Java allows you to select an application's look and feel.

Most operating systems' GUIs have their own unique appearance and style conventions. For example, if a Windows user switches to a Macintosh, UNIX, or Linux system, the first thing he or she is likely to notice is the difference in the way the GUIs on each system appear. The appearance of a particular system's GUI is known as its *look and feel*.

Java allows you to select the look and feel of a GUI application. The default look and feel for Java is called *Ocean*[1]. This is the look and feel that you have seen in all of the GUI applications that we have written in this book. Some of the other look and feel choices are Metal, Motif, and Windows. Metal was the default look and feel for previous versions of Java. Motif is similar to a UNIX look and feel. Windows is the look and feel of the Windows operating system.[2] Figure 12-31 shows how the `TempConverterWindow` class window, presented earlier in this chapter, appears in each of these looks and feels.

Figure 12-31   Metal, Motif, and Windows looks and feels

To change an application's look and feel, you call the `UIManager` class's static `setLookAndFeel` method. Java has a class for each look and feel, and this method takes the fully qualified class name for the desired look and feel as its argument. The class name must be passed as a string. Table 12-1 lists the fully qualified class names for the Metal, Motif, and Windows looks and feels.

Table 12-1   Look and Feel Class Names

Class Name	Look and Feel
`"javax.swing.plaf.metal.MetalLookAndFeel"`	Metal
`"com.sun.java.swing.plaf.motif.MotifLookAndFeel"`	Motif
`"com.sun.java.swing.plaf.windows.WindowsLookAndFeel"`	Window

When you call the `UIManager.setLookAndFeel` method, any components that have already been created need to be updated. You do this by calling the `SwingUtilities.updateComponentTreeUI` method, passing a reference to the component that you want to update as an argument.

The `UIManager.setLookAndFeel` method throws a number of exceptions. Specifically, it throws `ClassNotFoundException`, `InstantiationException`, `IllegalAccessException`, and `UnsupportedLookAndFeelException`. Unless you want to trap each of these types of

---

[1]Ocean is actually a special theme of the Metal look and feel.
[2]Currently the Windows look and feel is available only on computers running the Microsoft Windows operating system.

exceptions, you can simply trap exceptions of type `Exception`. Here is an example of code that can be run from a `JFrame` object that changes its look and feel to Motif:

```
try
{
    UIManager.setLookAndFeel(
            "com.sun.java.swing.plaf.motif.MotifLookAndFeel");
    SwingUtilities.updateComponentTreeUI(this);
}
catch (Exception e)
{
    JOptionPane.showMessageDialog(null, "Error setting the look and feel.");
    System.exit(0);
}
```

And here is an example of code that can be run from a `JFrame` object that changes its look and feel to Windows:

```
try
{
    UIManager.setLookAndFeel(
            "com.sun.java.swing.plaf.windows.WindowsLookAndFeel");
    SwingUtilities.updateComponentTreeUI(this);
}
catch (Exception e)
{
    JOptionPane.showMessageDialog(null, "Error setting the look and feel.");
    System.exit(0);
}
```

12.11 Common Errors to Avoid

The following list describes several errors that are commonly made when learning this chapter's topics.

- **Only retrieving the first selected item from a list component in which multiple items have been selected.** If multiple items have been selected in a list component, the `getSelectedValue` method returns only the first selected item. Likewise, the `getSelectedIndex` method returns only the index of the first selected item. You should use the `getSelectedValues` or `getSelectedIndices` methods instead.
- **Using 1 as the beginning index for a list or combo box.** The indices for a list or combo box start at 0, not 1.
- **Forgetting to add a list or text area to a scroll pane.** The `JList` and `JTextArea` components do not automatically display scroll bars. You must add these components to a scroll pane object in order for them to display scroll bars.
- **Using the `add` method instead of the constructor to add a component to a scroll pane.** To add a component to a scroll pane, you must pass a reference to the component as an argument to the `JScrollPane` constructor.
- **Adding a component to a scroll pane and then adding the component (not the scroll pane) to another container, such as a panel.** If you add a component to a scroll pane

and then intend to add that same component to a panel or other container, you must add the scroll pane instead of the component. Otherwise, the scroll bars will not appear on the component.

- **Forgetting to call the `setEditable` method to give a combo box a text field.** By default, a combo box is the combination of a button and a list. To make it a combination of a text field and a list, you must call the `setEditable` method and pass `true` as an argument.

- **Trying to open an image file of an unsupported type.** Currently, an `ImageIcon` object can open image files that are stored in JPEG, GIF, or PNG formats.

- **Loading an image into an existing `JLabel` component and clipping part of the image.** If you have not explicitly set the preferred size of a `JLabel` component, it resizes itself automatically when you load an image into it. The `JFrame` that encloses the `JLabel` does not automatically resize, however. You must call the `JFrame` object's pack method or `setPreferredSize` method to resize it.

- **Assigning the same mnemonic to more than one component.** If you assign the same mnemonic to more than one component in a window, it works only for the first component that you assigned it to.

- **Forgetting to add menu items to a `JMenu` component, and `JMenu` components to a `JMenuBar` component.** After you create a menu item, you must add it to a `JMenu` component in order for it to be displayed on the menu. Likewise, `JMenu` components must be added to a `JMenuBar` component in order to be displayed on the menu bar.

- **Not calling the `JFrame` object's `setJMenuBar` method to place the menu bar.** To display a menu bar, you must call the `setJMenuBar` method and pass it as an argument.

- **Not grouping `JRadioButtonMenuItems` in a `ButtonGroup` object.** Just like regular radio button components, you must group radio button menu items in a button group in order to create a mutually exclusive relationship between them.

Review Questions and Exercises

Multiple Choice and True/False

1. You can use this method to make a text field read-only.
   a. setReadOnly
   b. setChangeable
   c. setUneditable
   d. setEditable

2. A JList component generates this type of event when the user selects an item.
   a. action event
   b. item event
   c. list selection event
   d. list change event

3. To display a scroll bar with a JList component, you must do this.
   a. nothing—the JList automatically appears with scroll bars if necessary
   b. add the JList component to a JScrollPane component
   c. call the setScrollBar method
   d. you cannot display a scroll bar with a JList component

4. This is the `JList` component's default selection mode.
    a. single selection
    b. single interval selection
    c. multiple selection
    d. multiple interval selection

5. A list selection listener must have this method.
    a. `valueChanged`
    b. `selectionChanged`
    c. `actionPerformed`
    d. `itemSelected`

6. The `ListSelectionListener` interface is in this package.
    a. `java.awt`
    b. `java.awt.event`
    c. `javax.swing.event`
    d. `javax.event`

7. This `JList` method returns −1 if no item in the list is selected.
    a. `getSelectedValue`
    b. `getSelectedItem`
    c. `getSelectedIndex`
    d. `getSelection`

8. A `JComboBox` component generates this type of event when the user selects an item.
    a. action event
    b. item event
    c. list selection event
    d. list change event

9. You can pass an instance of this class to the `JLabel` constructor if you want to display an image in the label.
    a. `ImageFile`
    b. `ImageIcon`
    c. `JLabelImage`
    d. `JImageFile`

10. This method can be used to store an image in a `JLabel` or a `JButton` component.
    a. `setImage`
    b. `storeImage`
    c. `getIcon`
    d. `setIcon`

11. This is text that appears in a small box when the user holds the mouse cursor over a component.
    a. mnemonic
    b. instant message
    c. tool tip
    d. pop-up mnemonic

12. This is a key that activates a component just as if the user clicked on it with the mouse.
    a. mnemonic
    b. key activator
    c. tool tip
    d. click simulator

13. To display an open file or save file dialog box, you use this class.
    a. `JFileChooser`
    b. `JOpenSaveDialog`
    c. `JFileDialog`
    d. `JFileOptionPane`

14. To display a dialog box that allows the user to select a color, you use this class.
    a. `JColor`
    b. `JColorDialog`
    c. `JColorChooser`
    d. `JColorOptionPane`

15. You use this class to create a menu bar.
    a. `MenuBar`
    b. `JMenuBar`
    c. `JMenu`
    d. `JBar`

16. You use this class to create a radio button menu item.
    a. `JMenuItem`
    b. `JRadioButton`
    c. `JRadioButtonItem`
    d. `JRadioButtonMenuItem`

17. You use this method to place a menu bar on a `JFrame`.
    a. `setJMenuBar`
    b. `setMenuBar`
    c. `placeMenuBar`
    d. `setJMenu`

18. The `setPreferredSize` method accepts this as its argument(s).
    a. a `Size` object
    b. two `int` values
    c. a `Dimension` object
    d. one `int` value

19. Components of this class are multiline text fields.
    a. `JMultiLineTextField`
    b. `JTextArea`
    c. `JTextField`
    d. `JEditField`

20. This method is inherited from `JComponent` and changes the appearance of a component's text.
    a. `setAppearance`
    b. `setTextAppearance`
    c. `setFont`
    d. `setText`

21. This method sets the intervals at which major tick marks are displayed on a `JSlider` component.
    a. `setMajorTickSpacing`
    b. `setMajorTickIntervals`
    c. `setTickSpacing`
    d. `setIntervals`

22. **True or False:** You can use code to change the contents of a read-only text field.

23. **True or False:** A `JList` component automatically appears with a line border drawn around it.

24. **True or False:** In single interval selection mode, the user may select multiple items from a `JList` component.

25. **True or False:** With an editable combo box, the user may only enter a value that appears in the component's list.

26. **True or False:** You can store either text or an image in a `JLabel` object, but not both.

27. **True or False:** You can store large images as well as small ones in a `JLabel` component.

28. **True or False:** Mnemonics are helpful for users who are good with the keyboard.

29. **True or False:** A `JMenuBar` object acts as a container for `JMenu` components.

30. **True or False:** A `JMenu` object cannot contain other `JMenu` objects.

31. **True or False:** A `JTextArea` component does not automatically display scroll bars.

32. **True or False:** By default, a `JTextArea` component does not perform line wrapping.

33. **True or False:** A `JSlider` component generates an action event when the slider knob is moved.

34. **True or False:** By default, a `JSlider` component displays labels and tick marks.

35. **True or False:** When labels are displayed on a `JSlider` component, they are displayed on the major tick marks.

Find the Error

1. ```
   // Create a read-only text field.
   JTextField textField = new JTextField(10);
   textField.setEditable(true);
   ```

2. ```
   // Create a black 1-pixel border around list, a JList component.
   list.setBorder(Color.BLACK, 1);
   ```

3. ```
   // Create a JList and add it to a scroll pane.
   // Assume that array already exists.
   JList list = new JList(array);
   JScrollPane scrollPane = new JScrollPane();
   scrollPane.add(list);
   ```

4. ```
   // Assume that nameBox is a combo box and is properly set up
   // with a list of names to choose from.
   // Get value of the selected item.
   String selectedName = nameBox.getSelectedIndex();
   ```

5. ```
   JLabel label = new JLabel("Have a nice day!");
   label.setImage(image);
   ```
   ```

6. `// Add a menu to the menu bar.`
   `JMenuBar menuBar = new JMenuBar(menuItem);`

7. `// Create a text area with 20 columns and 5 rows.`
   `JTextArea textArea = new JTextArea (20, 5);`

Algorithm Workbench

1. Give an example of code that creates a read-only text field.

2. Write code that creates a list with the following items: Monday, Tuesday, Wednesday, Thursday, Friday, Saturday, and Sunday.

3. Write code that adds a scroll bar to the list you created in your answer to Question 2.

4. Assume that the variable `myList` references a `JList` component, and `selection` is a `String` variable. Write code that assigns the selected item in the `myList` component to the `selection` variable.

5. Assume that the variable `myComboBox` references an uneditable combo box, and `selectionIndex` is an `int` variable. Write code that assigns the index of the selected item in the `myComboBox` component to the `selectionIndex` variable.

6. Write code that stores the image in the file `dog.jpg` in a label.

7. Assume that `label` references an existing `JLabel` object. Write code that stores the image in the file `picture.gif` in the label.

8. Write code that creates a button with the text "Open File". Assign the O key as a mnemonic and assign "This button opens a file" as the component's tool tip.

9. Write code that displays a file open dialog box. If the user selects a file, the code should store the file's path and name in a `String` variable.

10. Write code that creates a text area displaying 10 rows and 15 columns. The text area should be capable of displaying scroll bars, when necessary. It should also perform word style line wrapping.

11. Write the code that creates a menu bar with one menu named File. The File menu should have the F key assigned as a mnemonic. The File menu should have three menu items: Open, Print, and Exit. Assign mnemonic keys of your choice to each of these items. Register an instance of the `OpenListener` class as an action listener for the Open menu item, an instance of the `PrintListener` class as an action listener for the Print menu item, and an instance of the `ExitListener` class as an action listener for the Exit menu item. Assume these classes have already been created.

12. Write code that creates a `JSlider` component. The component should be horizontally oriented and its range should be 0 through 1000. Labels and tick marks should be displayed. Major tick marks should appear at every 100th number, and minor tick marks should appear at every 25th number. The initial value of the slider should be set at 500.

Short Answer

1. What selection mode would you select if you want the user to only select a single item in a list?

2. You want to provide 20 items in a list for the user to select from. Which component would take up less space, a `JList` or a `JComboBox`?

3. What is the difference between an uneditable combo box and an editable combo box? Which is the default type of combo box?

4. Describe how you can store both an image and text in a `JLabel` component.

5. What is a mnemonic? How does the user use it?

6. What happens when the mnemonic that you assign to a component is a letter that appears in the component's text?

7. What is a tool tip? What is its purpose?

8. What do you do to a group of radio button menu items so that only one of them can be selected at a time?

9. When a checked menu item shows a check mark next to it, what happens when the user clicks on it?

10. What fonts does Java guarantee you have?

11. Why would a `JSlider` component be ideal when you want the user to enter a number, but you want to make sure the number is within a range?

12. Name three GUI looks and feels that are available in Java.

Programming Challenges

1. Scrollable Tax Calculator

Create an application that allows you to enter the amount of a purchase and then displays the amount of sales tax on that purchase. Use a slider to adjust the tax rate between 0% and 10%.

2. Image Viewer

deoNote
he Image
iewer
roblem

Write an application that allows the user to view image files. The application should use either a button or a menu item that displays a file chooser. When the user selects an image file, it should be loaded and displayed.

3. Dorm and Meal Plan Calculator

A university has the following dormitories:

> Allen Hall: $1,500 per semester
> Pike Hall: $1,600 per semester
> Farthing Hall: $1,200 per semester
> University Suites: $1,800 per semester

The university also offers the following meal plans:

> 7 meals per week: $560 per semester
> 14 meals per week: $1,095 per semester
> Unlimited meals: $1,500 per semester

Create an application with two combo boxes. One should hold the names of the dormitories, and the other should hold the meal plans. The user should select a dormitory and a meal plan, and the application should show the total charges for the semester.

4. Skateboard Designer

The Skate Shop sells the skateboard products listed in Table 12-2.

Table 12-2 Skateboard Products

Decks	Truck Assemblies	Wheels
The Master Thrasher $60	7.75-inch axle $35	51 mm $20
The Dictator $45	8-inch axle $40	55 mm $22
The Street King $50	8.5-inch axle $45	58 mm $24
		61 mm $28

In addition, the Skate Shop sells the following miscellaneous products and services:

Grip tape: $10
Bearings: $30
Riser pads: $2
Nuts & bolts kit: $3

Create an application that allows the user to select one deck, one truck assembly, and one wheel set from either list components or combo boxes. The application should also have a list component that allows the user to select multiple miscellaneous products. The application should display the subtotal, the amount of sales tax (at 6%), and the total of the order.

5. Shopping Cart System

Create an application that works like a shopping cart system for an online book store. In the book's source code (available at www.pearsonhighered.com/gaddis) you will find a file named BookPrices.txt. This file contains the names and prices of various books, formatted in the following fashion:

I Did It Your Way, 11.95
The History of Scotland, 14.50
Learn Calculus in One Day, 29.95
Feel the Stress, 18.50

Each line in the file contains the name of a book, followed by a comma, followed by the book's retail price. When your application begins execution, it should read the contents of the file and store the book titles in a list component. The user should be able to select a title from the list and add it to a "shopping cart," which is simply another list component. The application should have buttons or menu items that allow the user to remove items from the shopping cart, clear the shopping cart of all selections, and check out. When the user checks out, the application should calculate and display the subtotal of all the books in the shopping cart, the sales tax (which is 6% of the subtotal), and the total.

6. Cell Phone Packages

Cell Solutions, a cell phone provider, sells the following packages:

300 minutes per month: $45.00 per month
800 minutes per month: $65.00 per month
1500 minutes per month: $99.00 per month

The provider sells the following phones. (A 6% sales tax applies to the sale of a phone.)

Model 100: $29.95
Model 110: $49.95
Model 200: $99.95

Customers may also select the following options:

Voice mail: $5.00 per month
Text messaging: $10.00 per month

Write an application that displays a menu system. The menu system should allow the user to select one package, one phone, and any of the options desired. As the user selects items from the menu, the application should show the prices of the items selected.

7. Shade Designer

A custom window shade designer charges a base fee of $50 per shade. In addition, charges are added for certain styles, sizes, and colors as follows.

Styles:

Regular shades: Add $0
Folding shades: Add $10
Roman shades: Add $15

Sizes:

25 inches wide: Add $0
27 inches wide: Add $2
32 inches wide: Add $4
40 inches wide: Add $6

Colors:

Natural: Add $5
Blue: Add $0
Teal: Add $0
Red: Add $0
Green: Add $0

Create an application that allows the user to select the style, size, color, and number of shades from lists or combo boxes. The total charges should be displayed.

8. Conference Registration System

Create an application that calculates the registration fees for a conference. The general conference registration fee is $895 per person, and student registration is $495 per person. There is also an optional opening night dinner with a keynote speech for $30 per person. In addition, the optional preconference workshops listed in Table 12-3 are available.

Table 12-3 Optional Preconference Workshops

Workshop	Fee
Introduction to E-commerce	$295
The Future of the Web	$295
Advanced Java Programming	$395
Network Security	$395

The application should allow the user to select the registration type, the optional opening night dinner and keynote speech, and as many preconference workshops as desired. The total cost should be displayed.

9. Dice Simulator

Write a GUI application that simulates a pair of dice, similar to that shown in Figure 12-32. Each time the button is clicked, the application should roll the dice, using random numbers to determine the value of each die. (This chapter's source code folder contains images that you can use to display the dice.)

Figure 12-32   Dice Simulator

10. Card Dealer

This chapter's source code folder contains images for a complete deck of poker cards. Write a GUI application, similar to the one shown in Figure 12-33, that randomly selects a card from the deck and displays it each time the user clicks the button. When a card has been selected, it is removed from the deck and cannot be selected again. Display a message when no more cards are left in the deck.

Figure 12-33   Card Dealer

11. Tic-Tac-Toe Simulator

Create a GUI application that simulates a game of tic-tac-toe. Figure 12-34 shows an example of the application's window. The window shown in the figure uses nine large `JLabel` components to display the Xs and Os.

One approach in designing this application is to use a two-dimensional `int` array to simulate the game board in memory. When the user clicks the *New Game* button, the application should step through the array, storing a random number in the range of 0 through 1 in each element. The number 0 represents the letter O, and the number 1 represents the letter X. The `JLabel` components should then be updated to display the game board. The application should display a message indicating whether player X won, player Y won, or the game was a tie.

Figure 12-34   The Tic-Tac-Toe application

13 Applets and More

TOPICS

13.1 Introduction to Applets
13.2 A Brief Introduction to HTML
13.3 Creating Applets with Swing
13.4 Using AWT for Portability
13.5 Drawing Shapes

13.6 Handling Mouse Events
13.7 Timer Objects
13.8 Playing Audio
13.9 Common Errors to Avoid

13.1 Introduction to Applets

CONCEPT: An applet is a Java program that is associated with a Web page and is executed in a Web browser as part of that Web page.

Recall from Chapter 1 that there are two types of programs you can create with Java: applications and applets. An *application* is a stand-alone program that runs on your computer. So far in this book we have concentrated exclusively on writing applications.

Applets are Java programs that are usually part of a Web site. If a user opens the Web site with a Java-enabled browser, the applet is executed inside the browser window. It appears to the user that the applet is part of the Web site. This is how it works: Applets are stored on a Web server along with the site's Web pages. When a user accesses a Web page on a server with his or her browser, any applets associated with the Web page are transmitted over the Internet from the server to the user's system. This is illustrated in Figure 13-1. Once the applets are transmitted, the user's system executes them.

Applets are important because they can be used to extend the capabilities of a Web page. Web pages are normally written in Hypertext Markup Language (HTML). HTML is limited, however, because it merely describes the content and layout of a Web page and creates links to other files and Web pages. HTML does not have sophisticated abilities such as performing math calculations and interacting with the user. A programmer can write a Java applet to perform these types of operations and associate it with a Web page. When someone visits the Web page, the applet is downloaded to the visitor's browser and executed.

Figure 13-1 Applets are transmitted along with Web pages

Web Server   User with a Web browser

Figure 13-2 shows an example of a Web page that has an applet. In the figure, the Web page is being viewed with Internet Explorer. This Web page briefly explains the Fahrenheit and Celsius temperature scales. The area with the text boxes and the button at the bottom of the page is generated by an applet. To see a Fahrenheit temperature converted to Celsius, the user can enter the Fahrenheit temperature into the top text box and click the Convert button. The Celsius temperature will be displayed in the read-only text box.

NOTE: An applet does not have to be on a Web server in order to be executed. The Web page shown in Figure 13-2 is in the source code folder *Chapter 13\TempConverter*. Open the *TempConverter.html* file in your Web browser to try it. Later in this chapter we will take a closer look at this Web page and its applet.

Figure 13-2 A Web page with an applet

> **Fahrenheit and Celsius Temperatures** - Windows Internet Explorer
>
> C:\Users\Tony\Documents\Books\Java\Java - Control Structures to C | Search Google
>
> Google | Go | Bookmarks » | Settings▾ | Snagit
>
> Fahrenheit and Celsius Temperatures
>
> # Fahrenheit and Celsius Temperatures
>
> Fahrenheit and Celsius are two temperature scales in use today. The **Fahrenheit** scale was developed by the German physicist Daniel Gabriel Fahrenheit (1686 - 1736). In the Fahrenheit scale, water freezes at 32 degrees and boils at 212 degrees. The **Celsius** scale was developed by Swedish astronomer Andres Celsius (1701 - 1744). In the Celsius scale, water freezes at 0 degrees and boils at 100 degrees. The Celsius to Fahrenheit conversion formula is:
>
> $C = (5/9) * (F - 32)$
>
> where F is the Fahrenheit temperature. You can also use this Web page to convert Fahrenheit temperatures to Celsius. Just enter a Fahrenheit temperature in the text box below, then click on the Convert button.
>
> Fahrenheit Temperature: [   ]
>
> Celsius Temperature:
>
> [Convert]
>
> Applet TempConverter started | Computer | Protected Mode: Off | 100%

This part of the Web page is generated by an applet.

Most Web browsers have a special version of the JVM for running applets. For security purposes, this version of the JVM greatly restricts what an applet can do. Here is a summary of the restrictions placed on applets:

- Applets cannot delete files, read the contents of files, or create files on the user's system.
- Applets cannot run any other program on the user's system.
- Applets cannot execute operating system procedures on the user's system.
- Applets cannot retrieve information about the user's system, or the user's identity.
- Applets cannot make network connections with any system except the server from which the applet was transmitted.
- If an applet displays a window, it will automatically have a message such as "Warning: Applet Window" displayed in it. This lets the user know that the window was not displayed by an application on his or her system.

These restrictions might seem severe, but they are necessary to prevent malicious code from attacking or spying on unsuspecting users. If an applet attempts to violate one of these restrictions, an exception is thrown.

Checkpoint

13.1   How is an applet that is associated with a Web page executed on a user's system?

13.2   Why do applets run in a restricted environment?

13.2 A Brief Introduction to HTML

CONCEPT: When creating a Web page, you use Hypertext Markup Language (HTML) to create a file that can be read and processed by a Web browser.

Hypertext Markup Language (HTML) is the language that Web pages are written in. Although it is beyond the scope of this book to teach you everything about HTML, this section will give you enough of the fundamentals so that you can write simple Web pages. You will need to know a little about HTML in order to run Java applets. If you are already familiar with HTML, this section is optional.

Before we continue, let's look at the meanings of the terms "hypertext" and "markup language."

Hypertext

Web pages can contain regular text and hypertext, which are both displayed in the browser window. In addition, *hypertext* can contain a link to another Web page, or perhaps another location in the same Web page. When the user clicks on the hypertext, it loads the Web page or the location that the hypertext is linked to.

Markup Language

Although HTML is called a language, it is not a programming language like Java. Instead, HTML is a *markup language*. It allows you to "mark up" a text file by inserting special instructions. These instructions tell the browser how to format the text and create any hypertext links.

To make a Web page, you create a text file that contains HTML instructions, which are known as *tags*, as well as the text that should be displayed on the Web page. The resulting file is known as an *HTML document*, and it is usually saved with the *.html* file name extension. When a Web browser reads the HTML document, the tags instruct it how to format the text, where to place images, what to do when the user clicks on a link, and more.

Most HTML tags come in pairs. The first is known as the opening tag and the second is known as the closing tag. The general format of a simple tag is as follows:

```
<tag_name>
Text
</tag_name>
```

In this general format, `tag_name` is the name of the tag. The opening tag is `<tag_name>` and the closing tag is `</tag_name>`. Both the opening and closing tags are enclosed in angle brackets (< >). Notice that in the closing tag, the tag name is preceded by a forward slash (/). The `Text` that appears between the opening and closing tags is text that is formatted or modified by the tags.

Document Structure Tags

Some of the HTML tags are used to establish the structure of an HTML document. The first of the structure tags that you should learn is the `<html></html>` tag. This tag marks the beginning and ending of an HTML document. Everything that appears between these tags, including other tags, is the content of the Web page. When you are writing an HTML document, place an `<html>` tag at the very beginning, and a `</html>` tag at the very end.

The next tag is `<head></head>`. Everything that appears between `<head>` and `</head>` is considered part of the document head. The *document head* is a section of the HTML file that contains information about the document. For example, key words that search engines use to identify a document are often placed in the document's head. The only thing that we will use the document head for is to display a title in the Web browser's title bar. You do this with the `<title></title>` tag. Any text that you place between `<title>` and `</title>` becomes the title of the page and is displayed in the browser's title bar. Code Listing 13-1 shows the contents of an HTML document with the title "My First Web Page".

Notice that the `<title></title>` tag is inside of the `<head></head>` tag. The only output displayed by this Web page is the title. Figure 13-3 shows how this Web page appears when opened in a browser.

Code Listing 13-1   `(BasicWebPage1.html)`

```
<html>
<head>
    <title>My First Web Page</title>
</head>
</html>
```

Figure 13-3   Web page with a title only

After the document head comes the document body, which is enclosed in the <body></body> tag. The *document body* contains all of the tags and text that produce output in the browser window. Code Listing 13-2 shows an HTML document with text placed in its body. Figure 13-4 shows the document when opened in a browser.

Code Listing 13-2   `(BasicWebPage2.html)`

```
<html>
<head>
    <title>Java Applications and Applets</title>
</head>
<body>
    There are two types of programs you can create with Java: applications
    and applets. An application is a stand-alone program that runs on your
    computer. Applets are Java programs that are usually part of a Web site.
    They are stored on a Web server along with the site's Web pages. When a
    remote user accesses a Web page with his or her browser, any applets
    associated with the Web page are transmitted over the Internet from the
    server to the remote user's system.
</body>
</html>
```

Figure 13-4   Web page produced by *BasicWebPage2.html*

Text Formatting Tags

The text displayed in the Web page in Figure 13-4 is unformatted, which means it appears as plain text. There are many HTML tags that you can use to change the appearance of text. For example, there are six different header tags that you can use to format text as a heading of some type. The `<h1></h1>` tag creates a level one header. A level one header appears in boldface, and is much larger than regular text. The `<h2></h2>` tag creates a level two header. A level two header also appears in boldface, but is smaller than a level one header. This pattern continues with the `<h3></h3>`, `<h4></h4>`, `<h5></h5>`, and `<h6></h6>` tags. The higher a header tag's level number is, the smaller the text that it formats appears. For example, look at the following HTML:

```
<h1>This is an H1 Header</h1>
<h2>This is an H2 Header</h2>
<h3>This is an H3 Header</h3>
<h4>This is an H4 Header</h4>
<h5>This is an H5 Header</h5>
<h6>This is an H6 Header</h6>
This is regular unformatted text.
```

When this appears in the body of an HTML document, it produces the Web page shown in Figure 13-5.

You can use the `<center></center>` tag to center a line of text in the browser window. To demonstrate, we will add the following line to the document that was previously shown in Code Listing 13-2:

```
<center><h1>Java</h1></center>
```

Figure 13-5   Header levels

This will cause the word "Java" to appear centered and as a level one header. The modified document is shown in Code Listing 13-3, and the Web page it produces is shown in Figure 13-6.

Code Listing 13-3   `(BasicWebPage3.html)`

```html
<html>
<head>
    <title>Java Applications and Applets</title>
</head>
<body>
    <center>
        <h1>Java</h1>
    </center>
    There are two types of programs you can create with Java: applications
    and applets. An application is a stand-alone program that runs
    on your computer. Applets are Java programs that are usually
    part of a Web site. They are stored on a Web server along with
    the site's Web pages. When a remote user accesses a Web page
    with his or her browser, any applets associated with the Web
    page are transmitted over the Internet from the server to the
    remote user's system.
</body>
</html>
```

Figure 13-6 Web page produced by *BasicWebPage3.html*

Notice that in the HTML document, the word "Java" is enclosed in two sets of tags: the <center> tags and the <h1> tags. It doesn't matter which set of tags is used first. If we had written the line as follows, we would have gotten the same result:

```
<h1><center>Java</center></h1>
```

You can display text in boldface by using the <b></b> tag, and in italics by using the <i></i> tag. For example, the following will cause the text "Hello World" to be displayed in boldface:

```
<b>Hello World</b>
```

The following will cause "Hello World" to be displayed in italics:

```
<i>Hello World</i>
```

The following will display "Hello World" in boldface and italics:

```
<b><i>Hello World</i></b>
```

Creating Breaks in Text

We will look at three HTML tags that are used to create breaks in a document's text. These three tags are unique from the ones we previously studied because they do not occur in pairs. When you use one of these tags, you insert only an opening tag.

The <br> tag causes a line break to appear at the point in the text where it is inserted. It is often necessary to insert <br> tags in an HTML document because the browser usually ignores the newline characters that are created when you press the Enter key. For example, if the following line appears in the body of an HTML document, it will cause the output shown in Figure 13-7.

```
First line<br>Second line<br>Third line
```

Figure 13-7   Line breaks in an HTML document

The <p> tag causes a paragraph break to appear at the point in the text where it is inserted. A paragraph break typically inserts more space into the text than a line break. For example, if the following line appears in the body of an HTML document, it will cause the output shown in Figure 13-8.

```
First paragraph<p>Second paragraph<p>Third paragraph
```

Figure 13-8   Paragraph breaks in an HTML document

The <hr> tag causes a horizontal rule to appear at the point in the text where it is inserted. A horizontal rule is a thin, horizontal line that is drawn across the Web page. For example, if the following text appears in the body of an HTML document, it will cause the output shown in Figure 13-9.

```
This is the first line of text.
<hr>
This is the second line of text.
<hr>
This is the third line of text.
```

Figure 13-9 Horizontal rules in a Web page

The HTML document shown in Code Listing 13-4 demonstrates each of the tags we have discussed. The Web page it produces is shown in Figure 13-10.

Code Listing 13-4 (BasicWebPage4.html)

```
<html>
<head>
    <title>Java Applications and Applets</title>
</head>
<body>
    <center>
        <h1>Java</h1>
    </center>
    There are two types of programs you can create with Java: applications
    and applets.
    <p>
    <b>Applications</b>
    <br>
    An <i>application</i> is a stand-alone program that runs on
    your computer.
    <p>
    <b>Applets</b>
    <br>
    <i>Applets</i> are Java programs that are usually part of a
    Web site. They are stored on a Web server along with the site's
    Web pages. When a remote user accesses a Web page with his or
    her browser, any applets associated with the Web page are
    transmitted over the Internet from the server to the remote
    user's system.
    <hr>
</body>
</html>
```

Figure 13-10 Web page produced by *BasicWebPage4.html*

Inserting Links

As previously mentioned, a link is some element in a Web page that can be clicked on by the user. When the user clicks the link, another Web page is displayed, or some sort of action is initiated. We now look at how to insert a simple link that causes another Web page to be displayed. The tag that is used to insert a link has the following general format:

```
<a href="Address">Text</a>
```

The *Text* that appears between the opening and closing tags is the text that will be displayed in the Web page. When the user clicks on this text, the Web page that is located at *Address* will be displayed in the browser. This address is often referred to as a *uniform resource locator (URL)*. Notice that the address is enclosed in quotation marks. Here is an example:

```
<a href="http://www.gaddisbooks.com">Click here to go to
the textbook's Web site.</a>
```

The HTML document shown in Code Listing 13-5 uses this link, and Figure 13-11 shows how the page appears in the browser.

Code Listing 13-5 **(LinkDemo.html)**

```
<html>
<head>
    <title>Link Demonstration</title>
</head>
<body>
```

```
    This demonstrates a link.
    <br>
    <a href="http://www.aw.com/gaddis">Click here to go to
    the textbook's web site.</a>
</body>
</html>
```

The text that is displayed by a link is usually highlighted in some way to let the user know that it is not ordinary text. In Figure 13-11, the link text is underlined. When the user clicks on this text, the browser displays the Web page at `www.gaddisbooks.com`.

Figure 13-11 Web page produced by *LinkDemo.html*

Checkpoint

13.3 What tag marks the beginning and end of an HTML document?

13.4 What tag marks the beginning and end of an HTML document's head section?

13.5 What statement would you use in an HTML document to display the text "My Web Page" in the browser's title bar? What section of the HTML document would this statement be written in?

13.6 What tag marks the beginning and end of an HTML document's body section?

13.7 What statement would you write in an HTML document to display the text "Student Roster" as a level one header?

13.8 What statement would you write in an HTML document to display the text "My Resume" in bold and centered on the page?

13.9 What statement would you write in an HTML document to display the text "Hello World" in bold and italic?

13.10 What tag causes a line break? What tag causes a paragraph break? What tag displays a horizontal rule?

13.11 Suppose you wanted to display the text "Click Here" as a link to the Web site `http://java.sun.com`. What statement would you write to create the text?

13.3 Creating Applets with Swing

CONCEPT: You extend a class from `JApplet` to create an applet, just as you extend a class from `JFrame` to create a GUI application.

By now you know almost everything necessary to create an applet. That is because applets are very similar to GUI applications. You can think of an applet as a GUI application that runs under the control of a Web browser. Instead of displaying its own window, an applet appears in the browser's window. The differences between GUI application code and applet code are summarized here:

- A GUI application class inherits from `JFrame`. An applet class inherits from `JApplet`. The `JApplet` class is part of the `javax.swing` package.
- A GUI application class has a constructor that creates other components and sets up the GUI. An applet class does not normally have a constructor. Instead, it has a method named `init` that performs the same operations as a constructor. The `init` method accepts no arguments and has a `void` return type.
- The following methods, which are commonly called in a GUI application's constructor, are not called in an applet:

```
setTitle
setSize
setDefaultCloseOperation
pack
setVisible
```

The methods listed here are used in a GUI application to affect the application's window in some way. They are not usually applicable to an applet because the applet does not have a window of its own.

- There is no static `main` method needed to create an instance of the applet class. The browser creates an instance of the class automatically.

Let's look at a simple applet. Code Listing 13-6 shows an applet that displays a label.

Code Listing 13-6   (`SimpleApplet.java`)

```java
 1  import javax.swing.*;
 2  import java.awt.*;
 3
 4  /**
 5   * This is a simple applet.
 6   */
 7
 8  public class SimpleApplet extends JApplet
 9  {
10     /**
11      * The init method sets up the applet, much
12      * like a constructor.
13      */
```

```
14
15    public void init()
16    {
17       // Create a label.
18       JLabel label =
19             new JLabel("This is my very first applet.");
20
21       // Set the layout manager.
22       setLayout(new FlowLayout());
23
24       // Add the label to the content pane.
25       add(label);
26    }
27 }
```

This code is very much like a regular GUI application. Although this class extends `JApplet` instead of `JFrame`, you still add components to the content pane and use layout managers in the same way.

Running an Applet

The process of running an applet is different from that of running an application. To run an applet, you create an HTML document with an `applet` tag, which has the following general format:

```
<applet code="Filename.class" width=Wide height=High></applet>
```

In the general format, *Filename.class* is the name of the applet's *.class* file. This is the file that contains the compiled byte code. Note that you do not specify the *.java* file, which contains the Java source code. You can optionally specify a path along with the file name. If you specify only the file name, it is assumed that the file is in the same directory as the HTML document. *Wide* is the width of the applet in pixels, and *High* is the height of the applet in pixels. When a browser processes an `applet` tag, it loads specified byte code and executes it in an area that is the size specified by the *Wide* and *High* values.

The HTML document shown in Code Listing 13-7 uses an `applet` tag to load the applet shown in Code Listing 13-6. This document specifies that the applet should be displayed in an area that is 200 pixels wide by 50 pixels high. Figure 13-12 shows this document when it is displayed in a Web browser.

Code Listing 13-7   (`SimpleApplet.html`)

```
<html>
<head>
   <title>A Simple Applet</title>
```

```
</head>
<body>
    <applet code="SimpleApplet.class" width="200" height="50">
    </applet>
</body>
</html>
```

Figure 13-12 The Web page produced by *SimpleApplet.html*

NOTE: When you load a Web page that uses an applet into your browser, you will most likely get a security warning. For example, Figure 13-13 shows the warning you get from Internet Explorer. To run the applet, click the warning message and then select Allow Blocked Content... from the pop-up menu that appears.

Figure 13-13 Security warning in Internet Explorer

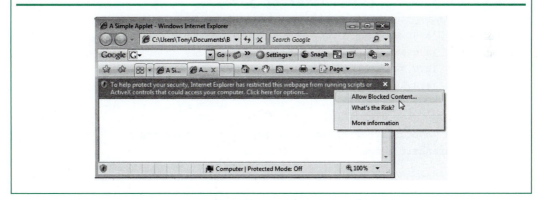

Running an Applet with `appletviewer`

The Sun JDK comes with an applet viewer program that loads and executes an applet without the need for a Web browser. This program can be run from a command prompt with the `appletviewer` command. When you run the program, you specify the name of an HTML document as a command line argument. For example, the following command passes `SimpleApplet.html` as the command line argument:

```
appletviewer SimpleApplet.html
```

This command executes any applet that is referenced by an `applet` tag in the file *SimpleApplet .html*. The window shown in Figure 13-14 will be displayed.

Figure 13-14 Applet executed by `appletviewer`

NOTE: The applet viewer does not display any output generated by text or tags in the HTML document. It only executes applets. If the applet viewer opens an HTML document with more than one `applet` tag, it will execute each applet in a separate window.

Handling Events in an Applet

In an applet, events are handled with event listeners exactly as they are in GUI applications. To demonstrate, we will examine the `TempConverter` class, which is shown in Code Listing 13-8. This class is the applet displayed in the Web page we examined at the beginning of this chapter. It has a text field where the user can enter a Fahrenheit temperature and a Convert button that converts the temperature to Celsius and displays it in a read-only text field. The temperature conversion is performed in an action listener class that handles the button's action events.

Code Listing 13-8 (`TempConverter.java`)

```
1   import javax.swing.*;
2   import java.awt.*;
3   import java.awt.event.*;
4   import java.text.DecimalFormat;
5
6   /**
7    * The TempConverter class is an applet that converts
8    * Fahrenheit temperatures to Celsius
9    */
10
11  public class TempConverter extends JApplet
12  {
13     private JPanel fPanel;        // Fahrenheit panel
14     private JPanel cPanel;        // Celsius panel
15     private JPanel buttonPanel;   // Button panel
16     private JTextField fahrenheit; // Fahrenheit temperature
17     private JTextField celsius;   // Celsius temperature
18
19     /**
20      * init method
21      */
22
```

```
23      public void init()
24      {
25         // Build the panels.
26         buildFpanel();
27         buildCpanel();
28         buildButtonPanel();
29
30         // Create a layout manager.
31         setLayout(new GridLayout(3, 1));
32
33         // Add the panels to the content pane.
34         add(fPanel);
35         add(cPanel);
36         add(buttonPanel);
37      }
38
39      /**
40       * The buildFpanel method creates a panel with a text
41       * field in which the user can enter a Fahrenheit
42       * temperature.
43       */
44
45      private void buildFpanel()
46      {
47         // Create a panel to hold other components.
48         fPanel = new JPanel();
49
50         // Create a label for instructions.
51         JLabel message1 = new JLabel("Fahrenheit Temperature: ");
52
53         // Create a text field for the Fahrenheit temperature.
54         fahrenheit = new JTextField(10);
55
56         // Create a layout manager for the panel.
57         fPanel.setLayout(new FlowLayout(FlowLayout.RIGHT));
58
59         // Add the label and text field to the panel.
60         fPanel.add(message1);
61         fPanel.add(fahrenheit);
62      }
63
64      /**
65       * The buildCpanel method creates a panel that
66       * displays the Celsius temperature in a read-only
67       * text field.
68       */
69
70      private void buildCpanel()
71      {
```

```
 72              // Create a panel to hold other components.
 73              cPanel = new JPanel();
 74
 75              // Create a label for instructions.
 76              JLabel message2 = new JLabel("Celsius Temperature: ");
 77
 78              // Create a text field for the Celsius temperature.
 79              celsius = new JTextField(10);
 80
 81              // Make the text field read-only.
 82              celsius.setEditable(false);
 83
 84              // Create a layout manager for the panel.
 85              cPanel.setLayout(new FlowLayout(FlowLayout.RIGHT));
 86
 87              // Add the label and text field to the panel.
 88              cPanel.add(message2);
 89              cPanel.add(celsius);
 90          }
 91
 92          /**
 93           * The buildButtonPanel method creates a panel with
 94           * a button that converts the Fahrenheit temperature
 95           * to Celsius.
 96           */
 97
 98          private void buildButtonPanel()
 99          {
100              // Create a panel to hold the button.
101              buttonPanel = new JPanel();
102
103              // Create a button.
104              JButton convButton = new JButton("Convert");
105
106              // Register an actionlistener.
107              convButton.addActionListener(new ButtonListener());
108
109              // Add the button to the panel.
110              buttonPanel.add(convButton);
111          }
112
113          /**
114           * The private inner class handles the action event
115           * that is generated when the user clicks the Convert
116           * button.
117           */
118
119          private class ButtonListener implements ActionListener
120          {
121              public void actionPerformed(ActionEvent e)
```

```
122         {
123             double ftemp;   // Fahrenheit temperature
124             double ctemp;   // Celsius temperature
125
126             // Create a DecimalFormat object for formatting.
127             DecimalFormat formatter = new DecimalFormat("0.0");
128
129             // Get the temperature entered by the user.
130             ftemp = Double.parseDouble(fahrenheit.getText());
131
132             // Convert the temperature to Celsius.
133             ctemp = (5.0 / 9.0) * (ftemp - 32);
134
135             // Display the Celsius temperature in the
136             // read-only text field.
137             celsius.setText(formatter.format(ctemp));
138         }
139     }
140 }
```

Code Listing 13-9 shows the contents of `TempConverter.html`, an HTML document that uses this applet. Figure 13-15 shows the Web page produced by this document. In the figure, the user has entered a Fahrenheit temperature and converted it to Celsius.

Code Listing 13-9   **(TempConverter.html)**

```
<html>
<head>
    <title>Fahrenheit and Celsius Temperatures</title>
</head>
<body>
    <center>
        <h1>Fahrenheit and Celsius Temperatures</h1>
    </center>
    Fahrenheit and Celsius are two temperature scales in use today.
    The <b>Fahrenheit</b> scale was developed by the German physicist
    Daniel Gabriel Fahrenheit (1686 - 1736). In the Fahrenheit scale,
    water freezes at 32 degrees and boils at 212 degrees. The <b>Celsius</b>
    scale was developed by Swedish astronomer Andres Celsius (1701
    - 1744). In the Celsius scale, water freezes at 0 degrees and
    boils at 100 degrees. The Celsius to Fahrenheit conversion formula
    is:
    <p>
    <i>C</i> = (5/9) * (<i>F</i> - 32)
    <p>
```

```
where <i>F</i> is the Fahrenheit temperature. You can also use
this Web page to convert Fahrenheit temperatures to Celsius.
Just enter a Fahrenheit temperature in the text box below, then
click on the Convert button.
<p>
<applet code="TempConverter.class" width="300" height="150">
</applet>
<hr>
</body>
</html>
```

Figure 13-15 Web page produced by *TempConverter.html*

Checkpoint

13.12 Instead of `JFrame`, an applet class is extended from what class?

13.13 Instead of a constructor, an applet class uses what method?

13.14 Why is there no need for a static `main` method to create an instance of an applet class?

13.15 Suppose the file *MyApplet.java* contains the Java source code for an applet. What tag would you write in an HTML document to run the applet in an area that is 400 pixels wide by 200 pixels high?

13.4 Using AWT for Portability

CONCEPT: Applets that use Swing components may be incompatible with some browsers. If you want to make sure that an applet is compatible with all Java-enabled browsers, use AWT components instead of Swing.

Java provides two libraries of classes that GUI components may be created from. Recall from Chapter 7 that these libraries are AWT and Swing. AWT is the original library that has been part of Java since its earliest version. Swing is an improved library that was introduced with Java 2. All of the GUI applications in Chapters 11 and 12, as well as the applets we have studied so far in this chapter, use Swing classes for their components.

Some browsers, such as Microsoft Internet Explorer and older versions of Netscape Navigator, do not directly support the Swing classes in applets. These browsers require a *plug-in*, which is software that extends or enhances another program, in order to run applets that use Swing components. Fortunately, this plug-in is automatically installed on a computer when the Sun JDK is installed. If you have installed the JDK, you should be able to write applets that use Swing and run them with no problems.

If you are writing an applet for other people to run on their computers, however, there is no guarantee that they will have the required plug-in. If this is the case, you should use the AWT classes instead of the Swing classes for the components in your applet. Fortunately, the AWT component classes are very similar to the Swing classes, so learning to use them is simple if you already know how to use Swing.

There is a corresponding AWT class for each of the Swing classes that you have learned so far. The names of the AWT classes are the same as those of the Swing classes, except the AWT class names do not start with the letter J. For example, the AWT class to create a frame is named `Frame`, and the AWT class to create a panel is named `Panel`. Table 13-1 lists several of the AWT classes. All of these classes are in the `java.awt` package.

Table 13-1 Several AWT classes

AWT Class	Description	Corresponding Swing Class
Applet	Used as a superclass for all applets. Unlike `JApplet` objects, `Applet` objects do not have a content pane.	JApplet
Frame	Creates a frame container that may be displayed as a window. Unlike `JFrame` objects, `Frame` objects do not have a content pane.	JFrame
Panel	Creates a panel container.	JPanel
Button	Creates a button that may be clicked.	JButton
Label	Creates a label that displays text.	JLabel
TextField	Creates a single line text field, which the user may type into.	JTextField
Checkbox	Creates a check box that may be selected or deselected.	JCheckBox

The Swing classes were intentionally designed with constructors and methods that are similar to those of their AWT counterparts. In addition, events are handled in the same way for each set of classes. This makes it easy for you to use either set of classes without learning a completely different syntax for each. For example, Code Listing 13-10 shows a version of the `TempConverter` applet that has been rewritten to use AWT components instead of Swing components.

Code Listing 13-10 (`AWTTempConverter.java`)

```java
 1  import java.applet.Applet;
 2  import java.awt.*;
 3  import java.awt.event.*;
 4  import java.text.DecimalFormat;
 5
 6  /**
 7   * The AWTTempConverter class is an applet that converts
 8   * Fahrenheit temperatures to Celsius.
 9   */
10
11  public class AWTTempConverter extends Applet
12  {
13     private Panel fPanel;         // Fahrenheit panel
14     private Panel cPanel;         // Celsius panel
15     private Panel buttonPanel;    // Button panel
16     private TextField fahrenheit; // Fahrenheit temperature
17     private TextField celsius;    // Celsius temperature
18
19     /**
20      * init method
21      */
22
23     public void init()
24     {
25        // Build the panels.
26        buildFpanel();
27        buildCpanel();
28        buildButtonPanel();
29
30        // Create a layout manager.
31        setLayout(new GridLayout(3, 1));
32
33        // Add the panels to the applet.
34        add(fPanel);
35        add(cPanel);
36        add(buttonPanel);
37     }
38
```

```
39      /**
40       * The buildFpanel method creates a panel with a text
41       * field in which the user can enter a Fahrenheit
42       * temperature.
43       */
44
45      private void buildFpanel()
46      {
47         // Create a panel to hold other components.
48         fPanel = new Panel();
49
50         // Create a label for instructions.
51         Label message1 = new Label("Fahrenheit Temperature: ");
52
53         // Create a text field for the Fahrenheit temperature.
54         fahrenheit = new TextField(10);
55
56         // Create a layout manager for the panel.
57         fPanel.setLayout(new FlowLayout(FlowLayout.RIGHT));
58
59         // Add the label and text field to the panel.
60         fPanel.add(message1);
61         fPanel.add(fahrenheit);
62
63      }
64
65      /**
66       * The buildCpanel method creates a panel that
67       * displays the Celsius temperature in a read-only
68       * text field.
69       */
70
71      private void buildCpanel()
72      {
73         // Create a panel to hold other components.
74         cPanel = new Panel();
75
76         // Create a label for instructions.
77         Label message2 = new Label("Celsius Temperature: ");
78
79         // Create a text field for the Celsius temperature.
80         celsius = new TextField(10);
81
82         // Make the text field read-only.
83         celsius.setEditable(false);
84
85         // Create a layout manager for the panel.
86         cPanel.setLayout(new FlowLayout(FlowLayout.RIGHT));
```

```
87
88          // Add the label and text field to the panel.
89          cPanel.add(message2);
90          cPanel.add(celsius);
91
92      }
93
94      /**
95       * The buildButtonPanel method creates a panel with
96       * a button that converts the Fahrenheit temperature
97       * to Celsius.
98       */
99
100     private void buildButtonPanel()
101     {
102         // Create a panel to hold the button.
103         buttonPanel = new Panel();
104
105         // Create a button.
106         Button convButton = new Button("Convert");
107
108         // Register an actionlistener.
109         convButton.addActionListener(new ButtonListener());
110
111         // Add the button to the panel.
112         buttonPanel.add(convButton);
113     }
114
115     /**
116      * The private inner class handles the action event
117      * that is generated when the user clicks the Convert
118      * button.
119      */
120
121     private class ButtonListener implements ActionListener
122     {
123         public void actionPerformed(ActionEvent e)
124         {
125             double ftemp;   // Fahrenheit temperature
126             double ctemp;   // Celsius temperature
127
128             // Create a DecimalFormat object for formatting.
129             DecimalFormat formatter = new DecimalFormat("0.0");
130
131             // Get the temperature entered by the user.
132             ftemp = Double.parseDouble(fahrenheit.getText());
133
134             // Convert the temperature to Celsius.
135             ctemp = (5.0 / 9.0) * (ftemp - 32);
```

```
136
137          // Display the Celsius temperature in the
138          // read-only text field.
139          celsius.setText(formatter.format(ctemp));
140        }
141     }
142  }
```

The only modifications that were made were as follows:

- The `JApplet`, `JPanel`, `JLabel`, `JTextField`, and `JButton` classes were replaced with the `Applet`, `Panel`, `Label`, `TextField`, and `Button` classes.
- The import `javax.swing.*;` statement was removed.

To run the applet in a browser, the `applet` tag in the *TempConverter.html* file must be modified to read as follows:

```
<applet code="AWTTempConverter.class" width=300 height=150>
</applet>
```

Once this change is made, the *TempConverter.html* file produces the Web page shown in Figure 13-16.

Figure 13-16   Web page running the `AWTTempConverter` applet

Checkpoint

13.16 To create an applet using AWT, what class do you inherit your applet class from?

13.17 In Swing, if an object's class extends `JFrame` or `JApplet`, you add components to its content pane. How do you add components to an object if its class extends `Frame` or `Applet`?

13.5 Drawing Shapes

CONCEPT: Components have an associated `Graphics` object that can be used to draw lines and shapes.

In addition to displaying standard components such as buttons and labels, Java allows you to draw lines and graphical shapes such as rectangles, ovals, and arcs. These lines and shapes are drawn directly on components. This allows a frame or a panel to become a canvas for your drawings. Before we examine how to draw graphics on a component, however, we must discuss the *XY* coordinate system. You use the *XY* coordinate system to specify the location of your graphics.

The *XY* Coordinate System

The location of each pixel in a component is identified with an *X* coordinate and a *Y* coordinate. The coordinates are usually written in the form (*x, y*). The *X* coordinate identifies a pixel's horizontal location, and the *Y* coordinate identifies its vertical location. The coordinates of the pixel in the upper-left corner of a component are usually (0, 0). The *X* coordinates increase from left to right, and the *Y* coordinates increase from top to bottom. For example, Figure 13-17 illustrates a component such as a frame or a panel that is 300 pixels wide by 200 pixels high. The *X* and *Y* coordinates of the pixels in each corner, as well as the pixel in the center of the component, are shown. The pixel in the center of the component has an *X* coordinate of 149 and a *Y* coordinate of 99.

Figure 13-17 *X* and *Y* coordinates on a 300 pixel wide by 200 pixel high component

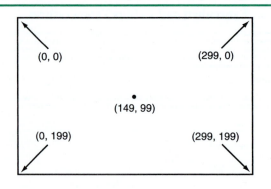

When you draw a line or shape on a component, you must indicate its position using *X* and *Y* coordinates.

Graphics Objects

Each component has an internal object that inherits from the `Graphics` class, which is part of the `java.awt` package. This object has numerous methods for drawing graphical shapes on the surface of the component. Table 13-2 lists some of these methods.

Table 13-2 Some of the graphics class methods

Method	Description
`void setColor(Color c)`	Sets the drawing color for this object to that specified by the argument.
`Color getColor()`	Returns the current drawing color for this object.
`void drawLine(int x1, int y1,` `    int x2, int y2)`	Draws a line on the component starting at the coordinate (*x1, y1*) and ending at the coordinate (*x2, y2*). The line will be drawn in the current drawing color.
`void drawRect(int x, int y,` `    int width, int height)`	Draws the outline of a rectangle on the component. The upper-left corner of the rectangle will be at the coordinate (*x, y*). The *width* parameter specifies the rectangle's width in pixels, and *height* specifies the rectangle's height in pixels. The rectangle will be drawn in the current drawing color.
`void fillRect(int x, int y,` `    int width, int height)`	Draws a filled rectangle. The parameters are the same as those used by the `drawRect` method. The rectangle will be filled with the current drawing color.
`void drawOval(int x, int y,` `    int width, int height)`	Draws the outline of an oval on the component. The shape and size of the oval is determined by an invisible rectangle that encloses it. The upper-left corner of the rectangle will be at the coordinate (*x, y*). The *width* parameter specifies the rectangle's width in pixels, and *height* specifies the rectangle's height in pixels. The oval will be drawn in the current drawing color.
`void fillOval(int x, int y,` `    int width, int height)`	Draws a filled oval. The parameters are the same as those used by the `drawOval` method. The oval will be filled in the current drawing color.

`void drawArc(int x, int y,`
`    int width, int height,`
`    int startAngle,`
`    int arcAngle)`
	This method draws an arc, which is considered to be part of an oval. The shape and size of the oval are determined by an invisible rectangle that encloses it. The upper-left corner of the rectangle will be at the coordinate (*x, y*). The *width* parameter specifies the rectangle's width in pixels, and *height* specifies the rectangle's height in pixels. The arc begins at the angle *startAngle*, and ends at the angle *arcAngle*. The arc will be drawn in the current drawing color.

`void fillArc(int x, int y,`
`    int width, int height,`
`    int startAngle,`
`    int arcAngle)`
	This method draws a filled arc. The parameters are the same as those used by the `drawArc` method. The arc will be filled with the current drawing color.

`void drawPolygon(int[] xPoints,`
`    int[] yPoints,`
`    int numPoints)`
	This method draws the outline of a closed polygon on the component. The *xPoints* array contains the X-coordinates for each vertex, and the *yPoints* array contains the Y coordinates for each vertex. The argument passed into *numPoints* is the number of vertices in the polygon.

(table continues next page)

Table 13-2 Some of the graphics class methods (continued)

Method	Description
`void fillPolygon(int[] xPoints, int[] yPoints, int numPoints)`	This method draws a filled polygon. The parameters are the same as those used by the `drawPolygon` method. The polygon will be filled with the current drawing color.
`void drawString(String str, int x, int y)`	Draws the string passed into *str* using the current font. The bottom left of the string is drawn at the coordinates passed into *x* and *y*.
`void setFont(Font f)`	Sets the current font, which is used by the `drawString` method.

In order to call any of these methods, you must get a reference to a component's `Graphics` object. One way to do this is to override the `paint` method. You can override the `paint` method in any class that extends as follows:

- `JApplet`
- `JFrame`
- Any AWT class, including `Applet` and `Frame`

The `paint` method is responsible for displaying, or "painting," a component on the screen. This method is automatically called when the component is first displayed and is called again any time the component needs to be redisplayed. For example, when the component is completely or partially obscured by another window, and the obscuring window is moved, then the component's `paint` method is called to redisplay it. The header for the paint method is:

```
public void paint(Graphics g)
```

Notice that the method's argument is a `Graphics` object. When this method is called for a particular component, the `Graphics` object that belongs to that component is automatically passed as an argument. By overriding the `paint` method, you can use the `Graphics` object argument to draw your own graphics on the component. For example, look at the applet class in Code Listing 13-11.

Code Listing 13-11 (`LineDemo.java`)

```
1   import javax.swing.*;
2   import java.awt.*;
3
4   /**
5    * This class is an applet that demonstrates how lines
6    * can be drawn.
7    */
8
9   public class LineDemo extends JApplet
10  {
11      /**
```

```
12        * init method
13        */
14
15       public void init()
16       {
17          // Set the background color to white.
18          getContentPane().setBackground(Color.WHITE);
19       }
20
21       /**
22        * paint method
23        */
24
25       public void paint(Graphics g)
26       {
27          // Call the base class paint method.
28          super.paint(g);
29
30          // Draw a red line from (20, 20) to (280, 280).
31          g.setColor(Color.RED);
32          g.drawLine(20, 20, 280, 280);
33
34          // Draw a blue line from (280, 20) to (20, 280).
35          g.setColor(Color.BLUE);
36          g.drawLine(280, 20, 20, 280);
37       }
38    }
```

This class inherits from `JApplet`, and it overrides the `paint` method. The `Graphics` object that is passed into the `paint` method's `g` parameter is the object that is responsible for drawing the entire applet window. Notice that in line 28 the method first calls the superclass version of the `paint` method, passing the object `g` as an argument. When overriding the `paint` method, you should always call the superclass's `paint` method before doing anything else. This ensures that the component will be displayed properly on the screen.

In line 31 the method sets the drawing color to red. In line 32 a line is drawn from the coordinates (20, 20) to (280, 280). This is a diagonal line drawn from the top-left area of the applet window to the bottom-right area. Next, in line 35, the drawing color is set to blue. In line 36 a line is drawn from (280, 20) to (20, 280). This is also a diagonal line. It is drawn from the top-right area of the applet window to the bottom-left area.

We can use the *LineDemo.html* file, which is in the same folder as the applet class, to execute the applet. The following line in the file runs the applet in an area that is 300 pixels wide by 300 pixels high:

```
<applet code="LineDemo.class" width=300 height=300>
</applet>
```

Figure 13-18 shows the applet running in the applet viewer.

Figure 13-18 LineDemo applet

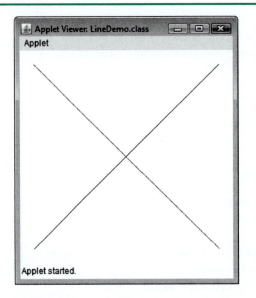

Notice that the paint method is not explicitly called by the applet. It is automatically called when the applet first executes. As previously mentioned, it is also called any time the applet window needs to be redisplayed.

Code Listing 13-12 shows the RectangleDemo class, an applet that draws two rectangles: one as a black outline and one filled with red. Each rectangle is 120 pixels wide and 120 pixels high. The file *RectangleDemo.html*, which is in the same folder as the applet class, executes the applet with the following tag:

```
<applet code="RectangleDemo.class" width=300 height=300>
</applet>
```

Figure 13-19 shows the applet running in the applet viewer.

Code Listing 13-12   **(RectangleDemo.java)**

```
 1  import javax.swing.*;
 2  import java.awt.*;
 3
 4  /**
 5   * This class is an applet that demonstrates how
 6   * rectangles can be drawn.
 7   */
 8
 9  public class RectangleDemo extends JApplet
10  {
```

```
11        /**
12         * init method
13         */
14
15        public void init()
16        {
17            // Set the background color to white.
18            getContentPane().setBackground(Color.WHITE);
19        }
20
21        /**
22         * paint method
23         */
24
25        public void paint(Graphics g)
26        {
27            // Call the superclass paint method.
28            super.paint(g);
29
30            // Draw a black unfilled rectangle.
31            g.setColor(Color.BLACK);
32            g.drawRect(20, 20, 120, 120);
33
34            // Draw a red-filled rectangle.
35            g.setColor(Color.RED);
36            g.fillRect(160, 160, 120, 120);
37        }
38    }
```

Figure 13-19 RectangleDemo applet

Code Listing 13-13 shows the OvalDemo class, an applet that draws two ovals. An oval is enclosed in an invisible rectangle that establishes the boundaries of the oval. The width and height of the enclosing rectangle defines the shape and size of the oval. This is illustrated in Figure 13-20.

When you call the drawOval or fillOval methods, you pass the X and Y coordinates of the enclosing rectangle's upper-left corner, and the width and height of the enclosing rectangle as arguments.

Code Listing 13-13   (OvalDemo.java)

```
1   import javax.swing.*;
2   import java.awt.*;
3
4   /**
5    * This class is an applet that demonstrates how
6    * ovals can be drawn.
7    */
8
9   public class OvalDemo extends JApplet
10  {
11     /**
12      * init method
13      */
14
15     public void init()
16     {
17        // Set the background color to white.
18        getContentPane().setBackground(Color.WHITE);
19     }
20
21     /**
22      * paint method
23      */
24
25     public void paint(Graphics g)
26     {
27        // Call the superclass paint method.
28        super.paint(g);
29
30        // Draw a black unfilled oval.
31        g.setColor(Color.BLACK);
32        g.drawOval(20, 20, 120, 75);
33
```

```
34          // Draw a green-filled rectangle.
35          g.setColor(Color.GREEN);
36          g.fillOval(80, 160, 180, 75);
37      }
38  }
```

Figure 13-20   An oval and its enclosing rectangle

Enclosing rectangle

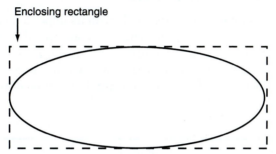

NOTE: The file *OvalDemo.html*, which is in the same folder as the applet class, executes the applet with the following tag:

```
<applet code="OvalDemo.class" width=300 height=255>
</applet>
```

Figure 13-21 shows the applet running in the applet viewer.

Figure 13-21   OvalDemo applet

TIP: To draw a circle, simply draw an oval with an enclosing rectangle that is square. In other words, the enclosing rectangle's width and height should be the same.

The drawArc method draws an arc, which is part of an oval. You pass the same arguments to drawArc as you do to drawOval, plus two additional arguments: the arc's starting angle and ending angle. The angles are measured in degrees, with 0 degrees being at the 3 o'clock position. For example, look at the following statement:

```
g.drawArc(20, 20, 100, 100, 0, 90);
```

This statement creates an enclosing rectangle with its upper-left corner at (20, 20) and with a width and height of 100 pixels each. The oval constructed from this enclosing rectangle is a circle. The arc that is drawn is the part of the oval that starts at 0 degrees and ends at 90 degrees. Figure 13-22 illustrates this arc. The dashed lines show the enclosing rectangle and the oval. The thick black line shows the arc that will be drawn.

Figure 13-22   An arc

Code Listing 13-14 shows the ArcDemo class, which is an applet that draws four arcs: two unfilled and two filled. The filled arcs are drawn with the fillArc method.

 NOTE: The file *ArcDemo.html*, which is in the same folder as the applet class, executes the applet with the following tag:

```
<applet code="ArcDemo.class" width=300 height=220>
</applet>
```

Figure 13-23 shows the applet running in the applet viewer.

Code Listing 13-14   (ArcDemo.java)

```
1  import javax.swing.*;
2  import java.awt.*;
3
```

```
 4  /**
 5   * This class is an applet that demonstrates how
 6   * arcs can be drawn.
 7   */
 8
 9  public class ArcDemo extends JApplet
10  {
11     /**
12      * init method
13      */
14
15     public void init()
16     {
17        // Set the background color to white.
18        getContentPane().setBackground(Color.WHITE);
19     }
20
21     /**
22      * paint method
23      */
24
25     public void paint(Graphics g)
26     {
27        // Call the superclass paint method.
28        super.paint(g);
29
30        // Draw a black unfilled arc from 0 degrees
31        // to 90 degrees.
32        g.setColor(Color.BLACK);
33        g.drawArc(0, 20, 120, 120, 0, 90);
34
35        // Draw a red-filled arc from 0 degrees
36        // to 90 degrees.
37        g.setColor(Color.RED);
38        g.fillArc(140, 20, 120, 120, 0, 90);
39
40        // Draw a green unfilled arc from 0 degrees
41        // to 45 degrees.
42        g.setColor(Color.GREEN);
43        g.drawArc(0, 120, 120, 120, 0, 45);
44
45        // Draw a blue-filled arc from 0 degrees
46        // to 45 degrees.
47        g.setColor(Color.BLUE);
48        g.fillArc(140, 120, 120, 120, 0, 45);
49     }
50  }
```

Figure 13-23   ArcDemo applet

The drawPolygon method draws an outline of a closed polygon, and the fillPolygon method draws a closed polygon filled with the current drawing color. A polygon is constructed of multiple line segments that are connected. The point where two line segments are connected is called a *vertex*. These methods accept two int arrays as arguments. The first array contains the *X* coordinates of each vertex, and the second array contains the *Y* coordinates of each vertex. The third argument is an int that specifies the number of vertices, or connecting points.

For example, suppose we use the following arrays as arguments for the *X* and *Y* coordinates of a polygon:

```
int[] xCoords = {60, 100, 140, 140, 100, 60, 20, 20};
int[] yCoords = {20, 20, 60, 100, 140, 140, 100, 60};
```

The first point specified by these arrays is (60, 20), the second point is (100, 20), and so forth. A total of eight points are specified by these arrays, and if we connect each of these points we get the octagon shown in Figure 13-24.

Figure 13-24   Points of each vertex in an octagon

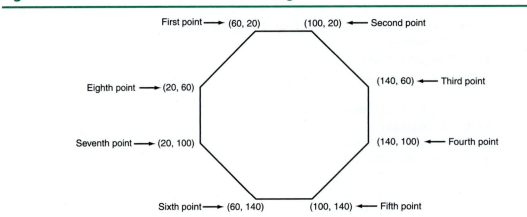

If the last point specified in the arrays is different from the first point, as in this example, then the two points are automatically connected to close the polygon. The PolygonDemo class in Code Listing 13-15 draws a filled polygon using these arrays as arguments.

Code Listing 13-15   (PolygonDemo.java)

```
1   import javax.swing.*;
2   import java.awt.*;
3
4   /**
5    * This class is an applet that demonstrates how a
6    * polygon can be drawn.
7    */
8
9   public class PolygonDemo extends JApplet
10  {
11     /**
12      * init method
13      */
14
15     public void init()
16     {
17        // Set the background color to white.
18        getContentPane().setBackground(Color.WHITE);
19     }
20
21     /**
22      * paint method
23      */
24
25     public void paint(Graphics g)
26     {
27        int[] xCoords = {60, 100, 140, 140, 100, 60, 20, 20};
28        int[] yCoords = {20, 20, 60, 100, 140, 140, 100, 60};
29
30        // Call the superclass paint method.
31        super.paint(g);
32
33        // Set the drawing color.
34        g.setColor(Color.RED);
35
36        // Draw the polygon.
37        g.fillPolygon(xCoords, yCoords, 8);
38     }
39  }
```

NOTE: The file *PolygonDemo.html*, which is in the same folder as the applet class, executes the applet with the following tag:

```
<applet code="PolygonDemo.class" width=160 height=160>
</applet>
```

Figure 13-25 shows the applet running in the applet viewer.

Figure 13-25 `PolygonDemo` applet

The `drawString` method draws a string as a graphic. The string is specified by its first argument, a `String` object. The *X* and *Y* coordinates of the lower-left point of the string are specified by the second and third arguments. For example, assuming that `g` references a `Graphics` object, the following statement draws the string "Hello World", starting at the coordinates 100, 50:

```
g.drawstring("Hello World", 100, 50);
```

You can set the font for the string with the `setFont` method. This method accepts a `Font` object as its argument. Here is an example:

```
g.setFont(new Font("Serif", Font.ITALIC, 20));
```

The `Font` class was covered in Chapter 12. Recall that the `Font` constructor's arguments are the name of a font, the font's style, and the font's size in points. You can combine font styles with the + operator, as follows:

```
g.setFont(new Font("Serif", Font.BOLD + Font.ITALIC, 24));
```

The `GraphicStringDemo` class in Code Listing 13-16 demonstrates the `drawString` method. It draws the same octagon that the `PolygonDemo` class drew, and then draws the string "STOP" over it to create a stop sign. The string is drawn in a bold 35-point sans serif font.

Code Listing 13-16   **(GraphicStringDemo.java)**

```
1   import javax.swing.*;
2   import java.awt.*;
3
```

```
4   /**
5    * This class is an applet that demonstrates how a
6    * string can be drawn.
7    */
8
9   public class GraphicStringDemo extends JApplet
10  {
11     /**
12      * init method
13      */
14
15     public void init()
16     {
17        // Set the background color to white.
18        getContentPane().setBackground(Color.WHITE);
19     }
20
21     /**
22      * paint method
23      */
24
25     public void paint(Graphics g)
26     {
27        int[] xCoords = {60, 100, 140, 140, 100, 60, 20, 20};
28        int[] yCoords = {20, 20, 60, 100, 140, 140, 100, 60};
29
30        // Call the superclass paint method.
31        super.paint(g);
32
33        // Set the drawing color.
34        g.setColor(Color.RED);
35
36        // Draw the polygon.
37        g.fillPolygon(xCoords, yCoords, 8);
38
39        // Set the drawing color to white.
40        g.setColor(Color.WHITE);
41
42        // Set the font and draw "STOP".
43        g.setFont(new Font("SansSerif", Font.BOLD, 35));
44        g.drawString("STOP", 35, 95);
45     }
46  }
```

> **NOTE:** The file *GraphicStringDemo.html*, which is in the same folder as the applet class, executes the applet with the following tag:
>
> ```
> <applet code="GraphicStringDemo.class" width=160 height=160>
> </applet>
> ```

Figure 13-26 shows the applet running in the applet viewer.

Figure 13-26   `GraphicStringDemo` applet

The `repaint` Method

As previously mentioned, you do not call a component's `paint` method. It is automatically called when the component must be redisplayed. Sometimes, however, you might want to force the application or applet to call the `paint` method. You do this by calling the `repaint` method, which has the following header:

```
public void repaint()
```

The `repaint` method clears the surface of the component and then calls the `paint` method. You will see an applet that uses this method in a moment.

Drawing on Panels

Each of the preceding examples uses the entire `JApplet` window as a canvas for drawing. Sometimes, however, you might want to confine your drawing space to a smaller region within the window, such as a panel. To draw on a panel, you simply get a reference to the panel's `Graphics` object and then use that object's methods to draw. The resulting graphics are drawn only on the panel.

Getting a reference to a `JPanel` component's `Graphics` object is similar to the technique you saw in the previous examples. Instead of overriding the `JPanel` object's `paint` method, however, you should override its `paintComponent` method. This is true not only for `JPanel` objects, but also for all Swing components except `JApplet` and `JFrame`. The `paintComponent` method serves for `JPanel` and most other Swing objects the same purpose as the `paint` method: It is automatically called when the component needs to be redisplayed. When it is called, the component's `Graphics` object is passed as an argument. Here is the method's header:

```
public void paintComponent(Graphics g)
```

When you override this method, first you should call the superclass's `paintComponent` method to ensure that the component is properly displayed. Here is an example call to the superclass's version of the method:

```
super.paintComponent(g);
```

After this you can call any of the `Graphics` object's methods to draw on the component. As an example, we look at the `GraphicsWindow` class in Code Listing 13-17. When this applet is run (via the *GraphicsWindow.html* file, which is in the same source code folder as the applet class), the window shown in Figure 13-27 is displayed. A set of check boxes is displayed in a `JPanel` component on the right side of the window. The white area that occupies the majority of the window is a `DrawingPanel` object. The `DrawingPanel` class inherits from `JPanel`, and its code is shown in Code Listing 13-18. When one of the check boxes is selected, a shape appears in the `DrawingPanel` object. Figure 13-28 shows how the applet window appears when all of the check boxes are selected.

Code Listing 13-17   (`GraphicsWindow.java`)

```java
1   import javax.swing.*;
2   import java.awt.*;
3   import java.awt.event.*;
4
5   /**
6    * This class displays a drawing panel and a set of check
7    * boxes that allow the user to select shapes. The selected
8    * shapes are drawn on the drawing panel.
9    */
10
11  public class GraphicsWindow extends JApplet
12  {
13     // The following will reference an array of check boxes.
14     private JCheckBox[] checkBoxes;
15
16     // The titles array contains titles for the check boxes.
17     private String[] titles = { "Line", "Rectangle",
18                 "Filled Rectangle", "Oval", "Filled Oval",
19                 "Arc", "Filled Arc" };
20
21     // The following will reference a panel to contain
22     // the check boxes.
23     private JPanel checkBoxPanel;
24
25     // The following will reference an instance of the
26     // DrawingPanel class. This will be a panel to draw on.
27     private DrawingPanel drawingPanel;
28
```

```
29      /**
30       * init method
31       */
32
33      public void init()
34      {
35         // Build the check box panel.
36         buildCheckBoxPanel();
37
38         // Create the drawing panel.
39         drawingPanel = new DrawingPanel(checkBoxes);
40
41         // Add the check box panel to the east region and
42         // the drawing panel to the center region.
43         add(checkBoxPanel, BorderLayout.EAST);
44         add(drawingPanel, BorderLayout.CENTER);
45      }
46
47      /**
48       * The buildCheckBoxPanel method creates the array of
49       * check box components and adds them to a panel.
50       */
51
52      private void buildCheckBoxPanel()
53      {
54         // Create the panel.
55         checkBoxPanel = new JPanel();
56         checkBoxPanel.setLayout(new GridLayout(7, 1));
57
58         // Create the check box array.
59         checkBoxes = new JCheckBox[7];
60
61         // Create the check boxes and add them to the panel.
62         for (int i = 0; i < checkBoxes.length; i++)
63         {
64            checkBoxes[i] = new JCheckBox(titles[i]);
65            checkBoxes[i].addItemListener(new CheckBoxListener());
66            checkBoxPanel.add(checkBoxes[i]);
67         }
68      }
69
70      /**
71       * A private inner class that responds to changes in the
72       * state of the check boxes.
73       */
74
75      private class CheckBoxListener implements ItemListener
76      {
```

```
77            public void itemStateChanged(ItemEvent e)
78            {
79                drawingPanel.repaint();
80            }
81        }
82    }
```

Figure 13-27   GraphicsWindow applet

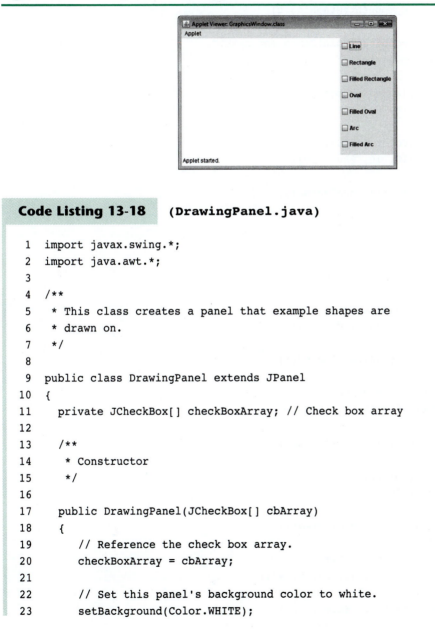

Code Listing 13-18   **(DrawingPanel.java)**

```
1    import javax.swing.*;
2    import java.awt.*;
3
4    /**
5     * This class creates a panel that example shapes are
6     * drawn on.
7     */
8
9    public class DrawingPanel extends JPanel
10   {
11      private JCheckBox[] checkBoxArray; // Check box array
12
13      /**
14       * Constructor
15       */
16
17      public DrawingPanel(JCheckBox[] cbArray)
18      {
19         // Reference the check box array.
20         checkBoxArray = cbArray;
21
22         // Set this panel's background color to white.
23         setBackground(Color.WHITE);
```

```
24
25          // Set the preferred size of the panel.
26          setPreferredSize(new Dimension(300, 200));
27     }
28
29     /**
30      * paintComponent method
31      */
32
33     public void paintComponent(Graphics g)
34     {
35          // Call the superclass paintComponent method.
36          super.paintComponent(g);
37
38          // Draw the selected shapes.
39          if (checkBoxArray[0].isSelected())
40          {
41              g.setColor(Color.BLACK);
42              g.drawLine(10, 10, 290, 190);
43          }
44          if (checkBoxArray[1].isSelected())
45          {
46              g.setColor(Color.BLACK);
47              g.drawRect(20, 20, 50, 50);
48          }
49          if (checkBoxArray[2].isSelected())
50          {
51              g.setColor(Color.RED);
52              g.fillRect(50, 30, 120, 120);
53          }
54          if (checkBoxArray[3].isSelected())
55          {
56              g.setColor(Color.BLACK);
57              g.drawOval(40, 155, 75, 50);
58          }
59          if (checkBoxArray[4].isSelected())
60          {
61              g.setColor(Color.BLUE);
62              g.fillOval(200, 125, 75, 50);
63          }
64          if (checkBoxArray[5].isSelected())
65          {
66              g.setColor(Color.BLACK);
67              g.drawArc(200, 40, 75, 50, 0, 90);
68          }
69          if (checkBoxArray[6].isSelected())
70          {
71              g.setColor(Color.GREEN);
```

```
72              g.fillArc(100, 155, 75, 50, 0, 90);
73          }
74      }
75  }
```

Figure 13-28 GraphicsWindow applet with all graphics selected

Let's take a closer look at these classes. First, notice in lines 14 through 19 of the GraphicsWindow class that two of the class's fields are array reference variables. The checkBoxes variable references an array of JCheckBox components, and the titles variable references an array of strings. The strings in the titles array are the titles that the check boxes will display.

The first statement in the init method, line 36, is a call to the buildCheckBoxPanel method, which creates a panel for the check boxes, creates the array of check boxes, adds an item listener to each element of the array, and adds each element to the panel.

After the buildCheckBoxPanel method executes, the init method creates a DrawingPanel object with the statement in line 39. Notice that the checkBoxes variable is passed to the DrawingPanel constructor. The drawingPanel object needs a reference to the array so its paintComponent method can determine which check boxes are selected and draw the corresponding shape.

The only times that the paintComponent method is automatically called is when the component is initially displayed and when the component needs to be redisplayed. In order to display a shape immediately when the user selects a check box, we need the check box item listener to force the paintComponent method to be called. This is accomplished by the statement in line 79, in the CheckBoxListener class's itemStateChanged method. This statement calls the drawingPanel object's repaint method, which causes the drawingPanel object's surface to be cleared, and then causes the object's paintComponent method to execute. Because it is in the item listener, it is executed each time the user clicks on a check box.

Checkpoint

13.18 In an AWT component, or a class that extends JApplet or JFrame, if you want to get a reference to the Graphics object, do you override the paint or paintComponent method?

13.19 In a JPanel object, do you override the paint or paintComponent method to get a reference to the Graphics object?

13.20 When are the paint or paintComponent methods called?

13.21 In the paint or paintComponent methods, what should be done before anything else?

13.22 How do you force the paint or paintComponent methods to be called?

13.23 When using a Graphics object to draw an oval, what invisible shape is the oval enclosed in?

13.24 What values are contained in the two arrays that are passed to a Graphics object's drawPolygon method?

13.25 What Graphics class methods do you use to perform the following tasks?
   a.   draw a line
   b.   draw a filled rectangle
   c.   draw a filled oval
   d.   draw a filled arc
   e.   set the drawing color
   f.   draw a rectangle
   g.   draw an oval
   h.   draw an arc
   i.   draw a string
   j.   set the font

13.6 Handling Mouse Events

CONCEPT: Java allows you to create listener classes that handle events generated by the mouse.

Handling Mouse Events

The mouse generates two types of events: mouse events and mouse motion events. To handle mouse events you create a *mouse listener* class and/or a *mouse motion listener* class. A mouse listener class can respond to any of the following events:

- The mouse button is pressed.
- The mouse button is released.
- The mouse button is clicked (pressed, then released without moving the mouse).
- The mouse cursor enters a component's screen space.
- The mouse cursor exits a component's screen space.

A mouse listener class must implement the MouseListener interface, which is in the java.awt.event package. The class must also have the methods listed in Table 13-3.

Table 13-3   Methods required by the `MouseListener` interface

Method	Description
`public void mousePressed(MouseEvent e)`	If the mouse cursor is over the component and the mouse button is pressed, this method is called.
`public void mouseClicked(MouseEvent e)`	A mouse click is defined as pressing the mouse button and releasing it without moving the mouse. If the mouse cursor is over the component and the mouse is clicked on, this method is called.
`public void mouseReleased(MouseEvent e)`	This method is called when the mouse button is released after it has been pressed. The `mousePressed` method is always called before this method.
`public void mouseEntered(MouseEvent e)`	This method is called when the mouse cursor enters the screen area belonging to the component.
`public void mouseExited(MouseEvent e)`	This method is called when the mouse cursor leaves the screen area belonging to the component.

Notice that each of the methods listed in Table 13-3 accepts a `MouseEvent` object as its argument. The `MouseEvent` object contains data about the mouse event. We will use two of the `MouseEvent` object's methods: `getX` and `getY`. These methods return the *X* and *Y* coordinates of the mouse cursor when the event occurs.

Once you create a mouse listener class, you can register it with a component using the `addMouseListener` method, which is inherited from the `Component` class. The appropriate methods in the mouse listener class are automatically called when their corresponding mouse events occur.

A mouse motion listener class can respond to the following events:

- The mouse is dragged (the button is pressed and the mouse is moved while the button is held down).
- The mouse is moved.

A mouse motion listener class must implement the `MouseMotionListener` interface, which is in the `java.awt.event` package. The class must also have the methods listed in Table 13-4. Notice that each of these methods also accepts a `MouseEvent` object as an argument.

Table 13-4 Methods required by the `MouseMotionListener` interface

Method	Description
`public void mouseDragged(MouseEvent e)`	The mouse is dragged when its button is pressed and the mouse is moved while the button is held down. This method is called when a dragging operation begins over the component. The `mousePressed` method is always called just before this method.
`public void mouseMoved(MouseEvent e)`	This method is called when the mouse cursor is over the component and it is moved.

Once you create a mouse motion listener class, you can register it with a component using the `addMouseMotionListener` method, which is inherited from the `Component` class. The appropriate methods in the mouse motion listener class are automatically called when their corresponding mouse events occur.

The `MouseEvents` class, shown in Code Listing 13-19, is an applet that demonstrates both a mouse listener and a mouse motion listener. The file *MouseEvents.html*, which is in the same source code folder as the applet class, can be used to start the applet. Figure 13-29 shows the applet running. The window displays a group of read-only text fields that represent the different mouse and mouse motion events. When an event occurs, the corresponding text field turns yellow. The last two text fields constantly display the mouse cursor's *X* and *Y* coordinates. Run this applet and experiment by clicking the mouse inside the window, dragging the mouse, moving the mouse cursor in and out of the window, and moving the mouse cursor over the text fields.

Code Listing 13-19   (`MouseEvents.java`)

```
1   import javax.swing.*;
2   import java.awt.event.*;
3   import java.awt.*;
4
5   /**
6    * This applet shows the mouse events as they occur.
7    */
8
9   public class MouseEvents extends JApplet
10  {
11     private JTextField[] mouseStates;
12     private String[] text = { "Pressed", "Clicked", "Released",
13                               "Entered", "Exited", "Dragged",
14                               "X:", "Y:" };
```

```
15
16      /**
17       * init method
18       */
19
20      public void init()
21      {
22          // Create a layout manager for the content pane.
23          setLayout(new FlowLayout());
24
25          // Create the array of text fields.
26          mouseStates = new JTextField[8];
27          for (int i = 0; i < mouseStates.length; i++)
28          {
29              // Create a text field.
30              mouseStates[i] = new JTextField(text[i], 10);
31              // Make it read-only.
32              mouseStates[i].setEditable(false);
33              // Add it to the content pane.
34              add(mouseStates[i]);
35          }
36
37          // Add a mouse listener to this applet.
38          addMouseListener(new MyMouseListener());
39
40          // Add a mouse motion listener to this applet.
41          addMouseMotionListener(new MyMouseMotionListener());
42      }
43
44      /**
45       * The clearTextFields method sets all of the text
46       * backgrounds to light gray.
47       */
48
49      public void clearTextFields()
50      {
51          for (int i = 0; i < 6; i++)
52              mouseStates[i].setBackground(Color.LIGHT_GRAY);
53      }
54
55      /**
56       * The following private inner class handles mouse events.
57       * When an event occurs, the text field for that event
58       * is given a yellow background.
59       */
60
```

```
61      private class MyMouseListener implements MouseListener
62      {
63         public void mousePressed(MouseEvent e)
64         {
65            clearTextFields();
66            mouseStates[0].setBackground(Color.YELLOW);
67         }
68
69         public void mouseClicked(MouseEvent e)
70         {
71            clearTextFields();
72            mouseStates[1].setBackground(Color.YELLOW);
73         }
74
75         public void mouseReleased(MouseEvent e)
76         {
77            clearTextFields();
78            mouseStates[2].setBackground(Color.YELLOW);
79         }
80
81         public void mouseEntered(MouseEvent e)
82         {
83            clearTextFields();
84            mouseStates[3].setBackground(Color.YELLOW);
85         }
86
87         public void mouseExited(MouseEvent e)
88         {
89            clearTextFields();
90            mouseStates[4].setBackground(Color.YELLOW);
91         }
92      }
93
94      /**
95       * The following private inner class handles mouse motion events.
96       */
97
98      private class MyMouseMotionListener
99                          implements MouseMotionListener
100     {
101        public void mouseDragged(MouseEvent e)
102        {
103           clearTextFields();
104           mouseStates[5].setBackground(Color.YELLOW);
105        }
```

```
106
107        public void mouseMoved(MouseEvent e)
108        {
109            mouseStates[6].setText("X: " + e.getX());
110            mouseStates[7].setText("Y: " + e.getY());
111        }
112    }
113 }
```

Figure 13-29   MouseEvents applet

Using Adapter Classes

Many times when you handle mouse events, you will not be interested in handling every event that the mouse generates. This is the case with the DrawBoxes applet, which handles only mouse pressed and mouse dragged events.

This applet lets you draw rectangles by pressing the mouse button and dragging the mouse inside the applet window. When you initially press the mouse button, the position of the mouse cursor becomes the upper-left corner of a rectangle. As you drag the mouse, the lower-right corner of the rectangle follows the mouse cursor. When you release the mouse cursor, the rectangle stops following the mouse. Figure 13-30 shows an example of the applet's window. You can run the applet with the *DrawBoxes.html* file, which is in the same source code folder as the applet class. Code Listing 13-20 shows the code for the DrawBoxes class.

> **NOTE:** To draw the rectangle, you must drag the mouse cursor to the right and below the position where you initially pressed the mouse button.

Figure 13-30   DrawBoxes applet

Code Listing 13-20   (DrawBoxes.java)

```
 1   import javax.swing.*;
 2   import java.awt.event.*;
 3   import java.awt.*;
 4
 5   /**
 6    * This applet demonstrates how mouse events and mouse
 7    * motion events can be handled. It lets the user draw
 8    * boxes by dragging the mouse.
 9    */
10
11   public class DrawBoxes extends JApplet
12   {
13     private int currentX = 0; // Current X coordinate
14     private int currentY = 0; // Current Y coordinate
15     private int width = 0;    // Rectangle width
16     private int height = 0;   // Rectangle height
17
18     /**
19      * init method
20      */
21
22     public void init()
23     {
24       // Add a mouse listener and a mouse motion listener.
25       addMouseListener(new MyMouseListener());
26       addMouseMotionListener(new MyMouseMotionListener());
27     }
```

```
28
29      /**
30       * paint method
31       */
32
33      public void paint(Graphics g)
34      {
35         // Call the superclass's paint method.
36         super.paint(g);
37
38         // Draw a rectangle.
39         g.drawRect(currentX, currentY, width, height);
40      }
41
42      /**
43       * Mouse listener class
44       */
45
46      private class MyMouseListener implements MouseListener
47      {
48         public void mousePressed(MouseEvent e)
49         {
50            // Get the X and Y coordinates of the mouse cursor.
51            currentX = e.getX();
52            currentY = e.getY();
53         }
54
55      /**
56       * The following methods are unused, but still
57       * required by the MouseListener interface.
58       */
59
60         public void mouseClicked(MouseEvent e)
61         {
62         }
63
64         public void mouseReleased(MouseEvent e)
65         {
66         }
67
68         public void mouseEntered(MouseEvent e)
69         {
70         }
71
72         public void mouseExited(MouseEvent e)
73         {
74         }
75      }
76
```

```
 77    /**
 78     * Mouse Motion listener class
 79     */
 80
 81    private class MyMouseMotionListener
 82                      implements MouseMotionListener
 83    {
 84       public void mouseDragged(MouseEvent e)
 85       {
 86          // Calculate the size of the rectangle.
 87          width = e.getX() - currentX;
 88          height = e.getY() - currentY;
 89
 90          // Repaint the window.
 91          repaint();
 92       }
 93
 94    /**
 95     * The following method is unused, but still
 96     * required by the MouseMotionListener interface.
 97     */
 98
 99       public void mouseMoved(MouseEvent e)
100       {
101       }
102    }
103 }
```

Notice in the mouse listener and mouse motion listener classes that several of the methods are empty. Even though the applet handles only two mouse events, the MyMouseListener and MyMouseMotionListener classes must have all of the methods required by the interfaces they implement. If any of these methods are omitted, a compiler error results.

The Java API provides an alternative technique for creating these listener classes, which eliminates the need to define empty methods for the events you are not interested in. Instead of implementing the MouseListener or MouseMotionListener interfaces, you can extend your classes from the MouseAdapter or MouseMotionAdapter classes. These classes implement the MouseListener and MouseMotionListener interfaces and provide empty definitions for all of the required methods. When you extend a class from one of these adapter classes, it inherits the empty methods. In your extended class, you can override the methods you want and forget about the others. Both the MouseAdapter and MouseMotionAdapter classes are in the java.awt.event package.

The DrawBoxes2 class shown in Code Listing 13-21 is a modification of the DrawBoxes class previously shown. In this version, the MyMouseListener class extends MouseAdapter and the MyMouseMotionListener class extends MouseMotionAdapter. This applet operates exactly the same as the DrawBoxes applet. The only difference is that this class does not have the empty methods in the listener classes.

NOTE: Java provides an adapter class for all of the interfaces in the API that have more than one method.

Code Listing 13-21   (`DrawBoxes2.java`)

```java
 1   import javax.swing.*;
 2   import java.awt.event.*;
 3   import java.awt.*;
 4
 5   /**
 6    * This applet demonstrates how the mouse adapter
 7    * classes can be used.
 8    */
 9
10   public class DrawBoxes2 extends JApplet
11   {
12      private int currentX = 0; // Current X coordinate
13      private int currentY = 0; // Current Y coordinate
14      private int width = 0;    // Rectangle width
15      private int height = 0;   // Rectangle height
16
17      /**
18       * init method
19       */
20
21      public void init()
22      {
23         // Add a mouse listener and a mouse motion listener.
24         addMouseListener(new MyMouseListener());
25         addMouseMotionListener(new MyMouseMotionListener());
26      }
27
28      /**
29       * paint method
30       */
31
32      public void paint(Graphics g)
33      {
34         // Call the superclass's paint method.
35         super.paint(g);
36
37         // Draw a rectangle.
38         g.drawRect(currentX, currentY, width, height);
39      }
40
```

```
41      /**
42       * Mouse listener class
43       */
44
45      private class MyMouseListener extends MouseAdapter
46      {
47         public void mousePressed(MouseEvent e)
48         {
49            // Get the mouse cursor's X and Y coordinates.
50            currentX = e.getX();
51            currentY = e.getY();
52         }
53      }
54
55      /**
56       * Mouse Motion listener class
57       */
58
59      private class MyMouseMotionListener
60                                    extends MouseMotionAdapter
61      {
62         public void mouseDragged(MouseEvent e)
63         {
64            // Calculate the size of the rectangle.
65            width = e.getX() - currentX;
66            height = e.getY() - currentY;
67
68            // Repaint the window.
69            repaint();
70         }
71      }
72   }
```

Checkpoint

13.26 What is the difference between a mouse press event and a mouse click event?

13.27 What interface would a listener class implement to handle a mouse click event? A mouse press event? A mouse dragged event? A mouse release event? A mouse move event?

13.28 What type of object do mouse listener and mouse motion listener methods accept? What methods do these types of objects provide for determining a mouse cursor's location?

13.29 If a class implements the MouseListener interface but does not need to use all of the methods specified by the interface, can the definitions for those methods be left out? If not, how are these methods dealt with?

13.30 What is an adapter class, and how does it make some programming tasks easier?

13.7 Timer Objects

CONCEPT: A `Timer` object regularly generates action events at programmer-specified time intervals.

`Timer` objects automatically generate action events at regular time intervals. This is useful when you want a program to perform an operation at certain times or after an amount of time has passed.

`Timer` objects are created from the `Timer` class, which is in the `javax.swing` package. Here is the general format of the `Timer` class's constructor:

```
Timer(int delay, ActionListener listener)
```

The argument passed into the *delay* parameter is the amount of time between action events, measured in milliseconds. A millisecond is a thousandth of a second, so a *delay* value of 1,000 causes an action event to be generated every second. The argument passed into the *listener* parameter is a reference to an action listener that is to be registered with the `Timer` object. If you want to add an action listener at a later time, you can pass `null` as this argument, then use the `Timer` object's `addActionListener` method to register an action listener. Table 13-5 lists the `Timer` class's methods.

Table 13-5 Timer class methods

Method	Description
void addActionListener (ActionListener *listener*)	Registers the object referenced by *listener* as an action listener.
int getDelay()	Returns the current time delay in milliseconds.
Boolean isRunning()	Returns `true` if the `Timer` object is running. Otherwise, it returns `false`.
void setDelay(int *delay*)	Sets the time delay. The argument is the amount of the delay in milliseconds.
void start()	Starts the `Timer` object, which causes it to generate action events.
void stop()	Stops the `Timer` object, which causes it to stop generating action events.

An application can use a `Timer` object to execute code automatically at regular time intervals. For example, a `Timer` object can be used to perform simple animation by moving a graphic image across the screen by a certain amount at regular time intervals. This is demonstrated in the `BouncingBall` class, shown in Code Listing 13-22. This class is an applet that displays a bouncing ball, as shown in Figure 13-31.

Figure 13-31 BouncingBall applet

Code Listing 13-22   (BouncingBall.java)

```
 1  import javax.swing.*;
 2  import java.awt.event.*;
 3  import java.awt.*;
 4
 5  /**
 6   * This applet uses a Timer object to animate a bouncing ball.
 7   */
 8
 9  public class BouncingBall extends JApplet
10  {
11     private final int X = 109;         // Ball's X coordinate
12     private final int WIDTH = 40;      // Ball's width
```

```
13      private final int HEIGHT = 40;          // Ball's height
14      private final int TIME_DELAY = 30;      // Time delay (milliseconds)
15      private final int MOVE = 20;            // Pixels to move the ball
16      private final int MINIMUM_Y = 50;       // Minimum height of ball
17      private final int MAXIMUM_Y = 400;      // Maximum height of ball
18      private int y = 400;                    // Ball's Y coordinate
19      private Timer timer;                     // Timer object
20      private boolean goingUp = true;          // Direction indicator
21
22      /**
23       * init method
24       */
25
26      public void init()
27      {
28          // Create a Timer object and register an ActionListener.
29          timer = new Timer(TIME_DELAY, new TimerListener());
30
31          // Start the timer.
32          timer.start();
33      }
34
35      /**
36       * paint method
37       */
38
39      public void paint(Graphics g)
40      {
41          // Call the superclass paint method.
42          super.paint(g);
43
44          // Set the drawing color to red.
45          g.setColor(Color.RED);
46
47          // Draw the ball.
48          g.fillOval(X, y, WIDTH, HEIGHT);
49      }
50
51      /**
52       * The "following" private inner class handles the Timer object's
53       * action events.
54       */
55
56      private class TimerListener implements ActionListener
57      {
```

```
58        public void actionPerformed(ActionEvent e)
59        {
60           // Update the ball's Y coordinate.
61           if (goingUp)
62           {
63              if (y > MINIMUM_Y)
64                 y -= MOVE;
65              else
66                 goingUp = false;
67           }
68           else
69           {
70              if (y < MAXIMUM_Y)
71                 y += MOVE;
72              else
73                 goingUp = true;
74           }
75
76           // Force a call to the paint method.
77           repaint();
78        }
79     }
80  }
```

The `BouncingBall` class's init method creates a `Timer` object with the following statement in line 29:

```
timer = new Timer(TIME_DELAY, new TimerListener());
```

This initializes the object with a time delay of 30 milliseconds (the value of `TIME_DELAY`) and registers an instance of the `TimerListener` class as an action listener. This means that once the object is started, every 30 milliseconds it generates an action event, causing the action listener's `actionPerformed` method to execute. The next statement in the `init` method, in line 32, starts the `Timer` object as follows:

```
timer.start();
```

This causes the `Timer` object to start generating action events. The `TimerListener` class's `actionPerformed` method calculates the new position of the bouncing ball and repaints the screen.

 Checkpoint

13.31 What type of events do `Timer` objects generate?

13.32 How are the time intervals between a `Timer` object's action events measured?

13.33 How do you cause a `Timer` object to begin generating action events?

13.34 How do you cause a `Timer` object to cease generating action events?

13.8 Playing Audio

CONCEPT: Sounds that have been stored in an audio file can be played from a Java program.

Java applets can play audio that is stored in a variety of popular sound file formats. The file formats directly supported are as follows:

- *.aif* or. *aiff* (Macintosh Audio File)
- *.au* (Sun Audio File)
- *.mid* or *.rmi* (MIDI File)
- *.wav* (Windows Wave File)

In order to play audio files, your computer must be equipped with a sound card and speakers. One way to play an audio file is to use the `Applet` class's `play` method. The version of the method that we will use is as follows:

```
void play(URL baseLocation, String fileName)
```

The argument passed to *baseLocation* is a URL object that specifies the location of the file. The argument passed to *fileName* is the name of the file. The sound that is recorded in the file is played one time.

When calling the `play` method, it is common to use either the `getDocumentBase` or `getCodeBase` methods, which are in the `Applet` class, to get a URL object for the first argument. The `getDocumentBase` method returns a URL object containing the location of the HTML file that invoked the applet. Here is an example of a call to the `play` method, using a call to `getDocumentBase` for the first argument:

```
play(getDocumentBase(), "mysound.wav");
```

This statement will load and play the *mysound.wav* sound file, stored at the same location as the HTML file that invoked the applet.

The `getCodeBase` method returns a URL object containing the location of the applet's *.class* file. Here is an example of its use:

```
play(getCodeBase(), "mysound.wav");
```

This statement will load and play the *mysound.wav* sound file, stored at the same location as the applet's *.class* file. The *AudioDemo1* folder, in the book's source code, contains an example applet that plays a sound file using the `play` method.

NOTE: If the sound file specified by the arguments to the play method cannot be found, no sound will be played.

Using an `AudioClip` Object

The `Applet` class's `play` method loads a sound file, plays it one time, and then releases it for garbage collection. If you need to load a sound file to be played multiple times, you should use an *AudioClip object*.

An `AudioClip` object is an object that implements the `AudioClip` interface. The `AudioClip` interface is in the `java.applet` package, and it specifies the following three methods: `play`, `loop`, and `stop`. The `play` method plays a sound one time. The `loop` method repeatedly plays a sound, and the `stop` method causes a sound to stop playing.

The `Applet` class's `getAudioClip` method can be used to create an `AudioClip` object for a given sound file as follows:

```
AudioClip getAudioClip(URL baseLocation, String fileName)
```

The argument passed to *baseLocation* is a `URL` object that specifies the location of a sound file, and the argument passed to *fileName* is the name of the file. The method returns an `AudioClip` object that can be used to play the sound file.

As before, we can use the `getDocumentBase` or `getCodeBase` method to get a `URL` object for the first argument. Here is an example of a statement that uses the `getAudioClip` method:

```
AudioClip clip = getAudioClip(getDocumentBase(), "mysound.wav");
```

This statement declares `clip` as an `AudioClip` reference variable. The object returned by the `getAudioClip` method will load the *mysound.wav* file, stored at the same location as the HTML file that invoked the applet. The address of the object will be assigned to `clip`. The following statement can then be used to play the sound file:

```
clip.play();
```

The sound file can be played repeatedly with the following statement:

```
clip.loop();
```

Any time the sound file is being played, the following statement can be used to stop it:

```
clip.stop();
```

The `AudioDemo2` class shown in Code Listing 13-23 is an applet that uses an `AudioClip` object to play a sound file. The file *AudioDemo2.html* can be used to start the applet. Figure 13-32 shows the applet running. The Play button calls the `AudioClip` object's `play` method, causing the sound file to play once. The Loop button calls the `loop` method, causing the sound file to be played repeatedly. The Stop button stops the sound file from playing. The sound file that is played is a famous NASA transmission from the Moon. NASA provides a wealth of public domain audio, video, and image files. You can find such items by going to www.nasa.gov, and then search the site using search terms such as "audio clips", "video clips", etc.

Code Listing 13-23   (`AudioDemo2.java`)

```java
1   import java.awt.*;
2   import java.applet.*;
3   import java.awt.event.*;
```

```
4   import javax.swing.*;
5
6   /**
7    * This applet uses the AudioClip class to play a
8    * sound. Sound source: NASA
9    */
10
11  public class AudioDemo2 extends JApplet
12  {
13     private JLabel credit;      // Displays NASA credit
14     private JButton playButton; // Plays the sound clip
15     private JButton loopButton; // Plays the clip in a loop
16     private JButton stopButton; // Stops the clip
17     private AudioClip sound;     // Holds the sound clip
18
19     /**
20      * init method
21      */
22
23     public void init()
24     {
25        // Create a layout manager.
26        setLayout(new FlowLayout());
27
28        // Make the credit label and add it.
29        credit = new JLabel("Audio source: NASA");
30        add(credit);
31
32        // Make the buttons and add them.
33        makeButtons();
34
35        // Get an AudioClip object for the sound file.
36        sound = getAudioClip(getDocumentBase(), "step.wav");
37     }
38
39     /**
40      * The makeButtons method creates the Play, Loop, and
41      * Stop buttons, and adds them to the content pane.
42      */
43
44     private void makeButtons()
45     {
46        // Create the Play, Loop, and Stop buttons.
47        playButton  = new JButton("Play");
48        loopButton  = new JButton("Loop");
49        stopButton  = new JButton("Stop");
50
```

```
51        // Register an action listener with each button.
52        playButton.addActionListener(new ButtonListener());
53        loopButton.addActionListener(new ButtonListener());
54        stopButton.addActionListener(new ButtonListener());
55
56        // Add the buttons to the content pane.
57        add(playButton);
58        add(loopButton);
59        add(stopButton);
60     }
61
62     /**
63      * The following private inner class handles the action event
64      * that is generated when the user clicks one of the
65      * buttons.
66      */
67
68     private class ButtonListener implements ActionListener
69     {
70        public void actionPerformed(ActionEvent e)
71        {
72           // Determine which button was clicked and
73           // perform the selected action.
74           if (e.getSource() == playButton)
75              sound.play();
76           else if (e.getSource() == loopButton)
77              sound.loop();
78           else if (e.getSource() == stopButton)
79              sound.stop();
80        }
81     }
82  }
```

Figure 13-32 AudioDemo2 applet

Playing Audio in an Application

The previous examples show how to play an audio file in an applet. You can play audio in an application as well. The process of getting a reference to an AudioClip object is different, however, in a class that does not extend JApplet. In the *Chapter 13\AudioDemo3* source code folder you will find a Swing application named *AudioFrame.java* that demonstrates how to do it. The following code segment is from the application.

```
43   // Create a file object for the step.wav file.
44   File file = new File("step.wav");
45
46   // Get a URI object for the audio file.
47   URI uri = file.toURI();
48
49   // Get a URL for the audio file.
50   URL url = uri.toURL();
51
52   // Get an AudioClip object for the sound
53   // file using the Applet class's static
54   // newAudioClip method.
55   sound = Applet.newAudioClip(url);
```

In line 44 we create a File object representing the audio file. Then, in line 47 we call the File class's toURI method to create a URI object representing the audio file. The URI class is in the java.net package. (URI stands for Uniform Resource Identifier.)

Then, in line 50 we call the URI class's toURL method to create a URL object representing the audio file. Note that if this method cannot construct a URL, it throws a checked exception—MalformedURLException. The MalformedURLException class is in the java.net package.

Last, in line 55 we call the Applet class's static newAudioClip method, passing the URL object as an argument. The method returns a reference to an AudioClip object that can be used as previously demonstrated to play the audio file.

✔ Checkpoint

13.35 What Applet method can you use to play a sound file?

13.36 What is the difference between using the Applet method asked for in Checkpoint 13.35 and using an AudioClip object to play a sound file?

13.37 What methods do an AudioClip object have? What do they do?

13.38 What is the difference between the Applet class's getDocumentBase and getCodeBase methods?

13.9 Common Errors to Avoid

The following list describes several errors that are commonly made when learning this chapter's topics.

- **Forgetting a closing tag in an HTML document.** Most HTML tags have an opening tag and a closing tag. The page will not appear properly if you forget a closing tag.
- **Confusing the `<head></head>` tag with `<h1></h1>` or another header tag.** The `<head></head>` tag marks a document's head section, whereas the `<h1></h1>` tag marks a header, which is large bold text.
- **Using X and/or Y coordinates that are outside of the component when drawing a shape.** If you use coordinates that are outside the component to draw a shape, the shape will not appear.
- **Not calling the superclass's `paint` or `paintComponent` method.** When you override the `paint` or `paintComponent` methods, the overriding method should call the superclass's version of the method before doing anything else.
- **Overriding the `paint` method with a component extended from `JComponent`.** You should override the `paint` method only with AWT components, `JFrame` components, or `JApplet` components.
- **Not calling the `repaint` method to redisplay a window.** When you update the data used to draw shapes on a component, you must call the `repaint` method to force a call to the `paint` or `paintComponent` methods.
- **Not providing empty definitions for the unneeded methods in a mouse listener or mouse motion listener class.** When writing mouse listeners or mouse motion listeners, you must provide definitions for all the methods specified by the listener interfaces. To avoid this you can write a listener as a class that inherits from an adapter class.
- **Forgetting to start a `Timer` object.** A `Timer` object does not begin generating action events until it is started with a call to its `start` method.

Review Questions and Exercises

Multiple Choice and True/False

1. This section of an HTML document contains all of the tags and text that produce output in the browser window.
   a. head
   b. content
   c. body
   d. output

2. You place the `<title></title>` tag in this section of an HTML document.
   a. head
   b. content
   c. body
   d. output

3. Everything that appears between these tags in an HTML document is the content of the Web page.
   a. `<content></content>`
   b. `<html></html>`
   c. `<head></head>`
   d. `<page></page>`

4. To create a level one header you use this tag.
   a. `<level1></level1>`
   b. `<header1></header1>`
   c. `<h1></h1>`
   d. `<head></head>`

5. When using Swing to write an applet, you extend the applet's class from this class.
   a. `Applet`
   b. `JApplet`
   c. `JFrame`
   d. `JAppletFrame`

6. When using AWT to write an applet, you extend the applet's class from this class.
   a. `Applet`
   b. `JApplet`
   c. `JFrame`
   d. `JAppletFrame`

7. This applet method is invoked instead of a constructor.
   a. `startUp`
   b. `beginApplet`
   c. `invoke`
   d. `init`

8. The Sun JDK comes with this program, which loads and executes an applet without the need for a Web browser.
   a. `applettest`
   b. `appletload`
   c. `appletviewer`
   d. `viewapplet`

9. A class that inherits from `Applet` or `Frame` does not have one of these.
   a. an add method
   b. an `init` method
   c. a content pane
   d. a layout manager

10. What location on a component usually has the coordinates (0, 0)?
   a. upper-right corner
   b. upper-left corner
   c. center
   d. lower-right corner

11. In a class that extends `JApplet` or `JFrame` you override this method to get a reference to the `Graphics` object.
    a. `paint`
    b. `paintComponent`
    c. `getGraphics`
    d. `graphics`

12. In a class that extends `JPanel` you override this method to get a reference to the `Graphics` object.
    a. `paint`
    b. `paintComponent`
    c. `getGraphics`
    d. `graphics`

13. The `drawLine` method is a member of this class.
    a. `JApplet`
    b. `Applet`
    c. `JFrame`
    d. `Graphics`

14. To force the `paint` method to be called to update a component's display, you _____.
    a. call the `paint` method
    b. call the `repaint` method
    c. call the `paintAgain` method
    d. do nothing; you cannot force the `paint` method to be called

15. A class that implements this interface can handle mouse-dragged events.
    a. `MouseListener`
    b. `ActionListener`
    c. `MouseMotionListener`
    d. `MouseDragListener`

16. A class that implements this interface can handle mouse-click events.
    a. `MouseListener`
    b. `ActionListener`
    c. `MouseMotionListener`
    d. `MouseDragListener`

17. This `MouseEvent` method returns the X coordinate of the mouse cursor at the moment the mouse event is generated.
    a. `getXCoord`
    b. `getMouseX`
    c. `getPosition`
    d. `getX`

18. If a class implements a standard API interface that specifies more than one method but does not need many of the methods, this should be used instead of the interface.
    a. your own detailed versions of the needed methods
    b. an adapter class
    c. a different interface
    d. there is no other choice

19. A `Timer` object's time delay between events is specified in this unit of time.
    a. seconds
    b. microseconds
    c. milliseconds
    d. minutes

20. A `Timer` object generates this type of event.
    a. action events
    b. timer events
    c. item events
    d. interval events

21. The following `Applet` class method returns a `URL` object with the location of the HTML file that invoked the applet.
    a. `getHTMLlocation`
    b. `getDocumentBase`
    c. `getAppletBase`
    d. `getCodeBase`

22. The following `Applet` class method returns a `URL` object with the location of the applet's *.class* file.
    a. `getHTMLlocation`
    b. `getDocumentBase`
    c. `getAppletBase`
    d. `getCodeBase`

23. **True or False:** Applets cannot create files on the user's system.

24. **True or False:** Applets can read files on the user's system.

25. **True or False:** Applets cannot make network connections with any system except the server from which the applet was transmitted.

26. **True or False:** Applets can retrieve information about the user's system or the user's identity.

27. **True or False:** The `<H6>` tag produces larger text than the `<H1>` tag.

28. **True or False:** You use a static `main` method to create an instance of an applet class.

29. **True or False:** In a class that extends `JApplet`, you add components to the content pane.

30. **True or False:** In an applet, events are handled differently than in a GUI application.

31. **True or False:** An object of the `Frame` class does not have a content pane.

32. **True or False:** In an overriding `paint` method, you should never call the superclass's version of the `paint` method.

33. **True or False:** Once a `Timer` object has been started, it cannot be stopped without shutting down the program.

34. **True or False:** The `Applet` class's play method loads and plays an audio file once and then releases the memory it occupies for garbage collection.

35. **True or False:** The `loop` and `stop` methods, for use with audio files, are part of the `Applet` class.

Find the Error

Find the errors in the following code:

1. ```
   <applet code="MyApplet.java" width=100 height=50>
   </applet>
   ```

2. ```
   public void paint(Graphics g)
   {
       drawLine(0, 0, 100, 100);
   }
   ```

3. ```
   // Force a call to the paint method.
   paint();
   ```

4. ```
   public class MyPanel extends JPanel
   {
       public MyPanel()
       {
           // Constructor code...
       }

       public void paint(Graphics g)
       {
           // paint method code...
       {
   }
   ```

5. ```
   private class MyMouseListener implements MouseListener
   {
       public void mouseClicked(MouseEvent e)
       {
           mouseClicks += 1;
       }
   }
   ```

6. ```
   private class MyMouseListener implements MouseAdapter
   {
       public void mouseClicked(MouseEvent e)
       {
           mouseClicks += 1;
       }
   }
   ```

Algorithm Workbench

1. Write the text and HTML tags necessary to display "My Home Page" as a level one header, centered in the browser window.

2. You have written an applet and saved the source code in a file named *MyApplet.java*. Write the HTML tag needed to execute the applet in an area that is 300 pixels wide by 200 pixels high. Assume that the compiled applet code is stored in the same directory as the HTML document.

3. Look at the following GUI application class and indicate by line number the changes that should be made to convert this to an applet using Swing:

```
1   public class SimpleWindow extends JFrame
2   {
3       public SimpleWindow()
4       {
5           // Set the title.
6           setTitle("A Simple Window");
7
8           // Specify what happens when the close button is clicked.
9           setDefaultCloseOperation(JFrame.EXIT_ON_CLOSE);
10
11          // Add a label.
12          JLabel label = new JLabel("This is a simple window.");
13          add(label);
14
15          // Pack and display the window.
16          pack();
17          setVisible(true);
18      }
19  }
```

4. Assume that g references a Graphics object. Write code that performs the following:
   a. Draws an outline of a rectangle that is 100 pixels wide by 200 pixels high, with its upper-left corner at (50, 75).
   b. Draws a filled rectangle that is 300 pixels wide by 100 pixels high, with its upper-left corner at (10, 90).
   c. Draws a blue outline of an oval with an enclosing rectangle that is 100 pixels wide by 50 pixels high, with its upper-left corner at (10, 25).
   d. Draws a red line from (0, 5) to (150, 175).
   e. Draws the string "Greetings Earthling". The lower-left point of the string should be at (80, 99). Use a bold, 20-point serif font.
   f. Draws a polygon with vertices at the following points: (10, 10), (10, 25), (50, 25), and (50, 10). What shape does this code result in?

5. Rewrite the following mouse motion listener so it uses an adapter class:

```
private class MyMouseMotionListener implements MouseMotionListener
{
    public void mouseDragged(MouseEvent e)
    {
    }

    public void mouseMoved(MouseEvent e)
    {
        mouseMovments += 1;
    }
}
```

6. Assume that a class has an inner class named `MyTimerListener` that can be used to handle the events generated by a `Timer` object. Write code that creates a `Timer` object with a time delay of one half second. Register an instance of `MyTimerListener` with the class.

Short Answer

1. When a user accesses a Web page on a remote server with his or her browser, and that Web page has an applet associated with it, is the applet executed by the server or by the user's system?

2. List at least three security restrictions imposed on applets.

3. Why are applets sometimes necessary in Web page development?

4. Why isn't it necessary to call the `setVisible` method to display an applet?

5. Why would you ever need to use the older AWT library instead of Swing to develop an applet?

6. A panel is 600 pixels wide by 400 pixels high. What are the X and Y coordinates of the pixel in the upper-left corner? The upper-right corner? The lower-left corner? The lower-right corner? The center of the panel?

7. When is a component's `paint` or `paintComponent` method called?

8. What is an adapter class? How does it make some programming tasks more convenient? Under what circumstances does the Java API provide an adapter class?

9. Under what circumstances would you want to use an `AudioClip` object to play a sound file, rather than the `Applet` class's play method?

Programming Challenges

1. `FollowMe` Applet

VideoNote
The House
Applet
Problem

Write an applet that initially displays the word "Hello" in the center of a window. The word should follow the mouse cursor when it is moved inside the window.

2. `House` Applet

Write an applet that draws the house shown on the left in Figure 13-33. When the user clicks on the door or windows, they should close. The figure on the right shows the house with its door and windows closed.

Figure 13-33   House drawing

House with door and windows open.   House with door and windows closed.

3. `WatchMe` **Applet**

Write an applet that displays a drawing of two eyes in the center of its window. When the mouse cursor is not inside the window, the eyes should look ahead. When the mouse cursor is inside the window, the eyes should follow the cursor. This is illustrated in Figure 13-34.

Figure 13-34 Eyes following the mouse cursor

Mouse not in the window,
eyes looking ahead.

Mouse below the eyes,
eyes looking down.

Mouse above the eyes,
eyes looking up.

Mouse to the left of the eyes,
eyes looking left.

Mouse to the right of the eyes,
eyes looking right.

4. Thermometer Applet

Write an applet that displays a thermometer. The user should be able to control the temperature with a slider component. When the user moves the slider, the thermometer should show the corresponding temperature.

5. Polygon Drawer

Write an applet that lets the user click on six points. After the sixth point is clicked, the applet should draw a polygon with a vertex at each point the user clicked.

6. `GridFiller` **Applet**

Write an applet that displays a 4×4 grid. When the user clicks on a square in the grid, the applet should draw a filled circle in it. If the square already has a circle, clicking on it should cause the circle to disappear.

7. `DrinkMachine` **Applet**

Write an applet that simulates a soft drink vending machine. The simulated machine dispenses the following soft drinks: cola, lemon-lime soda, grape soda, root beer, and bottled water. These drinks cost $0.75 each to purchase.

When the applet starts, the drink machine should have a supply of 20 of each of the drinks. The applet should have a text field where the user can enter the amount of money he or she is giving the machine. The user can then click on a button to select a drink to dispense. The applet should also display the amount of change it is giving back to the user. The applet should keep track of its inventory of drinks and inform the user if he or she has selected a drink that is out of stock. Be sure to handle operator errors such as selecting a drink with no money entered and selecting a drink with an inadequate amount of money entered.

8. Stopwatch Applet

Write an applet that simulates a stopwatch. It should have a Start button and a Stop button. When the Start button is clicked, the applet should count the seconds that pass. When the Stop button is clicked, the applet should stop counting seconds.

9. Slideshow Application

Write an application that displays a slideshow of images, one after the other, with a time delay between each image. The user should be able to select up to 10 images for the slide show and specify the time delay in seconds.

Creating GUI Applications with JavaFX

14

TOPICS

14.1 Introduction
14.2 Scene Graphs
14.3 Using Scene Builder to Create JavaFX Applications

14.4 Writing the Application Code
14.5 RadioButtons and CheckBoxes
14.6 Displaying Images
14.7 Common Errors to Avoid

14.1 Introduction

CONCEPT: In Java, you can use the JavaFX library to create GUI and graphical applications. JavaFX is the next generation GUI toolkit for Java developers.

In this chapter we discuss the basics of creating a Java application with a *graphical user interface* or *GUI* (pronounced "gooey") using JavaFX. *JavaFX* is a standard Java library for developing rich applications that employ graphics. It is fully integrated into Java, beginning with Java 7. You can use it to create GUI applications, as well as applications that display 2D and 3D graphics. You can use JavaFX to create standalone graphics applications that run on your local computer, applications that run from a remote server, or applications that are embedded in a Web page. This chapter introduces you to JavaFX as a tool for creating standalone GUI applications.

Compared with Swing (which is covered in Chapters 11 and 12), JavaFX is a relatively new part of the Java library. Although JavaFX does not replace Swing, it is the next generation of GUI toolkit for Java.

NOTE: It is not required that you read Chapters 11 and 12 before reading this chapter. This book is designed so you can choose either approach: Swing or JavaFX. If you have already read Chapter 11, you can skip the rest of this section, and jump directly to Section 14.2.

A GUI is a graphical window or a system of graphical windows presented by an application for interaction with the user. In addition to accepting input from the keyboard, GUIs typically accept input from a mouse, or a touch screen.

A window in a GUI commonly consists of several *components* that present data to the user and/or allow interaction with the application. Some of the common GUI components are Buttons, Labels, TextFields, CheckBoxes, and RadioButtons. Figure 14-1 shows an example of a window with a variety of components. Table 14-1 describes the components that appear in the window.

Figure 14-1 Various GUI components

Table 14-1 Some GUI components

Component	Description
AnchorPane	A container for other components. The components that are contained inside an AnchorPane can be "anchored" at a certain distance from one or more of the AnchorPane's edges.
Button	A button that can cause an action to occur when it is clicked.
CheckBox	A component that has a box that may be checked or unchecked.
ComboBox	A component that displays a drop-down list of items from which the user may select. A ComboBox also provides a TextField in which the user may type input. It is called a ComboBox because it can behave as the combination of a list and a TextField.
Label	An area that can display text.
List	A list from which the user may select an item.
RadioButton	A component that can be either selected or deselected. RadioButtons usually appear in groups and allow the user to select one of several options.
Slider	A component that allows the user to select a value by moving a slider along a track.
TextField	An area in which the user may type a single line of input from the keyboard.
TitledPane	A container for other components. A TitledPane has a title bar at its top, in which a title can be displayed. A TitledPane may also be closed or opened.

Event-Driven Programming

Programs that operate in a GUI environment must be *event-driven*. An *event* is an action that takes place within a program, such as the clicking of a button. Part of writing a GUI application is creating event listeners. An *event listener* is a method that automatically executes when a specific event occurs. If you wish for an application to perform an operation when a particular event occurs, you must create an event listener that responds when that event takes place.

Checkpoint

14.1   What is a GUI?

14.2   What is JavaFX?

14.3   What is a component?

14.4   What is an event? What is an event listener?

14.2 Scene Graphs

> **CONCEPT:** A scene graph is a tree-like hierarchical data structure that is used to organize the components in a JavaFX GUI.

In JavaFX, the components that are in a GUI are organized as a scene graph. A *scene graph* is a tree-like, hierarchical data structure that contains nodes. Figure 14-2 shows an example.

Figure 14-2   Nodes in a scene graph

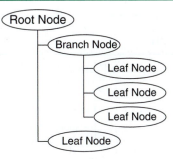

A scene graph can have three types of nodes:

- *Root Node*: The scene graph can have only one root node, which is the parent of all the other nodes in the scene graph. It is the first node in the structure.
- *Branch Node*: A branch node can have other nodes as children.
- *Leaf Node*: A leaf node cannot have children.

In a nutshell, the root node and branch nodes can have children, but leaf nodes cannot. But, how does that relate to components in a GUI? In JavaFX, a node that can have children is a *container*. It is a component that can hold other components inside of it. The JavaFX library provides several different types of containers. The AnchorPane container (which was described in Table 14-1) is commonly used as a GUI's root node.

A branch node is a container that is placed inside the root node or inside another branch node. For example, you might have a Pane (one of the simplest JavaFX containers) inside of an AnchorPane. A leaf node is a component that is not a container. For example, Button components and Label components are leaf nodes.

For example, look at the GUI shown in Figure 14-3. The outermost container is an AnchorPane. Inside the AnchorPane are a Pane and a Button. Inside the Pane are a Label and two RadioButton components. The scene graph that describes this GUI appears in Figure 14-4. Notice the following characteristics of the scene graph:

- The AnchorPane is the root node.
- The Pane is a branch node, and the Button is a leaf node.
- The Label and RadioButton components are leaf nodes, inside the Pane.

Figure 14-3 Example GUI

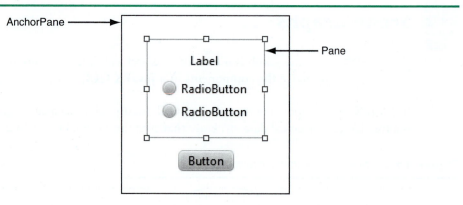

Figure 14-4 Example scene graph

Figure 14-5 shows a more complex GUI in the left image. It has:

- An AnchorPane, which is the root node
- A TitledPane, which is a child of the AnchorPane (it is contained inside the AnchorPane)
- Another AnchorPane, which is a child of the TitledPane (it is contained inside the TitledPane)
- Three RadioButtons, which are children of the innermost AnchorPane
- A Button that is a child of the root node AnchorPane.

The image on the right shows how the GUI's scene graph is organized. The AnchorPane is the root node. It has two children: the TitledPane and the Button.

Figure 14-5 A more complex GUI and its scene graph

 Checkpoint

14.5   What is a scene graph?

14.6   What are the three types of nodes in a scene graph?

14.7   What type of scene graph node can have children? What type cannot?

14.3 Using Scene Builder to Create JavaFX Applications

CONCEPT: Scene Builder is a free design tool from Oracle for visually creating GUIs.

You can write a JavaFX GUI application using nothing but Java code. The process is similar to the way you write Swing applications. As an alternative, Oracle provides a free design tool named *Scene Builder* that you can use to visually create a GUI. It works like this: You use Scene Builder to construct a GUI by dragging and dropping the components that you need onto a blank window. You visually arrange the components on the window and set various component properties to create the appearance that you want for the GUI. Then, you save the GUI to an FXML file.

FXML is a markup language that describes the components in a JavaFX scene graph. FXML uses tags to organize data, in a manner similar to the way that HTML uses tags to format text in a Web browser. If you know anything about HTML (there is a brief introduction to HTML in Chapter 13), you can probably look at the contents of an FXML file and understand how it describes a scene graph. For example, the following FXML describes the GUI shown in Figure 14-6:

```
<?xml version="1.0" encoding="UTF-8"?>

<?import java.lang.*?>
<?import java.util.*?>
<?import javafx.scene.control.*?>
<?import javafx.scene.layout.*?>
<?import javafx.scene.paint.*?>
```

```
<AnchorPane id="AnchorPane" maxHeight="-Infinity" maxWidth="-Infinity"
        minHeight="-Infinity" minWidth="-Infinity" prefHeight="130.0"
        prefWidth="173.0" xmlns:fx="http://javafx.com/fxml/1"
        xmlns="http://javafx.com/javafx/2.2">
  <children>
    <Label fx:id="myLabel" layoutX="53.0" layoutY="31.0"
        text="Hello World!" />
    <Button fx:id="myButton" layoutX="53.0" layoutY="80.0"
        mnemonicParsing="false" text="Click Me" />
  </children>
</AnchorPane>
```

Figure 14-6 Simple GUI

In this book, we will not modify the FXML files that Scene Builder creates. However, once you understand the contents of an FXML file, you can open it in a text editor and make changes to it to tweak the appearance of your GUI.

Visually creating a GUI with Scene Builder is only part of the process. Once you save a GUI's scene graph to an FXML file, the next step is to write Java code that reads the FXML file and displays the GUI on the screen and handles any events that occur while the application is running. In this section, we will introduce Scene Builder. In the next section, we discuss the Java code that you need to write to make a JavaFX application work.

Starting Scene Builder

You can download Scene Builder from the following location:

```
www.oracle.com/technetwork/java/javafx/downloads/
```

When you install Scene Builder in Windows, a shortcut is automatically created on the desktop. You can launch Scene Builder either by double-clicking the shortcut, or by going to *All Programs > JavaFX Scene Builder* and clicking *JavaFX Scene Builder x.x* (where *x.x* will be a version number such as 1.1 or 2.0).

If you installed Scene Builder on a Mac, go to the Applications folder and double-click the shortcut for *JavaFX Scene Builder x.x* (where *x.x* will be a version number such as 1.1 or 2.0).

The Scene Builder Main Window

The Scene Builder main window consists of a number of screen elements that you will use on a regular basis. Figure 14-7 shows the main window, with the locations of its panels.

Figure 14-7 The Scene Builder main window

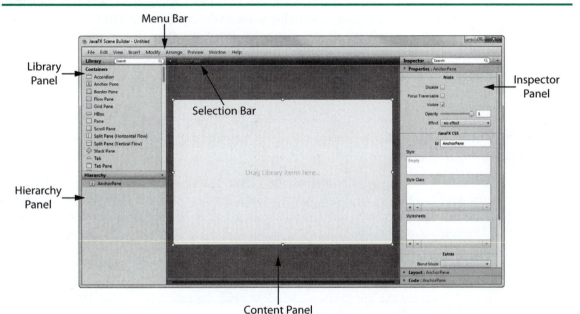

Here is a brief summary of each part of the main window:

- *Menu Bar*: Scene Builder's commands are located on the menus that access the menu bar at the top of the main window.
- *Library Panel*: The Library Panel provides a list of JavaFX components that you can use in an application. To place a component in a GUI, you simply drag it from the Library Panel, and drop it into the Content Panel.
- *Content Panel*: The Content Panel is where you visually design an application's GUI. It initially shows an AnchorPane as the GUI's root node. You create other components in the GUI by dragging them from the Library Panel and dropping them onto the root node component.
- *Hierarchy Panel*: The Hierarchy Panel shows the GUI's scene graph. As you add components to the Content Panel, nodes appear in the Hierarchy Panel. You can use the Hierarchy Panel to select nodes that you want to edit.
- *Selection Bar*: This area of the screen shows the hierarchical path of the currently selected node in the scene graph.

VideoNote

Using Scene
Builder to
Create the
Kilometer
Converter GUI

- *Inspector Panel*: The Inspector Panel is divided into three sections: Properties, Layout, and Code. The *Properties section* allows you to view and edit the values of the selected component's properties, which are values that determine the component's appearance. The *Layout section* lets you specify values that control the way the component is displayed when the GUI's window is resized. The *Code section* allows you to assign an `fx:id` to a component, which is similar to assigning a variable name to the component. The Code section also allows you to designate event handlers to execute when specific events happen to the selected component.

To get started with Scene Builder, perform the steps in the following tutorial.

Tutorial 14-1:
Using Scene Builder to Create the Kilometer Converter GUI

In this tutorial, and the next two, you will create the Kilometer Converter application. When the application is complete, it will present a window in which the user will be able to enter a distance in kilometers, and then click on a button to see that distance converted to miles. The conversion formula is:

$$Miles = Kilometers \times 0.6214$$

Figure 14-8 shows how the completed Kilometer Converter application will work. The image on the left shows the application's window after the user has entered 1000 as the distance in kilometers. The image on the right shows the window after the user has clicked the *Convert to Miles* button, and the distance is displayed, converted to miles.

Figure 14-8 The Kilometer Converter application

In this tutorial you will use Scene Builder to create the application's GUI. As shown in Figure 14-9, you will use the following components:

- An AnchorPane, as the root node
- A Label to display the prompt *Enter a distance in kilometers:*
- A TextField in which the user will enter a distance
- A Label to display a message showing the distance converted to miles
- A Button that performs the conversion

Figure 14-9 The GUI components

Step 1: Start Scene Builder. A new user interface project is started, and an AnchorPane is automatically created in the Content panel as shown in Figure 14-10. The AnchorPane is the root node in the scene graph.

Figure 14-10 A new user interface with an AnchorPane automatically created

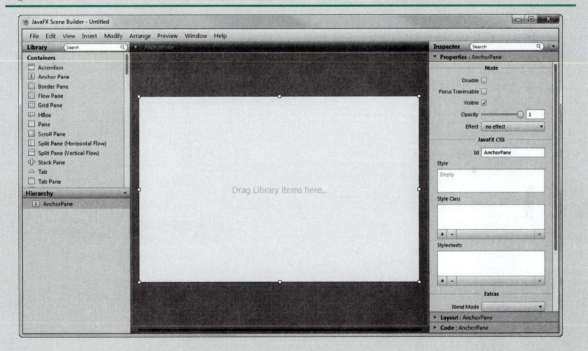

Step 2: The AnchorPane's default size is 600 pixels wide by 400 pixels high, which is too large for the application. You want to make the AnchorPane much smaller than it currently is. There are two ways to resize a component in Scene Builder:

- The first way to resize a component is with the component's sizing handles. When a component is selected in the Content panel, sizing handles appear along the component's edges. Figure 14-11 shows an example. When you position the mouse cursor over a sizing handle, the cursor changes to a two-headed arrow (⟺). When the mouse cursor becomes a two-headed arrow, you can click and drag the mouse to resize the component.

Figure 14-11 A resizing handle

Resizing Handle

- The second way to resize a component is with the Layout section of the Inspector panel. Make sure the Inspector panel's sections are displayed by clicking the dropdown arrow shown in Figure 14-12 and confirming that View Sections is selected. Then, click the Layout section to open it, and as shown in Figure 14-13, change the *Pref Width* and *Pref Height* fields to the desired width and height.

Use one of these techniques to resize the AnchorPane to 280 pixels wide by 135 pixels high, as shown in Figure 14-14.

Figure 14-12 Make sure View Sections is selected

Figure 14-13   Changing a component's width and height in the Layout section

Open the Layout section.

Change the preferred width
and preferred height to the
desired values.

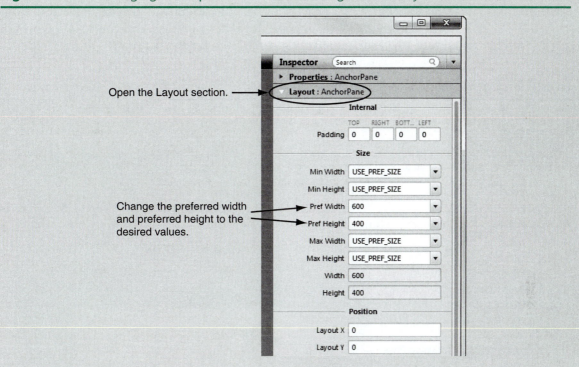

Figure 14-14   The resized AnchorPane

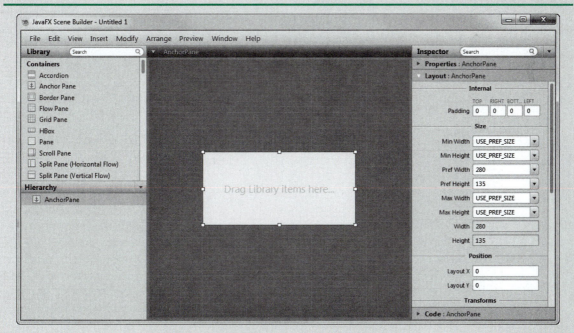

Step 3: Now you will create the Label that prompts the user to enter a distance in kilometers. The Library panel is divided into several different groups. Scroll down until you see the *Controls* group, and then find the Label control. As shown in Figure 14-15, drag the Label control onto the AnchorPane.

Figure 14-15 Dragging a Label component to the AnchorPane

Step 4: The text that is displayed by a Label component is determined by the Label's Text property. When you change the value of the component's Text property, you change the text that it displays. The Label component that you created in Step 3 currently displays the word *Label*. You need to change this to *Enter the distance in kilometers:*. With the component selected in the Content panel (as shown in Figure 14-16) open the Properties section of the Inspector panel and locate the Text property. Change the value of the Text property to *Enter the distance in kilometers:* as shown in Figure 14-17. Notice that when you change the Label's Text property, the text that it displays on the AnchorPane changes accordingly.

TIP: A quick way to change a Label's Text property is to double-click the component in the Content panel, and edit the text.

Figure 14-16   Locating the Label's Text property

Figure 14-17   The Label's Text property changed

Step 5: Now you will assign an `fx:id` to the Label component. An `fx:id` is a name that identifies a component in the FXML file that you will generate when you save your GUI. The component's `fx:id` will also become a variable name that you can use later in the Java code that you will write to run the application.

With the Label component selected in the Content panel (as shown in Figure 14-18) open the Code section of the Inspector panel, and locate the `fx:id` field. Change the value of the `fx:id` field to `promptLabel` as shown in Figure 14-18.

Figure 14-18 The Label's `fx:id` changed

Step 6: If necessary, reposition the Label component so it is in the upper-left area of the AnchorPane, as shown in Figure 14-19. (To move the component, simply click and drag it with the mouse.)

Figure 14-19 The Label repositioned

Step 7: Now you will create the TextField component in which the user will enter a distance in kilometers. In the Library panel you will find Text Field listed in the Controls group. As shown in Figure 14-20, drag the Text Field component onto the AnchorPane. (Drop the Text Field anywhere on the AnchorPane. You will resize it and move it in the next step.)

Figure 14-20   Dragging a Text Field to the AnchorPane

> **Step 8:** With the TextField component selected, use its sizing handles to resize it, and then drag the component approximately to the position shown in Figure 14-21.

Figure 14-21   The TextField component resized and repositioned

> **Step 9:** Now you will assign an `fx:id` to the TextField component. With the TextField component selected in the Content panel (as shown in Figure 14-22) open the Code section of the Inspector panel, and locate the `fx:id` field. Change the value of the `fx:id` field to `kilometerTextField` as shown in Figure 14-22.

Figure 14-22 The Label's `fx:id` changed

Step 10: Now you will create the Label component that will display the output message when the user clicks the *Convert to Miles* button. Perform the following:

- Drag a Label component from the Library panel (in the Controls section) onto the AnchorPane.
- With the Label selected, open the Properties section of the Inspector panel, and delete the contents of the Text property. (This causes the Label to display no text.)
- Resize and reposition the Label component similar to that shown in Figure 14-23.

Figure 14-23 The Label created, resized, and repositioned

- With the Label selected, open the Code section of the Inspector panel, and change the `fx:id` field to `outputLabel`.

Step 11: Now you will create the Button component that will convert the user's input to miles. Perform the following:

- Drag a Button component from the Library panel (in the Controls section) onto the AnchorPane.
- With the Button selected, open the Properties section of the Inspector panel, and change the Text property to *Convert to Miles*.
- Resize and reposition the Label component similar to that shown in Figure 14-24.
- With the Button selected, open the Code section of the Inspector panel, and change the `fx:id` field to `convertButton`.

Figure 14-24   The Button created, resized, and repositioned

Step 12: Notice that the Hierarchy panel, shown in Figure 14-25, displays the components that you have added to the GUI's scene graph. Clicking on a component in the Hierarchy panel selects that component in the Content panel.

If you want to see each component's `fx:id` in the Hierarchy panel, click the down-arrow that appears at the top of the panel, and select *Show fx:id*. The image on the left in Figure 14-26 shows an example. The image on the right in Figure 14-26 shows the Hierarchy panel with the `fx:ids` displayed.

Figure 14-25 The Hierarchy panel

Figure 14-26 Showing component `fx:ids` in the Hierarchy panel

Step 13: Now you will save the GUI as an FXML file. On the menu bar, click File, then click Save As . . . Select a location on your system, and save the file as KilometerConverter.fxml. (Remember where you save the file. You will need to save some Java files in the same location in the next two tutorials.)

Step 14: Although you haven't written the application's Java code yet, you can preview the way the GUI will appear. On the menu bar, click Preview, then click Show Preview in Window. You will see the preview window appear, as shown in Figure 14-27. Close the preview window. You will resume building the application in the next tutorial.

Figure 14-27 The GUI displayed in a preview window

Checkpoint

14.8 What is FXML?

14.9 What type of file does Scene Builder save a GUI to?

14.10 Which Scene Builder panel provides a list of JavaFX components?

14.11 Which Scene Builder panel do you use to visually design an application's GUI?

14.12 Which Scene Builder panel shows the scene graph?

14.13 Which Scene Builder panel allows you to work with a component's properties, layout, and code?

14.14 What is an `fx:id`?

14.4 Writing the Application Code

CONCEPT: Once you have saved an application's GUI to an FXML file, you can write the Java code that runs the application. A simple JavaFX application uses a main application class, and a controller class.

The Main Application Class

Once you have created a GUI with Scene Builder, and saved it to an FXML file, you need to write a Java class that performs the following:

- Loads the FXML file
- Builds the scene graph in memory
- Displays the GUI

We will refer to this class as the *main application class*. Code Listing 14-1 shows the main application class for the Kilometer Converter application.

Code Listing 14-1   `(KilometerConverter.java)`

```
1   import javafx.application.Application;
2   import javafx.fxml.FXMLLoader;
3   import javafx.scene.Parent;
4   import javafx.scene.Scene;
5   import javafx.stage.Stage;
6
7   public class KilometerConverter extends Application
8   {
9      public void start(Stage stage) throws Exception
10     {
11        // Load the FXML file.
12        Parent parent = FXMLLoader.load(
13                getClass().getResource("KilometerConverter.fxml"));
14
15        // Build the scene graph.
16        Scene scene = new Scene(parent);
17
18        // Display our window, using the scene graph.
19        stage.setTitle("Kilometer Converter");
20        stage.setScene(scene);
21        stage.show();
22     }
23
24     public static void main(String[] args)
25     {
26        // Launch the application.
27        launch(args);
28     }
29  }
```

VideoNote

Learning More About the Main Application Class

Let's take a closer look at the code:

- Lines 1 through 5 import the necessary JavaFX classes.
- The class declaration begins in line 7. The name of the class is `KilometerConverter`, and it extends the `Application` class. (The `Application` class is an abstract class in the JavaFX library. It is in the `javafx.application` package.)
- The `start` method appears in lines 9 through 22. This is the main entry point for the application. The `start` method is an abstract method in the `Application` class, and we must override it. Notice that the method has a parameter named `stage`. The `stage` variable will reference the window that the GUI will be displayed in.
  - Lines 12 through 13 load the KilometerConverter.fxml file.
  - Line 16 creates the scene graph in memory. The root node is referenced by the scene variable.

- Line 19 sets the text that will be displayed in the window's title bar.
- Line 20 specifies the scene graph that is to be displayed in the window.
- Line 21 displays the application's window.
- The main method appears in lines 24 through 28. Line 27 calls the launch method (which is inherited from the Application class) to launch the application.

All of the main application classes that you will see in this chapter will look like Code Listing 14-1, except the name of the class (in line 7), the name of the FXML file (in line 13), and the text that is displayed in the window's title bar (line 19) will be different.

In the following tutorial you will write and test the main application class for the Kilometer Converter application.

Tutorial 14-2:

Writing the Main Application Class For the Kilometer Converter GUI

VideoNote

Writing the Main Application Class For the Kilometer Converter GUI

Step 1: Open your Java editor and create a new source code file named KilometerConverter.java.

Step 2: Type the code for the `KilometerConverter` class exactly as it is shown in Code Listing 14-1.

Step 3: Save the KilometerConverter.java file in the same location as the KilometerConverter.fxml file that you created in the previous tutorial.

Step 4: Compile the KilometerConverter.java file, and run it. You should see the window shown in Figure 14-28. At this point the application only displays the GUI. Although you can type input into the TextField, the application does nothing when you click the *Convert to Miles* button. That is because you have not written an event handler that will execute when the button is clicked. You will write an event handler for the Button component in the next tutorial.

Figure 14-28   The Kilometer Converter application

The Controller Class

The main application class is responsible for building the scene graph and displaying the GUI. The *controller class* is responsible for handling events that occur while the application is running. The controller class contains the following items:

- The necessary import statements
- Private variables to reference the components that have an fx:id in the scene graph
- An initialize method that is automatically called after the FXML file is loaded
- Event listener methods

Code Listing 14-2 shows the controller class for the Kilometer Converter application.

Code Listing 14-2   (`KilometerConverterController.java`)

```
 1  import javafx.fxml.FXML;
 2  import javafx.scene.control.Button;
 3  import javafx.scene.control.Label;
 4  import javafx.scene.control.TextField;
 5
 6  public class KilometerConverterController
 7  {
 8     @FXML
 9     private Button convertButton;
10
11     @FXML
12     private TextField kilometerTextField;
13
14     @FXML
15     private Label outputLabel;
16
17     @FXML
18     private Label promptLabel;
19
20     // This method is called when the FXML file is loaded
21     public void initialize()
22     {
23        // Perform any necessary initialization here.
24     }
25
26     // Event listener for the convertButton
27     public void convertButtonListener()
28     {
29        final double CONVERSION_FACTOR = 0.6214;
30
31        // Get the kilometers from the TextField.
32        String str = kilometerTextField.getText();
33
```

```
34          // Convert kilometers to miles.
35          double miles = Double.parseDouble(str) * CONVERSION_FACTOR;
36
37          // Display the converted distance.
38          outputLabel.setText(str + " kilometers is " + miles + " miles.");
39      }
40  }
```

Let's take a closer look at the code:

VideoNote
Learning More
About the
Controller
Class

- Lines 1 through 4 import the necessary JavaFX classes:
  - Line 1 imports `javafx.fxml.FXML`, which is necessary to make the connection between the controller class and the application's FXML file.
  - Line 2 imports the `javafx.scene.control.Button` class. This is the class for the Button component.
  - Line 3 imports the `javafx.scene.control.Label` class. This is the class for the Label component.
  - Line 4 imports the `javafx.scene.control.TextField` class. This is the class for the TextField component.
- The class declaration begins in line 6. The name of the class is `KilometerConvertercontroller`.
- Lines 8 through 18 declare private field variables for the GUI components. The names of the variables are the same as the components' `fx:id`s. Specifically:
  - Line 9 declares the `convertButton` variable to reference the Button component. Recall that you assigned `convertButton` as the component's `fx:id` in Scene Builder.
  - Line 12 declares the `kilometerTextField` variable to reference the TextField component. Recall that you assigned `kilometerTextField` as the component's `fx:id` in Scene Builder.
  - Line 15 declares the `outputLabel` variable to reference the Label component that will display the converted distance. Recall that you assigned `outputLabel` as the component's `fx:id` in Scene Builder.
  - Line 18 declares the `promptLabel` variable to reference the Label component that will prompt the user to enter a distance. Recall that you assigned `promptLabel` as the component's `fx:id` in Scene Builder.

    Notice that each of the field declarations is preceded with a line that reads *@FXML*. (See lines 8, 11, 14, and 17.) This is a special *annotation* that must precede any nonpublic field declaration or nonpublic method definition that is used by the FXML file.
- The `initialize` method appears in lines 21 through 24. This method is automatically called as soon as the FXML file is loaded. If you have any initialization code to write, you write it in the `initialize` method.
- The `convertButtonListener` method appears in lines 27 through 39. This method is the event listener for the Button component. Here are some details about the method:
  - Line 29 declares a constant named `CONVERSION_FACTOR` that we will use in the calculation to convert kilometers to miles.
  - Line 32 calls the `kilometerTextField.getText()` method to get text that the user has entered into TextField. The text is assigned to a `String` variable named `kiloStr`.
  - Line 35 converts the kilometers to miles, and assigns the results to a `double` variable named `miles`.

- Line 38 calls the `outputLabel.setText` method to display a message in the `outputLabel` component. The message is the concatenated string that is passed as an argument to the method.

Once you have written and compiled the controller class, you must go back into Scene Builder and register the controller class to the application's GUI. Tutorial 14-3 provides the steps for writing the controller class, registering it with the GUI, and running the application.

Tutorial 14-3:
Registering the Controller Class with the Application's GUI

Step 1: Open your Java editor and create a new source code file named KilometerConverterController.java.

Step 2: Type the code for the `KilometerConverterController` class exactly as it is shown in Code Listing 14-2.

Step 3: Save the KilometerConverterController.java file in the same location as the KilometerConverter.fxml file that you created in Tutorial 14-1.

Step 4: Compile the KilometerConverterController.java file.

Step 5: Open the KilometerConverter.fxml file in Scene Builder.

Step 6: Select the root node by clicking its entry in the Hierarchy panel (as shown in Figure 14-29).

Figure 14-29   Select the AnchorPane

Step 7: With the AnchorPane selected, open the Code section of the Inspector panel. Near the top of the Code section, you will see a dropdown list for the controller class. As shown in Figure 14-30, click the dropdown list and select the `KilometerConverterController` class.

Figure 14-30   Select the controller class

Step 8:   At this point, the controller class is registered with the GUI, but you still need to register the event listener for the Button component. As shown in Figure 14-31, select the Button component in the Hierarchy panel.

Figure 14-31   Select the Button component

Step 9:   In the Code section of the Inspector panel you will see a dropdown list named *On Action*. As shown in Figure 14-32, click the dropdown and select #convertButtonListener. Recall that convertButtonListener is the name of the event listener method that you wrote in the controller class. This registers the convertButtonListener method as the event listener for the Button component.

Figure 14-32   Select the event listener method

Step 10: Save the FXML file by clicking the File menu, then clicking Save.

Step 11: At this point, all of the pieces of the application are in place. Run the code for the main application class (`KilometerConverter`). The application's window should appear. As shown in Figure 14-33, enter a value into the TextField and then click the Button. A message should appear displaying the value, converted from kilometers to miles.

Figure 14-33   The application running

Using the Sample Controller Skeleton

As an alternative for manually typing the code for the controller class, Scene Builder can provide a sample "skeleton" for the controller class. To see the sample controller skeleton, click the *View* menu, then click *Show Sample Controller Skeleton*, as shown in Figure 14-34. A window appears, as shown in Figure 14-35, containing the controller skeleton. You can click the Copy button to copy the sample code to the clipboard, and then paste it into an editing window in your IDE.

The obvious benefit of using the sample skeleton controller is that a lot of the code is written for you. The skeleton has all of the necessary import statements, and the class already has private field declarations for all of the components that have an `fx:id`. You just need to change the name of the class, and write the code for the event listener methods.

Figure 14-34   Accessing the sample controller skeleton

Figure 14-35   A sample controller skeleton

```
Sample Skeleton for "Untitled 1" Controller Class

import java.net.URL;
import java.util.ResourceBundle;
import javafx.fxml.FXML;
import javafx.scene.control.Button;
import javafx.scene.control.Label;
import javafx.scene.control.TextField;


public class PleaseProvideControllerClassName {

    @FXML
    private ResourceBundle resources;

    @FXML
    private URL location;

    @FXML
    private Button convertButton;

    @FXML
    private TextField kilometerTextField;

    @FXML
    private Label outputLabel;

    @FXML
    private Label promptLabel;
```

Add comments

Copy   Close

Summary of Creating a JavaFX Application

Here is a broad summary of the steps that you take when creating a JavaFX application in this chapter:

- Use Scene Builder to design the GUI. Be sure to give an `fx:id` to all of the components that you plan to access in your Java code. Save the GUI as an FXML file.
- Write the code for the main application class, which loads the FXML file and launches the application. Save and compile the code in the same location as the FXML file.
- Write the code for the controller class, which contains the event handler methods for the GUI. Save and compile the code in the same location as the FXML file.
- In Scene Builder, register the controller class, then register an event handler method for each component that needs to respond to events. Save the FXML file again.

Checkpoint

14.15 In general, what operations does the main application class perform?

14.16 What is the controller class?

14.17 What is an event listener?

14.18 How do you register a controller class to an application's GUI in Scene Builder?

14.19 How do you register an event listener to a component in Scene Builder?

14.5 RadioButtons and CheckBoxes

CONCEPT: RadioButtons normally appear in groups of two or more and allow the user to select one of several possible options. CheckBoxes, which may appear alone or in groups, allow the user to make yes/no or on/off selections.

RadioButtons

RadioButtons are useful when you want the user to select one choice from several possible options. Figure 14-36 shows a group of RadioButtons. A RadioButton may be selected or deselected. Each RadioButton has a small circle that appears filled-in when the RadioButton is selected and appears empty when the RadioButton is deselected.

Figure 14-36 RadioButtons

To create a RadioButton, you simply drag it from the Library panel and drop it onto the Content panel. (The RadioButton component is found in the Controls section of the Library panel.) RadioButtons have a Text property that determines the text they display. You change a RadioButton's Text property in the same way that you change a Label or a Button's Text property:

VideoNote
JavaFX
RadioButtons

- You select the component, and then change the Text property in the Properties section of the Inspector panel.

  Or

- You double-click the RadioButton in the Content panel, and edit the text that it displays. This changes the component's Text property.

RadioButtons normally are in a *toggle group*. Only one of the RadioButtons in a toggle group may be selected at any time. Clicking on a RadioButton selects it and automatically deselects any other RadioButton in the same toggle group. Because only one RadioButton in a toggle group can be selected at any given time, the buttons are said to be *mutually exclusive*.

Here are the steps for adding RadioButtons to a toggle group:

- Create the first RadioButton component in the Content panel.
- Open the Properties section of the Inspector Panel, and find the Toggle Group property. Enter the name you wish to give the toggle group. Figure 14-37 shows an example.
- Create the next RadioButton. For its Toggle Group property, you should be able to click the down-arrow and select the toggle group that you created for the first RadioButton. Repeat this for each subsequent RadioButton that you want in the same toggle group.

Figure 14-37 Creating a toggle group

If you want a RadioButton to initially appear selected, just check its Selected property as shown in Figure 14-38. Keep in mind that only one RadioButton in a toggle group can be selected. If you select a RadioButton, any previously selected RadioButton in the same toggle group will be unselected.

NOTE: The name *radio button* refers to the old car radios that had push buttons for selecting stations. Only one of the buttons could be pushed in at a time. When you pushed a button in, it automatically popped out any other button that was pushed in.

Figure 14-38   Making a RadioButton initially selected

Check the Selected property
to initially select the RadioButton.

Determining in Code Whether a RadioButton Is Selected

In the controller class, you can use the RadioButton's `isSelected` method to determine whether the RadioButton is selected or not. The `isSelected` method returns a `boolean` value. If the RadioButton is selected, the method returns `true`. Otherwise, it returns `false`. In the following code, assume the `radio` variable references as a RadioButton component. The `if` statement calls the `isSelected` method to determine whether the RadioButton is selected.

```
if (radio.isSelected())
{
   // Code here executes if the radio
   // button is selected.
}
```

The RadioButtonDemo application is an example. Figure 14-39 shows the application's GUI, which was created in Scene Builder. The name of the FXML file is RadioButtonDemo.fxml. The three RadioButtons are in a toggle group, so only one of them can be selected at a

Figure 14-39   The RadioButtonDemo application's GUI

AnchorPane

RadioButton (fx:id is veganRadioButton)
RadioButton (fx:id is vegetarianRadioButton)
RadioButton (fx:id is carnivoreRadioButton)

Label (fx:id is outputLabel)

Button
(fx:id is showChoiceButton)

time. When the user selects a RadioButton and then clicks the *Show Choice* button, a message appears in the outputLabel component indicating the user's selection. For example, in Figure 14-40 the user has selected Vegetarian, and then clicked the *Show Choice* button. The message *Vegetarian* is displayed in the outputLabel component.

Figure 14-40 The RadioButtonDemo application

Code Listing 14-3 shows the main application class, and Code Listing 14-4 shows the controller class. In the controller class, the showChoiceListener method in lines 34 through 44 is the event listener for the showChoiceButton component.

Code Listing 14-3 (RadioButtonDemo.java)

```java
1  import javafx.application.Application;
2  import javafx.fxml.FXMLLoader;
3  import javafx.scene.Parent;
4  import javafx.scene.Scene;
5  import javafx.stage.Stage;
6
7  public class RadioButtonDemo extends Application
8  {
9     public void start(Stage stage) throws Exception
10    {
11       // Load the FXML file.
12       Parent parent = FXMLLoader.load(
13               getClass().getResource("RadioButtonDemo.fxml"));
14
15       // Build the scene graph.
16       Scene scene = new Scene(parent);
17
18       // Display our window, using the scene graph.
19       stage.setTitle("RadioButtons");
20       stage.setScene(scene);
21       stage.show();
22    }
```

```
23
24     public static void main(String[] args)
25     {
26        // Launch the application.
27        launch(args);
28     }
29  }
```

Code Listing 14-4   (RadioButtonDemoController.java)

```
1   import javafx.fxml.FXML;
2   import javafx.scene.control.Button;
3   import javafx.scene.control.Label;
4   import javafx.scene.control.RadioButton;
5   import javafx.scene.control.ToggleGroup;
6
7
8   public class RadioButtonDemoController
9   {
10     @FXML
11     private RadioButton carnivoreRadioButton;
12
13     @FXML
14     private ToggleGroup myToggleGroup;
15
16     @FXML
17     private Label outputLabel;
18
19     @FXML
20     private Button showChoiceButton;
21
22     @FXML
23     private RadioButton veganRadioButton;
24
25     @FXML
26     private RadioButton vegetarianRadioButton;
27
28     public void initialize()
29     {
30        // Nothing to initialize.
31     }
32
```

```
33      // Event listener for the showChoiceButton component
34      public void showChoiceListener()
35      {
36          if (veganRadioButton.isSelected())
37              outputLabel.setText("Vegan");
38
39          if (vegetarianRadioButton.isSelected())
40              outputLabel.setText("Vegetarian");
41
42          if (carnivoreRadioButton.isSelected())
43              outputLabel.setText("Carnivore");
44      }
45  }
```

Responding to RadioButton Events

In many situations you want an action to take place at the time the user clicks a RadioButton. When this is the case, you must write an event listener method in the controller class for each RadioButton and then select the appropriate method as the event listener in Scene Builder. The process is the same as selecting an event listener for a Button component.

To demonstrate, we will look at the RadioButtonEvent application. This is very similar to the RadioButtonDemo application that we just looked at. This application does not have a Button component, however. Immediately after the user clicks one of the RadioButtons, a message is displayed in the outputLabel component. Figure 14-41 shows the application's GUI, which was created in Scene Builder. The name of the FXML file is RadioButtonEvent.fxml. In Figure 14-42 the user has selected Vegetarian, and the message *Vegetarian* is immediately displayed in the outputLabel component.

Figure 14-41 The RadioButtonEvent application's GUI

Figure 14-42 The RadioButtonEvent application

Code Listing 14-5 shows the main application class, and Code Listing 14-6 shows the controller class. The controller class contains the following event listener methods:

- The veganListener method in lines 34 through 37 is the event listener for the veganRadioButton component.
- The vegetarianListener method in lines 41 through 45 is the event listener for the vegetarianRadioButton component.
- The carnivoreListener method in lines 48 through 52 is the event listener for the carnivoreRadioButton component.

Code Listing 14-5 **(RadioButtonEvent.java)**

```
1   import javafx.application.Application;
2   import javafx.fxml.FXMLLoader;
3   import javafx.scene.Parent;
4   import javafx.scene.Scene;
5   import javafx.stage.Stage;
6
7   public class RadioButtonEvent extends Application
8   {
9       public void start(Stage stage) throws Exception
10      {
11          // Load the FXML file.
12          Parent parent = FXMLLoader.load(
13                  getClass().getResource("RadioButtonEvent.fxml"));
14
15          // Build the scene graph.
16          Scene scene = new Scene(parent);
17
18          // Display our window, using the scene graph.
19          stage.setTitle("RadioButtons");
20          stage.setScene(scene);
21          stage.show();
22      }
23
24      public static void main(String[] args)
25      {
26          // Launch the application.
27          launch(args);
28      }
29  }
```

Code Listing 14-6 (`RadioButtonEventController.java`)

```java
1  import javafx.fxml.FXML;
2  import javafx.scene.control.Button;
3  import javafx.scene.control.Label;
4  import javafx.scene.control.RadioButton;
5  import javafx.scene.control.ToggleGroup;
6
7
8  public class RadioButtonEventController
9  {
10     @FXML
11     private RadioButton carnivoreRadioButton;
12
13     @FXML
14     private ToggleGroup myToggleGroup;
15
16     @FXML
17     private Label outputLabel;
18
19     @FXML
20     private Button showChoiceButton;
21
22     @FXML
23     private RadioButton veganRadioButton;
24
25     @FXML
26     private RadioButton vegetarianRadioButton;
27
28     public void initialize()
29     {
30        // Nothing to initialize.
31     }
32
33     // Event listener for the veganRadioButton
34     public void veganListener()
35     {
36        if (veganRadioButton.isSelected())
37           outputLabel.setText("Vegan");
38     }
39
40     // Event listener for the vegetarianRadioButton
41     public void vegetarianListener()
42     {
43        if (vegetarianRadioButton.isSelected())
44           outputLabel.setText("Vegetarian");
45     }
```

```
46
47      // Event listener for the carnivoreRadioButton
48      public void carnivoreListener()
49      {
50         if (carnivoreRadioButton.isSelected())
51            outputLabel.setText("Carnivore");
52      }
53   }
```

CheckBoxes

A *CheckBox* is a small box with text appearing next to it. The window shown in Figure 14-43 has three CheckBoxes.

Figure 14-43   CheckBoxes

☑ Choice 1

☑ Choice 2

☑ Choice 3

Like RadioButtons, CheckBoxes may be selected or deselected at run time. When a CheckBox is selected, a small check mark appears inside the box. Although CheckBoxes are often displayed in groups, they are not usually grouped in a toggle group like RadioButtons are. This is because CheckBoxes are not normally used to make mutually exclusive selections. Instead, the user is allowed to select any or all of the CheckBoxes displayed in a group.

VideoNote
JavaFX
CheckBoxes

To create a CheckBox, you simply drag it from the Library panel and drop it onto the Content panel. (The CheckBox component is found in the Controls section of the Library panel.) CheckBoxes have a Text property that determines the text they display. You change a CheckBox's Text property in the same way that you change a Label or a Button's Text property:

- You select the component, and then change the Text property in the Properties section of the Inspector panel.

  Or

- You double-click the CheckBox in the Content panel, and edit the text that it displays. This changes the component's Text property.

If you want a CheckBox to initially appear selected, just check its Selected property as shown in Figure 14-44.

Figure 14-44 Making a CheckBox initially selected

Inspector — Properties : CheckBox

Text

Text	Click the box.
Font	System 12px
Text Fill	#292929
Wrap Text	☐
Text Alignment	
Text Overrun	ELLIPSIS
Ellipsis String	...
Underline	☐

Specific

Allow Indetermi...	☐
Indeterminate	☐
Selected	☑ ← Check the Selected property to initially select the CheckBox.

Determining in Code Whether a CheckBox Is Selected

In the controller class, you can use the CheckBox's isSelected method to determine whether the CheckBox is selected or not. The isSelected method returns a boolean value. If the CheckBox is selected, the method returns true. Otherwise, it returns false. In the following code, assume the checkbox variable references a CheckBox component. The if statement calls the isSelected method to determine whether the CheckBox is selected.

```
if (checkbox.isSelected())
{
    // Code here executes if the
    // CheckBox is selected.
}
```

The CheckBoxDemo application is an example. Figure 14-45 shows the application's GUI, which was created in Scene Builder. The name of the FXML file is CheckBoxDemo.fxml. When the user clicks the *OK* button, a message appears in the outputLabel component indicating whether the CheckBox is selected or not. Figure 14-46 shows examples of the application running.

Figure 14-45 The CheckBoxDemo application's GUI

AnchorPane

CheckBox (fx:id is myCheckBox)

Label (fx:id is outputLabel)

Button
(fx:id is okButton)

Figure 14-46 The CheckBoxDemo application running

Code Listing 14-7 shows the main application class, and Code Listing 14-8 shows the controller class. In the controller class, the okButtonListener method in lines 23 through 29 is the event listener for the okButton component.

Code Listing 14-7 **(CheckBoxDemo.java)**

```
1   import javafx.application.Application;
2   import javafx.fxml.FXMLLoader;
3   import javafx.scene.Parent;
4   import javafx.scene.Scene;
5   import javafx.stage.Stage;
6
7   public class CheckBoxDemo extends Application
8   {
9      public void start(Stage stage) throws Exception
10     {
11        // Load the FXML file.
12        Parent parent = FXMLLoader.load(
13                getClass().getResource("CheckBoxDemo.fxml"));
14
15        // Build the scene graph.
16        Scene scene = new Scene(parent);
17
18        // Display our window, using the scene graph.
19        stage.setTitle("CheckBoxes");
20        stage.setScene(scene);
21        stage.show();
22     }
23
24     public static void main(String[] args)
25     {
26        // Launch the application.
27        launch(args);
28     }
29  }
```

Code Listing 14-8 (`CheckBoxDemoController.java`)

```
 1  import javafx.fxml.FXML;
 2  import javafx.scene.control.Button;
 3  import javafx.scene.control.Label;
 4  import javafx.scene.control.CheckBox;
 5
 6  public class CheckBoxDemoController
 7  {
 8     @FXML
 9     private CheckBox myCheckBox;
10
11     @FXML
12     private Label outputLabel;
13
14     @FXML
15     private Button okButton;
16
17     public void initialize()
18     {
19        // Nothing to initialize.
20     }
21
22     // Event listener for the okButton component
23     public void okButtonListener()
24     {
25        if (myCheckBox.isSelected())
26           outputLabel.setText("The CheckBox is selected.");
27        else
28           outputLabel.setText("The CheckBox is not selected.");
29     }
30  }
```

Responding to CheckBox Events

Sometimes you want an action to take place at the time the user clicks a CheckBox. When this is the case, you must write an event listener method in the controller class for the CheckBox and then select the method as the event listener in Scene Builder. The process is the same as selecting an event listener for a Button component, or a RadioButton component.

To demonstrate, we will look at the CheckBoxEvent application. This is very similar to the CheckBoxDemo application that we just looked at. This application does not have a Button component, however. Immediately after the user clicks the CheckBox, a message is displayed in the outputLabel component. Figure 14-47 shows the application's GUI, which was created in Scene Builder. The name of the FXML file is CheckBoxEvent.fxml. Figure 14-48 shows examples of the application running.

Figure 14-47   The CheckBoxEvent application's GUI

Figure 14-48   The CheckBoxEvent application running

Code Listing 14-9 shows the main application class, and Code Listing 14-10 shows the controller class. In the controller class, the myCheckBoxListener method in lines 19 through 25 is the event listener for the myCheckBox component.

Code Listing 14-9   (**CheckBoxEvent.java**)

```
1   import javafx.application.Application;
2   import javafx.fxml.FXMLLoader;
3   import javafx.scene.Parent;
4   import javafx.scene.Scene;
5   import javafx.stage.Stage;
6
7   public class CheckBoxEvent extends Application
8   {
9      public void start(Stage stage) throws Exception
10     {
11        // Load the FXML file.
12        Parent parent = FXMLLoader.load(
13                getClass().getResource("CheckBoxEvent.fxml"));
14
15        // Build the scene graph.
16        Scene scene = new Scene(parent);
17
18        // Display our window, using the scene graph.
19        stage.setTitle("CheckBoxes");
20        stage.setScene(scene);
21        stage.show();
22     }
23
```

```
24      public static void main(String[] args)
25      {
26         // Launch the application.
27         launch(args);
28      }
29   }
```

Code Listing 14-10 (`CheckBoxEventController.java`)

```
1    import javafx.fxml.FXML;
2    import javafx.scene.control.Label;
3    import javafx.scene.control.CheckBox;
4
5    public class CheckBoxEventController
6    {
7       @FXML
8       private CheckBox myCheckBox;
9
10      @FXML
11      private Label outputLabel;
12
13      public void initialize()
14      {
15         // Nothing to initialize.
16      }
17
18      // Event listener for myCheckBox
19      public void myCheckBoxListener()
20      {
21         if (myCheckBox.isSelected())
22            outputLabel.setText("The CheckBox is selected.");
23         else
24            outputLabel.setText("The CheckBox is not selected.");
25      }
26   }
```

 Checkpoint

14.20 You want the user to be able to select only one item from a group of items. Which type of component would you use for the items, RadioButtons or CheckBoxes?

14.21 You want the user to be able to select any number of items from a group of items. Which type of component would you use for the items, RadioButtons or CheckBoxes?

14.22 What is the purpose of a toggle group?

14.23 Do you normally add RadioButtons or CheckBoxes to a toggle group?

14.6 Displaying Images

CONCEPT: Use the ImageView component to display images in a JavaFX application.

You can use the ImageView component to display images in an application's GUI. You simply drag the component from the Library panel (you will find it in the Controls section) and drop it onto the Content Panel. This creates an empty ImageView component, as shown in Figure 14-49. Although the component does not yet display an image, it has sizing handles that reveal its size and location when it is selected.

Figure 14-49 An empty ImageView component

ImageView component

Once you have created a ImageView control, you use its Image property to specify the image that it will display. Figure 14-50 shows the Image property in the Properties section of the Inspector panel. Click the ellipses button (⠄⠄) to browse your file system for an image file to display. Figure 14-51 shows an example of an image displayed in an ImageView component.

Figure 14-50 The Image property

Click here to browse for an image file.

Image property

Figure 14-51 An image displayed in an ImageView component

Displaying an Image with Code

Sometimes you might need to write code that will change the image being displayed in an ImageView component, as the application is running. In your controller class, you can call the ImageView component's `setImage` method to do this.

First, you must create an instance of the `Image` class, which can read the contents of an image file. The `Image` class is in the `javafx.scene.image` package. The `Image` class constructor accepts a `String` argument that is the name of an image file. Here is an example:

```
Image myImage = new Image("Dog.jpg");
```

This statement creates an `Image` object that reads the contents of the file Dog.jpg. Because no path was given, it is assumed that the file is in the current directory or folder. Here is an example that uses a path.

```
Image myImage = new Image ("C:\\Chapter 14\\Images\\Dog.jpg");
```

Once you have created an `Image` object, you pass a reference to that object to the ImageView component's `setImage` method. The following is an example. Assume that `myImageView` references an ImageView component, and `myImage` references an `Image` object.

```
myImageView.setImage(myImage);
```

To demonstrate how this works, we will look at the ImageViewDemo application. The application's GUI is shown in Figure 14-52. Initially, the ImageView component displays an image of a dog, and the *Dog* RadioButton is selected. If the user clicks the `catRadioButton`, the image changes to a photo of a cat. If the user clicks the `dogRadioButton`, the image changes back to the photo of the dog. Figure 14-53 shows the application running.

Figure 14-52   The ImageViewDemo application's GUI

AnchorPane

ImageView
(fx:id is myImage)

RadioButton
(fx:id is dogRadioButton)

RadioButton
(fx:id is catRadioButton)

Figure 14-53   The ImageViewDemo application running

Code Listing 14-11 shows the main application class, and Code Listing 14-12 shows the controller class.

Code Listing 14-11   **(ImageViewDemo.java)**

```
1   import javafx.application.Application;
2   import javafx.fxml.FXMLLoader;
3   import javafx.scene.Parent;
4   import javafx.scene.Scene;
5   import javafx.stage.Stage;
6
```

```
 7  public class ImageViewDemo extends Application
 8  {
 9     public void start(Stage stage) throws Exception
10     {
11        // Load the FXML file.
12        Parent parent = FXMLLoader.load(
13                   getClass().getResource("ImageViewDemo.fxml"));
14
15        // Build the scene graph.
16        Scene scene = new Scene(parent);
17
18        // Display our window, using the scene graph.
19        stage.setTitle("ImageViewDemo");
20        stage.setScene(scene);
21        stage.show();
22     }
23
24     public static void main(String[] args)
25     {
26        // Launch the application.
27        launch(args);
28     }
29  }
```

Code Listing 14-12   (`ImageViewDemoController.java`)

```
 1  import javafx.fxml.FXML;
 2  import javafx.scene.image.Image;
 3  import javafx.scene.image.ImageView;
 4  import javafx.scene.control.RadioButton;
 5  import javafx.scene.control.ToggleGroup;
 6
 7  public class ImageViewDemoController
 8  {
 9     // Private fields for components
10     @FXML
11     private ImageView myImage;
12
13     @FXML
14     private ToggleGroup myToggleGroup;
15
16     @FXML
17     private RadioButton dogRadioButton;
18
19     @FXML
20     private RadioButton catRadioButton;
21
```

```
22     // Private fields for the dog and cat images
23     private Image dogImage;
24     private Image catImage;
25
26     // Initialize method
27     public void initialize()
28     {
29        // Load the dog and cat images
30        dogImage = new Image("Dog.jpg");
31        catImage = new Image("Cat.jpg");
32     }
33
34     // Event listener for the dogRadioButton
35     public void dogRadioButtonListener()
36     {
37        if (dogRadioButton.isSelected())
38           myImage.setImage(dogImage);
39     }
40
41     // Event listener for the catRadioButtonListener
42     public void catRadioButtonListener()
43     {
44        if (catRadioButton.isSelected())
45           myImage.setImage(catImage);
46     }
47  }
```

Let's take a closer look at the controller class. Lines 10 through 20 declare the variables that will reference the components in the GUI. Lines 23 and 24 declare two Image variables to reference two Image objects. Notice that these two declarations are not preceded by the @FMXL annotation. That is because the Image variables will not reference any components in the GUI. For that reason, it is not necessary to precede the declarations by the @FMXL annotation.

The initialize method appears in lines 27 through 32. Recall that this method is automatically called after the FXML file is loaded. We will use the initialize method to create two Image objects. Line 30 creates an Image object, using the Dog.jpg image file that is in the same folder as the application. Line 31 creates another Image object, using the Cat.jpg image file that is also in the same folder as the application.

The dogRadioButtonListener method appears in lines 35 through 39. This is the event listener for the dogRadioButton component. If the dogRadioButton is selected, line 38 sets the ImageView component's Image property to the dog image.

The catRadioButtonListener method appears in lines 42 through 46. This is the event listener for the catRadioButton component. If the catRadioButton is selected, line 45 sets the ImageView component's Image property to the cat image.

Checkpoint

14.24 What ImageView property do you set in the Inspector panel to display an image?

14.25 What method do you call to change an ImageView's image?

14.7 Common Errors to Avoid

- **Not assigning an `fx:id` to a component.** If you need to access a GUI component in your Java code, you have to assign the component an `fx:id` in Scene Builder.
- **Forgetting to select the controller class for the root node in Scene Builder.** Before you can select event listener methods for a GUI's components, you must select the controller class that contains those event listeners, for the root node.
- **Forgetting to register the event listener for a component.** After you have registered the controller class for the root node, you have to select the event listener methods for each component that must respond to events.
- **Forgetting to write an event listener for each event you wish an application to respond to.** To respond to an event, you must write an event listener of the proper type registered with the component that generates the event.
- **Leaving out the `@FXML` attribute in private declarations in the controller class.** If you declare a private field in the controller class, and that declaration refers to a component in the FXML file, the declaration must be preceded with the `@FXML` annotation.
- **Not placing RadioButtons in a toggle group.** If you have a set of RadioButtons and you want the user to be able to select only one at a time, you must place the RadioButtons in a toggle group.

Review Questions and Exercises

Multiple Choice and True/False

1. A(n) _____ is a method that automatically executes when a specific event occurs.
   a. controller
   b. event listener
   c. `initialize` method
   d. autoresponder

2. A _____ is a tree-like hierarchical data structure that contains the components of a JavaFX GUI.
   a. directory tree
   b. node tree
   c. node graph
   d. scene graph

3. A _____ is the parent of all the other nodes in a scene graph.
   a. root node
   b. branch node
   c. leaf node
   d. primary node

4. A _____ can contain other nodes.
   a. root node
   b. branch node
   c. leaf node
   d. mother node

5. A _____ cannot have children.
   a. root node
   b. branch node
   c. leaf node
   d. terminal node

6. _____ is a markup language that describes a JavaFX scene graph.
   a. FXML
   b. JFXMarkUp
   c. HTML
   d. SceneXML

7. The _____ panel in Scene Builder provides a list of JavaFX components that you can use in an application.
   a. Content
   b. Inspector
   c. Library
   d. Hierarchy

8. The _____ panel in Scene Builder is where you visually design an application's GUI.
   a. Content
   b. Inspector
   c. Library
   d. Hierarchy

9. The _____ panel in Scene Builder shows the scene graph.
   a. Content
   b. Inspector
   c. Library
   d. Hierarchy

10. The _____ panel in Scene Builder allows you to work with a component's properties, layout, and code.
    a. Content
    b. Inspector
    c. Library
    d. Hierarchy

11. A(n) _____ is a name that identifies a component in the FXML file.
    a. `fx:name`
    b. `fx:id`
    c. `fx:component`
    d. `fx:variable`

12. In a JavaFX application, the _____ class loads the FXML file and builds the scene graph.
    a. main application
    b. controller
    c. event listener
    d. Loader

13. In a JavaFX application, the _____ class is responsible for handling events that occur while the application is running.
    a. main application
    b. controller
    c. event listener
    d. Loader

14. A _____ is a component that can be either selected or deselected. These components usually appear in a group so that only one of them in the group can be selected at a time.
    a. Button
    b. CheckBox
    c. RadioButton
    d. RadioBox

15. You call the _____ method to determine whether a RadioButton is selected.
    a. isRadioSelected
    b. isOn
    c. isSelected
    d. isClicked

16. You call the _____ method to determine whether a CheckBox is selected.
    a. isCheckBoxSelected
    b. isOn
    c. isSelected
    d. isClicked

17. You can use the _____ component to display images in an application's GUI.
    a. ImageView
    b. Image
    c. PictureBox
    d. GraphicBox

18. You call the _____ method to change an ImageView component's image.
    a. image
    b. changeImage
    c. showImage
    d. setImage

19. **True or False:** A mutually exclusive relationship is automatically created between all RadioButton components that are in the same toggle group.

20. **True or False:** A component's fx:id can become a variable name that you can use in an application's controller class.

21. **True or False:** The controller class usually loads the FXML file and builds the scene graph.

22. **True or False:** You can use Scene Builder to register a controller class to a GUI.

23. **True or False:** Registering a controller class to a GUI automatically registers event listeners to all of the GUI's components.

24. **True or False:** You can register an event listener to a RadioButton. The event listener will execute when the user clicks the RadioButton.

25. **True or False:** You cannot register an event listener to a CheckBox.

Find the Error

1. The following import statements are in a controller class that uses a Button component and a Label component.

```
import java.fxml.FXML;
import java.scene.control.Button;
import java.scene.control.Label;
```

2. Find the errors in the following controller class.

```
1   import javafx.fxml.FXML;
2   import javafx.scene.control.Button;
3
4   public class MyControllerClass
5   {
6       private Button okButton;
7
8       private Label outputLabel;
9
10      // This method is called when the FXML file is loaded
11      public void initialize()
12      {
13          // Perform any necessary initialization here.
14      }
15
16      // Event listener for the okButton
17      public void okButtonListener()
18      {
19        // Display "Hello World" in the outputLabel.
20        outputLabel.text("Hello World!");
21      }
22   }
```

Algorithm Workbench

1. You created a GUI in Scene Builder and saved it to a file named MyGUI.fxml. Write a main application class that loads the FXML file, builds the scene graph, and displays the GUI.

2. You created a GUI in Scene Builder and saved it to a file named Testing.fxml. The GUI has a Button component with the fx:id myButton, and a Label component with the fx:id myLabel. You have already written the main application class. Write the code for the controller class. The controller class should have an event listener for the Button component that displays the string "Testing 1, 2, 3" in the Label component.

3. In a controller class, the variable `radio1` references a RadioButton component, and `outputLabel` references a Label component. Write an `if` statement that determines whether the RadioButton is selected. If the RadioButton is selected, display "Selected" in the `outputLabel`. Otherwise, display "Not selected" in the `outputLabel`.

Short Answer

1. What is a scene graph?
2. List and describe the three types of nodes that can appear in a scene graph.
3. What is FXML?
4. What is an `fx:id`? Why is it important that you assign an `fx:id` to a component in Scene Builder?
5. What is the purpose of the main application class in a JavaFX application?
6. What is the purpose of the controller class in a JavaFX application?
7. What is an event listener?
8. Describe the steps for registering a controller class to an application's GUI in Scene Builder, and then registering event listeners to specific components.
9. Why should a group of RadioButtons belong to the same toggle group?

Programming Challenges

VideoNote
The Retail Price Calculator Problem

1. Retail Price Calculator

Create a JavaFX application where the user enters the wholesale cost of an item and its markup percentage into TextFields. (For example, if an item's wholesale cost is $5 and its markup percentage is 100%, then its retail price is $10.) The application should have a button that displays the item's retail price when clicked.

2. Latin Translator

Look at the following list of Latin words and their meanings.

Latin	English
sinister	left
dexter	right
medium	center

Create a JavaFX application that translates the Latin words to English. The GUI should have three Buttons, one for each Latin word. When the user clicks a Button, the application should display the English translation in a Label.

3. Name Formatter

Create a JavaFX application that lets the user enter the following pieces of data:

- The user's first name
- The user's middle name
- The user's last name
- The user's preferred title (Mr., Mrs., Ms., Dr., etc.)

Assume the user has entered the following data:

- First name: *Kelly*
- Middle name: *Jane*
- Last name: *Smith*
- Title: *Ms.*

The application should have buttons that display the user's name formatted in the following ways:

Ms. Kelly Jane Smith
Kelly Jane Smith
Kelly Smith
Smith, Kelly Jane, Ms.
Smith, Kelly Jane
Smith, Kelly

4. Tip, Tax, and Total

Create a JavaFX application that lets the user enter the food charge for a meal at a restaurant. When a button is clicked, the application should calculate and display the amount of an 18 percent tip, 7 percent sales tax, and the total of all three amounts.

5. Distance Traveled

Assuming there are no accidents or delays, the distance that a car travels down an interstate highway can be calculated with the following formula:

$$Distance = Speed \times Time$$

Create an application that allows the user to enter a car's speed in miles per hour. The application should have buttons that display the following:

- The distance the car will travel in 5 hours
- The distance the car will travel in 8 hours
- The distance the car will travel in 12 hours

6. Heads or Tails

Create a JavaFX application that simulates a coin being tossed. When the user clicks a button, the application should generate a random number in the range of 0 to 1. If the number is 0, the coin has landed on "heads," and if the number is 1, the coin has landed on "tails." Use an ImageView component, and the coin images that you will find in this book's Student Sample Programs to display the side of the coin when it is tossed.

7. Celsius and Fahrenheit Temperature Converter

Assuming that *C* is a Celsius temperature, the following formula converts the temperature to Fahrenheit:

$$F = 1.8 \times C + 32$$

Assuming that *F* is a Fahrenheit temperature, the following formula converts the temperature to Celsius:

$$C = (5/9) \times (F - 32)$$

Create a JavaFX application that allows the user to enter a temperature. The application should have Button components described as follows:

- A button that reads *Convert to Fahrenheit*. If the user clicks this button, the application should treat the temperature that is entered as a Celsius temperature and convert it to Fahrenheit.
- A button that reads *Convert to Celsius*. If the user clicks this button, the application should treat the temperature that is entered as a Fahrenheit temperature, and convert it to Celsius.

8. Dice Simulator

Create a JavaFX application that simulates the rolling of a pair of dice. When the user clicks a button, the application should generate two random numbers, each in the range of 1 through 6, to represent the value of the dice. Use ImageView component to display the dice. (In the Student Sample Programs you will find six images named Die1.png, Die2.png, Die3.png, Die4.png, Die5.png, and Die6.png that you can use in the ImageView components.)

9. Rock, Paper, Scissors Game

Create a JavaFX application that lets the user play the game of rock, paper, scissors against the computer. The program should work as follows.

1. When the program begins, a random number in the range of 1 through 3 is generated. If the number is 1, then the computer has chosen rock. If the number is 2, then the computer has chosen paper. If the number is 3, then the computer has chosen scissors. (Do not display the computer's choice yet.)
2. The user selects his or her choice of rock, paper, or scissors by clicking a Button. An image of the user's choice should be displayed in an ImageView component. (You will find rock, paper, and scissors image files in the book's Student Sample Files.)
3. An image of the computer's choice is displayed.
4. A winner is selected according to the following rules:
   - If one player chooses rock and the other player chooses scissors, then rock wins. (Rock smashes scissors.)
   - If one player chooses scissors and the other player chooses paper, then scissors wins. (Scissors cut paper.)
   - If one player chooses paper and the other player chooses rock, then paper wins. (Paper wraps rock.)
   - If both players make the same choice, the game must be played again to determine the winner.

10. Tic-Tac-Toe Simulator

Create a JavaFX application that simulates a game of tic-tac-toe. Figure 14-54 shows an example of the application's GUI. The window shown in the figure uses nine ImageView components to display the Xs and Os. (You will find images for the X and the O in the book's Student Sample Files.)

The application should use a two-dimensional int array to simulate the game board in memory. When the user clicks the *New Game* button, the application should step through the array, storing a random number in the range of 0 through 1 in each element. The number 0 represents the letter O, and the number 1 represents the letter X. The application's window should then be updated to display the game board. The application should display a message indicating whether player X won, player Y won, or the game was a tie.

Figure 14-54   The Tic-Tac-Toe application

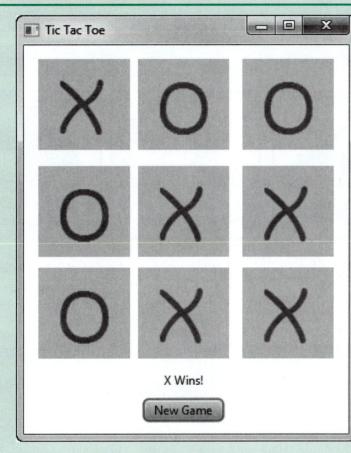

11. Slot Machine Simulation

A slot machine is a gambling device into which the user inserts money and then pulls a lever (or presses a button). The slot machine then displays a set of random images. If two or more of the images match, the user wins an amount of money that the slot machine dispenses back to the user.

Create a JavaFX application that simulates a slot machine. Figure 14-55 shows an example of how the GUI should look. The application should let the user enter into a TextField the amount of money he or she is inserting into the machine. When the user clicks the *Spin* button, the application should display three randomly selected symbols. (Slot machines traditionally display fruit symbols. You will find a set of fruit symbol images in the Student Sample Programs.) The program should also display the amount that the user won for the spin, and the total amount won for all spins.

The amount won for a spin is determined in the following way:

- If none of the randomly displayed images match, the user has won $0.
- If two of the images match, the user has won two times the amount entered.
- If three of the images match, the user has won three times the amount entered.

Figure 14-55 Slot Machine application

TOPICS

15.1 Introduction to Recursion

15.2 Solving Problems with Recursion

15.3 Examples of Recursive Methods

15.4 A Recursive Binary Search Method

15.5 The Towers of Hanoi

15.6 Common Errors to Avoid

15.1 Introduction to Recursion

CONCEPT: A recursive method is a method that calls itself.

You have seen instances of methods calling other methods. Method A can call method B, which can then call method C. It's also possible for a method to call itself. A method that calls itself is a *recursive method*. Look at the message method in Code Listing 15-1.

Code Listing 15-1 (`EndlessRecursion.java`)

```java
1  /**
2   * This class has a recursive method.
3   */
4
5  public class EndlessRecursion
6  {
7     public static void message()
8     {
9        System.out.println("This is a recursive method.");
10       message();
11    }
12 }
```

This method displays the string "This is a recursive method.", and then calls itself. Each time it calls itself, the cycle is repeated. Can you see a problem with the method? There's no way to stop the recursive calls. This method is like an infinite loop because there is no code to stop it from repeating.

Like a loop, a recursive method must have some way to control the number of times it repeats. The class in Code Listing 15-2 has a modified version of the message method. It passes an integer argument, which holds the number of times the method should call itself.

Code Listing 15-2   (`Recursive.java`)

```
 1  /**
 2   * This class has a recursive method, message, that displays
 3   * a message n times.
 4   */
 5
 6  public class Recursive
 7  {
 8     public static void message(int n)
 9     {
10        if (n > 0)
11        {
12           System.out.println("This is a recursive method.");
13           message(n - 1);
14        }
15     }
16  }
```

This method contains an `if` statement that controls the repetition. As long as the n parameter is greater than zero, the method displays the message and calls itself again. Each time it calls itself, it passes n - 1 as the argument. For example, look at the program in Code Listing 15-3.

Code Listing 15-3   (`RecursionDemo.java`)

```
 1  /**
 2   * This class demonstrates the Recursive.message method.
 3   */
 4
 5  public class RecursionDemo
 6  {
 7     public static void main(String[] args)
 8     {
 9        Recursive.message(5);
10     }
11  }
```

Program Output

```
This is a recursive method.
This is a recursive method.
This is a recursive method.
This is a recursive method.
This is a recursive method.
```

In line 9, the main method in this class calls the `Recursive.message` method with argument 5, which causes the method to call itself five times. The first time the method is called, the `if` statement displays the message and then calls itself with 4 as the argument. Figure 15-1 illustrates this.

Figure 15-1 First two calls of the method

The diagram in Figure 15-1 illustrates two separate calls of the message method. Each time the method is called, a new instance of the n parameter is created in memory. The first time the method is called, the n parameter is set to 5. When the method calls itself, a new instance of n is created, and the value 4 is passed into it. This cycle repeats until, finally, zero is passed to the method. This is illustrated in Figure 15-2.

As you can see from Figure 15-2, the method is called a total of six times. The first time it is called from the main method of the RecursionDemo class, and the other five times it calls itself. The number of times that a method calls itself is known as the *depth of recursion*. In this example, the depth of recursion is five. When the method reaches its sixth call, the n parameter is set to 0. At that point, the `if` statement's conditional expression is false, so the method returns. Control of the program returns from the sixth instance of the method to the point in the fifth instance directly after the recursive method call. This is illustrated in Figure 15-3.

Because there are no more statements to be executed after the method call, the fifth instance of the method returns control of the program back to the fourth instance. This repeats until all instances of the method return.

Figure 15-2   Total of six calls to the `message` method

The method is first called from the `main` method of the `RecursionDemo` class.

First call of the method

Value of n: 5

The second through sixth calls are recursive.

Second call of the method

Value of n: 4

Third call of the method

Value of n: 3

Fourth call of the method

Value of n: 2

Fifth call of the method

Value of n: 1

Sixth call of the method

Value of n: 0

Figure 15-3   Control returns to the point after the recursive method call

```
public static void message(int n)
{
    if (n > 0)
    {
        System.out.println("This is a recursive method.");
        message(n - 1);
    }
}
```

Recursive method call ⟶

Control returns here from the recursive call. There are no more statements to execute in this method, so the method returns.

15.2 Solving Problems with Recursion

CONCEPT: A problem can be solved with recursion if it can be broken down into successive smaller problems that are identical to the overall problem.

VideoNote
Reducing a
Problem with
Recursion

The `Recursive` and `RecursionDemo` classes shown in the previous section demonstrate the mechanics of a recursive method. Recursion can be a powerful tool for solving repetitive problems and is an important topic in upper-level computer science courses. What might not be clear to you yet is how to use recursion to solve a problem.

First, it should be noted that recursion is never absolutely required to solve a problem. Any problem that can be solved recursively can also be solved iteratively, with a loop. In fact, recursive algorithms are usually less efficient than iterative algorithms. This is because a method call requires several actions to be performed by the JVM. These actions include allocating memory for parameters and local variables, and storing the address of the program location where control returns after the method terminates. These actions, which are sometimes referred to as *overhead*, take place with each method call. Such overhead is not necessary with a loop.

Some repetitive problems, however, are more easily solved with recursion than with iteration. Whereas an iterative algorithm might result in faster execution time, the programmer might be able to design a recursive algorithm faster.

In general, a recursive method works like this:

- If the problem can be solved now, without recursion, then the method solves it and returns.
- If the problem cannot be solved now, then the method reduces it to a smaller but similar problem and calls itself to solve the smaller problem.

In order to apply this approach, we first identify at least one case in which the problem can be solved without recursion. This is known as the *base case*. Second, we determine a way to solve the problem in all other circumstances using recursion. This is called the *recursive case*. In the recursive case, we must always reduce the problem to a smaller version of the original problem. By reducing the problem with each recursive call, the base case will eventually be reached and the recursion will stop.

Let's take an example from mathematics to examine an application of recursion. In mathematics, the notation $n!$ represents the factorial of the number n. The factorial of a nonnegative number can be defined by the following rules:

If $n = 0$ then $n! = 1$
If $n > 0$ then $n! = 1 \times 2 \times 3 \times \ldots \times n$

Let's replace the notation $n!$ with factorial(n), which looks a bit more like computer code, and rewrite these rules as:

If $n = 0$ then   factorial(n) $= 1$
If $n > 0$ then   factorial(n) $= 1 \times 2 \times 3 \times \ldots \times n$

These rules state that when n is 0, its factorial is 1. When n is greater than 0, its factorial is the product of all the positive integers from 1 up to n. For instance, factorial(6) is calculated as $1 \times 2 \times 3 \times 4 \times 5 \times 6$.

When designing a recursive algorithm to calculate the factorial of any number, we first identify the base case, which is the part of the calculation that we can solve without recursion. That is the case where n is equal to 0:

If $n = 0$ then   factorial(n) $= 1$

This tells how to solve the problem when n is equal to 0, but what do we do when n is greater than 0? That is the recursive case, or the part of the problem that we use recursion to solve. This is how we express it:

If $n > 0$ then   factorial(n) $= n \times$ factorial($n - 1$)

This states that if n is greater than 0, the factorial of n is n times the factorial of $n - 1$. Notice how the recursive call works on a reduced version of the problem, $n - 1$. So, our recursive rule for calculating the factorial of a number might look like this:

If $n = 0$ then   factorial(n) $= 1$
If $n > 0$ then   factorial(n) $= n \times$ factorial($n - 1$)

The following code shows how this might be implemented in a Java method.

```java
private static int factorial(int n)
{
    if (n == 0)
        return 1;    // Base case
    else
        return n * factorial(n - 1);
}
```

The program in Code Listing 15-4 demonstrates the method.

Code Listing 15-4   (`FactorialDemo.java`)

```java
 1  import java.util.Scanner;
 2
 3  /**
 4   * This program demonstrates the recursive factorial method.
 5   */
 6
 7  public class FactorialDemo
 8  {
 9     public static void main(String[] args)
10     {
11        int number;    // To hold a number
12
13        // Create a Scanner object for keyboard input.
14        Scanner keyboard = new Scanner(System.in);
15
16        // Get a number from the user.
17        System.out.print("Enter a nonnegative integer: ");
18        number = keyboard.nextInt();
19
20        // Display the factorial.
21        System.out.println(number + "! is " + factorial(number));
22     }
23
24     /**
25      * Recursive factorial method. This method returns the
26      * factorial of its argument, which is assumed to be a
27      * nonnegative number.
28      */
29
30     private static int factorial(int n)
31     {
```

```
32          if (n == 0)
33              return 1;    // Base case
34          else
35              return n * factorial(n - 1);
36      }
37  }
```

Program Output with Example Input Shown in Bold

Enter a nonnegative integer: **4 [Enter]**
4! is 24

In the example run of the program, the factorial method is called with the argument 4 passed into n. Because n is not equal to 0, the `if` statement's `else` clause executes the statement in line 35. Although this is a `return` statement, it does not immediately return. Before the return value can be determined, the value of `factorial(num - 1)` must be determined. The `factorial` method is called recursively until the fifth call, in which the n parameter will be set to zero. The diagram in Figure 15-4 illustrates the value of n and the return value during each call of the method.

Figure 15-4 Recursive calls to the `factorial` method

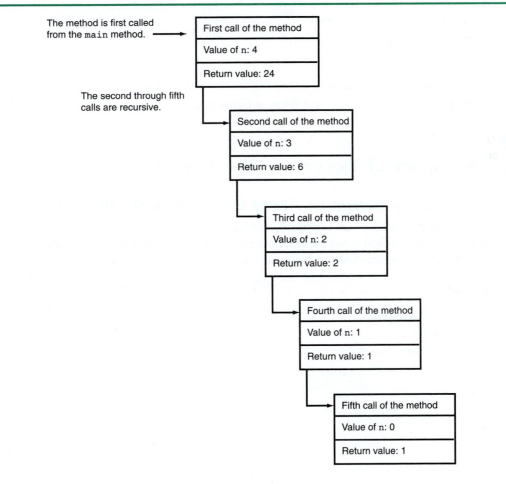

This diagram illustrates why a recursive algorithm must reduce the problem with each recursive call. Eventually the recursion has to stop in order for a solution to be reached. If each recursive call works on a smaller version of the problem, then the recursive calls work toward the base case. The base case does not require recursion, so it stops the chain of recursive calls.

Usually, a problem is reduced by making the value of one or more parameters smaller with each recursive call. In our factorial method, the value of the parameter n gets closer to 0 with each recursive call. When the parameter reaches 0, the method returns a value without making another recursive call.

Direct and Indirect Recursion

The examples we have discussed so far show recursive methods that directly call themselves. This is known as *direct recursion*. There is also the possibility of creating *indirect recursion* in a program. This occurs when method A calls method B, which in turn calls method A. There can even be several methods involved in the recursion. For example, method A could call method B, which could call method C, which calls method A.

Checkpoint

15.1   It is said that a recursive algorithm has more overhead than an iterative algorithm. What does this mean?

15.2   What is a base case?

15.3   What is a recursive case?

15.4   What causes a recursive algorithm to stop calling itself?

15.5   What is direct recursion? What is indirect recursion?

15.3 Examples of Recursive Methods

Summing a Range of Array Elements with Recursion

In this example we look at a method, rangeSum, that uses recursion to sum a range of array elements. The method takes the following arguments: an int array that contains the range of elements to be summed, an int specifying the starting element of the range, and an int specifying the ending element of the range. Here is an example of how the method might be used:

```
int[] numbers = {1, 2, 3, 4, 5, 6, 7, 8, 9};
int sum;
sum = rangeSum(numbers, 3, 7);
```

This code specifies that `rangeSum` should return the sum of elements three through seven in the numbers array. The return value, which in this case would be 30, is stored in `sum`. Here is the definition of the `rangeSum` method:

```java
public static int rangeSum(int[] array, int start, int end)
{
    if (start > end)
        return 0;
    else
        return array[start] + rangeSum(array, start + 1, end);
}
```

This method's base case is when the `start` parameter is greater than the `end` parameter. If this is true, the method returns the value 0. Otherwise, the method executes the following statement:

```java
return array[start] + rangeSum(array, start + 1, end);
```

This statement returns the sum of `array[start]` plus the return value of a recursive call. Notice that in the recursive call, the starting element in the range is `start + 1`. In essence, this statement says "return the value of the first element in the range plus the sum of the rest of the elements in the range." The program in Code Listing 15-5 demonstrates the method.

Code Listing 15-5   **(RangeSum.java)**

```java
 1  /**
 2   * This program demonstrates the recursive rangeSum method.
 3   */
 4
 5  public class RangeSum
 6  {
 7      /**
 8       * main method
 9       */
10
11      public static void main(String[] args)
12      {
13          int[] numbers = {1, 2, 3, 4, 5, 6, 7, 8, 9};
14
15          System.out.print("The sum of elements 2 through 5 is " +
16                          rangeSum(numbers, 2, 5));
17      }
18
19      /**
20       * The rangeSum method returns the sum of a specified
21       * range of elements in array. The start parameter
22       * specifies the starting element and the end parameter
23       * specifies the ending parameter.
24       */
25
```

```
26      public static int rangeSum(int[] array, int start, int end)
27      {
28         if (start > end)
29            return 0;
30         else
31            return array[start] + rangeSum(array, start + 1, end);
32      }
33   }
```

Program Output

```
The sum of elements 2 through 5 is 18
```

Drawing Concentric Circles

In this example we look at the `Circles` applet, which uses recursion to draw concentric circles. Concentric circles are circles of different sizes, one inside another, all with a common center point. Figure 15-5 shows the applet's output. The applet code is shown in Code Listing 15-6.

Figure 15-5 Circles applet

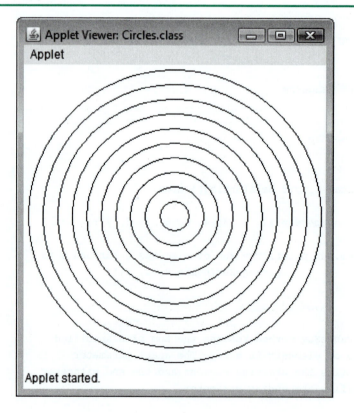

Code Listing 15-6   `(Circles.java)`

```java
1  import javax.swing.*;
2  import java.awt.*;
3
4  /**
5   * This applet uses a recursive method to draw
6   * concentric circles.
7   */
8
9  public class Circles extends JApplet
10 {
11    /**
12     * init method
13     */
14
15    public void init()
16    {
17       // Set the background color to white.
18       setBackground(Color.WHITE);
19    }
20
21    /**
22     * paint method
23     */
24
25    public void paint(Graphics g)
26    {
27       // Draw 10 concentric circles. The outermost circle's
28       // enclosing rectangle should be at (5, 5), and it
29       // should be 300 pixels wide by 300 pixels high.
30       drawCircles(g, 10, 5, 300);
31    }
32
33    /**
34     * The drawCircles method draws concentric circles.
35     * It accepts the following arguments:
36     * g, a Graphics object
37     * n, the number of circles to draw
38     * topXY, the top-left coordinates of the
39     *        outermost circle's enclosing rectangle
40     * size, the width and height of the outermost
41     *        circle's enclosing rectangle
42     */
43
```

```
44    private void drawCircles(Graphics g, int n, int topXY, int size)
45    {
46       if (n > 0)
47       {
48          g.drawOval(topXY, topXY, size, size);
49          drawCircles(g, n - 1, topXY + 15, size - 30);
50       }
51    }
52 }
```

The drawCircles method, which is called from the applet's paint method, uses recursion to draw the concentric circles. The n parameter holds the number of circles to draw. If this parameter is set to 0, the method has reached its base case. Otherwise, it calls the g object's drawOval method to draw a circle. The topXY parameter holds the value to use as the *X* and *Y* coordinate of the enclosing rectangle's upper-left corner. The size parameter holds the value to use as the enclosing rectangle's width and height. After the circle is drawn, the drawCircles method is recursively called with parameter values adjusted for the next circle.

The Fibonacci Series

Some mathematical problems are designed to be solved recursively. One well-known example is the calculation of *Fibonacci numbers*. The Fibonacci numbers, named after the Italian mathematician Leonardo Fibonacci (born circa 1170), are the following sequence:

   0, 1, 1, 2, 3, 5, 8, 13, 21, 34, 55, 89, 144, 233, …

Notice that after the second number, each number in the series is the sum of the two previous numbers. The Fibonacci series can be defined as:

If $n = 0$ then	$\text{Fib}(n) = 0$
If $n = 1$ then	$\text{Fib}(n) = 1$
If $n >= 2$ then	$\text{Fib}(n) = \text{Fib}(n - 1) + \text{Fib}(n - 2)$

A recursive Java method to calculate the *n*th number in the Fibonacci series is shown here:

```
public static int fib(int n)
{
   if (n == 0)
     return 0;
   else if (n == 1)
     return 1;
   else
     return fib(n - 1) + fib(n - 2);
}
```

Notice that this method actually has two base cases: when n is less than 0, and when n is equal to 1. In either case, the method returns a value without making a recursive call. The program in Code Listing 15-7 demonstrates this method by displaying the first 10 numbers in the Fibonacci series.

Code Listing 15-7   `(FibNumbers.java)`

```
1   /**
2    * This program demonstrates the recursive fib method.
3    */
4
5   public class FibNumbers
6   {
7       /**
8        * main method
9        */
10
11      public static void main(String[] args)
12      {
13          System.out.println("The first 10 numbers in the " +
14                              "Fibonacci series are:");
15
16          for (int i = 0; i < 10; i++)
17              System.out.print(fib(i) + " ");
18
19          System.out.println();
20      }
21
22      /**
23       * The fib method returns the nth
24       * Fibonacci number.
25       */
26
27      public static int fib(int n)
28      {
29          if (n == 0)
30              return 0;
31          else if (n == 1)
32              return 1;
33          else
34              return fib(n - 1) + fib(n - 2);
35      }
36  }
```

Program Output

```
The first 10 numbers in the Fibonacci series are:
0 1 1 2 3 5 8 13 21 34
```

Finding the Greatest Common Divisor

Our next example of recursion is the calculation of the greatest common divisor, or GCD, of two numbers. The GCD of two positive integers, x and y, is:

if y divides x evenly, then $gcd(x, y) = y$
Otherwise, $gcd(x, y) = gcd(y,$ remainder of $x/y)$

This definition states that the GCD of x and y is y if x/y has no remainder. This is the base case. Otherwise, the answer is the GCD of y and the remainder of x/y. The program in Code Listing 15-8 shows a recursive method for calculating the GCD.

Code Listing 15-8   (`GCDdemo.java`)

```
 1   import java.util.Scanner;
 2
 3   /**
 4    * This program demonstrates the recursive gcd method.
 5    */
 6
 7   public class GCDdemo
 8   {
 9      /**
10       * main method
11       */
12
13      public static void main(String[] args)
14      {
15         int num1, num2;   // Two numbers
16
17         // Create a Scanner object for keyboard input.
18         Scanner keyboard = new Scanner(System.in);
19
20         // Get two numbers from the user.
21         System.out.print("Enter an integer: ");
22         num1 = keyboard.nextInt();
23         System.out.print("Enter another integer: ");
24         num2 = keyboard.nextInt();
25
26         // Display the GCD.
27         System.out.println("The greatest common divisor " +
28                            "of these two numbers is " +
29                            gcd(num1, num2));
30      }
31
32      /**
33       * The gcd method returns the greatest common divisor
34       * of the arguments passed into x and y.
35       */
36
```

```
37    public static int gcd(int x, int y)
38    {
39       if (x % y == 0)
40          return y;
41       else
42          return gcd(y, x % y);
43    }
44 }
```

 ## 15.4 A Recursive Binary Search Method

CONCEPT: The recursive binary search algorithm is more elegant and easier to understand than its iterative version.

In Chapter 7 you learned about the binary search algorithm and saw an iterative example written in Java. The binary search algorithm can also be implemented recursively. For example, the procedure can be expressed as:

> If array[middle] *equals the search value, then the value is found.*
> Else if array[middle] *is less than the search value, perform a binary search on*
> *the upper half of the array.*
> Else if array[middle] *is greater than the search value, perform a binary search on*
> *the lower half of the array.*

When you compare the recursive algorithm to its iterative counterpart, it becomes evident that the recursive version is much more elegant and easier to understand. The recursive binary search algorithm is also a good example of repeatedly breaking a problem down into smaller pieces until it is solved. Here is the code for the method:

```
public static int binarySearch(int[] array, int first,
                               int last, int value)
{
    int middle;        // Mid point of search

    // Test for the base case where the value is not found.
    if (first > last)
       return -1;

    // Calculate the middle position.
    middle = (first + last) / 2;
```

```
              // Search for the value.
              if (array[middle] == value)
                 return middle;
              else if (array[middle] < value)
                 return binarySearch(array, middle + 1, last, value);
              else
                 return binarySearch(array, first, middle - 1, value);
       }
```

The first parameter, array, is the array to be searched. The next parameter, first, holds the subscript of the first element in the search range (the portion of the array to be searched). The next parameter, last, holds the subscript of the last element in the search range. The last parameter, value, holds the value to be searched for. Like the iterative version, this method returns the subscript of the value if it is found, or −1 if the value is not found. Code Listing 15-9 demonstrates the method.

Code Listing 15-9   (RecursiveBinarySearch.java)

```
1   import java.util.Scanner;
2
3   /**
4    * This demonstrates the recursive binary search method.
5    */
6
7   public class RecursiveBinarySearch
8   {
9      public static void main(String [] args)
10     {
11        // The values in the following array are sorted
12        // in ascending order.
13        int numbers[] = {101, 142, 147, 189, 199, 207, 222,
14                         234, 289, 296, 310, 319, 388, 394,
15                         417, 429, 447, 521, 536, 600};
16
17        int result;       // Result of the search
18        int searchValue;  // Value to search for
19        String again;     // User input
20
21        // Create a Scanner object for keyboard input.
22        Scanner keyboard = new Scanner(System.in);
23
24        do
25        {
26           // Get a value to search for.
27           System.out.print("Enter a value to search for: ");
28           searchValue = keyboard.nextInt();
29
30           // Search for the value
31           result = binarySearch(numbers, 0,
32                        (numbers.length - 1), searchValue);
```

```
33
34              // Display the results.
35              if (result == -1)
36              {
37                  System.out.println(searchValue +
38                                       " was not found.");
39              }
40              else
41              {
42                  System.out.println(searchValue +
43                                       " was found at " +
44                                       "element " + result);
45              }
46
47              // Consume the remaining newline.
48              keyboard.nextLine();
49
50              // Does the user want to search again?
51              System.out.print("Do you want to search again? " +
52                                   "(Y or N): ");
53              again = keyboard.nextLine();
54
55          } while (again.charAt(0) == 'y' || again.charAt(0) == 'Y');
56      }
57
58      /**
59       * The binarySearch method performs a binary search on an
60       * integer array. The array is searched for the number passed
61       * to value. If the number is found, its array subscript is
62       * returned. Otherwise, -1 is returned indicating the value was
63       * not found in the array.
64       */
65
66      public static int binarySearch(int[] array, int first,
67                                     int last, int value)
68      {
69          int middle;     // Mid-point of search
70
71          // Test for the base case where the value is not found.
72          if (first > last)
73            return -1;
74
75          // Calculate the middle position.
76          middle = (first + last) / 2;
77
78          // Search for the value.
79          if (array[middle] == value)
80            return middle;
```

```
81            else if (array[middle] < value)
82                return binarySearch(array, middle + 1, last, value);
83            else
84                return binarySearch(array, first, middle - 1, value);
85    }
86  }
```

Program Output with Example Input Shown in Bold

```
Enter a value to search for: 289 [Enter]
289 was found at element 8
Do you want to search again? (Y or N): y [Enter]
Enter a value to search for: 388 [Enter]
388 was found at element 12
Do you want to search again? (Y or N): y [Enter]
Enter a value to search for: 101 [Enter]
101 was found at element 0
Do you want to search again? (Y or N): y [Enter]
Enter a value to search for: 999 [Enter]
999 was not found.
Do you want to search again? (Y or N): n [Enter]
```

See Appendix K, available at www.pearsonhighered.com/gaddis, for a discussion of the recursive QuickSort algorithm.

15.5 The Towers of Hanoi

CONCEPT: The repetitive steps involved in solving the Towers of Hanoi game can be easily implemented in a recursive algorithm.

The Towers of Hanoi is a mathematical game that is often used in computer science textbooks to illustrate the power of recursion. The game uses three pegs and a set of discs with holes through their centers. The discs are stacked on one of the pegs as shown in Figure 15-6.

Figure 15-6 The pegs and discs in the Towers of Hanoi game

Notice that the discs are stacked on the leftmost peg, in order of size with the largest disc at the bottom. The game is based on a legend where a group of monks in a temple in Hanoi have a similar set of pegs with 64 discs. The job of the monks is to move the discs from the

first peg to the third peg. The middle peg can be used as a temporary holder. Furthermore, the monks must follow these rules while moving the discs:

- Only one disc can be moved at a time.
- A disc cannot be placed on top of a smaller disc.
- All discs must be stored on a peg except while being moved.

According to the legend, when the monks have moved all of the discs from the first peg to the last peg, the world will come to an end.

To play the game, you must move all of the discs from the first peg to the third peg, following the same rules as the monks. Let's look at some example solutions to this game, for different numbers of discs. If you have only one disc, the solution to the game is simple: Move the disc from peg 1 to peg 3. If you have two discs, the solution requires three moves:

- Move disc 1 to peg 2.
- Move disc 2 to peg 3.
- Move disc 1 to peg 3.

Notice that this approach uses peg 2 as a temporary location. The complexity of the moves continues to increase as the number of discs increase. To move three discs requires the seven moves shown in Figure 15-7.

Figure 15-7   Steps for moving three pegs

Original setup.

First move: Move disc 1 to peg 3.

Second move: Move disc 2 to peg 2.

Third move: Move disc 1 to peg 2.

Fourth move: Move disc 3 to peg 3.

Fifth move: Move disc 1 to peg 1.

Sixth move: Move disc 2 to peg 3.

Seventh move: Move disc 1 to peg 3.

The following statement describes the overall solution to the problem:

Move n discs from peg 1 to peg 3 using peg 2 as a temporary peg.

The following algorithm can be used as the basis of a recursive method that simulates the solution to the game. Notice that in this algorithm we use the variables *A*, *B*, and *C* to hold peg numbers.

To move n discs from peg A to peg C, using peg B as a temporary peg:
If n > 0 Then
     Move n − 1 discs from peg A to peg B, using peg C as a temporary peg.
     Move the remaining disc from peg A to peg C.
     Move n − 1 discs from peg B to peg C, using peg A as a temporary peg.
End If

The base case for the algorithm is reached when there are no more discs to move. The following code is for a method that implements this algorithm. Note that the method does not actually move anything, but displays instructions indicating all of the disc moves to make.

```java
private void moveDiscs(int num, int fromPeg, int toPeg, int tempPeg)
{
    if (num > 0)
    {
        moveDiscs(num - 1, fromPeg, tempPeg, toPeg);
        System.out.println("Move a disc from peg " + fromPeg +
                           " to peg " + toPeg);
        moveDiscs(num - 1, tempPeg, toPeg, fromPeg);
    }
}
```

This method accepts arguments into the following four parameters:

num	The number of discs to move.
fromPeg	The peg to move the discs from.
toPeg	The peg to move the discs to.
tempPeg	The peg to use as a temporary peg.

If num is greater than 0, then there are discs to move. The first recursive call is:

```java
moveDiscs(num - 1, fromPeg, tempPeg, toPeg);
```

This statement is an instruction to move all but one disc from `fromPeg` to `tempPeg`, using `toPeg` as a temporary peg. The next statement is:

```java
System.out.println("Move a disc from peg " + fromPeg +
                   " to peg " + toPeg);
```

This simply displays a message indicating that a disc should be moved from `fromPeg` to `toPeg`. Next, another recursive call is executed:

```java
moveDiscs(num - 1, tempPeg, toPeg, fromPeg);
```

This statement is an instruction to move all but one disc from `tempPeg` to `toPeg`, using `fromPeg` as a temporary peg. Code Listing 15-10 shows the `Hanoi` class, which uses this method.

Code Listing 15-10   (Hanoi.java)

```java
 1  /**
 2   * This class displays a solution to the Towers of
 3   * Hanoi game.
 4   */
 5
 6  public class Hanoi
 7  {
 8     private int numDiscs;    // Number of discs
 9
10     /**
11      * Constructor. The argument is the number of
12      * discs to use.
13      */
14
15     public Hanoi(int n)
16     {
17        // Assign the number of discs.
18        numDiscs = n;
19
20        // Move the number of discs from peg 1 to peg 3
21        // using peg 2 as a temporary storage location.
22        moveDiscs(numDiscs, 1, 3, 2);
23     }
24
25     /**
26      * The moveDiscs method accepts the number of
27      * discs to move, the peg to move from, the peg
28      * to move to, and the temporary peg as arguments.
29      * It uses recursion to display the necessary
30      * disc moves.
31      */
32
33     private void moveDiscs(int num, int fromPeg,
34                            int toPeg, int tempPeg)
35     {
36        if (num > 0)
37        {
38           moveDiscs(num - 1, fromPeg, tempPeg, toPeg);
39           System.out.println("Move a disc from peg " +
40                          fromPeg + " to peg " + toPeg);
41           moveDiscs(num - 1, tempPeg, toPeg, fromPeg);
42        }
43     }
44  }
```

The class constructor accepts an argument that is the number of discs to use in the game. It assigns this value to the numDiscs field, and then calls the moveDiscs method in line 22. In a nutshell, this statement is an instruction to move all the discs from peg 1 to peg 3, using peg 2 as a temporary peg. The program in Code Listing 15-11 demonstrates the class. It displays the instructions for moving three discs.

Code Listing 15-11   (`HanoiDemo.java`)

```
1   /**
2    * This class demonstrates the Hanoi class, which
3    * displays the steps necessary to solve the Towers
4    * of Hanoi game.
5    */
6
7   public class HanoiDemo
8   {
9      static public void main(String[] args)
10     {
11        Hanoi towersOfHanoi = new Hanoi(3);
12     }
13  }
```

Program Output

```
Move a disc from peg 1 to peg 3
Move a disc from peg 1 to peg 2
Move a disc from peg 3 to peg 2
Move a disc from peg 1 to peg 3
Move a disc from peg 2 to peg 1
Move a disc from peg 2 to peg 3
Move a disc from peg 1 to peg 3
```

15.6 Common Errors to Avoid

The following list describes several errors that are commonly made when learning this chapter's topics.

- **Not coding a base case.** When the base case is reached, a recursive method stops calling itself. Without a base case, the method will continue to call itself infinitely.
- **Not reducing the problem with each recursive call.** Unless the problem is reduced (which usually means that the value of one or more critical parameters is reduced) with each recursive call, the method will not reach the base case. If the base case is not reached, the method will call itself infinitely.
- **Writing the recursive call in such a way that the base case is never reached.** You might have a base case and a recursive case that reduces the problem, but if the calculations are not performed in such a way that the base case is ultimately reached, the method will call itself infinitely.

Review Questions and Exercises

Multiple Choice and True/False

1. A method is called once from a program's `main` method, and then it calls itself four times. The depth of recursion is
   a. one
   b. four
   c. five
   d. nine

2. This is the part of a problem that can be solved without recursion.
   a. base case
   b. solvable case
   c. known case
   d. iterative case

3. This is the part of a problem that is solved with recursion.
   a. base case
   b. iterative case
   c. unknown case
   d. recursion case

4. This is when a method explicitly calls itself.
   a. explicit recursion
   b. modal recursion
   c. direct recursion
   d. indirect recursion

5. This is when method A calls method B, which calls method A.
   a. implicit recursion
   b. modal recursion
   c. direct recursion
   d. indirect recursion

6. This refers to the actions taken internally by the JVM when a method is called.
   a. overhead
   b. set up
   c. clean up
   d. synchronization

7. **True or False:** An iterative algorithm will usually run faster than an equivalent recursive algorithm.

8. **True or False:** Some problems can be solved only through recursion.

9. **True or False:** It is not necessary to have a base case in all recursive algorithms.

10. **True or False:** In the base case, a recursive method calls itself with a smaller version of the original problem.

Find the Error

1. Find the error in the following program.

```java
public class FindTheError
{
    public static void main(String[] args)
    {
        myMethod(0);
    }

    public static void myMethod(int num)
    {
        System.out.print(num + " ");
        myMethod(num + 1);
    }
}
```

Algorithm Workbench

1. Write a method that accepts a `String` as an argument. The method should use recursion to display each individual character in the `String`.

2. Modify the method you wrote in Question 1 so it displays the `String` backwards.

3. What will the following program display?

```java
public class Checkpoint
{
    public static void main(String[] args)
    {
        int num = 0;
        showMe(num);
    }

    public static void showMe(int arg)
    {
        if (arg < 10)
            showMe(arg + 1);
        else
            System.out.println(arg);
    }
}
```

4. What will the following program display?

```java
public class ReviewQuestion4
{
    public static void main(String[] args)
    {
        int num = 0;
        showMe(num);
    }
```

```java
    public static void showMe(int arg)
    {
        System.out.println(arg);
        if (arg < 10)
            showMe(arg + 1);
    }
}
```

5. What will the following program display?

```java
public class ReviewQuestion5
{
    public static void main(String[] args)
    {
        int x = 10;
        System.out.println(myMethod(x));
    }

    public static int myMethod(int num)
    {
        if (num <= 0)
            return 0;
        else
            return myMethod(num - 1) + num;
    }
}
```

6. Convert the following iterative method to one that uses recursion.

```java
public static void sign(int n)
{
    while (n > 0)
    {
        System.out.println("No Parking");
        n--;
    }
}
```

7. Write an iterative version (using a loop instead of recursion) of the `factorial` method shown in this chapter.

Short Answer

1. What is the difference between an iterative algorithm and a recursive algorithm?

2. What is a recursive algorithm's base case? What is the recursive case?

3. What is the base case of each of the recursive methods listed in Algorithm Workbench Questions 3, 4, and 5?

4. What type of recursive method do you think would be more difficult to debug: one that uses direct recursion or one that uses indirect recursion? Why?

5. Which repetition approach is less efficient: a loop or a recursive method? Why?

6. When recursion is used to solve a problem, why must the recursive method call itself to solve a smaller version of the original problem?

7. How is a problem usually reduced with a recursive method?

Programming Challenges

1. Recursive Multiplication

Write a recursive function that accepts two arguments into the parameters x and y. The function should return the value of x times y. Remember, multiplication can be performed as repeated addition:

$$7 * 4 = 4 + 4 + 4 + 4 + 4 + 4 + 4$$

2. isMember Method

Write a recursive `boolean` method named `isMember`. The method should accept two arguments: an array and a value. The method should return `true` if the value is found in the array, or `false` if the value is not found in the array. Demonstrate the method in a program.

3. String Reverser

Write a recursive method that accepts a string as its argument and prints the string in reverse order. Demonstrate the method in a program.

4. maxElement Method

Write a method named `maxElement` that returns the largest value in an array that is passed as an argument. The method should use recursion to find the largest element. Demonstrate the method in a program.

5. Palindrome Detector

A palindrome is any word, phrase, or sentence that reads the same forward and backwards. Here are some well-known palindromes:

Able was I, ere I saw Elba
A man, a plan, a canal, Panama
Desserts, I stressed
Kayak

Write a `boolean` method that uses recursion to determine whether a `String` argument is a palindrome. The method should return `true` if the argument reads the same forward and backwards. Demonstrate the method in a program.

6. Character Counter

Write a method that uses recursion to count the number of times a specific character occurs in an array of characters. Demonstrate the method in a program.

7. Recursive Power Method

Write a method that uses recursion to raise a number to a power. The method should accept two arguments: the number to be raised and the exponent. Assume that the exponent is a nonnegative integer. Demonstrate the method in a program.

8. Sum of Numbers

Write a method that accepts an integer argument and returns the sum of all the integers from 1 up to the number passed as an argument. For example, if 50 is passed as an argument, the method will return the sum of 1, 2, 3, 4, . . . 50. Use recursion to calculate the sum. Demonstrate the method in a program.

9. Ackermann's Function

Ackermann's function is a recursive mathematical algorithm that can be used to test how well a computer performs recursion. Write a method `ackermann(m, n)` that solves Ackermann's function. Use the following logic in your method:

> If m = 0 then return n + 1
> If n = 0 then return ackermann(m - 1, 1)
> Otherwise, return ackermann(m - 1, ackermann(m, n - 1))

Test your method in a program that displays the return values of the following method calls:

```
ackermann(0, 0)    ackermann(0, 1)    ackermann(1, 1)    ackermann(1, 2)
ackermann(1, 3)    ackermann(2, 2)    ackermann(3, 2)
```

10. Recursive Population Class

In Programming Challenge 6 of Chapter 5 you wrote a population class that predicts the size of a population of organisms after a number of days. Modify the class so it uses a recursive method instead of a loop to calculate the number of organisms.

16 Databases

TOPICS

16.1   Introduction to Database Management Systems
16.2   Tables, Rows, and Columns
16.3   Introduction to the SQL SELECT Statement
16.4   Inserting Rows
16.5   Updating and Deleting Existing Rows
16.6   Creating and Deleting Tables
16.7   Creating a New Database with JDBC
16.8   Scrollable Result Sets
16.9   Result Set Meta Data
16.10 Displaying Query Results in a JTable
16.11 Relational Data
16.12 Advanced Topics
16.13 Common Errors to Avoid

16.1   Introduction to Database Management Systems

CONCEPT: A database management system (DBMS) is software that manages large collections of data.

If an application needs to store only a small amount of data, text and binary files work well. These types of files, however, are not practical when a large amount of data must be stored and manipulated. Many businesses keep hundreds of thousands, or even millions of data items in files. When a text or binary file contains this much data, simple operations, such as searching, inserting, and deleting, become cumbersome and inefficient.

When developing applications that work with an extensive amount of data, most developers prefer to use a *database management system*, or *DBMS*. A DBMS is software that is specifically designed to store, retrieve, and manipulate large amounts of data in an organized and efficient manner. Once the data is stored using the database management system, applications may be written in Java or other languages to communicate with the DBMS. Rather than retrieving or manipulating the data directly, applications can send instructions to the DBMS. The DBMS carries out those instructions and sends the results back to the application. Figure 16-1 illustrates this.

Figure 16-1 A Java application interacts with a DBMS, which manipulates data

Although Figure 16-1 is simplified, it illustrates the layered nature of an application that works with a database management system. The topmost layer of software, which in this case is written in Java, interacts with the user. It also sends instructions to the next layer of software, the DBMS. The DBMS works directly with the data and sends the results of operations back to the application.

For example, suppose a company keeps all of its product records in a database. The company has a Java application that allows the user to look up information on any product by entering its product ID number. The Java application instructs the DBMS to retrieve the record for the product with the specified product ID number. The DBMS retrieves the product record and sends the data back to the Java application. The Java application displays the data to the user.

The advantage of this layered approach to software development is that the Java application does not need know about the physical structure of the data. It only needs to know how to interact with the DBMS. The DBMS handles the actual reading, writing, and searching of data.

JDBC

Figure 16-1 gives a simple illustration of a Java application communicating with a DBMS. The technology that makes this communication possible is known as *JDBC*, which stands for *Java Database Connectivity*. The Java API contains numerous JDBC classes that allow your Java applications to interact with a DBMS. This is illustrated in Figure 16-2.

Figure 16-2 A Java application uses the JDBC classes to interact with a DBMS

SQL

SQL, which stands for *Structured Query Language*, is a standard language for working with database management systems. It was originally developed by IBM in the 1970s. Since then, SQL has been adopted by most every database software vendor as the language of choice for interacting with their DBMS.

SQL consists of several key words. You use the key words to construct statements, which are also known as *queries*. These statements, or queries, are submitted to the DBMS and are instructions for the DBMS to carry out operations on its data. When a Java application interacts with a DBMS, the Java application must construct SQL statements as strings and then use an API method to pass those strings to the DBMS. In this chapter you will learn how to construct simple SQL statements and then pass them to a DBMS using API method call.

NOTE: Although SQL is a language, you don't use it to write applications. It is intended only as a standard means of interacting with a DBMS. You still need a general programming language, such as Java, to write an application for the ordinary user.

Using a DBMS

In order to use JDBC to work with a database, you will need a DBMS installed on your system, or available to you in a school lab environment. There are many commercial DBMS packages available. Oracle, Microsoft SQL Server, DB2, and MySQL are just a few of the popular ones. In your school's lab, you may already have access to one of these, or perhaps another DBMS.

Java DB

If you do not have access to a DBMS in a school lab, you can use Java DB, which is included with the JDK. Java DB is an open source distribution of Apache Derby, a pure Java DBMS. It is automatically installed on your system when you install the JDK version 7 or higher. All of the examples in this chapter were created with Java DB. If you wish to use Java DB, see Appendix J—Configuring Java DB, available for download on this book's companion Web site, at www.pearsonhighered.com/gaddis.

Creating the `CoffeeDB` Database

In this chapter we will use a database named `CoffeeDB` as our example. The `CoffeeDB` database is used in the business operations of The Midnight Roastery, a small coffee roasting company. After you have installed the Java DB DBMS, perform the following steps to create the `CoffeeDB` database:

1. Make sure you have downloaded Student Source Code files from the book's companion Web site.
2. In this chapter's source code files, locate a program named `CreateCoffeeDB.java`.
3. Compile and execute the `CreateCoffeeDB.java` program. If Java DB is properly installed, this program will create the `CoffeeDB` database on your system.

 NOTE: If you are in a school lab environment using a DBMS other than Java DB, consult with your instructor on how to modify the program to work with your specific DBMS.

Connecting to the `CoffeeDB` Database

After installing Java DB and creating the `CoffeeDB` database, you should attempt to connect to the database with a Java program. A program can call the static JDBC method `DriverManager.getConnection` get a connection to a database. There are overloaded versions of this method, but the simplest one has the following general format:

```
DriverManager.getConnection(DatabaseURL);
```

The method returns a reference to a `Connection` object, which we will discuss in a moment. In the general format, *DatabaseURL* is a string known as a *database URL*. URL stands for Uniform Resource Locator. A database URL lists the protocol that should be used to access the database, the name of the database, and potentially other items. A simple database URL has the following general format:

```
protocol:subprotocol:databaseName
```

In this very simple general format, three items are listed, separated by colons: *protocol*, *subprotocol*, and *databaseName*. Let's take a closer look at each one.

- *protocol* is the database protocol. When using JDBC, the protocol will always be jdbc.
- The value for *subprotocol* will be dependent upon the particular type of DBMS you are connecting to. If you are using Java DB, the subprotocol is derby.
- *databaseName* is the name of the database you are connecting to.

If we are using Java DB, the URL for the CoffeeDB database is:

```
jdbc:derby:CoffeeDB
```

The DriverManager.getConnection method searches for and loads a JDBC driver that is compatible with the database specified by the URL. A *JDBC driver* is a Java class that is designed to communicate with a specific DBMS. Each DBMS usually comes with its own JDBC driver. Typically, when you install a DBMS, you also update your system's CLASSPATH variable to include the JDBC driver's location. This will enable the JVM to find the driver class when you call the DriverManager.getConnection method.

When the DriverManager.getConnection method finds a compatible driver, it returns a Connection object. Connection is an interface in the java.sql package. You will need to use this Connection object to perform various tasks with the database, so save the reference in a variable. Here is an example of code that we can use in a Java application to get a connection to the CoffeeDB database using Java DB:

```
final String DB_URL = "jdbc:derby:CoffeeDB";
Connection conn = DriverManager.getConnection(DB_URL);
```

In the second statement shown here, we call the DriverManager.getConnection method, passing the URL for the CoffeeDB database. The method returns a reference to a Connection object, which we assign to the conn variable. If the DriverManager.getConnection method fails to load an appropriate driver for the specified database, it will throw an SQLException.

Before going any further, compile and execute the TestConnection.java program shown in Code Listing 16-1. It demonstrates what we've covered so far. (This program assumes that Java DB has been installed, and that the CoffeeDB database has been created.)

Code Listing 16-1   **(TestConnection.java)**

```
 1  import java.sql.*;    // Needed for JDBC classes
 2
 3  /**
 4   * This program demonstrates how to connect to
 5   * a Java DB database using JDBC.
 6   */
 7
 8  public class TestConnection
 9  {
10     public static void main(String[] args)
11     {
12        // Create a named constant for the URL.
13        // NOTE: This value is specific for Java DB.
```

```
14              final String DB_URL = "jdbc:derby:CoffeeDB";
15
16          try
17          {
18              // Create a connection to the database.
19              Connection conn = DriverManager.getConnection(DB_URL);
20              System.out.println("Connection created to CoffeeDB.");
21
22              // Close the connection.
23              conn.close();
24              System.out.println("Connection closed.");
25          }
26          catch(Exception ex)
27          {
28              System.out.println("ERROR: " + ex.getMessage());
29          }
30      }
31  }
```

Program Output

```
Connection created to CoffeeDB.
Connection closed.
```

Notice that line 1 imports all of the classes in the java.sql package. This package contains many of the necessary JDBC classes. Line 14 creates a string constant containing the URL for the CoffeeDB database.

JDBC methods throw an SQLException if they encounter a problem with a database. For that reason, we use a try-catch statement to handle any such exceptions. Let's take a closer look at the statements inside the try block:

- Line 19 does the following:
  - It declares a Connection variable named conn.
  - It calls the DriverManager.getConnection method to get a connection to the CoffeeDB database.
  - The DriverManager.getConnection method returns a reference to a Connection object. The reference is assigned to the conn variable.
- Line 20 displays a message indicating that a connection was created.
- Line 23 calls the Connection object's close method, which simply closes the database connection.
- Line 24 displays a message indicating that the connection is closed.

If a connection cannot be created in line 19, or the connection cannot be closed in line 23, an exception will be thrown. The catch clause in line 26 will handle the exception, and line 28 will display the exception object's default error message.

Connecting to a Password-Protected Database

If the database that you are connecting to requires a user name and a password, you can use the following form of the `DriverManager.getConnection` method:

```
DriverManager.getConnection(DatabaseURL, Username, Password);
```

In this general format, *Username* is a string containing a valid username, and *Password* is a string containing the password.

✓ Checkpoint

16.1 Why do most businesses use a DBMS to store their data instead of creating their own text files or binary files to hold the data?

16.2 When a Java application uses a DBMS to store and manipulate data, why doesn't the Java application need to know specific details about the physical structure of the data?

16.3 What is the technology that makes it possible for a Java application to communicate with a DBMS?

16.4 What is the standard language for working with database management systems?

16.5 What is a database URL?

16.6 Suppose you have a Java DB database on your system named `InventoryDB`. What database URL would you use in a Java program to get a connection to the database?

16.7 What static JDBC method do you call to get a connection to a database?

16.2 Tables, Rows, and Columns

CONCEPT: Data that is stored in a database is organized into tables, rows, and columns.

A database management system stores data in a *database*. Your first step in learning to use a DBMS is to learn how data is organized inside a database. The data that is stored in a database is organized into one or more tables. Each *table* holds a collection of related data. The data that is stored in a table is then organized into rows and columns. A row is a complete set of information about a single item. The data that is stored in a row is divided into columns. Each column is an individual piece of information about the item.

The `CoffeeDB` database has a table named `Coffee`, which holds records for all of the different coffees sold by the company. Table 16-1 shows the contents of the table.

Table 16-1 The `Coffee` database table

Description	ProdNum	Price
Bolivian Dark	14-001	8.95
Bolivian Medium	14-002	8.95
Brazilian Dark	15-001	7.95
Brazilian Medium	15-002	7.95
Brazilian Decaf	15-003	8.55
Central American Dark	16-001	9.95
Central American Medium	16-002	9.95
Sumatra Dark	17-001	7.95
Sumatra Decaf	17-002	8.95
Sumatra Medium	17-003	7.95
Sumatra Organic Dark	17-004	11.95
Kona Medium	18-001	18.45
Kona Dark	18-002	18.45
French Roast Dark	19-001	9.65
Galapagos Medium	20-001	6.85
Guatemalan Dark	21-001	9.95
Guatemalan Decaf	21-002	10.45
Guatemalan Medium	21-003	9.95

As you can see, the table has 18 rows. Each row holds data about a type of coffee. The rows are divided into three columns. The first column is named `Description`, and it holds the description of a type of coffee. The second column is named `ProdNum`, and it holds a coffee's product number. The third column is named `Price`, and it holds a coffee's price per pound. As illustrated in Figure 16-3, the third row in the table holds the following data:

Description: Brazilian Dark
Product Number: 15-001
Price: 7.95

Figure 16-3   The Coffee database table

This row contains data about
a single item.
Description: Brazilian Dark
Product Number: 15-001
Price: 7.95

Description	ProdNum	Price
Bolivian Dark	14-001	8.95
Bolivian Medium	14-002	8.95
Brazilian Dark	15-001	7.95
Brazilian Medium	15-002	7.95
Brazilian Decaf	15-003	8.55
Central American Dark	16-001	9.95
Central American Medium	16-002	9.95
Sumatra Dark	17-001	7.95
Sumatra Decaf	17-002	8.95
Sumatra Medium	17-003	7.95
Sumatra Organic Dark	17-004	11.95
Kona Medium	18-001	18.45
Kona Dark	18-002	18.45
French Roast Dark	19-001	9.65
Galapagos Medium	20-001	6.85
Guatemalan Dark	21-001	9.95
Guatemalan Decaf	21-002	10.45
Guatemalan Medium	21-003	9.95

Description   ProdNum   Price
Column   Column   Column

Column Data Types

The columns in a database table are assigned a data type. Notice that the Description and ProdNum columns in the Coffee table hold strings, and the Price column holds floating-point numbers. The data types of the columns are not Java data types, however. Instead, they are SQL data types. Table 16-2 lists a few of the standard SQL data types and shows the Java data type that each is generally compatible with.

Table 16-2   A few of the SQL data types

SQL Data Type	Description	Corresponding Java Data Type
INTEGER or INT	An integer number	int
CHARACTER(n) or CHAR(n)	A fixed-length string with a length of n characters	String
VARCHAR(n)	A variable-length string with a maximum length of n characters.	String
REAL	A single-precision floating point number	float
DOUBLE	A double-precision floating point number	double
DECIMAL(t, d)	A decimal value with t total digits and d digits appearing after the decimal point.	java.math.BigDecimal
DATE	A date	java.sql.Date

There are many other standard data types in SQL. When the `Coffee` table was created, the following data types were used for the columns:

- The data type for the `Description` column is `CHAR(25)`. This means that each value in the `Description` column is a string with a fixed length of 25 characters, compatible with the `String` type in Java.
- The data type for the `ProdNum` column is `CHAR(10)`. This means that each value in the `ProdNum` column is a string with a fixed length of 10 characters, compatible with the `String` type in Java.
- The data type for the `Price` column is `DOUBLE`. This means that each value in the `Price` column is a double-precision floating-point number, compatible with the `double` data type in Java.

Primary Keys

Most database tables have a *primary key*, which is a column that can be used to identify a specific row in a table. The column that is designated as the primary holds a unique value for each row. If you try to store duplicate data in the primary key column, an error will occur.

In the `Coffee` table, the `ProdNum` column is the primary key because it holds a unique product number for each type of coffee. Here are some other examples:

- Suppose a table stores employee data, and one of the columns holds employee ID numbers. Because each employee's ID number is unique, this column can be used as the primary key.
- Suppose a table stores data about a cell phone company's inventory of phones, and one of the columns holds cell phone serial numbers. Because each phone's serial number is unique, this column can be used as the primary key.
- Suppose a table stores invoice data, and one of the columns holds invoice numbers. Each invoice has a unique invoice number, so this column can be used as a primary key.

> **NOTE:** It is possible for a table's primary key to be the combination of several columns in the table.

Checkpoint

16.8 Describe how the data that is stored in a table is organized.

16.9 What is a primary key?

16.10 What Java data types correspond with the following SQL types?
- `INTEGER`
- `INT`
- `REAL`
- `CHAR`
- `CHARACTER`
- `VARCHAR`
- `DOUBLE`

16.3 Introduction to the SQL SELECT Statement

CONCEPT: The SELECT statement is used in SQL to retrieve data from a database.

The first SQL statement we will discuss is the SELECT statement. You use the *SELECT statement* to retrieve the rows in a table. As its name implies, the SELECT statement allows you to select specific rows. We will start with a very simple form of the statement, as shown here:

```
SELECT Columns FROM Table
```

In the general form, *Columns* is one or more column names, and *Table* is a table name. Here is an example SELECT statement that we might execute on the CoffeeDB database:

```
SELECT Description FROM Coffee
```

This statement will retrieve the Description column for every row in the Coffee table. Figure 16-4 shows an example of the results.

Figure 16-4 Description Column

Description
Bolivian Dark
Bolivian Medium
Brazilian Dark
Brazilian Medium
Brazilian Decaf
Central American Dark
Central American Medium
Sumatra Dark
Sumatra Decaf
Sumatra Medium
Sumatra Organic Dark
Kona Medium
Kona Dark
French Roast Dark
Galapagos Medium
Guatemalan Dark
Guatemalan Decaf
Guatemalan Medium

Figure 16-4 shows the results of a SELECT statement, but what happens to these results? In a Java program, the results of a SELECT statement are returned to the program in a ResultSet object. A *ResultSet object* is simply an object that contains the results of an SQL statement. The process of sending an SQL statement to a DBMS can be summarized in the following steps:

1. Get a connection to the database.
2. Pass a string containing an SQL statement to the DBMS. If the SQL statement has results to send back, a ResultSet object will be returned to the program.
3. Process the contents of the ResultSet object, if one has been returned to the program.
4. When finished working with the database, close the connection.

You previously saw, in Code Listing 16-1, an example of how to perform step 1 (get a connection to the database) and step 4 (close the connection). Let's look at the details of how an SQL statement is sent to the DBMS and its results are processed in steps 2 and 3.

Passing an SQL Statement to the DBMS

Once you have gotten a connection to the database, you are ready to issue SQL statements to the DBMS. First, you must get a `Statement` object from the `Connection` object, using its `createStatement` method. Here is an example:

```
Statement stmt = conn.createStatement();
```

After this code executes, the `stmt` variable will reference a `Statement` object. `Statement` is an interface in the `java.sql` package. `Statement` objects have a variety of methods that can be used to execute SQL queries. To execute a `SELECT` query, you use the `executeQuery` method. The method returns a `ResultSet` object. Here is an example:

```
String sqlStatement = "SELECT Description FROM Coffee";
ResultSet result = stmt.executeQuery(sqlStatement);
```

The first statement creates a string containing an SQL query. The second statement passes this string as an argument to the `executeQuery` method. The method returns a reference to a `ResultSet` object containing the results of the query. The reference is assigned to the `result` variable. Figure 16-5 illustrates how the `result` variable references the `ResultSet` object.

Figure 16-5   A `ResultSet` object contains the results of an SQL query

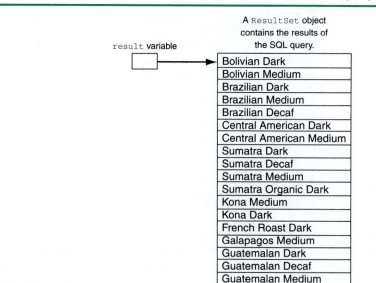

A `ResultSet` object contains a set of rows and columns. The `ResultSet` object in Figure 16-5 has eighteen rows and one column. The rows in a `ResultSet` are numbered, with the first row being row 1, the second row being row 2, and so forth. The columns are also numbered, with the first column being column 1, the second column being column 2, and so forth. Figure 16-6 shows the same `ResultSet` with the row and column numbers labeled.

Figure 16-6 ResultSet rows and columns

Column 1

Row 1	Bolivian Dark
Row 2	Bolivian Medium
Row 3	Brazilian Dark
Row 4	Brazilian Medium
Row 5	Brazilian Decaf
Row 6	Central American Dark
Row 7	Central American Medium
Row 8	Sumatra Dark
Row 9	Sumatra Decaf
Row 10	Sumatra Medium
Row 11	Sumatra Organic Dark
Row 12	Kona Medium
Row 13	Kona Dark
Row 14	French Roast Dark
Row 15	Galapagos Medium
Row 16	Guatemalan Dark
Row 17	Guatemalan Decaf
Row 18	Guatemalan Medium

Getting a Row from the ResultSet Object

A ResultSet object has an internal *cursor* that points to a specific row in the ResultSet. The row that the cursor points to is considered the *current row*. The cursor can be moved from row to row, and this provides you with a way to examine all of the rows in the ResultSet.

At first, the cursor is not pointing to a row, but is positioned just before the first row. This is illustrated in Figure 16-7.

Figure 16-7 The cursor is initially positioned before the first row

Initially the cursor is positioned just before the first row in the ResultSet.

Cursor ⟶ Column 1

Row 1	Bolivian Dark
Row 2	Bolivian Medium
Row 3	Brazilian Dark
Row 4	Brazilian Medium
Row 5	Brazilian Decaf
Row 6	Central American Dark
Row 7	Central American Medium
Row 8	Sumatra Dark
Row 9	Sumatra Decaf
Row 10	Sumatra Medium
Row 11	Sumatra Organic Dark
Row 12	Kona Medium
Row 13	Kona Dark
Row 14	French Roast Dark
Row 15	Galapagos Medium
Row 16	Guatemalan Dark
Row 17	Guatemalan Decaf
Row 18	Guatemalan Medium

To move the cursor to the first row in a newly created ResultSet, you call the object's next method. Here is an example:

```
result.next();
```

Assuming that result references a newly created ResultSet object, this statement moves the cursor to the first row in the ResultSet. Figure 16-8 shows how the cursor has moved to the first row in the ResultSet after the next method is called the first time.

Figure 16-8 The next method moves the cursor forward

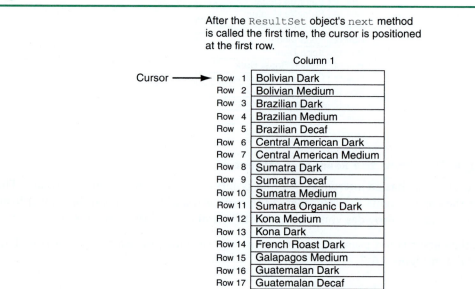

After the ResultSet object's next method is called the first time, the cursor is positioned at the first row.

Column 1

Cursor ──→	Row 1	Bolivian Dark
	Row 2	Bolivian Medium
	Row 3	Brazilian Dark
	Row 4	Brazilian Medium
	Row 5	Brazilian Decaf
	Row 6	Central American Dark
	Row 7	Central American Medium
	Row 8	Sumatra Dark
	Row 9	Sumatra Decaf
	Row 10	Sumatra Medium
	Row 11	Sumatra Organic Dark
	Row 12	Kona Medium
	Row 13	Kona Dark
	Row 14	French Roast Dark
	Row 15	Galapagos Medium
	Row 16	Guatemalan Dark
	Row 17	Guatemalan Decaf
	Row 18	Guatemalan Medium

Each time you call the next method, it moves the cursor to the next row in the ResultSet.

The next method returns a boolean value. It returns true if the cursor successfully moved to the next row. If there are no more rows, it returns false. The following code shows how you can move the cursor through all of the rows of a newly created ResultSet.

```
while (result.next())
{
    // Process the current row.
}
```

There are other ResultSet methods for navigating the rows in a ResultSet object. We will look at some of them later in this chapter.

Getting Columns in a ResultSet Row

You use one of the ResultSet object's "get" methods to retrieve the contents of a specific column in the current row. When you call one of these methods, you can pass either the column number or the column name as an argument. There are numerous "get" methods defined in the ResultSet interface. Table 16-3 lists a few of them.

Table 16-3   A few of the `ResultSet` methods

`ResultSet` Method	Description
double getDouble(int colNumber) double getDouble(String colName)	Returns the `double` that is stored in the column specified by *colNumber* or *colName*. The column must hold data that is compatible with the `double` data type in Java. If an error occurs, the method throws an `SQLException`.
int getInt(int colNumber) int getInt(String colName)	Returns the `int` that is stored in the column specified by *colNumber* or *colName*. The column must hold data that is compatible with the `int` data type in Java. If an error occurs, the method throws an `SQLException`.
String getString(int colNumber) String getString(String colName)	Returns the string that is stored in the column specified by *colNumber* or *colName*. The column must hold data that is compatible with the `String` type in Java. If an error occurs, the method throws an `SQLException`.

Recall that columns have an SQL data type. The SQL data types are not the same as the Java data types, but are compatible with them. To retrieve the contents of a column, you call the method that is designed to work with that column's data type. For example, if the column contains a string, you would use the `getString` method to retrieve its value. If the column contains an integer, you would use the `getInt` method. Likewise, if the column contains a `double`, you would call the `getDouble` method.

When you call one of the "get" methods, you must tell it which column in the current row you want to retrieve. These methods accept either an integer argument, which is a column number, or a `String` holding the column name.

The `ResultSet` that we have been looking at in our example has only one column: the `Description` column. The `Description` column's data type is `CHAR(25)`, which means it is a fixed-length string of 25 characters. This is compatible with the `String` type in Java. To display the contents of the `Description` column in the current row, we could use the following statement:

```
System.out.println(result.getString("Description"));
```

The `Description` column holds values that are compatible with the `String` type, so we use the `getString` method to retrieve its contents. We could also use the column number to retrieve the column contents. Here is an example:

```
System.out.println(result.getString(1));
```

 NOTE: Column names in a database table are not case sensitive. The column names `DESCRIPTION`, `description`, and `Description` are all the same.

Let's look at a complete program that demonstrates what we have covered so far. Code Listing 16-2 displays the `Description` column from all of the rows in the `CoffeeDB` database.

Code Listing 16-2 (`ShowCoffeeDescriptions.java`)

```java
1  import java.sql.*;    // Needed for JDBC classes
2
3  /**
4   * This program demonstrates how to issue an SQL
5   * SELECT statement to a database using JDBC.
6   */
7
8  public class ShowCoffeeDescriptions
9  {
10    public static void main(String[] args)
11    {
12       // Create a named constant for the URL.
13       // NOTE: This value is specific for Java DB.
14       final String DB_URL = "jdbc:derby:CoffeeDB";
15
16       try
17       {
18          // Create a connection to the database.
19          Connection conn = DriverManager.getConnection(DB_URL);
20
21          // Create a Statement object.
22          Statement stmt = conn.createStatement();
23
24          // Create a string with a SELECT statement.
25          String sqlStatement = "SELECT Description FROM Coffee";
26
27          // Send the statement to the DBMS.
28          ResultSet result = stmt.executeQuery(sqlStatement);
29
30          // Display a header for the listing.
31          System.out.println("Coffees Found in the Database");
32          System.out.println("-----------------------------");
33
34          // Display the contents of the result set.
35          // The result set will have three columns.
36          while (result.next())
37          {
38             System.out.println(result.getString("Description"));
39          }
40
41          // Close the connection.
42          conn.close();
43       }
```

```
44          catch(Exception ex)
45          {
46              System.out.println("ERROR: " + ex.getMessage());
47          }
48      }
49  }
```

Program Output

```
Coffees Found in the Database
-----------------------------
Bolivian Dark
Bolivian Medium
Brazilian Dark
Brazilian Medium
Brazilian Decaf
Central American Dark
Central American Medium
Sumatra Dark
Sumatra Decaf
Sumatra Medium
Sumatra Organic Dark
Kona Medium
Kona Dark
French Roast Dark
Galapagos Medium
Guatemalan Dark
Guatemalan Decaf
Guatemalan Medium
```

Let's take a closer look at the code. Line 14 declares a string constant, initialized with the URL for the CofeeDB database. The statements that access the database are written inside the try block that appears in lines 18 through 43. Line 19 gets a connection to the database. After line 19 executes, the conn variable will reference a Connection object that can be used to access the database.

At this point in the program, we have a connection to the CoffeeDB database, but we are not ready to send a SELECT statement to the database. In order to send a SELECT statement to the database, we must have a Statement object. Line 22 calls the Connection object's createStatement method, which returns a reference to a Statement object. The reference is assigned to the stmt variable.

Line 25 declares a String variable named sqlStatement, initialized with the string "SELECT Description FROM Coffee". This is the SQL statement that we want to submit to the database. Line 28 passes this string as an argument to the Statement object's executeQuery method, which executes the statement. The method returns a reference to a ResultSet object, which is assigned to the result variable. The ResultSet object contains the results of the SELECT statement.

The while loop that appears in lines 36 through 39 displays the contents of the ResultSet object. It works like this:

- The while statement in line 36 calls the ResultSet object's next method to advance the internal cursor. If the cursor is successfully advanced, the method returns true, and the loop iterates. If the cursor is at the end of the ResultSet object's rows, the method returns false and the loop terminates.
- Each time the loop iterates, the ResultSet object's internal cursor will be positioned at a specific row. The statement in line 38 gets the value of the Description column and displays it.

Line 42 closes the connection to the database.

More About the SELECT Statement

You can specify more than one column in a SELECT statement by separating the column names with commas. Here is an example:

```
SELECT Description, Price FROM Coffee
```

This statement will retrieve the Description column and the Price column for every row in the Coffee table. The program in Code Listing 16-3 displays the coffee descriptions and their prices.

Code Listing 16-3   (ShowDescriptionsAndPrices.java)

```java
 1  import java.sql.*;    // Needed for JDBC classes
 2
 3  /**
 4   * This program displays the coffee descriptions
 5   * and their prices.
 6   */
 7
 8  public class ShowDescriptionsAndPrices
 9  {
10     public static void main(String[] args)
11     {
12        // Create a named constant for the URL.
13        // NOTE: This value is specific for Java DB.
14        final String DB_URL = "jdbc:derby:CoffeeDB";
15
16        try
17        {
18           // Create a connection to the database.
19           Connection conn = DriverManager.getConnection(DB_URL);
20
21           // Create a Statement object.
22           Statement stmt = conn.createStatement();
23
```

```
24              // Create a string with a SELECT statement.
25              String sqlStatement =
26                 "SELECT Description, Price FROM Coffee";
27
28              // Send the statement to the DBMS.
29              ResultSet result = stmt.executeQuery(sqlStatement);
30
31              // Display the contents of the result set.
32              // The result set will have three columns.
33              while (result.next())
34              {
35                 System.out.printf("%25s %.2f\n",
36                                   result.getString("Description"),
37                                   result.getDouble("Price"));
38              }
39
40              // Close the connection.
41              conn.close();
42          }
43      catch(Exception ex)
44          {
45              System.out.println("ERROR: " + ex.getMessage());
46          }
47      }
48  }
```

Program Output

```
Bolivian Dark              8.95
Bolivian Medium            8.95
Brazilian Dark             7.95
Brazilian Medium           7.95
Brazilian Decaf            8.55
Central American Dark      9.95
Central American Medium    9.95
Sumatra Dark               7.95
Sumatra Decaf              8.95
Sumatra Medium             7.95
Sumatra Organic Dark      11.95
Kona Medium               18.45
Kona Dark                 18.45
French Roast Dark          9.65
Galapagos Medium           6.85
Guatemalan Dark            9.95
Guatemalan Decaf          10.45
Guatemalan Medium          9.95
```

The program in Code Listing 16-3 is very similar to Code Listing 16-2. The differences between the two programs are summarized here:

- Lines 25 and 26 initialize the sqlStatement variable with the string "SELECT Description, Price FROM Coffee". This is a SELECT statement that will retrieve the Description and Price columns from the database table.
- Inside the while loop, in lines 33 through 38, we call result.getString to get the current row's Description column, and we call result.getDouble to get the current row's Price column. These items are displayed with the System.out.printf method.

If you wish to retrieve every column, you can use the * character instead of listing column names. Here is an example:

```
SELECT * FROM Coffee
```

This statement will retrieve every column for every row in the Coffee table. The program in Code Listing 16-4 displays all the columns in the Coffee table.

Code Listing 16-4 (ShowCoffeeData.java)

```java
 1  import java.sql.*;    // Needed for JDBC classes
 2
 3  /**
 4   * This program displays all of the columns in the
 5   * Coffee table of the CoffeeDB database.
 6   */
 7
 8  public class ShowCoffeeData
 9  {
10     public static void main(String[] args)
11     {
12        // Create a named constant for the URL.
13        // NOTE: This value is specific for Java DB.
14        final String DB_URL = "jdbc:derby:CoffeeDB";
15
16        try
17        {
18           // Create a connection to the database.
19           Connection conn = DriverManager.getConnection(DB_URL);
20
21           // Create a Statement object.
22           Statement stmt = conn.createStatement();
23
24           // Create a string with a SELECT statement.
25           String sqlStatement = "SELECT * FROM Coffee";
26
27           // Send the statement to the DBMS.
28           ResultSet result = stmt.executeQuery(sqlStatement);
29
30           // Display the contents of the result set.
31           // The result set will have three columns.
```

```
32              while (result.next())
33              {
34                  System.out.printf("%25s %6s %5.2f\n",
35                                    result.getString("Description"),
36                                    result.getString("ProdNum"),
37                                    result.getDouble("Price"));
38              }
39
40              // Close the connection.
41              conn.close();
42          }
43          catch(Exception ex)
44          {
45              System.out.println("ERROR: " + ex.getMessage());
46          }
47      }
48  }
```

Program Output

```
Bolivian Dark              14-001      8.95
Bolivian Medium            14-002      8.95
Brazilian Dark             15-001      7.95
Brazilian Medium           15-002      7.95
Brazilian Decaf            15-003      8.55
Central American Dark      16-001      9.95
Central American Medium    16-002      9.95
Sumatra Dark               17-001      7.95
Sumatra Decaf              17-002      8.95
Sumatra Medium             17-003      7.95
Sumatra Organic Dark       17-004     11.95
Kona Medium                18-001     18.45
Kona Dark                  18-002     18.45
French Roast Dark          19-001      9.65
Galapagos Medium           20-001      6.85
Guatemalan Dark            21-001      9.95
Guatemalan Decaf           21-002     10.45
Guatemalan Medium          21-003      9.95
```

SQL statements are free-form, which means that tabs, newlines, and spaces between the key words are ignored. For example, the statement

```
SELECT * FROM Coffee
```

works the same as:

```
SELECT
    *
FROM
    Coffee
```

In addition, SQL key words and table names are case insensitive. The previous statement could be written as:

```
select * from coffee
```

Specifying a Search Criteria with the WHERE Clause

Occasionally you might want to retrieve every row in a table. For example, if you wanted a list of all the coffees in the Coffee table, the previous SELECT statement would give it to you. Normally, however, you want to narrow the list down to only a few selected rows in the table. That's where the WHERE clause comes in. The WHERE clause can be used with the SELECT statement to specify a search criteria. When you use the WHERE clause, only the rows that meet the search criteria will be returned in the result set. The general format of a SELECT statement with a WHERE clause is:

```
SELECT Columns FROM Table WHERE Criteria
```

In the general format, *Criteria* is a conditional expression. Here is an example of a SELECT statement that uses the WHERE clause:

```
SELECT * FROM Coffee WHERE Price > 12.00
```

The first part of the statement, SELECT * FROM Coffee, specifies that we want to see every column. The WHERE clause specifies that we only want the rows in which the contents of the Price column is greater than 12.00. Figure 16-9 shows the results of this statement. Notice that only two coffees meet this search criterion.

Figure 16-9 Rows where Price is greater than 12.00

Description	ProdNum	Price
Kona Medium	18-001	18.45
Kona Dark	18-002	18.45

Standard SQL supports the relational operators listed in Table 16-4 for writing conditional expressions in a WHERE clause.

Table 16-4 SQL relational operators

Operator	Meaning
>	Greater than
<	Less than
>=	Greater than or equal to
<=	Less than or equal to
=	Equal to
<>	Not equal to

Notice that the equal-to and not equal-to operators in SQL are different from those in Java. The equal to operator is one equal sign, not two equal signs. The not equal-to operator is <>.

Let's look at a few more examples of the SELECT statement. The following statement could be used to retrieve the product numbers and prices of all the coffees that are priced at 7.95:

```
SELECT ProdNum, Price FROM Coffee WHERE Price = 7.95
```

The results of this statement are shown in Figure 16-10.

Figure 16-10   Results of SQL statement

ProdNum	Price
15-001	7.95
15-002	7.95
17-001	7.95
17-003	7.95

The following SELECT statement retrieves all of the columns for the row where the description is "French Roast Dark". The results returned from this statement are shown in Figure 16-11.

```
SELECT * FROM Coffee WHERE Description = 'French Roast Dark'
```

Figure 16-11   Results of SQL statement

Description	ProdNum	Price
French Roast Dark	19-001	9.65

If you look carefully at the previous statement you will notice another difference between SQL syntax and Java syntax. In SQL, string literals are enclosed in single quotes, not double quotes.

> **TIP:** If you need to include a single quote as part of a string, simply write two single quotes in its place. For example, suppose you wanted to search the Coffee table for a coffee named Joe's Special Blend. You could use the following statement:
>
> ```
> SELECT * FROM Coffee WHERE Description = 'Joe''s Special Blend'
> ```

Let's look at an example program that uses a WHERE clause in a SELECT statement. The program in Code Listing 16-5 lets the user enter a minimum price, and then search the Coffee table for rows where the Price column is greater than or equal to the specified price.

Code Listing 16-5   **(CoffeeMinPrice.java)**

```java
1  import java.util.Scanner;
2  import java.sql.*;
3
4  /**
5   * This program lets the user search for coffees
6   * priced at a minimum value.
7   */
```

```
 8
 9     public class CoffeeMinPrice
10     {
11       public static void main(String[] args)
12       {
13          double minPrice;        // To hold the minimum price
14          int coffeeCount = 0;    // To count coffees that qualify
15
16          // Create a named constant for the URL.
17          // NOTE: This value is specific for Java DB.
18          final String DB_URL = "jdbc:derby:CoffeeDB";
19
20          // Create a Scanner object for keyboard input.
21          Scanner keyboard = new Scanner(System.in);
22
23          // Get the minimum price from the user.
24          System.out.print("Enter the minimum price: ");
25          minPrice = keyboard.nextDouble();
26
27          try
28          {
29             // Create a connection to the database.
30             Connection conn = DriverManager.getConnection(DB_URL);
31
32             // Create a Statement object.
33             Statement stmt = conn.createStatement();
34
35             // Create a string containing a SELECT statement.
36             // Note that we are incorporating the user's input
37             // into the string.
38             String sqlStatement =
39                "SELECT * FROM Coffee WHERE Price >= " +
40                Double.toString(minPrice);
41
42             // Send the statement to the DBMS.
43             ResultSet result = stmt.executeQuery(sqlStatement);
44
45             // Display the contents of the result set.
46             // The result set will have three columns.
47             while (result.next())
48             {
49                // Display a row from the result set.
50                System.out.printf("%25s %6s %5.2f\n",
51                                     result.getString("Description"),
52                                     result.getString("ProdNum"),
53                                     result.getDouble("Price"));
54
```

```
55                // Increment the counter.
56                coffeeCount++;
57            }
58
59            // Display the number of qualifying coffees.
60            System.out.println(coffeeCount + " coffees found.");
61
62            // Close the connection.
63            conn.close();
64        }
65        catch(Exception ex)
66        {
67            System.out.println("ERROR: " + ex.getMessage());
68        }
69    }
70 }
```

Program Output

```
Enter the minimum price: 12.00 [Enter]
Kona Medium              18-001      18.45
Kona Dark                18-002      18.45
2 coffees found.
```

Program Output

```
Enter the minimum price: 10.00 [Enter]
Sumatra Organic Dark     17-004      11.95
Kona Medium              18-001      18.45
Kona Dark                18-002      18.45
Guatemalan Decaf         21-002      10.45
4 coffees found.
```

Program Output

```
Enter the minimum price: 20.00 [Enter]
0 coffees found.
```

There are a few things in Code Listing 16-5 that deserve some explanation. In lines 24 and 25 the program prompts the user to enter a minimum price, and the user's input is assigned to the double variable minPrice. Then, notice in lines 38 through 40 that the minPrice variable is converted to a string and concatenated onto the string containing the SELECT statement. When the program runs, if the user enters 10.00, the SELECT statement that is created in lines 38 through 40 will be:

```
SELECT * FROM Coffee WHERE Price >= 10.00
```

Or, if the user enters 12.00, the SELECT statement that is created in lines 38 through 40 will be:

```
SELECT * FROM Coffee WHERE Price >= 12.00
```

Programs commonly need to use techniques such as this to create SQL statements that incorporate user input.

String Comparisons in a SELECT Statement

String comparisons in SQL are case sensitive. If you ran the following statement against the CoffeeDB database, you would not get any results:

```
SELECT * FROM Coffee WHERE Description = 'french roast dark'
```

However, you can use the UPPER() function to convert a string to uppercase. Here is an example:

```
SELECT * FROM Coffee WHERE UPPER(Description) = 'FRENCH ROAST DARK'
```

This statement will return the same results as shown in Figure 16-11. SQL also provides a LOWER() function, which converts its argument to lowercase.

Using the LIKE Operator

Sometimes searching for an exact string will not yield the results you want. For example, suppose we want a list of all the decaf coffees in the Coffee table. The following statement will not work. Can you see why?

```
SELECT * FROM Coffee WHERE Description = 'Decaf'
```

This statement will search for rows where the Description field is equal to the string "Decaf". Unfortunately, it will find none. If you glance back at Table 16-1, you will see that none of the rows in the Coffee table have a Description column that is equal to "Decaf". You will see, however, that the word "Decaf" does appear in the Description column of some of the rows. For example, in one row you will find "Brazilian Decaf". In another row you will find "Sumatra Decaf". In yet another row you will find "Guatemalan Decaf". In addition to the word "Decaf" each of these contains other characters.

In order to find all of the decaf coffees, we need to search for rows where "Decaf" appears as a substring in the Description column. You can perform just such a search using the LIKE operator. Here is an example of how to use it.

```
SELECT * FROM Coffee WHERE Description LIKE '%Decaf%'
```

The LIKE operator is followed by a string that contains a character pattern. In this example, the character pattern is '%Decaf%'. The % symbol is used as wildcard character. It represents any sequence of 0 or more characters. The pattern '%Decaf%' specifies that the string "Decaf" must appear with any sequence of characters before or after it. The results of this statement are shown in Figure 16-12.

Figure 16-12 Results of SQL statement

Description	ProdNum	Price
Brazilian Decaf	15-003	8.55
Sumatra Decaf	17-002	8.95
Guatemalan Decaf	21-002	10.45

Likewise, the following statement will result in all the rows where the Description column starts with the word "Sumatra".

```
SELECT * FROM Coffee WHERE Description LIKE 'Sumatra%'
```

The underscore character (_) is also used as a wildcard. Unlike the % character, the underscore represents a single character. For example, look at the following statement.

```
SELECT * FROM Coffee WHERE ProdNum LIKE '2_-00_'
```

This statement will result in all the rows where the ProdNum column begins with "2", followed by any single character, followed by "-00", followed by any single character. The results of this statement are shown in Figure 16-13.

Figure 16-13   Results of SQL Statement

Description	ProdNum	Price
Galapagos Medium	20-001	6.85
Guatemalan Dark	21-001	9.95
Guatemalan Decaf	21-002	10.45
Guatemalan Medium	21-003	9.95

You can use the NOT operator to disqualify a character pattern in a search criteria. For example, suppose you want a list of all the coffees that are not decaf. The following statement will yield just those results.

```
SELECT * FROM Coffee WHERE Description NOT LIKE '%Decaf%'
```

Using AND and OR

You can use the AND and OR logical operators to specify multiple search criteria in a WHERE clause. For example, look at the following statement:

```
SELECT * FROM Coffee WHERE Price > 10.00 AND Price < 14.00
```

The AND operator requires that both of the search criteria be true in order for a row to be qualified as a match. The only rows that will be returned from this statement are those where the Price column contains a value that is greater than 10.00 and less than 14.00. Figure 16-14 shows the results of the statement.

Figure 16-14   Results of SQL statement

Description	ProdNum	Price
Sumatra Organic Dark	17-004	11.95
Guatemalan Decaf	21-002	10.45

Here's an example that uses the OR operator:

```
SELECT * FROM Coffee
WHERE Description LIKE '%Dark%' OR ProdNum LIKE '16%'
```

The OR operator requires that either of the search criteria be true in order for a row to be qualified as a match. This statement searches for rows where the Description column contains the string "Dark" at any position, or where the ProdNum column starts with "16". Figure 16-15 shows the results of the query.

Figure 16-15 Results of the SQL statement

Description	ProdNum	Price
Bolivian Dark	14-001	8.95
Brazilian Dark	16-001	7.95
Central American Dark	16-001	9.95
Central American Medium	16-002	9.95
Sumatra Dark	17-001	7.95
Sumatra Organic Dark	17-004	11.95
Kona Dark	18-002	18.45
French Roast Dark	19-001	9.65
Guatemalan Dark	21-001	9.95

Sorting the Results of a SELECT Query

If you wish to sort the results of a SELECT query, you can use the ORDER BY clause. Here is an example:

```
SELECT * FROM Coffee ORDER BY Price
```

This statement will produce a list of all the rows in the Coffee table, ordered by the Price column. The list will be sorted in ascending order on the Price column, meaning that the lowest priced coffees will appear first.

Here's a SELECT statement that uses both a WHERE clause and an ORDER BY clause:

```
SELECT * FROM Coffee
    WHERE Price > 9.95
    ORDER BY Price
```

This statement will produce a list of all the rows in the Coffee table where the Price column contains a value greater than 9.95, listed in ascending order by price.

If you want the list sorted in descending order (from highest to lowest), use the DESC operator, as shown here:

```
SELECT * FROM Coffee
    WHERE Price > 9.95
    ORDER BY Price DESC
```

Mathematical Functions

SQL provides several functions for performing calculations. For example, the AVG function calculates the average value in a particular column. Here is an example SELECT statement using the AVG function:

```
SELECT AVG(Price) FROM Coffee
```

This statement produces a single value: the average of all the values in the Price column. Because we did not use a WHERE clause, it uses all of the rows in the Coffee table in the calculation. Here is an example that calculates the average price of all the coffees having a product number that begins with "20":

```
SELECT AVG(Price) FROM Coffee WHERE ProdNum LIKE '20%'
```

Another of the mathematical functions is SUM, which calculates the sum of a column's values. The following statement, which is probably not very useful, calculates the sum of the values in the Price column:

```
SELECT SUM(Price) FROM Coffee
```

The MIN and MAX functions determine the minimum and maximum values found in a column. The following statement will tell us the minimum value in the Price column:

```
SELECT MIN(Price) FROM Coffee
```

The following statement will tell us the maximum value in the Price column:

```
SELECT MAX(Price) FROM Coffee
```

The COUNT function can be used to determine the number of rows in a table, as demonstrated by the following statement:

```
SELECT COUNT(*) FROM Coffee
```

The * simply indicates that you want to count entire rows. Here is another example, which tells us the number of coffees having a price greater than 9.95:

```
SELECT COUNT(*) FROM Coffee WHERE Price > 9.95
```

Queries that use math functions, such as the examples shown here, return only one value. So, when you submit such a statement to a DBMS using JDBC, the ResultSet object that is returned to the program will contain one row with one column. The program shown in Code Listing 16-6 shows an example of how you can use the functions to display the MIN, MAX, and AVG functions to find the lowest, highest, and average prices in the Coffee table.

Code Listing 16-6   (CoffeeMinPrice.java)

```
1   import java.sql.*;
2
3   /**
4    * This program demonstrates some of the SQL math functions.
5    */
6
7   public class CoffeeMath
8   {
9      public static void main(String[] args)
10     {
11        // Variables to hold the lowest, highest, and
12        // average price of coffee.
13        double lowest = 0.0,
14               highest = 0.0,
15               average = 0.0;
```

```
16
17          // Create a named constant for the URL.
18          // NOTE: This value is specific for Java DB.
19          final String DB_URL = "jdbc:derby:CoffeeDB";
20
21          try
22          {
23             // Create a connection to the database.
24             Connection conn = DriverManager.getConnection(DB_URL);
25
26             // Create a Statement object.
27             Statement stmt = conn.createStatement();
28
29             // Create SELECT statements to get the lowest, highest,
30             // and average price from the Coffee table.
31             String minStatement = "SELECT MIN(Price) FROM Coffee";
32             String maxStatement = "SELECT MAX(Price) FROM Coffee";
33             String avgStatement = "SELECT AVG(Price) FROM Coffee";
34
35             // Get the lowest price.
36             ResultSet minResult = stmt.executeQuery(minStatement);
37             if (minResult.next())
38                lowest = minResult.getDouble(1);
39
40             // Get the highest price.
41             ResultSet maxResult = stmt.executeQuery(maxStatement);
42             if (maxResult.next())
43                highest = maxResult.getDouble(1);
44
45             // Get the average price.
46             ResultSet avgResult = stmt.executeQuery(avgStatement);
47             if (avgResult.next())
48                average = avgResult.getDouble(1);
49
50             // Display the results.
51             System.out.printf("Lowest price: $%.2f\n", lowest);
52             System.out.printf("Highest price: $%.2f\n", highest);
53             System.out.printf("Average price: $%.2f\n", average);
54
55             // Close the connection.
56             conn.close();
57          }
58          catch(Exception ex)
59          {
60             System.out.println("ERROR: " + ex.getMessage());
61          }
62       }
63    }
```

Program Output

```
Lowest price: $6.85
Highest price: $18.45
Average price: $10.16
```

Lines 31 through 33 declare three strings: minStatement, maxStatement, and avgStatement. Each of these strings contains a SELECT statement that uses a math function.

The code in lines 36 through 38 get the lowest price in the table. Here is a summary of how the code works:

- Line 36 executes the contents of minStatement, and the ResultSet reference that is returned is assigned to the minResult variable.
- The if statement in line 37 advances the ResultSet object's cursor, and line 38 gets the value of column 1 and assigns it to the lowest variable.

The code in lines 41 through 43 get the highest price in the table. Here is a summary of how the code works:

- Line 41 executes the contents of maxStatement, and the ResultSet reference that is returned is assigned to the maxResult variable.
- The if statement in line 42 advances the ResultSet object's cursor, and line 43 gets the value of column 1 and assigns it to the highest variable.

The code in lines 46 through 48 get the average price in the table. Here is a summary of how the code works:

- Line 46 executes the contents of avgStatement, and the ResultSet reference that is returned is assigned to the avgResult variable.
- The if statement in line 47 advances the ResultSet object's cursor, and line 48 gets the value of column 1 and assigns it to the average variable.

Checkpoint

16.11 What is a ResultSet object?

16.12 Look at the following SQL statement.

```
SELECT Id FROM Account
```

What is the name of the table that this statement is retrieving data from?
What is the name of the column that is being retrieved?

16.13 Assume that a database has a table named Inventory, with the following columns:

Column Name	Type
ProductID	CHAR(10)
QtyOnHand	INT
Cost	DOUBLE

   a. Write a SELECT statement that will return all of the columns from every row in table.
   b. Write a SELECT statement that will return the ProductID column from every row in table.

   c. Write a `SELECT` statement that will return the `ProductID` column and the `QtyOnHand` column from every row in table.
   d. Write a `SELECT` statement that will return the `ProductID` column only from the rows where `Cost` is less than 17.00.
   e. Write a `SELECT` statement that will return all of the columns from the rows where `ProductID` ends with "ZZ".

16.14 What is the purpose of the `LIKE` operator?

16.15 What is the purpose of the `%` symbol in a character pattern used by the `LIKE` operator? What is the purpose of the underline (_) character?

16.16 How to sort the results of a `SELECT` statement on a specific column?

16.17 Assume that the following declarations exist:

```
final String DB_URL = "jdbc:derby:CoffeeDB";
String sql = "SELECT * FROM Coffee";
```

   Write code that uses these `String` objects to get a database connection and execute the SQL statement. Be sure to close the connection when done.

16.18 How do you submit a `SELECT` statement to the DBMS?

16.19 Where is a `ResultSet` object's cursor initially pointing? How do you move the cursor forward in the result set?

16.20 Assume that a valid `ResultSet` object exists, populated with data. What method do I call to retrieve column 3 as a string? What do I pass as an argument to the method?

16.4 Inserting Rows

CONCEPT: You use the `INSERT` statement in SQL to insert a new row into a table.

In SQL, the `INSERT` statement is used to insert a row into a database table.

```
INSERT INTO TableName VALUES (Value1, Value2, etc...)
```

In the general format, *TableName* is the name of the database table. *Value1, Value2, etc...* is a list of column values. After the statement executes, a row containing the specified column values will be inserted into the table. Here is an example that inserts a row into the `Coffee` table, in our `CoffeeDB` database:

```
INSERT INTO Coffee VALUES ('Honduran Dark', '22-001', 8.65)
```

Notice that the string values are enclosed in single-quote marks. Also, notice the order that the values appear in the list. The first value, 'Honduran Dark', is inserted into the first column of the table, which is `Description`. The second value, '22-001' is inserted into the second column of the table, which is `ProdNum`. The third value, 8.65, is inserted into the third column of the table, which is `Price`. After this statement executes, a new row will be inserted into the `Coffee` table containing the following column values:

```
Description: 'Honduran Dark'
ProdNum: 22-001
Price: 8.95
```

If you are not sure of the order in which the columns appear in the table, you can use the following general format of the INSERT statement to specify the column names and their corresponding values.

```
INSERT INTO TableName
    (ColumnName1, ColumnName2, etc...)
VALUES
    (Value1, Value2, etc...)
```

In this general format `ColumnName1, ColumnName2, etc...` is a list of column names and `Value1, Value2, etc...` is a list of corresponding values. In the new row, `Value1` will appear in the column specified by `ColumnName1`, `Value2` will appear in the column specified by `ColumnName2`, and so forth. Here is an example:

```
INSERT INTO Coffee
    (Description, ProdNum, Price)
VALUES
    ('Honduran Dark', '22-001', 8.65)
```

This statement will produce a new row containing the following column values:

```
Description: 'Honduran Dark'
ProdNum: 22-001
Price: 8.95
```

If we rewrote the INSERT statement in the following manner, it would produce a new row with the same values:

```
INSERT INTO Coffee
    (ProdNum, Price, Description)
VALUES
    ('22-001', 8.65, 'Honduran Dark')
```

NOTE: If a column is a primary key, it must hold a unique value for each row in the table. No two rows in a table can have the same value in the primary key column. Recall that the ProdNum column is the primary key in the Coffee table. The DBMS will not allow you to insert a new row with the same product number as an existing row.

Inserting Rows with JDBC

To issue an INSERT statement with JDBC, you must first get a Statement object from the Connection object, using its createStatement method. You then use the Statement object's executeUpdate method. The method returns an int value representing the number of rows that were inserted into the table. Here is an example:

```
String sqlStatement = "INSERT INTO Coffee " +
                "(ProdNum, Price, Description) " +
                "VALUES ('22-001', 8.65, 'Honduran Dark')";
int rows = stmt.executeUpdate(sqlStatement);
```

The first statement creates a string containing an INSERT statement. The second statement passes this string as an argument to the executeUpdate method. The method should return the int value 1, indicating that one row was inserted into the table. The program in Code

Listing 16-7 shows an example. It prompts the user for the description, product number, and price of a new coffee and inserts that data into the Coffee table.

Code Listing 16-7   (CoffeeInserter.java)

```java
 1   import java.util.Scanner;
 2   import java.sql.*;
 3
 4   /**
 5    * This program lets the user insert a row into the
 6    * CoffeeDB database's Coffee table.
 7    */
 8
 9   public class CoffeeInserter
10   {
11      public static void main(String[] args)
12      {
13         String description;  // To hold the coffee description
14         String prodNum;      // To hold the product number
15         double price;        // To hold the price
16
17         // Create a named constant for the URL.
18         // NOTE: This value is specific for Java DB.
19         final String DB_URL = "jdbc:derby:CoffeeDB";
20
21         // Create a Scanner object for keyboard input.
22         Scanner keyboard = new Scanner(System.in);
23
24         try
25         {
26            // Create a connection to the database.
27            Connection conn = DriverManager.getConnection(DB_URL);
28
29            // Get the data for the new coffee.
30            System.out.print("Enter the coffee description: ");
31            description = keyboard.nextLine();
32            System.out.print("Enter the product number: ");
33            prodNum = keyboard.nextLine();
34            System.out.print("Enter the price: ");
35            price = keyboard.nextDouble();
36
37            // Create a Statement object.
38            Statement stmt = conn.createStatement();
39
40            // Create a string with an INSERT statement.
41            String sqlStatement = "INSERT INTO Coffee " +
42                     "(ProdNum, Price, Description) " +
43                     "VALUES ('" +
```

```
44                            prodNum + "', " +
45                            price + ", '" +
46                            description + "')";
47
48          // Send the statement to the DBMS.
49          int rows = stmt.executeUpdate(sqlStatement);
50
51          // Display the results.
52          System.out.println(rows + " row(s) added to the table.");
53
54          // Close the connection.
55          conn.close();
56       }
57       catch(Exception ex)
58       {
59          System.out.println("ERROR: " + ex.getMessage());
60       }
61    }
62 }
```

Program Output

Enter the coffee description: **Honduran Dark [Enter]**
Enter the product number: **22-001 [Enter]**
Enter the price: **8.65 [Enter]**
1 row(s) added to the table.

 Checkpoint

16.21 Write an SQL statement to insert a new into the Coffee table containing the
following data:

> Description: Eastern Blend
> ProdNum: 30-001
> Price: 18.95

16.22 Rewrite the following INSERT statement so it specifies the Coffee table's column
names.

> INSERT INTO Coffee
> VALUES ('Honduran Dark', '22-001', 8.65)

 16.5 **Updating and Deleting Existing Rows**

CONCEPT: You use the UPDATE statement in SQL to change the value of an existing
row. You use the DELETE statement to delete rows from a table.

In SQL, the UPDATE statement is used to change the contents of an existing row in a
table. For example, if the price of Brazilian Decaf coffee changes, we could use an

UPDATE statement to change the `Price` column for that row. Here is the general format of the UPDATE statement:

```
UPDATE Table
    SET Column = Value
    WHERE Criteria
```

In the general format, `Table` is a table name, `Column` is a column name, `Value` is a value to store in the column, and `Criteria` is a conditional expression. Here is an UPDATE statement that will change the price of Brazilian Decaf coffee to 9.95:

```
UPDATE Coffee
    SET Price = 9.95
    WHERE Description = 'Brazilian Decaf'
```

Here's another example:

```
UPDATE Coffee
    SET Description = 'Galapagos Organic Medium'
    WHERE ProdNum = '20-001'
```

This statement locates the row where `ProdNum` is `'20-001'` and sets the `Description` field to `'Galapagos Organic Medium'`.

It's possible to update more than one row. For example, suppose we wish to change the price of every Guatemalan coffee to 12.95. If you look back at Table 16-1 you will see that the product number for each of the Guatemalan coffees begins with '21'. All we need is an UPDATE statement that locates all the rows where the `ProdNum` column begins with '21', and changes the `Price` column of those rows to 12.95. Here is such a statement:

```
UPDATE Coffee
    SET Price = 12.95
    WHERE ProdNum LIKE '21%'
```

 WARNING! Be careful that you do not leave out the WHERE clause and the conditional expression when using an UPDATE statement. It's possible that you will change the contents of every row in the table! For example, look at the following statement:

```
UPDATE Coffee
    SET Price = 4.95
```

Because this statement does not have a WHERE clause, it will change the `Price` column for every row in the `Coffee` table to 4.95!

Updating Rows with JDBC

The process of issuing an UPDATE statement in JDBC is similar to that of issuing an INSERT statement. First, you get a `Statement` object from the `Connection` object, using its `createStatement` method. You then use the `Statement` object's `executeUpdate` method to issue the UPDATE statement. The method returns an int value representing the number of rows that were affected by the UPDATE statement. Here is an example:

```
String sqlStatement = "UPDATE Coffee " +
                      "SET Price = 9.95 " +
                      "WHERE Description = 'Brazilian Decaf'";
int rows = stmt.executeUpdate(sqlStatement);
```

The first statement creates a string containing an UPDATE statement. The second statement passes this string as an argument to the executeUpdate method. The method returns an int value indicating the number of rows that were changed.

Code Listing 16-8 demonstrates how to update a row in the Coffee table. The user enters an existing product number, and the program displays that product's data. The user then enters a new price for the specified product and the program updates the row with the new price.

Code Listing 16-8 **(CoffeePriceUpdater.java)**

```java
 1  import java.util.Scanner;
 2  import java.sql.*;
 3
 4  /**
 5   * This program lets the user change the price of a
 6   * coffee in the CoffeeDB database's Coffee table.
 7   */
 8
 9  public class CoffeePriceUpdater
10  {
11     public static void main(String[] args)
12     {
13        String prodNum;      // To hold the product number
14        double price;        // To hold the price
15
16        // Create a named constant for the URL.
17        // NOTE: This value is specific for Java DB.
18        final String DB_URL = "jdbc:derby:CoffeeDB";
19
20        // Create a Scanner object for keyboard input.
21        Scanner keyboard = new Scanner(System.in);
22
23        try
24        {
25           // Create a connection to the database.
26           Connection conn = DriverManager.getConnection(DB_URL);
27
28           // Create a Statement object.
29           Statement stmt = conn.createStatement();
30
31           // Get the product number for the desired coffee.
```

```
32              System.out.print("Enter the product number: ");
33              prodNum = keyboard.nextLine();
34
35              // Display the coffee's current data.
36              if (findAndDisplayProduct(stmt, prodNum))
37              {
38                 // Get the new price.
39                 System.out.print("Enter the new price: ");
40                 price = keyboard.nextDouble();
41
42                 // Update the coffee with the new price.
43                 updatePrice(stmt, prodNum, price);
44              }
45              else
46              {
47                 // The specified product number was not found.
48                 System.out.println("That product is not found.");
49              }
50
51              // Close the connection.
52              conn.close();
53           }
54        catch(Exception ex)
55        {
56           System.out.println("ERROR: " + ex.getMessage());
57        }
58     }
59
60     /**
61      * The findAndDisplayProduct method finds a specified coffee's
62      * data and displays it. The stmt parameter is a Statement
63      * object for the database. The prodNum parameter is the
64      * product number to search for. The method returns true or
65      * false indicating whether the product was found.
66      */
67
68     public static boolean findAndDisplayProduct(Statement stmt,
69                                                 String prodNum)
70                                                 throws SQLException
71     {
72        boolean productFound; // Flag
73
74        // Create a SELECT statement to get the specified
75        // row from the Coffee table.
76        String sqlStatement =
77           "SELECT * FROM Coffee WHERE ProdNum = '" +
78           prodNum + "'";
79
```

```
80           // Send the SELECT statement to the DBMS.
81           ResultSet result = stmt.executeQuery(sqlStatement);
82
83           // Display the contents of the result set.
84           if (result.next())
85           {
86               // Display the product.
87               System.out.println("Description: " +
88                                   result.getString("Description"));
89               System.out.println("Product Number: " +
90                                   result.getString("ProdNum"));
91               System.out.println("Price: $" +
92                                   result.getDouble("Price"));
93
94               // Set the flag to indicate the product was found.
95               productFound = true;
96           }
97           else
98           {
99               // Indicate the product was not found.
100              productFound = false;
101          }
102
103          return productFound;
104      }
105
106      /**
107       * The updatePrice method updates a specified coffee's price.
108       * The stmt parameter is a Statement object for the database.
109       * prodNum is the product number for the desired coffee.
110       * price The product's new price.
111       */
112
113      public static void updatePrice(Statement stmt, String prodNum,
114                                     double price) throws SQLException
115      {
116          // Create an UPDATE statement to update the price
117          // for the specified product number.
118          String sqlStatement = "UPDATE Coffee " +
119                          "SET Price = " + Double.toString(price) +
120                          "WHERE ProdNum = '" + prodNum + "'";
121
122          // Send the UPDATE statement to the DBMS.
123          int rows = stmt.executeUpdate(sqlStatement);
124
125          // Display the results.
126          System.out.println(rows + " row(s) updated.");
127      }
128  }
```

Program Output

```
Enter the product number: 17-001 [Enter]
Description: Sumatra Dark
Product Number: 17-001
Price: $7.95
Enter the new price: 9.95 [Enter]
1 row(s) updated.
```

In the main method, line 26 gets a connection to the database, and line 29 creates a Statement object. Lines 32 and 33 prompt the user for a product number, which is assigned to the prodNum variable.

Before we let the user change the specified product's price, we want to display the product's current information. So, line 36 calls a method named findAndDisplayProduct, passing the Statement object and the prodNum variable as arguments. The findAndDisplayProduct method (which is shown in lines 68 through 104) queries the database table for the row with the specified product number. If the row is found, the method displays the row's contents and then returns true. If the row is not found, the method simply returns false.

If the specified product is found, lines 39 and 40 prompt the user for the product's new price, and the user's input is assigned to the price variable. Then, line 43 calls a method named updatePrice, passing the Statement object, the prodNum variable, and the price variable as arguments. The updatePrice method (which is shown in lines 113 through 127) updates the row containing the specified product number with the new price.

Notice that neither the findAndDisplayProduct method nor the updatePrice method handle any SQLExceptions that might occur. If an SQLException happens in either of those methods, it gets passed up to the main method, where it is handled by the try-catch statement.

Deleting Rows with the DELETE Statement

In SQL you use the DELETE statement to delete one or more rows from a table. The general format of the DELETE statement is:

```
DELETE FROM Table WHERE Criteria
```

In the general format, *Table* is a table name and *Criteria* is a conditional expression. Here is a DELETE statement that will delete the row where ProdNum is 20-001:

```
DELETE FROM Coffee WHERE ProdNum = '20-001'
```

This statement locates the row in the Coffee table where the ProdNum column is set to the value '20-001', and deletes that row.

It is possible to delete multiple rows with the DELETE statement. For example, look at the following statement:

```
DELETE FROM Coffee WHERE Description LIKE 'Sumatra%'
```

This statement will delete all rows in the Coffee table where the Description column begins with 'Sumatra'. If you glance back at Table 16-1 you will see that four rows will be deleted.

WARNING! Be careful that you do not leave out the WHERE clause and the conditional expression when using a DELETE statement. It's possible that you will delete every row in the table! For example, look at the following statement:

```
DELETE FROM Coffee
```

Because this statement does not have a WHERE clause, it will delete every row in the Coffee table!

Deleting Rows with JDBC

The process of issuing a DELETE statement in JDBC is similar to that of issuing an INSERT statement or an UPDATE statement. First, you get a Statement object from the Connection object, using its createStatement method. You then use the Statement object's executeUpdate method to issue the DELETE statement. The method returns an int value representing the number of rows that were deleted. Here is an example:

```
String sqlStatement = "DELETE FROM Coffee " +
                      "WHERE ProdNum = '20-001'";
int rows = stmt.executeUpdate(sqlStatement);
```

The first statement creates a string containing a DELETE statement. The second statement passes this string as an argument to the executeUpdate method. The method returns an int value indicating the number of rows that were deleted.

The program shown in Code Listing 16-9 demonstrates how a row can be deleted from the Coffee table.

Code Listing 16-9   **(CoffeeDeleter.java)**

```java
 1  import java.util.Scanner;
 2  import java.sql.*;
 3
 4  /**
 5   * This program lets the user delete a coffee
 6   * from the CoffeeDB database's Coffee table.
 7   */
 8
 9  public class CoffeeDeleter
10  {
11     public static void main(String[] args)
12     {
13        String prodNum;    // To hold the product number
14        String sure;       // To make sure the user wants to delete
15
16        // Create a named constant for the URL.
17        // NOTE: This value is specific for Java DB.
18        final String DB_URL = "jdbc:derby:CoffeeDB";
19
```

```
20          // Create a Scanner object for keyboard input.
21          Scanner keyboard = new Scanner(System.in);
22
23       try
24       {
25          // Create a connection to the database.
26          Connection conn = DriverManager.getConnection(DB_URL);
27
28          // Create a Statement object.
29          Statement stmt = conn.createStatement();
30
31          // Get the product number for the desired coffee.
32          System.out.print("Enter the product number: ");
33          prodNum = keyboard.nextLine();
34
35          // Display the coffee's current data.
36          if (findAndDisplayProduct(stmt, prodNum))
37          {
38             // Make sure the user wants to delete this product.
39             System.out.print("Are you sure you want to delete " +
40                              "this item? (y/n): ");
41             sure = keyboard.nextLine();
42
43             if (Character.toUpperCase(sure.charAt(0)) == 'Y')
44             {
45                // Delete the specified coffee.
46                deleteCoffee(stmt, prodNum);
47             }
48             else
49             {
50                System.out.println("The item was not deleted.");
51             }
52          }
53          else
54          {
55             // The specified product number was not found.
56             System.out.println("That product is not found.");
57          }
58
59          // Close the connection.
60          conn.close();
61       }
62       catch(Exception ex)
63       {
64          System.out.println("ERROR: " + ex.getMessage());
65       }
66    }
67
```

```
68      /**
69       * The findAndDisplayProduct method finds a specified coffee's
70       * data and displays it.
71       * The stmt parameter is a Statement object for the database.
72       * prodNum is the product number. The method returns true or
73       * false to indicate whether the product was found.
74       */
75
76      public static boolean findAndDisplayProduct(Statement stmt,
77                                                    String prodNum)
78                                                    throws SQLException
79      {
80         boolean productFound; // Flag
81
82         // Create a SELECT statement to get the specified
83         // row from the Coffee table.
84         String sqlStatement =
85            "SELECT * FROM Coffee WHERE ProdNum = '" +
86            prodNum + "'";
87
88         // Send the SELECT statement to the DBMS.
89         ResultSet result = stmt.executeQuery(sqlStatement);
90
91         // Display the contents of the result set.
92         if (result.next())
93         {
94             // Display the product.
95             System.out.println("Description: " +
96                             result.getString("Description"));
97             System.out.println("Product Number: " +
98                             result.getString("ProdNum"));
99             System.out.println("Price: $" +
100                            result.getDouble("Price"));
101
102            // Set the flag to indicate the product was found.
103            productFound = true;
104        }
105        else
106        {
107           // Indicate the product was not found.
108           productFound = false;
109        }
110
111        return productFound;
112     }
113
```

```
114      /**
115       * The deleteCoffee method deletes a specified coffee.
116       * The stmt parameter is a Statement object for the database.
117       * prodNum The product number for the desired coffee.
118       */
119
120      public static void deleteCoffee(Statement stmt, String prodNum)
121                                  throws SQLException
122      {
123         // Create a DELETE statement to delete the
124         // specified product number.
125         String sqlStatement = "DELETE FROM Coffee " +
126                            "WHERE ProdNum = '" + prodNum + "'";
127
128         // Send the DELETE statement to the DBMS.
129         int rows = stmt.executeUpdate(sqlStatement);
130
131         // Display the results.
132         System.out.println(rows + " row(s) deleted.");
133      }
134  }
```

Program Output

```
Enter the product number: 20-001 [Enter]
Description: Galapagos Medium
Product Number: 20-001
Price: $6.85
Are you sure you want to delete this item? (y/n): y [Enter]
1 row(s) deleted.
```

 Checkpoint

16.23 The Midnight Roastery is running a special on decaf coffee. Write an SQL statement that changes the price of all decaf coffees to 4.95.

16.24 The sale on decaf coffee didn't do too well, so the Midnight Roastery has decided to stop selling decaf. Write an SQL statement that will delete all decaf coffees from the Coffee table.

16.6 Creating and Deleting Tables

CONCEPT: In SQL, the CREATE TABLE statement can be used to create a database table. The DROP TABLE statement can be used to delete a table.

The CoffeeDB database that we have been using as our example is very simple. It has only one table, Coffee, which holds product information. The usefulness of this database is limited to looking up coffee descriptions, product numbers, and prices.

Suppose we want to store other data in the database, such as a list of customers. To do so, we would have to add another table to the database. In SQL you use the CREATE TABLE statement to create a table. Here is the general format of the CREATE TABLE statement:

```
CREATE TABLE TableName
    (ColumnName1 DataType1,
     ColumnName2 DataType2,
     etc... )
```

In the general format, TableName is the name of the table. ColumnName1 is the name of the first column, and DataType1 is the SQL data type for the first column. ColumnName2 is the name of the second column, and DataType2 is the SQL data type for the second column. This sequence repeats for all of the columns in the table. Here is an example:

```
CREATE TABLE Customer
    ( Name CHAR(25),
      Address CHAR(25),
      City CHAR(12),
      State CHAR(2),
      Zip CHAR(5) )
```

This statement creates a new table named Customer. The columns in the Customer table are Name, Address, City, State, and Zip.

You may also specify that a column is a primary key by listing the PRIMARY KEY qualifier after the column's data type. Recall from our earlier discussion on database organization that a primary key is a column that holds a unique value for each row and can be used to identify specific rows. When you us the PRIMARY KEY qualifier with a column, you should also use the NOT NULL qualifier. The NOT NULL qualifier specifies that the column must contain a value for every row. Here is an example of how we can create a Customer table, using the CustomerNumber column as the primary key:

```
CREATE TABLE Customer
    ( CustomerNumber CHAR(10) NOT NULL PRIMARY KEY,
      Name CHAR(25),
      Address CHAR(25),
      City CHAR(12),
      State CHAR(2),
      Zip CHAR(5) )
```

This statement creates a new table named Customer. It has the same structure as the table created by the previous example, with one additional column, CustomerNumber, which is the primary key. Because CustomerNumber is the primary key, this column must hold a unique value for each row in the table.

TIP: Remember, a primary key is used to identify a specific row in a table. When selecting a column as a primary key, make sure it holds a unique value that cannot be duplicated for two rows in the table.

Take a look at the program in Code Listing 16-10. When you run this program, it creates the Customer table in the CoffeeDB database, and then inserts the three rows shown in Table 16-5.

Code Listing 16-10   (`CreateCustomerTable.java`)

```
1   import java.sql.*;    // Needed for JDBC classes
2
3   /**
4    * This program creates a Customer
5    * table in the CoffeeDB database.
6    */
7
8   public class CreateCustomerTable
9   {
10     public static void main(String[] args)
11     {
12        // Create a named constant for the URL.
13        // NOTE: This value is specific for Java DB.
14        final String DB_URL = "jdbc:derby:CoffeeDB";
15
16        try
17        {
18           // Create a connection to the database.
19           Connection conn = DriverManager.getConnection(DB_URL);
20
21           // Get a Statement object.
22           Statement stmt = conn.createStatement();
23
24           // Make an SQL statement to create the table.
25           String sql = "CREATE TABLE Customer" +
26              "( CustomerNumber CHAR(10) NOT NULL PRIMARY KEY, " +
27              "  Name CHAR(25)," +
28              "  Address CHAR(25)," +
29              "  City CHAR(12)," +
30              "  State CHAR(2)," +
31              "  Zip CHAR(5) )";
32
33           // Execute the statement.
34           stmt.execute(sql);
35
36           // Add some rows to the new table.
37           sql = "INSERT INTO Customer VALUES" +
38                 "('101', 'Downtown Cafe', '17 N. Main Street'," +
39                 " 'Asheville', 'NC', '55515')";
40           stmt.executeUpdate(sql);
41
42           sql = "INSERT INTO Customer VALUES" +
43                 "('102', 'Main Street Grocery'," +
44                 " '110 E. Main Street'," +
45                 " 'Canton', 'NC', '55555')";
46           stmt.executeUpdate(sql);
```

```
47
48              sql = "INSERT INTO Customer VALUES" +
49                   "('103', 'The Coffee Place', '101 Center Plaza'," +
50                   " 'Waynesville', 'NC', '55516')";
51              stmt.executeUpdate(sql);
52
53              // Close the connection.
54              conn.close();
55          }
56          catch (Exception ex)
57          {
58              System.out.println("ERROR: " + ex.getMessage());
59          }
60      }
61  }
```

Table 16-5 Rows inserted into the `Customer` table

CustomerNumber	Name	Address	City	State	Zip
101	Downtown Cafe	17 N. Main Street	Asheville	NC	55515
102	Main Street Grocery	110 E. Main Street	Canton	NC	55555
103	The Coffee Place	101 Center Plaza	Waynesville	NC	55516

Removing a Table with the DROP TABLE Statement

Should the need arise to delete a table from a database, you can use the DROP TABLE statement. Here is the statement's general format:

```
DROP TABLE TableName
```

In the general format, *TableName* is the name of the table you wish to delete. For example, suppose that after we created the `Customer` table, we discovered that we selected the wrong data type for many of the columns. We could delete the table and then recreate it with the proper data types. The SQL statement to delete the table would be:

```
DROP TABLE Customer
```

Checkpoint

16.25 Write the SQL statement to create a table named `Book`. The `Book` table should have the columns to hold the name of the publisher, the name of the author, the number of pages, and a 10 character ISBN number.

16.26 Write a statement to delete the `Book` table you created in Checkpoint 16.24.

16.7 Creating a New Database with JDBC

CONCEPT: Creating a new database with JDBC is as simple as adding an attribute to the database URL and then using SQL to create a table in the database.

In the previous section you learned about the CREATE TABLE statement, which is used to create a new table in an existing database. But, suppose you wish to create a completely new database. With JDBC, all you must do is append the attribute `;create=true` to the database URL. For example, suppose you wish to create a new database named EntertainmentDB, to hold data on your collection of DVDs. In Java DB, the URL you would use would be:

```
"jdbc:derby:EntertainmentDB;create=true"
```

Because we have appended the attribute `;create=true` to the database URL, the program will create the database when it runs. Then, we can use a CREATE TABLE statement to create a table in the database. The program in Code Listing 16-11 demonstrates how to create a database using Java DB.

Code Listing 16-11 (**BuildEntertainmentDB.java**)

```java
 1  import java.sql.*;
 2
 3  /**
 4   * This program shows how to create a new database
 5   * using Java DB.
 6   */
 7
 8  public class BuildEntertainmentDB
 9  {
10      public static void main(String[] args)
11                      throws Exception
12      {
13          final String DB_URL =
14              "jdbc:derby:EntertainmentDB;create=true";
15
16          try
17          {
18              // Create a connection to the database.
19              Connection conn =
20                      DriverManager.getConnection(DB_URL);
21
22              // Create a Statement object.
23              Statement stmt = conn.createStatement();
24
```

```
25                // Create the Dvd table.
26                System.out.println("Creating the Dvd table...");
27                stmt.execute("CREATE TABLE Dvd ("     +
28                             "Title CHAR(25), "   +
29                             "Minutes INTEGER, " +
30                             "Price DOUBLE)");
31
32                // Close the resources.
33                stmt.close();
34                conn.close();
35                System.out.println("Done");
36            }
37            catch(Exception ex)
38            {
39                System.out.println("ERROR: " + ex.getMessage());
40            }
41        }
42  }
```

When this program runs, the EntertainmentDB database will be created. This is because the database URL, in line 13, has the ;create=true attribute. Lines 27 through 30 then create a table named Dvd.

> **NOTE:** When you create a new database using Java DB, you will see a folder appear on your system with the same name as the database. This folder holds the database. To delete the entire database, simply delete the folder.

16.8 Scrollable Result Sets

CONCEPT: A scrollable result set allows random cursor movement. By default, a result set is not scrollable.

By default, ResultSet objects allow you to move the cursor forward only. Once the cursor has moved past a row, you cannot move the cursor backward to read that row again. If you need to move the cursor backward through the result set, you can create a *scrollable result set*. You do this when you create a Statement object by using an overloaded version of a Connection object's createStatement method. The method accepts two arguments. The first specifies the result set's scrolling type. You can use any of the following constants for this argument:

```
ResultSet.TYPE_FORWARD_ONLY
```

This is the default scrolling type. It specifies that the result set's cursor should move only forward.

```
ResultSet.TYPE_SCROLL_INSENSITIVE
```

This specifies that the result set should be scrollable, allowing the cursor to move forward and backward through the result set. In addition, this result set is insensitive to changes made to the database. This means that if another program or process makes changes to the database, those changes will not appear in this result set.

```
ResultSet.TYPE_SCROLL_SENSITIVE
```

This specifies that the result set should be scrollable, allowing the cursor to move forward and backward through the result set. In addition, this result set is sensitive to changes made to the database. This means that if another program or process makes changes to the database, those changes will appear in this result set as soon as they are made.

The second argument specifies the result set's concurrency level. You can use any of the following constants for this argument:

```
ResultSet.CONCUR_READ_ONLY
```

This is the default concurrency level. It specifies that result set contains a read-only version of data from the database. You cannot change the contents of the database by altering the contents of the result set.

```
ResultSet.CONCUR_UPDATEABLE
```

This specifies that the result set should be updateable. Changes can be made to the result set, and then those changes can be saved to the database. The `ResultSet` interface specifies several methods that may be used to update the result set, and then save those updates to the database. These methods allow you to make changes to the database without issuing SQL statements. For more information on these methods, see the Java API documentation.

Assuming that conn references a `Connection` object, here is an example of the method call:

```
Statement stmt =
    conn.createStatement(ResultSet.TYPE_SCROLL_INSENSITIVE,
                         ResultSet.CONCUR_READ_ONLY);
```

The `Statement` object created by this code will be scrollable, insensitive to changes made to the database by other processes, and will not be updateable.

ResultSet **Navigation Methods**

Once you have created a scrollable result set, you can use the following `ResultSet` methods to move the cursor:

`first()`	Moves the cursor to the first row in the result set.
`last()`	Moves the cursor to the last row in the result set.
`next()`	Moves the cursor to the next row in the result set.
`previous()`	Moves the cursor to the previous row in the result set.
`relative(rows)`	Moves the cursor the number of rows specified by the argument *rows*, relative to the current row. For example, the call `relative(2)` will move the cursor 2 rows forward from the current row, and `relative(-1)` will move the cursor 1 row backward from the current row.
`absolute(row)`	Moves the cursor to the row specified by the integer *row*. Remember, row numbering begins at 1, so the call `absolute(1)` will move the cursor to the first row in the result set.

NOTE: Scrollable result sets are not supported by all JDBC drivers. If your driver does not support scrollable result sets, it will throw an exception when you try to use an unsupported navigation method.

The following code shows a simple, yet practical use of some of these methods: determining the number of rows in a result set.

```
resultSet.last();                      // Move to the last row
int numRows = resultSet.getRow();      // Get the current row number
resultSet.first();                     // Move back to the first row
```

This code would be useful when you need to determine the number of rows in the result set before processing any of its data. The first statement moves the cursor to the last row. The second statement calls the `ResultSet` method `getRow`, which returns the row number of the current row. The third statement then moves the cursor to the first row for subsequent processing.

16.9 Result Set Meta Data

CONCEPT: Result set meta data describes the contents of a result set. The meta data can be used to determine which columns were returned when a query that is not known in advance is executed.

The term *meta data* refers to data that describes other data. A `ResultSet` object has meta data, which describes the data stored in the `ResultSet`. You can use result set meta data to determine several things about a result set, including the number of columns it contains, the names of the columns, the types of each column, and much more. Result set meta data can be very useful if you are writing an application that will submit an SQL query, and you don't know in advance what columns will be returned.

Once you have a `ResultSet` object, you can call its `getMetaData` method to get a reference to a `ResultSetMetaData` object. Assuming `resultSet` references a `ResultSet` object, here is an example:

```
ResultSetMetaData meta = resultSet.getMetaData();
```

`ResultSetMetaData` is an interface in the `java.sql` package. It specifies numerous methods, a few of which are described in Table 16-6.

Table 16-6   A few `ResultSetMetaData` methods

Method	Description
`int getColumnCount()`	Returns the number of columns in the result set.
`String getColumnName(int col)`	Returns the name of the column specified by the integer `col`. The first column is column 1.
`String getColumnTypeName(int col)`	Returns the name of the data type of the column specified by the integer `col`. The first column is column 1. The data type name returned is the database-specific SQL data type.
`int getColumnDisplaySize(int col)`	Returns the display width, in characters, of the column specified by the integer `col`. The first column is column 1.
`String getTableName(int col)`	Returns the name of the table associated with the column specified by the integer `col`. The first column is column 1.

The program in Code Listing 16-12 demonstrates how meta data can be used. It asks the user to enter a SELECT statement for the CoffeeDB database, and then displays information about the result set as well as the result set's contents.

Code Listing 16-12   (MetaDataDemo.java)

```java
 1  import java.sql.*;
 2  import java.util.Scanner;
 3
 4  /**
 5   * This program demonstrates result set meta data.
 6   */
 7
 8  public class MetaDataDemo
 9  {
10     public static void main(String[] args) throws Exception
11     {
12        // Create a named constant for the URL.
13        // NOTE: This value is specific for Java DB.
14        final String DB_URL = "jdbc:derby:CoffeeDB";
15
16        try
17        {
18           // Create a Scanner object for keyboard input.
19           Scanner keyboard = new Scanner(System.in);
20
21           // Get a SELECT statement from the user.
22           System.out.println("Enter a SELECT statement for " +
23                              "the CoffeeDB database:");
24           String sql = keyboard.nextLine();
25
26           // Create a connection to the database.
27           Connection conn =
28                 DriverManager.getConnection(DB_URL);
29
30           // Create a Statement object.
31           Statement stmt = conn.createStatement();
32
33           // Execute the query.
34           ResultSet resultSet = stmt.executeQuery(sql);
35
36           // Get the result set meta data.
37           ResultSetMetaData meta = resultSet.getMetaData();
38
39           // Display the number of columns returned.
40           System.out.println("The result set has " +
41                              meta.getColumnCount() +
42                              " column(s).");
```

```
43
44              // Display the column names and types.
45              for (int i = 1; i <= meta.getColumnCount(); i++)
46              {
47                  System.out.println(meta.getColumnName(i) + ", " +
48                                      meta.getColumnTypeName(i));
49              }
50
51              // Display the contents of the rows.
52              System.out.println("\nHere are the result set rows:");
53              while (resultSet.next())
54              {
55                  // Display a row.
56                  for (int i = 1; i <= meta.getColumnCount(); i++)
57                  {
58                      System.out.print(resultSet.getString(i));
59                  }
60                  System.out.println();
61              }
62
63              // Close the statement and the connection.
64              stmt.close();
65              conn.close();
66          }
67          catch(Exception ex)
68          {
69              System.out.println("ERROR: " + ex.getMessage());
70          }
71      }
72  }
```

Program Output with Example Input Shown in Bold

```
Enter a SELECT statement for the CoffeeDB database:
SELECT * FROM Coffee WHERE Price > 10.00 [Enter]
The result set has 3 column(s).
DESCRIPTION, CHAR
PRODNUM, CHAR
PRICE, DOUBLE

Here are the result set rows:
Sumatra Organic Dark    17-004      11.95
Kona Medium             18-001      18.45
Kona Dark               18-002      18.45
Guatemalan Decaf        21-002      10.45
```

Program Output with Example Input Shown in Bold

```
Enter a SELECT statement for the CoffeeDB database:
SELECT ProdNum FROM Coffee WHERE Price > 10.00 [Enter]
The result set has 1 column(s).
PRODNUM, CHAR

Here are the result set rows:
17-004
18-001
18-002
21-002
```

Line 34 submits the query to the DBMS and gets a `ResultSet` object. Line 37 gets a `ResultSetMetaData` object. The statement in lines 40 through 42 displays the number of columns contained in the result set. It uses the `ResultSetMetaData` object's `getColumnCount` method to get this value. The loop in lines 45 through 49 iterates once for each column in the result set. Each iteration displays the column name and column data type. The `ResultSetMetaData` object's `getColumnName` and `getColumnTypeName` methods are used to retrieve this information. The `while` loop in lines 53 through 61 displays the contents of the result set. It has a nested `for` loop, in lines 56 through 59, which iterates once for each column in the result set. Each iteration gets the column value as a string and displays it.

16.10 Displaying Query Results in a `JTable`

CONCEPT: The `JTable` component is a Swing class that can be used to display a table of data. It is ideal for displaying result set data in a GUI application.

The `JTable` class is a Swing component that displays data in a two-dimensional table. The class has several constructors, but the one we will use has the following format:

```
JTable(Object[][] rowData, Object[] colNames)
```

The *rowData* parameter is a two-dimensional array of `Object`s. This array contains the data that will be displayed in the table. Each row in the array becomes a row of data in the table, and each column in the array becomes a column in the table. The `JTable` component calls the `toString` method of each object in the array to get the value to store in each column of the table.

The *colNames* parameter is a one-dimensional array of `Object`s. It contains the column names to display. Once again, the `JTable` component calls the `toString` method of each object in the array to get a value.

The following code shows an example of how to set up a simple `JTable` component.

```
        String[] colNames = {"Name", "Telephone" };
        String[][] rowData = {{ "Jean",  "555-2222" },
                              { "Tim",   "555-1212" },
                              { "Matt",  "555-9999" },
                              { "Rose",  "555-4545" },
                              { "Geri",  "555-5214" },
                              { "Shawn", "555-7821" },
                              { "Renee", "555-9640" },
                              { "Joe",   "555-8657" } };

        JTable myTable = new JTable(rowData, colNames);
        JScrollPane scrollPane = new JScrollPane(JTable);
```

In this code, the `colNames` array contains the column names, and the `rowData` array contains the data to display in the table. After the `JTable` object is constructed, it is added to a `JScrollPane` object. Figure 16-16 shows an example of how this table will appear when displayed in a frame.

Figure 16-16 A JTable displaying data

Now, let's look at how a `JTable` can be used to display the results of a database query. We will use three classes to build an application that allows the user to enter a `SELECT` statement, and then displays the results of the query in a `JTable`. The three classes are `TableFormatter`, `CoffeeDBQuery`, and `CoffeeDBViewer`. Code Listing 16-13 shows the `TableFormatter` class, which inherits from `JFrame`. When you instantiate this class, you pass a two-dimensional array containing table data, and a single-dimensional array containing column names to the constructor. The object creates a `JTable` containing the data, and displays the `JTable` in a `JFrame` that is 400 pixels wide by 200 pixels high.

Code Listing 16-13   **(TableFormatter.java)**

```
1   import javax.swing.*;
2   import java.awt.*;
3
4   /**
5    * The TableFormatter class displays a populated JTable.
6    */
7
```

```
 8   public class TableFormatter extends JFrame
 9   {
10      // Constants for size.
11      private final int WIDTH = 400;
12      private final int HEIGHT = 200;
13
14      /**
15       *  Constructor
16       */
17
18      public TableFormatter(Object[][] data, Object[] colNames)
19      {
20         // Specify an action for the close button.
21         setDefaultCloseOperation(JFrame.DISPOSE_ON_CLOSE);
22
23         // Create a JTable with the results.
24         JTable table = new JTable(data, colNames);
25
26         // Put the table in a scroll pane.
27         JScrollPane scrollPane = new JScrollPane(table);
28
29         // Add the table to the content pane.
30         add(scrollPane, BorderLayout.CENTER);
31
32         // Set the size and display.
33         setSize(WIDTH, HEIGHT);
34         setVisible(true);
35      }
36   }
```

Let's look at the constructor. In line 18 it accepts a two-dimensional Object array, data, and a one-dimensional Object array, colNames. These arrays contain the data and the column names to display in the table. In line 24 they are passed to the JTable constructor. Also notice in line 21 that we pass JFrame.DISPOSE_ON_CLOSE to the setDefaultCloseOperation method. Because this JFrame will be instantiated by another class, we do not want to shut down the entire application when the user clicks the standard close button. Instead, we merely want to dispose of this JFrame.

Code Listing 16-14 shows the CoffeeDBQuery class. The class constructor accepts a String containing an SQL query. It creates a database connection, executes the query, and then makes the result set data and its column names available through accessor methods.

Code Listing 16-14 (CoffeeDBQuery.java)

```
1   import java.sql.*;
2
3   /**
4    * This class executes queries on the CoffeeDB database
5    * and provides the results in arrays.
6    */
```

```
7
8    public class CoffeeDBQuery
9    {
10       // Database URL Constant
11       public final String DB_URL =
12             "jdbc:derby:CoffeeDB";
13
14       private Connection conn;        // Database connection
15       private String[][] tableData;   // Table data
16       private String[] colNames;      // Column names
17
18       /**
19        *  Constructor
20        */
21
22       public CoffeeDBQuery(String query)
23       {
24          // Get a connection to the database.
25          getDatabaseConnection();
26
27          try
28          {
29             // Create a Statement object for the query.
30             Statement stmt =
31                conn.createStatement(
32                      ResultSet.TYPE_SCROLL_INSENSITIVE,
33                      ResultSet.CONCUR_READ_ONLY);
34
35             // Execute the query.
36             ResultSet resultSet =
37                      stmt.executeQuery(query);
38
39             // Get the number of rows
40             resultSet.last();                  // Move to last row
41             int numRows = resultSet.getRow();  // Get row number
42             resultSet.first();                 // Move to first row
43
44             // Get a meta data object for the result set.
45             ResultSetMetaData meta = resultSet.getMetaData();
46
47             // Create an array of Strings for the column names.
48             colNames = new String[meta.getColumnCount()];
49
50             // Store the column names in the colNames array.
51             for (int i = 0; i < meta.getColumnCount(); i++)
52             {
53                // Get a column name.
54                colNames[i] = meta.getColumnLabel(i+1);
55             }
56
```

```
57              // Create a 2D String array for the table data.
58              tableData =
59                  new String[numRows][meta.getColumnCount()];
60
61              // Store the columns in the tableData array.
62              for (int row = 0; row < numRows; row++)
63              {
64                  for (int col = 0; col < meta.getColumnCount(); col++)
65                  {
66                      tableData[row][col] = resultSet.getString(col + 1);
67                  }
68
69                  // Go to the next row in the ResultSet.
70                  resultSet.next();
71              }
72
73              // Close the statement and connection objects.
74              stmt.close();
75              conn.close();
76          }
77          catch (SQLException ex)
78          {
79              ex.printStackTrace();
80          }
81      }
82
83      /**
84       *  The getDatabaseConnection method loads the JDBC
85       *  and gets a connection to the database.
86       */
87
88      private void getDatabaseConnection()
89      {
90          try
91          {
92              // Create a connection to the database.
93              conn = DriverManager.getConnection(DB_URL);
94          }
95          catch (Exception ex)
96          {
97              ex.printStackTrace();
98              System.exit(0);
99          }
100     }
101
102     /**
103      *    The getColumNames method returns the column names.
104      */
105
```

```
106        public String[] getColumnNames()
107        {
108           return colNames;
109        }
110
111        /**
112         *    The getTableData method returns the table data.
113         */
114
115        public String[][] getTableData()
116        {
117           return tableData;
118        }
119 }
```

In line 22 the constructor accepts a `String` referenced by the `query` parameter variable. This `String` should contain a `SELECT` statement. In line 25, the constructor calls the `getDatabaseConnection` method. This method, which appears in lines 88 through 100, establishes a connection with the database.

Lines 30 through 33 create a `Statement` object, specifying a scrollable result set. Lines 36 and 37 execute the query that was passed as an argument to the constructor and gets a reference to a `ResultSet` object. In lines 40 through 42 we determine the number of rows in the result set. This involves moving the cursor to the last row, getting the row number (which is stored in the `numRows` variable), and then moving the cursor to the first row for subsequent processing.

Line 45 gets a `ResultSetMetaData` object. Line 48 creates a `String` array, referenced by the `colNames` variable, to hold the column names. This statement uses the `ResultSetMetaData` object's `getColumnCount` method to determine the size of the array. The `for` loop in lines 51 through 55 retrieves the column names from the `ResultSetMetaData` object and stores the names in the `colNames` array.

Lines 58 through 59 create a two-dimensional `String` array, referenced by the `tableData` variable, to hold the table data. It uses the `numRows` variable to determine number of rows, and the `ResultSetMetaData` object's `getColumnCount` method to determine the number of columns.

The `for` loop in lines 62 through 71 stores the result set data in the `data` array. This loop iterates once for each row in the result set. Inside the loop, in lines 64 through 67, a nested `for` loop iterates once for each column in the result set. It retrieves the value of each column, as a string, and stores it as an element in the `tableData` array. Lines 74 and 75 call the `Statement` and `Connection` objects' `close` method.

The `getColumnNames` method, in lines 106 through 109, is an accessor method that returns a reference to the `colNames` array. The `getTableData` method, in lines 115 through 118, is an accessor method that returns a reference to the `tableData` array.

Code Listing 16-15 shows the `CoffeeDBviewer` class, which allows the user to enter any sort of `SELECT` statement for the `CoffeeDB` database and then displays the result in an instance of the `TableFormatter` class.

Code Listing 16-15   (`CoffeeDBviewer.java`)

```java
1   import javax.swing.*;
2   import java.awt.*;
3   import java.awt.event.*;
4
5   /**
6    *  The CoffeeDBViewer class is a simple database viewer for
7    *  the CoffeeDB database.
8    */
9
10  public class CoffeeDBViewer extends JFrame
11  {
12     JPanel queryPanel;        // A panel to hold the query
13     JPanel buttonPanel;       // A panel to hold the buttons
14     JTextArea queryTextArea;  // The user enters a query here
15     JButton submitButton;     // To submit a query
16     JButton exitButton;       // To quit the application
17
18     /**
19      *   Constructor
20      */
21
22     public CoffeeDBViewer()
23     {
24        // Set the window title.
25        setTitle("CoffeeDB Viewer");
26
27        // Specify an action for the close button.
28        setDefaultCloseOperation(JFrame.EXIT_ON_CLOSE);
29
30        // Build the Query Panel.
31        buildQueryPanel();
32
33        // Build the Button Panel.
34        buildButtonPanel();
35
36        // Add the panels to the content pane.
37        add(queryPanel, BorderLayout.NORTH);
38        add(buttonPanel, BorderLayout.SOUTH);
39
40        // Pack and display.
41        pack();
42        setVisible(true);
43     }
44
```

```
45      /**
46       *   The buildQueryPanel method builds a panel to hold the
47       *   text area that the user will enter a query into.
48       */
49
50      private void buildQueryPanel()
51      {
52         // Create a panel.
53         queryPanel = new JPanel();
54
55         // Create a text area, 8 rows by 50 columns.
56         queryTextArea = new JTextArea(8, 50);
57
58         // Turn line wrapping on.
59         queryTextArea.setLineWrap(true);
60
61         // Add a scroll pane to the text area.
62         JScrollPane qaScrollPane =
63                         new JScrollPane(queryTextArea);
64         qaScrollPane.setHorizontalScrollBarPolicy(
65             JScrollPane.HORIZONTAL_SCROLLBAR_NEVER);
66         qaScrollPane.setVerticalScrollBarPolicy(
67             JScrollPane.VERTICAL_SCROLLBAR_AS_NEEDED);
68
69         // Add the text area to the panel.
70         queryPanel.add(qaScrollPane);
71      }
72
73      /**
74       *   The buildButtonPanel method builds a panel
75       *   to hold the Submit and Exit buttons.
76       */
77
78      private void buildButtonPanel()
79      {
80         // Create a panel.
81         buttonPanel = new JPanel();
82
83         // Create the Submit button.
84         submitButton = new JButton("Submit");
85
86         // Register an action listener for the Submit button.
87         submitButton.addActionListener(new SubmitButtonListener());
88
89         // Create the Exit button.
90         exitButton = new JButton("Exit");
91
```

```
 92              // Register an action listener for the Exit button.
 93              exitButton.addActionListener(new ExitButtonListener());
 94
 95              // Add the two buttons to the panel.
 96              buttonPanel.add(submitButton);
 97              buttonPanel.add(exitButton);
 98        }
 99
100        /**
101         *    The SubmitButtonListener class is an action listener
102         *    for the Submit button.
103         */
104
105        private class SubmitButtonListener implements ActionListener
106        {
107           public void actionPerformed(ActionEvent e)
108           {
109              // Get the user's statement.
110              String userStatement = queryTextArea.getText();
111
112              // Qualify that it is a SELECT statement.
113              if (userStatement.trim().toUpperCase()
114                                      .startsWith("SELECT"))
115              {
116                 // Create a CoffeeDBQuery object for the query.
117                 CoffeeDBQuery dbQuery =
118                              new CoffeeDBQuery(userStatement);
119
120                 // Get the column names.
121                 String[] colNames = dbQuery.getColumnNames();
122
123                 // Get the table data.
124                 String[][] data = dbQuery.getTableData();
125
126                 // Display the results in a table.
127                 TableFormatter table =
128                              new TableFormatter(data, colNames);
129              }
130              else
131              {
132                 JOptionPane.showMessageDialog(null,
133                              "Only enter SELECT statements.");
134              }
135           }
136        }
137
```

```
138        /**
139         *    The ExitButtonListener class is an action listener
140         *    for the Exit button.
141         */
142
143        private class ExitButtonListener implements ActionListener
144        {
145           public void actionPerformed(ActionEvent e)
146           {
147              // End the application.
148              System.exit(0);
149           }
150        }
151
152        /**
153         *    The main method creates an instance of the class.
154         */
155
156        public static void main(String[] args)
157        {
158           new CoffeeDBViewer();
159        }
160     }
```

In line 25 the title bar text is set, and in line 28 an action for the standard close button is established. In line 31, the buildQueryPanel method is called. This method, which appears in lines 50 through 71, creates a panel with a JTextArea component. The user will enter SELECT statements into this JTextArea.

In line 34 the buildButtonPanel method is called. This method, which appears in lines 78 through 98, creates a panel with a Submit button and an Exit button. In lines 37 and 38, the query panel and the button panel are added to the JFrame's content pane, and in lines 41 and 42 the JFrame is packed and displayed.

The SubmitButtonListener class, in lines 105 through 136, is registered as an action listener for the Submit button. When the user clicks the Submit button, the actionPerformed method, in lines 107 through 135 executes. In line 110 the text entered by the user into the JTextArea component is retrieved. The if statement which begins at line 113 determines whether the text begins with "SELECT". Because this application is only designed to execute SELECT statements, we want to reject any other types of statements. If the text does begin with "SELECT", we proceed. Otherwise, an error message is displayed in lines 132 and 133.

Lines 117 and 118 create an instance of the CoffeeDBQuery class, passing the user's SQL statement as an argument to the constructor. Line 121 calls the CoffeeDBQuery method getColumnNames to retrieve an array containing the column names. Line 124 calls the CoffeeDBQuery method getTableData to retrieve a two-dimensional array containing the table data. Lines 127 and 128 create an instance of the TableFormatter class, passing the arrays containing the table data and column names as arguments to the constructor.

The ExitButtonListener class, in lines 143 through 150, is registered as an action listener for the Exit button. When the user clicks the Exit button, this class's actionPerformed method ends the application.

The main method in lines 156 through 159 creates an instance of the CoffeeDBViewer class, which starts the application running. Figure 16-17 shows the application's window. In the figure, the user has entered the statement SELECT * FROM Coffee. When the user click the Submit button, the window at the bottom appears, showing the results of the query. Note that the JTable has a scroll bar, and not all of the rows are visible.

Figure 16-17 Interaction with the CoffeeDBViewer application

This window appears first. The user enters a SELECT statement and clicks the Submit button.

This window appears next. It displays the results of the SELECT statement in a JTable component.

Figure 16-18 shows another session with the application. In the figure, the user has entered the following statement:

```
SELECT
    ProdNum, Price
FROM
    Coffee
WHERE
    Price > 9.0
ORDER BY
    ProdNum
```

When the user clicks the Submit button, the window at the bottom appears, showing the results of the query.

Figure 16-18   Interaction with the `CoffeeDBViewer` application

This window appears first. The user enters a SELECT statement and
clicks the Submit button.

```
CoffeeDB Viewer                                    [ _ ][ □ ][ X ]

SELECT
   ProdNum, Price
FROM
   Coffee
WHERE
   Price > 9.0
ORDER BY
   ProdNum


                        [ Submit ]  [ Exit ]
```

This window appears next. It displays the results of the SELECT
statement in a JTable component.

```
Query Results                              [ _ ][ □ ][ X ]

   PRODNUM              │         PRICE
16-001                  │  9.95                         ▲
16-002                  │  9.95
17-004                  │  11.95
18-001                  │  18.45
18-002                  │  18.45                        ▬
19-001                  │  9.65
21-001                  │  9.95
21-002                  │  10.45
21-003                  │  9.95                         ▼
```

16.11 Relational Data

CONCEPT: In a relational database, a column from one table can be associated
with a column from other tables. This association creates a relationship
between the tables.

In the last section we added a `Customer` table to the `CoffeeDB` database. This made the
database more useful by giving us the ability to look up customer information, as well as
the product information held in the `Coffee` table.

Suppose we want to make the database even more useful by storing information about
unpaid customer orders. That way, we can get a list of all the customers with outstanding
balances. To do this, we will need to add an additional table and more data to the database.
Here is a summary of the `UnpaidOrder` table, which we will create to hold order data. (We
will explain what a foreign key is momentarily.)

`UnpaidOrder` table:

CustomerNumber	CHAR(10)	*Foreign Key*
ProdNum	CHAR(10)	*Foreign Key*
OrderDate	CHAR(10)	
Quantity	DOUBLE	
Cost	DOUBLE	

The first column, CustomerNumber, identifies the customer that placed the order. Notice, however, that the Order table does not hold any other customer data. It holds only the customer number. When designing a database, it is important that you avoid unnecessary duplication of data. Because the customer data is already stored in the Customer table, we need only to store the customer number in the Order table. We can use that number to look up the rest of the customer's data in the Customer table.

In the UnpaidOrder table, the CustomerNumber column is considered a foreign key. A *foreign key* is a column in one table that references a primary key in another table. Recall that CustomerNumber is the primary key in the Customer table. When we add a row to the UnpaidOrder table, the value that we store in the CustomerNumber column must match a value in the CustomerNumber column of the Customer table. This creates a relationship between the rows in the UnpaidOrder table and the rows in the Customer table.

The next column, ProdNum, is also a foreign key because it identifies a product in the Coffee table. This is the item that the customer ordered. Once again, it is not necessary to store all of the product data in the UnpaidOrder table. We need only to store the product number, and then we can use that number to look up the product data in the Coffee table.

The next column in the UnpaidOrder table is OrderDate. This will hold the date that the order was placed.[1] The Quantity column holds the number of pounds of coffee that the customer ordered. The Cost column holds the total cost of the item. We will use the following SQL statement to create the Order table:

```
CREATE TABLE UnpaidOrder
( CustomerNumber CHAR(10) NOT NULL REFERENCES Customer(CustomerNumber),
  ProdNum CHAR(10) NOT NULL REFERENCES Coffee(ProdNum),
  OrderDate CHAR(10),
  Quantity DOUBLE,
  Cost DOUBLE )
```

Notice that this statement introduces a new qualifier, REFERENCES, which is used with both the CustomerNumber and ProdNum columns. Here is the way it is used with the CustomerNumber column:

```
REFERENCES Customer(CustomerNumber)
```

This indicates that the column references the CustomerNumber column in the Customer table. Because of this qualifier, the DBMS performs a check when you insert a row into the UnpaidOrder table. It will only allow you to insert a row if the CustomerNumber column contains a valid value from the CustomerNumber column of the Customer table. This ensures *referential integrity* between the two tables.

The REFERENCES qualifier is also used with the ProdNum column:

```
REFERENCES Coffee(ProdNum)
```

This indicates that the column references the ProdNum column in the Coffee table. When you insert a row into the Order table, its ProdNum column must contain a valid value from the ProdNum column of the Coffee table.

---

[1] In SQL there is a DATE data type which is used to hold dates. It corresponds to the java.sql.Date class. To keep the example simple, however, we will merely store the invoice date as a string.

System designers commonly use *entity relationship diagrams* to show the relationships between database tables. Figure 16-19 shows an entity relationship diagram for the CoffeeDB database. In the diagram, the primary keys are denoted with (PK). The lines that are drawn between the tables show how the tables are related. In this diagram, there are two types of relationships:

- A *one to many relationship* means that for each row in table *A* there can be many rows in table *B* that reference it.
- A *many to one relationship* means that many rows in table *A* can reference a single row in table *B*.

Notice that the ends of each line show either a 1 or an infinity symbol (∞). You can interpret the infinity symbol as meaning *many*, and the number 1 as meaning *one*. Look at the line that connects the Customer table to the UnpaidOrder table. The 1 is at the end of the line near the Customer table, and the infinity symbol is at the end near the UnpaidOrder table. This means that one row in the Customer table may be referenced by many rows in the UnpaidOrder table. This makes sense because a customer can place many orders. (In fact, this is what management hopes for!)

If we look at the relationship in the other direction, we see that many of the rows in the UnpaidOrder table can reference one row in the Customer table. Here is a summary of all the relationships shown in the diagram:

- There is a one to many relationship between the Customer table and the UnpaidOrder table. One row in the Customer table may be referenced by many rows in the UnpaidOrder table.
- There is a many to one relationship between the UnpaidOrder table and the Customer table. Many rows in the UnpaidOrder table may reference a single row in the Customer table.
- There is a one to many relationship between the Coffee table and the UnpaidOrder table. One row in the Coffee table may be referenced by many rows in the UnpaidOrder table.
- There is a many to one relationship between the UnpaidOrder table and the Coffee table. Many rows in the UnpaidOrder table may reference a single row in the Coffee table.

Figure 16-19 Entity relationship diagram

Joining Data from Multiple Tables

When related data is stored in multiple tables, as in the CoffeeDB database, it is often necessary to pull data from different tables in a SELECT statement. For example, suppose we want to see information about all the unpaid orders. Specifically, for each unpaid order, we want to see the customer number, customer name, order date, coffee description, and cost. This involves columns from the Customer, UnpaidOrder, and Coffee tables. Because some of these tables have columns with the same name, we have to use qualified column names in our SELECT statement. A *qualified column name* takes the following form:

TableName.ColumnName

For example, `Customer.CustomerNumber` specifies the `CustomerNumber` column in the `Customer` table, and `UnpaidOrder.CustomerNumber` specifies the `CustomerNumber` column in the `UnpaidOrder` table. Take a look at the following query:

```
SELECT
    Customer.CustomerNumber,
    Customer.Name,
    UnpaidOrder.OrderDate,
    Coffee.Description,
    UnpaidOrder.Cost
FROM
    Customer, UnpaidOrder, Coffee
WHERE
    UnpaidOrder.CustomerNumber = Customer.CustomerNumber AND
    UnpaidOrder.ProdNum = Coffee.ProdNum
```

The first part of the query specifies the columns we want:

```
SELECT
    Customer.CustomerNumber,
    Customer.Name,
    UnpaidOrder.OrderDate,
    Coffee.Description,
    UnpaidOrder.Cost
```

The second part of the query, which uses the FROM clause, specifies the tables we want to pull the data from:

```
FROM
    Customer, UnpaidOrder, Coffee
```

Notice that the table names are separated by commas. The third part of the query, which uses the WHERE clause, specifies a search criteria:

```
WHERE
    UnpaidOrder.CustomerNumber = Customer.CustomerNumber AND
    UnpaidOrder.ProdNum = Coffee.ProdNum
```

The search criteria tell the DBMS how to link the rows in the tables. Recall from our earlier discussion that `UnpaidOrder.CustomerNumber` column references the `Customer.CustomerNumber` column, and the `UnpaidOrder.ProdNum` column references the `Coffee.ProdNum` column.

 WARNING! When joining data from multiple tables, be sure to use a WHERE clause to specify a search criteria that links the appropriate columns. Failure to do so will result in a large set of unrelated data.

An Order Entry System

Now, let's look at an example application that uses a relational database. In order to use this application, you will need the Coffee table, the Customer table, and the UnpaidOrder table in the CoffeeDB database. Back in Section 16.6 you saw a program named CreateCustomerTable.java. This program created the Customer table in the CoffeeDB database and added three sample rows. If you haven't already run that program, do so now. After running the program, you can run the CoffeeDBViewer application presented earlier in this chapter, and enter the statement SELECT * FROM Customer. You should see the data shown in Figure 16-20.

Figure 16-20   Customer table

Next, you should run the program CreateUnpaidOrderTable.java. This program is in the source code folder for this chapter, and it will create the UnpaidOrder table we discussed earlier in this chapter. The table will have no data stored in it, however.

Now that we have the necessary tables set up in our database, we will examine an order entry application that allows the user to place an order for coffee. The application is built from a number of classes. The first class we will look at is the CoffeeDBManager class, shown in Code Listing 16-16. This class performs a variety of operations on the CoffeeDB database, which we will need in our order entry system.

Code Listing 16-16   (**CoffeeDBManager.java**)

```
 1  import java.sql.*;
 2
 3  /**
 4   *  The CoffeeDBManager class performs operations
 5   *  the CoffeeDB database.
 6   */
 7
 8  public class CoffeeDBManager
 9  {
10     // Constant for database URL.
11     public final String DB_URL =
12              "jdbc:derby:CoffeeDB";
13
14     // Field for the database connection
15     private Connection conn;
16
```

```
17      /**
18       *  Constructor
19       */
20
21      public CoffeeDBManager() throws SQLException
22      {
23          // Create a connection to the database.
24          conn = DriverManager.getConnection(DB_URL);
25      }
26
27      /**
28       *   The getCoffeeNames method returns an array
29       *   of Strings containing all the coffee names.
30       */
31
32      public String[] getCoffeeNames()
33                          throws SQLException
34      {
35          // Create a Statement object for the query.
36          Statement stmt =
37            conn.createStatement(
38                    ResultSet.TYPE_SCROLL_SENSITIVE,
39                    ResultSet.CONCUR_READ_ONLY);
40
41          // Execute the query.
42          ResultSet resultSet = stmt.executeQuery(
43                      "SELECT Description FROM Coffee");
44
45          // Get the number of rows
46          resultSet.last();                  // Move to last row
47          int numRows = resultSet.getRow(); // Get row number
48          resultSet.first();                 // Move to first row
49
50          // Create an array for the coffee names.
51          String[] listData = new String[numRows];
52
53          // Populate the array with coffee names.
54          for (int index = 0; index < numRows; index++)
55          {
56              // Store the coffee name in the array.
57              listData[index] = resultSet.getString(1);
58
59              // Go to the next row in the result set.
60              resultSet.next();
61          }
62
63          // Close the connection and statement objects.
64          conn.close();
65          stmt.close();
66
```

```
67          // Return the listData array.
68          return listData;
69      }
70
71      /**
72       *   The getProdNum method returns a specific
73       *   coffee's product number. The coffeeName
74       *   parameter is the specified coffee.
75       */
76
77      public String getProdNum(String coffeeName)
78                              throws SQLException
79      {
80          String prodNum = ""; // Product number
81
82          // Create a connection to the database.
83          conn = DriverManager.getConnection(DB_URL);
84
85          // Create a Statement object for the query.
86          Statement stmt = conn.createStatement();
87
88          // Execute the query.
89          ResultSet resultSet = stmt.executeQuery(
90                          "SELECT ProdNum " +
91                          "FROM Coffee " +
92                          "WHERE Description = '" +
93                          coffeeName + "'");
94
95          // If the result set has a row, go to it
96          // and retrieve the product number.
97          if (resultSet.next())
98              prodNum = resultSet.getString(1);
99
100         // Close the Connection and Statement objects.
101         conn.close();
102         stmt.close();
103
104         // Return the product number.
105         return prodNum;
106     }
107
108     /**
109      *   The getCoffeePrice method returns the price
110      *   of a coffee. The prodNum parameter is the
111      *   specified product number.
112      */
113
```

```
114      public double getCoffeePrice(String prodNum)
115                                    throws SQLException
116      {
117         double price = 0.0;   // Coffee price
118
119         // Create a connection to the database.
120         conn = DriverManager.getConnection(DB_URL);
121
122         // Create a Statement object for the query.
123         Statement stmt = conn.createStatement();
124
125         // Execute the query.
126         ResultSet resultSet = stmt.executeQuery(
127                          "SELECT Price " +
128                          "FROM Coffee " +
129                          "WHERE ProdNum = '" +
130                          prodNum + "'");
131
132         // If the result set has a row, go to it
133         // and retrieve the price.
134         if (resultSet.next())
135            price = resultSet.getDouble(1);
136
137         // Close the connection and statement objects.
138         conn.close();
139         stmt.close();
140
141         // Return the price.
142         return price;
143      }
144
145      /**
146       *    The getCustomerNames method returns an array
147       *    of Strings containing all the customer names.
148       */
149
150      public String[] getCustomerNames() throws SQLException
151      {
152         // Create a connection to the database.
153         conn = DriverManager.getConnection(DB_URL);
154
155         // Create a Statement object for the query.
156         Statement stmt =
157            conn.createStatement(
158                    ResultSet.TYPE_SCROLL_SENSITIVE,
159                    ResultSet.CONCUR_READ_ONLY);
160
161         // Execute the query.
162         ResultSet resultSet =
163            stmt.executeQuery("SELECT Name FROM Customer");
```

```
164
165        // Get the number of rows
166        resultSet.last();                    // Move last row
167        int numRows = resultSet.getRow(); // Get row number
168        resultSet.first();                   // Move to first row
169
170        // Create an array for the customer names.
171        String[] listData = new String[numRows];
172
173        // Populate the array with customer names.
174        for (int index = 0; index < numRows; index++)
175        {
176           // Store the customer name in the array.
177           listData[index] = resultSet.getString(1);
178
179           // Go to the next row in the result set.
180           resultSet.next();
181        }
182
183        // Close the connection and statement objects.
184        conn.close();
185        stmt.close();
186
187        // Return the listData array.
188        return listData;
189     }
190
191     /**
192      *    The getCustomerNum method returns a specific
193      *    customer's number. The name parameter is the
194      *    specified customer's name.
195      */
196
197     public String getCustomerNum(String name)
198                                  throws SQLException
199     {
200        String customerNumber = "";
201
202        // Create a connection to the database.
203        conn = DriverManager.getConnection(DB_URL);
204
205        // Create a Statement object for the query.
206        Statement stmt = conn.createStatement();
207
208        // Execute the query.
209        ResultSet resultSet =
210          stmt.executeQuery("SELECT CustomerNumber " +
211                            "FROM Customer " +
212                            "WHERE Name = '" + name + "'");
213
```

```
214              if (resultSet.next())
215                  customerNumber = resultSet.getString(1);
216
217              // Close the connection and statement objects.
218              conn.close();
219              stmt.close();
220
221              // Return the customer number.
222              return customerNumber;
223          }
224
225          /**
226           *    The submitOrder method submits an order to
227           *    the UnpaidOrder table in the CoffeeDB database.
228           *    The custNum parameter is the customer number.
229           *    The prodNum parameter is the product number.
230           *    The quantity parameter is the quantity ordered.
231           *    The price parameter is the price.
232           *    The orderDate parameter is the order date.
233           */
234
235          public void submitOrder(String custNum, String prodNum,
236                                     int quantity, double price,
237                                     String orderDate) throws SQLException
238          {
239              // Calculate the cost of the order.
240              double cost = quantity * price;
241
242              // Create a connection to the database.
243              conn = DriverManager.getConnection(DB_URL);
244
245              // Create a Statement object for the query.
246              Statement stmt = conn.createStatement();
247
248              // Execute the query.
249              stmt.executeUpdate("INSERT INTO UnpaidOrder VALUES('" +
250                                     custNum + "', '" +
251                                     prodNum + "', '" + orderDate + "', " +
252                                     quantity + ", " + cost + ")");
253
254              // Close the connection and statement objects.
255              conn.close();
256              stmt.close();
257          }
258      }
```

Here is a summary of the methods in the `CoffeeDBManager` class:

- The constructor, in lines 21 through 25, establishes a connection to the database. The `getCoffeeNames` method, in lines 32 through 69, returns an array of strings containing the names of all the coffees in the `Coffee` table.

- The getProdNum method, in lines 77 through 106, accepts a String argument containing the name of a coffee. The method returns the coffee's product number.
- The getCoffeePrice method, in lines 114 through 143, accepts a String argument containing a coffee's product number. The method returns the price of the specified coffee.
- The getCustomerNames method, in lines 150 through 189, returns an array of strings containing the names of all the customers in the Customer table.
- The getCustomerNum method, in lines 197 through 223, accepts a String argument containing a customer's name. The method returns that customer's customer number.
- The submitOrder method in lines 235 through 257 creates a row in the UnpaidOrder table. It accepts arguments for the customer number, the product number of the coffee being ordered, the quantity being ordered, the coffee's price per pound, and the order date. Line 240 calculates the cost of the order by multiplying the quantity by the price per pound. Line 243 opens a connection to the database, and line 246 creates a Statement object. Lines 249 through 252 execute an INSERT statement on the UnpaidOrders table.

The next class we will look at is the CustomerPanel class, which is shown in Code Listing 16-17. This class, which inherits from JPanel, uses a JList component to display all of the customer names in the Customer table. Figure 16-21 shows an example of how the panel will appear when it is displayed in a GUI application.

Code Listing 16-17   **(CustomerPanel.java)**

```java
1   import java.sql.*;
2   import javax.swing.*;
3
4   /**
5    *  The CustomerPanel class is a custom JPanel that
6    *  shows a list of customers in a JList.
7    */
8
9   public class CustomerPanel extends JPanel
10  {
11     private final int NUM_ROWS = 5; // Number of rows to display
12     private JList customerList;      // A list for customer names
13     String[] names;                  // To hold customer names
14
15     /**
16      *   Constructor
17      */
18
19     public CustomerPanel()
20     {
21        try
22        {
23           // Create a CoffeeDBManager object.
24           CoffeeDBManager dbManager = new CoffeeDBManager();
25
```

```
26              // Get a list of customer names as a String array.
27              names = dbManager.getCustomerNames();
28
29              // Create a JList object to hold customer names.
30              customerList = new JList(names);
31
32              // Set the number of visible rows.
33              customerList.setVisibleRowCount(NUM_ROWS);
34
35              // Put the JList object in a scroll pane.
36              JScrollPane scrollPane =
37                           new JScrollPane(customerList);
38
39              // Add the scroll pane to the panel.
40              add(scrollPane);
41
42              // Add a titled border to the panel.
43              setBorder(BorderFactory.createTitledBorder(
44                               "Select a Customer"));
45          }
46      catch (SQLException ex)
47      {
48          ex.printStackTrace();
49          System.exit(0);
50      }
51   }
52
53   /**
54    *   The getCustomer method returns the customer
55    *   name selected  by the user.
56    */
57
58   public String getCustomer()
59   {
60      // The JList class's getSelectedValue method returns
61      // an Object reference, so we will cast it to a String.
62      return (String) customerList.getSelectedValue();
63   }
64 }
```

Figure 16-21 Customer panel

Line 24 in the constructor creates an instance of the `CoffeeDBManager` class. Line 27 calls the `getCustomerNames` method to get a `String` array containing the customer names. Line 30 creates a `JList` component, passing the array of customer names as an argument to the constructor. This will cause the `JList` component to be populated with the names of all the customers in the `Customer` table. Line 33 sets the number of visible rows for the `JList` component, and lines 36 through 37 put the `JList` in a scroll pane. Line 40 adds the scroll pane to the panel, and lines 43 through 44 create a titled border around the panel.

The `getCustomer` method, in lines 58 through 63, returns the customer name that is currently selected in the `JList` component.

The next class, `CoffeePanel`, is shown in Code Listing 16-18. This class, which inherits from `JPanel`, uses a `JList` component to display all of the coffee names in the `Description` column of the `Coffee` table. Figure 16-22 shows an example of how the panel will appear when it is displayed in a GUI application.

Code Listing 16-18   **(CoffeePanel.java)**

```java
1   import java.sql.*;
2   import javax.swing.*;
3
4   /**
5    *  The CoffeePanel class is a custom JPanel that
6    *  shows a list of coffees in a JList.
7    */
8
9   public class CoffeePanel extends JPanel
10  {
11     private final int NUM_ROWS = 5; // Number of rows to display
12     private JList coffeeList;       // A list for coffee descriptions
13     String[] coffeeNames;           // To hold coffee names
14
15     /**
16      *   Constructor
17      */
18
19     public CoffeePanel()
20     {
21        try
22        {
23           // Create a CoffeeDBManager object.
24           CoffeeDBManager dbManager = new CoffeeDBManager();
25
26           // Get a list of coffee names as a String array.
27           coffeeNames = dbManager.getCoffeeNames();
28
```

```
29                 // Create a JList object to hold the coffee names.
30                 coffeeList = new JList(coffeeNames);
31
32                 // Set the number of visible rows.
33                 coffeeList.setVisibleRowCount(NUM_ROWS);
34
35                 // Put the JList object in a scroll pane.
36                 JScrollPane scrollPane = new JScrollPane(coffeeList);
37
38                 // Add the scroll pane to the panel.
39                 add(scrollPane);
40
41                 // Add a titled border to the panel.
42                 setBorder(BorderFactory.createTitledBorder(
43                                         "Select a Coffee"));
44             }
45         catch (SQLException ex)
46         {
47             ex.printStackTrace();
48             System.exit(0);
49         }
50     }
51
52     /**
53      *   The getCoffee method returns the coffee
54      *   description selected  by the user.
55      */
56
57     public String getCoffee()
58     {
59         // The JList class's getSelectedValue method returns
60         // an Object reference, so we will cast it to a String.
61         return (String) coffeeList.getSelectedValue();
62     }
63 }
```

Figure 16-22 Coffee panel

Line 24 in the constructor creates an instance of the `CoffeeDBManager` class. Line 27 calls the `getCoffeeNames` method to get a `String` array containing coffee names. Line 30 creates a `JList` component, passing the array of coffee names as an argument to the constructor. This will cause the `JList` component to be populated with the names of all the coffees in the `Coffee` table. Line 33 sets the number of visible rows for the `JList` component, and line 36 puts the `JList` in a scroll pane. Line 39 adds the scroll pane to the panel, and lines 42 through 43 create a titled border around the panel.

The `getCoffee` method, in lines 57 through 62, returns the coffee name that is currently selected in the `JList` component.

The next class, `QtyDatePanel`, is shown in Code Listing 16-19. This class, which inherits from `JPanel`, simply displays `JTextField` components for the quantity of coffee being ordered (in pounds) and the date of the order. Figure 16-23 shows an example of how the panel will appear when it is displayed in a GUI application.

Code Listing 16-19   **(QtyDatePanel.java)**

```java
 1   import javax.swing.*;
 2   import java.awt.*;
 3
 4   /**
 5    *    The QtyDatePanel presents text fields for the
 6    *    quantity of coffee being ordered and the order
 7    *    date.
 8    */
 9
10   public class QtyDatePanel extends JPanel
11   {
12      private JTextField qtyTextField;    // Order quantity
13      private JTextField dateTextField;   // order date
14
15      /**
16       *    Constructor
17       */
18
19      public QtyDatePanel()
20      {
21         // Create a label prompting the user
22         // for a quantity.
23         JLabel qtyPrompt = new JLabel("Quantity");
24
25         // Create a text field for the quantity.
26         qtyTextField = new JTextField(10);
27
28         // Create a label prompting the user
29         // for a date.
30         JLabel datePrompt = new JLabel("Order Date");
31
```

```
32          // Create a text field for the date.
33          dateTextField = new JTextField(10);
34
35          // Create a grid layout manager, 4 rows, 1 column.
36          setLayout(new GridLayout(4, 1));
37
38          // Add the components to the panel.
39          add (qtyPrompt);
40          add (qtyTextField);
41          add (datePrompt);
42          add (dateTextField);
43       }
44
45       /**
46        *   The getQuantity method gets the quantity
47        *   entered by the user into the qtyTextField
48        *   component and returns it as an int.
49        */
50
51       public int getQuantity()
52       {
53          return Integer.parseInt(qtyTextField.getText());
54       }
55
56       /**
57        *   The getDate method gets the date
58        *   entered by the user into the dateTextField
59        *   component and returns it as a String.
60        */
61
62       public String getDate()
63       {
64          return dateTextField.getText();
65       }
66
67       /**
68        *   The clear method clears the text fields.
69        */
70
71       public void clear()
72       {
73          qtyTextField.setText("");
74          dateTextField.setText("");
75       }
76    }
```

Figure 16-23   QtyDate panel

Quantity

Order Date

The constructor creates text fields into which the user can enter the quantity of an order and the order date. It also creates labels that prompt the user for the correct information for each text box. A GridLayout manager is then created, and these components are added to the panel.

The getQuantity method, in lines 51 through 54, returns the quantity entered by the user as an integer. The getDate method in lines 62 through 65 returns the order date entered by the user as a String. The clear method, in lines 71 through 75, clears the text fields of any data.

Now let's look at the PlaceOrder class, shown in Code Listing 16-20. This application presents the GUI interface shown in Figure 16-24 for order entry.

Code Listing 16-20   (PlaceOrder.java)

```java
1   import java.sql.*;
2   import javax.swing.*;
3   import java.awt.*;
4   import java.awt.event.*;
5
6   /**
7    *   The PlaceOrder class is a simple order entry system.
8    */
9
10  public class PlaceOrder extends JFrame
11  {
12     CustomerPanel customerPanel; // Panel for customers
13     CoffeePanel coffeePanel;     // Panel for coffees
14     QtyDatePanel qtyDatePanel;   // Panel for quantity and date
15     JPanel buttonPanel;          // Panel for buttons
16
17     /**
18      *   Constructor
19      */
20
21     public PlaceOrder()
22     {
23        // Set the window title.
24        setTitle("Place Order");
25
```

```
26          // Specify an action for the close button.
27          setDefaultCloseOperation(JFrame.EXIT_ON_CLOSE);
28
29          // Create a CustomerPanel object.
30          customerPanel = new CustomerPanel();
31
32          // Create a CoffeePanel object.
33          coffeePanel = new CoffeePanel();
34
35          // Create a QtyDatePanel object.
36          qtyDatePanel = new QtyDatePanel();
37
38          // Build the ButtonPanel object.
39          buildButtonPanel();
40
41          // create a BorderLayout manager.
42          setLayout(new BorderLayout());
43
44          // Add the panels to the content pane.
45          add(customerPanel, BorderLayout.WEST);
46          add(coffeePanel, BorderLayout.CENTER);
47          add(qtyDatePanel, BorderLayout.EAST);
48          add(buttonPanel, BorderLayout.SOUTH);
49
50          // Pack and display the window.
51          pack();
52          setVisible(true);
53      }
54
55      /**
56       *   The buildButtonPanel method builds a panel for
57       *   the Submit and Exit buttons.
58       */
59
60      public void buildButtonPanel()
61      {
62          // Create a panel for the buttons.
63          buttonPanel = new JPanel();
64
65          // Create a Submit button and add an action listener.
66          JButton submitButton = new JButton("Submit");
67          submitButton.addActionListener(new SubmitButtonListener());
68
69          // Create an Exit button.
70          JButton exitButton = new JButton("Exit");
71          exitButton.addActionListener(new ExitButtonListener());
72
```

```
73          // Add the buttons to the panel.
74          buttonPanel.add(submitButton);
75          buttonPanel.add(exitButton);
76      }
77
78      /**
79       *    Private inner class that handles submit button events
80       */
81
82      private class SubmitButtonListener implements ActionListener
83      {
84          public void actionPerformed(ActionEvent e)
85          {
86              try
87              {
88                  // Get the customer name from the CustomerPanel object.
89                  String customerName = customerPanel.getCustomer();
90
91                  // Get the coffee description from the CoffeePanel.
92                  String coffee = coffeePanel.getCoffee();
93
94                  // Get the quantity from the QtyDatePanel object.
95                  int qty = qtyDatePanel.getQuantity();
96
97                  // Get the order date from the QtyDatePanel object.
98                  String orderDate = qtyDatePanel.getDate();
99
100                 // Create a CoffeeDBManager object.
101                 CoffeeDBManager dbManager = new CoffeeDBManager();
102
103                 // Get the customer number.
104                 String customerNum =
105                     dbManager.getCustomerNum(customerName);
106
107                 // Get the coffee product number.
108                 String prodNum = dbManager.getProdNum(coffee);
109
110                 // Get the coffee price per pound.
111                 double price = dbManager.getCoffeePrice(prodNum);
112
113                 // Submit the order.
114                 dbManager.submitOrder(customerNum, prodNum, qty,
115                                       price, orderDate);
116
117                 // Clear the text fields for quantity and order date.
118                 qtyDatePanel.clear();
119
```

```
120                // Let the user know the order was placed.
121                JOptionPane.showMessageDialog(null, "Order Placed.");
122            }
123         catch (SQLException ex)
124         {
125             ex.printStackTrace();
126             System.exit(0);
127         }
128     }
129  }
130
131  /**
132   *   Private inner class that handles exit button events
133   */
134
135  private class ExitButtonListener implements ActionListener
136  {
137     public void actionPerformed(ActionEvent e)
138     {
139         System.exit(0);
140     }
141  }
142
143  /**
144   *   main method
145   */
146
147  public static void main(String[] args)
148  {
149     new PlaceOrder();
150  }
151 }
```

Figure 16-24 Order entry GUI

In the constructor, lines 24 through 27 set the JFrame's title and specify an action for the close button. Lines 30, 33, and 36 create instances of the CustomerPanel, CoffeePanel, and QtyDatePanel classes. Line 39 calls the buildButtonPanel method. The buildButtonPanel method, which appears in lines 60 through 76, creates a panel with two JButton components: a Submit button and an Exit button. We will look at these buttons' event handlers in a moment. Back in the constructor, line 42 creates a BorderLayout manager. Lines 45 through 49 add the panels to appropriate regions of the content pane. Lines 51 and 52 pack and display the JFrame.

The SubmitButtonListener class, in lines 82 through 129, is the event handler for the submit button. Line 89 retrieves the customer name from the CustomerPanel object. Line 92 retrieves the coffee description from the CoffeePanel object. Lines 95 and 98 retrieve the quantity and order date from the QtyDatePanel object. Line 101 creates an instance of the CoffeeDBManager class, which we will use to submit the order.

We have the name of the customer placing the order and the name of the coffee being ordered, but to submit an order we need the customer number and the product number. Lines 104 through 105 call the CoffeeDBManager object's getCustomerNum method to retrieve the customer number. Line 108 calls the CoffeeDBManager object's getProdNum method to retrieve the product number. We also need the price of the coffee. Line 111 calls the CoffeeDBManager object's getCoffeePrice method to retrieve this information. Lines 114 through 115 call the CoffeeDBManager object's submitOrder method to submit the order. After the order is submitted, line 118 clears the text fields holding the quantity and order date, making it easier to enter the next order. Line 121 displays a dialog box indicating that the order was placed.

Figure 16-25 shows the order entry GUI with a customer selected, a coffee selected, a quantity entered, and an order date entered.

Figure 16-25   Order data entered

After we submit the order shown in Figure 16-25, we can run the CoffeeDBViewer application and enter the following SELECT statement to pull data from various tables relating to the order. Figure 16-26 shows the CofeeDBViewer application's opening screen with the SELECT statement already filled in and the results of the statement.

```
SELECT
    Customer.CustomerNumber,
    Customer.Name,
    UnpaidOrder.OrderDate,
    Coffee.Description,
    UnpaidOrder.Cost
FROM
    Customer, UnpaidOrder, Coffee
WHERE
    UnpaidOrder.CustomerNumber = Customer.CustomerNumber AND
    UnpaidOrder.ProdNum = Coffee.ProdNum
```

Figure 16-26 Order information viewed in `CoffeeDBViewer`

This window appears first in the CoffeeDBViewer application. The user enters a SELECT statement and clicks the Submit button.

This window appears next. It displays the results of the SELECT statement in a JTable component.

 16.12 Advanced Topics

Transactions

Sometimes an application must perform several database updates to carry out a single task. For example, suppose you have a checking account and a car loan at your bank. Each month, your car payments are automatically taken from your checking account. For this operation to take place, the balance of your checking account must be reduced by the amount of the car payment, and the balance of the car loan must also be reduced.

An operation that requires multiple database updates is known as a *transaction*. In order for a transaction to be complete, all of the steps involved in the transaction must be performed. If any single step within a transaction fails, then none of the steps in the transaction should be performed. For example, imagine that the bank system has begun the process of making your car payment. The amount of the payment is subtracted from your checking account balance, but then some sort of system failure occurs before the balance of the car loan is reduced. You would be quite upset to learn that the amount for your car payment was withdrawn from your checking account, but never applied to your loan!

Most database systems provide a means for undoing the partially completed steps in a transaction when a failure occurs. When you write transaction-processing code, there are two concepts you must understand: commit and rollback. The term *commit* refers to making a permanent change to a database, and the term *rollback* refers to undoing changes to a database.

By default, the JDBC `Connection` class operates in auto commit mode. In *auto commit* mode, all updates that are made to the database are made permanent as soon as they are executed. When auto commit mode is turned off, however, changes do not become permanent until a commit command is executed. This makes it possible to use a rollback command to undo changes. A rollback command will undo all database changes since the last commit command.

In JDBC, you turn autocommit mode off with the `Connection` class's `setAutoCommit` method, passing the argument `false`. Here is an example:

```
conn.setAutoCommit(false);
```

You execute a commit command by calling the `Connection` class's commit method, as shown here:

```
conn.commit();
```

A rollback command can be executed with the `Connection` class's rollback method, as shown here:

```
conn.rollback();
```

Let's look at an example. Suppose we add a new table named `Inventory` to the `CoffeeDB` database, for the purpose of storing the quantity of each type of coffee in inventory. The table has two rows: `ProdNum`, which is a coffee product number, and `Qty`, which is the quantity of each type of coffee. When an order is placed, we want to update both the `Inventory` table and the `UnpaidOrder` table. In the `Inventory` table we want to subtract the quantity being ordered from the quantity in inventory. In the `UnpaidOrder` table we want to insert a new row representing the order. Here is some example code that might be used to process this as a transaction.

```
Connection conn = DriverManager.getConnection(DB_URL);
conn.setAutoCommit(false);
Statement stmt = conn.createStatement();
// Attempt the transaction.
try
{
    // Update the inventory records.
    stmt.executeUpdate("UPDATE Inventory SET Qty = Qty - " +
                qtyOrdered + " WHERE ProdNum = " + prodNum);
    // Add the order to the UnpaidOrder table.
    stmt.executeUpdate("INSERT INTO UnpaidOrder VALUES('" +
                custNum + "', '" +
                prodNum + "', '" + orderDate + "', " +
                qtyOrdered + ", " + cost + ")");
```

```
        // Commit all these updates.
        conn.commit();
    }
    catch (SQLException ex)
    {
        // Roll back the changes.
        conn.rollback();
    }
```

Notice that inside the try block, after the statements to update the database have been executed, the `Connection` class's `commit` method is executed. In the catch block, the `rollback` method is executed in the event of an error.

Stored Procedures

Many commercial database systems allow you to create SQL statements and store them in the DBMS itself. These SQL statements are called *stored procedures*, and they can be executed by other applications using the DBMS. If you have written an SQL statement that is used often in a variety of applications, it might be helpful to store it as a stored procedure in the DBMS. Then, you can call the stored procedure from any of your applications when you need to execute the SQL statement. Because stored procedures are already in the DBMS, they usually execute faster than SQL statements that are submitted from applications outside the DBMS.

We won't go into the details of stored procedures in this book, but we will point you in the right direction if you want to learn more. Each DBMS has its own syntax for creating a stored procedure in SQL, so you will have to consult your DBMS documentation to determine the format. Once you have properly written a stored procedure in SQL, you simply submit it to the DBMS using the `Statement` class's `execute` method. To execute a stored procedure, you must create a `CallableStatement` object. `CallableStatement` is an interface in the `java.sql` package. To create a `CallableStatement` object, you call the `Connection` class's `prepareCall` statement.

16.13 Common Errors to Avoid

- **Using the == operator instead of the = operator in an SQL statement.** The equal-to operator in SQL is one = sign, instead of two.
- **Using double quotes around strings instead of single quotes.** String literals in SQL are enclosed in single quotes instead of double quotes.
- **Using && and || in an SQL statement.** The logical AND and logical OR operators in SQL are the words AND and OR, not the && and || symbols.
- **Not using the correct WHERE clause in an UPDATE statement.** Be careful that you do not leave out the WHERE clause and the conditional expression when using an UPDATE statement. It's possible that you will change the contents of every row in the table!
- **Not using the correct WHERE clause in a DELETE statement.** Be careful that you do not leave out the WHERE clause and the conditional expression when using a DELETE statement. It's possible that you will delete every row in the table!
- **Not using the correct WHERE clause when joining data.** When joining data from multiple tables, be sure to use a WHERE clause to specify a search criteria that links the appropriate columns. Failure to do so will result in a large set of unrelated data.

Review Questions and Exercises

Multiple Choice and True/False

1. This is the technology that makes it possible for a Java application to communicate with a DBMS.
   a. DBMSC
   b. JDBC
   c. JDBMS
   d. JDSQL

2. This is a standard language for working with database management systems.
   a. Java
   b. COBOL
   c. SQL
   d. BASIC

3. The data that is stored in a table is organized in
   a. rows
   b. files
   c. folders
   d. pages

4. The data that is stored in a row is divided into
   a. sections
   b. bytes
   c. columns
   d. tables

5. This is a column that holds a unique value for each row and can be used to identify specific rows.
   a. ID column
   b. public key
   c. designator column
   d. primary key

6. This type of SQL statement is used to retrieve rows from a table.
   a. RETRIEVE
   b. GET
   c. SELECT
   d. READ

7. This contains the results of an SQL SELECT statement.
   a. select set
   b. result set
   c. SQL set
   d. collection set

8. This clause allows you to specify a search criteria with the SELECT statement.
   a. SEARCH
   b. WHERE
   c. AS
   d. CRITERIA

9. This is a Java class that is designed to communicate with a specific DBMS.
   a. JDBC driver
   b. DBMS Superclass
   c. DBMS Subclass
   d. Stream converter

10. This is a string listing the protocol that should be used to access a database, the name of the database, and potentially other items.
    a. JDBC driver
    b. JDBC locator
    c. Database URL
    d. Database specifier

11. This method is specified in the `Statement` interface and should be used to execute a `SELECT` statement.
    a. `execute`
    b. `executeUpdate`
    c. `executeQuery`
    d. `executeSelect`

12. This method is specified in the `Statement` interface and should be used to execute an `UPDATE` statement.
    a. `execute`
    b. `executeUpdate`
    c. `executeQuery`
    d. `executeSelect`

13. This method is specified in the `Statement` interface and should be used to execute an `INSERT` statement.
    a. `execute`
    b. `executeUpdate`
    c. `executeQuery`
    d. `executeSelect`

14. This SQL statement is used to insert rows into a table.
    a. `INSERT`
    b. `ADD`
    c. `CREATE`
    d. `UPDATE`

15. This SQL statement is used to remove rows from a table
    a. `REMOVE`
    b. `ERASE`
    c. `PURGE`
    d. `DELETE`

16. This SQL statement is used to delete an entire table.
    a. `REMOVE`
    b. `DROP`
    c. `PURGE`
    d. `DELETE`

17. This is a column in one table that references a primary key in another table.
    a. secondary key
    b. fake key
    c. foreign key
    d. duplicate key

18. True/False: Java comes with its own DBMS.

19. True/False: A Java application that uses a DBMS to store data does not need know about the physical structure of the data.

20. True/False: You use SQL instead of Java to write entire applications, including the user interface.

21. True/False: In SQL, the not-equal-to operator is !=, which is the same as in Java.

22. True/False: When a `ResultSet` object is initially created, its cursor is pointing at the first row in the result set.

23. True/False: In a transaction, it is permissible for only some of the database updates to be made.

24. True/False: The term *rollback* refers to undoing changes to a database.

Find the Error

1. Find the error in the following SQL statement.

   ```
   SELECT * FROM Coffee WHERE Description = "French Roast Dark"
   ```

2. Find the error in the following SQL statement.

   ```
   SELECT * FROM Coffee WHERE ProdNum != '14-001'
   ```

3. Find the error in the following Java code. Assume conn references a valid `Connection` object.

   ```
   // This code has an error!!!
   String sql = "SELECT * FROM Coffee";
   Statement stmt = conn.createStatement();
   ResultSet result = stmt.execute(sql);
   ```

Algorithm Workbench

1. What SQL data types correspond with the following Java types?

   * `int`
   * `float`
   * `String`
   * `double`

2. Look at the following SQL statement.

   ```
   SELECT Name FROM Employee
   ```

   What is the name of the table that this statement is retrieving data from?

   What is the name of the column that is being retrieved?

For Questions 3 through 11, assume that a database has a table named Stock, *with the following columns:*

Column Name	Type
TradingSymbol	CHAR(10)
CompanyName	CHAR(25)
NumShares	INT
PurchasePrice	DOUBLE
SellingPrice	DOUBLE

3. Write a SELECT statement that will return all of the columns from every row in table.

4. Write a SELECT statement that will return the TradingSymbol column from every row in table.

5. Write a SELECT statement that will return the TradingSymbol column and the NumShares column from every row in table.

6. Write a SELECT statement that will return the TradingSymbol column only from the rows where PurchasePrice is greater than 25.00.

7. Write a SELECT statement that will return all of the columns from the rows where TradingSymbol starts with "SU".

8. Write a SELECT statement that will return the TradingSymbol column only from the rows where SellingPrice is greater than PurchasePrice and NumShares is greater than 100.

9. Write a SELECT statement that will return the TradingSymbol column and the NumShares column only from the rows where SellingPrice is greater than PurchasePrice and NumShares is greater than 100. The results should be sorted by the NumShares column, in ascending order.

10. Write an SQL statement that will insert a new row into the Stock table. The row should have the following column values:

    TradingSymbol: XYZ
    CompanyName: "XYZ Company"
    NumShares: 150
    PurchasePrice: 12.55
    SellingPrice: 22.47

11. Write an SQL statement that does the following: For each row in the Stock table, if the TradingSymbol column is "XYZ", change it to "ABC".

12. Write an SQL statement that will delete rows in the Stock table where the number of shares is less than 10.

13. Assume that the following declaration exists.

    ```
    final String DB_URL = "jdbc:derby:CoffeeDB";
    ```

    The string referenced by DB_URL is a database URL. Write a statement that uses this string to get a connection to the database.

14. Assuming that conn references a valid Connection object, write code to create a Statement object. (Do not be concerned about result set scrolling or concurrency.)

15. Look at the following declaration.

```
String sql = "SELECT * FROM Coffee WHERE Price > 10.00";
```

Assume also that `stmt` references a valid `Statement` object. Write code that executes the SQL statement referenced by the `sql` variable.

16. Assume that the following code is used to retrieve data from the `CoffeeDB` database's `Coffee` table. Write the code that should appear inside the loop to display the contents of the result set.

```
String sql = "SELECT * FROM Coffee";
Connection conn = DriverManager.getConnection(DB_URL);
Statement stmt = conn.createStatement();
ResultSet result = stmt.executeQuery(sql);
while (result.next())
{
    // Finish this code!!
}
stmt.close();
conn.close();
```

17. Write the SQL statement to create a table named `Car`. The `Car` table should have the columns to hold a car's manufacturer, year model, and a 20-character vehicle ID number.

18. Write an SQL statement to delete the `Car` table you created in Question 17.

Short Answer

1. If you are writing an application to store the customer and inventory records for a large business, why would you not want to use traditional text or binary files?

2. You hear a fellow classmate say the following: "JDBC is a standard language for working with database management systems. It was invented at IBM." Are these statements correct, or is he confusing JDBC with something else?

3. When we speak of database organization, we speak of such things as rows, tables, and columns. Describe how the data in a database is organized into these conceptual units.

4. What is a primary key?

5. What is a result set?

6. What are the relational operators in SQL for the following comparisons?

   Greater than
   Less than
   Greater than or equal to
   Less than or equal to
   Equal to
   Not equal to

7. What is the number of the first row in a table? What is the number of the first column in a table?

8. What is meta data? What is result set meta data? When is result set meta data useful?

9. What is a foreign key?

Programming Challenges

1. Customer Inserter

Write an application that connects to the CoffeeDB database and allows the user to insert a new row into the Customer table.

2. Customer Updater

Write an application that connects to the CoffeeDB database and allows the user to select a customer, then change any of that customer's information. (You should not attempt to change the customer number because it is referenced by the UnpaidOrder table.)

3. Unpaid Order Sum

Write an application that connects to the CoffeeDB database, then calculates and displays the total amount owed in unpaid orders. This will be the sum of each row's Cost column.

4. Unpaid Order Lookup

Write an application that connects to the CoffeeDB database and displays a JList component. The JList component should display a list of customers with unpaid orders. When the user clicks on a customer, the application should display a summary all the unpaid orders for that customer.

5. Population Database

Make sure you have downloaded the book's source code from the companion Web site at www.pearsonhighered.com/gaddis. In this chapter's source code folder you will find a program named CreateCityDB.java. Compile and run the program. The program will create a Java DB database named CityDB. The CityDB database will have a table named City, with the following columns:

Column Name	Data Type
CityName	CHAR (50) *Primary key*
Population	DOUBLE

The CityName column stores the name of a city, and the Population column stores the population of that city. After you run the CreateCityDB.java program, the City table will contain 20 rows with various cities and their populations.

Next, write a program that connects to the CityDB database and allows the user to select any of the following operations:

- Sort the list of cities by population, in ascending order.
- Sort the list of cities by population, in descending order.
- Sort the list of cities by name.
- Get the total population of all the cities.
- Get the average population of all the cities.
- Get the highest population.
- Get the lowest population.

6. `Personnel` **Database Creator**

Write an application that creates a database named `Personnel`. The database should have a table named `Employee`, with columns for employee ID, name, position, and hourly pay rate. The employee ID should be the primary key. Insert at least five sample rows of data into the `Employee` table.

7. Employee Inserter

Write a GUI application that allows the user to add new employees to the `Personnel` database you created in Programming Challenge 6.

8. Employee Updater

Write a GUI application that allows the user to look up an employee in the `Personnel` database you created in Programming Challenge 6. The user should be able to change any of the employee's information except employee ID, which is the primary key.

9. `PhoneBook` **Database**

Write an application that creates a database named `PhoneBook`. The database should have a table named `Entries`, with columns for a person's name and phone number.

Next, write an application that lets the user add rows to the `Entries` table, look up a person's phone number, change a person's phone number, and delete specified rows.

Getting Started with Alice 2

Alice is an innovative software system that allows you to create 3D animations and computer games while learning fundamental programming concepts. With Alice you place graphical objects such as people, animals, buildings, cars, and so on inside 3D virtual worlds. Then you create programming statements that make the objects perform actions. Alice's drag-and-drop program editor makes it easy to create animations with rich interactions between objects.

This appendix serves as a quick reference for using Alice version 2. If you need a complete text that teaches programming using the Alice software, see *Starting Out with Alice: A Visual Introduction to Programming*, also published by Pearson.

Downloading and Installing Alice

Alice is free software, available from Carnegie Mellon University. You can download the latest version from http://www.alice.org. When you download Alice 2 to your system, you get a file named *Alice2.x.zip*. (The *2.x* will be a version number. For example, the file will have a name such as *Alice2.4.zip*.) There is no installation wizard with Alice; you simply extract the contents of this file in the location where you want to install the software.

When you extract the contents of *Alice2.x.zip* you will get a folder named *Alice2.x*. Inside this folder you will find an executable file named *Alice.exe*. Double-click this file to run Alice.

TIP: You will probably want to create a shortcut to the *Alice.exe* file on your desktop. Right-click the file and then select *Send To→Desktop (create shortcut)* from the menu. To start Alice double-click the shortcut that appears on the desktop.

Using the *Welcome to Alice!* Dialog Box

When you start Alice the splash screen shown in Figure A-1 will display for a few seconds. When the software is fully loaded you should see the *Welcome to Alice!* dialog box, as shown in Figure A-2.

Figure A-1 The Alice splash screen

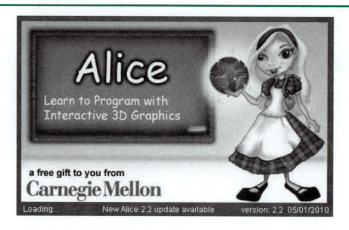

Figure A-2 The *Welcome to Alice!* dialog box

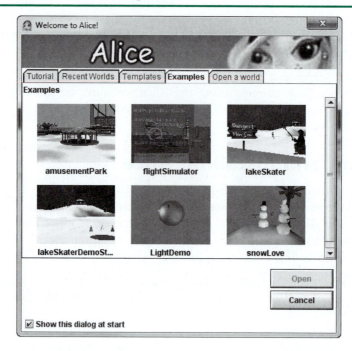

> **NOTE:** If you do not see the *Welcome to Alice!* dialog box on your system, then Alice has been configured so it will not display the dialog box at startup, which might be the case in a shared computer lab. You can display the dialog box by clicking *File* on the menu bar, and then clicking the *New World* or *Open World...* menu items.
>
> Note that at the bottom of the *Welcome to Alice!* dialog box there is a *Show this dialog at start* check box. Make sure this check box is checked so the dialog box will be displayed each time you start Alice.

Near the top of the *Welcome to Alice!* dialog box you will see a set of tabs labeled *Tutorial, Recent Worlds, Templates, Examples,* and *Open a world.* The following are brief descriptions of what you get when you click these tabs:

Tutorial—Click this tab and you will see a set of four Alice worlds that work as tutorials. These tutorial worlds guide you through the basic features of Alice. If you want to run the tutorials, click the *Start the Tutorial* button to execute them in order, or select and open any of the worlds individually.

Recent Worlds—Click this tab and you will see thumbnail images of the worlds that were most recently opened on your system. You can quickly open any world shown in this tab by selecting its thumbnail image and then clicking the *Open* button. You will not see any worlds listed here if you have not yet opened any worlds.

Templates—Click this tab and you will see a set of templates that you can use to create a new world. The templates are named *dirt, grass, sand, snow, space,* and *water.* Each template gives you a ground surface and a sky color.

Examples—Click this tab and you will see thumbnail images of example worlds that have been created by the developers of Alice.

Open a world—Click this tab and you will see a dialog box that allows you to open an Alice world. With this tab you can browse your local system or any attached network drive for Alice worlds. Note that Alice worlds are saved in files that end with the *.a2w* extension. (The *.a2w* extension signifies that the file contains an Alice version 2 world.)

The Alice Environment

In Alice the screen that you work with is referred to as the *Alice environment.* The Alice environment is divided into the following areas: the Toolbar, the World View Window, the Object Tree, the Details Panel, the Method Editor, and the Events Editor. In addition, the toolbar area provides a trashcan icon and one or more clipboard icons. The locations of these different areas and icons are shown in Figure A-3. In the figure, *SnowLove,* one of the example worlds, is opened. Brief descriptions of each area in the Alice environment follow:

Toolbar—The toolbar provides a *Play* button that plays your virtual world, an *Undo* button that undoes the previous operation, and a *Redo* button that repeats the operation that was most recently undone.

Trashcan—Next to the buttons on the toolbar there is a trashcan icon. You delete items by dragging them to the trashcan.

Clipboards—The clipboard provides a place to store a copy of something. In Alice clipboards you can store copies of objects, instructions, methods, and events. To store a copy of an item in a clipboard, you click and drag the item to the clipboard. When a clipboard contains an item, it appears as if it has a white sheet of paper on it. In Figure A-3 the leftmost clipboard shows an example. To paste the item that is stored in a clipboard, you click and drag the clipboard icon to the location where you want to paste the item. If you want to empty a clipboard, you click and drag it to the trashcan.

Figure A-3 Parts of the Alice environment

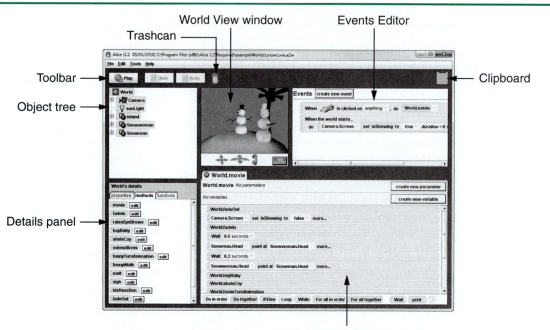

By default, Alice shows only one clipboard. To change the number of available clipboards you click the *Edit* menu and then click *Preferences*. On the dialog box that appears, you click the *Seldom Used* tab and then change the number that appears next to *number of clipboards*.

World View Window—The World View Window shows a view of your virtual world. Each virtual world has a camera; the World View Window acts as the camera's viewfinder and also provides controls for moving and rotating the camera.

Object Tree—The Object Tree holds a list of all the objects in the world. Each object in the world is represented by a *tile*, which is simply a small rectangular icon. Tiles are used extensively in the Alice environment to represent numerous things.

Details Panel—The Details Panel shows detailed information about an object that has been selected in the World View Window or in the Object Tree.

Method Editor—The Method Editor is where you create methods (a set of instructions that causes some action to take place). You create methods by arranging tiles in the Method Editor.

Events Editor—An event is some action that takes place while the world is playing, such as clicking the mouse or pressing a key. Alice is able to detect when various events take place. You can use the Events Editor to specify an action that is to take place when a specific event occurs.

Playing a World

When you click the *Play* button, a separate *World Running...* window appears and the world's animation will play out in that window. For example, Figure A-4 shows the *Snow-Love* example world playing.

Figure A-4   The *SnowLove* world playing

Notice the toolbar at the top of the *World Running...* window. The following are brief descriptions of the items that appear on the toolbar:

Speed Slider Control—This controls the speed at which the world is played. When the slider is set to 1×, the world plays at normal speed. Moving the slider to the right increases the speed up to 10 times its normal speed.

Pause Button—Clicking the *Pause* button causes the world to pause.

Play Button—Once a world has been paused with the *Pause* button, you can click the *Play* button to resume playing.

Restart Button—Clicking the *Restart* button causes the world to start playing again.

Stop Button—Clicking the *Stop* button causes the world to stop playing and closes the *World Running...* window.

Take Picture Button—Clicking the *Take Picture* button captures an image from the world and saves it in a file. The dialog box that appears when you click the *Take Picture* button reports the name and path of the file containing the image.

Creating a New World and Adding Objects to It

To create a new world, you click *File* on the menu bar and then click the *New World...* menu item. This displays the *Welcome to Alice!* dialog box, as shown in Figure A-2. (By default, this dialog box is also displayed when you start Alice.) Make sure the *Templates* tab is selected, as shown in Figure A-5.

Figure A-5   The *Welcome to Alice!* dialog box

The *Templates* tab shows a set of templates named *dirt*, *grass*, *sand*, *snow*, *space*, and *water* that you can use to create a new world. When you select a template from this dialog box and then click the *Open* button, Alice will create a ground surface and set the color of the sky. For example, Figure A-6 shows a world that was created with the sand template.

Figure A-6 shows the *Add Objects* button just below the World View Window. When you click this button the Alice environment changes to scene editor mode and opens a gallery, as shown in Figure A-7. A *gallery* is an assortment of different *types* of objects and is organized into various collections of objects such as animals, buildings, furniture, and people.

Alice provides two galleries: a local gallery and a Web gallery. The *local gallery* is stored on your computer and is installed with the Alice software. It provides a good sampling of object types and should be adequate for many of your projects. The *Web gallery* is maintained by the creators of Alice and may be accessed if your computer is connected to the Internet. It provides a much more extensive collection of object types than the local gallery.

Figure A-6   A world created with the sand template

Click the Add Objects button
to add objects to the world.

Figure A-7   Alice in scene editor mode

The navigation bar
indicates we are
in the local gallery.

The collections
in the gallery
are shown here.

Figure A-7 points out a navigation bar that indicates which gallery and collection is currently displayed. Below the navigation bar are thumbnail images for the collections in the gallery. To open a collection and see the object types it contains, you click the collection's thumbnail image. For example, one of the collections is named *People*. It contains various types of people objects, as shown in Figure A-8.

Figure A-8   Some of the object types in the `People` collection

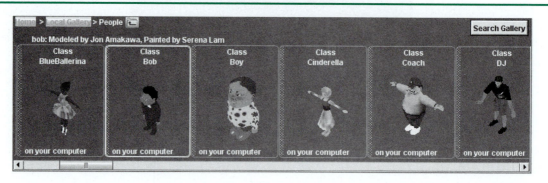

One way to add an object to the world is to click the thumbnail for that object type. You will then see an information window for the object. For example, if you click the thumbnail for the `Coach` object type, you will see the information window shown, as shown in Figure A-9. Click the *Add instance to world* button to add an object of this type to the world.

Figure A-9   Information window for the `Coach` object type

Another way to add an object to the world is to click and drag the thumbnail for the object type into the World View Window. When you release the mouse button (with the mouse pointer inside the World View Window) an object will be created.

After you add an object to a world, you should see a tile for the object in the Object Tree, as shown in Figure A-10. Each object in a world has a name, and the object's tile will show the name that Alice assigned to the object. You can rename the object by right-clicking its tile and then selecting *rename* on the menu that appears.

Figure A-10   An object is added to the world

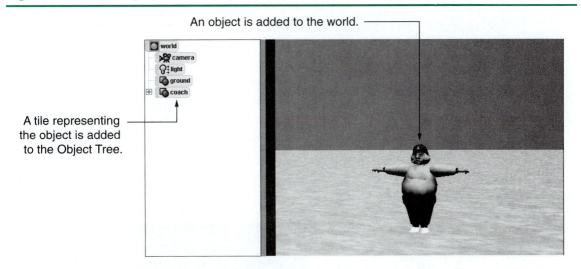

A tile representing the object is added to the Object Tree.

Moving the Camera in the Alice Environment

The three camera controls shown in Figure A-11 appear just below the World View Window. You use these controls to move the camera around in the world and point it in different directions. The control on the left moves the camera up, down, left, and right. The control in the center moves the camera forward and backward and rotates the camera left and right. The control on the right tilts the camera up and down.

Figure A-11   Camera controls

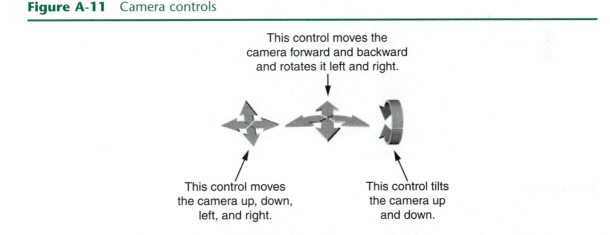

Notice that each of the controls shows a set of arrows. You manipulate these controls by clicking and dragging the arrow that points in the direction that you want to move, rotate, or tilt the camera. You can make the camera move faster by dragging the mouse pointer away from the center of the camera control. The farther you drag the pointer away from the center of the camera control, the faster the camera will move.

Selecting Objects

To work with an object in the Alice environment, often you first have to select the object. The following are the ways to select an object:

- Click its tile in the Object Tree
- Click the object in the World View Window

When you select an object, a box appears around it in the World View Window, as shown in Figure A-12. (On your screen the box will be yellow.) This *bounding box* indicates that the object is selected. Also, the object's tile in the Object Tree will appear highlighted, as shown in the figure.

Figure A-12   The coach object is selected

Object Subparts

Objects are commonly made of other objects, which are referred to as *subparts*. When a plus sign appears next to an object tile in the Object Tree, it means that the object is made of subparts. For example, look at the Object Tree shown in Figure A-12 and notice that a plus sign appears next to the tile for the coach object. You can click the plus sign next to an object to expand the tree and see the tiles for the subparts. The plus sign then turns into a minus sign, which hides the inner objects when clicked.

Figure A-13 shows the Object Tree expanded to reveal that the coach object is composed of numerous subparts. One of these subparts, the head, is selected.

Properties

Each object in an Alice world has *properties*, which are values that specify the object's characteristics. Once you have placed an object in an Alice world, you can adjust its properties until it has the characteristics you desire. To change an object's property you perform the following steps:

- Select the object
- In the Details Panel select the *properties* tab, as shown in Figure A-14
- Change the value of the desired property (to change a property's value, click the down-arrow that appears next to the property's value)

Figure A-13   An object subpart selected

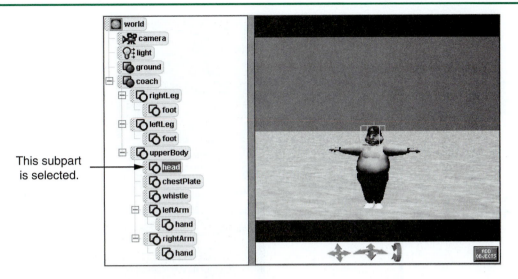

This subpart is selected.

Figure A-14   Properties displayed in the Details Panel

Primitive Methods

A *method* is a set of instructions that causes some action to take place. In Alice all objects have a common set of built-in methods for performing basic actions. These methods, which are known as *primitive methods*, cause objects to move, turn, change size, and do other fundamental operations.

While you are creating an Alice world you can immediately execute an object's primitive methods by right-clicking the object in the World View Window or the object's tile in the Object Tree. Then you select *methods* from the menu that appears. Another menu appears showing a list of methods that you can immediately execute in the World View Window. Figure A-15 shows an example of these menus. Table A-1 describes each of the primitive methods shown on the menu.

Figure A-15   Selecting a primitive method

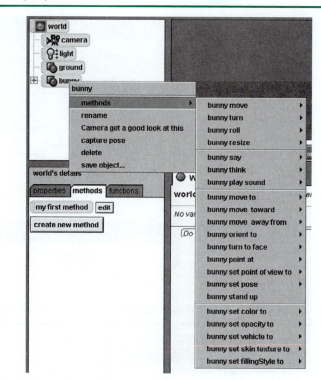

Table A-1   Primitive methods

Method Name	Description
move	This method causes the object to move up, down, left, right, forward, or backward. You specify the direction and distance that you want the object to move.
turn	This method causes the object to turn toward the left, right, forward, or backward. You specify the amount you want the object to turn in revolutions.
roll	This method causes the object to roll toward the left or the right. You specify the amount you want the object to roll in revolutions.
resize	This method changes the object's size by a specified amount.
say	This method causes a cartoon-like speech bubble containing a message to be displayed, as if the object were saying the message.
think	This method causes a cartoon-like thought bubble containing words to be displayed, as if the object were thinking the words.
play sound	This method plays a sound. You can specify one of the sounds that Alice provides or you can import any MP3 or WAV file.

(continues)

Table A-1   Primitive methods (*continued*)

Method Name	Description
move to	This method causes the object to move to another object. When the method completes, both objects' center points will be in the same location.
move toward	This method causes the object to move in the direction of another object. You specify the distance to move in meters.
move away from	This method causes the object to move away from another object. You specify the distance to move in meters.
orient to	This method orients the object in the same direction as another specified object. When this method executes, the object will turn so its up, right, and forward axes are aligned with the axes of the specified object.
turn to face	This method causes the object to turn so it is facing another object.
point at	This method is similar to the turn to face method, except the object will be tilted so its forward axis is "aiming" at the specified object's center point.
set point of view to	This method sets the object's point of view to that of another object. It is commonly used with the camera to move it to the location of another object and give a view from that object's point of view.
set pose	Alice allows you to position an object and its subparts in a certain way and then capture that as a pose. This method causes the object to assume a pose that was previously captured.
stand up	This method makes the object "stand up" by aligning the object's up axis with the world's up axis.
set color to	This method sets the object's color property to a specified color, making the object appear in that color.
set opacity to	This method sets the object's opacity property, which determines the object's transparency. You set this property to some value between 0 percent and 100 percent, where 0 is completely invisible and 100 is completely opaque.
set vehicle to	This method sets the object's vehicle property. The vehicle property couples the object with another object. When the other object moves, this object moves with it.
set skin texture to	This method sets the object's skin texture property. The skin texture property specifies a graphic image to be displayed on the object.
set fillingStyle to	The fillingStyle property determines how the object is displayed. It has three settings: solid, wireframe, and points. The default setting is solid, which causes the object to be displayed as a solid. When the fillingStyle property is set to wireframe, the object is displayed as a wire skeleton that you can see through. When the fillingStyle property is set to points, the object is displayed as a set of points.

Most of the primitive methods require that you specify additional pieces of information. For example, the move method causes the object to move, and it requires that you specify two pieces of information: a direction and an amount. These pieces of information are known as arguments—pieces of information that a method requires in order for it to execute.

Deleting Objects

You can delete an object in an Alice world by performing any of the following operations:

- Right-click the object in the World View Window and then select delete from the menu that appears
- Right-click the object's tile in the Object Tree and then select delete from the menu that appears
- Click and drag the object's tile from the Object Tree to the trashcan

Modifying Objects in Scene Editor Mode

When you click the *Add Objects* button, which appears below the World View Window, Alice goes into scene editor mode, in which you can use the mouse to modify the objects in your Alice world. For example, you can use the mouse to move objects, resize objects, rotate objects, and copy objects. Figure A-16 shows the location of the *mouse mode buttons*, which determine the action that can be performed with the mouse.

Figure A-16 Location of the mouse mode buttons

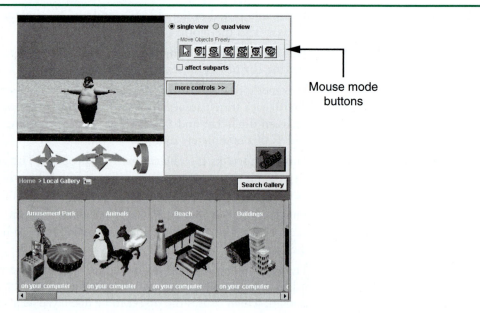

Figure A-17 shows the purposes of the buttons. The following are brief descriptions of each:

 Move Freely—When this button is selected the mouse can be used to move an object freely in the world. Here are the actions that you can perform:

- To move an object horizontally within the world you simply click and drag it
- To move an object straight up or down, you hold down the ⟨Shift⟩ key while clicking and dragging the object
- To rotate an object left or right, you hold down the ⟨Ctrl⟩ key while clicking and dragging the object
- To tumble an object (rotate it left, right, forward, backward, or any combination of these directions), you hold down the ⟨Ctrl⟩ and ⟨Shift⟩ keys while clicking and dragging the object

 Move Up and Down—When this button is selected you can move an object straight up or straight down by clicking and dragging the object.

Turn Left and Right—When this button is selected you can rotate an object toward the left or the right by clicking and dragging the object.

Turn Forward and Backward—When this button is selected you can rotate an object forward or backward by clicking and dragging the object.

Tumble—When this button is selected you can tumble an object by clicking and dragging the object. This means you can rotate the object right, left, forward, backward, or in any combination of these directions.

Resize—When this button is selected you can make an object larger or smaller by clicking and dragging the object.

Copy—When this button is selected you can make a copy of an object by clicking the object.

Figure A-17   The purposes of the mouse mode buttons

Notice that just below the buttons a check box labeled *affect subparts* appears. By default, this is not checked. When it is not checked the modifications that you make to an object using the *mouse mode* buttons are applied to the entire object. However, if you check the *affect subparts* check box, the modifications are applied only to one of the object's subparts.

Single View and Quad View Modes

When Alice is in scene editor mode, you can switch the display of the world between single view mode and quad view mode. So far we have been using *single view mode*, which is the default display mode. In single view mode you have one view of the world—the World View Window. In *quad view mode* you have four views of the world: the World View Window, a view from the top, a view from the right, and a view from the front. Figure A-18 shows an example of these views and points out the *quad view* button, which you click to switch to quad view mode.

Figure A-18 Quad view

You can use the mouse to modify objects in any of the views. If you look carefully at the *mouse mode* buttons while in quad view mode, you'll notice that the *Move Up and Down* button no longer appears because the right and front viewing windows support up and down movement. If you want to move an object up or down while in quad view mode, you simply select the *Move Objects Freely* button and then move the object up or down in either the right view or the front view.

You will also notice that two new buttons appear while in quad view mode: The *Scroll View* button and the *Zoom* button. Often, when you switch to quad view mode the objects in the world will not be fully visible in all of the views. To remedy this you can use the *Scroll View* button to scroll the top, right, or front view. To use the button, follow these steps:

1. Select the *Scroll View* button; the mouse pointer changes into a hand tool
2. Move the mouse pointer into the view you wish to scroll
3. Click and drag the view in the direction you wish to scroll

The *Zoom* button allows you to zoom into or out of the top, right, and front views. To use it, follow these steps:

1. Select the *Zoom* button; the mouse pointer changes into a zoom tool
2. Move the mouse pointer into the desired view and position it over the point that you wish to zoom into or zoom out from
3. Zoom by clicking and dragging; if you want to zoom in, drag down or to the right, if you want to zoom out, drag up or to the left

Writing Methods in Alice

Recall that a method is a set of instructions that causes some action to take place. If you want an action to take place when an Alice world is played, you have to write a method. Figure A-19 shows the location of the Method Editor in the Alice environment, where you write the methods that perform actions in an Alice world.

Figure A-19   The Method Editor

Notice that a *world.my first method* tab appears at the top of the Method Editor in Figure A-19. All methods have a name, and `world.my first method` is the name of the method that is currently open in the editor. When you create a new world Alice automatically creates an empty method named `world.my first method`. By default, this method is automatically executed when you play the world.

In Figure A-19 notice that a group of tiles appears at the bottom of the Method Editor. Each of these tiles is an instruction that you can place in the method. Table A-2 describes the instructions represented by these tiles.

Table A-2 Alice instructions

Instruction	Description
Do in order	You place other instructions inside a `Do in order` instruction. The instructions that you place inside a `Do in order` instruction are executed in the order that they appear.
Do together	You place other instructions inside a `Do together` instruction. The instructions that you place inside a `Do together` instruction are executed simultaneously.
If/Else	The `If/Else` instruction tests a condition, which is anything that gives a true or false value. If the value is true, then one set of instructions is executed. If the value is false, then a different set of instructions is executed.
Loop	The `Loop` instruction causes one or more other instructions to repeat a specific number of times.
While	The `While` instruction causes one or more other instructions to repeat as long as a condition is true.
For all in order	The `For all in order` instruction steps through the items in a list, one item at a time, performing the same operation on each item.
For all together	The `For all together` instruction performs the same operation on all the items in a list simultaneously.
Wait	The `Wait` instruction causes the method to pause for a specified number of seconds.
print	The `print` instruction displays a message in a special area at the bottom of the *World Running…* window.
//	The `//` tile allows you to insert a comment into a method.

In Alice you place instructions in a method by dragging tiles into the Method Editor. For example, if you want to place a `Wait` instruction in the method that you are currently writing, you simply click and drag the `Wait` tile into the Method Editor, as shown in Figure A-20. When you drop the tile (by releasing the mouse button) the `Wait` instruction will be created in the method.

In addition to using the instructions that you see at the bottom of the Method Editor, you can also create instructions that execute an object's primitive methods. Once you have added an object to a world, you can see tiles for all of the methods that the object can perform by doing the following:

1. Select the object
2. In the Details Panel select the *methods* tab to display a set of tiles representing the object's methods

Figure A-20   Dragging the `Wait` instruction into the Method Editor

For example, Figure A-21 shows an Alice world with an instance of the `Hare` class (which is in the *Animals* collection). The object, which is named `hare`, is selected. The *methods* tab is selected in the Details Panel, and a set of tiles for the `hare` object's primitive methods is displayed.

Figure A-21   Methods displayed in the Details Panel

To create an instruction that executes a primitive method in the method that you are currently writing, simply drag the primitive method's tile and drop it into the Method Editor.

For example, Figure A-22 shows tile for the `hare` object's `move` method being dragged into the Method Editor.

Figure A-22 Dragging the `hare.move` method tile into the Method Editor

Most of the primitive methods require that you specify arguments. For example, when you drop the tile for the `move` method into the Method Editor, a pop-up menu appears allowing you to select a direction. The allowable directions are up, down, left, right, forward, and backward. After you select a direction, another menu appears allowing you to select an amount, which is the distance that the object moves. In Alice distances are always measured in meters.

Figure A-23 shows an example of `world.my first` method after three instructions have been created. When the world containing this method is played, the `hare` object will move up 1 meter, then turn left 1 revolution, and then move down 1 meter.

Figure A-23 Three instruction tiles

First, the `hare` moves up 1 meter. ⟶

Second, the `hare` turns left 1 revolution. ⟶

Third, the `hare` moves down 1 meter. ⟶

Copying and Deleting Instructions

To make a copy of an instruction tile within the same method, you right-click the tile and then select *make copy* from the menu that appears. To copy an instruction so that you can paste it into a different method, you drag the instruction to the clipboard. Then you open the method that you want to paste the instruction into, and click and drag the clipboard icon to the location where you want to paste the instruction. To delete an instruction tile that you have created in the Method Editor, you drag the tile to the trashcan.

Creating Methods

When you first create an Alice world, a method named world.my first method is automatically created in the world object. You are not limited to this one method in the world, however. Follow these steps to create a new method in the world:

1. Select the world in the Object Tree.
2. In the Details Panel, under the *methods* tab, click the *create new method* button, as shown in Figure A-24.
3. A dialog box will appear asking for the new method's name. Enter a name in the dialog box and click the *OK* button. A tile for the new method will appear in the Details Panel, above the *create new method* button. For example, the Details Panel in Figure A-25 shows three world-level methods.
4. Create the instructions for the method in the Method Editor.

Figure A-24 The *create new method* button

Figure A-25 An example of a world with three world-level methods

Once you have created the new method, you can call it from other methods by dragging the new method's tile from the Details Panel into the Method Editor and dropping it at the point where you wish to call the method.

You can also create your own custom methods in the objects that you place in your world. In Alice the methods that are part of an object are referred to as *class-level methods*. If an object doesn't provide all of the methods that you need, you can easily add your own methods for that object. You write custom class-level methods in Alice by following these steps:

1. Create the desired object.
2. Select the object.
3. In the Details Panel, under the *methods* tab, click the *create new method* button.
4. A dialog box will appear asking for the new method's name. Enter a name in the dialog box and click the *OK* button. A tile for the new method will appear in the Details Panel, above the *create new method* button.
5. Create the instructions for the method in the Method Editor.

Once you have created the new method, you can call it from other methods in the usual way: by dragging the new method's tile into the Method Editor and dropping it at the point where you wish to call the method.

Renaming Methods

To rename a method, you simply right-click the method's tile and select *Rename* from the menu that appears. After you do this, you will be able to edit the name that appears on the method's tile directly.

Creating Variables and Parameters

A variable is a storage location that is represented by a name. Like traditional programming languages, Alice allows you to use variables to store data. The following variable categories are available in Alice:

- Local Variables—A *local variable* belongs to a specific method and can be used only in the instructions in that method. When a method stops executing, its local variables cease to exist in memory.
- World-Level Variables—A *world-level variable* belongs to the world object, and exists as long as the world is playing.
- Class-Level Variables—A *class-level variable* belongs to a specific object, and exists as long as the object exists. Class-level variables are like properties.
- Parameter Variables—A *parameter variable* is used to hold an argument that is passed to a method when the method is called. Once you create a parameter variable in a method, you must provide an argument for that parameter whenever you call the method.

Before you can use a variable, you have to create it. To create a local variable or a parameter variable in a method, you open the method in the Method Editor and then you click the *create new variable* button or the *create new parameter* button. Figure A-26 shows the locations of these buttons.

Figure A-26 The *create new variable* button

Click here to create a new parameter variable.

world.my first method

world.my first method *No parameters*   create new parameter

No variables   create new variable

(*Do Nothing*

Click here to create a new local variable.

When you click either of these buttons, a dialog box appears requiring you to enter more information about the variable. In the dialog box you enter the variable's name and select the variable's type and initial value. Figure A-27 shows the *Create New Local Variable* dialog box, which appears when you click the *create new variable* button. When you click the *create new parameter* button, a dialog box that is virtually identical to the one in Figure A-27 is displayed.

Figure A-27 The *Create New Local Variable* dialog box

The variable's name ⟶ Name:

The variable's type ⟶ Type: ● Number
                                ○ Boolean
                                ○ Object
                                ○ Other... String

The variable's initial value ⟶ Value: 1 ⊟   ☐ make a List

OK   Cancel

After you provide a name for the variable, select its type, specify its initial value, and click the *OK* button, a tile for the variable is created in the method.

To create a world-level variable you perform the following steps:

1. Select the world object in the Object Tree.
2. In the Details Panel select the *properties* tab.

3. Click the *create new variable* button, which appears at the top of the *properties* tab, as shown in Figure A-28.
4. Enter the variable's name, type, and initial value in the *create new variable* dialog box, which is similar to the one shown in Figure A-27. When you click the dialog box's *OK* button, a tile for the variable will be created in the Details Panel, under the *properties* tab.

Figure A-28 Creating a world-level variable

To create a class-level variable in an object you perform the following steps:

1. Select the object in the Object Tree.
2. In the Details Panel select the *properties* tab.
3. Click the *create new variable* button, which appears at the top of the *properties* tab, as shown in Figure A-29.
4. Enter the variable's name, type, and initial value in the *create new variable* dialog box, which is similar to the one shown in Figure A-27. When you click the dialog box's *OK* button, a tile for the variable will be created in the Details Panel, under the *properties* tab.

Figure A-29 Creating a class-level variable

Variable Assignment

When you create a variable, you give it an initial value. The initial value will remain in the variable until you store a different value in the variable. In an Alice method you can create *set instructions* that store different values in the variable. A set instruction simply "sets" a variable to a new value.

To create a set instruction for a variable, you drag the variable tile and drop it into the Method Editor at the point where you want the set instruction to occur. A menu appears, and you select *set value*. Another menu appears that allows you to specify the value you wish to store in the variable. As a result, a set instruction is created.

Events

An event is an action that takes place while a program is running. When Alice worlds are running, they are capable of detecting several different types of events. For example, an event occurs when the user clicks an object with the mouse. An event also occurs when the user types a key on the keyboard. Table A-3 describes all of the events that an Alice world can detect while it is running.

Table A-3   Events that Alice can detect

Event	Description
`When the world starts`	This event occurs immediately when the world is started. It happens only once, each time the world is played.
`When a key is typed`	When the user types a key on the keyboard, this event occurs when the key is released.
`When the mouse is clicked on something`	This event occurs when the user clicks an object in the world with the mouse.
`While something is true`	When a condition that you have specified becomes true, this event occurs as long as the condition remains true.
`When a variable changes`	This event occurs when a variable's value changes.
`Let the mouse move <objects>`	This event allows the user to move an object in the world by clicking and dragging it with the mouse.
`Let the arrow keys move <subject>`	This event allows the user to move an object in the world by typing the arrow keys on the keyboard.
`Let the mouse move the camera`	This event allows the user to move the camera through the world by clicking and dragging the mouse.
`Let the mouse orient the camera`	This event allows the user to change the camera's orientation (the direction in which it is pointing) by clicking and dragging the mouse.

When any of the events listed in Table A-3 occur, your Alice world can perform an action in response to that event, such as calling a method.

At the top right of the screen in the Alice environment, you see an area labeled *Events*, as shown in Figure A-30. This area is called the *Events Editor*. When you create an Alice world, a tile appears in the Events Editor that reads as follows:

```
When the world starts, do world.my first method
```

This tile specifies that when the world starts, the method `world.my first method` will be executed. The left portion of the tile shows the name of an event, `When the world starts`, and the right portion of the tile is a drop-down box that shows the name of the method that will be executed when the event occurs. You can click the down arrow on the drop-down box to select a different method. Any method that is selected in this tile will be automatically executed when the world starts.

Figure A-30 The Events Editor

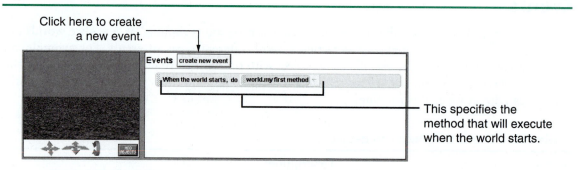

The process of responding to an event is commonly called *handling the event*. In order for an Alice world to handle an event, a tile for that event must appear in the Events Editor. When a world is first created, the only tile that appears in the Events Editor is for the `When the world starts` event. If you want the world to handle any other events, you must create a new tile for the event in the Events Editor. To create a new event tile, you click the *create new event* button, as shown in Figure A-30. A menu of available events will appear next. You select the event that you want to handle from this menu. A tile for the event will then be created in the Events Editor.

Most event tiles require that you specify additional arguments, such as the method that you want to execute in response to the event. A method that is executed in response to an event is commonly referred to as an *event handler*. For example, the event tile that is shown in Figure A-30 specifies that when the world starts, `world.my first method` is called. The method `world.my first method` is the event handler.

Figure A-31 shows another example of an event tile. Assume that this tile appears in a world that has an object named `fridge` (a refrigerator object). The event tile specifies that when the mouse is clicked on the `fridge` object's `fridgeDoor` subpart, the `fridgeDoor` will turn left 0.25 revolutions.

Figure A-31 Example of an event tile

Index

Symbols

- (subtraction operator), 60, 61
-- (decrement operator), 279–282
-= (combined assignment), 69–70
! (logical NOT operator), 222, 227
!= (not equal to operator), 196, 197
% (modulus operator), 60, 61
%= (combined assignment), 69–70
&& (logical AND operator), 222, 223–225
( ) (parentheses), 35, 64
* (multiplication operator), 11, 60, 61
*= (combined assignment), 69–70
, (comma separators), 111–112
/ (division operator), 60, 61
/* */ (comment symbols), 84–85
/** */ (comment symbols), 85–86
// (comment symbol), 32, 35, 83
/= (combined assignment), 69–70
; (semicolon), 11, 34–35, 200
;create=true attribute, 1114
\ (backslash), 40
\\ (backslash escape sequence), 42
\' (single quote escape sequence), 42
\" (double quote escape sequence), 42
\b (backspace escape sequence), 42
\n (newline escape sequence), 40–42
\r (return escape sequence), 42
\t (tab escape sequence), 41, 42
{ (opening braces), 33–35
||(OR logical operator), 222, 225–226
} (closing braces), 33–35
' (single quotation marks), 55–56
" " (double quotation marks), 35, 46
+ (addition operator), 60, 62
+ (string concatenation operator), 45, 392, 565
++ (increment operator), 279–282
+= (combined assignment), 69–70
< (less than operator), 195, 196, 1088
<= (less than or equal to operator), 195, 196, 1088
<> (diamond operator), 534
<> (not equal to operator), 1088
= (assignment operator), 11, 44, 137, 197
= (equal to operator), 1088
== (equal to operator), 195, 196, 197
> (greater than), 195, 196, 1088
>= (greater than or equal to operator), 195, 196, 1088

A

abstract classes, 651–657
abstract methods, 651–657
Abstract Windowing Toolkit (AWT), 739, 740–741
    Applet class, 929, 936
    Button class, 929
    Checkbox class, 929
    Frame class, 929, 936
    hierarchy, 774–775, 808
    Label class, 929
    Panel class, 929
    for portability, 929–933
    TextField class, 929
AbstractButton class, 871
    setMnemonic method, 871
access specification, 147
access specifier, 32
    private, 133, 134, 638
    protected, 632–638
    public, 32, 133, 134, 638
    in UML diagram, 637
accessor methods, 146
accumulator variable, 307
action command, 774
action events, 763, 799, 859
action listeners
    handling events with, 763–770
    registering, 765–770
ActionEvent class, 770
    getActionCommand()method, 770
    getSource()method, 770, 774
ActionListener interface
    actionPerformed method, 763–765, 768
actionPerformed method, 763–765, 768
adapter classes, 959
addActionListener method, 765, 769
address, 4
aggregation, 401–414
    security issues, 409–411
    in UML, 408–409
algorithm, 6
algorithm decomposition, 258–259
Alice, 1163–1188
ALU. *See* arithmetic and logic unit (ALU)
AnchorPane component, JavaFX GUI, 984, 986
AND operator (SQL), 1093–1094
anonymous object, 769
API (Application Programmer Interface), 37–38
Applet class, 929
    getAudioClip method, 970
    getCodeBase method, 969
    getDocumentBase method, 969
    newAudioClip method, 973
    paint method, 936
    play method, 969
    repaint method, 948
applets, 8–9, 909–911
    creation with AWT, 929–933
    creation with Swing, 921–928
    handling events in, 924–928
    playing audio in, 969–972
    plug-in, browser, 929
    running, 922–924
appletviewer command, 923–924
Application Programmer Interface (API), 37–38
application software, 5
applications, Java, 8–9

argument, 38, 149–151
  arrays, 472–475
  command-line, 522–523
  `main` methods, 522–523
  objects, 376–389
  passed by value, 151
  passing multiple, 149–151
  variable-length, 523–526
arithmetic and logic unit (ALU), 3
arithmetic operators, 60–68
`ArrayList` class, 526–534
  add method, 531–532
  autoboxing and unboxing, 590
  capacity, 532–533
  creating an object of, 526–528
  diamond operator (<>), 534
  enhanced for loop method, 528–529
  `get` method, 527–528
  `remove` method, 529–530
  `size` method, 527–528
  `toString` method, 529
arrays:
  arguments, as, 472–475
  averaging the values of, 478
  binary search, 505–508, 1053–1056
  bounds checking, 456–457
  comparing, 476–477
  concept, 449
  content, 460–471
  copying, 469–471
  declaration, 449–450
  declaration, alternate notation, 459–460
  elements, 451–452
  enhanced for loop, 465–466
  files and, 487–488
  highest value in, finding, 478–479
  initialization, 457–459
  initialization list, 458
  inputting and outputting contents, 452–456
  introduction to, 449–460
  length, 465
  lowest value in, finding, 478–479
  objects, of, 494–498
  off-by-one error, 457
  partially filled, 486–487
  ragged, 520–521
  reference variables, 468–469
  returning from methods, 488–490
  selection sort, 501–504
  sequential search, 498–500
  size declarator, 450–451
  size, user specified, 466–468
  `String` objects, 490–494
  subscript, 451
  summing contents of, 1046–1048
  summing values of, 477
  three or more dimensions, 521–522
  two-dimensional, 509–521
assignment statement, 44
associativity, operator, 63–64
attributes, 19, 129, 132–133
audio, playing, 969–973
  in applet, 969–972
  in application, 973
`AudioClip` interface, 970–972
  `loop` method, 970

play method, 970
  stop method, 970
auto commit mode, JDBC, 1153
autoboxing, 589–590
`AVG` function (SQL), 1094–1095
AWT (Abstract Windowing Toolkit), 739,
  740–741
  `Applet` class, 929, 936
  `Button` class, 929
  `Checkbox` class, 929
  for portability, 929–933
  `Frame` class, 929, 936
  hierarchy, 774–775, 808
  `Label` class, 929
  `Panel` class, 929
  `TextField` class, 929

B

BankAccount class, 161–167
base class, 606
BASIC programming language, 7
binary digit, 4
binary files, 321, 712–718
  appending data to, 718
  reading data from to, 715–717
  writing data to, 713–715
binary number, 712–713
  converting to, 588–589
binary operator, 60
binary search algorithm, 505–508
  recursive version, 1053–1056
binding, 366
bit, 4
block, 200–201
block comments, 85, 135
blueprint metaphor, 131
boolean data type, 54–55
Border class, 810
BorderFactory class, 810–812
  `createCompoundBorder` method, 811
  `createEmptyBorder` method, 811
  `createEtchedBorder` method, 811
  `createLineBorder` method, 811–812
  `createLoweredBevelBorder` method, 811
  `createMatteBorder` method, 811
  `createRaisedBevelBorder` method, 811
  `createTitledBorder` method, 811, 812
BorderLayout class, 781, 784–791
  `CENTER` constant, 785
  and components resizing, 788
  constructor, 788
  `EAST` constant, 785
  `NORTH` constant, 785
  `SOUTH` constant, 785
  `WEST` constant, 785
borders, 810–812
  compound border, 811
  empty border, 811
  etched border, 811
  line border, 811–812
  lowered bevel border, 811
  matte border, 811
  placing around list component, 848
  raised bevel border, 811
  titled border, 811, 812

branch node, scene graph, 985, 986
break statement, 320
buffer:
  file, 322
  keyboard, 95
Button class, 929
button component, 740. *See also* JButton class
Button component, JavaFX GUI, 984
ButtonGroup class, 798–799
byte, 4
byte code, 8, 12–14
Byte class, 587
  parseByte method, 588
  toString method, 588
byte data type, 50–51, 73

C

C programming languages, 7
C# programming languages, 7
C++ programming languages, 7
call stack, 699
Car class, 181
case key word, 239–245
case-sensitive language, 33, 35
cast operators, 71–73
catch clause, 684, 690
  multiple exceptions, handling,
    700–702
CD (compact disc), 5
CellPhone class, 168–171
central processing unit (CPU), 2, 3–4
ChangeListener interface
  stateChanged method, 892
char data type, 55–57
character(s), 55–57
  comparing, 201–202
  conversion, 553–554
  literals, 55–56
  reading from keyboard, 93–94
  testing, 548–552
Character class, 548–554
  isDigit method, 548
  isLetter method, 548
  isLetterOrDigit method, 548
  isLowerCase method, 548
  isSpaceChar method, 548
  isUpperCase method, 548
  isWhiteSpace method, 548
  toLowerCase method, 553
  toUpperCase method, 553
CHARACTER/CHAR data type (SQL), 1075
check box component, 740, 797, 804–808
Checkbox class, 929
CheckBox component, JavaFX GUI, 984,
    1019–1024
  events, responding to, 1022–1024
  isSelected method, 1020
  Text property, 1019
checked exceptions, 703–704
class, 21–22, 129–148
  abstract, 651–657
  adapter, 959
  body, 33
  building, step by step, 132–134
  collaboration, 431–435

constructors, 155–161
constructors, copy, 400–401
constructors, default, 159, 622
constructors, overloaded, 369–375
definition, 32
exceptions, 682–683, 708–711
field, 129, 134
finding, 174–182
header, 32
hierarchy, 644
inheritance from subclasses, 639–644
inner, 417–420
instance field, 152–155
instance method, 152–155
instance of, 22, 76, 130–132
key word, 32
layout of members, 148
members, 133
names, 48
no-arg constructor, 160, 622
Object, 644–646
overloaded methods, 364–369
protected members, 632–638
static fields, 358–360
static members, 357–363
static methods, 358, 360–363
type variable, 77
wrapper, 547–548
.class file extension, 14
class-type variables, 77
close() method
  DataInputStream class, 716
  DataOutputStream class, 714
COBOL programming languages, 7
collaboration, class, 431–435
color chooser, 875–876. *See also* JColorChooser class
Color class, 776
  constants, 776
colors, background and foreground, 776
columns, DBMS, 1073–1076
  content retrieval, ResultSet object and,
    1080–1081
combined assignment operators, 69–70
  %=, 69–70
  *=, 69–70
  +=, 69–70
  -=, 69–70
  /=, 69–70
combo box component, 740, 859–864. *See also* JComboBox
    class
ComboBox component, JavaFX GUI, 984
comma (,) separators, 111–112
comma separated value file format, 591
command-line arguments, 522–523
comments, 32
  /* */ symbols, 84–85
  /** */ symbols, 85–86
  // symbols, 83
  documentation, 85–87
  multiline, 84–85
  single-line, 83–84
commit, transaction-processing code, 1153
compact disc, 5
compilers, 12
compiling and running a program, 14
component, 739

Component class, 775
  addMouseListener method, 955
  addMouseMotionListener method, 956
  setBackground method, 776
  setForeground method, 776
component reusability, of OOP, 20
compound border, 811
compound operator, 69
concatenation, 45, 392, 565
conditional loop, 296
conditional operator, 237–238
conditionally-executed code, 195, 199–201, 212, 218
confirm dialog box, 742, 747–749
Connection class
  commit method, 1153
  createStatement method, 1078, 1099, 1102, 1107, 1115
  rollback method, 1153
  setAutoCommit method, 1153
console, 37
  output, 827–830
console output, 37
constants, enum, 420
constants, named, 74–76
constructors, 155–161
  BorderLayout class, 788
  copy, 400–401
  default, 159, 371–372, 622
  FileOutputStream class, 718
  Font class, 889
  Image class, 1026
  JButton class, 866
  JCheckBox class, 804
  JFileChooser class, 874
  JFrame class, 754, 756
  JLabel class, 762, 865, 866
  JList class, 842
  JRadioButton class, 798
  JRadioButtonMenuItem class, 884
  JScrollPane class, 849
  JSlider class, 891–892
  JTextArea class, 886
  no-arg, 160, 622
  overloaded, 369–375
  RandomAccessFile class, 719
  superclass, 614–623
  Timer class, 965
  UML in, 160
container, GUI, 753
  adding layout manager to, 781
Container class, 781
  setLayout method, 781
content pane, 759, 787
  background color, changing, 779–780
continue statement, 320
control character, 40
control unit, 3
controller class, JavaFX
  sample skeleton, 1009–1010
  writing code for, 1004–1008
conversion, data type, 70–74
  strings to numbers, 100–103
COUNT function (SQL), 1095
count-controlled loop, 296–297
CPU. *See* central processing unit (CPU)
CRC cards, 434–435

CREATE TABLE statement, 1110–1113
Customer class, 180–181

D
data hiding, 19–20, 146–147
data type, 49–59
  boolean, 54–55
  byte, 50–51, 73
  char, 55–57
  conversion, 70–74
  float, 52, 53
  floating-point, 52–54
  int, 50–51, 73
  integer, 50–52
  long, 50–51
  primitive, 49–59
  ranking, 71
  short, 50–51, 73
  UML, 147–148
database management system (DBMS), 1067–1076
  columns, 1073–1076
  Java DB, 1070
  JDBC, 1068–1069
  password-protected database, connecting, 1073
  primary keys, 1076
  rows, 1073–1075
  SQL, 1069
  SQL statement passing to, 1078–1088
  stored procedures, 1154
  tables, 1073–1076
  usage, 1069–1070
DataInputStream class, 715–716
  close methods, 716
  readBoolean method, 716
  readByte method, 716
  readChar method, 716
  readDouble method, 716
  readFloat method, 716
  readInt method, 716
  readLong method, 716
  readShort method, 716
  readUTF method, 717–718
DataOutputStream class, 713–714
  close method, 714
  writeBoolean method, 714
  writeByte method, 714
  writeChar method, 714
  writeDouble method, 714
  writeFloat method, 714
  writeInt method, 714
  writeLong method, 714
  writeShort method, 714
  writeUTF method, 714, 717–718
DATE data type (SQL), 1075, 1132
DECIMAL data type (SQL), 1075
DecimalFormat class, 248–253
  format method, 248–253
decision structure, 194–195
declaration, variable, 44, 50–51
decomposition, algorithm, 258–259
decorations, window, 754
decrement operator (--), 279–282
  postfix mode, 281–282
  prefix mode, 281–282
deep copy, 409, 410
default, 159, 371–372, 622

default exception handler, 682
DELETE statement, 1106–1107
delimiter, 323, 579
   multiple, using, 583–584
depth, of recursion, 1041
derived class, 606
deserialization, 725
design, object-oriented, 174–182, 431–435
diagnostic messages, 827
dialog boxes, 97–104, 742–752, 753
   confirm dialog, 742, 747–749
   defined, 742
   file chooser, 873–875
   input dialog, 97–99, 742, 746–747
   message dialog, 97–98, 742–746
   modal, 746
Diamond operator (), 534
Dimension class, 884
direct recursion, 1046
discounts, calculating, 65–57
disk drive, 4
division, integer, 62–63
division by zero, 203–204
documentation comments, 85–87
Double class, 587
   MAX_VALUE constant, 589
   MIN_VALUE constant, 589
   parseDouble method, 588
   toString method, 588
DOUBLE data type (SQL), 1075
double data type, 50, 52–54
do-while loop, 293–296
DriverManager.getConnection method, 1073
DROP TABLE statement, 1113
DVD drive, 5
dynamic binding, polymorphism and, 647–648

E

E notation, 53–54
editable combo box, 863–864
elements, of arrays, 451–452
else clause, 204
   trailing, 218
EmbeddedMain class, 758
empty border, 811
encapsulation, 19
entity relationship diagrams, 1133
enum constants, 420
enum key word, 420
enumerated types, 420–428
   compareTo method, 422–423
   equals method, 422
   ordinal method, 422
   ordinal value, 422
   switching on, 427–428
EOFException class, 683, 716
equals method, 422, 645–646
Error class, 683, 703
errors
   logical, 17
   syntax, 12, 14
escape sequence, 40–42
   \\, 40
   \', 42
   \", 42

\b, 42
\n, 40–42
\r, 42
\t, 41, 42
control character, 40
etched border, 811
event handler, 1188
event listener, 742, 763, 985
   registering, 765
event-driven programming, 742
events, 985
   action, 763
   change, 892
   CheckBox, responding to, 1022–1024
   defined, 763
   firing, 763
   handling, with action listeners, 763–770
   item, 804–805
   list selection, 844
   object, 763, 770
   RadioButton, responding to, 1016–1019
   source, 763
Excel spreadsheet, 591
Exception class, 683, 690, 705
exceptions, 324, 681–711
   checked, 703–704
   classes, 682–683, 708–711
   default error message for, 688–690
   default handler, 682
   defined, 682
   handler, 682
   handling, 682, 684–687
   multiple, handling, 690–692, 700–702
   polymorphic references to, 690
   throw statement, 704–705
   throwing, 704–711
   unchecked, 703
   when not caught, 702
executable file, 12
exit code, 752
exit method, 752, 755
explicit import statements, 173
extends key word, 611, 644
external drives, 5

F

factorial algorithm, 1043–1046
fetch/decode/execute cycle, 4
Fibonacci series, 1050–1051
field, 129, 134, 172
   instance, 152–155, 358–360
file chooser, 873–875. *See also* JFileChooser class
File class, 875
   toURI method, 973
FileInputStream class, 715, 725
FileNotFoundException class, 683, 686, 690, 695, 703, 719
FileOutputStream class, 713, 725
   constructor, 718
files
   appending data to, 327–328
   binary, 321, 712–718
   checking for existence, 337–340
   closing, 321
   detecting the end of, 332–334

files (*continued*)
  input, 321
  location, specifying, 328
  opening, 321
  output, 321
  pointer, 721–724
  random access, 718–724
  read position, 330
  reading data from, 329–337
  reading primitive values from, 334–336
  sequential access, 718
  text, 321
final key word, 74–75, 632
finally clause, 697–698
flags, 111–114. *See also* numbers
  if statement, 201
flash memory, 5
Float class, 587
  MAX_VALUE constant, 589
  MIN_VALUE constant, 589
  parseFloat method, 588
  toString method, 588
FlowLayout class, 781–784
  alignment, 783–784
  CENTER constant, 783–784
  component gaps, 784
  LEFT constant, 783–784
  RIGHT constant, 783–784
Font class, 889
  constructor, 889
fonts, 889–890
for loop, 296–306
  counter variable, 298, 300
  initialization expression, 297, 301, 303–304
  pretest, 300
  test expression, 297–298
  update expression, 297, 300–301, 303–304
  user controlled, 301–303
foreign key, 1131
format specifier
  flags, 111–114
  minimum field width, 108–110
  precision, 108, 109–110
  string argument, 114–116
  syntax for, 107
formatting numbers, 248–253
  DecimalFormat class, with, 248–253
FORTRAN programming languages, 7
Frame class, 929
  paint method, 936
  repaint method, 948
frame, GUI, 753
FXML, 987–988

G

garbage collection, 429–430
  finalize method, 430
"garbage in, garbage out," 290
generalization and specialization, 605–606
getActionCommand() method, 770
getArea method, 144–146
getLength method, 140–143
getMessage method, 688–690, 704, 706
getSource() method, 770, 774
getWidth method, 140–143
Gosling, James, 8

graphical shapes, 934–954
graphical user interface (GUI), 37, 739
  application, debugging, 827–830
  classes, equipping with main method, 757–758
  components, 739–740, 984
  event-driven programming, 985
  JavaFX applications, 983–1030
  windows, creation of, 753–780
Graphics class, 934–936
  drawArc method, 935, 942
  drawLine method, 935
  drawOval method, 935, 940
  drawPolygon method, 935, 944
  drawRect method, 935
  drawString method, 936, 946
  fillArc method, 935, 942
  fillOval method, 935, 940
  fillPolygon method, 936, 944
  fillRect method, 935
  getColor method, 935
  setColor method, 935
  setFont method, 936, 946
greatest common divisor, finding, 1052–1053
Green Team, 8
GridLayout class, 781, 791–797
GUI (graphical user interface), 37
  application, debugging, 827–830
  classes, equipping with main method, 757–758
  components, 739–740, 984
  event-driven programming, 985
  JavaFX applications, 983–1030
  windows, creation of, 753–780

H

hard drive, 4–5
hardware
  central processing unit (CPU), 2, 3–4
  components, 2, 3
  defined, 2
  input devices, 2, 5
  main memory, 2, 4
  output devices, 2, 5
  secondary storage, 2, 4–5
"has a" relationship, 406
header
  class, 32
  loop, 283, 297
  method, 33, 135–136
heavyweight components, 741
hex numbers, converting to, 588–589
hierarchy, class, 644
HTML. *See* Hypertext Markup Language (HTML)
hypertext, 911
hypertext markup language (HTML), 8–9, 911–920
  <a href=. . .> tag, 919
  <applet code=. . .> tag, 922
  <b>/<b> tag, 916
  <body>/<body> tag, 912

 tag, 916
   tag, 914
  <h1>. . .<h6> tag, 914
  <head></head> tag, 912
  <hr> tag, 917
  <html>/<html> tag, 912
  <i>/<i> tag, 916
  <p> tag, 917

`<title></title>` tag, 912
document body, 913
document head, 912
document structure tags, 912–914
links, 919
text formatting tags, 914–916

I

IDE. *See* integrated development environments (IDE)
identifiers, 9, 47–48
if statement, 193–202
   comparing characters, 201–202
   conditionally executed statements, 200–201
   flags, 201
   nested, 209–216
   programming style, 199–200
   relational operators, 195–197
   semicolons, 200
if-else statement, 202–204
if-else-if statement, 217–220
IllegalArgumentException class, 697, 706, 792
Image class, 1026
   constructor, 1026
ImageIcon class, 865
images, displaying, 865–870, 1025–1030
ImageView component, JavaFX GUI, 1025–1030
   setImage method, 1026
implements key word, 658, 662
import statement, 92, 173–174, 683
increment operator (++), 279–282
   postfix mode, 281–282
   prefix mode, 281–282
indirect recursion, 1046
inheritance, 22–23, 605–616
   and "is a" relationship, 606
   chain of, 639–644
   constructors, superclass, 614–623
   generalization and specialization, 605–606
   in UML diagram, 613, 643
   interface, 666
   subclass, 606
   superclass, 606
initialization, 57–58
   variables, 57–58
inner class, 417–420
input devices, 2, 5
input dialog box, 742, 746–747
InputMismatchException class, 690, 695, 701
INSERT statement, 1098–1101
   format of, 1099
   with JDBC, 1099–1100
instance, of class, 22
instanceof operator, 649–650
Integer class, 587
   MAX_VALUE constant, 589
   MIN_VALUE constant, 589
   parseInt method, 588
   toBinaryString method, 588–589
   toHexString method, 588–589
   toOctalString method, 588–589
   toString method, 588
INTEGER data type (SQL), 1075
integer division, 62–63
integrated development environments (IDE), 14, 15

interface key word, 657
interfaces, 657–668
   ActionListener, 763–765
   AudioClip, 970–972
   ChangeListener, 892
   fields in, 662
   implementing, 658
   in UML, 662–663
   inheritance, 666
   ItemListener, 804–805
   ListSelectionListener, 844
   MouseListener, 954–955
   MouseMotionListener, 955–956
   multiple, implementing, 662
   polymorphism and, 663–668
   Serializable, 724
InventoryItem class, 372–375
IOException class, 683, 701, 719
"is a" relationship, 606, 649
isSelected method
   CheckBox, 1020
   RadioButton, 1013
item events, 804–805
ItemListener interface, 804–805
   itemStateChanges method, 804–805
itemStateChanges method, 804–805

J

JApplet class, 921–928
   handling events in, 924–928
   init method, 921
   paint method, 936
   repaint method, 948
Java DB, 1070
Java Foundation Classes (JFC), 739, 740–741
Java programming language
   applets, 8–9
   applications, 8–9
   defined, 7
   history, 8
   key words, 10
   overview, 1
Java Virtual Machine (JVM), 12–14
java.applet package, 174, 970
java.awt package, 174
java.awt.event package, 764, 805, 871, 954, 962
java.io package, 174, 683, 719, 724, 875
java.lang package, 644, 683
java.lang packages, 174
java.net package, 174, 973
java.security package, 174
java.sql package, 174, 1078
java.swing package, 174
java.text package, 174
java.util package, 174, 690
JavaFX
   controller class, writing code for, 1004–1008
   display images in, 1025–1030
   GUI applications, 983–1030
   main application class, writing code for, 1001–1003
   Scene Builder, 987–1001
   scene graph, 985–987
   Swing classes *vs.*, 983
javafx.scene.image package, 1026
JavaScript programming languages, 7
javax.awt package, 741, 775

`javax.swing` package, 741, 742, 754, 775, 810, 844, 859, 865, 874, 876, 878, 921, 965
`javax.swing.event` package, 844, 892
`JButton` class, 758, 761, 764, 768
  `addActionListener` method, 765, 769
  constructor, 866
  image, displaying, 866–870
  `setActionCommand` method, 774
  `setIcon` method, 867
`JCheckBox` class, 804–808
  constructors, 804
  `doClick` method, 808
  `isSelected` method, 805
  item event, responding to, 804–805
`JCheckBoxMenuItem` class, 878
`JColorChooser` class, 876
  `showDialog` method, 876
`JComboBox` class, 859–864
  action events, responding to, 859
  constructor, 859
  editable, 863–864
  `getSelectedIndex` method, 860, 864
  `getSelectedItem` method, 860, 864
  `setEditable` method, 863–864
  uneditable, 863
`JComponent` class, 810
  `setFont` method, 889
  `setPreferredSize` method, 884
  `setToolTipText` method, 873
JDBC (Java Database Connectivity), 1068–1069
  auto commit mode, 1153
  deleting rows with, 1107
  inserting rows with, 1099–1100
  new database creation with, 1114–1115
  updating rows with, 1102–1106
JFC (Java Foundation Classes), 739, 740–741
`JFileChooser` class, 874–875
  `APPROVE_OPTION` constant, 875
  `CANCEL_OPTION` constant, 875
  constructors, 874
  `ERROR_OPTION` constant, 875
  `showOpenDialog` method, 875
  `showSaveDialog` method, 875
`JFrame` class, 753–754, 761, 787, 812
  constructor, 754, 756, 762
  content pane color, 779–780
  `EXIT_ON_CLOSE` constant, 755
  extending, 755–756
  `getContentPane` method, 780
  `HIDE_ON_CLOSE` constant, 755
  `paint` method, 936
  `repaint` method, 948
  `setDefaultCloseOperation` method, 755
  `setLayout` method, 781
  `setSize` method, 755, 762
  `setVisible` method, 755, 762
`JLabel` class, 758, 761
  constructor, 762, 865, 866
  image, displaying, 865–870
  `setIcon` method, 866
`JList` class, 842–858
  `addListSelectionListener` method, 844
  border, placing around, 848
  constructor, 842
  `getSelectedIndex` method, 844–845, 854
  `getSelectedValue` method, 844, 854

list selection events, responding to, 844
  multiple interval selection mode, 843–844, 854–855
  `MULTIPLE_INTERVAL_SELECTION` constant, 844, 854–855
  selection modes, 843–844
  `setListData` method, 853–854
  `setSelectionMode` method, 844, 854
  single interval selection mode, 843–844, 854
  single selection mode, 843–844
  `SINGLE_INTERVAL_SELECTION` constant, 844, 854
  `SINGLE_SELECTION` constant, 844
`JMenu` class, 878
`JMenuBar` class, 878
`JMenuItem` class, 878
`JOptionPane` class, 97–104, 742–752, 753, 769
  `CANCEL_OPTION` constant, 749
  `ERROR_MESSAGE` constant, 744–745
  `INFORMATION_MESSAGE` constant, 744–745
  input dialog, 97–99
  input dialog box, 742, 746–747
  message dialog, 97–98
  message dialog box, 742–746
  `NO_OPTION` constant, 749
  `PLAIN_MESSAGE` constant, 744–745
  `QUESTION_MESSAGE` constant, 744–745
  `showConfirmDialog` method, 747–749
  `showInputDialog` method, 99, 100, 746–747
  `showMessageDialog` method, 98, 742–746
  `WARNING_MESSAGE` constant, 744–745
  `YES_OPTION` constant, 749
`JPanel` class, 759, 761, 762, 948–949
  extending, 812–825
  `paintComponent` method, 948–949, 953
`JRadioButton` class, 797–803
  action events, responding to, 799–803
  constructor, 798
  `doClick` method, 803
  `isSelected` method, 803
`JRadioButtonMenuItem` class, 878
  constructor, 884
`JScrollPane` class, 849–853
  constructor, 849
  `HORIZONTAL_SCROLLBAR_ALWAYS` constant, 887
  `HORIZONTAL_SCROLLBAR_AS_NEEDED` constant, 887
  `HORIZONTAL_SCROLLBAR_NEVER` constant, 887
  `setHorizontalScrollBarPolicy` method, 887
  `setVerticalScrollBarPolicy` method, 887
  `VERTICAL_SCROLLBAR_ALWAYS` constant, 888
  `VERTICAL_SCROLLBAR_AS_NEEDED` constant, 887
  `VERTICAL_SCROLLBAR_NEVER` constant, 888
`JSlider` class, 891–895
  change event, responding to, 892
  constructor, 891–892
  `getValue` method, 892
  `setMajorTickSpacing` method, 892
  `setMinorTickSpacing` method, 892
  `setPaintLabels` method, 892
  `setPaintTicks` method, 892
`JTable` class, 1120–1131
  `colNames` parameter, 1120
  `rowData` parameter, 1120
`JTextArea` class, 886–888
  constructors, 886
  `getText` method, 887
  `setLineWrap` method, 888
  `setText` method, 887
  `setWrapStyleWord` method, 888

JTextField class, 758, 761, 762, 769, 841–842
  setEditable method, 841–842
JVM. *See* Java Virtual Machine (JVM)

K
key words, 9, 10, 47
keyboard buffer, 95
keyboard input, reading, 89–97
KeyEvent class, 871, 872

L
Label class, 929
label component, 740. *See also* JLabel class
Label component, JavaFX GUI, 984, 986
late binding, 647–648
layout managers, 780–797
  adding to container, 781
  BorderLayout class, 781, 784–791
  FlowLayout class, 781–784
  GridLayout class, 781, 791–797
leading zeros, padding numbers with, 112–113
leaf node, scene graph, 985, 986
left to right associativity, 63–64
left-justified numbers, 114
lexicographical comparison, 233
lightweight components, 741
LIKE operator (SQL), 1092–1093
line border, 811–812
line wrapping, 888
lines, 11
list component, 740, 842–858, 984. *See also* JList class
  adding scroll bar to, 849–853
  border around, placing, 810
ListSelectionListener interface
  valueChanged method, 844
ListSelectionModel class, 844
literal(s), 46–47
  character, 55–56
  floating-point, 53
  integer, 52
  string, 34, 76
local variable, 82, 172
logical errors, 17
logical operators, 222–229, 1093–1094
  ! (NOT), 222, 227
  && (AND), 222, 223–225
  || (OR), 222, 225–226
  associativity, 227–228
  checking numeric ranges, 228–229
  precedence, 227–228
  short-circuit evaluation, 223
Long class, 587
  MAX_VALUE constant, 589
  MIN_VALUE constant, 589
  parseLong method, 588
  toBinaryString method, 588–589
  toHexString method, 588–589
  toOctalString method, 588–589
  toString method, 588
look and feel, 895–897
loop
  arrays, with, 465–466
  body, 284
  control variable, 286
  count-controlled, 296–297
  deciding which to use, 320
  defined, 283
  do-while, 293–296
  for, 296–306
  header, 283, 297
  infinite, 286–287
  iteration, 285
  nested, 312–319
  pretest, 286
  programming style, 287–288
  user-controlled, 296
  while, 283–293
lowered bevel border, 811

M
main application class, JavaFX
  writing code for, 1001–1003
main memory, 2, 4
main method
  GUI classes equipping with, 757–758
MalformedURLException class, 973
many to one relationship, 1133
markup language, 912
Math class, 67–68, 363
  PI constant, 75–76
  pow method, 67–68
  sqrt method, 68
matte border, 811
MAX function (SQL), 1095
MAX_VALUE constant, 589
menus, 877–885
  check box menu item, 877. *See also* JCheckBoxMenuItem class
  menu bar, 877. *See also* JMenuBar class
  menu item, 877. *See also* JMenuItem class
  radio button menu item, 878. *See also*
    JRadioButtonMenuItem class
  separator bar, 878
  submenu, 878
message dialog box, 742–746
meta data, 1117–1120
method(s), 19, 33–34, 129
  accessor, 146
  abstract, 651–657
  binding, 647–648
  DataInputStream class, 716
  DataOutputStream class, 714
  equals, 645–646
  exit, 752, 755
  final, 632
  getMessage, 688–690, 704, 706
  Graphics class, 935–936
  header, 33
  main. *See* main method
  mutator, 146
  overloading *vs.* overriding, 629–631
  overriding, 624–632
  recursive. *See* recursion
  ResultSet class, 1116
  setDefaultCloseOperation, 755, 762
  setSize, 755, 762
  setVisible, 755, 762
  showConfirmDialog, 747–749
  showInputDialog, 746–747
  showMessageDialog, 742, 743
  signature, 627
  toString, 645–646

`Metric` class, 363
`MIN` function (SQL), 1095
`MIN_VALUE` constant, 589
minimum field width, 108–110
mnemonics, 871–872
modal dialog box, 746
mouse events, 954–964
mouse listener, 954
mouse motion listener, 954
`MouseAdapter` class, 962
`MouseEvent` class, 956
  `getX` method, 955
  `getY` method, 955
`MouseListener` interface, 954–955
  `mouseClicked` method, 955
  `mouseEntered` method, 955
  `mouseExited` method, 955
  `mousePressed` method, 955
  `mouseReleased` method, 955
`MouseMotionAdapter` class, 962
`MouseMotionListener` interface, 955–956
  `mouseDragged` method, 956
  `mousemoved` method, 956
multi-catch, 701
multiline comments, 84–85
multithreaded application, 578
mutator methods, 146

N

named constants, 74–76
names, programmer-defined, 9–10, 47–48
naming rules, 47–48
narrowing conversion, 71
negation operator, 60
nested `if` statement, 209–216
nested `if-else` statement, 220
nested loops, 312–319
`new` key word, 137
newline character, 95–97, 323
`nextLine` method, 329–332
no-arg constructors, 160, 622
nodes, scene graph, 985–986
nouns, 175–180
`null` references, 411–414
null statement, 200
`NumberFormatException` class, 689–690, 696–697, 701
numbers
  formatting, 248–253
  left-justified, 114
  padding, with leading zeros, 112–113
  right-justified, 114
  with comma separators, 111–112

O

`Object` class, 644–646
  `equals` method, 645–646
  `toString` method, 645–646
object-oriented design, 174–182, 431–435
  class collaboration, 431–435
  finding the classes, 174–182
  problem domain, 175–180
  responsibilities, identifying, 180–182
object-oriented programming (OOP), 19–23
  attributes, 19

  component reusability, 20
  data hiding, 19–20
  encapsulation, 19
  inheritance, 22–23. *See* inheritance
  methods, 19
`ObjectOutputStream` class, 725
objects, 19, 21–22
  as arguments, 376–389
  copy, 398–401
  defined, 19
  everyday example of, 21
  returning from methods, 389–392
  serialization, 724–728
  subparts, 1172
octal numbers, converting to, 588–589
off-by-one error, 457
one to many relationship, 1133
OOP. *See* object-oriented programming (OOP)
operands, 9, 11
operating system, 5
operators, 9, 11
  AND, 1093–1094
  `-` (subtraction operator), 279–282
  `--` (decrement operator), 279–282
  `-=` (combined assignment), 69–70
  `!` (logical NOT operator), 222, 227
  `!=` (not equal to operator), 196, 197
  `%` (modulus operator), 60, 61
  `%=` (combined assignment), 69–70
  `&&` (logical AND operator), 222, 223–225
  `( )` (parentheses), 35, 64
  `*` (multiplication operator), 11, 60, 61
  `*=` (combined assignment), 69–70
  `,` (comma separators), 111–112
  `/` (division operator), 60, 61
  `/* */` (comment symbols), 84–85
  `/** */` (comment symbols), 85–86
  `//` (comment symbol), 32, 35, 83
  `/=` (combined assignment), 69–70
  `;` (semicolon), 11, 34–35, 200
  `;create=true` attribute, 1114
  `\` (backslash), 40
  `\\` (backslash escape sequence), 42
  `\'` (single quote escape sequence), 42
  `\"` (double quote escape sequence), 42
  `\b` (backspace escape sequence), 42
  `\n` (newline escape sequence), 40–42
  `\r` (return escape sequence), 42
  `\t` (tab escape sequence), 41, 42
  `{` (opening braces), 33–35
  `||` (OR logical operator), 222, 225–226
  `}` (closing braces), 33–35
  `'` (single quotation marks), 55–56
  `" "` (double quotation marks), 35, 46
  `+` (addition operator), 60, 62
  `+` (string concatenation operator), 45, 392, 565
  `++` (increment operator), 279–282
  `+=` (combined assignment), 69–70
  `<` (less than operator), 195, 196, 1088
  `<=` (less than or equal to operator), 195, 196, 1088
  `<>` (diamond operator), 534
  `<>` (not equal to operator), 1088
  `=` (assignment operator), 11, 44, 137, 197
  `=` (equal to operator), 1088
  `==` (equal to operator), 195, 196, 197
  `>` (greater than), 195, 196, 1088

>= (greater than or equal to operator), 195, 196, 1088
  arithmetic, 60–68
  associativity, 63–64, 227–228
  binary, 60
  cast, 71–73
  combined assignment, 69–70
  compound, 69
  conditional, 237–238
  instanceof, 649–650
  LIKE, 1092–1093
  logical, 222–229
  mixed, in expressions, 73–74
  negation, 60
  OR, 1093–1094
  precedence, 63–64, 227–228
  relational, 195–197
  ternary, 60
  unary, 60
OR operator (SQL), 1093–1094
output devices, 2, 5
overhead, 1043
overloaded methods, 364–369
  constructors, 369–375
overloading, methods
  overriding *vs.*, 629–631
overriding methods, 624–632
  overloading *vs.*, 629–631
  preventing, 632

P
package access, 637–638
packages, 173–174
  java.applet, 174, 970
  java.awt, 174
  java.awt.event, 764, 805, 871, 954, 962
  java.io, 174, 683, 719, 724, 875
  java.lang, 174, 644, 683
  java.net, 174, 973
  java.security, 174
  java.sql, 174, 1078
  java.swing, 174
  java.text, 174
  java.util, 174, 690
  javafx.scene.image, 1026
  javax.awt, 741, 775
  javax.swing, 741, 742, 754, 775, 844, 859, 865, 874, 878, 921, 965
  javax.swing.event, 844, 892
padding numbers, with leading zeros, 112–113
Panel class, 929
panel component, 759. *See also* JPanel class
parameter variable, 135–136, 138–139, 149–151, 172
  UML, in, 147–148
parse methods, 587–588
Pascal programming languages, 7
pass by value, 151
password-protected database, connecting, 1073
Payroll class, 205–208
peer classes, 741
percentages, calculating, 65–57
Perl programming languages, 7
PHP programming languages, 7
pixels, 754
plug-in, browser, 929
polymorphism, 646–650
  and dynamic binding, 647–648
  and exceptions, 690
  and interfaces, 663–668
portability, 12–13
postfix mode, 281–282
precedence, operator, 63–64
precision, 108, 109–110
preferred size, 884
prefix mode, 281–282
primary keys, 1076, 1111, 1133
priming read, 291
primitive data type, 49–59
primitive-type variables, 77
print method, 37–42
printf method, 104–107
println method, 34, 37–42
PrintWriter class
  print method, 323
  println method, 322–323
private access specifier, 134, 258–259, 638
private methods, 21
problem domain, 175–180
procedural programming, 19
procedure, 19
programmer-defined names, 9, 10, 47–48
programming languages, 6–9
  BASIC, 7
  C, 7
  C#, 7
  C++, 7
  COBOL, 7
  elements, 9–11
  FORTRAN, 7
  Java. *See* Java programming language
  JavaScript, 7
  Pascal, 7
  Perl, 7
  PHP, 7
  Python, 7
  Ruby, 7
  Visual Basic, 7
programming process, 16–18
programming style, 87–89, 199–200, 287–288
protected access specifier, 632–638
pseudocode, 17
public access specifier, 32, 133, 135, 638
public methods, 21
punctuation, 9, 11
Python programming languages, 7

Q
queries, 1069
quotation marks, double ("), 35, 46
quotation marks, single ('), 55 – 56

R
radio button component, 740, 797–803.
  See also JRadioButton class
RadioButton component, JavaFX GUI, 984, 986, 1011–1019
  events, responding, 1016–1019
  isSelected method, 1013
  selection of, 1013–1014
  Text property, 1011
ragged arrays, 520–521
raised bevel border, 811

RAM. *See* random-access memory (RAM)
random access files, 718–724
    sequential files access *vs.,* 719
Random class, 261–263
    nextDouble method, 262
    nextFloat method, 262
    nextInt method, 262
    nextLong method, 262
random numbers, 261–263
random-access memory (RAM), 4, 11
RandomAccessFile class, 719–724
    constructor, 719
    files pointer, 721–724
    readByte method, 721
    readInt method, 721
    seek method, 721
    writeChar method, 720
ranges, checking, 228–229
ranking, data type, 71
raw binary format, 713
read, priming, 291
read-only text field, 841–842
REAL data type (SQL), 1075
realization relationship, 662–663
recursion, 1039–1060
    base case, 1043
    binary search algorithm, 1053–1056
    concentric circles, drawing, 1048–1050
    depth of, 1041
    direct, 1046
    factorial algorithm, 1043–1046
    Fibonacci series, 1050–1051
    greatest common divisor, finding, 1052–1053
    indirect, 1046
    introduction, 1039–1042
    problem solving with, 1042–1046
    recursive case, 1043
    summing array elements, 1046–1048
    Towers of Hanoi, 1056–1060
reference, null, 411–414
reference copy, 399
reference variables, 77, 137
    arrays, 468–469
    this, 414–416
    uninitialized, 159
referential integrity, 1132
regular expression, 585
relational data, 1131–1152
    joining data from multiple tables, 1133–1134
    order entry system, 1135–1152
relational operators, 195–197, 1088
    >= (greater than or equal to), 195, 196, 1088
    > (greater than), 195, 196, 1088
    <= (less than or equal to), 195, 196, 1088
    < (less than), 195, 196, 1088
    != (not equal to), 196, 197, 1088
    == (equal to), 195, 196, 197, 1088
relationship
    "has a," 406
    "is a," 606, 649
    realization, 662–663
reserved words. *See* key words
responsibilities, identifying, 180–182
result sets
    meta data, 1117–1120
    scrollable, 1115–1117

ResultSet class, 1078–1081
    absolute() method, 1116
    and column content retrieval, 1080–1081
    and row content retrieval, 1079–1080
    first() method, 1116
    getDouble method, 1081
    getInt method, 1081
    getMetaData method, 1117
    getRow method, 1117
    getString method, 1081
    last() method, 1116
    next method, 1080
    next() method, 1116
    previous() method, 1116
    relative() method, 1116
    TYPE_CONCUR_READ_ONLY constant, 1116
    TYPE_CONCUR_UPDATEABLE constant, 1116
    TYPE_FORWARD_ONLY constant, 1115
    TYPE_SCROLL_INSENSITIVE constant, 1115
    TYPE_SCROLL_SENSITIVE constant, 1116
ResultSetMetaData class, 1117
    getColumnCount method, 1117
    getColumnDisplaySize method, 1117
    getColumnName method, 1117
    getColumnTypeName method, 1117
    getTableName method, 1117
return statement, 140
reusability, component, 20
right to left associativity, 63–64
rollback, transaction-processing code, 1153
root node, scene graph, 985, 986
rows, 1073–1075
    content retrieval, ResultSet object and, 1079–1080
    deleting, 1106–1107
    inserting, 1098–1101
    updating, 1101–1106
Ruby programming languages, 7
running a program, 14
running total, 307–309
RuntimeException class, 683, 703, 706

S

SalesCommission class, 254–260
SalesData class, 479–482
Scanner class, 89–97, 336
    close method, 329, 336–337
    hasNext method, 332–333, 337
    nextByte method, 91, 334
    nextDouble method, 91, 334
    nextFloat method, 91, 334
    nextInt method, 91, 334
    nextLine method, 91, 94–97, 337
    nextLong method, 92, 334
    nextShort method, 92, 334
    reading from a file, 329–337
Scene Builder, and JavaFX applications, 987–1001
    main window, 989–990
    starting, 988
    tutorial, 990–1001
scene graph, 985–987
    nodes, 985
scientific notation, 53–54
scope, 81–83, 172–173, 235–236
scroll bars, 849–853. *See also* JScrollPane class
scrollable result sets, 1115–1117

search algorithm:
  binary, 505–508
  sequential, 498–501
secondary storage, 2, 4–5
security, 9
security warning, applet, 923
seek()method, 721
selection sort algorithm, 501–504
SELECT statement, 1077–1097
  string comparisons in, 1092
  WHERE clause, 1088–1094
self-documenting programs, 47
semicolon, 11, 34–35, 200
sentinel value, 310–311
sequence structure, 194
sequential access, files, 718
  random file access *vs.*, 719
sequential search algorithm, 498–501
Serializable interface, 724
serialization, object, 724–728
ServiceQuote class, 182
setActionCommand method, 774
setBorder method, 810
setDefaultCloseOperation method, 755, 762
setLength method, 135–139
setSelectionMode method, 844
setSize method, 755, 762
setVisible method, 755, 762
setWidth method, 139–140
shadowing, 172–173
shapes, drawing, 934–954
  arcs, 942–944
  lines, 936–938
  ovals, 940–941
  polygons, 944–946
  rectangles, 938–939
  strings, 946–948
  XY coordinate system, 934
Short class, 587
  MAX_VALUE constant, 589
  MIN_VALUE constant, 589
  parseShort method, 588
  toString method, 588
showConfirmDialog method, 747–749
showInputDialog method, 746–747
showMessageDialog method, 742, 743
signature, method, 627
single-line comments, 83–84
slider component, 740, 891–895, 984. *See also* JSlider class
Slider component, JavaFX GUI, 984
software, 5
  application, 5
  engineering, 23
  operating system, 5
solid-state drives, 4–5
sorting algorithm, 501
source code, 12
source file, 12
splash screen, 826
SQL (Structured Query Language), 1069
  AVG function, 1094–1095
  COUNT function, 1095
  CREATE TABLE statement, 1110–1113
  data types, 1075–1076, 1081
  DELETE statement, 1106–1107
  DROP TABLE statement, 1113

INSERT statement, 1098–1101
LIKE operator, 1092–1093
mathematical functions, 1094–1095
MAX function, 1095
MIN function, 1095
ORDER BY clause, 1094
relational operators, 1088
SELECT statement, 1077–1097
statement, passing to DBMS, 1078–1088
stored procedures, 1154
string comparisons in, 1092
SUM function, 1095
syntax, 1089
UPDATE statement, 1101–1106
WHERE clause, 1088–1094
square root, getting, 68
stack trace, 699–700
stale data, 147
standard input device, 89
standard output device, 37
Statement class, 1078, 1115, 1116
  executeQuery method, 1078
  executeUpdate method, 1099, 1102–1103, 1107
statements, 11
static class members, 357–363
  fields, 358–360
  methods, 358, 360–363
stored procedures, 1154
string
  comparing, 230–235
  comparisons in SQL, 1092
  concatenation operator, 45, 392, 565
  converting to numbers, 100–103
  literal, 34, 76
  substring, 555
  tokenizing, 578–586
  writing and reading, 717–718
string argument, formatting, 114–116
String class, 76–81, 130
  charAt method, 80
  compareTo method, 232–234
  compareToIgnoreCase method, 234–235
  comparing objects of, 230–235
  concat method, 565–566
  conversion to numbers, 100–103
  creating an object of, 78–79
  endsWith method, 556
  equals method, 230–232
  equalsIgnoreCase method, 234–235
  getChars method, 563–565
  indexOf method, 559–562
  lastIndexOf method, 559–562
  length method, 79, 80
  regionMatches method, 558
  replace method, 566
  split method, 585–586
  startsWith method, 555–556
  substring method, 562–563
  toCharArray method, 563–565
  toLowerCase method, 80
  toUpperCase method, 80
  trim method, 566
  valueOf method, 567
StringBuffer class, 578

`StringBuilder` class, 569–578
  append methods, 571
  `charAt` method, 571
  constructors, 570
  delete method, 573–574
  `deleteCharAt` method, 573–574
  `getChars` methods, 571
  `indexOf` methods, 571
  insert methods, 571–572
  `lastIndexOf` methods, 571
  length methods, 574
  replace methods, 572–573
  `setCharAt` method, 573–574
  substring method, 571
  toString methods, 574
`StringTokenizer` class, 579–584
  constructors, 580
  `countTokens` method, 581
  `hasMoreTokens` method, 581
  `nextTokens` method, 581
strongly typed language, 53, 70
subclass, 23, 606
subscript, 451–452
substring, 555–565
`SUM` function (SQL), 1095
Sun Microsystems, 8
`super` key word, 616–623, 627
superclass, 23, 606
  constructor, 614–623
  method overriding, 624–632
Swing classes, 740–741
  applets creation with, 921–928
  hierarchy, 774–775, 808
  JavaFX *vs.*, 983
  `JTable` class, 1120–1131
`switch` statement, 238–246
  break key word, 239–243
  case key word, 239–245
  enumerated types, with, 427–428
syntax, 9
syntax errors, 12, 14
`System` class, 38
  exit method, 100, 752, 755
  in object, 89
  out object, 38
`System.out.print` method. *See* print method
`System.out.println` method. *See* println method

T

tables, 1073–1076
  creating, 1110–1113
  deleting, 1113
  multiple, joining data from, 1133–1134
tabs, in output, 41–42
tags, markup, 912
telephone numbers, formatting, 574–577
ternary operator, 60
`TestScoreReader` class, 591–594
text areas component, 886–888. *See also* `JTextArea` class
text editor, 12
text field component, 740, 841–842, 1147. *See also* `JTextField` class
Text property
  CheckBox component, 1019
  RadioButton component, 1011

`TextField` class, 929
TextField component, JavaFX GUI, 984
`this` reference variable, 414–416
thread, 100, 752
throw statement, 704–705
`Throwable` class, 683
throws clause, 324, 703–704, 705
tile, for event, 1188
time sharing, 5
`Timer` class, 965–968
  `addActionListener` method, 965
  constructor, 965
  `getDelay` method, 965
  `isRunning` method, 965
  `setDelay` method, 965
  start method, 965
  stop method, 965
titled border, 811, 812
TitledPane component, JavaFX GUI, 984, 986
tokenizing strings, 578–587
tokens, defined, 579
tool tip, 871, 872–873
`toString` method, 392–395, 645–646
Towers of Hanoi, 1056–1060
trailing `else`, 218
transactions, 1152–1154
truncation, floating-point, 72
`try` statement, 684–687
  catch block, 684
  catch clause, 684, 700–702
  finally block, 698
  `finally` clause, 697–698
  try block, 684, 690
two-dimensional arrays
  arguments, as, 518–520
  declaration, 509–510
  displaying the elements in, 516–517
  initializing, 513–514
  `length` `field`, 514–516
  ragged arrays, 520–521
  rows and columns, 509
  subscripts, 510–511
  summing all the elements in, 517
  summing the columns in, 518
  summing the rows in, 517–518

U

UML. *See* Unified Modeling Language (UML)
unary operator, 60
unboxing, 589–590
unchecked exceptions, 703
uneditable combo box, 863
Unicode, 56–57
Unified Modeling Language (UML), 132–133
  abstract classes and methods, 657
  access specification, 147, 637
  aggregation, 408–409
  class, diagram for, 132–133
  constructors, 160
  data type, 147–148
  inheritance, 613, 643
  interfaces in, 662–663
  parameters, 147–148
uninitialized reference variables, 159
Universal Serial Bus (USB) drives, 5

UNIX, 5, 13
UPDATE statement, 1101–1106
URI class
   toURI method, 973
   toURL method, 973
URL class, 969
user-controlled loop, 296, 301
USB drives. *See* Universal Serial Bus (USB) drives
UTF-8 encoding, 717

V

VARCHAR data type (SQL), 1075
variable-length argument lists, 523–526
variable(s), 11–12, 43–48
   assignment, 57–58
   class-type, 77
   declarations, 44
   defined, 11
   initialization, 57–58
   local, 82, 172
   parameter, 135–136, 138–139, 147–151, 172
   primitive-type, 77
   reference, 77
   scope, 81–83, 172–173, 235–236
   shadowing, 172–173
   value hold one at a time by, 58–59
vertex, 944
Visual Basic programming language, 7

W

WHERE clause, 1088–1094, 1102, 1107
while loop
   input validation, used for, 290–293
   programming style, 287–288
widening conversion, 71–73
wildcard import statements, 173–174
window
   adding components to, 758–763
   creation of, 753–763
   decorations, 754
Windows operating system, 5, 13
word wrapping, 888
wrapper classes, 547–548
   Byte, 587
   Character, 548–555
   Double, 587
   Float, 587
   Integer, 587
   Long, 587
   Short, 587

X

XY coordinate system, 934

Credits

Figure 14.22: The Label's fx:id changed, Scene Builder, Oracle Corporate Counsel

Figure 14.23: The Label created, resized, and repositioned, Scene Builder, Oracle Corporate Counsel

Figure 14.24: The Button created, resized, and repositioned, Scene Builder, Oracle Corporate Counsel

Figure 14.25: The Hierarchy panel, Scene Builder, Oracle Corporate Counsel

Figure 14.26: Showing component fx:ids in the Hierarchy panel, Scene Builder, Oracle Corporate Counsel

Figure 14.27: The GUI displayed in a preview window, Scene Builder, Oracle Corporate Counsel

Figure 14.29: Select the AnchorPane, Scene Builder, Oracle Corporate Counsel

Figure 14.30: Select the controller class, Scene Builder, Oracle Corporate Counsel

Figure 14.31: Select the Button component, Scene Builder, Oracle Corporate Counsel

Figure 14.32: Select the event listener method, Scene Builder, Oracle Corporate Counsel

Figure 14.34: Accessing the sample controller skeleton, Scene Builder, Oracle Corporate Counsel

Figure 14.37: Creating a toggle group, Scene Builder, Oracle Corporate Counsel

Figure 14.38: Making a RadioButton initially selected, Scene Builder, Oracle Corporate Counsel

Figure 14.44: Making a CheckBox initially selected, Scene Builder, Oracle Corporate Counsel

Figure 14.50: The Image property, Scene Builder, Oracle Corporate Counsel